Remote, beautiful and culturally hospitable, these oft-dreamed-of islands are the place to enjoy the world's whitest sands between your toes and its clearest waters at your doorstep.

(left) Tonga's Vava'u islands (p451) seen from the air
(below) Children playing, Solomon Islands (p316)

enous spread of palm trees and warm ocean – if you escape your resort you'll find cultures and experiences as rich as coconut cream.

Ready for Action

Life moves slowly out here so it's no wonder plop-yourself-on-the-beach-and-do-nothing holidays are popular. But what if you like action? This is the South Pacific's wildcard. Of course there's world-class surfing, snorkelling and diving but how about hiking to crumbling *tiki* (sacred) statues in the jungle, swimming with whales, trekking to the top of a volcano, rappelling down a waterfall or kayaking to forgotten beaches? Adventure travel

has scarcely been tapped here and, other than a few mechanised experiences like jet boating in Fiji or 4WD tours, what's on offer is authentic, uncrowded and something you'll never likely forget.

Hospitality

No one knows how to treat guests better than Melanesians and Polynesians. This doesn't mean they'll always be in top form – working for minimum wage at a hotel can bring out the mediocre in the nicest of people – but it's their culture to generously offer the best of everything they have, be warm, gentle and make sure your stay is sublimely comfortable. There is pride that you'll go home with a gigantic smile.

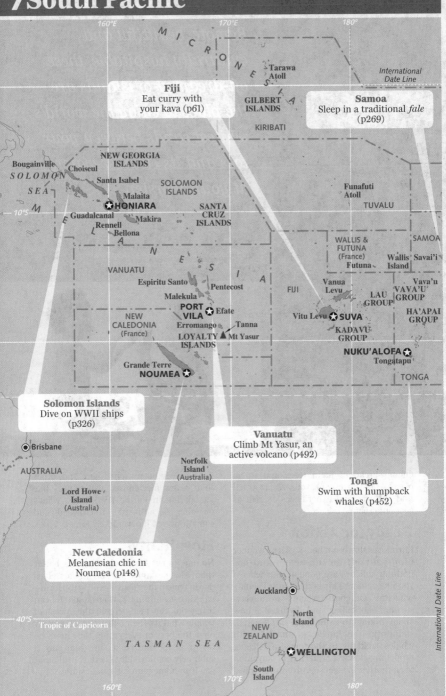

South Pacific

Fiji
Eat curry with your kava (p61)

Samoa
Sleep in a traditional *fale* (p269)

Solomon Islands
Dive on WWII ships (p326)

Vanuatu
Climb Mt Yasur, an active volcano (p492)

Tonga
Swim with humpback whales (p452)

New Caledonia
Melanesian chic in Noumea (p148)

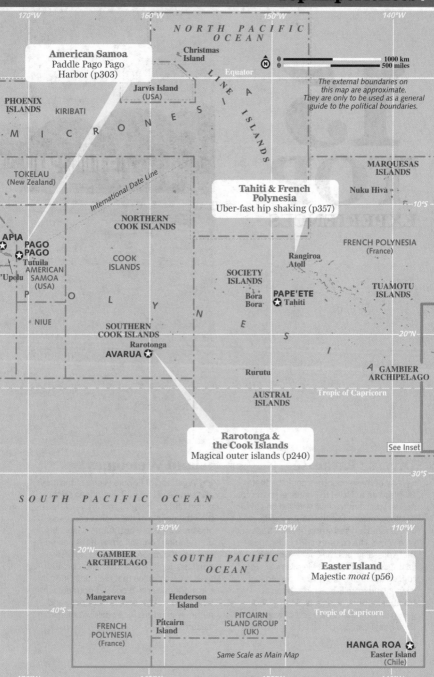

American Samoa
Paddle Pago Pago
Harbor (p303)

Tahiti & French
Polynesia
Uber-fast hip shaking (p357)

Rarotonga &
the Cook Islands
Magical outer islands (p240)

Easter Island
Majestic *moai* (p56)

NORTH PACIFIC
OCEAN

Christmas
Island

Equator

Jarvis Island
(USA)

0   1000 km
0   500 miles

*The external boundaries on
this map are approximate.
They are only to be used as a general
guide to the political boundaries.*

PHOENIX
ISLANDS   KIRIBATI

M I C R O N E S I A

TOKELAU
(New Zealand)

International Date Line

MARQUESAS
ISLANDS

Nuku Hiva

APIA

PAGO
PAGO

Tutuila
AMERICAN
SAMOA
(USA)

'Upolu

NIUE

NORTHERN
COOK ISLANDS

COOK
ISLANDS

P O L Y N E S I A

FRENCH POLYNESIA
(France)

Rangiroa
Atoll

SOCIETY
ISLANDS

Bora
Bora

PAPE'ETE
Tahiti

TUAMOTU
ISLANDS

SOUTHERN
COOK ISLANDS

Rarotonga

AVARUA

Rurutu

AUSTRAL
ISLANDS

Tropic of Capricorn

GAMBIER
ARCHIPELAGO

See Inset

SOUTH PACIFIC OCEAN

GAMBIER
ARCHIPELAGO

Mangareva

FRENCH
POLYNESIA
(France)

SOUTH PACIFIC
OCEAN

Henderson
Island

Pitcairn
Island

PITCAIRN
ISLAND GROUP
(UK)

Same Scale as Main Map

Easter Island
Majestic *moai* (p56)

Tropic of Capricorn

HANGA ROA
Easter Island
(Chile)

15 TOP
EXPERIENCES

Diverse Paradise

1 Any of these countries could be that place on a 'Travel to Paradise' poster that makes you want to leave your job and live in flip flops forever. But the South Pacific isn't just a homogenised string of palm trees and blue water. The cultures and landscapes that spread across the Pacific Ocean's vastness hold an incredible diversity, from rugged atolls to mangrove-encircled high islands and from Euro-chic capitals to traditional tribes in jungles. Each island group is home to its own sort of wonderful. Bora Bora Pearl Beach Resort & Spa (p389)

Island Welcomes

2 A garland of flowers is one of the most simple yet beautiful offerings on the planet and no one gives out more of these than the people of the Pacific. Loudness and brashness are out, subtle hospitality and genuine goodwill are in. If they could give you the moon they would, so please don't ask for it. There's a selfless beauty to island welcomes that feels untainted by the modern world. It doesn't pour out with fanfare but rather comes out slowly and naturally in return for a smile. Women from a *kastom* village on Tanna (p490), Vanuatu

MICHAEL PATRICK O'NEILL / GETTY IMAGES ©

MARK DAFFEY / LONELY PLANET IMAGES ©

Whales in Tonga

3 Tonga is an important breeding ground for humpback whales, which migrate to its warm waters between June and October; it's one of the few places in the world where you can swim with these magnificent creatures. They can be seen raising their young in the calm reef-protected waters and engaging in elaborate mating rituals. Humpbacks are dubbed 'singing whales' because the males sing during courtship routines, and the low notes of their 'songs' can carry 100km through the open ocean. There are whale-watch and whale-swim operators in all of Tonga's island groups.

Inland Treks

4 Most people travel to the South Pacific for the beaches but no one should go this far without heading inland. Imagine arriving to the tip of a knife-edged peak to watch seabirds fly by at eye level, plunging into massive waterfall pools, or finding petroglyphs hidden by hibiscus next to a rushing river. And these are everyday examples. Hiking is a hot and often muddy endeavour and the trails aren't in the best shape but the payoff is worth every discomfort and there are endless adventures to be had. Hiking through Hakaui Valley (p408), Nuku Hiva, French Polynesia

Easter Island's Moai

5 The strikingly enigmatic *moai* are the most pervasive image of Rapa Nui (p44). Dotted all around the island, these massive carved figures on stone platforms emanate a mystical vibe, like colossal puppets on a supernatural stage. It is thought that they represent clan ancestors. The biggest question is, how were these giant statues moved from where they were carved to their platforms? It's a never-ending debate among specialists. Never mind the answer, they have plenty to set your camera clicking without it.

Diving

6 The South Pacific offers world-class diving, with an irresistible menu of underwater treasures: luscious reefs festooned with huge sea fans, warm waters teeming with rainbow-coloured species and bizarre critters, eerie drop-offs that tumble into the abyss, and lots of pelagics, including sharks and manta rays – not to mention the thrill of diving uncrowded sites. And as on land, there's a sense of adventure to spice up the diving. Another clincher is the mind-boggling array of wrecks – of ships, aircraft and even submarines, mainly from WWII.

Tahitian Dance & Tattoos

7 Tahitians love to dance. The best dance performances in the country take place at the annual Heiva Festival (p351), which is held in Pape'ete in July. During the rest of the year, professional groups offer performances at the big resorts. Men stamp, gesture and knock their knees together, while women shake and gyrate their hips in an unmistakeably suggestive manner. Tattooing, another strong cultural trait, has enjoyed a revival since the early 1980s. For many people, it's a symbol of identity. Marquesan tattooists rank among the best in the South Pacific.

Indo-Fijian Culture

8 Fabulous festivals and food provide visitors with a peek into Indo-Fijian culture. Diwali, the Festival of Lights, is celebrated nationwide in October or November. It's ushered in with nightly displays, from multicoloured spotlit extravaganzas to delicate candlelit driveways and households. Fireworks are obligatory. Fire of another sort takes centre stage during the remarkable fire-walking festival at Suva's Mariamma Temple in July or August. And fantastic curry feasts and an astonishing array of sweetmeats accompany all Indo-Fijian events.
Hindu temple in Nadi (p64)

New Caledonian Coasts

9 With sunny bays for swimming in, waterside restaurants and resorts for living it up, and a thumping, invigorating nightlife, Noumea is a city of stylish splendour. Nearby, Île des Pins is the place for authentic seafood feasts, dining under the trees after a wind-in-your-hair scoot on a bay in a traditional *pirogue* (outrigger canoe). Smell the vanilla on the lovely Loyalty Islands; stay in tribal accommodation by white-sand beaches and sparkling blue waters and soak up the rich, friendly and relaxed Kanak culture.
Noumea (p148)

NEIL FARRIN / JAI / CORBIS ©

Vanuatu's Volcanoes

10 Staring down into a real-life, lava-spouting volcano is exactly the nerve-wracking experience you might assume it is, and Mt Yasur on Tanna is one of the most accessible in the world. Set yourself up in a simple bungalow or lofty banyan-tree tree house at its base, and sleep as it rumbles and spurts; climb the road in the evening to see the planet's best natural light show. Earthly delights include blue holes for swimming and snorkelling in and hot springs for bathing. Active volcano Mt Yasur (p492)

OCEAN / CORBIS ©

Outer Cook Islands

11 Welcome to one of the South Pacific's most accessible and versatile destinations. Ease into island time with Rarotonga's laid-back, family-friendly combination of spectacular snorkelling and hiking, fun day trips, excellent markets and restaurants, and vibrant island nightlife. Invest in a few days' discovering the Cooks' traditional outer islands. See the birdlife and explore the underground cave systems of 'Atiu, paddle your own kayak to deserted islets around Aitutaki's lagoon, or go local in a village homestay on remote Ma'uke or Mitiaro. Caving on 'Atiu (p228)

Beach Fale in Samoa

12 It's a brilliant idea: elongated, wall-free huts on stilts take in the entire view of the luscious turquoise sea and glowing white sands while letting in cool breezes. Few other South Pacific countries have retained their traditional architecture to the point that it's what they offer tourists, without design or modern fanfare, but Samoa does this, making for one of the most authentic sleeping experiences in the region. Pull down the thatched louvres for privacy or rain protection. *Fale* are rustic but the surroundings are pure luxury. 'Upolu Island (p252), Samoa

GRANT DIXON / LONELY PLANET IMAGES ©

PETER HENDRIE / LONELY PLANET IMAGES ©

Surfing

13 Polynesians invented surfing and yet, apart from Tahiti, Samoa and Fiji, the South Pacific remains largely unexplored by surfers. Intrepid board riders are making inroads into other Pacific islands and finding brilliant uncrowded waves in warm, crystal-clear tropical waters. In some places the swell is seasonal: the cyclone season from November to April brings waves from the north, and during winter (May to August) low pressure systems in the Southern Ocean and Tasman Sea bring big swells to islands with exposed southern coastlines.

Solomons' WWII Relics

14 The Solomon Islands has history in spades. Above the surface, WWII relics in the jungle will captivate history buffs. Outside Honiara (p320), you can visit poignant WWII battlefields and memorials as well as abandoned amtracks (small amphibious landing vehicles), a Sherman tank, Japanese field guns and the remains of several US aircraft. In New Georgia, Marovo Lagoon (p328) is the world's finest double-barrier-enclosed lagoon. Here is where you can visit villages where nothing happens in a hurry, picnic on a deserted island and meet master carvers. Kasi Maru wreck, Solomon Islands (p316)

Pago Pago Harbour

15 Yes Pago (p297), as it's affectionately called, is a gritty working town of fishermen and canneries. But perhaps that's what makes the setting that much more surprising. Vertical green peaks with jagged silhouettes plunge dramatically to frame an elongated bay of dark teal silk. Take out a kayak to experience the bay at its best, at sunrise or sunset when the light plays off the mountains. You have an equal chance of passing children playing at a beach park as you do stacks of shipping containers.

need to know

» For detailed information please see the chapter opening pages for each island nation.

Planes
» The most efficient (and sometimes only) way to island hop but flights can be expensive.

When to Go

Tropical climate, wet & dry seasons

Vanuatu GO Apr–Oct

Samoa GO May–Oct

French Polynesia GO May–Oct

Tonga GO May–Oct

Fiji GO Jun–Sep

New Caledonia GO Apr–Jun

The Cook Islands GO Aug–Oct

Your Daily Budget

Less than
US$100
» Guesthouse bed: US$12–50

» Markets for self-catering

» Bicycle rental, local buses and cargo ship travel keep costs low

Midrange
US$80–400
» Double room in a boutique hotel or small resort: $US80–250

» Snorkelling tour: US$25–60

» Meal in a local cafe: US$8–20

Top end over
US$400
» Night in an over-the-water bungalow: US$500–3500

» Dinner at a restaurant with international chef: US$50–200

» Two-tank dive: US$120

High Season
(Jun–Aug & Dec–Jan)

» Many islanders living abroad come home to visit family.

» Book flights well in advance.

» June to August is dry, December and January are wet. Cyclone season is November to April.

Shoulder Season
(May, Sep)

» Trade winds wick the humidity and keep temperatures pleasant.

» Flights are cheaper and less likely to be booked.

» Travel with company but no crowds.

Low Season
(Feb–Apr & Oct–Nov)

» Expect hot temperatures and high humidity.

» Search the web for deals on resorts looking to fill empty rooms.

» Diving visibility can be reduced due to heavy rains.

Driving

» Car hire available on large islands; in remote areas it may be possible through a friendly local or not at all.

Ferries & Boats

» Ferries ply short distances between main islands, while cargo ships make longer hauls.

Language

» English is common in tourist hubs while local languages prevail in remote regions. French in French territories. Spanish on Easter Island.

Mobile Phones

» Local SIM cards available. Reception is variable but available even on surprisingly remote islands.

Websites

» **South Pacific Tourism Organisation** (www.spto.org) Intergovernmental tourism organisation.

» **Pacific Islands Report** (www.pireport. org) Biggest news stories.

» **Te Puna Web Directory** (www. webdirectory.natlib. govt.nz/dir/en/pacific) Excellent list of links.

» **Pacific Magazine** (www.pacificmagazine. net) Regional magazine.

» **Lonely Planet** (www.lonelyplanet. com/pacific) Destination info, hotel bookings, traveller forum and more.

Money

Exchange money or use ATMs on main islands; it's cash only on most outer islands.
Chilean peso (CH$) Easter Island
Cour de Franc Pacific (CFP) French Polynesia, New Caledonia
Fijian dollar (F$) Fiji
New Zealand dollar (NZ$) Cook Islands
Samoan tala (ST) Samoa
Solomon Islands dollar (S$) Solomon Islands
Tongan pa'anga (T$) Tonga
US dollar (US$) American Samoa
Vatu (Vt) Vanuatu

Visas

» One to three month visas are usually issued on arrival in most South Pacific nations.

» EU nationals may apply for longer stays or work visas in French Polynesia and New Caledonia.

» Americans with onward tickets can stay visa-free in American Samoa.

» New Zealanders don't need an entry permit to the Cook Islands and New Zealand pensioners may be granted 12-month visitor permits.

Arriving

» **Nadi International Airport**
Frequent buses and plentiful taxis to downtown.

» **Faa'a International Airport, Pape'ete**
Arrange for your hotel to pick you up or hire a car. Local bus hours don't match most flights and taxis are expensive.

» **Tontouta International Airport, Noumea**
Regular public and private buses run transfers to town, 45km away.
For more information see Getting There & Away sections in the country chapters.

What to Take

☐ easy-to-remove shoes for visiting homes and clothes that cover knees and elbows

☐ seasickness medication, your prescription drugs and the names of generic equivalents

☐ insect repellent, box-style mosquito net, and anti-malarials where required (see p590)

☐ mask, snorkel, rash vest and reef shoes; PADI card and logbook if you're diving

☐ umbrella or rain poncho that covers your backpack, hat, sunglasses, high-UV-protection sunscreen

☐ good footwear, light trousers and long-sleeved shirt for sun and mosquito protection

☐ torch (flashlight) for exploring caves and late-night village toilet expeditions

☐ Lonely Planet's *South Pacific Phrasebook* and a stash of books or an electronic reading device

if you like...

Beaches

With so much coastline in these parts you can be assured of beaches, many of them dazzling white. Don't expect huge, spacious swaths of sand however. The South Pacific specialises in small, pretty and deserted.

Ofu (American Samoa) It's difficult to get here but this beach-laden isle is the definition of stunning (p308)

Aitutaki (Cook Islands) Broad sandy beaches on this 'almost atoll's' many islets are the stuff of daydreams (p221)

Vava'u Group (Tonga) With 61 islands, many with sheltered coves, there's a deserted beach here for everyone (p451)

Ouvéa (New Caledonia) Twenty-five kilometres of perfect white, backed by tropical flowers (p178)

The Tuamotus (French Polynesia) A massive chain of atolls with endless white- and pink-sand beaches (p395)

'Upolu (Samoa) The south coast holds every sort of beach you could fancy, from the wide and white to tiny, private and surrounded by black lava rock formations (p270)

Remote Escapes

Out here, finding an empty island paradise can be as easy as finding a cold beer. Some of these nations are remote by definition while others may require a flight or boat trip from the main island to go Crusoe.

Raivavae (French Polynesia) As beautiful as Bora Bora but with some of the most authentic culture in the country (p418)

Mitiaro (Cook Islands) Experience traditional Polynesian life and duck into limestone caves (p234)

The Maskelynes (Vanuatu) Friendly paradise to watch or join villagers in their daily life, hit up kava bars and dine on mud crab (p500)

Ouvéa (New Caledonia) A thin sliver of land over-endowed with beaches and blue water (p178)

Uoleva Island (Tonga) A beach-bum escape with whales breaching offshore (p450)

Lao Group (Fiji) Blaze a trail through these little-visited gems, renowned for their natural beauty (p135)

Diving & Snorkelling

The Pacific Ocean covers 28% of the Earth's surface so, yeah, there's a lot going on underwater in this balmy southern half. Coral and fish are more diverse to the east, while the western regions are known for big fauna.

Rainbow Reef (Fiji) Soft corals galore, fish aplenty and visits by hammerheads and turtles (p127)

Solomon Islands Hundreds of sunken WWII ships and aircraft have sat undisturbed for nearly 70 years, plus the corals are superb (p316)

Rangiroa (French Polynesia) Shark week is every week on this massive coral atoll. Drift the passes with a snorkel or bottle for big thrills and possible dolphin sightings (p397)

Espiritu Santo (Vanuatu) Dive on bright corals, one of the region's best wrecks and WWII artefacts (p504)

Muri Lagoon (Cook Islands) Snorkellers rejoice: pristine waters and sheltered coves (p210)

GLENN VAN DER KNUFF / LONELY PLANET IMAGES ©

» Coconut palms overhang an Aitutaki beach, Cook Islands (222)

Archaeology & History

Palm thatch doesn't preserve well and missionaries destroyed anything Pagan or naughty, so archaeological remains are the exception rather than the rule. What's left, however, is straight out of an Indiana Jones adventure. WWII buffs will also find some happiness.

Marquesas Islands (French Polynesia) Giant moss-covered *tikis* (sacred statues) (p406)

Taputapuatea (French Polynesia) One of the region's most important meeting places is beautifully restored, massive and lovely for a picnic (p377)

Burial Caves (Cook Islands) Explore several burial caverns on 'Atiu and Mangaia that may contain human bones (p237)

Ha'amonga 'a Maui Trilithon (Tonga) The 'Stonehenge of the South Pacific' sits in an eastern Tongatapu field (p442)

Pulemeilu Mound (Samoa) Lost in vines, this abandoned pyramid is the largest ancient structure in Polynesia (p282)

Espiritu Santo (Vanuatu) A treasure trove of WWII history (p504)

Moai (Easter Island) The iconic stone faces offer more mystery than answers (p47)

Hiking, Caves & Volcanoes

Lava and limestone form conical or jagged peaks, caves of stalactites and stalagmites and otherworldly lava tubes cut by subterranean rivers... and then there's Vanuatu's volcanoes. Hiking all of this is as taxing as it is thrilling.

Tanna, Ambae, Ambrym (Vanuatu) Head to Tanna's active volcano by 4WD, explore Ambae's crater lakes or hike Ambrym's moonscapes (p472)

The Dog's Head (Vanuatu) Amble through a veritable cultural documentary, passing magnificent scenery, caves and waterfalls (p498)

Hitiaa Lava Tubes (French Polynesia) Swim and hike through elongated, river-filled tunnels of cooled lava (p359)

Savai'i (Samoa) Hike to vertiginous craters or head down into subterranean lava tubes (p274)

Cross-Island Track (Rarotonga) Waterfalls, peaks and fern-filled valleys (p211)

'Eua (Tonga) A beautiful, varied 'forgotten island', perfect for hiking and caving (p443)

Marquesas Islands (French Polynesia) Tackle barren to lush landscapes on foot or by horseback (p406)

Luxurious Retreats

Opulence is hard won in the South Pacific. Everything needs to be imported, bug control and weeds need constant attention and a cyclone can wipe out years of work in minutes. But when it's done right, this luxury can't be bettered.

St Régis (French Polynesia) An exclusive bubble with casual elegance that lets the luxury sneak up on you (p389)

The Havannah (Vanuatu) Child-free bliss set in a magnificent, remote bay; dive in or dip in your private infinity pool (p487)

Vahine Private Island (French Polynesia) Intimate boutique resort with an outrageous setting that makes up for its relative simplicity (p383)

Explora (Easter Island) An eco-chic and gorgeously designed pad from which to watch the sun slink into the Pacific (p50)

Etu Moana (Cook Islands) Aitutaki's super-relaxed and understated yet downright plush hideaway (p224)

If you like... deep-sea fishing, head to the Great Astrolabe Reef off Kadavu for phenomenal poppering and jigging (p133)

Traditional Dance & Music

From wood-drum percussion to ukuleles and panpipes, music is a huge part of Pacific-island cultures. Each island group also has its own form of dance, from the warp-speed hips of Tahiti to the slow sway of Fiji.

Heiva (French Polynesia)
Expect unbelievably fast hips, outrageous costumes, complex percussion and soothing harmonies at the song-and-dance competitions of this July festival (p422)

Traditional Dance Show (Easter Island) Authentic shows with brilliant costumes are performed regularly at hotels (p53)

Island Nights (Cook Islands) Traditional evening show with everything from song and dance to fire juggling and acrobatics – plus a grand meal (p220)

Fiafia (Samoa) Fire dancing, traditional 'slap' dancing, singing and a Samoan-sized buffet (p287)

ROM Dance (Vanuatu) Watch feet pounding the dirt in this hypnotic, vibrant dance involving magic and custom (p503)

Tongan Fire Dance (Tonga) Enthusiastically performed in the Hina Cave at Oholei Beach on Tongatapu (p441)

Island Cuisine

Traditional island food is a hearty feast of roots and tubers alongside fish and meat, often swimming in a coconut milk concoction. The best meals are cooked in earth ovens. International flair comes via Indian, Chinese, French and New Zealand influences.

Sunday Lunch (Samoa) Sundays in Samoa are devoted to eating massive feasts with the family – make friends and you may get invited (p278)

Indian curries (Fiji) Delicious curry and vegie dishes are ubiquitous in this ethnically diverse island nation (p60)

Vaiete Square Roulottes (French Polynesia) The *roulotte* (mobile food van) capital of the country has everything from raw fish to *steak frites* in an outdoor setting (p354)

Plantation Dining Experience (Cook Islands) The best of Rarotonga's local and organic flavours (p217)

Île des Pins (New Caledonia) Lobster in a rustic, breezy setting by the bay (p181)

Mangoes Restaurant (Vanuatu) Local ingredients, from coconut crab to Santo beef (p483)

Sea Kayaking

'Take it slow' is a South Pacific–wide motto and what better way to heed the advice than by slipping into a sea kayak. Explore dreamy deserted islands where the only sounds are rippling water and wind through the palms.

Aitutaki Lagoon (Cook Islands) Sea kayak to your own deserted *motu* (island) (p222)

Lifou (New Caledonia) Guests can grab a free kayak at Hotel Drehu Village, Wé's main resort, and take on the local waves (p177)

Vava'u & Ha'apai Groups (Tonga) Hire the experts at Friendly Island Kayaks Paddle to explore these pristine waters (p454)

Kadavu (Fiji) Take a several-day tour around this wild and almost road-free island (p133)

'Upolu (Samoa) Paddle with a guide through aqua waters to flax-coloured beaches (p257)

Pago Pago Harbour (American Samoa) Rent a kayak for a DIY cruise around this magnificent harbour (p301)

month by month

February

It's hot and it might be raining, so duck inside to see a sure-to-impress documentary or indulge in some celebrations. The rest of us will be cooling off in the water.

✦ Tapati Rapa Nui
For two weeks at the beginning of February, Easter Island holds its spectacular cultural celebration that includes music, dance and sport. The highlights are the banana-tree sled races (Haka Pei) and bareback horse racing.

✦ Chinese New Year
The date changes each year (it's based on the Chinese lunar calendar) but the two-week-long celebrations on islands that have a Chinese community can include dancing, martial-arts displays and fireworks. Celebrations are biggest in Tahiti.

✦ Fifo Pacific International Documentary Film Festival
In early February comes this fantastic festival in Tahiti, with screenings (many in English) of the year's best Pacific documentary films from Australia to Hawai'i. You can also catch the films at other times of the year with 'Travelling Fifo' (http://en.fifo-tahiti.com) around the islands.

April

Easing out of the cyclone season, April can be hit or miss as far as weather is concerned but it's a good time to avoid travel crowds.

✦ Dancer of the Year
Dance displays are held throughout April in the Cook Islands, culminating in the hotly debated Dancer of the Year Competition. There are events for all ages from juniors to 'Golden Oldies'.

✦ Naghol
From April to July, awesome land-diving rituals are held on Pentecost in Vanuatu to ensure a plentiful yam harvest. A precursor to bungee jumping, in land diving the men jump from heights of up to 30m and their heads must touch the ground (for more information, see p515).

May

The southeast trade winds start to pick up this month, making it the ideal time to windsurf, kite surf or island-hop by sailboat. They also provide all-natural air-conditioning.

✦ Stag & Prawn Festival
This festival attracts thousands of visitors to the country town of Broussard, New Caledonia. Expect sausage-eating, shrimp-peeling and stag-calling competitions, canine demonstrations, traditional and modern singing and dancing, and a 'Miss' competition.

June

Many islanders are gearing up for festival month and you may hear the thumping of drums coming from gymnasiums and see young people practising sport or dance.

✦ Miss Tahiti
Tahiti has been known for its beautiful

vahine (women) for centuries and these stunning contestants are the crème de la crème. But the winner must have more than great looks – she must exemplify the Polynesian traditions this flashy show highlights. It's a cultural treat.

Pacific Nations Cup

Fiji, Tonga and Samoa join New Zealand's Junior All Blacks, Japan and sometimes the Australia A team, in play-offs for this annual rugby prize. The games are held from May to late June in venues of all the participating countries (www.irb.com/pacificnationscup).

July

This is festival month on many islands, highlighted by sports competitions, beauty pageants, traditional song and dance and lots of partying. You can also expect booked-up hotels – reserve early.

Festival of Pacific Arts

This vibrant festival (http://pacartsas.com) showcases traditional arts from around the Pacific and is held every four years in a different country. The next festival will be held in Guam in 2016.

Heiva I Tahiti

Held in Pape'ete, French Polynesia's most important festival lasts an entire month and is so impressive it's almost worth timing your trip around it. The best dancers and singers perform, and there are parades and traditional sports competitions.

Bula Festival

One of Fiji's biggest and longest-running festivals – held in Nadi – with rides, music, cultural shows and the crowning of 'Miss Bula'. Contestants are sponsored by companies to raise funds for charitable organisations.

Miss Galaxy Pageant

This international *fakaleiti* (transvestite) beauty pageant held in Nuku'alofa, Tonga, is riotous fun and always sells out. The three-night celebration is usually kicked off with a float parade.

Heilala Festival

Music from hip hop to church bands plays on block-party stages, plus modern and traditional dance, talent shows, parades and a beauty pageant mark Tonga's biggest festival. The date falls around the deceased King Taufa'ahau Tupou IV's birthday.

Independence Day

The Solomon Islands celebrate their independence from Great Britain with traditional dance performances, a parade organised by the police band, sports and lots of family gatherings. The biggest events take place in Honiara.

August

The July festivities spill over into August with music festivals and cultural happenings. This is the height of the tourist season so you'll enjoy it all with plenty of company.

Tahiti Billabong Pro

This is one of the biggest events (www.billabongpro.com) in surfing because the wave at Teahupoo is as beautiful as it is scary. Including the trials, the event spans about a month – you can take a boat ride to watch surfers boldly ride the tube.

Hindu Fire Walking

Indo-Fijian devotees pierce their tongues, cheeks and bodies with skewers and smear their faces with yellow turmeric before dancing 3km to a temple where they walk over beds of hot embers. This is the culmination of a 10-day ascetic period meant to cleanse before the acts of devotion and self-sacrifice.

Te Maeva Nui

Originally called the Constitution Celebrations, this festival's new name translates to 'The Most Important Celebration'. Marking the Cook Islands' self-rule from New Zealand, festivities include traditional song and dance, a parade, arts and sporting events.

Live en Août

New Caledonia's biggest music festival takes local acts and those from around the world to the stage in venues in and around Noumea. Expect everything from ska to jazz. The festival lasts two weeks.

September

September can be a lovely time to visit the South Pacific. School holidays are over and the cyclone season has yet to start.

Pacific Games
In September 2015 Port Moresby (Papua New Guinea) will host the Pacific Games, held every four years. Twenty-two Pacific nations take part in 32 sporting events – about 4000 athletes in all.

Teuila Festival
Samoa's capital Apia reels in the tourists with canoe races, food and craft stalls, traditional dancing and a beauty pageant.

October
You never know what weather you'll encounter in October. While it's the official beginning of the cyclone season they're rare at this time and temperatures aren't too high.

Rise of Palolo
It's not everywhere you get to celebrate worms rising at midnight (see p271). The celebrations are observed in Samoa and Fiji in October or November, seven days after the full moon.

Pacific Island Sevens Tournaments
Held annually in the Cook Islands, Fiji and Samoa, these games feature as much dance and celebration as they do rugby (www.oceaniarugby.com).

Hawaiki Nui Canoe Race
French Polynesia's major sporting event of the year, this is a three-day *pirogue* (canoe) race from Huahine to Ra'iatea, Taha'a and Bora Bora. Expect lots of people and ringside events on the beaches, and a fun ambience.

November
Pessimists call this the beginning of the rainy season but Pacific Islanders know it as the beginning of the season of abundance. The fishing is great and most fruits start to come in season.

Fest'Napuan
This annual four-day music festival in Port Vila, Vanuatu, showcases Pacific contemporary and traditional music (www.vanuatuculture.org).

Vaka Eiva
Held in Rarotonga, Vaka Eiva is the Cooks' biggest sporting event. Outrigger-canoe races are the feature of this week-long festival.

Diwali (Festival of Lights)
Hindus worship Lakshmi (the goddess of wealth and prosperity); houses are decorated and business is settled. Candles and lanterns are set on doorsteps to light the way for the goddess. Held in late October or early to mid-November in Fiji.

South Pacific World Music Festival
Acclaimed Fijian and international musicians treat Savusavu to five days of global harmony. Held in late November.

December
Melanesians and Polynesians are fervent about celebrating Christmas and, as in many places in the world, this month is marked by heavy shopping and lots of churchgoing.

Marquesas Arts Festival
This outrageously visceral arts festival celebrating Marquesan art and identity is held every four years, the next in 2015. Fortunately, there are usually 'mini' festivals held in between the major events – the next is scheduled for December 2013.

itineraries

Whether you've got six days or 60, these itineraries provide a starting point for the trip of a lifetime. Want more inspiration? Head online to lonelyplanet. com/thorntree to chat with other travellers.

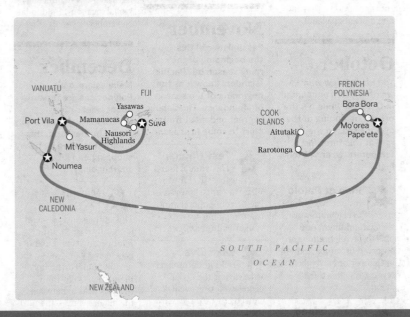

Two Months
Le Grande Tour

> Fly to Fiji, the South Pacific's biggest hub and catch a boat to the **Yasawas** or **Mamanucas** where countless islets offer fantastic digs and brilliant beaches. Back on Viti Levu, take a bus to the **Nausori Highlands** to experience traditional Fiji and then go onto **Suva**, where shopping malls and markets coexist in a distinctly Pacific style.
>
> Fly to Vanuatu to join a kava session in a *nakamal* (men's clubhouse) around **Port Vila** and see **Mt Yasur** glow in the dark on a night visit to one of the world's most accessible volcanoes. Your next stop will be **Noumea**, fronting the world's second largest coral reef lagoon. Pacific cultures are showcased at the wonderful Tjibaou Cultural Centre and don't miss an outrigger canoe *(pirogue)* trip around Île des Pins.
>
> Keep saying *bonjour* for French Polynesia. Start with some hip-shaking nightlife in **Pape'ete**. Take the ferry to **Mo'orea** for hiking, snorkelling with stingrays and dolphin watching or fly to **Bora Bora** to live it up with the jet-setters in an over-the-water bungalow.
>
> Finish your trip with the fun nightlife and restaurants on **Rarotonga** and unwind by **Aitutaki's** idyllic lagoon.

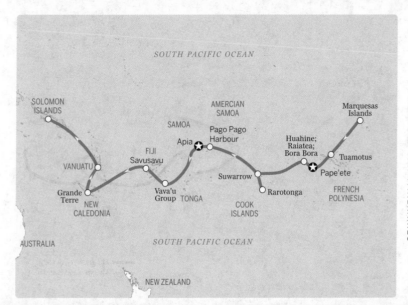

Six Months
Sailing The South Pacific

> The southeast trade wind makes this trip fairly predictable if sailed westward outside the December-to-March cyclone season. In fact the route is considered so easy by cruising standards that it's been dubbed the 'coconut milk run'. The **Marquesas Islands** are the targets after a stop at the Galapagos Islands or Hawai'i.

After the majestic peaks of the Marquesas where you can hopefully fill the coffers with fruit, the barren but beautiful **Tuamotus**, the largest group of atolls in the world, are next. This is the time to put down your daiquiri and pay attention – this is known as the Dangerous Archipelago and it has wrecks on the reefs to prove it.

Pape'ete in Tahiti becomes the natural hub to switch crew, stock up on Hinano beer and get a fix of civilisation. Cruising the Society Islands from here to the lagoons of **Huahine**, **Raiatea** and **Bora Bora** is a highlight, but an expensive one. Leaving Bora Bora, drop in on **Suwarrow** before deciding on **Samoa**, **Rarotonga** or **Tonga**.

Rarotonga is the closest stop from French Polynesia and the sailors who do stop here often cite it as one of their favourite stops. **Pago Pago Harbor** in American Samoa is a good place to restock and run errands in scenic surrounds while **Apia** in nearby Samoa is less organised but has a bit more soul. The jewel-like islands of the **Vava'u Group** in Tonga are hard to pass up.

Depending on your choice of hiding place during the cyclone season (many yachts head to New Zealand), you could extend the trip by exploring **Fiji**, including the favourite yachty anchorages at **Savusavu**, or casting off for French Melanesia and the never-ending lagoon around **Grande Terre** in New Caledonia. **Vanuatu** gets you to wilder terrain, including volcanoes and the culture that invented bungee jumping, which is only mild preparation for the numerous adventurous islands of the **Solomon Islands**.

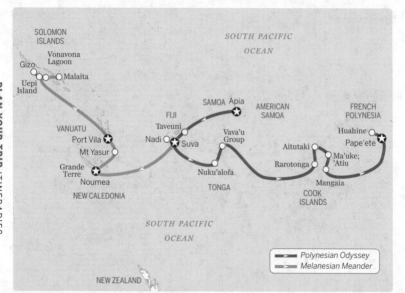

SOLOMON ISLANDS
Vonavona Lagoon
Gizo
Malaita
Uepi Island

SOUTH PACIFIC OCEAN

SAMOA Apia
AMERICAN SAMOA
FRENCH POLYNESIA

VANUATU
Port Vila
Mt Yasur
Grande Terre
Noumea
NEW CALEDONIA

FIJI
Taveuni
Nadi Suva
Vava'u Group
Nuku'alofa
TONGA

Huahine
Pape'ete
Aitutaki
Rarotonga
Ma'uke; 'Atiu
Mangaia
COOK ISLANDS

SOUTH PACIFIC OCEAN

NEW ZEALAND

Polynesian Odyssey
Melanesian Meander

One Month
Melanesian Meander

Start in **Nadi** and fly to **Taveuni** for Fiji's best hiking along the coast at Lavena then dive walls of willowing soft corals at the Rainbow Reef. Go back to Viti Levu via cosmopolitan **Suva** and chow down at an Indo-Fijian curry house.

Next fly to New Caledonia's capital **Noumea**, which blends Melanesia with French chic. Classy restaurants and boutique shopping aside, don't miss exploring the vast main island, **Grande Terre**, with its mangroves, silent forests and barren vistas.

Fly to Vanuatu's colourful **Port Vila** with its rich English and French colonial history. Swim in the pools of Mele-Maat Cascades and have a few shells of kava before trying some of Port Vila's restaurants and nightlife. Go to see the active **Mt Yasur** volcano and take the two-day trek across Malekula's Dog's Head, past the cannibal site, caves and traditional villages. On to Pentecost where yam farmers invented bungee jumping. Then Espiritu Santo for world-class diving.

Ride a boat through the Solomon Islands' stunning **Vonavona Lagoon**, snorkel or dive off **Uepi Island** and chill out in **Gizo**. Travel to **Malaita** where people summon sharks and live on artificial islands.

One Month
Polynesian Odyssey

Start in **Apia**, **Samoa**, to visit the dreamy Robert Louis Stevenson Museum before taking the bus or a car around 'Upolu and spend at least one night on the beach in a traditional *fale*. Take the ferry to Savai'i to visit underground cave tunnels, lava fields and glowing white beaches before trying to find the forest-engulfed and forgotten Pulemelei Mound, Polynesia's largest ancient monument.

Fly to **Nuku'alofa** in the Kingdom of Tonga, via **Fiji**. See the Royal Palace (not open to commoners) on the way to lively Talamahu Market. Mu'a (Lapaha) is rich in archaeological ruins. Head to the Ha'apai Group for beachside living in a thatched *fale* or the **Vava'u Group** for active adventures like sea kayaking, surfing, caving and cycling.

You'll also have to reach the Cook Islands' capital **Rarotonga** via Fiji. Once in the Cooks, walk the cross-island track and snorkel at sublime Muri Beach. Catch a plane to **Aitutaki** to see its exquisite lagoon. Explore the caves of the *makatea* islands of **'Atiu**, **Mangaia** and **Ma'uke**.

Fly to **Pape'ete**, the chic capital of the French Pacific, and lastly squeeze in a visit to sleepy **Huahine** and the Polynesian spiritual capital of Raiatea.

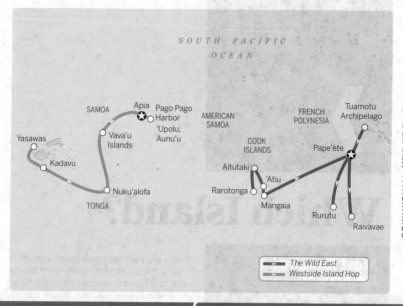

Westside Island Hop

It's ridiculously easy to island hop the western central region of the South Pacific from Australia or New Zealand. Start with a week to 10 days in Fiji exploring the blissful small islands and beaches of the **Yasawas** before heading off the beaten path a few days to dive, hike and relax in an eco-responsible resort on **Kadavu**.

Fly to Tonga for the next five days to a week, with a short stop in **Nuku'alofa** before heading for the **Vava'u Islands** for whale watching (between June and November) and kayaking to deserted beaches.

Spend the final week or more in the Samoas, driving around **'Upolu** for a few days to find empty white-sand beaches and enjoying the friendly bustle of **Apia**. Spend the last two to three days around the glorious **Pago Pago Harbor** in American Samoa, where tall mountains plunge to a mix of colonial architecture and fishing industry humbleness. While here, make sure to visit the spectacularly placed traditional villages of remote north bays of the island as well as walking around the relaxing and near car-free isle of **Aunu'u**.

The Wild East

This is an island galaxy far, far away, even from the rest of the South Pacific so while you're here, make the most of it. First fly to **Rarotonga** to swim in the dreamy lagoon and hike the island's many inland trails. Take a side trip either to kayak the nooks and crannies of **Aitutaki's** turquoise lagoon, go birdwatching on **'Atiu** or visit the mysterious limestone burial caves on **Mangaia**.

Take the short Air Tahiti flight to **Pape'ete** and quickly fly out to either the **Tuamotu Archipelago** for diving, snorkelling and *la vida* coral atoll or to the Austral Islands: **Rurutu** for whale watching and cave exploration or **Raivavae** for traditional island culture, hiking and scenery to rival Bora Bora's.

If you're not ready for the adventure to end yet, continue your journey eastward with a long flight to **Easter Island**.

Which Island?

Most Romantic Resorts

Vahine Island (French Polynesia)
Navutu Stars (Fiji)
Etu Moana (Cook Islands)
The Havannah (Vanuatu)
L'escapade Island Resort (New Caledonia)

Best for Backpackers

Wayalailai EcoHaven Resort (Fiji)
Namu'a Island Beach Fales (Samoa)
Chez Guynette (French Polynesia)
Traveller's Budget Motel (Vanuatu)
Aremango Guesthouse (Rarotonga)
Hideaway (Tonga)

Top Eco-Resorts

'Eua'iki Island Eco-Resort (Tonga)
Tetepare Descendants' Association (Solomon Islands)
Papageno Eco-Resort (Fiji)
Bokissa Eco Island Resort (Vanuatu)
Jean-Michel Cousteau Fiji Islands Resort (Fiji)

Dreamiest Locations

Erakor Island Resort (Vanuatu)
Aitutaki Lagoon Resort (Cook Islands)
Le Meridien Île des Pins (New Caledonia)
Virgin Cove (Samoa)

From a distance, the South Pacific appears to be a big string of similar palm-covered islands surrounded by blue water. In reality this is one of the world's most vast and diverse regions. While the postcards look strikingly similar, these nations have dramatically different cultures, landscapes and infrastructure. Doing a little homework can ensure you find exactly the type of island bliss you're looking for.

Resort Experience

Despite the stereotype, luxe resorts take up only a fraction of the South Pacific's accommodation. International chains have moved into tourist hot spots like Fiji, French Polynesia and Vanuatu, but you'll also find charming boutique resorts that blend local style and warmth with comfort and opulence.

Resorts: Which Island?

Cook Islands A good mix of international standards and boutique charm. Families are well catered for and there's plenty of activities and fun nightlife.

Easter Island This island has a handful of surprisingly posh choices – although few have pools or beaches and all are geared towards getting out to see the sights more than lounging on site.

Fiji Got kids? Fiji is the best family-resort destination in the region. It also caters well to active honeymooners and value seekers. Friendly service has been perfected.

New Caledonia On par with Tahiti for price, but with a modern Melanesian twist, resorts here

cater less to the masses and usually offer sublime lagoon-front locations.

Samoa There's nothing too luxurious here but the beaches are so stunning and the atmosphere so sweet and authentic that stress will ooze out of you with or without the swanky spa.

Solomon Islands Honiara and Western Province are the only places with real resorts. The best, found at the latter, are diving and ecology oriented. Think: total disconnection from the world.

Tahiti & French Polynesia If you are ever going to pamper yourself silly, this is the place to do it. Many top hotels are on isolated *motu* (islets).

Tonga Head out to the Ha'apai or Vava'u Groups for a scant number of eclectic, though not necessarily fancy, resorts in remote island settings. Many have an eco bent and offer whale watching.

Vanuatu Port Vila is swarming with sumptuous resorts to suit every style. Beyond the capital, Espiritu Santo has some decadent choices well placed for diving, and Tanna has a fun resort scene geared for climbs up Mt Yasur.

Resorts: What to Expect

You can expect restaurants, bars and a swimming pool at bigger places, a shop or two and an activities desk. While there are a number of room-block-style resorts, most feature individual bungalows (*fale, fare, bure* etc, depending on the local lingo) and super swanky places may have over-water bungalows (particularly in French Polynesia).

You'll be met at the airport and transferred to your resort by speedboat, aeroplane or van. From registration onwards you'll be given the choice to partake in organised activities or to chill and explore the island on your own.

Resort Food & Drink

All resorts have at least one restaurant, serving a mix of Western, Polynesian or Melanesian, Asian and fusion specialities and usually with an international chef. The bar will be stocked and, in the French territories, Vanuatu, Samoa and Fiji, a good wine selection

may be available. Some bigger hotels put on a traditional dance performance and buffet a few times a week. Breakfast is often a buffet, other meals á la carte, with simple options like burgers and sandwiches at lunch.

Local Experience

The South Pacific has a wide range of sleeping options, from camping upwards. If you want to travel independently and experience the culture at ground level, go local and you won't be sorry. Think ahead in terms of money when staying at smaller, family-owned places, especially on remote islands, as many do not take credit cards.

Local: Which Island?

Each country has its own accommodation style, from the humble family *pensions* of Tahiti and New Caledonia to the open traditional *fale* of Samoa. Yet it's not all budget: small boutique hotels and guesthouses are increasingly popular. If you're up for an adventure, foregoing resorts allows you to explore remote and fascinating islands.

Cook Islands On Rarotonga and Aitutaki stay at laid-back backpackers – complete with activities aplenty – or in good-value, self-contained holiday rentals. On the Cooks' smaller outer islands, go local at a family-run homestay.

Easter Island Easter Island has about 90 places to stay but *hostales* and *residenciales* (homestays) are the bulk of what's on offer. Usually small and social, these range from a few bare rooms in someone's house to simple, comfortable bungalows.

Fiji You can find almost anything from bare-bones backpackers, to cultural-connection homestays and gorgeously designed, upscale beach bungalows. There's a young party scene

in tourist hot spots, while things get quieter but pleasantly chummy on less-visited islands like Kadavu and Taveuni.

New Caledonia Even basic, dirt-cheap accommodation in New Caledonia comes with power points, lights, pristine cotton sheets and, often, gardens, restaurants and pools. Campsites take up some of the best beachy spots on the islands.

Samoa Samoa's signature accommodation is the beach *fale*, an elongated octagonal hut on stilts with no walls but coconut-thatch louvres that can be let down or drawn up depending on how much privacy or ventilation you want.

Solomon Islands Resthouses and hostels are inexpensive, have shared bathrooms and most patrons are local; 'lodges', mostly in Marovo, are simple but authentic and have loads of character. Some villages have a leafhouse (a bungalow made with natural materials and a thatched roof) set aside for visitors.

Tahiti & French Polynesia Family *pensions* or hotel-like *fare d'hôte* are found everywhere and are often the only choice on remote islands. These range from a hard bed in someone's back room with shared cold-water bathroom to stylish but homey boutique hotels.

Tonga Has a wide variety of sleeping options. For a cultural experience, stay at Tongan-run places, such as Port Wine Guest House in Vava'u, Hideaway on 'Eua, or Winnie's Guest House in Nuku'alofa.

Vanuatu Around 90% of accommodation here is simple, with thin foam mattresses adding some comfort. You'll choose between guesthouses or bungalows – the former usually being rooms in a concrete building and the latter more atmospheric thatched houses. Bathrooms are usually separate and food is served in another hut.

HOLIDAY RENTALS

Holiday rentals (private homes or rooms rented by an individual) are becoming more popular in the South Pacific, particularly in Fiji. These often self-catering options can be fun and economical for families or groups that plan on staying in one place for more than a night or two. We've listed our favourites under the Sleeping headings in this book. To search further, good sites include: www.homeaway.com, www.vrbo.com and www.airbnb.com.

Local: What to Expect

Some small lodgings on main islands may have air-con; many will be fan cooled and provide mosquito nets and coils; few have pools. All but the most rudimentary should have towels and linen, and most can provide an airport transfer if you arrange it in advance.

On the main islands you'll find everything from simple guesthouses to boutique hotels and most offer a decent level of comfort. On remote islands, however, you may encounter faulty plumbing, cold showers, unreliable electricity and a rustic set up. If you need wi-fi or internet, check in advance to make sure your place will have it.

Local Food & Drink

Many options on outer islands may offer (and sometimes insist on) half board, which usually means breakfast and dinner with other guests. Full board includes all meals. In many cases, the food is delicious and special needs are catered for where possible.

Activities

Resorts, upscale boutique places and even hardcore budget lodges usually have activities available for their guests or work with independent operators they know and trust.

Millions of square kilometres of warm tropical water, pristine lagoons and long stretches of beach are the most obvious attraction and almost everyone comes here to get wet. But there's more to the Pacific than watery pursuits. Opportunities abound for hiking, cycling, horse riding, bird and whale watching, as well as visiting archaeological or sacred sites and WWII relics. Caving is big in the Cook Islands (p244) and Tonga (p459).

Diving Many resorts have dive centres and local accommodation can usually hook you up with diving if it's available on the island. In fact, diving is such a big deal we've devoted a whole chapter to it. See p31 for details.

Going to Sunday Service The Pacific is a devoutly Christian region and Sunday is solemnly observed as a day of rest – some activities in some parts might be regarded as disrespectful. But most areas that are accustomed to the ways of tourists are pretty relaxed about their pursuits whatever day it happens to be. Attending a Sunday church service to listen to the beautiful singing is, for many, a highlight of their Pacific travels.

Fishing The South Pacific is a dream destination for anglers, with great sport fishing and excellent

» (above) Snorkelling past corals and seashells, Tonga
» (left) L'escapade Island Resort (p155), Noumea, New Caledonia

big-game fishing. Common catches include yellowfin and skipjack tuna, wahoo, barracuda, sailfish, and blue, black and striped marlin. For more information, see the following chapters: Fiji (p133), New Caledonia (p169), Rarotonga & Cook Islands (p244), Samoa (p289), Tonga (p453) and Vanuatu (p522).

Hiking The higher Pacific islands offer terrific opportunities to hike magnificent forested interiors, waterfalls, lava-formed coastal trails, archaeological sites and even live volcanoes. Some of the walks mentioned in this guide require the services of a local guide – resorts and guesthouses will know who they are. Since many tracks cross land under customary ownership, you may need permission or possibly have to pay a small fee. Countries that offer substantial hiking are Fiji (p140), French Polynesia (p346), New Caledonia (p190), Samoa (p289), Tonga (p430) and the Cook Islands (p196). Walking in the heat has the potential to be a truly miserable or even dangerous experience. Take sun protection, insect repellent and plenty of water.

Island & Lagoon Tours Buses, private cars or 4WDs may take you around to see the sights. More often than not though, the real adventure is on the water and boats (posh catamarans, ferries or old outboard skiffs) that tour the lagoons can whisk you away to deserted beaches of unimaginable beauty – plus you'll often get a picnic.

Sailing For information about taking your own yacht into the Pacific or getting a berth on someone else's, see p586. All Pacific countries have yacht clubs and many people charter yachts in French Polynesia (p346), with or without a crew.

Snorkelling Snorkellers are well-catered for via boat trips and excursions but it's a good idea to bring your own gear since rental equipment may be in poor shape. Some of the best spots include Somosomo Strait (p133) and Great Astrolabe Reef (p133) in Fiji, Motu Nui (p47) in Easter Island, the Loyalty Islands (p172) and Île aux Canards (p150) in New Caledonia, Tikehau (p403) and Bora Bora (p384) in French Polynesia, and Rarotonga's lagoon (p210) in the Cooks. Perhaps the best of the lot is off Uepi Island (p328) in the Solomons' Marovo Lagoon, where reef sharks, giant clams, fish and corals are dizzying in their abundance.

Spas The spa craze hasn't hit the South Pacific as much as you might suspect. Internationally owned and larger resorts will often have dedicated spas offering massage and a menu of exotic treatments but these are touted as perks more than a central aspect of what's on offer. Some smaller boutique resorts may also have spas, some with unique and creative offerings but this is an exception rather

than the rule. Local business-targeted, service-oriented day spas in island capitals can be less expensive than those geared towards tourists.

Surfing Polynesians invented surfing and surfers come in droves to French Polynesia (p366), which hosts the Billabong Tahiti Pro (www.aspworldtour.com) at Teahupoo. Fiji (p140), too, is popular with surfers. However, the uncrowded waves are to be found in the Solomon Islands (p343), Samoa (p290), the Cooks Islands (p196), Vanuatu (p493) and Tonga (p442). Surfers need to be intermediate at least, and should seek local advice before heading out. Since waves break outside lagoon reefs the paddle out can be long and reefs are unforgiving if you get that take-off wrong. Few islands have surfboards for sale, so surfers must come equipped.

Water Sports Most resorts have a water sports centre (check before booking). These vary enormously – some offer a basic array of canoes and windsurfing, while others run the gauntlet from waterskiing to kite surfing and wakeboarding. Sea kayaking is popular, and tours are offered in a handful of countries, including Fiji (p140), Tonga (p454) and Samoa (p290). Kite surfers have discovered the wonders of Aitutaki's superb lagoon in the Cook Islands (see p222) and French Polynesia, particularly Mo'orea (p363).

Wildlife Watching Migrating humpback whales spend much of the second half of the year in Pacific waters, and several countries, including New Caledonia (p190), the Cook Islands (p209) and Rurutu (p418) in French Polynesia, offer excellent opportunities to view them. Tonga offers great whale-watching experiences (p454), as well as opportunities for even closer experiences – see the boxed text on p452. Dive and tour centres on many islands offer dolphin and whale watching – some of these places are affiliated with resorts. There are also plenty of independent whale, dolphin, turtle-spotting, swimming-with-stingrays and birdwatching tours depending on the area.

Planning & Choosing

Outside high season (June through August and mid-December through mid-January) you could arrive just about anywhere in the South Pacific without any idea of where you're going or what you're doing and have an amazing trip. During the seasonal rush, the better places will be booked out so it's wise to plan in advance. For transport and tour options, see the transport chapter p582.

RESPONSIBLE DIVING

The Pacific islands and atolls are ecologically vulnerable. By following these guidelines while diving, you can help preserve the ecology and beauty of the reefs:

» Encourage dive operators in their efforts to establish permanent moorings at appropriate dive sites.

» Practise and maintain proper buoyancy control.

» Avoid touching living marine organisms with your body or equipment.

» Take great care in underwater caves, as your air bubbles can damage fragile organisms.

» Minimise your disturbance of marine animals.

» Take home all your rubbish and any litter you may find as well.

» Never stand on corals, even if they look solid and robust.

45m and the *Aaron Ward* in 65m) and are accessible to experienced divers only. Visibility is not the strong point here; expect 10m to 15m on average. There are also awesome reef dives, such as Twin Tunnels, which features two chimneys that start on the top of a reef in about 12m. Another signature dive, Sandfly Passage, is an exhilarating wall drift dive. And there's Manta Passage, near Maravagi, one of the Solomons' best-kept secrets, with regular sightings of huge manta rays.

New Georgia

While Munda offers a good balance of wreck and reef dives, the hot spot is Marovo Lagoon. South Marovo rewards divers with a host of scenic sites off Kicha, Mbulo and Male Male Islands. North Marovo Lagoon has a vibrant assemblage of dramatic walls (on the ocean side), exhilarating passages and uncomplicated reef dives, all within close reach of Uepi Island Resort.

Another not-to-be-missed area is Ghizo Island, further west. Here again the diving is superlative, with a stunning mix of WWII wrecks (bookmark the *Toa Maru*, a virtually intact WWII Japanese freighter), superb offshore reefs and plummeting walls. The 2007

beat. Here, divers will feel like pioneers – literally. The only dive centre on 'Upolu offers divers the opportunity to name the sites they find.

Solomon Islands
Guadalcanal

Guadalcanal has a number of world-class sunken WWII vessels lying close to the shore. Most sites can be reached by car from Honiara. A few favourites include Bonegi I and II, about 12km west of Honiara. Bonegi I, a giant-sized Japanese merchant transport ship, also known as the *Hirokawa Maru,* lies in 3m of water descending to 55m, just a few fin strokes offshore. About 500m further west, the upper works of Bonegi II, or *Kinugawa Maru,* break the surface, a towel's throw from the beach.

Tulagi

Tulagi, in the Central Province, is another must for wreck enthusiasts. It has superb sunken WWII shipwrecks, including the monster-sized USS *Kanawha,* a 150m-long oil tanker that sits upright, and the USS *Aaron Ward,* a 106m-long US Navy destroyer noted for its arsenal of big guns. The catch? They lie deep, very deep (the *Kanawha* in

THE FIRST TIME

The South Pacific provides ideal and safe conditions for beginners, with its warm, crystalline waters and prolific marine life. Arrange an introductory dive with a dive centre to give you a feel for what it's like to swim underwater. It will begin on dry land, where the instructor will run through basic safety procedures and show you the equipment.

The dive itself takes place in a safe location and lasts between 20 and 40 minutes under the guidance of the instructor, who will hold your hand if need be and guide your movements at a depth of between 3m and 10m. Some centres start the instruction in waist-high water in a hotel swimming pool or on the beach.

There is no formal procedure, but you shouldn't dive if you have a medical condition such as acute ear, nose and throat problems, epilepsy or heart disease (such as infarction), if you have a cold or sinusitis, or if you are pregnant.

earthquake/tsunami did wreak havoc on a few charismatic sites, but overall it's not too bad in other places and corals are slowly recovering. Kennedy Island is a lovely spot to learn to dive, with a parade of reef fish on the sprawling reef.

Tonga

Whale watching is so popular in Tonga that it has stolen the show. While Tongan waters will never be mistaken for those of, say, French Polynesia, there's some excellent diving off Ha'apai and Vava'u. The reefs are peppered with caves that make for atmospheric playgrounds and eerie ambience. In some places, you'll feel as though you're swimming in an underwater cathedral. Off Vava'u, the wreck of the *Clan MacWilliam* adds a touch of variety.

Vanuatu

A few fin strokes from the shore, the legendary SS *President Coolidge* is trumpeted as the world's best wreck dive. The sheer proportions of this behemoth are overwhelming: resting on its side in 20m to 67m of water off Luganville (Santo), the *Coolidge* is 200m long and 25m wide. Amazingly, more than 50 years after its demise it's still in good shape. You'll see numerous fittings and artefacts, including weaponry, gas masks, trenching tools, trucks, rows of toilets, a porcelain statue (the 'Lady'), a pool, personal belongings abandoned by 5000 soldiers, and all the fixtures of a luxury cruise liner. A minimum of five dives is recommended to get a glimpse of the whole vessel. Although nearly all dives on the *Coolidge* are deep (more than 30m), it is suitable for novice divers. The only downside is that the *Coolidge* has overshadowed

other sites in Vanuatu, such as the *Tui Tewate* and the USS *Tucker*.

If you need a break from wrecks, sample some truly excellent reef dives off Santo. Cindy's Reef is a favourite, as is Tutuba Point, but we found Million Dollar Point much more eye-catching. Thousands of tonnes of military paraphernalia were discarded here by the US Navy when they left the country. Divers swim among the tangle of cranes, bulldozers, trucks and other construction hardware in less than 30m and finish their dive exploring a small shipwreck in the shallows.

And what about the diving in Efate? It can't compete with Santo, but we found Hat Island as well as Paul's Rock pretty appealing. The seascape is top notch, and you'll see a smorgasbord of reef fish. For experienced divers, the *Corsair – WWII Fighter Plane* rests in 30m of water near Pele Island.

Dive Centres

In most cases, the standards of diving facilities are high in the South Pacific.

» All dive centres are affiliated to internationally recognised certifying agencies (PADI, NAUI, CMAS, SSI).

» Dive centres welcome divers provided they can produce a certificate from an internationally recognised agency.

» They offer a range of services, such as introductory dives, Nitrox dives, night dives, exploratory dives and certification programs.

» In general, you can expect well-maintained equipment, well-equipped facilities and friendly, knowledgeable, English-speaking staff.

» Be aware that each dive centre has its own personality and style. Visit the place first to get the feel of the operation.

» Dive centres are open year-round. Most are land-based and many are attached to a hotel. They typically offer two to four dives a day.

» Diving in the South Pacific is expensive compared with most destinations in Asia, the Caribbean or the Red Sea; expect to pay US$100 for an introductory dive and US$110 for a single dive (without gear). Dive packages (eg five or 10 dives) are usually cheaper.

» Gear hire may or may not be included in the price of the dive, so bring your own equipment if you plan to dive a lot.

» Almost all dive centres accept credit cards.

LIVE-ABOARDS

For hardcore divers, there are also a few live-aboard dive boats operating out of various countries to access remote locations. Check operator websites for itineraries.

Here's a selection:

» **Aqua Polynésie** (www.aquatiki.com) Tuamotu Islands, French Polynesia

» **Bilikiki** (www.bilikiki.com) Solomon Islands

» **Nai'a** (www.naia.com.fj) Fiji

Travel with Children

Best Regions for Kids

Fiji
Plenty of family-oriented resorts on mellow beaches, two cultures to explore (Fijian and Indo-Fijian) and magnificent interior landscapes make Fiji our top pick for families.

Vanuatu
Happy people and adventures to volcanoes and cannibal caves may lure you away from the idyllic coasts. European-tinged Port Vila is one of the best capitals for families.

French Polynesia
High-end resorts offer luxury family vacations while locally run places, filled with Polynesian and French families, will ease you into the gentle culture.

Rarotonga & the Cook Islands
Beyond the beach, there's ice cream aplenty and entertainment, from glass-bottom-boat tours to 'The Coconut King' who climbs trees, conjures fire from twigs and more.

New Caledonia
An aquarium, a cultural centre and cool critters like fruit bats are great fun when you need a break from the sun and surf of the impressive lagoon.

South Pacific For Kids

Few regions in the world are as family friendly as the South Pacific. With endless sunshine, sandy beaches, swimming and snorkelling, there's plenty to keep kids active and interested. Family is profoundly important here and children are prized. Child-rearing is a communal responsibility – you might well find your toddler on the hip of a motherly eight-year-old or see older kids absorbed into games with local children.

Water Activities

Diving, Snorkelling & Swimming Toddlers will be happy on a soft beach with a hermit crab to hassle, and anywhere with a shallow, sandy bottom is great for learning to swim. Seasoned swimmers can cruise the lagoon in areas free of currents and boat traffic. Many dive centres offer 'Bubble Maker' courses for kids aged eight and up, while good swimmers over nine can enrol in Junior PADI Open Water courses. In some cases they can even get school credit for it (see www.padi.com).

Wildlife Watching Whale and dolphin watching will thrill kids but if it's rough out, the unpleasantness of seasickness may outweigh the excitement. Sea turtles and birdlife abound and, in the Solomon Islands and Vanuatu, there are saltwater crocodiles. Giant fruit bats (flying foxes) are found from the Cook Islands east; and the further east

WHAT TO PACK

All ages need sunscreen (expensive on many islands), insect repellent and rain gear.

Babies & Toddlers

☐ A folding pushchair is practical for most areas. A baby carrier is better for hiking or exploring archaeological sites.

☐ Portable change mat, handwash gel (baby-change facilities are rare)

☐ Nappies (diapers) are available but pricey

6–12 years

☐ Binoculars for young explorers to zoom in on wildlife, surfers etc

☐ A camera to inject fun into 'boring' grown-up sights and walks

☐ Field guides to flora and fauna

Teens

☐ Local language phrasebook

☐ Mask, snorkel and flippers

☐ *Mutiny on the Bounty* or region-specific novel

you head, the more interesting the reptilian life becomes.

Surfing & Boogie Boarding It can be hard to find rental boards on many islands but some hotels have them for guests. Boogie boards are often sold in local shops; if you can, buy one and make a local kid's year by leaving it with them when you leave. The best waves for kids will be beach breaks; reef-breaking monsters are only for advanced surfers.

Land Lubbers

Hiking & Adventure Over-eights will love tropical interiors, choc-a-block with waterfalls with icy pools, dark caves, lakes and – on Vanuatu, Tonga and American Samoa – active volcanoes (check conditions).

Archaeology These sites can be fun because there's open space, you can climb on almost anything and the surrounding jungles often hold discoveries like wild passionfruit.

Horse Riding & Cycling There are several places for trail riding in all the larger countries. The routes, through hilly regions and plantations, are geared to all ages. Bicycles

can be rented on most islands and traffic is light, but child-sized bicycles can be harder to find.

Eating Out

Kids can happily munch on fish and fruit, chicken and coconut. Most places have kid pleasers, such as hamburgers and rice dishes, on their menus, and local cuisine is often soft enough for children to try new foods, such as taro or breadfruit. Baby supplies are available in all but the most remote places and ice cream is frequently available.

Don't expect high chairs but do expect a welcoming atmosphere in most eateries. Don't be afraid to ask for assistance in finding certain foods or cooking facilities.

Teen-Dream Nightlife

It's normal for whole families to party together here; teens are welcome at any sort of local dance or show. Areas where there are discotheques, such as Pape'ete and Suva, swarm with high-schoolers. Be warned though, alcohol flows freely and it's a meat-market atmosphere.

Children's Highlights
Beach Yourself

» **Fiji** Swimming and water sports on Treasure Island

» **Fiji** Snorkelling just offshore in the Yasawas

» **Vanuatu** Playing on the sandy stretches of Erakor Island

Get Cultured

» **Easter Island** Larger-than-life archaeology

» **Vanuatu** Cultural shows at Ekasup Cultural Village

» **French Polynesia** Visiting the Musée De Tahiti Et Des Îles

Budding Naturalists

» **Vanuatu** Critter Encounters at Secret Garden

» **Fiji** Sliding down rock chutes at Waitavala Water Slide

» **French Polynesia** Whale and dolphin watching in Mo'orea

Hotels & Discounts

Some hotels and resorts have no-children policies (especially under 12s) but others let kids stay for free – ask when booking. Some tours and activities are discounted for kids.

countries at a glance

It would take a lifetime to visit all of the vast South Pacific so chances are you'll have to pick and choose. Most countries have regions that are ideal for families, romance, diving and culture so the trick is to see what else sparks your fancy. Like history? Try Easter Island or the Marquesas Islands of French Polynesia. Want to swim with whales? Head to Tonga or French Polynesia. Vegetarians and spicy food lovers will enjoy Fiji while meat eaters will revel in the South American beef on Easter Island. Another surprise is that not all islands are loaded with beaches. Sand loungers should beeline for Samoa, New Caledonia, Tonga and Vanuatu.

Easter Island

History ✓✓✓
Outdoors ✓✓
Scenery ✓✓

Open-Air Museum
Easter Island is a mind-boggling open-air museum, with a wealth of pre-European archaeological remains, all shrouded with a palpable historical aura.

Outdoor Adventures
Outdoorsy types will be in seventh heaven, with hiking, diving, cycling, snorkelling and horse riding widely available.

Dramatic Landscapes
Hold on to your hat and lift your jaw off the floor as you stand on the edge of Ranu Kau, a lake-filled crater, or walk across the ruggedly beautiful Península Poike.

p44

Fiji

Diving ✓✓✓
Beaches ✓✓
Culture ✓✓✓

Dive-vana
Fiji's underwater landscapes wave with soft corals. More thrills come from manta ray, shark and turtle encounters, schools of barracudas, jacks and much more.

Slim & Sexy
Think svelte. There aren't many wide stretches of sand but the skinny beaches on offer are white, soft and lead into blue water bliss.

Kava to Curry
If the kava-offering, fire-dancing and friendly Fijian culture isn't enough for you, get into Indo-Fijian culture by visiting Hindu temples, eating delicious curries or catching a fire-walking ceremony.

p60

New Caledonia

Diving ✓✓
Beaches ✓✓
Food ✓✓

Endless Reef
With dive operators ready and willing to take you under on most of its islands, there are plenty of opportunities to explore its World Heritage–listed reef.

Off the Beachy Path
It's not just white-sand beaches leading to sky-blue waters that impress, it's natural aquariums, blue holes and just-off-the-beach coral gardens that make getting wet a joy here.

Bon Appétit
The French influence has rubbed off in New Caledonia; bakeries bake amazing goodies in Noumea, while even the simplest meal has a flavour you're unlikely to forget. Fresh, local, French: all keys to the food in New Caledonia.

p145

Rarotonga & The Cook Islands

Scenery ✓✓✓
Food ✓✓✓
History ✓✓

Mountains to the Sea
Explore the mountainous interior before discovering your own slice of Pacific perfection, sea kayaking Aitutaki's stunning lagoon. On isolated 'Atiu, Ma'uke and Mangaia, rugged sea cliffs conceal impossibly compact beaches.

Culinary Sophistication
Be surprised by Rarotonga's dining scene. There's an emphasis on all things organic and traditionally grown, and a highlight is dining in a restored colonial plantation house.

Ancient Polynesia
Discover the spiritual and historical significance of Avana harbour – departure point for the 14th-century Great Migration to New Zealand. On Mangaia and 'Atiu, burial caves are equally fascinating.

p196

Samoa

Beaches ✓✓✓
Hiking ✓✓
Culture ✓✓✓

Beaches at Every Turn
Beaches here offer spectacular variety. Choose from wide, white beauties that tumble into aqua lagoons to pockets of heaven between contrasting black lava formations.

Journey to the Centre of the Earth
Hike to spectacular waterfalls, along lava-shaped coasts and amble the lush grounds of Robert Louis Stevenson's villa. Or head downwards, via extensive lava tubes that gush with subterranean rivers.

The Heart of Polynesia
Independent and proud of it, most Samoans live the old way, in villages with meeting-houses, chiefs and strict customs. They'll invite you in to discover this authentic warmth too.

p250

American Samoa

Hiking ✓✓✓
Scenery ✓✓✓
Culture ✓✓

National Park & Beyond
National parks are rare in the South Pacific but the National Park of American Samoa covers a huge swath of the country. There are maintained trails here, from short nature walks to all-day adventures from mountain to sea.

Dreamy Silhouette
Sky-piercing peaks look more like a Disney ideal of paradise than reality. Surround this with lava-formed coves, blue water and ribbons of sparkling cream-coloured beach.

Village Life
Get out of Pago Pago and around the airport and American Samoa becomes ruled by church bells, village customs and welcoming smiles. All in sublime settings of course.

p295

Solomon Islands

Diving ✓✓✓
Adventure ✓✓✓
History ✓✓

Wreck Diving
The country offers an unbeatable repertoire of diving adventures, including world-class sunken WWII vessels lying close to the shore and incredibly healthy reefs.

Indiana Jones Land
Live out your Indiana Jones fantasies and blaze a trail of your own amid wild jungles. Be prepared for a culture shock, too. These islands are home to tiny villages where people lead lives that have changed little over centuries.

WWII to Jungles
The Solomons are blessed with a compelling history. Rusting relics of WWII are scattered in the jungle throughout the archipelago.

p316

Tahiti & French Polynesia

Diving ✓✓✓
Outdoors ✓✓
Culture ✓✓

Big Fauna
These 117 islands scattered over a marine area the size of Europe are paradise for diving enthusiasts and snorkellers. Expect fauna – you will see sharks.

Lagoon & Mountains
There's plenty to keep you busy in French Polynesia, on land and at sea – think lagoon excursions, hiking, horse riding, kite surfing, surfing and kayaking.

Past & Present
For culture buffs, French Polynesia will impress with flower garlands and smiles, fast-shaking hips and earth-oven feasts. Be awed by the well-preserved yet moss-covered *tikis* (sacred statues) and temples.

p346

Tonga

Watersports ✓✓✓
Islands ✓✓✓
Activities ✓✓✓

Pristine Waters
Tonga is close to heaven for those who love playing in and on warm crystal-clear water. Take your pick from sublime sailing, sea-kayaking, swimming, snorkelling and diving.

Islands Galore
Picture-perfect tropical islands abound, many uninhabited. Surrounded by spectacular turquoise waterways, particularly in Vava'u and Ha'apai, Tonga is an island lover's paradise. It's possible to stay in semi-luxury or be an all-out beach bum.

Hikes & Whales
There's plenty to do in Tonga, whether you prefer hiking on 'Eua, karting (in off-road buggies) on Vava'u, or sightseeing, fishing and whale watching throughout the islands. Listening to Tongans sing in church is an uplifting experience in itself!

p430

Vanuatu

Diving ✓✓✓
Culture ✓✓✓
Beaches ✓✓

Wreck Diving Spectacular
Most of Luganville's accommodation is geared to divers because a luxury-liner wreck, a WWII dumping ground for military paraphernalia and stunning coral are just minutes offshore.

Hang with the Ni-Van
Watch a traditional dance and buy stunning carvings to take home, but you'll learn most about the Ni-Van culture by hanging with them as they go smilingly about their daily lives.

The Coast in Black & White
Check out stunning Champagne Bay, a sweet horseshoe of azure and white, and enjoy the country's other black and white sand beaches. Some you'll have to yourself and others you'll share with laughing, splashing Ni-Van kids.

p472

Every listing is recommended by our authors, and their favourite places are listed first

Look out for these icons:

 Our author's top recommendation

 A green or sustainable option

 No payment required

See the Index for a full list of destinations covered in this book.

On the Road

Easter Island (Rapa Nui)

Best Places to Stay

» Explora en Rapa Nui (p50)

» Te Ora (p50)

» Aloha Nui (p51)

» Cabañas Christophe (p50)

» Cabañas Mana Ora (p50)

Best Places to Eat

» Au Bout du Monde (p52)

» Te Moana (p52)

» Kanahau (p52)

» Mikafé (p52)

Why Go?

Easter Island (Rapa Nui to its native Polynesian inhabitants) is like nowhere else on earth. Historically intriguing, culturally compelling and scenically magical, this tiny speck of land looks like it's fallen off another planet. In this blissfully isolated, unpolished gem it's hard to feel connected even to Chile, over 3700km to the east, let alone the wider world. It's just you, the indigo depths and the strikingly enigmatic *moai* (giant statues) scattered amid an eerie landscape.

When the *moai* have finished working their magic on you, there's a startling variety (for such a small island) of adventure options available. Diving, snorkelling and surfing are fabulous. On land, there's no better ecofriendly way to experience the island's savage beauty than on foot, from a bike saddle or on horseback. But if all you want to do is recharge the batteries, a couple of superb expanses of white sand beckon.

Although Easter Island is world famous and visitors are on the increase, everything remains small and personable – it's all about eco-travel.

When to Go
Easter Island

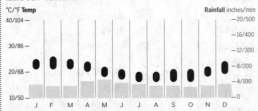

Jan–Mar Expect high prices and scarce accommodation, especially during Tapati Rapa Nui festival.

Jul–Aug A bit chilly. It's not the best time for the beach, but is ideal for hiking or horse riding.

Apr–Jun & Oct–Dec The shoulder season is not a bad time to visit; the climate is fairly temperate.

Connections

Short of sailing your own boat, the only way to and from Easter Island is by air. Flights between Easter Island and Santiago are frequent and last about five hours. There are also less frequent flights to/from Lima (Peru) and to/from Pape'ete (French Polynesia). Public transport is nonexistent on the island. Private minibuses, rental cars and bicycles are the most convenient ways to get around.

ITINERARIES

Four Days

Start the day by visiting the Museo Antropológico Sebastián Englert for some historical background. Next, take a half-day tour to Rano Kau and Orongo ceremonial village and soak up the lofty views. On day two take a full-day tour to marvel at Rano Raraku and Ahu Tongariki. On your return to Hanga Roa head straight to an atmosphere-laden bar on Av Atamu Tekena for the night vibe. Day three is all about Hanga Roa. Hit the *mercado* (market) to put a dent in the wallet and amble down Av Te Pito o Te Henua to enjoy the sunset at Ahu Tahai. Attend a traditional dance show later in the evening. Day four should see you lazing the day away at Anakena beach.

One Week

Follow the four-day agenda then make the most of the island's outdoor adventures. Book a horse-riding excursion along the north coast, spend a day diving off Motu Nui, scramble up and down Maunga Terevaka, and explore Península Poike.

Sustainable Travel

Easter Island is a superb open-air museum, but it's under threat due to the growing number of visitors. A few rules:

» Don't walk on the *ahu*, as they are revered by locals as burial sites.

» It's illegal to remove or relocate rocks from any of the archaeological structures.

» Don't touch petroglyphs, as they're very fragile.

» Stay on designated paths to limit erosion.

» Motor vehicles are not allowed on Península Poike or Terevaka.

» Don't pitch your tent in the park.

AT A GLANCE

Currency Chilean peso (CH$)

Language Spanish, Rapa Nui

Mobile phones Local SIM cards are available and can be used with unlocked GSM phones. Roaming agreements with most operators.

Money A few ATMs

Visas Not required for visitors from most Western countries

Fast Facts

» **Country code** ☎56 32
» **Land area** 117 sq km
» **Main city** Hanga Roa
» **Population** 6700

Exchange Rates

Australia	A$1	CH$517
Canada	C$1	CH$496
Europe	€1	CH$641
Japan	¥100	CH$642
New Zealand	NZ$1	CH$404
UK	UK£1	CH$795
USA	US$1	CH$509

For current exchange rates see www.xe.com.

Set Your Budget

» **Car rental** CH$35,000
» **Guesthouse** CH$40,000
» **Island tour** CH$25,000
» **Pisco sour** CH$2500
» **Two-course dinner** CH$15,000

HANGA ROA

POP 6700

Hanga Roa is the island's sole town. Upbeat it ain't, but with most attractions almost on its doorstep and nearly all the island's hotels, restaurants, shops and services lying within its boundaries, it's the obvious place to anchor oneself.

It features a picturesque fishing harbour, a couple of modest beaches and surf spots, as well as a scattering of archaeological sites.

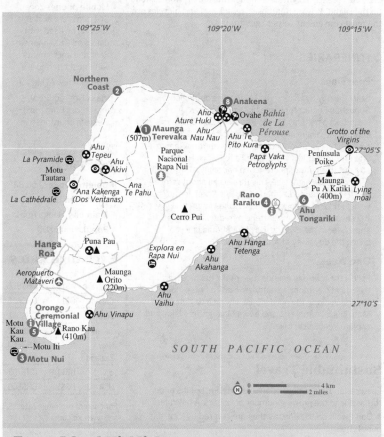

Easter Island Highlights

1 Clip-clop on the flanks of the extinct volcano **Maunga Terevaka** (p54) and feast your eyes on the mesmerising 360-degree views

2 Hike along the ruggedly beautiful **northern coast** (p50)

3 Ogle the stunning limpid blue waters of **Motu Nui** (p47) on a snorkelling or diving trip

4 Take a lesson in archaeology at **Rano Raraku** (p56), the 'nursery' of the *moai*

5 Ponder over the island's mysterious past at spellbinding **Orongo ceremonial village** (p55), perched on the edge of Rano Kau

6 Watch the sun rise at the row of enigmatic statues

at **Ahu Tongariki** (p56) while enjoying breakfast

7 Be hypnotised by the furious and sensual **dance performance** (p53) of a Rapa Nui group

8 Take a snooze under the swaying palms at **Anakena** (p55)

◉ Sights

TOP CHOICE **Museo Antropológico Sebastián Englert** MUSEUM
(☏255-1020; www.museorapanui.cl; Sector Tahai; admission CH$1000; ⊘9.30am-5.30pm Tue-Fri, 9.30am-12.30pm Sat & Sun) This well-organised museum explains the island's history and culture. It displays basalt fishhooks, obsidian spearheads and other weapons, and a *moai* head with reconstructed fragments of its eyes, among others.

Caleta Hanga Roa & Ahu Tautira ARCHAEOLOGICAL SITE
Your first encounter with the *moai* will probably take place at Ahu Tautira, which overlooks Caleta Hanga Roa, the fishing port in Hanga Roa at the foot of Av Te Pito o Te Henua. Here you'll find a platform with two superb *moai*.

Ahu Tahai & Ahu Akapu ARCHAEOLOGICAL SITE
Ahu Tahai, in the vicinity of Museo Antropológico Sebastián Englert, is a highly photogenic site that contains three restored *ahu*. Ahu Tahai proper is the *ahu* in the middle, supporting a large, solitary *moai* with no topknot. On the north side of Ahu Tahai is Ahu Ko Te Riku, with a topknotted and eyeballed *moai*. On the other side is Ahu Vai Uri, which supports five *moai* of varying sizes and shapes. Along the hills are foundations of *hare paenga* (traditional houses resembling an upturned canoe, with a single narrow doorway).

Continue further north along the coast and you'll soon come across Ahu Akapu, with its solitary *moai*.

Caleta Hanga Piko & Ahu Riata HARBOUR
Easily overlooked by visitors, the little Caleta Hanga Piko is used by local fishermen. Come in the early morning, when freshly caught fish are landed and sold on the quay. Facing the *caleta*, the restored Ahu Riata supports a solitary *moai*.

Iglesia Hanga Roa CHURCH
(Av Tu'u Koihu s/n) The unmissable Iglesia Hanga Roa, the island's Catholic church, is well worth a visit for its spectacular wood carvings, which integrate Christian doctrine with Rapa Nui tradition. It also makes a colourful scene on Sunday morning.

Playa Pea BEACH
For a little dip, the tiny beach at Playa Pea, on the south side of Caleta Hanga Roa, fits

BEST PLACES FOR...

Sunrise Wake up very early and arrive before dawn at Ahu Tongariki just in time to watch the sun rise behind the superb row of *moai*. Afterwards enjoy breakfast near the *ahu* – this is the life!

Sunset Be sure to come to Ahu Tahai at dusk and watch the big yellow ball sink behind the silhouetted statues – a truly inspiring sight.

Plane Spotting Keen plane spotters should position themselves on the coastal road to Rano Kau, at the western end of the runway, near the landing lights. Find out the exact arrival times of the Santiago–Easter Island plane on the Facebook page of Aeropuerto Mataveri.

the bill. There's another postage-stamp-sized beach near Pea restaurant.

🏃 Activities

Diving & Snorkelling
There's excellent diving on Easter Island, with gin-clear visibility in excess of 40m and a dramatic seascape. However, don't expect swarms of fish.

It's diveable year-round. Water temperatures vary from as low as 21°C in winter to almost 27°C in summer.

Most sites are scattered along the west coast. A few favourites include Motu Nui and the very scenic La Cathédrale (The Cathedral) and La Pyramide (The Pyramid). See p32 for more information.

There are three diving centres in Easter Island. Prices start at CH$30,000 for a single dive and CH$40,000 for an introductory dive. All operators also offer snorkelling trips to Motu Nui.

Atariki Rapa Nui DIVING, SNORKELLING
(☏255-0227; www.atarikirapanui.com; Caleta Hanga Piko s/n; ⊘Mon-Sat) A small outfit.

Mike Rapu Diving Center DIVING, SNORKELLING
(☏255-1055; www.mikerapu.cl; Caleta Hanga Roa s/n; ⊘Mon-Sat) A well-established operator.

Orca Diving Center DIVING, SNORKELLING
(☏255-0877; www.seemorca.cl; Caleta Hanga Roa s/n; ⊘Mon-Sat) Has good credentials.

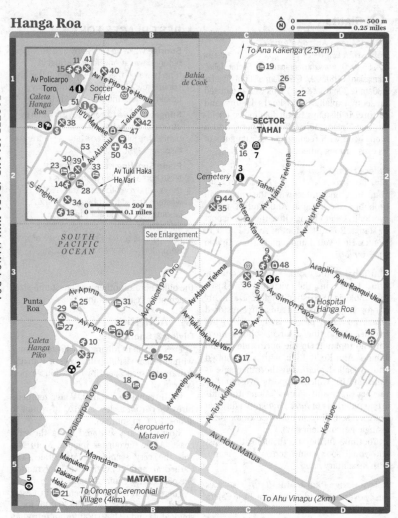

Surfing

Easter Island is hit with powerful swells from all points of the compass throughout the year, offering irresistible lefts and rights – mostly lava-reef breaks, with waves up to 5m. The most popular spots are scattered along the west coast. For beginners, there are a couple of good waves off Caleta Hanga Roa.

A handful of seasonal (usually from December to March) outfits based on the seafront offer surfing courses and also rent surfboards.

Hare Orca   SURFING

(☎255-0877; Caleta Hanga Roa s/n; rental per half day CH$11,000) This shop next to the Orca Diving Center rents body boards and surfboards.

Horseback Riding

A network of trails leading to some of the most beautiful sites can be explored on horseback – a typical Rapa Nui experience.

Reliable operators include **Pantu** (☎210-0577; www.pantupikerauri.cl; Sector Tahai s/n) and **Piti Pont** (☎210-0664). Expect to pay about CH$30,000 for a half-day tour and up to CH$70,000 for a full-day tour with a guide.

Hanga Roa

Hiking
You can take some fantastic trails through the island. A memorable walk is the way marked Ruta Patrimonial, which runs from Museo Antropológico Sebastián Englert up to Orongo ceremonial village (about four hours, 7km). Other recommended walks are the climb to Maunga Terevaka from near Ahu Akivi (about three hours) and the walk around Península Poike (one day). You can also follow the path along the northern coastline from Ahu Tepeu to Anakena beach (see p50). Bring water and food and have a detailed map at hand.

Boat Excursions
Seeing Easter Island from the sea is an exhilarating experience. A couple of operators organise customised tours along the coast. Prices depend on duration and distance. Bookings can be made through your hotel or *residencial*.

AHU TEPEU TO ANAKENA BEACH

The coastline between Ahu Tepeu and Anakena beach is extremely alluring: vast expanses of chaotic boulders, towering sea cliffs, barren landscapes and sensational ocean views. There are also plenty of archaeological sites dotted along the way as well as caves adorned with impressive petroglyphs. From Ahu Tepeu (p47) it takes six to seven hours to reach Anakena beach on foot. Then hitch back or arrange a taxi back to Hanga Roa. It's not marked and the archaeological sites are not signed; you'll definitely need a guide. Contact the tourist office or your lodging to secure one.

Cycling

Cycling is a superb way of seeing the island at your leisure, provided you're ready to come to grips with the steep and winding roads around the southern parts. An easy loop is from Hanga Roa up to Ahu Tepeu, then east to Ahu Akivi and back to Hanga Roa (about 17km).

Makemake Rentabike   BICYCLE RENTAL
(☑255-2030; Av Atamu Tekena; ⊙9am-1pm & 4-8pm) This venture rents mountain bikes in tip-top condition.

☞ Tours

We recommend joining an organised tour since you get the benefit of an English-speaking guide who can explain the cultural significance of the archaeological sites.

Plenty of operators do tours of the sites, typically charging CH$40,000 for a full day and CH$25,000 for a half day. Entrance fees to Parque Nacional Rapa Nui (CH$30,000) aren't included.

Aku Aku Turismo   CULTURAL TOUR
(☑210-0770; www.akuakuturismo.cl; Av Tu'u Koihu s/n) A well-established company that employs competent guides.

Haumaka Tours   CULTURAL TOUR
(☑210-0274; www.haumakatours.com; cnr Avs Atamu Tekena & Hotu Matua) Offers customised tours.

Kava Kava Tours   CULTURAL TOUR
(☑210-0243; www.kavakavatour.cl; Av Tu'u Koihu s/n) A recent company.

Kia Koe Tour   CULTURAL TOUR
(☑210-0852; www.kiakoetour.cl; Av Atamu Tekena s/n) Has good credentials and uses knowledgeable guides.

Rapa Nui Travel   CULTURAL TOUR
(☑210-0548; www.rapanuitravel.com; Av Tu'u Koihu) Run by a Rapa Nui–German couple.

🛌 Sleeping

Unless otherwise stated, most places come equipped with private bathroom, and breakfast is included. Air-con is scarce but fans are provided in the hottest months. Airport transfers are included.

Te Ora   CABIN $$
(☑255-1038; www.rapanuiteora.com; Av Apina s/n; r CH$40,000-70,000; ☜) Although it feels a bit cramped, Te Ora is fine value. All three rooms mix hardwoods and volcanic stones, but the Teora Ora, with sweeping views over the ocean, is a firm favourite. If she's around, the Canadian owner, Sharon, will give you the lowdown on all that's worth seeing on the island – in perfect English, of course. No breakfast is served, but there's a communal kitchen.

Explora en Rapa Nui   LUXURY HOTEL $$$
(☑395-2800 in Santiago; www.explora.com; 3-night all-inclusive packages from s/d US$3360/4770; ✳@☜🏊) This ultraluxurious and green property blends unobtrusively into a small forested patch of volcanic-singed countryside. Rooms, all overlooking the roaring Pacific and fiery sunsets, are abundant with indigenous materials. Prices include excursions. One proviso: it feels a bit cut off from the rest of the island (it's about 6km east of Hanga Roa).

Cabañas Christophe   BUNGALOW $$
(☑210-0826; www.cabanaschristophe.com; Av Policarpo Toro s/n; d CH$60,000-70,000; ☜) This charming venue seduces those seeking character and comfort, with three meticulously maintained rooms that blend hardwoods and volcanic stones. Angle for the upstairs room, which is spacious and inundated with natural light. It's at the start of the Orongo trail, about 1.5km from the centre.

Cabañas Mana Ora   BUNGALOW $$
(☑210-0769; www.manaora.cl; Sector Tahai; d CH$80,000) This is an adorable nest with two attractively decorated cottages perched on a slope overlooking the ocean. They come equipped with a handy kitchenette and a

terrace with sea views. One grumble: bathrooms are miniscule. It's a bit of a schlep from the centre (you'll need a bike).

Hare Swiss
BUNGALOW **$$**

(255-2221; www.hareswiss.com; Sector Tahai; s/d CH$40,000/60,000;) Just behind the Altiplanico, Hare Swiss is a solid option, with three immaculate bungalows, great sea views and a communal kitchen. If you don't fancy cooking, the driver can drive you to various eateries at dinner.

Hanga Roa
Eco Village & Spa
LUXURY HOTEL **$$$**

(957-0300; www.hotelhangaroa.cl; Av Pont s/n; s incl breakfast from CH$145,000, d incl breakfast from CH$200,000;) After a complete makeover in 2012, this sprawling establishment ranks as one of the best hotels on the island, with an array of creatively designed rooms and suites facing the sea. All units are built of natural materials and their layout is inspired by caves, with curving lines and shapes. They're not just posh and huge, they also blend into the environment. The on-site restaurant serves refined food and the spa is a stunner. It's eco-friendly: there's a water and electricity saving system.

Altiplanico
HOTEL **$$$**

(255-2190; www.altiplanico.cl; Sector Tahai; s/d US$350/390; @) The best thing about this well-run venture with a boutique feel is its excellent location on a gentle slope in Tahai. Try for bungalows 1, 2, 3, 10, 11 or 17, which have panoramic sea views. The 17 units are all sparkling clean and quirkily decorated, but they're fairly packed together and we found the prices somewhat inflated. The on-site restaurant is elegant but pricey (starters cost US$20). It runs on solar energy.

Aloha Nui
GUESTHOUSE **$$**

(210-0274; haumakatours@gmail.com; Av Atamu Tekena s/n; s/d CH$35,000/70,000;) After a complete makeover in 2011, this agreeable place now features six well-equipped rooms and a vast, shared living room. But the real reason you're staying here is to discuss Rapa Nui archaeology in flawless English with Josefina Nahoe Mulloy, who leads reputable tours.

Gomero
HOTEL **$$**

(210-0313; www.hotelgomero.com; Av Tu'u Koihu s/n; s from CH$60,000, d from CH$80,000; @) This reputable abode has a well-tended little pool nestled in lush gardens, which makes this place a restful spot in summer. Angle for the superior rooms in the new wing (20 to 23), which are more modern and have aircon, or for the 'standards' (4 to 6, 9 to 11, 16 to 18).

Atavai – Chez Antoine y Lolita
CABIN **$$**

(210-0145; www.hotel-atavai.com; s/d CH$50,000/65,000;) This venture offers a soothing collection of white bungalows (nine rooms in total). Quarters are a bit cramped, but otherwise it's serviceable. Evening meals are available on request. The only downside: its location near the aiport is not *that* exceptional – you'll need a bike to get to the centre. Look for deals on the website.

Mihinoa
CAMPGROUND **$**

(255-1593; www.mihinoa.com; Av Pont s/n; campsites per person CH$5000, dm CH$9000, d CH$20,000-25,000;) Cheap and sometimes cheerful, this backpacker crash pad is a popular spot for budgeteers. You have options here: one of the smallish but well-scrubbed rooms in the two buildings, a six-bed dorm or a campsite on a grassy plot (no shade). The dorm is cramped but serviceable and, joy of joys, has hot showers (mornings and evenings). Perks include tent hire (CH$5500), wi-fi access (CH$5000 for the duration of your stay), a well-equipped communal kitchen and laundry service. And you're just a pebble's throw from the seashore.

Tau Ra'a
HOTEL **$$**

(210-0463; www.tauraahotel.cl; Av Atamu Tekena s/n; s/d CH$60,000/75,000;) The 10 rooms are spotless and flooded with natural light, and they come equipped with firm beds and functional bathrooms. Alas, no sea views. The substantial breakfast is a plus. Bill, the

TAPATI RAPA NUI

Easter Island's premier festival, the Tapati Rapa Nui, lasts about two weeks in the first half of February and is so impressive that it's almost worth timing your trip around it (contact the tourist office for exact dates). Expect a series of music, dance, cultural and sport contests between two clans that put up two candidates who stand for the title of Queen of the Festival.

Aussie owner, is a treasure trove of local information.

Teanui
CABIN $$

(255-1990; www.teanui.cl; Av Pont s/n; s/d CH$35,000/65,000;) This well-maintained establishment offers comfortable motel-style rooms as well as two self-contained bungalows in a garden-like setting.

Inaki Uhi
CABIN $

(255-1160; www.inakiuhi.com; Av Atamu Tekena s/n; s/d CH$35,000/70,000;) The 15 boxy rooms here occupy two rows of low-slung buildings facing each other. They feel sterile and the decor is bland but there are four shared kitchens and it's conveniently located on the main drag.

Cabañas Nuae Koro
CABIN $

(255-1418; www.nuaekoro.com; off Av Atamu Tekena; s/d CH$20,000/35,000) This budget option doesn't offer much privacy – the wall that separates the two adjoining units is particle board – but it's central and good value.

Hostal Tojika
GUESTHOUSE $

(099-358-0810; Av Apina s/n; dm/s/d CH$10,000/20,000/30,000;) Has four rooms, a five-bed dorm and a communal kitchen in a single building overlooking the sea. The rooms lack natural light but the dorm is an excellent bargain.

Vaianny
GUESTHOUSE $

(210-0650; www.residencialvaianny.com; Av Tuki Haka He Vari; s/d CH$25,000/35,000;) A good bet for budgeteers, with basic but clean rooms. Mattresses are saggy and bathrooms tiny. It's within hollering distance of some the town's best bars and restaurants.

✖ Eating

For self-caterers, there are a couple of super-markets on Av Atamu Tekena.

Mikafé
CAFETERIA, SANDWICHES $

(Caleta Hanga Roa s/n; ice creams CH$1500-2500, sandwiches & cakes CH$2500-4500;9am-8pm) Hmm, the *helados artesanales* (homemade ice creams)! Oh, the damn addictive banana cake! Other treats include paninis and sandwiches.

Te Moana
CHILEAN $$

(Av Atamu Tekena s/n; CH$10,000-17,000;lunch & dinner Mon-Sat) This buzzy restaurant and bar with a cosy interior is renowned for its delectable grilled meat and fish dishes.

Au Bout du Monde
INTERNATIONAL $$$

(Av Policarpo Toro s/n; mains CH$10,000-16,500;lunch & dinner Wed-Mon) In this agreeable venue run by a Rapa Nui–Belgian couple, every visitor ought to try the tuna in vanilla sauce, the homemade tagliatelle or the beef fillet. Leave room for dessert – the Belgian chocolate mousse is divine.

Haga Piko
SEAFOOD $

(Caleta Hanga Piko; mains CH$5500-7700;11am-4pm Mon-Sat) This simple family-run establishment is excellent value. The fish on offer is determined by what's in the nets that day, and the terrace overlooking Caleta Hango Piko is a good place to soak up the atmosphere of the seafront.

Kanahau
SEAFOOD, CHILEAN $$

(Av Atamu Tekena s/n; mains CH$8000-16,000;lunch & dinner) Whether you satisfy yourself with outstanding *ceviche* or sample the *lomo kanahau* (beef with a homemade sauce), among a variety of hearty dishes, you'll be pleased with the careful preparation and attentive service.

Donde El Gordo
CHILEAN, SANDWICHES $

(Av Te Pito o Te Henua s/n; mains CH$6000-11,000;lunch Tue-Sun, dinner Tue-Sat) Simple and satisfying are words that come to mind when dining here. The menu consists of generous sandwiches, *empanadas* (from CH$1800), pizzas and copious salads, as well as vitamin-packed fruit juices. A good surprise.

Haka Honu
CHILEAN $$

(Av Policarpo Toro s/n; mains CH$6000-16,000;lunch & dinner Tue-Sun) Fish dishes, steaks, pasta and salads round out the menu at this buzzy eatery. The outside terrace catches every wisp of breeze and is perfect for watching the world surf by.

La Kaleta
SEAFOOD, CHILEAN $$

(Caleta Hanga Roa; mains CH$6500-16,000;lunch & dinner) In a lovely location over-looking the sea, breezy La Kaleta is your spot for salads, pasta, steaks and fish dishes.

Ariki o Te Pana – Tia Berta
CHILEAN $

(Av Atamu Tekena s/n; mains CH$2000-10,000;lunch & dinner Mon-Sat) Surrender to some melt-in-your-mouth *empanadas* prepared mamma-style in this no-frills den.

Mahina Nui
SEAFOOD, CHILEAN $$

(Av Atamu Tekena s/n; mains CH$6000-16,000;lunch & dinner Mon-Sat) With its flashy facade on the main drag, Mahina Nui is

sure to draw your attention. There's a varied menu; the *ceviche* is recommended.

Kuki Varua SEAFOOD, CHILEAN $
(Av Te Pito o Te Henua s/n; mains CH$6500-8000; ☺lunch Tue-Sun, dinner Tue-Sat) This place has a wide assortment of set menus. Good sea views from the upstairs terrace.

 Drinking

Most restaurants feature a bar section.

Te Moana BAR
(Av Atamu Tekena s/n; ☺11am-late Mon-Sat) One of Hanga Roa's hottest spots at the time of writing. Come for the good fun, good mix of people and good cocktails.

Topa Tangi Pub PUB
(Av Atamu Tekena s/n; ☺6pm-late Wed-Sat) Can get really lively on weekends.

Marau BAR
(Av Atamu Tekena s/n; ☺6.30pm-late) Another hang-out of choice, with a loungy feel.

Haka Honu BAR
(Av Policarpo Toro s/n; ☺11am-late Tue-Sun) A cool spot where you can cut loose over some sunset cocktails in pleasant surrounds.

Kanahau BAR
(Av Atamu Tekena s/n; ☺11am-late) Kick off the night with a strong mojito at this cheerful hang-out decked in wood.

Mikafé CAFE
(Caleta Hanga Roa s/n; ☺9am-8pm) In search of a real espresso? Mikafé is your answer.

Vai Te Mihi BAR
(Av Policarpo Toro s/n; ☺6pm-late) Gets lively on Friday and Saturday nights. Also features traditional dance shows.

Explora en Rapa Nui BAR
(☺9am-late) Order a pisco sour and watch the sun set – a magical experience.

 Shopping

Hanga Roa has numerous souvenir shops, mostly on Av Atamu Tekena and on Av Te Pito o Te Henua.

Feria Municipal CRAFT
(cnr Avs Atamu Tekena & Tu'u Maheke; ☺Mon-Sat) Good prices.

Mercado Artesanal CRAFT
(cnr Avs Tu'u Koihu & Ara Roa Rakei; ☺Mon-Sat) Across from the church. Has a bit of everything.

DON'T MISS

TRADITIONAL DANCE SHOWS

If there's one thing you absolutely have to check out while you're on Easter Island it's a traditional dance show. There are about six groups that usually perform three times a week. Shows cost about CH$10,000. A few favourites:

Kari Kari (☎210-0767; Av Atamu Tekena s/n) Performs at a venue called Ma'ara Nui.

Matato'a (☎255-2060; www.matatoa .com) At the Au Bout du Monde restaurant, upstairs.

Te Ra'ai (☎255-1460; www.teraai.cl) Includes an *umu* (underground oven) feast and cultural demonstrations.

El Baul del To CRAFT
(Av Pont; ☺10am-8.30pm) This 'cultural centre' sells locally made handicrafts and traditional Rapa Nui costumes. Also offers body painting.

Mokomae TATTOO PARLOUR
(☎099-292-1591; Av Atamu Tekena s/n; ☺by appointment) For traditionally designed tattoos head to this highly rated tattoo studio. Mokomae also sells woodcarvings.

 Information

Banco Santander (Av Apina; ☺8am-1pm Mon-Fri) On the waterfront. Currency exchange, and has two ATMs that accept Visa and MasterCard. Also has an ATM at the airport (departure area).
BancoEstado (Av Pont s/n; ☺8am-1pm Mon-Fri) Changes US dollars and euros. Charges a CH$1500 commission on travellers cheques. There's also an ATM but it only accepts MasterCard. Visa holders can get cash advances at the counter during opening hours (bring your passport); the bank charges a CH$2000 fee for the service.
Farmacia Cruz Verde (Av Atamu Tekena; ☺9am-7.30pm Mon-Sat) Large and well-stocked pharmacy.
Hospital Hanga Roa (☎210-0215; Av Simon Paoa s/n)
Mana@net (Av Atamu Tekena s/n; per hr CH$1200; ☺9am-10pm) Internet cafe and call centre.
Omotohi Cybercafé (Av Te Pito o Te Henua s/n; per hr CH$1000; ☺9am-10pm) Internet and wi-fi access, and call centre.

LEARN YOUR AHU FROM YOUR MOAI

You don't need a university degree to appreciate the archaeological remains in Easter Island. The following explanations should suffice.

Ahu – *Ahu* were village burial sites and ceremonial centres and are thought to derive from altars in French Polynesia. Some 350 of these stone platforms are dotted around the coast. *Ahu* are paved on the upper surface with more or less flat stones, and they have a vertical wall on the seaward side and at each end.

Moai – Easter Island's most pervasive image, the enigmatic *moai* are massive carved figures that probably represent clan ancestors. From 2m to 10m tall, these stony-faced statues stood with their backs to the Pacific Ocean. Some *moai* have been restored, while others have been re-erected but are eroded. Many more lie toppled on the ground.

Topknots – Archaeologists believe that the reddish cylindrical *pukao* (topknots) that crown many *moai* reflect a male hairstyle once common on Rapa Nui.

Police (☎133)

Post office (Av Te Pito o Te Henua s/n; ⊙9am-1pm & 2.30-6pm Mon-Fri, 9am-12.30pm Sat)

Puna Vai (Av Hotu Matua; ⊙8.30am-1pm & 3-8pm Mon-Sat, 9am-1pm Sun) This petrol station also doubles as an exchange office. Much more convenient than the bank (no queues, better rates, longer opening hours, no commission on travellers cheques). There's an ATM inside (MasterCard only).

Sernatur (☎210-0255; ipascua@sernatur.cl; Tu'u Maheke s/n; ⊙9am-6pm Mon-Fri, 10am-5pm Sat) Has various brochures and maps of the island. Staff speak some English.

PARQUE NACIONAL RAPA NUI

Since 1935, much of Rapa Nui's land and all of the archaeological sites have been a **national park** (admission non-Chileans CH$30,000) administered by **Conaf** (☎210-0236; www.conaf.cl), which charges admission at Orongo and Rano Raraku that is valid for the whole park for five days as of the first day of entrance. In theory, you're allowed one visit to Orongo and one visit to Rano Raraku; in practice, most rangers allow repeat visits if you ask nicely. There are ranger information stations at Orongo, Anakena and Rano Raraku.

◉ Sights

NORTHERN CIRCUIT

North of Ahu Tahai, the road is rough but passable if you drive slowly. Your best bet is to explore the area on foot, on horseback or by mountain bike, but there are no signs marking the sites.

Ana Kakenga CAVE
About 2km north of Tahai is Ana Kakenga, or Dos Ventanas. This site comprises two caves opening onto the ocean (bring a torch).

Ahu Tepeu ARCHAEOLOGICAL SITE
This large *ahu* has several fallen *moai* and a village site with foundations of *hare paenga* (elliptical houses) and the walls of several round houses.

Ana Te Pahu CAVE
Off the dirt road to Akivi, Ana Te Pahu is a former cave dwelling with an overgrown garden of sweet potatoes, taro and bananas.

Ahu Akivi ARCHAEOLOGICAL SITE
Unusual for its inland location, Ahu Akivi, restored in 1960, sports seven restored *moai*. They are the only ones that face towards the sea, but, like all *moai,* they overlook the site of a village, traces of which can still be seen.

TOP CHOICE **Maunga Terevaka** MOUNTAIN
Maunga Terevaka is the island's highest point (507m). This barren hill is only accessible on foot or on horseback (see p48).

Puna Pau ARCHAEOLOGICAL SITE
The volcanic Puna Pau quarry was used to make the reddish, cylindrical *pukao* (topknots) that were placed on many *moai*.

SOUTHWEST CIRCUIT

Ana Kai Tangata CAVE
Past the Hotel Iorana in Hanga Roa, a sign points the way to Ana Kai Tangata, a vast cave carved into black cliffs that sports beautiful rock paintings. However, entrance is forbidden due to falling rocks.

TOP CHOICE Rano Kau CRATER LAKE

Nearly covered in a bog of floating *totora* reeds, this crater lake resembles a giant witch's cauldron – awesome!

Perched 400m above, on the edge of the crater wall on one side and abutting a vertical drop plunging down to the cobalt-blue ocean on the other side, **Orongo ceremonial village** (admission CH$30,000; ☺9am-5pm) boasts one of the South Pacific's most dramatic landscapes. It overlooks several small *motu* (offshore islands), including Motu Nui, Motu Iti and Motu Kau Kau. Built into the side of the slope, the houses have walls of horizontally overlapping stone slabs, with an earth-covered arched roof of similar materials, making them appear partly subterranean. Orongo was the focus of an island-wide bird cult linked to the god Makemake in the 18th and 19th centuries. Birdman petroglyphs are visible on a cluster of boulders between the cliff top and the edge of the crater.

Orongo is either a steepish climb or a short scenic drive 4km from the centre of town.

Ahu Vinapu ARCHAEOLOGICAL SITE

Beyond the eastern end of the airport runway, a road heads south past some large oil tanks to this ceremonial platform, with several toppled *moai*.

NORTHEAST CIRCUIT

TOP CHOICE Anakena BEACH

Beach bums in search of a place to wallow will make a beeline for this picture-postcard-perfect, white-sand beach. It also forms a perfect backdrop for **Ahu Nau Nau**, which comprises seven *moai,* some with topknots. On a rise south of the beach stands **Ahu Ature Huki** and its lone *moai.*

Ovahe BEACH

This beach offers more seclusion than Anakena for wannabe Robinson Crusoes but is considered dangerous because of falling rocks.

Ahu Te Pito Kura ARCHAEOLOGICAL SITE

Beside Bahía de La Pérouse, a nearly 10m-long *moai* lies face down with its neck broken; it's the largest *moai* moved from Rano Raraku and erected on an *ahu.*

Papa Vaka Petroglyphs ARCHAEOLOGICAL SITE

About 100m off the coastal road (look for the sign), you'll find a massive basaltic slab decorated with prolific carvings.

TOP CHOICE Península Poike PENINSULA

At the eastern end of the island, this high plateau is crowned by the extinct volcano **Maunga Pu A Katiki** (400m) and bound in by steep cliffs. The landscape is stark, with huge fields of grass, free-roaming horses and intimidating cows.

The best way to soak up the primordial rawness of Península Poike is to take a two-day horseback excursion from Hanga Roa, or a day hike from the main road. Ask your guide to show you a series of small *moai* that lie face down, hidden amid the grass, as well as the **Grotto of the Virgins** (Ana O Keke), carved into the cliffs.

LOCAL KNOWLEDGE

SERGIO RAPU, ARCHAEOLOGIST

A former governor of Rapa Nui, Sergio Rapu is one of the island's most respected archaeologists and has conducted numerous experiments and measurements in the field.

What special experience do you recommend? Go to the crater rim at Rano Kau half an hour before sunset and bring a bottle of pisco sour. If you're lucky, you'll see the moon rising.

Most powerful archaeological site on the island? Rano Raraku has special vibes – come here early morning or late afternoon and you could almost feel the presence of spooky beings watching you...

Best time for a visit? February, when the Tapati Rapa Nui festival is held. This truly genuine cultural event is a great chance for foreigners to immerse themselves in local culture. My favourite contest is the Haka Pei: on the flanks of the Cerro Pui, a dozen male contestants run downhill on a makeshift sled at a speed that can reach 70km/h. Just thinking about it makes my spine tingle!

TOP CHOICE **Ahu Tongariki** ARCHAEOLOGICAL SITE

The monumental Ahu Tongariki has plenty to set your camera's flash popping, with 15 imposing statues, the largest *ahu* ever built. The statues gaze over a large, level village site, with ruined remnants scattered about and some petroglyphs nearby.

TOP CHOICE **Rano Raraku** ARCHAEOLOGICAL SITE

Known as 'the nursery', the volcano of Rano Raraku, about 18km from Hanga Roa, is the quarry for the hard tuff from which the *moai* were cut. You'll feel as though you're stepping back into early Polynesian times, wandering among *moai* in all stages of progress studded on the southern slopes of the volcano. At the top the 360-degree view is truly awesome. Within the crater are a small, glistening lake and about 20 standing *moai*.

UNDERSTAND EASTER ISLAND

Easter Island Today

In 2008 Easter Island was granted a special status. It is now a *territoria especial* (special territory) within Chile, which means greater autonomy for the islanders. But independence is not the order of the day – ongoing economic reliance on mainland Chile renders this option unlikely in the foreseeable future.

The main claim is for the return of native lands, and the new status should help settle these matters in the forthcoming years. Indigenous Rapa Nui control almost no land outside Hanga Roa. A national park (designated in 1935) comprises more than a third of the island, and nearly all the remainder belongs to Chile. Native groups have asked the Chilean government and the UN to return the park to aboriginal hands. In 2010 a land dispute opposed one Rapa Nui clan to the owners of the Hanga Roa hotel. The occupation of the hotel and several administrative buildings by Rapa Nui individuals was followed by violent confrontations between police and demonstrators.

The Rapa Nui are also concerned about the development and control of the tourism industry. Mass tourism it ain't, but the rising number of visitors – approximately 65,000 tourists each year – has an impact on the environment.

The recent influx of mainland Chileans (mostly construction workers) has fostered tensions with some locals, who see mainland Chileans as 'troublemakers'. In August 2009 a group of Rapa Nui people blocked the airport for a few days to protest against what they perceive as 'uncontrolled immigration'.

History

The first islanders arrived either from the Marquesas, the Mangarevas, the Cooks or Pitcairn Island between the 4th and 8th centuries.

The Rapa Nui developed a unique civilisation, characterised by the construction of the ceremonial stone platforms called *ahu* and the famous Easter Island statues called *moai* (see p54). The population probably peaked at around 15,000 in the 17th century. Conflict over land and resources erupted in intertribal warfare by the late 17th century, only shortly before the arrival of Europeans, and the population started to decline. More recent dissension between different clans led to bloody wars and cannibalism, and many *moai* were toppled from their *ahu*. Natural disasters – earthquakes and tsunamis – may have also contributed to the destruction. The only *moai* standing today were restored during the last century.

European Arrival

When the Dutch admiral Jacob Roggeveen arrived on Easter Sunday 1722, many of the great *moai* were still standing, but there was no sign of any modern implements, suggesting the islanders did not trade with the outside world.

In 1774 the celebrated English navigator James Cook led the next European expedition to land on Rapa Nui. His account is the first to mention that many *moai* had been damaged, apparently as a result of intertribal wars.

Fourteen years later French explorer La Pérouse found the people prosperous and calm, suggesting a quick recovery.

European Takeover

Contact with outsiders nearly annihilated the Rapa Nui people. A raid by Peruvian blackbirders (slavers) in 1862 took 1000 islanders away to work the guano (manure) deposits of Peru's Chincha islands. After intense pressure from the Catholic Church,

some survivors were returned to Easter Island, but disease and hard labour had already killed about 90% of them.

A brief period of French-led missionary activity saw most of the surviving islanders converted to Catholicism in the 1860s. Commercial exploitation of the island began in 1870, when French adventurer Jean-Baptiste Dutroux-Bornier introduced the wool trade to Rapa Nui and sent many islanders to work on plantations in Tahiti. Conflicts arose with the missionaries, who were at the same time deporting islanders to missions on Mangareva (in the Gambier Archipelago). Dutroux-Bornier was assassinated by an islander in 1877.

Annexation by Chile

Chile officially annexed the island in 1888 during a period of expansion that included the acquisition of territory from Peru and Bolivia after the War of the Pacific (1879–84).

By 1897 Rapa Nui had fallen under the control of a single wool company, which became the island's de facto government, continuing the wool trade until the middle of the 20th century.

In 1953 the Chilean government took charge of the island, continuing the imperial rule to which islanders had been subject for nearly a century. With restricted rights, including travel restrictions and ineligibility to vote, the islanders felt they were treated like second-class citizens. In 1967, the establishment of a regular commercial air link between Santiago and Tahiti, with Rapa Nui as a refuelling stop, opened up the island to the world and brought many benefits to Rapa Nui people.

The Culture

Rapa Nui is a fairly conservative society, and family life, marriage and children still play a central role in everyday life, as does religion.

A third of the population is from mainland Chile or Europe. The most striking feature is the intriguing blend of Polynesian and Chilean customs. Although they will never admit it overtly, the people of Rapa Nui have one foot in South America and one foot in Polynesia.

Despite its unique language and history, contemporary Rapa Nui does not appear to be a 'traditional' society – its continuity was shattered by the near extinction of the population in the last century. However, although

they have largely adapted to a Westernised lifestyle, Rapa Nui people are fiercely proud of their history and culture, and they strive to keep their traditions alive.

Language

See the Language chapter on p591 for Easter Island basics.

Arts

As in Tahiti, traditional dancing is not a mere tourist attraction but one of the most vibrant forms of expression of traditional Polynesian culture. A couple of talented dance groups perform regularly at various hotels. Tattooing is another aspect of Polynesian culture, and it has enjoyed a revival among the young generation since the late 1980s.

There are also strong carving traditions on Easter Island. Carvings incorporate human, bird, fish and other animal motifs, often in combination.

Environment

Easter Island is roughly triangular in shape, with an extinct volcanic cone in each corner – Maunga (Mt) Terevaka, in the northwest corner, is the highest point at 507m. The island's maximum length is just 24km, and it is only 12km across at its widest point. Much of the interior of Easter Island is grassland, with cultivable soil interspersed with rugged lava fields. Wave erosion has created steep cliffs around much of the coast, and Anakena, on the north shore, is the only broad sandy beach.

Erosion, exacerbated by overgrazing and deforestation, is the island's most serious problem. To counteract the effects of erosion, a small-scale replanting program is under way on Península Poike.

SURVIVAL GUIDE

Directory A–Z

Accommodation

If you come here from mainland Chile, be prepared for a shock. Despite a high number of establishments – about 90 when we visited – accommodation on Easter Island is fairly pricey for what you get. All

PRACTICALITIES

» **Media** *Mercurio,* the national daily newspaper, can be purchased in Hanga Roa. Easter Island also has its own newspaper, *El Correo del Moai.*

» **Television** Chilean programs of the government-owned Television Nacional (TVN) are beamed to the island via satellite.

» **DVDs/Videos** NTSC system

» **Electricity** 240V, 50Hz AC

» **Weights & Measures** Metric system

accommodation options are located in Hanga Roa except the Explora en Rapa Nui. *Residenciales* (homestays) form the bedrock of accommodation on the island but there's a growing number of luxury options. At the other end of the scale, there are also a couple of camping grounds in Hanga Roa. Note that wild camping is forbidden in the national park.

The following review price ranges refer to a double room.

$ less than CH$40,000

$$ CH$40,000–80,000

$$$ more than CH$80,000

Business Hours

The following are normal opening hours for Easter Island. Reviews do not list business hours unless they differ from these standards.

Offices 9am to 5pm Monday to Friday.

Restaurants 9am to 9pm Monday to Saturday.

Food

Restaurant review price indicators are based on the cost of a main course.

$ less than CH$8000

$$ CH$8000–12,000

$$$ more than CH$12,000

Internet Access

You'll find internet cafes in Hanga Roa. Wi-fi is also available at most hotels and guesthouses but connections can be slow at times.

Internet Resources

Easter Island Foundation (www.islandheritage.org)

Easter Island home page (www.netaxs.com/trance/rapanui.html)

Lonely Planet (www.lonelyplanet.com/chile/rapa-nui-easter-island)

Money

ATMs Easter Island has only five ATMs, two of which accept only MasterCard. Don't rely solely on your credit card and make sure you keep some cash in reserve.

Credit Cards Many *residenciales,* hotels, restaurants and tour agencies accept credit cards but they usually charge an additional 5% to 10% commission.

Currency The local currency is the Chilean peso (CH$). A number of businesses on Rapa Nui, especially *residenciales,* hotels and rental agencies, accept US cash (and euros, albeit at a pinch). Travellers from Tahiti must bring US cash (or euros) as Tahitian currency is not accepted.

Moneychangers There are two banks and an exchange office in Hanga Roa. US dollars are the best foreign currency to carry, followed by euros. Note that exchange rates on Easter Island are lower than those offered in mainland Chile.

Taxes All prices given in this book are inclusive of tax.

Tipping & Bargaining Tipping and bargaining are not traditionally part of Polynesian culture.

Telephone

Easter Island's international telephone code is the same as Chile's (☎56), and the area code (☎32) covers the whole island. International calls (dial ☎00) start at around US$0.50 per minute. You'll find several private call centres in town. Entel offers GSM mobile phone service, and prepaid SIM cards are available for purchase.

Getting There & Away
Air

The only airline serving Easter Island is **LAN** (☎210-0920; www.lan.com; Av Atamu Tekena s/n; ☺9am-4.30pm Mon-Fri, 9am-12.30pm Sat). It has daily flights to/from Santiago, one weekly flight to/from Pape'ete (Tahiti) and twice weekly flights to/from Lima (Peru). A standard economy round-trip fare from Santiago can range from US$600 to US$900.

Sea

Few passenger services go to Easter Island. A few yachts stop here, mostly in January, February and March. Anchorages are not well sheltered.

Getting Around

Outside Hanga Roa, nearly the entire east coast road and the road to Anakena are paved. Other roads are not paved but are in decent enough condition.

To/From the Airport

The airport is just on the outskirts of Hanga Roa. Accommodation proprietors wait at the airport and will shuttle you for free to your hotel or *residencial*.

Bicycle

Mountain bikes can be rented in Hanga Roa for about CH$12,000 per day. Ask at your *residencial* or hotel.

Car & Motorcycle

Some hotels and agencies rent 4WDs for CH$25,000 to CH$45,000 per eight-hour day, and CH$35,000 to CH$60,000 for 24 hours depending on the vehicle. A word of warning: insurance is *not* available, so you're not covered should the vehicle get any damage. Don't leave valuables in your car.

Scooters and motorcycles are rented for about CH$20,000 to CH$25,000 a day.

You can contact the following outfits.

Haunani (☎210-0353; Av Atamu Tekena s/n)

Oceanic Rapa Nui Rent a Car (☎210-0985; www.rapanuioceanic.com; Av Atamu Tekena s/n)

Rent a Car Insular (☎210-0480; www.rentainsular.cl; Av Atamu Tekena s/n)

Taxi

Taxis cost a flat CH$1500 for most trips around town. Longer trips around the island can be negotiated.

Fiji

Includes »

Best Places to Stay

» Likuliku Lagoon (p103)

» Wayalailai Eco Haven Resort (p105)

» Caqalai Island Resort (p114)

» Castaway Island Resort (p103)

Best Places to Eat

» Blue Bure (p71)

» Guava (p92)

» Daikoku (p71 and p92)

» Navutu Stars (p110)

» Mantaray Island Resort (p107)

Why Go?

With alabaster beaches, cloudless skies and kaleidoscopic reefs, Fiji is the embodiment of the South Pacific dream. Most who head here want little more than to fall into a sun-induced coma under a shady palm, and with over 300 islands to choose from, the decision on where to unfurl your beach towel isn't easy. While some may find that anything more than two snorkelling excursions a day and half an hour on the volleyball court is not in keeping with Fiji's famously languid sense of time, there is more to these isles than can ever be seen from a deckchair or swim-up bar.

In a (coco)nut shell, Fiji is arguably the easiest place in the South Pacific to travel around. The population adopts you on your arrival, and there are two robust cultures, a surprisingly diverse landscape and accommodation to suit most budgets.

When to Go
Suva

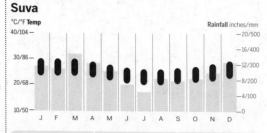

Jun–Sep High season, with costs peaking in June and July.

May & Oct Shoulder season and the beginning and end of the dry season.

Nov–Apr Expect wet and humid weather.

Connections

The Mamanuca Group and Yasawa Group are reached by ferry or high-speed catamaran from Nadi. Ovalau has boat and bus transfers via Suva but these take several hours. Ovalau and further-flung islands like Vanua Levu, Taveuni and Kadavu are most quickly reached by plane, although interisland services are cancelled at the hint of bad weather. Cargo ships are another option and the new *Lomaiviti Princess* has made this a cleaner and more reliable option.

ITINERARIES

One Week

From **Nadi** follow the Coral Coast Hwy south to the **Momi Guns**, and **Natadola Beach** for horse riding. Chug into the verdant interior on the **Coral Coast Scenic Railway** or trek to the top of the **Sigatoka Sand Dunes**. Make your way to **Pacific Harbour** for diving with sharks in **Beqa Lagoon**. Don't miss the chance to raft the canyons of the **Navua River** before heading to **Suva**. Complete your loop via the Kings Rd, windsurfing at **Nananu-i-Ra** or scuba diving at **Rakiraki**. Head back to sugar country and visit **Lautoka**, the second-largest city and a great base for exploring the **Nausori Highlands**. If you have an extra night, spend it at the traditional village of **Navala** before heading back to Nadi.

Two Weeks

Thanks to a high-speed catamaran that weaves daily from **Port Denarau** through the **Yasawas** and back, this chain is readily explored. The boat passes a few of the **Mamanucas** on the way, so these islands are a good place to start. Spend the next few days on the sliver of sand that connects **Wayasewa** to **Waya** before drifting north to **Naviti** to snorkel with manta rays. Dash up to **Nacula**, or **Nanuya Lailai**, where you can paddle in the **Blue Lagoon**. From here, leapfrog back down the chain, stopping at **Matacawalevu** and Naviti once more.

Essential Food & Drink

» **Yaqona** Also called kava or grog, this mildly narcotic drink is a muddy tea made from a root.

» **Lovo** Traditional Fijian oven where food is cooked in a pit on hot stones.

» **Kokoda** A raw-fish salad marinated in lime juice, mixed with vegetables and topped with coconut cream.

» **Palusami** Corned beef or onions with coconut cream, all wrapped and baked in young taro leaves.

» **Thali** Set Indian meals with several curries.

» **Roti** Literally this is an Indian flatbread, but the term often refers to the bread stuffed with a dry curry dish – a great quick meal.

AT A GLANCE

Currency Fijian dollar (F$)

Language Fijian, Fijian Hindi, English

Mobile phones Prepaid SIM cards

Money ATMs on main islands only

Visas Free

FIJI

Fast Facts

» **Capital** Suva (Viti Levu)
» **Country code** ☏679
» **Emergency** ☏911
» **Land area** 18,274 sq km
» **Population** 849,000

Exchange Rates

Australia	A$1	F$1.85
Canada	C$1	F$1.80
Europe	€1	F$2.30
Japan	¥100	F$2.30
New Zealand	NZ$1	F$1.45
UK	UK£1	F$2.85
USA	US$1	F$1.85

For current exchange rates see www.xe.com.

Set Your Budget

» **Local restaurant main course** F$15–20
» **Half-day snorkelling** F$15–20
» **Bunch of bananas** F$2
» **Yasawa Flyer (seven-day pass)** F$321
» **Car hire** from F$125 per day

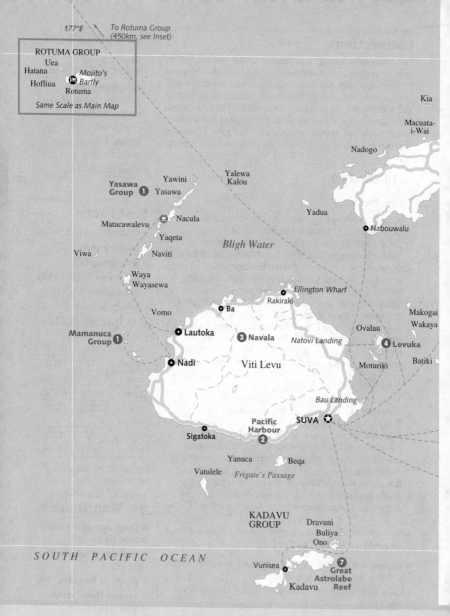

ROTUMA GROUP
Uea
Hatana
Hofliua
Rotuma
Mojito's
Barfly
Same Scale as Main Map

177°E
*To Rotuma Group
(450km, see Inset)*

Kia
Macuata-
i-Wai
Nadogo
Nabouwalu

Yasawa
Group ➊
Yawini
Yasawa
Yalewa
Kalou
Yadua

Matacawalevu
Nacula
Yaqeta

Viwa
Naviti

Bligh Water

Waya
Wayasewa
Vomo

Ellington Wharf
Rakiraki
Makogai
Wakaya

Mamanuca
Group ➊
Ba
Lautoka
➌ Navala
Natovi Landing
Ovalau
➍ Levuka
Batiki

Nadi
Viti Levu
Moturiki

Bau Landing

Sigatoka
Pacific
Harbour
➋
SUVA ✪

Yanuca
Beqa
Vatulele
Frigate's Passage

KADAVU
GROUP
Dravuni
Buliya
Ono

SOUTH   PACIFIC   OCEAN

Vunisea
➐
Great
Astrolabe
Reef
Kadavu

Fiji Highlights

➊ Relaxing in the cobalt waters and somniferous sun of the **Mamanuca** (p99) and **Yasawa** (p105) islands

➋ Remembering to breathe when the first bull shark swims

into view in the waters off **Pacific Harbour** (p84)

➌ Having a drink at the *tanoa* bowl in the traditional village of **Navala** (p75)

➍ Strolling around the colonial architecture of Fiji's first capital, **Levuka** (p112)

➎ Dropping anchor with the yachties at **Savusavu Bay** (p115)

180° Cikobia

178°W

16°S

N 0 _____ 100 km
   0 _____ 50 miles

Vetauua

Quelevu

Nukusemanu

Nukubasage
Nukubalati

Drua
Drua

Mali

Labasa

Vanua Levu

Rabi   Cobia

Kioa   Yanuca

Buca Bay

Matei

Nanuku
Lailai

Nanuku
Levu

Wailagi Lala

⑤ Savusavu

Somosomo
Strait

⑥ Somosomo

Savusavu
Bay

⑧ Lavena
   Coastal
   Walk

Taveuni

Nanuku
Passage

Naitaba

Malima

Vanua
Balavu

Avea

Koro

Nukutolu

Yacata

Kaidu

Kanacea

Cikobia-i-Lau

Moana's Guesthouse

Namalata

Susui

Munia

LOMAIVITI
GROUP

Vatu Vara

Mago

Karafaga

Vekai

Nairai

Tuvuca

LAU GROUP

Yarous

Gau

KORO SEA

Cicia

Nayau

Lakeba

Aiwa

Vanua Vatu

Oneata

Moala

Olorau

Moce

Komo

Tavua Na Sici

Namuka-i-Lau

Vuaqava

Same Scale as
Main Map

MOALA
GROUP

Totoya

Kabara

Navutu-i-Ra

Yagasa

19°S

Marabo

Navutu-i-Loma

Ono-i-Lau

Same Scale as
Main Map

To Vatoa
(140km,
see Inset)

Fulaga

Ogea Levu

To Ono-i-Lau
(290km, see Inset)

Matuku

Vatoa

⑥ Donning a mask, fins
and maybe a tank to explore
Taveuni's **Somosomo Strait**
(p133)

⑦ Diving or snorkelling with
manta rays at Kadavu's **Great
Astrolabe Reef** (p133)

⑧ Hiking or kayaking
Taveuni's **Lavena Coastal
Walk** (p132) then staying the
night in Lavena village

VITI LEVU

POP 600,000 / AREA 10,400 SQ KM

Like a grand chief presiding over a tribal council, Viti Levu, the largest of the Fijian islands, is the pivotal point around which the wheels of industry, commerce and politics turn. The 'mainland's' beaches may run a distant second to those of the outer islands, but Viti Levu's lush interior and steamy highlands offer dramatic vistas and some of the country's best trekking. The hinterland is framed by the resort-rich Coral Coast on its southern side and by the less-visited and more rugged Kings Rd to the north. Befitting its status as the largest South Pacific city, Suva is a sultry hub of culture, cuisine and urban activity, and it offers an engaging glimpse into a nation far different from that depicted by Fiji's promotional adverts.

ⓘ Information

Suva, the country's capital, largest city and main port, is in the southeast. Most travellers arrive in the west of the island at Nadi International Airport, 9km north of central Nadi and 24km south of Lautoka.

Nadi and Suva are linked by the sealed Queens Rd that runs along the southern perimeter of Viti Levu (221km) and contains the scattering of villages and resorts known as the Coral Coast.

Heading north from Suva, the Kings Rd is mostly sealed and travels for 265km through Nausori (where Suva's airport is located), the eastern highlands, Rakiraki, Ba (on the north coast), and Lautoka. South of Rakiraki is Fiji's highest point – Tomanivi (Mt Victoria) at 1323m.

Three roads head up from the coast to the Nausori Highlands villages of Navala and Bukuya (via Ba, Nadi and Sigatoka).

ⓘ Dangers & Annoyances

Travelling around Viti Levu is easy and safe, and most visitors will encounter a warm reception, particularly in rural areas. Walking around towns during daylight hours is a perfectly safe exercise; however, as soon as night descends it's a no-go. This is particularly pertinent in Suva – from dusk onwards, locals will catch a taxi, even for a distance of 300m, and you should as well. Muggings and sexual assaults are a common risk, especially for solo travellers.

ⓘ Getting There & Away

Most travellers arrive in Fiji at Nadi International Airport. Nadi and Suva are both domestic transport hubs, with flights to many of the other islands, as well as boat services and cruises to offshore islands. See p142 and individual island sections for information on interisland flights and ferry details.

ⓘ Getting Around

AIR For those in a hurry or after a scenic flight, there are cheap, regular light-plane flights between Nadi and Suva for around F$180.

BUS Viti Levu also has a cheap and frequent bus network. Express buses operated by Pacific Transport and Sunbeam Transport link the main centres of Lautoka, Nadi and Suva, along both the Queens Rd and the Kings Rd. Slower local buses also operate throughout the island, and even remote inland villages have regular (though less-frequent) services. Before heading to an isolated area, check that there is a return bus, as sometimes the last bus of the day stays overnight at the final village.

Companies and services available:

Coral Sun Fiji (☑672 3105; www.coralsun fiji.com) Runs comfortable, air-conditioned coaches between Nadi's airport and Suva (F$22, four hours, twice daily), stopping at resorts on the Coral Coast.

Feejee Experience (☑672 5950; www.feejee experience.com) Offers hop-on-hop-off coach packages from F$449.

Pacific Transport Limited Lautoka (☑666 0499); Nadi (☑670 0044); Sigatoka (☑650 0088); Suva (☑330 4366) About six express buses run daily between Lautoka and Suva (F$14.25, five/six hours for express/regular services) via the Coral Coast.

Sunbeam Transport Limited Lautoka (☑666 2822); Suva (☑338 2122, 338 2704) Nine Lautoka–Suva express services go daily via the Queens Rd (F$17.74, five hours). In addition, about nine services daily travel via the Kings Rd (F$20.70).

MINIBUS, CAR & TAXI Minibuses and carriers (small trucks) also shuttle locals along the Queens Rd. Taxis are plentiful, but drivers don't always use meters, so confirm the price in advance. Viti Levu is also easy to explore by car or motorbike, although for the unsealed highland roads you'll generally need a 4WD.

Nadi

POP 31,400

Nadi is Fiji's revolving door, the neck in the hourglass through which everyone must pass. Its proximity to the airport and Port Denarau ensures a constant flow of travellers arriving and departing, and consequently this town-cum-business-centre is littered with hotels, shops and eateries. While Nadi is a convenient base from which to organise trips around Viti Levu and to offshore islands, there are no real 'must-sees' in Nadi itself. The most common advice you'll hear from seasoned travellers is to get in,

get stocked up and get out. Nadi makes no bones about this – in fact, it specialises in helping people do just that.

Sights

Sri Siva Subramaniya Swami Temple
TEMPLE

(Map p72; admission F$3.50; ☺5.30am-7pm) Striking a vibrant pose against a dramatic mountainous backdrop, this peaceful Hindu temple leaves the hustle of Main St far in its wake. The temple itself is decorated with carved wooden deities that travelled all the way from India, along with the artists who painted the multihued exterior and vivid frescoes. It is one of the few places outside India where you can see traditional Dravidian architecture, and there is usually a temple custodian on hand to help answer those curly questions about Lord Shiva's various reincarnations.

Visitors are welcome as long as they're dressed modestly, leave their shoes at the entrance and take photos only from the outside.

Garden of the Sleeping Giant
GARDENS

(Map p76; Wailoko Rd; adult/child F$14.50/7.50; ☺9am-5pm Mon-Sat, 9am-noon Sun) This beautiful garden is a tribute to the orchid, boasting dozens of varieties of the colourful flower amid a sea of tropical vegetation. Tucked beneath the foothills of the Sabeto mountain range, the garden offers visitors a network of walking tracks, lily ponds and perfect picnic spots. To get here, travel along the Queens Rd for about 6km north of Nadi airport and turn east onto Wailoko Rd for a further 2km. A taxi from Nadi will cost around F$13.

Sabeto Hot Springs
SPRING

(Map p76; admission F$12; ☺9am-5pm Mon-Sat) A few kilometres further inland from the Garden of the Sleeping Giant are the Sabeto Hot Springs; a series of geothermal hot pools with floors of soft and silty, knee-deep mud. The pools are very informal – just a few ponds in a field – but they are fun. What starts as a few playful smears invariably turns into a full-on fight with mud slinging from all quarters.

Activities & Tours

Nadi is a good base from which to explore the west side of Viti Levu (check out p72 for a rundown on the tours offered by Nadi travel agents) and take day trips to the closer of the Mamanuca and Yasawa islands.

Sleeping

The black-sand New Town and Wailoaloa beaches will disappoint anyone with visions of white sands and aqua oceans, but they are quiet and peaceful and the best beaches Nadi has to offer. Closer to town, there's a scattering of hotels along the Queens Rd that have easy access to buses in and out of downtown. Most accommodation offers free transfers from the airport if they know to expect you.

NEW TOWN BEACH

Smugglers Cove Beach Resort & Hotel
HOSTEL $

(Map p73; ☑672 6578; www.smugglersbeachfiji. com; Wasawasa Rd; dm incl breakfast F$28-38, r F$135-195; ✳@☒) This modern resort straddles the backpacker–midrange market with clean and simple rooms for the latter

---

HINDU SYMBOLISM

Tiny Hindu temples and shrines dot the Fijian countryside, each one symbolising the body or residence of the soul. For Hindus, union with God can be achieved through prayer and by ridding the body of impurities – hence no meat in the belly or shoes on the feet when entering a temple.

Inside the temples, Hindus give symbolic offerings and blessings to their many gods. Water and flowers symbolise the Great Mother who personifies nature, while burning camphor represents the light of knowledge and understanding. Smashing a coconut denotes cracking humans' three weaknesses: egotism (the hard shell), delusion (the fibre) and material attachments (the outermost covering). The white kernel and sweet water represent the pure soul within.

Hindus believe that a body enslaved to the spirit and denied all comforts will become one with the Great Mother. Life is compared to walking on fire: a disciplined approach, like that required in the fire-walking ceremony, leads to balance, self-acceptance and the ability to see good in all.

66

Viti Levu

FIJI NADI

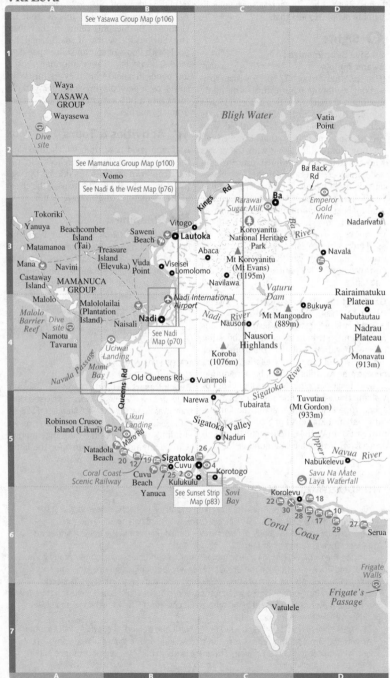

See Yasawa Group Map (p106)

See Mamanuca Group Map (p100)

See Nadi & the West Map (p76)

See Nadi Map (p70)

See Sunset Strip Map (p83)

Waya
YASAWA
GROUP
Wayasewa

Dive
site

Bligh Water

Vatia
Point

Ba Back
Rd

Emperor
Gold
Mine

Nadarivatu

Vomo

Kings Rd

Rarawai
Sugar Mill

Ba

Ba River

Tokoriki
Yanuya
Beachcomber
Island
(Tai)
Matamanoa
Treasure
Island
(Elevuka)
Mana
Navini
Castaway
Island
MAMANUCA
GROUP
Malolo
Malololailai
(Plantation
Island)

Vitogo
Saweni
Beach
Lautoka
Abaca
Viseisei
Vuda
Point
Lomolomo
Navilawa

Koroyanitu
National Heritage
Park
Mt Koroyanitu
(Mt Evans)
(1195m)

Navala
9

Malolo
Barrier
Reef
Dive
site
Namotu
Tavarua

Naisali

Nadi

Nadi International
Airport

Nadi River

Nausori

Vaturu
Dam

Mt Mangondro
(889m)

Bukuya

Rairaimatuku
Plateau
Nabutautau
Nadrau
Plateau

Navula Passage

Uciwai
Landing

Momi
Bay

Queens Rd

Old Queens Rd

Vunimoli

Koroba
(1076m)

Nausori
Highlands

1

Sigatoka River

Monavatu
(913m)

Narewa

Tubairata

Tuvutau
(Mt Gordon)
(933m)

Robinson Crusoe
Island (Likuri)

Likuri
Landing

Maro Rd

24

Sigatoka Valley

Naduri

Upper Navua River

Natadola
Beach

20

12

19

26

Sigatoka

Cuvu

4

Nabukelevu

Cuvu
Beach

Coral Coast
Scenic Railway

25

2

Kulukulu

Korotogo

Savu Na Mate
Laya Waterfall

Yanuca

See Sunset Strip
Map (p83)

Sovi
Bay

Korolevu

22

30

28

7

17

18

10

Coral Coast

29

27

Serua

Frigate
Walls

Vatulele

Frigate's
Passage

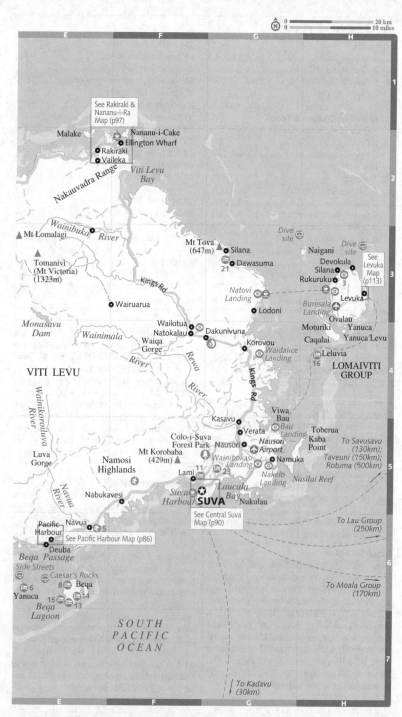

0 20 km
0 10 miles

Malake
See Rakiraki &
Nananu-i-Ra
Map (p97)
Nananu-i-Cake
Ellington Wharf
Rakiraki
Vaileka
Viti Levu
Bay
Nakauvadra Range

Mt Lomalagi
Wainibuka River

Tomanivi
(Mt Victoria)
(1323m)
Kings Rd
Mt Tova
(647m)
Silana
Dawasuma
21
Dive
site
Naigani
Dive
site
See
Levuka
Map (p113)
Devokula
Silana
Rukuruku
3
Levuka

Wairuarua
Natovi
Landing
Lodoni
Buresala
Landing
Ovalau
Yanuca
Moturiki
Yanuca Levu

Monasavu
Dam
Wainimala
Wailotua
Natokalau
Dakunivuna
Waiqa
Gorge
Rewa
Korovou
Waidalice
Landing
Caqalai
Leluvia
16
LOMAIVITI
GROUP

VITI LEVU
Wainimala
River
River

Wainikoroiluva River
Kasavu
Viwa
Bau
Bau
Landing
Toberua
Kaba
Point
To Savusavu
(130km);
Taveuni (150km);
Rotuma (500km)

Luva
Gorge
Namosi
Highlands
Colo-i-Suva
Forest Park
Mt Korobaba
(429m)
Verata
Nausori
Nausori
Airport
Wainibokasi
Landing
Namuka
Nakelo
Landing
Nasilai Reef

Nabukavesi
Lami
11
23
Suva
Harbour
SUVA
Laucala
Bay
Nukulau

Navua
River
Navua
5
See Central Suva
Map (p90)
To Lau Group
(250km)

Pacific
Harbour
Deuba
See Pacific Harbour Map (p86)
Beqa Passage
Side Streets
Caesar's Rocks
Yanuca
6
8
Beqa
15
14
13
Beqa
Lagoon
To Moala Group
(170km)

SOUTH
PACIFIC
OCEAN

To Kadavu
(30km)

Viti Levu

and a range of dorm options from four to 34 beds. It's popular with the younger crowd who take advantage of the tour desk, restaurant, minimart, coin-operated laundry and free use of the Nadi Airport Golf Course.

Bluewater Lodge   HOSTEL $
(Map p73; ☑672 8858; bluewaterfiji@connect.com. fj; New Town Beach; dm incl breakfast F$15-40, d incl breakfast F$135; ☯❋☎) This spick-and-span house has been converted into a trendy little backpackers. Each dorm has only three or four beds and there's a small pool in the garden. It's a 500m walk to the beach but, for those wanting a little peace and quiet, this is the pick of the bunch. The wee restaurant (mains F$16 to F$25) and bar opens for dinner only.

Aquarius Fiji   HOSTEL $
(Map p73; ☑672 6000; www.aquarius.com.fj; 17 Wasawasa Rd; dm incl breakfast F$32-36, d F$126-138; ☯❋@☎) This professional set-up attracts backpackers by the planeload. There's a good restaurant, lively bar, and a beachside pool area with enough hammocks for the sun-starved masses. Double rooms are cheerful and sunny, and those upstairs have balconies overlooking the beach. The cheaper dorms sleep 12 and are slightly airless and cramped when full.

Tropic of Capricorn   HOSTEL $
(Map p73; ☑672 6607; www.tropicofcapricorn fiji.com; dm F$20-25, d F$90-120; ☯❋☎) This place gets good reviews from those seeking a home-away-from-home. The older, fan-cooled rooms are still here, while a newer three-storey block occupies the prime beachfront location; the pool is sandwiched between the two. The meals (mains F$10 to F$18) are good value and Mama cooks up a mean mash – reason enough for many to stay.

WAILOALOA BEACH
Beachside Resort   RESORT $
(Map p70; ☑670 3488; www.beachsideresortfiji. com; Wailoaloa Beach Rd; r incl breakfast F$78-155; ☯❋@☎) The moniker's a tad misleading, but this compact and private resort (away from the beach) provides more comfort than a backpackers and is easier on the wallet than a resort. The rooms are stylish and immaculate and dressed with cheery Fijian prints. Cheaper rooms are tucked behind the main complex, while others have balconies overlooking the central pool. Windows have flyscreens and wooden shutters (no glass), which makes it dark when the air-con's on. The in-house Coriander Cafe (mains F$20 to F$25) has an inventive blackboard menu.

Club Fiji Resort
RESORT $$

(Map p70; ✆672 0150; www.clubfiji-resort.com; Wailoaloa Beach Rd; bungalows F$118-173, villas F$186; ⊝❄☒) Making the most of its beachside location, Club Fiji feels more like a resort and less like a transit stop than most other options around Nadi. Daily activities include good-value fishing trips (F$30 per person per hour; minimum two people) and free nonmotorised water sports. In the accommodation stakes you can choose between Mediterranean-style villas, ocean-view *bure* (bungalows) or smaller timber and thatched *bure*.

QUEENS ROAD

Mercure Hotel Nadi
HOTEL $$

(Map p73; ✆672 2255; www.mercure.com; Queens Rd, Martintar; r F$135-175; ⊝❄@☒) Renovated and fancied-up into a flashy haven of creature comforts, the Mercure offers deluxe or modern superior rooms, all of which have bar fridges, TVs and sassy bathrooms. Families populate the grassy grounds, which include a small pool and al fresco restaurant (mains F$30 to F$45).

Nadi Bay Resort Hotel
RESORT $

(Map p73; ✆672 3599; www.fijinadibayhotel.com; Wailoaloa Rd, Martintar; dm F$35-36, r without bathroom F$75-89, s/d with bathroom F$110/185; ⊝❄@☒) One of Nadi's best-equipped budget resorts, this serves a mixed bag of package-tour guests and backpackers in its wide range of rooms, two excellent restaurants (mains F$15 to F$35), two bars, palm-fringed pools and small movie theatre. Some rooms are better value than others but the standard is fairly good.

Hexagon International
HOTEL $

(Map p73; ✆672 0044; www.hexagonfiji.com; Queens Rd, Martintar; r F$66-77, apt F$163; ❄@☎☒) This complex contains a series of rooms surrounding a total of three pools, the largest of which is beside the apartments. While standard and deluxe rooms are sparsely furnished, they offer excellent value for the budget traveller, and the self-contained apartments are sizeable and comfortable. There's a poolside bar and restaurant (dinner F$21 to F$27), and massage facilities are available at the beauty spa next door.

NEAR THE AIRPORT

Raffles Gateway Hotel
RESORT $$

(Map p70; ✆672 2444; www.rafflesgateway.com; d & tw F$103-175; ⊝❄@☒☞) Directly opposite the airport, behind the mock-colonial entrance, Raffles is a sound choice. Those with kids will appreciate the pool's water slide and the fact that children under 16 stay free. Cheaper standard rooms are pinchy but cool and crisp, while the superior rooms are a leap in value with their lounge furniture, TVs and private patios. There's a poolside restaurant (mains F$20 to F$35) and a grassed central courtyard flanked by massive bougainvilleas that give an accurate idea of the age of this long-time favourite.

Tanoa Skylodge
LODGE $

(Map p70; ✆672 2200; www.tanoahotels.com; Queens Rd, Namaka; dm F$31-36, r F$80-120; ⊝❄@☒) Set well off the main road in a grassy compound, the Skylodge has enough space to accommodate a small army of holidaymakers. Like most accommodation at this price level, the dorms and basic singles and doubles are fairly spartan, although for a bit more you can get air-conditioning, a private bathroom, phone and TV. On-site facilities include a restaurant (mains F$15 to F$20), volleyball courts, a games room, a tour desk and a large pool.

Novotel Nadi
RESORT $$

(Map p70; ✆672 2000; www.novotel.com; Namaka; r from F$178; ⊝❄@☎☒☞) The Novotel (once the Mocambo) underwent a major overhaul with the name change and now features the brown-on-beige colour scheme so popular with Fiji's hip hotels. The rooms aren't huge, but many enjoy mountain views and all come with flat-screen TVs and internet connections. In addition to the usual facilities you'd expect at a top hotel – like shops, business centre and swimming pool – there is also a nine-hole golf course and day spa. Children under 16 stay free, and decent same-day discounts are offered depending on availability.

Tanoa International
RESORT $$

(Map p70; ✆672 0277; www.tanoahotels.com; r from F$178; ⊝❄@☒☞) The Tanoa International is the flagship of the Tanoa chain and by far its finest hotel; its 148 rooms still include some of the best this side of Denarau. Guests here enjoy tennis courts, a beauty spa, gym, lush gardens, swanky cafes and Saturday curry and Sunday roast buffets. Again, substantial same-day discounts are likely for walk-ins. Kids aged 12 and under stay free.

Nadi

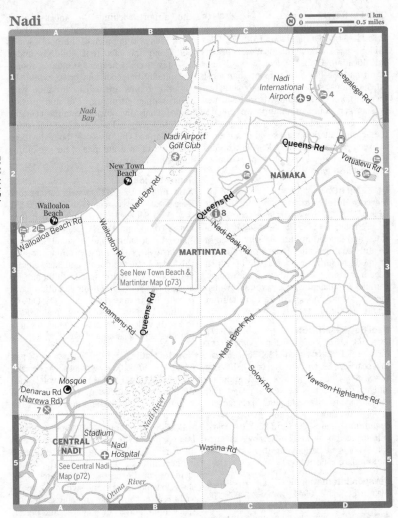

NADI OUTSKIRTS

Stoney Creek Resort RESORT $

(Map p76; ☎620 3644; www.stoneycreekfiji.net; Sabeto Rd; dm incl breakfast F$45, r with shared bathroom incl breakfast F$85, r with bathroom incl breakfast F$150-180; @⚊) Hidden at the base of the highlands, this resort has a taste of the Wild West with cosy dorms in mock train carriages and doubles with sweeping views in cute and private *bure*. There's a saloon-style bar and restaurant (meals F$13 to F$25) and a good range of activities on offer, plus free internet. The resort also pays airport transfers for two-night and longer stays. Regular 'Sabeto' buses

run from Nadi bus station (F$1.90, one every 1½ hours between 8am and 5.30pm).

Eating

Although small, Nadi caters to travellers' palates well with a decent variety of Indian, Chinese and Western cuisine. Most hotels and resorts have restaurants where nonguests are welcome.

The bottom end of Main St in downtown Nadi has a number of cheap curry houses, all of which expend far more energy on the cheap nosh than on the dim surrounds. You can lunch there for around F$5.

Nadi

Nadi has a large **produce market** (Map p72; Hospital Rd) with lots of fresh fruit and vegetables, as well as several bakeries and large supermarkets on Main St.

TOP CHOICE Blue Bure
FUSION $$
(Map p70; 670 7030; cnr Narewa & Queen's Rd; mains F$15-25; ⊙lunch & dinner Mon-Sat) Tropical green and blue walls and eclectic decor feature in this low-key, funky bar-restaurant. Food is fresh, delicious and fusion, reflecting the American/Italian/Tunisian/Fijian mix of the family that runs it; chicken, coconut and ginger tortellini followed by a shisha pipe and mint tea, perhaps? (Oh – and a visit to the loo is, in the nicest possible way, a must.) Light lunches are around F$10.

Daikoku
JAPANESE $$$
(Map p73; 670 3622; cnr Queens Rd & Northern Press Rd, Martintar; mains F$30-52; ⊙lunch & dinner Mon-Sat) Perched around large hotplates, patrons sip Asahi beer while their individual chef performs the sometimes gentle, sometimes energetic, but always entertaining art of teppanyaki. There's also delicate sushi or sashimi and good-value lunch specials (F$15).

Small Plates
CHINESE $
(Map p73; Queens Rd, Martintar; dishes from F$6; ⊙dinner) Think Chinese tapas and you've got the measure of this low-key bar-restaurant set back in a garden off the main road. An odd-seeming mix, perhaps, but it works – and full marks to the crisp and delicious salt-and-pepper squid. It opens at 4pm, for a happy hour that stretches until 8pm.

Bulaccino
CAFE $
(Map p72; 672 8638; Main St, Nadi; light meals & snacks F$5-20; ⊙breakfast & lunch; ⊛⊛@) This place has the perfect antidote to shoppers' fatigue – riverside tables, strong coffee and scrummy cakes. Healthy options include salads, roti wraps, Bircher muesli and fresh tropical juices.

Saffron & Corner Cafe
INDIAN $$
(Map p72; 670 1233; Jacks Mall, Sagayam Rd, Nadi; mains F$15-25; ⊙lunch & dinner Mon-Sat, dinner Sun; ⊛⊛) This place has a split personality. On one side is a cafe serving regular light lunches and burgers, while the other half is an upmarket Indian restaurant specialising in fine Indian cuisine.

Mama's Pizza
PIZZERIA $$
(Map p72; 670 0221; Main St, Nadi; mains F$9-22; ⊙lunch & dinner; ⊛⊛) Traditionalists may want to stick to the proven crowd-pleasers, but everyone else should check out the flip side of the menu for the gourmet varieties. This downtown store (there are a few shops around town) is rather dark and uninviting, although the wood-fired pizzas here are the best around.

Drinking

Most travellers seem content to drink at the hotel bars and restaurants, but to rub shoulders with locals head to either of these pubs in Martintar, on the way to the airport.

Bounty Restaurant & Bar
SPORTS BAR
(Map p73; 79 Queens Rd, Martintar) This convivial bar-restaurant is named after the local rum (not the chocolate bar) and is thick with seafaring kitsch. Even though it hosts a solid drinking phase somewhere between dinner and the live music, most drunken sailors are well behaved.

Ed's Bar
PUB
(Map p73; Lot 51, Queens Rd, Martintar) Ed's is the other long-time favourite and, like Bounty across the road, you'll need to get your beer boots on early if you want a table to rest your Fiji Bitter on. On Friday and Saturday nights live bands often hit the boards; otherwise, the music favours the jazz, hip-hop and rap genres.

Shopping

Nadi's Main St is a tribute to souvenir and duty-free shops, and their mass-produced products are aimed unashamedly at mass tourism. Some of the strong-arm tactics

Central Nadi

Fiji Visitors Bureau (FVB; Map p70; ☑672 2433; www.fijime.com; ste 107, Colonial Plaza, Namaka; ⊙8am-4.30pm Mon-Thu, to 4pm Fri) Fiji's official tourism bureau is geared more to marketing to travel agents than to assisting walk-in visitors.

Police (Map p72; ☑emergency 917, 670 0222; Koroivolu Ave)

Post office Airport (Nadi International Airport); Downtown (Map p72; Sahu Kahn Rd, Nadi)

Travel Agencies

The travel agents at the airport will find you before you've had time to hail a taxi. The major and more reputable companies have offices and representatives on the ground, while the 13 agencies upstairs are smaller local operators that take turns pouncing on anyone with a backpack. They can offer good deals but their advice isn't impartial.

Some agencies:

Rosie Holidays (Map p70; ☑672 2755; www. rosiefiji.com; Nadi airport concourse) The largest and best resourced agency in Fiji. Rosie Holidays manages the tour desks at many resorts and organises group multiday treks into the central highlands and the Sigatoka Valley, and day treks to the Nausori Highlands, as well as busloads of road tours to Sigatoka Valley/ Kula Eco Park, Viseisei village/Garden of the Sleeping Giant, and Pacific Harbour. It is also the agent for Thrifty Car Rental.

Tourist Transport Fiji (Map p70; ☑672 2074; www.touristtransportfiji.com; Nadi airport concourse) This company operates the twice-daily Coral Sun Nadi–Suva/Suva–Nadi scheduled bus services; Feejee Experience bus transfers and package tours; and Great Sights Fiji small-group 4WD tours to destinations including Navilawa in Koroyanitu National Heritage Park (F$139 per person) and to Navala in the Nausori Highlands (F$215 per person).

employed in the smaller shops can be a bit tiring, although it's nothing compared with Asia or India.

Nadi Handicraft Market   HANDICRAFTS
(Map p72; Koroivolu Ave, Nadi) The market offers the best chance of finding something unique, but it's wise to check the prices in the major shops beforehand.

ℹ Information

You won't have any trouble finding banks and ATMs in central Nadi and Martintar, and there is an ANZ bank (with ATM) at the airport. It opens for all international flights. Internet is also thick on the ground in Nadi and costs around F$3 per hour.

DSM Medical Centre (Map p72; ☑670 0240; www.dsmcentrefiji.com.fj; 2 Lodhia St; ⊙8.30am-4.30pm Mon-Fri, 8.30am-12.30pm Sat) Specialising in travel medicine, with radiology and physiotherapy departments.

❶ Getting Around

BUS Nadi International Airport is 9km north of downtown Nadi; there are frequent local buses just outside the airport that travel along the Queens Rd to town (F$0.65). Buses travel regularly between New Town Beach and downtown Nadi (F$0.80, 15 minutes, Monday to Saturday).

TAXI Taxis are plentiful in Nadi, but they generally don't use meters; agree on a price before getting in.

Around Nadi

DENARAU ISLAND

Like a cruise ship docked at a port, Denarau Island (2.55 sq km) is an artificial enclave of top-end resorts, manicured gardens, heavenly pools and professionally run tourist facilities. Although it bears little resemblance to the rest of Fiji, it's a popular place to indulge in some pampering at one of the international resorts here. Be warned – what the brochures and websites don't advertise is that Denarau is built on reclaimed mangrove mudflats, and the beach has dark-grey sand and murky water unsuitable for snorkelling.

⚡ Activities

Adrenalin Watersports   WATER SPORTS
(Map p74; ☎675 0061; www.adrenalinfiji.com) This company has the licence to run the water-sports shops at all of the Denarau resorts and at **Port Denarau Retail Centre**. It specialises in jet-ski tours to Beachcomber, Castaway or Malolo islands (F$500 solo riders), and offers parasailing, wakeboarding, hot-air ballooning and more.

Denarau Golf & Racquet Club   GOLF, TENNIS
(Map p74; ☎675 9711; info@denaraugolf.com.fj; ⊙6.30am-6.30pm) This club has an immaculately groomed 18-hole golf course with bunkers in the shape of sea creatures. Green fees are F$145/95 for 18/nine holes; tennis courts cost F$35 per hour.

🛏 Sleeping & Eating

Proving that money loves company, seven resorts have opened in Denarau and more are planned. They each have four or five restaurants and a bevy of bars, and welcome their competitors' guests with open arms. The inter-resort 'bula' bus (F$7 per person, unlimited daily travel) trundles between them (and the port) on a continuous circuit.

Radisson Blu Resort Fiji   RESORT $$$
(Map p74; ☎675 6677; www.radisson.com/fiji; r from F$442; ❄✳@🛜🏊👶) The Radisson has

New Town Beach & Martintar

taken pool design to new heights. Faced with an unappealing beach, the architects have spared no expense with this mammoth free-form pool. Its waterfall can be seen from the reception, and it boasts lagoons, sandy beaches, a white-water tunnel, adult areas and an island containing a day spa. The kids club here is F$20 per day and there are free kayaks, windsurfers and catamarans. There are 270 rooms.

Denarau Island

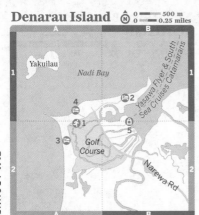

N   0 |———| 500 m
    0 |———| 0.25 miles

Denarau Island

◉ Sights
Adrenalin Watersports .... (see 5)

✦ Activities, Courses & Tours
1 Denarau Golf & Racquet Club A2
   Island Hoppers .... (see 5)
   PJ's Sailing & Snorkelling .... (see 5)
   Seaspray .... (see 5)

🛏 Sleeping
2 Fiji Beach Resort & Spa
   Managed by Hilton B1
3 Radisson Blu Resort Fiji A2
4 Westin Denarau Island A1

🛍 Shopping
5 Port Denarau Retail Centre B2

ℹ Transport
Awesome Adventures .... (see 5)
Bus to Nadi; Resorts Shuttle .... (see 5)
Captain Cook Cruises .... (see 5)
Malolo Cat I & II .... (see 5)
Port Denarau Marina .... (see 5)
South Sea Cruises .... (see 5)

Fiji Beach Resort & Spa
Managed by Hilton   RESORT $$$
(Map p74; ☑675 6800; www.hilton.com; r from F$480; ☒✳@☏☒🐾) A series of seven rectangular, interlocking pools surrounded by artistically simple daybeds is a nice architectural change from the other resorts. The long beachfront (the best Denarau has to offer) can be seen from all 273 rooms (most with kitchens), and renowned restaurant

Nuku (mains from F$40) is on-site. The kids club here is free.

Westin Denarau Island   RESORT $$$
(Map p74; ☑675 0000; www.starwoodhotels.com; r from F$390; ☒✳@☏☒🐾) The Westin's elegant lobby features a beautiful blend of dark timber, pale sandstone and alternating low and vaulted ceilings. The small artificial beach here is a nice spot to relax, as is the resort's day spa. After some serious pampering, you can sit back and relax while taking in one of the twice-weekly fire-walking demonstrations. Children are welcome – the kids club has a one-time F$55 fee.

ℹ Getting There & Away
West Bus Transport (☑675 0777) runs frequently (less so on Sunday) between Nadi bus station and Denarau Island. A taxi from the airport/downtown costs F$24/12.

SONAISALI ISLAND
There's plenty of white sand at **Sonaisali Island Resort** (Map p76; ☑670 6011; www.sonaisali.com; r incl breakfast F$495-682, ste incl breakfast from F$891; ☒✳@☒🐾), but unfortunately none of it's on the beach. Like Denarau, Sonaisali is on the edge of mangroves, and the dark sand disappoints some. To compensate there is a large pool with a swim-up bar and an endless array of activities including a free kids club, and it remains a popular destination for antipodean package tourists. The meal plan (per day adult/child F$96/48) is the way to go for big eaters, but bring plenty of duty-free booze – the drinks are pricey (cocktails F$22). The hotel rooms in the double-storey building are getting tired, whereas the semi-detached *bure* are far nicer, with spa baths built into the verandahs.

Sonaisali is a 25-minute drive, followed by a three-minute boat shuttle (free for guests), south from Nadi airport. A taxi from the airport costs F$32, the resort shuttle F$55.

UCIWAI LANDING
Uciwai Landing, used by surfers to access the Mamanuca surf-breaks, is 25km southwest of Nadi. Surfing is really the only reason to head here, and the only place to stay is **Rendezvous Beach Resort** (Map p76; ☑628 1216; www.surfdivefiji.com; campsite per person F$33, dm F$40, r F$75-150, prices incl breakfast & internet; ✳@☒), where the air is thick with surfing lingo and the scent of board wax and sunblock. It's fairly basic and the staff are as languid as the seasoned surfers who visit,

but they will organise trips to Mamanuca surf-breaks. Resort transfers from Nadi/airport are F$40/60, or local buses to Uciwai from Nadi bus station (F$2) depart a couple of times a day Monday to Saturday.

VISEISEI & VUDA POINT

About 12km north of Nadi is Viseisei village, which, according to local lore, is the oldest settlement in Fiji. The story goes that *mataqali* (kinship groups) here are descendants of the first ocean-going Melanesians who landed 1km north of here circa 1500.

The **Vuda Point Marina** (Map p76; 666 8214; www.vudamarina.com.fj) is a well-organised and thriving boaties' lure. Facilities include free showers, an excellent noticeboard, coin-operated laundry, sailmakers, berths, a general store and cafe, and yacht-repair specialists and chandlery.

Perched on the water's edge and dripping with palms and colourful foliage, **First Landing Resort** (Map p76; 666 6171; www.firstlandingfiji.com; r incl breakfast from F$374, 2-bedroom villas incl breakfast from F$740;) is made to order for those who enjoy package holidays. The *bure* and villas are like cheerful hotel rooms with bright, tiled bathrooms and mosquito-screened verandahs. The more expensive villas have private plunge pools and, although the beach isn't great, there's an artificial island in the shape of a footprint. The restaurant serves excellent seafood (mains F$25 to F$38), pasta and wood-fired pizza.

KOROYANITU NATIONAL HERITAGE PARK

Just an hour's drive from Nadi or Lautoka, and deep within Viti Levu's interior, the beautiful Koroyanitu National Heritage Park seems a world away.

Sights & Activities

The area has a landscape of native dakua forests and grasslands, with many birds and several archaeological sites. Easiest access to the park is from tiny Navilawa village, north of the Sabeto Rd above Nadi – there are waterfalls and swimming holes along the road in.

After arrival (visitors should take a *sevusevu*, a gift to present to the village chief), take a short rainforest hike to a cave shelter that the villagers use during hurricanes, beside a clear-flowing creek. The village itself is set in an old volcanic crater, with forest and mountains around – a photographer's delight.

Self-sufficient visitors could spend an interesting couple of days staying here, being part of village life. A small, simple, self-contained **lodge** (Map p76; per person F$35) with six beds (and shower and flush toilet) is the only accommodation option; bedding is provided, but bring your own food.

Abaca (Am-*ba*-tha) village, southeast of Lautoka, is another, more logistically challenging, access option for the park. From here it's possible to make longer day hikes if guides are available.

Getting There & Away

4WD There is no local transport to Navilawa or Abaca, and getting to both villages requires 4WD; drivers would be wise to check directions with anyone on the road, as there are many small turnings.

To Navilawa from Nadi, take the Sabeto Rd and turn off left, 3.9km beyond Stoney Creek Resort; it's a further 9.3km to Navilawa. To Abaca from Lautoka, take Tavakubu Rd and turn off right, 4.7km from the main road. It's a further 10km of gravel road to Abaca.

TOURS A good option is to take a half-day guided tour (F$139 per person) to Navilawa with **Great Sights Fiji** (672 2074; www.touristtransportfiji.com).

NAUSORI HIGHLANDS & NAVALA

The grassy slopes of the Nausori Highlands snake their way into the mountainous interior, leaving the coastline and panoramic views in their wake. This region is one of the best places to experience traditional Fijian culture and hospitality, and although the region shares the same name as the airport town of Nausori near Suva, its small villages and scattered settlements are quite different.

HAVE YOUR SAY

Found a fantastic restaurant that you're longing to share with the world? Disagree with our recommendations? Or just want to talk about your most recent trip?

Whatever your reason, head to lonelyplanet.com, where you can post a review, ask or answer a question on the Thorntree forum, comment on a blog, or share your photos and tips on Groups. Or you can simply spend time chatting with like-minded travellers. So go on, have your say.

Nadi & the West

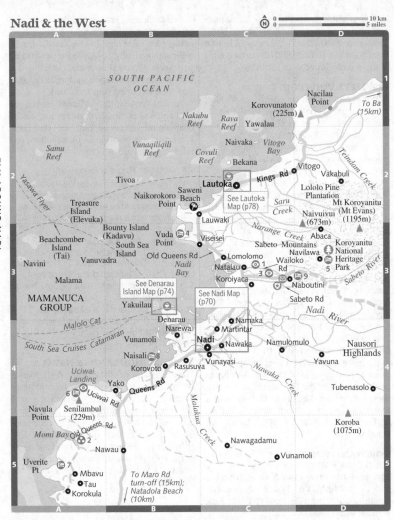

On the banks of the Ba River, tiny **Navala** (Map p66) is by far Fiji's most picturesque village. The houses here are all traditional *bure*, built with local materials using time-honoured techniques. Navala is a photographer's delight, but you need to get permission and pay the F$15 entrance fee before wandering around. If arriving independently, ask the first person you meet to take you to the *turaga-ni-koro* (the chief-appointed headman who collects the entrance fee). A traditional *sevusevu* is not required, although all other village etiquette applies.

Sleeping & Eating

Bulou's Eco Lodge
LODGE $

TOP CHOICE

(Map p66; ☑628 1224; dm/bungalows per person incl meals F$75/180) On the river's edge a kilometre south of Navala, Bulou N Talili and her son Tui have established a grass-roots ecolodge. There are two traditional, slightly tatty *bure* in the garden and a 10-bed dorm attached to the house with cold-water showers, flush toilets and limited electricity. Tui is a hereditary chief and excellent guide and he accompanies guests around the village introducing them to his relatives and friends. His mother is an excellent cook and

Nadi & the West

◎ Sights

takes her responsibility of keeping guests well fed seriously.

ⓘ Getting There & Away

BUS The local buses from Ba to Navala (F$3) leave Ba bus station at 12.30pm, 4.30pm and 5.15pm Monday to Saturday. Buses return to Ba at 6am, 7.30am and 1.45pm Monday to Friday. Ring Bulou's Eco Lodge in advance and they will pick you up from Navala.

CAR & 4WD If driving from Ba, there are a couple of turns to watch out for: at the police post turn left, passing a shop on your right, and at the next fork in the road keep left. The road is rough and rocky, but usually passable.

TOURS Several tour companies run day tours from Nadi to Navala.

Lautoka

POP 52,900

Sweet Lautoka is 'Sugar City' and its colonial history is entwined with the cane it's nicknamed after. The Lautoka Sugar Mill has been operating here since 1903 and the local economy still relies heavily on diminishing returns. During the cutting season, sugar trains putt along the main street and in September the city crowns a Sugar Queen at the annual Sugar Festival.

From a traveller's perspective, there's not much to do. If you wander the wide streets amid swaying saris and aromatic curry houses, stroll along the picturesque esplanade towards the sugar mill or take a peek at the small botanical gardens and the Hare Krishna **Sri Krishna Kaliya Temple** (Map p78; 5 Tavewa Ave; ⊙8am-6pm), you have

pretty much seen the best of the city. Banks and internet access are plentiful.

🛏 Sleeping

Sea Breeze Hotel   HOTEL **$**
(Map p78; ☑666 0017; seabreezefiji@connect.com.fj; Bekana Lane; r F$54-76; ⊛❄✿) Sequestered down an alley near the city centre, this hotel has cool, white and piously austere rooms that provide a spotless and tranquil sanctuary. The more expensive sea-view rooms with air-con are the nicest. There's also a TV lounge where breakfast is available (F$6.60 to F$8.80).

Cathay Hotel   HOTEL **$**
(Map p78 ☑666 0566; www.fiji4less.com; Tavewa Ave; dm F$24-26, r F$64-71; ❄✿) Easy on the wallet and with a handy central location, the Cathay's dorms and simple rooms are good value. There are only four beds to a dorm and the spacious rooms come with air-con or are fan-cooled, with or without private bathrooms.

Tanoa Waterfront   HOTEL **$$**
(Map p78 ☑666 4777; www.tanoawaterfront.com; Marine Dr; r F$168-188; ⊛❄@✿) Lautoka's top hotel has a top waterfront location. The cheapest rooms are spotlessly clean and have the ambience and trimmings of a mid-range US hotel chain. The more expensive rooms have contemporary interiors, flat-screen TVs and small balconies overlooking two pools. On-site is a gym, coin-operated laundry, small children's playground, a bar and restaurant.

🍴 Eating

Lautoka has fewer restaurants than Nadi or Suva but lots of inexpensive lunchtime eateries.

TOP CHOICE **Blue Ginger Café**   CAFE **$**
(Map p78; Post Office Roundabout; breakfast from F$6; ⊙breakfast & lunch Mon-Sat; ⊛❄) Delicious breakfasts (the menu includes homemade yoghurt, fruit and poached eggs) and lunches of wholemeal sandwiches, interesting wraps, fresh salads and buttery cakes and biscuits. It's run by a Swiss-Filipina couple; there's also truly good coffee (and/or a decent glass of wine) to go with the food.

Chilli Bites   INDIAN **$**
(Map p78; Yasawa St; meals from F$10-15; ⊙breakfast, lunch & dinner Mon-Sat, lunch & dinner Sun; ⊛❄) Ignore the scratched Formica tables

Lautoka

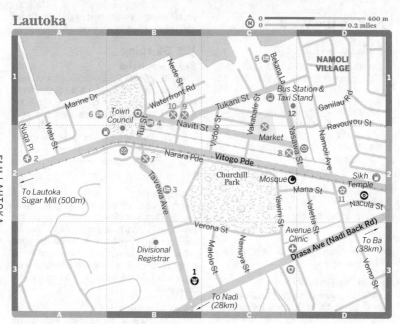

0 — 400 m
0 — 0.2 miles

Lautoka

⊙ Sights
1 Sri Krishna Kaliya Temple	B3

⊕ Activities, Courses & Tours
2 Blue Lagoon Cruises	A2

🛏 Sleeping
3 Cathay Hotel	B2
4 Lautoka Hotel	B1
5 Sea Breeze Hotel	C1
6 Tanoa Waterfront	A1

✕ Eating
7 Blue Ginger Café	B2
8 Chilli Bites	C2
9 Chilli Tree Cafe	B1
10 Nang Ying	B1

✪ Entertainment
Ashiqi Nightclub	(see 4)
11 Damodar Village Cinemas	D2

ⓘ Transport
Pacific Transport	(see 12)
12 Sunbeam Transport	C1

and enjoy this authentic North Indian food made by authentic North Indian Indians. The tandoor breads, rich and flavoursome curries, and sweet or salty yoghurt lassis are cheap and delicious.

Chilli Tree Cafe CAFE $
(Map p78; 3 Tukani St; meals F$6-12; ⊗breakfast & lunch Mon-Sat; ⊛) This corner cafe is the best place to grab a newspaper and coffee, build a sandwich and settle into a chair behind the plate-glass window for some serious people-watching.

Nang Ying CHINESE $$
(Map p78; Nede St; mains F$13-30; ⊗lunch & dinner Mon-Sat, dinner Sun; ⊛) Twinkly lights, backlit pictures and fake flowers give this place an air of Chinatown kitsch that would do San Francisco proud. Fragrant poultry and noodle dishes, sizzling seafood hotplates and fried rice specials demonstrate that these cooks know their way around their chopsticks.

 Drinking & Entertainment

Lautoka has a limited number of pubs and clubs, which generally veer towards the

seedier side. The best place for a relaxing drink is the bar at Tanoa Waterfront hotel (p77); for a loud Friday or Saturday night out, head to **Ashiqi Nightclub** (Map p78; Tui St) in the Lautoka Hotel.

Hollywood and Bollywood are screened in harmony at **Damodar Village Cinemas** (Map p78; Namoli Ave; adult/child F$5.50/4.50).

❶ Getting There & Around

BUS Local buses shuttle between Lautoka and Nadi every 15 minutes (F$2.50, one hour). Sunbeam Transport and Pacific Transport also have frequent bus services to and from Suva via both the Queens Rd (F$16, six hours) and the Kings Rd (F$18, seven hours). Both companies have offices in Yasawa St, opposite the market.

TAXI Taxis are plentiful but drivers are loath to use their meters.

Southern Viti Levu & the Coral Coast

Skirting the southern half of the mainland, the Queens Rd winds through cane fields and snakes over dry hills along the stretch of shore known as the Coral Coast. This region is peppered with small towns, all manner of accommodation options, and some interesting local attractions. Despite the name, the Coral Coast doesn't offer particularly good snorkelling and the coral shelf is often exposed at low tide. Further east the weather turns more inclement, and the road near Pacific Harbour is flanked by waves of green hills on one side and a fringing reef that drops off dramatically into the deep blue of the ocean on the other.

MOMI BAY

The first of the Coral Coast attractions are the **Momi Guns** (Map p76; adult/child/family F$3/1/6; ⊗9am-5pm), an evocative WWII battery built to defend Fiji against the Japanese Imperial Army; an army that had already swept through Papua New Guinea, the Solomon Islands and parts of what is now Vanuatu. A quick scan of the horizon will reveal why this spot was chosen for the installation. The guns (and now tourists) have unobstructed views to Malolo Barrier Reef, the Mamanuca islands and Navula Passage – the only entry point into western Fiji for large ships.

🛌 Sleeping & Eating

Seashell@Momi RESORT $
(Map p76; ☑670 6100; www.seashellresort.com; dm/s/d/bungalow/apt F$27/$70/80/128/176;

⊜❄@⊠) Accommodation comes in all shapes and sizes at Seashell, from self-contained *bure* and apartments to spacious suites, inexpensive lodges and roomy dorms. On-site facilities include a tennis court, two pools, a restaurant (mains F$10 to F$20), Nadi transfers (F$30 per person, minimum charge F$60), a dive operator (two-tank dive/PADI Open Water Course F$205/780), and boat access to the Mamanuca surfbreaks (F$65 per person, minimum of two people).

❶ Getting There & Away
The turn-off to Momi is about 20km from Nadi. Seashell@Momi is 13km from the main road; on the way there watch for the sign to Momi Guns; they're 4km along a gravel road.

A bus leaves Nadi for Momi Bay at 8am, 12.30pm, 2.30pm and 4pm and costs F$2. The 11.15am bus from Sigatoka costs F$3.80. Both buses pass the Momi Guns and the resort, but do not operate on Sunday.

ROBINSON CRUSOE ISLAND

Robinson Crusoe Island Resort (Map p66; ☑628 1999; www.robinsoncrusoeislandfiji.com; dm F$39-45, bungalows F$79-150, lodges F$189; ❄🍴) is a hit with families. Every Tuesday, Thursday and Sunday the island becomes anything but deserted when it is besieged by day trippers (adult/child F$149/75, including Nadi and Coral Coast transfers). From start to finish, expect a fairly intense entertainment program loosely themed along cultural lines.

The rest of the week is far quieter. Small, simple *bure* and 'lodges' – very smart, light and airy stand-alone rooms with private bathrooms – had a facelift in 2011, and the dorms were about to go under the knife. Bucket showers in the shared bathrooms remain a source of entertainment and/ or frustration. The beautiful white-sand beach isn't great for snorkelling, although there is an on-site dive operator (two-tank dive F$120) who can get you to better reefs. Transport to and from Nadi costs F$99.

NATADOLA BEACH

Natadola's wide stretch of sand is lauded throughout Fiji as the mainland's best beach. Unlike elsewhere, this beach isn't nearly as tidal, and the absence of coral allows for enough surf to satisfy beginners and bodysurfers. Rather persistent locals offer **horse riding** (F$25) along the beach to some nearby caves. It's a picturesque ride but be prepared to bargain hard.

🍴 Sleeping & Eating

Natadola Beach Resort   RESORT $$
(Map p66; 🕿672 1001; www.natadola.com; r F$195; 🌐) This adults-only resort injects a soft splash of Spain into Fiji and skips the mod cons in favour of spacious bathrooms, small private courtyards and tiled interiors. The archways and stucco walls give it a Mediterranean feel, although the lush gardens and meandering pool are Fijian tropical through and through. The restaurant-bar (mains F$38 to F$50) is open to nonguests and it's a popular lunch stop with day trippers (lunches F$20).

InterContinental Resort Fiji   RESORT $$$
(Map p66; www.intercontinental.com; r from F$720; 🌐❄🌐🌐) This mammoth resort, a conglomeration of slate-grey buildings somewhat at odds with the tropical land- and seascape, occupies a prime piece of real estate on the beach. The 271 rooms and 91 suites are beautifully furnished, with spa baths on each balcony and three indoor-outdoor restaurants all offering sunset views. The attached 18-hole golf course is spruiked as the finest in the southern hemisphere – a sentiment echoed by golfers we met who'd played it.

Yatule Beach Resort   RESORT $$
(Map p66; 🕿672 8004; http://yatule-resort. com.fj; villas F$200-$320, f villa F$530; 🌐❄@) Originally built to accommodate the executives involved in the building of the InterContinental, Yatule has been remodelled into a decent midrange resort. All the thatched-roof villas have minikitchens, bedrooms and separate lounges. The family villa has four separate bedrooms and is ideal for teenage kids who need privacy. The bar on the beach is a top spot for a beer.

ℹ️ Getting There & Away
Paradise Transport buses head to and from Sigatoka (F$3, one hour, four daily Monday to Friday), although most travellers arrive on organised day trips from Nadi or on the Coral Coast Scenic Railway. Keen walkers could follow this track from Yanuca to Natadola Beach (about 3½ hours) and catch the train or bus back.

For those with a rental car, turn off the Queens Rd onto Maro Rd 36km from Nadi.

YANUCA & AROUND
Past the turn-off to Natadola, the Queens Rd continues southeast, winding through hills and down to the coast at Cuvu Bay and blink-and-you'll-miss-it Yanuca, about 50km from Nadi.

🏃 Activities

Coral Coast Scenic Railway   SCENIC RAILWAY
(Map p66; 🕿652 0434; Queens Rd) An old sugar train makes a scenic run from Yanuca to Natadola Beach, a 14km trip that takes about 1¼ hours, leaving at 10am on Monday, Wednesday and Friday and returning at 4pm (adult/child F$92/46 including barbecue lunch). On Tuesday, Thursday and Saturday a Sigatoka shopping trip runs east and costs F$46/23. The station is at the causeway entrance to Shangri La's Fijian Resort.

🍴 Sleeping & Eating

Namuka Bay Resort   RESORT $$
(Map p66; 🕿670 0243; www.namukabayresort. com; dm incl meals F$95, villas F$200) Eight roomy beachfront villas with shared verandahs are tucked 6km down a bumpy side road. The resort fronts a lagoon and 2km of beach, with a historic (deserted) village site on the hill behind, and a cave-walk just along the coast. It's very secluded and you'd want good weather – or a good supply of books – to fully enjoy it. The turn-off is about 5km west of Shangri-La's Fijian Resort.

Gecko's Resort & Kalevu Cultural Centre   RESORT $$
(Map p66; 🕿652 0200; www.fijiculturalcentre.com; r/f F$130/250; 🌐❄@🌐) Directly opposite the scenic railway station, this resort has 35 simple, spacious hotel rooms. The restaurant (mains F$25 to F$50) is recommended and is often busy with dining escapees from the Shangri-La. In the landscaped grounds is a purpose-built cultural centre showcasing a collection of traditionally built huts and *bure*, pottery, *masi* (bark cloth) and carvings (one-hour guided tour F$20 per person, open 9.30am to 4pm).

Shangri-La's Fijian Resort   RESORT $$$
(The Fijian; Map p66; 🕿652 0155; www.shangri-la. com; r incl breakfast from F$490; 🌐❄@🌐🏊) Occupying its own tiny island and linked to the mainland by a private causeway, this massive resort occupies one of the Coral Coast's prime spots. The 442 rooms come in a variety of configurations and packages – some of which include free breakfasts and children's meals. For big kids there's golf, a posh day spa, excellent restaurants, bars, tennis courts and wedding chapel. For little kids there's a kids club, three swimming pools, snorkelling and babysitters.

ⓘ Getting There & Away

The Fijian and Gecko's are about a 45-minute drive from Nadi and 11km west of Sigatoka.

SIGATOKA & AROUND
POP 9500

Sigatoka is a neat and orderly town that serves as the commercial hub for the farming communities that live in the fertile Sigatoka Valley. It's also a popular day trip for tourists in the area and, while all its major attractions are a short taxi ride out of town, its riverside location, bustling produce market, supermarket, souvenir shops and local mosque mean that it's a pleasant place to while away a few hours. There are no great places to stay in Sigatoka town but options are plentiful at nearby Korotogo on the coast.

◉ Sights

Sigatoka Sand Dunes   HISTORIC SITE
(Map p66; adult/child/family F$10/5/25, children under 6yr free; ⊙8am-4.30pm) Windswept and peppered with sheets of grey sand, these impressive dunes are one of Fiji's natural highlights. For millions of years, sediment brought down by the Sigatoka River has been washed ashore and blown inland by prevailing winds to form giant dunes. They now stand around 5km long, up to 1km wide and 10m to 60m high. A mahogany forest was planted in the 1960s to halt the dunes' slow expansion onto the Queens Rd, and in 1989 the state-owned part of the area was declared Fiji's first national park. Archaeological excavations suggest that this area has been occupied for thousands of years, and human skeletal remains and pottery shards suggest that concealed beneath the shifting sands is one of the largest burial sites in the Pacific.

Tavuni Hill Fort   HISTORIC SITE
(Map p66; adult/child F$12/6; ⊙8am-5pm Mon-Sat) This defensive fort was built in the 18th century by Tongan chief Maile Latumai, who was seeking to escape an era of political and social upheaval in his homeland. He and his entourage arrived in 1788 in a double-hulled canoe and, although it took some time, they were eventually accepted and given this land on which to build their fort. The steep limestone ridge here was an obvious strategic location because of its commanding views.

The site has been restored as a means of income for villagers and it's the most accessible fort of its kind in Fiji. The information centre, a number of gravesites, a *rara* (ceremonial grounds) and a *vatu ni bokola* (head-chopping stone) all help to provide an insight into the strong precolonial links between Tonga and Fiji.

The fort is about 4km northeast of Sigatoka on the eastern side of the river, above Naroro village. Occasional local carriers make the trip past the entrance gate but most visitors drive themselves or hire a taxi to wait while they visit.

Naihehe Cave   CAVE
(Map p66) The Naihehe Cave, about an hour's drive upriver from Sigatoka, was once used as a fortress by hill tribes and has the remains of a ritual platform and cannibal oven. Adventures in Paradise offers guided tours here.

⚡ Activities
For surfers, Sigatoka has Fiji's only beach break, over a large, submerged rock platform covered in sand and at the point break at the mouth of the Sigatoka River.

☞ Tours

Adventures in Paradise   TOURS
(☏652 0833; www.adventuresinparadisefiji.com; tours per person incl Coral Coast/Nadi hotel transfers F$99/119, child 5-12yr half-price) Offers day trips upriver to Naihehe Cave and its large cathedral-like chamber.

Sigatoka River Safari   BOAT TOURS
(☏650 1721; www.sigatokariver.com; jet-boat tours per person incl Coral Coast/Nadi hotel transfers F$245/265, child 4-15yr F$120/130) The half-day jet-boating trips include a 45km whirl up the Sigatoka River, a village visit and lunch.

🛏 Sleeping, Eating & Drinking
You'll find a grubby hotel room in Sigatoka if you're stuck, but you're better off heading to the superior accommodation in nearby Korotogo (p82).

Vilisite's Seafood Restaurant   SEAFOOD $$
(Map p66; Queens Rd; mains F$15-20; ⊙breakfast, lunch & dinner) Tuck into fabulous seafood in kitschy tropicana surrounds at this popular Fijian eatery. The extensive menu includes curries and Chinese dishes but you'd be nuts to bypass the shellfish.

True Blue Hotel & Restaurant
& Sigatoka Club   BAR
(Map p66) The draw at this local hang-out is its elevated position and lovely views from the cavernous, dance-hall-like restaurant and balcony along the mangrove-lined Sigatoka

River. Grab a seat in one of the waterfront booths or help prop up the horseshoe-shaped bar with the locals.

ⓘ Getting There & Around

Pacific Transport and Sunbeam Transport run several express buses a day between Nadi and Sigatoka (F$5, 1¼ hours) and between Sigatoka and Suva (F$9, three hours).

KOROTOGO & KOROLEVU

The Coral Coast begins its dazzling thread in earnest at the small village of Korotogo. From here the road winds along the shore, skirting clear blue bays and scaling progressively greener hills as it heads east. Unexpected glimpses of coral reefs and deserted beaches make this the most photogenic stretch of the Queens Rd highway. Villages are plentiful and each is announced by a series of judder bars designed to slow traffic and reduce accidents. East of Korolevu, the road turns away from the shore and climbs over the southern end of Viti Levu's dividing mountain range towards Pacific Harbour.

◉ Sights

Kula Eco Park   ZOO
(Map p83; www.fijiwild.com; adult/child F$25/12.50; ⏱10am-4pm) Supported by the National Trust for Fiji and several international parks and conservation bodies, this wildlife sanctuary is a must for fans of the furred, feathered and scaled. Wooden walkways traverse streams, Fijian flora and a menagerie of hawksbill sea turtles (hand-fed at 11am, 1pm and 3.30pm daily), reptiles, birds (including Fiji's national bird, the kula parrot), fruit bats, tropical fish and live coral. The park runs invaluable breeding programs for Fiji's only remaining duck species, the Pacific black duck, and the crested and banded iguana.

🏃 Activities

The Korolevu stretch of coast offers some spectacular diving, and most of the resorts in the area are serviced by **Dive Away Fiji** (Map p66; ☑650 0100; www.diveaway-fiji.com) or **South Pacific Adventure Divers** (Map p66; ☑653 0555, ext 609; www.spadfiji.com). Both operators will collect guests from any place that doesn't have an on-site concession, and both are similarly priced at around F$190/700 for a two-tank dive/PADI Open Water Course.

🛏 Sleeping

The resort stretch of coast at Korotogo is locally known as Sunset Strip.

TOP CHOICE Wellesley Resort   RESORT $$
(Map p66; ☑603 0664; www.wellesleyresort.com. fj; Man Friday Rd, Korolevu; d incl breakfast from F$179; ❄✳@✉) Offering top-end style at midrange prices, this adults-only resort oozes comfort, style and tranquillity. The 15 suites saddle a small valley that leads to a pretty cove and even the most ardent adrenalin junkie will soon rediscover their inner sloth. If they don't, they may find this place a little isolated without a rental car (even though tours are available), as it's 4.5km down a dirt road.

Sandy Point Beach Cottages   HOLIDAY RENTALS $
(Map p83; ☑650 0125; www.sandypointfiji.com; Sunset Strip; s/d/f F$100/120/160; ✉) Five ageing beachside cottages (fully self-contained) built in the style of roomy Kiwi baches (holiday homes) from the '60s. They're quiet, low-key and perfect for independent self-caterers, and a rental car is a good idea if you're staying for more than a couple of days. Owner Bob Kennedy is a communications nut, and satellite dishes hidden in the grounds provide an interesting array of TV channels.

Tubakula Beach Bungalows   RESORT $
(Map p83; ☑650 0097; www.fiji4less.com/tuba. html; Sunset Strip; dm/s/tw F$26/58/63, ste F$115-164; ❄✉) If it weren't for the palm trees, swimming pool and waterfront setting, this low-key resort would be right at home in the mountains. Simple dorms, singles and twins have shared facilities, and the excellent A-frame chalets have strapping timber frames, modern kitchens, and verandahs with slouchy wooden seats. It's perfect for self-driving, self-catering, self-sufficient types wishing to escape the crowds.

Waidroka Surf & Dive Resort   RESORT $$
(Map p66; ☑330 4605; www.waidroka.com; Korolevu; r F$210, bungalows F$270-330; @✉) Over a hilly 4.5km of dirt road, Waidroka caters to serious surfers and divers. A small flotilla of boats takes guests to local breaks and the resort runs the only dive operation to Frigate Walls. Nonsurfing/diving partners are also well catered for with free snorkelling and kayaking, game fishing (from F$250), shopping trips, beachside massages and an excellent restaurant (meal packages F$95). Guests stay in either bright orange *bure* or the adjoining terrace rooms – both are very smart.

Sunset Strip

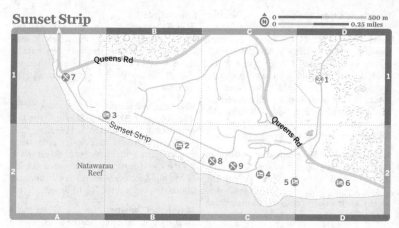

Mango Bay Resort HOSTEL **$**

(Map p66; ☑653 0069; www.mangobayresort fiji.com; Korolevu; dm/d/bungalow incl breakfast F$36/200/280; ☺@☎☒) The dorm, cabins and *bure* are scattered through parklike grounds. Facilities are far better than those found in your average backpackers: the dorms are modern and new, the *bure* have atrium showers and the beach is one of the best on the Coral Coast. Mango Bay targets the 18- to 35-year-old set with plenty of activities of the full-moon-party and sunset-bonfire variety.

Bedarra Beach Inn INN **$$**

(Map p83; ☑650 0476; www.bedarrafiji.com; Sunset Strip; r F$167-180; ☒@☎☒) This modern hotel is a gem. It offers spacious, spotlessly clean rooms with tiled floors and plenty of natural light, and most have ocean views. There's a good balance between resort-style comfort and DIY practicality; everyone who stays here seems to rave about it and most guests are returning Australians. The bar is uniquely designed so that social types can face each other as they sip cocktails, and wi-fi is (erratically) available in most rooms.

Beachhouse HOSTEL **$**

(Map p66; ☑653 0500; www.fijibeachouse.com; Korolevu; campsite per person/dm/d incl breakfast F$25/40/119; ☺@☎☒) Aimed squarely at backpackers, this long-time favourite combines simple digs with heady social activities in a winning formula. The dorms (including a women-only dorm) are in two-storey houses and the doubles are in colourful duplex bungalows. Buses will stop right outside, and

Sunset Strip

⊚ Sights

1 Kula Eco Park D1

🛏 Sleeping

2 Bedarra Beach Inn B2
3 New Crow's Nest Resort B1
4 Outrigger on the Lagoon C2
5 Sandy Point Beach Cottages C2
6 Tubakula Beach Bungalows D2

✕ Eating

7 Koko's Café A1
8 Le Café C2
9 Mayshaars Cuisine C2

there's a pretty pool, a cheap cafe and on-site cooking facilities. Activities include horse riding (F$25 per hour) and a recommended 'jungle trek' to the local waterfall (F$10).

Outrigger on the Lagoon RESORT **$$$**

(Map p83; ☑650 0044; www.outrigger.com/fiji; Sunset Strip; r from F$567; ☺☒@☎☒☝) The 7m outrigger canoe suspended from the ceiling in the lobby creates a powerful first impression of this much-touted resort. From the main building, an artificial stream meanders through lush gardens to a huge, lagoon-style pool – it can get noisy with excited kids and the pool loungers are in hot demand. The *bure* (from F$990), with their high, hand-painted *masi* ceilings are fabulous, as is the day spa with its superb hilltop location. There's a kids club and children dine for free – depending on which package you have.

New Crow's Nest Resort
RESORT $

(Map p83; ☎650 0230; www.crowsnestfiji.com; Sunset Strip; r F$135-145; ⊝❋@☒) Nautical terms abound at these split-level timber bungalows. Each has a lovely balcony and ocean views, and they're in good nick and are good value. The slightly more expensive rooms are self-contained, but all can accommodate a family of four (kids stay free). The restaurant (mains F$17 to F$25) faces the hillside pool and has a cosmopolitan menu.

Namatakula Village Homestay
HOMESTAY $

(Map p66; www.fijibure.com/namatakula/index. htm; per adult/child incl meals F$130/100) For simple accommodation, generous meals and an authentic window onto traditional village life.

Warwick Fiji Resort & Spa
RESORT $$$

(Map p66; ☎653 0555; www.warwickfiji.com; Korolevu; s & d incl breakfast F$350-550, ste incl breakfast F$740; ⊝❋@☒) Owned by the same crowd that owns the Naviti Resort, the Warwick is another feature-laden, activity-rich resort. Five restaurants, seven bars and lagoons with all-tide swimming areas.

Crusoe's Retreat
RESORT $$

(Map p66; ☎650 0185; www.crusoesretreat. com; Korolevu; r incl breakfast from F$235; @☒) Tucked into a fold between two hills on the coast, Crusoe's pretty and remote location is the draw for many guests. There are 28 fan-cooled *bure* and a fabulous restaurant.

Naviti Resort
RESORT $$$

(Map p66; ☎653 0444; www.navitiresort.com. fj; Korolevu; r incl breakfast F$285-799; ⊝❋@☎☒) Heavy on the greenery and light on the concrete, the colossal Naviti has all the goodies – four restaurants, five bars, a nine-hole golf course, swim-up bar, health spa and kids club.

✖ Eating

Most of the resorts listed under Sleeping have restaurants and bars – in some cases, multiple restaurants and bars – and they all welcome the opportunity to steal a few clients from their neighbours.

Le Café
BISTRO $$

(Map p83; Sunset Strip; mains F$10-25; ⊙breakfast, lunch & dinner) Just west of the Outrigger on the Lagoon, pretty Le Café has a Swiss chef who cooks European-style food – tasty pastas and pizzas are the speciality. There's also a daily happy hour from 5pm to 8pm.

Koko's Café
CAFE $$

(Map p83; Sunset Strip; mains F$10-20; ⊙breakfast, lunch & dinner) Good coffee and a decent steak sandwich are among the things on offer at this low-key cafe, newly opened when we visited. A liquor licence was pending; in the meantime, BYO.

Vilisite's Restaurant
FISH & CHIPS $$

(Map p66; Queens Rd; mains F$15-40; ⊙breakfast, lunch & dinner) If you have a Hawaiian shirt you'll feel right at home, as this place drips tropical garb. With its sweeping ocean views, it's the nicest restaurant in the area outside of the big Korolevu resorts – it's a couple of kilometres beyond the Naviti Resort.

Mayshaars Cuisine
FAST FOOD $

(Map p83; Sunset Strip; mains F$8-18; ⊙lunch & dinner) Diners take their seats on picnic tables in front of a small supermarket with an outdoor pool table. While the setting is utterly unsophisticated, you name the cuisine, they've got it – Chinese, Fijian, Italian and Western. You may hear it called by its former names: Johnny's, Beachside Restaurant or Ice Bar.

ⓘ Getting There & Away

The Korotogo area is about 8km east of Sigatoka, and Korolevu village is 31km east of Sigatoka. Regular buses ply the Queens Rd and will drop guests off outside most resorts. For the more isolated resorts it is best to phone ahead and arrange collection or a taxi once you have reached the Coral Coast vicinity.

PACIFIC HARBOUR

The unseemly swamp that was once Pacific Harbour has been tamed, drained, subdivided and pedicured into a brochure-perfect housing development quite unlike the rest of Fiji. The wide cul-de-sac streets, flawless lawns and ordered river setting might seem incongruous to some but local residents love it. Pacific Harbour markets itself as the 'Adventure Capital of Fiji' on the basis of a number of adrenalin-fuelled activities including shark diving in nearby Beqa (*ben*-ga) Lagoon, and rafting and trekking in the Namosi Highlands.

⊙ Sights

Arts Village
CULTURAL CENTRE

(Map p86; ☎345 0065; tours per adult/child from F$66/33; ⊙9am-4pm Wed-Sat) This faux village is unashamedly 'Fiji in a theme park', and within its Disneylike confines are a temple, chiefly *bure*, cooking area with utensils and weaving hut. Fijian actors dressed in

traditional costumes carry out mock battles, preach pagan religion and demonstrate traditional arts. Tours include an Island Boat Tour (for the kids), Island Temple Tour and Arts Village Show, and fire-walking. It's good fun for families, but a far cry from authentic village life.

Attached to the Arts Village, the **Marketplace** is a congregation of eateries, supermarkets and souvenir shops, and is a pleasant spot in which to kill an hour or so.

Activities

The beach at nearby Deuba is reasonable for swimming.

Freedive Fiji FISHING
(☎973 0687; www.freedivefiji.com; half-day per person F$225) If spear- and game fishing are your thing, this is the outfit for you. Offers charters too.

Fishing Charters & Pleasure Cruises BOATING
(☎345 0020; www.fcpcfiji.com) Lower-key and lower-priced than Freedive Fiji, this mob will take you on options including a gentle lake cruise (from F$130), an inland fishing trip (from F$150) and a snorkelling/fishing combination (from F$200).

Rivers Fiji KAYAKING, RAFTING
(Map p86; ☎345 0147; www.riversfiji.com; Pearl South Pacific; day tours per person from F$205) Rivers Fiji offers excellent kayaking and rafting trips through the scenic gorges of the Namosi Highlands and Upper Navua River.

Pearl Championship Golf Course GOLF
(Map p86; ☎345 0905; 9 holes with/without club hire F$47/24) On the outskirts of town, this course can provide a challenging game on a bunker-peppered course.

Zip Fiji ADVENTURE SPORTS
(off Map p86; ☎930 0545; www.zip-fiji.com; adult/child F$210/105; ⊗8am-8pm) For something a little faster, try swinging through the jungle attached to a tree-top zipline.

DIVING
There are more than 20 excellent dive sites near Pacific Harbour, mostly within **Beqa Lagoon** (Map p66), but these are overshadowed by the opportunity to dive with 4m-long tiger sharks and massive, barrel-chested bull sharks without being caged (or sedated). The dives are well organised (they would have to be), and not nearly as intimidating as many imagine. The tigers

don't always show but the bulls are regularly seen between February and early September.

Aqua-Trek Beqa (Map p86; ☎345 0324; www.aquatrek.com; Club Oceanus) and **Beqa Adventure Divers** (Map p86; ☎345 0911; www.fiji-sharks.com; Studio 6 on the Lake, formerly Lagoon Resort) both specialise in this activity, and their prices average around F$210 for a two-tank dive, F$245 for a two-tank shark-feeding dive and F$750 for the PADI Open Water Course.

Tours

Discover Fiji Tours TOURS
(Map p66; ☎345 0180; www.discoverfijitours.com) Based just outside Pacific Harbour at Navua, this outfit has several day tours (from F$115 per person) to the Navua River area, which include waterfall visits, 4WD trips and kayaking.

Beqa Island Trips BOAT TOURS
(Map p86; ☎345 0910; www.beqaislandtrips.com) These day tours to Beqa Lagoon offer a family-friendly beach barbecue/swimming/snorkelling day at Yanuca island (Thursday and Sunday; F$190 per person) and a *meke* (dance performance that enacts stories and legends), *lovo* (earth oven) lunch and snorkel in the locally managed marine protected zone at Lawaki Beach House on Beqa island (Tuesday and Saturday; F$210 per person).

Sleeping

Uprising Beach Resort RESORT $$
(Map p86; ☎345 2200; www.uprisingbeachresort.com; Queens Rd; dm incl breakfast F$38, bungalows incl breakfast F$255-470, villas incl breakfast F$375-510; ❄@≋) The Uprising continues to give other resorts a run for their money, recently raising the bar with 12 very swish villas to add to the 12 spacious *bure*. There are nifty outdoor showers and bifolding doors to catch the ocean breeze. The 'tree house' dorm is spotlessly clean and although it isn't in a tree, it does afford beautiful views from the verandah. The restaurant serves global cuisine, and there are usually enough barflies buzzing around to give the bar a cheery vibe.

Nanette's Accommodation B&B $
(Map p86; ☎345 2041; www.nanettes.com.fj; 108 River Dr; r incl breakfast F$150; ❄≋) This four-bedroom villa with swimming pool makes for terrific home-from-home accommodation. Rooms all have private bathrooms and are big, light and airy, and the shared lounge and kitchen are comfortable and vibrantly decorated.

Pacific Harbour

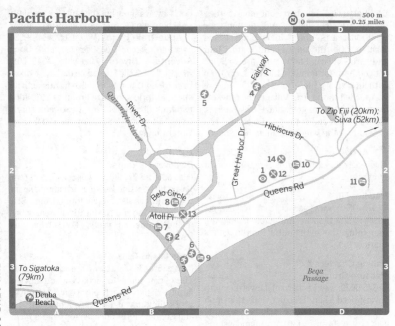

Pacific Harbour

Pearl South Pacific RESORT $$$
(Map p86; ☎345 0022; www.thepearlsouth
pacific.com; Queens Rd; r F$372-452, ste F$698-
792; ❄✳@🖥☎) No expense has been spared
in this, one of Fiji's finest hotels. Style gurus
will overdose on the marble bathrooms,
low-slung beds and private decked alcoves
with cushioned sunloungers, and on the
six extraordinary Fijian-Asian fusion rooms
themed in colours (including Red Passion
and Moody Blues). There's no kids club here
(a nanny service is available) but there are
plenty of activities to keep adults happy.

**Tsulu Backpackers
& Apartments** HOSTEL $
(Map p86; ☎345 0065; dm F$35, d F$65-88, apt
F$99-293; ✳@☎) Attached to the Arts Village
(p84), the Tsulu has picked up the artistic
gauntlet and really, and we mean really, run
with it. The walls (and in some cases the
ceilings) of the dorms, double rooms and
self-contained apartments are painted in
vibrant murals. One room is bright blue with
life-size fish, coral gardens and a snorkeller
painted on the ceiling above. It's ridiculously
good value.

Club Oceanus
MOTEL **$**

(Map p86; 📞345 0498; www.cluboceanus.com; 1 Atoll Pl; dm/d/f F$30/120/130; 🌐❄🍽) This waterside accommodation has 10 clean and comfortable rooms in a long, compact block, with kitchen facilities in the dorm. It's good value, located in a convenient spot on the canal within walking distance of the Arts Village complex, with a small cafe on-site.

✖ Eating

Baka Blues Cafe
FUSION **$$**

(Map p86; Arts Village Marketplace; mains F$20-30; ⏱lunch & dinner Mon-Sat) Bluesy music accompanies the Cajun-influenced menu at this restaurant, which has well and truly lifted the bar for food and wine in the Marketplace. Spicy Cajun-style fish with snappy beans is a great combination.

Mantarae Restaurant
FUSION **$$$**

(Map p86; 📞345 0022; Pearl South Pacific; mains F$28-40; ⏱dinner Tue-Sat) This place offers interesting contemporary, fusion-style cuisine with a hint of Southeast Asia that has diners licking their lips from starters to dessert. The dining experience involves white linen and lots of glass.

Water's Edge
PIZZERIA **$$**

(Map p86; Arts Village Marketplace; mains F$8-28; ⏱lunch & dinner) The deckside dining at Water's Edge is surrounded by the water-lily pond and makes a scenic lunch stop. The menu is strong on pizza and Indian (tandoori chicken pizza F$20).

Oasis Restaurant
INTERNATIONAL **$$**

(Map p86; Arts Village Marketplace; mains F$16-36; ⏱breakfast, lunch & dinner; 🌐❄@) Burgers, sandwiches, tortillas, curries and a whole lot of seafood is served at this long-time local favourite. The secondhand books for sale may not be great literature but go really well on a sunlounger.

Sakura House
JAPANESE **$$$**

(Map p86; 📞345 0256; River Dr; mains F$25-40; ⏱dinner) Although it features other Asian dishes, the Japanese tempura, sashimi, *shabu-shabu* (thinly sliced meat and vegetables cooked tableside in a pot of boiling water) and teriyaki are Sakura House's speciality.

ⓘ Getting There & Away
Pacific Harbour is about an hour's express bus ride from Suva (F$4.15) and around 3½ hours from Nadi (F$15). A taxi to Suva costs about F$40.

NAMOSI HIGHLANDS
The steamy Namosi Highlands, north of Pacific Harbour, have Fiji's most spectacular scenery, complete with rainforests, steep ranges, deep river canyons and tall waterfalls. The simplest way to see these highlands is to sign up with one of the Pacific Harbour tour companies (see p85) that specialise in this remote area or, if you have your own wheels (preferably 4WD), take a detour inland from Nabukavesi.

OFFSHORE ISLANDS
Offshore from Pacific Harbour, a 64km-long barrier reef encloses the exquisite **Beqa Lagoon** (Map p66), world-famous for its dizzying dive sites including Side Streets and Caesar's Rocks. Divers are joined by avid surfers, who test their mettle on the powerful left-hand breaks at **Frigate's Passage** (Map p66). Anchored amid the lagoon are Beqa and Yanuca islands, untouched except for a handful of inconspicuous resorts.

BEQA
AREA 36 SQ KM

The volcanic and rugged island of Beqa is best known for its villagers, who practise traditional fire-walking – but the best place to see them isn't on Beqa; they now perform chiefly for tourists at the Coral Coast resorts.

The cosy and relaxed **Lawaki Beach House** (Map p66; 📞992 1621, 368 4088; www.lawakibeachhouse.com; campsite per tent incl meals F$70, dm/tw incl meals F$130/280; @) comprises two double *bure* with en suites and a six-bed dorm. There is good snorkelling off the secluded, pristine white-sand beach, as well as visits to the nearby village, diving and surfing (F$225 for the boat, plus F$25 per hour). Meals are served in the communal TV lounge, and the resort can organise boat transfers from Pacific Harbour for F$220 per person one way. Alternatively you can catch the small public ferry from the Navua jetty. The ferry usually leaves between noon and 2.30pm from Monday to Saturday, and costs F$40 per person one way. It returns to Navua at 7am every day except Sunday.

A second option is **Beqa Lagoon Resort** (Map p66; 📞330 4042; www.beqalagoonresort.com; ❄@🍽), comprising 25 *bure* with classy bathrooms and traditional interiors. It's decidedly upmarket, catering mostly to US diving groups.

Two other smaller, top-end resorts on Beqa specialise in diving for couples, who may also choose to get married or honeymoon in them: **Lalati Resort** (Map p66;

www.lalati-fiji.com) and **Kulu Bay Resort** (Map p66; www.kulubay.com).

YANUCA

Compact and beautiful Yanuca is a mass of green hills, interrupted by a village and a couple of surf camps. The beaches here are lovely, but it's Yanuca's proximity to the surf-breaks of Frigate's Passage that lures travellers here.

Many a surfer hits **Batiluva Beach Resort** (Map p66; ☑345 1019, 939 1975; www. batliuva.com; dm/d incl meals F$200/400) for a week, only to wake a month later in a hammock wondering where the time went. Spotless and airy dorms and semi-private double rooms are rented on a per-person basis, with couples getting dibs on the doubles. 'Gourmet jungle meals' are included in the tariff but, more importantly, so is the daily boat out to Frigate's Passage for the surf-til-you-drop clientele. Transfers from Pacific Harbour are F$60 return, per person.

Tiny, locally run surf camp **Yanuca Island Resort** may also be open; ask around.

Suva

POP 168,000

Suva (pronounced soo-va) is more than just the Fijian capital; it is the largest city in the South Pacific, an important regional centre and a cosmopolitan milieu of cultures and influences. This is partly due to the University of the South Pacific, which is jointly owned by 12 Pacific nations and attracts a vibrant potpourri of island students. The compact downtown grid is equally diverse, with grand colonial buildings, modern high-rises and shiny shopping plazas flanked by a breezy esplanade.

Beyond downtown Suva, a string of pretty suburbs dribbles along the hills that crowd the capital's busy port. On the city outskirts lie the ballooning settlement camps of tin sheds, home to around half of Suva's inhabitants.

On a less serious but equally grey note, clouds tend to hover over Suva and frequently dump rain on the city (around 300mm each year), which accounts for the lush tropical plants and comparative lack of tourists.

⊙ Sights

Fiji Museum   MUSEUM

(Map p90; www.fijimuseum.org.fj; Ratu Cakobau Rd; adult/child F$7/5; ☺9am-4.30pm Mon-Sat) Situated in the middle of **Thurston Gardens**, this small but excellent museum delves into Fiji's archaeological, political, cultural and linguistic evolution. The museum features original examples of musical instruments, cooking apparatus, jewellery and a daunting array of Fijian war clubs. The section exhibiting cannibal utensils provides a vivid insight into traditional life. The massive Ratu Finau, Fiji's last *waqa tabus* (double-hulled canoe), is the museum's showpiece, although some of the smaller exhibits, like the well-chewed – but ultimately inedible – shoe of Thomas Baker (a Christian missionary eaten for his indiscretions in 1867), are just as interesting.

The gardens outside are all that remains of the original village of Suva and, although they have grown more haphazard with every passing coup, the stately fig trees are still a great spot to picnic beneath and ponder your newfound knowledge.

Colo-i-Suva Forest Park   FOREST

(Map p66; adult/child F$5/1; ☺8am-4pm) This lush rainforest park is a cool and peaceful respite about 9km north of downtown Suva. It is only 2.5 sq km in size but boasts 6.5km of walking trails that navigate clear, natural pools and gorgeous vistas. Many of the trails follow the Waisila Creek as it slips and slides its way towards the Waimanu River. The creek gives rise to natural swimming holes, some of which have rope swings and are guaranteed to bring out the Tarzan in anyone.

You can buy your ticket and pick up a map from the visitor information centre on the left side of the road as you approach from Suva. It's worth asking about the security situation and, if it is of concern, forking out extra to have a guard show you around the park.

To get here, take the Saweni bus from Suva bus station (F$2, 30 minutes, half-hourly) or a taxi (F$8).

Government Buildings   LANDMARK

The forbidding and handsome Government Buildings (built in 1939 and 1967) at the end of Carnarvon St are set on heavy foundations atop reclaimed land. Opened in 1992, the **parliament buildings** (Map p90; ☑330 5811; www.parliament.gov.fj; Battery Rd; admission free) are far more aesthetic and adorned with traditional Fijian tapa cloths and works of art. Depending on political events at the time, they may or may not be open to the public: it's advisable to call ahead.

University of the South Pacific   UNIVERSITY

Set in a breadth of breezy gardens east of Central Suva, the University of the South Pacific's main **Laucala Campus** (USP; www.usp.ac.fj; Laucala Bay Rd) is a pleasant spot for a stroll and a bout of people-watching. Students from islands throughout the Pacific attend the university, and the cultural diversity is a curio in itself.

Suva Municipal Market   MARKET

(Map p94; Usher St; ⊙6am-6pm Mon-Fri, 6am-4.30pm Sat) The beating heart of Suva and a great place to spend an hour or so poking around with a camera. Besides the recognisable tomatoes, cabbages and chillies, look out for bitter gourds, kava, jackfruit, *dalo* (a taro-like root vegetable), *rourou* (*dalo* leaves) and sweet potatoes.

🏃 Activities

The **Suva Olympic Swimming Pool** (Map p90; 224 Victoria Pde; adult/child F$3/1.50; ⊙10am-6pm Mon-Fri, 8am-6pm Sat) is, handily, slap bang in the middle of town. Other sports open to the public include golf and lawn bowls, and a brisk walk along the waterfront promenade (in daylight hours only) is a must.

Royal Suva Yacht Club   SAILING

(off Map p94; ☑331 2921; www.rsyc.org.fj; ⊙office 8am-5pm Mon-Fri, 9am-4pm Sat) A popular watering hole for yachties and locals alike, and the noticeboard here is a good place to find crewing positions. The marina has dockside fuel and water. Anchorage fees are F$5 per day or F$50 if you prefer to overnight in one of the six berths. There are laundry and shower facilities for those who have just arrived, and the office should be able to advise on immigration procedures.

🛏 Sleeping

In addition to the reviewed options, there is also a swag of budget and midrange hotels along Robertson Rd (Map p94), particularly the loop it forms between Anand St and Waimanu Rd.

Five Princes Hotel   BOUTIQUE HOTEL $$

(Map p66; ☑338 1575; www.fiveprinceshotel.com; 5 Princes Rd; d/bungalows/villas F$199/230/335; ❄@🛜🏊) The aged 1920s exterior belies the transformation that this one-time colonial villa has undergone on the inside. Solid teak furniture, polished timber floors, power showers and satellite TV are all to be had in timelessly appointed rooms. Set in beautifully landscaped gardens, the stand-alone villas are similarly decorated. It's a 10-minute drive from the centre of town.

Quest Serviced Apartments   APARTMENTS $$

(Map p90; ☑331 9117; www.questsuva.com; Thomson St; studios/1-bedroom apt F$185/237) You'd never know these gems of apartments were here, tucked away on the 6th and 7th floor of the Suva Central building. Central, quiet, well maintained and secure, there are usually a few units available for overnight and short stays. There's an air-con gym on-site too, and breakfast included at the coffee shop on the building's 2nd floor.

South Seas Private Hotel   HOSTEL $

(Map p90; ☑331 2296; www.fiji4less.com; 6 Williamson Rd; s/d without bathroom F$39/51, r with bathroom F$64; ⊝) The art deco sign out front sets the scene for this grand old dame, set on a quiet street just a step away from the museum. The sweeping interior verandah, high ceilings and wide halls speak of a bygone era. There are simple, clean rooms, comfortably ageing lounge furniture and a shared kitchen.

Suva Apartments   APARTMENTS $

(Map p90; ☑330 4280; www.fijiolympiccommittee.com; 17 Bau St; apt F$76-92; ❄) These small, neat, self-contained one-bedroom apartments are great value and well located, just a five-minute bus ride from town, and a five-minute walk from shops. They are one of the income-generating ventures of the Fiji Olympic Committee, so your stay supports Fiji's athletes.

Nanette's Accommodation   B&B $

(off Map p94; ☑331 6316; www.nanettes.com.fj; 56 Extension St; r incl breakfast F$119, apt incl breakfast F$145-195; ⊝❄@) Resort-weary travellers can find solace here in unassuming comfort, set in tranquil residential surrounds only a 15-minute walk to downtown Suva. The four upstairs rooms of varying size share a communal TV lounge and kitchen and all have bathrooms. Downstairs are three comfortable self-contained apartments.

Novotel Suva Lami Bay   HOTEL $$$

(off Map p94; ☑336 2450; www.novotelsuva.com.fj; Queens Rd, Lami; r from F$300; ⊝❄@🏊) Reopened with a sleek new look and under new management in 2009, these 108 rooms offer business-style accommodation. Popular with the regional conference set, the hotel

Central Suva

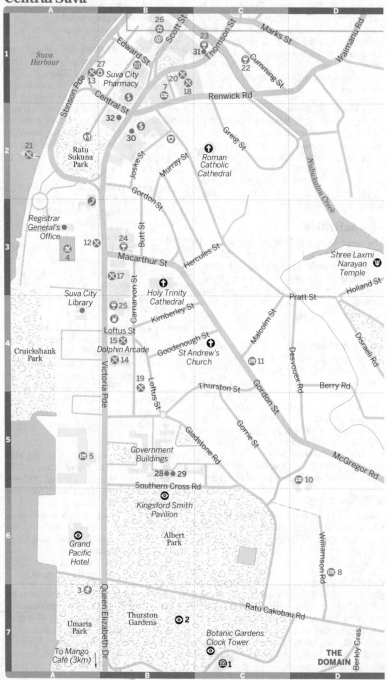

See North Central Suva Map (p94)

FIJI SUVA

has a great waterfront location with views across Draunimbota Bay, and is a 10-minute drive from central Suva.

Suva Motor Inn HOTEL **$$**
(Map p90; ☏331 3973; www.hexagonfiji.com; cnr Mitchell & Gorrie Sts; d F$119-187; ❋@☎♠) Fab for families, the Suva Motor Inn is a little humble with its title. The four-storey hotel (no lift) is shaped like a 'U' around a small pool into which snakes a water slide. All rooms have balconies (the best with views to Albert Park) and the larger two-bedroom apartments sleep four and have kitchens. It's a solid midrange choice.

Holiday Inn HOTEL **$$**
(Map p90; ☏330 1600; reservations@holidayinn-suva.com.fj; Victoria Pde; r F$272-497; ⊝❋@☎☎) This inn occupies a great location on the harbour shore, across from the Government Buildings and near the museum. Rooms are generically spacious, cool and comfortable and will please picky travellers. The inn patently appeals to business travellers and those on coach tours and it has the facilities to match.

Tanoa Plaza Hotel HOTEL **$$**
(Map p90; ☏331 2300; www.tanoahotels.com; cnr Gordon & Malcolm Sts; r F$248-276, ste F$494; ⊝❋@☎☎) Rooms here are comfortable, functional and forgettable; sleek and sophisticated in a minibar and pamper-products-in-the-bathroom kind of way. The views, though, are impressive and service is among Suva's best.

Peninsula International Hotel HOTEL **$**
(Map p90; ☏331 3711; www.peninsula.com.fj; cnr McGregor Rd & Pender St; r F$90-130, apt $165; ⊝❋☎) Set on a leafy hill just above the city.

OUT OF TOWN
Raintree Lodge LODGE **$**
(Map p66; ☏332 0113; www.raintreelodge.com; Princes Rd, Colo-i-Suva; dm/d/bungalow F$25/65/165; ⊝@☎) Set against a backdrop of tranquil, rainforest-fringed lake, the lodge seems a world away from the city; in fact it's only 11km. The three dormitories, communal kitchen and double and twin rooms with shared bathrooms are clean and comfortable; there are also five *bure* set among the trees and these offer excellent value with plump beds, private decks, TV and DVD players. The lakeside bar-restaurant (mains F$15 to F$28) is a pretty place to hang out.

Central Suva

⊚ Sights

⊛ Activities, Courses & Tours

⊜ Sleeping

⊗ Eating

⊝ Drinking

⊗ Entertainment

⊝ Shopping

ⓘ Information

ⓘ Transport

The only drawback is the taxi ride (F$8) to town. Alternatively, the Tacirua Transport bus to Sawani passes the Raintree Lodge (F$2, 30 minutes), half-hourly from Monday to Saturday.

✕ Eating

For a compact city, Suva offers a relatively diverse array of eateries. Besides the restaurants listed here, you will find excellent hole-in-the-wall curry houses dotted all over town, late-night barbecue stands beside the handicraft market, and a good selection of cheap eats in the shopping-mall food courts.

TOP CHOICE Guava FUSION $$
(Map p90; ☎362 1051; 22 Marion St; lunch specials F$15; ☺breakfast & lunch; ☻) Check out this restaurant in a beautifully restored cottage a five-minute taxi ride above town. There's great fresh food served in interesting Pacific and Western combinations, with several salads and hot dishes of the day on offer.

Old Mill Cottage FIJIAN $
(Map p90; ☎331 2134; 49 Carnarvon St; dishes F$5-12; ☺breakfast & lunch Mon-Sat; ☻) Workers from the nearby embassies cram the front verandah of this cheap and cheerful Suva institution to dabble in authentic Fijian fare. Dishes including *palusami* (meat, onion and *lolo* – coconut cream – wrapped in *dalo* leaves) are served, alongside Indian curries and vegetarian dishes.

Daikoku Restaurant JAPANESE $$$
(Map p90; ☎330 8968; Victoria Pde; mains F$25-40; ☺lunch & dinner Mon-Sat) Upstairs past the closet-sized bar, the acrobatic culinary skills of Daikoku's teppanyaki chefs are reason enough to spend an evening here. It's the partner restaurant to Daikoku in Nadi; the F$15 lunch specials are popular here too, so arrive promptly at midday or be prepared to wait.

Mango Café SANDWICHES $
(off Map p90; Ratu Sukuna Rd, Nasese; mains from F$10; ☺breakfast, lunch & dinner; ☻✷) This

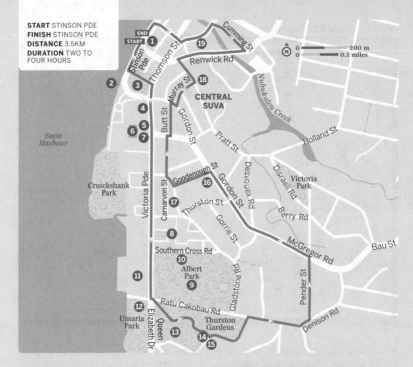

Suva

Downtown Suva has a scattering of colonial buildings and places of interest, making it a pleasant place to wander around.

Start on Stinson Pde at the ❶ **Suva Curio & Handicraft Market**. Cross the street and follow the esplanade south, enjoying the views of Suva Harbour and Joske's Thumb. Once you reach ❷ **Tiko's Floating Restaurant**, cross the road and amble through the tree-lined ❸ **Ratu Sukuna Park**. Continue south down Victoria Pde, past the 1926 ❹ **Fintel building** and the 1904 ❺ **old town hall**. The ❻ **Suva Olympic Swimming Pool** is set back between this building and the 1909 ❼ **Suva City Library**.

Continue down Victoria Pde. On your left are the stately ❽ **Government Buildings**. Just south is ❾ **Albert Park**, a large sporting field. The ❿ **Kingsford Smith Pavilion**, named after the famous aviator who landed here, is on Southern Cross Rd. Opposite the park is the once-glorious ⓫ **Grand Pacific Hotel**. Just past Ratu Cakobau Rd is ⓬ **Umaria Park & Suva Bowls Club**, where you can take a breather with a cold drink.

Cross the road at Queen Elizabeth Dr and enter ⓭ **Thurston Gardens**. Meander through this colourful park, stopping at the ⓮ **Botanic Gardens Clock Tower** and the ⓯ **Fiji Museum**.

Continue east, then turn left at Pender St and left again at McGregor Rd, which turns into Gordon St. Turn left at ⓰ **St Andrew's Church**, follow Goodenough St and dog-leg onto Carnarvon St. If you need a pick-me-up, drop into the ⓱ **Old Mill Cottage** or **Rave Bistro** for a traditional Fijian feast and/or a good coffee.

Stroll north past the bars and clubs to the ⓲ **Roman Catholic Cathedral**, one of Suva's most prominent landmarks.

Turn left, then right and window-shop your way to Cumming St, then turn left to immerse yourself in Suva's little India.

Make your way past the stately ⓳ **Garrick Hotel**, then head back to the Curio & Handicraft Market. If you've got any energy left, spend it on a bout of souvenir shopping.

North Central Suva

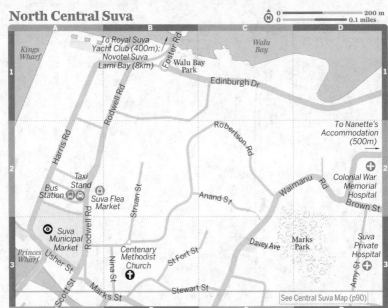

groovy little cafe is the place to stop during a walk or drive along the Suva waterfront. It serves good coffee and fresh salad wraps, with comfortable cool indoor tables and a garden forecourt.

Esquires Coffee House
CAFE $

(Map p90; ☑330 0828; Renwick Rd; cakes & sandwiches F$3-9; ⊗breakfast, lunch & dinner; ⊜⊛) Popular for informal work meetings, this air-con cafe serves good coffee (F$4 to F$5.50) and ordinary cakes and sandwiches to government and international workers from the offices opposite.

Tiko's Floating Restaurant
INTERNATIONAL $$$

(Map p90; ☑331 3626; off Stinson Pde; mains F$25-40; ⊗lunch & dinner Mon-Fri, dinner Sat; ⊜⊛) The only way you could be any more harbourside would be if you were standing in the water. This permanently moored, former Blue Lagoon cruise ship serves excellent surf-and-turf fare, including NZ steak, fresh local fish (*walu* and *pakapaka*) and an extensive wine list, all served on white linen.

Ashiyana
INDIAN $$

(Map p90; ☑331 3000; Old Town Hall Bldg, Victoria Pde; mains F$10-20; ⊗lunch & dinner Tue-Sat, dinner Sun) This pint-sized restaurant is a long-standing Indian favourite with some of the best butter chicken in town, and curries so spicy even the taxi drivers consider them hot.

Maya Dhaba
INDIAN $$

(Map p90; ☑331 0045; 281 Victoria Pde; mains F$13-22; ⊗lunch & dinner; ⊜⊛) Maya Dhaba looks ready for a refurb, but still screens hip-gyrating Bollywood musicals on flat-screen TVs in Suva's most urbane restaurant. The meals are excellent and you can wrap your *naan* around any number of familiar and maybe not-so-familiar Indian classics – like goat masala.

Shanghai Seafood House
CHINESE $$

(Map p90; ☑331 4865; 6 Thomson St; mains F$13-20; ⊗lunch & dinner) In the heart of the shopping district, this 1st-floor restaurant is plush in a kitschy, fake-flower kind of way. The encyclopaedic menu and al fresco seating on the 1914 building's balcony induce long and lazy lunches.

Suva Municipal Market
MARKET $

(Map p94; Usher St) The best place for fresh fish, fruit and vegetables.

MHCC Department Store
SUPERMARKET $

(Map p90; Thomson St) The best supermarket in town is Superfresh in the MHCC Department Store, where you can also pick up fresh

bread and muffins from the bakery on the ground floor.

Drinking

Suva's drinking and dancing dens get happy and loaded on Friday and Saturday nights when Victoria Pde swarms with clubbers and bar-hoppers. Happy hours usually last from 6pm to 8pm, and many clubs charge an entrance fee (no more than a few dollars) by 10pm. Dress standards aren't high but you won't be admitted wearing flip-flops and shorts.

If you're looking for something to wash down a picnic, try **Victoria Wines & Spirits** (Map p90; Victoria Pde; ⊙11am-9pm Mon-Fri, to 2pm Sat).

Friends (Map p90; Terry Walk) and **Liquids** (Map p90; Harbour Centre, upstairs) are recommended by locals as having an interesting local and international mix both of music and people, drawn by cheaper drinks than at O'Reilly's and Traps.

TOP CHOICE **O'Reilly's**   PUB
(Map p90; ☎331 2322; cnr Macarthur St & Victoria Pde) A combination of O'Reilly's nightclub, Shenanigans bar (a nonsmoking area) and Bad Dog Café, O'Reilly's kicks the evening off in relatively subdued fashion: relaxed punters eating, playing pool or watching sport on the numerous TVs. But it brews quite a party as the hours tick by and come 11pm-ish the place is generally throbbing with a diverse crowd shaking their bits to Europop, soft metal, techno, peppy rock-pop...basic-ally anything that keeps the crowd moving. It is one of the few pubs where a reasonably smart dress code prevails, so dig out your best threads. It's an expat and professional-Fijian haunt more than a welcome-all-comers place.

Traps Bar   LIVE MUSIC
(Map p90; Victoria Pde) Something of a subterranean saloon bar with a series of cavelike, dimly lit rooms. Take a seat in the pool room with wide-screen TV (yes, with sports) or join the happy din at the main bar. The crowd is generally young, trendy, relatively affluent and dancing by 11pm. Live music is frequent (usually on Thursdays), as are Bob Marley singalongs.

☆ Entertainment

Check out the entertainment section of the *Fiji Times* for upcoming events, cinema listings and what's on at nightclubs.

Fijians are fanatical about their rugby, and even if you aren't that keen on the game it's worth going to a match. The season lasts from April to September, and teams tough it out at the **National Stadium** (Laucala Bay Rd, Laucala) east of central Suva. The atmosphere is huge.

Damodar Village Cinema (Map p90; Scott St; adult/child F$6/5) shows recently released Hollywood and Bollywood films.

Shopping

There are a number of tourist-oriented shops along Victoria Pde and in the

FIJI SUVA

MOVING TO THE BEAT OF A DIFFERENT DRUM

Dancers pay homage to the steady beat of the drums, seemingly oblivious to the spectators. The poorly lit room is crowded with both tourists and locals yelling '*bula*' to one another over the din. As a big, indigenous Fijian man – who should be playing the chief in this scene – approaches with a flower behind his ear and a pitcher of beer on his tray, you don't need any reminding that this is no *meke*. This is Saturday night in Suva, when the country's urban youth let down their hair and pole-dance to pop music.

Fiji's urban youth face many of the same difficulties as young people around the globe: teenage parenthood, crime, drugs and skyrocketing unemployment (only one in eight school-leavers finds a job). However, these youths also find themselves straddling two opposing worlds – the traditional, conservative society of the villages many have left behind, where life was filled with cultural protocols, and the liberal, individualistic lifestyle of the modern and increasingly Westernised city.

The rising club and cafe culture is bringing together youths from indigenous and Indo-Fijian backgrounds, in the midst of a city filled with ethnic strife. Many face the near impossibility of surviving unemployment. Although it's not the Fiji of postcards, Fiji's rising urban youth culture is an intrinsic aspect of the country and an unexpected eye-opener.

downtown shopping malls. They mostly stock mass-produced souvenirs so you have a better chance of finding something more distinctive at one of the local markets.

Suva Curio & Handicraft Market
HANDICRAFTS

(Map p90; Stinson Pde) The endless stalls are thick with throwing clubs, masks, cannibal forks, *tanoa* bowls and *masi*. If you know your stuff it is possible to get some excellent buys here, although you will have to bargain well to do so.

Suva Flea Market
HANDICRAFTS

(Map p94; Rodwell Rd) Less touristy than the Suva Curio & Handicraft Market, this is another great place to buy *masi* and traditional crafts. There is also a second-hand bookstall near the back that is worth checking out.

USP Book Centre
BOOKS

(www.uspbookcentre.com; USP Laucala Campus) Stocks the country's best selection of local and international novels, Lonely Planet guides and Pacific nonfiction.

ℹ Information

Internet access is cheap (F$3 per hour) and abundant in Suva, and many of the cybercafes along Thomson St are open 24 hours. There are also plenty of banks, ATMs and Western Union–affiliated currency exchange shops scattered along the same street.

ATS Pacific Holiday Inn (☑330 1600; Victoria Pde); Novotel Suva Lami Bay (☑336 4086; Queens Rd, Lami) Books local tours and activities, including those at nearby Pacific Harbour.

Connect Internet Café (Map p90; Scott St; per hr F$3; ☺8am-10pm Mon-Fri, 9am-10pm Sat, 9am-8pm Sun) Central with reliable connections.

Police (Map p90; ☑911, 331 1222; Pratt St)

Post office (Map p90; Thomson St)

Suva Private Hospital (Map p94; ☑330 3404; Amy St)

ℹ Getting There & Away

Suva is well connected to the rest of the country by air and interisland ferries. These are detailed in the Getting Around section on p142.

TO/FROM THE AIRPORT Nausori International Airport is 23km northeast of central Suva. **Nausori Taxi & Bus Service** (☑347 7583) has regular shuttle buses between the airport and the Holiday Inn hotel in Suva (F$10). A taxi between the airport and Suva costs around F$28.

BUS Frequent local buses operate along the Queens Rd and the Kings Rd from Suva's **main bus station** (Map p94; Rodwell Rd), although it's worth waiting for a **Sunbeam Transport** (☑338 2122) or **Pacific Transport** (☑330 4366) express bus if you are going some distance. Sample adult fares include: Pacific Harbour (F$3.60), Korolevu (F$6.70), Sigatoka (F$8.50), Nadi (F$9.35) and Lautoka (F$14.20). **Coral Sun Fiji** (☑620 3086) buses leave the Holiday Inn twice daily, calling at the major Coral Coast resorts as they travel to Nadi International Airport.

ℹ Getting Around

It is easy to get around central Suva on foot. Metered taxis are cheap for short trips.

Viti Levu's Kings Road

While the Kings Rd may lack the coastal scenery of the faster and more popular Queens Rd, it makes amends with ribboning, highland ascents, gorgeous views over the Wainibuka River and, from Viti Levu Bay, a coast-skirting run to Lautoka past rugged cliffs and sugar-cane fields. The price to be paid for this relatively untrammelled scenery is a slow trip on a bumpy road. In the wet season a 4WD is recommended, particularly on the short unsealed portion west of Korovou, but buses ply this route no matter what the road's condition. A coastal road runs parallel to Natovi Landing (about a 20-minute drive from Korovou), from where there are combined bus and ferry services to Levuka on Ovalau (p112). Beyond the landing, village-based **Natalei Eco-Lodge** (Map p66; ☑949 7460; nataleiecolodge@gmail.com; dm/r incl meals F$80/120) offers access to fabulous **Moon Reef** and its spinner dolphins (boat trips F$40 per person).

NAUSORI

On the eastern bank of the Rewa River, Nausori (population 47,600) is a bustling service centre for the area's agricultural and industry workers. Its only draw for travellers is its airport – the country's second largest. The airport, about 3km southeast of Nausori, is primarily a domestic hub.

VAILEKA, RAKIRAKI & ELLINGTON WHARF

Northwest from Korovou, the Kings Rd slides alongside Wainibuka River, past small villages, towards Viti Levu Bay. West of Rakiraki junction, a turn-off leads past the sugar mill to the small service town of Vaileka

Rakiraki & Nananu-i-Ra

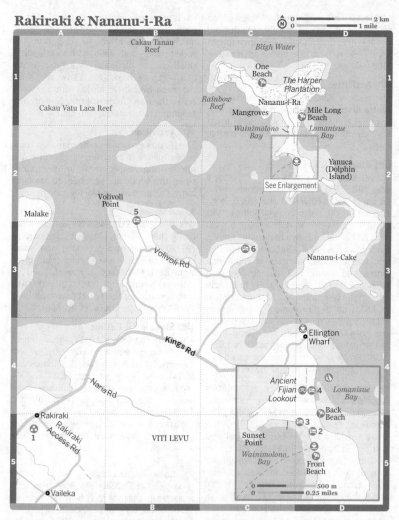

(Map p97). This is where buses arrive and depart from, and it's a good place to stock up on provisions before heading offshore. Town amenities include a supermarket, taxi rank, internet, produce market, banks with ATMs and several fast-food restaurants.

Heading out of Rakiraki towards Nadi, look out for **Udreudre's Tomb** (Map p97), the resting place of Fiji's most notorious cannibal, whose personal tally reached at least 872 corpses. It's about 100m west of the Vaileka turn-off, on the left, and resembles a rectangular slab of concrete.

Rakiraki & Nananu-i-Ra

◎ Sights
1 Udreudre's Tomb.................................A5

✪ Activities, Courses & Tours
Safari Island Lodge.......................(see 4)

⌂ Sleeping
2 Betham's Beach Cottages...................D5
3 McDonald's Beach Cottages...............D5
4 Safari Island Lodge............................D4
5 Volivoli Beach....................................B2
6 Wananavu Beach Resort....................C3

The turn-off to **Ellington Wharf** (Map p97) is about 5km east of Rakiraki junction, and it is here that resorts collect their guests for the short boat ride across to Nananu-i-Ra.

Activities

The reefs of Rakiraki offer some excellent **scuba diving** with dense marine life and beautiful coral gardens. Both resorts listed have on-site dive shops and knowledgeable staff.

Sleeping & Eating

Volivoli Beach RESORT $

(Map p97; ☏669 4511; www.volivoli.com; Volivoli Rd; dm F$31.50 d F$126-250 villas F$320; ❋ ⛱) Located on the northernmost point of Viti Levu, the eight-person dorms share a huge deck and come with two bathrooms apiece. Further up the hill is another lodge divided into four doubles that share a communal lounge and a wide hall that doubles as a kitchen. Removed from the noisy backpackers and the restaurant and bar (mains F$20 to F$35) are self-contained, two-bedroom villas with sweeping ocean views and modern, crisp interiors. If you are disappointed by the mangrove-lined beach you'll be pleasantly surprised by the picturesque sand spit only a minute's walk around the corner.

Wananavu Beach Resort RESORT $$$

(Map p97; ☏669 4433; www.wananavu.com; bungalows incl breakfast from F$470; ❋ @ ⛱) The restaurant (mains F$18 to F$39) here has gorgeous views over the beautiful pool area and out to Nananu-i-Ra island. Each *bure* has timber floors, panelled walls, air-con and a small deck surrounded by bougainvillea-filled gardens. The beach here is artificial and, although the landscapers have done an excellent job with strategically placed palm trees, most guests end up swimming in the pool.

Getting There & Away

Sunbeam Transport has regular express buses along the Kings Rd from Suva (F$12.90, 4½ hours) and Nadi (F$11.50, 2¼ hours) that stop at Vaileka and the turn-off to Ellington Wharf. To avoid lugging groceries and gear 1.3km to the wharf, get off at Vaileka and catch a taxi (F$15) to the jetty.

NANANU-I-RA

AREA 3.5 SQ KM

Tiny and perfectly formed, Nananu-i-Ra is only a hop and a skip from the mainland but quite different in character. There are no roads or villages, most residents are of European descent, and cattle grazing has cleared much of the island's dense vegetation. The wide beaches and scalloped bays support a small enclave of upmarket holiday homes and backpacker cottages. Those who walk the grassy hills are rewarded with fine views across the water to the volcanic Nakauvadra mountain range on the mainland.

Activities

The island's exposure to the southeast trade winds makes it ideal for windsurfing and kite boarding, especially from May to July when the winds are generally 10 knots or more. Offshore reefs make for good diving.

Safari Island Lodge WATER SPORTS

(Map p97; ☏628 3332, 948 8888; www.safarilodge.com.fj) This is the only place with kiteboarding (F$220/580 per two/six hours) and windsurfing gear for hire (beginner/advanced equipment F$350/500 per week) and an experienced instructor. It's also the only PADI dive operator on the island (two-tank dive/PADI Open Water Course F$185/690).

Sleeping & Eating

Most places accept credit cards (check before you go) and are well set up for self-caterers. Safari Island Lodge, Betham's and McDonald's Beach Cottages have indoor-outdoor cafes with limited menus and small stores selling the basics. Fresh fruit and vegetables can be limited.

Expect cold-water showers and the generator to be switched off around 10pm at most places.

Safari Island Lodge LODGE $

(Map p97; ☏628 3332, 948 8888; www.safarilodge.com.fj; campsite per tent F$10, dm/d/r F$30/95/150, bungalows F$195-320) There's a terrific variety of accommodation here, to suit all styles and budgets, with meal plans (F$65) or facilities for self-caterers. Together with the great range of outdoor activities (p98), it's the place to stay for the wind- and water-sports inclined. The wind-and-water theme continues throughout – a wind turbine provides 24-hour power and solar panels provide hot water.

Betham's Beach Cottages HOLIDAY RENTALS $

(Map p97; ☏669 4132; www.bethams.com.fj; dm/tw/cottages F$28/85/145) Betham's has some sound, old-fashioned beach-house accommodation options. The duplex beachfront cottages have kitchens, tiled floors and can

sleep up to five people. The double rooms are good value and the large communal kitchen is shared by those in the spacious eight-bed dorm.

McDonald's Beach Cottages   CABINS **$**
(Map p97; ✆628 3118; www.macsnananu.com; dm/tw F$26/90, bungalows F$135-145) McDonald's offers a scattering of supertidy self-contained cabins on a nicely landscaped property right in front of the jetty. The cute blue and yellow cottages are self-contained and it's popular with DIY types.

ℹ Getting There & Away
Nananu-i-Ra is a 15-minute boat ride from Ellington Wharf, and each resort runs its own transfers (around F$40 per person return). Arrange your pick-up in advance.

MAMANUCA GROUP

Reliably sunny and basking in a lagoon cradled by the Malolo Barrier Reef, the white-sand beaches of these 20 or so islands in a crystalline sea need little introduction. They make less contribution to the national culture than to the national economy – the Mamanuca Group is a tourist magnet. Whether you prefer to spend your days poolside getting intimate with a Fiji Bitter or making the most of the world-class snorkelling, diving and surfing, you'll find it all here.

ℹ Getting There & Away
Thanks to their proximity to both Port Denarau and Nadi airport, the Mamanuca islands are easily reached by catamaran, **speedboat** (www.mamanucaexpress.com), **seaplane** (www.fijiseaplanes.com) or **helicopter** (www.helicopters.com.fj).

Most people arrive on one of the high-speed catamarans departing Port Denarau, and tickets include courtesy pick-up from hotels in the Nadi region. Prices are for one-way adult fares. Children aged five to 15 are half-price.
Awesome Adventures (Map p74; ✆675 0499; www.awesomefiji.com) The *Yasawa Flyer* calls at South Sea Island (F$68), Bounty Island (F$60), Beachcomber Island(F$68) and Vomo (F$135) on its way north to the Yasawas.
Malolo Cat I & II (Map p74; ✆675 0205) Fast catamarans run to Malololailai (Musket Cove and Plantation Island resorts) three times daily (F$120).
South Sea Cruises (Map p74; ✆675 0500; www.ssc.com.fj) Six daily catamaran transfers to South Sea Island (F$50), Bounty Island (F$60), Beachcomber Island (F$68), Treasure

Island (F$68), Mana (F$83), Matamanoa (F$105), Castaway Island (F$78), Malolo (F$78) and Tokoriki (F$105).

South Sea Island
South Sea Island is the smallest of the island resorts and little more than a bump of sand with some trees on top. You can circumnavigate the whole island in three minutes, two if you hurry.

Many backpackers spend a night at **South Sea Island** (✆675 0500; www.ssc.com.fj/South_Sea_Island.aspx; dm F$89; ☒) on their way to or from the Yasawas. The only accommodation is in the 32-bed dorm above a communal lounge.

Bounty Island
AREA 0.2 SQ KM
Bounty (Kadavu) is bigger than its immediate neighbours but still takes only 20 minutes to walk around or, if you don't stop to tease clownfish, 1½ hours to snorkel. The white-sand beach attracts both endangered hawksbill turtles and the all-too-common day tripper.

Bounty Island Resort (✆628 3387; www.fiji-bounty.com; dm incl meals F$110-120, bungalows incl meals F$334-386; ✳☒) is a notch above South Sea Island in terms of quality and a few decibels quieter than Beachcomber. The ageing *bure* with tiled floors, air-conditioning and attached bathrooms are fairly basic by Mamanuca standards but those returning from the Yasawas will appreciate the hot showers and round-the-clock electricity.

Beachcomber Island
AREA 0.2 SQ KM
Tiny Beachcomber (Tai) has the reputation of being *the* Pacific party island, and tales of drunken debauchery are told far and wide. But truly in recent years some of the shine has rubbed off Beachcomber's disco ball. Nonetheless, the huge bar, live music and activities involving the inappropriate use of alcohol mean that this island isn't about to put away its boogie shoes anytime soon.

Accommodation options at **Beachcomber Island Resort** (✆666 1500; www.beachcomberfiji.com; dm/s/d incl meals F$122/282/374, bungalows incl meals F$409-542; ☺@☒) include rooms in a lodge, some clean, no-frills beach huts and a double-storey

Mamanuca Group

FIJI TREASURE ISLAND

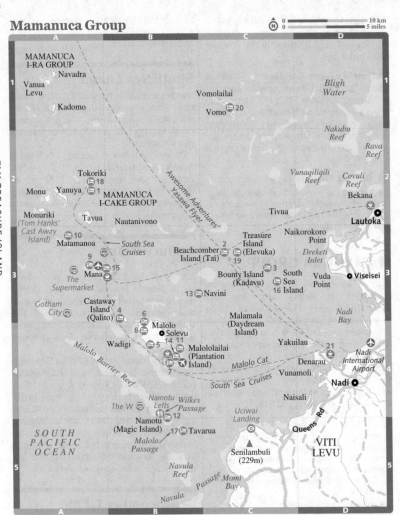

bure that sleeps 120. This may sound like dormitory hell but it is actually quite nice. The food at Beachcomber is generally good, particularly the enormous buffet breakfasts.

Treasure Island

AREA 0.06 SQ KM

Treasure Island (Elevuka) is another tiny island that takes mere minutes to walk around and is no more than a flyspeck on most maps. It's covered in tropical gardens and ringed by a white-sand beach.

Treasure Island Resort (☎666 6999; www.fiji-treasure.com; bungalows from F$474; ✳@✉☂) caters for families. The new pool has plenty of sloping 'beaches' for toddlers, and the turtle-feeding and mini-putt course are ideal for older kids. It has 66 comfortable, recently refurbished air-conditioned units housed in 34 duplex *bure* with roofs that resemble witches' hats. It's resolutely midrange despite its top-end prices and relies heavily on repeat guests who keep coming back for more – so it must be doing something right.

Mamanuca Group

FIJI VOMO

Vomo

AREA 0.09 SQ KM

This wedge-shaped island rises to a magnificent high ridge and has two lovely beaches (one or the other will be sheltered if it's windy) and some of the best snorkelling in the group.

The *bure* at **Vomo Island Resort** (☑666 7955; www.vomofiji.com; bungalows from F$1675; ❄@⊠) feature stylish Pacificana touches, indigenous wooden floors and separate living areas. Rates include divine meals (all of which are three courses), daily snorkelling trips, access to the nine-hole pitch 'n' putt golf course, and nonmotorised water sports. Unlike many five-star resorts, Vomo accepts children.

Navini

AREA 0.25 SQ KM

Fringed by a reef, surrounded by a beautiful beach and topped with tall trees, teeny Navini looks like a wafer topped with pesto and is just as delicious.

TOP CHOICE **Navini Island Resort** (☑666 2188; www.navinifiji.com.fj; bungalows F$595-790, villas F$890; @) has only 10 *bure*, all within 10m of the beach, each with private hammocks and sunloungers. All rooms are sizeable; the honeymoon *bure* has a courtyard and a private spa; the villa will likely make you want to move in for good. A three-meal plan of fresh and fabulous food costs F$110 and, as

there are more staff than guests, the service can't be faulted.

Return transfers by resort speedboat (adult/child/family F$270/130/780) allow you to maximise your time on the island no matter what your flight schedule.

Malololailai

AREA 2.4 SQ KM

Tranquil Malololailai is the second-largest island of the Mamanuca Group and encompasses three resorts, a marina and an airstrip. The lagoon offers protected anchorage for yachties but the beach is extremely tidal and not ideal for swimmers.

◉ Sights

Musket Cove Marina MARINA
(☑666 2215, ext 1279; VHF channel 68; mcyc@musket covefiji.com) Facilities include 27 moorings (F$15 per day), 25 marina berths (F$2 per metre, per day), dockside fuel and water, postal services, laundry, rubbish disposal, hot showers, bookswap, noticeboard and limited repair services.

In September each year, the Musket Cove Yacht Club hosts **Fiji Regatta Week** and the Musket Cove to Port Vila yacht race.

⬛ Sleeping & Eating

The **Musket Cove Trader & Coffee Cove** (General Store; ☑666 2215; ⊘store 8am-7pm, cafe 10am-6pm) is probably the best-stocked shop in the Mamanucas (but don't expect

MAMANUCAS DIVING & SURFING

Diving

Mamanuca diving sites teem with fantastically gaudy fish circling impossibly psychedelic corals. The visibility here astounds first-time divers and you can see forever – well, 30m to 40m for much of the year. The companies listed below are the big fish in the diving pond, with multiple dive shops on multiple islands; some resorts operate their own dive shops for similar prices.

Reef Safari (☑675 0566; www.reefsafari.com.fj) Has dive shops at South Sea Island, Bounty Island Resort and Amunuca Resort. A two-tank dive costs F$205 and a PADI Open Water Course is F$700.

Subsurface Fiji (☑666 6738; www.subsurfacefiji.com) Runs the dive shops at Malolo and Beachcomber, Musket Cove and Treasure Island. It also offers diving with free pick-ups for guests at Namotu, Navini and Tavarua Island resorts, Resort Walu Beach, Funky Fish and Likuliku. A two-tank dive costs F$210, and a PADI Open Water Course is F$790.

Surfing

The reefs off the southern Mamanuca islands have some of the world's most formidable breaks, including legendary left-handers **Cloudbreak**, **Restaurants** and **Namotu Lefts**.

Fiji's surfing guru Ian Muller is at **Fiji Surf Company** (Map p72; ☑670 5960; www.fiji surfco.com; 2nd fl, cnr Main St & Hospital Rd, Nadi). Ian and his crew offer surf trips and surf school for all levels, from family friendly to highly experienced. Resorts on Malololailai and Malolo will also get you out to the breaks (around F$50 per person).

mainland prices) and makes a decent coffee in the attached cafe.

Lomani Island Resort RESORT $$$
(☑666 8212; www.lomaniisland.com; bungalows incl breakfast F$674-840; ✳🖥🌊) Lomani is David to the Goliath of Plantation next door. This small, adults-only resort has a huge pool, a classy colonial-style bar and a decent outdoor restaurant (meal plans F$224 per person). The rooms have a Mediterranean feel to them; think stucco walls and arched doorways.

Musket Cove Island Resort RESORT $$
(☑666 2215; www.musketcovefiji.com; r F$276, bungalows from F$590, villas F$820; ✳@🌊) Musket Cove offers several types of accommodation, from hotel rooms to self-catering thatched *bure*. The newer villas – clustered on an artificial island – have over-water verandahs and a private pool.

Named after the owner, Dick's Place (mains F$35 to F$45) often hosts theme nights including the popular 'pig-on-a-spit' (although this isn't so popular with the pig). The casual Ratu Nemani Island Bar is linked to the resort by a walkway and is the place for DIY barbecues, cold beers and salty banter with visiting yachties.

Plantation Island Resort RESORT $$$
(☑666 9333; www.plantationisland.com; r F$316-650; ✳@🌊🛝) There are kids spilling out everywhere here; they're in the sea, in the pool, painting T-shirts, climbing plaster cows, egg-and-spoon racing, watching TV and eating chips in the free Club Coconut. This place is huge (850 people can stay here) and has a slight holiday-camp feel about it – you may have to line up for your buffet or set meal (adult/child full meal packages are F$91/51). The rooms come in a dizzying array of options including hotel-style, two-bedroom garden *bure* and beachfront.

❶ Getting There & Away

The *Malolo Cat* catamaran operates transfers from Port Denarau (p142).

Malolo

The big daddy of the Mamanuca Group has two villages, several resorts, mangroves and coastal forest. The island's highest point, **Uluisolo** (218m), offers panoramic views of the Mamanucas and southern Yasawas.

🛏 Sleeping & Eating

Funky Fish Beach Resort RESORT $
(☑651 3180; www.funkyfishresort.com; dm/d F$35/108, 1-/2-bedroom bungalows F$170/340; ❋@❋) Funky Fish is popular with surfers and is run by former Fiji rugby coach and All Black, Brad Johnston. The 12-bed dorm is modern, clean and partitioned into groups of four. The 'rock lobster' *bure* are tiny with thatched roofs and outdoor showers, while the larger, beachside 'grand grouper' *bure* can accommodate four. Tasty meals (mains F$18 to F$25) are served in an impressive hillside *bure* that enjoys panoramic views over the extremely tidal beach.

Malolo Island Resort RESORT $$$
(☑672 0978; www.maloloisland.com; bungalows F$730-911; ➖❋@❋⚞) Malolo had a stylish renovation in 2010 and the 49 *bure* are in great shape. It's lively and compact, and families who stay here love the white-sand beach, lush tropical gardens and free kids club. There are two restaurants (mains from F$35), a day spa, an adults-only pool and lounge, walking trails and dive shop.

Likuliku Lagoon LUXURY HOTEL $$$
(☑672 4275; www.likulikulagoon.com; bungalows F$1674-2810; ➖❋@🛜❋) For couples with cash to splash, the intimacy and privacy to be had here extend almost scurrilously far beyond a do-not-disturb sign on the door. The top-of-the-line over-the-water *bure* are the only ones of this kind in Fiji, and even Likuliku's second-tier accommodation boasts private plunge pools, thatched lounging pavilions, his-and-hers closets and inside

and outside showers. As you would expect in this five-star-plus category, a gourmet chef prepares ambrosial food.

Castaway Island

AREA 0.7 SQ KM
Reef-fringed Castaway Island (Qualito) is 27km west of Denarau and just short of paradise.

TOP CHOICE ⭐ Castaway Island Resort (☑666 1233; www.castawayfiji.com; bungalows F$740-985; ❋@❋⚞) is the oldest and still one of the best family destinations in the Mamanucas. The 66 spacious *bure* have two sections to accommodate those with children (kids stay free), small verandahs and intricate *masi* ceilings; all bathrooms were renovated in 2011. There's a swimming-pool bar, an open-air pizza shack and a great dining terrace overlooking the ocean where dinner costs F$30 to F$40 (or F$118/59 adult/child per day for the unrestricted meal plan). The excellent kids club will take three- to 12-year-olds off your hands, leaving you free to enjoy the complimentary nonmotorised water sports.

Mana

Beautiful Mana has a good selection of beaches and a peppering of hills with spectacular views. Upmarket Mana Island Resort stretches for over 80 hectares between the north and south beaches, while the budget resorts are sewn into the folds of the island's only village. For an interesting snorkelling

---

TOUR THE MAMANUCAS

Day cruises to the Mamanucas from Nadi are exceedingly popular and generally include transfers from Nadi hotels, lunch, nonmotorised water activities and as much sunburn as you can handle.

Captain Cook Cruises (Map p74; ☑670 1823; www.captaincook.com.au) Offers a day sailing cruise to tiny Tivua island (adult/child F$139/70), a dinner cruise for F$99/50 per adult/child, and three-day, two-night trips to the Mamanucas and southern Yasawas.

South Sea Cruises (Map p74; ☑675 0500; www.ssc.com.fj) Ferries day trippers from Port Denarau to various islands, with prices ranging from F$149 to F$185 per adult and F$75 to F$140 per child. Half-day options are also available.

PJ's Sailing & Snorkelling (Map p74; Sailing Adventures Fiji; ☑623 2011; www.sailing adventuresfiji.com) Popular PJ's takes up to 25 people for a day of Mamanuca cruising, snorkelling, singing and lunch at Plantation Island (adult/child F$160/80).

Seaspray (Map p74; ☑675 0500; www.ssc.com.fj) Travel by catamaran to Mana, from where the two-masted schooner *Seaspray* sails (or motors when it's calm) to Monuriki. Cruises cost F$165/89 per adult/child.

experience check out the south beach pier, where the fish go into a frenzy under the night lights.

🛏 Sleeping & Eating

A manned guard post and a high fence separate the three backpacker places from the Mana Island Resort and, like a mini Berlin Wall, divide the wealthy west from the ragged poor in the east. Escapees from the resort's dining rooms are welcome at Ratu Kini's but it's harder to move in the other direction.

Ratu Kini Backpackers HOSTEL $
(☎672 1959; www.ratukini.com; dm incl breakfast/all meals F$32/66, d incl breakfast/all meals F$120/189; @) No-fuss, no-frills dorms share cold-water showers; the big doubles are in a long block that's almost indistinguishable from the village. The restaurant-cum-bar sits out over the water and is a prime spot for sunset viewing and socialising.

Mana Island Resort RESORT $$$
(☎665 0423, 666 1455; www.manafiji.com; bungalow F$320-750, honeymoon ste incl breakfast F$900; ➋❉@☎☎🚹) One of the oldest and largest island resorts in Fiji; the 82 rooms and 70 *bure* come in a variety of configurations and are constantly being refurbished with polished wood and cool stone evident. Stylish split-level hotel-style suites are winners, each with a bedroom on the mezzanine floor.

Food gets mixed reviews; some guests choose to eat à la carte – or down the beach at Ratu Kini's – rather than go for the meal plans. There are two beautifully sited indoor-outdoor restaurants, a kids club for three- to 12-year-olds (a one-time fee of F$25 applies), and a creche for the littlies.

ℹ Getting There & Away

Mana is serviced by South Sea Cruises catamarans (see p142), and guests of Mana Lagoon Backpackers and Ratu Kini Backpackers can use the resorts' own (small) *Mana Flyer* transfer boat (F$120 return).

Matamanoa

Covered in dense vegetation, dotted with coconut palms and surrounded by white-sand beaches, Matamanoa is a secluded and hilly island just north of Mana.

The adults-only **Matamanoa Island Resort** (☎672 3620; www.matamanoa.com; d unit/bungalow incl breakfast F$465/755; ❉@☎) has 20 *bure* overlooking a lovely, white-sand beach. All *bure* have a verandah and beach views (half facing sunrise, half sunset). There are also 14 good-value, but not nearly as nice, air-conditioned hotel-style units with garden views. Young professionals and honeymooners are much in evidence.

Monuriki

Tiny uninhabited Monuriki (and ironically not Castaway Island) featured in the 2000 Tom Hanks movie *Cast Away,* and every resort worth its cabanas and cocktails sells day trips to what is increasingly referred to as the **Tom Hanks Island**. The trips cost around F$50 to F$80 depending on how far the boat has to travel to get there and what kind of lunch, if any, is included.

Tokoriki

The small, hilly island of Tokoriki has a beautiful, fine white-sand beach facing west to the sunset and is the northernmost island in the Mamanuca Group.

Dripping with orchids, **Tokoriki Island Resort** (☎672 5926; www.tokoriki.com; d bungalows/villas from F$1092/1535; ❉@☎) is the ideal romantic getaway. There are queen-sized beds with old-fashioned mosquito-net canopies and a gorgeous island-style wedding chapel of stone, wood and stained glass. The 30 beachfront *bure* have indoor and outdoor showers, and it's only a few steps past the hammock to the beach. Five villas have private plunge pools, beautiful interiors and large sandstone terraces. Lunch is served in the pleasant terrace and pool area while the gourmet candlelit dinners (mains from F$40) are served on white linen in the restaurant.

Also on the island is **Amunuca Resort** (☎664 0642; www.amunuca.com; bungalows F$323-794; ❉@☎🚹), whose facilities of late have gone up and down like the tide at its beachfront.

Namotu & Tavarua

Namotu and Tavarua are islands at the southern edge of the Malolo Barrier Reef, which encloses the southern Mamanucas. Namotu is a tiny (1.5 hectares) and pretty island, home to **Namotu Island Resort**

(www.namotuislandfiji.com). The bigger Tavarua is 12 hectares, rimmed by beautiful white sand, and is home to **Tavarua Island Resort** (www.tavarua.com). Both islands are primarily package surf resorts, geared to the American market. There is no public access.

YASAWA GROUP

Washed in dazzling sunshine and strung along 90km of reef, these 20 volcanic islands represent Fiji at its picture-postcard best. The Yasawas, rich in blue lagoons and alluring beaches encourage a welcome sojourn from life's hectic pace. This island chain has long been a backpacker favourite, but a new tide of midrange and top-end accommodation options is enticing an increasingly diverse crowd, and now tourism, along with agriculture, forms the backbone of the local economy.

The Yasawas are still remote and isolated and there are no shops, banks, postal or medical services. Although increased mobile-phone range has made communication somewhat easier for locals (and visitors), it can still be a bit erratic when there's a mountain in the way. Electricity is intermittent at best in many resorts (it is usually off overnight). Dorms are seldom full but it's worth prebooking double rooms and private *bure;* most places accept credit cards.

There are no restaurants in the Yasawas, and in the budget resorts quality, quantity and choice of food can be limited. There is little fussy eaters can do to minimise this, other than work the grapevine on the *Yasawa Flyer* and pack snacks.

ⓘ Getting There & Around

Half the fun of staying in the Yasawas is getting on and off the comfortable *Yasawa Flyer* as it works its way up the chain towards Nacula. The catamaran is operated by **Awesome Adventures Fiji** (☑675 0499; www.awesomefiji.com), and with an accommodation booking desk on-board (credit cards accepted), island-hopping travellers are able to book their beds as they go. (Having said that, the resorts appreciate direct bookings and in peak season it pays to book ahead.) The boat departs Denarau at 8.30am daily, calling into South Sea Island, Bounty Island, Beachcomber Island and Vomo in the Mamanucas before reaching the Yasawa Group. From Denarau, it takes about 1¾ hours to Kuata or Wayasewa (F$123 per person, one way), two hours to Waya (F$130), three hours to Naviti

(F$136) and 4½ hours to the lagoon shared by Tavewa, Nanuya Lailai and Nacula (F$148). In the afternoon it follows the same route back to the mainland, calling into all the resorts once more. Island-hoppers should consider a 'Bula Pass' (seven/14/21 days F$321/385/483) that enables unlimited travel but only one return to Denarau.

Awesome Adventures also offers five or more nights' travel and accommodation packages from F$771 per person, but if you're looking for flexibility you're better off booking your accommodation separately.

Pacific Island Air & Seaplanes (www.pacificislandair.com) charters are another option for travel from Nadi.

Kuata

Petite Kuata is the first Yasawa stop for the *Flyer* and, with its unusual volcanic rock formations, it makes a fine introductory impression. The best snorkelling is off the southern end of the island, and the summit can be conquered in a hot and sticky 20 minutes.

Sitting on a coarse sandy beach with Wayasewa hovering in the foreground, **Kuata Natural Resort** (Map p106; ☑862 8262; campsite per person incl meals F$50, dm/d incl meals F$72/172) appeals to unfussy backpackers with a 20-bed and 10-bed dorm and traditional en suite *bure* tightly arranged around the gardens. Standards are modest, and the price range quoted above reflects the age and quality of the *bure*.

Wayasewa

Also known as Wayalailai (Little Waya), Wayasewa is dominated by Vatuvula, a volcanic rock plug that dramatically towers over the beaches below. The hike to the top is an hour's hard scramble, and views take in the whole Yasawa Group. A 35-minute boat ride away is a local reef renowned for its **shark snorkelling** (without/with equipment F$25/40). The sharks, which are mostly white-tip reef sharks, are totally harmless, but their sleek looks and stealth-like appearance make a thrilling outing. The trips can be arranged through **Dive Trek Wayasewa** (two-tank dive/PADI Open Water Course F$180/650), which is based at the Wayalailai Eco Haven Resort.

Wayalailai Eco Haven Resort (Map p106; ☑603 0215; www.wayalailairesort.com; campsite per person incl meals F$60, dm incl meals F$80, d incl meals F$180-200) is owned and operated

Yasawa Group

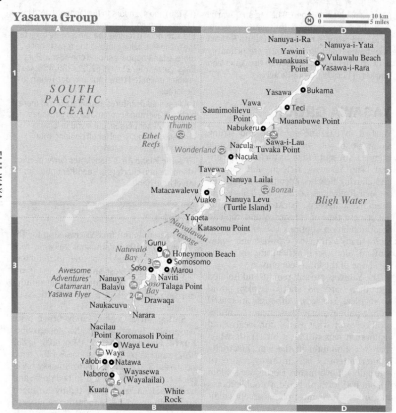

Yasawa Group

entirely by villagers. This two-tiered budget resort is tucked squarely beneath Vatuvula's granite facade, with bamboo and thatched *bure* overlooking the beach, thin-walled double rooms, and simple dorms. Buffet meals are served in a raised bar-restaurant overlooking the beach.

A few minutes' boat ride further along the beach, **Naqalia Lodge** (Map p106; ☑977 4696; www.naqalialodge-yasawa.com; dm/d incl meals F$117/234) has four airy *bure*, covered in wildly colourful artwork.

Waya

With rugged hills, beautiful lagoons and a periphery of long sandy beaches, Waya is easy on the eyes. Walkers can tackle the summit of **Ului Nakauka** (three hours return from Octopus Resort) and snorkellers can explore the thick rim of coral that traces the island.

The only place to stay is **Octopus Resort** (Map p106; ☑666 6337; www.octopusresort.com; dm F$45-55, d F$255-479; ⊖✳@✱🛜), with its breezy bar-restaurant, swaying hammocks and a wide sandy beach peppered with thatched sun huts and padded sunloungers. It's a mostly midrange option of stand-alone

thatched and fan-cooled *bure*; there's also a small air-con dorm and several decidedly top-end villas. The compulsory meal package (F$77) includes excellent à la carte lunches and set dinners in a sand-floored restaurant. Octopus also offers direct boat transfers from Vuda Point marina (adult/child F$150/110 one way, 1¼ hours), south of Lautoka, for guests who don't wish to island-hop the *Flyer*'s route.

Naviti & Around

AREA 33 SQ KM

One of the largest and highest (up to 380m) of the Yasawa islands, Naviti has a rugged volcanic profile and a dazzling snorkelling site where you can swim with manta rays. The best time to see the giant rays is between June and August. All the resorts in the area offer snorkelling trips for around F$35 per person plus snorkel hire, but only Mantaray Island Resort employs spotters, sending the boat out only when they are assured of a successful encounter.

Korovou Eco-Tour Resort and White Sandy Beach resort share a protected stretch of white-sand beach, but the swimming is only marginal here due to a bank of ugly, dead reef. Fortunately, a short track (around a 10-minute walk) provides access to the pretty and secluded Honeymoon Beach.

🛏 Sleeping & Eating

TOP CHOICE **Mantaray Island Resort** RESORT $
(Map p106; 603 0202; www.mantarayisland.com; dm F$41, d F$139-250;) Mantaray occupies its own wee island, spreading through and over a small hill between two pretty beaches. The modern dorm is divided into cubicles of four bunk beds, and each contains its own fan and light. The cheaper 'treehouse' *bure* share the self-composting toilets and hot showers with the dorm, while the very comfortable 'jungle' *bure* have private bathrooms. Food is fusion and delicious in the restaurant, and there's a pizza oven on the beach.

Korovou Eco-Tour Resort HOSTEL $$
(Map p106; 603 0050; www.korovoufiji.com; dm/d/villas incl meals F$120/286/330;) Korovou can accommodate about 70 travellers and can be packed with young and sociable troops. Two 20-bed dorms have wooden bunks and fans; stone and wooden villas each have a separate lounge, fridge and stone bathroom; doubles have their own verandahs and bathrooms, and are spotlessly clean.

Barefoot Lodge LODGE $
(Map p106; 777 5250; www.captaincook.com.au; bungalows per person incl meals F$99) This is a mellow, very low-key resort on tiny Drawaqa island. Small, clean and simple

FIJI NAVITI & AROUND

YASAWA ISLANDS TOURS

Captain Cook Cruises (670 1823; www.captaincook.com.au) Captain Cook Cruises offers an all-inclusive cruise ranging from three to seven nights (from F$1295 per person) on board *Reef Endeavour*. The 68m cruiseboat has a swimming pool, bars, lounges and air-conditioned accommodation for 135 people spread over three decks. Cruises depart from Denarau Marina. The company also runs sailing trips to the southern Yasawas aboard the tall ship SV *Spirit of the Pacific*. Swimming, snorkelling, fishing, village visits, *lovo* and more are all part of the deal. Accommodation is in simple *bure* ashore at Barefoot Lodge. Twin-share prices, per person, are F$599.

Blue Lagoon Cruises (Map p78; 666 1662; www.bluelagooncruises.com; 183 Vitogo Pde, Lautoka) Offers a variety of cruise combinations including three-day (single/double F$2068/3136) and seven-day (single/double F$3513/6027) trips to the Yasawas aboard motor-cruisers and catamarans. Transfers, on-board activities and food are included but drinks, snorkelling and diving are extra. Cruises depart from Lautoka, north of Nadi.

Awesome Adventures Fiji (675 0499; www.awesomefiji.com) Offers the only scheduled day tour to the Yasawas, to Botaira Beach Resort on Naviti (adult/child F$103/57).

Southern Sea Ventures (www.southernseaventures.com) Australian-operated, this company offers eight-day kayaking safaris between May and October along the Yasawa chain of islands (A$1995 per person).

FAST FOOD

On 29 April 1789, Captain William Bligh and 18 loyal crew members were set adrift by mutineers of HMS *Bounty* in an open boat just 7m long and 3m wide. The epic journey that followed passed through treacherous water littered with shallow reefs and islands inhabited by cannibals. As they passed the Yasawas, two war canoes put to sea and began pursuit. Fortunately a squall swept in some much-needed wind to raise the mainsail and blew Bligh and his crew to the safety of the open sea. This body of water is known as Bligh Water today and, while the Yasawas remain relatively undeveloped, the locals are considerably friendlier.

bure made with lattice walls and thatched roofs are owned and operated by Captain Cook Cruises.

Tavewa

AREA 3 SQ KM

This small, low island houses some of the Yasawa Group's northernmost resorts. A pleasant beach unfurls itself on the southeastern coast but it's often plagued by buffeting trade winds. Head to Savutu Point, just around the bend, for relief from the gales and some lovely snorkelling.

Based at Coral View Resort, **Dive Yasawa Lagoon** (Map p109; ☑666 2648, marine VHF channel 72; www.diveyasawalagoon.com) will also pick up from other resorts (transfer fees apply) on nearby islands. Every Wednesday and Saturday, Dive Yasawa Lagoon operates a shark dive where you are likely to see resident lemon sharks and grey reef sharks. A two-tank dive/PADI Open Water Course costs F$180/750 including equipment.

Sleeping & Eating

Coral View Resort HOSTEL $
(Map p109; ☑922 2575; www.coralviewfiji.com; dm/s/d incl meals F$76/140/185; ✳@) This well-run budget resort can be full to the brim with young Brits intent on drinking the island dry, and the nightly entertainment often features beach parties and bonfires. Accommodation options range from air-con 20-bed dorms to good-value stone

cottages with high-pitched roofs and *masi* and bamboo-lined interiors – and there's 24-hour electricity.

Otto & Fanny's HOMESTAY $
(Map p109; ☑996 3108; ottofanny@connect.com.fj; dm/d incl meals F$100/210; @) On a sprawling property, among a former copra plantation, this quiet place has several *bure* with private bathrooms and a spacious, 12-bed dorm. The flat, grassy grounds are inundated with coconut trees that offer plenty of wide-open spaces and there's decent beach just around the corner. It's more quiet homestay than hostel, and sees returning guests of all ages.

Nacula

Blanketed with rugged hills and soft peaks, the interior of the third-largest island in the Yasawas is laced with well-trodden paths leading to villages and small coves. Beach devotees will be happy to know that Nacula's Long Beach is ideal for swimming.

Sleeping & Eating

TOP CHOICE **Blue Lagoon Beach Resort** RESORT $$
(Map p109; ☑603 0223; www.bluelagoonbeach resort.com.fj; Long Beach; dm/d F$45/179, villas F$329-879; ✳) Blue Lagoon ticks all the right boxes. It's small enough to be low-key and relaxed, but big enough (about 70 guests when full) to have a bit of a buzz. It caters for all budgets in a compatible way: *bure* are stylish, the 16-bed air-con dorm is clean as a whistle, and inventive food (meal plans F$79 per person) is served in a groovy sand-floored restaurant-bar.

Safe Landing Resort HOSTEL $
(Map p109; ☑948 2180; www.safelandingfiji.com; South Coast; campsite per person incl meals F$50, dm/d incl meals F$70/180; @) Several small *bure* dot the waterfront here, overlooking the resort's pretty little beach framed between two rocky outcrops. It's one of few places to welcome BYO campers, with flat and shady sites under coconut palms, and an airy dorm was under construction when we visited.

Nanuya Lailai

Ever since a young, bikini-clad Brooke Shields thrilled moviegoers in *The Blue Lagoon,* Nanuya Lailai's **Blue Lagoon** has been a magnet for snorkellers, divers, luxury

cruiseboat passengers and yachties – all keen to dabble in its gorgeous depths.

On the exposed eastern side of the island is the settlement of Enadala and several budget resorts. Connecting the Blue Lagoon and Enadala beaches is a well-trodden track. Diving is provided by **Westside Watersports** (Map p109; ☎666 1462; www.fiji-dive.com) at Nanuya Island Resort; it caters to guests at resorts on nearby islands, as well as Blue Lagoon Cruises' passengers. A two-

tank dive/PADI Open Water Course costs F$180/750.

🛏 Sleeping & Eating

TOP CHOICE **Nanuya Island Resort** BOUTIQUE HOTEL **$$**
(Map p109; ☎666 7633; www.nanuyafiji.com; d incl breakfast F$275-415; @) A short walk, even in flippers, to the azure waters of the Blue Lagoon, this swish and understated resort is the kind of place you picture when you

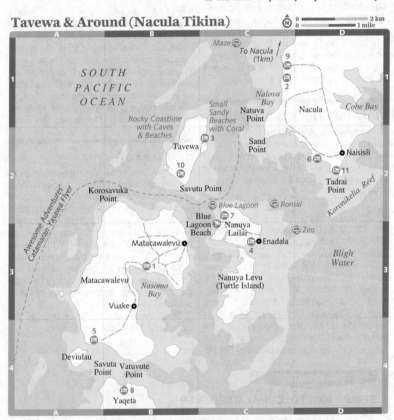

Tavewa & Around (Nacula Tikina)

dream of indulgence, beachside cocktails and exquisite vistas. The *bure* are Fiji-nouveau; the roofs may be thatched but the interiors are chic and elegant. All are fan-cooled, with solar-heated hot water. This place oozes romance and it's a favourite spot for couples (no children under seven). The beachside restaurant is very atmospheric and the à-la-carte fare (F$25 to F$35) deliciously inventive.

Gold Coast Inn
HOMESTAY **$**

(Map p109; ☑665 1580; Enadala; dm/d incl meals F$82/185) Offering the only budget accommodation on the island, the private timber *bure* here have a double and single bed as well as bathrooms. This is a smallish affair – there are only six bungalows and a small dormitory – but it's run by a family with a big heart.

Matacawalevu & Yaqeta

Matacawalevu is a 4km-long hilly volcanic island protected by the large Nasomo Bay on its eastern side. Nanuya Levu (Turtle Island) is to the east, and to the south, across a protected lagoon used for seaweed farming, is Yaqeta.

TOP CHOICE ### Navutu Stars
BOUTIQUE HOTEL **$$$**

(Map p109; ☑664 0553; www.navutustarsfiji.com; d F$525-892; ❂❄@☒) This boutique hotel specialises in opulent decadence Pacific-style, with petal-sprinkled baths, intimate sunset dining and complimentary massages on arrival. The whitewashed villas have king-sized beds, exquisitely detailed 7m-high roofs and fantastic views north from their private decks. Children under 14 are not permitted and the fabulous food is Italian-inspired (à la carte or meal packages F$120).

Long Beach Backpackers
HOSTEL **$**

(Map p109; ☑603 1020; longbeach_vuaki@yahoo.com; campsite/dm/d incl bfast F$60/70/250) Low-key and mellow, this welcoming family-run hostel has several double *bure* with private bathrooms, and a clean eight-bed dorm with a tired bathroom. The big draw here is the long, horseshoe-shaped beach, and a breezy deck overlooks tiny Deviulau island – you can wade over at low tide and scramble to the top for great views.

Bay of Plenty Lodge
HOSTEL **$**

(Map p109; ☑995 1341; bayofplentylodge@yahoo.com; dm/d incl meals F$72/165) Five small hillside villas have tiled floors and attached bathrooms with excellent views. The mangrove-fringed beach has brownish sand and, being extremely tidal, resembles an estuary for much of the day – but an optional bonus is helping the cook wade out with nets to catch fish for dinner.

Sawa-i-Lau

At Sawa-i-Lau, underwater limestone rocks are thought to have formed a few hundred metres below the surface and then uplifted over time. Shafts of daylight enter the great dome-shaped **cave** (Map p106), looming 15m above the water surface, where you can swim in the natural pool. With a guide, a torch and a bit of courage, you can also swim through an underwater passage into an adjoining chamber. The limestone walls have mysterious indecipherable carvings, paintings and inscriptions.

Most Yasawa resorts offer trips to the caves for around F$45 per person.

LOCAL KNOWLEDGE

SERUVI IOSEFO: CORAL GARDENER

As activities' coordinator at Navutu Stars resort in the Yasawas – and as a local villager – Seruvi is a passionate advocate of coral gardening. After all, as he says, it may be slow going but it's not rocket science. 'It's just like planting cassava. You break a bit off, find a good place to put it, make sure the new conditions are right. If the bottom's attached after a couple of weeks, you know it'll survive!' It's a great way to explain the simplicity of the process to visitors.

Armed with snorkel, mask and flippers, Seruvi swims off. Pointing out the bright blue tips of a healthy staghorn coral, he snaps a piece off, fins away to a bleached, barren patch of tired reef and pokes the just-picked stem into a crevice. He indicates small, single-stemmed corals next to it that were transplanted recently and are growing well, grins, and gives a thumbs-up before swimming on.

OVALAU & THE LOMAIVITI ISLANDS

POP 12,064 / AREA 409 SQ KM

Lomaiviti literally means 'Middle Fiji' and although the group is just off Viti Levu's east coast, it really does feel like the middle of nowhere. It is therefore hard to believe that this is where the Fijian nation was made, and picturesque Levuka, Ovalau's main town, was Fiji's earliest European settlement and the country's first capital. Today it's laid-back and the political machinations long departed, but with the right wind you may yet catch a whiff of the town's wild and immoral colonial days.

South of Ovalau, the tiny coral islands of Leleuvia and Caqalai have sandy beaches, good snorkelling and simple budget resorts.

Getting There & Around

From Suva **Northern Air** (☑347 5005; www.northernair.com.fj) flies to Ovalau (F$80 one way, 12 minutes, Monday to Saturday) at 8am and returns to Suva at 8.40am. Book online or at the airport when there are departing or incoming flights. The airstrip is about 40 minutes' drive from Levuka. Minibuses to the airstrip (F$10 per person) will pick you up from your hotel on request. A taxi costs about F$40.

Patterson Brothers Shipping (Map p113; ☑344 0125; Beach St, Levuka; ⊙8.30am-4.30pm Mon-Fri, to noon Sat) has a bus-ferry-bus service from Levuka to Suva via Natovi Landing (F$35, four to six hours, gather at 4.30am for 5am departure daily from Levuka; from Suva arrive at the far lot of Suva's bus terminal at 1pm for a 1.30pm departure). You can also opt to stay on the boat from Natovi to Nabouwalu (on Vanua Levu) and then continue by bus to Labasa (F$65). **Venu Shipping** (☑339 5000; Rona St, Walu Bay, Suva) has direct services from Levuka to Walu Bay in Suva a couple of times a week but the timetable can be erratic. The *Lomaiviti Princess*, run by **Goundar Shipping** (☑330 1035), makes occasional stops in Levuka during busy periods on its Savusavu–Taveuni–Koro–Suva–Kadavu route.

The resorts on the islands near Ovalau (all except Koro) offer private transfers in their own boats to either Natovi, Bau or Waidalice landings on Viti Levu and to Levuka. See each island's section for details.

Ovalau

Ovalau is the largest island in the Lomaiviti Group. The island itself is not as pretty as the little brothers and sisters scattered around

it, but the capital, Levuka, is captivating and is the only place in the Lomaiviti Group with decent banks, shops and services.

🏃 Activities

CYCLING

Levuka and its surrounding area are compact, and it is easy to get around by bike. If you're reasonably fit it will take you about a day to cycle around the island. No one was officially renting out bikes at the time of research, but ask around and you're sure to find someone who will rent or lend you one.

DIVING & SNORKELLING

The Lomaiviti waters offer some wonderful, little-visited dive sites where you can encounter manta rays, hammerheads, turtles, white-tip reef sharks and lionfish. Blue Ridge, off Wakaya island, is famous for its bright-blue ribbon eels. There is stunning soft coral at Snake Island, just off Caqalai, in the Moturiki Channel, and excellent hard coral at Waitovu Passage.

Wakaya Club, Naigani Island Resort and Caqalai Island Resort all offer diving.

YACHTING

Levuka is a port of entry into Fiji for yachties and there are a few good spots to put down anchor in the Lomaiviti Group. You can anchor in Levuka harbour to explore Ovalau, and good desert-island spots to park include

---

DON'T MISS

EPI'S MIDLAND TOUR

Visit Lovoni village in the crater of an extinct volcano deep in the heart of Ovalau (although it resembles a flat valley floor surrounded by hills rather than anything else). Epi, who runs the full-day tour (per person F$80), is a Lovoni and will take you through forest and past streams, pointing out all kinds of plants, bush food and local medicine along the way. Once you've reached the village and presented your *sevusevu* (gift) to the village chief – assuming the chief is around – you can take a dip in the river. A delicious lunch in one of the village homes is laid on. Price includes transfers and lunch but requires a minimum of two people; the per-person price goes down with each additional person. Book through Ovalau Watersports (see p112).

Leleuvia island and Dere Bay on Koro island. Try VHF marine channel 16 to reach the appropriate authorities if entering the country at Levuka, but if no one answers, anchor near Queen's Wharf and make your way ashore.

☞ Tours

Aside from the following agents, Ovalau Tourist Information Centre (see p114) offers a historical, two-hour **walking tour** (per person F$10) around Levuka.

Ovalau Watersports ISLAND TOURS
(Map p113; ☑960 9136) Serai is the mover and shaker of the Lomaivitis' small tourism world and many guesthouses, resorts and tours use her as their booking agent. The office is officially at Levuka Holiday Cottage out near Gun Rock, but Serai can often be found at the back of the unnamed shop on the corner of Hennings and Beach Sts. She is the person to seek out for round-the-island 4WD tours as well as arranging all of the tours listed here.

Silana Village Tour VILLAGE TOURS
(Map p66; per person F$35) Requires a minimum group of six, with a few days' notice, and includes a *meke* (dance performance that enacts stories and legends), a *lovo* (feast cooked in a pit oven) and a chance to make your own handicrafts from coconut and pandanus leaves. The guide, Seru, will also take you around Silana any time for F$15 (including lunch).

LEVUKA
POP 3750

There's no denying Levuka's visual appeal. It's one of the few places in the South Pacific that has retained its colonial buildings: along the main street, timber shopfronts straight out of a Hollywood western are sandwiched between blue sea and fertile green mountains. The effect is quite beguiling – you can almost taste the wild frontier days of this former whaling outpost.

◎ Sights

Cession Site HISTORIC SITE
About 10 minutes' walk south of town is Cession Site, where the Deed of Cession was signed in 1874. Across the road the **Provincial Bure** sits like a loaf of wholemeal bread covered in straw.

Former Morris Hedstrom Trading Store HISTORIC SITE
(Map p113) Downtown stands the first trading store (1868) in Fiji. Behind its restored facade is a branch of the **Fiji Museum** (admission F$2; ⊙8am-1pm & 2-4.30pm Mon-Fri, 9am-1pm Sat), which holds a small exhibition detailing the history of Levuka, including some wonderful old colonial photos.

Notable Buildings ARCHITECTURE
(Map p113) Other buildings to keep an eye out for include the **Sacred Heart Church** (1858); Levuka's **original police station** (1874); the **Ovalau Club** (1904), Fiji's first private club; and the **former town hall** (1898). You'll also find the stone shell of the South Pacific's first **Masonic Lodge** (1875) and Levuka's only Romanesque building. It was burnt to a husk in the 2000 coup by villagers egged on by their church leaders.

199 Steps of Mission Hill VIEWPOINT
(Map p113) The 199 Steps of Mission Hill are worth climbing for the fantastic view. The simple coral and stone Gothic-style **Navoka Methodist Church** (1864) near the foot of the steps is one of Fiji's oldest churches.

🛏 Sleeping

TOP CHOICE Levuka Homestay B&B $
(Map p113; ☑344 0777; www.levukahomestay. com; Church St; s/d incl breakfast F$126/148, extra person F$42) Far and away the most chic choice in Levuka: a multilevel house with four large, comfortable, light-filled rooms with terraces, each one on its own level. Guests come to eat a spectacular breakfast or share a drink with the owners on their enormous deck overlooking the harbour (spot whales while imbibing from May to October).

TOP CHOICE Royal Hotel HOTEL $
(Map p113; ☑344 0024; www.royallevuka.com; s/d/tw F$29/43/43, cottages from F$85; ✻@☎) The Royal is the oldest hotel in the South Pacific, dating back to the 1860s (though it was rebuilt in the early 1900s after a fire) and it's got the character to back it up. Each room in this colonial-atmosphere building is different and full of quirky old furniture, with iron bedsteads and sloping floors.

Levuka Holiday Cottage CABIN $
(Map p113; ☑344 0166; cottage@owlfiji.com; d F$80) About a 15-minute walk north of town (F$3 by taxi), this is the only self-catering option close to Levuka. There's a well-equipped kitchen, hot water, and it's right in the middle of a pretty, tropical garden under Gun Rock cliff.

Levuka

Levuka

FIJI OVALAU

✕ Eating

Whale's Tale   INTERNATIONAL $
(Map p113; ✆344 0235; Beach St; breakfast F$6, lunch sandwiches F$8, mains $12; ⊙lunch & dinner Mon-Sat) This is a perennial favourite serving 'the best fish and chips in Fiji', as one local resident told us. There are excellent burgers, sandwiches and set meals. It's a cute little place with big windows for watching the world go by, and a small, bamboo-thatched kitchen area at the back.

Kim's Paak Kum Loong   CHINESE $
(Map p113; ✆344 0059; Beach St; mains F$8; ⊙lunch & dinner) This is the best place to get Chinese food in Levuka. There are two menus here – one with standard Chinese dishes, another with a mixture of Fijian-style fish and meat dishes and a selection of Thai curries.

Koro Makawa Restaurant

INTERNATIONAL **$**

(Map p113; ☑344 0429; Beach St; pizzas from F$9; ☺breakfast, lunch & dinner) You can get curries, fish and chips, and other European meals here, but locals recommend it because of the pizza, which is, apparently, very hit and miss – 'either one of the best pizzas you've ever tasted or a total disaster' was one comment.

🍷 Drinking & Entertainment

There are a number of pool halls where locals like to pot balls to pop music.

Ovalau Club

BAR

(Map p113; Nasau Park; ☺4-9.30pm Mon-Thu, 2pm-midnight Fri, 10am-midnight Sat, 10am-9.30pm Sun) This is the main place in town to go for a drink. Fiji's first gentlemen's club, it's extremely atmospheric and the white timber colonial-style building is a sight in its own right. It's no longer a colonial club in any respect, but local residents (mostly expats) get together for a drink at 6pm every Tuesday and tourists are always welcome to join them.

ℹ Information

There are Westpac and BSP Bank ATMs right next to each other on Beach St.

Levuka Hospital (Map p113; ☑344 0221; Beach St; ☺outpatient treatment 8am-1pm & 2-4pm Mon-Fri, to noon Sat, emergencies only after hours) A good, new hospital at the northern end of town.

Ovalau Tourist Information Centre (Map p113; ☑330 0356; Levuka Community Centre, Morris Hedstrom Bldg; ☺8am-1pm & 2-4.30pm Mon-Fri, to 1pm Sat) Has an information board detailing Ovalau's accommodation and food options, and also organises Levuka town tours.

Police station (Map p113; ☑344 0222; Totoga Lane)

Post office (Map p113; Beach St) Near Queen's Wharf at the southern end of town; there's a cardphone outside.

Caqalai

Teeny little Caqalai island (pronounced 'Thangalai') lies just south of Moturiki. It only takes 15 minutes to walk around the island perimeter's beautiful golden-sand beaches, which are fringed with palms, electric-blue water and spectacular reef.

TOP CHOICE Caqalai Island Resort (☑343 0366; www.fijianholiday.com; campsite/dm/bungalows per person incl meals F$50/65/75) is a gem of a backpackers run by Moturiki's Methodist Church, but don't let that scare you – you'll find more kava here than kumbaya, although you'll have to bring your own alcohol if you prefer that to the muddy stuff. Accommodation is in big, basic thatched or wooden *bure*, scattered between the palm trees and hibiscus. Cold-water showers are in a shared block and toilets are in brightly painted stalls that are strategically placed near all the *bure*. Snorkelling right off the beach is fantastic, but for some of the best snorkelling in Fiji walk out about 10 minutes to Snake Island at low tide and swim around the reef. There's a dive centre with a hodgepodge of ageing equipment and a local divemaster can be found on demand.

ℹ Getting There & Away

If you're coming from Levuka, you can book transport and accommodation from Ovalau Watersports (p112) or call for a pick-up. One-way transfers cost F$30 per person. Transfers from Caqalai to Bureta airstrip on Ovalau cost F$50 for one person, or F$25 per person for two or more.

From Suva, catch a bus heading down the Kings Rd from the main bus terminal and get off at Waidalice Landing, which is next to Waidalice Bridge. You need to call ahead for a boat from Caqalai to pick you up here (F$30 per person).

Leleuvia

Just south of Caqalai sits beautiful Leleuvia, another stunning palm-fringed coral island (slightly larger than Caqalai) wrapped in white, powdery beaches with outstanding views out to sea.

TOP CHOICE Leleuvia Island Resort (Map p66; ☑973 0339; www.leleuvia.com; dm incl meals F$50, bungalows F$110; ⚑) is less backpacker-y than nearby Caqalai, making it a better choice for couples looking for more comfort, and it's a fantastic choice for families thanks to the sandy bottom and shallow swimming at the island's point. Thatched *bure* here are basic but classy with views of the sea and trade winds pouring through for natural ventilation. A large, open, sand-floored bar and restaurant area serves cold beer and tasty meals (three meals per day F$32 per person; the Saturday *lovo* is a favourite), and at the resort's 'entrance' is a gorgeous wide stretch of beach with sunloungers and kayaks. While the snorkelling is not on a par

with Caqalai, it is still excellent and you can hire equipment.

❶ Getting There & Away

Boat transfers to/from Waidalice or Bau Landing are F$25 each way (call in advance for a pick-up). Waidalice is about a 1½-hour bus ride from Suva. Transfers to/from Levuka (one hour) also cost F$30 each way. Call in advance for a pick-up or you can book via Ovalau Watersports (p112).

VANUA LEVU

POP 130,000

The few who make it to Fiji's second-biggest island smile smugly – they know they're onto one of the tropic's best-kept secrets. Many roads on the east and west sides are rutted dirt and Labasa, the island's largest 'city', is a one-road strip of shops. Still, the island's few settlements are hard-working places filled with folks farming sugar cane and copra. Outside the small pockets of relative hustle are remote villages, mountain passes streaming with waterfalls, endless swaths of forest and an ever-changing coastline forgotten by the world. Take it slow, keep a smile on your face and enjoy exploring rural Fiji on its grandest scale.

❶ Getting There & Around

AIR

Flying is the best way to get to Vanua Levu and Pacific Sun has regular flights from Labasa to Nadi, Suva and perhaps in the future, Taveuni (check the website, www.airpacific.com). In Savusavu the office of **Pacific Sun** (☑885 2214) is in the Copra Shed; in Labasa, **Pacific Sun** (Map p123; ☑881 1454; Northern Travel Service office, Nasekula Rd) is off the main drag.

The Labasa airport is about 11km southwest of Labasa. There's a bus that passes the airport about every hour but it doesn't link up with flights and you'll have to go out to the main road to flag it down. A taxi from Labasa costs F$16.

Savusavu airstrip is 3km south of town but only charter airlines were using it at the time of writing. Labasa is the main airport for Vanua Levu.

BOAT

TO/FROM TAVEUNI A bus leaves Savusavu every morning at 7am, arriving at the pier at Natuva around 11am where a small boat leaves for Lovonivonu (Taveuni), arriving at around 1pm. In the reverse direction, boats leave Lovonivonu at 9am and connect to the bus at Natuva at 11am. On Tuesday, Thursday, Friday and Sunday, this service (F$20) is run by Grace Shipping – buy tickets at Mum's Country Kitchen (p120). On other days you'll have to hop on the bus without a reservation but the boat (the *Sunny*) is cheaper and slightly faster – on these days the bus costs F$5 and the boat is F$10.

The *Lomaiviti Princess* run by Goundar Shipping (see below) also crosses between Taveuni and Savusavu a few days a week as part of its Suva route.

TO/FROM SUVA Bligh Water Shipping (Map p123; ☑885 3192), **Consort Shipping** (Map p123; ☑885 0279) and **Goundar Shipping** (Map p119; ☑883 3085) offer boat services to and from Vanua Levu via Koro, Taveuni and/or Ovalau. The best by far is the *Lomaiviti Princess* operated by Goundar; the office is located in Kong's Shop on Main St in Savusavu.

CHARTERS & CRUISES For those looking to charter their own boat, **SeaHawk Yacht Charters** (☑885 0787; www.seahawkfiji.com) rents out a beautiful 16m yacht with captain and cook or crew from US$150 per person per day. You can go practically anywhere in Fiji and the crew can help you arrange activities such as diving.

CAR

Vanua Levu's remote, tropical roads are crying out to be explored by 4WD. Hire cars are available in Labasa (see p124) and Savusavu (p122). Petrol stations are scarce and usually closed on Sundays, so plan to fill up in Labasa, Savusavu or Seaqaqa.

It's also possible to navigate the island by bus, but timetables can be erratic and journeys take far longer.

Just remember, you cannot wander on foot through the countryside without permission from the landowners.

Savusavu & Around

If you ever dreamed of a sweetly scented South Pacific port nestled against a sweeping bay, backed by sloping green hills and filled with hibiscus flowers, chances are your image looks a lot like Savusavu (population 4970). It's a timeless little town where everyone smiles and says '*bula*', and there are several good restaurants, bars and well-stocked stores. The stunning looks and ease of living continue to seduce folks to stay longer than planned and many foreigners have snapped up land to build second homes and lodges in the hills and surrounding coast. As such, there's an uncommonly large but very laid-back expat community.

FIJI SAVUSAVU & AROUND

Vanua Levu

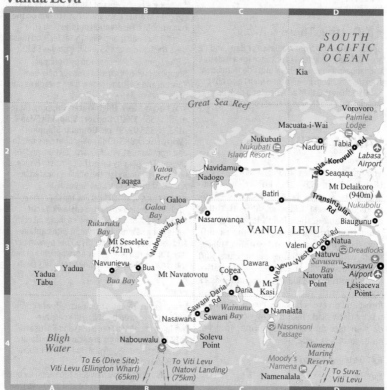

SOUTH PACIFIC OCEAN

Kia

Great Sea Reef

Vorovoro
Palmlea Lodge

Macuata-i-Wai

Nukubati
Nukubati Island Resort Naduri Tabia
Tabia-Korovuli Rd
Labasa Airport

Vatoa Reef Navidamu Seaqaqa
Yaqaga Nadogo

Batiri Mt Delaikoro (940m) ▲
Transinsular Rd Nukubolu

Galoa
Galoa Bay Nasarowanqa **VANUA LEVU** Biaugunu

Rukuruku Bay Valeni Natua
Mt Seseleke (421m) ▲ *Vanua West Coast Rd* Natuvu *Dreadlocks*
Navunievu Dawara *Savusavu Bay* Savusavu
Yadua Yadua Bua Cogea Natovatu Point Savusavu Airport
Yadua Tabu Mt Navatovotu ▲ Mt Kasi ▲ Lesiaceva Point
Bua Bay Daria

Sawani-Daria Rd Namalata
Nasawana Sawani *Wainunu* *Sawani Bay*
Nasonisoni Passage

Bligh Water Nabouwalu Solevu Point *Namena Marine Reserve*
Moody's Namena
To E6 (Dive Site); To Viti Levu Namenalala To Suva;
Viti Levu (Ellington Wharf) (Natovi Landing) Viti Levu
(65km) (75km)

⊙ Sights & Activities

Diving & Snorkelling

Far and away the best diving, perhaps in all of Fiji, is about a two-hour boat ride from Savusavu at **Namena Marine Reserve**, a protected reserve (park fee is an additional F$30 per person, valid for one year) of corals so vibrant and marine life so plentiful, it's become the poster child for Fiji's underwater world.

The best sites closer in are just outside Savusavu Bay (about a 20-minute boat ride) and include **Dreamhouse**, where you'll search for hammerheads in the blue before seeing great schools of barracuda, jacks and tuna at a coral outcrop; **Dungeons and Dragons**, which is a towering maze of dive-throughs; and **Nasonisoni Passage**, an incredible drift dive where you'll be sucked along by a strong current. The interior of Savusavu Bay itself has unfortunately been plagued by crown of thorns starfish recently,

and the corals of the once-famous sites will take several years to grow back.

KoroSun Dive DIVING
(⌂885 2452, 934 1033; www.korosundive.com; Hibiscus Hwy) Colin and Janine run an attentive and professional centre, ideally located on the Hibiscus Hwy about 15km from Savusavu and near the best dives outside of Savusavu Bay (at Koro Sun Resort, p120). Two-tank dives/PADI Open Water Courses, including all gear, cost F$190/750. They'll pick you up and drop you off free of charge from anywhere around Savusavu.

Aboard a Dream DIVING
(⌂828 3030; www.aboardadream.com; charters from per person A$400) A live-aboard is the best way to dive the Namena Marine Reserve and fortunately this highly recommended outfit can take you there, as well as to other little-known sites, on three- to seven-day charters. The 15m ship takes maximum six passengers

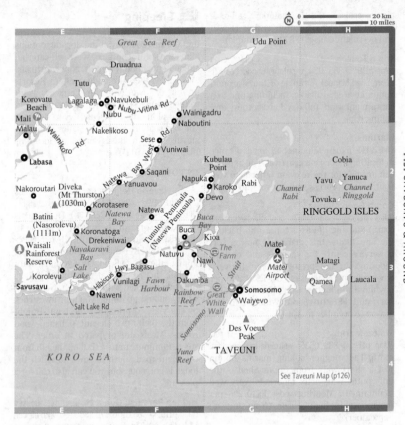

and your charming hosts have spent nearly a decade diving Fijian waters.

L'Aventure Diving   DIVING
(☎885 0188; laventurefiji@connect.com.fj) This is a top-notch centre but, since it doesn't provide pick-up, there's no point paying for the extra transport unless you're staying at the Jean-Michel Cousteau Fiji Islands Resort (p119) or want to dive Nasonisoni Passage (this is the only centre that often goes there). Two-tank dives/PADI Open Water Courses cost F$280/860 with gear included.

J Hunter Pearls   SNORKELLING
(Map p119; ☎885 0821; www.pearlsfiji.com) Learn all about how black pearls are farmed before being boated out to the farm (now a floating structure since the grafting house was destroyed in a cyclone). If you want to snorkel the oyster lines, bring your own gear and jump in; otherwise you can check everything out from the glass bottom of the

boat. Tours depart at 9am weekdays (F$25, 1½ hours). Afterwards you can head to the shop to buy pearls and shell jewellery.

Other Activities
There are **hot springs** (Map p119) behind the playing field and near the wharf. The shallow streams are literally boiling and locals come to cook food in them. You'll scald yourself if you touch them.

Rock n' Downunder Divers   RENTALS, CRUISES
(Map p119; ☎885 3447, 932 8363; Waitui Marina) Rents out kayaks (F$40 per day) and mountain bikes (F$35 per day) and has catamarans. Also arranges a number of activities including village visits (F$60 per person), beach cruises (F$70), sunset cruises (F$40) and boat charters (F$60 per hour).

SeaHawk Yacht Charters   CRUISES
(☎885 0787; www.seahawkfiji.com) Offers cruises around Savusavu Bay, including full-day

picnic cruises (F$85), half-day sail-and-snorkel trips (F$55), sunset cruises (F$50) and overnight cruises (F$720 per couple).

Trip n Tour ISLAND TOURS
(Map p119; ☎885 3154; tripntour@connect.com.fj; Copra Shed Marina) A range of tours around Vanua Levu is available, including one to a copra plantation, full-day Labasa tours and fishing trips.

Marinas

Use VHF marine channel 16 for assistance in locating moorings on arrival. The marinas can arrange for the relevant officials to visit your boat to process your arrival into Fiji.

Copra Shed Marina MARINA
(Map p119; ☎885 0457; coprashed@connect.com.fj) Starting life as a copra mill back in the late 1800s, this marina is now a sort of service centre for yachties and visitors. Moorings in the pretty harbour between Savusavu and Nawi islet cost F$10/260 per day/month in high season (June to September), and F$8/210 per day/month in low season (November to April).

Waitui Marina MARINA
(Map p119; ☎885 0536; waituimarina@connect.com.fj) The rougher-looking marina option just a short walk from Copra Shed is the only outfit with helix moorings (very well maintained). Moorings cost F$10/225 per day/month in high season (from June to September).

THE TUI TAI

A trip with **Tui Tai Adventure Cruises** (☎885 3032; www.tuitai.com) combines the comfort, relaxation, fantastic food and luxury of an intimate, upscale resort with an ever-changing South Pacific backdrop. Setting off from Savusavu, a typical itinerary includes Taveuni, Kioa and Rabi islands, and provides the only way of reaching the Ringgold Isles (a beautiful, mostly uninhabited group of islands east of Vanua Levu), although your itinerary may vary. All accommodation is in cabins with private bathroom and air-con. A five-night cruise costs from US$2567/3851 per person single/double, including all meals and activities except diving.

🛏 Sleeping

Savusavu caters to long-term (often returning) visitors, so many of the sleeping options along the scenic south coast are self-catering single-home holiday rentals; some are luxurious while others are budget affairs. Resorts are out of town, either on Lesiaceva Point to the southwest, Savusavu Rd to the northwest or along the Hibiscus Hwy to the east; you can soak up South Sea sailor charm by staying in town. Buses service all locations regularly (see p121).

IN TOWN

TOP CHOICE **Naveria Heights Lodge** B&B $$
(off Map p119; ☎885 0348; www.naveriaheightsfiji.com; r incl breakfast F$210; 🖥) This B&B is owned by some of the most fun people in the area – Sharon and Scott lead yoga classes, take you river-tubing, mountain biking, hiking...the list goes on. Or if you just want to chill, they're good at that too, and keep the fridge stocked with cold beer. No matter what you end up doing, you'll be awestruck by the view (overlooking the bay) straight from the B&B's two elegant, polished-wood rooms. Meals are prepared to order. The steep, 15-minute nature trail up the hill from the main road south of town to reach the lodge is gorgeous, but you can also call for a pick-up.

Hidden Paradise Guest House GUESTHOUSE $
(Map p119; ☎885 0106; s/d F$30/60, with air-con F$40/70; ❄) This is the best place to meet other budget travellers. It's a no-frills deal, with a shared bathroom and cold-water showers, but the rooms are spotless and the smiling owner Elenoa is often found playing a lively game of cards with her friends in the courtyard. A cooked breakfast is included in the price and you can watch life pass by from the Sea View Café at the front of the guesthouse.

Hot Springs Hotel HOTEL $
(Map p119; ☎885 0195; www.savusavufiji.com; Nakama Rd; r with fan/air-con incl breakfast F$55/125; ❄🖥🏊) Every room has a little balcony with fantastic, picture-postcard views over Savusavu Bay. The rooms are clean and spacious, but have a whiff of identikit motel about them (it *did* used to be a Travelodge). Lower-level rooms are fan-cooled while the upper ones – with slightly better views – have air-con. The hotel also has a bar, cafe and a pool with a view.

Savusavu

Savusavu

◎ Sights
1 Copra Shed Marina.................................C1
2 Hot Springs...B2
3 J Hunter Pearls.....................................A1
4 Waitui Marina.......................................B1

◉ Activities, Courses & Tours
Rock n' Downunder Divers.............(see 4)
Trip n Tour.......................................(see 1)
5 Tui Tai Adventure Cruises.....................A1

🛏 Sleeping
6 Hidden Paradise Guest House...............B1
7 Hot Springs Hotel.................................B2

✕ Eating
Captain's Table..............................(see 1)
8 Decked Out Café....................................C1

Mum's Country Kitchen...................(see 1)
Surf and Turf....................................(see 1)

🍸 Drinking
9 Planters' Club.......................................A1
10 Savusavu Wines & Spirits.....................B1
Savusavu Yacht Club.......................(see 1)
Waitui Marina.................................(see 4)
White Stork.....................................(see 9)

✪ Entertainment
11 Uros...D1

ℹ Information
12 Hot Springs Medical Centre..................B2

ℹ Transport
13 Goundar Shipping.................................D2

LESIACEVA ROAD

Lesiaceva Rd runs southwest along the peninsula from Savusavu about 12km and is home to several white beaches and supremely relaxing places to stay.

TOP CHOICE Fiji Beach Shack HOLIDAY RENTALS $$$
(☑885 1002; www.fijibeachshacks.com; Lesiaceva Rd; houses per day/week from F$350/2380; 🛜🏊) These are seriously glam: the two-level 'House of Bamboo' has two bedrooms and a fabulous bathroom complete with a sunken bath and sea views from two large windows. The 'Pod House' is an extremely private one-bedroom overlooking the bay. Both have a plunge pool, a deck and a daybed. You can

snorkel out to gorgeous Split Rock from the beachfront across the road.

Hans' Place HOLIDAY RENTALS $
(☑885 0621; www.fiji-holiday.com; Lesiaceva Rd; Yasiyasi studio per week F$450, Yaka cottage per week F$550) Sitting up on Lesiaceva Point, a skip and a jump away from the ocean, are two excellent-value, cosy, self-contained cottages with comfortable decks. Both sleep two people. Each has a kitchenette, is fan-cooled and has a hot shower. Bikes are available for hire at F$10 a day.

Jean-Michel Cousteau Fiji Islands Resort RESORT $$$
(☑885 0188; www.fijiresort.com; Lesiaceva Rd; d bungalows from F$1000; @🏊👨‍👩‍👧) This

outstanding, luxury eco-resort was started by the son of Jacques Cousteau. As you'd expect, it attracts divers, but it also has one of the best kids clubs we've ever seen. The *bure* are massive and feature handmade furnishings, large decks and private garden areas. Great gourmet meals are included in the price. The thin white beach is a bit rocky but OK and there's a pier to dive off into deeper water. All activities, except diving, are included in the rate.

Daku Resort RESORT $$
(off Map p119; ☑885 0046; www.dakuresort. com; Lesiaceva Rd; bungalows/villas from F$195/ 320; @≋) A resort-cum-self-improvement- centre, Daku attracts guests to participate in a surprisingly diverse array of courses, from gospel singing to watercolour painting, meditation and yoga. There's neat accom- modation (in *bure*), a sweeping sea view, a pleasant pool and a good restaurant and bar. The beach across the road is pebble rather than sand, but at high tide you can swim out and find top-notch fish-viewing.

Bayside Backpacker Cottage HOLIDAY RENTAL $
(☑885 3154; tripntour@connect.com.fj; Lesiaceva Rd; s/d F$40/50) This sweet little cottage is in the grounds of travel agent Eddie Bower's home, sleeps two and has a decent kitchen with a gas stove, TV and DVD player. There's a beach across the road but it's not fantastic; bring a snorkel, though, as underwater it's a different story. You can borrow mountain bikes to cycle the 3km to town and there's a minimum two-night stay.

HIBISCUS HIGHWAY
The Hibiscus Hwy runs along the south coast of Vanua Levu starting about 5km from Savusavu. The following places to stay are around 8km along on coast that's both scenic with white sand beaches and relatively near to some of the better diving spots. **Dolphin Bay Divers Retreat** (p128) is southeast of Buca Bay. Accessible only by boat, it is most easily reached from Taveuni.

Namale Resort RESORT $$$
(☑885 0435; www.namalefiji.com; Hibiscus Hwy; bungalows US$1170-2200; ⊕≋) Namale is a hugely exclusive and pricey resort right by the water, 9km from Savusavu. Accommodation ranges from tropically delicious *bure,* hidden among the rain- forest and reached by wooden walkways, to a jaw-droppingly luxurious grand villa

complete with a mini movie theatre, and private stretch of beach. The price includes all meals and activities except diving.

Koro Sun Resort RESORT $$$
(☑885 0262; www.korosunresort.com; Hibiscus Hwy; bungalows F$400-1200; ✳⊕≋⊞) The homey and welcoming Koro Sun has a hand- ful of lavish two-storey *bure* over a clear, blue lagoon; some bigger family-style units look out over a shady lily pond and a string of rather dated units sit on the hillside. Food is included in the price, as are numerous activities. Diving is available through Koro- Sun Dive (see p116).

✕ Eating

Surf and Turf INTERNATIONAL $$$
(Map p119; ☑885 0511; Copra Shed Marina; mains F$25-40; ⊕lunch & dinner) This is the poshest restaurant in Savusavu town, with a lovely outside space overlooking the water. There are great wines available by the bottle or the glass, and tasty pasta, steaks, lobster and crayfish dishes and daily specials. Lunch is a lighter affair with burgers and sandwiches on offer.

Captain's Table INTERNATIONAL $$
(Map p119; ☑885 0511; Copra Shed Marina; pizza from F$15, lunch/dinner F$8/16; ⊕breakfast, lunch & dinner) Dine overlooking the bay (from the Copra Shed Marina) on a creative assortment of international and Indian fare like chicken stuffed with spinach, steaks and seafood. If you're feeling more casual, try Captain's Café on the street side, which serves pizzas, pancakes, quesadillas and sandwiches from F$9.

Decked Out Café INTERNATIONAL $$
(Map p119; ☑885 0195; meals around F$15; ⊕lunch & dinner; ⊕) Across the street from the Copra Shed Marina, this no-frills, semi- outdoor pad has become one of the more popular yachtie hang-outs. It serves pizzas, salads, fish and chips and much more. Happy hour (5pm to 7pm) beers are F$3 and there's live music (6pm to 11pm) Thurs- day through Saturday. Wi-fi is free with a tab of F$10 or more.

Mum's Country Kitchen INDIAN $
(Map p119; ☑927 1372; breakfast F$2-3, meals F$6; ⊕breakfast, lunch & dinner) One step up from a hole-in-the-wall, this place is popular with local Indo-Fijians for its curries – it's always packed.

🍷 Drinking

Savusavu Yacht Club
BAR

(Map p119; ☑885 0685; Copra Shed Marina; ⏱10am-10pm Sun-Thu, to midnight Fri & Sat) Tourists are considered temporary members of this friendly little drinking hole. There are tables out by the waterside, plenty of cold beer, and some mingling yachties and expats.

Waitui Marina
BAR

(Map p119; ☑885 0536; ⏱10am-10pm Mon-Sat) Sit on the balcony upstairs to enjoy classic South Pacific views of the yacht-speckled, palm-lined bay. The bar is well stocked and all foreigners on holiday are considered temporary members. Expect locals playing guitars, and heavy drinking as the night wears on.

Planters' Club
BAR

(Map p119; ☑885 0233; ⏱10am-10pm Mon-Sat, to 8pm Sun) This was traditionally a place for planters to come and drink when they brought in the copra, and some of their descendants can still be found clustered around the bar today. It has a whiff of colonialism and is teeming with expats. Happy hour is from 5.30pm to 6.30pm. Once a month, the club holds a Sunday-lunch *lovo*. You're allowed two visits as a nonmember.

Savusavu Wines & Spirits
WINE SHOP

(Map p119; ⏱8am-6pm Mon-Fri, to 1pm Sat) It's amazing what you can find in this little bottle shop: a great wine and international spirits selection as well as imported gourmet coffees, cheeses, cereals and more. There are a couple of tables outside if you wish to sit down and imbibe – and many do.

☆ Entertainment

Uros
CLUB

(Map p119; admission F$5; ⏱8pm-midnight) Meaning 'Sexy' in Fijian, the only viable clubbing option in town is where anyone and everyone goes to bump and grind to local and international music. It's a smallish room up a dark flight of stairs and great fun.

ℹ Information

Being an official point of entry for yachts, there are customs, immigration, health and quarantine services available. ANZ, Colonial National and Westpac banks all have branches in the main street.

Customs (☑885 0727; ⏱8am-1pm & 2-5pm Mon-Fri) West of the marinas on the main street.

Hospital (☑885 0444) Located 1.5km east of town on the road to Labasa. Call the hospital if an ambulance is required.

Hot Springs Medical Centre (Map p119; ☑885 0721) Brand new and the best place to go.

Police (☑885 0222) Located 600m past the Buca Bay Rd turn-off.

Post office At the eastern end of town near Buca Bay Rd.

ℹ Getting There & Around

For information on air and boat travel see p115.

BUS The Savusavu bus station is in the centre of town, near the market. Buses travelling the scenic, sealed (yet bumpy) highway from Savusavu over the mountains to Labasa (F$8, three hours, four times daily) depart from 7.30am to 3.30pm. Some buses take the longer route from Savusavu to Labasa along Natewa Bay, and these depart at 9am (F$15, six hours).

Buses from Savusavu to Napuka (F$7, 4½ hours), at the tip of the Tunuloa Peninsula, depart at 10.30am, 1pm and 2.30pm daily. The afternoon bus stays there overnight and returns at 7am. A 4pm bus only goes as far as Naweni (F$3). There is no bus from Savusavu to Nabouwalu in the west; you have to catch a morning bus to Labasa and change buses there.

From Monday to Saturday there are five bus services from Savusavu to Lesiaceva Point (F$1, 15 minutes) between 6am and 5pm. For

---

WORTH A TRIP

NUKUBOLU

Deep in the mountains north of Savusavu, reachable by 4WD, lie the ruins of **Nukubolu**, an ancient Fijian village, whose old stone foundations, terraces and thermal pools are in surprisingly good condition. The setting is lovely: a volcanic crater with steaming hot springs in the background. Nukubolu has myriad uses for the local villagers, who dry kava roots on corrugated-iron sheets laid over the pools, and use the hot springs as a healing aid. The ruins are on the property of the village of Biaugunu, so take a *sevusevu* (gift) for the chief and ask permission before wandering around. The turn-off is about 20km northwest of Savusavu; continue about 8km inland and over a couple of river crossings. You can also rent a carrier from town to take you there; combine it with a trip to Waisali Rainforest Reserve.

confirmation of bus timetables in the south, call **Vishnu Holdings** ([☎]885 0276).

CAR Cars can be booked through Trip n Tour (p118); prices start at F$110 a day for a two-door 4WD.

TAXI Taxis are easy to find in Savusavu and the main taxi stand is right next to the bus station. Flagfall is F$1.70 and each 100m costs 10 cents.

Namenalala

The volcanic island of Namenalala rests on the Namena Barrier Reef, now one of the most spectacular protected marine reserves in the country, 25km off the southeastern coast of Vanua Levu and about 40km from Savusavu. Namenalala has the best diving and snorkelling in the region, lovely beaches, and it's a natural sailors' refuge. There's just one small, upmarket resort.

TOP CHOICE **Moody's Namena** (Map p116; [☎]881 3764; www.moodysnamenafiji.com; 5-night all-inclusive packages per person sharing from F$1875; [☺]closed Apr) is an outrageously located dive and snorkel eco-retreat that has six bamboo-and-timber *bure* on a forested ridge. Diving here is the best of the best and costs F$300 for six tanks (divers must be certified). Other activities (which include windsurfing, fishing, snorkelling, and use of canoes and paddleboards) are included in the rate. The island has a nature reserve for birdwatching and trekking and is home to seabirds, red-footed boobies and a giant-clam farm. From November to February hawksbill and green turtles lay their eggs on Namenalala beaches. There is a five-night minimum stay, and packages include transfers from Savusavu. No children under 16 years old are allowed.

Labasa

POP 24,100

Labasa (pronounced 'Lambasa'), Vanua Levu's biggest settlement, is a bustling and dusty sugar and timber town. Sitting about 5km inland on the sweltering banks of the Labasa River and reclaimed mangrove swamps, the star attractions are a large sugar mill on the outskirts of town and a 'sugar-railway' that ka-chunks bushels of cane through Labasa centre. Labasa's population is predominantly Indo-Fijian, many of whom are descendants of *girmityas* (indentured labourers brought from India to work on the plantations).

Out of town are nearly-undeveloped coastal areas that are rumoured to get great surf and have awesome diving.

⊙ Sights & Activities

Wasavula Ceremonial Site   HISTORIC SITE
(off Map p123; Vunimoli Rd) At the entrance to the site, just south of town, is a sacred monolith that villagers believe grew from the ground. Behind the standing stone is the village cemetery. Beyond is the area that was used during cannibalistic ceremonies, and has a flat *vatu ni bokola* (head-chopping stone), another rock where the severed head was placed, and a bowl-like stone in which the brain was placed for the chief. Unless you are given a guided tour you could probably walk right past most of these stones without noticing.

⌇ Sleeping

Palmlea Lodge   BUNGALOWS $$
(Map p116; [☎]828 2220; www.palmleafarms.com; Tabia–Naduri Rd; villas from F$259; [❋][≋]) This remote-feeling eco-resort is only 14km west of town off a dirt road and overlooks the Great Sea Reef. Simple bamboo-thatched *bure* with verandahs sit on a gentle green slope a short walk to the resort's jetty – from here you can kayak to a private white-sand beach or just jump in for fantastic snorkelling. Fruit and veg is grown on an on-site organic farm and every effort is made to manage the resort in an eco-friendly fashion. Buses run past the resort five times a day, making it easy to get to Savusavu.

Grand Eastern Hotel   HOTEL $
(Map p123; [☎]881 1022; grest@connect.com.fj; Rosawa St; r F$100-130; [❋][☏][≋]) This is the plushest and most convenient hotel in Labasa, located just off the main road. There's an airy, somewhat-colonial atmosphere and the staff are wonderful. Standard rooms have porches facing the river, but it's worth paying extra for the deluxe rooms that open out onto the courtyard swimming pool. All room interiors are plain and slightly careworn, however. There's also a decent restaurant and bar.

Friendly North Inn   HOTEL $
(Map p123; [☎]881 1555; fni@connect.com.fj; Butinikama–Siberia Rd; r F$70-90; [❋]) For peace and quiet, head to the Friendly North Inn, which is a better deal than the Grand Eastern if you don't mind the 20-minute walk to

Labasa

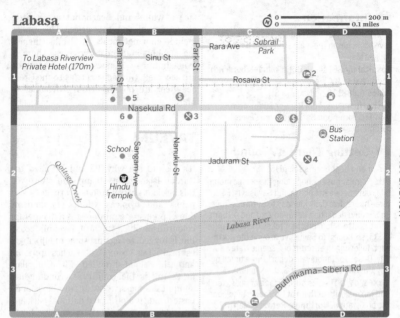

town. There are several surprisingly classy duplex villas set in a mellow, flower-studded garden; less-expensive, pink 'apartments' share a common kitchen and lounge area between two or three rooms. The hotel has a large, open bar and restaurant, but meals need to be ordered in advance. A taxi into town will cost F$5.

Labasa Riverview
Private Hotel   GUESTHOUSE $
(off Map p123; ☎881 1367; fax 881 4337; Nadawa St; r without/with air-con F$55/70; ❄) This is an un-assuming house with ageing but cute rooms with cold-water bathrooms. A lounge area with a pool table overlooks a calm, murky river and the vibe is sweet. It's F$3 for a taxi to town.

🍴 Eating

Labasa is full to the brim with basic cafes serving cheap plates of Indian and Chinese food. Note: most restaurants, although open for dinner, close by 7pm. There's also a cavernous market next to the bus station and a few well-stocked supermarkets.

Oriental Bar & Restaurant   CHINESE $
(Map p123; ☎881 7321; Jaduram St; meals F$8; ☺lunch & dinner Mon-Sat, dinner Sun; ⊛) Look for the bright-orange door and pink balcony

Labasa

🛏 Sleeping
1 Friendly North Inn	C3
2 Grand Eastern Hotel	D1

🍴 Eating
3 Gopal's	B1
4 Oriental Bar & Restaurant	D2

ℹ Information
5 Northpole Rentals	B1

ℹ Transport
6 Bligh Water Shipping	B1
Consort Shipping	(see 7)
7 Pacific Sun	B1

overlooking the bus station. Although you wouldn't guess it from the outside, this is one of Labasa's most upmarket and atmospheric restaurants, with a well-stocked bar and a wide choice of tasty Chinese dishes, including plenty of vegies and a few Fijian options.

Gopal's   VEGETARIAN $
(Map p123; Nasekula Rd; thali F$10; ☺breakfast, lunch & dinner; ✍) Specialises in vegetarian Indian food, and has fantastic thalis. There's also a sweets counter with a nice selection of sinful Indian treats.

❶ Information

ANZ, Colonial National and Westpac banks all have branches in the main street and have 24-hour ATMs.

Hospital (☏881 1444; Butinikama–Siberia Rd) Southeast of the river.

Police (☏881 1222; Nadawa St)

Post office (Nasekula Rd; ⊙7.30am-4pm Mon-Fri, 8am-noon Sat) There are several cardphones outside.

❶ Getting There & Around

For air and boat tickets see p115).

BUS Regular buses chug along the scenic mountain route between Labasa and Savusavu (F$8, three hours, five daily Monday to Saturday, four on Sunday) departing between 7am and 4.15pm. There is also a 9am bus that takes the long route (F$15, six hours) to Savusavu around the northeast, following the even-more-scenic Natewa Bay. Buses to Nabouwalu depart three times per day Monday to Saturday (F$10, six hours).

TAXI & 4WD There is no shortage of taxis. You'll find the majority of them at the main stand near the bus station. **Northpole Rentals** (Map p123; ☏881 8008; www.northpole.com.fj/rentals. html) has an office at the hotel of the same name on the main drag. You can rent 4WD Suzuki Jimmys from F$100 per day, and it offers free airport pick-up and drop-off.

Around Labasa

The area around Labasa is a great place to explore by 4WD. There are a few points of interest; however, it's definitely the adventure of finding them rather than the sights themselves that make it worthwhile. For all of these sights, you'll need to turn left onto Wainikoro Rd, just past the sugar mill and across from a secondary school. This is the main road out of town to the east.

🛌 Sleeping & Eating

Tribe Wanted   VILLAGE STAY **$$**
(☏992 0428; www.tribewanted.com) A 'unique community tourism project' founded by two young English entrepreneurs who, in 2006, signed a three-year lease on Vorovoro island, offshore from Vanua Levu. Guests love it, but the lease ran out and in late 2011 the project was closed. It was scheduled to reopen under new management in 2012.

🖊 Nukubati Island Resort   RESORT **$$$**
(Map p116; ☏881 3901; www.nukubati.com; d bungalow incl meals & activities from US$710) *Bure*

face a white-sand beach but are a little old-fashioned for the price. The prices include gourmet meals, all drinks (including alcohol) and most activities. There is a maximum of 14 guests and only adults are accepted. Guided surf trips to the Great Sea Reef are possible from November to March.

TAVEUNI

POP 12,000

It's easy to see why Taveuni is called the Garden Island. Hot, steamy and often wet, this luscious strip of land is a carpet of green palms and tropical wildflowers, and its dense, prehistoric rainforest is a magnet for colourful birdlife. Much of Taveuni's coastline is rugged, set against some of Fiji's highest peaks. Des Voeux Peak reaches up 1195m and the cloud-shrouded Mt Uluigalau, at 1241m, is the country's second-highest summit. A massive swath of the island's eastern side is a protected national park and here you can get sweaty on hillside hikes, cool off under a waterfall or enjoy a coastal walk along an impossibly beautiful beach trail. Dotted around the island's perimeter are black-sand beaches.

The island's beauty descends below the water's surface, attracting divers from across the globe, all eager to explore the dazzling corals and diverse marine life of the world-famous Somosomo Strait with its profusion of fish and the occasional shark, turtle or even pilot whale from September to November.

The most famous of the vibrant soft-coral sites is **Rainbow Reef** (Map p126), which fringes the southwest corner of Vanua Levu but is most easily accessed from Taveuni. Highlights include the luminescent Great White Wall. See p32 for details. The island is especially hot and humid in January and February and the water clarity is reduced due to plankton blooms and northerly winds from the equator.

There is plenty for snorkellers, too. **Vuna Reef** (Map p126), off southern Taveuni, boasts dazzling coral and improbable creatures. The three small islands immediately offshore from Naselesele Point also have good snorkelling (the third is known as the local 'Honeymoon Island'). You can also snorkel happily at Prince Charles or Beverly beaches.

ℹ Getting There & Away

AIR At Matei airport, **Pacific Sun** (☑6720 888) has two flights a day to/from Nadi (F$300 one way, 1½ hours) and Suva (F$260 one way, 45 minutes), but be aware that routes are often heavily booked and are cancelled at the hint of bad weather. At the time of research there were no direct flights between Vanua Levu and Taveuni but this may change in the future. See p142 for more details on travelling by air in Fiji.

BOAT The Wairiki Wharf, for large vessels such as the MV *Suliven* and *Lomaviti Princess*, is about 1km south of Waiyevo. Smaller boats depart from the Korean Wharf, about 2km north. **Goundar Shipping** (Map p119; ☑in Savusavu 330 1035), **Consort Shipping** (☑in Suva 330 2877) and **Bligh Water Shipping** (☑888 0261, in Suva 331 8247) have regular Suva–Savusavu–Taveuni ferries with competitive rates – a ticket between Taveuni and Savusavu should cost around F$35. Goundar is by far the more comfortable and reliable service. Bus-boat trips run to Savusavu and Labasa (F$20 to F$25; see p115). The boat departs from the Korean Wharf at 9am. The booking office is in Naqara.

For more information about these ferries see p143.

ℹ Getting Around

The one main road in Taveuni follows the coast, stretching from Lavena in the east, up north and around to Navakawau in the south. It is sealed from Matei to Wairiki, and there's also a sealed (though slightly potholed) section through Taveuni Estates. Getting around Taveuni involves a bit of planning – the main disadvantage being the sporadic bus service. To get around cheaply and quickly you need to combine buses with walking, or take taxis – the driver will probably act as a tour guide too!

TO/FROM THE AIRPORT From Matei airport expect to pay about F$30 to Waiyevo, and F$90 to Vuna (about one hour) in a taxi. Most upmarket resorts provide transfers for guests.

BUS Pacific Transport (☑888 0278) has a depot in Naqara, opposite the Taveuni Central Indian School. From Monday to Saturday, buses run from Wairiki to Bouma at 8.30am, 11.30am and 4.20pm. The last bus continues to Lavena, where the first bus of each morning starts out at 5.45am. On Tuesday and Thursday all buses go as far as Lavena. On Sunday there is one bus at 3.30pm from Wairiki to Lavena, and one from Lavena to Wairiki at 6.45am.

Going south from Naqara, buses run to Navakawau at 9am, 11.30am and 4.45pm Monday to Saturday, returning at 5.30am and 8.15am. On Sunday a bus departs Navakawau at 6.45am and returns from Naqara at 4pm. From Matei, buses run to Wairiki at 11.30am Monday to Saturday and also at 7am and 3pm Monday to Friday during school terms.

The bus schedule is very lax: buses may show up early or an hour late. Be sure to double-check the time of the return bus when you board, just to make sure there is one.

CAR At the time of research there were no official car-rental agencies on Taveuni, although locals are often willing to hire out their cars for around F$125 per day. This of course means that there is no rental agreement and you will not be insured.

TAXI It's easy to find taxis in the Matei, Waiyevo and Naqara areas, though on Sunday you might have to call one in advance. Hiring a taxi should cost around F$120 for the day, or more, depending on how far you want to go. For destinations such as Lavena you can go one way by bus and have a taxi pick you up at the end at a designated time (but arrange this before you go).

Waiyevo, Somosomo & Around

This isn't the most beautiful part of Taveuni but it is a good place to get things done and holds most of the island's facilities. It's also politically important – Somosomo is the largest village on Taveuni and headquarters for the Tui Cakau (high chief of Taveuni). The **Great Council of Chiefs' meeting hall** *(bure bose)* was built here in 1986 for the gathering of chiefs from all over Fiji. Just south of Somosomo is Naqara, Taveuni's metropolis – if you take metropolis to mean a few supermarkets, a budget hotel and the island's only bank. Head another 2km down the coast and you'll hit Waiyevo, which is Taveuni's administrative centre and home to the hospital, police station, more ferry links and a resort. About

---

WORTH A TRIP

WAIRIKI CATHOLIC MISSION

Peering over the Somosomo Strait, the Wairiki Catholic Mission is best visited during the 7am, 9am or 11am Sunday Mass. Join the congregation sitting cross-legged on the floor beneath an impressive beam ceiling and stained-glass windows (reputedly from France) as they belt out a few hymns. In the presbytery, there's a painting of a famous battle in which a Catholic missionary helped Taveuni's warriors develop a strategy to defeat their Tongan attackers.

Taveuni

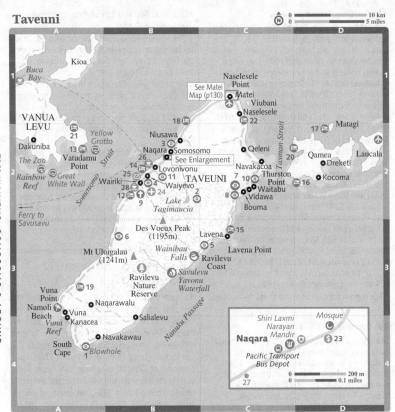

2km further south of Waiyevo is Wairiki village, which has a general store and a beautiful old hilltop Catholic mission.

⊙ Sights

180-Degree Meridian
Survey Beacon   LANDMARK
(Map p126) Although the International Date Line officially dog-legs Fiji, the 180-degree meridian cuts straight through Taveuni, about a 10-minute walk south of Waiyevo. A red survey beacon marks the spot along the water and there's an info board on the field above.

Waitavala Water Slide   OUTDOORS
(Map p126) Before sliding down the natural rock chutes, ask a local kid for a demo first and study their technique with care. Locals warn that unless you have a death wish do not even consider starting from the top, and be prepared to be dumped unceremoniously in the small pool with at least a couple of

bruises. To get here, head north from Waiyevo, take the first right at the bus stop, take another right at the branch in the road, pass a shed and then go left down a hill. You'll see a 'waterfall' sign. This is private property so if you pass anyone, ask permission.

Des Voeux Peak   MOUNTAIN
(Map p126) On a clear day the views from the top (at 1195m) are fantastic – it's possible to see Lake Tagimaucia and perhaps even the Lau Group. Allow three to four hours to walk the steep and arduous 6km ascent and at least two hours to return. From Waiyevo, take the inland track just before Wairiki Catholic Mission. Alternatively, arrange for a lift up and then walk back at your leisure.

Lake Tagimaucia   LAKE
(Map p126) In the mountains above Somosomo rests in an old volcanic crater some 823m above sea level. Fiji's national flower, the rare tagimaucia, grows on the lake's

Taveuni

shores and blooms from late September to late December. The hike is overgrown and muddy; start from Somosomo, where you need to present the chief with a *sevusevu* and ask permission. Take lunch and preferably a guide; allow eight hours for the round trip.

◎ Activities

Diving

Taveuni Ocean Sports DIVING
(Map p126; ☎888 1111; www.taveunioceansports.com) Based at Nakia Resort & Dive, this well-equipped, professional place gets top reviews from guests around the island. Each dive starts with a short lesson on local marine biology and the centre is dedicated to protecting the environment.

Other Activities

Taveuni Adventures TOURS
(Map p126; ☎888 1700; www.taveuni.com.au; 1st fl, Garden State Price Point Bldg) Based in Naqara, this place can organise a range of activities including birdwatching excursions, hiking trips to Des Voeux Peak or Lake Tagimaucia, village tours and sunset cruises. It

also acts as a booking agent for several accommodation options on the island.

Taveuni Estates GOLF
(Map p126; ☎888 0441) Visitors are welcome to this nine-hole golf course (F$40 green fee), plus the four tennis courts (F$15) and a swimming pool.

🛏 Sleeping & Eating

Nakia Resort & Dive BUNGALOWS $$
(Map p126; ☎888 1111; www.nakiafiji.com; bungalows US$220; ☜) Four simple, dark yet comfortable *bure* sit on a cheerful, grassy hillside looking out to sea at this raved-about eco-resort. These guys use alternative energy wherever possible, are into composting and recycling, and have a large organic garden where they get fresh fruit and veg for their restaurant. The dive shop is excellent and takes the same eco-bent.

Aroha Resort BUNGALOWS $$
(Map p126; ☎888 1882; www.arohataveuni.com; bungalows from F$216; ☜☎⊞) Simple but elegant varnished-wood rooms with louvred windows look out over a black-sand beach.

Two rooms can be adjoined for families and each unit has its own airy kitchen and open-to-sky bathroom. There's a small infinity pool, barbecue, bikes and kayaks, all for free use by guests. It's a short walk to Wairiki and its shops and restaurants.

Garden Island Resort HOTEL $$$
(Map p126; ✆888 0286; www.gardenislandresort.com; r F$350-500; ✳🖥🌊) A plain block-like exterior opens to a surprisingly chic nest streamlined with white tile and hip black furniture. Rooms are luxe, the pool beckons you with stylish lounging chairs, and the snorkelling off the rocky beach is great, but what we like the most is the magnificent tree dripping with sleeping bats at the water's edge. Get the best deals with online packages.

ⓘ Information

Colonial National Bank (Naqara; ⊙9.30am-4pm Mon, from 9am Tue-Fri) The only bank on the island will exchange currency and travellers cheques and has an ATM.

Hospital (✆888 0444; Waiyevo)

Police (✆888 0222; Waiyevo) The main police station is at the government compound behind the Garden Island Resort in Waiyevo. There is also a police station in Naqara.

Post office (Waiyevo; ⊙8am-1pm & 2-4pm Mon-Fri) Among the shops beneath the First Light Inn.

Southern Taveuni

The southern part of the island isn't well serviced by public transport but it's a beautiful place to visit. Check out the **blowhole** on the dramatic, windswept South Cape. Southern Taveuni is also home to Vuna Reef, which is perfect for snorkellers and novice divers. The main villages in southern Taveuni are Naqarawalu (in the hills) and, on the southern coast near Vuna Reef, Kanacea, Vuna and Navakawau.

🏃 Activities

Diving

Taveuni Dive DIVING
(Map p126; ✆828 1063; www.taveunidive.com) This long-running team operates recommended centres at Paradise Taveuni, and at the upscale housing development Taveuni Estates – so they can easily pick up from anywhere on the island. A two-tank dive/PADI Open Water Course costs F$270/660 including equipment.

Dolphin Bay Divers DIVING
(Map p126; ✆992 4001, 828 3001; www.dolphinbaydivers.com) Over at Dolphin Bay Divers Retreat (p128), which is located on Vanua Levu but is more easily accessed from Taveuni. It offers two-tank dives/PADI Open Water Courses for F$195/650 including equipment. The gear is in excellent condition.

🛏 Sleeping

Remote Resort RESORT $$$
(Map p126; ✆9201 334; www.theremoteresort.com; Vanua Levu; villas from F$1600; 🖥✳🌊🍴) Private villas on the doorstep of the Rainbow Reef make this luxury diving heaven. It's on Vanua Levu but accessed via Taveuni and only 10 minutes' boat ride to the White Wall.

⌖ Dolphin Bay Divers Retreat BUNGALOWS $
(Map p126; ✆828 3001, 926 0145; www.dolphinbaydivers.com; Vanaira Bay, Vanua Levu; campsites per person F$15, d safari tents/bungalows F$55/115; @) Just a bay over from Sau Bay on Vanua Levu (but most easily accessed from Taveuni), this is a friendly place with simple *bure,* space for camping and some permanent safari tents. It's very popular with divers, who make up most of the guests, but there's also good snorkelling from the beach. Transfers from Matei cost F$60 one way. Meal plans are F$75 per day with snacks. Important: this is a very remote location and you'll have to organise transfers in advance. Transfers from Vanua Levu are discouraged. Dives cost F$195/650 for a two-tank dive/PADI Open Water Course.

Paradise Taveuni RESORT $$$
(Map p126; ✆888 0125; www.paradiseinfiji.com; d incl all meals & transfers F$650-700; ✳🖥🌊) Set on a former plantation, this oceanfront place has stunning sunset views and plenty of strategically placed hammocks and sunloungers from which to enjoy them. The *bure* and *vale* (rooms) are luxury all the way with large decks, locally handmade daybeds, separate living and sleeping quarters, and huge bathrooms, some with the added bonus of outdoor Jacuzzis and rock showers. There's diving through Taveuni Dive and incredible snorkelling right off the shore on the house reef, although there's not much of a beach.

Matei

A residential area on Taveuni's northern point, Matei is the main tourist hub, if you can call it that, with a scarcely visible string

of guesthouses, hotels and rental properties strewn along a long stretch of road crowned by stately palm trees and skirted by beach. Only a couple of beaches are suitable for swimming and sunbathing, but this is a good place to base yourself for diving and activities.

🏃 Activities

Tango Fishing Adventures   FISHING
(Map p130; ☎332 4303, 888 0680; makaira@ connect.com.fj) Book through Makaira by the Sea in Matei. These folks will take you fishing for big game aboard the *Tango* with Captain John Llanes Jr, who has over 30 years' experience. The boat has GPS, VHF and seven rod holders. A half/full day costs F$600/1000.

Peckham Pearl Farm Tours   SNORKELLING
(Map p130; ☎888 2789) Snorkel the island's only saltwater black-pearl farm, in the Naselesele lagoon. Tours leave at 10am Monday to Friday from Audrey's Beach in Matei (opposite Audrey's Island Coffee & Pastries) and last for 1½ hours (F$25/12 per adult/child). You can then browse the wares (pearls F$24 and up).

🛌 Sleeping

TOP CHOICE **Tuvununu**   HOSTEL $
(Map p126; ☎625 0582; tuvununu@gmail.com; dm/s/d F$30/60/80; 🛜) Backpacker bliss with a long stretch of hammocked, waterfront deck, guitar-playing locals and a magically refilling kava bowl. Rooms are clean and comfy but a bit loud and nothing special. What you come here for is the convivial ambience, the huge home-cooked meals around a big table, and the majestic view over offshore islands (grab a kayak to get a little closer). Wi-fi is free. The backpackers is about a 10-minute walk through forest and a scenic village to Matei, and many folks stay here as a jumping-off point for Maqai Resort on Qamea (p132).

TOP CHOICE **Taveuni Palms**   VILLAS $$$
(Map p130; ☎888 0032; www.taveunipalmsfiji.com; d villas all-inclusive except alcohol US$1400-2000; ❄🛜🐾) Breathtakingly beautiful, completely tasteful and private, Taveuni Palms boasts three villas, each on their own beach and equipped with their own swimming pool and staff, including a personal chef and one babysitter per child if you bring the kids. All the fruit and vegies are organic-

ally grown on the sprawling, manicured property.

Bibi's Hideaway   BUNGALOWS $
(Map p130; ☎888 0443; bungalows F$32-118) A rambling, quiet, 2-hectare hillside plot hides a selection of adorable, colourful *bure* in varying sizes amongst the fruit and palm trees. Pick a pineapple for breakfast and papayas for lunch – if you don't your charming host Pauline will probably bring you fruit anyway. There are self-catering facilities here and plenty of room for exploring.

Coconut Grove Beachfront Cottages   B&B $$$
(Map p130; ☎888 0328; www.coconutgrovefiji.com; bungalows F$300-390; 🛜) A stone path studded with fish mosaics leads down to three calm, tasteful and bright cottages and a gorgeous slice of golden sandy beach. The American owner Ronna likes to let her staff run things for a more Fijian feel – although she stays firmly on the sidelines. This place doesn't accept children under 12.

Tovu Tovu Resort   BUNGALOWS $
(Map p130; ☎888 0560; www.tovutovu.com; bungalows from F$95; 🛜) This is a friendly place with a selection of ageing wooden *bure* with wooden verandahs, kitchenettes, hot-water bathrooms and fans. The best thing is the vibe – it's very welcoming. The resort is a 20-minute walk southeast of Matei airport. Even if you don't stay here, you should stop by for the restaurant (p130).

Taveuni Island Resort   RESORT $$$
(Map p130; ☎888 0441; www.taveuniislandresort. com; bungalows from US$500, honeymoon villa US$1800; 🛜🍽) Reminiscent of a sort of late-1960s minimalist chic, Taveuni Island Resort has 12 *bure* with polished-wood walls, white tiled floors, wicker furniture, outdoor rock showers and complete privacy, balanced on a hill. Meals are a gourmet's delight; they're included in the price and can be taken by the pool or in your *bure*. No children under 15 allowed.

Beverly Campground   CAMPGROUND $
(Map p130; ☎888 0381; campsites per person F$17, permanent tents/dm F$20/40) One of those magical spots where everybody makes friends easily, this small site is set on a white-sand beach, beneath fantastic, huge poison-fish trees. The camp has very basic facilities including flush toilets, showers and

Matei

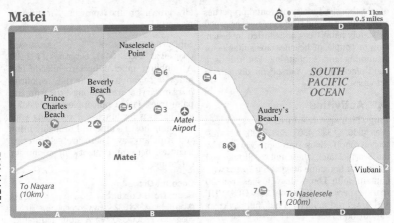

Matei

a sheltered area for cooking and dining. The owner sometimes brings around fresh fruit and vegetables in the morning. He can also provide equipment for snorkelling, fishing and kayaking.

✖ Eating & Drinking

There are several good choices in Matei. If you're here on a Wednesday, try the *lovo* or buffet (complete with entertainment) at Naselesele village (your accommodation will be able to arrange this for you). Profits go to the local school.

Really good rotis (F$1.50) can be bought at Matei airport.

TOP CHOICE Audrey's Island Coffee and Pastries   CAFE $

(Map p130; ☑888 0039; coffee & cake F$10; ⊙10am-6pm) You can sit on the deck of US-born Audrey's house and enjoy fabulous cakes (moist chocolate cake and white-chocolate coconut slabs are just a couple of the possibilities – it depends on what she's been baking) and coffee while looking down the sweeping coast road and out to sea. If you're lucky, she may break out the Kahlua and offer you a shot or three.

Restaurant Tramonto   INTERNATIONAL $$

(Map p130; ☑888 2224; pizza from F$25, meals F$20-25; ⊙lunch & dinner) If you're in the market for a pizza then Tramonto won't disappoint – they're huge and mightily topped. There are also a couple of other well-prepared dishes available daily, including fish and chips and lamb shanks. On Sunday there's a buffet dinner and on Wednesday, a barbecue; reservations are required.

Coconut Grove Restaurant   INTERNATIONAL $$

(Map p130; ☑888 0328; lunch F$7-22, dinner F$14-35; ⊙breakfast, lunch & dinner) Take off your shoes and enjoy the sea views from the deck of this guesthouse's lovely restaurant. The menu includes wonderfully fresh vegetarian dishes, homemade pasta, soups, salads and fish. You can just turn up for breakfast or lunch but you'll have to let them know you're coming for dinner.

Vunibokoi Restaurant   FIJIAN $$

(Map p130; ☑888 0560; dinner mains F$18; ⊙breakfast, lunch & dinner) Tovu Tovu Resort's restaurant has large windows overlooking

the island of Viubani. At lunch there are burgers and sandwiches, and there are a few choices (usually changing daily) on the dinner board in the evenings, including delights such as crab curry, stir-fried prawns and soup of *rourou* (boiled taro leaves in coconut cream). On Friday, there's a popular 'buffet and music night' (F$20).

Eastern Taveuni

The local landowners of beautiful eastern Taveuni have rejected logging in favour of ecotourism, under the banner of the Bouma Environmental Tourism Project. Scenes for the 1991 movie *Return to the Blue Lagoon* were filmed at Bouma National Heritage Park's Tavoro Waterfalls and at Lavena Beach.

⊙ Sights

**Bouma National
Heritage Park**   NATIONAL PARK
(Map p126; www.bnho.org; admission F$15) Taveuni still retains large amounts of pristine forest and the national park protects around 80% of this, and covers about 150 sq km of coastal forest and rainforest. Within are several kilometres of bushwalks and the three beautiful **Tavoro Waterfalls** (Map p126). The walking track begins opposite the reception *bure,* south of the river in Bouma.

If you are a keen walker, try the **Vidawa Rainforest Trail**. Beginning at Vidawa village, it passes through the historic fortified village site of Navuga and cuts through tropical rainforests rich with birds before linking with the Tavoro Waterfalls. You can only do this walk with a guide and need to book in advance. The trip runs Monday to Saturday and can take a maximum of eight people (F$40). The price includes guides, lunch, afternoon tea and park admission fee. Book through **Tavoro Waterfalls Visitor Centre** (Map p126; ☎888 0390; ⊙9am-4pm).

Waitabu Marine Park   MARINE RESERVE
This area offers excellent snorkelling off a white-sand beach. You can visit the park only with a guide. The village of Waitabu has set up a half-day **tour** (Map p126; ☎888 0451; per person F$40, for groups of 4 or more per person F$35), which includes a guided snorkel, *bilibili* (bamboo raft) ride and morning or afternoon tea in the village. There's also a backpackers' tour with guided snorkelling and boat transfers (F$20 per person).

✷ Activities

Birdwatching
Taveuni is one of Fiji's best areas for birdwatching. More than 100 species of bird can be found here. Try Des Voeux Peak at dawn for a chance to see the rare orange dove (the male is bright orange with a green head, while the female is mostly green) and the silktail. The forested Lavena coast is also a good spot to see orange or flame doves, Fiji goshawk, wattled honeyeater, and grey and white heron.

Hiking
Taveuni's wild interior makes it perfect for exploring on foot. Bouma National Heritage Park is the place to head for hiking action. Here you can amble beachside on the Lavena Coastal Walk (p132), hike up and down hills to the Tavoro Waterfalls or take in the guided Vidawa Rainforest Trail. If that's not hard-core enough you can slog it up Des Voeux Peak (p126) or around Lake Tagimaucia (p126).

🛏 Sleeping & Eating

Lavena Lodge   GUESTHOUSE $
(Map p126; ☎888 0116; tw per person incl Lavena Coastal Walk F$30) Run by friendly, informative staff, the lodge has basic, clean rooms and a shared kitchen and bathroom. Electricity is supplied in the evening. Meals are available (F$7 breakfast, F$10 lunch or dinner). There's a tiny shop in the village, but if you're planning to cook, bring your own supplies.

Offshore Islands

Qamea, Laucala and Matagi are a group of islands just east of Thurston Point, across the Tasman Strait from northeastern Taveuni. All three of the islands have lovely, white-sand beaches.

MATAGI
Tiny, horseshoe-shaped Matagi (1 sq km), formed by a submerged volcanic crater, is 10km off Taveuni's coast and just north of Qamea. Its steep rainforest sides rise to 130m. The bay faces north to open sea and there is a fringing reef on the southwest side of the island.

At **Matangi Island Resort** (Map p126; ☎888 0260; www.matangiisland.com; bungalows incl all meals & nonmotorised activities US$730-1250; 🖥⛴), the *bure* are huge, vaulted-ceilinged

LAVENA COASTAL WALK

The 5km Lavena Coastal Walk is well worth the effort. The trail follows the forest edge along the beach, past peaceful villages, and then climbs up through the tropical rainforest to a gushing waterfall. There's some good snorkelling and kayaking here and Lavena Point is fine for swimming.

The path is clearly marked and well maintained. To reach the falls at the end of the trail you have to clamber over rocks and swim a short distance through two deep pools. If you're visiting in the rainy season, the rocks near the falls can be slippery, if not flooded. It can be difficult and dangerous to reach the falls at this time.

The park is managed through Lavena Lodge (p131). Park entrance is F$15. You can also take a guided sea-kayak journey and coastal walk for F$50 (including lunch). You can also arrange to take a boat one way and walk back (F$200 for the whole boat).

Lavena village is about 15 minutes' drive past Bouma, 35 minutes from Matei. However, by local bus it takes about one hour from Matei or just under two from Waiyevo. Expect to pay about F$75 for a taxi to/from Matei.

affairs with massive beds, tons of windows to let in the light, and separate seating areas. Each *bure* is surrounded by a neat tropical garden. It's romance run amok in the 'treehouse', perched 5m up in the tree canopy with wraparound decks, views to the beach, outdoor Jacuzzis, lanterns aplenty and daybeds. Matangi boasts 30 dive spots within 10 to 30 minutes of the island; a two-tank dive is F$225 (including gear) at the resort's dive shop. The resort is not suitable for children under the age of 12.

QAMEA

The closest of the three islands to Taveuni is Qamea (34 sq km), only 2.5km east of Thurston Point. Its coastline is riddled with deep bays and lined with white-sand beaches; the interior is fertile, green and rich in birdlife. The island is also notable for the *lairo* (annual migration of land crabs). For a few days from late November to early December, at the start of their breeding season, masses of crabs move from the mudflats towards the sea.

🛏 Sleeping

TOP CHOICE **Maqai Resort**   HOSTEL **$**
(Map p126; ☑990 7900; www.maqai.com; campsite per person F$20, dm/bungalows from F$35/60; @) A private white-sand beach, excellent snorkelling, a fickle but sometimes epic surfing wave, and nightly entertainment (from music around the kava bowl to fire shows) – and believe it or not, this is a backpackers. Accommodation is in sturdy, clean safari tents and meals are taken in a Crusoe-like common area with sand floors. Three (huge) meals per

day cost F$50, and return transfer to Tuvununu (p129) on Taveuni are F$50 per person.

Qamea Resort & Spa   RESORT **$$$**
(Map p126; ☑888 0220; www.qamea.com; bungalows US$690-950; ✳✿) The magnificently thatched *bure* lie on a long stretch of beautiful, white-sand beach. The huge, air-conditioned *bure* are decorated with Fijian art, and some have plunge pools, spa baths or rock showers. Rates include meals and transfers to and from Taveuni; children under 16 are not accepted. There is excellent snorkelling just offshore as well as tons of activities. There's a dive shop where two-tank dives/PADI Open Water Courses cost F$260/950 including gear.

KADAVU

This is where you wish you were right now. Remote and authentic yet easily accessed from Viti Levu (it's 100km to the south) and home to comfortable, eco-friendly resorts, Kadavu blends Fiji's best assets. Your flight to the tiny airstrip will be followed by a long, and sometimes bumpy, boat ride to your resort past prehistoric-looking coves chirping with rare birds and fringed by the world's fourth-largest barrier reef. Handsome stretches of long, sandy beach and sheltered coves ring the islands' perimeters.

The group is made up of several islands including Kadavu (Fiji's fourth-largest island), Ono, Galoa and Yaukuve Levu.

Most visitors stay on Kadavu, where you'll find the bulk of the accommodation and the group's only town, petite Vunisea.

✦ Activities

The Kadavu Group's rich landscape and underwater seascapes make it a perfect destination for nature lovers, divers, hikers and birdwatchers.

Hiking

Kadavu's hilly rainforest interior is sprinkled with waterfalls and hiking trails. There are good treks into the interior from several of the resorts.

Diving & Snorkelling

Buliya island, just north of Ono, is a great manta snorkelling site, where you're pretty much guaranteed an amazing encounter with the rays; Matava Resort takes people diving at a site off Kadavu accurately called Manta Reef. For novice divers, Yellow Wall and the Pacific Voyager wreck dive are on the more-protected western side of the island. All the resorts have either a dedicated dive centre or will find an outfit to take you out.

Fishing

Australia's *Modern Fishing* magazine has stated that the area around the Great Astrolabe Reef 'may well be the hottest poppering and jigging locations on the planet'. Many of Kadavu's resorts will take you out beyond the reef for some serious fishing action.

Sea Kayaking

Organised kayaking trips take place from May to September and all of the resorts have two-person ocean kayaks free or for hire.

Tamarillo Sea Kayaking KAYAKING
(☏761 6140; www.tamarillo.co.nz/fiji) These recommended, interesting and well-organised jaunts run from five to seven days and cost from F$2400 per person. All tours include meals and accommodation as well as a village stay. The operator also offers day and overnight trips. There's a two-person minimum.

Birdwatching

The lush rainforests, especially on Kadavu's eastern side, are home to a wide variety of birdlife, including the indigenous Kadavu honeyeater, Kadavu fantail, velvet fruit dove and the colourful Kadavu musk parrot. Most of the resorts will be able to arrange a guide but you'll see many of the birds fluttering around the resorts as well.

🛏 Sleeping

Take into account the time and cost of transfers when choosing your accommodation.

In Kadavu, most of the places to stay are a fair way from the airport, and the only way to get there is by boat. Most places have a three-night minimum and offer package rates from their websites that are more economical than per-night rates.

KADAVU

TOP CHOICE Papageno Eco-Resort RESORT $$$
(☏603 0466; www.papagenoresortfiji.com; s/d incl meals & transfers from F$355/540; 🛜🎣) Large, dark-wood *bure,* with decks looking out to sea, are spread sparingly around manicured tropical gardens. All rooms are decked out with local artwork and have bigger-than-average bathrooms. The resort prides itself on its eco-credentials, using solar and microhydro energy to complement its generator, composting organic waste on-site, and investing heavily in environmental-development and local community projects. The food is excellent and plentiful.

TOP CHOICE Matava Resort RESORT $$$
(☏333 6222; www.matava.com; d per person incl meals & transfers from F$305; 🛜) Anything you want to do on Kadavu – from diving to sportfishing, birding or hiking – the enthusiastic team here can set you up and you'll have plenty of new friends to enjoy your outing with. Meanwhile stay in spacious and clean hardwood *bure* with tons of windows to maximise the views, and good solid beds. The resort runs on solar power, has

> **DON'T MISS**
>
> ## THE GREAT ASTROLABE REEF
>
> The famous Great Astrolabe Reef, which is a major pull for most visitors to Kadavu and is the fourth-largest barrier reef in the world, hugs the eastern side of the Kadavu island group, and is bisected by the Naiqoro Passage. It's home to brilliantly coloured soft and hard corals; a fantastic assortment of tunnels, caverns and canyons; and a variety of marine life, including plenty of reef sharks and graceful manta rays. Particularly recommended dive sites are Eagle Rock and Broken Stone. The weather often dictates which sites are suitable to dive, and visibility can range from 15m to 70m. Most of the resorts will also take snorkellers out to the reef.

Kadavu

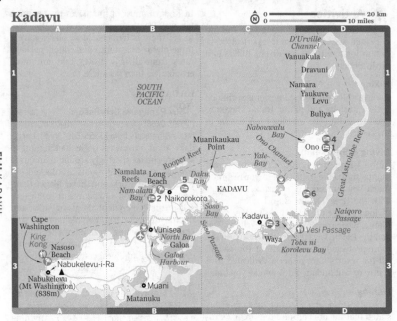

a large organic garden and employs strict recycling policies. Fantastic meals are eaten communally in the big restaurant-bar *bure*.

Matana Beach Resort Dive Kadavu
RESORT $$

(☎368 3502; www.divekadavu.com; per person incl meals & transfers s/d/tr/q F$290/225/198/180; 🛜📶) This resort has *bure* with comfortable beds, verandahs, hot water and tidy bathrooms – the brighter choices are the smaller units at the southern end. Diving is the main reason folks come here (this sheltered side of the island has less fickle conditions than the Great Astrolabe Reef) but there are myriad other activities available. Sheltered from the prevailing southeasterly winds, it boasts an excellent beach where the snorkelling

and swimming is wonderful, regardless of the tide.

🌿 Waisalima Beach Resort
BUNGALOWS $$$

(☎331 7281; www.waisalima.com; d bungalows incl meals & transfers from F$345) Adorable, large thatched *bure* grace a remote stretch of white sand lined by coconut palms.

ONO

TOP CHOICE Oneta Resort
RESORT $$$

(☎603 0778; www.onetafiji.com; dm/d per person incl meals & transfers F$280/467; 🛜) The architecturally lovely thatched *bure* with hardwood floors, woven walls and louvred, netted windows are among this region's most luxurious and are definitely the classiest. All this wonderfulness sits in an artfully landscaped garden complete with fruit trees and organic vegies and there's a lush white-sand beach out front. This place is mostly meant to be a fishing lodge but diving (with nearby Mai Dive) and so many other activities are on offer, meaning that anyone would be happy here.

TOP CHOICE Mai Dive Astrolabe Reef Resort
RESORT $$

(☎603 0842; www.maidive.com; campsite per person incl meals F$75, s/d incl meals F$180/270; 🛜)

Pretty bungalows line the beach at this very tidy, streamlined resort run by an Australian-Fijian family. All *bure* have polished-timber floors and wooden verandahs, and are right by the water; they are simple but stylish and have an incredibly happy feel to them. The dive centre here has become one of the island's most respected – serious divers should make this their first choice. There's a one-week minimum stay.

ⓘ Information

Some resorts, especially the more upmarket ones, accept credit cards but check before you fly out. You can't change foreign currency in Vunisea and there's no ATM so bring as much money as you'll need. Many resorts offer wi-fi but service is very slow.

Hospital (☎333 6008) Vunisea's hospital only has limited services. For more serious ailments, you're better off heading back to Viti Levu.

Police (☎333 6007) In Vunisea.

ⓘ Getting There & Away

AIR Pacific Sun (☎672 0888; www.airpacific. com) has daily flights to Kadavu from Suva (F$185 one way, 40 minutes) and Nadi (F$220 one way, 50 minutes). It is advisable to check timetables and confirm flights the day before departure as they are often late or cancelled.

BOAT Goundar Shipping (☎330 1035; one way F$50) runs the clean and reliable MV *Lomaiviti Princess*, which departs Suva late Wednesday night and arrives at Vunisea four to five hours later; it departs Kadavu Thursday afternoon and arrives in Suva that night, connecting onwards to Vanua Levu and Taveuni. **Venu Shipping** (☎in Suva 339 5000, 330 7349; Rona St, Walu Bay, Suva) operates the much less reliable MV *Sinu-i-Wasa* to Suva from F$55 one way on Tuesday nights.

ⓘ Getting Around

There are a few roads in the Vunisea area and one rough, unsealed road to Nabukelevu-i-Ra around the western end of Kadavu. Small boats are the island group's principal mode of transport. Each resort has its own boat and will pick up guests from Vunisea airstrip. Be sure to make arrangements in advance. Boat trips are expensive due to fuel costs. In rough weather it can be a wet and bone-crunching trip to the more-remote resorts.

LAU GROUP

Fiji's final frontier, the 57 Lau islands are strewn across the southeast corner of Fiji's vast archipelago like a rash of green spots on the skin of the Pacific. Few people visit here, but those who do report countless bays, deserted, reef-rimmed atolls and sparsely populated islands with hilly interiors.

Lau islanders are known for their wood-carving and *masi* crafts, and have been greatly influenced by neighbouring Polynesian cultures. Although the climate here is drier than most parts of Fiji, storms can be fierce and some of the bays are used as hurricane shelters by visiting yachts.

ⓘ Getting There & Away

AIR Pacific Sun (☎347 8077; www.airpacific. com) flies between Suva and Vanua Balavu on Wednesdays (F$225 one way, one hour) and to Lakeba on Thursdays (F$225 one way, 1½ hours).

BOAT Bligh Water Shipping (☎331 8247; www. blighwatershipping.com.fj) has slow monthly trips from Suva to Vanua Balavu and Cicia. One-way fares, including meals, are F$135.

At the time of writing, the more-reliable **Goundar Shipping** (☎330 1035) was planning to start servicing Vanua Balavu and Lakeba via Cicia once a month as well.

Vanua Balavu

AREA 53 SQ KM

This beautiful island, averaging about 2km wide, has lots of sandy beaches and rugged limestone hills. The celebrated **Bay of Islands**, also known as Qilaqila, sits in the northwest pocket and is a spectacular site for diving, kayaking and swimming.

Lomaloma, the largest village, was Fiji's first port, regularly visited by sailing ships trading in the Pacific. Today the people of Vanua Balavu rely largely on copra and *bêche-de-mer* (sea cucumber) for their income.

The hospitable **Moana's Guesthouse** (☎822 1148, 820 1125; www.moanasguesthouses. com; r per person incl meals F$95; @) covers all the basics with beach *bure* and guesthouse options. Moana's can arrange boat, snorkelling and fishing trips, and collects travellers from the airstrip for F$60 return. There is internet but it's slow and not always working.

ROTUMA

POP 3000 / AREA 43 SQ KM

Far-flung and isolated, the tiny volcanic island of Rotuma drifts in the Pacific 636km northwest of Suva. The vast distance between

its tiny frame and the mainland may be an accident of geography, but this divide has allowed Rotumans to evolve ethnically and linguistically independent of the mainland. The best time to visit is during **Fara**, an annual six-week festival beginning on 1 December that sees Rotumans toss aside their strong work ethic for dancing, parties and general revelry. There are no banks or shops here.

The easiest way to stay on Rotuma is through a Rotuman contact (try www.rotuma.net). Alternatively, contact the Rotuman Island Council via the Fiji Visitors Bureau in Nadi.

Mojito's Barfly (☑889 1144; Motusa) has simple rooms with shared facilities, but they're generally reserved for government workers. Meals are also available, given plenty of notice.

❶ Getting There & Away

Western Shipping (☑331 4467; Narain's Wharf, Walu Bay, Suva) operates the *Cagi Mai Ba* to Rotuma (deck/seat/cabin F$118/165/180) the first Saturday of every month. The journey takes 36 hours and the conditions on board are very basic.

Visiting yachts must obtain permission to anchor from the Ahau government station in Maka Bay, on the northern side of the island.

UNDERSTAND FIJI

Fiji Today

In early 2012 the Public Emergency Regulations (PER), which had been put in place during the 2009 political turmoil, were lifted. These restricted people's freedom of speech, freedom of assembly and freedom of the media. While this may smack of the tyrannical rule of a dictator, Bainimarama maintains that he's only doing what's necessary to stamp out the corruption and systemic racism that characterised previous governments. He's said it before (in 2010) and he may well say it again, he's 'committed to free and fair elections'. It's just the date that's proving tricky to pin down. Recently 2014 has been earmarked as the year Fiji returns to democracy.

History

Vitians

'Fiji' is actually the Tongan name for these islands, which was adopted by the Europe-

ans. The inhabitants formerly called their home Viti.

Vitian culture was shaped by Polynesian, Melanesian and Micronesian peoples over 35 centuries of settlement. The Lapita people arrived from Vanuatu and the eastern Solomon Islands in about 1500 BC (see p539), and for about a thousand years they lived along the coasts and fished to their hearts' (and stomachs') content. Around 500 BC they became keen on agriculture and as a result the population shot up, tribal feuding got nasty and cannibalism became common.

European Arrival & Settlement

In the early 19th century Fiji was known to European whalers, sandalwood and *bêche-de-mer* traders. By the 1830s a small whaling and beachcomber settlement had been established at Levuka on Ovalau. It became one of the main ports of call in the South Pacific, and was the centre of the notorious blackbirding trade (see p547).

The introduction of firearms by the Europeans resulted in an increase in violent tribal warfare, particularly from the late 1840s to the early 1850s. The eventual victor, Ratu Seru Cakobau of Bau, became known to foreigners as Tui Viti (King of Fiji), despite having no real claim over most of Fiji.

By the mid-19th century, London Missionary Society pastors and Wesleyan Methodist missionaries had found their way to Fiji, having entered the southern Lau Group from Tahiti and Tonga in the 1830s. They gradually displaced the priests of the old religion and assumed privileged positions in island society, instilling a legacy of influence.

In 1871 Cakobau formed a Fiji-wide government but, unable to maintain peace, it quickly crumbled. Two years later Britain agreed to annex Fiji, citing blackbirding as its principal justification. Fiji was pronounced a British crown colony on 10 October 1874.

Colonial Period & Independence

Fiji's economy became depressed following the slump in the cotton market at the end of the US Civil War. Unrest and epidemics ensued, with measles wiping out a third of the indigenous population. Fearing a racial war, the colonial government sought the support of the chiefs in order to control the masses. The existing Fijian hierarchy was incorporated into the colonial administration and, in order to curb quibbling, the sale of land to foreigners was forbidden.

Under increasing pressure to make the Fijian economy self-sufficient, the colonial government turned to plantation crops, which demanded large pools of cheap labour. Indentured labour seemed the perfect solution, and between 1879 and 1916 more than 60,000 Indians were transported to Fiji. Many came with hopes of escaping poverty, but were faced with heavy work allocations, low wages, unjust treatment and rationed food. Despite the hardship, the vast majority of *girmityas* (indentured labourers) decided to stay in Fiji once they had served their contract, and many brought their families across from India to join them. They were prohibited from buying land and discouraged from interacting with Fijians.

On 10 October 1970, Fiji regained its independence after 96 years of colonial administration. The new constitution followed the British model, although political seats and parties were racially divided.

Fiji's first postindependence election was won by the indigenous Fijian Alliance Party (FAP), and Fijians were at first optimistic about their future. However, underlying racial tensions grew as the economy worsened.

Era of the Coups

Greater unity among workers led to the formation of the Fiji Labour Party (FLP), and in April 1987 an FLP government was elected in coalition with the National Federation Party (NFP). Despite having a Fijian prime minister and majority indigenous-Fijian cabinet, the new government was labelled 'Indian dominated' and racial tensions rose. On 14 May 1987, only a month after the elections, Lieutenant Colonel Sitiveni Rabuka took over the elected government in a bloodless coup and formed a civil interim government supported by the Great Council of Chiefs.

In September 1987 Rabuka again intervened with military force. The 1970 constitution was invalidated, Fiji was declared a republic and dismissed from the Commonwealth, and Rabuka proclaimed himself head of state.

The coups, which were supposed to benefit all indigenous Fijians, in fact caused immense hardship. The economy's two main sources of income, sugar and tourism, were seriously affected, overseas aid was suspended and about 50,000 people – mostly Indo-Fijian skilled tradespeople and professionals – emigrated.

In the elections of May 1999 the FLP formed a coalition with the Fijian Associa-tion Party. Indo-Fijian Mahendra Chaudhry became prime minister, and indigenous Fijians were far from pleased. On 19 May 2000, armed men entered parliament in Suva and took 30 hostages, including Prime Minister Chaudhry. Failed businessman George Speight quickly became the face of the coup, claiming to represent indigenous Fijians. He demanded the resignation of both Chaudhry and President Ratu Sir Kamisese Mara and that a 1997 multiethnic constitution be abandoned.

Support for Speight's group was widespread, and Indo-Fijians suffered such harassment that many fled the country. Both Chaudhry and Mara eventually stepped down, the head of Fiji's military, Commander Frank Bainimarama, announced martial law and the 1997 constitution was revoked – but not for long.

In March 2001, the appeal court decided to uphold the 1997 constitution and ruled that Fiji be taken to the polls. Lasenia Qarase, heading the Fijian People's Party (SLD), won 32 of the 71 parliamentary seats in the August 2001 elections but defied the constitution by including no FLP members in his cabinet.

By 2004 the country was once again divided, this time by the Qarase government's draft *Promotion of Reconciliation, Tolerance and Unity (PRTU) Bill*, whose opponents saw the amnesty provisions for those involved in the coup as untenable. Backed by the military, Commodore Frank Bainimarama presented a list of demands to the Qarase government, which included dropping the PRTU and other controversial bills.

Although Qarase met several of the demands, it wasn't enough. On 5 December 2006, President Ratu Josefa Iloilo dissolved Parliament on Bainimarama's order and Qarase was put under house arrest. Several key groups, including the Methodist Church and the Great Council of Chiefs, did not approve of Bainimarama's coup and refused to meet without the presence of Qarase and President Iloilo (whom Bainimarama had ousted in declaring a state of emergency). Taking matters into his own hands, Bainimarama dissolved the council and has acted as interim prime minister since.

Bainimarama Secures His Position

The international reaction was scornful. New Zealand Prime Minister Helen Clark

compared Bainimarama to Zimbabwean dictator Robert Mugabe and refused to allow him to attend Pacific Islands Forum events in NZ.

Meanwhile, Bainimarama has strengthened his power base and attempted to legitimise his position as Fiji's rightful prime minister in a series of political manoeuvrings best described as gymnastic. In 2009, when the Court of Appeal declared Bainimarama's interim government illegal, Bainimarama and his entire government immediately stepped down so that President Iloilo was free to appoint 'a distinguished person' as a caretaker prime minister.

President Iloilo then surprised everyone – well, perhaps not Bainimarama – when he promptly dismissed the Court of Appeal, suspended the constitution and declared a new legal order with himself as Fiji's head of state. His first order of business: to reinstate Bainimarama as interim prime minister; in turn, Bainimarama reinstated his cabinet. The shuffle effectively restored Bainimarama to power but without the annoying thorn in his side he seemingly found the courts and constitution to be.

The Culture

The National Psyche

The Fijian people are the country's greatest asset. A smile goes a long way here, and Fijians of all backgrounds go to great lengths to make visitors feel welcome. Sometimes, however, these lengths can be too great. Not wishing to disappoint, a Fijian 'yes' might mean 'maybe' or 'no', which can be disconcerting if not confusing for visitors. Face-to-face confrontation is rare, but debate is a healthy component of daily life (just scan the readers' letters of any newspaper and you'll get the gist). The different challenges facing indigenous Fijians and Indo-Fijians remain key to a sense of national identity, and you're likely to hear both sides of the story in complete candour during any visit.

Multiculturalism

Fiji's population is the most multiracial in the South Pacific. Indigenous Fijians are predominantly of Melanesian origin, but there are Polynesian aspects in both their physical appearance and their culture. Most Indo-Fijians are descendants of indentured labourers. They constitute around 37% of the population, although large numbers continue to emigrate.

The government categorises people according to their racial origins, as you will notice on the immigration arrival card. 'Fijian' means indigenous Fijian, and while many Indo-Fijians have lived in Fiji for several generations they are still referred to as 'Indian', just as Chinese-Fijians are 'Chinese'. Fijians of other Pacific island descent are referred to by the nationality of their ancestors. Australians, Americans, New Zealanders – and Europeans – are referred to as 'Europeans'. Mixed Western and Fijian heritage makes a person officially 'part-European'.

INDIGENOUS FIJIANS

Most indigenous Fijians live in villages in *mataqali* (extended family, or kinship, groups) and acknowledge a hereditary chief, who is usually male. Each *mataqali* is allocated land for farming and also has communal obligations. Village life is supportive but also conservative; being different or too ambitious is seen to threaten the village's stability, and traditional gender roles are still very much in evidence.

Concepts such as *kerekere* (obligatory sharing) and *sevusevu* (a gift in exchange for an obligatory favour) are still strong, especially in remote areas. The consumption of *yaqona,* or kava, remains an important social ritual, and clans gather on special occasions for traditional *lovo* (feast cooked in a pit oven) and *meke* (dance and song performance that enacts stories and legends).

INDO-FIJIANS

Most of this group are fourth- or fifth-generation descendants of indentured labourers. The changes these labourers were forced to undergo, such as adapting to living communally with Indians from diverse backgrounds, created a relatively unrestricted, enterprising society distinct from the Indian cultures they left behind. This is the basis for the Indo-Fijian culture of today.

Extended families often live in the same house, and in rural areas it's common for girls to have arranged marriages at an early age. Many women wear traditional dress, although dress codes are more cosmopolitan in Suva.

Religion

Religion is extremely important in all aspects of Fijian society. Of the country's 52% Christians, about 37% are Methodists.

Hinduism is practised by 38% and Islam by about 8%.

Language

See the Language chapter on p591 for Fijian basics.

Arts

Indigenous Fijian villagers practise traditional arts and crafts, such as woodcarving and pottery, dance and music, and making *masi* (bark cloth). Some arts remain an integral part of the culture, while others are practised solely to satisfy tourist demand. Indo-Fijians, Chinese Fijians and other cultural groups also retain many of their traditional arts.

Contemporary art includes fashion design, pottery and, though not common, painting and photography. The most likely place to see contemporary work displayed is Suva.

Dance

Visitors are often welcomed with an indigenous *meke,* a dance and song performance enacting stories and legends. They vary from touristy performances accompanied by a disco-Fijian soundtrack (common in resorts) to traditional and low-key.

One of the best places to see contemporary dance in Fiji is the Oceania Centre for Arts and Culture at the USP Laucala Campus in Suva.

Music

Unsurprisingly, reggae has been a major influence on contemporary Fijian music, and you're likely to hear Bob Marley and his Fijian counterparts recycled continuously on popular radio stations.

Young Fijians have embraced hip hop and rap. Music from Bollywood films and Indian dance and pop music are understandably popular. It's not an entirely one-sided relationship – Indo-Fijian singer Aiysha is a big hit in India.

Choral CDs are also extremely popular, thanks to the tradition of enthusiastic Sunday service attendance. Missing out on the rousing but dulcet tones of a Fijian mass would be a crime.

Bark Cloth

You'll most likely become acquainted with tapa (also known as *masi* or *malo),* the

FIJIAN LITERATURE

» **Moving Through the Streets** (Joseph C Veramu) An eye-opener about disaffected youth in Suva.

» **Fiji** and **Stalker on the Beach** (Daryl Tarte) Historical saga that looks at the influence of outsiders on the country.

» **Kava in the Blood** (Peter Thomson) Evocative autobiography of a white Fijian who became a senior civil servant and was imprisoned by Rabuka during the 1987 coup.

Fijian art of making bark cloth, during your first shopping expedition. The cloth is made from the inner bark of the paper mulberry bush. Intricate rust and brown patterns are printed either by hand or stencil, often carrying symbolic meaning. For more information about tapa, see p567.

Environment
Geography

The Fiji archipelago has about 332 islands, varying from mere bumps a few metres in diameter to Viti Levu ('Great Land') at 10,400 sq km. Only about a third are inhabited. The smaller islands are generally of coral or limestone formation, while the larger ones are of volcanic origin; hot springs continue to boil on Vanua Levu. Fiji's highest peak is Viti Levu's majestic Tomanivi (Mt Victoria) at 1323m.

Ecology

Fiji's tropical forests are home to some of the richest natural communities in the South Pacific. Unfortunately, economic progress and the wheels of industry have seen around 15% of these forests cleared since the 1960s. Logging remains a constant, but many villages are turning to ecotourism as an alternative means of income. However, while remote villages can benefit from the income brought by low-impact tourism, even sensitive developments bring additional pollution and rapid cultural change.

Waste management is a national problem and marine pollution near Suva is severe. Overfishing and destructive fishing techniques are commonly employed and global warming has contributed to extensive coral bleaching.

SURVIVAL GUIDE

Directory A–Z

Accommodation

All room prices include bathrooms unless specified otherwise. When meals or breakfasts are included, 'incl breakfast' or 'incl meals' is shown in the accommodation listing. Price ranges are for twin or double rooms during peak season (July to September) and include Fiji's 15% value-added tax (VAT) and the 5% hotel turnover tax. Hotel websites commonly quote prices in various currencies (US$, A$, NZ$) although we have quoted prices in Fijian dollars throughout this guide for ease of comparison.

Price ranges are defined as follows:

$ less than F$150

$$ F$150–350

$$$ more than F$350

Activities

Diving & Snorkelling Fiji offers some spectacular snorkelling. Among the best spots are Nananu-i-Ra off Viti Levu's northern coast, as well as islands in the Mamanuca and Yasawa Groups. Fiji is also a diver's mecca, with magnificent reefs and a raft of operators, so getting to some premium sites is easy. An introductory dive costs about F$130, a two-tank dive between F$200 and F$245 including equipment rental, and Open Water certification courses cost between F$700 and F$850. See p32 for further information on diving in the region.

Hiking Viti Levu and Taveuni are the best islands for hiking. Suva's Colo-i-Suva Forest Park and Taveuni's Lavena Coastal Walk have marked trails that don't require guides or permission. Hiking hot spots in the Viti Levu highlands include Mt Batilamu and Koroyanitu National Heritage Park.

Kayaking Sea-kayaking tours are available during the drier months (between May and November), and combine paddling with hiking, snorkelling, fishing and village visits. Two prime areas for kayaking safaris are the Yasawa and Kadavu Groups.

Surfing Surfing usually requires boat trips as the majority of breaks are on offshore reefs. The best spots are in barrier-reef passages along southern Viti Levu (Frigate's Passage) and in the southern Mamanucas (Cloudbreak, Namotu Left and Wilkes Passage). These should be tackled only by experienced surfers. The dry season (May to October) is the best time to surf due to low pressures bringing in big waves.

Business Hours

Most businesses open weekdays from 8am to 5pm, and some from 8am to 1pm on Saturday. Many places close for lunch from 1pm to 2pm and practically nothing happens on Sunday.

Government offices 8am to 4.30pm Monday to Friday (to 4pm on Friday).

Restaurants 11am to 2pm and 6pm to 9pm Monday to Saturday, dinner Sunday.

Children

Fiji is a major family destination and very child-friendly. Many resorts cater specifically for children, with babysitting, cots and high chairs, organised activities, children's pools and kids clubs. In many resorts children stay, and in some cases eat, for free.

Embassies & Consulates

All embassies and consulates in Fiji are found in Suva. A complete list can be found at www.fiji.gov.fj. For a list of Fijian missions abroad also visit www.fiji.gov.fj. Choose 'Directory' in the menu and then 'Fiji Overseas Missions' in the submenu.

Food

The following price ranges refer to the prices for standard main dishes:

$ less than F$15

$$ F$15–25

$$$ more than F$25

Internet Access

Internet cafes are fairly prolific in Suva, Lautoka and Nadi, and you can jump online with broadband access for as little as F$3 per hour. Access outside urban centres is more limited and pricier (up to F$8 per hour).

If you have your own laptop or iPad you can sign up for a prepay account with a service provider such as **Connect** (www.connect.com.fj), **Unwired Fiji** (www.unwired.com.fj) or **Vodafone** (www.vodafone.com.fj). The latter sells modem sticks for F$79. 1GB of data costs F$15.

Maps

The **Map Shop** (Map p90; Rm 10, Department of Lands & Surveys, Government Buildings) in Suva sells big (1:50,000) and detailed topographic maps of each island or island group, as well as maps of Suva. The front of the telephone book has a series of excellent city and town maps. The Hema map of Fiji is the most useful for tourists.

Money

The local currency is the Fiji dollar (F$); it's fairly stable relative to Australian and NZ dollars. The dollar is broken down into 100 cents. Bank notes come in denominations of F$50, F$20, F$10, F$5 and F$2. There are coins to the value of F$1, F$0.50, F$0.20, F$0.10, F$0.05, F$0.02 and F$0.01. See www.xe.com for up-to-date exchange rates.

ATMs ATMs are common in urban areas and most accept the main international debit cards, including Cirrus and Maestro, as well as Visa and MasterCard. Before you head out to remote parts of Fiji, check in the appropriate section to find out if you will be able to access money, exchange currency or cash travellers cheques.

Taxes All prices quoted in this chapter are inclusive of VAT (value-added tax; a 15% sales tax on goods and services) and, for accommodation listings, the 5% hotel turnover tax.

Tipping Not a traditional part of Fijian culture although it is welcomed in top-end resorts.

Telephone

There are no area codes within Fiji. To dial a Fijian number from outside Fiji, dial the country code ☎679 followed by the local number. To use International Direct Dial (IDD), dial ☎00 plus the country code.

You'll find a phone in most midrange and top-end hotel rooms. While local calls are often free, hefty surcharges are added to long-distance calls.

Collect (reverse-charge) calls are more expensive and a surcharge applies when using operator assistance ☎010 or international operator assistance ☎022. Outer islands are linked by cable and satellite to worldwide networks.

Mobile Phones Vodafone (www.vodafone.com.fj) operates a GSM digital service and has roaming agreements with Vodafone in Australia, NZ and the UK, as well as Optus in Australia. Cheap mobile phones are readily available in urban areas from F$20, and SIM cards start at F$10, including F$10 free talk-time.

Time

Fiji is 12 hours ahead of GMT. When it's noon in Suva it's midnight the previous day in London, 5pm the previous day in Los Angeles, noon the same day in Auckland and 10am the same day in Sydney.

Tourist Information

The head office of the **Fiji Visitors Bureau** (Map p70; ☎672 2433; www.fijime.com; ste 107, Colonial Plaza, Namaka) is in Nadi. The **South Pacific Tourism Organisation** (Map p90; ☎330 4177; www.spto.org; 3rd fl, Dolphin Plaza, cnr Loftus St & Victoria Pde, Suva; ⊙9am-4pm Mon-Fri) is a useful source for regional information.

Alternatively, head to Lonely Planet (www.lonelyplanet.com/fiji) for planning advice, author recommendations, traveller reviews and insider tips.

Visas

A free tourist visa for four months is granted on arrival to citizens of more than 100 countries. You can check www.fiji.gov.fj for a full list (click on 'Travel' under 'About Fiji'). You are required to have an onward ticket and a passport valid for at least three months longer than your intended stay.

Nationalities from countries excluded from this list will have to apply for visas through a Fijian embassy prior to arrival.

Tourist visas can be extended for up to six months by applying through the Department of Immigration. You will need to show an onward ticket and proof of sufficient funds, and your passport must be valid for three months after your proposed departure.

You will need to apply at the **Immigration Department** (Map p90; ☑331 2672; Government Buildings, Suva).

Those entering Fiji by boat are subject to the same visa requirements as those arriving by plane. Yachts can enter only through the designated ports of Suva, Lautoka, Savusavu and Levuka. Yachts have to be cleared by immigration, customs and quarantine, and are prohibited from visiting any outer islands before doing so.

Getting There & Away

Air

Most international flights to Fiji arrive at Nadi International Airport, with a few flights landing at Nausori International Airport near Suva.

Nausori International Airport, about 23km northeast of downtown Suva, is principally used for domestic flights by Pacific Sun.

See p583 for details of air passes that include Fiji.

The following international airlines fly to and from Fiji:

Aircalin (☑672 2145; www.aircalin.nc)

Air New Zealand (☑331 3100; www.airnew zealand.co.nz)

Air Niugini (☑670 0870; www.airniugini.com.pg)

Air Vanuatu (☑672 2521, 331 5055; www. airvanuatu.com)

Fiji Airways (formerly Air Pacific; ☑672 0888, 330 4388; www.airpacific.com)

Jetstar Airways (www.jetstar.com)

Korean Air (☑672 1043; www.koreanair.com.au)

Qantas Airways (☑672 2880, 331 3888, 331 1833; www.qantas.com.au)

Solomon Airlines (☑672 2831; www.fly solomons.com)

Virgin Australia (☑672 0777; www.virgin australia.com)

Sea

Travelling to Fiji by sea is difficult unless you're on a cruise ship or yacht.

Yachts need to head for the designated ports of entry at Suva, Lautoka, Levuka or Savusavu, to clear customs, immigration and quarantine. Present a certificate of clearance from the previous port of call, a crew list and passports.

You must email or fax a completed Advanced Notice of Arrival Form (C.2.C) to **FRCA** (Fiji Revenue & Customs Authority; ☑324 3000; www.frca.org.fj; yachtsreport@frca.org. fj) Suva (fax 330 2864); Lautoka (fax 666 7734); Levuka (fax 344 0425); Savusavu (fax 885 0728) a minimum of 48 hours prior to arriving. Forms can be downloaded from the website.

In 2011 a port health quarantine fee (F$172.50) and a biosecurity levy (F$102) were introduced. On arrival, contact port control on VHF channel 16 to be directed to quarantine and await the arrival of customs officials.

Getting Around

By using local buses, carriers and ferries, you can get around Fiji's main islands relatively cheaply and easily. If you'd like more comfort, or are short of time, you can use air-conditioned express buses, rental vehicles, charter boats and small planes.

Air

Pacific Sun (☑330 4388; www.pacificsun. com.fj) runs most of the regular interisland flights by light plane. Tiny **Northern Air** (☑3475 005; www.northernair.com.fj) has a few scheduled flights from Suva to Levuka, Kadavu, Moala, Labasa and Koro. It also supplies charter services.

PACIFIC SUN FLIGHTS DEPARTING SUVA

DESTINATION	PRICE ONE-WAY
Cicia	F$265
Kadavu	F$185
Labasa	F$240
Lakeba	F$225
Nadi	F$180
Savusavu	F$265
Taveuni	F$260
Vanua Balavu	F$225

PACIFIC SUN FLIGHTS DEPARTING NADI

DESTINATION	PRICE ONE-WAY
Kadavu	F$220
Labasa	F$225
Rotuma	F$632
Savusavu	F$310
Suva	F$180
Taveuni	F$300

CHARTER SERVICES

Charter services are most commonly used by those wishing to maximise their time at island resorts.

Island Hoppers (☎675 0670; www.helicopters .com.fj) Helicopter transfers to most of the Mamanuca resort islands. A flight to Vomo, Castaway Island, Waidigi and Tokoriki resorts by helicopter costs F$294 one way per person.

Turtle Airways (☎672 1888; www.turtle airways.com) Charters a five-seater Cessna and a seven-seater de Havilland Canadian Beaver. Contact the company for rates.

Pacific Island Air (☎672 5644; www.pacific islandair.com) Offers transfers to islands in the Mamanuca, Yasawa and Lau Groups.

Boat

With the exception of the upmarket resort islands, often the only means of transport to and between islands is by small local boats. Life jackets are rarely provided; if the weather looks ominous or the boat is overcrowded, seriously consider postponing the trip!

High-speed, comfortable catamarans link Viti Levu to the Yasawas and Mamanucas. Less-reliable services link the mainland to Vanua Levu, Taveuni and Ovalau. Irregular boats also take passengers from Suva to the Lau Group, Rotuma and Kadavu. The fast catamarans aside, ferry timetables are notorious for changing frequently, and there is often a long wait at stopovers. Toilets can become filthy, so take your own toilet paper.

Note that most car-rental agencies won't let you take their car on board.

NADI–MAMANUCA GROUP

See p99 for details on the following companies.

Awesome Adventures (☎675 0499; www. awesomefiji.com) Calls into four Mamanuca islands on its daily run to the Yasawas.

Malolo Cat I & II (☎675 0205) Both owned by Plantation and Musket Cove resorts and travel between Port Denarau and Malololailai.

South Sea Cruises (☎675 0500; www.ssc. com.fj) Operates two fast catamarans from Denarau Marina to most of the Mamanuca islands.

NADI–YASAWA GROUP

Awesome Adventures (☎675 0499; www. awesomefiji.com) Runs a large yellow catamaran called the *Yasawa Flyer* to all of the Yasawa Group islands, plus several of the Mamanuca Group islands daily. See p99 for more information.

SUVA–VANUA LEVU/TAVEUNI

The three ferry companies listed below connect Suva and Savusavu, often via Koro, Taveuni and/or Ovalau.

It takes around 12 hours to reach Savusavu. For those bound for Labasa, a bus often meets the boats at Savusavu and tickets can be bought in Suva that include the Labasa bus transfer. Sometimes the boats depart from Natovi Landing, a half-hour bus ride north of Suva.

Bligh Water Shipping (☎in Suva 331 8247; 1-2 Matua St, Walu Bay; www.blighwatershipping. com.fj) Regular Suva–Savusavu–Taveuni departures aboard the MV *Suliven* in five classes.

Consort Shipping (Map p90; ☎in Suva 330 2877; fax 330 3389; consortship@connect.com. fj; Ground fl, Dominion House Arcade, Thomson St, Suva) Also runs Suva–Savusavu–Taveuni service.

Goundar Shipping (☎in Savusavu 330 1035; Kong's Shop, Main St, Savusavu) Began operations in 2011. The *Lomaiviti Princess* brings a new level of comfort and much-needed professionalism to the Suva–Vanua Levu route.

SUVA–KADAVU

Viti Levu is connected to Kadavu by only two companies. Both sail out of Suva. See p135 for details.

Goundar Shipping (☎in Savusavu 330 1035; Kong's Shop, Main St, Savusavu)

Venu Shipping (☎339 5000; Rona St, Walu Bay, Suva)

OUTER ISLANDS

The Lau, Moala and Rotuma Groups only receive one ferry a month, making this an unreliable option for anyone on any kind of schedule. There are rumours of a new Goundar Shipping plan to service Vanua Balavu and Lakeba via Cicia once a month.

If you are planning on travelling to any of the remote outer islands contact Tomi Finau or Atelaite Cama at **Procure Fiji** (☎in Suva 331 8151; procurefiji@gmail.com; Shop 8, Port of Mua-i-Walu no 2, Walu Bay). They run the procurement office for the outer islands and know exactly what boats are going where, when and whether it will take

passengers. They can also hook up outer-island homestays.

Bus

Catching a local bus on Fiji's larger islands is an inexpensive and fun way of getting around. While they can be fairly noisy, the buses are perfect for the tropics, with un-glazed windows and pull-down tarpaulins for when it rains. There are bus stops but you can often just hail buses, especially in rural areas.

Car & Motorcycle

Ninety per cent of Fiji's 5100km of roads are on Viti Levu and Vanua Levu (about 20% are sealed). Both islands are fun to explore by car.

Driving Licence If you hold a current driving licence from an English-speaking country, you are entitled to drive in Fiji. Otherwise, you will need an international driving permit, which should be obtained in your home country before travelling.

Hire Rental cars are relatively expensive in Fiji. Despite this, it is a good way to explore the larger islands, especially if you can split the cost with others. Expect to pay about F$125 per day for a short-term rental. It's usual to pay a deposit by credit card; if you don't have one, you'll need to leave a hefty cash bond. Generally, the larger, well-known companies have better cars and support, but are more expensive. A valid overseas or international driving licence is required. The minimum age requirement is 21 or, in some cases, 25.

Insurance Third-party insurance is compulsory, and all car-rental companies add it onto the daily rental rate (count on F$22 to F$30 depending on the size of the vehicle). Personal accident insurance is highly recommended if you are not already covered by travel insurance. Renters are liable for the first F$500 damage. Common exclusions, or problems that won't be paid for by the insurance company, include tyre damage, underbody and overhead damage, windscreen damage and theft of the vehicle.

Road Rules Driving is on the left-hand side of the road. The speed limit is 80km/h, which drops to 20km/h in towns. Many villages have speed humps to force drivers to respect the village pace. Seat belts are compulsory for front-seat passengers. Should you pick up a parking fine in Suva it's likely to be around F$2.

Tours

Fiji has many companies providing tours within the country, including hiking, kayaking, diving, bus and 4WD tours. Cruises to the outer islands such as the Mamanucas and Yasawas are extremely popular.

Feejee Experience (☑672 5950; www.feejeeexperience.com) offers popular coach transport on Viti Levu geared to budget-oriented 20-somethings, with four-day packages including lodging starting at F$499. This fun, party-ready outfit gets rave reviews, however a local bus will take you on the same route around the island for F$38.45.

New Caledonia

Includes »

Best Places to Stay

» Le Lagon (p154)

» Auberge de Jeunesse (p154)

» Relais de Poingam (p169)

» À La Petit Baie (p177)

» Tour de Monde (p154)

Best Places to Eat

» Chez Toto (p156)

» Sushi Hana (p157)

» Restaurant Finemem (p177)

» Chez Mamie (p165)

» Zanzibar (p156)

Why Go?

Dazzling – yes, New Caledonia is dazzling. Its lagoon surrounds it with every colour of blue. So the light and the space delight your senses. The 2008 prestigious listing of the lagoon as a World Heritage site has brought the people together to celebrate and protect it, from village level through to government.

New Caledonia isn't just a tropical playground. There's a charming mix of French and Melanesian: warm hospitality sitting beside European elegance, gourmet food beneath palm trees, sand, resorts, bungalows, concrete, bamboo. Long gorgeous beaches are backed by cafes and bars, with horizons that display tiny islets to attract day trippers. Be lured into kayaks, rock climb, sail, dive into a world of corals, canyons, caves and heritage shipwrecks, go whale watching or snorkelling, or relax on the warm sand of a deserted isle. Natural wonders and manmade delights are at your fingertips.

When to Go
Noumea

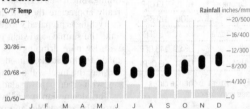

Apr–May Fresh from the heat and rains, the country is sparkling again.

Jul It may be too cool for beach-goers, but that bodes well for hikers.

Oct–Nov Catch life on the islands before folk head off on their annual summer vacation.

AT A GLANCE

Currency Cour de Franc Pacifique (CFP)

Language French, Melanesian-Polynesian

Mobile phones Liberté SIMs (6130 CFP from post offices) work in unlocked European and Australian phones. Public phones available.

Money ATMs on the Grande Terre, one on each of the Loyalty Islands and Île des Pins.

Visas Not needed for stays up to three months for EEC, US, Australia, New Zealand, Japan and South Korea passport holders.

Fast Facts

» **Area** 18,575 sq km
» **Capital** Noumea
» **Country code** ☎687
» **Emergency** ambulance ☎15, fire ☎18, police ☎17
» **Population** 260,000

Exchange Rates

Australia	A$1	96 CFP
Canada	C$1	92 CFP
Europe	€1	119 CFP
Japan	¥100	119 CFP
New Zealand	NZ$1	75 CFP
UK	UK£1	148 CFP
USA	US$1	95 CFP

For current exchange rates see www.xe.com.

Set Your Budget

» **Hotel room** 14,000 CFP
» **Museum visit** 400 CFP
» **Bottle of beer** 350 CFP
» **Transport ticket** 210 CFP

Connections

It's a breeze travelling to New Caledonia's islands; the Betico passenger ferry links them with Noumea twice a week, and offers day trips to Île des Pins. You can fly from island to island, with the exception of Maré, which is linked to Lifou and Ouvéa by ferry only, and Île des Pins, which connects only to Noumea. If planning to transfer from an international to a domestic flight take into account the 1.5 hr travel time between the international and domestic airports.

ITINERARIES

One Week

Practise your swimming at **Noumea**'s beaches (Anse Vata and Baie des Citrons) and indulge in French pastries and bistro meals. Loll around the hotel pool, but emerge to see the gorgeous **aquarium** and, further out, the **Tjibaou Cultural Centre**. Ferry it to **Île des Pins**, pick up your awaiting rental car and drive to **La Piscine Naturelle**. Walk in and along a river to a simple beachside restaurant where you can eat lobster. Return the car, catch the ferry back and dance like there's no tomorrow at an over-water nightclub.

Two Weeks

As above, then head north for a week of cultural exploration. Stay waterside or journey into the depths of deer hunting, cowboy country on a farmstay. Book ahead for a couple of magic days at **Relais de Poingam**, right at the tip, before heading down the east coast, buying up carvings and tropical fruits. Still time? Duck south and explore the **Parc Provincial de la Rivière Bleue** by canoe.

Essential Food & Drink

New Caledonian restaurants are famous for their fine dining. But it's at the *snacks* (eateries) and cafes that you really appreciate the flare and flavour of French cuisine: everything is prepared with delicious sauces and marinades. Take the simple sandwich. It's a very long, crusty baguette with leg ham dripping out the sides, or perhaps a homemade terrine stacked inside. If a restaurant serves Pacific cuisine, the meal will be simple but elegant: fish in lemon, say, with green papaya salad.

The Melanesian speciality is *bougna:* yam, sweet potato, taro, other vegetables and meat, fish or seafood covered in coconut milk, wrapped in banana leaves and cooked on hot stones in an earth oven for two hours. Most Melanesian-run gîtes can prepare a *bougna* but you must order 24 hours in advance.

GRANDE TERRE

POP 210,000 / AREA 16,500 SQ KM

A chain of mountains sweeps down the middle of Grande Terre, and the wide plains that stretch along its west coast are dotted with country towns where cattle breeders stroll down the street in Stetsons and cowboy boots. On the east coast fruit stalls dot the area where the mountains descend to the sea, their lush vegetation meeting the steep and sinuous coastline. Waterfalls rush down the mountainsides into deep pools and out into the famously colourful lagoon, where the islands' inhabitants spend much

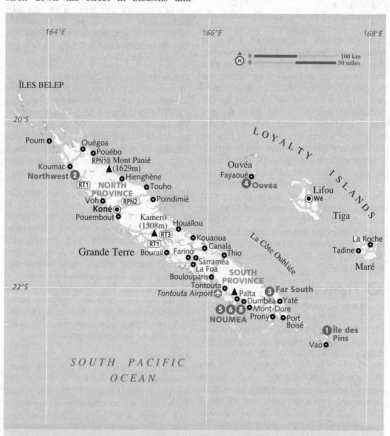

New Caledonia Highlights

1 Swimming in a 'natural swimming pool' after a lobster lunch on **Île des Pins** (p181)

2 Driving up to the wild **northwest coast** (p167) of the Grande Terre and donning a cowboy attitude for a night at a farmstay

3 Heading into the surprisingly isolated **far south** (p159) of the Grande Terre for a full-moon kayak tour

4 Admiring the coral reefs, lunching on freshly caught fish then feeding a nearby shark colony on **Ouvéa** (p178)

5 Drinking black coffee with the locals at Noumea's **market** (p148) while listening to a local Kanak band singing by the water

6 Day tripping it to one of the tiny **islands off Noumea** (p150) with a snorkel and picnic lunch sourced from one of Noumea's bakeries

7 Scuba diving (p171) at any of the terrific sites in the World Heritage lagoon

8 Dancing till the early hours at an **over-water disco** in Noumea (p158)

of their leisure time fishing, boating and enjoying other water sports. Grande Terre is not only New Caledonia's major island, but also the third-largest island in the Pacific after Papua New Guinea and New Zealand.

Noumea

POP 92,000

With its cheerful multi-ethnic community, New Caledonia's cosmopolitan capital is both sophisticated and uncomplicated, classy and casual. The relaxed city sits on a large peninsula, surrounded by picturesque bays, and offers visitors a variety of experiences. Diners can eat out at sassy French restaurants hidden in the latin quarter, dine at bold water-fronting bistros or grab a bargain meal from a nocturnal van in a car park. Meanwhile, shopaholics can blow their savings on the latest Parisian fashions or go bargain hunting for imported Asian textiles.

Central Noumea revolves around Place des Cocotiers, a large, shady square with landscaped gardens, a couple of blocks in from the waterfront. The main leisure area where locals and tourists hang out lies south of the city centre at Baie des Citrons and Anse Vata, with beaches, restaurants, bars and nightclubs.

◎ Sights

Place des Cocotiers   SQUARE
This is the heart of the city. The square (Map p152) slopes gently from east to west and at the top is a band rotunda, a famous landmark dating back to the late 1800s. Place des Cocotiers is the perfect spot to watch the world go by. Near the band rotunda there's a popular *pétanque* pitch and a giant chessboard. Down the other end it's like a lush botanical garden, with palms and large spreading trees.

Regular concerts and street markets are held in Place des Cocotiers. The popular **Jeudis du Centre Ville** (⊘Thu evenings Apr-Nov) street market has a different theme each week, outlined in *NC Pocket* (free from the Office du Tourisme). Stalls sell arts and crafts, fresh produce, cakes and local dishes, and entertainment includes live music and traditional dance.

Musée de la Ville de Noumea   MUSEUM
(Noumea Museum; Map p152; Rue Jean Jaurès; admission 100 CFP; ⊘9am-5pm Mon-Fri, open 9am-11am & 2-5pm Sat Mar-Dec) The beautiful colonial-style Musée de la Ville de Nou-

mea, which overlooks Place des Cocotiers, is dwarfed by towering palm trees. It features temporary and permanent displays on the early history of Noumea.

Cathédrale St Joseph   CHURCH
(Map p152; 3 Rue Frédérick Surleau) The cathedral was built in 1888 by convict labour and is one of Noumea's landmarks. It has beautiful stained-glass windows and an elaborately carved pulpit, altar panels and confessional. The main entrance is generally locked, but you should find the side doors open.

Musée de Nouvelle-Calédonie   MUSEUM
(Museum of New Caledonia; Map p152; www.musee nouvellecaledonie.nc; 42 Av du Maréchal Foch; adult 200 CFP; ⊘9-11.30am & 12.15-4.30pm Wed-Mon) The Musée de Nouvelle-Calédonie provides an excellent introduction to traditional Kanak and regional Pacific culture. Local exhibits are displayed on the ground floor and regional artefacts on the mezzanine level.

Mwâ Ka   MONUMENT
(Map p152) The magnificent Mwâ Ka is erected in a landscaped square opposite Musée de Nouvelle-Calédonie. The 12m totem pole is topped by a *grande case* (chief's hut), complete with *flèche faîtière* (carved rooftop spear), and its carvings represent the eight customary regions of New Caledonia. The Mwâ Ka is mounted as the mast on a concrete double-hulled *pirogue*, steered by a wooden helmsman, and celebrates Kanak identity as well as the multi-ethnic reality of New Caledonia.

Le Marché   MARKET
(Map p152; ⊘5-11am) This colourful multi-hexagonal-shaped market is beside the marina at Port Moselle. Fishermen unload their catch; trucks offload fruit, vegetables and flowers; and there's fresh-baked bread and cakes, plus delights like terrines and olives. The arts and crafts section includes a central cafe. On Saturday and Sunday a local string band keeps shoppers entertained. The market is at its busiest early in the morning.

Musée de l'Histoire Maritime   MUSEUM
(Maritime Museum; Map p149; ☑26 34 43; 11 Av James Cook) The Musée de l'Histoire Maritime was closed at the time of research, but was scheduled to open again by the time you read this.

Parc Zoologique et Forestier   ZOO
(Zoological & Botanical Gardens; Map p149; ☑27 89 51; Rte de Laubarède; adult/child 400 CFP/

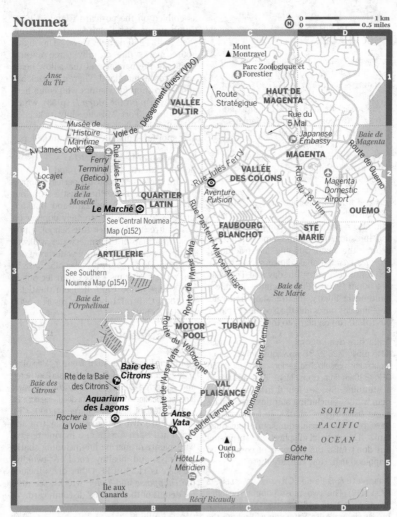

free; ⊙10.15am-5.45pm Tue-Sun, to 5pm May-Aug) Wander along a network of paths through gardens of native shrubs and trees, cactus and forest with a changing backdrop of sea views in the distance. You'll come across native species such as the flightless *cagou*, *roussette*, *notou* pigeon and various parakeets right in front of you. Speed around the Parc Zoologique et Forestier on a **Segway** (☑86 46 83; per person 7500 CFP) for something different.

Le Petit Train (p152) and Noumea Explorer buses (p159) run here from the city centre, or it's a quick taxi ride out.

Tjibaou Cultural Centre   ARTS CENTRE

(☑41 45 45; www.adck.nc; Rue des Accords de Matignon; adult/child 500 CFP/free, guided tours 1000 CFP; ⊙9am-5pm Tue-Sun) The cultural centre is a tribute to a remarkable man, pro-independence Kanak leader Tjibaou who was assassinated in 1989. It sits in a peaceful woodland and mangrove setting on Tina Peninsula. Displays include sculpture, paintings and photographs representing Kanak culture, as well as other cultures from around the Pacific. The main buildings are a series of tall, curved wooden structures which rise majestically above the trees. The harmony

ONE PASS, SIX PLACES

On your first visit to a Noumea museum or site, ask about buying the 'Pass to Nature & Culture'. It costs 1700 CFP but it gives you entry to three museums, the aquarium, the Tjibaou Cultural Centre and the zoo and botanical gardens. However, those aged over 60 get much better individual entry discounts. Get to all the places on the hop-on, hop-off Noumea Explorer (p159).

between this contemporary architecture (designed by Italian architect Renzo Piano, who also designed Paris' Pompidou Centre) and the surrounding landscape is amazing. Behind the main building are traditional *grandes cases;* Kanak dance shows by We Ce Ca are held every Tuesday and Thursday at 2.30pm (2500 CFP). Amenities include a multimedia library, theatre, shop and cafe. Blue-line city buses and the Noumea Explorer bus (p159) run regularly to the centre.

Aquarium des Lagons AQUARIUM
(Map p154; ☑26 27 31; www.aquarium.nc; Rte de l'Aquarium; adult/child/senior 1000/500/750 CFP; ☑10am-5pm, closed Mon) This aquarium is stunning. Species found in New Caledonian waters – including nautilus, sea snakes, stone fish, turtles, sharks and stingrays – have realistic surroundings in their huge tanks. Living coral displays are surprising but don't miss the emperor of coral reefs: Napoleon fish. How cute are these?

Anse Vata & Baie des Citrons BEACHES
(Map p149) The two most popular beaches are at Anse Vata and Baie des Citrons. On a breezy day at Anse Vata, you can watch the colourful kite- and windsurfers skimming up and down the bay. The best thing: as they face different directions, one of these beaches is always free of wind for the sun loungers.

Amédée Islet ISLAND
(Map p160) The waters around Noumea are sprinkled with beautiful islets. Most are marine reserves and the clear waters surrounding them are great for snorkelling. This islet, about 20km south of Noumea, is famous for its tall white lighthouse, **Phare Amédée** (admission 200 CFP), which was built in France, shipped out in pieces, and

assembled on the postcard island in 1865. Climb up its spiral staircase to a narrow shelf with 360-degree views. The lighthouse marks one of only three natural breaks in the barrier reef that allow boats access to the mainland. There's a snack bar and curio shop for visitors who come here on a day trip on the *Mary D* (p153), which leaves from Port Moselle. Buy tickets at Palm Beach or Port Moselle. It's also a popular spot for scuba divers and snorkellers.

Île aux Canards & Îlot Maître ISLAND
Île aux Canards (Map p154) and Îlot Maître are the cutest postcard-perfect poppets of islets. You can see them just a swim out from Anse Vata, sitting 2km and 1km offshore. Kite surfing is extremely popular on Îlot Maître (try Noumea Kite School, p190). Pick up a map of the underwater walkway on Île aux Canards, or buy a waterproof one at the kiosk. **L'escapade** (Map p152; ☑28 53 20; Port Moselle) runs a boat transfer out to Îlot Maître (3000 CFP). Redeem the ticket for 1000 CFP off L'escapade resort's 5900 CFP lunch buffet.

🏃 Activities

Diving

Noumea dive clubs **Alizé Diving** (Map p154; ☑26 25 85; www.alizedive.com; Nouvata Park Hôtel) and **Amédée Diving Club** (☑264 029; www.amedee.sponline.com, www.amedeediving.nc; 28 Rue du Général Mangin) charge 11,000 CFP for an intro dive along with a day trip and lunch at **Phare Amédée**, a marine reserve with plenty of marine life including sharks and rays and healthy coral. A two-dive package is 14,500 CFP. Other dives include the *Dieppoise* and *TohoV* wrecks; see p190 for details of the 'Plongée' discount card.

Abyss Plongée DIVING
(Map p154; ☑79 15 09; www.abyssnc.com; Marina Port du Sud, Baie de l'Orphelinat) Dives at many sites around Grande Terre and charges 7000 CFP for an intro dive and 11,000 CFP for a double dive, plus transport costs. Dive clubs all offer PADI courses.

Water Activities

See p190 for information on boats to hire, or get a full list of companies from the Office du Tourisme.

Noumea Yacht Charter and Pacific Charter (see p190) rent fishing boats from Noumea. **New Caledonia Fishing Safaris** (☑25 19 40; www.newcaledoniafishing safaris.nc), also

based in Noumea, runs sportfishing safaris around Poum and other spots.

La Maison du Lagon
LAGOON TOUR

(Map p154; ☎27 27 27; www.maisondulagon.nc; Port Moselle) Book boat tours, whale-watching trips and anything else lagoon-related here.

Plages Loisirs
BOAT TOUR, WATER SPORTS

(Map p154; ☎26 90 00; www.plagesloisirs.nc; 110 Promenade Roger Laroque; ⏱7.30am-5.30pm) Rents out equipment and runs a taxi boat to Île aux Canards and Îlot Maître.

Centre Nautique Vata Plaisirs
WATER SPORTS

(Map p154; ☎78 13 00, 76 59 09; www.mdplaisirs. com) Offers introductory lessons (2900 CFP). Ask about the MD Plaisirs Card, which gives you 40% discount (eg catamaran 1550 CFP, kayak 750 CFP) and is usable here, and in Poé.

Locajet
JET SKIING

(Map p149; ☎77 79 79; www.locajet.info; all day 25,000 CFP) In Nouville on the western side of Baie de la Moselle, rents jet skis. Do a circular whiz from Île de la Moselle to Île aux Canards, Îlot Maitre, a few more islets and back to the northern side of the Nouville peninsula.

Dumbéa River
CANOEING

The RT1 crosses Dumbéa River at Parc Fayard, 16km north of Noumea. It's popular during the hot summer months as the shady park is a good picnic area, the river offers good swimming, and there are hiking tracks along two branches of the river: north takes you to a canyon, south to a dam. **Terra Incognita** (☎77 70 78, 78 94 46; terincognita@canl.nc) rents out canoes, and runs full-moon kayaking trips down the river (two hours, 5200 CFP).

Aquanature
SNORKELLING

(Map p152; ☎26 40 08, 78 36 66; quanature@canl. nc; Port Moselle; half/full day 6900/8200 CFP) Bernard takes you out from Port Moselle to snorkel on the reef; he finds the best spots and you get coffee and cakes as well.

Noumea Kite School
KITE SURFING

(Map p154; ☎79 07 66; www.noumeakiteschool. com; Port du Sud; ⏱9am-noon & 3-7pm Mon-Sat) One-hour lessons are 8900 CFP including transport to the islands. You'll need a medical certificate to say you're fit to kite surf.

Noumea Yacht Charter
YACHT CHARTER

(Map p152; ☎28 66 66; www.nyc.nc; Port Moselle) Skippered or bare-boat 11m catamarans and monohulls from 74,000 CFP and 63,000 CFP a day on 'the best lagoon in the world'.

Land-Based Activities

You'll find all your favourite sporting activities are available in Noumea, or around Grande Terre: golf, squash, clay-pigeon shooting; just ask at the Office du Tourisme.

The Office du Tourisme produces a folder, *Randonnées en Nouvelle-Calédonie,* of helpful brochures describing many small or grand walks, cycling trips and climbs across islands, through forests and up many creeks.

Le Circuit Historique, a lovely booklet produced by the **Hôtel de Ville** (Town Hall; ☎27 31 15; www.ville-noumea.nc; 16 Rue du Général Mangin), takes you on a fascinating history tour past Noumea's old buildings (from 1856 on).

Noumea Fun Ride
BICYCLE RENTAL

(Map p152; ☎26 96 26, 78 40 25; noumeafun ride.org@canl.nc; Gare Maritime; scootcars 1/2hr 5500/7500 CFP; 👶) Rents fun movable vehicles including miniature cars (7000/8500 CFP per one/two hours) if you're over 16 years of age. There's also mountain and beach bikes (1100 CFP half-day), helmets, child seats and roller blades.

☞ Tours

One of the most popular tours of Noumea is organised by *Le Petit Train* (p152). Aventure Pulsion and Caledonia Tours (p163) run

---

NOUMEA FOR CHILDREN

Face it, the children want to stay on the beach, swimming and building sand castles at **Anse Vata** or **Baie des Citrons** beaches (p173). But if anything will drag them away, it's a ride on **Le Petit Train** (p152).

There's a shady **children's playground** (Map p154) at Baie de l'Orphelinat off Rue du Général de Gaulle, and next to the public swimming pool at Ouen Toro near Anse Vata. Or head to **Le Marché** (p148). There's a buzz of activity, plenty to buy, and opposite, in the car park, children's **fair rides** (200 CFP; ⏱from 3pm Mon-Sun).

A visit to the **aquarium** (p150) is a must: endlessly entertaining and the perfect introduction to a trip out in a glass-bottom boat. And when Thursday evening comes around (March to December), go by **Place des Cocotiers** (p148), where traditional dances will entrance kids.

Central Noumea

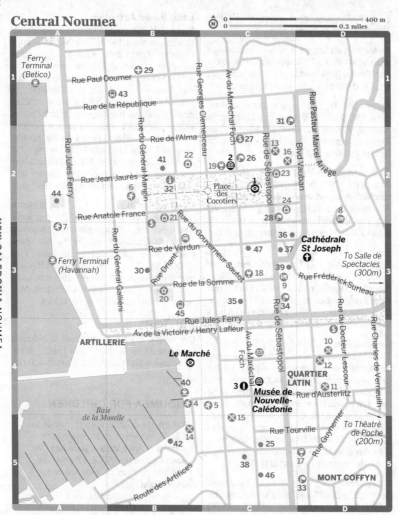

NEW CALEDONIA NOUMEA

day excursions to the far south. There are tours to Monts Koghis, tours on the deep blue and tours up north. See p195 for a few ideas, or contact the Office du Tourisme for recommendations.

Helicopters fly a maximum of three people over Noumea's bays, the islets sprinkled across the lagoon, shipwrecks and the barrier reef. A longer flight takes in the incredible inlets of the far south. Take the flight to the Île des Pins between June and August and perhaps spot whales. The honeymoon flight (48,000 CFP) includes a 30-minute champagne stop on an island.

Operators include **Helicocean** (☎25 39 49; helicocean@mls.nc; 30min flight 43,500 CFP) and **Hélisud** (☎26 96 62; www.helisud.nc; 30min flight 43,500 CFP).

Le Petit Train   TOUR
(Map p154; ☎77 80 73; www.petit-train.nc; adult/child 1400/700 CFP) Yes, that was a train you saw. It's very cute and entertaining, and a big photo opportunity. 'Le Petit Train' Touristique de Noumea makes two large loops a day (except Sunday) leaving Palm Beach at 9.30am and 1pm, passing through Baie de Citron, the city centre and out to Parc

Central Noumea

Zoologique et Forestier, offering grand views as you return inland to Palm Beach. Purchase tickets from the driver.

Colleen Excursions   BOAT TOUR
(Map p154; ☏79 59 29; cruellas@offratel.nc; 56 Promenade Roger Laroque) Go out in a glass-bottom taxi boat (2500 CFP per 45 minutes), located at Fun Beach. Or head for Île aux Canards (1000 CFP), or Îlot Maître (2500 CFP),

watching the sea life on the way. Rent snorkel gear and wet suits (500 CFP) or go reef fishing (three hours 6200 CFP).

Mary D   BOAT TOUR
(Map p154; ☏26 31 31; www.amedeeisland.com; Galerie Palm Beach, departs from Port Moselle, Anse Vata; 14,100 CFP; ⊙8.30am Thu-Sun) A grand day on one of Mary D's launches out to Amédée Islet. Visit the lighthouse, snorkel offshore or

from the glass-bottom boat, feed sharks on the reef, indulge in a luscious three-course buffet lunch, and see fun dance and cultural shows.

Alpha International   BOAT TOUR
(Map p154; ☑27 24 20; www.alpha-tourisme.com; 143 Rte de l'Anse Vata) Catamaran trips to islets and day trips in the far south. Tours to Mont-Dore and Monts Koghis cost 10,500 CFP and to Parc Provincial de la Rivière Bleue cost 6300 CFP.

🛏 Sleeping

Noumea has few budget options and a good midrange selection.

Le Lagon   HOTEL $$
(Map p154; ☑26 12 55; www.lelagon.nc; 149 Rte de l'Anse Vata; studio/ste 11,000/15,000 CFP; ✱@🛜🌊) A bright aquarium welcomes guests and lovely staff make all the difference. The one-bedroom suites are double the size of the studios but all have mod-

ern kitchenettes, lovely king-sized beds and bathrooms with bath and shower. The pool's not huge, but popular Anse Vata beach is nearby.

TOP CHOICE Auberge de Jeunesse   HOSTEL $
(Map p152; ☑27 58 79; www.yhanoumea.lagoon.nc; 51bis Rue Pasteur Marcel Ariège; dm/d 1700/3900 CFP; @🛜) This sparkling-clean hostel, behind St Joseph's Cathedral, has a fantastic view of the city and Baie de la Moselle. The energy here is exciting. It's an extra 400 CFP for nonmembers of HI; wi-fi or computer use is 200 CFP an hour. Linen is provided. You'll get stacks of tourist info. The quickest way to get there from the centre of town on foot is up the 103 steps at the top of rue Jean Jaurès. Advance bookings are recommended.

TOP CHOICE Tour de Monde   B&B $$
(Map p160; No 4 Les Fougeres, Col de Katiramona, Dumbea; s/d 4800/5800 CFP; ✱🛜🌊) You

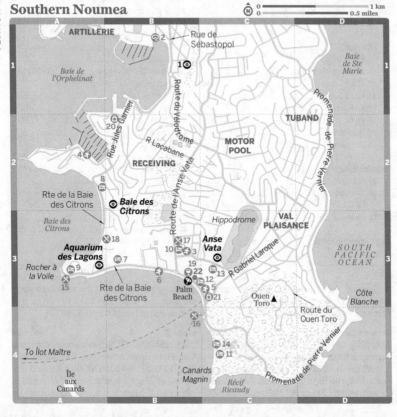

Southern Noumea

can't get much more wordly than this; each cute cabin is themed with pictures of the owner's travels, so take your pic of the Orient, Broussard (think cowboy) or Melanesian cabin. There's a hot tub and small pool in a lovely communal/dining area; taking the half-board option is recommended. Jean-Claude speaks English and is excellent help for those planning New Caledonian adventures. It may seem a suburban location, and it is out of town, but you're in another world when you get through the gates. The Noumea–Tontouta (airport) bus stops nearby.

L'escapade
RESORT $$$

(☑26 05 12; Îlot Maître; garden-/beach-view bungalows 22,600/27,000 CFP, over-water bungalows 52,000 CFP; ❋�❋) Skip the garden view rooms and head straight for the over-water bungalows; they're divine. Sure, this means you can't bring the kids, but really, this is what island life should be like. Walls of windows, your own private deck and, well, what feels like your own private lagoon. Transfers are 3000 CFP.

Hôtel Beaurivage
HOTEL $$

(Map p154; ☑26 20 55; www.grands-hotels.nc; 7 Promenade Roger Laroque; standard/seaview 6500/7500 CFP; ❋led) Talk about position. This rather faded retro hotel is just across the road from the beach at Baie des Citrons and a quick step away from the restaurant strip. Yet it's a quiet spot and rooms are airy.

Royal Tera Beach Resort & Spa
RESORT $$$

(Map p154; ☑29 64 00; resa.royal@tera.nc; 140 Promenade Roger Laroque; d with breakfast 21,600 CFP; ❋❋led❋) There's a cool, calm ambience to this resort, from its gigantic entrance to its lounge bar and its rooms, which are modern affairs with two TVs, modern fittings and balconies. It fronts a popular patch of beach, or laze away from the sand in the beachside pool.

Hôtel Le Surf
CASINO HOTEL $$

(Map p154; ☑28 66 88; www.grands-hotels.nc; Rocher à la Voile; r 13,500 CFP; ❋led❋) Two large hotel sections with a network of private balconies bridge together across an access road with a casino and restaurant below. Rooms with sea views are an extra 1500 CFP, and it's

NEW CALEDONIA NOUMEA

Southern Noumea

an easy stroll to either Anse Vata beachfront or Baie de Citrons. The breakfast buffet is 2700 CFP, the evening seafood buffet 6400 CFP. Stay a week and the tariff is 9500 CFP per night.

Le Méridien Noumea   RESORT $$$

(Map p154; ☎26 50 00; www.lemeridien.com; Pointe Magnin; classic/superior/executive with breakfast 40,000/45,000/48,000 CFP; ❄ ⚹ ⚛) This stunning hotel by Anse Vata beach has landscaped grounds, a hypnotic pool area (the best in town) and several restaurants. You have transport to all sites and activities, should you ever wish to drag yourself off the premises. Check out the special deals on the website.

Hôtel Le Paris   HOTEL $$

(Map p152; ☎28 17 00; www.bestwestern-leparis hotel.com; 45 Rue de Sébastopol; s/d with breakfast 9100/10,350 CFP; ⚹) It's good to be in the centre of Noumea, a short stroll into the French atmosphere of Place des Cocotiers. The rooms are sea-blue and spacious.

Nouvata Hôtel Complex   HOTEL $$

(Map p154; ☎26 22 00; 123 Promenade Roger Laroque; r garden/beach view 14,400/22,900 CFP; ❄ ⚹ ⚛) This grand hotel, in the middle of the tourist atmosphere at Anse Vata, has all the facilities you could possibly need. It's divided into three different sections, starting with cheaper rooms at Le Pacifique. It also offers deluxe rooms and suites (from 27,900 CFP). The lounging areas, pool area and restaurants are welcoming, making for good places to meet other guests.

Ramada Plaza   HOTEL $$$

(Map p154; ☎23 90 00; www.ramadaplaza-noumea. nc; Rue Boulari; studios 20,900 CFP, deluxe 29,200 CFP) The rooms and suites at the twin-towered Ramada Plaza are tastefully decorated in contemporary Pacific style. Rooms have racecourse or sea views and the revolving restaurant features fine dining with fine views.

Casa del Sole   HOTEL $$

(Map p154; ☎25 87 00; www.casadelsole.nc; 10 Rte de l'Aquarium; 1-/2-bedroom apt 10,350/ 13,350 CFP; ⚹ ⚛) This hard-to-miss skyscraper houses spacious and modern apartments with bright kitchenettes, comfy furnishings and private terraces filled with views. It's a couple of minutes' walk from the beach, shops and restaurants.

✖ Eating

Noumea has fabulous restaurants specialising in French and international cuisine as well as seafood. The hotels all have excellent restaurants as well. Many places are closed on Sunday or Monday.

CITY CENTRE

Chez Toto   FRENCH $$

(Map p152; ☎28 80 42; 15 Rue August Brun, Quartier Latin; mains 2700 CFP; ☺dinner) Head to this buzzing little restaurant for terrific French meals; it is truly so Frenchy, so classically chic, and, not surprisingly, often full to the brim.

Zanzibar   RESTAURANT $$

(Map p152; ☎25 28 00; 51 Rue Jean Jaurès; mains 1900-2700 CFP; ☺lunch Mon-Fri, dinner Mon-Sat) It's all atmospheric timber and cloth, with a tiny upstairs verandah and a range of dishes like duck with lavender. It's famous for its desserts.

La Chaumière   FRENCH $$

(Map p152; ☎27 24 62; 13 Rue du Docteur Guégan; menus lunch/dinner 2300/3400 CFP; ☺lunch Sun-Fri, dinner Mon-Sat) The atmosphere is warm and uncluttered in this old colonial building where fabulous fine dining makes it very popular. French favourites like fish soup or confit of duck come with traditional accompaniments it's hard to find elsewhere. Come for lunch, share the menu, whatever – just don't miss out.

La Kasbah   MIDDLE EASTERN $$

(Map p152; ☎27 88 61; 15 Rue de Sébastopol; mains 1900-3300 CFP; ☺lunch & dinner Tue-Sun) Enter another universe in this fascinating spot, where the *tajines* are large and full of glorious flavours that almost match the exotic decor. Sharing a *tajine* is totally acceptable.

Roulottes   TAKEAWAY $

(Map p152; Rue Georges Clémenceau; dishes around 650 CFP; ☺dinner) These food vans gather in the large car park opposite the market at night and serve great takeaway meals.

Le Bout du Monde   RESTAURANT $$

(Map p152; 4 Rue de la Frégate Nivôse; mains 1600-2900 CFP; ☺7am-11pm) This relaxed bar and restaurant that spills out towards the marina at Port Moselle serves a lunchtime salad buffet (1600 CFP) daily, but you can also order à la carte.

Best Cafe   CAFE $$

(Map p152; 47 Rue de Sébastopol; mains 600-2950 CFP; ☺6.30am-11pm) It looks a bit ordinary,

but the food is delicious. The chef edges the prawns with a salt that makes them burst with flavour, and the *plat du jour* is often a roast.

BAIE DES CITRONS
The electric strip at Baie des Citrons has some neat shops tucked between an oft-changing line-up of restaurants clamouring to be noticed: Italian, seafood, steak – you name it. Wander along, join all the other people soaking up the atmosphere, enjoying a drink or two, then pick your spot, but be good and leave the ice-cream bar till last. Main meals cost between 1500 CFP and 3300 CFP.

Sushi Hana JAPANESE $$
(Map p154; ✆23 88 87; 25 Promenade Roger Laroque, Mirage Plaza, Baie des Citrons; mains 2000 CFP; ✆ lunch & dinner Tue-Sun) Cool, quiet and frequently booked out, this restaurant has Japanese food brimming with fresh flavour. Try a couple of starters (500 CFP each) before a simply divine main.

ANSE VATA
Fun Beach Restaurant & Grill GRILL $$
(Map p154; mains 1300-2800 CFP; ✆11am-2pm & 6-11pm) Up the other end, away from the main restaurant drag, this is all Western-style pasta, fish and steak, served on a deck by the bay. And it's a pleasant spot for a drink in the evening.

Le Roof RESTAURANT $$$
(Map p154; ✆25 07 00; 134 Promenade Roger Laroque; mains 2900-4700 CFP; ✆lunch & dinner) Out on the pier, spacious and open, Le Roof has a large central backlit hole so that you can see ocean, fish and perhaps even a turtle. Add two large aquariums, delicate white china, majestic wine glasses, delicious fish dishes and it's like fine dining for mermaids.

Snack Ulysse TAKEAWAY $
(Map p154; Rte de l'Anse Vata; sandwiches 450-880 CFP; ✆lunch & dinner) A popular *snack* that serves generously filled hot or cold sandwiches, burgers, chips and rice dishes. Eat in or take away.

🍷 Drinking
Everywhere, your drinks are served with a bowl of peanuts or marinated olives. So nice.

Art Cafe BAR
(Map p152; 30 Rue Duquesne, Quartier Latin; ✆6.30am-10.30pm Mon-Fri) Don't miss a drink

at this terrific indoor/outdoor bar. You may chance upon live acoustic music while you eat pizza or drink cocktails on the terrace, and the crowd is friendly.

Les 3 Brasseurs BREWERY
(Map p154; ✆to midnight Sun-Thu, to 2am Fri & Sat) A popular microbrewery, where you can choose your poison, blonde, amber or brown, from the stainless-steel brewing equipment. There's live music on the weekends.

Bodega Del Mar BAR
(Map p154; 134 Promenade Roger Laroque) In Anse Vata, a trendy bar on the pier with DJs most nights.

Le Bilboquet Plage WINE BAR
(Map p154; Palm Beach; ✆11am-2pm & 6.30pm-1am) This upstairs French brasserie serves tasty meals and snacks (from 650 CFP) and has a spacious verandah that's a relaxing place for a drink amidst plenty of potted palms (well, green stuff).

L'Etrave BAR
(Map p154; Promenade Roger Laroque; ✆9am-midnight) If you prefer to drink in a bar with comfy lounge chairs and mood music, the friendly staff here makes this stylish place both casual and fun.

Le Bout du Monde BAR
(Map p152; 4 Rue de la Frégate Nivôse; ✆7am-11pm) In the city centre, at the Port Moselle marina, a pleasant place for a drink as well as a meal (see p156). Frequently has live music, too.

Le Muzz' Bar BAR
(Map p152; 37 Rue Jean Jaurès; ✆6pm-late Tue-Sun) This spot oozes atmosphere and features popular live music (from 9pm Thursday to Saturday). There's tapas and bruschetta on Wednesdays and Thursdays.

Nakamal du Col KAVA BAR
(Dumbéa; kava per shell 100 CFP; ✆2-7pm Mon-Fri, 3-7pm Sat) For a South Pacific experience, head out to Dumbéa to this kava house on the RT1. It has small *farés* on a terraced hillside with panoramic views over Noumea and its bays. Don't miss the sunset.

Malecon Café BAR
(Map p154; ✆to 11pm) Busy spot throughout the day and night, serving quiche and pizza (650 CFP) to help you drink more.

Le Bilboquet Village BAR
(Map p152; 45 Av du Maréchal Foch; ✆9am-11pm Mon-Sat) Back in the city, serves drinks and

meals in the charming courtyard of an old courthouse at Le Village.

☆ Entertainment

The Office du Tourisme publishes the *NC Pocket* (www.sortir.nc) entertainment guide.

The nightlife mostly happens naturally: the buzz along Baie des Citrons as young people and music fill the bars and spill across to the beach; the slightly older group that park their cars along the Anse Vata foreshore and make the most of the heavenly nights and music drifting or beating across the bay.

The **entertainment centre** (Salle de Spectacles, FOL; off map p152; ☎27 21 40; 51 Rue Olry) and lovely old theatres **Théâtre de Poche** (Centre d'Art; ☎25 07 50; www.ville-noumea.nc/pratique/culture_centre_art.asp; 6 Blvd Extérieur) and **Théâtre de l'Île** (☎25 50 50; www.theatre delile.nc) have local groups, amateur theatre and stand-up comedy nights. Ask for the programs at Office du Tourisme or visit www.sortir.nc.

Pop Light   NIGHTCLUB
(Map p154; Anse Vata) It's fun, bright and as close to the water as you can get (without getting wet).

Ciné City   CINEMA
(Map p152; 18 Rue de la Somme; admission 1050 CFP) Twelve theatres screen a large range of movies in French. During La Foa Film Festival (June/July) movies are screened, both here and at La Foa's Cinéma Jean-Pierre Jeunet, in their original language.

🔒 Shopping

You'll find shops selling French designer labels as well as prêt-à-porter outlets along Rue de Sébastopol, Rue de l'Alma and Rue Jean Jaurès. There are also duty-free shops in this area.

Galerie Commercial Port Plaisance (Map p154) and **Galerie Noumea Centre** (Map p152) are pleasant malls; tiny **Palm Beach shopping mall** (Map p154) has loads of boutiques and cafes.

Terre d'Origine   CLOTHING
(Map p152; 48 Rue Anatole France) Sells local brands.

Librairie Montaigne   BOOKS
(Map p152; 23 Rue de Sébastopol) Has a selection of books and travel guides in English.

Librairie Calédo Livres   BOOKS
(Map p152; 21 Rue Jean Jaurès) Specialises in books on New Caledonia and the Pacific.

❶ Information

Internet Access
Cyber Espace (Map p152; Rue Duquesne; per 30min 250 CFP)

Maps
Bookshops and major supermarkets sell IGN maps with scales ranging from 1:50,000 to 1:500,000. The Office du Tourisme (p159) has excellent free maps of Noumea, New Caledonia and individual maps of the main islands.

Medical Services
Pharmacies, identified by a green cross, are dotted all over Noumea. On Saturday afternoons and Sundays, only one emergency pharmacy is open, according to a rotating schedule.

Decompression Chamber (Map p152; ☎26 45 26) A Comex 1800 decompression chamber, next to the hospital, is available 24/7, accessible by land, sea or air.

Hôpital Gaston Bourret (Map p152; ☎25 66 66, emergencies 256 767; 7 Rue Paul Doumer) Noumea's main hospital.

Money
ATMs are outside most banks, and they accept most major credit cards. There are several banks on Av de la Victoire/Henry Lafleur (aka Bankers Rd).

Banque BNP Paribas (Map p154; ☎26 21 03; 111 Promenade Roger Laroque) At the Anse Vata shops.

Banque Calédonienne d'Investissement (BCI; Map p152; ☎24 20 60; 20 Rue Anatole France)

Banque Société Générale (Map p152; ☎25 63 00; 44 Rue de l'Alma & 56 Av de la Victoire/Henry Lafleur) Western Union representative.

Post
Main post office (Map p152; 7 Rue Eugène Porcheron) The main office of the Office des Postes et Télécommunications (OPT) has a poste restante and fax service, and there's an ATM outside the building. There's also a post office on Route de Anse Vata, on the way to the beach. Buy SIM cards here.

Tourist Information
First, pick up the free *Weekly* from airports, tourist sites, hotels, Office du Tourisme etc. It is spot on, with everything to do that week including the theme for Thursday's festivities. Also get the monthly entertainment guide *NC Pocket* (www.sortir.nc) for the month's festivals, exhibitions, concerts and Jeudis du Centre Ville themes.

Next collect a fantastic range of information, plus maps, brochures, booklets and DVDs for the entire country from the following offices:

Office du Tourisme (Map p152; 28 75 80, free call 057 580; www.office-tourisme.nc; Place des Cocotiers; ⊙8am-5.30pm Mon-Fri, 9am-noon Sat) The very friendly staff offer practical information in English or French, make bookings for you, and have walls layered with pamphlets about every activity and service.

Office du Tourisme, Anse Vata (Map p154; ⊘27 73 59; 113 Promenade Roger Laroque; ⊙9am-5pm) It's a little smaller than the office in the city centre, but the service is just as good.

Travel Agencies

Companies that organise transport, tours and accommodation within New Caledonia:

Air Calédonie (Map p152; ⊘25 21 77; www.air-caledonie.nc; 39 Rue de Verdun)

Alpha International (Map p154; ⊘27 24 20; www.alpha-tourisme.com; 143 Rte de l'Anse Vata)

Arc en Ciel Voyages (Map p152; ⊘27 19 80; www.arcenciel.nc; 59 Av du Maréchal Foch)

ⓘ Getting There & Away

Air

The domestic airport at Magenta is 4km to the east of the city centre.

Air Calédonie (Map p152; ⊘25 21 77; www.air-caledonie.nc; 39 Rue de Verdun; ⊙8am-4pm Mon-Fri, to 3pm Sat) is the domestic airline, with flights to northern Grande Terre, Île des Pins and the Loyalty Islands. It also has a **ticket office** (⊘25 03 82) at the domestic airport in Magenta.

Boat

The friendly and efficient **Capitainerie** (Harbour Master's Office; Map p152; ⊘27 71 97; www.sodemo.nc) is at Port Moselle's southern end. Noumea is connected to the Loyalty Islands and Île des Pins by the fast *Betico* ferry and the *Havannah*, a slower cargo boat (see p194).

ⓘ Getting Around

To/From the Airport

Tontouta International Airport is 45km northwest of Noumea. Public buses operated by **Carsud** (⊘25 16 15; 400 CFP) run there from the corner of Rues Georges Clémenceau and Paul Doumer (Line C). Several private companies, including **Philo Tours** (⊘28 99 57; philo@canl.nc) and Arc en Ciel Voyages (p159), run airport transfers (one-way 3000 CFP). **Taxis** (⊘28 35 12) into Noumea cost 11,000 CFP (shared).

Magenta domestic airport is serviced by Blueline Karuia buses (210 CFP) and a taxi to the city or beaches costs around 1700 CFP (shared).

Bus

Red-and-white buses (210 CFP) operate around the city from 6am to 7pm. The ticket office is at Place des Cocotiers (tickets are 190 CFP there, 210 CFP when purchased on the bus). The routes are colour coded.

Bleue (Blue) Tjibaou Cultural Centre–Magenta–city centre

Jaune (Yellow) Faubourg Blanchot–city centre–Gare de Montravel

Orange (Orange) Val Plaisance–Anse Vata–city centre

Verte (Green) Kuendu–city centre–Baie de L'Orphelinat–Baie des Citrons–Anse Vata

Violette (Purple) Magenta–Vallée des Colons–city centre

The hop-on, hop-off **Noumea Explorer** (Map p154; ⊘27 19 80; day pass adult/child 1500/750 CFP; ⊙8.30am-5pm Tue-Sun) does four circuits per day running from Anse Vata into the city via Baie des Citrons and then on to the Maritime Museum in Nouville, the Parc Zoologique et Forestier and the Tjibaou Cultural Centre before returning to Anse Vata.

Car & Scooter

The Office du Tourisme has a comprehensive list of car- and scooter-hire companies; also see p194 for some suggestions. Car rental costs from 3500 CFP per day, including free 150km per day – go for unlimited if you plan to tour the north or south.

Taxi

Noumea's taxis are operated by **Radio Taxis de Noumea** (⊘28 35 12). They can be hard to find on the street, so call or head to the **main taxi rank** (Map p152) which is on Rue d'Austerlitz, adjacent to the Galerie Noumea Centre. There's also one near the aquarium.

The Far South

The far south feels like a remote wilderness. The vast, empty region is characterised by its hardy scrub vegetation and red soil, and offers a wide range of activities including hiking, kayaking, abseiling and mountain biking. If you are looking for a bit of action and adventure, head to the far south. If you're looking for a peaceful, isolated spot by a river, head to the far south. The presence of a massive nickel-cobalt mine has resulted in sediments and toxic metals being discharged into the lagoon offshore, almost alongside the south's specially protected Merlet Marine Reserve.

Southern Grande Terre

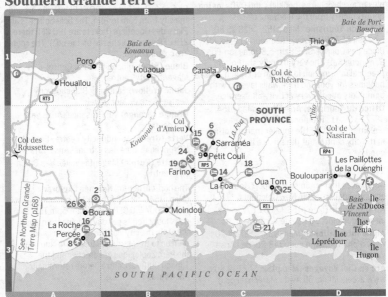

Southern Grande Terre

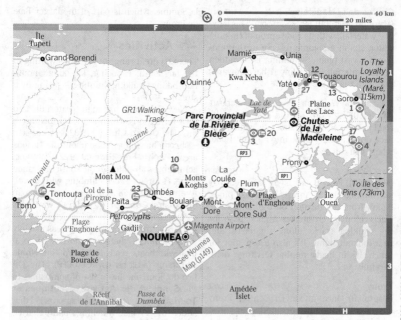

Sights

Monts Koghis   MOUNTAIN
(Map p160) Monts Koghis are clad in rainforest and rich native flora, and they have several walking trails; the **Direction des Ressources Naturelles** (Map p152; ✏24 32 60; env@province-sud.nc; 19 Av du Maréchal Foch) publishes a free walking map. Or take a tree-top trail on swinging bridges and rope walks with **Koghi Parc Aventure** (Map p160; ✏82 14 85; talon@mls.nc; trail 2500 CFP; ⊙10am-4pm Sat & Sun, by reservation Mon-Fri), behind the *auberge* (p163). Fun. The turn-off to these mountains is on the RT1, 14km north of central Noumea.

**Parc Provincial de la
Rivière Bleue**   WILDLIFE RESERVE
(Map p160; ✏43 61 24; adult/student 400/200 CFP; ⊙7am-5pm Tue-Sun, entry closes 2pm) Spacious protected Blue River Park is a reserve for many bird species, including the *cagou*. The landscape is a mixture of the far south's typical scrub vegetation and dense rainforest, and includes gigantic kaori trees, at least 1000 years old with trunks up to 2.7m across. Take the RP3 from La Coulée to get to the western end of the hydroelectric dam, **Lac de Yaté**, where you enter lovely Parc Provincial de la Rivière Bleue.

There is a **visitor information centre** by the entrance gate which has good displays in English and French on the park's flora and fauna. At the entrance you will also find free maps that outline the park's many walks. A bus departs almost hourly (7.30am to o3.15pm, 400 CFP) from Port Perignon to Vieux Refuge.

One of the park's famous features is a drowned kaori forest, the trunks reaching, ghostlike, out of the clear blue water. Go on a moonlit paddle to become part of it.

To the west and northwest of the park are the Rivière Blanche and Rivière Bleue, Lac de Yaté's main tributaries. You can drive along the banks of Rivière Blanche to the end of the road, walk or bike along the Rivière Bleue side, or kayak up the river.

Site de Netcha   LOOKOUT
(Map p160; day entry adult 400 CFP) Here, there are wooden diving platforms over the river and shelters and tables overlooking the water where you can picnic. Best of all, there's a kid's playground and you can rent canoes. To get here from the RP3, take the sign-posted road turning towards the eastern end of the Lac de Yaté.

NEW CALEDONIA THE FAR SOUTH

Chutes de la Madeleine   WATERFALL
(Map p160; adult 400 CFP; ⊗8am-5pm) This lady-like waterfall, with its wide apron of tinkling water, sits in a botanic reserve in the middle of a vast plain. Swimming is forbidden at the waterfall, but allowed back towards the main road.

Cascade de Wadiana   WATERFALL
(Map p160) At Goro on the east coast the road passes beside Wadiana falls, which cascade down a rocky slope into a natural pool where you can swim.

Port Boisé   BEACH
(Map p160) Port Boisé is an isolated bay surrounded by a forest of Cook pines, 6.5km from the turn-off on the main road. The ecolodge here makes a good base for the walking tracks along the coast and to a lookout point. It's also a top spot for lunch. It's in heavy mining territory; drive carefully.

Prony   VILLAGE
(Map p160) Once a convict centre, Prony sits in a lush hollow surrounded by forest beside Baie de Prony. No cars are allowed, but it's only a few minutes' walk from the car park. A stream runs through the village of corrugated-iron cottages and overgrown stone ruins. A plaque tells about Capitaine Sebert landing here in 1887. He found rose-wood – wanted in Europe for walking sticks, pipes and clogs – ebony, koup and kaori. Across the stream a banyan has sculpted its roots to the edge of the cliff. Look for the little purple mushrooms and brilliant orange fungi. There's a 14km walk from here; expect it to take four to five hours.

Baie de Prony is a good place for yachts to hide from the Westerlies. Whale-watching trips leave from here between July and September; book through La Maison Du Lagon (see p151). The GR1 walking track also starts about 500m south of the village at Baie de la Somme, which is part of the larger Baie de Prony.

Activities

There's a great range of activities waiting in the far south: canoeing, kayaking, mountain biking, walking, hunting – sitting by a stream.

New Caledonia has many waterfalls and rock formations which are ideal for abseiling. The **Gecko Club** (☑78 32 58; www.gecko-club.com) has information about the various areas. **Pacific Free Ride** (☑79 22 02; www.pfr.nc) arranges abseiling in the south of Grande Terre. Go tree or rock climbing with **Escal' Aventure** (☑74 78 37; www.escalaventure.com) or **Loisirs Concept** (☑83 90 12; www.loisirsconcept.com).

During the whale-watching season (July to September), there are dozens of local men with boats, ready to take you out **whale watching** (adult per day 8500 CFP). The Office du Tourisme has a list of companies in the **Syndicat des Activités Nautiques et Touristiques** (www.maisondulagon.nc) that adhere to its Whale-Watching Quality charter.

Aventure Pulsion   KAYAKING
(Map p149; ☑26 27 48; www.aventure-pulsion.nc; kayaks half/full day 3000/6000 CFP) Rent your kayak in Noumea (carried on your own car), or take a guided sea-kayak tour to a hot spring, a moonlit paddle over the drowned forest, or a river or lake (5000 CFP, see the website for dates).

Sud Loisirs   BICYCLE RENTAL
(Map p160; ☑77 81 43; www.sudloisirs.nc) Hire a mountain bike (2800 CFP) on weekends, in Parc Provincial de la Rivière Bleue. Ask the ranger at the park entrance for directions to the kiosk.

Pacific Free Ride   ADVENTURE SPORTS
(☑79 22 02; www.pfr.nc; per person from 6000 CFP) Go abseiling down the falls at Yaté or kayak in Baie de Prony and Baie des Pirogues.

Terra Incognita   KAYAKING
(Map p160; ☑78 94 46) Kayak rental at Parc Provincial de la Rivière Bleue (5500 CFP). Full-moon kayaking (4200 CFP); park nature tour by foot, bike, kayak and 4WD (11,000 CFP).

GR1 Walking Track   HIKING
(Map p160; Grande Randonnée 1; www.trekking-gr-sud-nc.com) The GR1 is a five-day (123.4km) walk (Great Walk) between Prony through

---

THE CAGOU

The *cagou (Rhynochetos jubatus)* is a much-loved New Caledonian bird and an unofficial national symbol. It is about 50cm tall with soft grey plumage and crest, red eyes and an orange beak. Its call sounds like a dog barking; ironically, dogs are its main predator as the *cagou* cannot fly. It mates for life and females have one chick a year.

SLEEP IN A TREE

Climbers Alan Waterneaux and Cedrick Beckers run Loisirs Concept/Escal' Aventure, which operates a variety of sports activities and offers unusual tree-tent accommodation.

What gave you the idea to put tents in trees for accommodation? I've been living in New Caledonia for 10 years, and Cedrick for five years, so we have a good knowledge of the country. We've been climbing for a long time. We chose to organise our concept in this location [close to La Rivière Bleue] because the trees in the south allow this kind of activity, and this place was ready to host campers with toilets, showers and *fares*.

Where's the best place in New Caledonia to get close to nature? The south and the east coast are our favourite places to stay in nature. The relaxing places in New Caledonia are the islands, but they're full of people by the weekends, so the south is the best option close to Noumea!

Where do you eat and drink when you're in Noumea? Our favourite restaurant in Noumea is Zanzibar (p156), and our favourite bar is Le Bout du Monde (p156). But we are not so often in Noumea to be honest. When we're not climbing trees we spend our time on other activities like kayaking, mountain biking and trekking.

Parc Provincial de la Rivière Bleue and on northwest to Dumbéa. It's possible to continue north to La Foa. Trek from the sea through plains, forests, hills and streams, along mule tracks and into pond or marsh. The air might be moist, acrid or crisply alpine; the views are always magnificent. Bunk down in a hut along the way; download the route and hut details from the website. Drop-offs or pick-ups need to be arranged either through the office at Site de Netcha (p161) or Aventure Pulsion has a taxi service to and from the different legs of the walk (around 15,000 CFP for up to eight people).

Tours

The following tours of the far south are based on a minimum of two adults.

Aventure Pulsion   4WD TOUR
(Map p149; ☑26 27 48; www.aventure-pulsion. nc; 4WD per adult per day 18,000 CFP) A grand adventure in a 4WD, visiting waterfalls, tribal villages, bays and mountain tops. Lunch is a three-course feast and you'll learn heaps from your driver/guide. Tours leave at 8am. Other tours, including half-day kayak tours, cost from 8200 CFP.

Caledonia Tours   BUS TOUR
(☑25 94 24; caledoniatours@lagoon.nc; adult/ child 11,500/7500 CFP) Specialises in day tours through the Blue River Park. Swim, walk through rainforest, bird watch and listen to a rich commentary about geology, botany,

wildlife and history. Lunch is a BBQ by the river. Tours leave at 8.15am.

Sleeping

Accommodation places serve meals to non-guests but you must book in advance.

Auberge du Mont Koghi   BUNGALOW $$
(Map p160; ☑41 29 29; koghi land@offratel.nc; Dumbéa; chalets/half board 8500/17,500 CFP) Overlooking Noumea and its bays, 476m above sea level, the *auberge* has chalets and more remote huts about a 10-minute walk into the forest. The restaurant is open for lunch and dinner. It has a fireplace, warm timber interior, and specialises in melted-cheese *raclette* (4500 CFP).

TOP CHOICE Loisirs Concept   CAMPGROUND $$$
(Map p160; ☑89 50 88; Les Bois du Sud; entrance 400 CFP, camping/incl tent 500/10,000 CFP) Camp here in this peaceful, wooded spot, or better still, reserve a tent hanging from a tree (☑83 90 13; escalaventure@gmail.com) Prices vary depending on whether you can get down from the tent yourself (10,000 CFP); or if you prefer stay higher (2m to 12m up), this involves a professional tree climber teaching you how to get up (and down) from your tent (18,000 CFP). Crazy stuff.

Site de Netcha Camping Site CAMPGROUND $
(Map p160; ☑46 98 00; camping 1000 CFP) Cute little roofed campsites are set by the river. Camp fires, tables and benches sit between the bushes, the toilet is swish and there's a

shower and basin. There's no electricity and you must take drinking water.

Kanua Tera Ecolodge
BUNGALOW $$$

(Map p160; ☑46 90 00; www.tera.nc; r with breakfast 20,400 CFP; ☎) Port Boisé seems so isolated, on the edge of a magical forest of Cook pines. Then you come down a narrow road into a lovely garden with nestled bungalows and a restaurant that meets the calm bay. The beach is shallow but you can snorkel on the edge of the fringing reef. Not great value.

Gîte Iya
BUNGALOW $

(Map p160; ☑46 90 80; camping 1500 CFP, bungalows 5000 CFP) The rustic but comfortable bungalows are in a coconut grove beside a small private beach. Meals are from 2100 CFP (closed for dinner on Sunday), or 4600 CFP for lobster. You can snorkel along the fringing reef not far from the beach. There's a signpost to the gîte, just south of Wao.

Gîte St Gabriel
BUNGALOW $$

(Map p160; ☑46 42 77; camping per person 1000 CFP, bungalows half board 15,000 CFP) The turn-off to St Gabriel is signposted about 3km south of Touaourou. It's a peaceful spot and you can go for long walks along the beach. There are five bungalows. Meals are good; expect seafood platters, *bougna* and other local dishes (set menu from 2860 CFP, order in advance) in the open-air restaurant.

ⓘ Information

A small **visitor information centre** (☺8am-12.30pm, 1.30-5pm Mon-Fri, 8am-12.30pm Sat) at Yaté (next to the market) has information on accommodation and activities, including walking-track brochures.

ⓘ Getting There & Around

To get to the far south, head east out of Noumea towards Mont-Dore. The easiest route is to follow the Voie Express out of Noumea to the RP1. The road forks when it reaches the mountain at La Coulée: take either the RP3 across to Yaté or continue along the RP1 south to Prony and Port Boisé, then the two routes eventually meet at the Chutes de la Madeleine. Ask about road conditions before you start as they can be pretty bad due to traffic from the nickel processing plant.

You'll need to hire a car to explore the far south; see p194 for car-rental agents in Noumea. It's about a 1½-hour drive to Yaté from Noumea. Buses to Yaté (600 CFP, two hours) leave from Noumea's Gare Routière at 11.30am Monday to Saturday but don't connect with a return

service. Tours which include a commentary plus lunch are always a good option (see p163). There are newly carved bike paths in the area; pick up a brochure at the information centre or see www.province-sud.nc for details.

Boulouparis

Not far from the bustling cosmopolitan capital, central Grande Terre offers enriching cultural experiences, coastal scenery and mountain treks.

Just north of Tontouta airport is Boulouparis, a west-coast settlement with a *gendarmerie* (police station), pharmacy, post office, bank, supermarket and little cinema that screens the latest films in French on Wednesday and weekend evenings.

A turn-off to Bouraké beach takes you to the departure point for trips to Îlot Ténia, a beautiful sandy islet surrounded by clear waters near the barrier reef. The islet is a popular surfing, diving and snorkelling spot.

Bouts-d'Brousse (Map p160; ☑76 42 38; www.ilot-tenia.com; to island return 5500 CFP) organises trips to the island which include dolphin watching; great fun, especially for children. Take your own picnic lunch. Trips depart at 8am, 9am or 10am. **Scuba diving** (☑77 40 40; intro dive 7000 CFP) includes exploring a magnificent coral massif that rises from the reef face.

La Foa & Around

On Grande Terre's west central coast you can stay in a Kanak *tribu* (clan community) or a Caldoche farm and explore the countryside by foot or on horseback. The west-coast settlement of La Foa (Map p160) is a neat little town 1½ hours from Noumea.

The friendly and efficient staff at **La Foa Tourisme** (☑41 6911; www.lafoatourisme.asso.nc; ☺8.15am-5pm Mon-Sat, 8.15am-11am Sun), the visitors information centre, can advise on accommodation and activities in La Foa, Farino and Sarraméa. A major event on New Caledonia's social calendar is the June/July film festival where international films, screened in their own language, are shown at La Foa's **Cinéma Jean-Pierre Jeunet** (☑41 69 11). Each year, the festival is presided over by a famous person from the film industry.

The **sculpture garden** (☺8am-8pm Sep-Apr, to 6pm May-Aug) behind La Foa Tourisme features wonderful sculptures by art-

ists from throughout New Caledonia. The garden is a pleasant place for a picnic, with a children's playground and public toilets.

Sarraméa, 15 minutes' drive north of La Foa, sits in a lush valley surrounded by mountains. At the end of the road a path continues through a farm gate to **Trou Feuillet**, also known as *la cuve*, a refreshing rock pool in a mountain stream. On the main road, just past the Sarraméa turn-off, is **tribu de Petit Couli**, where a beautiful old *grande case* stands at the end of a row of tall araucaria pines.

Farino is a mountain village in primary tropical forest, known for its produce and craft markets held every second Sunday of the month. The real crowd-puller is its Vers de Bancoule market day in September, which culminates in a contest to see who can eat the most fat, wriggling white grubs. Ask your host about horse riding adventures.

🏃 Activities

Sarraméa Randonnées   HORSE RIDING
(Map p160; ☎76 60 45; www.sarramearandonnees. com; ☺8am-5pm) A ride starts at 2800 CFP for an hour, or take a half-day tour for 11,000 CFP. If horses sound like too much work, hire a quad bike (one hour 7700 CFP) or hike a clearly marked path (entry 500 CFP per person).

🛏 Sleeping & Eating

Les Bancouliers de Farino   LODGE $$
(Map p160; ☎41 20 41; www.bancouliers.blogspot. com; Farino; camping per tent 1500 CFP, half board per person 6500 CFP) A lovely timber bungalow with a mezzanine looks out over a river and sleeps six, or stay in one of the brightly decorated rooms that are attached to the house. It's friendly, rustic and you'll love the homemade (and often home-grown) food.

Refuge de Farino   BUNGALOW $$
(Map p160; ☎44 37 61; refuge.farino@lagoon.nc; camping 1400 CFP, bungalows 8100 CFP; ☎) On a hillside in Farino's forest, these timber bungalows have a kitchenette and forest views from their decks. There are barbecues, a hot tub (2100 CFP to use) and a playground. Breakfast is 850 CFP. BYO food, order meals 24 hours before, or eat at Chez Mamie's, 1km back down the road.

Ouano Surf Camp   BUNGALOW $$
(Map p160; ☎46 90 90; www.ouanosurf.com; camping 1050 CFP, safari tent/bungalows 6500/8000 CFP; ☎☒) It's not exactly cheap to go out

for a surf, but everything's here, including a laundry, modern but basic bungalows (or cool safari tents) and good meals. It's a 20-minute boat ride (7000 CFP) out to surf the reef breaks.

La Petite Ferme   BUNGALOW $
(Map p160; ☎44 34 05; lafoatourisme@canl.nc; full board for 2 people 16,200 CFP) This prefab bungalow with bunks makes a base to go hunting; your host, Jean Louis, runs 4WD night spins to see the deer. Meals (included in the rates) are served in the garden, but book 48 hours ahead (six days ahead if you're a large group wanting *cassoulet*).

Tontoutel Hotel   HOTEL $$
(Map p160; ☎35 11 11; ecotel@canl.nc; s/d/f 7300/9000/13,600 CFP; ☎☒) It's five minutes from Tontouta International Airport, so it's perfect if you're catching an early morning flight. Rooms are large and comfortable with timber ceilings and there's a pleasant restaurant.

Hôtel Banu   BUNGALOW $$
(Map p160; ☎44 31 19; s/d/f 4400/5200/7600 CFP, bungalows s/d 6400/7200 CFP; ☒☎☒) This hotel is in the middle of town and looks quaint, but the bungalows behind the hotel are just right. The restaurant is open for all meals except Sunday dinner, and the cheerful staff serve the best *plat du jour* (1600 CFP) and other delicious meals (1300 CFP to 6500 CFP) using local produce. Or have a gourmet sandwich on the porch (550 CFP) then try counting the 5000 caps on the bar's ceiling.

Hotel Evasion   HOTEL $$
(Map p160; ☎44 55 77; www.hotel-evasion.com; r/ bungalows incl breakfast 9200/17,600 CFP; ☒@☒) Smart bungalows with little verandahs overlook a stream at the end of the road in Sarraméa. The cheaper motel-style rooms are up a hill behind the hotel, but it's all heading for renovation so this will change. Meals (2500 CFP to 4500 CFP) are terrific.

Chez Mamie   RESTAURANT $$$
(Map p160; ☎43 23 14; meals 2500-3500 CFP) Mamie's *table d'hôte* is very popular. Enjoy filling Caldoche cuisine including venison, wild pig, fish and duck dishes. It's 3km from the Farino *mairie* (town hall).

Aux Délices des Jumelles   RESTAURANT $$$
(Map p160; ☎43 46 65; set menus from 3000 CFP) In a gorgeous garden near the chapel in Sarraméa, Bernadette serves four courses of

Kanak cuisine that delight her guests. Try her special *mamarènü* (coffee with coconut jam). Book 24 hours ahead and dinner is available by arrangement (BYO drinks).

Chez Marie-Georgette   RESTAURANT $$$
(Map p160; ☎44 38 17; set menu 3000-3500 CFP) This *table d'hôte* adjacent to the *tribu* de Oua Tom serves Kanak cuisine including *bougna,* and chicken or prawn dishes. Book 48 hours in advance and take your tent so you can stay the night (camping 1000 CFP).

❶ Getting There & Around

Several buses a day from Noumea stop in the west-coast towns (see p194).

Bourail & Around

With a rural atmosphere and strong Cal-doche community, Bourail is the next biggest town on Grande Terre after Noumea. The main road crosses the Néra River bridge at the southern end of town, and the turn-off to La Roche Percée, New Caledonia's only surf beach, and Poé beach is immediately after the bridge.

An old stone building 500m south of the centre houses the **Musée de Bourail** (adult/student 250/100 CFP; ☺9am-noon & 1-5pm Mon-Sat). Its displays include objects relating to the presence of US and NZ troops in Bourail during WWII and a guillotine complete with the basket where the decapitated head was placed. The guillotine was brought to New Caledonia in 1867. Behind the museum there's a *case.*

Bourail holds a hugely popular **country fair** (admission 500 CFP) over the weekend closest to 15 August: there are farm animals on display; produce, arts and crafts for sale; children's rides; food stalls; and, the high-light, a rodeo. Campsites are available, and 25,000 people are expected. With contests, races and demonstrations, it is one grand weekend.

About 9.5km east of Bourail is the well-tended **New Zealand War Cemetery** (Map p160), where over 200 NZ soldiers killed in the Pacific during WWII are buried. NZ troops set up a hospital in the area dur-ing the war, and many locals received free medical care there. A ceremony is held at the cemetery on the Saturday closest to Anzac Day (25 April) and local children place a flower on each grave.

La Roche Percée has two famous rock formations: **La Roche Percée** (pierced rock) and **Le Bonhomme,** shaped like a tubby man. A walking track begins at the base of the cliff near the rocks and follows the coast for 4km past Baie des Tortues (Turtle Bay) to Baie des Amoureux (Lover's Bay).

There's a panoramic viewing point above Le Bonhomme where you can often spot turtles in the Baie des Tortues below. With its bent araucarias and wide beach, Baie des Tortues is a beautiful spot but beware of the strong currents. To get there, follow the main road round to the right instead of turning left to La Roche Percée. As you ascend the hill, turn onto the dirt road to the left.

🏃 Activities

The surf at La Roche Percée is caused by a break in the fringing reef, so you don't have to go out to the reef to catch a wave. The best spot is at the mouth of the Néra river. When you've conquered the shore breaks, Nëkwéta offers trips to the barrier reef to surf (four hours for 5300 CFP), snorkel (half-day 5500 CFP) or explore Île Vert (3100 CFP).

Plage de Poé is a beautiful, long white-sand beach 9km north of La Roche Percée. It's all happening on the beach at Poé.

Bourail Sub Loisirs   DIVING
(☎44 20 65, 78 20 65; butterfly.diving@lagoon.nc; 2-dive package 12,000 CFP) The dive club, also at the Néra river mouth, will take you to see magnificent corals along vertical drops and canyons with abundant sharks, rays and Napoleon fish. Surfing trips to the barrier reef and boat trips (from 3000 CFP) can be arranged.

Glass-Bottom Boat Tours   BOAT TOUR
(☎41 28 78; www.campingdepoe.com; 1800 CFP) Head out on a glass-bottom boat tour with the folk from Le Camping de Poé.

Poé Kite School   KITE SURFING
(☎77 60 59; www.poekiteschool.com; 3½hr 13,000 CFP) Learn how to kite surf at this picturesque spot.

Poé Plaisirs   WATER SPORTS
(☎75 00 01; www.mdplaisirs.com) Rents out kayaks (1200 CFP per hour), windsurfers (beginners/intermediate 4800/6500 CFP per hour) and funboards (1200 CFP per hour). Ask about the MD Plaisirs discount card.

Sleeping & Eating

TOP CHOICE **Nëkwéta** BUNGALOW $$
(Map p160; 43 23 26, 78 40 26; www.nekweta.
com; d 10,150 CFP) Choose from an attractive
case (bungalow) or one of the rooms in a
new two-storey building being built from
scratch by owner Manu. It's at La Roche
Percée, one block back from the beach.

Chez Catherine et Pascal GUESTHOUSE $$
(Map p160; 43 98 06, 79 57 82; s/d 6100/6500
CFP) Another sweet tropical garden in La Roche Percée with attractive prefab bungalows,
private space and charming hosts who'll cook
for you if you ask (breakfast 1000 CFP, three-
course dinner with wine 4100 CFP).

Hôtel La Néra MOTEL $$
(Map p160; 44 16 44; s/d 7150/8150 CFP;
❊❞❉) This Bavarian-style hotel with a river
view is by the Néra River bridge. Dishes in-
cluding deer curry cost between 1900 CFP
and 2300 CFP at the hotel's cosy restaurant
(breakfast is 800 CFP). Head out on a night
tour of the farm (1000 CFP).

Gîte du Cap BUNGALOW $$
(Map p168; 46 90 09, 76 66 17; gitesducap@
tropik.nc; maisonnettes/chalets incl breakfast
10,900/6900 CFP) A further 24km up the RT1
from Bourail, turn at the sign on col du Cap
and it's 8km towards the sea to Gîte du Cap.
The well-equipped maisonnettes sleep five –
the chalets three – on this 70-hectare farm.
Germaine cooks traditional meals (3800
CFP) with local produce while Yann takes
you around·the farm, or to fish, canoe and
hike.

Snack Hibiscus CAFE $$
(Map p160; dishes 1400 CFP, snacks 450-600 CFP;
❉7am-6pm) It's orange, busy and serves good
paninis, toasted sandwiches and burgers, or
copious fish or chicken dishes.

Northwest Coast

Much of the northwest coast and its rolling
plains are taken up by cattle ranches. The
coast is not great for swimming, as it has
mangrove swamps and shallow bays, so it
makes more sense to head inland for horse
trekking or staying on a Caldoche farm or in
a Kanak homestay.

KONÉ & AROUND

Koné, the Northern Province capital, has a
post office, *gendarmerie,* clinic, pharmacy,
supermarkets and banks with ATMs. It
is noted for its excellent horse-trekking
opportunities.

North of Koné, in Voh, there's a mangrove
swamp which has developed some un-
usual natural designs. The most intriguing
is a perfect heart shape, **La Cœur de Voh**
(Map p168), which is on the cover of *Earth
from Above,* the book of aerial photography
by famous photographer Yann Arthus-
Bertrand.

There's a track up to a viewing point on
a mountain but the heart is best seen from
the air. **Alain Nouard** (47 25 93; 30min
flight 6000 CFP) takes microlight flights on
weekends. Book well in advance.

For guided horse treks into the foothills
or to the summits of the central mountain
range contact **Eric Tikarso** (47 23 68, 79 36
80; per 2/4hr 2000/3000 CFP).

Sleeping & Eating

Paddock de La Boutana HOMESTAY $$
(Map p168; 47 16 17; www.paddockboutana.com;
adult/child half board 8500/4500 CFP) Marie-
Claude is your host at this peaceful farmstay

FROM 12 TO 120,000

You never know, do you? Take deer: Bambi, cute as. Back in 1862, 12 rusa deer were
introduced to New Caledonia when the then governor's wife brought them from the
Philippines, but today their numbers are estimated at over 100,000. The deer have
reproduced to such an extent that they pose a significant threat to local plant species
and forest ecosystems.

As a result, deer hunting has become an intrinsic part of local life and some
visitors also come to New Caledonia with this in mind. Venison, as well as trophies
(stuffed by a local taxidermist), can be taken overseas depending on the destination
country's quarantine laws, but requires an invoice to prove it's been obtained
through proper channels. A hunting licence is required to borrow a gun and
ration of ammunition.

Hôtel Banu (44 31 19) and **Hôtel La Nero** (44 16 44) can offer advice.

Northern Grande Terre

Northern Grande Terre

20km inland from Pouembout. The rates include breakfast and dinner, tours of the farm and deer-spotting trips. Go hiking, swim in the rivers and creeks.

Hôtel Koniambo
HOTEL **$$**

(Map p168; ☎47 39 40; www.grands-hotels.nc; r 13,800 CFP; ❄) Named after the mountain range behind it and recently rebuilt, this makes a very comfortable base to explore the surrounding 'stockman's country'. The restaurant's buffet features regional dishes, such as venison, and international cuisine.

Tumbala Café
CAFE **$$**

(Map p168; snacks 450-650 CFP, mains 1500-2400 CFP; ⏱6am-11pm Mon-Fri) It's all about music at the bright and popular Tumbala Café. It serves light snacks, fish and meat dishes like veal escalope and chicken with caramel, and there's a busy bar.

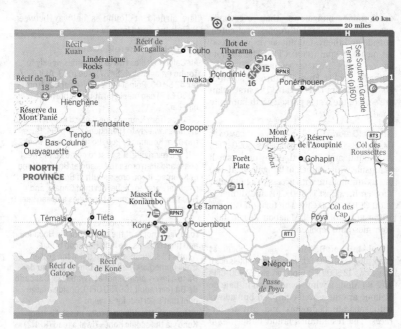

KOUMAC

Koumac, further north than Koné, is quite big. Like Koné, it has a post office, *gendarmerie,* clinic, pharmacy, supermarkets and banks with ATMs. **Koumac Tourisme** (☑42 78 42; www.koumac-tourisme.com; ⊘9am-noon & 1-4pm Mon-Fri, 9am-noon Sat), the information centre, is at the northern end of town opposite the post office. Elsa will give you lots of local advice.

Located near the roundabout, eye-catching **Église Ste Jeanne d'Arc** was constructed in 1950 out of a WWII aircraft hangar. Take a peek inside at its stained-glass windows and traditionally inspired wood carvings.

Head to Koumac's lovely marina, La Marina de Pandop, where the dive club, **Reve Bleu** (Map p168; ☑42 45 64, 97 83 12; www.revebleucaledonie.com), is geared up to provide a grand professional experience. It's a 15-minute boat ride to the reef with your PADI divemaster. Intro dives are 8000 CFP, double explorative dives 13,000 CFP.

Monitel Koumac (Map p168; ☑47 66 66; monitelkoumac@lagoon.nc; bungalows s/d 9100/10,500 CFP, chalets s/d 10,500/11,500 CFP; ☒) has timber and stone bungalows or Western-style units that are timber lined and well equipped. They look out on the pool with its inviting deck chairs. The restaurant meals (eat inside or out) are great (mussels 2300 CFP).

The Far North

The remote region north of Koumac is known as the far north. Up here, fishermen wade around the endless white with their lines and nets, thinking they're in heaven. The area is considered one of the world's top five for fly-fishing; the world record is from here. Richard Bertin of **New Caledonia Fishing Safaris** (Map p168; ☑78 62 00; www.fishinpeace.com) organises sportfishing tours to Poingam. Don't worry: it's catch, tag and release. You can also go big-game fishing in Richard's Boston Whaler, deer hunting (see p167) or birdwatching.

🛏 Sleeping & Eating

Stock up on supplies before heading to the Far North as there's not much available in the tiny town of Poum.

TOP CHOICE **Relais de Poingam**   BUNGALOW $$
(Map p168; ☑47 92 12; camping per person 1000 CFP, bungalows 10,000 CFP; ☒) On a long beach at the northern tip of Grande Terre are these

comfortable bungalows that everybody loves. The private bathrooms are cutely outside and the restaurant serves very good set-meals at 8pm (3300 CFP). The shallow lagoon is not great for swimming, but the saltwater pool is. From the turn-off south of Poum, it's 23km to Poingam. The first 10km are sealed; the rest is packed earth but quite good.

Gîte de Golone   BUNGALOW **$$**
(Map p168; ☑472 000; bungalows 6000 CFP) A tranquil and isolated place on a small peninsula with a bunch of bungalows. It also has a camping site with access to a hot water shower. Breakfast is 800 CFP, and dinner is 2200 CFP to 2500 CFP. The turn-off is about 400m north of Hôtel Malabou Beach. Take your mosquito repellent.

Hôtel Malabou Beach   HOTEL **$$**
(Map p168; ☑47 60 60; www.grands-hotels.nc; d bungalows 12,500 CFP, 6-person ste 22,900 CFP; ❖ ⑤ ⑧ ⑥) Along a white-sand beach in Baie de Néhoué are these well-equipped bungalows with separate bedrooms and private terraces. The restaurant's grand buffet (3900 CFP) specialises in seafood straight from the lagoon. There is no end of activities – kayaks, treks, tennis, minigolf. The hotel is signposted on the main road.

❶ Getting There & Around

Air Calédonie flies twice weekly from Noumea to **Koné** (☑agency 472 113) and **Koumac** (☑agency 475 390); see p193. There are daily buses from Noumea (see p194). The **gare routière** (bus station; Rue Roger Trouillot), 300m from the roundabout in Koumac, has schedules for buses going north to Poum and northeast to Ouegoa and Pouébo.

Northeast Coast

The stunning coastline here is edged by foothills covered in lush vegetation, gentle rivers, fascinating rock formations, waterfalls and deserted beaches. Visitors can experience traditional Kanak life in a *tribu* plus there are nature trails to suit all levels of fitness, from 20-minute walks to hikes lasting several days. Keen hikers can climb Mont Panié (1629m), New Caledonia's highest peak.

Poindimié and Hienghène are the two main towns on the northeast coast. Both have grocery stores, a post office, clinic, pharmacy, bank and ATM, and *gendarmerie*.

The airfield at Touho is halfway between Poindimié and Hienghène.

❶ Getting There & Around

Air Calédonie flies two to four times weekly to **Touho** (☑agency 428 787); see p193. **ALV** (☑/fax 42 58 00; Poindimié; car hire per day from 5000 CFP) can meet you at the airport with a hire car.

Buses from Noumea run daily to Poindimié and six times weekly to Hienghène; see p194. Buses run from Koumac to Pouébo four times a week.

If you're driving, it's best to come up the west coast and then cross the island at Bourail, Koné or Koumac. If you cross south of Bourail the road between Kouaoua, north of Canala, and Houaïlou winds through the mines and can seem very long.

Driving on the RT3 across from Bourail, the road veers north at the roundabout in Houaïlou, and then crosses the long Houaïlou bridge. Another 13.5km north, turn down the gravel track immediately after the bridge at **tribu de Bâ** to a lovely picnic spot at a waterfall, **Cascade de Bâ** (car/adult 100/50 CFP), beside a large pool that's perfect for a swim.

However, the drive not to be missed is from Koné via the scenic Koné–Tiwaka road (RPN2) that winds through the mountains over high river bridges and past forested slopes, to the Tiwaka river mouth, 14km north of Poindimié. Halfway through the mountains you can detour via **tribu de Bopope**, with its charming bark-and-thatch *cases* perched on the edge of steep slopes.

POINDIMIÉ

The largest town on the coast, Poindimié has a picturesque coastline and, stretching inland, the peaceful valleys of Ina, Napoémien and Amoa River, where you can admire the lush vegetation and magnificent treeferns of the natural bush or pretty *tribu* gardens. These valleys are delightful places for a walk or a scenic drive. Ina valley is at the southern end of town. To get to Napoémien, turn inland at the *mairie*. In Amoa valley, turn at the bridge just before the church at Tié Mission.

Poindimié overlooks Îlot de Tibarama, an islet just offshore. **Tiéti Diving** (Map p168; ☑42 42 05; www.tieti-diving.com; dives 7000 CFP) is run by a friendly instructor who also offers transfers to Îlot de Tibarama (per person full day 2000 CFP) – a great spot to relax, snorkel and swim.

🍴 Sleeping & Eating

Relais le Mo.Sa.Sa   CAMPGROUND **$$**
(Map p168; ☑42 48 66 www.mo-sa-sa.com; Tribu d'Ina, Poindimié; camping d 1200 CFP, bungalows

s/d 6300/7100 CFP; ☎) Five new tile-floored bungalows sit under coconut trees fronting a rocky beach, while campsites spread out to the north. Hire a canoe or snorkel gear or play a game of *pétanque*.

Tiéti Tera Beach Resort   RESORT $$$
(Map p168; ☑42 64 00; www.tera.nc; r/ste B&B 20,600/31,750 CFP; ✳☎✱) A little more 'motel' than you might expect for its prices, however it is spacious and features stacks of timber beams and carvings for a rich atmosphere. Plus you're an easy walk away from charming Poindimié. Dinner dishes like *confit de canard* cost from 2500 CFP to 2900 CFP. Or choose a three-course menu (lunch/dinner 3700/4300 CFP).

Snack Naautea   CAFE $$
(Map p168; dishes 1200-1700 CFP) Two large banyan trees watch over this friendly place where an excellent chef oversees the *paninis* and toasted sandwiches, then cooks tasty veal, fish or chicken dishes.

Chez Simone   RESTAURANT $$
(Map p168; ☑42 74 84; http://chezsimone.lagoon. nc; meals 2000 CFP) You may like to book in for the night (single/double 4500/7000 CFP) after your feast of home-cooked Kanak cuisine. Dishes are based around wild deer, pig or fish. The turn-off is 4km south of Poindimié and it's another 3.5km to Simone's in *tribu* de Nessapoé. Reserve 12 hours in advance.

HIENGHÈNE

This serene village with its fairy-tale buildings is tucked into the foothills on the shores of Baie de Hienghène, at the mouth of the Hienghène River. The area has fascinating rock formations, and it is also important historically as it was the home of Jean-Marie Tjibaou, New Caledonia's pro-independence leader. People speak of Tjibaou with great respect, and he is buried in Tiendanite, a *tribu* 20km up the Hienghène valley.

Hienghène's renowned **Poule Couveuse** (Brooding Hen) rock formation sits on one side of the entrance to Baie de Hienghène, facing the **sphinx** on the other. You can view these two rock formations from the signposted lookout, 2km south of the village. There's a better profile of the sphinx about 1.5km north of the village.

The **Lindéralique rocks** are towering black limestone rocks with jagged edges, which begin about 10km south of Hienghène.

The **visitor information centre** (☑42 43 57; hienghen-tourism@mls.nc; Hienghène; ⊗8am-noon & 1-5pm Mon-Fri, 8am-3pm Sat) looks over the Hienghène marina (which is also the bus terminal. Staff can book accommodation in *tribus*, help you contact **Association Dayu Biik** (☑42 87 77; dayubiik@lagoon.nc; ⊗8.30am-5.30pm Mon-Fri) for trekking in the area, and arrange traditional meals and dances in local *tables d'hôte*.

🏃 Activities

There are dozens of excellent local guides in Hienghène, waiting to take you on the hike of your life, through and over this stunning region of mountain, forest, river, waterfall, beach, lagoon and extraordinary rock formation.

At Lindéralique village, about 4km south of Hienghène, you can kayak beneath the overhanging rocks.

Centre Culturel
Goa Ma Bwarhat   CULTURAL CENTRE
(☑42 80 74; culturehienghene@mls.nc) Closed for restoration during research, but usually houses exhibitions, a museum and a sculptor's workshop.

Babou Côté Océan   DIVING
(Map p168; ☑42 83 59; www.babou-plongee. com) Go diving around unique cliff faces of gorgonia and sheltered coral massifs (intro/ double dives cost 8000/11,600 CFP), on island trips which include snorkelling (3800 CFP), or on a river walk (3500 CFP). It's based at Koulnoué Camping.

Nord Aventure   KAYAKING
(☑42 84 28; nord.aventure@canl.nc) Tour the Poule Couveuse by kayak.

🛏 Sleeping & Eating

In the Hienghène valley there are many *accueil en tribu* (per person around 3000 CFP), traditional homestays with Kanak families. Visitors usually take part in everyday activities and meals. Book through Hienghène's visitor information centre at least a day in advance.

TOP CHOICE **Koulnoué Camping**   CAMPGROUND $
(Map p168; ☑42 83 59; camping per person 400 CFP, tent hire 1000 CFP) Just past Koulnoué Village is this pretty campsite on its own tiny bay where you can swim and picnic for 100 CFP. Sleep beneath the towering rock formations. The Babou Côté Océan dive club is based here.

Koulnoué Village
BUNGALOW $

(Map p168; ✆42 81 66; bungalows 12,900 CFP; ❄🛜🏊) Feel young again at this ex–Club Med establishment that still has plenty of good vibes. The bungalows are well equipped and have private porches out to the beach. The traditional *case* is along the beach. Play tennis, canoe, go horse riding. Meals are buffet style (breakfast 1900 CFP, dinner 3900 CFP). The turn-off is 8.5km south of Hienghène.

Gîte Ka Waboana
BUNGALOW $$

(Map p168; ✆42 47 03; r/bungalows 5300/8400 CFP) These colourful bungalows with kitchenettes perch on a hill opposite the marina, with views of the bay. The on-site cafe is open daily (breakfast 1050 CFP).

NORTH OF HIENGHÈNE

This is the wildest and most stunning stretch of the northeast coast. It's covered in tropical vegetation, and waterfalls and streams rush down the mountains to join the sea.

A **punt** carries vehicles across the wide Ouaïème River, 17km northwest of Hienghène. It's free and runs 24 hours a day. The crossing is one of the highlights of the east coast.

The rugged coastal scenery changes to rolling hills, plains and mangrove swamps at **Pouébo**. Inside Pouébo's large Catholic church there's a marble **mausoleum** where the remains of Bishop Douarre, who set up New Caledonia's first Catholic mission, are interred. The first Europeans arrived in New Caledonia at Balade and Bishop Douarre arrived in 1843. The stained-glass windows in the small church here tell the story from the first Catholic mass. In 1853 France officially laid claim to New Caledonia at Balade, the same year in which Douarre died.

An altar beneath an enormous banyan at **Mahamat beach** commemorates that first Catholic mass on Christmas Day 1843. The turn-off to the altar is 1.5km north of the church.

🕴 Activities

The area north of Hienghène is an amazing drawcard for trekking enthusiasts and nature lovers. However, all activities require a guide and authorisation for you to enter tribal territories. Guides and permissions are arranged by **Association Dayu Biik** (✆42 87 77; dayubiik@lagoon.nc; ⏰8.30am-5.30pm Mon-Fri), including authorisation from the **Direction du Développement Economique et de L'Environnement** (DDEE; ✆42 72 52; Poin-

dimié). It takes one to two weeks for arrangements to be finalised, so get your requests in as early as possible.

Mont Panié includes about 5000 hectares of botanical reserve. Its peak is New Caledonia's highest and the climb to the top is a magical two-day hike (19,000 CFP, maximum four people) out of Tao, passing giant kaoris, mountain araucarias, magnificent coloured rocks, waterfalls and creeks. Other guided walks cost around 12,900 CFP for one day.

You can also go on a half-day adventure around the **Cascade de Tao** (3/12 people 4200/7350 CFP), which plummets down a mountainside 7km north of the Ouaïème River ferry. A path leads to the bottom of the falls starting at the cottage just after Tao bridge.

🛏 Sleeping & Eating

There are a couple of **campsites** (camping 1000 CFP) north of the Tao River ferry where you can simply turn up. Stock up on groceries before you go.

TOP CHOICE **Relais de Ouane Batch**
BUNGALOW $

(Map p168; ✆42 47 92, 96 70 72; ouanebatch@lagoon.nc; camping 1100 CFP, bungalows with/without bathroom 5000/3500 CFP) Run by a friendly family, located 16km north of the river ferry. The new bungalows with mosquito nets are terrific and the *table d'hôte* serves very good meals (2500 CFP); book 24 hours in advance (closed Monday and Wednesday afternoon). Activities include canoe hire (half/full day 600/1000 CFP).

LOYALTY ISLANDS

POP 17,000 / AREA 1980 SQ KM

Maré, Lifou and Ouvéa. Such fairy-tale names for fairy-tale islands, each with their own characteristics: Maré is known for its deep rock holes, rugged coastal scenery and serene beaches; Lifou for its breathtaking cliff-top views and small secret beaches; Ouvéa for its unending beach and tranquil lagoon stretching to the horizon. They're all sparsely populated with secluded beaches, hidden caves and deep holes. They all have large tracts of impenetrable bush, but their roads are so good that driving around is a dream. Loyalty Islands? Captain Cook named them that, perhaps because the people are so friendly.

The locals blend traditional and modern lifestyles with ease, offering tourists a

charming experience. You'll need to take cash (although each island has a bank with an ATM). You must book meals 24 hours in advance; seafood is a speciality and most places offer lobster or crab platters.

You'll find a shop with limited groceries in each village. Most places offer camping but only a couple have tents for hire.

ⓘ Getting There & Away
Air Calédonie flies at least twice a day between Noumea and each island (p193).

The *Betico* and *Havannah* sail from Noumea to the islands, and between the islands, once or twice a week; see p194.

ⓘ Getting Around
The islands have limited public transport so it's best to hire a car and have it waiting for you on arrival. Car-rental companies drop off vehicles at the airport, wharf or accommodation places for free.

Hitchhiking is common everywhere but it can take a while for a car to come along. As well as the usual precautions for hitching, watch out for drunk drivers.

Maré

POP 5400 / AREA 641 SQ KM

With its scenic coastline of stunning beaches and rugged coral cliffs and an interior that hides impressive sunken pools and a mysterious ancient rock edifice, it is small wonder that Maré's geographical features have inspired legends. The island was rocked by violence in 2011, though the situation was quickly calmed.

◎ Sights

TADINE & WESTERN MARÉ
The main road runs beside the coast for almost the entire length of western Maré. It's a picturesque drive, taking you past beaches, cliffs, *tribus* and forests.

Beaches   BEACH
The southwest coast has several gorgeous beaches where you can swim or snorkel during the day and watch the glorious sunsets in the evening. The small beach at Eni is the southernmost beach where you might spot **humpback whales** between July and September. Between Cengéité and Wabao is a fabulous beach beside a small enclosed lagoon whose water is an exquisite turquoise.

Keep going to the long white beach at Hôtel Nengone Village (p175) or continue to la plage de Pede, a sheltered beach protected by the headland at Cap Wabao. A path to the beach leads through a gate from the main road at the sharp bend where it joins the coast.

Le Bone de la Léproserie   CAVE
Inland from Medu there is a *trou bleu* known as Le Bone de la Léproserie; there was once a leper hospital nearby which explains the name. This enormous hole in the limestone rock, hidden by thick vegetation, drops vertically to a pool of still water. It's one of the largest drowned cavities in the world. Ask for permission to visit, and ask what condition the track is in after you turn at the signposted turn-off. The *trou bleu* is 1.5km down the track beside some solar panels.

Aquarium Naturelle   AQUARIUM
About 3km south of Tadine is a large Aquarium Naturelle, a rock pool sunk in the cliffs and linked to the sea by an underground channel. Watch for Napoleon fish, perroquettes, picods and sometimes turtles swimming in the translucent water (take bread so that they come quickly). It is signposted by a parking area beside the main road.

Trou de Bone   CAVE
About 3km off the La Roche–Tadine Rd, on the road to Thogone, is Trou de Bone, a deep rock cavity which drops to a lush tropical garden and a pool. It's on the right-hand side of the road as you're heading to Thogone, about 1.5km from the turn-off. It isn't signposted, so look out for a metal guardrail beside the road. Yell out to let off some steam and hear your echo.

LA ROCHE & EASTERN MARÉ
Paths lead through the forest to the coast in the northeast of Maré; you can enquire about them at the various *tribus*. Maré's south-eastern coastline is rugged and windswept.

Centre Culturel Yeiwene Yeiwene   MUSEUM, RUINS
(☎45 44 79; ⊙7.30-11.30am & 1-4pm Mon-Fri) There is a small exhibition of Kanak artefacts here, about 2km out of La Roche. Behind it, and more interesting because of their mysterious nature, are the stone ruins known as the **Hnaenedr wall**. This ancient rock fortification dates back to AD 250. The origins of the people who built the wall and its purpose are not entirely clear but legend

Maré

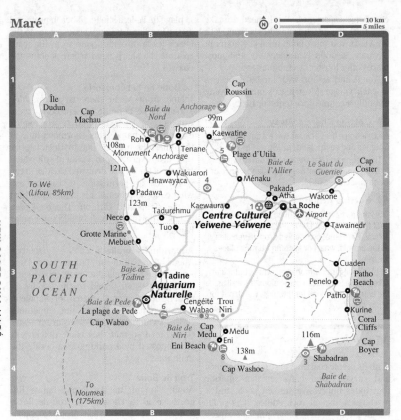

Maré

◉ Top Sights

◎ Sights

🛌 Sleeping

ℹ Transport

tells of two warring tribes who agreed to construct walls for protection.

La Roche   HILL

A huge limestone rock covered in vegetation near the coast gives the surrounding area of La Roche (the Rock) its name. The rock, known locally as Titi, rises above an attractive Catholic church with a red steeple. You can climb to the top of the rock with a local guide. Make enquiries in the *tribu*.

Le Saut du Guerrier   LOOKOUT

(Warrior's Leap) East of La Roche is this gap in the cliffs, 5m wide and 30m above the pounding surf. Legend tells of a warrior who escaped his enemies by leaping across the abyss. Try to imagine the jump as you look down at the rocks and waves below.

Shabadran   FOREST

An isolated, sheltered spot at the very south of Maré surrounded by cliffs and forest. The

curved sandy beach is cut off from the sea by a reef, where waves crash and send foaming water cascading over coral terraces into a small sparkling lagoon.

🏃 Activities

Follow the pleasant 6km **coastal walk** that links the beach at the northern end of Hôtel Nengone Village with that at Pede. It is mostly flat and shady as the path follows the shoreline through the trees. Near Cap Wabao, it veers inland and meanders through a forest beneath a small cliff. Turn left at the end of the cliff and follow the wide path straight ahead through a wooded paddock to Baie de Pede.

Possibly the best walk on the islands is the coastal walk to Shabadran. Of course, Shabadran's beauty is enhanced by the effort of clambering along steep cliffs. But the views are amazing, and after a two-hour walk you descend to the exquisite beach: take plenty of water, a picnic lunch and wear sturdy footwear. You must have a **guide** (☑45 05 96; 1/2 days 3700/12,600 CFP), so contact Leon Bearune in Kurine, the last *tribu* before the end of the road. Book in advance; you need to be relatively fit.

☞ Tours

The hotels and gîtes organise tours of the island for around 3000 CFP per person. Local entrepreneurs include the following:

Boniface Wahaga SNORKELLING
(☑45 45 00) Runs guided snorkelling excursions to the coral beds up north (1700 CFP).

Jone Peu HIKING
(☑45 03 49) Explore the forest and cliffs at La Asicen (2000 CFP).

Lakoredine Transport TOUR
(☑45 42 44, 45 45 00) Marcel Lakoredine takes round-island tours (3050 CFP).

🛏 Sleeping & Eating

Hôtel Nengone Village RESORT $$$
(☑45 45 00; www.hotelnengonevillage.nc; bungalows/ste 14,700/27,300 CFP; ❄🛜💥) Bungalows sit along a boardwalk looking quaint and tropical, yet modern, featuring local timbers. An infinity pool flows below the restaurant, there's some coral a few steps out from the shore and kayaks are available. Meals (breakfast 1700 CFP, dinner mains 1200 CFP to 2600 CFP) are served in a pleasant room overlooking the ocean; airport/wharf transfers cost 2800/1600 CFP.

Chez Nath BUNGALOW $
(☑45 10 93; Tribu de Kaewatine; s 2100 CFP) Head through the casual open-air restaurant (meals from 2000 CFP) and follow the coral paths to two smart traditional *cases* with a separate bathroom. There's electricity, friendly faces and guides for local walks too, though the beach is a good 40-minute walk away.

Seday BUNGALOW $
(☑45 02 25; camping 1200 CFP, case per person 2000 CFP) Up north, in the quiet *tribu* of Roh, is a little honeymoon bungalow (5000 CFP) set on a rock in the water, plus three bungalows near the rocky coast. Sit on the wooden platform over the water, or slither

NEW CALEDONIA MARÉ

KANAK GRANDE CASE

The *grande case* (chief's hut) is one of the strongest symbols of the Kanak community. It was traditionally home to the chief. Nowadays the *grande case* is the political centre of the district where the chief, who inherits his position, gathers with the village representatives to discuss the running of the community and affairs they want discussed in parliament.

Where possible, the *grande case* is built on a knoll above the rest of the village. The central pillar, an immense tree trunk, is erected first. It will support the entire *case* and symbolises the chief. A stone hearth is laid between the central pillar and the entrance which is via a low doorway flanked by carved posts.

Inside, the walls and ceiling are lined with wooden posts or beams, lashed to the frame with strong vines, all of which lean against the central pillar to symbolise the clan's close link to the chief. Finally, the roof is topped with a *flèche faîtière*, a carved wooden spear that becomes home to ancestral spirits.

A *grande case* is always surrounded by large spiked tree-trunk fences. Only enter these areas with a guide and ask permission before taking photos.

between the rocks where it's great to snorkel. The restaurant serves excellent meals (1800 CFP) based on fish and home-grown vegetables. Transfers are 2900 CFP.

Waterloo BUNGALOW $
(☑45 18 02, 87 05 93; Eni; bungalows/camping d 4200/1260 CFP) There are two lovely *cases* here in pretty gardens beside the family home. Dinner is likely to be fish (2500 CFP), served with a delicious papaya salad. There are two bathrooms and shaded camping spots. Lovely Eni beach is a short walk away.

ⓘ Information

The small coastal town of Tadine is Maré's main centre; if you're travelling by ferry you'll arrive or leave from the wharf there. Tadine has shops, a petrol station, a pharmacy and a market on Tuesday and Friday.

Air Calédonie (☑45 55 10; ☺8-11am & 2-5pm Mon-Fri) Has an office at the airport.

BCI bank (☑45 40 62; ☺7.15am-noon & 1.15-4pm Mon-Fri) Has an external ATM.

Post office (☑45 41 05; ☺7.45-11.15am & 12.15-3pm Mon-Fri)

ⓘ Getting Around

You can try cycling around the island if you are fit but roads are long, straight and monotonous. Hôtel Nengone Village hires bicycles (half/full day 650/1100 CFP).

The best way to get around Maré is by car. Car hire companies:

ETTM (☑45 42 73; per day from 6300 CFP)

Golf Location (☑45 09 42, 95 02 13; Wabao; per day from 6300 CFP)

Lifou

POP 8320 / AREA 1207 SQ KM

Lifou is home to magnificent cliff-top views, sheltered bays with coral shelfs teeming with colourful tropical fish, secluded beaches, fascinating caves and a rich traditional culture. It's no wonder it's also a cruise-ship destination.

⊙ Sights

Chapelle Notre Dame de Lourdes CHURCH
At the large white cross at Easo, a sealed road turns off to a parking area on the Easo peninsula beneath the small Chapelle Notre Dame de Lourdes that's topped by a statue of the Virgin Mary. Steps lead up the hill to the chapel from where there are fantastic views of Baie de Jinek to the west and Baie

du Santal to the east and south. The chapel was built in 1898 to commemorate the arrival of the first Catholic missionaries in 1858.

Peng BEACH
Don't miss the blissful and secluded beach at Peng on Baie du Santal, 3.5km off the Wé–Drueulu Rd; turn off at the *tribu* Hapetra.

Luengoni Beach BEACH
A stretch of fine white sand bordering a stunning lagoon. Locals boast that it is New Caledonia's most beautiful beach. The sheltered bay is a renowned turtle haunt.

Grotte les Joyaux de Luengoni GROTTO
Just before Luengoni beach are limestone caves both above and below ground; the underground caves have beautiful deep rock pools which shimmer emerald green when you shine a torch on the water.

🏃 Activities

Jokin Cliffs SNORKELLING
Lifou's northernmost *tribu* sits on the cliff tops overlooking a vast bay with brilliant sunset views; the footpath to the left of the church here leads to a cove where you can snorkel among the coral formations.

Baie de Jinek SNORKELLING
About 200m before the chapel a road heads off to Baie de Jinek, where steps from a wooden platform built above sharp coral rocks lead down to the water. It's a great place for snorkelling as the bay's clear and the water teems with small tropical fish.

Lifou Diving DIVING
(☑45 40 60, 78 94 72; www.lifou-diving.com; 2-dive package 11,000 CFP) Based at Easo, organises dive trips to the sheltered Shoji and Gorgones reefs. The club also offers night dives (7000 CFP).

☞ Tours

Vanilla Plantations TOUR
The road from Jokin to Easo winds through a cool green forest past Mucaweng, a *tribu* known for its vanilla plantations. Félix Bolé shows visitors around his plantation for a small fee; sample vanilla tea or coffee and buy beans (200 CFP each). The farm is down the track next to the white water tower in Mucaweng.

Noël Pia TREKKING
(☑45 09 53; per person 1600 CFP) Takes guided treks to the Grotte les Joyaux de Luengoni.

🛏 Sleeping & Eating
WÉ

TOP CHOICE **Hôtel Drehu Village** BUNGALOWS $$$
(📞45 02 70; www.hoteldrehuvillage.nc; bungalows/ste 14,700/26,250 CFP; ❀🛜🖤) Turn down towards Châteaubriand beach and you're in this lovely garden where comfortable bungalows spread through to the grass and white-sand beach. The restaurant tables are romantically situated around a pool and under a *faré* (dinner mains 2300 CFP to 3400 CFP).

Chez Jeannette BUNGALOWS $$
(📞45 45 05; bungalows d 5600 CFP, case 2100 CFP) Jeannette's homestay buzzes with energy as adventurers organise their day. It's right on the beach at the end of Baie de Châteaubriand. Jeannette only caters for house guests (meals from 3500 CFP), so you'll need to stay to enjoy her famous crab dish. Follow the unsealed road in front of *tribu* Luecilla along the waterfront.

Restaurant Finemem RESTAURANT $
(⊙Mon-Fri 8am-3pm & 6-9pm) By day it's *paninis* (try the prawn, yum), but by night this spot is the life of Lifou, with its pizza, great evening specials and delicious desserts like *crème brûlée à la vanille de Lifou*.

Snack Makanu TAKEAWAY $
(dishes 600-1000 CFP; ⊙7.30am-7pm Mon-Fri, 8am-2pm Sat) You know the food's good when everyone wants to eat there. It's outside Korail Alimentation and offers a choice of meals with rice, slices of quiche and light snacks.

NORTHERN LIFOU
Lilorève BUNGALOWS $$
(📞45 14 23; camping 1250 CFP, bungalows s/d 4830/5400 CFP) Three thatched bungalows sit on a grassy property sloping down to Baie du Santal, with a wide view over the bay and a private sandy cove. A set menu is 2000 CFP to 3500 CFP. There's bike/car hire (1700/6800 CFP per day); airport/wharf transfers are 2000/3000 CFP.

Faré Falaise BUNGALOWS $$
(📞45 02 01; camping 2100 CFP, d bungalows 5775 CFP) Perched on the very edge of the cliffs at Jokin, these rustic bungalows have decks to see magnificent sunsets and the best views. A set menu is available for 1800 CFP. The beach is via 200 steps, but it's great snorkelling. The gîte accepts credit cards. Airport/wharf return transfers cost 1700/3000 CFP.

Le Servigny BUNGALOWS $$
(📞45 12 44; www.hotel-servigny.nc; r/bungalows 6900/8900 CFP; ❀❀) This fab place is actually only five minutes from the beach at Easo. It has a large swimming pool in a pleasant garden, so don't be put off by its position. The two-bedroom bungalows are spacious, with plenty of mod cons. Airport/harbour transfers are 700/2000 CFP.

SOUTHERN LIFOU
TOP CHOICE **À La Petit Baie** BUNGALOWS $
(📞45 15 25; Tribu de Joj; bungalow per person 2100 CFP) Its *case*, in lovely gardens, is one of the best you'll find, and the dining room and bar is by the sea (organise your simple meals the day before). There's a kayak club here, and ask Annette about her outrigger trips.

Chez Jeanne Forrest BUNGALOWS $
(📞45 16 56; camping 1100 CFP, case/bungalows 2100/4200 CFP) Bungalows squat around the spacious lawns that run down to magnificent Luengoni beach. Jeanne is charming and cooks tasty local dishes (from 2500 CFP), but don't forget to book. Jeanne also arranges hikes to cliffs and caves.

Hukekep BUNGALOWS $
(📞45 14 34; camping 1100 CFP, paillote without bathroom 4700 CFP) At the end of Luengoni beach, away from the main road, this gorgeous place is oh so peaceful, the breeze whispering between the coconut palms. The *paillotes* (huts) have both beds and mattresses; bathrooms are shared. It's self-catering.

L'Oasis de Kiamu RESORT $$
(📞45 15 00; www.hoteloasisdekiamu.nc; d/tr & f 10,800/17,200 CFP; ❀🛜🖤👪) Owner Didier Grava has created a little oasis here below a cliff; smart rooms suit singles, couples, groups and families – check out the variety. Dinner mains are 2000 CFP, and the family room has a kitchenette. Airport/wharf transfers are 2850/1450 CFP.

ℹ Information
The main centre in Lifou is Wé, where the Loyalty Island's provincial offices are based. Wé stretches for about 2km along the main road beside Baie de Châteaubriand. You can people-watch or relax on the white and aqua beach, there's a market Wednesdays and Fridays and a good supermarket.

Air Calédonie (⊙7.30-11.30am & 12.30-5.15pm Mon-Fri, 8-11.30am Sat) airport (📞45 55 20);

Lifou

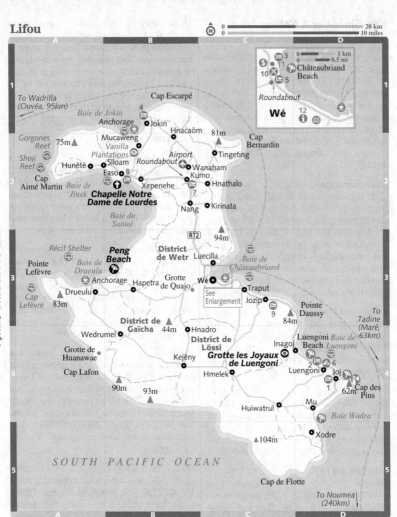

Wé (☎45 55 50) An office in Wé and a desk at the airport.

BCI bank (☎45 13 32; ⊙7.20am-noon & 1-3.45pm Mon-Fri) On the main road opposite Air Calédonie. It has an external ATM.

Marina (☎45 10 62; dae@loyalty.nc; ⊙6am-6pm Mon-Fri) Customs and immigration clearance.

Post office (☎45 11 00; ⊙7.45am-3pm Mon-Fri) Behind the provincial offices.

Visitor information centre (CEMAID; ☎45 00 32; cemaid@lagoon.nc; ⊙7.30-11.30am & 12.30-4.30pm Mon-Fri) Next to the *mairie*. There's also a CEMAID booth at the airport with maps and stacks of info.

❶ Getting Around

The best way to get around is by car, though you can split the island and take it on with a bike. Car rental companies include the following:

Aéro Location (☎45 04 94; contact@aeroloc.nc; per day from 7400 CFP)

Loca V (☎45 07 77; locav@lagoon.nc; per day from 5700 CFP)

Ouvéa

POP 3360 / AREA 132 SQ KM

Think 25km of perfect white beach backed with grass and wild tropical flowers. Look

Lifou

out, over an exquisite lagoon stretching as far as you can see. Add a chain of tiny islets, the Pléiades. Sound unreal? Nope, it's just Ouvéa.

◎ Sights

Trou Bleu d'Anawa CAVE
The deep Trou Bleu d'Anawa is sunk in the coral rock and connected to the sea underground. You can see fish and turtles in the blue water. Turn left along a track just past the Anawa shop, where the road curves sharply away from the coast. The pool is behind some abandoned bungalows.

Pont de Mouli BRIDGE
Here Ouvéa's tip is cut off by a wide channel that flows out of Baie de Lékiny into the lagoon. From the bridge, the display of dazzling white sand and different shades of blue is broken by outlines of sharks, rays, turtles and fish swimming beneath you (unless it's the weekend, when all you'll see are kids jumping off).

Les Falaises de Lekiny CLIFFS
These grey cliffs are 12km south from Fayaoue, explore them with a guide **Felix Alosio** (☏92 55 12; per person 2100 CFP).

Grotte de Kong Houloup CAVE
This cave is in the bush behind the airport at Houloup. Drive or walk to the bottom of the cliff where the cave is set in the cliff wall. Stop en route to locate a **guide** (per person 1100 CFP).

Memorial MEMORIAL
The large white memorial in Wadrilla is a tribute to 19 Kanaks who died in 1988, when French military personnel stormed a cave to free French *gendarmes* being held hostage by the pro-independence movement. Tragically, pro-independence leaders Jean-Marie Tjibaou and Yeiwene Yeiwene were assassinated opposite the memorial at the first-year memorial ceremony. The perpetrator believed they had ceded too much to France.

🏃 Activities

Canio WATER SPORTS
(☏75 45 457; ⊙8-11.30am & 1-4.30pm Mon-Sat) The interesting new building on the beach in Fayaoué is the sailing club. Canio rents per one/two hours windsurfers (1500/2500 CFP), hobby cats (from 2000/3500 CFP) and kayaks (1000/1700 CFP).

Randonée Pedestre WALKING TOUR
(☏98 72 05, 97 76 99; St Joseph; per person 2100 CFP) Antoine Omei takes northern discovery walks around the very old primary forest and to Nimek where it's a magical 6km walk to see the shark nursery (BYO lunch). Walks leave from in front of St Joseph Church.

Mio Palmo Plongée DIVING
(☏84 47 38; aquamarina-ouvea@yahoo.fr; 2-dive package 12,000 CFP) A friendly scuba-diving club just before the bridge. Take an intro dive for 8000 CFP, or a PADI Open Water Course for 49,000 CFP.

Jeoffrey Prebin Tours BOAT TOUR
(☏92 90 95; ouveamoto@gmail.com; half/full day per person 6000/10,000 CFP) Explore the waters with English-speaking Joe; a fish lunch is 2000 CFP extra.

Charly Aema Tours BOAT TOUR
(☏45 07 60; incl lunch tour 5000 CFP) Head out on a boat tour from Moague with Charly Aema. Late each year large sharks give birth in the warm shallow waters. Their hormones kick in, making them quiet (so they don't eat their offspring), and not dangerous to tourists. Beforehand you'll be taken to Pléiades du Sud where you can snorkel and fish and enjoy a picnic.

Ouvéa

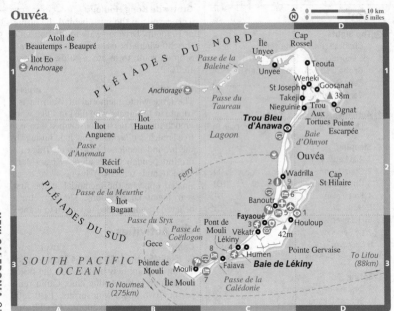

🛏️ Sleeping & Eating

Moague BUNGALOW $$

TOP CHOICE

(☑️45 07 60, 75 08 89; Mouli; camping 2500 CFP, bungalows s/d 5100/6000 CFP) This friendly beachside accommodation is run by Charly Aema, who is famous for his boat excursions (see p179). There's a tasty set menu for 1780 CFP, and coconut crabs, lobster or *bougna* on request for around 4000 CFP per person. Airport/wharf transfers are 2500/3500 CFP.

Gîte Cocotier BUNGALOW $$

(☑️45 70 40, 79 43 57; camping 1300 CFP, bungalows from 5000 CFP) Sammy is your host at this homestay about 500m north of the church in Mouli. It's across the road from the beach, but you can pitch your tent on the beachfront. Hire bikes for 2000 CFP a day, or take an island tour for 4000 CFP. A set menu is 2200 CFP. Airport/wharf transfers cost 2500/3800 CFP.

Chez Dydyce BUNGALOW $

(☑️45 72 87, 94 78 21; champagne@lagoon.nc; camping 1500 CFP, bungalows 4700 CFP; @) This spot has a good camp kitchen, clean bathrooms and sunny camping spots. The restaurant Snack Champagne (complete with sand floor) is on-site, offering three-course

meals for 1900 CFP and you can hire bikes here too (per day 1500 CFP).

Hôtel Paradis d'Ouvéa RESORT $$$

(☑️45 54 00; hotelouvea@canl.nc; cottages 52,500 CFP, 2-/4-person villas 34,700/52,500 CFP; 🛜🏊) Step out of your luxurious spacious cottage onto a stunning white-sand beach, or lie on your private deck and think about swimming in the azure sea. The tropical restaurant has soaring ceilings. Hire bikes for 1050 CFP per four hours. Airport return transfers are 2000 CFP and around-island tours 4200 CFP.

Gîte Beaupré BUNGALOW $$

(☑️45 71 32; bungalows 11,600 CFP, studios 6300 CFP) Three bright wooden bungalows in a large garden are across the road from the beach. The basic studio rooms are airy and have shared bathrooms. The restaurant is open to anyone (closed Sunday lunch), but you must book (breakfast 850 CFP, main meals from 1600 CFP, lobster 3800 CFP). Airport/wharf transfers are 1000/1500 CFP. The helpful owner, Willy, takes guests on tours with/without a crab lunch for 7500/3500 CFP.

Snack Fassy RESTAURANT $

(chicken or fish main 750 CFP; ⏰7am-8pm) A fun place with tables set under a thatched roof.

Ouvéa

Nine local tribes take week-long turns to run the *snack*, and obviously enjoy it. Order in advance for specials, like lobster or lagoon crab (2500/1800 CFP).

ⓘ Information

Ouvéa is a thin sliver of land with administrative centres at Wadrilla and Fayaoué. However, the facilities in these villages are so spread out that nowhere can really be described as a centre. There's a clinic and pharmacy near the airport.

Air Calédonie (☉7.30-11am & 1.30-4pm Mon-Fri; Airport (☎45 55 30); Office (☎45 70 22) Has an office in Wadrilla and a desk at the airport in Houloup.

BCI bank (☎45 71 31; Wadrilla; ☉7.20am-noon Mon-Fri, plus 1-3pm Wed) Has an internal ATM.

Post office (☎45 71 00; Fayaoué; ☉7.45-11.15am & 12.15-3pm Mon-Fri)

Tourist Information (☎94 97 14; Wadrilla; ☉7.30-11am & 12.30-4.30pm Mon-Fri) Has info on tours and accommodation on the island. The office is on the beach road in Wadrilla.

ⓘ Getting Around

Car-hire companies:
Julau Location (☎45 45 30; per day from 5500 CFP)
Ouvéa Location (☎45 73 77, 79 55 58; per day from 6300 CFP)

There's one **private bus** (☎45 70 77; 250 CFP; ☉Mon-Sat) that leaves St Joseph at 6.30am, passes through Fayaoué at 7.30am, arrives at Mouli at 9am, then returns to Fayaoué by 10.30am and St Joseph by 11.30am. The driver stops anywhere along the route if you flag him down.

ÎLE DES PINS

POP 1900 / AREA 152 SQ KM

A tranquil paradise of turquoise bays, white-sand beaches and tropical vegetation, Île des Pins (Isle of Pines) is also a haunting place where dark caves hide in the forest and the bush invades the crumbling ruins of a convict prison. The Kuniés, as the island's inhabitants are known, have kept alive the tradition of sailing *pirogues,* and you'll see these ancient craft gliding elegantly across the calm lagoon. Île des Pins' *escargots* (snails) are a local speciality and most places serve them. Seafood, in particular lobster, is another popular dish. All restaurants attached to gîtes or hotels accept nonguests, but you must book in advance. Restaurants can also prepare sandwiches if you'd like a picnic.

Vao is the main administrative centre. Kuto is the main tourist area, although hotels and gîtes are all around the island; most organise car rental and island

PIROGUE EXCURSION

Its scenery aside, Île des Pins' most famous attraction is its wooden *pirogues* with their triangular sails that glide you softly over the deep blue. *Pirogues* leave Baie de St Joseph at 8am, heading for Baie d'Oro where a path leads through the forest to magical *La Piscine Naturelle* (natural pool; p185). Laze on the sand around the pool or snorkel above a kaleidoscope of fish in its clear waters. Bring your picnic lunch or indulge your senses further by booking into one of Baie d'Oro's wonderful eating options, all just a five-minute stroll along the waterway (see p185).

Organised *pirogue* excursions, including transfers to Baie de St Joseph and from Baie d'Oro, cost around 3800 CFP. Or just turn up before 8am (sail 1800 CFP) and arrange your lift back from Baie d'Oro.

Île des Pins

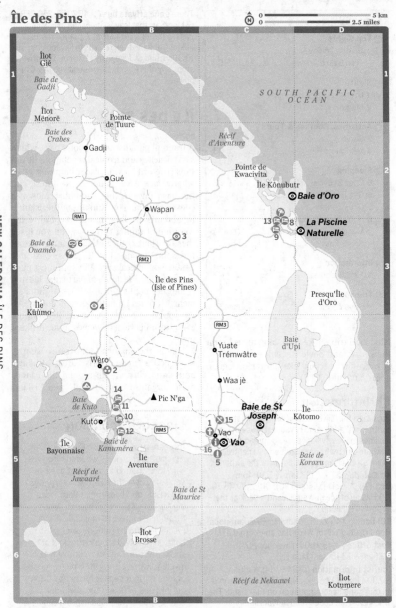

or lagoon excursions. The Office du Tourisme in Noumea (p159) can also book accommodation, car rental and activities.

Do not climb the taboo rock in Baie de Kanuméra (Le Rocher). This is the large vegetation-covered rock with wooden stairs

up the side that is separated from the beach at high tide. It is OK to swim around it or sit on the sand beneath it.

It's forbidden to kite surf near Île des Pins (though you can ask permission from Gaby at Camping Les Rouleaux, p184), or

Île des Pins

for yachts to sail through St Joseph, Upi and Koroxu bays.

ⓘ Getting There & Away

Air Calédonie (☉7.30-11am & 2-5pm Mon-Fri, 7.30-11.30am Sat) airport (☏44 88 40); Vao (☏44 88 50) flies to Île des Pins from Noumea at least twice daily (see p193).

The *Betico* (☏44 22 42) sails from Noumea at 7am most Wednesdays, Saturdays and Sundays, docking at the wharf in beautiful Baie de Kuto. It returns to Noumea at 5pm (16,000 CFP).

ⓘ Getting Around

It is important to arrange a hire car, transfer or tour in advance, so you're not stranded at the airport or wharf, especially if you're on a day trip.
Taxis (☏79 19 26, 76 84 50) Book well in advance.
Some rental companies that drop your car where you want it:
Location (☏35 35 94; per day 7000 CFP)

Khon Moere (☏93 55 66; per day from 7500 CFP)

Kou-Bugny and Kodjeue hotels, and Gîte Nataiwatch hire cars (per day from 7000 CFP).
Other rental options:
Bikes Gîte Nataiwatch, Oure and Hôtel Kodjeue (per half/full day 1200/1800 CFP). Cycling is excellent: not many steep climbs and short distances between places.
Boats Le Méridien (per half/full day 50,000/80,000 CFP).
Electric bikes Hôtel Kodjeue and Gîte Nataiwatch (half-/full day 1000/1500 CFP).
Kayaks Hôtel Kodjeue (half/full day 750/1500 CFP).
Scooters Hôtel Kou-Bugny (per half/full day 4000/5500 CFP).

Vao

Île des Pins' main village, Vao, is a serene place with several interesting sights and activities in the town and the surrounding area.

The attractive 19th-century **Catholic church** dominates Vao. It was established by the Marist priest Father Goujon, who managed to convert most of the island's population in just over 30 years following his arrival in 1848. A path behind the church leads up to a small chapel from where you can admire the view over the village to the lagoon.

The **Statue de St Maurice** at (signposted) Baie de St Maurice commemorates the arrival of the first missionaries on the island and is also a war memorial. You don't need permission to photograph the solemn circle of wooden totem poles guarding a statue of Christ, just above the beach.

Baie de St Joseph, 2km east of Vao, is also referred to as Baie des Pirogues. Early morning, when the *pirogues* are out on the water, is the best time to visit. Later in the day you can watch sailors building their *pirogues* on the beach under the coconut palms. A trip on one of these crafts is a must if you're visiting Île des Pins; see the boxed text, p181.

Vao Market (☉6-11am Wed & Sat) sells local produce. It's opposite the visitor information centre 100m south of the church.

Snack Kohu (dishes 750-1450 CFP; ☉9.30am-3pm Mon-Fri) is a pleasant place to stop, with tables under thatched shelters and everyone very friendly. Meals include chicken or steak and chips, sandwiches (from 450 CFP) and

a *plat du jour* (1650 CFP). Try the delicious fruit salads.

BCI bank (☑46 10 45; ⊙7.30am-noon & 1-3.30pm Mon & Fri, 8am-noon Tue & Wed, 1-3.30pm Thu) Has an outside ATM.

Post office (☑46 11 00; ⊙7.45-11.15am & 12.30-3.30pm Mon-Fri) It also has a public telephone; there are other phones at the airport and wharf.

Visitor information centre (☑46 10 27, 93 55 98; www.ile-des-pins.com; ⊙8-11.30am Mon-Sat & 2-4pm Mon-Fri, 8.30-11.30am Wed & Sat) Opposite the market. There's an information desk (☑46 14 00) at the airport which opens for flights.

Kuto

Kuto has two gorgeous aquamarine bays, separated by the narrow neck of Kuto peninsula. **Baie de Kuto** is the perfect place to lie on the beach or swim in the calm sea. Leafy trees grow to the edge of the beach, so you're always guaranteed some shade. For snorkelling go to **Baie de Kanuméra**, where coral grows not far from the shore. Transfers to your accommodation around Kuto are airport/wharf 2000/600 CFP.

Just north of Baie de Kuto, beside the main road, are the crumbling, overgrown ruins of an old **convict prison** built in the late 19th century. Île des Pins was initially used as a place of exile for convicts, including Paris Communards and Algerian deportees in the 1870s.

Feeling energetic? Take a 45-minute climb up **Pic N'ga** (262m), the island's highest point. The path is mostly exposed, so it's best to go early morning or late afternoon. From the summit there are fantastic views over the entire island and its turquoise bays. The signposted path begins from the main road 200m south of Relais Le Kuberka.

🛏 Sleeping & Eating

Camping Les Rouleaux CAMPGROUND $ (☑46 11 16, 94 54 20; camping 1600 CFP; ☎) A popular spot for kite surfers, this large, shady campsite also has a great self-contained bungalow (8750 CFP). It fronts on to the sandy beach at Baie des Rouleaux; heading north, turn left at the kiosk, take the right fork and follow the power lines for 1km.

Hôtel Oure RESORT $$$ (☑43 13 15; www.tera.nc; garden/lagoon/beach bungalows 31,000/48,000/48,000 CFP; ✳@☎☒)

This is so delightful. Step off your wide verandah, across the grass, to amazing Baie de Kanuméra, closed in by pine-covered islands so you're in your own aquamarine paradise with coral gardens a flipper-kick from the sand. The open bar and dining room (mains 2800 CFP to 3600 CFP) open on to a curving pool area.

Relais Le Kuberka HOTEL $$ (☑46 11 18; camping 1600 CFP, s/d 7500/9400 CFP, bungalows 10,400 CFP; ☎☒) A short walk from the beach is this home-away-from-home. Rooms and bungalows are set around a small tidy garden and pool. The restaurant serves an excellent range of meals (dishes 2100 CFP). Airport/wharf transfers 1500/500 CFP.

Gîte Nataiwatch BUNGALOWS $$ (☑46 11 13; www.nataiwatch.com; camping 1800 CFP, bungalows 10,900 CFP, B&B s/d 9700/10,900 CFP; ☎) A relaxed and popular gîte in a wooded area towards the eastern end of Baie de Kanuméra. Modern concrete bungalows have bathrooms, traditional ones have kitchens but share bathrooms. Meals cost 1700 CFP.

Hôtel Kou-Bugny HOTEL $$$ (☑46 18 00; www.kou-bugny.com; std/deluxe bungalows 24,600/25,600 CFP; ☎☒) Kou-Bugny spreads across the quiet road from Kuto beach: traditional-inspired bungalows under spreading branches of trees by a small pool; restaurant and boutique all glass on the beachfront.

The West Coast

As you travel north there are open areas and patches of forest. A couple of roads lead to beaches. About 8km from Kuto a signposted turn-off leads down a dirt track to the sunken **Grotte de la Troisième**. Stop when you come to a clearing where cars can turn around; the cave is 30m down a path. If you climb into the cave's wide opening, you can peer into its depth. With a torch and a sense of adventure, you can go down the steep slippery floor of the cave to the bottom, which is filled with fresh water. Experienced divers can venture even further into the underground caves.

Kunié Scuba Centre (☑46 11 22; www.kunie-scuba.com; intro/2 dives from 8800/13,000 CFP), based at Hôtel Kodjeue, organises dives to the caves and sites off the northern tip of the

island, especially Vallée des Gorgones, to see soft and hard corals, eagle rays and leopard sharks (ask about the accommodation-and-dive packages). Snorkelling trips with gear and picnic lunch are 4200 CFP. Fishing trips can also be arranged for 8500 CFP per person.

Baie d'Oro & Around

North of Vao the road climbs gradually towards the central plateau, where you have views over the dense forests of the east coast to the sea. Turn east opposite a small cemetery to beautiful secluded Baie d'Oro, its long white-sand beach enclosed on one side by a reef and on the other by tall araucaria pines. The area is best known for **La Piscine Naturelle**, a pool of exquisite turquoise water sheltered behind the reef. It is part of a waterway leading from the open sea to Baie d'Oro: follow the sandy waterway from Le Méridien or Chez Regis. Another waterway leads north back to Baie d'Oro, coming out near Chez Emile and Camping/Restaurant Le Kou-gny.

Just north of the airport road turning is **Grotte de la Reine Hortense** (admission 250 CFP), an impressive cave which tunnels into a limestone cliff. A path leads through a beautiful wild tropical garden to the wide entrance. This cave was where Queen Hortense, wife of a local chief, is believed to have taken refuge for several months during intertribal conflict in 1855; there's a smooth rock ledge where she slept. The friendly lady who maintains the cave can tell you its history and that of the island in general.

The cave's earth floor is slippery; take a torch (flashlight) if you have one. The sealed road down to the cave is signposted.

🛏 Sleeping & Eating

Le Méridien RESORT **$$$**
📞46 15 15; www.lemeridien.com; r/ste/bungalows incl breakfast 66,000/76,000/86,000 CFP; 🛜🐾)
Tropical luxury: cool timber floors flowing through to private decks, idyllic forest all round, views across Baie d'Oro to araucarias silhouetted against the sky, a swimming pool that seems to flow into the lagoon. Central lounge, bar and restaurant areas invite you to relax, enjoy. Transfers are 2400 CFP. Dinner mains are 2900 CFP to 3500 CFP.

Camping/Restaurant
Le Kou-gny CAMPGROUND, RESTAURANT **$**
(📞75 81 31, 46 95 45; camping 1200 CFP) This rustic campsite and restaurant has an excellent reputation for its lobster meals (4300 CFP) and fish menu (2200 CFP). Tables are set under the trees on the beach overlooking a dreamy lagoon. It's a 20-minute walk along the water, or five minutes from Le Méridien.

Chez Emilen BUNGALOW, RESTAURANT **$**
(📞93 63 40; bungalow per person 2000 CFP) Between the Riviere de Sable waterway leading to *La Piscine Naturelle* and Le Kou-gny is a casual little spot where fish, chicken and *escargots* are barbecued to perfection (menu 3500 to 4000 CFP). Camping (1200 CFP) is available and they have one lovely *case* that sleeps six.

Gîte d'Oro Chez Régis BUNGALOW **$**
(📞43 45 55; camping 1500 CFP, bungalows B&B 10,500 CFP) This shady campsite has four bungalows sitting along the waterway leading to *La Piscine Naturelle*. Book lunch early to enjoy chicken *bougna* (3000 CFP).

UNDERSTAND NEW CALEDONIA

New Caledonia Today

New Caledonia is certainly a country with two personalities: its nickel mines dot the east coast and south coast of Grande Terre, sitting side-by-side with a heritage-listed lagoon system that equals or overtakes Australia's much larger Great Barrier Reef in terms of coral and fish diversity. There is still an obvious divide between Kanak and European descendents, and there are several areas where Europeans avoid, such as the Canala region on the Grande Terre's east coast. Kanaks, for the most part, still have a lower social economic status than their European country-folk. Recent disputes have had some effect on tourism, as an inter-tribal conflict on Maré led to the island's best resort being used as a base by police who were brought in to quell the dispute and conduct investigations.

Travellers may find that there's a feeling of change in the air. Though New Caledonia is currently an overseas territory of France (its chief of state is currently Francois Hollande), a new referendum is scheduled to take place between 2014 and 2019. Currently, the chief of state is represented by High Commissioner Albert Dupuy and the President of Government is Harold Martin.

The French tricolour was the country's flag until 2010, when the independence movement's flag also obtained official status.

History

New Caledonia was first populated by a hunter-gatherer people known as the Lapita, who arrived from the islands of Vanuatu around 1500 BC; see p539 for more on Lapita. From about the 11th century AD until the 18th century, groups of Polynesians also migrated to New Caledonia.

Early Europeans

English explorer James Cook spotted Grande Terre in 1774, naming it New Caledonia because the terrain reminded him of the highlands of Scotland (which was called Caledonia by the Romans).

During the 19th century British and US whalers, followed by sandalwood traders, were the first commercial Westerners to land on the islands.

The first missionaries, two Protestant Samoans from the London Missionary Society, arrived on Île des Pins in 1841. A little later, French Catholic missionaries established a mission at Balade on the northeast coast of Grande Terre in 1843.

French Colonisation

France officially claimed New Caledonia in 1853, initially establishing it as a penal colony. The first shiploads of convicts arrived at Port-de-France (present-day Noumea) in 1864. In 1871 they were joined by political prisoners from the Paris Commune uprising and the Arab revolt of 1870 against the French colonial government in Algeria.

Having served their sentences, many former convicts were given concessions to farm and a shipload of orphans was dispatched to be their wives. They landed at Baie de l'Orphelinat, hence its name. As more settlers arrived an increasing amount of Melanesian land was taken over. This resulted in the revolt of 1878, led by chief Ataï, which lasted several months and was eventually quashed by the French, aided by allied clans.

WWI & WWII

During WWI male Caldoches (New Caledonia's European inhabitants) and Kanaks (the indigenous Melanesians) were recruited to fight on the French and Turkish fronts.

During WWII New Caledonian soldiers fought for the allied forces in North Africa, Italy and France. Meanwhile, 40,000 US and a smaller number of New Zealand soldiers set up a base in New Caledonia. The US headquarters was what's now La Promenade in Anse Vata. The influence of the US soldiers in particular ushered New Caledonia into the modern era with their dollars, Coca-Cola and tobacco. Shops were opened, and entertainment on the island was ramped up with wrestling, movies and the brief arrival of Hollywood actors.

Postwar

Between 1946 and 1956 Kanaks were progressively given the right to vote, and in 1953 the first political party involving Kanaks was formed.

A nickel boom in the 1960s and '70s saw many New Caledonians abandoning their professions to work in the nickel industry. The boom brought a large number of French migrants, seen as opportunists by the locals. After the boom a lot of people were left unemployed.

Independence became an increasingly important issue for Kanaks, and the majority of Kanak parties joined to form the Front Indépendentiste (Independence Front) in 1979. In 1977 Jacques Lafleur established the loyalist Rassemblement pour la Calédonie dans la République (RPCR), the main adversary of the pro-independence movement.

The Independence Movement

In 1984 other pro-independence parties joined the Front Indépendentiste to form the Front de Libération National Kanak et Socialiste (FLNKS), with Jean-Marie Tjibaou as its leader.

In that same year, mounting political tensions resulted in Les Événements (the Troubles), a period of violent confrontation between pro-independence Kanaks and loyalist supporters.

In 1986 the UN General Assembly voted in favour of adding New Caledonia to its decolonisation list.

Conflict & Resolution

In January 1987 the French National Assembly approved a new plan for the territory and an election was called for 24 April 1988, the same day as the first round of voting for the French presidency. Pro-independence supporters demanded that the date

be changed, and ended up boycotting the election. The disagreement led to the Ouvéa hostage drama (see p179).

The presidential elections saw the Socialists returned to power and a concerted effort was made to end the bloodshed in New Caledonia. Newly elected Prime Minister Michel Rocard brokered the Matignon Accords, a historic peace agreement signed by the two New Caledonian leaders, Jean-Marie Tjibaou and Jacques Lafleur.

Under the accords it was agreed that New Caledonia would be divided into three regions: the Southern, Northern and Loyalty Islands provinces. It was assumed that the latter two would come under Kanak control in an election. The accords also stated that a referendum on self-determination would be held in 1998, with all New Caledonians eligible to vote.

In May 1989 Jean-Marie Tjibaou and his second-in-command, Yeiwene Yeiwene, were assassinated (see p179). Their party split and lost power. Kanaks were discouraged. President Mitterand brought the French army home and brokered another deal which included education opportunities and economic benefits, and a clear path towards independence.

A Common Destiny

An agreement between the FLNKS, RPCR and French government was signed in Noumea in 1998. The Noumea Accord outlines a 15- to 20-year period of growth and development. It also calls for the establishment of a common destiny for New Caledonians, including symbols of national identity such as an anthem and flag. Three governing bodies in Parliament, the elected representatives of the three provinces, means there has to be consensus through discussion and understanding. Working together became a theme for both political and racial harmony. Where, just decades before, there were two societies, gradually European and Melanesian people began to socialise more readily, Kanak youth began to attend university and interracial marriages became totally acceptable in many circles.

The Culture
The National Psyche

New Caledonia is a mix of Western efficiency and Pacific casualness with an unmistakable Frenchness. Noumea is where many French,

Caldoches and people of Asian origin have made their fortunes in business, and they love displaying that wealth with shiny cars and flash houses. Noumeans are also very sporty: you'll see them cycling, jogging and walking along the city's picturesque southern bays.

Outside the capital, rural Caldoches are called Broussards (people from the bush). They are great storytellers, while rural Kanaks may be shy at first. However, the one thing all rural New Caledonians have in common is their generosity and warm hospitality.

Lifestyle

The lifestyles enjoyed by Kanaks and Caldoches are similar in many ways as both groups are family oriented and enjoy being outdoors in their leisure time. What sets them apart are cultural differences such as *la coutume,* the essential component of Kanak society.

La coutume is a code for living that encompasses rites, rituals and social interaction between and within clans. During important events such as birth, marriage and mourning, symbolic offerings are made and discussions are held.

Population

New Caledonia's population of around 260,000 includes 44% indigenous Kanaks, 34% Europeans, plus Polynesians, Asians and other minority groups. Two-thirds of the population live in the greater Noumea region.

All New Caledonians are French citizens, but are divided into various groups.

Kanaks, the indigenous Melanesians, belong to clan communities known as *tribus,* and though many move to Noumea for education and employment, they maintain strong ties with their *tribus,* returning for holidays and cultural and family celebrations.

New Caledonia's European population has two distinct groups: the Caldoches and the Métros. Caldoches were born in New Caledonia and have ancestral ties to the penal colony or the early French settlers. Many Broussards are cattle breeders who have forged a culture of their own, similar to that of outback Australia.

The term Métro comes from Métropolitain, as in metropolitan France, and refers to those who were born in France and migrated.

There is a large Polynesian population in New Caledonia, mainly from the French territory of Wallis and Futuna. In fact, more Wallisians live in New Caledonia than in their homeland and they make up 9% of the population.

People of Asian origin, including Indonesians, Vietnamese and Chinese, began arriving in New Caledonia in the early 20th century. Today they are mainly involved in the trade sector.

Language

See the Language chapter on p591 for French basics.

Sport

Pétanque, a game inherited from the French and sometimes called boules, is played mainly by men on a *boulodrome,* a smooth, hard pitch. Soccer, volleyball and a local version of cricket are also popular.

Arts

Wood sculpture is a popular form of artistic expression in New Caledonia, particularly in Kanak culture. Île des Pins is famous for its sculpted wooden posts. A few workshops on Lifou are open to the public. Soapstone sculpture is popular on the northeast coast of Grande Terre around Pouébo.

Several art galleries in Noumea sell paintings by local artists; for an overview of Kanak arts, visit the Tjibaou Cultural Centre (p149).

Dance

Many dance styles are popular in New Caledonia, including *pilou* (traditional Kanak dance), Tahitian, Vietnamese and Indonesian. Performances are held regularly at festivals and public events check with the local tourism offices.

Literature

New Caledonia has a dynamic literary scene made up of several publishers and many authors.

Déwé Gorodey is a Kanak politician and writer who evokes the struggle for independence in her writing and gives a feminist view of Kanak culture. *The Kanak Apple Season* is a collection of short stories, exploring Kanak political and cultural issues.

Pierre Gope is another Kanak writer whose works include poetry and plays. Caledonian Nicolas Kurtovitch writes poetry, short stories and plays. *Les Dieux sont borgnes* is a play co-written by Gope and Kurtovitch. The first half is set in the 18th century at the arrival of Captain James Cook. The second half is set in contemporary New Caledonia. Bernard Berger, also Caledonian, is a cartoonist whose *Brousse en Folie* comic-book series is immensely popular.

Louis-José Barbançon, a Caledonian historian, has written books on the penal-colony history and the difficult political climate of the 1980s. *L'Archipel des Forçats* looks at the convict history of New Caledonia.

Music

In addition to popular Western music and hip hop, reggae has a huge following in New Caledonia, along with music from Tahiti, Vanuatu and Fiji. The immensely popular local music known as Kaneka is a mixture of reggae and traditional Kanak rhythms.

Dick and HNatr Buama have both produced solo albums. Edou, leader of the band Mexem from Lifou, produces albums, both solo and with his band. Gulaan, former lead singer of OK! Ryos, sings beautiful melodies in his clear, mellow voice. Tim Semeke and his cultural dance troupe We Ce Ca have produced several albums and perform at the Tjibaou Cultural Centre (p149; at 2.30pm on Tuesday and Thursday).

There's great live music at Bodega, Le Muzz' Bar and Bout du Monde, or, for a terrific souvenir, buy a copy of *Carnet de Voyage,* a CD with some 27 vibrant songs and poems from the different areas of New Caledonia.

Environment

Despite its small size, New Caledonia has a rich endemic biodiversity. The main threats to its natural environment are mining, deforestation, cattle farming, deer and wildfires. The barrier reef that surrounds New Caledonia is 1600km long and ranges from 200m to 1km in width. Inside the reef, the lagoon is seldom more than 25m deep and provides the country with a fabulous aquatic-based lifestyle. The ocean is 1km deep outside the reef.

Traditionally, Kanaks had a very sensible relationship with the environment, considering it their *garde-manger* (food

safe), which meant the territory had to be managed properly in order to provide a sustainable food supply.

Open-cut nickel mining has caused deforestation, erosion, water pollution and reef damage. The last has occurred particularly along the midsection of the east coast of Grande Terre, as the run-off from the stripped mountains pours straight into the sea.

The emissions released from the nickel smelter in Noumea are another serious issue. International health and environmental agencies have classified nickel, a carcinogen, as an 'extremely hazardous substance' and have recognised that it can induce asthma. Measures to analyse the air in the greater Noumea region were introduced in 2005.

Vale Nouvelle-Calédonie Goro nickel processing plant in the far south is also causing controversy with new chemical extraction methods; breaks in its equipment in 2010 caused leaks of diluted hydrochloric acid and dispersed solvents, halting the plant's development.

Bushfires, which lead to erosion and desertification, are a huge problem despite public awareness campaigns calling for vigilance and responsible action. Fires are often deliberately lit to clear land for agriculture and for hunting wild pigs (in order to herd them into specific areas). Dry season fire bans have been introduced.

Geography

The territory is an archipelago that comprises the Grande Terre (16,500 sq km); Île des Pins (152 sq km); the Loyalty Islands (1980 sq km); and the tiny Îles Belep. Scattered around at considerable distances are various minuscule and uninhabited dependencies.

Grande Terre is 450km long with 400km of central ranges dividing the lush, mountainous east coast from the dry west coast and its savannah plains. It is rich in minerals and has one of the biggest nickel reserves in the world. The opencast mining used to extract nickel has left scarred mountains, blocked rivers, farmland turned to swamp and damaging run-offs into the lagoon. Thirty years after legislation was introduced to stop the environmental impact, the slow-growing endemic plants still haven't covered the gouged areas.

The Loyalty Islands and Île des Pins are uplifted, flat coral islands. New Caledonia has 1600km of reef enclosing a magnificent 23,500 sq km turquoise lagoon.

Ecology

New Caledonia's flora and fauna originated in eastern Gondwanaland, evolving in isolation when Grande Terre became separated 80 million years ago. As a result there are many unique plants and animals, especially birds, and per sq km New Caledonia boasts the world's richest diversity. Of the 3250 flowering plant species, 80% are native.

There's an estimated 68 species of land birds, about 20 of which are indigenous. The most renowned indigenous species is the endangered *cagou (Rhynochetus jubatus)*, New Caledonia's unofficial national bird (see p162). Of the few land mammals, only *roussettes* (members of the fruit-bat family), a traditional Kanak food source, are indigenous. Introduced mammals include rusa deer, which are causing major damage to native plants and the environment (see them on Caldoche farms on the west coast). Venison is served in local restaurants.

New Caledonia's waters are home to around 2000 species of fish. Humpback whales visit between July and September. New Caledonia's 14 species of sea snakes are often sighted on the water's surface or on land. The most commonly seen is the amphibious *tricot rayé* (banded sea krait). They are highly venomous but not aggressive and bites are extremely rare.

Parks & Reserves

There are many land and marine parks and reserves in New Caledonia. In the far south, Parc Provincial de la Rivière Bleue (p161) and Chutes de la Madeleine (p162) are easily accessible. The ascent of Mont Panié, at 1629m New Caledonia's highest peak, is suitable for fit hikers.

SURVIVAL GUIDE

Directory A–Z
Accommodation

Hotels everywhere have glorious garden and/or ocean views. Prices start around 7000/14,000/22,000 CFP per night for a room in a basic/midrange/top-end hotel for a single or double. Singles usually pay the same rate as a double.

Bungalow prices range from 4000 CFP to 21,000 CFP. Bungalows usually have private

bathrooms, an on-site restaurant and sometimes a communal kitchen.

There are homestays *(accueil en tribu)*, gîtes and campsites everywhere, except in Noumea. Campsites have toilets and showers of varying degrees of cleanliness (but usually with hot water) and cost between 1100 and 2100 CFP per tent (with two people). Homestays and farmstays are usually in a Melanesian family compound and have *cases* (with mattresses on the floor) or bungalows (with beds). They cost from 1000 CFP to 6000 CFP per person. It's best to bring your own towels and soap, as they're not usually provided. Meals are extra.

The following price ranges refer to a double room with bathroom. Unless otherwise stated tax of 5% is included in the price.

$ less than 5000 CFP

$$ 5000–15,000 CFP

$$$ more than 15,000 CFP

Activities

DIVING
Scuba diving is big here, with many dive sites, most reached by boat. Prices reflect this – a two-dive package costs from 10,000 CFP. Out on the barrier reef there are many shipwrecks and, closer, several intentionally sunk ships. There are dive centres at Boulouparis, Bourail, Hienghéne, Île des Pins, Lifou, Noumea, Ouvéa and Poindimié.

Nouvelle-Calédonie Plongée (www.nouvellecaledonieplongee.com) offers 'Plongée' cards which give a 15% (minimum) discount on dives. Cards (5000 CFP and valid for one year) can be purchased at member clubs; check the website for clubs and contact details.

HIKING
New Caledonia has diverse landscapes that are great for hiking, best done during the cooler mid-year months. Popular hiking areas around Noumea include Monts Koghis (p161), Parc Provincial de la Rivière Bleue (p161) and the GR1 walking track (p162).

Association **Dayu Biik** (☑42 87 77; dayu biik@lagoon.nc) organises guided walks in the Hienghène region.

The **Office du Tourisme** (www.office-tourisme.nc, www.trekking-gr-sud-nc.com) has fantastic brochures and maps detailing a selection of hikes. Or visit the **Direction des Ressources Naturelles** (Map p152; ☑24 32 60; env@province-sud.nc; 19 Av du Maréchal Foch) in Noumea.

HORSE RIDING
Many ranches and *tribus* on Grande Terre offer one- or multiple-day horse-riding trips into the central mountain ranges; check the Dumbéa, La Foa and Koné local tourism offices.

SAILING & BOATING
The **Cercle Nautique Calédonien** (yacht club; p193; www.cncnnc.fr) is a good place to enquire about yachting and sailing. **Pacific Charter** (Map p152; ☑/fax 26 10 55; www.pacificcharter.nc; Port Moselle) Hires out a range of motor boats, from a 6.5m flyer, departing from Port Moselle (per half/full day from 29,400/42,000 CFP).

WATER SPORTS
The best spots for **snorkelling** are the reefs around the Loyalty Islands, Île des Pins and the east coast of the Grande Terre. Bring your own gear and watch out for strong currents. In Noumea, take a boat to the Île aux Canards, Îlot Maître or Amédée Islet (p150) marine sanctuaries.

Windsurfing and **kite surfing** are extremely popular on Noumea's bays. Equipment can be rented at Anse Vata from Plages Loisirs (p150). **Noumea Kite School** (☑79 07 66; www.noumeakiteschool.com; Port du Sud) runs a kite school on Îlot Maitre. **Glisse Attitude** (☑28 90 69, 78 27 69; glisseattitude.com; per hr/half-day 4500/9000 CFP) in Noumea organises kite-surfing trips and courses.

Centre Nautique Vata Plaisirs Water Sports (Map p149; ☑78 13 00, 76 59 09; www.mdplaisirs.com) offers introductory lessons (2900 CFP). Ask about the MD Plaisirs Card, which gives you 40% discount (eg catamaran 1550 CFP, kayak 750 CFP) and is usable here, and in Noumea and in Poé.

Surfing trips to the reef are run by Nëkwéta (p167) in Bourail, Ouano Surf Camp (p165) near La Foa and Bouts-d'Brousse (p164) in Boulouparis.

WHALE WATCHING
Humpback whales cause a flurry of whale-watching excursions off Grande Terre's south coast (p162) and Lifou (p176) between July and September. You may even sight them from the beach in Maré or on a helicopter trip to Île des Pins.

Business Hours

Government offices & businesses
7.30am or 8am to 11.30am and 1.30pm to 4pm or 5pm Monday to Friday. Banks

in Noumea and most post offices remain open at lunchtime.

Shops 7.30am to 11am and 2pm to 6pm Monday to Friday, 8am to noon Saturday. Some supermarkets don't close for lunch and are open all day Saturday and Sunday morning. It's impossible to buy alcohol from supermarkets during the weekend.

Sunday is extremely quiet throughout New Caledonia.

Children

If you're travelling in Noumea with children, see p151 and check out Lonely Planet's *Travel with Children*. Infants under three years stay free at most places. Children under 12 pay half the adult rate for accommodation and activities.

It's handy to travel with a fold-out change bag, and in Noumea or on Île des Pins car-hire companies can provide a safety seat.

Dangers & Annoyances

In general, New Caledonia is very safe for travellers. Always check that you're not walking or swimming in a taboo area, or on somebody's property.

Embassies & Consulates

Australia (Map p152; ☎27 24 14; www.austral ianconsulatenoumea.embassy.gov.au; 19 Av du Maréchal Foch, Noumea)

Japan (Map p149; ☎25 37 29; 45 Rue du 5-Mai, Noumea)

Netherlands (Map p152; ☎28 48 58; 1st fl, 33 Rue de Sébastopol, Noumea)

New Zealand (Map p152; ☎27 25 43; 2nd fl, 4 blvd Vauban, Noumea)

UK (Map p152; ☎28 21 53; 14 Rue Générale Sarrail, Noumea)

Vanuatu (Map p152; ☎27 76 21; 1st fl, 53 Rue de Sébastopol, Noumea)

Festivals & Events

See p579 for details of regional holidays. The Office du Tourisme website (www.office -tourisme.nc) and www.visitnewcaledonia. com (agenda) have a calendar of events.

Festival of the Yam (March) Kanak festival marking the beginning of the harvest.

Giant Omelette Festival (April) At Dumbéa, a dozen chefs, 7000 eggs and many hands make a free-for-all 3.5m-diameter omelette. Held close to Easter at Parc Fayard.

Avocado Festival (May) Held in Nece, Maré. It's the island's biggest fair, celebrating the end of the harvest.

Fete du Lagon (early June) A day-long fishing festival in Ouvéa.

La Foa Film Festival (late June) A week celebrating film in La Foa and Noumea.

Bastille Day (14 July) France's national day. Fireworks on the 13th and a military parade in Noumea on the 14th.

Marathon Internationale de Noumea (July/August) Held annually, attracts top athletes from all over the world.

Live en Août (August) Noumea's annual music festival featuring foreign and local bands.

Foire de Bourail (August/September) Three-day fair featuring a rodeo, cattle show, horse racing and a beauty pageant.

Équinoxe (October) Held in Noumea. Biennial festival of contemporary theatre, dance and music.

Fête du Bœuf (October/November) Païta's popular fair and rodeo.

Sound & Light Show (October/November) Impressive light shows staged at Fort Teremba, near La Foa, over a fortnight.

Food

The following price ranges refer to a standard main course.

$ less than 1000 CFP
$$ 1000–2500 CFP
$$$ more than 2500 CFP

Gay & Lesbian Travellers

The following website has events and information for gay and lesbian travellers to New Caledonia: www.homosphere. asso.nc. Homosexuality is legal in New Caledonia and there should be no problems in being out.

Internet Access

Most hotels offer free wi-fi access, sometimes in guests' rooms but usually in the lobby. Internet cafes are few and far between, but free wi-fi is sometimes available at cafes.

InternetResources

Government of New Caledonia
(www.gouv.nc)

La Maison du Lagon
(www.maisondulagon.nc)

Lonely Planet (www.lonelyplanet.com/
new-caledonia)

Northern Province Tourism
(www.tourismeprovincenord.nc)

The Loyalty Islands (www.iles-loyaute.com)

Tourist Office of New Caledonia
(www.office-tourisme.nc)

Maps

The Office du Tourisme in Noumea (p159) and Anse Vata has good free maps of New Caledonia and detailed maps of each island, with useful contact information on the reverse side. Charts can be consulted at the Cercle Nautique Calédonien (p193); or you can buy them at **Marine Corail** (Map p152; ☑27 58 48; 28 Rue du Général Mangin, Noumea), along with excellent mariners' maps produced by the Service Hydrographique et Océanographique de la Marine (SHOM).

Money

Tipping is not expected.

Public Holidays

Don't be surprised if your accommodation has 'shut up shop' in December or January; many places close as owners head off on their own holidays.

New Year's Day 1 January

Easter Monday March/April

Labour Day 1 May

Victory Day 8 May

Ascension Day 17 May

Whit Monday 28 May

National Day 14 July

Assumption Day 15 August

New Caledonia Day 24 September

All Saints' Day 1 November

Armistice Day 11 November

Christmas Day 25 December

Telephone

New Caledonia's international telephone code is ☑687. You can dial ☑19 for a cheaper call to certain destinations, including France (33 CFP per minute), Australia and NZ (38 CFP), the UK (70 CFP) and Japan (60 CFP). To make a reverse-charge call *(en PCV)* dial ☑1050.

Mobile (Cell) Phones A local SIM card costs 6190 CFP and includes 3000 CFP credit. Make sure you buy the correct recharge card (Liberté; 1000 CFP), which is available from post offices and tobacconists stores. For assistance dial ☑1014 free call.

Phonecards To use a public phone, you need a *télécarte*. For a fixed/mobile phone you can use IZI cards (1000/3000 CFP). Both cards are available at post offices and some tobacconists' shops in Noumea.

Time

New Caledonia is 11 hours ahead of GMT. It's one hour ahead of Australian Eastern Standard Time (Sydney, Brisbane and Melbourne) and one hour behind NZ and Fiji.

Tourist Information

The visitor information centre is the **Office du Tourisme** (☑28 75 80; www.office-tourisme.nc; place des Cocotiers, Noumea).

Getting There & Away

Air

The following airlines fly into New Caledonia.

Air France (Map p152; ☑25 88 88; www.airfrance.com; 41 Rue de Sébastopol, Noumea) Air France flies code-share with Aircalin (Air Calédonie International).

Air New Zealand (Map p152; ☑28 66 77; www.airnewzealand.com; Axxess Travel, 22 Rue Duquesne, Noumea) There are four flights per week between Auckland and Noumea starting from US$700.

Air Vanuatu (Map p152; ☑28 66 77; www.airvanuatu.com; Axxess Travel, 22 Rue Duquesne, Noumea) You can fly between Port Vila (Vanuatu) and Noumea four times a week (from US$350 return) with Air Vanuatu.

Aircalin (Map p152; ☑26 55 00; www.aircalin.com; 8 Rue Frédéric Surleau, Noumea) Three direct flights per week from Osaka, four per week from Tokyo (US$1400 return), four from Auckland and Port Vila (Vanuatu), three from Brisbane and two from Seoul (South Korea). Also flies to Nadi (Fiji) twice a week (US$500 return)

and to Pape'ete once a week (US$1000 return).

Qantas (Map p152; ☑28 65 46; www.qantas. com; 35 Av du Maréchal Foch, Noumea) Access from Rue de Verdun. Qantas flights leave from Brisbane three times per week and Sydney daily. A return fare from Sydney/ Brisbane starts at US$850/900.

AIRPORTS
New Caledonia's redeveloped Tontouta International Airport has ATMs and a currency exchange office (exchange currency on arrival before clearing customs). Duty-free shopping is limited on arrival. The airport is 45km northwest of Noumea, it takes around an hour by public bus (see p159). The domestic airport is another 20-minute bus ride from Noumea.

Sea
The passenger and cargo boat **Havannah** (☑27 04 05; cmisa@lagoon.nc; one way 11,170 CFP) sails to Vanuatu (Port Vila, Malekula and Santo) every six weeks. There's no regular departure date; check with the office.

CRUISE SHIP
Like floating white cities, a seemingly never-ending parade of cruise ships visit New Caledonia each year, and all dock at Noumea's Gare Maritime where **Office du Tourisme** (www.office-tourisme.nc) opens a booth for them. The ships also often have stops at Lifou and the Île des Pins.

Pacific Sun, Pacific Dawn, Pacific Jewel and *Pacific Pearl* (www.pocruises.com.au) are the most regular visitors.

YACHT
New Caledonia welcomes thousands of yachties every year. There are marinas and customs/immigration clearing services in Noumea, Koumac, Hienghène and Wé in Lifou. One hour before arriving in Noumea, use VHF 67 to contact the **Capitainerie** (harbour master's office; Map p152; ☑27 71 97; www.sodemo.nc; ⊙8am-4pm Mon-Fri, to 11am Sat), who'll call in Quarantine, Immigration and Customs. There's berthing assistance, fuel, laundry and many services available. Rates for berthing at the marina start at 1500 CFP a day (live-aboard), or use the facilities from 1400 CFP for three days.

The **Cercle Nautique Calédonien** (CNC; Map p154; ☑26 27 27; www.cncnc.fr; VHF Channel 68; 2 Rue du Capitaine Desmier, Noumea) yacht club at Baie des Pêcheurs is a good source of information about yachting and sailing.

Cruising New Caledonia & Vanuatu, by Alan Lucas, gives details on many natural harbours and out-of-the-way anchorages. The *Cruising Guide to New Caledonia,* by Joël Marc, Ross Blackman and Marc Rambeau, is a general yachting guide that also provides an exhaustive list of possible anchorages around the islands.

Getting Around

Air
New Caledonia's domestic airline is **Air Calédonie** (Map p152; ☑28 78 88; www.air-caledonie.nc; 39 Rue de Verdun, Noumea; ⊙7.30am-5pm Mon-Fri, to 11am Sat), which flies out of Magenta airport in Noumea to airports at the following destinations:

» Koné and Koumac two and three times a week (from 25,000 CFP return).
» Each of the Loyalty Islands two to four times daily (23,500 CFP return); there are flights between islands three to four times a week (transit in Noumea for Maré).
» Île des Pins two to four times daily (17,00 CFP return).

The website has flight schedules, Air Pass details and booking facilities. There are Air Calédonie agencies at all flight destinations, and a **ticket office** (☑25 21 77) at Magenta airport.

AIR PASS
For international travellers, the Air Calédonie Pass (26,900/4650 CFP per four-flight coupon/extra coupon) offers roughly half-price domestic flights. It's great in theory, but is not available throughout the year, and there are a limited number of pass seats for each flight. This pass is sold through the Air Calédonie office in Noumea. You need to fax them your passport and international ticket to qualify.

Bicycle
You have to be pretty eager to cycle round 400km-long Grande Terre. However, Ouvéa and Île des Pins are ideal for cycling. Bikes can be transported on the *Betico* and *Havannah* ferries.

There are few bike lanes in Noumea, but drivers both in the capital and elsewhere are not necessarily courteous to cyclists, so you need to be vigilant.

Boat

The *Betico*, a fast passenger ferry, sails from Noumea to Île des Pins (2½ hours) at 7am most Wednesdays, Saturdays and Sundays. It returns for Noumea at 5pm (10,900 CFP return).

For the Loyalty Islands, on Mondays the *Betico* sails Noumea–Maré–Lifou–Noumea; on Fridays it sails Noumea–Lifou–Maré–Noumea (15,500 CFP return). Crossings take 3½/4½ hours to Maré/Lifou.

Tickets can be bought online (they will have a printout to give you as you board) or at the **Gare Maritime des Îles** (Map p152; ☑26 01 00; www.betico.nc; Ferry Terminal, 1 Av James Cook, Noumea; ☺7.30am-5.30pm Mon-Fri, 6-10am Sat).

The *Havannah*, a cargo boat, departs Noumea on Monday at 8pm, arriving at 6am in Maré, then 3pm on Lifou on Tuesday. It returns to Noumea at 7am Wednesday; one-way adult 5500 CFP. It is operated by **Compagnie Maritime des Îles** (☑27 36 73; cmisa@lagoon.nc; Ferry Terminal), which has an office at 2 Av Henri Lafleur, Quai des Caboteurs.

Bus

Nearly every town on Grande Terre is connected to the capital by bus, all leaving from Noumea's old **gare routière** (bus station; Map p152; ☑24 90 26; 36 Rue d'Austerlitz, Noumea; ☺7.30am-noon & 1.30-4pm), next to Ciné City. It is best to book in advance, especially if you are travelling on Friday or Sunday.

Carsud (Map p152; ☑25 16 15; Gare de Montravel, Rue Edouard Unger, Noumea) operates buses between Noumea and the greater Noumea region between 6am and 6pm. They go as far north as Tontouta (400 CFP), passing through Dumbéa (320 CFP) and Païta (360 CFP), and south to Plum in Mont-Dore (400 CFP).

On the other islands there are practically no buses. It's essential to prearrange transport (or hitchhike). If hitching, make sure your backpack isn't oversized as cars are generally small and, as well as taking the usual precautions, avoid getting in a car with a drunk driver.

AROUND GRANDE TERRE BY BUS

Fares range from 600 CFP to 2000 CFP. The following schedules are for services departing from Noumea:

DESTINATION	DURATION	FREQUENCY
Bourail	2½hr	Mon-Sat
Canala	3½hr	daily
Hienghène	6½hr	Mon-Sat
Koné	4hr	daily
Koumac	5½hr	daily
La Foa	1¾hr	Mon-Sat
Poindimié	5hr	daily
Pouébo	6½hr	Wed & Fri
Thio	2hr	daily
Yaté	2hr	Mon-Sat

Car, Scooter & Campervan

Touring New Caledonia by car allows you to explore places off the beaten track which aren't easy to reach by bus. Car-hire rates are reasonable and petrol is the same price no matter how remote you are. New Caledonia's major roads and most of its minor ones are sealed and in good condition. Road signs are sometimes missing or placed down the turn-off where they can't be seen, so a good map is essential.

Driving Licence

A valid licence from your own country will suffice to drive in New Caledonia.

Hire

Car-rental companies abound in Noumea and the larger ones have desks at the airport. The Office du Tourisme (p159) has a list of companies. Most companies rent small sedans from 4500 CFP including 150km per day. Per extra kilometre costs from 23 CFP. With unlimited kilometres it costs from 7000 CFP per day. Look for deals such as one-week's all-inclusive rental from 28,000 CFP.

In the Loyalty Islands and Île des Pins, prices start at 6500 CFP per day with unlimited kilometres (it's not like you can go far).

Reliable car rental companies include the following:

AB Location de Voitures (Map p152; ☑28 12 12; ablocation@mls.nc; 36 Ave du Maréchal Foch, Noumea) has a smart supply of zippy white Peugeots for rent from 4100 CFP per day.

Point Rouge (Map p152; www.pointrouge.nc; ☑28 59 20; 96 Rue du Général de Gaulle, Orphelinat) rents everything from small cars (3300 CFP, plus tax) to 4WDs (from 5500 CFP per day plus tax).

Insurance

No extra insurance is required when hiring a car. Some companies charge a security deposit of 100,000 CFP.

Road Rules

Driving in New Caledonia is on the right-hand side of the road. The speed limit on a main road is 110km/h and in residential areas 50km/h. Seat belts are compulsory.

The maximum permissible blood alcohol concentration is 0.05%, and random breath testing is carried out.

Taxi

Taxis are confined to Noumea, the larger towns on Grande Terre and a couple of islands. It's best to call and book, rather than stand and wait. They run on a meter.

Tours

Tour operators in Noumea organise tours and activities in and around the city, as well as throughout New Caledonia. The Office du Tourisme has details.

Outside Noumea, many places offering accommodation run tours such as guided walks or horse treks, usually on private or customary land.

Arc en Ciel Voyages (Map p152; ☎27 19 80; www.arcenciel-voyages.nc; 59 Av du Maréchal Foch, Noumea) Arranges tickets for travelling or touring anywhere, including day trips to the islands.

Aventure Pulsion (☎26 27 48; aventure@ canl.nc) Organises off-the-beaten-track tours by 4WD in the far south (see p162).

Caledonia Tours (☎25 94 24; caledonia-tours@lagoon.nc) Runs tours to Blue River Park (see p163).

Terraventure (☎77 88 19; www.terraventurenc. org; tours from 3000 CFP) Local adventures, discovery weekends: kayak on the Forgotten Coast, splodge in a hot pool out of Prony, check out Canala.

VIP Tours (☎43 53 08, 79 27 89; jbrighton@ mls.nc; trips 11,000 CFP) Day trips include the Once-upon-a-time Tour. It's in English and includes lots of jokes and banter.

Rarotonga & the Cook Islands

Best Places to Stay

» Sea Change (p214)

» Kura's Kabanas (p215)

» Aito Apartments (p214)

» Etu Moana (p224)

» Tiare Cottages (p233)

Best Places to Eat

» Plantation House Dining (p217)

» Vaima Restaurant & Bar (p216)

» Café Salsa (p205)

» Punanga Nui Market (p205)

» The Mooring (p218)

Why Go?

Fifteen droplets of land cast across 2 million sq km of wild Pacific blue, the Cook Islands are simultaneously remote and accessible, modern and traditional.

With a hip cafe culture, fine restaurants and funky nightlife, Rarotonga lives confidently in the 21st century. But beyond the island's tourist buzz and contemporary appearance is a robust culture, firmly anchored by traditional Polynesian values and steeped in oral history.

North of 'Raro', the sublime lagoon of Aitutaki is ringed with tiny deserted islands and is one of the Pacific's most improbably scenic jewels. Venture further and robust Polynesian traditions emerge nearer the surface. Drink home brew at a traditional 'Atiuan *tumunu* (bush-beer drinking club), explore the ancient *makatea* (raised coral cliffs) and taro fields of Mangaia, or swim in the underground cave pools of Mitiaro and Ma'uke. The even more remote Northern Group is a sublime South Seas idyll experienced only by a lucky few.

When to Go

Avarua

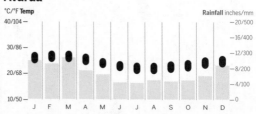

Mar–Apr The end of cyclone season usually brings clear, sunny days.	**Aug** Celebrate the nation's 1965 declaration of independence at the annual Te Maire Nui Festival.	**Sep–Oct** Look forward to warmer temperatures and reduced humidity.

Connections

If you're not crewing on a private yacht, air travel is the only practical way to connect from Rarotonga to the other Cook Islands. There are occasional cargo ships, but these are slow and usually run to somewhat flexible timetables. From Rarotonga there are regular flights to Aitutaki, 'Atiu, Ma'uke, Mitiaro and Mangaia. Three flights per week link Aitutaki to 'Atiu, and there are occasional unscheduled flights linking Ma'uke to Mitiaro. If you are planning an extended sojourn around several islands, you may well have to connect back through Rarotonga. Flights to the islands of the Northern Group are very expensive, and may be either booked out or cancelled due to insufficient passenger numbers. Book well ahead, but still prepare to be flexible.

ITINERARIES

One Week

Ease into Rarotonga's holiday spirit with a relaxed combination of snorkelling, hiking and casual dining, before hopping north to Aitutaki and exploring one of the South Pacific's finest lagoons. Definitely find time to attend a wildly entertaining 'island night'.

Two Weeks

From Aitutaki, fly to rocky and remote 'Atiu. Sample the local coffee and *tumunu* (bush beer), swim in shimmering underground pools, and discover 'Atiu's rare and idiosyncratic birdlife. If your budget permits, return to Rarotonga and fly south to sleepy Mangaia for reef fishing and to explore the island's fascinating burial caves.

Essential Food & Drink

» **Go local** Head to Avarua's excellent Punanga Nui Market and hunt down local delicacies including *ika mata* (raw fish marinated in lime and coconut), *rukau* (steamed taro leaves), *poke* (banana with arrowroot and coconut) and *mitiore* (fermented coconut with onion and seafood).

» **Refresh with nature** Quickly gain an appreciation of quite possibly the most refreshing drink on the planet, a chilled *nu* (young green coconut).

» **Drinking with the guys** Look forward to a few laughs with the friendly locals at an 'Atiuan *tumunu* (bush beer) session. It's a refreshing, slightly effervescent concoction, and you'll be required to introduce yourself to the group before drinking. Don't be surprised also if your local drinking buddies regale you with stories of relatives living in Auckland or Sydney.

AT A GLANCE

Currency NZ$

Languages English, Cook Islands Maori

Mobile phones GSM network through Telecom Cook Islands; international roaming and local SIM cards available.

Money Limited ATMs on Rarotonga and Aitutaki; credit cards widely accepted on Rarotonga and Aitutaki.

Visas Not required for stays up to one month.

Fast Facts

» **Capital** Avarua
» **Country code** ☑682
» **Emergency** police ☑999; ambulance ☑998
» **Land area** 241 sq km
» **Maritime area** 2 million sq km
» **Population** 19,569

Exchange Rates

Australia	A$1	NZ$1.30
Canada	CAN$	NZ$1.25
Europe	€1	NZ$1.60
Japan	¥100	NZ$1.60
UK	UK£1	NZ$1.95
USA	US$1	NZ$1.25

For current exchange rates see www.xe.com.

Set Your Budget

» **Midrange room** NZ$150
» **Two-course dinner** NZ$35
» **Island tour** NZ$60
» **Beer** NZ$5
» **Scooter hire** NZ$20

165°W   160°W

Penrhyn

10°S

Rakahanga

Manihiki

200 km
100 miles

Islands Not to Scale

Pukapuka

Nassau

**NORTHERN
GROUP**

Suwarrow

15°S   *SOUTH PACIFIC OCEAN*

Palmerston Atoll

Aitutaki's ⑤
Lagoon

Manuae

Takutea

**SOUTHERN
GROUP**

'Atiu ⑥   ⑧ Ma'uke

20°S

①②③④ AVARUA
Rarotonga ✪

⑦ Mangaia

Rarotonga & Cook Islands Highlights

① Snorkel, kayak or
paddleboard in the pristine
azure waters of Rarotonga's
Muri Lagoon (p210)

② Trek Rarotonga's **cross-
island track** (p211), inland
trails and valley walks

③ Feast on the freshest of
seafood and organic local

produce in Rarotonga's
excellent restaurants (p216)

④ Uncover Rarotonga's
rich history and heritage on a
circle-island tour (p214)

⑤ Explore **Aitutaki's
stunning lagoon** (p222)
by kayak, and find your own
deserted *motu* (island)

⑥ Spend time on **'Atiu**
(p228), exploring caves, coffee
plantations and unique birdlife

⑦ Learn about **Mangaia's**
(p237) ancient ways and
explore its mysterious
limestone burial caves

⑧ Discover the heritage and
architecture of the **Divided
Church** (p234) on Ma'uke

RAROTONGA

POP 13,100 / AREA 67.2 SQ KM

The most populous of the Cook Islands is stunning in its natural beauty and physical drama. A halo of flame-orange coral reef encircles the island, and Rarotonga's sapphire-blue lagoon is trimmed by sparkling white beaches. Beyond the reef, breakers foam and crash like distant thunder.

Rarotonga's settlements are nestled on the coastal flatlands, with the island rising spectacularly through lush fields and rural farmland to the mountainous and thickly forested interior. These silent, brooding peaks dominate the landscape from every angle.

Rarotonga has plenty of history, too, with ancient *marae* (traditional meeting places) and monuments to explore, and some of the best-preserved coral churches in the South Pacific.

History

Legend tells that Rarotonga was discovered by Io Tangaroa who arrived about 1400 years ago from Nuku Hiva in the Marquesas (French Polynesia). In the early 13th century two great warrior chiefs, Tangi'ia from Tahiti and Karika from Samoa, arrived in *vaka* (ocean-going canoes) to conquer the island and rule Rarotonga as joint kings. The land was divided among six tribes, each headed by an *ariki*. The first recorded European visitor was Philip Goodenough, captain of the *Cumberland,* who came in 1814 and spent three months looking for sandalwood. In 1823 missionaries John Williams and Papeiha set out to convert the Rarotongans, and in little more than a year Christianity had taken a firm hold.

ⓘ Getting There & Away

Air New Zealand (p247) links Rarotonga to Auckland, Sydney and Los Angeles, and Virgin Australia has flights between Auckland and Rarotonga. Air Rarotonga and Air Tahiti operate code-share flights linking Rarotonga with Tahiti.

ⓘ Getting Around

TO/FROM THE AIRPORT

Most hotels and hostels provide transfers from Rarotonga Airport (RAR). Raro Tours (p214) operates an airport-shuttle service (NZ$20 one-way to anywhere on the island).

BUS

Circle-island buses run around the coast road in both directions, departing from the **Cook's Corner Arcade bus stop** (Map p206) in Avarua. Daytime buses running clockwise depart hourly from 7am to 4pm Monday to Saturday, and from 8am to noon and from 2pm to 4pm Sunday. Buses running anticlockwise depart at 25 minutes past the hour, from 8.25am to 4.25pm Monday to Friday only. A night bus service runs clockwise Monday to Saturday from 6pm to 10pm, with extra hourly buses on Friday night from midnight to 2am.

Adult/child fares are NZ$4/3 for one ride, NZ$7/4 for a return trip (two rides) or NZ$25/13 for a 10-ride ticket. A family pass, valid for two

---

RAROTONGA IN...

Two Days

Take a **circle-island tour** or hire a scooter and buzz around the back roads to get acquainted with the island. Factor in kayaking or paddleboarding around **Muri Lagoon**, before settling in for sunset drinks at the **Shipwreck Hut** and a sand-between-your-toes dinner at **Vaima Restaurant & Bar**. Start your second day on an active note by conquering the **cross-island track** in the company of Pa Teuraa. After the South Pacific's best fish sandwiches at the **Mooring**, relax with swimming and snorkelling near **Fruits of Rarotonga**, before heading out for an exciting **island night** combining local food, singing and dancing. Look forward to a high level of audience interaction.

Four Days

Highland Paradise Cultural Centre is the place to go on day three for insights into traditional Cook Islands culture. Spend the evening exploring more contemporary local culture amid the **nightlife** of Avarua. Walk between the **Whatever Bar**, **Trader Jacks** and **Staircase**, and if you're in the mood for dancing, break out your best island moves at **Rehab**. After a well-earned lie in, head into Avarua for a lazy brunch at **Café Salsa** followed by exploring the town's shopping. If you're in town on a Monday or Thursday night, meet the locals on a **progressive dinner** around the island.

Rarotonga

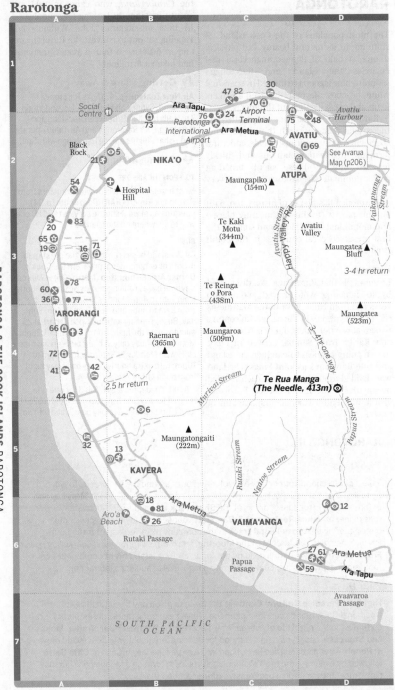

Social Centre

Ara Tapu

47 82
30

76 24
70
Airport Terminal
75 48

73
Rarotonga International Airport
Ara Metua
AVATIU
Avatiu Harbour

45
69
See Avarua Map (p206)

Black Rock

21 5

NIKA'O

ATUPA

54

Hospital Hill

Maungapiko (154m)

Avatiu Valley

20
83

Te Kaki Motu (344m)

65
19
16 71

Maungatea Bluff
3-4 hr return

60
36
78
77

Te Reinga o Pora (438m)

'ARORANGI

Maungatea (523m)

66 3

Raemaru (365m)

Maungaroa (509m)

72

41
42

Te Rua Manga (The Needle, 413m)

44

2.5 hr return

Murivai Stream

3-4 hr one way

6

Papua Stream

32

Maungatongaiti (222m)

13

Rutaki Stream

Ngatoe Stream

KAVERA

Ara Metua

18
81

12

Aro'a Beach

26

VAIMA'ANGA

Rutaki Passage

27 61
Ara Metua

Papua Passage

59
Ara Tapu

Avaavaroa Passage

SOUTH PACIFIC OCEAN

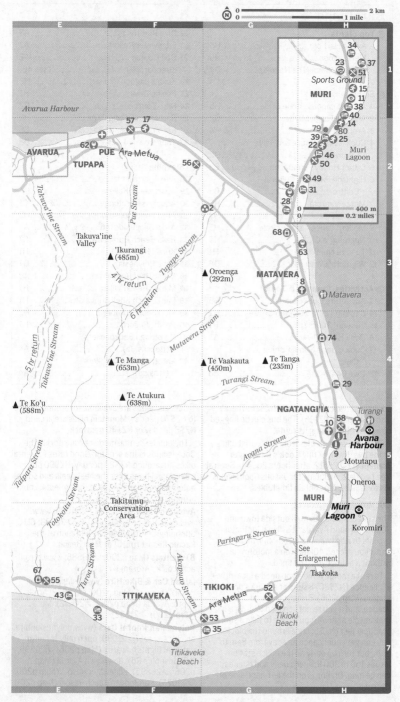

RAROTONGA & THE COOK ISLANDS RAROTONGA

Rarotonga

adults and two children, costs NZ$26. There's also a day pass (NZ$16). The bus can be flagged down anywhere along its route.

Pick up bus timetables from the tourist office or the bus driver, or ring **Cook's Passenger Transport** (☑25512, after hours 20349). Several free booklets, including the Jasons *Cook Islands Visitor Guide*, also contain timetables.

CAR, MOTORCYCLE & BICYCLE

The speed limit is 50km/h outside town and 30km/h around Avarua. It's illegal for motorcyclists to ride two abreast (though many do), and if you exceed 40km/h on a motorcycle without a helmet you'll be fined.

To rent a motor vehicle you need a local driving licence (NZ$20) issued at Avarua's police station (Map p206). Bring your home driving licence, and if you're not licensed to drive a motorcycle at home you'll have to take a short practical test (NZ$5; once around the block). You can get your licence any day from 8am to 3pm, but turn up early as the police station issues 150 to 200 licences daily and queues can be long. Driving is on the left-hand side of the road.

Cars and jeeps are available for around NZ$45 to NZ$70 per day. Mountain bikes are around NZ$6 per day or NZ$40 per week.

The quintessential mode of transport in the Cook Islands is the scooter. Good rates for rental bikes are around NZ$20 per day, NZ$90 per week. Local firms offer the best deals and some hotels offer cheap rentals to their guests. Look around for a good deal.

Avis Cook Islands Airport (☑21039; www.avis.co.ck); Avarua (Map p206; ☑22833; CITC Shopping Centre) Also has a branch at the Pacific Resort (p215) at Muri Beach.

BT Rentals (Map p200; ☑23586; www.btrentacar.co.ck; 'Arorangi)

Island Car & Bike Hire (www.islandcarhire.co.ck) 'Arorangi (Map p200; ☑22632; Ara Tapu); Avarua (Map p206; ☑24632; Muri (Map p200; ☑21632)

Polynesian Rental Cars (www.polynesianhire.co.ck) Airport (☑21039; open only for international flights); Avarua (Map p206; ☑20895; 2 St Joseph's Rd); downtown Avarua (Map p206; ☑26895); Edgewater Resort (Map p200; ☑21026); Rarotongan Beach Resort (Map p200;

20838); Pacific Resort (Map p200; 21838)

Rarotonga Rentals (Map p200; 22326; www.rarotongarentals.co.ck) Opposite the airport.

Tipani Rentals (Map p200; 22382; 'Arorangi) Opposite the Edgewater Resort in 'Arorangi.

TAXI

Rates are about NZ$2.50 per kilometre. From Muri to the airport will cost NZ$40.

Areiti Taxis & Tours (23012, 55752; Muri Beach; 24hr)

Aroa Taxi Shuttle (28144; 'Arorangi)

Doro's Taxi (21400, 52355; Avana; 24hr)

Kia Orana Taxis (20203, 50721; 24hr)

Muri Beach Taxis (21625; Muri Beach)

Avarua

Fronting a pretty bay on Rarotonga's north coast, Avarua is the Cook Islands' only proper town. Hardly an urban jungle, Avarua's largest buildings are barely the height of a coconut tree, and the atmosphere of shops and cafes is extremely laid-back. Avarua showcases the island's twin harbours, the main market and some intriguing sights, including the National Museum and the Para O Tane Palace.

There's one main road, the Ara Maire, running through town, and past the shops at the western end of Avarua is the Punanga Nui Market and Avatiu Harbour. This is where interisland passenger freighter ships depart from, and where the Port Authority is based. The airport is 1km further west.

⊙ Sights

Para O Tane Palace   HISTORIC BUILDING
(Map p206) On the inland side of the main road is this palace and its surrounding Taputapuatea *marae*. The palace is where Makea Takau, the paramount *ariki* (chief) of the area, signed the treaty accepting the Cook Islands' status as a British protectorate in 1888. The building has recently been renovated, but only the outside is accessible to the public.

SADDLE SORE?

We're not sure how many registered motorscooters there are in the Cooks, but we reckon – counting every man, woman and child – there'd be enough for about three or four each. This egalitarian form of transport is everywhere you look. To see a minister dressed in his flowing best white finery aboard his trusty Honda on the way to Sunday-morning church is a visionary sight indeed. People smoke and chat riding two-abreast, talk or text on the phone and maybe chew a sandwich at the same time. We've seen one gentleman riding with a 100L drinks cooler under one arm and another with a large extension ladder. Enormous Polynesian mamas visibly ooze over each side while tiny children cling on behind.

Locals prefer the manual 110cc 'postie bike' but the scooters hired to tourists are usually the automatic type. They're easy to ride with push-button ignitions, brakes and throttle, and rent for around NZ$20 per day. Even if you've never ridden a motorcycle before, after 10 minutes you'll be riding like a pro, and after a few days you'll be walking like a cowhand. Just be careful with the proximity of your suntanned legs to the hot exhaust pipe. Get too close and you'll be in danger of getting a 'Rarotongan Tattoo'.

TOP CHOICE Cook Islands

Christian Church   CHURCH

(CICC; Map p206; Makea Tinirau Rd) On the opposite side of the road is Avarua's white-washed church, built in 1853. The graveyard contains the graves of the author Robert Dean Frisbie and Albert Henry, the first prime minister of the Cook Islands. The main church service is at 10am on Sunday, and visitors are usually invited to stay for morning tea.

Beachcomber Gallery   HISTORIC BUILDING

(Map p206; Ara Tapu) This historical building was once an LMS missionary school. These days it houses Avarua's trendiest shops (p208) and a cafe (p206) worthy of your time.

Cook Islands Library
& Museum Society   MUSEUM

(Map p206; Makea Tinirau Rd; admission NZ$2; ⊙9am-1pm Mon-Sat, 4-8pm Tue) Inland behind the Para O Tane Palace, this collection of Pacific literature incorporates a small museum. Intriguing exhibits include an old whaling pot, spears and the island's first printing press. Nearby at the junction of Ara Metua and Takuva'ine Rd is the Papeiha Stone. This marks the spot where Tahitian preacher Papeiha preached the gospel in Rarotonga for the first time.

National Museum   MUSEUM

(Map p206; Victoria Rd; admission by donation; ⊙8am-4pm Mon-Fri) Inside the National Culture Centre, the National Museum showcases Cook Islands and South Pacific artefacts, and sometimes hosts temporary exhibitions.

🏃 Activities

Deep-sea fishing is popular in the Cook Islands, with catches of mahi-mahi fish and tuna (from October to May), wahoo and barracuda (April to October), and sailfish and marlin (November to March). The following operators have safety gear; contact them by telephone or down at the Avatiu wharf where the boats tie up. A five-hour tour, including lunch and refreshments, costs around NZ$150 to NZ$170 per person.

Akura Fishing Charters   FISHING

(☑54355; www.akurafishingcharters.com) Big-game fishing from NZ$170 per person.

Captain Moko's   FISHING

(☑20385; www.fishingrarotonga.com) Expect lots of Raro humour and the opportunity to eat your catch afterwards. Half-day trips from NZ$150 per person.

Marlin Queen   FISHING

(☑55202; www.marlinqueen.co.ck) Half- and full-day tours available.

Seafari Charters   FISHING

(☑55096; www.seafari.co.ck) On board the MV *Seafari*, a 1934 Canadian fishing trawler.

Wahoo Fishing Charters   FISHING

(☑25130, 73731; juscook@oyster.co.ck) Morning and afternoon 4½-hour trips available.

SV Southern Cross   SAILING

(☑24919; www.svsoutherncross.co.nz; Avatiu Harbour; adult/child NZ$60/30; ⊙Jul-Oct) This 58ft craft heads off whale watching daily from 2pm to 4pm. Two-hour sunset cruises from 4.30pm are also available.

Sail Tropicbird
SAILING

(☎23577, 55225; www.sailtropicbird.com; Avatiu Harbour) Board this sleek trimaran for discovery cruises including lunch (adult/child NZ$90/55), or sundowner cruises with snacks and a cocktail (adult/child NZ$70/40).

☞ Tours

Raro Reef Sub
BOAT TOUR

(Map p206; ☎55901; www.raroreefsub.com; adult/child NZ$65/35; ⊙daily 9am, 11am, 2pm & 4pm) Explore the outer reef on Raro's very own yellow submarine. Descend into the semi-submersible's underwater-viewing area to spy on shape-shifting shoals of giant trevally and the rusting hulk of the 1916 shipwreck of the SS *Maitai*. If you're lucky you might see turtles and eagle rays, and humpback whales are sometimes sighted from July to October.

Raro Safari Tours
GUIDED TOUR

(Map p206; ☎23629; www.rarosafaritours.co.ck; opposite Punanga Nui Market; morning & Sun tours adult/child NZ$75/37.50, afternoon tours adult/child NZ$60/30; ⊙9am & 1.15pm Mon-Fri & noon Sun) Just maybe Raro's most entertaining excursions are these three-hour expeditions around the island's rugged mountains, inland valleys and historical points of interest in safari-style jeeps. A fresh-fish beach barbecue lunch is included on the morning and Sunday departures, and costs include pick-up from your accommodation. Say hi to Mr Hopeless for us.

🛏 Sleeping

Paradise Inn
GUESTHOUSE $

(Map p206; ☎20544; www.rarotongamotelaccommodation.com; s NZ$70-95, d/tr/f NZ$115/135/150; 🖥) Paradise Inn was once Rarotonga's largest and liveliest dance hall, but has been refitted to provide simple, good-value accommodation with kitchen facilities. The old building is packed with character, featuring a huge lounge, polished-wood floors and a sea-view verandah. The location is terrific, just a few minutes' walk to Avarua's shops and restaurants.

Jetsave Travel
ACCOMMODATION SERVICES $$

(Map p206; ☎27707; www.jetsave.co.ck; Ara Maire, Avarua) Everything from rental houses through to luxury apartments.

Rarotonga Realty
ACCOMMODATION SERVICES $$

(Map p206; ☎26664; www.rarorealty.co.ck; Ara Tapu, Avarua) Includes houses for sale if you really get the itch to go troppo on Raro.

Shekinah Homes
ACCOMMODATION SERVICES $$

(Map p206; ☎26004; www.shekinah.com; Ara Tapu, Avarua) Options from simple beachfront studios to larger family villas.

✖ Eating

Café Salsa
CAFE $$

(Map p206; www.salsa.co.ck; Avarua; lunch NZ$13-24, dinner NZ$21-30; ⊙7.30am-3pm Mon-Sat, dinner Thu-Fri) This trendy cafe-restaurant next to CITC Shopping Centre is more Auckland-chic than Polynesian-rustic, and is one of Avarua's best spots for lunch or dinner. The diverse menu combines Mediterranean and Asian flavours with local produce, and standout dishes include the Thai-style *eke* (octopus) curry, and the wood-roasted mahi-mahi fillet with slow-roasted tomatoes, feta and pine nuts. There's also live music from 6pm on Thursday and Friday nights, perfect with a gourmet pizza (NZ$18).

Cafe Ariki
CAFE $$

(Map p206; Ara Metua, Avarua; mains NZ$18-26; ⊙lunch & dinner Mon-Sat) Tucked away inland behind Avarua township, this friendly cafe and bar is a big favourite with locals. Sashimi, *ika mata* (marinated raw fish) and huge burgers and salads for lunch give way to regular barbecues for dinner. Combine grilled tuna with a few beers, and definitely leave room for dessert of peach and yoghurt cake. Welcome to one of Rarotonga's best-value restaurants.

Punanga Nui Market
MARKET $

(Map p206; Ara Tapu, Avarua; ⊙6am-noon Sat) Head here for fresh fruit and vegetables, fish and seafood, barbecued snacks, and stalls selling fresh bread and traditional Polynesian food. Foodie stalls to discover include the Waffle Shack, and the stand selling freshly prepared crepes crammed with smoked marlin or *rukau* (steamed taro leaves). Don't miss trying the homemade ginger lemonade either.

Trader Jacks
PUB $$

(Map p206; www.traderjackscookislands.com; Ara Tapu, Avarua; mains NZ$20-35; ⊙lunch & dinner) Trader Jacks is one of Rarotonga's iconic watering holes, and panoramic sea views and good food also make it a great place to eat. The front bar has top-notch pizzas, while the restaurant is more stylish and classy with meals including excellent sashimi and smoked marlin salad. There's usually a live band on Friday and Saturday nights.

Avarua

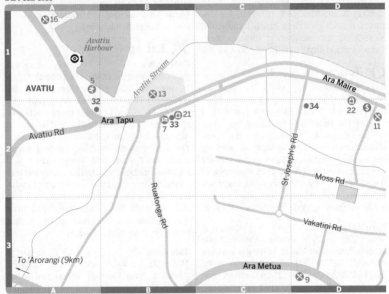

Tahiti Café SEAFOOD $$

(Map p206; Ara Tapu, Avarua; mains NZ$18, platters NZ$30; ☺lunch Mon-Fri) Secure a table on the breezy deck and tuck into tasty Tahitian- and Asian-style spins on sashimi and *ika mata*. The concise seafood-only menu also extends to fried fish and fish platters, and it's all good, and all very fresh.

Café CAFE $

(Map p206; Ara Tapu, Avarua; cakes & muffins NZ$2-6, lunch NZ$10-12; ☺8.30am-2pm Mon-Sat) This cosy cafe in the restored Beachcomber building serves up excellent juices, toasted sandwiches, and coffee and cake. There's usually a good selection of New Zealand newspapers and lifestyle magazines to browse.

Le Bon Vivant CAFE $

(Map p206; Ara Tapu, Avarua; ☺breakfast & lunch Sun-Fri) Pop in for a coffee and croissant and stock up on artisan breads, deli produce and other picnic-friendly goodies. Brunch and lunch is also available, and there's a similar offering at the associated **Deli Foods** (Map p200) in Muri Beach.

Waffle Shack CAFE $

(Map p206; Ara Tapu, Avarua; waffles NZ$5-8; ☺7.30am-2.30pm Tue-Fri) Life's pretty simple really. Some days all you need is good coffee and a freshly made waffle crammed with tropical fruit. Harbour views and simple outdoor tables seal the deal. On Saturday mornings, the Waffle Shack relocates to Avarua's Punanga Nui Market (p205).

Foodland SUPERMARKET $

(Map p206; Ara Maire; closed Sun) The best all-round supermarket is in the middle of Avarua's main shopping strip, with fresh bread, fruit and vegetables, packaged goods and a deli counter.

🍷 Drinking & Entertainment

The main after-dark action on Rarotonga is centred around Avarua. Raro's big night out is Friday, but Saturday is catching up in popularity. On Friday most places stay open to around 2am, but doors are bolted shut at midnight on Saturday out of respect for the Sabbath. Most restaurants double as bars, and resort bars are open to nonguests. Check out the *Cook Islands Sun* tourists' newspaper for what's on around the island.

For an organised Friday night out exploring Rarotonga's bars and clubs, join a Going Troppo tour (NZ$35 per person) with Raro Tours (p214). After-dark tours on Friday nights are also arranged by Rarotonga's bigger resorts and hostels.

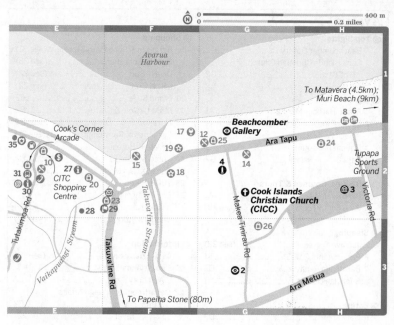

Listed under Eating, Trader Jacks and Cafe Ariki in Avarua, and Waterline Bar & Grill in 'Arorangi are also good spots for a few quiet ones.

Whatever Bar & Grill
BAR

(Map p206; Ara Tapu, Avarua) Who'd have thought – an open-air bar on a disused rooftop? Just out of Avarua, this place attracts trendy young things and gets lively on Friday and Saturday nights. There are DJs, and the 'No Strings Attached' string band is always fun on Wednesday. Nighttime views across town and the harbour are brilliant and there's also well-priced bar food, including gargantuan burgers and fish sandwiches.

Staircase Restaurant & Bar
CLUB

(Map p206; Ara Tapu, Avarua; ⊘Thu-Sat) Upstairs behind the Topshape Health & Fitness Centre building, the Staircase is always popular. The bar's decked out with atmospheric island decor and has regular live bands and DJs, as well as good-value island nights on Thursday and Friday.

Hidie's Bar
BAR

(Map p206; Cook's Corner Arcade; ⊘Tue-Sat) On busy weekend nights everyone crams into Hidie's to check out the live bands, and there are usually DJs a couple of nights a week. The courtyard garden bar is a great place to be on a warm tropical night.

Rehab
CLUB

(Map p206; Ara Tapu, Avarua; ⊘late Wed-Sat) House and electro grooves thump 'n' bump under ultraviolet and stroboscopic lights. Rehab is open late with occasional drinks specials if you arrive before 10pm.

🛍 Shopping

Shops around Avarua sell local basketwork, shell jewellery, necklaces, carvings and musical instruments. Many islands have their own speciality handicrafts, including *rito* (coconut-fibre) fans and hats from the Northern Group and *pupu ei* (shell necklaces) from Mangaia. Beware of cheap Asian imports. Most shops are closed on Sundays.

Printed *pareu* (sarongs) cost around NZ$15 to NZ$20, while handmade ones cost NZ$25 to NZ$35. There's always a good selection at Saturday morning's **Punanga Nui Market** (p205). Great local T-shirts are also sold at the Punanga Nui market and at surfwear shops.

And only the Cooks and French Polynesia produce black pearls, which are much rarer

Avarua

than their cream-coloured cousins. A single pearl could cost you anything from NZ$10 to well over NZ$2000.

Beachcomber Gallery ARTS & CRAFTS
(Map p206; Ara Tapu) Houses trendy shops selling pearls, clothing and designer homewares, and has a good cafe.

Island Craft SOUVENIRS
(Map p206; Ara Maire) The best-stocked souvenir shop is in Avarua.

Island Style ARTS & CRAFTS
(Map p206; Banana Court) Excellent selection of local craftwork.

M&M Ukalele & Crafts MUSIC
(Map p206; Ara Tapu, Avarua; ☺9.30am-4pm Mon-Fri) Located opposite the Punanga Nui market, M&M sells handmade ukuleles and has a great selection of local music on CD. On Saturday mornings you'll find it at the market. If you're feeling a tad tropical, it also has a good selection of traditional handmade fans.

Photo Studio PHOTOGRAPHY
(Map p206; Ara Tapu, Avarua; ⊘10am-5pm Mon-Fri, 10am-noon Sat) Local photographer Jeff Vinicombe's breezy studio doubles as a shop selling a range of large-format colour images of the Cook Islands. Also worth a look are the fascinating black-and-white photographs from the 1920s and 1930s.

Bergman & Sons Pearl Store JEWELLERY
(Map p206; www.icon.net.nz; Tutakimoa Rd) With unique and modern settings including necklaces, rings and bracelets.

Dive n' Surf CLOTHING, SPORTS
(Map p206; ✆27122; Ara Maire, Avarua) Sells good-quality fins, masks and snorkels and surfwear.

Vonnia's Store CLOTHING
(Map p206; Ara Maire) Centrally located.

Tuki's Pareu CLOTHING
(Map p206; Ara Maire) The local's choice.

Mareko CLOTHING
(Map p206; Ara Maire) Good for T-shirts.

Bounty Bookshop BOOKS
(Map p206; Ara Tapu, Avarua) Drop by for good historical and pictorial books about the Cook Islands.

Philatelic Bureau STAMPS & COINS
(Map p206; Ara Tapu, Avarua) Cook Islands coins and bank notes are sold here, plus sets of Cook Islands stamps (highly prized by philatelists). The unique $3 Cook Islands note is available in two designs.

University of the South Pacific BOOKS
(USP; Map p206; Makea Tinirau Rd) The best place for books on Cook Islands history, politics and culture.

ⓘ Information

Internet access is widely available on Rarotonga, and the average charge is about NZ$12 an hour. There are wi-fi hot spots all around the island, including most of the major resorts. Telecom sells pre-paid wi-fi cards in denominations of NZ$15 (50MB), NZ$36 (150MB), NZ$50 (250MB) and NZ$64 (400MB).

ANZ (www.anz.com/cookislands; ⊘closed Sun) ATMs at the main branch in Avarua, at Cook's Corner in Avarua, at Wigmore's Superstore at Vaimaanga, at Muri Beach, and at the Rarotongan Beach Resort at 'Arorangi.

CITC Pharmacy (Map p206; ✆22000; CITC Shopping Centre, Ara Maire) Part of the CITC department store.

Click Internet Lounge (Cook's Corner Arcade; ⊘9am-4pm Mon-Sat)

Cook Islands Tourist Authority (Map p206; ✆29435; www.cookislands.travel; Avarua; ⊘8am-4pm Mon-Fri) The main tourist office can help with everything from accommodation and nightspots to interisland flights and shipping services. Ask here about island nights around Rarotonga, and attractions and accommodation on the outer islands.

Jetsave Travel (Map p206; ✆27707; www.jetsave.co.ck; Ara Maire, Avarua) Has good airfare-and-accommodation packages and deals to the outer islands.

Post office (Map p206; ⊘8am-4pm Mon-Fri, 8am-noon Sat)

Telecom (Map p206; Tutakimoa Rd, Avarua; ⊘7am-11pm) Also has wi-fi access.

Telepost (Map p206; CITC Shopping Centre, Ara Maire) Wi-fi access and mobile phone services.

Westpac (Map p206; www.westpac.co.ck; ⊘closed Sun) The main branch is beside the Foodland supermarket in Avarua, and another airport branch opens for international flights – both have ATMs. Westpac ATMs are also at Oasis Service Centre (Nikao), JMC Store (Muri) and the Edgewater Resort ('Arorangi).

ⓘ Getting Around

See p227 for information on getting to and from Avarua from the airport and p248 for information on transport options around the island.

Around the Island

Though Rarotonga is the largest of the Cook Islands, it's still compact and accessible, and is circumnavigated by a 32km coastal road known as the Ara Tapu (Sacred Rd). Inland is a second road, the Ara Metua (Ancient Rd), built in the 11th century. The Ara Metua passes through farmland, taro plantations, and rambling homesteads in the foothills of Rarotonga's mountainous centre. The island's rugged interior can be crossed only on foot. There are no private beaches on Rarotonga, but take care not to cross private land in order to access the shoreline.

⊙ Sights

The sights listed here are anticlockwise from Avarua, and are all near the main coast road.

Cook Islands Whale & Wildlife Centre MUSEUM
(Map p200; ✆21666; www.whaleresearch.org; Ara Metua, Atupa; adult/child NZ$12/6; ⊘10am-

4pm Sun-Fri; ☎) Visit this recently expanded centre to learn about whales and other wildlife frequenting the Cook Islands. It's an essential stop if you're planning on going whale watching, and the centre's cosy Whale Tail Café has good coffee, snacks and wi-fi. Live critters include a giant centipede and coconut crabs, and there are also exhibits on sharks, turtles and shipwrecks.

Black Rock   LOOKOUT

On the coast just beyond the golf course is Black Rock (Turou), traditionally believed to be where the spirits of the dead commenced their voyage to 'Avaiki (the afterworld). It's also one of the island's best **snorkelling** spots. Look out for the sign to the Rarotonga Hospital from where there are commanding views of the island's west coast.

'Arorangi   HISTORIC SITE

On Rarotonga's west coast, 'Arorangi was the first missionary-built village, conceived as a model for other villages on the island. The missionary Papeiha is buried at the 1849 CICC (Map p200).

Highland Paradise
Cultural Centre   CULTURAL CENTRE

(Map p200; ☑21924; www.highlandparadise.co.ck; admission adult/child NZ$30/15, tours adult/child $60/30; ⊙9am-3pm Mon-Fri, tours 10am Mon-Fri) High above 'Arorangi, Highland Paradise stands on the site of the old Tinomana village with panoramic views over the west

and south coasts. Members of the Pirangi family, descendants of Tinomana Ariki, take visitors on a two-hour tour of the site, including gardens, *marae,* chief's throne and old lookout. Transport is included. On Wednesday and Friday fabulous sunset island nights are held.

Wigmore's Waterfall   WATERFALL

(Map p200) On the eastern edge of the abandoned Sheraton resort site, a road leads inland to Wigmore's Waterfall, a lovely cascade dropping into a fresh, cool swimming pool. Note that in the dry season, the cascade can be more of a trickle. The south coast also has the island's best beaches, with the best snorkelling to be found at **Aro'a**, **Titikaveka** and **Tikioki**.

⬛ TOP CHOICE Muri   BEACH

(inset Map p200) With its four *motu* (islets), Muri is the most beautiful section of Rarotonga's encircling lagoon. The vivid blue water is packed with tropical fish, especially around the *motu* (Taakoka, Koromiri, Oneroa and Motutapu), and out towards the reef. Taakoka is volcanic while the others are sand cays. The swimming is wonderful here over sparkling white sand. Watersports equipment and lagoon cruises are available from Muri through Captain Tama's (p213) and Koka's Lagoon Cruises (p213). Other attractions include kite surfing, paddleboarding and a few good restaurants.

EXPLORING MURI

Start at the northern end of Muri Beach at Avana Harbour, one of the only deep-water passages into Rarotonga's lagoon. Maybe grab a fruit smoothie or fish sandwich from the **Mooring** (p218) to set you up for the walk ahead.

The great ocean-going *vaka* (canoes) set off from here in the 14th century to settle New Zealand – the so-called 'Great Migration'. Walk a little north onto the small promontory to see **Marae Vaerota** (Map p200), the traditional *marae* of the Kainuku Ariki, where canoes were blessed and human sacrifices were made to the gods.

Head south to the picturesque **Ngatangi'ia CICC** (Map p200), where you'll find some interesting headstones. Opposite in the park there's the **ancient canoes' stone circle** (Map p200) and a plaque commemorating the seven canoes that completed the journey to New Zealand: *Takitumu, Tokomaru, Kurahaupo, Aotea, Tainui, Te Arawa* and *Mataatua*. There's a **modern stone circle** (Map p200) further south that commemorates the arrival of traditional Polynesian canoes during the sixth Festival of Pacific Arts in 1992.

To the south, glorious **Muri Beach** (p210) is one of the island's best snorkelling areas. It's a lovely walk along the shoreline with views over the four palm-covered *motu* (islets) in the lagoon. The remains of one of Rarotonga's oldest *marae* are on **Motutapu** (Map p200), but you'll need to kayak out there. Pick up coffee and cake at **Deli-licious** (p221) or a more leisurely lunch at **Sails Restaurant** (p218), before ambling down the main road to **Shells & Craft** (Map p200) to see some spectacular conch and clam shells.

Te Vara Nui Village CULTURAL BUILDING
(Map p200; ☑24006; www.tevaranui.co.ck; Muri;
village tour adult/child NZ$39/19, dinner & show
adult/child NZ$89/45; ☺village tour 5pm, dinner
& show 7.30pm Tue, Thu & Sat) Te Vara Nui
combines a purpose-built village showcasing local culture including traditional
medicine, carving, tapa making and
legends, with one of Rarotonga's most
spectacular island nights. After-dark shows
take place on pavilions and stages set in a
manmade lagoon, and dinner is a sprawling *umu* (earth oven) buffet. A combination
deal (adult/child NZ$109/59) for both the
two-hour village tour and the dinner and
show is also available.

Matavera CICC CHURCH
(Map p200) The old CICC is lovely at night
when the outside is lit up.

Arai-Te-Tonga Marae HISTORIC SITE
(Map p200) A small sign points off the road to
the island's most important *marae* site, Arai-
Te-Tonga. Situated just off the Ara Metua
there's a stone-marked *koutu* (ancient open-
air royal courtyard) site in front of you. This
whole area was a gathering place, and the
remains of the *marae,* the *koutu* and other
meeting grounds are still visible.

Cross-Island Track WALKING TRAIL
This three- to four-hour hike from the north
to south coasts via the 413m **Te Rua Manga**
(Needle; Map p200) is the most popular
walk on Rarotonga, and passes through
some of the island's most impressive natural
scenery. You shouldn't try to do the walk in
a south–north direction, as the chances of
taking a wrong turn are much greater. Wear
adequate shoes, take plenty of drinking
water, and slather on the mosquito repellent.
Parts of the walk get extremely slippery in
wet weather and the upper section is quite
rugged and overgrown. You're likely to get
muddy and sweaty, so don't make plans for a
flash lunch immediately afterwards.

The tourist office recommends walkers
join a guided tour (see p214), but it's possible
to do the walk on your own. The road to the
starting point is south of Avatiu Harbour.
Continue on the road up the valley by Avatiu
Stream until you reach a sign announcing
the beginning of the walk. A private vehicle
road continues for about 1km.

From the end of the vehicle road a footpath leads off and after 10 minutes drops
down and crosses a small stream. Don't
follow the white plastic power-cable track

up the valley, but instead pick up the track
beside the massive boulder on the ridge to
your left, after the stream crossing.

From here, the track climbs steeply up to
the Needle (about 45 minutes). At the first
sight of the Needle there's a boulder in the
middle of the path – a nice place for a rest.
A little further on is a T-junction; the Needle
is a 10-minute walk to the right. Don't try to
climb up to the Needle itself, as there have
been several rockfalls and landslides, and
there's a long and probably fatal drop on either side of the trail. Follow the track round
to the left instead and you'll begin the long,
slippery descent towards the south coast.

After 30 minutes the track meets the Papua Stream and follows it downhill, zigzag-
ging back and forth across the stream. After
about 45 minutes, the track emerges into
fernland. Be sure to stick to the main track,
as there are several places where minor
tracks seem to take off towards the stream
but these end at dangerous spots upstream
from the waterfall. Another 15 minutes further on, the main track turns back towards
the stream, bringing you to the bottom of
Wigmore's Waterfall (p210). A dirt road
leads from the south coast up to the waterfall. It's about a 15-minute walk to the coast
road, where you can flag down the circle-
island bus or cool off in the nearby lagoon.

🏃 Activities

Deep-Sea Fishing

Cook Islands Game Fishing Club FISHING
(Map p200) Just east of Avarua, anglers swap
yarns at this friendly club. Non-fishing types
are also welcome at one of the island's most
affordable bars, and adjacent is the excellent
Flying Boat Fish & Chips (p218).

Diving & Snorkelling

Diving is fantastic outside the reef, especially around the passages along the island's southern side. There are canyons,
caves and tunnels to explore, and outside
the lagoon the island drops off to around
4000m, although most diving is between
3m and 30m.

Rarotonga has several well-preserved
shipwrecks, including SS *Maitai* off the
northern shore. Other well-known diving
spots include Black Rock in the north; Sand-
river and Matavera Wall on the island's east
side; and the Avaavaroa, Papua and Rutaki
passages in the south (see p31).

Rarotonga has five accredited diving
operators, all offering twice-daily boat trips.

HELPING RAROTONGA'S ANIMALS

You'll probably spy the cute animals from the **Esther Honey Foundation** (www. estherhoney.org) at its stall at Saturday morning's Punanga Nui Market, but it's also worth visiting the main location (Map p200) to check out the excellent animal welfare work being undertaken.

Rarotonga has a much lower stray canine population compared to other Pacific islands, and significant credit is due to the Esther Honey Foundation. Dog numbers on the island have decreased from 6000 to around 2000, a reduction managed only by spaying and neutering animals, and the dog population of the Cook Islands is now noticeably healthier and more easygoing than in other Pacific destinations.

Drop by to have a chat with the international crew of vets and assistants, and there's also the chance to interact with a diverse menagerie of dogs, cats and other animals. Feeding times are in the morning. The foundation's always keen to hear from potential volunteers so, if you're interested, see the website for details.

Single-tank dives cost around NZ$95 and two-tank dives are about NZ$145 including gear. Introductory dives are available and four-day open-water courses cost around NZ$450. Dive trips are also offered by Adventure Cook Islands.

Rarotonga's spectacular lagoon is fantastic for snorkelling and swimming. The water is crystal clear, warm and packed with technicolour fish and coral. The beaches along the island's southern and western sides are all good for swimming, but the northern and upper-eastern sides are not as good. The best snorkelling is around Muri Lagoon, Aro'a Beach, Titikaveka and Tikioki (Fruits of Rarotonga) in the south of the island, and Black Rock in the northwest. Many of these areas are protected by *ra'ui* (traditional conservation areas).

Snorkelling gear is available from the island's diving operators, and most accommodation also provide free gear for guests' use. For night snorkelling in Muri Lagoon, see Pacific Divers.

Cook Island Divers   DIVING
(Map p200; ☑22483; www.cookislandsdivers.com; 'Arorangi) Offers introductory dives in the Tikioki Marine Sanctuary.

Dive Centre   DIVING
(Map p200; ☑20238; www.thedivecentre-raro tonga.com; Aro'a Beach) Also offers special 'Bubblemaker' scuba experiences for kids.

Dive Rarotonga   DIVING
(Map p200; ☑21873; www.diverarotonga.com; 'Arorangi) See the website for an interactive map of Rarotonga's dive sites.

Pacific Divers   DIVING
(Map p200; ☑22450; www.pacificdivers.co.ck; Muri Beach) Also offers night snorkelling around Muri Lagoon.

Adventure Cook Islands   SNORKELLING
(Map p200; ☑22212; www.adventurecookislands. com; Kavera) Excellent company that offers everything from mountain treks and mountain biking through to diving, snorkelling and spearfishing. Gear rental includes sea kayaks, mountain bikes, snorkelling gear and bodyboards.

Hiking

The island's mountainous centre is criss-crossed by walking tracks and trails. The top walk is the Cross-Island Track (p211), but there are lots of others to discover. The best guide is *Rarotonga's Mountain Tracks and Plants* by Gerald McCormack and Judith Künzlé, also authors of *Rarotonga's Cross-Island Walk*. Guided hiking trips are offered by Pa's Mountain Walk and Adventure Cook Islands.

Wear light, breathable clothing and sturdy boots, and check the weather forecast before you go. Tell someone where you're headed and when you expect to return.

Sailing & Water Sports

Muri Lagoon and the island's south coast are the best places for swimming, windsurfing, sailing and kayaking. Sailing races start at Muri Beach every Saturday and Sunday afternoon from around 1.30pm. Kayaks are readily available to explore the lagoon's deserted *motu* and many hotels provide them for guests' use.

Surfing is in its infancy on Rarotonga. Bodyboarding is popular but local board

riders are few and it's not the place to learn as the reef-breaks are steep and fast, and the water is shallow. See Adventure Cook Islands (p212) for bodyboard rentals. Raro surfing is dangerous – for intermediates and experts only – and too fast for longboarders. The island's north gets swells in the November-to-March cyclone season while the south works best during the May-to-August 'winter'. There are breaks at **Social Centre** in the northwest, off the **Rarotongan Beach Resort**, **Avaavaroa** and **Papua** on the south coast, and **Koromiri**, **Turangi** and **Matavera** on the east side. Since the waves break outside the lagoon it's a long paddle to the action. For local advice talk to the guys at Chillis Sports Bar (219).

Rarotonga Sailing Club SAILING
(Map p200; ☎27349; Muri Beach) Rents out kayaks and small sailing boats.

Learn to Sail SAILING
(☎26668; upwind@oyster.co.ck) Learn the ropes with Kiwi expat Ken Kingsbury on the super-sheltered waters of Muri Lagoon. Up to four people can share a two-hour lesson (NZ$141), and you can then hire his cute and compact sailboat for NZ$69 per hour. He can also hook you up with a treddlecat, a surprisingly speedy pedal-powered catamaran.

Captain Tama's Lagoon Cruises KAYAKING
(Map p200; ☎27350; www.captaintamas.com; Muri Beach) Beside the Rarotonga Sailing Club, Captain Tama's rents out kayaks (singles/doubles NZ$7/10 per hour), paddleboards

(NZ$15 per hour) and sailboats (NZ$30 per hour). Go local and hire a traditional wooden *vaka* (canoe) for NZ$20 per hour. Captain Tama's also has snorkelling gear for hire.

KiteboardHQ KITE SURFING
(Map p200; ☎52491, 55668; kiteboardhq@gmail. com; Muri) Head to Muri Beach for all your kite surfing essentials including lessons, gear hire and tours. The operators are also paddleboard enthusiasts.

Other Sports
Volleyball is often played on Muri Beach. **Tennis** courts are available at **Edgewater Resort** (Map p200) and **Rarotongan Beach Resort** (Map p200).

Golf course GOLF
(Map p200; ☎20621; www.rarotonga.nzgolf.net; ◷8am-2pm Mon-Fri, members only Sat) Rarotonga's nine-hole course is near the airport.

☞ Tours
Underwater Viewing
Captain Tama's Lagoon Cruises BOAT TOUR
(Map p200; ☎27350, 55002; www.captaintamas. com; Muri Beach; adult/child NZ$70/35; ◷11am-3.30pm Mon-Sat) The entertaining crew from Captain Tama's run glass-bottom boat tours, including snorkelling and a barbecue lunch on the tiny *motu* of Koromiri.

Koka Lagoon Cruises BOAT TOUR
(Map p200; ☎27769, 55769; www.kokalagoon cruises.co.ck; Muri Beach; adult/child NZ$70/35;

RAROTONGA FOR CHILDREN

Always check with the place you're staying about their policy on children, as some don't cater for kids under 12. For really little ones, you can hire strollers, car seats and porta-cots from **Coco Tots** (☎56986; www.cocotots.com). Ask at your accommodation or the tourist information office about babysitting services.

The top draw for kids is the island's colourful lagoon and the spectacular beach that stretches around the island. Good spots for snorkelling are Muri, Tikioki and Aro'a Beach, and **smoothies and ice creams** are never far away at Fruits of Rarotonga (p219) and the Saltwater Cafe (p218).

For an in-depth look at the island's underwater inhabitants, kids will adore a **glass-bottom boat tour** (p213) around Muri Lagoon from either Captain Tama's Lagoon Cruises or Koka Lagoon Cruises. An option to explore the **underwater world** beyond the reef is on the Raro Reef Sub (p205). From July to October they might be lucky enough to see **humpback whales** cruising past the island. If they're really keen on all things cetacean, drop by the excellent Cook Islands Whale & Wildlife Centre (p214).

Active kids will love exploring the island's **jungle-covered interior**, especially in the company of Pa Teuraa (p214). An entertaining **jeep ride** around the island with Raro Safari Tours (p205) will be sure to please, or you can take them for a **quad-bike** spin with Coconut Tours (p214). Only if they're 11 years or older, that is.

⊙10am-2.30pm Mon-Sat) Koka operates a similar operation around Muri including a barbecue fish lunch and snorkelling with friendly local guides. A percentage of all bookings is donated to support marine conservation.

Scenic Flights

Air Rarotonga   SCENIC FLIGHT
(☑22888; www.airraro.com; min 2, max 3; adult/child NZ$90/50; ⊙8.30am-4pm) Climb aboard for 20-minute scenic flights, complete with onboard commentary.

Walking Tours

Pa's Mountain Walk   HIKING
(☑21079; www.pastreks.com; per person NZ$70) A guided trek over the cross-island track is run by the dreadlocked Pa Teuraa. He's also a herbalist, botanist and traditional healer. Pa's cross-island walk runs on Monday, Wednesday and Friday (weather permitting), and he conducts nature walks on Tuesdays and Thursdays. A light lunch is included on both excursions and you'll need moderate fitness for the cross-island walk. See the website for more information.

Takitumu Conservation Area   BIRDWATCHING
(TCA; Map p200; ☑29906, 55228; kakerori@tca.co.ck; Ara Tapu, Avarua; guided tour adult/child NZ$50/30) This private forest reserve in Rarotonga's southeast corner runs guided tours where you might see the endangered *kakerori* (Rarotongan flycatcher).

Whale Watching

Humpback whales visit the Cook Islands from July to October. Most diving, sailing and fishing charters offer whale-watching trips in season. Visit the Cook Islands Whale and Wildlife Centre (p209) to learn more about whales.

Vehicle Tours

A round-the-island tour is a great way to see Rarotonga, especially if you're only here for a few days.

Tangaroa 4x4 Adventures   GUIDED TOUR
(Map p200; ☑22200; www.tangaroa4x4.co.ck; Ara Tapu, Vaima'anga; adult/child NZ$75/37.50) Tangaroa runs a tour of the island's main attractions, including the inland road, Avana Harbour, eastern heights, *marae*, library, power station and even the Rarotongan prison. The three-hour tour, which includes lunch and transfers, runs Monday to Saturday mornings and on Sunday afternoons.

Coconut Tours   GUIDED TOUR
(Map p200; ☑24004; www.coconuttours.co.ck; per person with/without lunch NZ$185/150) Lead a convoy of excited wannabe rally drivers on quad bikes through the backroads and streams of the island's rugged interior. Tours run rain or shine and 4WD adventure tours are also on offer (adult/child including lunch NZ$85/45). Kids from 11 to 16 years can ride pillion on the quad bikes with an adult.

Raro Tours   GUIDED TOUR
(Map p200; ☑25325; www.rarotours.co.ck; adult/child NZ$49/25; ⊙10am-1pm Mon-Fri) Join an Island Discovery Tour and explore ancient *marae* and the island's best snorkelling spots.

🛏 Sleeping

Rarotonga has accommodation options to suit all budgets, although postcard-perfect views can come at a premium. High-season prices are given here. Renting a house is often the best-value way to visit the island, especially for families. Fully furnished two-bedroom houses cost around NZ$800 to NZ$1200 per week.

For more options, try **Cook Islands Resorts** (www.cook.pacific-resorts.com), **Jetsave Travel** (www.jetsave.co.ck), **Jasons Travel** (www.jasons.com) or **Cook Islands Tourism** (www.cookislands.travel).

Aito Apartments   APARTMENTS $$
(Map p200; ☑20029; www.aitoapartmentsmuri.com; Ara Tapu, Muri; d NZ$160) These two modern apartments represent excellent value just a short walk from the cafes, restaurants and water sports of Muri Lagoon. The Cook Island-Tahitian owners are a real delight, and the spotless apartments feature spacious verandahs, designer bedrooms punctuated with Pacific textiles, and lovely bathrooms trimmed with natural river stones. Fire up the barbecue, prepare loads of tropical fruit in the self-contained kitchen and you'll quickly ease into island time.

Sea Change   BOUTIQUE HOTEL $$$
(Map p200; ☑22532; www.sea-change-rarotonga.com; Ara Tapu; villas NZ$535-850; ✳@☒) Many of Rarotonga's boutique hotels look to this place as a benchmark. The impeccably appointed free-standing thatched villas have fabulously appointed interiors with luxury king-size four-poster beds, entertainment systems, flat-screen TVs and private outdoor pools. The open-plan villas are finished in

earthy tones and traditional materials, offsetting the contemporary design elements.

Kura's Kabanas
BUNGALOWS $$

(Map p200; ☑27010; www.kkabanas.co.ck; Ara Tapu; units & cabanas NZ$200; ✳@☎) Shady palms, Muri Lagoon views and a glorious china-white beach are just steps from the doors of Kura's airy timber-framed cabanas. Two larger 1st-floor family studios can sleep four (children under 12 free). Fully equipped kitchens, queen beds, TVs and a great location make this hard to beat for the price. Check the website for details of Kura's two self-contained villas at the nearby Paku's Retreat (NZ$150 to NZ$200).

Aremango Guesthouse
GUESTHOUSE $

(Map p200; ☑24362; www.aremango.co.ck; Ara Tapu; s/d from NZ$45/69; @☎) Aremango has single and double fan-cooled rooms arranged along a central hallway. The common lounge, bathroom and kitchens are clean, comfortable and well fitted out, and there's a pleasant garden area to relax in. The guesthouse is exceptionally well run, and is a quieter alternative to a few of the other budget options around the island. Muri Beach and lots of good restaurants are a short walk away. Check the website for details of Aremango's private self-contained studio on the island's south coast. Bikes and kayaks are also available for use.

Aro'a Beachside Inn
BUNGALOWS $$

(Map p200; ☑22166; www.aroabeach.com; Ara Tapu, 'Arorangi; d NZ$205-290; ✳@☎) Choose from eight beachside units or three ocean-view units at this super-friendly spot on Rarotonga's sunset-friendly west coast. Rates include a tropical breakfast and free use of everything you need to explore the nearby reef. After you've invested holiday energy in kayaking, paddleboarding or snorkelling, kick back in the Shipwreck Hut bar.

Manea Beach Villas
BUNGALOWS $$

(Map p200; ☑25336; www.maneabeachrarotonga. com; Muri Beach; bungalows NZ$195, houses NZ$350-520; ✳☒) Down a quiet Muri road near the Flame Tree restaurant, Manea Beach combines spotless one-bedroom bungalows – some with lagoon views – and three larger three-bedroom houses that are perfect for families or groups of friends. The decor is a winning combination of modern and tropical, and there's a pleasant shared pool overlooking nearby Muri Lagoon.

WE DO

Many couples come to the Cook Islands to get married as it's a very romantic destination. Most hotels and resorts offer wedding packages and there are also several specialist wedding companies. Cook Islands marriages are legally binding worldwide. You'll need a copy of your birth certificate and passport. If you've been married before, you'll also need your divorce papers or a death certificate. The Marriage Registrar requires a minimum of four days before the wedding day to issue a marriage licence, otherwise an extra fee may be incurred.

Pacific Resort
RESORT $$$

(Map p200; ☑20427; www.pacificresort.com; units NZ$450-1050; ✳@☎☒) Right on Muri Beach and shaded by palm trees, the Pacific Resort's 64 self-contained units are smart and elegant, harnessing local elements of design and decor – the best have sitting rooms and private verandahs. Amenities include the beachfront Barefoot Bar, the open-air Sandals Restaurant and a good pizza restaurant (including takeaway) near the main island road.

Apartments Kakera
APARTMENTS $$$

(Map p200; ☑20532; www.apartmentskakera. com; Ara Tapu; apt NZ$300-430; ✳@☎☒) With three huge modern apartments blending sleek modern decor with lovely Polynesian touches, Kakera also boasts a long list of eco-credentials. The split-level apartments have high ceilings, private courtyard gardens with plunge pools, full kitchens and flat-panel TV/DVD and entertainment systems.

Little Polynesian
BOUTIQUE HOTEL $$$

(Map p200; ☑24280; www.littlepolynesian.com; Ara Tapu; villas NZ$550-950; ✳@☎☒) The 10 beachfront and four garden villas at Little Polynesian are a superb blend of traditional Polynesian design (with traditional Mangaian coconut-fibre sennit binding) and modern architecture, and the uninterrupted lagoon view from the foyer, pool and villas is sublime.

Muri Beachcomber
RESORT $$$

(Map p200; ☑21022; www.beachcomber.co.ck; Ara Tapu; per d unit NZ$285-395; ✳@☎☒) With a choice of garden and sea-view units and

luxury villas overlooking lovely grounds and a tropical lily pond, the Muri Beachcomber has a relaxed family-friendly village feel. The accommodation is modern – clean lines and tasteful appointments – and on-site facilities include guest lounge, laundry, pétanque court, free kayak use and snorkelling gear.

Sunhaven Beach Bungalows BUNGALOWS $$
(Map p200; ☑28465; www.mysunhaven.com; Ara Tapu; studios NZ$195-260, bungalows NZ$260-300; ☒☜☎) Sunhaven offers good value in some of the largest self-contained rooms on the island, set around a beachfront swimming pool on a quiet stretch of west-coast beach. The nine bungalows are sparkling clean and simply finished, with white-tile floors, cane furniture and functional fixtures. There's also an on-site licensed cafe, and lagoon kayaking and snorkelling on tap. Only children 15 years and older please.

Magic Reef Bungalows BUNGALOWS $$$
(Map p200; ☑27404; www.magicreef.co.nz; Ara Tapu; s & d NZ$295-395; ☒@☜☎) On a golden stretch of sand on the sunset side of the island, Magic Reef features tastefully decorated bungalows with four-poster beds, fans and air-con, galley kitchens, private outdoor showers and separate bathrooms with bathtubs.

Aquarius Rarotonga MOTEL $$
(Map p200; ☑21003; www.aquariusrarotonga.com; Ara Tapu; dm NZ$30, s & d NZ$155; ☒@☜☎) On the beachfront opposite the airport, the Aquarius offers ocean-view self-contained doubles and a large dorm area. A good choice for families, Aquarius is spotlessly clean and good value. There's a pizza and poolside barbecue restaurant on site, perfect for a cold beer and a final Cook Islands meal if you're leaving on an evening flight.

Bella Beach Bungalows BUNGALOWS $$
(Map p200; www.shekinahhomes.com; Ara Tapu; bungalows NZ$200) With the waves all but licking the stilts of these four functional units at Titikaveka on the island's south side, they're about as close to the beach as you can get. Inside are tiled floors, kitchens, small bathrooms and comfortable king-sized beds, while outside are large sundecks overlooking the beach and lagoon.

Rarotonga Backpackers HOSTEL $
(Map p200; ☑21590; www.rarotongabackpackers.com; Ara Tapu; dm NZ$20-25, s NZ$36-40, d NZ$44-150, bungalows NZ$72; @☜☎) Raro-

tonga Backpackers have a beachfront site and a recently renovated hillside site. Both offer accommodation from dorms to fully self-contained suites and a beachfront house. Dorms and rooms are set around a central pool, and there are self-contained units with private verandahs and fabulous views.

Vara's HOSTEL $
(Map p200; ☑23156; www.varas.co.ck; Ara Tapu; dm NZ$25-28, s NZ$48, d NZ$55-95, units NZ$85-130; @☜) Vara's on Muri Beach is popular with the young party set. It has a reputation for late-night revelry, so those seeking South Seas tranquillity should look elsewhere. The beachside accommodation can be cramped but the hillside lodge offers more room and great views.

Tiare Village Hostel HOSTEL $
(Map p200; ☑23466; www.tiarevillage.co.ck; Ara Metua; dm/s/d/poolside units NZ$20/25/45/70; @☜☎) Near Avarua, behind the airport, this hostel is a good choice for budget travellers, groups and families. Small dorm rooms inside the large main house share a kitchen, bathroom and comfortable lounge. Outside are three compact self-contained A-frame chalets and several roomier self-contained poolside units.

Muri Beach Shell Bungalows BUNGALOWS $
(Map p200; ☑22275; www.shellbungalows.co.ck; Ara Tapu; d/q NZ$100/110, flats NZ$100) In a great location 100m from Muri Beach behind the Shells & Craft shop, these two large self-contained bungalows with full kitchens are great value. One has a mezzanine level that sleeps an extra two, and next to the shop there's a huge flat that sleeps four.

✖ Eating

Vaima Restaurant & Bar POLYNESIAN $$
(Map p200; ☑26123; www.vaimarestaurant.com; Ara Tapu; mains NZ$24-32; ☺dinner Mon-Sun) Perched near a sandy beach on the island's south coast, Vaima is one of Rarotonga's best eateries and bookings are essential. The dining room has a tasteful island decor featuring local artworks, a beachfront patio and breezy outside terrace. Combine sumptuous Pacific cuisine with the sand between your toes for a quintessential Raro experience. Pizza (NZ$18 to NZ$22) is available for takeaway from 5pm.

RAROTONGA FOR FOODIES

After a successful career in restaurants in Australia, cook and food stylist Minar Purotu Henderson returned to Rarotonga to offer the island's Plantation Dining Experience (p217) in a restored 1850 colonial home. See her at her shop, Island Living (p220), for the latest on Rarotonga's growing scene for gourmet travellers.

Why is Rarotonga such a great destination for foodies? We've got some of the Pacific's best local fresh produce and our restaurants focus strongly on seasonal ingredients. Fresh fish is available daily and there's a growing range of artisan foods stalls at our weekly market. There's also a growing awareness of the importance of organic and traditional planting methods.

What are some of your favourite foodie spots around the island? At the **Cook Islands Coffee Company** (Map p200; Matavera; ⊙from 7.30am Sun-Fri), Neil Dearlove blends and roasts gourmet coffee at his home. Many locals stop in for their fix on the way into work. Le Bon Vivant (p206) is great for fresh pastries, artisan breads and deli essentials. It's a regular breakfast spot for us. Tahiti Café (p206) has the island's best sashimi. Go for lunch and try the 'Fishermans Plate' with five different styles of sashimi and Asian-inspired dipping sauces. Cafe Ariki (p205) is great for families and does good value and wholesome meals with an alfresco ambience. Try the fresh salads and local roast pork and vegetables.

What's Rarotonga's one essential destination for visiting foodies? Saturday morning at the Punanga Nui Market (p205) gives visitors one chance a week to explore and indulge in the island's great tastes.

What market stalls should visitors look out for? Ani Wichman's stall is called 'The Art', and she sells locally baked Turkish bread with grilled chicken, homemade yoghurt dressing and sweet chilli jam. Check out the tongue-in-cheek art covering her van. Josh and Renata at Waffle Shack (p206) have excellent espresso coffee and island-size waffles laden with fresh fruit salad and local ice cream. At Plantation House we get our pineapples from the Maoate family and, at the market, they sell pineapple juice and coconut-fed hot pork rolls with gravy and apple sauce. Make sure you leave room for Aunty Annie's pineapple meringue pie.

Everything sounds delicious, but what if we're still hungry? Michelle Finn – next to the coconut honey stall – sells sashimi trays with Asian-inspired *ika mata,* and also *firi firi,* Tahitian-style doughnuts with chocolate filling. Cook Islands dishes like *rukau, poke, mitiore* and octopus curry are also popular at her stall. The 'Noni Hut' is just nearby and sells amazing loaves made from freshly grated coconut, organic bananas, green pawpaw and nuts. They're perfect with a local coffee.

What about something to take away? Excellent 100% organic artisan bread is available from 'Varaua mata, e te Miti, Vai'. There's sourdough, croissants and wholegrain bread, and also locally made dips, sauces and chutneys.

Plantation House Dining   POLYNESIAN $$$
(Map p200; ☑25325; www.rarotours.com; Ara Tapu; per person NZ$95; ⊙dinner Thu) Join chef Minar Purotu Henderson for a three-course meal in a wonderfully restored colonial house. The evening kicks off with an informative walk around the villa's spacious gardens before settling in for foodie treats with a Polynesian and Asian spin. Dishes often include coconut-fed pork belly with caramelised pawpaw seed pepper, warm coconut and kaffir lime syrup cake, and lemongrass tea with coconut honey. Dinners run on Thursday, but other evenings can be requested subject to availability.

Progressive Dining   POLYNESIAN $$$
(☑20639; per person NZ$85; ⊙dinner Mon & Thu) Eat your way around the island during this progressive dinner held in locals' houses. The relaxed, easygoing occasions run to three courses across four to five hours and include live music and visits to gardens and plantations. It's a great way to meet the

locals and tuck into dishes including *ika mata* and pawpaw salad. Book at the Natura Holidays office in the CITC shopping centre.

The Mooring
SANDWICHES $

(Map p200; Avana Lagoon; sandwiches NZ$10; ⊘9.30am-3.30pm Mon-Fri, noon-4pm Sun) Tuck into tuna and mahi-mahi fish sandwiches on grilled Turkish bread at this funky blue shipping container on the edge of Avana Lagoon. Variations include Tijuana Tuna or Cajun Spiced, and other goodies include Rustys – marinated chicken pieces with pawpaw salsa. Refresh with one of Raro's best fruit smoothies (NZ$7), and donate any mortally wounded flip-flops to the 'Dead Chandals' hall of fame. The Mooring is handily open on Sunday afternoons.

Flame Tree
POLYNESIAN $$$

(Map p200; ✆25123; www.flametreerestaurant. com; Muri; mains NZ$29-37; ⊘dinner) In a quiet location near Muri Beach, Flame Tree combines Pacific ingredients with Mediterranean and Asian flavours. Order the gossamer-light mahi-mahi spring rolls or the seared yellowfin tuna. If you're really hungry after a day's Raro adventuring, the pork belly on roasted kumara (sweet potato) will *definitely* fill you up. Bookings are essential; choose between the casual outdoor courtyard or the more formal dining room.

Flying Boat Fish & Chips
FISH & CHIPS $

(Map p200; Game Fishing Club, Tupapa; snacks & meals NZ$5-15; ⊘lunch & dinner) Tuck into Raro's best fish and chips at this funky reconfigured fishing boat. The lagoon's waters are just metres away and cheap-as-chips drinks are available from the bar at the adjacent Game Fishing Club. The club's a good place to drop by if you're looking to watch live rugby action from New Zealand's mighty All Blacks.

Tamarind House
INTERNATIONAL $$$

(Map p200; ✆26487; www.tamarind.co.ck; Ara Tapu, Tupapa; mains NZ$25-35; ⊘9.30am-2.30pm Mon-Fri, 5.30-10.30pm Mon-Sat) Owner Sue Carruthers made her reputation with Flame Tree, but has since fitted out this sweeping colonial-style building on the island's north shore. Book a table on the grand verandah and enjoy the cool evening breeze with an inspired fusion of European, Asian and Pacific flavours. Try the Pacific seafood ragout or the subtle Burmese-style fish curry.

Saltwater Cafe
CAFE $$

(Map p200; Titikaveka; mains NZ$19-28; ⊘10am-2.30pm Mon-Thu & Sun) This colourful roadside eatery on the south coast at Titikaveka is a great place for lunch or a cold drink. New owners have invigorated the menu with tasty offerings including octopus curry, pad Thai and garlic prawns. The homemade chocolate cake (NZ$8) is excellent and it's a handy spot on Sundays when not much else is open.

Hidden Spirit Café & Grill
CAFE $$$

(Map p200; ✆22796; www.hiddenspirit.net; Ara Tapu; mains NZ$30; ⊘lunch & dinner Mon-Sat) Set in the verdant surroundings of the Maire Nui Gardens, this cafe showcases delicious cakes and desserts – try the lemon meringue pie (NZ$16) – and healthy salads. Later at night the focus shifts to classy grills, including marinated lamb rump and barbecued pork loin. Afterwards you can take a relaxing stroll around the gardens (NZ$4). Bookings for dinner are recommended.

Sails Restaurant
POLYNESIAN $$

(Map p200; ✆27349; www.sailsrestaurant.co.ck; Muri Beach; mains NZ$17-33; ⊘lunch & dinner) In a great location overlooking the sands and sea of Muri Lagoon, breezy Sails is an open-air bistro-bar serving light lunchtime fare and heartier evening meals daily. Try the island-style fries with the yellowfin tuna *ika mata*. Bookings are recommended for dinner, and brunch is available from 9.30am on the weekend.

Waterline Bar & Grill
INTERNATIONAL $$

(Map p200; ✆22161; www.waterlinerestaurant. com; 'Arorangi; mains NZ$25-36; ⊘lunch & dinner, closed Mon) Welcome to the South Pacific restaurant-bar of your dreams with a rustic beachfront pavilion and absolute waterfront tables and chairs. Book in for around 30 minutes before sunset to enjoy a cocktail with the sand between your toes, before graduating to a table in the restaurant for calamari, prawns and steak. Lunchtime's a more informal offering including BLT sandwiches and kebabs. Rarotonga's musos often get together here on a Wednesday night.

Kikau Hut
RESTAURANT $$

(Map p200; ✆26860; 'Arorangi; mains NZ$24-34; ⊘dinner Mon-Sun) Candles and dim lighting make this circular restaurant in 'Arorangi a great place for an evening meal. The international cuisine is well prepared and the welcome is friendly and convivial. There's

regular live music and a breezy relaxed atmosphere. Just come as you are and fast forward to an easygoing holiday state of mind.

Fruits of Rarotonga   CAFE $
(Map p200; breakfasts NZ$4-6; ⊘closed Sun) Homemade jams and tropical-flavoured chutneys are divine at this little shop opposite Tikioki beach, but it's good for breakfast, burgers, cakes and fruit juices too. Kayaks are available for hire (per hour NZ$5), and you can leave gear with them when you go snorkelling in the nearby lagoon. Don't leave without recharging on a creamy pawpaw-and-banana smoothie (NZ$6).

Deli-licious   CAFE $
(Map p200; www.delilicious.net; Muri Beach; lunch NZ$10-18; ⊘8am-5pm Mon-Sat; @) Right in the heart of the Muri, Deli-licious serves up cooked breakfasts, and salads and sandwiches for lunch. Excellent 'Atiu coffee is served along with shakes and smoothies. This place is always buzzing and has internet terminals and an alfresco deck.

Café Jireh   CAFE $$
(Map p200; Main Rd, opposite airport; ⊘8am-4pm Mon-Fri, from 1pm Sat) Near the airport, Café Jireh does excellent coffee and homestyle baking including creamy custard squares. It's also a popular spot for a lazy brunch.

CITC Supermarket   SUPERMARKET $
(Map p200; Ara Tapu; ⊘closed Sun) Halfway to the airport from Avarua, the huge CITC Supermarket is great for tinned and pack-aged produce. There's also a liquor store attached.

Wigmore's Superstore   SUPERMARKET $
(Map p200; Ara Tapu; ⊘6am-9pm) The south coast's only proper grocery store is more expensive than Avarua's supermarkets. It's the only large supermarket that trades on Sunday though and it has a small liquor store. Drop in on a Sunday afternoon for lots of still-warm freshly baked local produce.

Super Brown   SUPERMARKET $
(Map p200; Tupapa; ⊘24hr) Super Brown is Raro's only all-night convenience store and petrol station, with a fair selection of groceries and takeaway food.

🍷 Drinking & Entertainment

The Shipwreck Hut   BAR
(Map p200; 'Arorangi) Judged one of the planet's top beach bars in 2011 by CNN, the Shipwreck Hut is a wonderfully rustic spot with an absolute waterfront location. There's regular live music, great pub meals and barbecue dinners, and it's a top west-coast location to watch Rarotonga's incredible sunsets. Come along on a Thursday night for the dulcet tones of Jake Numanga. He's the ukulele whiz who welcomed you when you flew in.

Chillis Sports Bar   BAR
(Map p200; Ara Tapu) There's an interesting mix of people at Chillis, most drawn by the well-priced beer and the opportunity

KEEP YOUR COOL, RARO STYLE

Exploring Rarotonga can be thirsty work, so here's our top-five picks to cool down, island-style.

» Dive into nature's very own electrolyte, a **nu (young green coconut)**, chilled and ready to drink from the Punanga Nui Market (p205). Don't be surprised if it's also the drink of choice when you're served lunch on an island tour.

» Lots of tropical fruit equals lots of **tropical smoothies**. Recharge after snorkelling with huge servings of creamy, liquid goodness from Saltwater Cafe (p218) or Fruits of Rarotonga (p219).

» Pull up a bar stool at Trader Jacks (p205), and toast Raro's dedicated crews of outrigger paddlers with a frosty pint of **Cook's Lager**.

» Yes, the craft-beer movement has even washed up on Rarotongan shores. Head to the **Waterline Bar & Grill** (p218) and cool down a west coast sunset with **Matutu Kiva Pale Ale**.

» Discover the unique flavours of **banana wine** at Muri's **Koteka Winery** (Map p200; Muri) or visit the winery's stall at Avarua's weekly market. The wine is mixed with whatever fruit is in season – anything from passionfruit, mango or orange. See www. punanganuiculturalmarket.co.ck for details of its banana vodka too.

to watch their Aussie or Kiwi footy team of choice. Check the blackboard out front to see what's scheduled.

🔒 Shopping

Island Living   HOMEWARES
(Map p200; Matavera; ⊙9am-3pm Mon-Fri) Drop by the village of Matavera for interesting Pacific-style design and homewares, exquisite woven hats from the remote atoll of Manihiki, and handmade soaps.

Mike Tavioni   ARTS & CRAFTS
(Map p200; Ara Metua, Atupa) Visit the workshop of Rarotonga's most renowned sculptor and carver on the back road near Avarua. See his stone carvings at the Punanga Nui Market (p205) and the National Culture Centre.

Prison Craft Shop   ARTS & CRAFTS
(Map p200; 'Arorangi; ⊙8.30am-3pm Mon-Fri) A good spot for unique gifts including handmade ukuleles.

Tivaevae Collectables   ARTS & CRAFTS
(Map p200; www.tivaevaecollectables.com; Nikao) Visit for beautiful Cook Islands *tivaevae* (hand-sewn quilted fabrics) harnessing traditional designs like bedspreads and bed linen, but also reworked as cushion covers, tablecloths and women's clothing. Shopping online and worldwide shipping are both possible if you're concerned about excess baggage.

The Art Studio   ARTS & CRAFTS
(Map p200; www.theartstudiocookislands.com; 'Arorangi; ⊙10am-5pm Mon-Fri) Contemporary art from owners Ian and Kay George combines with works from other Pacific artists. Sculpture and handpainted or printed textiles are also available.

Akoa Night Market   MARKET
(Map p200; 'Arorangi; ⊙5-10pm every 2nd Wed) This bi-weekly night market is a proudly local affair with *pareu* and crafts for sale, and a good selection of cheap-and-cheerful alfresco Pacific eats.

Tokerau Jim   JEWELLERY
(Map p200; www.tokeraujim.com) Located in Matavera, Tokerau Jim does beautiful and incredibly fine carvings on pearls and pearl shell.

Turtles & Ocean/Earth   CLOTHING
(Map p200; Avatiu) Interesting designs spoofing global brands.

Perfumes of Rarotonga   GIFTS
(Map p200; www.perfumes.co.ck) Near the airport, this place makes its own perfumes, soaps, liqueurs and scented oils. There's another outlet (Map p206; Cook's Corner Arcade) in central Avarua.

Croc Ta Tatau   TATTOO PARLOUR
(Map p200; croctatau@gmail.com) Englishman 'Croc' is the only man on Rarotonga crafting *tata'u* (tattoos) the traditional way, using pigment and hand tools. Check out his blog (www.croctatau.wordpress.com) for information and photos. He's sometimes off the island working in Europe, so email him before you travel. You'll find other local tattooists offering traditional designs but modern techniques at Avarua's weekly Punanga Nui Market (p205).

DON'T MISS

ISLAND NIGHTS

Rarotonga's traditional form of evening entertainment is the island night – a spectacular showcase combining traditional dance and music *(karioi)* with a lavish buffet of local food *(kai)*. Dancing, drumming and singing are always on show, and fire juggling, acrobatics and storytelling are often thrown into the mix.

Island nights are held regularly at the large resorts, and every night except Sunday you can catch a show somewhere on the island. Extravagant affairs are featured at the **Pacific Resort** (p215), **Edgewater Resort** (Map p200; ☑25435), **Crown Beach Resort** (Map p200; ☑23953) and the **Rarotongan Beach Resort** (Map p200; ☑25800). You'll pay between NZ$15 and NZ$35 for the show on its own, or NZ$55 to NZ$89 for the show and buffet.

On Wednesday and Friday nights, **Highland Paradise** (p210) offers a NZ$89 show that includes transport, a cocktail and an *umukai* (underground oven) feast. Another *umukai* is provided at **Te Vara Nui Village** (p211) on Tuesday, Thursday and Saturday nights. On Thursday and Friday nights the **Staircase Restaurant & Bar** (p207) features a show costing just NZ$35 including food (NZ$6 for show only).

ℹ Information

Deli-licious (Map p200; Muri; ⊘9am-5pm) Internet access.

Hospital (Map p200; ✆22664; 24hr emergency) On a steep hill behind the golf course.

Island Hopper Vacations (Map p200; ✆22576; www.islandhoppervacations.com; Turama House, Nika'o) Has good airfare-and-accommodation packages and deals to the outer islands.

Kavera Central (Map p200; Kavera) Internet access.

Outpatient clinic (Map p200; ✆20065; ⊘8am-4pm Mon-Fri) About 1km east of Ava-rua. Also has emergency dental services.

ℹ Getting Around

See p247 for information on getting to and from the airport, and for information on transport options around the island.

AITUTAKI

POP 2035 / AREA 18.3 SQ KM

Aitutaki, the Cooks' second-most visited island, curls gently around one of the South Pacific's most stunning lagoons. The aqua water, foaming breakers around the perimeter reef and broad sandy beaches of its many small deserted islets make for a glorious scene. From the air or on the water, Aitutaki will take your breath away.

It's just 45 minutes by air from Rarotonga but it feels like another world. Although there are some impressive, plush resorts, this island is slower and much less commercialised. Many visitors come on Air Rarotonga's day tour or opt to stay at upmarket resorts, but there are still good-value accommodation options, and it's worth spending a few days to slow down to island time.

Sunday is solemnly observed as the day of prayer and rest. Take the opportunity to see a local church service, as the singing is spine-tingling. Sunday flights from Rarotonga continue to inspire protest from elements of the island's religious community, and you may see a few banners and placards when you arrive.

Aitutaki is shaped like a curved fishhook, and you'll fly into the north of the island near O'otu Beach and the private Aitutaki Lagoon Resort. On the west side are most of the hotels and Arutanga, the island's main town. On the east coast are the small villages of Tautu, Vaipae and Vaipeka. The

motu around the edge of Aitutaki's lagoon are uninhabited.

History

Legend tells that Ru from 'Avaiki (Ra'iatea in French Polynesia) arrived at Aitutaki by *vaka* (canoe). He came with four wives, four brothers and their wives, and 20 royal maidens at the Akitua *motu* (now the Aitutaki Lagoon Resort).

Aitutaki's first European visitor was Captain William Bligh, who arrived on the *Bounty* on 11 April 1789 (17 days before the famous mutiny). In 1821 John Williams left Tahitian preachers Papeiha and Vahapata here to convert the islanders to Christianity. Charles Darwin passed by on the 1835 *Beagle* voyage, and in the 1850s Aitutaki become a favourite port of call for whaling ships. During WWII American soldiers arrived to build two long runways, and in the 1950s the lagoon was used as a refuelling stopover for the Tasman Empire Air Line's (TEAL; Air New Zealand's predecessor) luxurious 'coral route' across the Pacific, flown by Solent flying boats. John Wayne and Cary Grant were just two of the celebrities who spent time on Akaiami *motu* while their Solent was re-fuelled. Most lagoon cruises stop at Akaiami where the crumbling foundations of TEAL's absolute waterfront terminal are still visible.

⊙ Sights

The lagoon may be what draws the tourists here, but Aitutaki's ancient *marae* are also notable for their large stones and cultural significance. **Marae Orongo** is today in the main village of Arutanga. The main road runs through another large *marae*, and on the inland road between Nikaupara and Tau-tu are the islands' most magnificent *marae* – including **Tokangarangi** and **Te Poaki O Rae** – mostly reclaimed by the jungle.

Arutanga TOWN

After you've been to Rarotonga, Arutanga, Aitutaki's only town, seems astonishingly quiet, with few signs of life even on week-days when the shops are open. The island's main harbour is by the Orongo Centre. The lovely weather-beaten **CICC** church near the Administration Centre was built in 1828, making it the oldest in the Cooks. Beauti-fully restored in 2010, the church has lovely stained-glass windows, fine carved-wood panelling and an old anchor precariously suspended from the ceiling. Try to attend a service on the first Sunday of every month

Aitutaki

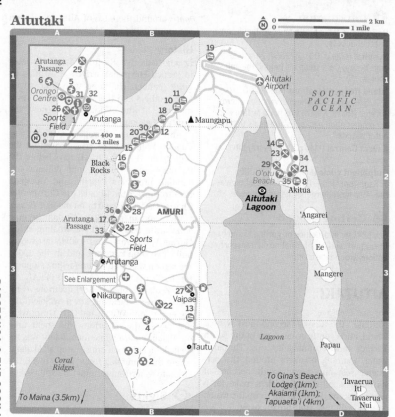

when Aitutaki's female parishioners wear pristine white dresses.

Maungapu   LOOKOUT

The 30-minute hike to the top of Maungapu (124m), Aitutaki's highest peak, provides splendid views over the entire atoll and the sapphire-blue lagoon. The track starts off pretty gently opposite the bungalows of Paradise Cove, but gets more challenging towards the summit.

Aitutaki Lagoon   LAGOON

Aitutaki's stunning lagoon, brimming with marine life and ringed by 15 palm-covered *motu*, is one of the treasures of the South Pacific. **Maina** (Little Girl) offers some of the best snorkelling spots and is home to the red-tailed tropicbird, once prized for its crimson feathers. Nearby is the wreck of cargo freighter *Alexander,* which ran aground in the 1930s. **Akaiami** is where the old TEAL flying boats landed to refuel on

the trans-Pacific 'Coral Route' between Fiji, Samoa and Tahiti – the remnants of the old jetty can still be seen. **Tapuaeta'i** (One Foot Island) is the best-known *motu,* fringed by white beaches and divided from its neighbour, Tekopua, by a deepwater channel that's teeming with tropical fish.

Activities

The best swimming, snorkelling and beaches are around the *motu,* especially near Maina, accessible by boat. The folks at **Aitutaki Glass Bottom Boat** (p224) offer snorkelling trips outside the perimeter reef where marine life is much more abundant. Just south of Black Rocks you can walk out to the outer reef on a coral causeway that starts 50m from the shore. The nicest swimming beaches on the main island are **O'otu Beach** and the wharves at **Vaipae** and **Tautu**. The island's east coast is mainly shallow mud and mangrove swamp.

Aitutaki

Scuba diving is fantastic in Aitutaki. The visibility is great, and features include drop-offs, multilevels, wall dives and cave systems. Many divers ask to dive on the wreck of the *Alexander,* but it sits in a mere metre of water and is just as suitable for snorkellers.

Bubbles Below (☑31537; www.diveaitutaki. com; 1/2 dives NZ$105/170, PADI discover/open-water course NZ$170/550) offers dive trips and courses. The entertaining manager Onu (Turtle) Hewett really knows the waters surrounding Aitutaki.

Check out www.aitutaki.net, www.aitutaki tourism.com and www.aitutaki.com for more activities listings.

☞ Tours

Most tour operators on Aitutaki don't have offices. Arrange a cruise by calling the operator or ask the people you're staying with to arrange it. The operator will collect you from your hotel.

Fishing

Find out about the fishing scene at **Aitutaki Game Fishing Club** (☑31379), by the wharf in Arutanga. It's also a good place for a cold beer from 5pm on Wednesday, Friday and Saturday nights. Bonefish are among the fastest and most exciting fighting fish in the world, and Aitutaki's lagoon has some of the biggest on the planet.

Black Pearl Charters   FISHING
(☑31125; www.blackpearlaitutaki.com) Hooking wahoo, giant trevally and mahi-mahi from NZ$180 per person. Spearfishing trips in the lagoon (half/full day NZ$250/500) are also available.

Bonefish E2   FISHING
(☑31686, 52077; www.e2sway.com) Local guide Itu Davey has been hooking Aitutaki's bonefish since he was a boy. Half-/full-day charters per two people are NZ$350/450.

Lagoon Cruises

For many travellers an Aitutaki lagoon cruise is a Cook Islands highlight. There are several operators that cruise around the *motu* and snorkelling spots. All provide snorkelling gear, a barbecue fish lunch and a stop at Tapuaeta'i (One Foot Island) – remember to

take your passport to get it stamped at the One Foot Island 'post office'.

Aitutaki Glass Bottom Boat BOAT TOUR
(☎57863, 72222) Aitutaki's glass-bottomed boat cruises outside the barrier reef to see turtles and rich marine life. Morning departures (adult NZ$50, child NZ$30; 10am to noon) focus on viewing only, while afternoon departures (adult NZ$60, child NZ$30; 2pm to 4pm) incorporate snorkelling beyond the reef. The boat moors at the wharf at Arutanga and bookings are recommended.

Aitutaki Adventures LAGOON TOUR
(☎31171; ⊗cruises Sun-Fri) Lagoon cruises include snorkelling, fish-feeding and a barbecue lunch on Tapuaeta'i.

Bishop's Cruises BOAT TOUR
(☎31009; www.bishopscruises.com; ⊗tours Mon-Sat) Tours visit Maina, Moturakau and Tapuaeta'i; there's a tour to Akaiami (NZ$35), as well as sunset, honeymoon cruises and *motu* drop-offs.

Kia-Orana Cruises LAGOON CRUISE
(☎31442; www.kiaoranacruise.com; per person NZ$85; ⊗Sun-Fri) The main tour visits Maina, Moturakau, Honeymoon Island and Tapuaeta'i. Snorkelling excursions (per person NZ$60), and dinner and overnight stays on Honeymoon Island are also available.

Vaka Cruise LAGOON CRUISE
(☎31398; www.aitutaki.net; per person NZ$85; ⊗10am-4pm daily) Cruises are on a Polynesian-style catamaran, the *Titi Ai Tonga* (Wind from the South), which has a roof and onboard bar. Look forward to lots of onboard entertainment and the company of a few day-trip visitors across from Rarotonga.

Teking LAGOON CRUISE
(☎31582; www.teking.co.ck) Offers a main 'Five Island' cruise (per person NZ$99) to Akaiami, Tapuaeta'i, Honeymoon Island, Moturakau and Maina. Other options include a champagne-brunch cruise (per person NZ$105) and a barbecue and sunset departure (per person NZ$95).

Other Tours

Aitutaki Discovery Safari Tours GUIDED TOUR
(☎31757; safari@aitutaki.net.ck; adult/child NZ$55/28) An interesting 'discovery safari' that visits the island's main historical sites in a yellow Jeep. The three-hour tours run at 9am and 1pm Sunday to Friday. Local guide Ngaa Pureariki is a keen archaeology buff.

Nane & Chloe's Tropicool Tour GUIDED TOUR
(☎31248; per person NZ$50) Runs morning and afternoon minibus tours to the villages and *marae* of Aitutaki from Monday to Sunday.

🛏 Sleeping

TOP CHOICE Etu Moana BOUTIQUE HOTEL $$$
(☎31458; www.etumoana.com; villas NZ$465-590; ❄@🖥🌊) These boutique beach villas have thatched roofs and luxurious furnishings showcasing gleaming Tasmanian oak floors, lofty ceilings, king-sized beds, private outdoor showers and teak sundecks. The design and decor are superb and very classy, and there's a tear-drop pool complete with rock garden, sun-shaded tables and a deluxe honesty bar. If you prefer your luxe resorts a little down-sized and understated, then this is the place. Sorry, no kids under 12.

Aretai Beach Villas APARTMENTS $$$
(☎31645; www.aretaibeachvillas.com; villas NZ$300; ❄@) The lovely two-bedroom villas at Aretai are the largest on the island, and definitely the best presented and best value for money in this price range. Halfway between Arutanga and the airport, with wonderful sea views and outstanding facilities – including full kitchens, dining areas, gorgeous furniture and huge patios – these villas are ideal for families or groups who want a little style in their lifestyle. The delightful Mama Tatui is the matriarch and genial host.

Amuri Sands BUNGALOWS $$
(☎31130, 50613; www.aitutaki-vacation.com; Amuri; s/d/tw $120/150/150) These two recently built beach bungalows offer all you need for an island sojourn; a lagoon-facing location, trade-wind-friendly decks and a grassy lawn studded with coconut palms. Decor is simple but trendy, and the bathrooms and self-contained kitchens are spotless and modern. Look forward to a central location near good restaurants and cafes.

Gina's Garden Lodges LODGE $
(☎31058; www.ginasaitutakidesire.com; s/d/tr NZ$75/120/150; 🌊) Set amid a peaceful garden of fruit trees and flowers in Tautu, these four large family-friendly lodges are the best value on Aitutaki. Queen Manarangi Tutai, one of Aitutaki's three *ariki* (high chiefs), is the proprietor here and one of the island's most gracious and charming hosts. The self-contained lodges have high

ceilings and large verandahs overlooking the gardens and decked swimming pool, and each has beds in a small loft that are perfect for kids. Gina's is a few kilometres from town, so you'll need transport. Queen Tutai also runs **Gina's Beach Lodge** (s/d/tr NZ$200/300/375 incl transfers) on Akaiami Island, and guests can choose to spend a while at each.

Pacific Resort
RESORT $$$

(☑31720; www.pacificresort.com; beachfront bungalows/ste/villas NZ$600/1190/1890; ✳@🛜🌊) Like its sister resort in Rarotonga, Pacific Resort Aitutaki is a benchmark in luxury Polynesian. From the Oriental lily ponds and enormous carved-timber reception desk of its sumptuous foyer to the rough-rendered walls and timber floors, decor and views of the split-level restaurant, the Pacific Resort is breathtaking. The rooms are superb, with commanding views, huge private beach decks and private garden bathrooms with outdoor showers. Even if you can't afford to stay, come and enjoy the resort's restaurants.

Tamanu Beach
RESORT $$$

(☑31810; www.aretamanu.com; bungalows NZ$340-550; ✳@🛜🌊) The elegant Tamanu Beach is another indicator of Aitutaki's ongoing evolution as a destination targeting more moneyed travellers. Chic bungalows range in size from studio to one-bedroom, all arrayed around a lush garden or with excellent lagoon views. 'Casual luxury' is the resort's slogan and we reckon that's pretty accurate.

Aitutaki Lagoon Resort
RESORT $$$

(☑31201; www.aitutakilagoonresort.com; beachfront/over-water bungalows NZ$600/1240; ✳@🛜🌊) Aitutaki Lagoon Resort, ensconced on its own Akitua Island, has everything the finicky glam jet-set patron would expect. It's truly beautiful, with great expanses of glistening white beach and a private ferryman to shunt you to and from the mainland. There are bars and restaurants, and a pool and day spa. The thatched garden and beachfront villas are large, light and comfortable, but the over-water bungalows and new premium beachfront bungalows are extra special. Nonguests are welcome, so drop in for a visit. The resort offers packages and discounts for extended stays – see the website.

Ranginui Sunset
BUNGALOWS $$

(☑31836; www.bookthecooks.com; d NZ$180) Look forward to a quiet, absolute beachfront location on the sleepy northern tip of the island near the airport and golf course. The three fan-cooled self-contained villas are simple, with large verandahs, queen beds and basic kitchen facilities. You'll need transport to get around the island and to restaurants.

Matriki Beach Huts
BUNGALOWS $

(☑31564; www.matrikibeachhuts.com; s NZ$62-68, d NZ$79-90, tr NZ$110) Three knocked-up beachfront fibro shacks with mural-painted walls and one self-contained garden unit comprise this most delightfully ramshackle place to stay. The split-level huts share toilet facilities but are otherwise self-contained with kitchenettes and showers and the most brilliant location. Matriki runs snorkelling trips outside the lagoon reef and can arrange fishing charters and activities.

Inano Beach Bungalows
BUNGALOWS $$

(☑31758; www.inanobeach.com; lagoon-view/beachfront bungalows NZ$130/160) Offering excellent value for money, Inano Beach Bungalows have been built using largely local materials and traditional methods. There are woven pandanus walls, ironwood balconies and mahogany tabletops. Near the end of the airport fronting a nice stretch of beach, Inano's self-contained bungalows are large with good kitchen facilities.

Amuri Guesthouse
GUESTHOUSE $

(☑31231; www.amuri-aitutaki.com; s/d/tr NZ$40/70/90) Amuri has six double bedrooms and two shared bathrooms with a large dining and kitchen area in the owner's house. Accommodation is very clean, friendly and excellent value, and fresh fruit is often supplied *gratis* for breakfast. You'll be around 100m from the beach, but handily placed for food shopping and a great little cafe.

Paradise Cove
BUNGALOWS $$

(☑31218; www.paradisecove.co.ck; bungalows & garden ste NZ$150) Paradise Cove features beachfront bungalows on a glorious beach shaded by coconut palms. The thatched pole-house bungalows offer uninterrupted views across the lagoon from private verandahs. Inside are king-sized beds, kitchenettes with fridges, bathrooms and ceiling fans. They're not huge, but the larger garden suites can sleep up to four – a good option for families.

Paparei Bungalows
BUNGALOWS **$$**

(☑31837; www.papareibungalows.com; d NZ$225) Paparei offers two modern self-contained beachfront bungalows near the centre of town. They're large, clean, well equipped and nicely decorated in an unfussy way. Owners Vicki and Peter Petero are lovely hosts.

✕ Eating

Koru Café
CAFE **$$**

(☑31110; www.korucafe.biz; O'otu Beach; meals NZ$10-30; ☺7am-3pm; @🖥) Located near the airport, Koru is a spacious and breezy Aitutaki spin on a trendy New Zealand cafe. All-day cooked breakfasts and lunches – including Caesar salad, steak sandwiches, BLT, pasta and salt-and-pepper calamari – all complement the island's best coffee. Wi-fi is available, along with a laptop, and you can call to arrange picnic lunches or barbecue packs. Locally made arts and crafts, including weaving, jewellery and ukuleles, are also available.

Kuku's
CAFE **$**

(Arutanga; snacks & meals NZ$10-15; ☺10am-4pm Mon-Sat, 6-8pm Fri & Sat) Pop into this funky cafe to recharge and refresh with great coffee and tropical-fruit smoothies. Grab an alfresco table under the sprawling breadfruit tree and tuck into all-day breakfasts, superior gourmet burgers and toasted sandwiches. Hands-down the best eatery in Arutanga, it's worth the trip even if you're staying near the airport.

Samade on the Beach
RESTAURANT **$$**

(O'otu Beach; lunch NZ$10-25, dinner NZ$15-30; ☺lunch & dinner) With a sand floor and a thatched roof, this is a cool and rustic place for a beer, lunch by the lagoon or an evening meal at sunset. The food is simple – fish, burgers, steaks and salads – but the view is serene and the ambience relaxed. Samade has regular island nights and a good Sunday afternoon barbecue (NZ$20, from noon to 9pm). Live music also kicks off at 6pm on Sundays.

Café Tupuna
POLYNESIAN **$$$**

(☑31678; Tautu; mains NZ$30-40; ☺dinner) Café Tupuna is the only independent restaurant on Aitutaki offering fine dining. It's in a lovely rural setting in the hills behind Arutanga. The menu features fresh local fish and seafood cooked with island flavours and exotic spices. Try the 'Trio of Fish'. The lush garden setting makes for a relaxed atmosphere and there's a good wine list. Prior booking is strongly recommended, and bringing insect repellent is often a wise move.

⚑ Tauono's
CAFE **$$**

(☑31562; www.tauonos.com; cakes NZ$4-8, lunch & dinner NZ$15-25; ☺lunch & afternoon tea Mon, Wed & Fri, dinner by arrangement; 🖥) Tauono's is a delight, a tiny garden cafe run by one-time Austrian Sonja and her hardworking team of travellers and WWOOFers (Willing Workers on Organic Farms). Renowned for its coconut cake, fruit smoothies (NZ$6) and afternoon teas, Tauono's offers brilliant home-cooked cuisine served alfresco. The food is prepared according to what's been freshly picked from their on-site organic garden. Stop by for homemade cake and fresh fruit and veg from Sonja's shop (open 10am to 5pm Monday to Friday), and ask about joining a plantation tour (per person NZ$35). Fresh and frozen meals are also available to take away.

Boatshed Bar & Grill
BAR, RESTAURANT **$$**

(☑31739; Popaara Beach; mains NZ$15-35; ☺lunch & dinner Mon-Sun; 🖥) A sprawling array of maritime memorabilia and classic country music makes the Boatshed a very laid-back spot. Try to secure a space on the deck for reef views, and feast on seafood classics like chowder, *ika mata* and curried prawns. The beer's cold, the wine's reasonably priced, and it's the kind of easygoing place where the guys that were there at 2pm might still be around hours later. Book for dinner.

Rapae Bay Restaurant
FUSION **$$$**

(☑31720; lunch from NZ$15, mains NZ$27-55; ☺lunch & dinner) The island's standout resort restaurant is in Pacific Resort. It offers superb Pacific fusion cuisine in a brilliant split-level patio setting. Look forward to interesting combinations of Pacific and Southeast Asian flavours including tuna sashimi and fresh spring rolls. The Pacific Resort's other eatery is the more informal Black Rock Café.

Tamanu Beachfront
POLYNESIAN **$$**

(Tamanu Beach; lunch NZ$15-25, dinner NZ$25-35; ☺breakfast, lunch & dinner) The in-house restaurant of the Tamanu Beach hotel is also open to outside guests. Here's your chance to dine at sunset on Pacific-style fresh fish, top-notch salads and other local dishes. Tamanu's island night on Thursday is renowned as one of Aitutaki's best.

Maina Traders Superstore SELF-CATERING **$**
(☑31055; ☺closed Sun) Centrally located in Arutanga.

Rerei's SELF-CATERING **$**
(☺closed Sun) Stock up on groceries at this Amuri store with a Heineken sign out the front. Unfortunately it's not a bar, but it does have a pretty good selection of beer and wine.

Neibaa SELF-CATERING **$**
(☺open daily) On the island's east side in Vaipae, Neibaa is the only shop that opens Sundays.

Market SELF-CATERING **$**
(Orongo Centre; ☺from 7am Mon-Sat) Self-caterers can stock up on fruit, vegetables and fruit at Aitutaki's market. Also good for organic fruit and vegetables is Tauono's (p226).

Drinking

Puffy's Bar BAR
(☺Mon-Sat) Puffy's is a tiny bar popular with locals and backpackers from nearby Paradise Cove. Simple meals – mainly burgers and fish and chips – and cheap booze are served, and there's also a really good weekly island night. Keep an eye on the noticeboard out the front.

❶ Information

Ask at your hotel if you should boil the water before drinking it. Many places get their drinking water from separate rain tanks.

There aren't any dogs on Aitutaki (the island's canine population was blamed for a leprosy outbreak) but there are plenty of roosters – bring earplugs if you're planning on sleeping in.

The main police station is behind the Orongo Centre near the wharf in Arutanga.

Aitutaki Tourism (☑31767; www.aitutakitourism.com; ☺8am-noon & 1-4pm Mon-Fri) A very helpful office in Arutanga.

ANZ Bank agent (☺8am-3pm Mon-Fri) Inside Mango Trading with an ATM outside.

Hospital (☑31002; ☺24hr) On the hill behind Arutanga.

Post office & Telecom (☺8am-4pm Mon-Fri) In the Administration Centre in Arutanga.

SpiderCo Internet Lounge (per min NZ$0.50) In Arutanga, this place also morphs into a pretty good local bar at night.

❶ Getting There & Away

AIR Air Rarotonga (☑in Arutanga 31888; in Rarotonga 22888; www.airraro.com;) operates

several flights to Aitutaki from Rarotonga Monday to Saturday, and one flight on Sunday. Regular one-way fares cost from NZ$109 to NZ$264. There's also a direct flight from Aitutaki to 'Atiu on Monday, Wednesday and Friday. One-way fares are priced from NZ$217. Also available is an Aitutaki/'Atiu combo fare combining travel from Rarotonga to Aitutaki to 'Atiu and back to Rarotonga. Check the Air Rarotonga website for the latest fares.

Air Rarotonga runs Aitutaki Day Tours from Monday to Saturday, leaving Rarotonga at 8am and returning at 5.30pm. The cost is NZ$459 per person, including hotel transfers, flights, a lagoon cruise with snorkelling gear and lunch.

BOAT Cargo ships travelling to the Northern Group occasionally stop at Aitutaki (see p248).

❶ Getting Around

TO/FROM THE AIRPORT Island Tours (☑31379) offers a minibus transfer service that costs NZ$15 to and from the airport. The larger resorts provide transfers for their guests.

CAR, MOTORCYCLE & BICYCLE Various places rent out bicycles (NZ$5 per day), scooters (NZ$25), cars and jeeps (NZ$70 to NZ$100). Try **Popoara Rentals** (☑31739; O'otu Beach), **Ranginui's Retreat** (☑31657; O'otu Beach) or, for the best range, **Rino's Beach Bungalows & Rentals** (☑31197; Arutanga).

PALMERSTON

POP 60 / AREA 2.1 SQ KM

Palmerston, 55km northwest of Rarotonga, is the Southern Group's only true atoll, halfway towards the Cooks' Northern Group. The lineage of all Palmerston Islanders can be traced to just one man – prolific Englishman William Masters, a ship's carpenter, who arrived from Manuae with two Polynesian wives in 1863. Having quickly added a third wife, over the next 36 years Masters created his own island dynasty. He came from Gloucester and his progeny spoke excellent English with a thick Gloucester accent. Today, there are three main families on Palmerston (who spell their name Marsters), and you'll find Marsterses scattered throughout the Cooks and the rest of Australasia – the total number of William's descendants is now well into triple figures.

There's no organised accommodation on Palmerston, but if you're planning to travel there, contact the island secretary **Tere Marsters** (☑37620, 37615; palmerstonisland@hotmail.com). The only way to reach

the island is by interisland freighter or private yacht.

'ATIU

POP 480 / AREA 27 SQ KM

In pre-European times 'Atiu was an important seat of regional power and its warriors were renowned for ferocious fighting and ruthlessness. By contrast, the rocky, reef-fringed island is now known for gentler pursuits. It's the Cooks' eco-capital and a haven for naturalists and bird lovers. It also attracts adventurous travellers in search of an island with a more traditional edge.

'Atiu's five main villages (Areora, Tengatangi, Mapumai, Te'enui and Ngatiarua) are clustered together on the island's central plateau, surrounded by a band of fertile swampland and lush taro plantations. The *makatea* – the dramatic ring of upthrust rock that's rich in marine fossils and was once the island's exterior reef – is just one of 'Atiu's natural features. The island is also covered with forest and honeycombed with limestone caves. 'Atiu's most famous cave is Anatakitaki Cave, the only known home of the *kopeka* ('Atiuan swiftlet).

History

'Land of Birds' or 'Land of Insects' is the translation of 'Atiu's traditional name 'Enua Manu. Along with its neighbours Ma'uke and Mitiaro, 'Atiu makes up the Nga Pu Toru (Three Roots). In the recent pre-European times, 'Atiuan *ariki* overlorded smaller Ma'uke and Mitiaro. 'Atiuan warriors also made incursions on Rarotonga and Aitutaki, but without success. James Cook was the first European to land on 'Atiu on 3 April 1777. Reverend John Williams landed on 19 July 1823. Rongomatane, the leading 'Atiuan chief, was converted to Christianity after Williams' missionaries boldly ate sugarcane from Rongomatane's sacred grove – he subsequently ordered all the idols on the island to be burnt. The arrival of missionaries Williams and Tahitian Papeiha is celebrated on Gospel Day (19 July).

⊙ Sights & Activities

Deep limestone caves, hidden away deep in the bush-covered *makatea,* are the most famous feature of 'Atiu. A torch and sturdy walking shoes are essential, and the coral is razor sharp. The main caves are on private land and you'll need a guide to visit them.

Many caves were used for burials – it's *tapu* (taboo) to disturb the bones, so unless you fancy taking home a curse…

Anatakitaki   CAVE

Eerie Anatakitaki is 'Atiu's most spectacular cave, a multichambered cavern surrounded by banyan roots and thick jungle. It's also home to the rare *kopeka,* or 'Atiuan swiftlet – listen for its distinctive echolocating clicks.

Te Ana O Rakanui   CAVE

Te Ana O Rakanui is a burial cave packed with musty old skulls and skeletal remains. It's a tight squeeze inside – claustrophobics be warned.

Rima Rau   CAVE

Another of 'Atiu's burial caves, Rima Rau is reached by a vertical pothole and still contains skeletal remains. You'll find it just as claustrophobic as Te Ana O Rakanui.

Lake Te Roto   LAKE

Lake Te Roto is noted for its *itiki* (eels), a popular island delicacy. On the western side of the lake, a cave leads right through the *makatea* to the sea.

Taunganui Harbour
& Oravaru Beach   SWIMMING

'Atiu's barrier reef is close to shore. The surrounding lagoon is rarely more than 50m wide and its waters quite shallow. Taunganui Harbour, on the west coast where the water is clear and deep, is the best spot for swimming. About 1km south is Oravaru Beach where Captain Cook's party made its landing.

Taungaroro & Tumai   BEACHES

Continue 1.5km further south from Ovararu to reach Taungaroro and Tumai, two of the most popular swimming beaches.

Takauroa Beach   BEACH

You can swim in the three lovely **sinkholes** west of Takauroa Beach only at low tide. Between Takauroa Beach and Matai Landing, the falling tide empties through the sinkholes and fish become trapped in a fascinating natural aquarium known as the Coral Garden.

Atiu Coffee   PLANTATION

(☑33031; www.atiu-coffee.com) Coffee was introduced to 'Atiu by early-19th-century traders and became a thriving export industry. By the 1980s, however, the coffee trade had declined and the plantations

TUMUNU

Christian missionaries took to eradicating kava drinking among Cook Islanders so 'Atiuans developed home-brewed alcohol, and the *tumunu* (bush-beer drinking clubs) were born. Men would retreat into the bush and imbibe 'orange beer'. *Tumunu* are still held regularly on 'Atiu; the *tumunu* is the hollowed-out stump of a coconut palm traditionally used for brewing beer. *Tumunus* retain some of the old kava-drinking ceremonies, but these days the vessel is likely to be plastic. Technically, bush-beer drinking sessions are still illegal.

The annual 'Atiu Tumunu Tutaka is held each December. Ten or more judges are selected from the island visitors to judge the best *tumunu* of 'Atiu – an award of great prestige.

Most tours of 'Atiu can also include a visit to a *tumunu*, or ask at your accommodation. Traditionally, it's for men only, but the rules are relaxed for tourists, and males and females are both welcome. Be warned – 'orange beer' can be pretty potent stuff.

were fallow. German-born Juergen Manske-Eimke moved to 'Atiu in the 1980s and re-established coffee production. Coffee is machine-roasted in the coffee factory in Mapumai village. Tours and coffee sampling are NZ$25 per person and include a visit to the Atiu Fibre Arts Studio (p232).

Atiu Island Coffee   GUIDED TOUR
(☑33088) Mata Arai, whose family had grown coffee in the 1950s, returned to 'Atiu in the 1990s and resumed production. Her coffee is hand picked, hand dried and hand roasted, using coconut cream to give the coffee its flavour. Tours are NZ$30 per person and include yummy pikelets and coconut cream.

Marae Orongo   HISTORIC SITE
Near Oravaru Beach, was once 'Atiu's most sacred *marae*, and it's still a powerfully atmospheric place – many locals are reluctant to go near it. You'll need a guide as it's on private land.

Marae Vairakai   HISTORIC SITE
Along a walking track north of Kopeka Lodge, Marae Vairakai is surrounded by 47 large limestone slabs, six of which have curious projections cut into their top edges.

Marae Te Apiripiri   HISTORIC SITE
This *marae* is where the Tahitian preacher Papeiha first spoke the words of the Gospel in 1823. There's not much left to see, but a stone commemorates the site.

☞ Tours

Atiu Tours   GUIDED TOUR
(☑33041; www.atiutoursaccommodation.com) Run by Englishman Marshall Humphreys, Atiu

Tours offers an informative 3½-hour circle-island tour (per person NZ$50) visiting *marae*, beaches and other historical points of interest. There's also an excellent 2½-hour tour to Anatakitaki (per person NZ$35) and Rima Rau burial cave (per person NZ$30). Don't miss having a candlelit swim in the beautiful underground pool in the Anatakitaki cave.

George Mateariki   BIRDWATCHING
(☑33047) Also known as Birdman George, George Mateariki is 'Atiu's resident ornithologist and a local celebrity thanks to his highly entertaining ecotour (per person NZ$50). George oversaw the release of the endangered *kakerori* (Rarotongan flycatcher) here from Rarotonga, and with luck you'll meet his favourite pair of birds (named George and Mildred after the 1970s UK sitcom). Ask him about having a tropical feast at his Restaurant at the Beach at 4pm on Sundays.

Paiere Mokoroa   GUIDED TOUR
(☑33034; macmokoroa@gmail.com) Historical tours taking in *marae* and battle sites around the island cost NZ$30 per person. Paiere Mokoroa is based at Taparere Lodge.

Andrew Matapakia   FISHING
(☑33825) Offers reef and lagoon fishing tours (NZ$30).

Ngere Tariu   FISHING
(☑33011) Takes anglers on deep-sea fishing cruises ($100).

Roi Viti   FISHING
(☑33076) Another local contact for deep-sea fishing (NZ$100).

RAROTONGA & THE COOK ISLANDS 'ATIU

'Atiu

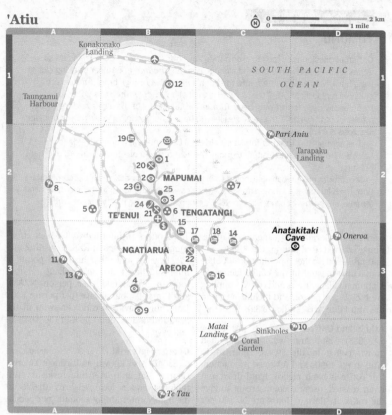

SOUTH PACIFIC
OCEAN

🛌 Sleeping

Atiu Bed & Breakfast
B&B **$$**

(📞33041; www.atiutoursaccommodation.com; r per person NZ$60; @) Tour provider Marshall Humphreys rents out rooms in his very comfortable family home near Areora. A double and a twin comprise the accommodation (with shared bathrooms), and guests have the run of the house. A tropical breakfast is complimentary, and evening meals and packed lunches can be arranged. Marshall's wife Jéanne is a celebrated local artist, and her colourful and tropical work is for sale (from NZ$30).

Atiu Villas
VILLAS **$$**

(📞33777; www.atiuvillas.com; bungalows NZ$180-220, extra persons NZ$20; @🛜🛏) The extra money goes a long way at Atiu Villas, which was built from local materials around 30 years ago by Roger Malcolm (one-time Doctor of Physics) and his 'Atiuan wife Kura. Six delightful villas are arrayed around a shady garden and have decks from where you can take in the valley views. There's a pool, tennis courts and a large bar-restaurant. Complimentary wi-fi is provided, as is internet access on resident computers. Prepaid bookings made 12 weeks in advance earn a 15% discount, and last-minute bookings (seven days in advance) attract a 40% discount.

Atiu Guesthouse
GUESTHOUSE **$**

(📞33031; www.atiu-guesthouse.com; Areora; dm/s/d/tr NZ$40/60/80/95) 'Atiu's only budget accommodation is this three-bedroom house in the centre of Areora village. There's a clean shared kitchen, living room and bathroom, but not much in the way of private space.

Kia Orana Bungalows
BUNGALOWS **$**

(📞33013; atiu.kiaoranabungalows@gmail.com; s/d NZ$60/80) Except for some gingerbread trim

'Atiu

you might reckon these dinky timber bungalows belonged to a Romanian gypsy caravan train. The bungalows inside are tiny, with a diminutive kitchen-and-bedroom area, but have nice views across a jungle valley from rear verandahs.

Kopeka Lodge
LODGE **$**

(☑33006; kopeka1@kopekalodges.co.ck; s/d NZ$85/100) Three rustic plywood chalets sit in rural grounds southeast of Areora village, with one single and two double units complete with self-contained kitchen. The stained-wood and pale-green colour scheme is simple, but the units are quite comfortable. On Rarotonga contact **Eddie Drollet** (☑52884).

Taparere Lodge
LODGE **$**

(☑33034; macmokoroa@gmail.com; s/d NZ$75/100) With two large breeze-block units, Taparere is bright, airy and cheerfully decorated. Accommodation is self-contained with kitchen facilities and (sometimes) hot-water showers. Shady verandahs overlook a pleasant valley.

✕ Eating & Drinking

Self-catering from the slim pickings at the grocery stores – largely tinned and frozen food – is the most reliable eating option. 'Atiu has a couple of restaurants, but they're closed unless there are a few tourists on the island. Ask George Mateariki (p229) about his regular Sunday afternoon 'Restaurant at the Beach'.

Kura's Kitchen
POLYNESIAN **$$**

(☑33777; Atiu Villas; dinner NZ$30) Kura at Atiu Villas cooks up evening vittles whenever there's a quorum, and sometimes there's an informal island night that kicks off in the thatched restaurant-bar area (NZ$30 with food, or NZ$40 including the show). Kura's Kitchen is open to outside guests, but booking before 3pm is essential. Bring along your favourite flag to add to the Pavilion Bar's growing collection.

Terangi-Nui Café
CAFE **$$**

(☑33101; Areora; dinner NZ$25; ⊘8am-3pm Tue-Sat & 7-10pm Sun-Sat) The lovely Parua Tavioni runs this cafe-restaurant serving breakfast, lunch and a two-course dinner (dependent on numbers). If the gates are open, pop in for some delightful 'Atiuan hospitality. Phone ahead or drop by for bookings for dinner. The cafe also hosts a small shop selling local crafts, gifts and *pareu*.

Akai Bakery
BAKERY **$**

(Mapumai) Fresh-baked bread is ready for the milling crowd by about 11am each day. Saturday is the Seventh-Day Adventist

Sabbath and the baking doesn't begin until dusk – at 11.30pm there's that milling crowd again.

Super Brown
FAST FOOD $

(Areora) Drop in for burgers, toasted sandwiches and fish and chips at this friendly spot in Areora village. You can even have a cold beer while you wait.

Shopping

Atiu Fibre Arts Studio
ARTS & CRAFTS

(☑33031; www.atiu-fibrearts.com; Te'enui; ☺9am-3pm Mon-Fri, 9am-1pm Sat) Andrea Eimke's studio specialises in *tivaevae* (appliqué work) and traditional textile arts. Machine-sewn double- to queen-size *tivaevae* cost around NZ$1250. Hand-sewn *tivaevae,* taking countless hours of work, cost upwards of NZ$4000. There's an on-site gallery, and Andrea's work has also expanded into jewellery and wonderfully delicate installations crafted from traditional *tapa* and gossamer-light lace. See the website for details of five-day workshops learning traditional Cook Islands techniques.

Information

ADC Shop (Areora) Provides cash advances on credit cards.

Post & Telecom (☺8am-4pm Mon-Fri) North of Mapumai village.

Visitor information Website www.atiu.info is an excellent information resource on 'Atiu. See also www.atiutourism.com.

Getting There & Around

TO/FROM THE AIRPORT Return airport transfers by accommodation owners are NZ$20 per person.

AIR Air Rarotonga (☑33888; www.airraro.com) flies between Rarotonga and 'Atiu Monday to Saturday. One-way fares cost from NZ$198. On Monday, Wednesday and Friday you can fly direct from Aitutaki to 'Atiu from NZ$217. Also available is an Aitutaki/'Atiu combo fare for travel from Rarotonga to Aitutaki to 'Atiu and back to Rarotonga. Check the website for the latest fares.

CAR, MOTORCYCLE & BICYCLE You'll need transport to get around 'Atiu. The circle-island road is fun for exploring by motorbike, and walking tracks lead down to the dramatic beach. Accommodation places can provide motorbikes (NZ$25 per day), and most also have mountain bikes. Atiu Villas rents a soft-top Jeep for NZ$65 a day.

MA'UKE

POP 310 / AREA 18.4 SQ KM

Although much flatter than 'Atiu and only slightly larger than Mitiaro, Ma'uke is also characterised by its *makatea* and thick coastal forest. Ma'uke is a sleepy and quietly charming island, traditional in its ways, and circled by a rough coastal track. It's pockmarked with many underground caverns, including Motuanga, a network of limestone chambers said to stretch right out underneath the reef. Known as the Garden Island, Ma'uke is one of the Cooks' main exporters of tropical flowers, which means your goodbye *'ei* is likely to be particularly impressive.

Sights

Like its sister islands, 'Atiu and Mitiaro, Ma'uke's raised-coral *makatea* is riddled with caves, many filled with cool freshwater pools. Interesting caves around the island include **Vai Ou**, **Vai Tukume**, **Vai Moraro**, **Vai Ma'u** and **Vai Moti**, reached by old coral pathways across the *makatea*.

Vai Tango
CAVE

Vai Tango is the best cave for swimming, a short walk from Ngatiarua village. Schoolkids often head there at weekends and afternoons after school and they can show you where to find it.

Motuanga
CAVE

Motuanga (the Cave of 100 Rooms) is a complex of tunnels and caverns in the island's southeast that's said to extend all the way under the reef and out to sea. The cave was used as a hiding place from 'Atiuan war parties. Access is via a small crawlspace into a surprisingly compact subterranean atrium complete with an underground pool.

Circle-Island Road
BEACHES

An 18km-long circle-island road takes you past Ma'uke's many secluded coves and beaches, which are some of the island's main attractions. One of the nicest is **One'unga**, on the east side, and **Teoneroa** and **Tukume** on the island's southwestern side are also delightful. **Anaraura** and Teoneroa have sheltered picnic areas that are popular with the island's pigs. **Kea's Grave** is on the cliffs above Anaiti, where the wife of Paikea (the Whale Rider) is said to have perished while waiting for her husband's return.

Just south of Tiare Cottages is **Kopupooki (Stomach Rock) Beach**, with a beautiful fish-filled cave that becomes accessible at low tide.

Around 3km south from Tiare Cottages, the fractured rusting hulk of the **Te Kou Maru** sits groaning on the edge of the reef. The cargo ship floundered in October 2010, but quick work from Ma'uke locals ensured most cargo was ferried by hand across the rugged *makatea* to safety. Walk towards the coast around 50m south of Ma'uke's rubbish tip to find the wreck.

Marae Rangimanuka   HISTORIC SITE
Marae Rangimanuka, the *marae* of Uke, is one of Ma'uke's many *marae* that are now overgrown, but you can still find it with a guide.

Marae Puarakura   HISTORIC SITE
Marae Puarakura is a modern *marae,* still used for ceremonial functions, complete with stone seats for the *ariki, mataiapo* and *rangatira* (subchief).

⚐ Tours

Tangata Ateriano   GUIDED TOUR
(☑35270) Based at Tiare Cottages, 'Ta' Ateriano takes visitors around the island (per person NZ$25), either in his 4WD or on a scooter tour. Highlights include the island's caves and beaches, and the Divided Church.

🛌 Sleeping

Tiare Cottages   GUESTHOUSE $$
(☑35192; www.maukeholiday.com; bungalows NZ$80, self-contained lodge NZ$90, house NZ$150) The old tin-roofed budget lodges are a little

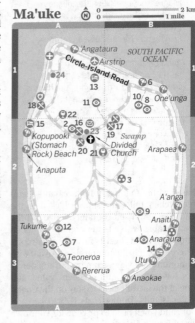

Ma'uke

Ma'uke

DON'T MISS

THE DIVIDED CHURCH

Ma'uke's CICC was built by two villages, Areora and Ngatiarua, in 1882. When the outside was completed, there was disagreement between the villages about how the inside should be decorated so they built a wall down the middle. The wall has since been removed, though the interior is decorated in markedly different styles. Each village has its own entrance, sits at its own side and takes turns singing the hymns. The minister stands astride the dividing line down the middle of the pulpit. Look for the Chilean coins that are set into the wooden altar. Chilean currency was frequently traded throughout the South Pacific in the 19th century.

basic, with a main sleeping area and a simple kitchen, toilet and shower tacked on the end. The newer self-contained lodge is more comfortable, with a better-equipped kitchen and an airy and cheerily furnished bedroom. There's also a brilliant house – O'Kiva – with panoramic sea views from its cliff-top perch. It's self-contained and excellent value, and one of the nicest places to stay on the Cooks' outer islands. Dinner costs NZ$20 per person, and you'll need to provide for your own breakfast and lunch.

Ri's Retreat   BUNGALOWS $$
(☎35181; keta-ttn@oyster.net.ck; bungalows NZ$120) Ri's Retreat has bungalows located near Anaraura Beach, and a few near the airport. The airport bungalows are all sparkling clean and brightly decorated, with large beds, modern bathrooms and verandahs. The seaside bungalows have the nicer location, built on stilts beside the gorgeous and remote Anaraura Beach, and are often enlivened by robust trade winds. You'll need to rent a scooter to get around the island from here.

🍴 Eating & Drinking

Guests at Tiare Cottages have the option of home-cooked dinners for NZ$20 per meal.

The best of Ma'uke's grocery stores is **Virginia's** near the Divided Church, and a less-well-stocked back-up option is the **Ariki Store**. **Kato's Store** is well stocked and is also the island's only bakery. Kato's also

hosts a **takeaway bar** (⊘11am-1pm & 5-9pm Mon-Sat) turning out good burgers, fish and chips and milkshakes. Pull up a chair in the adjacent gazebo and get chatting to the locals.

From 8.30am on Friday morning you can buy fresh produce at **Ma'uke's market**, near the wharf.

Tura's Bar   BAR
Liquid refreshment is available at this humble spot opposite Ma'uke College. Opening nights vary, so ask Ma'uke locals for the latest. Tuesday night is usually darts night and Ma'uke players are renowned across the Cooks.

Tua's Bar   BAR
Another option for a relaxed beer with the locals, Tua's is near the island's rugby field and normally open on a Friday and Saturday night.

ⓘ Information

Hospital (☎35664; ⊘8am-noon & 1-4pm Mon-Fri)
Police station (☎35086) Between the Administration Centre and the wharf.
Post office & Telecom office (⊘8am-noon & 1-4pm Mon-Fri) There's a 24-hour Kiaorana cardphone outside and pricey internet access.

ⓘ Getting There & Around

TO/FROM THE AIRPORT Transfers to/from the airport cost NZ$20.
AIR Air Rarotonga (airport ☎35120, Kimiangatau 35888; www.airraro.com) operates flights between Rarotonga and Ma'uke on Monday, Wednesday and Friday (NZ$508 return). There are occasionally unscheduled flights between Ma'uke and Mitiaro.
BOAT See p248 for details of travelling by cargo ship.
MOTORCYCLE & BICYCLE You can hire scooters for NZ$25 per day from Tiare Cottages and Ri's Retreat (p233). Tiare also rents out mountain bikes.

MITIARO

POP 180 / AREA 22.3 SQ KM

The tourism juggernaut that churns through Rarotonga and Aitutaki is a world away from sleepy Mitiaro. Here people live much the same way as their ancestors have for hundreds of years (except for electricity and motorscooters). Mitiaro may not be

classically beautiful in the traditional South Pacific sense – the beaches are small and, where the land's not covered with boggy swamp, it's mainly black craggy rock – yet it is an interesting slice of traditional Polynesian life and makes for a rewarding place to spend a few days.

Like on 'Atiu and Ma'uke, the *maketea* of Mitiaro has many deep and mysterious caves, including the brilliant underground pools of Vai Nauri and Vai Marere. Mitiaro also has the remains of the Cook Islands' only fort. The islanders on Mitiaro are great craftspeople and you'll discover that the weaving, woodcarving and traditional outrigger canoes are all beautifully made. Another highlight is staying a few days in a homestay, either in a local's private home or in one of the three *kikau* cottages being completed at the time of writing.

◎ Sights

Vai Marere
LANDMARK

The Cook Islands' only sulphur pool is Vai Marere, a 10-minute walk from Mangarei village on the Takaue road. From the main road it's barely visible and easy to miss, but as you duck into the cave it broadens out into a gloomy cavern covered with stalactites. According to locals, the water here has healing properties.

Vai Nauri
LANDMARK

A real highlight in this region is the deep sparkling-blue Vai Nauri, Mitiaro's natural swimming pool. Local women used to hold gatherings known as *terevai* at Vai Nauri and at nearby Vai Tamaroa, where they met to swim and sing the bawdy songs of their ancestors. With Mitiaro's declining population, the *terevai* tradition is now largely limited to holiday periods like Christmas and New Year when islanders return to Mitiaro from their homes in Australia and New Zealand.

Marae Takero
HISTORIC SITE

The *marae* of Mitiaro are largely consumed by jungle, but you are still able to see the stone seat of the *ariki* and several graves at Marae Takero, located near the abandoned Takaue village.

Te Pare Fort
HISTORIC SITE

The remains of Te Pare Fort, set deep in the *makatea*, are Mitiaro's most impressive ancient ruins. The fort was built as a defence against 'Atiuan raiders. In times of danger, people would assemble in the underground shelter, while above stood a lookout tower from which approaching canoes could be seen. The only tour guide to Te Pare Fort is **Julian Aupuni** (☑36180), who has permission to visit from the site's owner, Po Tetava Ariki. **Papa Neke** (☑36347) leads tours around the island's other historical sites. You'll most likely meet the affable patriarch when he picks you up at the airport.

Cook Islands Christian Church
CHURCH

The white-painted CICC is a fine sight, with its blue trim, stained-glass windows and parquet ceiling decorated with black-and-white stars. The Sunday church singing is inspirational.

Te Rotonui & Te Rotoiti
LAKES

Mitiaro is unique in the Cooks for its twin lakes, Te Rotonui (Big Lake) and Te Rotoiti (Small Lake). A rough track leads to the edge of Te Rotonui, where there's a boat landing and a pleasant picnic spot. Both lakes are stuffed with *itiki*, a local eel delicacy.

🛏 Sleeping & Eating

Accommodation on Mitiaro is limited to a couple of local homestays, or bedding down in one of the island's recently constructed **kikau bungalows** (per person incl meals NZ$100). Made from woven panels of *kikau* leaves, they're light and airy and feature en suite bathrooms and spacious verandahs. The bungalows are arrayed around the main village of Mangarei, and meals are provided by local families. For reservations and more information email office@cookislands connect.co.ck.

Limited food supplies are sold at the small village food shops and at **Pa's Store.**

Nane's Homestay
HOMESTAY $

(☑36107; per person incl meals NZ$100) One of Mitiaro's best places to stay is with Nane Pokoati, a local *mataiapo* and a bubbly, friendly host. There are no private rooms, just beds in a communal sleeping area in Nane's large, modern house. You'll probably get to meet a few friendly Cook Island government workers who also stay there when visiting the island.

Another friendly homestay, either in a bright and breezy two-bedroom standalone house or inside the main house with shared bathrooms, is with the delightful **Aunty Mii O'Brian** (☑36106; per person incl meals NZ$100).

Mitiaro

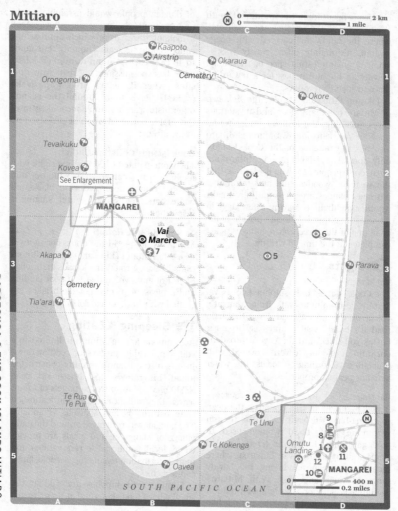

Bookings at Aunty Mii's are handled by Nane Pokoati.

ℹ Information

It's difficult to change money on Mitiaro so bring plenty of cash. Don't drink the tap water, and watch out for the island's vicious mosquitoes.

The **Administration Centre**, located near the wharf, houses the **post office** (⊙9am-4pm Mon-Fri), **Telecom** (☎36680; ⊙8-10am & 1-3pm), **police station** (☎36110, 36124), **island secretary** (☎36157, 36108) and the mayor.

Everybody knows everyone else on the tiny island, so ask at your accommodation if you'd like to go on a tour with either Julian Aupuni or Papa Neke. To conduct your own exploration of the island, bicycles and scooters can be hired from **Ngarouru Tou** (☎36148).

ℹ Getting There & Away

AIR Air Rarotonga (☎22888; www.airraro. com) flies to Mitiaro on Monday, Wednesday and Friday. The return cost is NZ$578/358. There are occasionally unscheduled flights linking Ma'uke and Mitiaro.

BOAT For information on interisland ships, see p248.

Mitiaro

MANGAIA

POP 573 / AREA 51.8 SQ KM

Next to Rarotonga, Mangaia (pronounced mung-EYE-ah) is the Cooks' most geographically dramatic island. It is the second largest of the islands – it's only slightly smaller than Rarotonga – with a towering circlet of black two-tiered raised-coral *makatea* (three-tiered in the island's north) concealing a huge sunken volcanic caldera that falls away on each side of the 169m Rangimotia ridge, the island's central spine. This sunken interior is swampland planted with taro fields and vegetables.

Mangaia is the Pacific's oldest island – at once craggy and lushly vegetated – and riddled with limestone caves that once served as sacred burial grounds and havens during tribal fighting. There are lakes in the island's centre, dramatic cliffs and many spectacular lookout points. Mangaians have a reputation for haughtiness and superiority, and they're perhaps a little less voluble on first meetings, but they are friendly, gracious and impeccably well mannered.

Mangaia's three main villages are on the coast: Oneroa in the west, Ivirua in the east and Tamarua in the south. Oneroa, the main village, has three parts: Tava'enga to the north and Kaumata to the south on the coast, and Temakatea high above the second *makatea* tier overlooking the ocean. The island's interior is cross-hatched by tracks and dirt roads, which are great for walking, but they can get very muddy after heavy rain. The airstrip is in the north of the island.

History

Mangaian legend tells that the island was not settled by voyagers on canoes, but that the three sons of the Polynesian god Rongo – Rangi, Mokoaro and Akatauira – lifted the island up from the deep, and became the first settlers and ancestors of the Nga Ariki tribe.

James Cook landed in 1777 but found the Mangaians were hostile and quickly moved on. Cannibalism had already been outlawed by Mangaian chief Mautara 100 years before the first missionaries arrived. John Williams was the first missionary to land in 1823 but, like James Cook, he was not welcome. Subsequent Polynesian missionaries had more success – the Mangaians were eventually converted to Christianity by the Rarotongan preacher Maretu.

◎ Sights

Mangaia has many spectacular caves, including **Te Rua Rere**, a huge burial cave that has crystalline stalagmites and stalactites, and some ancient human skeletons. Other caverns worth exploring include the multilevel **Tuatini Cave** and the long, maze-like **Toru a Poru Cave**.

Some of the finest old CICCs in the Cooks are on Mangaia. **Tamarua CICC** is especially beautiful, and still has its original roof beams, woodcarved interiors and sennit-rope binding. The interiors of the **Oneroa** and **Ivirua CICCs** were once even more impressive, but were sadly mostly removed in the 1980s.

The island also has 24 pre-missionary *marae,* but you'll need a guide to find them since they have been mostly overtaken by bush.

Avarua Landing   HARBOUR
Fishermen return from their morning's exploits around 8am or 9am in tiny outrigger canoes with several huge wahoo and tuna. Hang around for the cleaning and gutting

Mangaia

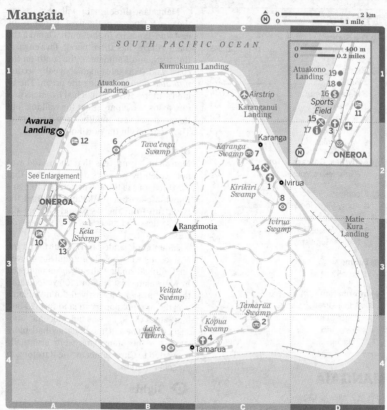

Mangaia

◎ Top Sights
Avarua Landing A2

◎ Sights
1 Ivirua CICC C2
2 Maumaukura Lookout C4
3 Oneroa CICC D2
4 Tamarua CICC C4
5 Te Pa'ata Lookout A3
6 Te Rua Rere Cave B2
7 Te-Toa-A-Morenga Lookout C2
8 Toru a Puru Cave C2
9 Tuatini Cave B4

⌂ Sleeping
10 Babe's Place A3
11 Mangaia Lodge D1
12 Mangaia Villas A2

⊗ Eating
13 Akeke Trading A3
   Babe's Store .... (see 16)
14 Kirikiri Store C2
15 Market D2

⊙ Drinking
   Babe's Bar .... (see 10)

ⓘ Information
16 Babe's Store D1
17 Visitor Information Centre D2

ⓘ Transport
18 Air Rarotonga D1
19 Moana Rentals D1

because there are three giant green turtles that come to feed on the entrails and off-cuts that are cast into the water. Whales pass just beyond the reef in the July-to-October season.

Rangimotia
LOOKOUTS

At 169m, Rangimotia is the highest point on the island with stunning coastal views. From the Oneroa side, a dirt road leads to the top. There are also several other stunning viewpoints around the island, including **Te-Toa-A-Morenga** lookout, just inland from Ivirua; the **Maumaukura** viewpoint, which has a glorious view inland from the top of the *makatea* cliff; and **Te Pa'ata** above Oneroa.

Tours

Doreen Tangatakino & Ura Herrmann
GUIDED TOUR

(☎34092; c/- Babe's Place) Takes visitors on a full-day island tour for NZ$50, which includes the inland taro plantations and Lake Tiriara. Tours to Tuatini Cave cost NZ$30. Doreen's husband **Moekapiti Tangatakino** (c/- Babe's Place) is the school history teacher and runs an informative three-hour tour that takes in the lookouts over the taro farms, lakes, the 1909 wreck site of the coal freighter *Saragossa* (only the anchor remains), the human *umu* (underground pit-oven used to cook human flesh), villages and *marae* for NZ$50.

Maui Peraua
FISHING

(☎34388) Maui Peraua leads tours to his family cave of Toru a Poru (NZ$35) and runs popular traditional pole-fishing tours on the reef (NZ$25) – you can have your catch cooked on the beach.

Sleeping

Mangaia Villas
VILLAS $$$

(☎29882; www.mangaiavillas.com; Oneroa; villas NZ$375) These six luxurious one-bedroom villas are hands-down the Cook Islands' finest accommodation beyond Rarotonga and Aitutaki. Spacious verandahs showcase ocean views, whale watching and tropical sunsets, and the villas are constructed of local Mangaia limestone with thatched roofs and shimmering hardwood floors. Modern touches include designer kitchens and bathrooms, and rates include a tropical breakfast. Lunch and dinner can also be provided for an extra charge.

Babe's Place
MOTEL $

(☎34092; www.babesplace.co.ck; Oneroa; s/d/tr incl meals NZ$75/120/150) With all meals included, a terrific location and four large comfortable motel-style rooms, Babe's Place is good value for money and definitely the best accommodation in Mangaia. Babe is the island's entrepreneur, owning the island's main store, liveliest bar and this motel. The units have mosquito nets, colourful bedspreads and small patio areas. Guests have 24-hour use of the main kitchen – with a fridge, tea and coffee – and the lounge area with a TV. Lively Babe's Bar, next door, parties on well into the night on Friday and Saturday.

Mangaia Lodge
LODGE $

(☎34324; Oneroa; s/d NZ$40/70) This tumbledown colonial-style lodge has three plain bedrooms and a sunny, enclosed terrace overlooking the gardens. The accommodation is basic but the old building has a rustic charm and million-dollar views over the ocean. The separate shared toilet/shower block is pretty rustic. Meals are included.

Eating & Drinking

There's no eating out on Mangaia, but meals are usually provided with accommodation. A weekly Friday-morning **market** kicks off at 8am beside the Oneroa post office.

Babe's Store
SELF-CATERING

(Tava'enga) The best-stocked shop.

Kirikiri Store
SELF-CATERING

North of Ivirua.

Akeke Trading
SELF-CATERING

Inland from Oneroa.

Babe's Bar
BAR

(Oneroa) Opens Friday and Saturday nights.

Shopping

Basketwork, tie-dyed *pareu,* stone pounders and *pupu ei* are Mangaia's most famous handicrafts.

Mangaia Airport Shop
ARTS & CRAFTS

This tiny shop opens for incoming flights. It also doubles as a booking office for tours and activities.

Information

Babe's Store (Oneroa) The island's ANZ agent.
Post & Telecom (internet access per 30min

NZ$10.50; ⊙7.30am-4pm Mon-Fri) On the hill above Oneroa.

Visitor information centre (☑34289) In the Administration Centre at the bottom of the Temakatea road cutting.

ⓘ Getting There & Around

AIR Air Rarotonga (☑34888; www.airraro. com) flies between Rarotonga and Mangaia three times a week for around NZ$400 return.

BOAT See p248 for details on shipping services from Rarotonga to Mangaia.

MOTORCYCLE You'll need a motorbike to get around Mangaia. There are some very rough sections of road in the island's south, and the cross-island roads are muddy and perilous after rains. **Moana Rentals** (☑34307) hires out motorcycles for NZ$25 per day.

NORTHERN GROUP

These sparsely populated tropical idylls are breathtaking in their beauty and remoteness. This sublime isolation inspired writers Tom Neale and Robert Dean Frisbie, who both lived as castaways on these far-flung coral atolls. Only the hardiest and most intrepid travellers ever make it to the Northern Group. Flights are few and mind-bogglingly expensive but, if you can surmount the financial and logistical challenges, the rewards are sublime.

ⓘ Getting There & Away

AIR Air Rarotonga (☑22888; www.airraro.com) Flights from Rarotonga to Manihiki once a week, and to Pukapuka occasionally. Flights take about 3½ hours, and the return fare is a staggering NZ$2700. Penrhyn is occasionally serviced for a return fare of NZ$3436. Bad weather, limited fuel supplies and too few bookings can cause the flights to be cancelled at short notice.

BOAT The only other regular transport to the Northern Group islands is on the Taio Shipping cargo ship. See p248. To reach Rakahanga, you must fly to Manihiki and then take a boat.

YACHT Suwarrow is accessible only by private yacht, although you can get passage on the research vessel **SRV Discovery** (☑23513, 52400; www.pacific-expeditions.com), which undertakes a two-week voyage every May from Rarotonga (per person US$3400). The expedition also visits Palmerston, Nassau and Pukapuka.

Manihiki

POP 243 / AREA 5.4 SQ KM

Manihiki, 1046km from Rarotonga, is where most of the Cooks' black pearls are farmed. It has a magnificent lagoon – one of the South Pacific's finest – and is a highlight of the Northern Group. Nearly 40 tiny *motu* encircle the enclosed lagoon, which is 4km wide at its broadest point. The island is the summit of a 4000m underwater mountain. The US ship *Good Hope* made the first European discovery in 1822, and Manihiki was a US territory until it was ceded in 1980.

Tauhunu is the main village, and the airstrip is at Tukao on this island's northern point. Black pearls are the island's economic mainstay and they're harvested from September to December. The lung-busting abilities of the island's pearl divers are legendary – they can dive to great depths and stay submerged for minutes at a time.

Beachside retreat **Manihiki Lagoon Villas** (☑43123; www.manihikilagoonvillas.co.ck; s/d incl all meals NZ$110/200) offers bungalows built on the water's edge of the lagoon. The accommodation is simple but the location is deluxe.

Rakahanga

POP 77 / AREA 4.1 SQ KM

With two major islands and many smaller *motu* dotted in a turquoise lagoon, Rakahanga is another idyllic island. The lagoon here is unsuitable for pearl farming and the few families who live here are concentrated in Nivano village in the southwestern corner. The only export is copra, although the island is still renowned for its fine *rito* (coconut-fibre) hats, which are mostly sold on Rarotonga.

Penrhyn

POP 203 / AREA 9.8 SQ KM

Penrhyn is the northernmost of the Cook Islands and boasts one of the largest lagoons in the country – so huge that the twin islands on opposite sides of the lagoon are barely visible from each other. Penrhyn has three deepwater passages that make excellent harbours, a fact that attracted whalers and traders in the 19th century. Peruvian blackbirders (slave traders) also visited the island in the 1860s. Penrhyn is another centre for black-pearl production and some interesting shell jewellery is produced on the island. The remains of a crashed B17 bomber are reminders of the WWII US servicemen who were stationed here and built the airstrip.

Soa's Guesthouse (☑42181; Omoka village; r NZ$95) is run by Soa Tini, a local fisherman and pearl farmer, who has a three-bedroom family house in the centre of Omoka village.

Pukapuka

POP 453 / AREA 5.1 SQ KM

Well known for both its sensuous dancers and beautiful girls, remote Pukapuka is in many ways closer to Samoa than to the rest of the Cook Islands. Pukapuka's most famous resident was the American travel writer Robert Dean Frisbie, who lived here in the 1920s and wrote several evocative accounts of his life on the islands. Pukapuka sustained severe damage during the 2005 cyclones.

Contact the **island secretary** (☑/fax 41712) or the **island council** (☑41034) to arrange homestay accommodation.

Suwarrow

POP 0 / AREA 0.4 SQ KM

The Cook Islands' only national park is a nature lover's paradise, home to huge colonies of seabirds and some of the country's richest marine life. Two atoll managers live here six months of the year to oversee the park. During cyclone season they head back to Rarotonga. Suwarrow is best known as the home of Tom Neale, who lived here for three long stints between 1952 and his death in 1977. You can relive his adventures in his classic book *An Island to Oneself,* and visit his old house on Anchorage Island – one room is still furnished just as it was when he lived here. The only way you're likely to be able to visit Suwarrow is by private yacht, or on the annual expedition on the SRV *Discovery* (p247).

UNDERSTAND RAROTONGA & THE COOK ISLANDS

Rarotonga & the Cook Islands Today

Welcome to one of the Pacific's most versatile destinations. Imbued with the cosmopolitan influence of Auckland, Rarotonga combines exciting holiday experiences with a burgeoning organic and artisan food scene. To the north, Aitutaki is morphing slowly into a more upmarket destination, while the nation's other outer islands are increasing the emphasis on authentic and eco-aware traveller experiences. Stay in a traditional *kikau* homestay on Mitiaro, discover 'Atiu's fascinating birdlife or go underground in the storied burial caves on Mangaia. All around the Cook Islands, the welcome for visitors continues to be friendly and gregarious, so remember to pack a good sense of humour.

History

Cook Islanders are Maori people closely related to indigenous New Zealanders and French Polynesians. The Maori had no written history, but historians believe that Polynesian migrations from the Society Islands in French Polynesia to the Cooks began around the 5th century AD. Oral histories speak of around 1400 years of Polynesian activity on Rarotonga. A *marae* (religious meeting ground) on tiny Motutapu in Rarotonga's Muri Lagoon is estimated to be around 1500 years old. In the 14th century great ocean-going *vaka* (canoes) departed from Rarotonga for Aotearoa (New Zealand), and the settlers were ancestors of present-day New Zealand Maori.

During his disastrous second voyage from Spanish-occupied Peru, Don Alvaro de Mendaña y Neyra came upon Pukapuka on 20 August 1595 – he would die just months later in the Solomon Islands. Eleven years later, Mendaña's chief pilot Pedro Fernández de Quirós led another Pacific expedition, stopping at Rakahanga. James Cook explored the Cooks in 1773 and 1779. Only ever setting foot on Palmerston and never finding Rarotonga, Cook named the group the Hervey Islands in honour of a British Lord of the Admiralty. In his 1835 *Atlas de l'Océan Pacifique,* Russian explorer and cartographer Admiral Adam Johann von Krusenstern renamed them in honour of Captain Cook.

Reverend John Williams of the London Missionary Society (LMS) arrived on Aitutaki in 1821. In 1823 Papeiha, a convert from Ra'iatea in the Societies, moved to Rarotonga and set about converting the islands to Christianity. Though many *marae* were destroyed and sacred artefacts were carted off to British museums, much of the

island's culture survived, including the traditional titles of *ariki* (chief) and *mataiapo* (subchief), the land-inheritance system and the indigenous language. The missionaries imposed a catalogue of strict rules and doctrines (known as the Blue Laws) and brought deadly diseases, such as whooping cough, measles, smallpox and influenza, leading to a long-term decline in population numbers.

The Cook Islands became a British protectorate in 1888, in response to fears of French colonisation. In 1901 the islands were annexed to New Zealand, and the Southern and Northern Groups together became known as the Cook Islands.

During WWII the US built airstrips on Penrhyn and Aitutaki, but the Cooks escaped the war largely unscathed, unlike many of their South Pacific neighbours. In 1965 the Cook Islands became internally self-governing in free association with New Zealand.

Since self-governance was achieved, successive Cook Islands governments have struggled to maintain fiscal balance. In the early 1990s a series of bad investments – including the failed Sheraton resort on Rarotonga's south coast – left the country almost NZ$250 million in debt, representing 113% of national GDP. An economic stabilisation plan in 1996 slashed public spending and the public sector workforce. Many Cook Islanders voted with their feet and left for greater opportunities in New Zealand and Australia.

Population decline and the country's national debt – estimated to be NZ$115 million in 2011 – remain the country's major issues. Growth in tourism is an ongoing opportunity, with 2011 visitor numbers of 115,000 expected to increase with the introduction of direct flights from Sydney.

The Culture

The National Psyche

Cook Islanders carry New Zealand passports, which allow them to live and work in New Zealand and, by extension (courtesy of the Special Category Visa), to live and work in Australia. This means many Cook Islanders are well travelled, worldly people. Rarotonga is a cosmopolitan place, yet beneath this Westernised veneer many Maori traditions remain, including traditional titles, family structure and the system of land inheritance. All native islanders are part of a family clan connected to the ancient system of *ariki*. Many still refer to themselves as from their 'home island' – Mangaian or Aitutakian.

But there is still a continuing exodus from the outer islands to Rarotonga, New Zealand and Australia, and some claim that Cooks Islands' nationhood is undermined by that Kiwi passport – when the going gets tough the islanders move away to Auckland or Melbourne. Tourism is the Cooks' only major industry, but few tourists go beyond Rarotonga and Aitutaki. The outer islands have a fraction of the populations they had a few decades ago.

Politics, sport, dance, music, land and inheritance remain important, as do community, family and traditional values. Christianity is taken very seriously.

Lifestyle

Islanders from Rarotonga are thoroughly First World in their lifestyles, with modern houses, regular jobs and reasonable salaries. Elsewhere in the Cooks, people live a more traditional lifestyle by fishing, growing crops and practising traditional arts and crafts. Family and the church are the two most influential elements in most islanders' lives, but people remain relaxed and informal about most aspects of day-to-day living. Like elsewhere in the Pacific, Cook Islanders are especially relaxed about timekeeping – things will happen when they do.

Population

The resident population of the Cook Islands is around 18,000, but around 80% of Cook Islanders live overseas. More than 50,000 Cook Islanders live in New Zealand, half that number in Australia, and several thousand more in French Polynesia, the Americas, Europe and Asia. Of those who do live in their country of origin, more than 90% live in the Southern Group, with 60% living on Rarotonga.

Like many Pacific islands, the Cooks are struggling with a long-term population drain, as islanders move overseas in search of higher wages. More than 90% of the population is Polynesian, though the people of some of the Northern Group islands are more closely related to Samoans than to other Cook Islanders.

Language

See the Language chapter on p591 for Cook Islands Maori basics.

Arts

Dance & Music

Cook Islanders love to dance and they're reputed to be the best dancers in Polynesia. Don't be surprised if you're invited to join them at an island night. Traditional dance forms include the *karakia* (prayer dance), *pe'e ura pa'u* (drum-beat dance), *ate* (choral song) and *kaparima* (action song). Men stamp, gesture and knock their knees together, while women shake and gyrate their hips in an unmistakeably suggestive manner.

The islanders are also great singers and musicians. The multi-part harmony singing at a Cook Islands church service is truly beautiful, but pop music is popular too. Polynesian string bands, featuring guitars and ukuleles, often perform at local restaurants and hotels.

Arts & Crafts

Traditional woodcarving and woven handicrafts (pandanus mats, baskets, purses and fans) are still popular in the Cooks. You'll see women going to church wearing finely woven *rito* (coconut-fibre) hats, mainly made on the Northern Group islands. Ceremonial adzes, stone taro pounders and *pupu ei* (snail-shell necklaces) are produced on Mangaia, and the best place to see traditional *tivaevae* (appliqué work, used for bedspreads, cushion covers and home decoration) is at the Atiu Fibre Arts Studio (p232) on 'Atiu. Black pearls are grown in the Northern Group and are an important export. *'Ei* (floral necklaces) and *'ei katu* (tiaras) are customarily given to friends and honoured guests. You're bound to receive a few, especially on the outer islands.

Traditional *tata'u* (tattooing) is also making a resurgence, with intricate designs often showcasing an individual's genealogy. See p220 to find local tattooists and ask at Avarua's bookshops for *Patterns of the Past: Tattoo Revival in the Cook Islands* by Therese Mangos and John Utanga.

Literature

Purchase these in Avarua's bookshops.

An Island to Oneself by Tom Neale is the classic desert-island read, written by a New Zealander who lived as a virtual hermit on Suwarrow during the 1950s and 1960s.

Robert Dean Frisbie ran a trading outpost on Pukapuka in the 1920s and wrote two evocative memoirs, *The Book of Pukapuka* and *The Island of Desire.*

Sir Tom Davis (Pa Tuterangi Ariki) was – among many things, including medical doctor and NASA scientist – the Cook Islands' prime minister for most of the 1980s (he died in 2007). His autobiography is called *Island Boy.*

If you're after local legends, pick up *Cook Islands Legends* and *The Ghost at Tokatarava and Other Stories from the Cook Islands,* both by the notable Cook Islands author Jon Tikivanotau Jonassen. Pukapukan poet Kauraka Kauraka published several books of poems including *Ta 'Akatauira: My Morning Star.*

Akono'anga Maori: Cooks Islands Culture, edited by Ron and Marjorie Tua'inekore Crocombe, is an excellent book that looks at culture manifested in traditional Polynesian tattooing, poetry, art, sport and governance. *Patterns of the Past: Tattoo Revival in the Cook Islands* by Therese Mangos and John Utanga is a beautifully illustrated title on *tata'u* in the Cook Islands.

Guide to Cook Islands Birds by DT Holyoak is a useful guide to the islands' native birds, with colour photos and tips for identification.

Environment

The Cook Islands' small land mass (just 241 sq km) is scattered over 2 million sq km of ocean, midway between American Samoa and Tahiti.

The 15 islands are divided into Northern and Southern Groups. Most of the Southern Group are younger volcanic islands, although Mangaia is the Pacific's oldest island. The Northern Group are 'low islands', coral atolls with outer reefs encircling lagoons, that have formed on top of ancient sunken volcanoes (see p552). 'Atiu, Ma'uke, Mitiaro and Mangaia are 'raised islands' characterised by *makatea* – rocky coastal areas formed by uplifted coral reefs.

Waste management is a major issue in the Cook Islands. Glass, plastic and aluminium are collected for recycling, but there's still a huge surplus of rubbish. Water supply is also a major concern.

Rising sea levels associated with global warming are a huge threat to the Cooks. Many of the islands of the Northern Group

are low lying and could be uninhabitable within the next 100 years (see the boxed text, p554). Climate scientists predict that severe cyclones are likely to become much more common.

In 2011, the Cook Islands government announced plans to become the Pacific's 'greenest' destination, and was targeting 100% reliance of solar and wind-generated energy by 2020.

Wildlife

Rarotonga's mountainous centre is covered with a dense jungle of ferns, creepers and towering trees, providing habitat for the island's rich birdlife. Coconut palms and spectacular tropical flowers grow almost everywhere in the Cook Islands, though the once-common pandanus trees are now rare on Rarotonga and 'Atiu.

The only native mammal is the Pacific fruit bat (flying fox), found on Mangaia and Rarotonga. Pigs, chickens and goats were introduced by the first Polynesian settlers, along with rats, which devastated the islands' endemic wildlife, especially native birds. The *kakerori* (Rarotongan flycatcher) was almost wiped out, but is now recovering thanks to the establishment of the Takitumu Conservation Area on Rarotonga. Other native birds include the cave-dwelling *kopeka* ('Atiu swiftlet) on 'Atiu, the *tanga'eo* (Mangaian kingfisher) and the *kukupa* (Cook Islands fruit dove).

SURVIVAL GUIDE

Directory A–Z

Accommodation

Officially, visitors are required to have booked accommodation before arriving in the Cook Islands, although you can usually arrange a hotel when you arrive at the airport. However, many places to stay on Rarotonga are booked up in advance, so it pays to plan ahead.

Rarotonga's accommodation includes hostels, motel-style units, self-contained bungalows and expensive top-end resorts. All the major Southern Group islands have organised accommodation. For families, renting a house can be a good way to cut costs.

Manihiki and Penrhyn are the only Northern Group islands with simple accommodation.

This book's Sleeping reviews are ordered in preference, and categorised by the average cost of accommodation for two people. For a dorm bed, budget travellers can expect to pay around NZ$30.

$ less than NZ$125

$$ NZ$125–250

$$$ more than NZ$250

 Activities

The Cook Islands are perfect for relaxation, but there's plenty of activities to keep energetic travellers busy. Rarotonga is an excellent place for hiking, and Aitutaki's backcountry roads and deserted beaches are good for exploring. 'Atiu, Ma'uke, Mitiaro and Mangaia have many trails winding through the *makatea*. History enthusiasts will enjoy visiting the historic *marae* on most of the islands. Many of these traditional religious meeting grounds are still used today for formal ceremonies, such as the investiture of a new *ariki* or *mataiapo*.

WATER SPORTS

The sheltered lagoons and beaches on Rarotonga and Aitutaki are great for swimming and snorkelling. Diving is also excellent, with good visibility and lots of marine life, from sea turtles and tropical fish to reef sharks and eagle rays. See p31 for more diving information. You can hire snorkelling gear on Aitutaki and Rarotonga, as well as kayaks, sailboards and other water-sports equipment.

Raro has just a handful of resident surfers, but there are serious waves outside Rarotonga's perimeter reef and a budding community of bodyboard riders.

Kite surfing, paddleboarding and small-boat sailing are popular in Rarotonga's Muri Lagoon. Glass-bottomed boats also operate from Muri Beach, and there are several lagoon-cruise operators in Aitutaki. Deep-sea fishing boats can be chartered on Rarotonga and Aitutaki, and bonefishing on Aitutaki lagoon is growing in popularity. From July to October, whale-watching trips are available on Rarotonga.

CAVING

The Cook Islands has some extraordinary caves to explore including Anatakitaki and Rima Rau on 'Atiu, Motuanga on Ma'uke,

Vai Nauri on Mitiaro, and Te Rua Rere on Mangaia.

Business Hours

Sunday is largely reserved for churchgoing and rest, although a few cafes and restaurants around Rarotonga and Aitutaki open in the afternoon.

Banks open to 3pm on weekdays. Only Avarua's Westpac is open on Saturday morning.

Businesses and shops 9am to 4pm Monday to Friday, most shops open until noon on Saturday.

Small grocery stores 6am or 7am until 8pm or 9pm.

Children

Travelling with kids presents no special problems in the Cook Islands, although many smaller hotels and bungalows don't accept children aged under 12 – ask about the policy before booking.

Customs

The following restrictions apply: 2L of spirits or wine or 4.5L of beer, plus 200 cigarettes or 50 cigars or 250g of tobacco. Quarantine laws are strictly enforced, and plants, animals or any related products are prohibited. Firearms, weapons and drugs are also prohibited.

Dangers & Annoyances

Swimming is very safe in the sheltered lagoons but be wary around reef passages, where currents are especially strong. Rarotonga's main passages are at Avana Harbour, Avaavaroa, Papua and Rutaki. They exist on other islands as well, often opposite streams.

Mosquitoes can be a real nuisance in the Cooks, particularly during the rainy season (around mid-December to mid-April). Use repellent, and mosquito coils are available everywhere.

Embassies & Consulates

COOK ISLANDS CONSULATES

See www.cook-islands.gov.ck for details on consular representation in Monaco, Belgium, Norway and the UK.

Australia (02-9907 6567; fax 9949 6664; Sir Ian Graham Turbott, 8/8 Lauderdale Ave, Fairlight, NSW 2094)

New Zealand Auckland (09-366 1100, mobile 027- 596 0602; cookconsul@ihug.co.nz; Mrs Rima Ngatoa, 1st fl, 127 Symonds St, PO Box 37-391, Auckland) Wellington (04-427 5126; Ms Tepaeru Hermann, 56 Mulgrave St, Thorndon, PO Box 12-242)

CONSULATES IN THE COOK ISLANDS

New Zealand High Commission (Map p206; 22201, 55201; nzhcraro@oyster.net.ck; PO Box 21, Avarua) is located above the Philatelic Bureau in Avarua. New Zealand the only country with diplomatic representation in the Cook Islands. Citizens from other countries seeking consular advice should talk to the Secretary of the **Department of Foreign Affairs & Immigration** (Map p206; 29347; www.mfai. gov.ck) on the 3rd floor of the Trustnet building in Avarua.

Festivals & Events

Dancer of the Year (April) Dance displays are held throughout April, culminating in the Dancer of the Year competition.

Gospel Day (July) The arrival of the gospel to the Cook Islands is celebrated with *nuku* (religious plays), held on 20 July on 'Atiu, 21 July on Mitiaro, 25 July on Rarotonga, and elsewhere on 26 October.

Constitution Celebration (Te Maire Nui; August) Celebrating the 1965 declaration of independence, this is the Cook Islands' major annual festival.

Tiare (Floral) Festival Week (August) Celebrated with floral-float parades and the Miss Tiare beauty pageant.

Vaka Eiva (November) This week-long canoe festival celebrates the great Maori migration from Rarotonga to New Zealand. There are many race events and celebrations of Cooks culture.

Food

Eating options in this chapter are listed in order of preference and categorised by the following indicators for the average cost of a main dish. Main meals at a restaurant are usually around NZ$25, but many cafes and fast-food places have options from NZ$10 or NZ$20.

$ less than NZ$15

$$ NZ$15–30

$$$ more than NZ$30

Internet Access

Rarotonga has internet cafes dotted around the island, and most accommodation offers wi-fi access on a prepaid basis. Telecom Cook Islands sells prepaid wi-fi access codes that can be used at hot spots around Rarotonga. Aitutaki has just one dedicated internet cafe, but wi-fi and internet access is available at the Koru Café (p226). Most Telecom offices on the outer islands have small cyberbooths, though the connections are slow and expensive.

Internet Resources

Aitutaki Tourism (www.aitutakitourism.com) Excellent website for accommodation and activities on Aitutaki.

Cook Islands Government Online (www.cook-islands.gov.ck) Government news and press releases.

Cook Islands Herald (www.ciherald.co.ck) Online edition of the popular weekly newspaper.

Cook Islands News (www.cinews.co.ck) Online edition of the daily Cook Islands newspaper.

Cook Islands Website (www.ck) Local business details including tourist operations.

Enjoy Cook Islands (www.enjoycookislands. com) Website for the *Cook Islands Sun* newspaper, including lots of traveller-friendly information.

Escape (www.escapemagazine.travel) Website for *Escape,* an excellent travel and lifestyle magazine covering the Cook Islands.

Lonely Planet (www.lonelyplanet.com/ rarotonga-and-the-cook-islands) Author recommendations, traveller reviews and insider tips.

Telecom Cook Islands (www.telecom.co.ck) Searchable telephone directories.

Tourism Cook Islands (www.cookislands. travel) Central information site for the main tourist office.

www.cookislands.org.uk Hosted out of the UK, this is the only noncommercial website covering the Cooks.

www.jasons.com New Zealand-based portal for Pacific travel including accommodation bookings.

Money

New Zealand dollars are used in the Cook Islands. You'll probably get a few Cook Islands coins in change (in denominations of 5c, 10c, 20c, 50c, $1, $2 and $5). The Cook Islands prints a $3 note that's quite collectable and available at the Philatelic Bureau in Avarua. Note that Cook Islands currency cannot be exchanged anywhere in the world.

There are ATMs and banks on Rarotonga and Aitutaki, and using credit cards and changing money is also widely accepted on the nation's main two islands. Credit cards are accepted at the larger hotels on Aitutaki

---

MEDIA & PRACTICALITIES

» **Newspapers** Rarotonga's *Cook Islands News* is published daily except Sunday, and the *Cook Islands Herald* comes out on Wednesday. Both feature local and international news.

» **Radio** Radio Cook Islands (630 kHz AM; www.radio.co.ck) reaches most islands and broadcasts local programs, Radio New Zealand news and Radio Australia's world news. The smaller KC-FM (103.8 MHz FM) station can be received only on Rarotonga.

» **TV** Cook Islands Television (CITV) screens across Rarotonga; international cable channels are available at some hotels. On outer islands, Sky Fiji is available and programming is usually controlled by each island's mayor. If you're engrossed in CNN or a wildlife documentary, there's every chance it will be switched mid-program to the rugby. Only in the Pacific! Aitutaki has a small station that broadcasts intermittently on local issues.

» **DVDs** Can be hired all over Rarotonga and many accommodation places can provide DVD players.

» **Electricity** 240V AC, 50Hz, using Australian-style three-blade plugs. Power is available 24 hours throughout the Southern Group.

» **Weights & Measures** Metric system.

and at some places on 'Atiu, but for other islands cash is essential.

Taxes A 12.5% VAT (value-added tax) is included in the price of most goods and services. All prices quoted include VAT. A departure tax of NZ$55 applies when leaving the Cook Islands. Children 12 years and under are exempt from the departure tax.

Tipping Not customary in the Cook Islands, but it's not frowned upon for exceptional service. Haggling over prices is considered rude.

Post

Poste-restante mail is held for 30 days at post offices on most islands. To collect mail at the post office in Avarua it should be addressed to you c/o Poste Restante, Avarua, Rarotonga, Cook Islands.

Public Holidays

New Year's Day 1 January

Good Friday & Easter Monday March/April

Anzac Day 25 April

Queen's Birthday First Monday in June

Gospel Day (Rarotonga only) 25 July

Constitution/Flag-Raising Day 4 August

Gospel Day (Cook Islands) 26 October

Christmas Day 25 December

Boxing Day 26 December

Telephone

All the islands, with the exception of Nassau, are connected to the country's modern telephone system. Each island has a Telecom office, usually incorporating a payphone and a (pricey) internet booth.

The country code for the Cook Islands is ☑682, and there are no local area codes. Dial ☑00 for direct international calls and ☑017 for international directory service. The local directory operator is ☑010. You can make collect calls from any phone by dialling ☑015.

Prepaid Kiaorana cards are available in NZ$5, NZ$10, NZ$20 and NZ$50 denominations from the post office, Telecom, Telepost and many shops and hotels. They can be used for local, interisland and international phone calls and work from both public and home telephones. See p197 for details of mobile (cell) phone coverage.

Time

The Cook Islands are east of the International Date Line, 10 hours behind Greenwich Mean Time (GMT). The country has no daylight-saving time. When it's noon in the Cooks it's 10pm in London, noon in Tahiti and Hawai'i, 2pm in LA, 10am the next day in Fiji and New Zealand, and 8am the next day in Sydney.

Tourist Information

Tourism Cook Islands (CITC; ☑29435; www.cookislands.travel; PO Box 14, Avarua) In the centre of Avarua on Rarotonga.

Australia (☑61-423 765 402; ausmanager@cookislands.travel; PO Box 3900, Robins Town Centre, QLD 4230)

Canada (☑604-541 9877; canadamanager@cookislands.travel; PO Box 75-188, Surrey, BC, V4A 0B1)

Northern Europe (☑49-892 1909 6513; rhett.lego@theconjointmarketinggroup.com; Fraunhoferstr.8, 82152 Martinsried, Germany)

New Zealand (☑09-366 1106; nzmanager@cookislands.travel; Level 1, 127 Symonds St, Parnell, Auckland)

UK (☑44-20 8237 7979; sarah@mccluskey.co.uk; McCluskey International, 1/4 Prince of Wales Tce, Chiswick, LON, W42EY)

USA (☑310-545 4200; usamanager@cookislands.travel; 1334 Parkview Ave, Suite 300, Manhattan Beach, California 90266)

Getting There & Away

Air

Rarotonga has international flights to Auckland, Sydney, Los Angeles and Tahiti. Low-season travel to the Cooks is from mid-April to late August, and the high season runs from December to February. There's heavy demand from New Zealand to the Cooks in December, and in the other direction in January. Demand for flights from New Zealand and Australia is also strong during those countries' respective school holiday periods.

AUSTRALIA

Air New Zealand (www.airnewzealand.com) Weekly direct flights between Sydney and Rarotonga on a Saturday (return fares from A$746).

Another option is to fly via Auckland on Air New Zealand or Virgin Australia.

NEW ZEALAND

Air New Zealand (www.airnewzealand.com) Regular flights between Auckland and Rarotonga (return fares from NZ$478).

Virgin Australia (www.virginaustralia.com) Regular flights between Auckland and Rarotonga (return fares from NZ$448).

NORTH AMERICA

Air New Zealand (www.airnewzealand.com) Weekly direct flights between Rarotonga and Los Angeles on a Saturday (return fares from US$1216).

TAHITI

Air Tahiti (www.airtahiti.aero) Direct codeshare flights on Thursday with Air Rarotonga linking Tahiti with Rarotonga (return fares from around NZ$800).

Sea

Rarotonga is a favourite port of call for South Pacific cruise ships but they don't take on passengers, typically arriving in the morning and departing in the afternoon after quick island tours and souvenir shopping.

YACHT

The Cooks are popular with yachties except during the cyclone season (November to March). Once you arrive at Rarotonga, fly your Q flag and visit the **Harbour Master** (Map p206; 28811; Avatiu Harbour, Rarotonga). There are other official ports of entry at Aitutaki, Penrhyn and Pukapuka, which have good anchorages. Virtually uninhabited, Suwarrow Atoll is a trophy destination for cruising yachties, but isn't an official entry.

There's a slim chance of catching a crewing berth on a yacht from the Cook Islands to Tonga, Samoa, Fiji, French Polynesia or New Zealand. You can ask at Rarotonga's **Ports Authority** (Map p206; Avatiu Harbour), where yachties leave messages if they are looking for crew.

Getting Around

Unless you're sailing your own yacht, travel between the Cook Islands is limited to slow cargo ships and Air Rarotonga flights. Flights to the Northern Group islands are expensive, and only Manihiki, Penrhyn and Pukapuka have airstrips.

Air

Air Rarotonga (22888; www.airraro.com), the only domestic airline in the Cook Islands, has several daily flights to Aitutaki, and several weekly flights between Rarotonga and the rest of the Southern Group. Other than the high-traffic Rarotonga–Aitutaki route, Air Rarotonga sometimes cancels or moves flights to consolidate passengers if there are too many empty seats.

Flights to the Northern Group are more erratic – there's a scheduled flight to Manihiki every second Tuesday, and flights to Penrhyn are flown only when there's sufficient demand.

The baggage allowance for the Southern Group is 16kg (excess NZ$3 per kilogram), for the Northern Group it's 10kg (excess NZ$6.50 per kilogram). Passengers are allowed one piece of hand luggage not exceeding 3kg.

Boat

Shipping schedules are notoriously unpredictable – weather, breakdowns and unexpected route changes can all put a kink in your travel plans. Ships stop off at each island for just a few hours, and only Rarotonga and Penrhyn have decent harbours. At all the other islands you go ashore by lighter or barge.

Taio Shipping (24905; taio@oyster.net.ck; Avatiu Wharf) is the only interisland shipping company and its vessels are far from luxury cruise liners: there's limited cabin space and some ships have no cabins at all. Showers and toilets are available to all passengers. Return trips to the islands of the Southern Group cost NZ$250. To the Northern Group, return fares are NZ$1200 in a cabin and NZ$450 for deck space. Ships only run one or two times per month.

The private research vessel **Bounty Bay** (23513, 52400; www.pacific-expeditions.com), based on Rarotonga, runs ecotrips around the more remote islands of the Cooks, including Palmerston, Nassau and Suwarrow.

Local Transport

All the islands are good for cycling. Rarotonga has a regular circle-island bus service, taxis and bicycles, motorcycles and cars for hire. Aitutaki has a taxi service and bicycles, motorcycles and cars for hire. 'Atiu has a taxi service, rental motorcycles and a couple of Jeeps. You can rent scooters and bicycles on Ma'uke, Mitiaro and Mangaia.

Hitchhiking is legal, though of course never entirely safe, and if you're walking along an empty stretch of road someone will stop and offer you a lift before too long.

☞ Tours

Circle-island tours on Rarotonga offer a good introduction to the island's history, geography and traditional culture. Guided tours are also offered on Aitutaki, 'Atiu, Ma'uke and Mangaia.

Rarotongan travel agencies can organise single-island or multi-island package tours. Day trips from Rarotonga to Aitutaki are available.

Samoa

Best Places to Stay

» Seabreeze Resort (p269)

» Namu'a Island Beach Fale (p269)

» Aggie Grey's Hotel & Bungalows (p256)

» Samoan Outrigger Hotel (p256)

» Virgin Cove Resort (p270)

Best Places to Eat

» Bistro Tatau (p262)

» Seabreeze Restaurant (p269)

» The Mangrove Garden (p271)

» Sunday lunch (p278)

Why Go?

Anchored at the heart of Polynesia, Samoa rises languidly from the sea, draped in jungle, dotted with flower-filled villages and surrounded by iridescent lagoons.

This tiny nation's proud history spans more than 3000 years and its people were the first Polynesians to reclaim independence following European colonisation. As such, Samoans have firmly held on to their customs. Village life is still the norm here, and traditional governance and communal ownership carry much legal weight. The result is sweet, safe and gentle; a trip to Samoa is like sipping the world's purest water on a warm day.

If your ideal for a South Pacific holiday involves spa treatments and jet skis, Samoa may not be for you. What Samoa excels in is affordable, unpretentious beachside accommodation, friendly people and a peace and quiet rare to this world. It's easy to get around, everyone speaks English and political stability is almost guaranteed.

When to Go

Apia

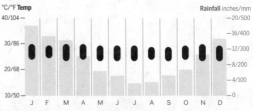

Dec–Jan Peak holiday period when Samoans living abroad visit home.

May–Oct Dry season and festival time.

Nov–Apr Wet weather and cyclone season.

Connections

Regular ferries ply the 22km between 'Upolu and Savai'i. Manono is reached by either a regular taxi boat that meets the bus, or by arrangement with your lodging. It's only possible to reach Namu'a with the owners of the beach *fale* operation on the otherwise deserted island. Getting around 'Upolu and Savai'i is easiest in a hire car but everyone should try and take the crowded, friendly and colourful bus at least once.

ITINERARIES

Five Days

Spend a day or two exploring **Apia**, making sure to visit **Palolo Deep Marine Reserve**, the **Robert Louis Stevenson Museum** and seeing a *fiafia* (dance performance) at **Aggie Grey's Hotel & Bungalows**. The following day begin the loop around 'Upolu, heading east and stopping for the sights and village calm. Spend your first night at **Namu'a Island Beach Fale** then continue on around the island, stopping two more nights at the resort or *fale* of your choice. Don't miss splashing around the **To Sua Ocean Trench** and stopping at **Aganoa** and **Matareva** beaches.

Ten Days

Start as above, then continue north up the coast of 'Upolu, stopping for a night on the island of **Manono**. The following day take the ferry to **Savai'i** and spend the next four days leisurely driving around the island counter-clockwise, making sure to get covered in mud at the **Dwarf's Cave**, take the eerie, scenic drive to **Fafa O Sauai'i**, and get blown away by the **Alofaaga Blowholes**. If you're keen on archaeology and adventure, search for the lost and mysterious **Pulemelei Mound**.

Essential Food & Drink

» **Umu** Traditional Samoan hot-stone ovens are built above ground and used to cook breadfruit, fish, *palusami* and more.

» **Oka** Tender chunks of raw fish are marinated in lime juice, mixed with vegetables and topped with coconut cream.

» **Palusami** Calorie bombs of coconut cream wrapped in young taro leaves and cooked in a stone oven. Find it at the market in Apia.

» **Fish & chips** Found on every menu. We thought the best was at Seafood Gourmet in Apia.

» **Koko Samoa** Strong coffee-like beverage made with hot water and ground Samoan cacao.

» **Vailima** One of the best beers in the Pacific. A crisp and refreshing lager.

AT A GLANCE

Currency Samoan tala (ST)

Language Samoan, English

Mobile phones Prepaid SIM cards

Money ATMs in and around Apia, at Salelologa and Manase.

Visas Free

Fast Facts

» **Area** 2934 sq km
» **Capital** Apia ('Upolu)
» **Country code** ☑685
» **Emergency** ☑999
» **Population** 183,081

Exchange Rates

Australia	A$1	ST2.45
Canada	C$1	ST2.35
Europe	€1	ST3.05
Japan	¥100	ST3.05
New Zealand	NZ$1	ST1.91
UK	UK£1	ST3.75
USA	US$1	ST2.40

For current exchange rates see www.xe.com.

Set Your Budget

» **Main course in a fine-dining restaurant** from ST25

» **Night in a Samoan fale** from ST30

» **'Custom fee' to access beaches** ST5-10

» **Ferry to Savai'i** ST12

» **Car hire** from ST120 per day

SAMOA

'UPOLU

POP 136,000 / AREA 1115 SQ KM

'Upolu is the smaller of Samoa's two main islands, but when it comes to population, development and tourist infrastructure, it's well on top.

If your first experience of Samoa is the 35km drive from the airport to Apia, you'll already have passed the bulk of the island's population who live in the procession of tidy northwest-coast villages that gradually join together to form the capital. The rest of 'Upolu has a charmingly rural feel. The main roads pass through small villages where locals wave cheerful greetings and speed bumps keep you at the speed of a jog.

Most visitors devote themselves to the dazzling strips of sand that skirt 'Upolu's southern shoreline, with regular forays into the pristine offshore lagoons to poke their noses into coral groves and schools of fish.

But you can also hike into tangled rainforest, visit rough coastal cliffs formed by the cooling of lava rivers, and enjoy the company and cultural teachings of the Samoans. Divers, experienced surfers and golfers will find plenty to keep themselves busy. The urban attractions of Apia shouldn't be neglected either – not if you fancy the odd boogie, movie, or a choice of eating and drinking establishments.

Whether your vision of Polynesian paradise is lying around a resort, cocktail in hand and nose buried in a Dan Brown novel, or whether it's shooting pool with the locals in a ramshackle pub, 'Upolu's got the options.

ⓘ Getting Around

TO/FROM THE AIRPORT

Faleolo Airport is on the coast, 35km west of Apia. Many of the larger resorts and hotels have minivans for transfers. Otherwise there's always

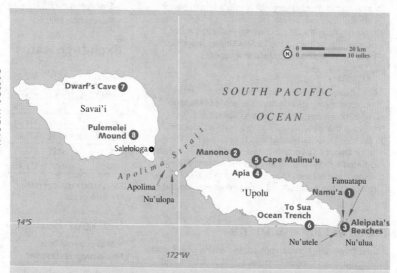

Samoa Highlights

❶ Sleeping in a traditional Samoan *fale* such as those on **Namu'a island** (p269)

❷ Soaking up the village vibe while strolling around the tiny white-sand-encircled island of **Manono** (p273)

❸ Stepping off the perfect flax-coloured sands into the blinding turquoise waters of **Aleipata's beaches** (p267)

❹ Partying with the locals in the bars and nightclubs of dinky but friendly **Apia** (p264)

❺ Admiring the sunset from the edge of the world at coral-ringed **Cape Mulinu'u** (p281)

❻ Bathing in the idyllic, near-underground isolation of the **To Sua Ocean Trench** (p267)

❼ Heading downward into an old lava tunnel, swimming and getting covered in mud at Savai'i's **Dwarf's Cave** (p280)

❽ Having a lost-world moment after battling overgrown weeds and lost trails, standing atop the mysterious **Pulemelei Mound** (p282)

an armada of taxis ready to ferry arrivals to the city or other 'Upolu destinations. The fare to Apia is around ST50 to ST60.

If you're travelling alone, it's cheaper to catch an airport shuttle. It pays to prebook, but you'll usually spot them waiting across from the terminal for all of the major international flights (they don't bother meeting the small planes from Pago Pago). Both **Samoa Scenic Tours** (☑26981) and **Go See Samoa** (☑44136) have shuttles that stop at any of Apia's hotels (each charges per person ST25) and take around 45 minutes.

Many of the international flights arrive and depart at ungodly hours, but if you're lucky enough to have one at a reasonable time, buses are an option. Walk out to the main road and hail any bus approaching from your right to get to Apia. To get to Faleolo Airport from Apia (ST3.10), take any bus marked 'Pasi o le Va'a', 'Manono-uta', 'Falelatai' or 'Faleolo'.

BUS

Buses connecting Apia with almost every other part of 'Upolu leave from both Maketi Fou (the main market) and from behind the Flea Market. Drivers circle between the two until the bus is full (this can take up to an hour) and are liable to veer off route to deposit locals at their front doors. There are set bus stops on the coastal road, but if you hail the driver they'll stop almost anywhere. Pay as you leave the bus. Buses begin running early in the morning and stop in the early afternoon.

A bus schedule for 'Upolu that includes fare information is available from the **Samoa Tourism Authority** (Map p258; ☑63500; www.samoa.travel; Beach Rd; ⊘9am-5pm Mon-Fri, to noon Sat).

To reach the Aleipata district at the eastern end of the island, catch the Lalomanu bus. To head east along the north coast, take the Falefa, Fagaloa or Lotofaga bus. For any point along The Cross Island Rd, take either the Si'umu or Salani bus. For Togitogiga and O Le Pupu-Pu'e National Park, take the Falealili or Salani bus.

CAR

The main roads in 'Upolu range from excellent to potholed tracks. The national speed limit maxes out at 70km/h but drops to 40km/h through villages, and frequent speed humps make sure that you never forget to slow down – since there are very few stretches of road that don't pass through villages, expect to be driving at 40km/h most of the time. The sealed Main Coast Rd winds its way around 'Upolu, while three roads cross over the island's east–west central ridge and divide it roughly into quarters.

A high-clearance 2WD vehicle should be adequate for all but the road to Uafato and to Aganoa Black Sand Beach, where a 4WD is a necessity. Outside of Apia and the road between the city and the airport, petrol stations are in short supply.

Apia

POP 37,240

Few people come to a Pacific paradise to hang around in a small city with not much in the way of beaches. That's a shame as Apia can be a lot of fun – and its position makes it a handy base to explore all parts of 'Upolu. It's the only place in Samoa big enough to have a decent selection of eateries, bars and entertainment, but it's still small enough that within a week you'll be recognising people on the street.

The only town of any note in Samoa, Apia has grown from a small harbourside settlement to sprawl along the coast and up the slopes of Mt Vaea, swallowing about 50 villages in the process. These villages still retain their own traditional forms of governance, but significant parcels of freehold land are also available for those wishing to escape the strictures of village life. This includes a significant expat community.

⊙ Sights

The closest beach to Apia is **Vaiala Beach** (Map p258), immediately east of the harbour. The currents can be strong, so take care and avoid the area marked by buoys where there's a dangerous whirlpool.

Maketi Fou   MARKET

(Map p258; Fugalei St) The town's three main markets are a lively cultural experience in themselves, especially the main market. This dirty, noisy, 24-hour bazaar is almost always jammed with locals lugging vegetables, meat and groceries, and devouring deep-fried delights. Family members of stallholders take turns to sleep overnight to make sure they don't lose their spot. Pretty much everything is sold here, from hair dye to bananas. Craft hunters will find *siapo* (decorated bark cloth), woodcarvings, coconut-shell jewellery, *kirikiti* (cricket) bats and balls, *lava-lava* (wraparound sarongs) and T-shirts. The ambience is somewhat enlivened by the fume-ridden chaos of the adjacent bus station.

FREE **Falemataaga –**
The Museum of Samoa   MUSEUM

(Vaitele St; ⊘10am-4.30pm Mon-Fri) The German-era school building looks abandoned from the outside, but inside is an

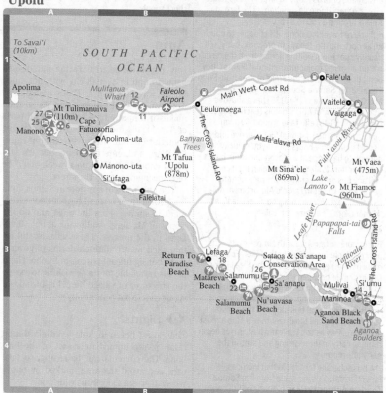

enchanting collection divided between four air-conditioned, themed rooms: history, culture, Pacific and environment. Donations are appreciated.

FREE Madd Gallery
GALLERY

(Map p258; Ifiifi St; ⊘9am-3pm Mon-Fri) A short walk up the road from Falemataaga – The Museum of Samoa, this small space displays local, contemporary art.

Flea Market
MARKET

(Map p258; Beach Rd) Down on the waterfront, a labyrinth of small stalls selling all of the aforementioned craftwork available at Maketi Fou (p253). Don't bother to test your bargaining skills here, however, as haggling is not an element of Samoan commerce.

Mormon Temple
CHURCH

(Map p258; Vaitele St) One of the most impressive buildings in Samoa is this massive temple taking up 1736 sq metres on the western approach to town. Completed in 2005 after a fire destroyed the previous building, the white granite edifice has an elegant art deco sensibility and is capped by a golden angel.

Fish Market
MARKET

(Map p258; off Beach Rd) A scramble takes place here at the crack of dawn every Sunday to snag the freshest catches for the post-church to'ona'i (Sunday lunch).

Mulivai Catholic Cathedral
CHURCH

(Map p258; Beach Rd) Looking over the harbour is the white, Madonna-topped cathedral, built in 1905 and a reliable landmark for sea-weary sailors until government and bank offices rose up in front of it. The white tiling around the sanctuary is reminiscent of a very religious butcher's shop, but the patterned woodwork of the ceiling is lovely.

🏃 Activities

Palolo Deep Marine Reserve   SNORKELLING
(Map p258; Vaiala Beach Rd; adult/child ST3/1, hire of mask & flippers/snorkel ST5/3; ☺8am-6pm) Between the beach and the harbour, this reserve is a magnificent stretch of shallow reef (best visited at high tide) that features a deep, coral-encrusted hole thronging with marine life. To reach the drop-off, swim out from the beach to the dark patch of water to the left of the marker stick. It's around 100m from the shore, and you'll need flippers and a snorkel to get you out there without damaging the coral (or your feet).

Le Spa   DAY SPA
(Map p266; ☑38601; off The Cross Island Rd, Vaoala; massage per 90min ST150) If you're after a less-active pursuit, this place is a haven of tranquillity, where you can pamper yourself with a beauty treatment or therapeutic massage, including the traditional Samoan *fofo* style. It also hosts yoga and guided meditation classes. You'll find it signposted from The Cross Island Rd opposite the large Shrine of Three Hearts.

Misiluki Day Spa   DAY SPA
(☑770 3434; www.misiluki.com; Falealili St; massage per 45min from ST50) For a massage closer to town as well as mani-pedis, waxing, facials and body treatment, this serene yet simple spa gets top marks from locals.

👉 Tours

TOP CHOICE Polynesian Xplorer   ISLAND TOURS
(Map p266; ☑26940; www.polynesianxplorer. com; Falealili St) Full-service boutique travel agency that runs recommended tours in 'Upolu (half-day ST79, full-day ST179 to ST199) and day tours to Manono (ST180) and Savai'i (ST269). Groups are small and you can design your own custom itinerary

'Upolu

SAMOA APIA

including lodging and transfers. Also has an airport office.

Samoa Adventure CRUISES
(☏777 0272; www.samoa-adventure.com; Aggie Grey's Hotel & Bungalows, Beach Rd) This lovely 35ft catamaran makes sunset tours, and a slew of other excursions including a Manono cruise (ST250 per person including fishing, food and drinks) and fishing trips (from ST1200 for a half-day for four people).

Samoa Scenic Tours ISLAND TOURS
(☏26981; www.samoascenictours.ws; Aggie Grey's Hotel & Bungalows, Beach Rd) Runs big bus-style tours around 'Upolu (half-/full day ST85/150) and to Manono (ST180).

🛌 Sleeping

TOP CHOICE **Aggie Grey's Hotel & Bungalows** HISTORIC HOTEL $$$
(Map p258; ☏22880; www.aggiegreys.com; Beach Rd; s US$120-165, d & tw US$130-175, ste US$350-900; ❄@⊗) If you ever wanted to step into a 1940s-era tale of the South Seas, this iconic hotel gives you the chance. The dated decor and breezy, near-colonial atmosphere is in pristine condition – although it's verging on dowdy, the look works, it's very comfortable

and it feels good to be here. You can easily imagine famous former guests such as James Michener, William Holden or Marlon Brando swaggering into view. The best rooms are the *fale*-inspired garden bungalows (positioned strangely on a busy path), followed by the standard rooms facing the pool. They're larger and quieter than the more expensive rooms in the ocean-view wing. Yes it is overpriced but the atmosphere is one of a kind.

TOP CHOICE **Samoan Outrigger Hotel** HOTEL $
(Map p266; ☏20042; www.samoanoutriggerhotel.com; Falealili St, Moto'otua; fale per person ST70, s/d ST120/170, all incl breakfast; ❄@⊛⊗) Set in a high-ceilinged, century-old timber building hidden behind a high hedge, this charming place has a hip periwinkle-blue lobby area for lounging as well as a lush garden with a pool. You get a choice of bright rooms with shared bathrooms in the house, or garden-side thatched traditional beach-hut-style *fale* with mattresses on the floor. Reception is sweet and there are good car-rental discounts for those staying four or more days. It's just a bit out of town but the quality is worth the short distance.

GET ACTIVE ON 'UPOLU

Diving

Diving is undeveloped in Samoa. On 'Upolu this means that more-experienced divers can partake in exploration trips with AquaSamoa Watersports and potentially get sites named after them! At the time of writing there were about 30 mapped sites around the island, the best being along the Manono Wall just off of Manono island. Top dives include Magic Mushrooms, where you'll find the namesake unique mushroom-shaped coral formations that are frequented by schools of sharks. Just next door is the *Noongamanda*, a long-liner wreck that sank in 2008 and has grown some lovely soft corals.

AquaSamoa Watersports (Map p254; ☎45662; www.aquasamoa.com; Aggie Grey's Lagoon Beach Resort, Main West Coast Rd) 'Upolu's only dive centre is a good one. There are plans to expand with a minibus that will be able to pick up guests from the south side of the island as well as around Apia. The centre also offers waterskiing, wakeboarding, snorkelling and island tours. Two-tank dives are ST320 and PADI Open Water Courses are ST1250.

Hiking

Shorter tracks that don't require a guide include the short but steep walk to Robert Louis Stevenson's grave near the summit of Mt Vaea (p265) and the Mt Matavanu crater walk (p278). Even on short walks, the sun and hot, humid conditions can take their toll. Good walking shoes are essential. For longer hikes a guide is imperative.

SamoaOnFoot (☎31252, 759 4199; samoaonfoot@gmail.com) Based in Apia, Eti offers expert guided hikes to Lake Lanoto'o (p266), Uafato Conservation Area (p267) and O Le Pupu-Pu'e National Park (p270). On Savai'i, Mt Silisili (p281) offers a challenging multiday trek.

Surfing

'Upolu has great surf but most of it is reef-breaking, far offshore and within limits of village's water rights, so you'll need permission. It's best to go with an operator. **Salani Surf Resort** (p271), **Maninoa Surf Camp & Beach Fales** (p272) and **Manoa Tours** (☎777 0007; manoatours@gmail.com) at Coconuts Beach Club Resort (p271) offer surf packages as well as shuttle service to the breaks for nonguests.

Offshore Adventures (☎750 8825; www.offshoreadventuressamoa.com) Brent offers transport to surf-breaks for ST100 per person, fishing from ST100 per person and snorkelling with shark- and turtle-watching (two to three hours) for ST70 per person. This outfit has a great reputation and resorts along the west coast book tours here – or you can just call and organise a trip yourself.

Other Activities

Island Explorer Kayak Samoa (☎777 1814; www.islandexplorer.ws) Caters to everyone from beginners to experienced paddlers, offering day trips, two-day tours to Namu'a and four-day south-coast expeditions (all ST180 per day; accommodation and meals extra).

Oceanic Sport Fishing Adventures (☎775 9606; www.grandermarlin.com) Go with Captain Chris to catch the big ones – from tuna to marlin – on his comfortable, sturdy 43ft *Southern Destiny*. Best from April to October.

Fagali'i Golf Club (Map p254; ☎20120; Royal Samoa Country Club, Plantation Rd, Fagali'i; per 9/18 holes ST10/20, club hire ST20 plus ST50 deposit; ⊙6am-6.30pm) An 18-hole, par-70 course.

Le Penina Golf Course (Map p254; ☎770 4653; Main West Coast Rd; per 9/18 holes ST81/135, equipment hire per 9/18 holes ST50/90; ⊙8am-5pm Mon-Sat, noon-5pm Sun) In front of Aggie's is the trim greenery of this par-72 course.

Apia

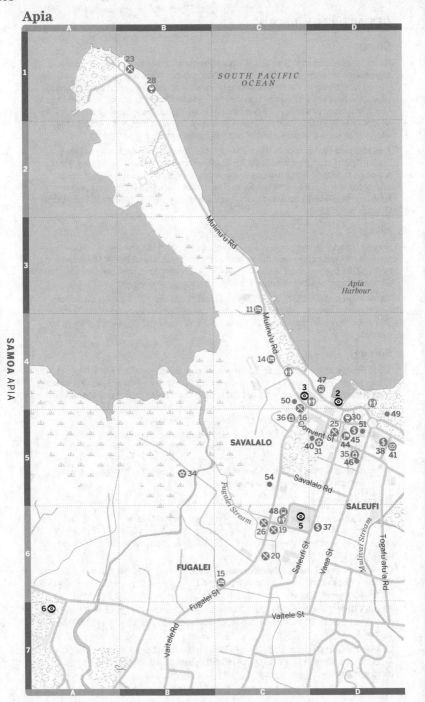

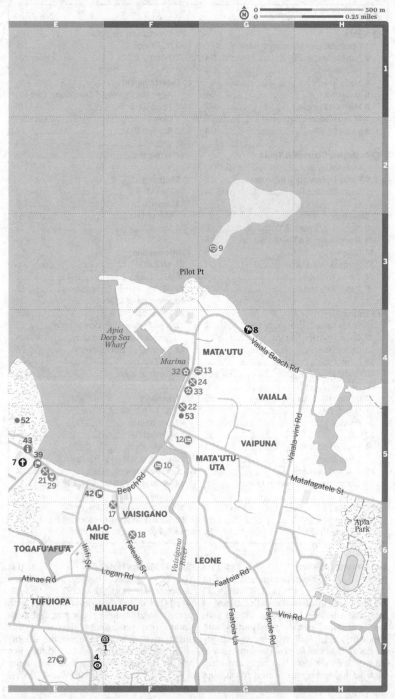

0 500 m
0 0.25 miles

SAMOA APIA

Pilot Pt

Apia Deep Sea Wharf

Marina

MATA'UTU

Vaiala Beach Rd

VAIALA

Vaiala-vini Rd

VAIPUNA

MATA'UTU-UTA

VAIPUNA

Matafagatele St

Beach Rd

VAISIGANO

Faleolii St

AAI-O-NIUE

Iliili St

Vaisigano River

LEONE

TOGAFU'AFU'A

Atinae Rd

Logan Rd

Faatoia Rd

Faipule Rd

Faatoia La

Vini Rd

Apia Park

TUFUIOPA

MALUAFOU

Apia

Le Manumea Resort HOTEL $$$

(Map p266; ☎27755; www.manumearesort.com; The Cross Island Rd, Vailima; r from ST280; ❄@🅿🛜🏊) Le Manumea inhabits the cooler climes of the slopes above Apia. Rooms are the prettiest you'll find outside the beaches with pandanus-woven wall panels, *siapo* lampshades and Samoan fabrics. The semi-outdoor showers are built from lava rocks and every unit has its own terrace with a couch, kept private by wooden lattices and ornate foliage.

Samoa Marina Hotel HOTEL $$

(Map p258; ☎22580, 771 4559; samoamarinahotel@gmail.com; Beach Rd; s ST99, d ST140-180; ❄🏊) One of the best deals in town, with a great location near the water and steps from great restaurants, the beach and nightlife. Rooms are cute, nautical-feeling and clean, albeit dark (a good thing when it's hot outside) with attached bathrooms, TVs, minifridges and tea- and coffee-making facilities. Taja and Lucy (sisters) are

supremely friendly and there's even a pool out the back.

Pasefika Inn
HOTEL **$$**

(Map p258; ☑20971; www.pasefikainn.ws; Matafagatele St; s ST140-160, d ST160-200; ✳✱) Carved beams, *siapo*-inspired bed runners and bunches of polished coconuts lining the stairway add Samoan touches to this casual, airy place that's bettered by its spacious communal lounge, guest kitchen and swimming pool. The good-looking rooms all have attached bathrooms. While the more-expensive rooms with terraces are bigger, they also pick up more noise from the busy road out front. It's in a fantastic central location.

Amanaki Hotel & Restaurant
HOTEL **$$**

(Map p258; ☑27889; www.amanakihotel.com; Mulinu'u Rd; d incl breakfast ST220-280; ✳✿✱) This new hotel is a two-storey block across from the sea wall. The huge rooms have a comfy minimalist design with white tiles and white-painted brick walls – they all face a nicely landscaped pool. The restaurant here is very popular with locals for its breezy atmosphere and high-quality meals (think burgers or fish and chips) at very reasonable prices (mains ST10 to ST25).

Tanoa Tusitala
HOTEL **$$$**

(Map p258; ☑21122; www.tanoahotels.com; Mulinu'u Rd; r from ST280; ✳✿✱) The swankiest place in town is a garden property across the street from the sea wall. The hotel has a huge and high traditional-roofed lobby backed by two, two-storey room blocks. Rooms are big and elegant with white tiles and dark-wood furniture, and the plush pool has plenty of lounge chairs and a bar-restaurant steps away.

Aniva's Place
GUESTHOUSE **$$**

(Map p266; ☑23431; anivas@lesamoa.net; off Falealili St, Moto'otua; s/d incl breakfast ST115/150; ✳✿✱) Owned by a wonderfully hospitable Samoan-Scottish family, this two-storey suburban dwelling offers a homey atmosphere with clean, comfortable rooms, an honesty bar and a small pool. All but the cheapest rooms have private bathrooms.

Valentine's Motel
GUESTHOUSE **$**

(Map p258; ☑22158; valentine@samoa.ws; Fugalei St; d from ST79; ✳@) This friendly place has the feel of a big family home, a perception reinforced by the prominent tomb of a family member on the back lawn. It's all a bit shabby but the best options are the bright

---

THERE'S SOMETHING ABOUT BLOODY MARY

Agnes Genevieve Swann was the daughter of William Swann, a Lincolnshire chemist who had migrated to Samoa in 1889, and Pele, a Samoan girl from Toamua village. In 1917 she married Gordon Hay-Mackenzie, the recently arrived manager of the Union Steamship Company. They had four children before Gordon died eight years later. Soon afterwards, Aggie married Charlie Grey, who was, unfortunately, a compulsive gambler. Charlie lost everything they had and Aggie had to look for some means of supporting the family.

In 1942 American soldiers arrived in Apia carrying 'unimaginable wealth', and Aggie saw an opportunity to earn a little money. She borrowed US$180, bought the site of a former hotel and began selling hamburgers and coffee to US servicemen. Response to her business was overwhelming and, although supplies were difficult to come by during WWII, Aggie built up an institution that became famous Pacific-wide as a social gathering place for war-weary soldiers. She even succeeded in getting through the New Zealand–imposed prohibition of alcoholic beverages.

When James Michener published his enormously successful *Tales of the South Pacific*, Aggie Grey was so well known throughout that realm that it was widely assumed she was the prototype for the character of Michener's Tonkinese madam, Bloody Mary. Michener has said that he did visit Aggie's place whenever he could from Pago Pago, where he was frequently stationed. However, he denies that anything but the good bits of Bloody Mary were inspired by Aggie Grey.

Over the next few decades, the snack bar expanded into a hotel where numerous celebrities stayed while filming or travelling in the area. (Many of the *fale* rooms are named after these famous people.) If you'd like to read more about Aggie Grey, who died in June 1988 at the age of 91, pick up a copy of her biography, *Aggie Grey of Samoa*, by Nelson Eustis.

and airy upstairs fan-cooled rooms with shared bathrooms.

Eating

Apia is the only place in Samoa where you won't be held hostage to the culinary abilities (or lack thereof) of your accommodation provider. There's a decent selection of eateries scattered around town, with most of the upmarket ones lining the waterfront.

TOP CHOICE Bistro Tatau
FUSION $$$

(Map p258; ☑22727; Beach Rd; mains ST48-65; ☺lunch Mon-Fri, dinner Mon-Sat; ✿☑) You'd be hard-pressed to find another menu as innovative as Tatau's in Samoa, fusing local favourites such as *palusami* into soufflé and ravioli. Polished floorboards, white tablecloths, vibrant local art, tropical floral arrangements and efficient barefoot waiters in *lava-lava* complete the experience.

Seafood Gourmet
SEAFOOD, BURGERS $

(Map p258; Beach Rd; mains ST10-22; ☺breakfast, lunch & dinner Mon-Sat) This local institution is favoured by Samoans and expats alike for its no-frills but tasty seafood meals and burgers. The open-sided dining areas let in the marina breezes to keep things cool and the fish is invariably fresh and cooked to perfection. In the morning there are omelettes and hotcakes.

Paddles
ITALIAN $$$

(Map p258; ☑21819; Beach Rd; mains ST22-53; ☺lunch Mon-Fri, dinner Mon-Sat) A delightful Italian-Samoan family serves delicious home cooking and ready conviviality at this attractive terrace restaurant across from the seafront. It has that perfect balance of laid-back and chic. Try the fish lasagne or the yummy vegetarian risotto.

Coffee Bean
CAFE $

(Map p258; Falealili St; mains ST12-22; ☺8am-4pm Mon-Fri, 8am-noon Sat & Sun; ☎) If the quality of your morning coffee affects how you cope with your day, head here for a wake-up call. Along with your espresso there are big breakfasts like eggs Benedict (ST22) or lighter choices and baked goods; at lunch choose from sandwiches, savoury pies and casseroles. It's tucked behind Misiluki Day Spa so a little hard to see from the road.

Giordano's
ITALIAN $$

(Map p266; ☑25985; off Falealili St, Moto'otua; mains ST19-40; ☺dinner Tue-Sun) Sit in the back courtyard with its Italian murals and thatched *fale*-style roof, and tuck into delicious pizza featuring such exotic (for Samoa) toppings as olives, blue cheese, parmesan, pepperoni and anchovies. It was the first pizza place to open in Samoa and many think it's still the friendliest and the best.

Tifaimoana Indian Restaurant
INDIAN $$

(Map p258; Fugalei St; dishes from ST12; ☺breakfast, lunch & dinner Mon-Sat; ☑) The chef here (from the Punjab region of India) orders ingredients from his homeland and you can taste it. The thali set meals (many vegetarian; prices from ST25) are Samoan-sized and include a lassi; if you're ordering à la carte, the chicken korma is memorably good. It's a small air-conditioned space at the Elava Hotel.

China Town Restaurant
CHINESE $$

(Map p258; ☑26177; Falealili St; dishes ST16-80; ☺lunch & dinner) A favourite with local Chinese (always a good sign), China Town offers a big range of delicious dishes, many of which will feed two with a side order of rice. The decor may be humble, but the salt-and-pepper lobster (ST80) is world-class.

Roko's
INTERNATIONAL $$

(Map p266; ☑20992; Ifiifi St; mains ST13-54; ☺breakfast, lunch & dinner) Roko's terrace tables gaze over a lush gully – it's a great spot for a cocktail. The menu lurches between Thai, Japanese, Samoan, French and Italian, but has a lightness of touch missing from many of its peers.

Sydney Side Cafe
CAFE $

(Map p258; ☑24368; Convent St; mains ST10-29; ☺breakfast & lunch) Staff aren't friendly but serve up coffee good and strong, along with breakfast scones, full breakfasts and sandwiches. The Samoan-style cocoa smoothie (with ground-up cocoa beans) is another delicious reason to stop by.

Sails
INTERNATIONAL $$

(Map p258; ☑20628; Mulinu'u Rd; mains ST26-48; ☺lunch & dinner Mon-Sat, dinner Sun) Canvas sails provide shelter at this upmarket waterside restaurant and bar. The menu is a mixture of Italian, Indian and island influences, with seafood at the fore.

Swashbucklers
INTERNATIONAL $$

(Map p258; ☑28584; Mulinu'u Rd; mains around ST30; ☺dinner) At Apia Yacht Club, there's a million-dollar view but the food's an oft-overcooked mix of fish and chips, steaks and grilled fish. Still, it's one of your few choices for a meal and a beer on Sundays.

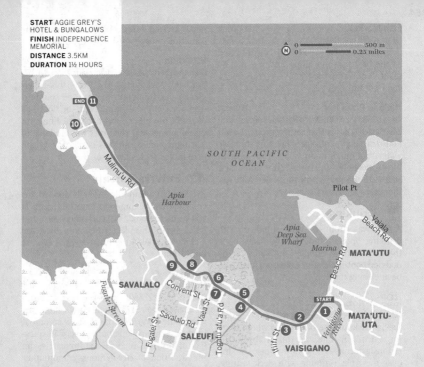

Walking Tour
Apia

❭ Start from ❶ **Aggie Grey's Hotel & Bungalows**, Samoa's most famous address. Founded in 1933, it became a popular haunt of American servicemen during WWII. The late Aggie Grey is said to have been the inspiration for the character of Bloody Mary in James Michener's novel *Tales of the South Pacific*.

Cross the road and walk west along the sea wall to the ❷ **John Williams monument**. It celebrates an early missionary who was killed and eaten in 1839 while evangelising in Vanuatu. His bones were recovered and buried under the church across the road. A little further along you'll pass the genteel wooden colonial-style ❸ **Supreme Court**.

As you continue along Beach Rd, gaze up at the recessed statues and twin turrets of the ❹ **Mulivai Catholic Cathedral** on your left and then the *fale*-style ❺ **Samoa Tourism Authority office** on your right. This and the large government buildings behind it were built on reclaimed land. Originally the ❻ **clock tower**, constructed in memory of those who fought and were killed in WWI, stood near the water's edge. Across the road are the elegant arches of the Spanish Mission–style ❼ **Chan Mow's building**.

From the clock tower, take the smaller road heading behind the library to check out the ❽ **Fish Market** and then the ❾ **Flea Market**.

Now amble north through the pretty park beside the sea wall that buttresses the eastern shore of the Mulinu'u Peninsula until you reach the large peach-hued bowler hat that is Samoa's parliament house, the ❿ **Fale Fono**. In case you had any doubts about Samoa's Christian leanings, cross the road to read the ⓫ **Independence Memorial**. It was built to celebrate the independence of Western Samoa on 1 January 1962 and bears the inscription 'Samoa is founded on God', with lengthy thanks paid to each member of the Holy Trinity.

Fish Market SEAFOOD $
(Map p258; off Beach Rd; fish & chips ST7.50;
⊘7am-3pm Mon-Fri, to noon Sat) Locally rated
as the best fish and chips, and you can be
assured of freshness. It's a very gritty, local-
style setting.

Italiano Pizza Bar ITALIAN $$
(Map p258; ☑24330; Beach Rd; small pizzas ST18-
24; ⊘lunch & dinner Mon-Sat, dinner Sun) Locals
and travellers converge on this humble
waterfront pizzeria to talk, drink jugs of
lurid alcoholic mixtures and add their
scrawl to the graffiti on the walls. And yes,
the pizzas are great.

 Drinking

Apia's waterfront is well supplied with
drinking options, though few places open
their doors on a Sunday and some of the
dodgier pool halls aren't pleasant places to
be at closing time.

Y-Not BAR
`TOP CHOICE`
(Map p258; Beach Rd; cover charge ST10; ⊘5-10pm
Tue-Sat) Ask anyone of any age where to go
for a drink in Apia and this is always the
enthusiastic answer. It's no wonder. Looking
over the Apia Harbour with deck seating,
live or DJ music on Friday and Saturday
nights and a reliable mix of expats, locals
and visitors, it's the most fun place in town.
Find it in the same building as Paddles
restaurant.

Apaula Heights BAR
(Map p258; ☑20836; off Vaitele St; mains ST20-
75; ⊘dinner Mon-Sat) High-altitude Apaula
Heights' signature dishes include tuna
steaks, garlic prawns and chilli bugs (that's
crustaceans, not insects) but its popularity
comes more for its sunset view (a perfect
match for exotic cocktails) and as the place
that stays open after the clubs are closed.
Look for the sign pointing up a small,
unnamed road from Vaitele St.

Apia Yacht Club BAR
(Map p258; ☑21313; Mulinu'u Rd; ⊘5-11pm Tue-
Sun) Its private-club status makes it one of
the few sure-fire places for a drink on a Sun-
day evening. The seaside seating literally on
the sea wall merely reinforces the relaxing
effects of a cold Vailima beer.

Cocktails on the Rocks BAR
(Map p258; ☑20736; Beach Rd; ⊘3pm-midnight
Mon-Sat) Known as 'Cocks on the Rocks',
this small bar is a favourite haunt of expats,

newly arrived *palagi* (Westerners) and their
sometimes suspiciously friendly admirers.

RSA Club BAR
(Returned Services Association; Map p258; ☑20171;
Beach Rd) Nicknamed 'the Rosa', this rough
place is anything but flowery: the standard
drink is a 750mL Vailima beer, the floor has
possibly the oldest, most scarred linoleum
on the planet and you don't want to be here
if a fight breaks out (it's best to avoid the
pool tables at closing time).

 Entertainment

By Samoan standards, Apia is spoiled for
choice when it comes to entertainment. If
you've had enough of beachside peace and
quiet, here's the place to catch a flick, see
a show or boogie the night away – at least
until 10pm.

**Aggie Grey's
Hotel & Bungalows** TRADITIONAL DANCE
(Map p258; ☑22880; www.aggiegreys.com; Beach
Rd; dinner & show ST75) Aggie Grey's stages ar-
guably the best *fiafia* dance show accompa-
nied by a sumptuous buffet every Wednes-
day at 6.45pm. Aggie Grey Jnr carries on
the tradition of her famous grandmother
by dancing the final *siva* (slow, fluid dance),
and the evening is capped off by a spectacu-
lar fire-dance where the pool is set alight.

Siva Afi TRADITIONAL DANCE
(Map p258; ☑26128; Beach Rd; dinner & show
ST55) Also called Laumei Faiaga, this place
has a commitment to training young per-
formers, especially in fire-dancing. It hosts
an exclusively Samoan show on Tuesdays
and a broader Polynesian show on Fridays
(buffet from 7.30pm, show 8.30pm).

Tropicana CLUB
(Map p258; ☑32332; Fugalei; admission ST5;
⊘6-10pm Wed-Sat) Tucked down a dubious-
looking road, Tropicana offers a genuine
slice of local nightlife. A wide age group
comes to party in this pretension-free zone,
either to a live band or DJ. Heading from
town on Fugalei St, turn right at the first
road after the bridge (before Tatiana Motel)
and veer left at the first intersection.

Rock da Boat CLUB
(Map p258; Beach Rd; admission ST20; ⊘6.30-
10pm Fri & Sat) This berthed party boat is a
fun place to get your boogie on before trying
to find somewhere else open past 10pm.
Expect DJs spinning hip hop.

Club X   CLUB
(Map p258; Beach Rd; admission ST15-20;
🕑6-10pm Wed-Sat) Head upstairs for sea views
and ice-cold beers. Later in the evening the
dance floor fills up with the young and
horny, both Samoan and *palagi* alike.

Apolo Cinemas   CINEMA
(Map p258; 🖉28126; Convent St; adult/child
ST12/8) Big Hollywood blockbusters often hit
the screens here before they reach Australia
or NZ and for a fraction of the price.

🛍 Shopping

Memorable souvenirs can be bought at
various shops around Apia, including *siapo*,
ie toga (fine mats) and finely made, multi-
legged *'ava* (kava) bowls. A treasure trove
of such crafts is available from **Maketi
Fou** (Fugalei St; 🕑24hr) and the **Flea Market**
(Beach Rd); for details, see p253 and p254.

Plantation House   HANDICRAFTS, GIFTS
(Map p266; Lotopa Rd, Alafua) The best place
for high-quality, locally made craft and gifts,
including hand-blocked fabric, *lava-lava*,
prints, tailored shirts, bedding and jewellery.

Mailelani   BEAUTY
(Map p266; www.mailelani-samoa.com; The Cross
Island Rd) Handmade and gorgeous smell-
ing, the soaps, creams and goodies here are
made with organic coconut oil and are simply sublime. Stop by and you'll probably get
a tour showing how the products are made.

Mena   CLOTHING
(Map p258; www.mena.com.ws; MacDonald Bldg,
Fugalei St) High Samoan fashion in the form
of well-cut dresses in traditional fabrics or
painted with floral patterns. It's a bit pricey
but there's something for all shapes and sizes.

Janet's   HANDICRAFTS, GIFTS
(Map p258; upstairs, Lotemau Centre, Vaea St) Not
all of its stock is locally made, but there's a
large range of woodcarvings, *siapo* and gifts.

ℹ Information

ANZ Bank (Map p258; Beach Rd) There are
also ATMs on Vaiala–Vini Rd and on Saleufi St
opposite Maketi Fou.
Main post office (Map p258; Post Office St)
For poste restante, go to the separate office,
two doors from the main post office. Have
mail addressed to you care of: Poste Restante,
Samoa Post, Apia, Samoa.
MedCen (Map p266; 🖉26519; The Cross Island
Rd, Vailima; 🕑9am-10pm Mon-Fri, 10am-1pm &

CLOSING TIME

Many of the unusual rules in Samoa are
linked. In 2009, driving changed from
the right-hand to left-hand side of the
road. The reason was so that the many
Samoans living in New Zealand could
import their cars to Samoa. When the
change took place there were worries
there would be more traffic accidents so
it was decided that closing time for bars
would temporarily be 10pm.

Well, by 2012 there weren't many
traffic accidents (the speed limit in
town *is* 40km/h) but everyone was
accustomed to the 10pm closing time
so it just may stick. That said, many
places do stay open later than they're
supposed to (perhaps even till the ungodly hour of midnight) and more out-
of-the-way places that can get away
with it sometimes stay open much later
if there's a crowd wanting to stay.

6-10pm Sat & Sun) Private clinic with a 24-hour
emergency department.
Samoa Tourism Authority (Map p258;
🖉63500; www.samoa.travel; Beach Rd;
🕑9am-5pm Mon-Fri, to noon Sat) Occupying a
prominently positioned *fale* in front of the government buildings. Usually well stocked with
brochures, but the service is hit and miss.
Westpac Bank (Map p258; Beach Rd) Has an
ATM out the front.

ℹ Getting Around

Apia has an extraordinary number of taxis and
fares are cheap. You shouldn't be charged more
than ST5 for a ride within town, though it pays to
check the fare before you get in.
Recommended companies:
City Central Taxis (🖉23600)
Malo Fou Taxis (🖉27861)

Around Apia

👁 Sights & Activities

**Robert Louis Stevenson Museum
& Mt Vaea Scenic Reserve**   MUSEUM
(Map p266; www.rlsmuseum.com; The Cross Island Rd, Vailima; adult/child ST20/10; 🕑9am-4pm
Mon-Fri, to noon Sat) This lovely museum occupies the Scottish author's former residence (see the boxed text, p268, for more
information).

Around Apia

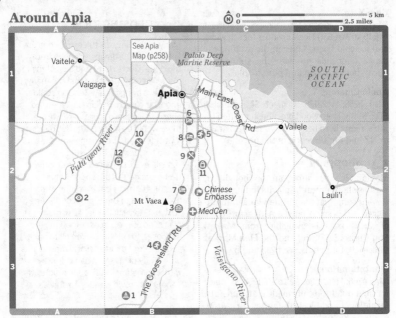

The estate is an enchanting place with a centrepiece lawn and perfectly manicured gardens. The house, substantially destroyed in the cyclones of 1991 and 1992, was lovingly rebuilt and opened as a museum in 1994 on the centenary of Stevenson's death. Access is by a half-hour tour that leads through rooms filled with antiques and sepia family photographs.

Stevenson is buried in the adjacent **Mt Vaea Scenic Reserve** (admission free). Look for the signs for the path to the tomb. At the first unmarked fork, turn left. After a short climb this path forks again: the right-hand trail (30 minutes) is steeper but shorter; the left-hand trail (45 minutes) is gentler but still involves a final slippery section. At the top you'll be greeted by a wonderful view of Apia, a stately Victorian tomb under a rain of yellow flowers, and clouds of vicious mosquitoes.

A taxi from Apia to the museum costs ST8, or take the Vaoala or Siumu bus (ST2) from Maketi Fou.

Papase'ea Sliding Rocks   NATURAL SLIDES
(Map p266; off Maugafolau Rd; admission ST20; ⏰7am-6pm) Kids and adults alike have a great time skimming down the waterfalls into cool rock pools at Papase'ea Sliding Rocks. If you visit during the dry season,

check that the water level is deep enough to be safe.

The site is 6km from central Apia, well signposted from the road past the Mormon Temple. Take the Se'ese'e bus (ST2.50) from Maketi Fou and ask to be dropped at the turn-off for Papase'ea.

Bahá'í House of Worship   RELIGIOUS
(Map p266; The Cross Island Rd, Tiapapata; ⏰6am-6pm) The architecturally interesting Bahá'í House of Worship sits in formal gardens near the highest point of The Cross Island Rd and is one of only eight such structures in the world – all are different except for being domed and having nine sides and entrances, reflecting the Bahá'í faith's central tenet of a basic unity of religions and peoples. Designed by Canadian Husayn Amanat and dedicated in 1984, its elegant white dome reaches 28m. Attendants in the adjoining information centre will happily answer any questions about the faith, which originated in Persia in 1844.

A taxi from Apia costs around ST24 or you can catch the Siumu bus (ST4) from Maketi Fou.

Lake Lanoto'o   LAKE
(Map p254) The pea-green crater of Lake Lanoto'o is about as removed from human

Around Apia

◎ Sights
1 Bahá'í House of Worship B3
2 Papase'ea Sliding Rocks.....................A2
3 Robert Louis Stevenson
   Museum B2

◉ Activities, Courses & Tours
4 Le Spa..B3
5 Polynesian Xplorer C2

◎ Sleeping
6 Aniva's Place B1
7 Le Manumea Resort............................B2
8 Samoan Outrigger Hotel.....................B2

◎ Eating
9 Giordano's B2
10 Roko's..B2

◎ Shopping
11 Mailelani..C2
12 Plantation House B2

habitation as you can get on 'Upolu. Its remote central-highlands location and alternating warm and cold currents lend it an eerie nature. It's also known as Goldfish Lake as it's full of wild goldfish.

The steep trail leading to the lake from the car park (located 3km along a very rough side road) is overgrown and forks repeatedly. Consequently, a number of hikers (including locals) have gotten lost. You would be foolish to attempt it without a guide. A dependable outfit is **SamoaOnFoot** (☑31252, 759 4199; samoaonfoot@gmail.com).

Papapapai-tai Falls   WATERFALL
(Map p254; The Cross Island Rd) About 3.5km south of the Bahá'í House of Worship is the lookout for Papapapai-tai Falls, a 100m waterfall that plunges into a forested gorge. Roughly 100m before the lookout, an unmarked track leads to the **Tiavi waterhole**, a blissful place to cool off on a hot day.

Eastern 'Upolu

The pointy end of 'Upolu is blessed with some of Samoa's best beaches, offering the winning combination of white sand, clear waters and excellent snorkelling. Heading east from Apia there's a succession of beautiful, sleepy villages along the surf-battered shoreline. The road turns sharply

inland not far past Piula Cave Pool and skirts rainforest and plantations before hitting the glorious white-sand-riddled Aleipata coast.

◉ Sights & Activities

Aleipata Beaches & Reefs   BEACHES
(Map p254) At the southeastern end of 'Upolu, Aleipata district has a reef system that's making a good comeback after being pummelled by the 2009 tsunami. It already has surprisingly good snorkelling, and the beaches here are some of the most spellbindingly beautiful you're likely to find anywhere in the world. Check out the area's submerged beauty by walking in off the spectacular white beach at **Lalomanu**. If you're lucky you might spot a turtle, but beware of strong currents.

The bus from Apia to Lalomanu (ST5.70) takes around two hours.

To Sua Ocean Trench   NATURAL POOL
(Map p254; Main South Coast Rd; adult/child ST10/5; ⊙7am-6pm) Not so much 'trenches' as two sinkhole-like depressions with sheer rock walls decorated in greenery – a magical aquamarine pool swishes, linked to both, at the bottom. You can swim under a broad arch of rock from the larger pool, serenaded by droplets of water hitting the surface, to the second large opening to the sky. The pool is fed by the waves surging through an underwater passageway – don't attempt to swim through it. The pools are accessed by a vertiginous but sturdy wooden ladder. Once you've descended the 20-odd metres into the crystalline waters of this fairy grotto, there's a most serene sense of being removed from the world.

When you've had your fill of this enchanted waterhole, take the short track to the wave-battered cliffs. The well-groomed garden is a great spot for a picnic.

Unfortunately there are no bathrooms or showers here so if you want to go for a dip, bring a freshwater rinse and a towel or you'll have to leave wet and salty.

Uafato Conservation Area   FOREST
(Map p254) The 14 sq km of wild and rugged terrain that comprise the Uafato Conservation Area boast untouched rainforest that marches down from 'Upolu's northeastern hills to dip its toes in the ocean. Flora lovers can track down a rare stand of *ifilele* (the tree used for carving *'ava* bowls), while fauna lovers can observe numerous bird and bat species going about their aerial

SAMOA EASTERN 'UPOLU

HERE HE LIES WHERE HE LONGED TO BE

In December 1889 the already famous Scottish author and poet Robert Louis Balfour Stevenson and his wife Fanny Osborne arrived in Apia aboard the schooner *Equator*. Stevenson had left Europe in search of relief from worsening tuberculosis and the general sickliness that had plagued him all his life. He was enchanted by Samoa and in 1890 he paid £200 for 126 hectares of land in the hills above Apia.

Stevenson's health improved and, with his family, he set sail for Australia. However, he became ill again in Sydney and it was decided that the climate of Samoa would be much better for him. The Stevenson family returned to Apia in September 1890 and constructed Vailima, the grandest home ever seen on the island. They imported furniture from Stevenson's native Scotland and dressed their Samoan employees in *lava-lava* patterned with the Stuart tartan.

In the 1890s, during the period of strife in Samoa between Britain, the USA and Germany, Stevenson became an activist for Samoan rights, maintaining that the people should be left to determine their own destiny in accordance with their customs. Most Europeans there would have liked to see him deported at the time, but this would have been very unpopular indeed; Stevenson came to be loved by the Samoans for his friendliness towards them and his ability to entertain with stories. They respectfully and affectionately referred to him as Tusitala (Teller of Tales).

On 3 December 1894 Stevenson died of a stroke at Vailima. When the Samoan chief Tu'imaleali'ifano spoke of Stevenson's death, he echoed the sentiments of many Samoans: 'Talofa e i lo matou Tusitala. Ua tagi le fatu ma le 'ele'ele,' he said. ('Our beloved Tusitala. The stones and the earth weep.') Just two months before his death, in gratitude for his kindness to them, a delegation of Samoan chiefs had arranged for a hand-dug road to be made between Apia and Vailima, which they called O Le Ala O Le Alofa, the Road of the Loving Heart.

Stevenson had stipulated that he wished to be buried at the top of Mt Vaea, part of the Vailima estate. And so, after a Christian burial service, the coffin was laid on a base of coral and volcanic pebbles and the grave lined with black stones, a practice normally reserved for Samoan royalty. You'll have to climb to the top of Mt Vaea to read his and his wife Fanny's poetic epitaphs.

business. Uafato village is known for its traditional carvers, who are usually willing to demonstrate their art to visitors.

Uafato can be reached via a rough road that winds around Fagaloa Bay from the turn-off at Falefa Falls. This route offers beautiful views, but don't go past Saletele without a high-clearance vehicle. Another option is the road (4WD only; 10km) signposted off Le Mafa Pass Rd to the village of Ta'elefaga.

SamoaOnFoot (☑31252, 759 4199; samoaon foot@gmail.com) offers 15km guided walks along Fagaloa Bay (per person ST100).

Piula Cave Pool   NATURAL POOL

(Map p254; Main East Coast Rd; adult/child ST5/3; ⊙8am-4pm Mon-Sat) Secreted beneath the campus of Piula Methodist Theological College, Piula Cave Pool consists of two blue-green, fish-filled freshwater grottoes side by side, only metres from the sea. The brave can swim between them via a creepy 3m under-water passage, although it's difficult to find in the darkness at the rear of the caves. The pools are concreted in so it's not a completely *au naturel* experience but it is refreshing and the college grounds are beautiful. There are bathrooms and a changing area.

From Apia, take the Falefa or Lalomanu bus (ST3.10).

Sopo'aga Falls   VIEWPOINT

(Map p254; Le Mafa Pass Rd; adult/child ST3/ free) The 54m-high Sopo'aga Falls empty themselves into an enormous gorge close to where the Main South Coast Rd meets Le Mafa Pass Rd. The well-signposted look-out is quite a distance from the falls, but the owners make an effort to give value for the entrance fee by touring visitors around their well-labelled kitchen garden. Traditional artefacts are also displayed, including drums and an *umukuka* (cooking house).

🛏 Sleeping & Eating

NAMU'A & LALOMANU

Lalomanu Beach stretches long and white in front of a lagoon so blue it looks radioactive.

Beach *fale* on this strip are all right next to each other, making this the most 'built up' (take this term lightly) strip outside of Apia. The accommodation is all simple and local style so, while it's not tops for privacy, it feels more social and fun than touristy or spoiled. There are several other very basic places besides the ones we've listed so you can easily go and shop around.

TOP CHOICE Namu'a Island Beach Fale   FALE $
(Map p254; ✆751 0231; Namu'a; fale incl 2 meals & return boat transfers per person ST90) Namu'a is only a short boat ride from Mutiatele, but once you're on this tiny private island you'll feel like 'Upolu is light years away (even though it's clearly visible across the strait). Do a circumnavigation of the shoreline (low tide only), clamber up the steep central peak and snorkel the surrounding reef. *Fale* are open, basic and right on the beach – there's no electricity so everything is lit by oil lamps at night. Meals are mostly local style (think fried fish and cassava for dinner, and spam and eggs for breakfast). Park your car (ST10 per day) at the shop with the Namu'a sign in Mutiatele and they'll call the resort to come pick you up.

Taufua Beach Fales   FALE $$
(Map p254; ✆844 1051; www.samoabeach fales.com; Main South Coast Rd, Lalomanu; open fale s/d ST120/180, closed fale s/d/tr/q ST140/240/330/440, all incl breakfast & dinner; @) Yellow and mint-green *fale* are as bright as the welcoming smiles of the owner and staff, and the spectacular Lalomanu beach is steps away. You get a choice of a basic open *fale* with a mattress on the floor or closed ones with walls, fans and proper beds. At its centre is an attractive dining *fale* where a *fiafia* (open to nonguests for ST30 including dinner) is held on Wednesday nights. Breakfast and dinner are both served as copious buffets.

Litia Sini's Beach Resort   FALE $$
(Map p254; ✆41050; www.litiasinibeach.ws; Main South Coast Rd, Lalomanu; fale s ST180, d ST260-280, incl breakfast & dinner) It's well worth paying the extra ST20 for the enclosed beachfront *fale* here, which have terraces right over the outrageous Lalomanu beach and are decorated in bright whites and blues. Nonbeachfront *fale* are older and drab. All have shared bathrooms and there's a big restaurant area overlooking the water. The prices are steep for *fale,* but you do get

a ceiling fan, electric light and lockable door. Reception lacks typical Samoan warmth.

Anita's Beach Bungalows   FALE $
(Map p254; ✆777 9673; www.samoabeach bungalows.ws; Main South Coast Rd, Lalomanu; fale per person ST40) One of the most basic budget options at Lalomanu, friendly Anita's offers simple open *fale* with pull-down plastic sheets and a mattress on the floor. There's a basic restaurant with meals from ST10 to ST20.

SALEAPAGA TO AUFAGA
There are several beach *fale* places along Saleapaga Beach – a stretch almost as gorgeous as Lalomanu (nitpickers may notice a few pebbles blemishing otherwise perfect white sand).

Notoriously stunning Vavau Beach, west from Aufaga, is rumoured to have an upscale resort coming soon. This has been talked about for more than eight years, but who knows? It may finally happen during the lifetime of this book.

TOP CHOICE Seabreeze Resort   RESORT $$$
(Map p254; ✆41391; www.seabreezesamoa.com; off Main South Coast Rd, Aufaga; d/tr/q incl breakfast from ST460/558/702; ✳@) Like the cocktail of the same name, you could easily become intoxicated by Seabreeze's cool, tropical charms. Set in a black-lava-rock bay lined with palm trees and scattered with tiny islands, this small resort offers beautifully built bungalows decorated with white tiles, neutral linens, Gauguin prints and fresh flowers. Kayaks are available or you can snorkel in front and swim to isolated patches of beach. Its excellent restaurant and bar will take care of your dining needs – including seabreezes. Some rooms here are wheelchair accessible and kids under 10 are not allowed.

Faofao Beach Fales   FALE $
(Map p254; ✆772 6693, 729 0775; birtwistlemark@ gmail.com; Main South Coast Rd, Saleapaga; fale per person incl breakfast & dinner ST70) Faofao treats guests like family. Mealtimes often feel more like social events, and the Saturday night *fiafia* (guests/nonguests free/ST30) is just one cause for celebration. The open *fale* are charming, all-natural thatch and are surrounded by short coconut palms.

Seabreeze Restaurant   INTERNATIONAL $$
(Map p254; ✆41391; off Main South Coast Rd, Aufaga; mains ST30-75; ⊘breakfast, lunch & dinner)

Beautifully decorated and idyllically situated on the edge of the bay, this restaurant offers the best food by far at this end of the island. The signature dish is slow-cooked smoky barbecue ribs, but you should also try the real Indian curries with fresh roti, or the surf and turf (porterhouse steak and prawns).

South Coast

The fact that Samoa's swankiest resorts are clumped on this stretch of coastline says much about its beauty. It's a delight to drive through the villages, the bright houses painted with the same stridency of colour as the native flora, which is particularly lush and tropical on this side of the island. You'll also find Samoa's only national park.

Many of the beaches are a bumpy drive from the main road, giving welcome seclusion after the road-hugging bays of Aleipata.

◉ Sights & Activities

South Coast Beaches & Reefs   BEACHES
The south coast of 'Upolu hosts numerous secluded beaches where you can play castaway amid leaning coconut palms and surf-lapped sand.

To the east of O Le Pupu-Pu'e National Park, there's a decent surfing spot at **Vaiula Beach**, accessed from Tafatafa village. West of the park is **Aganoa Black Sand Beach** (admission per car ST10, surf fee ST10), where the water is deep enough for swimming but there's no reef to protect you – the snorkelling, however, is some of the best on the island. There's a popular surf-break called **Boulders** here, just off Cape Niuato'i. The very rough 3km track to Aganoa is 150m east of the one-lane stone bridge in Sa'agafou – don't attempt it without a 4WD. The beach is a 10-minute walk to the east.

Near the bottom of The Cross Island Rd, there are several lovely beaches attached to resorts. Further on, **Salamumu** (admission per car ST10) is a beautiful set of beaches reached by a potholed 5.5km track. The approach to **Matareva** (admission per car ST20) is even better, leading to a series of delightful coves with shallow snorkelling areas and lots of rock pools.

At Lefaga village is **Return to Paradise Beach** (☏777 4986; admission per car ST10; ⊘Mon-Sat), which had a starring role in the 1951 Gary Cooper film *Return to Paradise*. This particular paradise is a little rough on swimmers, however.

O Le Pupu-Pu'e National Park   NATIONAL PARK
(Map p254) The 29-sq-km O Le Pupu-Pu'e National Park stretches 'from the coast to the mountaintop', which is what the park's name means. Experienced hikers can pick up a trail near the Togitogiga Recreation Reserve car park, which leads through thick rainforest to **Pe'ape'a Cave** (six hours return), a large lava tube inhabited by *pe'ape'a* (swiftlets); bring a torch. From here you can continue along a heavily overgrown trail to **Ofa Waterfall** (three days return). A guide, such as Eti from **SamoaOnFoot** (☏31252, 759 4199; samoaonfoot@gmail.com), is essential.

At the park's western boundary, a bumpy 3km unsealed access road (open 7am to 4pm) leads to the magnificently rugged **O Le Pupu Lava Coast**, where a rocky coastal trail leads along lava cliffs, the bases of which are constantly harassed by enormous waves.

Togitogiga Recreation Reserve   FOREST
(Map p254) The Togitogiga Recreation Reserve is a tropical oasis centred on a series of gentle waterfalls. Unless you visit on a Saturday, you'll probably have the sheltered swimming holes between the falls to yourself – although you won't get much of a swim if the weather's been particularly dry. To get here, take the access road for O Le Pupu-Pu'e National Park and stop at the parking area.

⌂ Sleeping

Virgin Cove Resort   FALE $$
(Map p254; ☏27085; www.virgin-cove.ws; Sa'anapu; fale s/d from ST140/200, beach bungalows s/d ST380/450, all incl breakfast) This is what Pacific Island dreams are made of – tiny soft white coves, iridescently blue water and picturesque *fale* poking out of lush, twisting mangroves. Accommodation ranges from traditional semi-enclosed *fale* with lockers and electricity, to large polished-wood houses (called 'beach bungalows') on stilts with full kitchens and cold-water bathrooms. All are well spaced out for privacy's sake. The shared stone-walled, open-air showers (cold-water only) are charming. The only downsides are the ever-present mosquitoes, flip-flop-stealing crabs, the extremely rough access road (only just doable in a high-clearance 2WD) and good but strangely posh and expensive meals (mains ST35 to ST45). To reach it, head to Sa'anapu (access fee per car ST10) and turn right. There's fantastic snorkelling at high tide.

Coconuts Beach Club Resort — RESORT $$$

(Map p254; ☑24849; www.coconutsbeachclub.
com; Main South Coast Rd, Maninoa; ste/fale/villas
from ST685/750/910; ❋@☎☂☒) Gorgeously
revamped post-tsunami, this is the hip-
pest resort in the country. The design takes
traditional architecture and adds modern
lines, tiled floors and plenty of windows.
Beach *fale* have big tiled decks, elevated
bamboo beds and bright cushioned bamboo
couches; many of the villas line a river and
are accessed via their own bridges. Balcony-
equipped 'treehouse' suites are back from
the beach but have good views. The snorkelling isn't great, but you can hire a kayak or
content yourself with lazing around the pool
and swimming up to the bar. Rates include a
free stocked minibar and transfers.

Mangrove Garden — FALE $

(Map p254; ☑774 7404, 844 7404; www.mangrove
gardensamoa.com; Sa'anapu; fale/treehouse per
person incl breakfast & dinner ST80/90) Unique
to the island, this place is a three-minute
walk to white-sand bliss but takes advantage
of cool and shady mangrove forests. The
best choices here are traditional *fale* with
terraces built over the river and kept private
by the surrounding jungle – but you can also
choose to sleep high, high up in a massive
banyan tree. The German-Samoan owners
offer tons of activities and serve one of the
best *umu* (traditional stone oven) feasts on
the island. An over-the-water bar was in the
planning stages when we passed.

Salani Surf Resort — BUNGALOWS $$$

(Map p254; ☑41069; www.surfsamoa.com; Salani;
nonsurfer/surfer package per d ST580/820; ❋@)
Located at the mouth of the Fupisia River
with excellent left- and right-hand breaks in
view, Salani caters primarily to experienced
surfers with packages that include transfers,
accommodation, meals, tours, guided surfing, and use of kayaking and snorkelling
gear. Numbers are limited to a total of 16
guests at any one time. Accommodation is
in swish and comfy wooden huts on stilts
with tiled hot-water bathrooms and decks
overlooking the river. It's a bit pricey but this
is hands down the best place to go if you're
serious about surfing. The resort will take
nonguests out to the surf for ST100.

Sinalei Reef Resort — RESORT $$$

(Map p254; ☑25191; www.sinalei.com; Main South
Coast Rd, Maninoa; d ST605-1450, presidential ste
ST2170; ❋@☎☂☒) If you like to laze around
the pool and be handed cocktails by charm-

ing waiters, Sinalei's the best place in Samoa
to do it. This beautifully landscaped plot by
the ocean offers well-appointed, stand-alone,
TV-free units, along with two restaurants,
tennis courts, a golf course, water-sports
centre and good snorkelling around an
ocean spring. The staff are delightful but
the rooms, though comfortable and packed
with amenities, are a bit plain for the price.
House-sized presidential suites take the luxe
up several notches but lack privacy. No kids
under 12 years are allowed.

Sa'moana Resort — RESORT $$

(Map p254; ☑28880; www.samoanaresort.com;
Salamumu; r from ST120; ❋☎☂☒⛱) Under new
ownership, this place was getting a major
remodel in 2012. The location, on white-
sand beach that tumbles past black lava
formations into a stunning lagoon, can't be
beat – it's one of the prettiest spots on the
island. A new saltwater infinity pool was
in the planning stages and, while upscale
bungalows will be built beachfront, a huge
lush garden at the back will be home to less
expensive options (about ST120). There will
also be a spa, gym and of course a full-scale
bar and restaurant.

Matareva Resort — FALE $

(Map p254; ☑779 1208; Matareva Beach; fale s/d
incl breakfast & dinner ST70/130) This place's

claim to fame is that the 2011 *Survivor* TV show was filmed here. When that's forgotten there will still be the beach – blindingly white and one of the widest on the island – that wraps around a stunning bay perfect for swimming and snorkelling. Day-use *fale* nab the beachfront (ST20 per day) so to stay overnight you'll have to check in to some very simple square bungalows (with proper beds) back near the road. The owners are super-welcoming and food is basic but plentiful.

Samoa Hideaway
Beach Resort   BUNGALOWS $$
(Map p254; ☑41517; www.samoahideawaybeach. ws; Matatufu; fale per person ST50, bungalows ST300-500; ⊕) Choose from large open beach *fale* with proper beds and tables and chairs inside, or new and shiny timber bungalows with tin roofs. One of the three bungalows is two-storey and great for families; all have bathrooms, TVs (with DVD player) and kitchens, and are right on a lovely white beach. The common area has a restaurant and a saltwater pool with slides. Plans were in the works to build more bungalows and land was being cleared for a flashier resort next door when we passed.

Vaiula Fales   FALE $
(Map p254; ☑779 2754; Tafatafa; fale incl breakfast & dinner per person ST60) There are three *fale* places on this beach, far removed from the road along a sand track, but this one is the longest-running. *Fale* have plastic blinds and sit on a skinny strip of perfect, palm-lined white sand. Nab the upper storey of a giant two-storey open *fale* under a big tree for ST70 per person.

Maninoa Surf Camp & Beach Fales   FALE $
(Map p254; ☑31200; maninoa.beachsurf@lesa moa.net; Main South Coast Rd, Maninoa; fale per person ST60) Squeezed between two luxury resorts, this humble collection of beach *fale* looks more ramshackle than it actually is. There's a chilled-out communal area where you can shoot pool, watch TV or raid the library. Surfers can add an extra ST90 for a daily boat trip to the breaks or it's ST100 for nonguests.

✕ Eating

Laumo'osi Fale Restaurant &
Ava i Toga Pier Restaurant   INTERNATIONAL $$$
(Map p254; ☑25191; Sinalei Reef Resort, Main South Coast Rd, Maninoa; mains ST25-70; ⊕8am-9pm)

Sinalei alternates evening meals between its two restaurants. The pier restaurant is the pick of the two, offering an eclectic menu of Samoan dishes, Japanese noodles, pasta dishes, salad and grills in a romantic waterside setting. Themed buffet dinners are served in the *fale* restaurant. Saturday night is Asian night (ST65) – you can eat as much as you like, but the food is lacklustre given the price. For ST15 more you get entertainment with your buffet at the Wednesday night *fiafia* (6.30pm).

Salani Cafe   CAFE $$
(Map p254; Salani Surf Resort; mains ST16-35; ⊕lunch & dinner; ☑) If you're touring the island it's worth the detour to lunch here. Try the excellent satay chicken wrap or fish burger (that's seared not fried). For dinner there's fresh sashimi and a tempting vegetarian risotto, as well as a whole menu of house-invented cocktails (ST24).

Mika's Restaurant   INTERNATIONAL $$
(Map p254; ☑24849; Coconuts Beach Club Resort, Main South Coast Rd, Maninoa; mains ST28-75; ⊕breakfast, lunch & dinner) The main restaurant at Coconuts travels the globe for inspiration, serving delicious Italian, French and Samoan dishes and a wonderful Hawaiian *ahi poke* salad (raw fish with sesame oil and chilli).

Northwestern 'Upolu

The main reason for staying here, in the least attractive part of 'Upolu, is to be near the airport, the ferries to Savai'i and the boats to the Apolima Strait islands. The coastline is quite built-up, particularly between Apia and the airport, and the brilliantly coloured lagoon is too shallow for a satisfying swim.

🛏 Sleeping & Eating

Aggie Grey's Lagoon
Beach Resort   RESORT $$$
(Map p254; ☑45611; www.aggiegreys.com; Main West Coast Rd; r from ST780; ✳🌐🌊⊕) The best things about this vast sprawling resort (which lacks the period charm of its famous Apia sister) are its large pool, spacious grounds and proximity to the airport. For these prices you might expect a little more luxury and design verve than the luridly painted concrete-block accommodation wings. And the lacklustre but expensive meals and cocktails wouldn't be quite so bad if you weren't trapped so far from alterna-

IT'S JUST NOT CRICKET

One of the primary requirements for any serious *kirikiti* player is the ability to dance and play cricket at the same time. *Kirikiti* is a unique South Pacific version of the English game of cricket, and is a great example of how an imported measure of civilisation has been adapted to suit Samoan needs. The willow bat became a three-sided club of a size that would make any warlord happy, and the ball was fashioned out of rubber – all the better to be catapulted into the local lagoon. This is a colourful game, too – Samoans keep their whites for church on Sunday; the runs are made in *lava-lava* and sandals.

And the rules? Well, it's just not cricket. There can be any number of players in a Samoan team, which means a game can continue for days, sometimes weeks, at a time. But there's none of that 'stand and watch the grass grow' stuff about this game either. As the batsman swings at every ball, the leader of the opposite team jumps up and down and blows his whistle incessantly in a kind of syncopated rhythm. The rest of the team also gyrates, clapping hands in rhythmic harmony, at the same time watching for an opportunity to catch out the rival. Only when all the batsmen of the opposing team have been dismissed does the other team get its chance.

It's energetic, exuberant and lots of fun. From June to September you'll see it in every village just before sunset.

---

tives. There's a dedicated kids club and a scintillating *fiafia* every Friday night.

Le Vasa Resort
RESORT $$$

(Map p254; ☑46028; www.levasaresort.com; Main West Coast Rd; r from ST535; ❄🖳🌊) A millennium ago the Tongans were booted out of Samoa at this grassy headland, but you can expect a warmer welcome. This personable little resort offers spacious ocean-facing bungalows, some sleeping up to six – there's no beach but there is a good pool. Kayaks and bikes are free, but meals aren't included (mains from ST25).

Manono

POP 1090 / AREA 3 SQ KM

If you'd like to temporarily escape engine noise and village dogs, the small island of Manono offers a tranquil option. Canines and cars have been banished, and the only things that might snap you out of a tropical reverie are occasional blasts from stereos and the tour groups that periodically clog the island's main trail.

It's obligatory for visitors to do the 1½-hour circumnavigation of the island via the path that wends its way between the ocean and people's houses. They're friendly sorts here, so expect to be greeted with a cheery '*malo*' a dozen or so times.

The trail winds through Lepuia'i, where you'll see the two-tiered **Grave of 99 Stones**. Translated from the Samoan the name is actually 'Grave of the Missing Stone'

and is dedicated to high chief Vaovasa, who was killed after an unsuccessful attempt to abduct his 100th wife from 'Upolu. The missing stone at the grave's centre represents the missing wife. The trail's most beautiful section is Manono's less-populated northern edge, where little bays offer terrific views of Apolima. Apai village has the island's best beach.

If you follow the path behind the women's committee building in Salua, you'll eventually end up on top of Mt Tulimanuiva (110m), where there's a large **star mound** (see boxed text, p300). Nearby is the **grave of Afutiti**, who was buried standing up to keep watch over the island. Allow 90 minutes to two hours for this side trip.

🛏 Sleeping

Sunset View Fales
FALE $$

(Map p254; ☑759 6240, 761 0733; info@samoa. travel; Lepuia'i; fale per person without/with bathroom ST100/130) Rustic but bright beach shacks are offered here (now up on the hill since the 2009 tsunami wiped out the waterfront ones), along with a daily boat trip out to the edge of the reef for memorable snorkelling stints. Price includes all meals and boat transfers, making this the better of the island's two options. The family that runs this place is charming although they often seem half-asleep.

The Sweet Escape
FALE $$

(Map p254; ☑726 1570; Faleu; thesweetescape 2009@live.com; fale per person incl breakfast &

dinner ST140) Facing 'Upolu, these enclosed, bright-yellow *fale* are closely clustered together on a sandy spit of landfill.

ⓘ Getting There & Away

Both **Samoa Scenic Tours** (☑26981; www. samoascenictours.ws; Aggie Grey's Hotel & Bungalows, Beach Rd, Apia) and **Polynesian Xplorer** (☑26940; www.polynesianxplorer.com; Falealili St, Apia) offer day tours of Manono; for details, see p255.

If you'd rather go it alone, head for the jetty just south of Le Vasa Resort (p273). Buses marked either 'Manono-uta' or 'Falelatai' (ST3.90) will get you here from Apia (allow 90 minutes). The boats leave when there are enough people (usually when the bus arrives) and the cost is ST3 each way. If you want to charter the whole boat expect to pay about ST30 to ST40 each way. Although the boats are small, Manono is inside the reef so the 20-minute trip isn't usually rough.

Apolima

POP 80 / AREA 1 SQ KM

Few travellers make the trip out to minuscule but ruggedly beautiful Apolima. From a distance, its steep walls look completely inaccessible. When you get closer you can spy the narrow gap in the northern cliffs, through which small boats can enter the crater and land on a sandy beach. The small settlement consists of a handful of buildings interspersed with pigpens, jungly foliage and (naturally) a large church. To get an overview of the island, climb up to the small **lighthouse** perched high on the crater's northern rim.

Getting to Apolima isn't easy. To start with, you'll need an invitation to stay with a local family. Leota, the *matai* (chief) from Manono's Sunset View Fales (p273) may be able to arrange this, along with a boat to come and collect you, but you'll have to negotiate a fee.

SAVAI'I

POP 43,100 / AREA 1700 SQ KM

Savai'i is a spectacular combination of plantations, lush jungle, sea-smashed cliffs, pristine waterfalls and ragged volcanic cones (around 450 of them). The volcanic nature of the largest island in Polynesia outside NZ and Hawai'i has resulted in some gargantuan lava overflows in Savai'i's northern reaches. The island has a leading role

in Samoan mythology, its rough landscape yielding numerous legendary formations and enigmatic archaeological sites.

In this scarcely developed, sparsely populated paradise, the *fa'a* Samoa (Samoan way) remains strong. Scattered around the coastline are breezy villages, where children sit atop the tombs of ancestors, men wander the roadside cheerfully swinging bush knives, and weather-beaten churches resound with the melodies of Sunday services.

ⓘ Getting There & Away

AIR

At the time of research there were no flights to Savai'i, but there is an airport so flights may start up again in future.

BOAT

Two car ferries tackle the 22km Apolima Strait between 'Upolu and Savai'i daily (per passenger ST12, car plus driver ST95). The larger of the two boats, the *Lady Samoa III*, is the more comfortable (see table for schedule). The smaller *Lady Samoa II* has departures from Salelologa at 6am, 10am and 2pm and from Mulifanua at 8am, noon and 4pm every day except Sunday and Wednesday.

Vehicles should be prebooked through the **Samoa Shipping Corporation** (☑20935; www. samoashipping.com). Before putting your car on the ferry at Mulifanua Wharf, you must have its underside cleaned (free) at the spraying station 100m before the boat terminal. This is done to prevent the spread of the giant African snail.

LADY SAMOA III 'BIG BOAT' FERRY DEPARTURES

Departs Salelologa	Departs Mulifanua
Sun 10am & 2pm	noon & 4pm
Mon 6am, 10am & 2pm	8am, noon & 4pm
Tue 6am & 2pm	8am & 4pm
Wed 6am, 10am & 2pm	8am, noon & 4pm
Thu 6am & 2pm	8am & 4pm
Fri 6am, 10am & 2pm	8am, noon & 4pm
Sat 6am & 2pm	8am & 4pm

ⓘ Getting Around

BUS

Salelologa's market is the main terminal for Savai'i's colourful, crowded buses. For the east-coast beaches take the Pu'apu'a bus or to continue on to Fagamalo, take the Lava Field Express. To carry on to Manase, take the Manase or Sasina bus. The Falealupo bus will take you around the Falealupo Peninsula, while the Salega or Fagafau buses trundle past the Alofaaga Blowholes and Satuiatua Beach. The most you'll

pay for a ride is ST8.60 (to Asau). Buses to out-of-the-way destinations are timed with the ferries.

CAR

It's a joy to drive the sealed Main Coast Rd that circles the island, but keep an eye out for stray children, pigs, dogs and chickens. Off the main road you'll encounter a few bumpy tracks where at the very least you'll need a high-clearance 2WD (if not a 4WD if there's been heavy rain). This includes the steep, rocky climb up Mt Matavanu.

There are several petrol stations around Salelologa but only a few others scattered around the island.

Cars can be hired on Savai'i but, as there's more competition on 'Upolu, if you're staying several days it works out cheaper and easier to bring a car over on the ferry. Prices for a small 2WD Hyundai cost ST130 per day.

TAXI

A small army of taxis congregates around the Salelologa Market and greets every boat that arrives.

Salelologa & the East Coast

Ragtag Salelologa stretches up from the ferry terminal, offering little of interest except for a bustling **market** (Map p276; ⊙early-late Mon-Sat), selling everything from groceries to colourful reef fish laid out on slabs. Salelologa is as close as Savai'i gets to a proper town, making it a useful place to stock up on supplies and cash before heading further afield.

Heading north you'll pass a tight series of villages fronting a shallow lagoon. It's only once you round the point at Tuasivi that things get exciting, as long white-sand beaches come into view, outlining the vivid aquamarine lagoon. The best of them, **Si'ufaga** and **Lano**, are among Savai'i's finest. The area also has numerous freshwater pools and springs for bathing.

🛏 Sleeping

There are several places to stay in Salelologa, but it's only once you head out of town that you really start to experience the restful charms of Savai'i.

SALELOLOGA

Lusia's Lagoon Chalets HOSTEL $
(Map p276; ☑51487; www.lusiaslagoonchalets.ws; fale per person ST55-65, d ST120-270; ⊛) Lusia's most basic options are small, square, plywood *fale* among the jungle-like shore

or rough wooden *fale* on stilts over the lagoon. Although the latter are seemingly cobbled together out of driftwood and have mattresses on the floor rather than beds, the cute sea-gazing decks make them the better option. The self-contained units are a large jump up in comfort, offering private bathroom, hot water and air-conditioning. Kayaks can be hired for ST20 and there's deep enough water for a proper swim off the pier.

Jet Over Hotel HOTEL $
(Map p276; ☑51565; www.jetoverhotel.ws; fale s/d ST60/80, r/ste ST100/260; ⊛☜⊛) 'Manned' almost exclusively by an efficient team of *fa'afafine* (men who live their lives as women), the cheapest rooms at this surprisingly stylish place are in the old wing and are plain and large with carpeting, air-con and cold-water bathrooms. Suites facing the beach are two-storey and more like mini-apartments, quite modern and comfortable. On the lawn are possibly the smartest *fale* in Samoa – with louvre windows and thatched roofs. There's also a pool, tour agency, very agreeable restaurant and kayaks for guests.

LALOMALAVA & SAPAPALI'I

Le Rosalote Guest Fales FALE $
(Map p276; ☑53568; Main North Coast Rd, Sapapali'i; fale per person ST60) Welcome to Samoa's answer to the over-the-water bungalow: adorable enclosed white-painted wooden *fale* on stilts right over the sea. Small terraces let you take in all the teal blue you can handle then plop in for a swim at any time. Plus there's a genuine village feel here, with the large *fale* used for community meetings and bingo

Savai'i

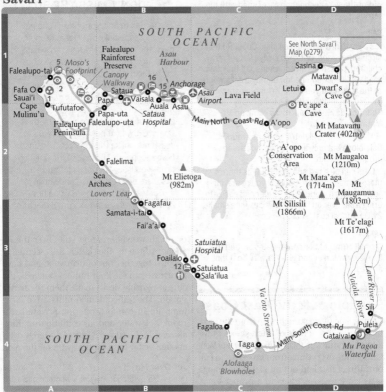

sessions. Meals are charged separately (breakfast/lunch/dinner ST20/30/40). If you're lucky the on-site catering business might invite you along for Sunday lunch. There's also a small shop run by the same people out front for all your cold Vailima needs.

Savaiian Hotel
RESORT $

(Map p276; ☎51296; http://savaiianhotel.com; Main North Coast Rd, Lalomalava; fale s/d/tr/q ST65/100/130/160, units s/d/tr ST130/160/190; ❄🛜🏊) The snazzy large bungalows that go by the name *fale* here are many steps above your standard beach *fale*. They have balconies, fans and private bathrooms for a start, not to mention walls, windows and doors – they are a fabulous bargain. The units add amenities including air-conditioning, but these are darker and not as fun. They're all set in a sparse garden between the village and the sea; although the water's too shallow for a decent swim there is a small pool. Service is excellent and bike rental (per

hour/day ST5/35), tours and well-priced car rental are also available.

Safua Hotel
FALE $

(Map p276; ☎51271; safuahotel@lesamoa.net; Lalomalava; s/d ST80/140) Savai'i's first hotel has seen better days but it retains a nostalgic Samoan family feel. It's situated well away from the ocean, but the staff are delightful, there are lovingly decorated common areas and the *fale*-style cottages have private bathrooms. A buffet dinner is available for ST30.

TUASIVI & LANO

Joelan Beach Fales
FALE $

(Map p276; ☎722 9588, 758 0979; joelanbeachfales@gmail.com; Main North Coast Rd, Lano; fale per person incl breakfast & dinner ST50) Long, languid Lano Beach easily rates as one of the best strips of sand on Savai'i, and Joelan's simple but well-kept thatched *fale* nab the best bit – some are so close to the water you could almost dangle your toes in the surf. It's

named after the friendly owner's youngest daughter.

Lauiula Beach Fales FALE $
(Map p276; ☑53897; www.lauiulabeachfales.com; Main North Coast Rd, Lano; fale per person incl breakfast & dinner ST70; ⏸) Right next to Joelan's, the beach here has eroded away quite a bit but close-together *fale* are more 'posh' thanks to linoleum floors and a more sturdy thatch enclosure. Plus there's a pro set-up with tours and transport on offer. Breakfast and dinner are served in a gorgeous carved, seafront dining *fale*.

Siufaga Beach Resort RESORT $$
(Map p276; ☑53518; www.siufaga.com; Main North Coast Rd, Tuasivi; s/d with fan ST210/250, with air-con ST320/350; ❋⏸❄) Siufaga Beach is a skinnier version of Lano Beach, and the resort, across the road from the palm trees and turquoise water, is positioned to capitalise on it. These large, relatively luxurious units hooked

around a lushly landscaped pool are the most upmarket choice on this coast.

Eating & Drinking

LeSogaimiti Restaurant & Bar INTERNATIONAL $$
(Map p276; ☑51296; Savaiian Hotel, Main North Rd, Lalomalava; lunch ST13-22, dinner ST20-45) At the Savaiian Hotel, this plain restaurant with water views serves some of the best and copious meals on the islands, from fish/chicken/sausages/steak and chips to Samoan and Thai dishes. Try the octopus in coconut milk if it's available.

Parenzo's Bar & Restaurant INTERNATIONAL $$$
(Map p276; ☑53518; Siufaga Beach Resort, Main North Coast Rd, Tuasivi; mains ST20-60) Parenzo's

SUNDAY LUNCH

On Sunday mornings you'll find the islands shrouded in smoke as villagers everywhere light fires to warm stones needed for the *umu* (ground ovens) used to bake *to'ona'i* (Sunday lunch). Visitors sometimes complain that nothing happens in Samoa on Sunday, but it's hardly true – after a small breakfast (on account of the looming lunch), Samoans go to church and sing their lungs out, at noon they eat an enormous roast dinner and in the afternoon they sleep.

You may be lucky enough to be invited to a family *to'ona'i*. A typical spread includes baked fish and other seafood (freshwater prawns, crabs, octopus cooked in coconut milk), suckling pig, baked breadfruit, bananas, *palusami* (coconut cream wrapped in taro leaves), salads and curry dishes.

commands the top floor of the reception building at Siufaga Beach Resort, providing a memorable setting for a pasta, steak, grilled fish or lobster meal.

Information

ANZ Bank (Map p276; Salelologa; ⊘8.30am-3pm Mon-Fri, to noon Sat) Beside the market. Only accepts ANZ cards.

Malietoa Tanumafili II Hospital (Map p276; ✆53511; Main North Coast Rd, Tuasivi) Has on-call doctors and a pharmacy. Other basic hospitals are at Safotu, Sataua and Satuiatua.

Post office (Map p276; Blue Bird Mall, Salelologa; ⊘8.30am-noon & 1-4pm Mon-Fri) Has telephones.

Westpac Bank (Map p276; Salelologa; ⊘9am-3pm Mon-Wed, to 4pm Thu-Fri) Accepts the usual wide range of cards.

Central North Coast

This is the most popular part of Savai'i and a great place to become laid-back, preferably all the way to horizontal. Once you pass the lava flows at Sale'aula, the white-sand beaches start again. Fagamalo has a nice lagoon with good snorkelling and swimming at high tide. There's a bottleneck of accommodation at lovely Manase, where numerous budget *fale* providers compete for the

beachfront business. The high chief here had the foresight to ban dogs, making this one of the most unstressful villages to explore outside of Manono. The bus from Salelologa to Manase costs about ST6.

Sights

Lava Field   SCENIC AREA
(Map p276) The Mt Matavanu eruptions between 1905 and 1911 created a moonscape in Savai'i's northeastern corner as a flow of lava 10m to 150m thick rolled through plantations and villages. The Main North Coast Rd crosses this dark, fractured lava field and provides access to several interesting sites.

The modern, iron-roofed *fale* of the village of **Mauga** encircle a shallow, almost perfectly circular crater populated by banana palms. The access road is guarded by an enormous Catholic church. Approach a villager if you'd like to be shown around.

In Sale'aula, 5km north of Mauga, are several **lava-ruined churches** (tour adult/child ST5/3). On the western side of the 'information *fale*' is a trail leading to the **LMS Church**, where 2m of lava flowed through the front door and was eerily imprinted by corrugated iron when the roof collapsed. Behind it a short trail leads over an expanse of twisted black rock stretching to the sea. North of the church is the **Virgin's Grave**, which purportedly marks the burial place of a girl so pure that the lava flowed around her grave, leaving it untouched.

Mt Matavanu Crater   HIKING
(Map p276) A visit to the volcano responsible for the devastation visited upon northeastern Savai'i a century ago is worth the price of admission, if only to meet 'Da World Famous Craterman', the larger-than-life Seu Api Utumapu, who maintains the **crater track** (✆724 5146; admission ST20; ⊘9am-4pm Mon-Sat) and collects the fee on behalf of his village.

From Safotu take the turn-off to Paia village and from there the signposted track up the mountain; you can walk the 8km route from Paia, or drive up in a high-clearance 2WD (though a 4WD is recommended). After a lengthy stint of bouncing over the old lava flow, you'll reach the *fale* that serves as Da Craterman's headquarters. If he's not around, just keep heading up and you'll doubtless find him. From here there's an even bumpier 2km to the car park, where a 10-minute trail leads to the crater's edge. Keep the kids tight at hand as there's a vertiginous drop into the lush greenness below. The whole route

North Savai'i

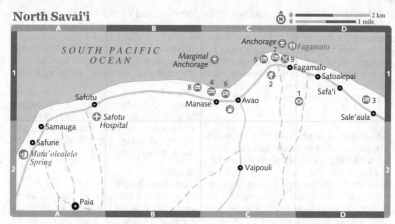

is lined with cheesy signs in Da Craterman's peculiar style of Pidgin English, representing the visitors from 110-and-counting countries who have made the trek.

Satoalepai Turtle Sanctuary
WILDLIFE SANCTUARY

(Map p279; off Main North Coast Rd; admission ST5; ⏰8am-5pm Mon-Sat) For those not fortunate enough to spot turtles in the wild, a turtle enclosure near Satoalepai has a dozen or so captive turtles on display and offers the chance to swim with them for ST5. This is not a conservation effort and neither is it a zoo. There's no expert on hand to ensure the creatures are fed a healthy diet, looked after when sick, or to carry out an effective breeding program. The shallow ponds and papaya diet are a far cry from the saltwater depths and jellyfish feasts that these creatures are used to. You'll either love it or find it extremely depressing.

Pe'ape'a Cave
CAVE

(Map p279; Main North Coast Rd; adult/child ST5/2; ⏰8am-5pm) This cave sits beside the coast road just south of Letui. A round-trip guided exploration of this small lava tube takes only 10 minutes, but you'll see white-rumped Polynesian swiftlets and their nests up close. Bring your own torch.

🏃 Activities

Dive Savai'i
DIVING

(Map p279; ☑54172; www.divesavaii.com; Main North Coast Rd, Fagamalo) This place had just changed hands when we passed and will now be run by a lovely German couple. Besides close-by diving to some very interesting

North Savai'i

⊙ **Sights**
1 Satoalepai Turtle Sanctuary D1

🚴 **Activities, Courses & Tours**
2 Dive Savai'i C1

🛏 **Sleeping**
3 Bayview Resort D1
4 Jane's Beach Fales C1
5 Le Lagoto Beach Resort C1
6 Regina's Beach Fales C1
7 Savai'i Lagoon Resort C1
8 Tanu's Beach Fales B1

⊗ **Eating**
9 Seki-a Pizza C1

sites including a Missionary-era shipwreck (two-tank dives ST260), the family-friendly outfit also runs half-day snorkelling tours (adult/child under 12 years ST60/30, snorkelling gear ST20) stopping at three different sites. They also hire snorkelling equipment on a casual basis (full set per 24 hours ST30).

🛏 Sleeping & Eating

All of the following options are on the Main North Coast Rd and they all include breakfast in the rates. Those in Manase throw in lunch and dinner as well.

SALE'AULA

Bayview Resort
RESORT $$

(Map p279; ☑54170; www.bayviewresort.ws; fale with fan/air-con ST200/250; ❄🖸) If you're a lava lover, this resort is perched on the solid river of rock and overlooks a stunning turquoise bay.

The best cottages have a big enclosed room area with bathroom plus a massive open *fale* extension for tons of shady lounging space. Escape from the heat of the black rocks on the small white-sand beach on the lagoon or borrow a kayak to explore this uniquely beautiful area. There's also a decent restaurant here that occasionally serves Samoan feasts.

FAGAMALO

TOP CHOICE **Savai'i Lagoon Resort** RESORT $$$
(Map p279; ☑54168; www.savaiilagoon.co.nz; d/tr/q ST320/410/500) Taking the plum spot on one of Savai'i's best and most protected beaches, these large, self-contained, modern units are comfortable and clean, but overpriced for the simplicity of the furnishings and lack of air-conditioning. That said, they are inviting enough that few people complain. Use of volleyball and *pétanque* courts, kayaks and dinghies are free, along with UV-filtered drinking water, which the resort provides free of charge to the local village. It's a friendly and supremely pleasant place to stay.

Le Lagoto Beach Resort RESORT $$$
(Map p279; ☑58189; www.lelagoto.ws; d US$200-250, tr US$230-280; ✳✳) Next door to Savai'i Lagoon Resort on the second-best part of the beach, the wooden bungalows at this boutique resort are the plushest you'll find on

WORTH A TRIP

DWARF'S CAVE

From Paia, you can visit this **cave** (Map p276; guide per group ST20; ⊙9am-5pm Mon-Sat), an intriguing subterranean lava tube that leads downwards as if to the centre of the earth. It's said that no one has reached the end of it (although we met a tourist who claimed he had after a few hours) and your guides (the village *matai* or local boys) will keep leading you through its prodigious depths, crossed by subterranean rivers, until you tell them to turn around. It's signposted off the Main North Coast Rd, just west of the Mt Matavanu turn-off. In Paia, look for the faded signpost on the right and wait outside the blue *fale* at this intersection; someone should appear to guide you to the cave. Bring your own torch and reliable footwear, and be prepared to swim and get seriously muddy.

the island and are wonderfully atmospheric with intricate Samoan roofs (although the outsides are shingled) and views of blue sea. The restaurant (mains ST20 to ST75) doesn't always get it right, but it's the best option on the north coast and open daily for nonguests.

Seki-a Pizza PIZZERIA $$
(Map p279; ☑54454; pizzas ST23-33; ⊙10am-8pm Mon-Sat, 11am-8pm Sun) Get good thin-crust pizzas a few steps east from Savai'i Lagoon Resort, including the 'diablo' made with home-grown chillies.

MANASE

Jane's Beach Fales FALE $
(Map p279; ☑54066; www.janesbeach.ws; fale per person incl breakfast & dinner ST70; @) Pretty bubblegum-pink-and-yellow Jane's is big enough to be social but small enough to take care of each of its guests. The beachfront *fale* are lockable, lined with Samoan print vinyl wallpaper and have double beds and small decks. This place has a small shop, bar, internet cafe, car rental, canoe hire and a good strip of sand and sea in front.

Regina's Beach Fales FALE $
(Map p279; ☑54054; fale per person incl breakfast & dinner ST55) It's nice to know that there are still small, welcoming, family-run operations like Regina's that don't charge the earth. The *fale* are of the traditional variety with woven blinds and mattresses on the floor, but they do have electric lights. Meals are more like low-key social events, with the substantial local dishes such as roast breadfruit and taro served up at a communal dining table.

Tanu's Beach Fales FALE $
(Map p279; ☑54050; tanubeach@samoa-experience.com; fale per person incl breakfast & dinner ST65, s/d ST90/160) Long-standing Tanu's is almost overwhelmingly huge, which is only fitting as it's owned by the village's *ali'i* (high chief; the man to be thanked for the dog ban). There are dozens of simple traditional *fale* dotting the beach. If you'd prefer a proper bed and solid walls, the accommodation block across the road offers simple, clean rooms with shared bathrooms.

Northwestern Savai'i

Jutting out from the western end of Savai'i is the beautiful Falealupo Peninsula, rich with sites associated with significant Samoan legends. The peninsula's remoteness and

protected tracts of rainforest lend it an almost unnerving calm.

In past years, burglars have targeted tourists in this area, so lock your car and don't leave anything of value in it or in your *fale*. Even if you don't have anything stolen, you'll feel robbed after having been asked for so many exaggerated 'custom fees' if you tour the sites. It's definitely one of the more beautiful areas of the island, though, so weigh the pros and cons of feeling swindled.

◉ Sights

Fafa O Sauai'i
SACRED SITE

(Map p276; Falealupo Rd; ⊙8.30am-5pm Mon-Sat) At Cape Mulinu'u you'll find the beautiful outlook of Fafa O Sauai'i, which was considered one of Samoa's most sacred spots in pre-Christian times (see boxed text, p282). Don't pass up a swim in the large rock pool, where you don't even have to enter the water to watch fish dart around the colourful corals at the base of the rocks.

Across the road are a star mound, Vaatausili Cave (which was filled with water when we passed, so it looked more like a pool) and the Via Sua Toto (the 'Blood Well' – named after the warrior Tupa'ilevaililigi, who threw his enemies' severed heads in here).

An elderly man named Tanu is the guardian who invariably asks for a high and mighty ST20 admission fee, but for a short visit he seemed happy enough when we offered him ST10.

Falealupo Rainforest Preserve
FOREST

(Map p276) In 1989 the 1200-hectare area of lowland rainforest on the peninsula's northern side became the first customary-owned conservation area in Samoa. This was thanks to the assistance of Dr Paul Alan Cox, an American ethnobotanist who was working with indigenous healers in Falealupo when he discovered that the area's *matai* had reluctantly signed a contract with a Japanese logging firm in order to pay for the construction of a primary school. After watching the whole village weeping over the loss of their sacred rainforest, Dr Cox personally guaranteed the money for the school. Upon learning this, chief Fuiono Senio ran 9km through the forest to stop the bulldozers.

A sign marked **Canopy Walkway** (Falealupo Rd; admission ST20; ⊙7am-6pm) leads to a *fale* beside a school, which is where you pay admission that apparently also covers you for Moso's Footprint and the Rock House, although this was a bit unclear when

WI-FI ON SAVAI'I

If you're travelling with a laptop, you're in luck. Many places to stay in Savai'i (except for places along the west coast) use LavaSpot hotspots (see p291). Strangely, the connection on Savai'i is faster than anywhere in the country outside of Apia.

we passed and no ticket was given. The walkway is a 24m jerry-built bridge strung 9m above the rainforest floor between two large trees. After you cross the walkway to the second tree, climb via a sturdy wooden ladder to a platform up a magical, nearly 230-year-old banyan tree.

A'opo Conservation Area & Mt Silisili
HIKING

(Map p276) The two- to three-day return trip to the summit of Mt Silisili (1866m), the highest point in Samoa, traverses some wonderful rainforested sections of the A'opo Conservation Area and Savai'i's mountainous backbone. To organise a guide speak to the *pulenu'u* (a combination of mayor and police chief) of A'opo (ask in the town's small shop for directions). You'll pay in the vicinity of ST40 per person per day and will need to supply food and water and all the requisite camping and hiking equipment.

Falealupo Ruins
RUINS

(Map p276) Cyclones Ofa and Val struck the peninsula in 1990 and 1991, completely destroying the village of Falealupo. The decision was made to rebuild the village further inland and the ruined village was left in tatters – until recently, when some families began to move back. The ruins of the **Catholic church** (Falealupo Rd) are particularly enigmatic and eerily beautiful. A group of elderly ladies tried to get us to pay ST20 just to stop and take a picture of the church ruins but quickly went down to ST10 when we asked nicely. This is still ridiculous just to take a photo, but they also offered to take us on a tour at the newly opened, unextraordinary Catholic church across the street.

Rock House
LAVA TUBE

(Map p276; Falealupo Rd; admission incl in Canopy Walkway ticket; ⊙7am-6pm) About 300m southwest of the ruins is the partly collapsed lava tube known as the Rock House. Legend says that it's the result of a house-building

GATEWAY TO THE UNDERWORLD

The natural beauty of the Falealupo Peninsula befits its spiritual significance. In pre-Christian times it was believed to be the gateway for souls into the next world. According to tradition, there are two entrances to the underworld: one for chiefs and another for commoners. One entrance is through a cave near Cape Mulinu'u and the other is on the trail made by the setting sun over the sea.

competition between Falealupo's men and women, a contest the women won. During the cyclones, whole families sheltered here. Like Moso's Footprint, the story is more interesting than the actual cave, and it's quite an effort to find – you'll probably have to pay to get one of the local kids to lead you to it (ST5 is plenty).

Moso's Footprint   SACRED SITE
(Map p276; Falealupo Rd; admission incl in Canopy Walkway ticket; ⊘7am-6pm) The ancient 1m by 3m rock depression called Moso's Footprint is decidedly unremarkable apart from the legend that surrounds it. The story goes that the giant Moso made the footprint when he stepped from Fiji to Samoa. You'll find it well signposted in front of a tidy *fale*.

🛏 Sleeping & Eating

Va-i-Moana Seaside Lodge   RESORT $$
(Map p276; ☑58140; vaimoana@ipasifika.net; off Main North Coast Rd, Asau; open fale incl breakfast s/d ST76/136, closed fale incl breakfast & dinner from s/d ST96/160, r ST264; ❄@) This hodgepodge of lodging is set on the old expat headquarters of a now defunct wood mill that was built in 1969. The family has reclaimed the land and its small white-sand beach, and transformed one old building into air-con rooms – but the more interesting options are the rickety, enclosed *fale*, some of which are perched on stilts over the surf. There's a good restaurant here, lots of effort to please customers, free kayaks and fishing tours on offer (from ST150 for three to four hours).

Vaisala Beach Hotel   HOTEL $
(Map p276; ☑58016; www.vaisalabeachresort. ws; off Main North Coast Rd, Vaisala; s/d/tr/q/f ST100/120/140/160/180; ❄) The strange and barracks-like Vaisala faces its own beautiful, deep-enough-for-a-decent-swim beach. The rooms are dated but comfortable; if you're lucky, you might get a shifting-image holy picture on the wall. All rooms have terraces and an extra ST20 will nab you the much better ones down near the beach. The hotel's restaurant also has an outdoor deck and serves filling set-menu dinners (ST45).

Falealupo Beach Fales   FALE $
(Map p276; ☑774 7420; www.falealupobeachfales. ws; Falealupo Rd, Falealupo; fale per person incl breakfast & dinner ST60) The beach is gorgeous, the *fale* simple and the family absent. We found no one here when we passed, and travellers who stayed here reported hardly seeing the owners.

South Coast

With less reef to protect it, Savai'i's south coast witnesses some dramatic confrontations between land and sea, resulting in blustering blowholes and some great surfing spots. If you thought the rest of Savai'i was chilled out, wait until you hit this sparsely populated stretch.

◉ Sights

Pulemelei Mound   ARCHAEOLOGICAL SITE
(Map p276; off Main South Coast Rd) Polynesia's largest ancient structure is the intriguing, pyramidal Pulemelei Mound, marked on some maps as Tia Seu Ancient Mound. It measures 61m by 50m at its base and rises to a height of more than 12m. It's a stirring place, with views from its stony summit both to the ocean and into thick, primordial jungle. On sunny days, colourful butterflies swarm across it and birds swoop overhead. For more information as to its possible purpose, see boxed text, p300. The surrounding area is presumably covered in house sites and other important archaeological finds but, for now, everything is covered in jungle.

Unfortunately it's very difficult to visit Pulemelei Mound as it's located on disputed land. As such, there's no sign and no upkeep – the path to the site and the mound itself are becoming very overgrown. Guides don't like to take people here because they worry that someone who has an ambiguous claim to the land may hassle them into handing over an exorbitant fee, or worse, just kick them off.

You can still try and go (we made it). To get here, head down the road flanked by

iron poles that starts about 300m beyond the iron-girder bridge on the opposite side of the river from Afu-A-Au Falls (there's no signage). Before long you'll reach a rocky ford over a stream – not worth risking unless you've got a good 4WD. If you park here, there's a flat but slow 2km walk along this plantation road through high grass (wear good shoes or your feet will get destroyed by thorny undergrowth) to the mound; veer left if you're ever in doubt. Shortly after crossing a culvert you'll see the old parking area marked with a broken sign on a tree and another rough sign on your left marking the start of the track. From here it's a 150m trek along a fern-filled path and up the mound. It's a little hard to see you're on the mound till you've actually reached the top to a virtual processional way of bright pink and blue flowers.

As both parking areas are secluded, don't leave any valuables in your car.

Afu-A-Au Falls
WATERFALL

(Map p276; off Main South Coast Rd; adult/child ST5/2; ⊘8am-5pm Mon-Sat, 11am-5pm Sun) Gorgeous Afu-A-Au Falls, also known as Olemoe Falls, offer visitors dreamy tropical seclusion and a refreshing swim in a 3m-deep waterhole. The waters are spring-fed so remain cool, green and deep even during the dry season. The falls weren't signposted from the main road when we passed but the turnoff is just east of an iron-girder bridge – ask anyone around Vailoa village and they may even hop in the car and show you there themselves. Pay admission at the *fale* near the entrance.

Tafua Peninsula Rainforest Preserve
NATURE PRESERVE

(Map p276; admission ST5) This preserve contains superb stands of rainforest and rugged stretches of lava coast studded with cliffs and sea arches. A highlight is the **Tafua Savai'i crater**: its sheer, deep walls are choked with vegetation, giving it a lost-world feel. You may catch glimpses of flying foxes napping in the trees far below.

To get here, take the side road signposted to Tafua opposite the now-defunct Ma'ota Airport and pay the 'custom fee' about 50m along. It's reasonably difficult to find the crater, so it's worth taking the services of a guide; however, be sure to agree on a price beforehand.

If you decide to go it alone, follow the road for 2.6km and park at the beginning of

the gated road on your left (if you reach the Tafua village sign, you've gone too far). After about 650m of flat road leading past taro and banana plantations, look for a small thatched *fale* on your right. The path to the crater is hard to discern in the long vegetation but it starts between this *fale* and a large dead tree, its white trunk blackened at the bottom. The rocky path becomes clearer as you head into the rainforest towards the crater's precipitous lip. Follow it around to the left for better views into the volcanic bowl and over the centre of the island.

Activities

At the western end of Fa'a'ala village, a track leads to lovely **Aganoa Beach** (Map p276; per person/surfer ST5/20). There are strong currents here, so swim with care. Pay the fee at Aganoa Beach Resort. This is the base for **Savai'i Surfaris** (Map p276; ☑50180; savaiisurfaris@samoa.ws; Aganoa Beach Resort, Fa'a'ala), which runs surf tours around the island; for details, see Aganoa Beach Resort.

Surfers will also find an excellent left-hand surf-break at **Satuiatua** (per person ST10); the fee is used to support the local school.

Sleeping & Eating

Satuiatua Beach Fales
FALE $

(Map p276; ☑56026, 846 4119; sbresort@lipacifika. net; Main South Coast Rd; fale per person incl breakfast & dinner ST75) Run by a family of women, this place is loaded with simple touches that make it stand out from other beach *fale* places. Open *fale* have drapy curtains, proper beds and well-maintained thatched louvres. The entire place is spotless and there are plans to build a beachfront treehouse. Self-sufficient surfers love this friendly place (there's a break out the front) and there's top-notch snorkelling here too. The restaurant (lunch ST20) is set up on a spacious outdoor deck and serves good, hearty meals. It's a good stop for lunch if you find yourself in these parts when the tummy rumbles.

Aganoa Beach Resort
FALE $$

(Map p276; ☑50180; www.aganoaretreat-samoa. com; Fa'a'ala; d fale without/with bathroom ST150/180, all incl breakfast & dinner; @⚑) This resort exploits the beauty of an exquisite little beach and four excellent associated surf-breaks (all within a paddleable distance) on the western edge of Tafua Peninsula. Nonsurfers can snuggle down in the bed-equipped *fale* after a long day of inactivity.

LOCAL KNOWLEDGE

ALOFAAGA BLOWHOLES

Blasting seawater tens of metres into the air, the biggest **blowhole** (Map p276; Taga; admission ST5; ⊙7am-6pm) here is truly spectacular if you catch it during a decent swell at high tide. There are several other less-impressive blowholes along this coast, as well as the 'washing machine' about 50m south of the main blowhole, that fills and empties like a giant flushing toilet with each wave (cooler than it sounds). Pay admission at the first *fale* and park your car at the second *fale*, near the main blowhole; if you drive into the accommodation compound, you'll be charged ST5 to park there and one of the attendants will perform the nifty trick of throwing coconuts into the blowhole at just the right time to have them shoot up with the water – this is well worth the price. Don't get too close to the blowholes as freak waves occasionally break over the rocks.

From here you can follow a track around the coast to the now-deserted village of Fagaloa (three to four hours return).

Meals are served at the resort's Kahuna Bar & Grill (mains ST20 to ST30), from which you can watch your friends surf. Surfers' packages start at ST250 per day, including transfers to surf spots around the island. The far left-hand break in front can even be good for beginners.

UNDERSTAND SAMOA

Samoa Today

In 2012 Samoa celebrated 50 years of independence with huge pomp and partying. But despite that Samoa is very much its own country it still relies heavily on foreign aid particularly from Australia and New Zealand with whom ties are very close. At the end of 2011 Samoa moved even closer to New Zealand by hopping over to the western side of the International Date Line.

History

Prehistory

The oldest evidence of human occupation in Samoa is Lapita village, partially submerged in the lagoon at Mulifanua on the island of 'Upolu. Carbon tests date the site to 1000 BC. For more on Lapita, see boxed text, p539.

Archaeologists have discovered more than a hundred star-shaped stone platforms across the islands. It's believed that these platforms, dubbed 'star mounds' (see boxed text, p300), were used to snare wild pigeons, which was once a favoured pastime of *matai* (chiefs). Savai'i's Pulemelei Mound is the largest ancient structure in the Pacific.

Around AD 950, warriors from Tonga established their rule on Savai'i, and then moved on to 'Upolu. They were eventually repelled by Malietoa Savea, a Samoan chief whose title, Malie toa (Brave warrior), was derived from the shouted tributes of the retreating Tongans. There was also contact with Fiji, from where legends say two girls brought the art of tattooing. The Samoans never really trusted their neighbours – *togafiti* (tonga fiji) means 'a trick'.

European Contact

Whalers, pirates and escaped convicts apparently introduced themselves to Samoa well before the first officially recorded European arrival in the region. This was the Dutchman Jacob Roggeveen, who approached the Manu'a Islands in American Samoa in 1722. Other visitors followed in his wake and over the next 100 years numerous Europeans settled in. The settlers established a society in Apia and a minimal code of law in order to govern their affairs, all with the consent of 'Upolu chiefs, who maintained sovereignty in their own villages. Along with technological expertise, the *palagi* (Europeans) also brought with them diseases to which the islanders had no immunity.

Missionaries

In August 1830 missionaries John Williams and Charles Barff of the London Missionary Society (LMS) arrived at Sapapali'i on Savai'i's eastern coast. They were followed by Methodist and Catholic missionaries, and in 1888 Mormons added to the competition for souls. Samoans were quite willing to accept Christianity due to the similarity of Christian creation beliefs to Samoan legend,

and because of a prophecy by war goddess Nafanua that a new religion would take root in the islands. Although interdistrict warfare was not abolished until the start of the 20th century, schools and education were eagerly adopted.

Squabbling Powers

There were (and still are) four paramount titles relating to four 'aiga (extended families), equivalent to royal dynasties, in what is now Samoa: Malietoa, Tupua Tamasese, Mata'afa and Tu'imaleali'ifano. During the 1870s a civil dispute broke out between two of these families, dividing Samoa. Much land was sold to Europeans by Samoans seeking to acquire armaments to settle the matter.

The British, Americans and Germans then set about squabbling over Samoan territory, and by the late 1880s Apia Harbour was crowded with naval hardware from all three countries. Most of it subsequently sunk – not because of enemy firepower, but because of a cyclone that struck the harbour in March 1889. After several attempted compromises, the Tripartite Treaty was signed in 1899, giving control of Western Samoa to the Germans and eastern Samoa to the Americans.

Foreign Administration

In February 1900 Dr Wilhelm Solf was appointed governor, and the German trading company DHPG began to import thousands of Melanesians and Chinese to work on its huge plantations. But although the Germans had agreed to rule 'according to Samoan custom', they didn't keep their word. In 1908, three years after the eruption of Savai'i's Mt Matavanu, there was an eruption of human discontent with the organisation of the Mau a Pule (Mau Movement) by Namulau'ulu Lauaki Mamoe. In January 1909 Namulau'ulu and his chief supporters were sent into exile.

In 1914, at the outbreak of WWI, Britain persuaded NZ to seize German Samoa. Preoccupation with affairs on the home front prevented Germany from resisting. Under the NZ administration, Samoa suffered a devastating (and preventable) outbreak of influenza in 1919; more than 7000 people (one-fifth of the population) died, further fuelling anger with the foreign rulers. Increasing calls for independence by the Mau Movement culminated in the authorities opening fire on a demonstration at the courthouse in Apia in 1929.

Following a change of government (and policy) in NZ, Western Samoa's independence was acknowledged as inevitable and even desirable, and in 1959 Prime Minister Fiame Mata'afa was appointed. The following year a formal constitution was adopted and, on 1 January 1962, independence was finally achieved.

Since Independence

The Human Rights Protection Party (HRPP) has been in power for most of the period since independence. Economic development has been excruciatingly slow or nonexistent, far below population growth, but at least the country has been politically stable.

'Upolu and Savai'i have been battered by several huge tropical storms over the past two decades, beginning with Cyclone Ofa in February 1990 and Cyclone Val in December 1991.

In 2009 the government switched driving from the right-hand side of the road to the left. The rationale was to allow access to cheap secondhand vehicle imports from NZ.

The Culture

Many visitors correctly sense that below the surface of the outwardly friendly and casual Samoan people lies a complex code of traditional etiquette. Beneath the lightheartedness, the strict and demanding fa'a Samoa (Samoan way) is rigorously upheld.

The National Psyche

'Aiga, or extended family groupings, are at the heart of the fa'a Samoa. The larger an 'aiga, the more powerful it is, and to be part of a powerful 'aiga is the goal of all tradition-minded Samoans. Each 'aiga is headed by a matai, who represents the family on the fono (village council). Matai are elected by all adult members of the 'aiga and can be male or female, but over 90% of current matai are male.

The fono consists of the matai of all of the 'aiga associated with the village. The ali'i (high chief of the village) sits at the head of the fono. In addition, each village has one pulenu'u (a combination of mayor and police chief) and one or more tulafale (orators or talking chiefs). The pulenu'u acts as an intermediary between the village and the national government, while the tulafale liaises between the ali'i and outside entities, carries out ceremonial duties and engages in ritual debates.

EARTHQUAKE & TSUNAMI DISASTER IN THE SAMOAS

On 29 September 2009, 'Upolu's southern and eastern coasts and the south coast of Tutuila in American Samoa were struck by a tsunami that killed approximately 190 people and left thousands homeless. It began with an 8.1 magnitude earthquake with its epicentre 190km south of Apia, which struck at 6.48am local time. Eight minutes later, a 10m-high wave demolished 'Upolu's south coast where people had little to no warning. On Tutuila, four tsunami waves between 4m and 6m were reported; these waves surged up to 1.6km inland, destroying homes and wiping out the electricity infrastructure.

By 2012 many of Samoa's damaged resorts had reopened, although the local residents of the village of Saleapaga had mostly moved to a location further inland out of fear. In American Samoa the damage was less cleaned-up, with abandoned houses rotting on the seafront, and in Leone there were still a few residents living in tents. Many people with new homes built from the US disaster funds were still without basic interior amenities such as kitchens and showers.

'Ava (kava) is a drink derived from the ground root of the pepper plant. The 'ava ceremony is a ritual in Samoa, and every government and matai meeting is preceded by one.

Beneath the matai, members of a village are divided into four categories. The society of untitled men, the aumaga, is responsible for growing food. The aualuma, the society of unmarried, widowed or separated women, provides hospitality and produces various goods such as siapo (decorated bark cloth) and the ie toga (fine mats) that are an important part of fa'alavelave (lavish gift-exchange ceremonies). Married women are called faletua ma tausi. Their role revolves around serving their husband and his family. The final group is the tamaiti (children). Close social interaction is generally restricted to members of one's own group.

Individuals are subordinate to the extended family. There is no 'I', only 'we'. The incapable are looked after by their family rather than by taxpayers, and with such onerous family (plus village and church) obligations, it's a struggle for any individual to become wealthy. Life is not about individual advancement or achievement, but about serving and improving the status of your 'aiga. The communal ownership of land and lack of reward for individual effort tend to stymie Western-style economic development, but have kept control of most of Samoa's resources in Samoan hands.

Lifestyle

Parents and other relatives treat babies with great affection, but at the age of three the children are made the responsibility of an older sibling or cousin. Fa'aaloalo is respect for elders, the most crucial aspect of the fa'a Samoa, and children are expected to obey not just their immediate relatives, but all the matai and adults in the village as well as older siblings. Parents rarely hug or praise their children, so the youth often suffer from low self-esteem and lack confidence and ambition. Fun family activities are few and far between; a rare exception is White Sunday in October, when children eat first, star in church services, and are bought new clothes and toys. Some teenagers resort to musu (refusing to speak to anybody) as a form of protest.

Overriding all else in Samoa is Christianity. Every village has at least one large church, ideally a larger one than in neighbouring villages. These operate as the village social centre, the place where almost everyone makes an appearance on Sunday, dressed up in their formal best. Sunday-morning church services are inevitably followed by to'ona'i (Sunday lunch), when families put on banquets fit for royalty.

Sa, which means 'sacred', is the nightly vespers, though it's not applied strictly throughout all villages. Sometime between 6pm and 7pm a gong sounds, signifying that the village should prepare for sa. When the second gong is sounded, sa has begun. All activity should come to a halt. If you're caught in a village during sa, stop what you're doing, sit down and quietly wait for the third gong, about 10 or 15 minutes later, when it's over.

A rigid approach to Christianity has led to conservative attitudes on many social issues, including homosexuality, but this is tempered by a generally tolerant attitude to fa'afafine – men who dress and behave like

women. The name *fa'afafine* means 'like a woman' and has no obvious parallel in Western society. *Fa'afafine* fulfil an important role in the social fabric, often helping out with the children and looking after their parents in old age. A *fa'afafine* may have a relationship with a man, but this isn't seen as homosexual. Neither are they seen as women, per se.

Population

Three-quarters of Samoans live on the island of 'Upolu. The urban area of Apia houses around 21% of the nation's population, with the rest sprinkled around the small villages that mainly cling to the coastline. Minorities include both expat and Samoan-born Europeans (called *palagi* in Samoan) and a small number of Chinese; both minorities are centred on Apia.

Language

See the Language chapter on p591 for Samoan basics.

Sport

Sport in Samoa is a community event, which might explain why this tiny nation turns out a disproportionate number of great sportspeople. Drive through any village in the late afternoon and you'll see people of all ages gathering on the *malae* (village green) to play rugby, volleyball and *kirikiti* (see boxed text, p273). *Fautasi* (45-person canoe) races are held on special occasions. Samoa's main obsession is rugby union and the members of the national team, Manu Samoa, are local heroes – as are the many Samoan players who fill the ranks of rugby union, rugby league and netball teams in NZ, Australia, the UK and France.

Arts

Architecture

Traditional (not to mention highly practical) Samoan architecture is exemplified by the *fale*, an oval structure with wooden posts but no walls, thus allowing natural airflow. It's traditionally built on a stone or coral foundation and thatched with woven palm or sago leaves. Woven coconut-leaf blinds can be pulled down to protect against rain or prying eyes, but in truth, privacy in such a building is practically impossible.

Palagi-style square homes with walls, louvre windows and doors, though uncomfortably hot and requiring fans, have more status than traditional *fale* and are becoming more common in Samoa.

Fiafia

Originally, the *fiafia* was a village play or musical presentation in which participants would dress in costume and accept money or other donations. These days the term *'fiafia* night'* usually refers to a lavish presentation of Samoan fire- and slap-dancing and singing, accompanied by a buffet dinner. But traditional *fiafia* are still performed during weddings, birthdays, title-conferring ceremonies and at the opening of churches and schools.

Drummers keep the beat while dancers sing traditional songs illustrated by coordinated hand gestures. A *fiafia* traditionally ends with the *siva,* a slow and fluid dance performed by the village *taupou* (usually the daughter of a high chief), dressed in *siapo* with her body oiled.

Literature

Towering over Samoan literature is Albert Wendt, a novelist, poet, academic and latterly visual artist, now resident in NZ. Many of his novels deal with the *fa'a* Samoa bumping against *palagi* ideas and attitudes, and the loss of Samoa's pre-Christian spirituality; try *Leaves of the Banyan Tree* (1979), *Ola* (1995) or *The Mango's Kiss* (2003). Perhaps some of the prose is too risqué for the Methodists who run most of Samoa's bookshops, as copies are hard to track down in Samoa – you'll have better luck overseas or online.

The Beach at Falesa by Robert Louis Stevenson is a brilliant short story set in Samoa by a master stylist with inside knowledge of the South Pacific. Stevenson spent the last four years of his life in Samoa; for details, see p268.

Music

Music is a big part of everyday life in Samoa, whether it be the exuberant drumming that accompanies *fiafia* nights, the soaring harmonies of church choirs or the tinny local pop blaring out of taxis.

Traditionally, action songs and chants were accompanied by drums and body slaps, but guitars, ukuleles and Western-style melodies are now a firm part of the *fiafia* repertoire. Songs were once written to

tell stories or commemorate events and this practice continues today. Love songs are the most popular, followed by patriotic songs extolling local virtues. *We are Samoa* by Jerome Grey is Samoa's unofficial national anthem.

Contemporary artists include the reggae-influenced Ben Vai and hip-hopper Mr Tee, both of whom write in Samoan and perform regularly around Apia. However, it's offshore that Samoan artists are hitting the big time, especially the new breed of NZ-based rappers such as King Kapisi, Scribe and Savage.

Siapo & Ie Toga

The bark cloth known as *siapo* is made from the inner bark of the *u'a* (paper mulberry tree) and provides a medium for some of the loveliest artwork in Samoa.

The fine mat called *ie toga* is woven from pandanus fibres split into widths of just a couple of millimetres and can involve years of painstaking work. *Ie toga,* along with *siapo,* make up 'the gifts of the women' that must be exchanged at formal ceremonies. Agricultural products comprise 'the gifts of the men'.

Tattooing

Samoa is the last of the Polynesian nations where traditional tattooing is still widely practised (albeit against the wishes of some religious leaders). The traditional *pe'a* (male tattoo) covers the man's body from the waist to the knees. Women can elect to receive a *malu* (female tattoo), but their designs cover only the thighs.

The skills and tools of the *tufuga pe'a* (tattoo artist) were traditionally passed down from father to son, and sharpened shark teeth or boar tusks were used to carve the intricate designs into the skin. It was believed that the man being tattooed must not be left alone in case the *aitu* (spirits) took him. In most cases the procedure takes at least a fortnight. Noncompletion would cause shame to the subject and his *'aiga.*

Environment

Geography

Samoa lies in the heart of the vast South Pacific, 3700km southwest of Hawai'i. Tonga lies to the south, Fiji to the southwest, Tuvalu to the northwest and Tokelau to the north, while to the southeast is the Cook Islands.

The country has a total land area of 2934 sq km and is composed primarily of high, eroded volcanic islands with narrow coastal plains. It has two large islands: Savai'i (1700 sq km) and 'Upolu (1115 sq km). The nation's highest peak, Mt Silisili on Savai'i, rises to 1866m. The small islands of Manono and Apolima lie in the 22km-wide Apolima Strait that separates 'Upolu and Savai'i. A few other tiny, uninhabited rocky islets and outcrops lie southeast of 'Upolu.

Ecology

On the heights of Savai'i and 'Upolu is temperate forest vegetation: tree ferns, grasses, wild coleus and epiphytic plants. The magnificent *aoa* (banyan tree) dominates the higher landscapes, while other areas are characterised by scrublands, marshes, pandanus forests and mangrove swamps. The rainforests of Samoa are a natural apothecary, home to some 75 known medicinal plant species.

Because Samoa is relatively remote, few animal species have managed to colonise it. The Lapita brought with them domestic pigs, dogs and chickens, as well as the ubiquitous Polynesian rat. But apart from two species of fruit bat (protected throughout the islands after being hunted close to extinction) and the small, sheath-tailed bat, mammals not introduced by humans are limited to the marine varieties. Whales, dolphins and porpoises migrate north and south through the islands, depending on the season.

Pili (skinks) and *mo'o* (geckos) can be seen everywhere, and various types of turtles visit the islands. The only land creature to beware of (besides the unloved and unlovely dogs) is the giant centipede, which packs a surprisingly nasty bite.

SURVIVAL GUIDE

Directory A–Z

Accommodation

It's fair to say that accommodation options in Samoa are limited. There's little budget accommodation outside the ubiquitous *fale;* and at the other end of the scale, only a handful of resorts qualify as truly luxurious. At both ends of the scale, many properties are overpriced given the quality offered.

SAMOA ENVIRONMENT

That said, much of the country's accommodation occupies idyllic settings on the beautiful sands that fringe the islands – this meets the minimum requirements for most visitors.

The accommodation in this chapter is listed according to author preference and any taxes are included in the price. The following price ranges refer to a double room, or *fale* where stated:

$ less than ST150

$$ ST150–300

$$$ more than ST300

An excellent source of accommodation information is the **Samoa Hotels Association** (Map p258; ☎30160; www.samoa-hotels.ws; Samoa Tourism Authority, Beach Rd, Apia). It also acts as a booking agent, taking its fee from the provider, not the guest.

Beach *fale* are the most interesting budget option (see boxed text). Hotel, motel and resort accommodation ranges from rooms in slightly dilapidated buildings with cold-water showers to well-maintained rooms with all the mod cons. There's sometimes access to a shared kitchen. Resorts tend to offer bungalow-style accommodation (sometimes called *fale* to sound exotic), with the bigger ones having swim-up cocktail bars and multiple restaurants.

Stays with families in local villages can be organised through **Safua Tours** (Map p276; ☎51271; Safua Hotel, Lalomalava, Savai'i).

Activities

Visiting Samoa is less about seeing sights as doing stuff – particularly things that involve tropical beaches. See the destination sections for further information on place-specific pursuits, as well as where to indulge in that other popular activity – ordering cocktails from the bar.

DIVING
While Samoa's reefs are far less developed than those of some of its neighbours, there are still some fantastic dive sites to explore, providing access to a multitude of tropical fish and larger marine creatures, such as turtles and dolphins. See p33 for information on the main dive sites, and p257 and p279 for regional details of the dive centre on each island. Two-tank dives start from ST260 and PADI Open Water Courses are ST1200. Prices are more expensive on 'Upolu because of the longer distances to get to dive sites.

FISHING
Samoan reefs and their fishing rights are owned by villagers, so you can't just drop a line anywhere; seek permission first. If you'd like to go fishing with locals, inquire at your hotel or beach *fale*, or speak to the *pulenu'u* of the village concerned.

Game fishing is becoming increasingly popular in the islands – in fact, Samoa has been rated one of the top 10 game-fishing destinations in the world. The **Samoa International Game Fishing Tournament** (www.fishing.ws) heads out from Apia Harbour in early May.

See p257 for details on fishing tours.

HIKING
Samoa's rugged coastal areas, sandy beaches, lush rainforests and volcanoes all invite exploration on foot. However, trails

SAMOA DIRECTORY A–Z

THE BEACH FALE: SAMOA'S SIGNATURE ACCOMMODATION

The simple structures called *fale* come in a variety of styles. At their most simple and traditional, they're just a wooden platform with poles supporting a thatched roof, surrounded by woven blinds that can be pulled down for privacy. Woven sleeping mats are laid on the floor, topped by a mattress with sheets and a mosquito net. From this basic model, various degrees of luxury can be added: electric lights, ceiling fans, proper beds, wooden walls (often with some trellis work to let a breeze flow through), lockable doors and decks. Avoid those with plastic-sheeting walls as these tend to flap around in the wind without letting much air through. Bathroom facilities are usually a communal block, with cold water being the norm. The price usually includes breakfast and often a set lunch and dinner as well.

Fale are usually priced per person, ranging from a reasonable ST50 (including meals) to well over ST100. As a result, couples or larger groups may find themselves paying much more than they would for a midrange hotel, for what is basically one step up from camping on the beach.

can quickly become obscured because of the lush tropical environment and half-hearted track maintenance. Combine this with the effects of heavy rain and there's often a good chance of getting lost (or at the very least covering yourself in mud). For more remote treks, it pays to take a guide with you.

Guiding costs vary enormously. Sometimes villagers will be happy to accompany you for nothing; at other times, they'll be seeking goods as a reward (like cigarettes), but mostly they'll be interested in cash.

See p257 for more details.

KAYAKING

Kayaks are perfect for pottering around the lagoons and several accommodation providers have them available to be borrowed and hired. See p257 for more details.

SNORKELLING & SWIMMING

The novice snorkeller will find Samoa's waters fascinating and filled with life. In places the reef has been damaged by cyclones, the tsunami and human contact, but will still reveal live corals and an abundance of colourful fish, often in a short walk straight out from the beach. Some particularly good and accessible spots are Lalomanu (p267), Namu'a (p268) and Palolo Deep Marine Reserve (p255). More and more places are hiring out snorkelling gear, but it's still well worth bringing your own mask and snorkel with you.

The majority of Samoan beaches are great for splashing about in, but too shallow for satisfying swimming. Always ask permission from local villagers before using their beach.

SURFING

Powerful conditions, sharp reefs and offshore breaks that are difficult to access mean that surfing in Samoa is challenging, to say the very least, and probably one of the worst places in the world to learn the sport! While the surf can be unbelievable at times, offering waves of a lifetime in glorious surroundings, conditions are generally difficult to assess, with some very dangerous situations awaiting the inexperienced or reckless. Despite all this, the islands have become an increasingly popular destination for experienced surfers. The wet season (November to April) brings swells from the north; the dry season (May to October) brings big swells from the south.

It's best to hook up with a surfing outfit. They know all the best spots and provide boat transport to them and, perhaps more importantly, they have established relationships with local villagers and understand the culture – they know where it is and isn't OK to surf. For details see p257.

Business Hours

On Sunday almost everything is closed, although ripples of activity appear in the evening. Markets normally get under way by about 6am; Maketi Fou in Apia is active more or less 24 hours a day.

We don't give opening hours for establishments mentioned in the text unless they differ greatly from the following standards:

Banks 9am to 3pm Monday to Friday, some open 8.30am to 12.30pm Saturday.

Bars noon to 10pm or midnight.

Government offices 8am to 4.30pm Monday to Friday.

Restaurants 8am to 4pm and 6pm to 9pm.

Shops 8am to 4.30pm Monday to Friday, 8am to noon Saturday (kiosks and convenience stores keep longer hours).

Children

The Samoan climate (except the long periods of heavy rain or the odd cyclone, of course), warm waters and dearth of poisonous creatures make the islands a paradise for children. You'll find that Samoans tend to lavish attention on very young children, which means that foreign toddlers will not be starved for attention or affection while visiting the islands.

Never leave your child unsupervised near beaches, reefs or on walking tracks, particularly those running along coastal cliffs (these are never fenced). Lonely Planet's *Travel with Children* has useful advice on family travel. Typically only the upmarket resorts provide cots, and bigger car-rental agencies have car seats, so it may pay to bring your own.

Embassies & Consulates

Following is a list of countries with diplomatic missions based in Apia:

Australia (Map p258; ☎23411; www.embassy.gov.au/ws.html; Beach Rd; ☒8.30am-4pm Mon-Fri) Canadian consular services are also provided here.

China (Map p266; ☎777 2479; The Cross Island Rd, Vailima; ☒8.30am-noon & 2-4.30pm Mon-Fri)

New Zealand (Map p258; ☎21711; Beach Rd; ⏱8am-4pm Mon-Fri)

USA (Map p258; ☎21631; 5th fl, ACC Bldg, Apia; ⏱9.30am-noon & 1-4pm Mon-Wed & Fri, 9.30am-noon Thu)

Festivals & Events

The main causes of celebration across Samoa include the country's **independence** festivities over the first three days of June; the **Teuila Festival** in Apia in September, when Samoa's capital reels in the tourists with canoe races, food and craft stalls, traditional dancing and a beauty pageant; and **White Sunday**, the day that Samoan children rule the roost, which is held on the second Sunday in October.

Another event to look out for is the **Palolo Rise** celebrations in October/November; see the boxed text, p271.

Food

The following price ranges refer to a meal. Unless otherwise stated tax is included in the price.

$ less than ST20

$$ ST20–35

$$$ more than ST30

Internet Access

Wi-fi in Samoa is offered almost exclusively through LavaSpot (www.samoa.ws) hotspots on a pay-by-the-minute basis. The cheapest option is to buy minutes directly online from the website. LavaSpot hotspots are found at restaurants and hotels all around Apia and at more-upmarket resorts around 'Upolu and Savai'i. The worst areas for finding any internet at all are the south coast of 'Upolu and west coast of Savai'i, but this may change in future.

Otherwise, your only option for accessing the web (assuming your accommodation provider doesn't have any terminals for guest use, which is rare) is an internet cafe. There are several internet cafes scattered around Apia but few elsewhere. Expect to pay anywhere between ST10 and ST30 for an hour's access.

Note that web connections can drop out with frustrating frequency on these remote islands.

Internet Resources

Lonely Planet (www.lonelyplanet.com/samoa) For planning advice, author recommendations, traveller reviews and insider tips.

Samoan Hotels Association (www.samoa hotels.ws) An extensive, regularly updated listing of Samoan places to stay, including photos of many of the properties.

Samoa Observer (www.samoaobserver.ws) The website of the country's main newspaper is a good resource for news and current affairs relating to Samoa, as well as the Pacific region as a whole.

Samoa Tourism Authority (www.visitsamoa. ws) A comprehensive website for independent Samoa, with an up-to-date events calendar and easy-to-browse information on activities, attractions and useful organisations.

Maps

The free Jasons *Samoa Visitor Map* is updated annually and is widely available. It's reasonably basic but should suit most visitors' needs. The more detailed 1:200,000 *Samoa* map published by Hema (ST17.50) can be purchased from various places in Apia, including Janet's (p265).

Money

The tala (dollar), divided into 100 sene (cents), is the unit of currency in use in Samoa. In this book, unless otherwise stated, all prices given are in tala (ST).

ATMs Several branches of the ANZ and Westpac banks are equipped with ATMs. Be aware that ATMs can be prone to running out of bills at the start of the weekend. Take plenty of cash with you (in small denominations) when you're heading outside the bigger settlements.

Tipping Not expected or encouraged in Samoa. It is, however, deemed acceptable for exceptional service at finer restaurants.

Public Holidays

For information about public holidays in the region, see p579.

Telephone

The country code for Samoa is ☎685. The nation does not use area codes.

State-owned SamoaTel is the main telecommunications provider. Collect (reverse-charge) and credit-card international calls can be made from public phones by dialling ☎956 from Apia, ☎957 from the rest of 'Upolu, ☎958 from Savaii and ☎959 from the airport.

SAMOA DIRECTORY A–Z

Mobile Phones Mobile-phone providers and outlets have mushroomed throughout Samoa. The big names are Digicel, SamoaTel and Bluesky. They'll test whether your phone is compatible before selling you a SIM card for around ST30 (usually including ST5 to ST10 worth of free minutes). Prepay top-ups can be purchased from dozens of shops around both islands. Reception is generally very good, especially on Digicel.

Time

At midnight on 29 December 2011, Samoa officially switched to the west side of the International Date Line. This means its dates are the same as those of NZ, Australia and Asia. Local time is Greenwich Mean Time/ Coordinated Universal Time (GMT/UTC) plus 13 hours. Therefore, when it's noon in Samoa, it's 11am the same day in Auckland.

Samoa also recently decided to adopt daylight saving time. In early October the clocks go forward (to GMT/UTC plus 14 hours), returning to normal in late March.

Visas

A free, 60-day visitor permit is granted to all visitors on arrival in Samoa – except for American Samoans, who must obtain a 30-day single-entry or multiple-entry permit – provided they have an onward ticket and a passport valid for at least another six months. You'll also be required to provide a contact address within the country, so have the name of a hotel ready upon arrival.

Samoan visitor permits may be extended by several weeks at a time by the country's **Immigration Office** (Map p258; ☑20291; www.samoaimmigration.gov.ws; Convent St, Apia; ☺8am-4pm Mon-Fri). Take along your passport, wallet and two passport-sized photos and don't make any other plans for the rest of the day. You may also need to have proof of hotel accommodation, onward transport and sufficient funds for your requested period of stay.

Getting There & Away

Air

Aside from a few flights from American Samoa, all flights to Samoa arrive at **Faleolo Airport** (airport code APW; Map p254; ☑21675; Main West Coast Rd, 'Upolu), 35km west of Apia. Many arrive and depart in the early hours of the morning, but airport transfer and accommodation providers are well used to this. **Fagali'i Airport** (Map p254), on Apia's eastern outskirts, is only used for American Samoan services on Inter Island Airways.

Direct flights head to Samoa from American Samoa, Fiji, Auckland, Brisbane and Sydney. If you're flying from the northern hemisphere, flights via Honolulu are likely to be the most straightforward. Samoa is often a stopover or cheap 'optional extra' on tickets between Europe/North America and NZ and on round-the-world fares.

Airlines that service Samoa include the following (all phone numbers mentioned here are for dialling from within Samoa, unless otherwise indicated):

Air New Zealand (airline code NZ; Map p258; ☑20825; www.airnz.com; cnr Convent & Vaea Sts, Apia; ☺8.30am-4.30pm Mon-Fri, 9am-noon Sat) Flights from Auckland.

Fiji Airways (airline code FJ; Map p258; ☑22172; www.airpacific.com; 5th fl, Central Bank Bldg, Beach Rd, Apia; ☺8.30am-5pm Mon-Fri, 8am-noon Sat) Flies from Nadi twice weekly with connections to Los Angeles, and once weekly direct to/from Honolulu.

Inter Island Airways (airline code IIA; ☑42580; www.interislandair.com; Faleolo Airport) Two to four daily flights to American Samoa.

Polynesian Airlines (airline code PH; Map p258; ☑21261; www.polynesianairlines.com; Beach Rd, Apia) The state carrier flies to American Samoa three to five times daily.

Virgin Samoa (airline code PLB; Map p258; www.virginsamoa.com; Beach Rd, Apia) Previously called Polynesian Blue. Samoa owns 49% of this airline in partnership with Virgin Australia. It flies from Auckland, Brisbane and Sydney.

Sea

SHIP

The **Samoa Shipping Corporation** (Map p258; ☑20935; www.samoashipping.com; Beach Rd, Apia) runs a car ferry/cargo ship called MV *Lady Naomi* between Apia and Pago Pago (American Samoa) once a week. It departs from Apia on Tuesday at 9am. The trip takes seven hours each way. Return deck fares are ST120/75 per adult/child; return cabin fares are ST190/120. Note that American passport holders can only buy one-way tickets from Apia. Book online.

Cargo ships sail between Apia and remote Tokelau about three times a month. Bookings for the 24- to 26-hour trip can be made in Apia at the **Tokelau Apia Liaison Office** (Map p258; ☎20822; Fugalei St, Apia; ⊗8am-5pm Mon-Fri). You must obtain a Tokelau visa before booking. Return deck fares are NZ$286/143 per adult/child; return cabin fares are NZ$528/266.

YACHT

Between May and October (outside the cyclone season), the harbours of the South Pacific swarm with yachts from around the world. Many follow the favourable winds west from the Americas, while others head north from NZ. Apia serves as the official entry point for private yacht owners visiting Samoa. In Savai'i, there are also anchorages at Fagamalo, Salelologa Wharf and Asau Harbour.

Visiting yachts must apply for clearance from the **Prime Minister's Department** (Map p258; ☎21339; 5th fl, Government Office Bldg, Beach Rd) in Apia; bear left as you exit the elevator and take the unmarked door straight through the archway. The captain will need to present crew passports and the boat's registration papers.

Getting Around

Air

There have been no scheduled domestic flights in Samoa since 2004. It's possible that Polynesian Airlines may recommence flights to Savai'i from 'Upolu at some point in the future.

Bicycle

Touring 'Upolu and Savai'i by bicycle is a scenic, reasonably relaxed option – we say 'reasonably' because aggressive dogs are a prevalent problem. The roads are generally in good condition and traffic is minimal. The major roads encircling the islands are sealed and relatively flat, but you'd need a sturdy mountain bike to tackle most of the trails to beaches and other coastal attractions. You can transport a bike between Samoa's two main islands on the ferry.

A big challenge for cyclists is the heat. Even during the coolest months of the year (July, August and September), afternoon temperatures will still be high. Plan to avoid cycling long stretches in the heat of the day. Also bear in mind that buses are unlikely to be able to accommodate bicycles should you run out of leg power.

Bikes are a common form of local transport in Samoa, so it shouldn't be hard to track down a bike repairer if you really need one. But it's obviously best to bring your own comprehensive bike repair kit, a decent lock and heavy-duty panniers. Some accommodation providers offer bike hire, but these are for day touring, not long-distance rides.

Boat

The ferry from Mulifanua Wharf is the only option for travel between 'Upolu and Savai'i (p274). Small boats leave from Cape Fatuosofia for Manono (p274). The Samoa Shipping Corporation operates scenic cruises out of Apia.

The **Apia Yacht Club** (Map p258; ☎21313; Mulinu'u Rd, Apia; ⊗5-11pm Tue-Sun) is a good place to share information on sailing around the islands over a cold beer (see p264).

Bus

Travelling by public bus in Samoa is an experience that shouldn't be missed. The buses are vibrantly painted (look out for the Bon Jovi–themed one), wooden-seated vehicles (prepare yourself for hard jolts) that blast Samoan pop music at deafening volumes (prepare yourself for endless reggaefied Christmas carols from October onwards). The drivers are often as unique as the vehicles and services operate completely at their whim. If a driver feels like knocking off at 1pm, he does, and passengers counting on the service are left stranded. Never rely on catching a bus after about 2pm. Buses are also scarce on Saturday afternoon and often only cater to church services on Sunday.

All buses prominently display the name of their destination in the front window. To stop a bus, wave your hand and arm, palm down, as the bus approaches. To signal that you'd like to get off the bus, either knock on the ceiling or clap loudly. Fares are paid to the driver – try to have as near to the exact change as possible.

Although most visitors don't notice it at first, there is a seating hierarchy on Samoan buses. Unmarried women normally sit together, while foreigners and older people must have a seat and sit near the front of the bus. Don't worry about arranging this yourself – the locals will see to it that everything is sorted out. The way in which Samoans stack themselves on top of each other on

crowded buses without losing any dignity is akin to a social miracle.

Details about specific routes and fares are provided at the start of the 'Upolu (p252) and Savai'i (p274) sections.

Car

Getting around by car in Samoa is quite straightforward. The coastal roads on both main islands are sealed and the general condition of most other main roads is also pretty good. A 4WD will make trips down rough, unsealed side roads much more comfortable, but nearly all of these side routes can be tackled in a high-clearance 2WD. After heavy rain, however, some roads will be inaccessible to 2WD vehicles.

DRIVING LICENCE

Visitors to Samoa need to obtain a temporary driving licence. Most car-hire companies can issue these, or you can call into the **Ministry of Works, Transport & Infrastructure** (Map p258; ☑21611; Beach Rd; licence per 1/2 months ST12/24; ☉9am-5pm Mon-Fri) in Apia. You'll need to present a valid overseas driving licence.

HIRE

There are literally dozens of car-hire agencies in Samoa and, on top of this, some of the larger accommodation providers also hire vehicles. Most of the agencies are in or around Apia and the airport, and the prices can be quite competitive. Note that you can usually take hire cars from 'Upolu over to Savai'i and back, but cars hired on Savai'i cannot be taken to 'Upolu. It's sometimes cheaper to hire in 'Upolu even given the ferry fee, especially if you obtain a discount for a longer booking.

When hiring a vehicle, check for any damage or scratches and note everything on the rental agreement, lest you be held liable for damage when the car is returned. Furthermore, fend off requests to leave your passport or a cash deposit against possible damages. Many places will require a credit card pre-authorisation by way of a deposit and it's usual to pay in advance.

Apia has numerous car-hire agencies. Prices start at around ST120 per day, with discounts offered for longer-term rentals. Hire cars are subject to a ST1000 to ST2000 insurance excess in the event of any accident.

INSURANCE

It's essential to have your hire car covered by insurance as repair costs are extremely high in Samoa. Insurance costs aren't always included in the price of a quote, so always double-check this. Hire cars are subject to a ST1000 to ST2000 insurance excess (non-reduceable).

ROAD RULES

In 2009 the Samoan government decided to change the law from driving on the right-hand side of the road to the left-hand side. Still, don't be surprised to see a mixture of left-hand-drive and right-hand-drive vehicles on the road, and you might even end up with an American hire car even though you'll have to drive on the left side of the road. The speed limit within central Apia and through adjacent villages is 40km/h; outside populated areas it's 55km/h.

Local Transport

On 'Upolu, taxis can be a useful transport option for day tripping (see p265); however, the same can't be said for taxis on Savai'i, which are only convenient for short trips. However, the impending move towards installing meters may even this out – but may also increase the rates. It always pays to have the correct change as drivers can be (perhaps too conveniently) relied upon not to have any.

If you find a driver you hit it off well with early on, it can be worth getting their telephone number and using their service during your stay. You may be able to negotiate a decent day rate that compares favourably with a hire car.

American Samoa

Best Places to Stay

» Moana O Sina (p304)

» Tee's Place (p305)

» Vaoto Lodge (p309)

» Tisa's Barefoot Bar (p305)

» Le Falepule (p303)

Best Beaches

» Ofu Beach (p308)

» Fagatele Bay National Marine Sanctuary (p302)

» Alega Beach (p302)

» Avaio Beach (p302)

Why Go?

Stick 'American' in front of a name and people think of McDonald's and shopping malls. While that hamburger chain does a brisk business in these islands, this is not what they're about. When you visit American Samoa, any preconceived notions are overridden by the country's exceptional beauty. Imagine steep, geometric peaks to rival French Polynesia, a natural harbour worthy of a New Age artist's daydream, and villages that some locals claim live more-traditional lifestyles than in independent Samoa next door. There may be fewer traditional *fale* here but this is because people have more money – can you blame them?

Pago Pago is a working fishing town but hike the lush trails of the National Park of American Samoa, visit the rest of spectacular Tutuila or get way off the beaten path to the dazzling Manu'a Islands and you'll find a Polynesia that's authentic, adventurous and virtually untouristed.

When to Go

Pago Pago

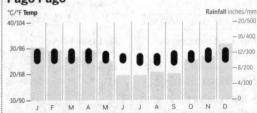

Dec–Jan Peak holiday period when Samoans living abroad visit home.	**May–Oct** Dry, cool season with minimal to no risk of cyclones.	**Oct** Festival month and whale season.

AT A GLANCE

Currency US$

Language Samoan, English

Mobile phones Prepaid SIM cards are US$20.

Money ATMs are found in commercial areas of Tutuila only. There's no ATM at the airport.

Visas Free entry to US citizens with a return ticket. Australian, New Zealand and UK citizens get 30-day visas on arrival; all other nationalities must apply for an entry pass.

Fast Facts

» **Area** 197 sq km

» **Capital** Pago Pago (on Tutuila)

» **Country code** ✆1-684

» **Emergency** ✆911

» **Population** 63,500

Exchange Rates

Australia	A$1	US$1.00
Canada	C$1	US$1.00
Europe	€1	US$1.25
Japan	¥100	US$1.25
New Zealand	NZ$1	US$0.80
UK	UK£1	US$1.55

For current exchange rates see www.xe.com.

Set Your Budget

» **Main course** from US$10

» **Night in a midrange hotel** US$135

» **Nine holes of golf** US$3

» **Ferry to Aunu'u** US$1

» **Car hire** from US$70 per day

Connections

American Samoa's only internal flight is between Pago Pago and Ta'u in the Manu'a Islands. A boat also plies this route twice a month, and makes additional stops at the group's two other islands (which are linked by a bridge), Ofu and Olosega. There is no regular transport between Ta'u and Ofu and Olosega so the only option is to get a local fisherman to take you; they charge US$150 each way.

ITINERARIES

Two Days

Begin with breakfast in **Pago Pago** and then spend the day exploring the eastern end of Tutuila. Stop for a swim at **Alega Beach** and lunch at **Tisa's Barefoot Bar** before catching the ferry to **Aunu'u** for the afternoon. Head back to Pago Pago Harbor for dinner. Start the next day at **Mom's Place** to fuel up Samoan-style before hiking the **Mt Alava Trail** – here you'll get a taste of all the landscapes Tutuila has to offer, from forest to reef. That night catch the *fiafia* (traditional dance performance) at the **Equator** restaurant at the Tradewinds Hotel in Tafuna.

Four Days

Take the supply boat to **Ofu** and spend the first two days snorkelling, lying around the beach and exploring **Olosega** by foot. Head back to Tutuila (via chartered boat and flight from Ta'u) then fill your last two days as above.

Essential Food & Drink

» **Palolo** Considered the caviar of the Pacific, these blue-green sea worms rise only twice per year and are considered a delicacy. The flavour is between crab and mussels and they have the texture of warm pudding. Ta'u is the place to get them.

» **Palusami** Calorie bombs of coconut cream wrapped in young taro leaves and cooked in a stone oven. Rich and delicious.

» **Fast food** Everything from Pizza Hut to Carl's Jr can be found blighting the landscape.

» **Kimchi** The Korean population has waned as the fishing fleets have moved elsewhere, but there are still enough people to support a healthy selection of Korean and Japanese restaurants.

» **Sashimi** Found on most menus, thinly sliced raw tuna is served on a bed of shredded cabbage with a side of soy sauce and wasabi.

» **American home-cooking** Pasta, burgers, fish and chips, steaks and Mexican dishes are found on many menus, usually in ridiculously large servings.

TUTUILA

POP 62,000 / AREA 132 SQ KM

Tutuila is a mass of sharp edges and pointy peaks, softened by a heavy padding of rainforest. At the island's spiky extremities you'll find shallow turquoise waters and white sands, all backed by those craggy green silhouettes. It's little wonder that the island's radio jocks insist on referring to it as 'The Rock'.

Whether arriving by sea or air, the island packs an explosive visual first impression. Unfortunately the first area you see on the ground – a string of fast-food joints and shabby deserted buildings – extinguishes some of the fireworks. Thankfully, colourful local buses await to spirit you with chaotic aplomb to areas that do live up to those first images: Pago Pago Harbor, Rainmaker Mountain and flower-scented villages tucked into white-sand coves.

◉ Sights

PAGO PAGO

There's a gritty charm to Pago Pago (population 6400). Spread along the coast of a deep bowl of water and overlooked by steep, South Pacific–sharp mountain ridges and peaks, you'd be hard-pressed to find a more gorgeous natural harbour on any other island in the world. Parks and white beaches are interspersed with busy shops and restaurants, but also abandoned buildings, many destroyed in the 2009 tsunami, which serve as a blunt reminder of that destructive day. A huge port filled with shipping containers sits amid it all and two tuna canneries blight the view at the far end of town. Sailors and fishermen, mostly from the USA, Korea and the Philippines, talk shop over beers in bars and cafes, Samoan children in their *lava-lava* school uniforms clog the streets after 3.30pm and the market overflows with fish, coconuts and

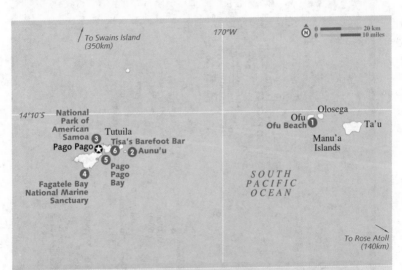

American Samoa Highlights

❶ Sighting rainforest-clad mountains and white sands as you lift your head out of the crystalline waters of **Ofu Beach** (p308)

❷ Strolling the plantations and crater lakes on the diminutive island of **Aunu'u** (p302)

❸ Hiking the jungle trails of the **National Park of American Samoa** (p301) from view-filled peak to a dip in the sea

❹ Alternating snorkelling and whale watching in **Fagatele Bay National Marine Sanctuary** (p302)

❺ Paddling the magnificent calm of **Pago**

Pago Harbor (p303) surrounded by vertical peaks

❻ Enjoying a traditional Samoan meal with a modern twist, beachside at **Tisa's Barefoot Bar** (p306)

❼ Touring **eastern and western Tutuila** (p299), their traditional villages and beaches

Tutuila

0   2 miles
0   4 km

SOUTH PACIFIC OCEAN

Cape Matatula
Tula
Onenoa
Sa'ilele
Masa'usi
Aoa
Au'asi
Mt Olomoana (327m)
Matuli Pt
Aunu'u
To Manu'a Islands (110km)

Nafanua Bank

Amouli
Alofau
Sinatau Pt

Nuusetoga

Masefau Bay
Masefau
Afono
Faga'itua
Faga'itua Bay
Avaio Beach

Cockscomb Pt
Pola Island
Vatia Bay
Amalau Bay
Afono Bay
Vatia
Tafeu Cove

Amalau Valley
Aua
Rainmaker Mountain (523m)
Laulii tuai
Ma'a
Kamela
To Alega Beach

National Park of American Samoa

See Pago Pago Harbor Map (p304)
Mt Alava (491m)
Fagatogo
Fagaalu
PAGO PAGO
Matafao Utulei Peak (653m) 20
Faga'alu
Faganeanea
Nu'uuli
Fagasa
Fagasa Bay
Fusaga Bay

Breakers Pt
Laufi
Fatu ma futi
Fatuoaia
Taema Bank

Lion's Park
Masepa
Pava'ia'i
Pala
Lagoon
Tafuna Coconut Pt
Tafuna International Airport
Fogagogo
Blowholes

Massacre Bay
A'asu

Mt Olotele (493m)
Leone Falls
A'oloaufou
'Ili'ili
Malaeloa
Vaitogi

Mt Lealataua (354m)
Nua
Asili
Leone
Leone Bay
Vailoa
Sliding Rock
Taputimu

Fagamalo
Maloata
Fagalii
Amanave
Poloa
Palagi Beach
Cape Taputapu

Fagatele Bay National Marine Sanctuary
Fogama'a Cove
Sail Rock Pt
Steps Pt

SOUTH PACIFIC OCEAN

Tutuila

bananas. It's a real working town, but that's what's refreshing about it.

Though pretty well stuck together, Pago Pago is technically a string of villages. Confusingly, 'Pago Pago' (pronounced *pung-o pung-o,* and often shortened to the singular) is used to describe the small village at the far end of the harbour, the harbour itself, the 'town' and, often, the whole island of Tutuila or even the whole of American Samoa.

Utulei is edged by a beach lined with day *fale,* where you can shelter from the sun between swims. Fagatogo is the administrative centre and contains the Fono, the traditionally inspired building that houses American Samoa's Senate and House of Representatives.

FREE **Jean P Hayden Museum** MUSEUM
(Map p304; ◎8am-4pm Mon-Fri) Has a small but interesting display of Samoan artefacts, including *va'a* (bonito canoes), *alia* (war canoes), coconut-shell combs, pigs' tusk armlets and native pharmacopoeia, plus information on traditional tattooing and a very informative display on native medicinal plants and Samoan medicine.

Fagatogo Market MARKET
(Map p304) This is the town's social centre on a Friday night. Locals come here to gossip, ransack food stalls and browse freshly

arrived coconuts, breadfruit and other produce. By Saturday, all the good stuff is gone and the market is hushed for another week. There are a few local-style 'fast-food' places at the back selling Samoan-sized plates of food (some with fresh fish) for US$5 for lunch on weekdays.

WESTERN TUTUILA
Most of the western end of Tutuila is taken up by the ruggedly beautiful, rainforest-wreathed mountains that line the northern coast. The bulk of the population inhabits the flat plains to the south, particularly the mildewed, strip-mall suburbs of Tafuna and Nu'uuli. However, once you pass Leone, a succession of cute villages lining pretty white-sand beaches reminds you that you're in a Polynesian paradise after all.

Nu'uuli Falls WATERFALL
(Map p298) Standing in stark relief to Nu'uuli's scruffy strip of restaurants and convenience stores, this secluded waterfall with a deliciously cool swimming hole at its base seems even more magical. The surrounding rainforest muffles the sound of the water cascading down 20m of jagged black lava rocks.

This is a local secret: there are no signposts and it's a little hard to find. Coming along the main road from the west, turn left

at the Nu'uuli Family Mart and follow this side road, veering left when you see the pig farm. At the end, park on the grass to the left (you'll see a house downhill on your right) and look for the start of the track in front of you. If you see anyone outside the house it would be polite to ask their permission to continue on, but you shouldn't have to pay any money.

The track is quite narrow and rough but should only take about 15 minutes. At the first juncture, veer to the left and continue until the trail reaches the stream. Stop here and look for the path leading steeply up the hill on the other side before wading across.

Tia Seu Lupe   ARCHAEOLOGICAL SITE
(Map p298) The most accessible of American Samoa's fascinating star mounds is secreted behind a statue of St Mary near the Catholic cathedral in Tafuna. Tia Seu Lupe has a viewing platform where you get a good look at the two distinct tiers of the structure, without disturbing the ancient site. The name literally means 'earthen mound to catch pigeons'.

To find it, head towards the Tradewinds Hotel and take the second road to the right; park by the statue at the very end of this road.

Holy Family Cathedral   CHURCH
(Map p298) The real beauty of Tafuna's imposing Catholic cathedral, with its space-age bell tower and dissected dome, lies inside.

Above the altar a larger-than-life-sized Samoan Christ offers an 'ava (kava) cup with outstretched hands, while a traditionally garbed man and woman sit cross-legged looking on. Outside a life-sized nativity scene swaps the stable for a *fale* and the manger for an 'ava bowl. In the foyer, Duffy Sheridan's large canvas entitled *The Holy Family* pictures an idyllic Samoan village scene with the mother opening a coconut while the father carves a canoe.

Turtle & Shark Site   SACRED SITE
(Map p298; Vaitogi; access fee US$2; ⊙Mon-Sat) The most famous of Tutuila's legends is set at this dramatic cliff-top site. According to just one of the myriad versions of this legend, an old blind lady and her granddaughter jumped into the sea after being turned out of their village during a time of famine. When their family learned what they'd done, they went to the shore, guilt-ridden, and called the pair by name. A turtle and shark appeared, and the family knew that their relatives had been miraculously transformed in the water and were OK.

Even if the turtle and shark have taken the day off, you'll enjoy the rugged character of the place, with its black lava cliffs, heavy surf and blowholes. Don't swim here though, as this is a sacred site; also, the currents are treacherous.

Leone   VILLAGE
(Map p298) The village of Leone welcomed the first missionary to Tutuila in 1832. John Williams subsequently erected the island's first **church**, garnishing it with three towers, some stunning woodwork and stained glass. Try to attend a service here on Sunday morning, when villagers congregate in their best whites to sing hymns before heading home for a lunchtime banquet.

STAR MOUNDS

More than 140 distinctive stone or earthen mounds dating back to late prehistoric times have been found scattered across the Samoan archipelago. Dubbed star mounds, the structures range from 6m to 30m in length, are up to 3m high and have from one to 11 raylike projections radiating from their base. Forty of these star mounds have been discovered (though not yet excavated) in Tutuila's east on the road between Amouli and Aoa.

The main theory regarding the star mounds is that they were used for pigeon-snaring, an extremely important sport of chiefs that was traditionally pursued from June through September. Villagers would follow their *matai* (chiefs) into the forest to observe and support competitions.

However, American archaeologists David Herdrich and Jeffrey Clark believe star mounds also served a much more complex function in Samoan society, including as sites for rituals related to marriage, healing and warfare. The archaeologists also believe the star mounds came to reflect the position of the *matai* and the notion of *mana* (supernatural power).

Between the church and the sea is a monument to Williams.

Cape Taputapu
SCENIC AREA

(Map p298) Cape Taputapu is Tutuila's westernmost point and received its name (*taputapu* means 'forbidden') after imaginatively fearful tales about it were spread by locals who wanted the cape's valuable grove of paper mulberry trees all to themselves. No such taboos prevent modern-day visitors from enjoying the cape's beautiful location.

Just past Amanave is a lovely white-sand beach known as **Palagi Beach**; ask for directions in the village store. Beyond Amanave, the road winds around valleys and over ridges to the small villages of Poloa, Fagali'i, Maloata and Fagamalo, revealing spectacular views of the coastline along the way.

EASTERN TUTUILA

Fale may have given way to clunky concrete-block houses, but otherwise the small villages cling to the shoreline as they've done for centuries.

Rainmaker Mountain
MOUNTAIN

(Map p298) Also known as Mt Pioa, 523m-high Rainmaker Mountain is the culprit that traps rain clouds and gives Pago Pago Harbor the highest annual rainfall of any harbour in the world. From afar it looks like a single, large peak, but a drive up Rainmaker Pass for close-up views reveals that the summit is actually three-pronged. The mountain and its base area are designated a national landmark site due to the pristine nature of the tropical vegetation on the slopes.

Masefau & Sa'ilele
SCENIC AREA

(Map p298) A cross-island road leads from the village of Faga'itua up over a pass before winding slowly down to Masefau, one of those villages that look too idyllic to be anything but a mirage.

Back at the pass, a turn-off takes you down a narrow, potholed road to Sa'ilele, which has one of the island's loveliest beaches: coconut palms are anchored into the sand by mounds of rocks and coral fragments, and the water is placid. The sandy area below the large rock outcrop at the beach's western end provides an excellent place for a picnic.

🏃 Activities

Hiking & Walking

Hiking is one of American Samoa's biggest drawcards, with decently maintained trails through extraordinary pristine rainforest and coastlines.

National Park of American Samoa
NATIONAL PARK

(Map p298) Created in 1988, the territory's sole national park protects huge swaths of pristine landscapes and marine environments on Tutuila, Ofu (see p308) and Ta'u (see p309). The 1000-hectare Tutuila section follows the north coast between the villages of Fagasa and Afono. The wonderful thing about trails within park boundaries is that they are often very well maintained.

The National Park Visitor Information Center (p306) in Pago Pago is an invaluable source of information. The best hikes within the park in order of difficulty (easy to challenging) include the following.

Pola Island Trail

(Map p298) Vatia is a peaceful village situated on a lovely, coral-fringed bay. Guarding the mouth of the bay, tiny Pola Island has magnificent, sheer, 120m-high cliffs populated by seabirds. For a close-up of soaring rocks and birds, head through the village and park at the school, then walk 300m to reach the wonderfully isolated beach at the base of the cliffs.

Amalau Valley

(Map p298) From Aua, a surfaced road switchbacks steeply up over Rainmaker Pass and down to Afono and Vatia. Between these two villages is the beautiful, secluded Amalau Valley, home to many forest bird species and to two rare species of flying fox. Stop at the lookout point just past the western side of Amalau Bay for some wonderful views.

Mt Alava

(Map p304) The NPS hiking trail that leads up Mt Alava (491m) and then down to the coast presents a wonderful way to experience the park's lowland and montane rainforests, its thriving birdlife, and the peacefulness that permeates it. On Mt Alava, a metal stairway leads up to a TV transmission tower and the rusted remains of a cable-car terminal that once ran 1.8km across Pago Pago Harbor to Solo Hill. The 5.5km ridge trail (1½ to two hours one way) starts from Fagasa Pass. Behind the rest *fale* at the end of this section, a very steep trail (including ladders in places) leads 2km down to Vatia; allow an additional two hours for the descent.

DON'T MISS

AUNU'U

The 3-sq-km, tangled confines of Aunu'u (Map p298) are perfect for a half-day of roaming and exploring on foot. Actually, there's no other choice as the island only has a handful of vehicles. The walking tracks are pretty good but you might still want to consider arranging a guide when you get off the ferry (US$8 is a reasonable fee for a tour of the island).

At the north end of the island is **Pala Lake**, a deadly-looking expanse of quicksand whose fiery red hue is best appreciated at low tide. Within Aunu'u's central volcanic crater lies **Red Lake**, filled with eels and suffused by a preternatural glow at dusk. On the island's eastern shore is rough-and-tumble **Ma'ama'a Cove**, a rocky bowl constantly pounded by large waves. Legend says that this is the site of Sina ma Tigila'u (Sina and Tigila'u), two lovers who were shipwrecked here. You can make out bits of crossed 'rope' and broken 'planks' embedded in the rocks.

Below the western slope of Aunu'u's crater are the **Taufusitele Taro Marshes**, which are planted Hawaiian-style with swamp taro. The safest place to swim on the island is in the little harbour, where the water's so clear that you can see the coral from the breakwater.

Small launches head to Aunu'u from the dock at Au'asi. If you catch a boat with other villagers, you pay US$1 each way. If you have to charter a boat, be prepared to pay around US$10 for the return trip. Boats don't run on Sunday.

Fagatele Bay National Marine Sanctuary
HIKING TRAIL

(Map p298; ☎633 7354; www.fagatelebay.noaa.gov) A submerged volcanic crater, Fagatele Bay is fringed by Tutuila's last remaining stretch of coastal rainforest and its cliff-side depths contain more than 140 species of coral. It's also visited by numerous turtle species and, between June and September, by migrating southern humpback whales. With these marvellous natural assets, it's little wonder that the bay was designated a marine sanctuary in 1986, although it does lie outside national-park boundaries.

A trail runs along this magical coastline between the village of Vailoa (there's a US$5 fee paid to the local family here) and the Turtle & Shark Lodge (see p305), which is much more difficult to access (you'll need a 4WD). In between are deserted white-sand beaches worthy of your wildest tropical fantasies and a variety of lush landscapes. The trail has some short uphill bits but other than that is fairly easy – it should take about four hours return.

Massacre Bay
HIKING TRAIL

(Map p298) A marvellous 4km hiking trail (four hours return) leads from the scenic village of A'oloaufou, high up on the rocky spine of Tutuila, down to A'asu on Massacre Bay. Massacre Bay's foreboding name is due to a skirmish between French sailors and Samoan villagers that occurred there in 1787, leaving 51 people dead.

The track begins near the community garden in A'oloaufou and is apparently maintained (or not, as the case may be) by the sole family residing in A'asu. It's often overgrown, extremely muddy and difficult to navigate, particularly on the climb back up. Hikers should seriously consider hiring a guide in A'oloaufou (between US$5 and US$10).

Swimming & Snorkelling

Many coastal areas are too rough or shallow for swimming but there are a number of easily accessible places to get in the water; you can get to all of the following beaches by bus. In most cases swimsuits are a no-no – wear a T-shirt and long shorts or a *lava-lava* (wraparound sarong).

Alega Beach
SNORKELLING

(Map p298) A short drive east of Pago Pago, this is a lovely stretch of sand that gets crowded with Samoan bodies on the weekend. It's not only a great place to swim and snorkel (check currents and conditions with locals first), but is also overlooked by Tisa's Barefoot Bar (p306), the perfect spot for a cold drink. You can waive the access fee for the beach (US$5) by simply buying a drink at Tisa's.

Avaio Beach
SNORKELLING

(Map p298; access fee US$2; ⊙7am-6pm) Just east of Alega Beach is this well-looked-after strip of white sand, which is also known as '$2 Beach' for obvious reasons. The water's shallow but it's a good spot for snorkelling and there's a little green island just offshore.

Faga'alu Park
SWIMMING

At the outer southern part of Pago Pago Harbor, this grassy park with picnic tables and a small white-sand beach is the most central place for a dip. The water here is much cleaner than the interior of the bay and the corals are in surprisingly good shape.

Kayaking & Canoeing

There are several outrigger canoe clubs that welcome guests to paddle with them on Pago Pago Harbor. A few leave from the beach at Sadie's by the Sea, so ask around about times and availability.

Sadie's by the Sea
KAYAKING

(Map p304; ☑633 5900; www.sadieshotels.com; Utulei) Kayaks and paddleboats are free for guests of this hotel, or US$10 per hour for nonguests, and are a highly recommended way to explore Pago Pago's scenic harbour. The beach fee for nonguests (where you'll have to launch from) is US$5 per day.

Golf

'Ili'ili Golf Course
GOLF

(Map p298; ☑699 2995; 'ili'ili; ⊙6am-6pm) This is a 'very forgiving' 72-par course with dramatic mountain peaks overlooking it to the north and a view of the Pacific to the east. Green fees for nine/18 holes are US$3/5 on weekdays and US$4/7 on weekends. Club hire costs US$8 and carts are US$18.

☞ Tours

North Shore Tours
HIKING

(☑731 8294; www.polynesianherbs.angelfire.com) Rory West is a true mountain man and has impressive knowledge of and passion for the island's plants, legends and best secret spots. He caters to all levels but his tendency veers towards hard-core – so if he suggests going off a trail be prepared for a real adventure.

Busy Corner Tours
ISLAND TOURS

(☑733 0833; http://amsamoa-busycorner.blog spot.com) John Wasko enthusiastically leads tours to the island's best sights as well as to lesser-known but fascinating spots, including an ancient seaside adze 'factory' where basalt was ground to fine tools that were prized throughout the precontact Pacific.

Tisa's Tours
ISLAND TOURS

(Map p298; ☑622 7447; www.tisasbarefootbar.com; Alega Beach) Island tours include lunch and swimming at Tisa's Barefoot Bar (see p306).

🛏 Sleeping

Since most people come to American Samoa on business, not for tourism, many places seem to set their rates based on the official government per diem allowance (about US$135), and there's an incredible range of value (from great to terrible) at that rate. There are surprisingly few waterside options but there are a handful of excellent and quirky places to stay.

PAGO PAGO

Le Falepule
B&B $$

(Map p298; ☑633 5264; isabel@blueskynet.as; Faga'alu; s/d US$135/145; ❋@☎) Sitting on the terrace of this luxury boutique B&B, sipping a beverage you've poured for yourself from the honesty bar, and gazing over the most sublime ocean views, you may never want to leave. Le Falepule ticks all the boxes – the staff are delightful, the breakfasts deliciously tropical, the rooms elegantly and comfortably furnished (with a gentle Samoan theme), and the location quiet and private but close to both Pago Pago and the airport. There's even a free laundry service and wireless internet. You'll find it at the end of a steep driveway 200m north of the hospital turn-off.

Sadie's by the Sea
HOTEL $$

(Map p304; ☑633 5900; www.sadieshotels.com; Utulei; r US$139; ❋☎☎) The 'by the sea' bit is the big drawcard here. It's one of the few places with a swimmable beach at its doorstep – but if you have qualms about bathing in Pago Pago Harbor, there's also a bat-shaped pool. Rooms are midrange-hotel ordinary but are the most convenient in town with microwaves, fridges and everything you need steps away. The great on-site restaurant, Goat Island Cafe (p305), is another big perk.

Evelani's Motel
HOTEL $

(Map p304; ☑633 7777; Pago Pago; r without bathroom US$60; ❋) Also known as Motu-O-Fiafiaga Motel, this friendly motel is owned by the once-top showgirl in a Polynesian dance spectacular in Las Vegas circa 1969. Evelani may have left Vegas but Vegas never left Evelani: the fabulously (and unintentionally) retro decor here could best be described as brothel-chic. Head down the creaky, scarlet-carpeted corridors, lined with 1980s-style mirrors and posters of Marilyn Monroe and James Dean, and you'll find that the bright rooms are very comfortable

Pago Pago Harbor

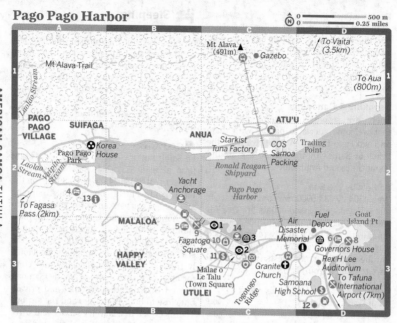

Pago Pago Harbor

for the price – although they do shake when trucks rumble along the road out the front.

Sadie Thompson Inn
HOTEL **$**
(Map p304; ☏633 5981; www.sadiethompsoninn.com; Malaloa; r US$98; ❋) People seem pretty convinced that this wooden inn edged with white verandahs was where the original Sadie Thompson (immortalised in Somerset Maugham's novel *Rain*) set up her red light.

Regardless, the dozen or so rooms here are large and comfortable, if not dull for all the hoopla surrounding them. Locals say skip the restaurant.

WESTERN TUTUILA

TOP CHOICE Moana O Sina
B&B **$$**
(Map p298; ☏699 8517; isobel@blueskynet.as; Fogagogo; s/d incl breakfast US$135/145; ❋🖥📶)

The seaside version of Le Falepule (p303), Moana O Sina shares the same owners, high standards and excellent Polynesian-inspired rooms for an amazing-value price. Beautiful lawns of Japanese grass slope down to a natural rock pool, where you can cool off in the water while tropical fish dart around and waves crash against the cliffs below. There's a small, stylish dipping pool at the edge of an expanse of sea spray and lava rocks surrounded by lounge chairs – all that could easily belong to a resort three times this price – and another full-sized swimming pool with an equally outrageous ocean view was about to be finished when we passed. An on-site bar and restaurant serving three meals per day should be finished by the time this book is published, as well as a relaxing central lounge *fale*.

Tee's Place B&B $$$
(Map p298; 699 5714, 733 5981; taalogatupai@ yahoo.com; Vaitogi; d without/with bathroom US$180/250;) Unique on the island, this B&B mixes high comfort with a classy Polynesian welcome on lush garden grounds. Four rooms are available in Tee's American-plush two-storey home, all with high-quality beds, flat-screen TVs and fridges. The real draw, however, is the airy, sofa-filled common verandah shaded by a giant banyan tree, plus the copious flowers and the long skinny swimming pool with a Japanese-style bridge running across it. Graceful and lovely Tee is known around the island for her cooking; a full breakfast is included in the price, and Tee will also make lunch or dinner on request.

Turtle & Shark Lodge LODGE $$
(Map p298; 699 3131; Vaitogi; r US$135;) Isolated down a long dirt track, this ageing but comfy self-catering house (with five rooms for rent and a kitchen for guest use) is on a cliff over an impressive blowhole and has views along the pristine Fagatele Bay National Marine Sanctuary. Hike the trail to deserted beaches, hang out with the lively Samoan family that runs the place (they live in the house next door) and, if you're lucky enough to be here from September to November, you may get to see whales giving birth in the bay below the house.

Tradewinds Hotel HOTEL $$
(Map p298; 699 1000; www.tradewinds.as; Main Ottoville Rd, Tafuna; r/ste from US$149/240;) Tradewinds has all the bells and whistles you'd expect from such a large business hotel – including an enticing resort pool, day spa, restaurant, internet room and an ATM in the high-ceilinged lobby – and like many such hotels it's opted for a bland, generic look for its spacious rooms and broad corridors. The location is handy to the airport but not the sea.

EASTERN TUTUILA
You may be able to arrange an overnight stay in Vatia through the National Park of American Samoa's homestay program; see p306.

Tisa's Barefoot Bar FALE $
(Map p298; 622 7447; www.tisasbarefootbar.com; Alega Beach; fale per person incl breakfast & dinner US$50) Unlike their cousins to the west, American Samoans have traded *fale*-life for the joys of concrete-block construction. Tisa's is the only place that offers travellers the traditional option, but even then the comfort is ratcheted up a notch. There are no mattresses on the floor in these babies, just comfy beds and decks for endless ocean-gazing. Plus you get the fun company of gorgeous Tisa and her boyfriend Candyman.

Eating
American Samoa's reputation for fatty fried foods is not generally contradicted by the eateries on Tutuila (steak and eggs with a side order of spam, anyone?). The main road leading from the airport is a tribute to America's fast-food giants and a testimony to the high esteem they hold in the Polynesian palate. A scattering of Asian restaurants (mainly Chinese, Korean and Japanese) provides a lighter alternative.

PAGO PAGO
Goat Island Cafe INTERNATIONAL $$
(Map p304; 633 5900; Sadie's by the Sea, Utulei; mains US$10-28; breakfast, lunch & dinner) If it's a reasonably healthy and comparatively inventive menu you're after, this resort restaurant is your best option. Plus it has the added bonus of offering waterside tables. Try the grilled curried-vegie wrap or a New York steak with shrimp.

DDW AMERICAN $$
(Don't Drink the Water; Map p304; 633 5297, Pago Pago; mains US$7-18; breakfast & lunch Mon-Sat) This relaxed, waterfront cafe gets superbusy at breakfast and lunchtime, when local workers stampede through the door to tuck into well-cooked burgers, omelettes, pasta, salads, steaks and tasty cakes and pies.

Evie's Cantina   MEXICAN $

(Map p304; ☑633 7781; Pago Pago; mains US$5-13; ☺lunch Tue-Fri, dinner Tue-Sun) Late at night this Mexican restaurant morphs into a nightclub, but until then it serves big, tasty burritos, enchiladas and other cheesy treats. Grab a booth and watch your stomach bulge once the food arrives.

Sook's Sushi Restaurant   JAPANESE $$

(Map p304; ☑633 5525; GHC Reid Bldg, Malaloa; mains US$10-20; ☺lunch & dinner Mon-Sat) The entrance of this one-room Japanese restaurant strangely leads from behind the cash register and all heads turn in shock if a non-Asian face appears. No one speaks much English (staff are Korean) but the food is good. Try the generous sushi dishes, or the Korean *kalbi* (ribs).

WESTERN TUTUILA

Manuia   KOREAN $$

(Map p298; ☑699 9927; Tafuna; meals US$7-25; ☺11am-10pm Mon-Sat) Tucked away in a Tafuna backstreet, this local eatery is well worth hunting out for its tasty selection of Korean, Japanese and Chinese dishes. Try the sashimi tuna and vegetables mixed in the chef's own chilli and red-pepper sauce, served with kimchi and rice. It's nearly as good as the zany mural of a giant squid and semiclad women adorning the walls.

Mom's Place   SAMOAN $

(Map p298; ☑699 9494; Tafuna; mains US$5-10; ☺breakfast & lunch Mon-Sat; ☻) Mom's rich, diner-style cooking won't help keep your waistline under control, but to hell with it. Try your luck at getting through a plate of *panikeke* (the round doughnuts that Samoans call pancakes), or go island-style with corned beef hash or spam and eggs.

EASTERN TUTUILA

TOP CHOICE Tisa's Barefoot Bar   SAMOAN $$

(Map p298; ☑622 7447; Alega Beach; meals US$12-18) The food at this beachside institution is superb, with vegetarians well catered for from the owner's organic garden. The opening hours can be sporadic, so it pays to call ahead. On Wednesday nights it fires up the *umu* (stone oven) for its legendary Samoan feast (US$30), where traditional fare is given an international twist.

🍷 Drinking

Evie's Polynesian Hut   BAR, NIGHTCLUB

(Map p304; ☑633 7781; Pago Pago; Tue-Thu admission free, Fri & Sat US$3) Sporting more

aliases than your average mobster (Evie's Cantina, Evelani's, Motu-O-Fiafiaga Motel), this vinyl-clad Pago Pago mainstay comes into its own on the weekends when DJs hit the decks. Hostesses wear fitted Polynesian gowns, all the interior building posts are made to look like palm trees and it all feels like a Disney ride, complete with twinkling fairy lights and videos on a big screen. Its Halloween parties are legendary.

Tisa's Barefoot Bar   BAR

(Map p298; ☑622 7447; Alega Beach) Tisa's driftwood bar is a sublime place to rest your elbows and sip a cold one while gazing out over some typical Polynesian beachfront beauty.

☆ Entertainment

For an all-singing, all-dancing, thigh-slapping Samoan *fiafia,* head to the Equator restaurant at Tradewinds Hotel (p305) on a Friday night. A buffet dinner is included in the price (US$25).

A handful of bars and cafes host local musicians, including Tisa's.

Karaoke bars tend to cater to the seedier side of the fishing industry via Chinese prostitutes.

Nu'uuli Place Cinemas   CINEMA

(Map p298; ☑699 9334; Nu'uuli; adult/child US$6.75/4) If local TV isn't floating your *bonito* canoe, you can always head here for some smash-'em-up Hollywood action.

🔒 Shopping

Don't expect Armani but most of your more humble purchasing requirements can be fulfilled in the shopping centres and strip malls of Tafuna, Nu'uuli and Pago Pago.

Off Da Rock Tattoos   TATTOOS

(Map p304; ☑252 8384, 252 4858; Fagatoga Sq, Pago Pago; ☺9am-4pm by appointment) The 'first and only tattoo shop on the island' takes it easy on tourists with a modern, electric needle.

Mr Lavalava   CLOTHING

Nu'uuli (Map p298; ☑699 7707; Laufou Shopping Center); Tafuna (Map p298; ☑699 1570) The name says it all.

ⓘ Information

Many of American Samoa's hotels offer free wi-fi. ATMs are found throughout commercial areas of the island but not at the airport.

ILLUSTRATING SAMOA

The full-bodied *pe'a* (male tattoo), which extends from the waist to just below the knees, is a prized status symbol in Samoa. It can take weeks to complete and is a very painful process. Thus, anyone who undergoes the ritual is considered to be extremely brave. Any adult member can, in effect, receive a *pe'a* if the *'aiga, tufuga* (tattoo artist) and village leaders agree that it is suitable. The *tufuga* is usually paid with traditional gifts of *ie toga* (fine mats) and food.

Tattooing was discouraged when the missionaries came, but as young Pacific islanders take more pride in their cultural heritage, there has been a revival of interest in the traditional designs, though with a modern twist.

The contemporary tattoo sported by many young, more Westernised Samoans comes without social and cultural restrictions. But the designs may signify a person's *'aiga,* ancestors, reference to nature or something very personal. The wrist and armband tattoos may have been originally developed for tourists, but they are now a popular Samoan fashion and many young Samoans sport a wrist, arm or ankle tattoo of their own design. Many Samoan men also have a family member or their own name tattooed in Gothic letters across their arms, backs or chests. They can be made with the modern machine or by the traditional comb.

American Samoa Historic Preservation Office (Ashpo; Map p298; ☑699 2316; www.ashpo.org; Nu'uuli) Excellent contact for history, sociology, anthropology and archaeology buffs. Produces the excellent, free *A Walking Tour of Historic Fagatogo* booklet (available from the office).

ANZ Amerika Samoa Bank Has branches in Fagatogo and Tafuna.

Bank of Hawai'i Has a branch in Utulei, and a second branch in Tafuna, on the main road from the airport.

Blue Sky (Map p298; www.blueskynet.as; Tafuna; ☺8am-4pm Mon-Fri) Blue Sky hotspots can be found all over Tutuila including at the airport and many restaurants (see the website for a list of spots). Get online at any hotspot to purchase time with a credit card; unlimited time for 24 hours is US$10 and one week costs US$20.

LBJ Tropical Medical Center (Map p298; ☑633 1222; Faga'alu; ☺emergency 24hr) American Samoa's only hospital.

National Park Visitor Information Center (Map p304; ☑633 7082; www.nps.gov/npsa; Pago Pago; ☺8am-4.30pm Mon-Fri) Best stop for tourist info with the only decent map we found of the island (free) plus a day-hikes pamphlet, information on WWII sites and a homestay program with choices on Tutuila and Ta'u (US$35 to US$50 per night). They also have updates on coral reef health, water quality and more. Plus staff are helpful and professional.

Office of Tourism (Map p298; ☑699 9411; www.amsamoa.com; Tasi St, Tafuna; ☺7.30am-4pm Mon-Fri) Getting information to tourists doesn't seem to be a high priority for this office, tucked away down a side street in Tafuna in a building with no signage.

Post office (Map p304) Located across from the Manu'a Ferry.

ⓘ Getting There & Away

All flights and boats to American Samoa head to Tutuila; see p314 for details. Flying is the most popular and painless option, but it's only possible from Samoa, Hawai'i and Los Angeles. For details on travel between Tutuila and the Manu'a Islands, see p308.

ⓘ Getting Around

To/From the Airport

Frequent buses from Pago Pago Harbor to Tafuna International Airport are marked 'Tafuna' and stop right outside the terminal (US$1.50). If arriving at night you'll need to get a cab into Pago Pago (between US$8 and US$15). There's a taxi stand just outside the airport entrance.

Bus

Riding Tutuila's colourful *'aiga* (extended family) buses – small pick-up trucks modified for public transport and equipped with ear-busting sound systems – is a highlight of a visit to American Samoa. These buses do unscheduled runs around Pago Pago Harbor and the more remote areas of the island from the main terminal at the market in Fagatogo (Map p304).

Buses regularly head east to Aua (US$1) and Tula (US$1.50), south to Tafuna (US$1.75) and west to Leone (US$2). Less frequently, buses go to Fagasa (US$1), A'oloaufou on the central ridge (US$1.75), Amanave (US$1.75) and Fagamalo in the far west (US$2); a trip to the northwest

villages often means disembarking at Leone and catching another bus from there. Buses also head over Rainmaker Pass to Vatia (US$2.25).

Car

A 2WD is fine for motoring around Tutuila. Car-hire agencies charge around US$70 per day. For insurance information, see p315.

The following are recommended companies:

Avis Car Rental (☑699 2746; res@avissamoa. com; Tafuna International Airport)

Sir Amos Car Rental (☑699 4554; siramos rental@yahoo.com; Tafuna International Airport) Nothing special but often the only booth open at the airport.

Taxi

Taxis are plentiful and convenient in Pago Pago, Nu'uuli and Tafuna. Charters cost US$10.50 per hour, waiting is US$2 per 15 minutes and there's a US$1 surcharge for each piece of luggage over two pieces.

MANU'A ISLANDS

POP 1310 / AREA 56 SQ KM

Sometimes the best things in life require a bit of effort, and that's certainly true of Manu'a. These three islands, anchored about 100km to the east of Tutuila, are some of the most remote and beautiful you could hope to encounter in the Pacific. Although the rest of your stay may suffer in comparison, plan to visit them near the beginning of your trip as any disruption in the weather could keep you here longer than you intended. That's hardly likely to be a hardship, as Ofu is the undisputed highlight of any visit to American Samoa.

Ofu, Olosega and Ta'u may be separate islands, but they all share the same marvellous natural characteristics: enormous cliffs sheltering seabird colonies; expired volcanic cones; undisturbed beaches that flow into lagoons stocked with a brilliant array of coral; and a sense of timelessness that makes watches completely redundant. The Manu'a Islands make the laid-back environs of Tutuila seem just about chaotic by comparison, so when you visit, pack plenty of extra reading material and a willingness to fall asleep in the middle of the day.

ⓘ Information

Ofu village has a basic medical clinic. Post offices can be found in Olosega village on Olosega and in Fiti'uta on Ta'u.

There are no banks in the Manu'a Islands but the internet connection is faster than anywhere else in the Samoan islands!

ⓘ Getting There & Away

AIR Inter Island Airways (☑in Tutuila 699 7100, in Ofu 655 7100, in Ta'u 677 7100; www. interislandair.com) flies four times weekly from Pago Pago (US$170 return; Monday, Wednesday, Friday and Sunday) to Ta'u. Ofu's airport was closed at the time of writing and it looked unlikely to reopen any time soon.

BOAT The **MV Sili** (☑633 5532, 633 4160) departs Tutuila every second Thursday at 10pm and one-way tickets cost US$35 (plus US$3 per piece of luggage); tickets are sold between 8am and 4pm on the day of departure. The journey takes nine to 12 hours and stops are made at both Ofu and Ta'u. This boat doesn't enter Manu'a harbours – rather, you transfer to a smaller boat at the harbour entrance.

ⓘ Getting Around

There are no established plane or boat services between individual Manu'a islands. Ofu and Olosega are joined by a bridge, but to get from either of them to Ta'u requires a **charter boat** (☑655 1104; one-way hire US$150) and the crossing can be rough.

Getting around on the islands themselves involves walking or sticking your thumb out. There are only a handful of vehicles on the islands but few drivers will pass a walker without offering a lift.

Ofu & Olosega

OFU POP 290 / AREA 5.2 SQ KM
OLOSEGA POP 220 / AREA 3 SQ KM

These twin islands, separated by a deep channel but linked by a bridge, are as close to paradise as anywhere you'll find on this blue planet. Ofu has its sole village at its western end, leaving the rest of the island delightfully unpopulated. Taking up its southern shoreline, **Ofu Beach** is 4km of shining, palm-fringed white sand, flanked by ridiculously picturesque jagged peaks that rise behind it like giant shark's teeth.

This, along with 140 hectares of offshore waters, comprises the Ofu section of the **National Park of American Samoa** (see p301). The reef here is considered to be one of the healthiest in all the Samoas. The water's wonderfully clear and the coral forms giant mushroom shapes only metres from the shoreline. Multitudes of coloured fish dart around, occasionally pursued by reef sharks (they're harmless fellows, to humans at least, but a little freaky for a novice snorkeller).

◉ Sights & Activities

Olosega shares the same marvellous encircling reef system as Ofu. The two islands

Ofu & Olosega

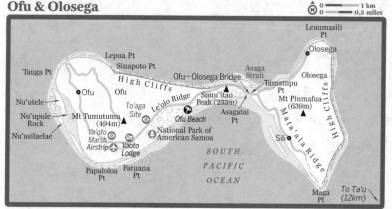

look conjoined, but are separated from each other by the 137m-wide Asaga Strait. From the cyclone-proof **bridge**, the water is impossibly clear. Local kids regularly jump off, letting the current carry them to shore. This isn't advised for travellers – if you get the wrong tides you could just as easily be carried straight out to sea.

To'aga Site
ARCHAEOLOGICAL SITE

Behind Ofu Beach is the To'aga site, where in 1987 archaeologists found an unprecedented array of artefacts ranging in age from the earliest times of Samoan prehistory to modern day. The excavations have been filled, so there's now nothing to actually see here. Samoans believe the area of bush between the road and the beach is infested with devilish *aitu* (spirits or ghosts). The upshot of this is that you're likely to have one of the world's best beaches all to yourself.

Mt Tumutumu
HIKING TRAIL

The 5.5km-long, often indistinct track (five hours return) to the summit of Mt Tumutumu (494m) begins just north of Ofu village wharf and twists up to the TV relay tower atop the mountain, where a large rock provides a handy viewpoint. You'll need sensible shoes, long trousers (to protect from cutting plants), heavy-duty mosquito repellent and a bush knife to hack through the foliage.

Maga Point
WALKING TRAIL

The 1.5km walk from Olosega village up to Maga Point on the island's southern tip is a highlight of a visit. The point's steep cliffs, the reefs marching out from the shore, and the view of distant Ta'u and the Pacific hori-

zon are simply unforgettable. To avoid local dogs, veer around Olosega village on the beach. After passing the rubbish tip, pick your way along the coral-strewn beach and look for the narrow trail that climbs up the hillside.

Sleeping & Eating

Both Ofu and Olosega villages have basic stores where you can stock up on provisions.

TOP CHOICE Vaoto Lodge
LODGE $

(655 1120; www.vaotolodge.com; s/d/tr/f US$75/85/95/110;) Fifty metres of green lawn away from the currently defunct airstrip, this is a slice of paradise. Sensational snorkelling can be found off the beach in front. The units are simple but clean and comfy, each with a bathroom and firm beds. The friendly family that runs the place provides bikes, snorkelling gear, board games and a book and DVD library (only the family cabin has a TV and the one in the lounge only gets one channel), and dishes up delicious meals (US$35 for three meals). Beer and other drinks are available. Bring plenty of insect repellent as the mosquitoes are vicious.

Ta'u

POP 800 / AREA 39 SQ KM

On the dramatic south coast of this remote, sparsely populated island, some of the highest sea cliffs in the world rise 966m to Mt Lata, the territory's highest point. Much of Ta'u is covered in dense rainforest and dotted with inactive cones and craters. If you

Ta'u

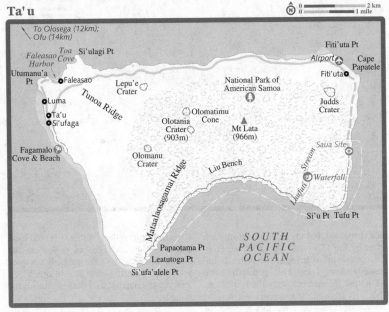

do venture out here, you'll invariably have the island's marvellous forests, volcanic remnants and numerous bird species mostly to yourself.

The main settlement on Ta'u consists of the villages of Ta'u, Luma and Si'ufaga in the island's northwest. From Ta'u village there's a good walk south to secluded **Fagamalo Cove**. It was in Luma that the young Margaret Mead researched her classic anthropological work, *Coming of Age in Samoa*, in 1925. Despite the permissive impression you may have gained from that text, visitors should be aware that Ta'u is the most conservative part of American Samoa. Bikinis are a definite no-no.

The Ta'u segment of the **National Park of American Samoa** (see p301) occupies 2160 hectares of land and 400 hectares of offshore waters. Its lowland and montane rainforests are home to flying foxes and numerous native birds, including black noddies, white terns, multicoloured fruit doves and the revered *lupe* (Pacific pigeon). Ta'u is also the only habitat of the Pacific boa.

About 2.5km from Fiti'uta is the legendary **Saua site**, where Tagaloa is said to have created the first humans before sending them out to Polynesia (see the boxed text, opposite). This sacred place is an atmospheric landscape of volcanic boulders, wild surf and windswept beach. Short trails lead to the main archaeological area and three *fale* have been erected for shelter. Keen hikers can continue via a rough track to Tufu Point. If you've arranged a guide you could plug on for another 2km to a waterfall on the **Laufuti Stream**.

Only very experienced, intrepid and/or foolhardy hikers tackle the island's jungly interior – and only the certifiable would do so without a guide. You should be able to hack your way to **Judds Crater** in Ta'u's northeast in about three hours from the road near Fiti'uta. A recent expedition to Mt Lata was forced to turn back after two days.

🛏 Sleeping & Eating

The best option is to arrange village-stay accommodation through the National Park of American Samoa (see p306).

Mauga's Homestay   LODGE $
(☏677 3414; Fiti'uta; r US$75) Offers simple rooms with shared bathrooms in an inland house near the airport. It also provides meals (breakfast and lunch US$7.50 each, dinner US$10).

UNDERSTAND AMERICAN SAMOA

American Samoa Today

The two tuna canneries in Pago Pago account for 80% of American Samoa's employment although the high costs of operation here as compared to more struggling economies makes the staying power shaky at best.

In 2009 an earthquake and devastating tsunami killed 200 people and destroyed uncountable homes and businesses. Although the US relief provided almost $25 million for the recovery, a few people were still living in tents as late as 2012 and some homes that replaced ones lost lack basic necessities like kitchens and bathrooms.

History

Prehistory

Archaeological finds near the villages of Tula and Aoa at the eastern tip of Tutuila, and at To'aga on Ofu, reveal that the islands have been inhabited for more than 3000 years. Traditionally Samoans believed that the Manu'a Islands were the first land to emerge at the hands of the god Tagaloa. The Tu'i Manu'a (paramount chief of the islands) was held in high esteem by Samoans. Although various conflicts ultimately split the islands, the paramount chief was still a proud and powerful figure at the time of cession to the US at the beginning of the 20th century.

European Contact

In 1722 Dutchman Jacob Roggeveen sighted the Manu'a Islands but sailed on without landing. In May 1768 French explorer Captain Louis-Antoine de Bougainville bartered with the inhabitants of Manu'a, but merely sighted Tutuila. The first expedition to set foot on Tutuila was headed by Frenchman Jean-François de Galaup, comte de la Pérouse, who landed at Fagasa in 1787. The encounter had a tragic finish, with the French and the Samoans fighting each other at A'asu: 12 sailors and 39 villagers were killed, and A'asu was christened Massacre Bay (see p302).

US Military Rule

A Samoan civil war in the 1870s and 1880s was co-opted by the US, Britain and Germany into an argument over which foreign power should rule the islands. By the time the dust had settled, control of western Samoa had been granted to Germany and, by 1900, the

AND GOD CREATED SAMOA

Samoans claim their land is the 'cradle of Polynesia', a place created by the sky god Tagaloa (Tangaroa). Before the sea, earth, sky, plants or people existed, Tagaloa lived in the expanse of empty space. He created a rock, commanding it to split into clay, coral, cliffs and stones. As the rock broke apart, the earth, sea and sky came into being. From a bit of the rock emerged a spring of fresh water.

Next, at Saua in the Manu'a Islands, Tagaloa created man and woman, whom he named Fatu and 'Ele'ele ('Heart' and 'Earth'). He sent them to the region of fresh water and commanded them to people the area. He ordered the sky, which was called Tu'ite'elagi, to prop itself up above the earth.

Tagaloa then created Po and Ao ('Night' and 'Day'), which bore the 'eyes of the sky' – the sun and the moon. At the same time he made the nine regions of heaven, inhabited by various gods.

In the meantime, Fatu and 'Ele'ele were 'peopling the area'. Reckoning that all these people needed some form of government, Tagaloa sent Manu'a, a son of Po and Ao, to be the people's chief. The Manu'a Islands were named after this chief, and from that time on, Samoan kings were called Tu'i Manu'a tele ma Samoa 'atoa (King of Manu'a and all of Samoa).

Next, the countries were divided into islands or groups of islands. The world now consisted of Manu'a, Viti (Fiji), Tonga and Savai'i. Tagaloa then went to Manu'a and noticed that a void existed between it and Savai'i. Up popped 'Upolu and then Tutuila.

Tagaloa's final command was: 'Always respect Manu'a; anyone who fails to do so will be overtaken by catastrophe.' Thus, Manu'a became the spiritual centre of the Samoan islands and, to some extent, of all Polynesia.

islands of eastern Samoa had been formally annexed to the US by a deed of cession signed by all local chiefs. Eastern Samoa became a naval station under the jurisdiction of the US Department of the Navy. In exchange, the US agreed to protect the traditional rights of indigenous Samoans. The inhabitants acquired the status of US nationals but were denied a vote or representation in Washington.

In 1905 the military commander of Tutuila was given the title of governor and the territory officially became known as American Samoa.

Increasing Democracy

Until the 1960s American Samoa retained its traditional social structure and subsistence economy. But under the orders of President Kennedy, American Samoa was swiftly modernised, with European-style homes replacing traditional *fale* (houses with thatched roofs and open sides), electrification and the construction of an international airport and tuna canneries.

Through the 1960s and 1970s a series of referenda resulted in the adoption of a constitution, a democratically elected governorship and a two-chamber legislature. In 1980 American Samoans were allowed, for the first time, to elect a delegate to serve in the US House of Representatives. However, this delegate doesn't have any voting rights in the house.

Recent Decades

In January 1987 the territory was hit by Cyclone Tusi, one of the worst storms in recorded history. The Manu'a Islands were particularly hard hit. Several more cyclones ploughed through the area between 1990 and 2009. Then, most of Tutuila (but particularly the south and west coasts) were pummelled by a massive tsunami approximately eight minutes after an offshore earthquake (see p286); there was no warning.

Even in early 2012 damage from the tsunami could be seen everywhere, and some people in villages around Leone Bay were still living in tents. Houses built by FEMA (the US Federal Emergency Management Agency) were often just shells without plumbing, kitchens or appliances, so other people were (and probably still are) essentially camping in concrete boxes. While Samoa next door received funds from around the world and cleaned up the mess rather quickly, it seems Uncle Sam wasn't as efficient. Many villages around the island look not unlike a war zone.

While American Samoa relies heavily on funding from the US Government, the relationship isn't as one-sided as it seems. Many a US sports team would be in a much poorer state without their Samoan players. American Samoans are very loyal to the US and many serve in the US military.

The Culture

More than most Polynesian peoples, Samoans have maintained their traditional way of life in their sauna of a climate, and still closely follow the social hierarchies, customs and courtesies established long before the arrival of Europeans.

For a profile of the Samoan psyche and a description of the Samoan lifestyle, see the cultural detail provided in the Samoa chapter (p285).

Population

Most of the 63,500-strong population live on the main island of Tutuila. The birth rate is high but this is offset by emigration to Hawai'i and the US mainland. Some 1500 foreigners reside in American Samoa, most of whom are Koreans or Chinese involved in the tuna or garment industries. About one-third are *palagi* (Westerners), many of whom hold government jobs, usually in the teaching or health fields.

Language

See the Language chapter on p591 for basic words and phrases.

Arts

American Samoa shares its artistic traditions with Samoa, from the energetic song-and-dance routines called *fiafia* and the satirisation of their elders by village youth in the skit-based *Faleaitu* (meaning 'House of Spirits'), to the breezy architecture of the *fale,* intricate tattoos (p307), and the lovely *siapo* (bark cloth) and *ie toga* (fine mats) used in customary gift exchanges. For more on these, see the Arts section of the Samoa chapter (p287).

Environment

Geography

American Samoa has a total land area of 197 sq km. The main island, Tutuila, is 30km long and up to 6km wide. The Manu'a

group, 100km east of Tutuila, consists of the islands of Ta'u, Ofu and Olosega, all wildly steep volcanic remnants.

The easternmost part of the territory is tiny Rose Atoll, two minuscule specks of land (plus a surrounding reef) that were declared a Marine National Monument in 2009. This special recognition by the US Government helps to protect the green turtle, as well as the extremely rare hawksbill turtle. Only scientific research expeditions are currently allowed to visit the atoll.

Equally tiny Swains Island is situated 350km north-northwest of Tutuila and consists of a 3.25-sq-km ring of land surrounding a brackish lagoon. Both culturally and geographically it belongs to Tokelau, but in 1925 the island's owner, the Jennings family, persuaded the US to annex it.

Ecology

The wild inhabitants of American Samoa includes two species of flying fox, *pili* (skinks), *mo'o* (geckos) and the harmless *gata* (Pacific boa), which is found only on Ta'u. The surrounding waters are home to pilot whales, dolphins and porpoises, while hawksbill turtles occasionally breed on remote beaches. Bird species include the nearly flightless banded rail, the barn owl and the superb *sega* (blue-crowned lory). While walking in rainforests, listen for the haunting calls of the rare multicoloured fruit doves (only 50 survive on Tutuila) and the beautiful green-and-white Pacific pigeons.

Tutuila is characterised by its broadleaf evergreen rainforest. Ofu, Olosega and Ta'u host temperate forest vegetation such as tree ferns, grasses, wild coleus and epiphytic plants.

SURVIVAL GUIDE

Directory A–Z

Accommodation

Fale accommodation for tourists has never quite caught on in American Samoa. Instead, beds are almost all found in generic motels, hotels and a handful of B&Bs.

The National Park of American Samoa operates a village homestay program; for details, see p306.

The sleeping options in this chapter are listed according to author preference and unless otherwise stated tax is included in the price. The following price ranges refer to a double room with bathroom:

$ less than US$100

$$ US$100–150

$$$ more than US$150

Business Hours

We don't give opening hours for establishments mentioned in the text unless they differ greatly from the following standards:

Banks 9am to 4pm Monday to Friday, some open 8.30am to 12.30pm Saturday

Bars noon to midnight.

Government offices 9am to 5pm Monday to Friday.

Restaurants 8am to 4pm and 6pm to 10pm.

Shops 8am to 4.30pm Monday to Friday, 8am to noon Saturday (village stores keep longer hours).

Embassies & Consulates

All American Samoan diplomatic affairs are handled by the US. There are no consulates or embassies in American Samoa and no places that are able to issue visas for the US.

Festivals & Events

Flag Day (17 April) American Samoa's main public holiday commemorates the raising of the US flag over the islands in 1900 with an arts festival and much traditional fanfare.

Tisa's Tattoo Festival Held in October, at Tisa's Barefoot Bar on Tutuila. The inaugural version took place in 2005.

White Sunday Also in October (on the second Sunday of the month), when kids get to celebrate being kids.

Moso'oi Festival A week of sporting and cultural events during the last week of October.

Food

The following price ranges refer to a standard main course.

$ less than US$10

$$ US$10–20

$$$ more than US$20

Internet Access

Many hotels and guesthouses offer internet access and wi-fi and there are a few internet

cafes. See p306 for the best-value wi-fi connection options via hotspot.

Internet Resources

American Samoa Historic Preservation Office (www.ashpo.org) This site includes information on Samoa's history and a good walking tour.

Busy Corner (http://amsamoa-busycorner. blogspot.com) Online magazine highlighting culture.

Lonely Planet (www.lonelyplanet.com/amer ican-samoa) For planning advice, author recommendations, traveller reviews and insider tips.

National Park of American Samoa (www. nps.gov/npsa) This excellent site has infor- mation on the park's homestay program, and local flora and fauna.

Office of Tourism (www.amsamoa.com)

Samoa News (www.samoanews.com) For the latest American Samoan news.

Maps

The maps in this book should be sufficient for navigating around the islands. The tour- ism and national park offices (p306) both produce free brochures with maps included, but they're less detailed.

Money

The US dollar, divided into 100 cents, is the unit of currency in use in American Samoa. In this chapter, unless otherwise stated, all prices given are in US dollars.

ATMs Provided by the ANZ Amerika Samoa Bank and the Bank of Hawai'i on Tutuila.

Tipping Not expected or encouraged in American Samoa. It is, however, deemed acceptable for exceptional service at finer restaurants.

Telephone

ASTCA (American Samoa Telecommunications Authority; ☑633 1121; Fagatogo) runs the terri- tory's telephone services. It has a large office in Pago Pago with banks of phones available.

A cheaper option for international calls is the Toa Com prepay cards, which allow you to call from any landline (local call rates ap- ply) via an internet-based service. Toa Com charges 7c per minute to the US and 10c per minute to the UK or NZ.

Mobile Phones You can hire phones or buy SIM cards for use in GSM 900-com- patible phones from **Blue Sky Commu- nications** (☑699 2759; www.blueskynet.as; Tafuna; ☺8am-5pm Mon-Fri, 9am-2pm Sat).

Time

The local time in American Samoa is Green- wich Mean Time/Coordinated Universal Time (GMT/UTC) minus 11 hours. There- fore, when it's noon in American Samoa, it's 11pm the same day in London, 3pm the same day in Los Angeles, 9am the following day in Sydney and, by complete lack of logic, 1pm the following day in Apia.

Visas

US citizens equipped with a valid passport and an onward ticket can visit American Samoa visa-free. Nationals of the following countries equipped with a passport (valid for at least 60 days) and an onward ticket will receive a free one-month visa on arrival: Australia, New Zealand and UK. Nationals of all other countries must apply in advance for their one-month visa (US$40).

Visa extensions are handled by the **Immi- gration Office** (Map p304; ☑633 4203; ground fl, Executive Office Bldg, Utulei; ☺8am-4pm Mon- Fri), located within the government building in Pago Pago. Visas can only be extended by one month; the fee for this varies depending on what country you hail from.

Getting There & Away

Air

There's no better illustration of the physical isolation of American Samoa than the fact that you can only fly directly to Tutuila from Samoa and Hawai'i.

All flights land at Tafuna International Airport, 15km southwest of Pago Pago Har- bor. Following are the airlines that service American Samoa (telephone numbers listed here are for dialling from within American Samoa). They all have offices at the airport. At the time of writing, America West Air- lines was considering starting services to American Samoa.

Hawaiian Airlines (airline code HA; ☑699 1875; www.hawaiianair.com) Flies twice a week to/from Honolulu; return fare from US$1373.

Inter Island Airways (airline code IIA; ☑699 7100; www.interislandair.com) Two daily

flights to/from Samoa; return fares from US$182.

Polynesian Airlines (airline code PH; ✈699 9126; www.polynesianairlines.com) Flies to/from Samoa three to five times a day.

Sea

FERRY

A car ferry/cargo ship called MV *Lady Naomi* runs between Pago Pago and Apia once a week. It departs Pago Pago each Thursday at 4pm for the seven-hour trip. Return deck fares are US$65; return cabin fares are US$130. Tickets must be purchased at least one day in advance from **Polynesia Shipping Services** (Map p304; www.samoashipping.com; ✆633 1211; Pago Pago).

YACHT

During the region's dry (and cyclone-free) season between May and October, yachts cruise all around the South Pacific. Pago Pago's deep, spectacular harbour serves as the official entry point for private yacht owners.

All yachts and boats are required to contact the Harbour Master before entering American Samoan waters on VHF channel 16, and permission from Pago Pago is needed to sail to other islands in the country. Yachts should be granted anchorage from US$7.50 per month in the harbour. Vessels arriving from Hawai'i will need to present a US customs clearance document from Honolulu.

Getting Around

Air

Inter Island Airways (✆in Tutuila 699 7100, in Ofu 655 7100, in Ta'u 677 7100; www.interislandair.com) flies the 30-minute air route from Tutuila to Ta'u.

Bicycle

Tutuila is not very conducive to a cycling tour. The island is mountainous, traffic can be heavy, and a complete circuit is impossible since there are no roads across the rugged north coast. Dogs can also be a major hassle here.

Boat

See individual islands for details.

Bus

Villages and towns on the island of Tutuila are serviced by '*aiga*-owned buses. The vehicles – modified pick-up trucks with deadly sound systems – theoretically run until early evening, but don't try to test this theory after 2pm on Saturday, or on Sunday at any time. All buses display the name of their final destination in the front window. To stop a bus, wave your hand and arm, palm down, as the bus approaches. To signal that you'd like to get off the bus, either knock on the ceiling or clap loudly. Pay the fare to the driver; try to have the exact fare.

Details of routes and fares are given on p307.

Car

Hiring a car allows you to explore Tutuila quickly and comfortably via the island's good sealed roads. That said, complete reliance on a hire car will rob you of the unique cultural experiences that can be gained on public transport.

When hiring a vehicle, check for any damage or scratches before you get into the car and note everything on the rental agreement, lest you be held liable for damage when the car is returned. For details of car-hire firms on Tutuila, see p308.

Vehicles drive on the right-hand side of the road. The speed limit is 40km/h (25mph) island-wide. A valid foreign driving licence should allow you to drive in American Samoa, though you can always get yourself an international driving licence to be absolutely certain.

INSURANCE

It's essential to have your hire car covered by insurance as repair costs are extremely high. Several local car-hire firms offer contracts where there's no option of accepting a CDW (collision/damage waiver). The lack of a CDW technically means that the car hirer is liable for *all* costs resulting from an accident, regardless of whose fault it is, so sign such contracts at your peril. You should insist on a CDW, for which you pay an extra fee of around US$10 per day.

Taxi

Taxis on Tutuila are expensive and are only convenient for short trips.

Solomon Islands

Best Historical Sites

» US War Memorial (p321)
» Mt Austen (p326)
» Vilu Open-Air Museum (p327)
» Skull Island (p333)

Best Places to Stay

» Tavanipupu Private Island Resort (p331)
» Tetepare Island (p335)
» Uepi Island Resort (p330)
» Sanbis Resort (p336)
» Oravae Cottage (p335)

Why Go?

For those seeking an authentic Melanesian experience or an off-the-beaten-track destination, the Solomons are hard to beat. From WWII relics scattered in the jungle to leaf-hut villages where traditional culture is alive, there's so much on offer. Then there's the visual appeal, with scenery reminiscent of a Discovery Channel documentary: volcanic islands that jut up dramatically from the cobalt-blue ocean, croc-infested mangroves, huge lagoons, tropical islets and emerald forests.

Don't expect white-sand beaches, ritzy resorts and wild nightlife – the Solomon Islands is not a beach-holiday destination. With only a smattering of traditional guesthouses and comfortable hideaways, it's tailor-made for ecotourists. For outdoorsy types, lots of action-packed experiences can easily be organised: climb an extinct volcano, surf uncrowded waves, snorkel pristine reefs or kayak across a lagoon. Beneath the ocean's surface, unbeatable diving adventures await.

The best part is, there'll be no crowds to mar the experience.

When to Go

Honiara

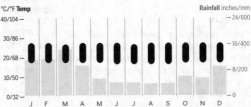

°C/°F Temp — 40/104, 30/86, 20/68, 10/50, 0/32
Rainfall inches/mm — 24/600, 16/400, 8/200, 0
J F M A M J J A S O N D

Dec–Mar Intervals of calm weather broken by storms makes for good reef breaks and diving.

Jun–Sep Mild weather (but rough seas); good for hiking, less ideal for diving. Great festivity time.

Apr–May & Oct–Nov The shoulder seasons are relatively dry and aren't a bad time to visit.

Connections

Solomon Airlines' domestic wing offers scheduled flights to about 20 airstrips throughout the archipelago. Honiara is the main hub. From the capital there are frequent flights to the main tourist gateways, including Seghe, Munda and Gizo.

There are regular passenger boat services between Honiara and Auki (Malaita). There's also a scheduled weekly service between Honiara and Gizo (via Marovo), but it's more erratic.

ITINERARIES

One Week

Go west! Skip Guadalcanal and the nearby islands (Savo and Tulagi) in favour of Marovo Lagoon, Munda and Gizo – the three unmissable destinations in 'the West'. Thanks to reliable interisland boat and plane services, they can easily be combined. That said, you won't cover more than two destinations in a week – Munda and Gizo are the easiest to tackle.

Two Weeks

Split your time between three provinces – Guadalcanal, Central Province and Western Province. Devote three days to Guadalcanal (four days if you're a diver), then catch a boat to Savo or Tulagi and settle in for a couple of days of relaxation. Grab a flight to Gatokae or Seghe for a few days of exploring Marovo Lagoon. Afterwards, fly to Gizo where two days can easily be spent messing around in and on the water. You might also make time for a hike on Kolombangara.

Three Weeks

Stretch the two-week itinerary into a saner 16 days. Use the extra time for a stay at Munda, which offers great diving options and excellent day tours to some must-see WWII relics, or book a back-to-nature trip to Tetepare Island. Fly back to Honiara and catch a boat to Malaita where you can chill out in Langa Langa Lagoon. Or you could round out your trip with a romantic stay at Tavanipupu Private Island Resort on Guadalcanal.

Resources

» **Solomon Islands Visitor Bureau** (www.visitsolomons.com.sb) Official tourism site with oodles of information about activities, accommodation and services.

» **Welkam Solomons** (www.welkamsolomons.com) Packed with loads of useful information about hotels, cultural sites, transport, history and activities.

» **Solomons Travel Portal** (www.solomonislands-hotels.travel) Has a wealth of information on accommodation, with online bookings, as well as other practical information for visitors.

SOLOMON ISLANDS

AT A GLANCE

» **Currency** Solomon Islands dollar (S$)

» **Language** Solomon Islands Pijin

» **Mobile phones** Local SIM cards are available and can be used with unlocked GSM phones.

» **Money** A few ATMs in major urban centres.

» **Visas** Not required for most Western countries for stays of up to one month.

Fast Facts

» **Capital** Honiara
» **Country code** ☑677
» **Emergency** ☑999
» **Land area** 27,540 sq km
» **Population** 538,000

Exchange Rates

Australia	A$1	S$7.00
Canada	C$1	S$6.80
Euro	€1	S$8.70
Japan	¥100	S$8.80
New Zealand	NZ$1	S$5.50
UK	UK£1	S$10.90
USA	US$1	S$6.95

For current exchange rates see www.xe.com.

Set Your Budget

» **Twin room in a resort** S$1200

» **Two-course evening meal** S$180

» **Ticket Honiara–Gizo (one-way)** S$1380

» **Two-tank dive** S$1300

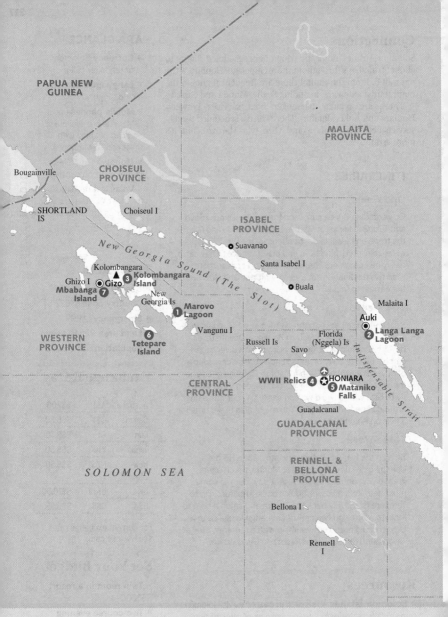

Solomon Islands Highlights

1 Diving and snorkelling in fish soup in **Marovo Lagoon** (p328)

2 Feeling free in an intimate lodge at **Langa Langa Lagoon** (p340)

3 Huffing to the top of the mount on **Kolombangara Island** (p336)

4 Spending the day spotting rusty **WWII relics** around Honiara (p326)

5 Taking a dip in a natural pool at **Mataniko Falls** (p327)

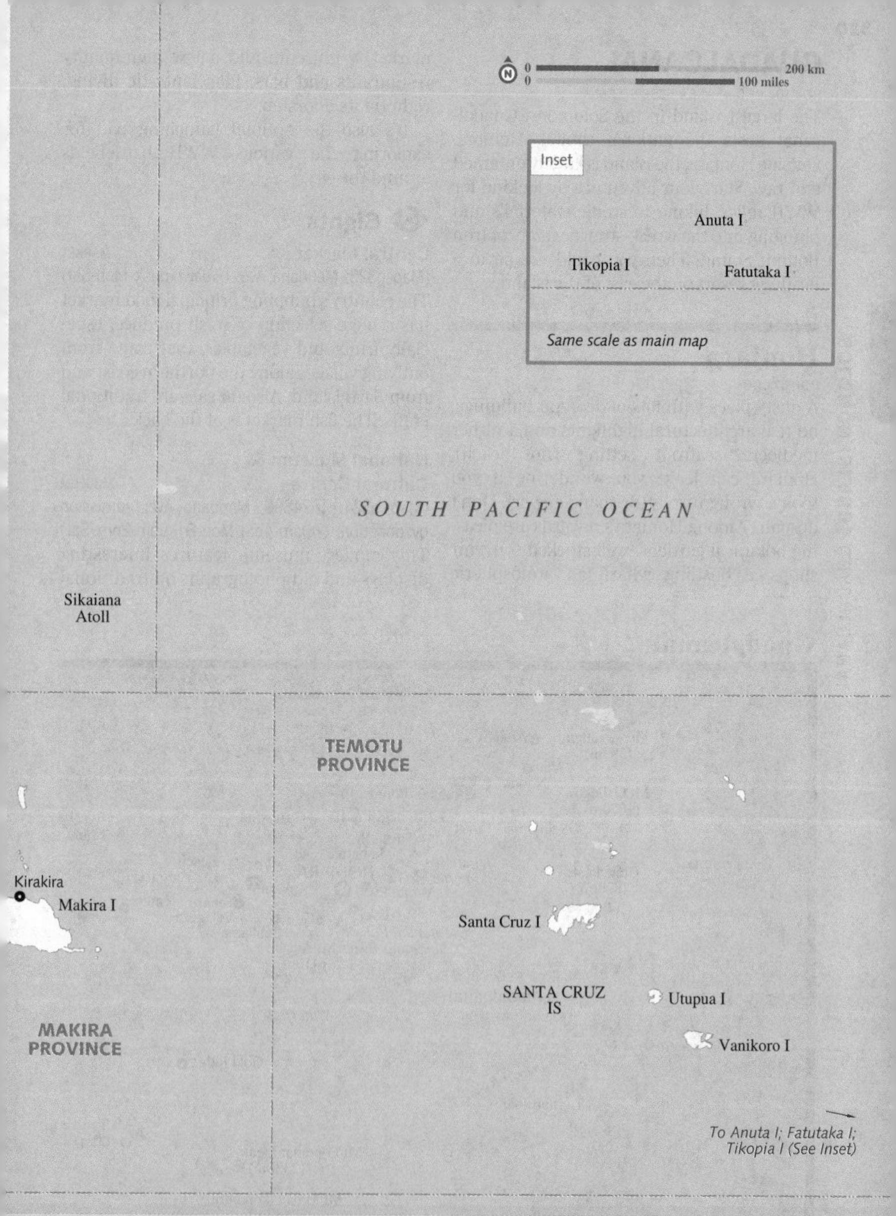

Inset

Anuta I

Tikopia I   Fatutaka I

Same scale as main map

SOUTH PACIFIC OCEAN

Sikaiana
Atoll

TEMOTU
PROVINCE

Kirakira
Makira I

Santa Cruz I

SANTA CRUZ   Utupua I
IS
                  Vanikoro I

MAKIRA
PROVINCE

*To Anuta I; Fatutaka I;
Tikopia I (See Inset)*

6 Assisting rangers   **7** Chilling out at a
in tagging marine turtles   laid-back resort on
on ecofriendly **Tetepare**   **Mbabanga Island** (p336)
Island (p335)

GUADALCANAL

POP 104,000 / AREA 5336 SQ KM

The largest island in the Solomons, Guadalcanal hosts the national capital, Honiara. Outside Honiara, the island is largely untamed and raw. Start your adventure by looking for WWII relics, hiking to scenic waterfalls and plunging into the wreck-strewn waters of Iron Bottom Sound. Then you could escape to a far-flung resort on the east of the island.

Honiara

POP 57,000

A dusty place with lots of decrepit buildings, no real architectural highlights and a rather mediocre seafront setting (no beach), Honiara can leave you wondering if you took a wrong turn at Brisbane airport. Don't despair! Among Honiara's rewards are pleasing botanical gardens, well-stocked souvenir shops, a bustling wharf, an atmospheric market, a museum and a few high-quality restaurants and bars. Plus fantastic diving, right on its doorstep.

It's also the optimal launching pad for exploring the various WWII battlefields around the city.

◉ Sights

Central Market MARKET
(Map p323; Mendana Ave; ◷dawn-dusk Mon-Sat) The country's bubbling principal food market has a huge selection of fresh produce, especially fruits and vegetables, that come from outlying villages along the northern coast and from Savo island. Also on sale are traditional crafts. The fish market is at the back.

**National Museum &
Cultural Centre** MUSEUM
(Map p324; ☑24896; Mendana Ave; admission by donation; ◷9am-4pm Mon-Fri, 9am-2pm Sat) This modest museum features interesting displays and old photographs on traditional

Guadalcanal

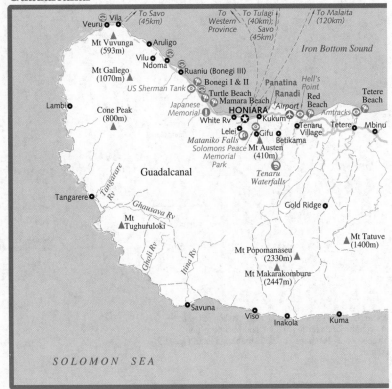

National Parliament — PUBLIC BUILDING
(Map p324; Lower Vayvaya Rd; ☺8am-4pm Mon-Fri) The conical-shaped concrete building that's perched on the hill above Hibiscus Ave is the National Parliament. Inside, the dome boasts a rich tapestry of traditional art, including arching frescoes.

US War Memorial — HISTORIC SITE
(Map p323) Skyline Dr has commanding views over the town and leads to the US War Memorial, a steep 30-minute walk up from Mendana Ave. The compound has marble slabs bearing detailed descriptions of battles fought during the Guadalcanal campaign.

Botanical Gardens — GARDENS
(Map p323; ☎24032; Lenggakiki; admission by donation; ☺8am-4.30pm) These lovely grounds on the hills located above the city provide a green haven for nature lovers.

🏃 Activities

Diving is Honiara's trump card, with a fantastic collection of WWII wrecks lying offshore in an area known as Iron Bottom Sound, including Bonegi I & II to the west, and the *John Penn* to the east. See p35 for more information on diving.

Tulagi Dive — DIVING, SNORKELLING
(off Map p323; ☎7475043, 26589; www.tulagidive.com.sb) This highly professional dive shop based in White River is run by Australian Neil Yates, who adheres to strict safety procedures for deep dives. Prices start at S$250 for a shore dive. He organises day trips to Florida Islands (S$1100 including two dives and lunch) and snorkel trips (S$150). Gear hire is S$550 per day.

🛌 Sleeping

Honiara is expensive and, excepting a few basic guesthouses, hotels catering mainly to business people dominate the market.

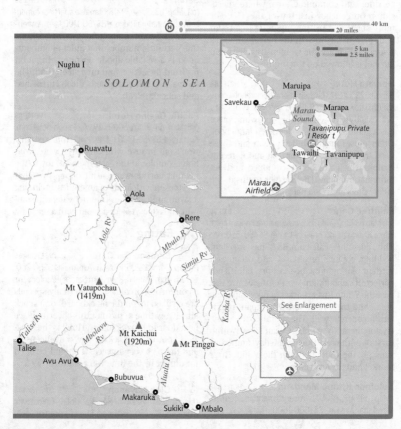

Heritage Park Hotel
HOTEL $$$

(Map p324; ☑24007; www.heritageparkhotel.com. sb; Mendana Ave; d S$2200-2400; ❄@🛜⛱) By some degree the fanciest big hotel in the Solomons, this hotel and conference centre is where you'll find the richest businesspeople and international consultants. It's right in the centre and on the waterfront. Nearly all the small but tastefully designed rooms have a sea view and a sunny balcony; angle for one on the upper floors for the most privacy and best views. Heritage Park offers plenty of amenities, including two restaurants, two bars, a small pool and a disco.

Chester Resthouse
GUESTHOUSE $

(Map p324; ☑26355; mbhches@solomon.com.sb; Lower Vayvaya Rd; r with shared/private bathroom S$220/500) This budget set-up is popular with travellers and local families because it's spitting distance from the action. In the older wing, fan-cooled rooms are tiny and lack privacy (windows open right onto the corridor and communal area, where guests slump on couches in front of the TV). For more space and privacy, upgrade to a room with private facilities in the newer wing. It's also a safe choice for women travellers. No alcohol is allowed on the premises.

Honiara Hotel
HOTEL $$

(Map p323; ☑21737; reservation@honiarahotel.com. sb; Chinatown; d S$750-1900; ❄🛜⛱) While it's not exactly city central, this sprawling place has a genuine ace up its sleeve – a large pool. Other pluses include a bar, a gym and three good restaurants. Go for the more recent rooms, which are better equipped and get more natural light. The cheaper rooms in the older wings aren't such a good deal.

Raintree Café
B&B $$

(off Map p323; ☑7444383; www.raintreehoniara.com; White River; s/d incl breakfast from S$450/550; 🛜) This fair-value cafe-cum-B&B has excellent bedding, copious breakfasts, and occupies a verdant plot right by the seashore, but it's not perfect: it's about 3km west of the centre just past the White River market (a not-so-inviting area), and the Orchid and Frangipani rooms face a concrete wall. The moral of the story: try for the aptly named Ocean View, within earshot of the sea. During the day, numerous vans ply the route between the White River market and the city centre.

Solomon Kitano Mendana
HOTEL $$$

(Map p324; ☑20071; reserv@mendana.com.sb; Mendana Ave; d S$1000-1600; ❄🛜⛱) The Mendana scores high on amenities, with two restaurants, a bar, an airy foyer and a small pool. All rooms have undergone a major renovation in 2011 and 2012 and are equipped to a high standard, so you can expect bright interiors, modern furnishings and prim bathrooms. Be sure to ask for a room with a sea view.

King Solomon
HOTEL $$$

(Map p324; ☑21205; www.kingsolomonhotel.info; Hibiscus Ave; d S$800-1300; ❄🛜⛱) Anchored on a steep hill with a kinky funicular that shunts people between the rooms and the reception area, this longstanding venture features a variety of spacious units scattered amid beautifully landscaped grounds and boasts a stress-melting swimming pool built into the hill. Most bungalows are self-contained. Not all rooms have an ocean view. Compared with its competitors, the 'King Sol' has a more laid-back feel. Avoid the onsite restaurant and instead head to Bamboo Bar Cafe next door.

Sanalae
APARTMENTS $$

(off Map p323; ☑39218; sanalae.apart@solomon. com.sb; Panatina Ridge; r S$750-1100; 🛜) A well-guarded secret among long-term visitors, this pert little number in a quiet neighbourhood is a reliable abode despite being a bit far from the action and up a steep road. The rooms are self-contained, nicely furnished and squeaky clean.

Pacific Casino Hotel
HOTEL $$

(off Map p323; ☑25009; www.solomon-hotel.com; Kukum; d S$750-1300; ❄@🛜⛱) You certainly won't fall in love with this large waterfront hotel complex at the eastern end of town (the neon-lit corridors are a bit oppressive), but it's stocked with loads of amenities, including a swimming pool, an internet cafe, a restaurant and a bar. Ask for a room with a sea view.

✕ Eating

TOP CHOICE Bamboo Bar Cafe
CAFETERIA $$

(Map p324; ☑21205; Hibiscus Ave; mains S$50-200; ⊙7am-4pm Mon-Fri, 8am-2pm Sat; 🛜) Perfect for a comforting breakfast, lunch (daily specials are chalked up on the blackboard) or a snack attack any time of the day, this cheerful place next door to King Solomon Hotel is the snazziest spot in town. Good news: it's licensed, and there's a cosy terrace. It should be open for dinner by the time you read this.

TOP CHOICE Club Havanah
FRENCH $$$

(Map p323; ☑21737; Honiara Hotel, Chinatown; mains S$180-350; ⊙dinner) The G-spot for local

Greater Honiara

gourmands. Georges, the adept French chef, is a true alchemist, judging from the ambitious *confit de canard maison* (duck cooked and preserved in its own fat). Leave room for the decadent *marquise aux deux chocolats* (white and black chocolate mousse). Next to the pool, a cheaper alternative is the **Oasis Restaurant** (mains S$75-270; ☺breakfast, lunch & dinner). The Sunday 'Buffet Roast Night' (S$180) is a steal. Honiara Hotel's third restaurant, **Mandarin** (mains S$70-150; ☺dinner) is well known for its mile-long menu featuring excellent Chinese dishes.

Lime Lounge
CAFETERIA $

(Map p324; ☎23064; off Mendana Ave; mains S$40-90; ☺7am-5pm Mon-Fri, 8am-3pm Sat, 9am-3pm Sun; ☎) Funky little Lime Lounge is popular with expats. There's everything from satisfying breakfasts to palate-pleasing salads, well-made sandwiches and yummy pastries. No view and no terrace, but the walls are adorned with paintings by local artists, which gives the place a splash of style.

Raintree Café
CAFETERIA $$

(off Map p323; ☎7444383; www.raintreehoniara. com; White River; mains S$60-220; ☺7am-9.30pm; ☎) A very relaxing spot. Picture a lovely waterfront location, ample views of Savo, and organic food with vegetarian options. It also

Greater Honiara

◎ Sights
1 Botanical Gardens	A2
2 Central Market	D2
3 US War Memorial	C3

⊟ Sleeping
4 Honiara Hotel	D3

✕ Eating
Club Havanah	(see 4)
Mandarin	(see 4)
Oasis Restaurant	(see 4)

ⓘ Information
5 Police Headquarters	A1

offers lovely tea, coffee and juices, though it's a shame the service is so slow. It's in White River, about 3km west of the centre.

Hakubai
JAPANESE $$

(Map p324; ☎20071; Solomon Kitano Mendana Hotel, Mendana Ave; mains S$90-300; ☺lunch & dinner) If you have a sashimi or yakitori craving that must be met, head to Hakubai inside the Mendana Hotel for authentic Japanese food. Next door, the **Capitana** (mains S$90-250; ☺lunch & dinner) serves classic Western dishes and boasts a terrace overlooking the sea.

Central Honiara

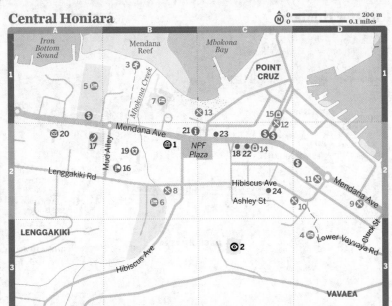

Central Honiara

◎ Sights
1 National Museum & Cultural
Centre...B2
2 National Parliament C3

☺ Activities, Courses & Tours
3 Extreme Adventures B1

🛏 Sleeping
4 Chester Resthouse..............................D3
5 Heritage Park Hotel............................A1
6 King Solomon.....................................B2
7 Solomon Kitano Mendana B1

✕ Eating
8 Bamboo Bar Cafe B2
Capitana...(see 7)
9 Frangipani Ice D2
Hakubai...(see 7)
10 Hong Kong Palace D2
11 Honiara Hot Bread Kitchen..................D2
12 Lime Lounge C2
13 Point Cruz Yacht Club..........................C1

🍸 Drinking
Bamboo Bar Cafe ....(see 8)
Lime Lounge ....(see 12)

✪ Entertainment
Club Xtreme...................................(see 5)

🛍 Shopping
14 King Solomon's Handicraft C2
15 Melanesian Handicrafts.......................C1

ℹ Information
16 Australian High Commission B2
17 Our Telekom..A2
18 Point Cruz Chemist.............................C2
19 Police Station B2
20 Post Office (Solomon Post) A2
21 Solomon Islands Visitors
Bureau (SIVB) B2

ℹ Transport
22 Guadalcanal Travel Services
(GTS)..C2
MV 360 Discovery.......................(see 14)
23 MV Lady Wakehurst............................C2
MV Pelican Express....................(see 15)
24 Solomon Airlines C2

Point Cruz Yacht Club FISH & CHIPS **$$**
(Map p324; 22500; Mendana Ave; mains S$60-90; ☺lunch & dinner) Frequented by crusty expats and yachties, the ageing Point Cruz Yacht Club is an interesting place to enjoy a cold Solbrew and well-prepared fish and chips. It's nothing fancy (think plastic chairs) and the choice is limited, but sizzling-hot value for what you get. There's a member fee of S$30, of which S$20 is deducted from your meal.

Ocean View Restaurant INTERNATIONAL **$$**
(off Map p323; 25009; Pacific Casino Hotel, Kukum; mains S$100-250; ☺breakfast, lunch & dinner) The big dining room lacks character, but the seafront terrace is inviting, with great views north over the Florida Islands. Pizzas, meat dishes and seafood feature prominently on the menu.

Hong Kong Palace CHINESE **$**
(Map p324; 23338; Hibiscus Ave; mains S$50-300; ☺lunch & dinner) For comforting Chinese fare, head to this unmissable blood-red pagoda on Hibiscus Ave.

Frangipani Ice ICE CREAM **$**
(Map p324; Mendana Ave; ice cream from S$4; ☺8am-6pm) This ice-cream parlour is very popular with locals.

Honiara Hot Bread Kitchen BAKERY **$**
(Map p324; Mendana Ave; ☺6am-7pm) Has freshly baked bread and buns. Come early; by 10am the buns are sold out.

Drinking & Entertainment

If you've just arrived in the Solomon Islands, you'll find the bar scene pretty dull in Honiara. But those who've just arrived from several weeks in the provinces will feel like they're in Ibiza.

Check out the bars at Honiara's top-end hotels, which are popular and often offer live entertainment once or twice a week – bamboo bands, Micronesian hula dancers and karaoke. For a fruit juice or a cuppa, head to Lime Lounge (p323) or Raintree Café (p323). Bamboo Bar Cafe (p322) is another mellow spot and, joy of joys, it's licensed.

Honiara's sole decent club is the elegant **Club Xtreme** (Map p324; ☺Wed-Sat), inside Heritage Park Hotel.

🔒 Shopping

There are a few prominent stores with better-than-average crafts on and around the main

drag, including **Melanesian Handicrafts** (Map p324; 22189; Point Cruz) and **King Solomon's Handicraft** (Map p324; Mendana Ave). It's also worth considering the gift shops at top-end hotels, as well as the shop at the National Museum (p320).

❶ Information

Dangers & Annoyances

Be sure to use your common sense and avoid walking alone in deserted streets. Beware of pickpockets at the market and in crowded areas. At night, take a taxi.

Internet Access

You'll find a few internet cafes in the NPF Plaza building. There's a small internet outlet at the post office, too. Rates average S$20 per hour. The Pacific Casino Hotel and the Heritage Park Hotel also offer internet access. Wi-fi is available at most hotels as well as at the Lime Lounge, Raintree Café and Bamboo Bar Cafe.

Medical Services

National Referral Hospital (off Map p323; 23600; Kukum)

Point Cruz Chemist (Map p324; 22911; Mendana Ave; ☺8am-5pm Mon-Fri, to 1pm Sat) A well-stocked pharmacy.

Money

You'll find a dozen or so 24-hour ATMs in the centre. There's a small bureau de change at the airport.

ANZ (Map p324; Mendana Ave; ☺9am-4pm Mon-Fri) Changes all major currencies. Has an ATM inside. Other ATMs are located outside the post office and next door to Lime Lounge.

Bank South Pacific (Map p324; BSP; Mendana Ave; ☺8.30am-3pm Mon-Fri) Changes all major currencies and has ATMs. Other ATMs are in the main BSP office near Heritage Park Hotel and beside the reception at Heritage Park Hotel.

Westpac (Map p324; Mendana Ave; ☺9am-4pm Mon-Fri) Changes all major currencies except euros. Has an ATM. Another ATM is outside the Our Telekom office.

Post

Solomon Post (Map p324; Mendana Ave; ☺8am-4.30pm Mon-Fri, 8am-noon Sat) Also houses a Western Union counter and a small internet cafe.

Telephone

Our Telekom (Map p324; Mendana Ave; ☺8.30am-4.30pm Mon-Fri, 9am-noon Sat) Next to the post office. Sells prepaid phonecards, Bumblebee cards (for wi-fi access) and prepaid mobile phonecards.

Tourist Information

Solomon Islands Visitors Bureau (SIVB; Map p324; ☑22442; www.visitsolomons.com.sb; Mendana Ave; ☺8am-4.30pm Mon-Fri) There's little printed material, but staff can provide advice and contact isolated lodges and villages (by two-way radio) to make bookings. Also sells a useful map of the country.

ⓘ Getting There & Away

Air

International flights land at Honiara's Henderson Airport, and all domestic routes begin and end in Honiara. See p345 for details of international flights. **Guadalcanal Travel Services** (GTS; Map p324; ☑22586; guadtrav@solomon.com. sb; Mendana Ave; ☺8am-4.30pm Mon-Fri, 9am-noon Sat) represents most international and regional airlines. From Honiara, **Solomon Airlines** (Map p324; ☑23562, 20031; www. flysolomons.com; Hibiscus Ave; ☺8am-4pm Mon-Fri, 8.30-11.30am Sat) flies to most islands in the country.

Boat

The passenger boat **MV Pelican Express** (Map p324; ☑28104) offers a weekly service between Honiara and Gizo via Marovo Lagoon (Seghe and Mbunikalo). The 12-hour Honiara–Gizo trip costs S$600. It generally plies this route on Sunday (return on Monday); check while you're there. The office is next door to Lime Lounge. The passenger boat **MV 360 Discovery** (Map p324; ☑20957, 7442802; City Centre Bldg) operates daily between Honiara and Auki (S$220 one-way, three to four hours); four days a week it makes a stop at Tulagi (S$160). The **MV Lady Wakehurst** (Map p324; ☑7592006; Solomon Motors, Mendana Ave) also travels between Honiara and Auki (S$150, five to six hours, twice weekly).

Island hopping on the cargo boats that sail between Guadalcanal, Malaita and the Western Province is an adventurous and inexpensive way to travel. Departure times and dates are unscheduled and the best way to find out what's available is to ask around at the docks. Try the **Kosco**, which runs between Honiara and the Western Province.

ⓘ GETTING AROUND THE NORTH COAST

Exploring the north coast by public transport is feasible, but it's not really convenient. Most sights are not signed and are not easy to find. We suggest hiring a taxi in Honiara; count on S$100 per hour.

ⓘ Getting Around

From the airport, the standard taxi fare into town is S$100.

Honiara's minibuses are cheap, frequent (in daylight hours) and safe. The flat S$3 fare will take you anywhere on the route, which is written on a placard behind the windscreen of the bus.

There are taxis everywhere in Honiara. They don't have meters, so agree on a fare before hopping in – S$10 per kilometre is reasonable.

Rental cars can be arranged through the Pacific Casino Hotel.

East of Honiara

One of the star attractions in Honiara's hinterlands is **Mataniko Falls**, which features a spectacular thundering of water down a cliff straight into a canyon below (see p327).

The road to Mt Austen begins in Kukum and climbs up to the historical sites where Japanese troops doggedly resisted the US advance. The **Solomons Peace Memorial Park**, about 3.5km from the main coastal road, was built by Japanese war veterans in 1981 to commemorate all who died in the WWII Guadalcanal campaign. Further south you'll go past the **Gifu**, named after a Japanese district by its wartime Japanese defenders, before reaching the summit of **Mt Austen** (410m). A dirt track leads to a former **Japanese Observation Point**. Americans in WWII dubbed this spot 'grassy knoll'. There's a plaque that explains the strategic importance of Mt Austen during WWII.

About 6.5km from Honiara is the turnoff south to the **Betikama SDA Mission**. The sprawling property comprises a large handicraft shop and a small **museum** (S$25) with an outdoor collection of WWII debris.

A memorial at **Henderson Airport** honours US forces and their Pacific islander allies. About 100m to the west of the terminal is the scaffold-style **US WWII control tower**.

About 4km past the airport is a marble monument on a private property near a deserted black-sand beach at **Hell's Point**. The Japanese Colonel Kiyono Ichiki and his 800 men 'died with courage' here on 20 August 1942 after a banzai attack from the eastern side of the creek against US machine guns and artillery on its western bank.

A few hundred metres further east, a road heads inland and follows the west bank of the Tenaru River. After 1.5km you'll come to Marine Hospital No 8, the first wartime hospital in Guadalcanal, in **Tenaru Village**.

Tenaru is the launching pad for the **Tenaru Waterfalls** (see p327).

Back to the main coastal road, continue further east until you reach **Red Beach**. Here you'll find a lonely, very rusted Japanese gun, placed here by US veterans and pointing forlornly out to sea. This is the only reminder of the US landings here in 1942.

Continue east to **Tetere**, where a dirt track leads to a **beach** and 30 or more abandoned **amtracks** (amphibious troop carriers). There's a S$50 *kastom* fee.

West of Honiara

Life becomes very sedate as one heads west through some of the north coast's delicious scenery. Urban existence is left behind once the road traverses White River and crawls its way along the scenic coastline.

The area boasts a high historical significance. The seas between Guadalcanal's northwestern coast and Savo island were the site of constant naval battles between August 1942 and February 1943. By the time the Japanese finally withdrew, so many ships had been sunk it became known as Iron Bottom Sound.

Popular with locals and expats at weekends, **Mamara Beach** (S$25) has black sand and is OK for swimming and bathing. About 1km further west is **Turtle Beach** (S$25), an appealing strip of white coral sand fringed with coconut trees.

Just past the Bonegi II site (see p328), there's a bush track that heads inland and runs about 400m to a well-preserved **US Sherman tank** (S$30) called *Jezebel*.

At **Ruaniu** (also known as Bonegi III), about 4.5km west from Bonegi II, there's a 6500-tonne Japanese transport ship, believed to be the *Kyushu Maru,* that lies just offshore – another superb playground for divers.

About 25km from Honiara, a turn to the south from the coastal road brings you to the **Vilu Open-Air Museum** (S$50). Here there are US and Japanese memorials, four large Japanese field guns and the remains of several US aircraft.

CENTRAL PROVINCE

Another world awaits just a two-hour boat ride from Honiara, either in the Nggela (Florida) group or on Savo.

DON'T MISS

TAKE A DIP!

Short of dreamy expanses of white sand on Guadalcanal, you can take a dip in lovely natural pools. But you've gotta earn these treats, as they are accessible only on foot.

Mataniko Falls

The hike starts in Lelei village with a steep ascent to a ridge, followed by an easier stretch amid mildly undulating hills. Then you'll tackle a gruelling descent on a slippery muddy path to reach the floor of the little canyon where the Mataniko flows. It takes roughly two hours return to do this walk. You'll find guides in Lelei.

Tenaru Waterfalls

The gorgeous Tenaru Waterfalls are a fairly easy four-hour walk (return) from a tiny settlement about 2km south of Tenaru Village. The path follows the floor of the river valley and cuts across the river's many bends. Guides are available at Tenaru Village.

❶ Getting There & Away

Small cargo boats take two hours to ply the route between Tulagi (or Savo) and Honiara, charging about S$250 one-way. In Honiara, they leave from the little beach next to Point Cruz Yacht Club. Lodgings can organise private transfers.

Florida (Nggela) Islands

POP 21,600 / AREA 1000 SQ KM

The Floridas' main draws? Diving, snorkelling, surfing and an ultra-chilled atmosphere. The two main islands, Tulagi and Nggela Sule, have rugged interiors, long white-sand beaches and mangrove swamps. In the middle of the Floridas, Tulagi was the Solomons' former capital; it was also a Japanese base during WWII.

🏃 Activities

There's superb **snorkelling** off Maravagi Resort and fabulous **diving** off Tulagi, including world-class wrecks (see p35). Contact **Tulagi Dive** (☑7475043, 26589; www.tulagidive.com.sb) in Honiara.

Maravagi is also an increasingly popular venue for **surfing**.

Extreme Adventures
BOAT TOURS

(☎23442, 749541; per person from S$1200) Based in Honiara, Extreme Adventures runs boat excursions to the Florida Islands most weekends. They include snorkel stops and a beach barbecue lunch.

🛌 Sleeping & Eating

Maravagi Resort
BUNGALOWS **$$**

(☎29065, 23179; www.maravagiresort.com.sb; Mangalonga Island; s/d A$60/102) Honiara's expats come to this small island near the northern end of the Florida group to enjoy the stunning location, with gorgeous coral pinnacles that extend just off the dining room. The rustic, beachfront leafhouse bungalows feature private bathrooms (cold-water showers), breezy terraces, mozzie nets and electricity. Avoid the six charmless, dorm-style rooms at the back. Meals (A$55 per day) are tasty. Village visits, surfing and snorkelling trips can be organised. Private boat transfers from Honiara cost from A$110 return. Credit cards are accepted.

Vanita Motel
GUESTHOUSE **$**

(☎32074; Tulagi; r without bathroom S$220, r with bathroom from S$350) A no-frills but well-kept guesthouse.

Savo

POP 3500 / AREA 31 SQ KM

Though lying just 14km north of Guadalcanal, Savo is a world away from the capital. Imagine an active volcano with a pair of dormant craters, coconut groves, a narrow strip of grey-sand beach and a few hot springs that are accessible by foot. The island also features a megapode field where hundreds of female birds lay their eggs in holes scratched into the hot sand.

Savo is also one of the most dependable locations in the Solomons to spot pods of dolphins, which usually congregate off the west coast.

🛌 Sleeping & Eating

Sunset Lodge
HOTEL **$$**

(☎22517, 28071, 7498347; Kuila; r per person incl meals S$500) Features 20 tidy rooms, some with private bathrooms, in a fairly bland concrete building on a hillside. The setting is enchanting, with the added appeal of tasty meals; transfers can be arranged from Honiara (from S$600). Various excursions and tours can be organised.

WESTERN PROVINCE

Marovo Lagoon, Munda and Gizo are the three unmissable destinations in the Western Province. Thanks to reliable interisland boat and plane services, they can easily be combined and toured at a comfortable, leisurely pace.

Marovo Lagoon

On New Georgia's eastern side, Marovo Lagoon is the world's finest double-barrier-enclosed lagoon, bordered by the large New Georgia and Vangunu Islands on one side and a double line of long barrier islands on the other. It contains hundreds of beautiful small islands, most of which are covered by coconut palms and rainforest, and surrounded by coral.

Here you can visit laid-back villages and explore *tambu* (sacred) sites, picnic on deserted islands, take a lagoon tour, meet master carvers, dive in fish soup, kayak across the lagoon or take a walk through the rainforest or up awesome summits.

Don't expect paradise on earth, though. Truly idyllic stretches of sand are almost nonexistent and years of intense logging have left their scars, literally.

🏃 Activities

Diving & Snorkelling

Marovo Lagoon offers plenty of exhilarating dives for both experts and novices. Here's the menu: channels, caves, drop-offs, coral gardens, clouds of technicolour fish and a few wrecks thrown in for good measure.

DON'T MISS

BONEGI

About 12km west from Honiara, **Bonegi** (S$25) is music to the ears of divers and snorkellers. Two large Japanese freighters sank just offshore on the night of 13 November 1942, and make for a magnificent playground for scuba divers, who call them Bonegi I and Bonegi II. As the upper works of Bonegi II break the surface, it can also be snorkelled. For more information on diving these sites, see p321 and p35. There's also a black-sand **beach** that is suitable for a picnic.

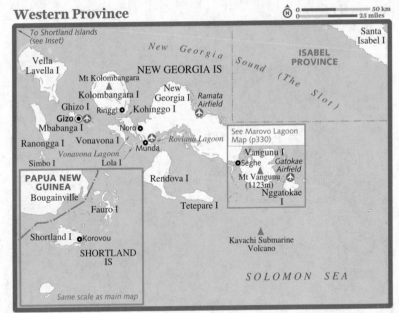

See the diving chapter (p35) for more information.

With hundreds of lovely sites scattered throughout the lagoon, snorkelling is equally impressive. Lodges can organise lagoon tours and snorkelling trips, which cost anything from S$50 to S$300 per person depending on distance and duration. Bring your own gear.

Solomon Dive Adventures
DIVING, SNORKELLING

(www.solomondiveadventures.com; Peava, Gatokae Island) This small outfit is based at Vuana Guesthouse in Peava (South Marovo). The ebullient American owner, Lisa Roquette, runs dive trips to Mbulo, Kicha and Male Male Islands. Introductory dives cost S$1000 (including gear), shore dives are S$400 and one-/two-tank dives run at S$550/1100. Two-tank outings to Kicha Island with a picnic lunch cost S$1300. Rental gear is available (S$240 per day). They also offer snorkelling excursions (from S$400). Cash only.

Uepi Island Resort
DIVING, SNORKELLING

(www.uepi.com; Uepi island; dives from A$75) This outfit has a great reputation for service and professionalism and offers stunning dives for all levels of proficiency throughout Marovo Lagoon. Equipment hire is A$40 per day. It's also renowned for its certification courses and dedicated snorkelling trips. It caters mainly to the resort's guests; non-guests may be accepted – space permitting and by prior arrangement only.

Dive Wilderness
DIVING

(www.thewildernesslodge.org; Peava, Gatokae Island) This operation, launched in early 2012, caters to guests staying at the Wilderness Lodge. A single dive costs A$75.

Kayaking

Kayaking is probably the most entrancing way to explore Marovo Lagoon. Uepi Island Resort can arrange multiday kayaking trips.

Walking

If you've got itchy feet, don't forget your walking shoes. Consider scaling Mt Mariu (887m) on Gatokae (two days), climbing the hill that lords over Chea Village on Marovo island (two hours) or tackling Mt Reku (520m) on Vangunu (half a day).

Tours

All kinds of tours and activities, including village visits, guided walks, picnic trips and lagoon excursions can be arranged through the region's lodges.

Marovo Lagoon

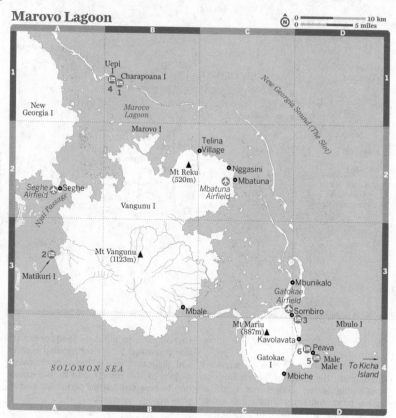

Marovo Lagoon

🌀 Activities, Courses & Tours

🛏 Sleeping

🛏 Sleeping

There's a small network of ecolodges on the lagoon. These rustic, family-run establishments are great places to meet locals and offer an authentic cultural experience. If you want to pamper yourself, opt for Uepi Island Resort or the Wilderness Lodge.

Most places overlook the lagoon, but there's no beach.

TOP **CHOICE** **Uepi Island Resort** RESORT $$$
(www.uepi.com; Uepi Island; s incl meals A$220-290, d incl 3 meals A$380-500; 🛜) This extremely well-run resort is very popular with Australian divers, who stay here to get thrilled by the sensational dive sites right on their doorstep. Snorkellers will get a buzz on the house reef that spreads from the end of the short jetty. The best thing is that it also appeals to honeymooners and families. The spacious bungalows are comfortable, but not flash (no air-con, ordinary furnishings), and are scattered amid lovely bush gardens and coconut palms. The ethos is laid-back, ecological and activity oriented. Perks include a bar, a breezy dining room with excellent meals, a full dive shop and a good excursion program. Boat transfers to Seghe are A$105 per person return.

TOP CHOICE Wilderness Lodge BUNGALOWS $$$
(www.thewildernesslodge.org; Peava, Gatokae Island; r/bungalow per person incl 3 meals A$155/185) Nestled in a coconut grove right by the lagoon, this 'lodge' features a large leafhouse with two bedrooms that share a bathroom as well as two luxurious seafront bungalows with private facilities. Meals incorporate locally grown fruit and vegetables and there's 24-hour solar-generated electricity. Adventurous travellers can forgo relaxing on the pontoon in favour of snorkelling along the magnificent house reef, spear fishing in the bay, diving off Kicha Island (there's a small onsite dive centre), hiking and crocodile-spotting – all of which can be organised by the lodge. Boat transfers to Gatokae airstrip cost A$56 per person return.

Matikuri Lodge BUNGALOWS $$
(☑7467177, 7541016; Matikuri Island; dm incl 3 meals S$350, bungalow per person incl 3 meals S$470) Matikuri Lodge's drawcard is its soothing sense of isolation, sitting on the western arc of Marovo Lagoon. Digs are in three island-style bungalows that face the sea; the four dorm-style rooms in the main house are rudimentary. There's good swimming just offshore. No electricity, but kerosene lamps are provided. The dining area has a large deck on stilts. A host of guided walks, village visits and lagoon tours can be organised, and there are kayaks for hire. One-way boat transfers to Seghe airstrip (20 minutes) are S$250 per person.

Vuana Guesthouse GUESTHOUSE $$
(www.solomondiveadventures.com; Peava, Gatokae Island; r per person incl 3 meals S$700-800) Divers couldn't ask for a better base than this well-run guesthouse with an onsite dive centre and a sensational house reef. There are two simple bungalows with fabulous water frontage as well as one room in the owner's house. Aim for the slightly dearer 'Breeze' unit, which is more charming and better laid out. Toilets and showers (cold water) are shared. Most guests are here on dive packages, though the guesthouse is also a great place to decompress. It takes a genuine interest in sustainability, composting food and supporting local projects. If only there was a beach! Instead of sand at the front, it's ironshore – a sharp rock made of coral and limestone. Not exactly a great tanning spot, but don't fret – there's a nice strip of sand a short walk away. Boat transfers to Seghe airstrip are S$250 (for two people) one way. Cash only.

WORTH A TRIP

TAVANIPUPU ISLAND

If you've ever dreamed of having your own island paradise, **Tavanipupu Private Island Resort** (☑36081, 36082; www.tavanipupu.com; d incl 3 meals A$550), off Guadalcanal's eastern tip, has all the key ingredients – exclusivity, seclusion and atmosphere. Digs are in six tastefully decorated, spacious bungalows scattered in a well-tended coconut grove that overlooks the beach. The restaurant uses only the freshest seafood. Snorkelling is excellent (gear provided), as is fishing, and you can work your tan on sandy beaches or pamper yourself in the spa. Solomon Airlines flies three times a week from Honiara to Marau (S$1600 return, 30 minutes), from where it's a 15-minute boat ride to the resort.

Charapoana Lodge BUNGALOWS $$
(☑30156, 7409634, 7403714; kanikilasana@gmail.com; Charapoana Island; r per person incl 3 meals S$370) Just across the passage from Uepi Island, this well-regarded ecolodge exudes a Melanesian family atmosphere. Guests are accommodated in a large wooden house with three basic rooms. There are also a few bungalows on a little stretch of sand, offering more privacy. The shared 'mangrove toilet' is something that has to be used to be believed (you'll see). Food is copious and varied. Sunbathing, swimming and snorkelling are top notch – there's even a manta ray cleaning station just a short swim away. Boat transfers to Seghe airstrip cost S$1100/700/570 for one/two/three people. Cash only.

Ropiko Lodge BUNGALOWS $$
(☑7495805, 28065; rolandpiko@yahoo.com; Gatokae Island; r per person incl 3 meals S$400) This charming place grows on you quickly, with a well-proportioned bungalow facing the lagoon. Lovely setting: the property is filled with colourful orchids and there's a small beach lapped by turquoise waters. The decent

DAY OFF

Take note that Marovo Lagoon is strongly Seventh Day Adventist, so you can't do much on Saturday.

ablution block has flush toilets. When we visited, the owner had started to build additional bungalows with private facilities. Enjoy excellent swimming and snorkelling on the nearby reef. Boat transfers to Gatokae airstrip cost S$200 per person return. Cash only.

❶ Information

The mobile phone network doesn't cover Marovo Lagoon entirely; at the time of writing, South Marovo wasn't yet covered. Bookings for resorts and lodges can be made online or through SIVB in Honiara (p326).

❶ Getting There & Away

AIR There are two main gateways to Marovo: Seghe (for North Marovo Lagoon) and Gatokae Island (for South Marovo Lagoon). **Solomon Airlines** (www.flysolomons.com) connects Seghe with Honiara (S$1200, daily), and Munda (S$685) and Gizo (S$790) about six days a week. Gatokae is serviced from Honiara (S$1200, three times weekly). All prices are one-way.

BOAT The passenger boat **MV Pelican Express** (☑28104 in Honiara) offers a weekly service between Honiara and Gizo via Marovo Lagoon; it stops at Mbatuna (one-way S$460) and Seghe (one-way S$500) on its way to Gizo. Check while in Honiara, as the schedule is erratic.

❶ Getting Around

If you have booked accommodation, your hosts will arrange airport transfers. Costs will depend on the distance travelled and the number of passengers.

Public transport does not exist. To get from South Marovo to North Marovo (or vice versa), you'll need to charter a boat; as an indication of price, a ride between Gatokae and Uepi should set you back around S$2000.

Munda

West New Georgia has its fair share of attractions as well as reliable accommodation options, a hatful of historic sites –

MONEY MATTERS

Marovo Lagoon has no ATMs and no banks, and credit cards are only accepted at Uepi Island Resort, so you'll need to bring a stash of cash to cover your entire bill (including accommodation, meals, activities and transport), plus some extra for surprise add-ons.

from WWII relics to skull shrines – and thrilling dive sites. The largest settlement, the little town of Munda on New Georgia itself, makes a convenient, if not glamorous, base for exploring the area's attractions.

◉ Sights & Activities

Museums   WWII RELICS
(S$25 each) History buffs should consider the two small private 'museums' of WWII relics. The one closest to Agnes Lodge is run by Gordon Beti (no sign; ask for exact location); the second, and most interesting, is further east along the road, near the soccer field, a 20-minute walk from Agnes Lodge. Run by Alphy Barney Paulson, it features lots of utensils, ammunition, machine guns, shells, crockery, helmets, shavers and knives, all left behind by the Japanese and Americans.

Dive Munda   DIVING, SNORKELLING
(☑62156; www.mundadive.com; Agnes Lodge) Munda is a destination of choice for demanding divers, who have the pick of lots of superlative dive sites (see p35), with an exciting selection of wrecks, drop-offs, reefs and underwater caves. Run by a friendly British couple, Dive Munda offers two-tank dives (A$200 with all equipment) and certification courses. At most dive sites snorkelling (A$50) is also possible.

☞ Tours

The easiest way to get a broad look at the delights around West New Georgia is to take a half- or one-day tour. Based at Agnes Lodge, **Go West Tours** (☑62180) offers a wide range of excursions. Prices start at S$800 for two people.

🛏 Sleeping & Eating

Agnes Lodge   INN $$
(☑62133, 62101; www.agneslodge.com.sb; s with shared bathroom S$220-280, d with shared bathroom S$440-550, d S$800-1100, ste S$1200-1400; ❋🛜) This long-established venture on the waterfront (no beach) has a variety of rooms for all budgets, from fan-cooled, two-bed rooms to comfy self-contained units with air-con. Downside: rooms are tightly packed together. It isn't luxurious but is in top nick, the onsite bar is good for discovering essential local gossip and the **restaurant** (mains S$80-300; ⊘breakfast, lunch & dinner) serves excellent food. It's a short walk from the airstrip. Credit cards are accepted.

Zipolo Habu Resort
RESORT $$$

([✓]62178, 7471105; www.zipolohabu.com.sb; Lola Island; bungalow with shared bathroom A$140-190, deluxe bungalow A$230-340; [❄]) On Lola Island, about 20 minutes by boat from Munda, this small resort with a casual atmosphere sates the white-sand beach, coconut-palm, azure-lagoon fantasy, with six spacious, fan-cooled bungalows. The cheaper ones are fairly basic leafhouses, while the two deluxe units boast private bathrooms and unobstructed views over the lagoon. The restaurant (meals per day A$80) gets good reviews. This place offers village tours, lagoon excursions, sport-fishing and surf charters. Return boat transfers to Munda cost A$120 per boatload. Divers can be picked up at the resort by Dive Munda. Credit cards are accepted.

Qua Roviana
GUESTHOUSE $$

([✓]62123; quaroviana@gmail.com; s with shared bathroom S$220, r with shared bathroom S$550; [❄][❄]) Just across the road from Agnes Lodge, this family-run abode is great value. The nine rooms are simply furnished but serviceable, and the common lounge, bathrooms and kitchen are clean, comfortable and well fitted out. Qua Roviana will accept cash only.

ⓘ Information

Check your emails at **Telekom** (per hr S$20; ⊙8am-noon & 1-4.30pm Mon-Fri).

The **Bank South Pacific** changes currency and has an ATM. The **ANZ** branch, near the post office, also has an ATM.

ⓘ Getting There & Away

AIR Solomon Airlines ([✓]62152; www.fly solomons.com) connects Munda with Honiara (S$1250, daily), Gizo (S$685, daily) and Seghe (S$685, six weekly).

BOAT Go West Transport ([✓]62180), based at Agnes Lodge, has a shuttle service to Gizo (S$240, two hours, two to three weekly) stopping at various places en route, including Zipolo Habu Resort and Lolomo Eco Resort.

Around West New Georgia

Fancy a dip? Head to the 10m **Holupuru Falls**, east of Munda. If you've got itchy feet, you can hike up **Mt Bau**, about 9km inland. You'll need a guide to show you the way (ask at Agnes Lodge, p332).

In Baeroko Bay you'll see the *Casi Maru,* a sunken **Japanese freighter** near the shore (and a dive site). Its rusty masts protrude from the water. It was bombed as its crane was loading cargo on to an adjacent barge. Enoghae, at the jutting northern lip of the bay, has several large **Japanese WWII anti-aircraft guns** still hidden in the scrub.

Skull Island, on Vonavona Lagoon, is the final resting place for the skulls of countless vanquished warriors, as well as a shrine for the skulls of Rendovan chiefs.

On Kohinggo Island, there is a wrecked **US Sherman tank** on the northern shore. It was lost in action in September 1943 when US marines overran a Japanese strongpoint.

🛏 Sleeping

Lolomo Eco Resort
BUNGALOWS $$

([✓]8519774, 22902; warren.paia@gmail.com; Kohinggo Island; r with shared bathroom S$660; [❄][❄]) Halfway between Munda and Gizo, this supremely relaxing place, opened in 2011, offers something different, with three large, smartly finished thatched-roof bungalows on stilts, but it's a bummer it's not suitable for swimming; the shore is fringed with mangroves. For a dip, the owners will happily take you to a nearby sandy island. The ablution block is squeaky clean and equipped with flush toilets and hot-water showers. The meals package costs S$300 per day. Lolomo is very isolated but convenient nonetheless, as the shuttle operated by Go West Transport stops here when it travels between Munda and Gizo. Private boat transfers to either Munda or Gizo cost S$1200 per boatload return. Cash only.

Gizo

Little Ghizo Island is dwarfed by its neighbours, but it has the Solomons' second-biggest 'city', Gizo (pronounced the same, spelt differently), the most developed area outside the capital.

Gizo is the hub around which the Western Province revolves. Sprawled along the waterfront with its steep hills behind, the town is not devoid of appeal, although the architecture is charmless. Most places of importance are on the main street. Apart from the bustling market on the waterfront, there are no specific sights, but there are some appealing lodgings a short boat ride away. Gizo is also a good base for divers, surfers and hikers.

Gizo

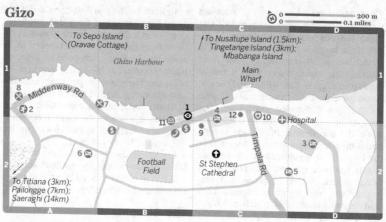

Gizo

◎ Sights

Market
MARKET

(☺Mon-Sat) Villagers from neighbouring islands (and even from the Shortland Islands) arrive each morning by boat to occupy their little stands under the shade of tall trees. It's at its liveliest Monday and Friday mornings.

World Fish Centre
CLAM FARM

(☎60022; Nusatupe island; ☺by reservation) On Nusatupe island (Gizo's airstrip), this clam farm and research centre is a good spot if you want to snorkel over giant clams of up to 1m long in the lagoon (bring your own gear). Boat transfers from Gizo cost about S$200, or you can take the Solomon Airlines shuttle (S$60 one-way).

⚹ Activities

Diving & Snorkelling

Gizo has made a name for itself in diving. Sure, large tracts of reefs were battered when the 2007 tsunami hit the Gizo area, but overall the level of destruction was relatively low and most sites have now recovered. Most dives are less than a 20-minute boat ride from Gizo and include wrecks and reef dives. See p35 for more information on dive sites.

In the mood for snorkelling? Kennedy Island, just off Fatboys (p336), is your answer. Take the shuttle to Fatboys (S$100), hire snorkelling gear at the resort and snorkel to your heart's content. Dive Gizo also runs snorkelling trips (S$40, including lunch and snorkel set).

Dive Gizo
DIVING, SNORKELLING

(☑60253; www.divegizo.com; Middenway Rd) This solid professional outfit at the western end of town charges A$140 for an introductory dive (including equipment hire) and A$150 for a two-tank dive, including picnic (add an extra A$30 for gear rental). An open-water certification is A$680. We love the two-tank dive organisation; you spend your surface interval picnicking on a secluded island or having lunch at Fatboys (p337).

Swimming & Surfing

The main road out of Gizo skirts the shore to **Saeraghi** at the island's northwestern end, which has lovely beaches. There's excellent point surfing off **Pailongge**, on Ghizo's southern coast. The October-to-April swell rises to 2m or more. There's a great left-hander near **Titiana** village, with a long paddle out to the reef's edge, and a right at Pailongge. Gizo Hotel is a good source of information. To get to the spots, take a taxi from Gizo. Bring your own boards.

Hiking

If you're a hiking fiend, we'd unhesitatingly recommend the climb up Kolombangara (see p336).

🛏 Sleeping

GIZO

Nagua Resthouse
GUESTHOUSE $$

(☑60012; s with shared bathroom S$150-350, r S$400-500) A short (uphill) walk from town, this family-run guesthouse features plain, functional well-scrubbed rooms with air-con, and there's a nice communal kitchen. Overall the whole place is well maintained, linen is fresh and the staff is friendly. A safe bet.

Cegily's Guesthouse
GUESTHOUSE $$

(☑60035, 60935, 7467982; r with shared bathroom S$290-350) This small guesthouse with only three fan-cooled rooms could just be the best choice for those on a tight budget. It's a study in simplicity, but it's also clean, calm and secure. There's a well-kept communal kitchen, a tidy lounge area and a terrace with good ocean views. It's just past the hospital, on a hillside.

Rekona Moamoa Lodge
GUESTHOUSE $$

(☑60368; dm S$160, d with shared bathroom S$250, d S$350-690; ❄🛜) Good value for its quiet and central location on a street which sees little traffic. The cheaper rooms are fairly Spartan, but at these rates you know you're not getting the Ritz. The dearer ones – especially rooms 16 to 20, upstairs – are much more inviting and come with private bathrooms and air-con. There's a kitchen area for common use.

Gizo Hotel
HOTEL $$$

(☑60199; www.gizohotel.com; Middenway Rd; r S$1000-1200; ❄🛜🏊) Gizo Hotel is a perennial favourite for its central location, salubrious yet unflashy rooms and wide array of facilities (wi-fi, air-con, gift shop, bar and restaurant). Popular with expats and businesspeople, it can't quite shake that just-a-motel feeling, despite a swimming pool amid lush vegetation at the back. Some rooms have sea views, others open onto the garden and the pool. Excursions to Kennedy Island are organised most Sundays.

SEPO ISLAND

🌿 Oravae Cottage
BUNGALOWS $$

(☑66621, 66619; www.oravaecottage.com; cottage incl 3 meals per person from A$100) Look at the homepage on the website: it's truly like this.

WORTH A TRIP

TETEPARE ISLAND

This large rainforest island is one of the Solomons' conservation jewels and a dream come true for ecotourists. The **Tetepare Descendants' Association** (☑62163 in Munda; www.tetepare.org; r per person incl meals S$500), which manages the island, welcomes visitors in its simple yet genuinely ecofriendly leafhouses (no air-con, solar power, shared facilities). There are plans to build another two bungalows with private facilities. What makes this place extra special is the host of environmental activities available, including snorkelling with dugongs, spotting crocodiles, birdwatching and turtle-tagging. They're free (except the ones that involve boat rides), and you'll be accompanied by trained guides. Food is fresh and organic. No alcohol is available, but it's BYO. Minuses: the cost and duration of transfers (S$1900 per boatload one-way, two hours from Munda), but there are plans to arrange cheaper transfers with Go West Transport (p338) – ask when you book.

HIKING IN KOLOMBANGARA

Growing weary of water activities? Consider climbing up to the crater's rim on Kolombangara (the big island facing Gizo). It's an exhilarating two-day/one-night hike. Take note that it's an arduous walk – it's wet and muddy all the way up, it's steep, and the path is irregular – so you'll need to be fit. But the atmosphere and views are surreal.

You'll need guides and porters. Dive Gizo (p335) and **Kolombangara Island Biodiversity Conservation Association** (KIBCA; ✆60230, 7400544; www.kolombangara.org) can arrange logistics. Plan on S$1600 to S$2000 per person, excluding boat transfers from Gizo (S$1600 per boatload return).

Kolombangara also has less challenging hikes, including crater walks and river walks.

Just 10 minutes from Gizo, this lovely retreat has two handsomely designed traditional houses with private facilities (cold-water showers). The bigger cottage can sleep up to eight people; the smaller one is suitable for couples. Both units have a terrace opening onto the lagoon. Luxury it ain't, but it has charm in spades. The atmosphere is delightfully chilled out and meals get high marks from travellers. Swimming and snorkelling are excellent.

TINGETANGE ISLAND

At the time of writing, a new resort was being built on this islet lying a five-minute boat ride from Gizo. The owners had plans to name it **Imagination Island** (ward_geoscience@yahoo.com). It will comprise seven bungalows, a six-room house, a bar and a restaurant.

MBABANGA ISLAND

A mere 10-minute boat ride south of Gizo, this island has a brochure-esque appeal, with an expansive lagoon and a string of white-sand beaches.

Sanbis Resort   RESORT $$$
(✆66313; www.sanbisresort.com; d S$1500, lodge A$1000; ☎) A place of easy bliss. Relax in your creatively designed bungalow, snorkel over healthy reefs just offshore, snooze in a hammock, treat yourself to a tasty meal at the laid-back over-the-water restaurant or kayak over translucent waters. The icing on the cake is the ultra-exclusive Lodge, which is outstandingly positioned at the tip of the island. No air-con, but the location benefits from cooling breezes. The beach is thin but attractive, and the whole place is ecofriendly. It's a good base for honeymooners, divers (there's a small on-site dive shop) and fisherfolk (professional equipment is available for rent). No kids under 12.

Fatboys   RESORT $$$
(✆60095, 7443107; www.fatboysgizo.com; d from A$230; ☎) This small complex has suffered in recent years from a lack of maintenance and TLC, but at the time of writing, capable new managers were working to get the place back into shape. It consists of five spacious waterfront bungalows that blend tropical hardwoods and traditional leaf. It's quite spread out so you can get a decent dose of privacy. The defining factor, however, is the lovely bar and restaurant directly over the exquisite waters of the lagoon. The narrow beach is average, but the snorkelling is sensational.

✕ Eating

Gizo has several well-stocked supermarkets, open Monday to Saturday.

Lamasa   SEAFOOD, CHINESE $$
(Middenway Rd; mains S$50-110; ⏰lunch & dinner Mon-Fri) Lamasa is nothing more than a few tables, but it's hygienically kept and the fish and chips are brilliant value. No alcohol, but the smoothies are to die for.

SB Bar   INTERNATIONAL $$
(✆66313; Sanbis Resort, Mbabanga Island; mains S$60-130; ⏰from 11am) Sanbis Resort's over-water restaurant is an atmospheric place to sample a well-executed pizza or a burger at lunchtime. Call the reception to arrange transfers from Gizo.

Nuzu Nuzu Restaurant   INTERNATIONAL $$
(✆60199; Gizo Hotel, Middenway Rd; mains S$90-150; ⏰breakfast, lunch & dinner) The breezy open-air dining room is suitably exotic, with wood-carved posts, wooden tables and wicker seating. The choice of dishes on offer is pretty limited, but fish is ultrafresh, the daily specials are well prepared and the wood-fired pizzas are tasty. Breakfast is average.

PT 109

SEAFOOD $

(Middenway Rd; mains S$60-120; ⊘lunch & dinner Mon-Fri) Named after John F Kennedy's WWII patrol boat that sank off Gizo, and situated in a great waterfront location, this place has a relaxed vibe. A blackboard displays a few simple dishes, such as local fish or chicken, as well as lobster.

Fatboys

INTERNATIONAL $

(☑60095; Mbabanga Island; mains S$50-120; ⊘lunch) What a sensational setting! The dining room is on a pier that hovers over the turquoise waters of Vonavona Lagoon. Food-wise, it's a bit less overwhelming – fish and chips, grilled fish and salads. There are billiard tables and a reading library. After your meal, rent snorkelling gear and swim over sandy shallows that extend to Kennedy Island. From Gizo, take the daily shuttle at 11am (S$60 one-way). It's best to reserve.

Market

MARKET $

(⊘Mon-Sat) For organic fruit and vegetables, as well as fresh fish, nothing can beat the market on the waterfront.

Drinking

The best drinking dens include the bar at the Gizo Hotel and PT 109. During the day, nothing can beat a frothy tropical cocktail or a cold beer at Sanbis Resort or Fatboys, on Mbabanga Island.

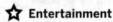 Entertainment

If you want to re-live *Saturday Night Fever* island-style, try **Bamboo**, which is part of the Gizo Hotel, or PT 109, which has a dance floor. Both get busy on Thursday, Friday and Saturday evenings.

Shopping

Dive Gizo and Gizo Hotel have a rather wide selection of stonework and woodcarvings.

Information

ANZ Bank (Middenway Rd; ⊘9am-4pm Mon-Fri) Currency exchange. Has an ATM.

Bank South Pacific (BSP; Middenway Rd; ⊘8.30am-3.30pm Mon-Fri) Currency exchange. Has an ATM.

Daltron BeMobile (Middenway Rd; per hr S$30; ⊘8.30am-4.30pm Mon-Fri, 8am-noon Sat) Internet access. Beside the entrance of Gizo Hotel.

Gizo Internet Cafe (per hr S$25; ⊘8am-8pm) Same location as Lamasa restaurant.

Hospital (☑60224; Middenway Rd)

Immigration Office (⊘8-11.30am & 1-4.30pm Mon-Fri) Behind ANZ Bank. Can issue a visitor's permit for yachties proceeding from PNG and the Shortland Islands.

BEST OF THE REST

If, after visiting Guadalcanal, Malaita, Central and Western Provinces, you still feel the urge for more off-the-beaten-track adventures, and if time is really no object, consider travelling to the other provinces.

Choiseul One of the least-visited provinces in the Solomons, Choiseul has two airfields, on Taro Island and in Kagau.

Shortland Islands Like Choiseul, the Shortland Islands are culturally closer to Bougainville in Papua New Guinea, which lies only 9km to the north.

Makira-Ulawa An untouched world only one hour from Honiara. Kirakira is the main gateway. Sensational surfing off Star Harbour.

Temotu Temotu Province lies at the Solomons' most easterly point. Lata, the provincial capital, on Santa Cruz Island, is the main launching pad for outlying islands, such as Reef Islands, Utupua and Vanikoro.

Rennell & Bellona Both islands are Polynesia outliers, sharing similar languages and cultures. Geologically they're both rocky, uplifted-coral atolls.

Isabel This province is a castaway's dream come true, especially if you can make it to the Arnavon Islands, off the northwestern tip of Isabel. This conservation area managed by **Nature Conservancy** (☑20940, 28095 in Honiara; www.nature.org) is one of the world's largest nesting grounds for the hawksbill turtle. Isabel has an excellent place to stay, **Papatura Island Retreat** (www.papatura.com), which offers snorkelling, fishing and surfing outings. The gateways to Isabel are Buala and Suavanao.

Our Telekom (Middenway Rd; per hr S$20; ☺8.30am-12.30pm &1-4.30pm) Sells phonecards, SIM cards and Bumblebee cards. Internet access is available, too (two computers only).

ⓘ Getting There & Away
Air
Solomon Airlines (☑60173; www.fly solomons.com; Middenway Rd; ☺8.30am-4pm Mon-Fri) has up to three daily flights between Gizo and Honiara (from S$1380). There are also daily flights between Gizo and Munda (from S$685), and three weekly flights between Gizo and Seghe (from S$790). From Gizo you can also fly to the Shortland Islands and Choiseul. The airfield is on Nusatupe island (boat transfer S$60).

Boat
The **MV Pelican Express** (☑28104 in Honiara) has a weekly service between Gizo and Honiara via Marovo Lagoon (S$600, 12 hours).

Go West Transport (☑62180; Agnes Lodge, Munda) runs a shuttle boat connecting Gizo to Munda (S$240, two hours, two to three weekly) stopping at various places en route, including Zipolo Habu Resort and Lolomo Eco Resort.

Islands Around Ghizo

A perfect cone-shaped volcano that rises to 1770m, **Kolombangara** looms majestically on the horizon northeast of Ghizo Island. It's a scenic two-day hike to the top and back if you are fit and have the energy (see p336). It rises from a 1km-wide coastal plain through flat-topped ridges and increasingly steep escarpments to the rugged crater rim of Mt Veve. For history buffs, there are WWII Japanese relics scattered around the island. **Vila Point** was an important WWII Japanese base and you can still see guns in the bush.

Definitely worth a visit is **Simbo Island** for its megapode hatcheries and its easily climbable volcano. There's also a sulphur-covered crater lake.

Both Kolombangara and Simbo offer accommodation in the form of village stays.

ⓘ Getting There & Away
The islands around Ghizo have no regular boat services. Your best bet is to find a shared ride at Gizo market. Dive Gizo (p335) can arrange excursions to Simbo and Kolombangara islands.

MALAITA

Malaita Province is named after the largest island in the region. Easily reached from Guadalcanal, Malaita is a hauntingly beautiful island with narrow coastal plains, secluded bays and a rugged highland interior. As well as having a host of natural features to explore, Malaita has an equally fascinating ethnic heritage. It's a rare combination of being both an adventure island as well as a stronghold of ancient Melanesian traditions and cultures.

Unlike in Guadalcanal and the Western Province, the development of tourism is still in its infancy here. In the main destinations (Auki and Langa Langa Lagoon) there's enough infrastructure to travel safely on your own. Elsewhere it's virtually uncharted territory.

Auki & Around

Curled around a wonderfully shaped bay and surrounded by jungle-clad hills, Auki is the Solomons' third-largest town. It's a nondescript little port town, with a few low-slung buildings and a smattering of houses on stilts. Everything moves slowly except at the lively market and the bustling wharf, at the town's southern end.

◉ Sights & Activities

Lilisiana   FISHING VILLAGE
With its traditional-style houses raised on stilts over the shore, the friendly fishing village of Lilisiana, about 1.5km from Auki, is photogenic to boot. Lilisiana's peaceful beach is a narrow, long, golden sand spit beside coral shallows. Beside the beach is **Osi Lake**, which is home to colonies of seabirds.

Riba Cave   CAVE
(S$25) An hour's walk east of Auki is Riba Cave, with stalagmites, several large subterranean chambers and an underground river.

Kwaibala Waterfall   WATERFALL
(S$25) If you need to refresh yourself, head to Kwaibala Waterfall, about 3km from Auki. Expect modest cascades with a few pools where you can take a bracing dip.

Marata Man   TOUR GUIDE
(☑7458201; marataman1@yahoo.com.au) You'll need a guide to visit Riba Cave and Kwaibala Waterfall, which are on private land

Malaita Province

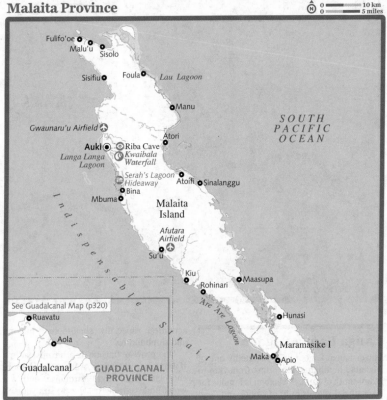

and difficult to find. Silas Diutee Malai is a freelance guide who charges S$200 for Riba Cave, S$200 for Kwaibala Waterfall and S$100 for Osi Lake. Make sure that *kastom* fees are included in the prices he quotes.

🛏 Sleeping & Eating

Auki Motel   HOTEL **$$**
(☎40014, 40208; Loboi Ave; r S$250-660; ❄🖥) Auki Motel has the best facilities in town. Bathrooms are in good nick and it features a range of rooms to suit all budgets. Downstairs rooms are a tad cramped but have private bathrooms and shared air-con. The menu at the **restaurant** (mains S$50-70; ⊙breakfast, lunch & dinner) varies according to what's available.

Rarasu   SEAFOOD **$**
(☎40280; off Maasina Rulu Pde; mains S$40-65; ⊙lunch & dinner Mon-Sat, dinner Sun) Choice is very limited, but the dishes are fresh and

copious. The vaguely barn-like surrounds ooze a ramshackle charm.

ℹ Information

Get online at **Telekom** (per hr S$20; ⊙8.30am-noon & 1-4pm Mon-Fri).

An **ANZ** (off Loboi Ave; ⊙9am-4pm Mon-Fri) and a **Bank South Pacific** (BSP; off Loboi Ave; ⊙8.30am-3pm Mon-Fri) are in the town centre and change major currencies. Both have an ATM (Visa and MasterCard).

ℹ Getting There & Away

Because of land disputes, flights were indefinitely suspended between Honiara and Auki at the time of writing.

The passenger boats **MV Pelican Express** (☎28104), **MV 360 Discovery** (☎20957, 7442802) and **MV Lady Wakehurst** (☎7592006) have regular services between Honiara and Auki (from S$150, four to six hours).

Auki

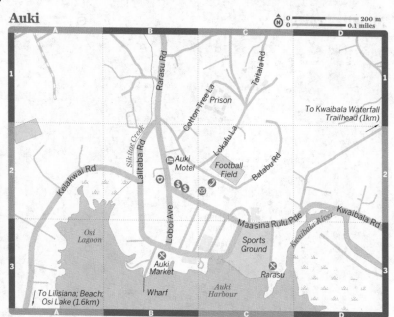

Langa Langa Lagoon

Langa Langa Lagoon is indisputedly one of Malaita's highlights. Extending from 7km to 32km south of Auki, the lagoon is famous for its artificial islands built of stones and dead corals. It's also a strong centre for traditional activities, especially shell-money making and shipbuilding.

One proviso: 'lagoon' is a bit misleading. If it has recently rained, waters may be more chocolate than bright turquoise, and you won't find stunning beaches to sun yourself on. People rather come here for the laid-back tempo and the magical setting.

SERAH'S LAGOON HIDEAWAY

Scene: Langa Langa Lagoon at dusk. Close up: you're sipping a glass of bush lime on your private terrace at **Serah's Lagoon Hideaway** (☎7472344; serah _kei@yahoo.com.au; r per person incl meals S$550-650). Run with flair by Serah Kei, this retreat comprises two bungalows on stilts embellished with a few feminine touches and a three-room house. The ablution block is tip top, with a proper shower and flush toilets, and the meals are memorable. Your host can arrange lagoon tours as well as cultural shows (from S$300). Call Serah to arrange transfers from Auki (about S$600 per boatload one-way).

UNDERSTAND THE SOLOMON ISLANDS

Solomon Islands Today

RAMSI (Regional Assistance Mission to Solomon Islands) remains in the Solomons in an ongoing capacity while the country slowly rebuilds, but it's hoped that all RAMSI police will have withdrawn by 2015.

Due to unstable parliamentary coalitions, changes of government are frequent in the Solomons. In August 2010, Danny Philip was elected Prime Minister by a majority of one. He resigned in November 2011 following a vote of no confidence, and his former Minister for Finance and Treasury, Gordon Darcy Lilo, was elected Prime Minister a week later. The next elections will be held in 2014.

With restored security and increased stability, the economic outlook is positive. Thanks to better air connections from Australia, tourism is slightly on the rise, and the Gold Ridge Mine, 40km southeast of Honiara, which was closed in 2000 due to civil unrest, recommenced commercial operations in 2011. The Solomon Islands hosted the 11th Festival of Pacific Arts in July 2012, a major cultural event in the region.

JFK

In 1960 John F Kennedy invited two Solomon Islanders to his presidential inauguration in Washington DC. They were turned away because they spoke no English. In 1943 these two islanders rescued 26-year-old skipper JFK and 10 survivors after their boat was sunk by Japanese during WWII.

History

Papuan-speaking hunter-gatherers from New Guinea were the only inhabitants of the Solomons for thousands of years, until Austronesian-speaking proto-Melanesians began moving in around 4000 BC. The Lapita people appeared between 2000 and 1600 BC. Polynesians from the east settled the outer islands such as Rennell, Bellona and Ontong Java between AD 1200 and 1600.

The first European visitor was Spaniard Don Alvaro de Mendaña y Neyra in 1568. He returned in 1595 with four ships and 450 would-be colonists. He came upon and named Santa Cruz, and established a settlement before dying there of malaria. After two months the settlement was abandoned and the survivors limped back to Peru.

There was almost no further contact with Europeans until 1767, when the British Captain Philip Carteret came upon Santa Cruz and Malaita. British, French and American explorers followed, and whalers began arriving in 1798. Sandalwood traders visited from the 1840s to late 1860s.

On 6 October 1893, Britain proclaimed a protectorate over the archipelago's southern islands, which was extended in 1897 and again in 1898. In 1899, Britain relinquished claims to Western Samoa, and in return Germany ceded the Shortlands, Choiseul, Ontong Java and Santa Isabel to Britain.

Between 1871 and 1903 blackbirders (slave traders) took 30,000 men from the Solomons to work in the cane fields of northern Australia and Fiji.

The year 1942 marked a turning point: in April the Japanese seized the Shortland Islands. Three weeks later Tulagi was taken and the Japanese began building an airstrip on Guadalcanal. United States troops landed on Guadalcanal in August 1942, but were severely defeated by a Japanese naval force that had left Rabaul in New Guinea to attack the US transports. However, the US forces gradually gained the upper hand. During the Guadalcanal campaign, six naval battles were fought and 67 warships and transports sunk – so many ships were sunk off the northern coast of Guadalcanal that this area is now called Iron Bottom Sound. Around 7000 American and 30,000 Japanese lives were lost on land and at sea. The Allies recovered all islands after the official Japanese surrender in 1945. (In 1965, after 20 years of hiding in the bush after the end of WWII, the last Japanese soldier surrendered on Vella Lavella island in the Solomons. He returned home to full military honours.) The town of Tulagi was gutted during the war and the Quonset-hut township of Honiara replaced it as the capital.

A proto-nationalist postwar movement called Marching Rule sprang up in Malaita, opposed to cooperation with the British authorities, whose rule had been restored after WWII. Britain began to see the need for local government, and a governing council was elected in 1970. The British Solomon Islands Protectorate was renamed the Solomon Islands five years later and independence was granted on 7 July 1978.

Ethnic tensions started to fester; the Gwale people (people from Guadalcanal) resented the fact that their traditional land was being settled by migrants from Malaita. Early in 1999, the inevitable happened. Civil war broke out, and hundreds died in the fighting. Following mediation by Australia and New Zealand, the Townsville Peace Agreement was signed between the two factions in October 2000. However, what began as ethnic tension descended into general lawlessness. Though the conflict was confined to Guadalcanal, 'events' started happening elsewhere, including in the Western Province. The whole country was crippled and traumatised, and the fragile economy collapsed.

On 24 July 2003, the RAMSI, an Australian-led coalition of police from Pacific island

states, was deployed throughout the whole country to restore law and order. However, this progress was seriously undermined in April 2006, when the election of controversial Snyder Rini as prime minister resulted in two days of rioting in the streets of Honiara, despite the presence of RAMSI. Australia flew in reinforcements for the RAMSI personnel. Rini resigned and the subsequent ascension of Manasseh Sogavare as prime minister brought calm to the Solomons' capital.

In early April 2007, a tsunami struck Western and Choiseul provinces. Gizo, the Solomons' second-largest city, was at the centre of the disaster, and Ghizo's south-west coast was worst hit, leaving Gilbertese villagers between Titiana and Saeraghi homeless. Aid workers arrived en masse to help rebuild the local economy. All things considered, the destruction was fairly limited and the effects of the tsunami are almost no longer visible on land.

The Culture

Solomon Islanders' obligations to their clan and village bigman (chief) are eternal and enduring, whether they live in the same village all their lives or move to another country. As in most Melanesian cultures, the *wantok* system is observed here. All islanders are born with a set of obligations to their *wantok,* but they're also endowed with privileges that only *wantok* receive. For most Melanesian villagers it's an egalitarian way of sharing the community assets. There's no social security system and very few people are in paid employment, but the clan provides economic support and a strong sense of identity.

Melanesian culture is deeply rooted in ancestor worship, magic and oral traditions. Villagers often refer to their traditional ways, beliefs and land ownership as *kastom;* it's bound up in the Melanesian systems of lore and culture.

The Solomons' 2005 population was estimated at 538,000. Melanesians represent 94% and Polynesians 4%. The large Micronesian communities who were resettled from Kiribati by the British in the 1960s are still called Gilbertese. The remainder of the population is made up of Asians and expats, mainly Aussies and Kiwis. Most of the population lives in rural villages.

About 96% of the population is Christian. Of these, 35% are members of the Anglican-affiliated Church of Melanesia and 20% are Roman Catholics.

Islanders still practise pre-Christian religions in a few remote areas, particularly on Malaita; in other places traditional beliefs are observed alongside Christianity.

Arts

Solomon Islanders are incredibly musical people – it's a must to go to a local church service to listen to the singing. The Malaitan pipe bands (or bamboo bands) are amazing. In ensembles of 12 or so members, the band plays bamboo pipes in all sizes bundled together with bushvine. They're played as panpipe and flutes, and as long tubes whose openings are struck with rubber thongs to make an unusual plinketty-plonk sound. One of the most famous panpipe groups is Narasirato (www.narasirato.com), from Malaita; this group has gained international recognition. They mix classic Malaitan panpipe music with contemporary beats.

There are also strong carving traditions in the Solomons. Carvings incorporate human, bird, fish and other animal motifs, often in combination, and they frequently represent deities and spirits. Woodcarvings are inlaid with nautilus or trochus shell. Carvings of *nguzunguzu* (canoe figure-heads, also carved in miniature) and animals are produced from kerosene wood and ebony. Decorated bowls and masks are widely available, as are stone replicas of traditional shell money.

Shell money is used in Malaita, while in the Temotu Islands red-feather coils are still used.

Environment

The country is largely covered by tropical rainforest, but much of it has been degraded by logging operations. Excessive logging threatens the rich diversity of flora and fauna as well as the traditional lifestyle of villagers. Other possible negative effects include erosion, climate changes, loss of water resources and disruption to coral reefs. In Marovo Lagoon, Isabel and other islands, the effects of logging are clearly being felt. That said, there are plans to encourage sustainable logging and thus reduce the pressure on the environment.

SOLOMONS ENDEMICS TIM FLANNERY

The Solomon Islands represent a whole other environment, for they are an ancient island archipelago that has never been connected to a continent. The cuscus (tree-dwelling marsupial) found there only reached the islands a few thousand years ago with people. The true endemics are giant rats, monkey-faced bats and unusual birds, such as the Guadalcanal honeyeater. The giant rats are rare now, but you might be fortunate enough to spot one of the half-dozen species in dense, virginal forest. One of the largest species makes nests like those constructed by eagles in the tallest rainforest trees. One other aspect of the Solomons fauna is a radiation of frogs that is unique. Some look like dead leaves, others like lumps of moss, while one genus, which is often found in caves, is gigantic, reaching over 20cm long.

Tim Flannery is a naturalist, ecologist, environmental activist and author. He is currently an adjunct professor at Macquarie University.

The spectacular marine environment is home to a rich variety of fish, corals, anemones and many other creatures, including eight species of venomous sea snakes. Several islands are breeding grounds for green and hawksbill turtles.

The Solomons has 173 bird species, 40 of them endemic.

Native reptiles include the 1.5m-long monitor lizard, freshwater crocodiles and the very dangerous saltwater crocodile.

More than 130 butterfly species are found locally, and 35 are endemic.

SURVIVAL GUIDE

Directory A–Z

Accommodation

Tourist-class hotels are confined to Honiara, Gizo and Munda. Although basic by international standards, these hotels generally have rooms with or without private shower and air-con. Most have restaurants and bars, offer wi-fi service (or internet facilities) and take credit cards. There's also a handful of plush resorts in Honiara and the Western Province. A few high-end places quote their rates in Australian dollars.

Elsewhere accommodation is offered in basic leafhouse-style lodges or private houses, usually with only basic shared bathrooms.

The visitor information centre in Honiara (p326) can make suggestions and organise bookings. Online bookings can be made with the **Solomons Travel Portal** (www.solomon islands-hotels.travel).

PRICE RANGES

The following price ranges refer to a double room with bathroom, unless specified otherwise in the accommodation listings:

$ less than S$250

$$ S$250 to S$800

$$$ more than S$800

Activities

Diving The highly reputable live-aboard dive boat **MV Bilikiki** (www.bilikiki.com) offers regular cruises around the Russell Islands and Marovo Lagoon. Australian-based specialist companies offering package dive tours include **Allways Dive Expeditions** (www.allwaysdive.com.au), **Dive Adventures** (www.diveadventures.com.au) and **Diversion Dive Travel** (www.diversionoz.com).

Surfing Two ecofriendly operators organise community-based surfaris to Guadalcanal, Malaita, Isabel and Makira islands: **Surf Solomons** (www.surfsolomons.com) and **Sol Surfing** (www.surfingsolomonislands.com).

Business Hours

The following are common business hours in the Solomons; exceptions are noted in reviews.

Banks & post offices 8.30am to 3pm Monday Friday.

Government offices 8am to noon and 1pm to 4pm Monday to Friday.

Restaurants 11am to 9pm.

Shops 8.30am to 5pm Monday to Friday, 8.30am to noon Saturday.

Embassies & Consulates

Australia (Map p324; ☎21561; www.solomon
islands.embassy.gov.au; Mud Alley, Honiara)

France & Germany (☎22588; tradco@
solomon.com.sb; Tradco Office, City Centre Bldg,
Honiara)

NZ (☎21502; www.nzembassy.com/solomon
-islands; City Centre Bldg, Honiara)

PNG (☎20561; Anthony Saru Bldg, Honiara)

UK (☎21705; www.ukinsolomonislands.fco.gov.
uk; Tanuli Ridge, Honiara)

Food

Tipping is not required or expected in the
Solomons and prices listed in this book
include tax. The following price ranges refer
to standard mains:

$ less than S$60

$$ S$60 to S$120

$$$ more than S$120

Holidays

New Year's Day 1 January

Easter March or April

Whit Monday May or June

Queen's Birthday First Monday in June

Independence Day 7 July

Christmas 25 December

National Thanksgiving Day 26 December

Internet Access

You'll find internet cafes in Honiara and in
Gizo. **Solomon Telekom** (www.solomon.com.
sb) has public email facilities in Honiara,
Gizo, Munda and Auki.

Wi-fi is also available at the better hotels
and at a few cafes in Honiara, Munda and
Gizo thanks to the prepaid Bumblebee card.

PRACTICALITIES

» **Newspapers & Magazines**
The *Solomons Star* (www.solomon
starnews.com), the *National Express*
and the web-only *Solomon Times
Online* (www.solomontimes.com)

» **Electricity** The Solomons uses
240V, 50Hz AC and Australian-style
three-pin plugs.

» **Weights & Measures** The imperial
system is used here.

It's available in some shops and hotels or at
Solomon Telekom offices.

Money

ATMs There are ATMs at ANZ, Bank South
Pacific (BSP) and Westpac in Honiara, as well
as in Auki, Munda and Gizo.

Credit cards The main tourist-oriented
businesses, the Honiara branch of Solomon Airlines, a few dive shops and most
upmarket hotels and resorts accept credit
cards (usually with a 5% surcharge), but
elsewhere it's strictly cash.

Currency The local currency is the Solomon Islands' dollar (S$). A supply of coins
and small-denomination notes will come
in handy in rural areas, at markets, and
for bus and boat rides.

Moneychangers The Bank South Pacific,
Westpac and ANZ will change money in
most major currencies.

Taxes There's a 10% government tax on
hotel and restaurant prices, but more basic
places often don't charge it. All prices
given in this book are inclusive of tax.

Tipping & bargaining Tipping and
bargaining are not traditionally part of
Melanesian culture.

Telephone

Solomon Telekom (www.telekom.com.sb)
operates the country's telephone system.
Public phones are reasonably common in
the larger centres and phonecards are widely
available. Solomon Islands' country code is
☎677; first hit ☎00 to dial out of the country.

Mobile Phones Solomon Telekom and
BeMobile offer GSM mobile phone service
in most areas (but Marovo isn't entirely
covered yet). Prepaid SIMs are available
for purchase. Both operators have international roaming agreements with Telstra
and Optus (Australia).

Visas

Citizens from most Western countries don't
need a visa to enter the Solomon Islands,
just a valid passport, an onward ticket and
sufficient funds for their stay. On arrival
at the airport, you will be given an entry
permit for up to one month.

Women Travellers

Exercise normal caution in Honiara – after
dark, take a taxi and stay in busy areas.

Melanesians are very sensitive about the show of female thighs, so shorts and skirts should be knee-length and swimwear should incorporate boardshorts rather than bikini bottoms.

Getting There & Away
Air

The Solomons' only international airport is Henderson Airport, 11km east of Honiara.

The following airlines have regular scheduled flights to the Solomon Islands.

Fiji Airways (www.airpacific.com) Connects Honiara with Nadi and Honiara with Vila. As we went to print, Fiji's national carrier was rebranding itself from Air Pacific, and the airline information in this book may be subject to change.

Air Niugini (www.airniugini.com.pg) Has flights between Port Moresby and Nadi to Honiara.

Our Airline (www.ourairline.com.au) Flies from Nauru to Honiara (and on to Brisbane).

Virgin Australia (www.virginaustralia.com) Has services to/from Brisbane. Formerly called Pacific Blue.

Solomon Airlines (www.flysolomons.com; Mendana Ave, Honiara) The national carrier. Has services between Honiara and Brisbane, Nadi, Port Moresby and Vila.

Sea

The Solomons is a favourite spot for yachties who take refuge in the lagoons during cyclone season. Along with Honiara, Korovou (Shortland Islands), Gizo, Ringgi, Yandina, Tulagi and Graciosa Bay are official ports of entry where you can clear customs and immigration.

Getting Around
Air

Solomon Airlines (www.flysolomons.com) services the country's 20-odd airstrips. The main tourist gateways, including Gizo, Seghe (for North Marovo Lagoon) and Munda are serviced daily from Honiara, but be sure to confirm your flight at least 24 hours before your departure.

The baggage allowance is set at 16kg per passenger.

Boat
DINGHIES
Outboard-powered dinghies are the most common means of transport in the Solomons. People pay a fare to travel a sector. Charters cost around S$1500 per day for the boat and a driver; fuel is often not included (S$20 per litre in remote areas).

PASSENGER BOATS
Go West Transport Operates a thrice-weekly shuttle between Munda and Gizo (Western Province).

MV 360 Discovery Has regular services between Honiara, Tulagi and Auki (Malaita).

MV Pelican Express Has a weekly service between Honiara and the Western Province (including Marovo Lagoon and Gizo).

Bus

Public minibuses are found only in Honiara. Elsewhere, people pile into open-backed trucks or tractor-drawn trailers.

Car & Motorcycle

The country has around 1300km of generally dreadful roads. International driving permits are accepted, as are most driving licences. Driving is on the left side of the road.

Hire cars are available only in Honiara. Contact Pacific Casino Hotel (p322).

Hitching

If you want a ride through the countryside, another option is to flag down a passing vehicle and ask the driver the cost of a lift. In rural areas most vehicles double as public transport but take the usual precautions.

Taxi

Taxis are plentiful in Honiara and there are small fleets in Gizo and Auki. They are meterless, so agree on the price before you set off.

Tahiti & French Polynesia

Best Places to Stay

» Ninamu Resort (p404)

» Tevahine Dream (p398)

» Sunset Beach Motel (p380)

» Vahine Island Private Island Resort (p383)

Best Places to Eat

» Bora Kaina Hut (p390)

» Le K (p370)

» Snack Te Anuanua (p403)

» Vaiete Square Roulottes (p354)

Why Go?

Just the name Tahiti conjures up centuries of legend and lifetimes of daydreams. Its 18th-century reputation as a wanton playground of flower-bedecked Polynesians in an Eden-like setting has morphed into a 21st-century image of a chic honeymoon haven. But there's more to the country than cocktails on the terrace of your over-water bungalow.

When you're not idling in the scent of gardenias, warm damp breezes and ukulele riffs by starlight, try hiking up a waterfall valley, paddling out on a turquoise lagoon or diving through sharky passes. While the resorts make headlines, the country's unsung heroes are the impressive collection of family pensions that range from rickety rooms in someone's home to luxurious boutique-style bungalows on private islets.

From the vast lagoons of the Tuamotu atolls, to the culturally intense Marquesas Islands and the scenic mountainscapes of the Society Islands (Tahiti, Mo'orea, Ra'iatea, Taha'a, Bora Bora and Maupiti), French Polynesia's 118 islands provide enough diversity and surprises for several voyages.

When to Go
Pape'ete

May–Jun & Sep–Nov Excellent times to visit. It's cool, dry and less windy than in July and August.

Jul–Aug Peak tourist season. Can be windy. The region comes to life for Heiva festival in July.

Dec–Apr The summer rainy season. It's often humid, cloudy and very wet.

Connections

Short of sailing your own boat, air travel is the most practical way to connect from Tahiti to other islands. Pape'ete is the transport hub for French Polynesia with regular flights to all archipelagos. Boat travel is a reliable option within the Society group. A number of boats shuttle back and forth between Tahiti and Mo'orea each day, and one catamaran serves the Society Islands. Island hopping on the cargo boats that sail between Tahiti and the other archipelagos is an adventurous and inexpensive way to travel but you'll need plenty of time.

ITINERARIES

One Week

Start on **Tahiti**. Spend day one driving around the island. Devote day two and three to **Mo'orea**, (considered by many to be the most beautiful isle in the Societies). Splash around in the lagoon or go on a whale- or dolphin-watching tour. Fly to **Bora Bora**, where cool hikes, boat tours on the vast turquoise lagoon and fancy restaurants await. Live it up for a couple of nights in an over-water bungalow. From Bora Bora, you can day trip to **Maupiti**, one of French Polynesia's hidden gems.

Two Weeks

Start with two days on **Tahiti** and the same on **Mo'orea** before flying to **Huahine** for a taste of Polynesian culture. Push on from here to **Bora Bora** where you can spend a few days. Then it's time to change scene. Fly to **Rangiroa**, the largest coral atoll in the country. You'll need three days to do the atoll justice. Next, hop to **Fakarava** or **Tikehau**, where you can dive, snorkel and relax for a few days before returning to Tahiti.

Essential Food & Drink

» **Ma'a Tahiti** Traditional Tahitian food. It's a mix of starchy taro and *uru* (breadfruit), raw or cooked fish, fatty pork, coconut milk and a few scattered vegetables.

» **Fish** Features prominently in Tahitian cuisine. *Poisson cru* (raw fish in coconut milk) is the most popular local dish. It can also be served grilled, fried or poached. It's usually tuna, bonito, wahoo, mahi mahi, parrotfish or jackfish.

» **Steaks** Hmm, lamb and beef from New Zealand!

» **Chow mein** This fried noodle dish is one of numerous Chinese specialities available.

» **Po'e** Baked, mashed fruit mixed with starch and doused with coconut milk.

» **Beer** Wash everything down with a cold Hinano.

» **Cocktails** Try mai tai, made with rum, fruit juices and coconut liqueur.

» **Wine** Good French wines and one local wine, Vin de Tahiti.

AT A GLANCE

Currency Cour de Franc Pacifique (CFP)

Language Tahitian, French

Mobile phones Local SIM cards are available and can be used with unlocked GSM phones. Roaming agreements with most operators.

Money ATMs on most islands; credit cards accepted on major islands

Visas Not required for most Western countries

Fast Facts

» **Capital** Pape'ete
» **Country code** ☎689
» **Land area** 3500 sq km
» **Population** 270,000

Exchange Rates

Australia	A$1	96 CFP
Canada	C$1	92 CFP
Europe	€1	119 CFP
Japan	¥100	119 CFP
New Zealand	NZ$1	75 CFP
UK	UK£1	148 CFP
USA	US$1	95 CFP

For current exchange rates see www.xe.com.

Set Your Budget

» **Pension** 8000 CFP
» **Two-course dinner** 3600 CFP
» **Boat excursion** 8500 CFP
» **Bottle of Hinano beer** 400 CFP
» **Car rental** 10,000 CFP

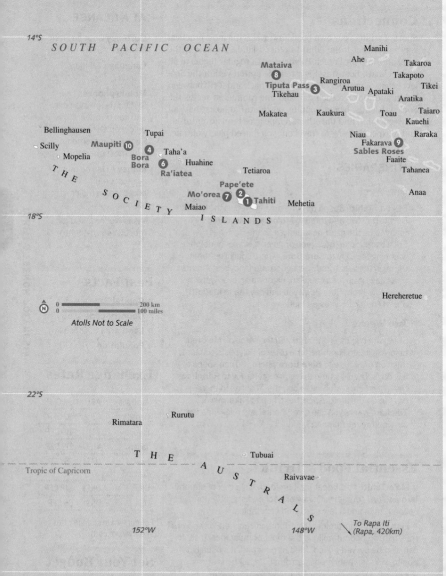

Tahiti & French Polynesia Highlights

1 Exploring by 4WD **Tahiti's** (p361) divinely lush and craggy interior

2 Watching the best of the best shake their hips and waggle their knees at

the Heiva festival's **dance competitions** (p351) in Pape'ete in July

3 Diving with sharks and manta rays in Rangiroa's fantastic **Tiputa Pass** (p397)

4 Pampering yourself on ultra-gorgeous and over-the-top luxurious **Bora Bora** (p387)

5 Exploring the wild green yonder of **Nuku Hiva's** (p408) wild and rugged interior

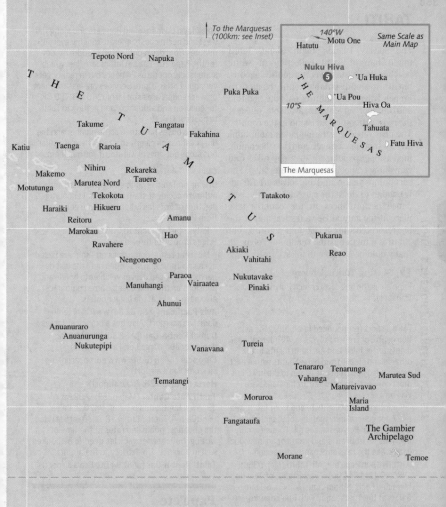

To the Marquesas
(100km: see Inset)

140°W
Hatutu   Motu One   Same Scale as
Main Map

Nuku Hiva
❺   'Ua Huka
'Ua Pou
10°S   Hiva Oa
              Tahuata
        Fatu Hiva

THE MARQUESAS

The Marquesas

THE TUAMOTUS

Tepoto Nord   Napuka

Puka Puka

Takume   Fangatau
              Fakahina
Katiu   Taenga   Raroia
Makemo   Nihiru   Rekareka
Motutunga   Marutea Nord   Tauere
        Tekokota   Tatakoto
Haraiki   Hikueru
    Reitoru
    Marokau   Amanu
Ravahere   Hao   Pukarua
                    Reao
    Nengonengo   Akiaki
              Vahitahi
        Paraoa   Nukutavake
    Manuhangi Vairaatea   Pinaki
        Ahunui

Anuanuraro
Anuanurunga
Nukutepipi   Tureia
        Vanavana
                Tenararo   Tenarunga
                Vahanga   Marutea Sud
    Tematangi   Matureivavao
              Moruroa   Maria
                    Island
        Fangataufa   The Gambier
                    Archipelago
        Morane   Temoe

SOUTH PACIFIC OCEAN

140°W   136°W

❻ Pondering over French
Polynesia's mysterious past at
Marae Taputapuatea (p377)
on Ra'iatea

❼ Driving around **Mo'orea**
(p362) and being awed

by its mesmerising
landscapes

❽ Leaving the world behind
on little-known **Mataiva** (p405)

❾ Finding your own slice of
beach heaven on the unspoilt

sands of **Sables Roses** (p403),
Fakarava's most idyllic spot

❿ Taking life at a slower pace
on **Maupiti** (p392), which is
packed with quiet charm

TAHITI

POP 185,000 / AREA 1045 SQ KM

The Society Islands' main island, Tahiti might have a scant collection of white beaches and vistas over turquoise lagoons, but it's the undisputable centre of modern French Polynesian culture; plus the nightlife and outdoor adventures available make it the most action-packed island in the country. The near vertical, waterfall-laden mountains are as inviting as ever and are becoming increasingly popular for lush day hikes and canyoning (rappelling down waterfalls). The surf pumps year-round and locals are friendly enough to share their breaks; and the best dance performances in the country take place at the annual Heiva festival and at the big resorts. It's not a Gauguin painting, but Tahiti is a myth-busting version of Polynesia that would be a shame to miss.

Getting There & Away

Pape'ete is the hub of all French Polynesian transport.

AIR

Faa'a airport (pronounced fa-ah-ah) is the aviation centre of French Polynesia. All international flights arrive here, and Air Tahiti flights to the other islands leave from here. Flights within each archipelago hop from one island to the next, but most connections between archipelagos are via Faa'a.

For international flights to and from Tahiti, see p427; for general information about air travel within French Polynesia, see p428; and for connections to/from an island group or an individual island, see the relevant chapter or section.

AIRLINES In Pape'ete, **Air Tahiti** (Map p356; ☑86 42 42, 47 44 00; www.airtahiti.pf; Rue du Maréchal Foch; ☺8am-5pm Mon-Fri, 8-11am Sat) is at the intersection with Rue Edouard Ahnne. It also has an **office** (☺6am-4.30pm Mon-Fri, 6am-4pm Sat & Sun) at the airport.

For international airline offices, see p427.

BOAT

All passenger boats to other islands moor at the **Gare Maritime** (Blvd Pomare). The numerous cargo ships to the different archipelagos work from the Motu Uta port zone, to the north of the city.

See p428 for general information on inter-island ships, or the individual island chapters or sections for specific information on travel to/from those destinations.

Getting Around

Public transport in Tahiti is limited so you're best off renting a car.

BUS

Weekdays, buses around Pape'ete and along the west and north coasts operate roughly every 15 minutes from dawn until about 5.30pm except for the Pape'ete–Faa'a–Outumaoro line, which supposedly operates 24 hours but in reality gets very quiet after 10pm. Services are less frequent on weekends. Fares start from 140 CFP (80 CFP for children and students), and getting to Tahiti Iti costs 500 CFP.

Tahiti's buses have their route number and the final destination clearly marked. There are official bus stops but drivers will stop if you hail them.

CAR

Driving on Tahiti is quite straightforward and, although accident statistics are not encouraging, the traffic is fairly light once you get away from Pape'ete.

Rates start at about 10,000 CFP per day. Prices drop after three days.

Most car-rental companies on Tahiti are based at Faa'a airport and stay open until the last departure. They can deliver vehicles to hotels and pensions on the west coast. Some companies also have desks at the bigger hotels:

Avis Pacificar (☑85 02 84; www.avis-tahiti. com; Faa'a airport) Also has a branch in Taravao.

Daniel Rent-a-Car (☑82 30 04, 81 96 32; daniel.location@mail.pf; Faa'a airport)

Europcar (☑86 61 96; www.europcarpolyne sie.com; Faa'a airport)

Hertz (☑82 55 86; Faa'a airport)

Tahiti Auto Center (Map p352; ☑82 33 33; www.tahitiautocenter.pf; PK20.2, Pa'ea; ☺7.30am-4.30pm Mon-Fri, 8-11.30am Sat) Had the cheapest published rates at the time of writing, but cheaper vehicles need to be booked well in advance. No delivery to the airport.

Tahiti Rent-a-Car (☑81 94 00; Faa'a airport)

Pape'ete

With Polynesian smiles, French-style sidewalk cafes and the occasional guy on the kerb strumming a ukulele, Pape'ete does feel exotic despite its lack of beaches and blue water. Yeah, the edges are grimy and it's a little seedy, but the waterfront's palm-fringed promenade makes the town prettier and the busy streets and lanes are dripping with well-regarded restaurants.

⊙ Sights

⌈TOP⌉
⌊CHOICE⌋ **Marché de Pape'ete**   MARKET
(Pape'ete Market; Map p356; cnr Rue Colette & Rue du 22 Septembre; ☺7am-5pm Mon-Fri, 4-9am Sun) Load up on colourful *pareu* (sarongs), shell

necklaces, woven hats and local produce at the famed Marché de Pape'ete – a Pape'ete must. The most fun time to visit is early Sunday morning when local residents flock in as early as 4am.

Temple de Paofai
CHURCH

(Blvd Pomare) The large pink Temple de Paofai makes a colourful scene on Sunday morning, when it is bursting at the seams with a devout congregation dressed in white and belting out rousing *himene* (hymns). The church is on the site of the first Protestant church in Pape'ete, which was built in 1818.

Jardins de Paofai
GARDENS

(Blvd Pomare) In these trimmed public gardens near Place To'ata, you'll find paved walking paths that meander past blooming planter boxes and the occasional tree. As you walk east there are racing *pirogues* (local outrigger canoes) lined up under on the pebbly shore.

Place Vaiete
SQUARE

(Vaiete Square; Map p356) Place Vaiete is home to multiple *roulottes* and occasional live-music performances at night but is quite peaceful during the day. There are plenty of public benches along here where you can sit and watch the world go by.

Cathédrale Notre-Dame
CATHEDRAL

(Map p356) Taking pride of place in the centre of town is the Cathédrale Notre-Dame, with its recently renovated facade. It dates from the 19th century.

FREE Musée de la Perle
MUSEUM

(Pearl Museum; ☑46 15 54; www.robertwan.com; Blvd Pomare; ☉9am-5pm Mon-Sat) This pearl museum was created by pearl magnate Robert Wan with aims of luring visitors into his glamorous shop. It's a worthwhile, small and modern museum that covers all facets of the pearl-cultivating business.

Parc Bougainville
PARK

(Bougainville Park; Map p356; Blvd Pomare) A great spot to just chill out, Parc Bougainville is a tropical oasis in the middle of the city. Lush and cool, it's fronted by a 1909 bust of the great French navigator.

🛌 Sleeping

Central Pape'ete is not the place to stay if you're looking for tranquillity or anything resembling a tourist brochure; the options on the outskirts of town offer more palm-fringed, beachlike choices.

THE HEIVA

If your visit is in July, stay on in Tahiti for the hugely popular Heiva, French Polynesia's premier festival, which is held at various venues in and near Pape'ete. It lasts about four weeks from late June to late July and is so impressive that it's almost worth timing your trip around it. Expect a series of music, dance, cultural and sporting contests.

TOP CHOICE Intercontinental Resort Tahiti
RESORT $$$

(Map p355; ☑86 51 10; www.tahitiresorts.intercontinental.com; PK8, Faa'a; r & bungalows d from 25,000 CFP; ✳🐾🛜🌊) The Intercontinental is as posh as Tahiti gets. Marble bathrooms, plush canopies and Mo'orea views from private balconies are standard both in the rooms and romantic over-water bungalows. The two swimming pools are fabulous and the water-sports centre is the best on the island.

Fare Suisse
GUESTHOUSE $

(☑42 00 30; www.fare-suisse.com; Rue des Poilus Tahitiens; d 10,200 CFP; ✳🛜) This pension (guesthouse) is in a spotless and stylish cement home in a quiet area not far from the centre of town. Beni the dynamic owner picks guests up free of charge at the airport, lets folks store their luggage and creates a super pleasant atmosphere. Breakfast is an extra 1200 CFP.

Sofitel Maeva Beach Resort
RESORT $$

(Map p355; ☑86 66 00; www.accorhotels.com; PK8, Faa'a; d from 15,000 CFP; ✳🐾🛜🌊) This resort is one of the better deals on the island, provided you keep your expectations in check. The '70s-style exterior could use a facelift, but rooms are comfortable enough.

Tiare Tahiti
HOTEL $$

(Map p356; ☑50 01 00; hoteltiaretahiti@mail.pf; Blvd Pomare; d from 15,500 CFP; ✳) This clean hotel overlooks the water in the hub of Pape'ete, but sadly is afflicted by the noise of traffic. A somewhat kitschy favourite with tour groups, it has 38 simply furnished, motel-like rooms that are overpriced; the cheaper ones are at the back and lack views but are quieter.

Tahiti Airport Motel
HOTEL $$

(Map p355; ☑50 40 00; www.tahitiairportmotel.com; PK5.5, Faa'a; d/q incl breakfast 14,000/22,000 CFP;

Tahiti

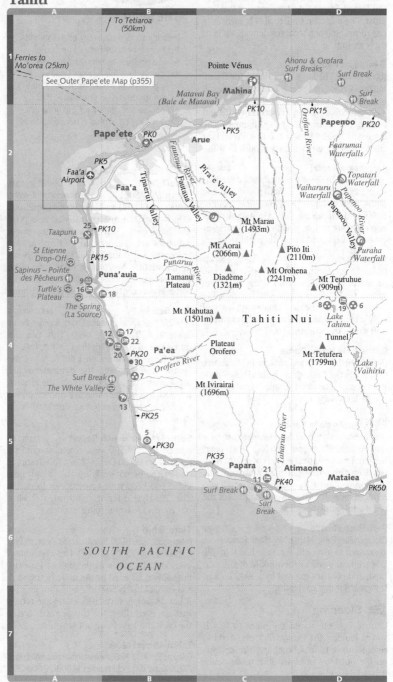

To Tetiaroa
(50km)

Ferries to
Mo'orea (25km)

Pointe Vénus

Ahonu & Orofara
Surf Breaks

Surf Break

Surf
Break

See Outer Pape'ete Map (p355)

Matavai Bay
(Baie de Matavai)

Mahina

PK10

PK15

Papenoo

PK20

Pape'ete

PK0

Arue

PK5

Orofara River

Faauta River

Fautaua River

Faarumai
Waterfalls

Faa'a
Airport

PK5

Faa'a

Tipaerui Valley

Fautaua Valley

Pira'e Valley

Topatari
Waterfall

Vaiharuru
Waterfall

Papenoo River

Papenoo Valley

Taapuna

25

PK10

Mt Marau
(1493m)

Puraha
Waterfall

St Etienne
Drop-Off

PK15

Puna'auia

Punaruu River

Mt Aorai
(2066m)

Pito Iti
(2110m)

Mt Orohena
(2241m)

Mt Teuruhue
(909m)

Sapinus – Pointe
des Pêcheurs

Turtle's
Plateau

9

16

18

Tamanu
Plateau

Diadème
(1321m)

Tahiti Nui

8

19

6

The Spring
(La Source)

Mt Mahutaa
(1501m)

Lake
Tahinu

Tunnel

12

17

Pa'ea

20

22

PK20

30

7

Plateau
Orofero

Orofero River

Mt Tetufera
(1799m)

Lake
Vaihiria

Surf Break

The White Valley

13

Mt Ivirairai
(1696m)

PK25

5

PK30

PK35

Papara

Taharuu River

21

Atimaono

11

PK40

Mataiea

Surf Break

Surf
Break

PK50

SOUTH PACIFIC
OCEAN

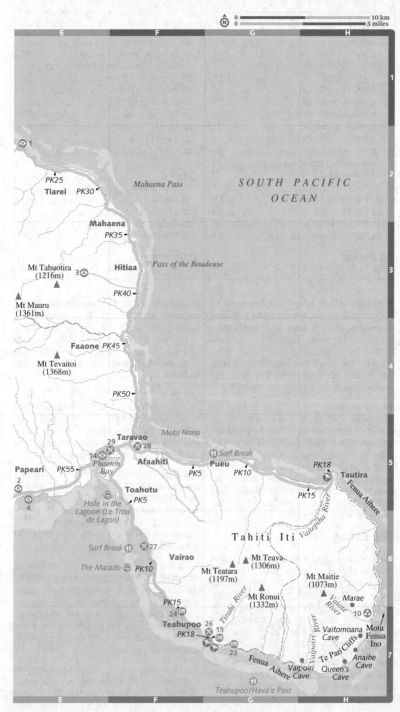

Tahiti

❈ ⓐ) Right across from Faa'a International Airport, this would appear to be the most convenient place to stay for a quick stop-over, but there's no shuttle so you have to drag your luggage across the car park then up the short but sometimes muddy hill. Rooms are impersonal but crisp and comfortable.

Teamo Pension GUESTHOUSE $
(Map p356; ✆42 47 26; www.teamoguesthouse.com; Rue du Pont-Neuf; dm 2600 CFP, d with shared bathroom 6600 CFP, d 7600-8600 CFP; ❈ⓐ) This place is a little depressing and the rooms need a freshen-up but the location is the saving grace – it's in a quiet area not far from the waterfront. The dearer rooms have private bathrooms and air-con while the dorm room has six beds.

🍽 Eating

TOP CHOICE Vaiete Square Roulottes POLYNESIAN $
(Map p356; Pl Vaiete; mains from 900 CFP; ❍dinner) The country's famous *roulottes* (literally 'caravans' in French) are a gastronomic pleasure. These little mobile stalls sizzle, fry and grill up a storm every evening from around 6pm; things don't quiet down until well into the night. Cash only.

Place Toata Snacks POLYNESIAN $
(Pl To'ata; mains 1300-2700 CFP; ❍lunch & dinner) This cluster of open-air *snacks* (snack bars) with outdoor seating near Place Toata is a

great place to chill with regulars and savour the most authentic and best-value food in town (but no alcohol is served).

Opening hours vary but there are usually at least two or three places serving lunch from 11am to 1.30pm and dinner from 6pm to 10pm. Cash only.

Le Lotus FUSION $$
(Map p355; ✆86 51 25; Intercontinental Resort Tahiti, PK8, Faa'a; mains 2000-4500 CFP; ❍lunch & dinner) Inside the Intercontinental Resort Tahiti, this uber-romantic restaurant on the edge of the lagoon is perfect for a special night out.

Lou Pescadou ITALIAN $
(Map p356; ✆43 74 26; Rue Anne-Marie Javouhey; mains 1200-2700 CFP; ❍Tue-Sat) A Pape'ete institution, this cheery restaurant has hearty pizza and pasta dishes. It's authentic Italian, right down to the red check tablecloths and carafes of red wine.

Le Rétro BISTRO $$
(Map p356; ✆50 60 25; Blvd Pomare; mains 1800-2500 CFP; ❍lunch & dinner) After an extensive renovation, this Pape'ete icon features trendy furnishings and a hip outdoor terrace overlooking the noisy boulevard. The wide-ranging menu covers enough territory to please most palates.

L'Oasis POLYNESIAN, FRENCH $$
(Map p356; ✆45 45 01; Centre Vaima; mains 1600-2500 CFP; ❍6am-3pm Mon-Sat) There's

Outer Pape'ete

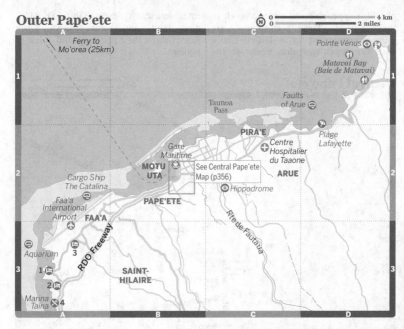

no contest about the most popular lunch spot in Pape'ete – this place is always busy. The range of daily specials on offer is well priced and filled with subtle flavours.

Patachoux   CAFETERIA **$**
(Map p356; ☎83 72 82; Rue Lagarde; mains 600-1200 CFP; ☺6am-4pm Mon-Sat) Takeaway sandwiches here are the deluxe version – fresh wholemeal or French bread stuffed with gourmet meats, fish and/or salads. Excellent pastries, too.

Morrison's Café   FRENCH, POLYNESIAN **$$**
(Map p356; ☎42 78 61; Vaima Centre; mains 1600-2800 CFP; ☺lunch Tue-Fri, dinner Wed-Sat) By far the trendiest spot in town, Morrison's Café is a casually elegant eatery on a rooftop and it makes a delightful escape from the main drag. Savour well-prepared fish and meat dishes as well as salads and pastas.

Les 3 Brasseurs   BRASSERIE **$$**
(Map p356; ☎50 60 25; Blvd Pomare; mains 1800-2500 CFP; ☺lunch & dinner) You can't miss the colourful facade of this lively brasserie in front of the Gare Maritime. It has good daily specials as well as more mainstream dishes.

Outer Pape'ete

⊕ Activities, Courses & Tours

Eleuthera Plongée	(see 4)
Fluid Dive Centre	(see 4)
Topdive	(see 1)

⊟ Sleeping

1	Intercontinental Resort Tahiti	A3
2	Sofitel Maeva Beach Resort	A3
3	Tahiti Airport Motel	A3

⊗ Eating

	Casa Bianca	(see 4)
	Le Lotus	(see 1)
4	Pink Coconut	A3
	Quai des Îles	(see 4)

♟ Drinking & Entertainment

After a stay on other islands, where nightlife is just about nonexistent, Pape'ete could almost pass itself off as a city of wild abandon. Many restaurants have a bar section, and you'll find some good watering holes on the main drag. Top-end hotel bars are also a focus of Pape'ete social life, especially on Friday and Saturday evenings.

Tahiti is a good island for tapping your toes along to some of the best Polynesian dance and music groups, many

of which appear several times a week in the big hotels. These performances are often accompanied by a buffet. Check with the hotel reception desks at the Intercontinental Resort Tahiti, Le Méridien Tahiti and Sofitel Maeva Beach Resort about their programs and entrance policies.

Central Pape'ete

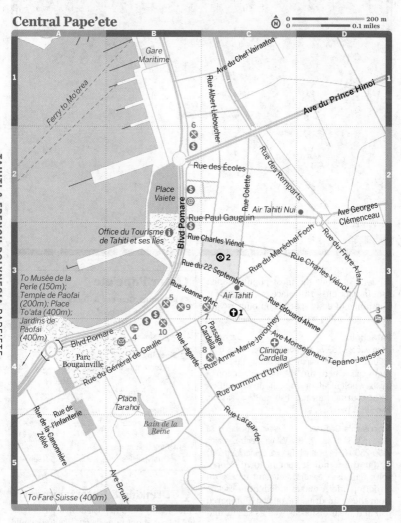

Central Pape'ete

🛍 Shopping

There's really not much to buy in Tahiti besides Tahitian pearls (and boy are there lots of pearl shops) and a few handicrafts. Your best bet for everything from *pareu* (sarong-type garment) to woven hats, pearls, vanilla and homemade *monoï* (fragranced coconut oil) is the Marché de Pape'ete. Watch out though – anything that seems to be mass produced probably is mass produced in China, Indonesia or the Philippines.

❶ Information

Emergency
Ambulance (☑15)
Police (☑17)

Internet Access
Cybernesia (Map p356; Vaima Centre; per hr 720 CFP; ☺8.30am-5pm Mon-Fri, 9am-1pm Sat)
Maison de la Presse (Map p356; Blvd Pomare; per hr 600 CFP; ☺8am-6pm Mon-Fri, 8.30am-1pm & 4.30-6pm)

Medical Services
Centre Hospitalier du Taaone (Map p355; ☑48 62 62, 24hr emergencies 42 01 01; Pira'e) The biggest hospital in French Polynesia, with good facilities and a range of medical specialities.
Clinique Cardella (Map p356; ☑42 04 25; Rue Anne-Marie Javouhey; ☺24hr) Private clinic behind the cathedral.

Money
There are banks (Banque Socredo, Banque de Tahiti and Banque de Polynésie) and ATMs scattered around Pape'ete and its suburbs. Banque Socredo has a branch at Faa'a airport, where there's also an ATM. See p426 for general information on banks and changing money.
Broadway (Map p356; Blvd Pomare; ☺7.30am-11pm Mon-Wed, 7-1am Thu-Sat, 8am-11pm Sun) Small bureau de change with longer opening hours next door to Les 3 Brasseurs. No commission on currency exchange but the rates offered are slightly lower than what you'll get at banks.

Post
Post office (OPT; Map p356; www.opt.pf; Blvd Pomare; ☺7.30am-5pm Mon-Fri, 7.30-11am Sat) Pape'ete's main post office is next to Parc Bougainville.

Tourist Information
Office du Tourisme de Tahiti et ses Îles (Map p356; ☑50 40 30; www.tahiti-tourisme.com; Fare Manihini, Blvd Pomare; ☺7.30am-5.30pm Mon-Fri, 8am-4pm Sat, 8am-noon Sun) Has information on all of French Polynesia. Although Mo'orea and Bora Bora have tourist offices, the more remote islands don't, so if you have any queries, ask here.

❶ Getting There & Around
To/From the Airport
The taxi drive to central Pape'ete will set you back 2000 CFP during the day and 2500 CFP at night (8pm to 6am).

If you arrive at a reasonable time of the day, you'll be able to catch any bus going towards town from the airport (northeast bound or to your left as you leave the airport), which will take you straight to the centre of Pape'ete in about 15 minutes for a flat fare of 140 CFP during the day and 250 CFP after 6pm. Walk straight across the car park outside the airport, up the steps to street level and across the road to hail a city-bound bus. From Pape'ete to the airport, take a bus heading to Faa'a and Outumaoro – the destination will be clearly posted on the front – from along Rue du Général de Gaulle.

Taxi
All the big hotels have taxi ranks, and there are plenty of taxis in central Pape'ete. Any trip of a reasonable length will approximate a day's car rental, so if you want wheels you may as well rent them.

Around Tahiti Nui

It's another world outside of Pape'ete; the sea is a deep blue, the jagged, green mountains frame the sky and cars putter along at 50km/h.

◉ Sights
The following is a 114km clockwise circuit around Tahiti Nui.

Pointe Vénus & Matavai Bay HISTORICAL SITE
(Map p355; PK10) Part of Captain Cook's mission on his three-month sojourn in 1769 was to record the transit of Venus across the face of the sun in an attempt to calculate the distance between the sun and the earth. Pointe Vénus, the promontory that marks the eastern end of Matavai Bay, was the site of Cook's observatory. Today it's a popular, shaded black-sand **beach** overlooked by an impressive **lighthouse**. It's unsigned; just turn off at VenuStar Supermarket at PK10.

Arahoho Blowhole NATURAL SITE
(Map p352; PK22) When the swell is big enough, huge sprays of water shoot out from the *trou du souffleur* (blowhole) by the road just before Tiarei at PK22, coming from Pape'ete. Just past the blowhole is a

fine sliver of black-sand **beach**, ideal for a picnic pause. There are sometimes fruit vendors here.

Faarumai Waterfalls
WATERFALLS

(Map p352; PK22.1) Through the village of Tiarei, you'll see a sign on the mountain side of the road for the exceedingly high Faarumai Waterfalls. It's a couple of hundred metres through a forest of *mape* trees to **Vaimahutu**, the first of the waterfalls. Another 20-minute stroll leads to the other two falls, **Haamarere Iti** and **Haamarere Rahi**, which stand almost side by side.

Taravao
TOWN

(PK54) Strategically situated at the narrow isthmus connecting Tahiti Nui with Tahiti Iti, the town of Taravao has been a military base on and off since 1844, when the first French fort was established. Although there is little of interest in the town, it does have shops, banks, petrol stations and a number of small restaurants. From Taravao, roads run along the north and south coasts of Tahiti Iti. If you're not going to Tahiti Iti, continue along the road that goes back to Pape'ete along the south and west coast of Tahiti Nui.

Jardins Botaniques
BOTANICAL GARDENS

(Map p352; PK51; admission 600 CFP; ⊘9am-5pm) Tahiti's Jardins Botaniques and Musée Gauguin share an entrance road and car park at PK51.2. The 137-hectare Jardins Botaniques has walking paths that wind their way through the garden past ponds, palms and a superb *mape* forest.

Bain de Vaima & Vaipahi Spring Gardens
BOTANICAL GARDENS

(Map p352; PK49) Vaima Pool is where locals come from all over to bathe in the icy but exceptionally clear waters that are thought to have healing properties.

The Vaipahi Spring Gardens further along is a beautifully landscaped garden with a magnificent natural waterfall. There's a small network of **hiking trails** that lead from a signpost with a map up to more waterfalls.

Plage de Taharuu
BEACH

(Map p352; PK39) Everybody loves Plage de Taharuu – locals taking the kids for a swim, tourists on day trips from Pape'ete and surfers catching some great waves. This gently curving black-sand beach is long, broad and fairly protected.

Maraa Grotto
CAVE

(Map p352; PK28.5) Lush gardens, overhung caverns, crystal-clear pools and ferny grottoes are all standard features at gorgeous Maraa Grotto.

Plage du PK23.5
BEACH

(Map p352; PK23.5) This rather wide (by Tahiti standards) beach is popular with families and has public facilities.

Marae Arahurahu
ARCHAEOLOGICAL SITE

(Map p352; PK22.5) Tranquil, huge and beautifully maintained, the *marae* (traditional temple) is undoubtedly the best-looking one on the island and even rivals those on other islands.

Plage du Mahana Park
BEACH

(Map p352; PK18.5) Plage du Mahana Park has calm waters and a snorkelling reef close to shore. On weekends there are kayaks for hire.

Plage du PK18
BEACH

(Map p352; PK18) Beloved by locals, Plage du PK18 is a stunning beach to sun yourself on, but not that great for swimming or snorkelling due to the shallow water.

TOP CHOICE Musée de Tahiti et des Îles
MUSEUM

(Museum of Tahiti & Its Islands; Map p352; ✆54 84 36; PK15.1; admission 800 CFP; ⊘9.30am-5.30pm Tue-Sun) This excellent museum in Puna'auia has one of the best collections in the Pacific, including dioramas about island geology, archaeological finds and ancient art. Outside is one of Tahiti's most popular surf breaks.

🏃 Activities

Diving & Whale Watching

There are some excellent diving opportunities to be had in Tahiti (see p32 for more information about the sites). Most dive shops lead whale-watching tours between July and October when humpbacks swim near the coasts. Half-day trips cost from 8000 CFP per person. Dolphin-watching tours run year-round and are slightly cheaper.

Eleuthera Plongée
DIVING

(Map p355; ✆42 49 29, 77 65 68; www.dive-tahiti. com; Marina Taina, PK9) A big outfit that also leads whale-watching excursions. It charges 7900/14,100 CFP for a single-/two-tank dive, 7600 CFP for an introductory dive and 35,000/60,000 CFP for a five-/10-dive package.

Fluid Dive Centre
DIVING, WHALE WATCHING

(Map p355; ☑85 41 46, 70 83 75; www.fluidtahiti. com; Marina Taina, PK9) Fluid offers introductory dives (10,000 CFP), single dives (7000 CFP) and two-tank dives (12,600 CFP), as well as 10-dive packages (48,000 CFP).

Topdive
DIVING, WHALE WATCHING

(Map p355; ☑53 34 96; www.topdive.com; Intercontinental Tahiti Resort, PK8) This large and efficient operation offers a full range of dives, from Nitrox dives to introductory dives (8000 CFP). Six- and 10-dive packages are 43,000/70,000 CFP.

Hiking

Tahiti's interior is home to some of the most exquisite, and challenging, hikes in French Polynesia. Most trails require a guide as there's no waymark and it's easy to get lost. For a DIY hike, consider the trail from the Vaipahi Spring Gardens. The following hikes are among the most popular.

Fautaua Valley Trail
HIKE

One of the most pleasant and accessible walks on Tahiti, on the east coast. Allow four to five hours return. It leads to the Fautaua Waterfall. In theory, the Fautaua Valley Trail doesn't require a guide, but we suggest hiring one.

Mt Aorai
HIKE

Mt Aorai (2066m) is the third-highest peak on Tahiti and its ascent is one of the island's classic climbs. It takes at least 4½ hours of steady walking to reach the top.

Lava Tubes
HIKE

At Hitiaa on the east coast, these lava tubes are elongated tunnels formed by the cooling and rapid hardening of lava. A river runs through the giant, wormlike caves so that hiking through them actually means lots of swimming in cold water. It's imperative to have a guide.

WALKING GUIDES

Mato-Nui Excursions
GUIDED HIKES

(☑78 95 47) Mato leads hiking excursions and camping trips as well.

Polynesian Adventure
GUIDED HIKES

(☑43 25 95, 77 24 37; www.polynesianadventure. com) Offers all kinds of hikes on the island.

Tahiti Evasion
GUIDED HIKES

(☑56 48 77; www.tahitievasion.com; all-day hikes per person from 5500 CFP) One of the most reputable operators in the country.

Tahiti Reva Trek
GUIDED HIKES

(☑74 77 20; www.tahitirevatrek.com) Run by a female guide who has lots of experience and offers a wide range of hikes for all levels.

Canyoning

Canyoning (rappelling down waterfalls) is an even more exhilarating way to explore the interior. Tahiti's canyoning hot spots are found in various valleys. All are very atmospheric; you can expect various jumps, leaps in natural pools and jaw-dropping rappelling. Plan on 10,000 CFP to 12,000 CFP per person, including gear and transfers. All canyoning outings are led by a qualified instructor. Contact **Rando Pacific** (☑70 56 18; www.randopacific.com) or **Mato Nui Excursions** (☑78 95 47).

Surfing

Tahiti offers some fabulous beginner breaks particularly at Papenoo and along the east coast. More advanced surfers can head to the Papara shore break and the reef breaks at Sapinus and Taapuna along the west coast, and the Tapuaeraha Pass (Big Vairao Pass) and Te Ava Iti (Small Viarao Pass) at Tahiti Iti. Tahiti's most radical wave is at Hava'e Pass in Teahupoo on Tahiti Iti, where there's a big international surf contest held each August.

🛏 Sleeping

There are a number of places to stay along the west coast, particularly around Puna'auia. All places listed here take credit cards.

Le Méridien Tahiti
RESORT $$$

(Map p352; ☑47 07 07; www.lemeridien-tahiti.com; PK15; d from 35,000 CFP; ❋@🖙🌊) Le Méridien has truly lovely grounds dotted with lily ponds and fronted by a natural white-sand beach that has Mo'orea views. The overwater bungalows are stylishly built with hard woods and natural materials, and most rooms have recently been spruced up.

Manava Suite Resort Tahiti
RESORT $$

(Map p352; ☑47 31 00; www.spmhotels.com/resort/tahiti; PK10.8; d from 18,000 CFP; ❋🖙🌊) Le Manava is a good choice – combining friendly informality with some class and style. It lacks a beach but has the biggest infinity pool on Tahiti. It sports smartly finished suites and studios with clean lines, ample space and heaps of amenities.

Taaroa Lodge
GUESTHOUSE $

(Map p352; ☑58 39 21; www.taaroalodge.com; PK18.2; dm/d/bungalows 2800/6000/10,000 CFP) Right on the waterfront, Taaroa Lodge features three categories of accommodation options: a dorm, a room and two bungalows. Kayaks are free, and the nearest public beach is a two-minute walk away.

Pension de la Plage
PENSION $

(Map p352; ☑45 56 12; www.pensiondelaplage. com; PK15.4; s/d from 8500/9000 CFP; ☜☒) Just across the road from a narrow white-sand beach, this impeccably maintained place offers comfortable motel-style rooms in several gardenside buildings around a swimming pool. There's a bit of street noise but nothing to lose sleep over. Breakfast is available for 1000 CFP, dinner for 2600 CFP.

Le Relais Fenua
STUDIOS $$

(Map p352; ☑45 01 98, 77 25 45; www.relais-fenua. pf; PK18.25; studios d 9500-12,000 CFP; ✳☜☒) A great option in Pa'ea, with seven clean and spacious rooms set around a little swimming pool. It's close to the main road, so expect some traffic noise during the day. Plage de Mahana Park is stumbling distance away. Prices go down by 10% after three nights.

Te Miti
PENSION $

(Map p352; ☑58 48 61; www.pensiontemiti.com; PK18.6; dm 2500 CFP, r from 6500 CFP; ✳) Run by a young, friendly French couple, this lively place has a low-key backpacker vibe. It's about 200m from a white-sand beach and prices include breakfast. There's an equipped communal kitchen, a few bicycles for guests' use and a laundry service; 24-hour airport transfers are available for 1500 CFP per person (1800 CFP at night).

Taharuu Lodge
GUESTHOUSE $

(Map p352; ☑74 79 32; PK39; s/d with shared bathroom 5000/7000 CFP; ☜) This traveller-savvy haven occupies a functional building amid tropical gardens. Location is ace – Plage de Taharuu is just across the road. The eight rooms are spartan but clean and have good mattresses. There are surfboards and bikes available for rent, a fully equipped kitchen for self-catering and a vast lounge area.

✖ Eating

Most of Tahiti Nui's restaurants are along the west coast not far from Pape'ete. Besides the following finer restaurants, there are plenty of tasty and inexpensive *roulottes* that open up along the roadside at night.

🔺 Blue Banana
FRENCH, POLYNESIAN $$

(Map p352; ☑41 22 24; http://bluebanana-tahiti. com; PK11.2; mains 1500-3500 CFP; ☺lunch Tue-Sun, dinner Mon-Sat) This is a hip lagoonside restaurant in Puna'auia. Feast on innovative French and Polynesian dishes (small portions but artistically presented) and fine French vintages from the air-conditioned cellar. Pizzas also grace the menu.

Pink Coconut
FRENCH $$$

(Map p355; ☑41 22 23; www.pinkcoconuttahiti.com; PK9, Marina Taina; mains 1800-3600 CFP; ☺lunch & dinner Mon-Sat) We love this lively spot right on Marina Taina with great views of stylish yachts at anchor. Dine on French-inspired fare with a contemporary twist.

Quai des Îles
FRENCH, CREOLE $$$

(Map p355; ☑81 02 38; PK9, Marina Taina; mains 2000-3600 CFP; ☺lunch & dinner Tue-Sun) Creole, French and Polynesian dishes populate the menu of this well-regarded restaurant, just next door to Pink Coconut. On Sunday it lays on an excellent Tahitian brunch (3800 CFP).

Casa Bianca
ITALIAN $$

(Map p355; ☑43 91 35; PK9, Marina Taina; mains 1300-2700 CFP; ☺lunch & dinner) If pasta offerings or pizzas make your stomach quiver with excitement, opt for this perky eatery with an outdoor dining area overlooking the marina.

Terre-Mer
POLYNESIAN $$

(Map p352; ☑57 08 57; PK58.8; mains 1400-2900 CFP; ☺lunch Tue-Sun, dinner Wed-Sat) This reputable eatery could hardly be better situated: the dining deck is right on the seashore. At night it's a romantic spot to enjoy succulent local seafood and meat dishes with a Tahitian twist.

Taumatai
FRENCH, POLYNESIAN $$

(Map p352; ☑57 13 59; Taravao; mains 1700-3000 CFP; ☺lunch & dinner Tue-Sat, lunch Sun) This delightful little place in Taravao serves the town's best French and Tahitian food in an elegant garden setting. The restaurant is hidden behind a stone wall so it's a little hard to find.

Tahiti Iti

If you're looking for old-school Tahiti this should be your first stop. Tahiti Iti is the quiet, unpretentious half of the island that attracts hikers, surfers and seekers of calm

INLAND THRILLS

Archaeological remains, mossy, velvet-green mountains and sensational vistas await you in Tahiti Nui's lush (and uninhabited) interior.

Papenoo to the Relais de la Maroto The 18km route from Papenoo on the north coast to the Relais de la Maroto follows the wide Papenoo Valley, the only valley to cut right through the ancient crater. The Papenoo River is the largest on Tahiti. There are several waterfalls along the valley, including the **Topatari Waterfall**, the **Vaiharuru Waterfall** and, further, the **Puraha Waterfall**. Between the Vaiharuru Waterfall and the Puraha Waterfall lies the **Marae Vaitoare**, a well-preserved sacred site. Then the track reaches the Relais de la Maroto.

Around the Relais de la Maroto The **Relais de la Maroto** (Map p352; ☑57 90 29; d 7000-10,000 CFP; bungalows d 13,000 CFP; mains 1400-2800 CFP) is the only place to stay and eat, smack in the lush heart of the island. The rooms and bungalows are simple yet tidy and offer sensational mountain views. The restaurant is a great spot to break the journey.

The restored **Marae Farehape** site is almost directly below the ridge line on which the Relais de la Maroto perches; you can see an archery platform from where arrows were shot up the valley. Another archaeological site, **Marae Anapua**, has also been beautifully restored and is worth a gander.

From Relais de la Maroto to Mataiea From Relais de la Maroto, the track makes a very steep and winding climb to a pass and a 200m-long tunnel, at a height of about 800m, before plunging down to **Lake Vaihiria** (450m). Most tours stop here before returning via the same route; at the time of research the road was closed further down the valley due to a barricade built by the area's residents.

The best way to explore the area is to join a 4WD tour. Full-day trips cost 6500 CFP; children under 10 are half-price and hotel pick-up is included. You'll stop at Relais de la Maroto for lunch (not included). A few 4WD tour favourites:

» **Tahiti Safari Expeditions** (☑42 14 15, 77 80 76; www.tahiti-safari.com) This is the biggest operator and has reliable standards.

» **Patrick Adventure** (☑83 29 29, 79 08 09; patrickadventure@mail.pf) Another experienced operator.

» **Ciao Tahiti** (☑81 03 17, 73 73 97; www.ciaotahiti.com) A fairly recent operation with good credentials.

» **Tahiti Adventures** (☑29 01 60; www.tahiti-aventures.net) Offers something different: guided ATV tours in the Papenoo Valley.

with its wild coastlines, clean lagoon and laid-back pace.

The road only goes as far as Teahupoo to the south and Tautira in the north, so you can't drive around the whole island. The north coast road from Taravao runs past steep hills and waterfalls to Tautira.

◉ Sights & Activities

The south coast road runs past beaches and bays to **Teahupoo**. The size and hollowness of the waves at Teahupoo have earned it an international reputation. The road stops abruptly at the Tirahi River at PK18; from here it's a two-hour walk to **Vaipoiri Cave** (Map p352); another kilometre and a half

along the coast from here the **Te Pari Cliffs** begin. You can hike the 8km of this coast dotted with archaeological treasures, waterfalls and caves, but only in good weather and if the swell isn't too big. A guide is essential (see p359).

Probably the most fun you can have in a day on Tahiti Iti is by taking a **boat excursion**, which invariably includes a picnic lunch, a visit to Vaipoiri Cave and, if the weather permits, Te Pari. All pensions in the area can arrange excursions.

Very few divers know that there's fantastic **diving** on Tahiti Iti. Most sites are scattered along the south coast, between Taravao and Teahupoo. You can expect pristine sites and fabulous drop-offs. **Tahiti Iti Diving** (Map

p352; ☑42 25 33, 71 80 77; www.tahiti-iti-diving. com; PK58.1; ⊘Tue-Sun) is based near Taravao on Tahiti Nui but runs dive trips to Tahiti Iti. It charges 5800 CFP for an introductory dive or single dive and 48,000 CFP for a 10-dive package.

🛏 Sleeping & Eating

TOP CHOICE **Vanira Lodge** BUNGALOW **$$**
(Map p352; ☑57 70 18; www.vaniralodge.com; PK15, Teahupoo; bungalows d/q 13,000/17,000 CFP; 🛜🍽) Drive up a steep driveway on this mini plateau to enjoy vast views of the lagoon. The seven bungalows are all built from a combination of bamboo, thatch, rustic planks of wood, glass, coral and rock. Cosy nooks, handcarved furniture, airy mezzanines and al fresco kitchens are unique touches. Breakfast costs 1400 CFP, but you're on your own for other meals. Bikes, kayaks and snorkel gear are available for rent. You'll need a car if you stay here.

Green Room Villa VILLA **$$**
(Map p352; www.greenroomvilla.com; PK18, Teahupoo; ❄🛜) Rent this exquisite four-bedroom house for a romantic getaway or bring up to seven other people (eight total) for a family or surfing get-together. At the bottom half of the large, fruit-tree-covered garden is the 'honeymoon bungalow' that's perched on stilts over a pond filled with purple water lilies. The quiet, private property is a five-minute walk to Teahupoo's beach and a minute's walk to a river bathing pool. Note that there's a three-day minimum stay.

Te Pari Village PENSION **$$**
(Map p352; ☑42 59 12; bungalows with full board per person 11,000 CFP) Ten minutes by boat from the Teahupoo pier, this option is in the middle of a magnificent coconut and fruit-tree grove beside the lagoon. The handful of simple wooden bungalows make a circle around tall red ginger flowers and the main eating area is a big Polynesian meeting hall-style building. Prices include one excursion to Vaipoiri Cave and transfers from Teahupoo. Cash only.

La Plage de Maui POLYNESIAN **$$**
(Map p352; ☑74 71 74; PK7.6, Vairao; mains 1600-2700 CFP; ⊘10am-5pm) On the beach of the same name, this place looks like a shack inside and out but the food is Polynesian haute cuisine. We found the meals tasty, yet overpriced, but the position overlooking the lagoon is sublime. Cash only.

Hinareva POLYNESIAN **$$**
(Map p352; ☑57 60 84; PK18, Teahupoo; mains 1200-2200 CFP; ⊘lunch & dinner Tue-Sun) At the end of the road in Teahupoo, this place serves good food. There's a great selection of fish, meats and burger plates every day, *ma'a Tahiti* (traditional Tahitian food; d; 500 CFP) all day on Sundays, and daily specials on other days of the week.

MO'OREA

POP 16,000 / AREA 53 SQ KM

If you've been dreaming of holiday-brochure turquoise lagoons, white-sand beaches, vertical peaks and lush landscapes you'd be hard-pressed to find better than this gem of an island. Hovering under 20km across the 'Sea of the Moon' from its big sister, Tahiti, Mo'orea absorbs its many visitors so gracefully that it feels surprisingly nontouristy. Dine on stylishly prepared fresh seafood, lounge on the svelte strips of sand or take part in the myriad outdoor activities available. Mo'orea has something for everyone.

⊙ Sights

The following circuit starts at the airport and moves in an anticlockwise direction, following the northern PK markers.

Teavaro & Temae Beaches BEACH
(Map p364; PK1 to PK0) The best beaches on the east coast, and the widest perhaps in all of French Polynesia, stretch from Teavaro round to the airport. The Sofitel Moorea Ia Ora Beach Resort occupies Teavaro Beach, where there's good snorkelling in the shallow water. The public section of Teavaro Beach, just north of the Sofitel, is usually referred to as Temae Beach.

TOP CHOICE **Cook's Bay** NATURAL SITE
(PK6 to PK11) The spectacular Cook's Bay is something of a misnomer because Cook actually anchored in Opunohu Bay. With Mt Rotui as a backdrop, Cook's Bay is a lovely stretch of water. There's no real centre to Cook's Bay; shops, restaurants and hotels are simply dotted along the road. At the base of Cook's Bay is the sleepy village of **Paopao.**

FREE Distillerie et Usine de
Jus de Fruits de Moorea DISTILLERY, FACTORY
(Map p364; ☎55 20 00; www.manuteatahiti.com;
PK11; ⊙8.30am-4.30pm Mon-Thu, 8.30am-3pm Fri,
9am-4pm Sat) About 300m inland from the
coastal road, this juice processing factory
and distillery is well worth a stop. Tours are
available at 9am and 2pm from Monday to
Thursday and last about 40 minutes. The gift
shop sells drinks, jams, honey and souvenirs.

Ta'ahiamanu (Mareto) Beach BEACH
(Map p364; PK14) This narrow stretch of white
sand is a popular spot for both tourists
and locals on weekends. Despite the lack
of facilities, it's ideal for splashing about,
sunbathing or picnicking.

TOP CHOICE **Opunohu Bay** NATURAL SITE
(PK14 to PK18) Magnificent Opunohu Bay feels
wonderfully fresh and isolated. There is less
development along here than around Cook's
Bay, and it's one of the more tranquil and
eye-catching spots on the island. At PK18,
a road turns off inland along the Opunohu
Valley to the valley *marae* and the *belvédère*
(lookout).

Moorea Tropical Garden ORGANIC FARM
(Map p364; ☎70 53 63; PK16; ⊙8am-5pm Mon-
Sat, 8am-3pm Sun) This delightfully peaceful property perched on a small plateau is
heaven on earth for the sweet-toothed. Here
they can sample (and buy) homemade organic jams and delicious ice creams. Freshly
squeezed juices are also on offer. Needless to
say, the lagoon views are fantastic.

Magical Mountain LOOKOUT
(Map p364; PK21) At PK21, a cement road
veers inland and makes a very steep climb
to a lookout called 'Magical Mountain',
at a height of 209m. The view over the
northern part of the island and the lagoon
is mesmerising.

Hauru Point BEACHES
(PK25 to PK30) The coastal road rounds
Hauru Point, the northwestern corner of
the island, between PK25 and PK30. This
is one of the island's major tourist enclaves,
although it has seen better days – a number
of shops, restaurants and hotels have closed
since 2008. Unlike Cook's Bay, Hauru Point
has a **beach**. Though narrow, it's pretty
spectacular with turquoise water and good
snorkelling. Immediately offshore are **Motu
Tiahura** and **Motu Fareone**, attractive lit-

tle islets so close to the shore you can easily
swim out to them and enjoy fine snorkelling
on the way.

Painapo Beach BEACH
(Map p364; PK33) You can't miss the huge
(though falling apart) statue of a tattooed
man holding a club at the entrance of this
private property overlooking a lovely strip of
white sand. In theory, there's an access fee to
get to the beach – ask around.

Haapiti VILLAGE
(PK24) The largest village on the west coast,
Haapiti is home to the huge twin-towered
Catholic **Église de la Sainte Famille**, which
is made of coral and lime. The **Protestant
Temple** is another notable building; it's at
PK23.5, on the lagoonside of the road.

Vaiare VILLAGE
(PK4) The constant toing and froing of ferry
boats and high-speed catamarans at the
ferry quay, the busy market scene and the
cars, taxis and *le trucks* (buses) shuttling
visitors around render the 100m or so near
the dock area the busiest patch of real estate
on Mo'orea.

Toatea Lookout LOOKOUT
(Map p364; PK0.6) Atop the hill north of the
Sofitel Moorea Ia Ora Beach Resort, this
lookout affords dazzling views of the hotel,
the lagoon mottled with coral formations,
the barrier reef and Tahiti in the background.

🏃 Activities
Diving & Snorkelling
Mo'orea is one of French Polynesia's main
underwater playgrounds, which is no surprise considering its high visibility and
clean waters. Most diving is focused along
the north coast, especially between Hauru
Point and Opunohu Bay. For details about
sites see p32.

For snorkelling, join an organised lagoon
tour or DIY around Hauru Point and its *motu*,
around the interior of the reef beyond Temae
beach or off Ta'ahiamanu (Mareto) beach.

Topdive DIVING
(Map p369; ☎56 31 44; www.topdive.com) At
Intercontinental Moorea Resort & Spa. This
well-established dive shop arranges controversial 'shark dives' involving shark-feeding
demonstrations. It charges 8000 CFP for an
introductory dive, 8000 CFP for a single dive
and 43,000/70,000 CFP for a six-/10-dive
package.

Mo'orea

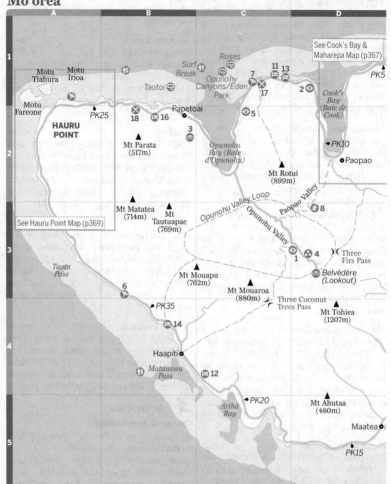

Ia Ora Diving DIVING

(Map p364; ☎56 35 78) At Sofitel Ia Ora Moorea Beach Resort. Due to its location on the northeastern corner of the island, it specialises in dive sites along the east coast. Count on 7500 CFP for an introductory dive and 7200 CFP for a single dive.

Moorea Blue Diving DIVING

(Map p367; ☎55 17 04; www.mooreabluediving. com) At Moorea Pearl Resort & Spa, this hotel dive shop gets good reviews. An introductory dive costs 7500 CFP, a single dive is 6900 CFP and five-/10-dive packages are 33,000/60,000 CFP.

Moorea Fun Dive DIVING

(Map p369; ☎56 40 38; www.moorea-fundive.com; PK26.7) At Hauru Point, on the beach. An introductory dive costs 7100 CFP, a single dive is 6400 CFP and six-/10-dive packages are 33,000/52,000 CFP.

Scubapiti DIVING

(Map p369; ☎56 20 38, 78 03 52; www.scubapiti. com) At Les Tipaniers. Introductory dives are 6500 CFP, single dives cost 6100 CFP. Prices drop by about 10% for more than two dives.

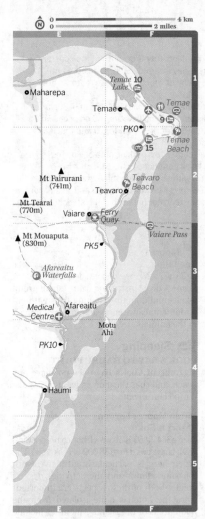

Lagoon Excursions

The best way to discover Mo'orea's magnificent lagoon is by joining a lagoon excursion. Tours typically visit the two bays, stop to feed the sharks, feed and swim with the rays at a spot off the Intercontinental Moorea Resort & Spa, and picnic and snorkel on Motu Fareone. Plenty of operators are available for day-long tours that usually include lunch and cost around 8000 CFP; check at your accommodation.

For boat rental, contact **Moorea Loca Boat** (Map p369; ☏78 13 39; 2/4/8hr incl fuel 7000/9000/11,000 CFP). This outfit right on the beach beside Les Tipaniers rents outboard-powered boats. No licence is required. It also has peddle boats.

Hiking

Exhilarating hikes of varying difficulty tackle the lush inland area. Most trails are infrequently used and poorly marked, so it's necessary to use a guide. For a DIY hike, consider the trails at the Lycée Agricole (p366).

Hiking Discovery GUIDED HIKES
(☏70 73 31) Can arrange hikes on Tahiti and Mo'orea.

Moorea Hiking GUIDED HIKES
(☏56 16 48, 79 41 54; meretmontagne@mail.pf) A Mo'orea-based guide with good credentials.

Polynesian Adventure GUIDED HIKES
(☏43 25 95, 77 24 37; www.polynesianadv.com) A well-established operator. Offers hikes on Tahiti and Mo'orea.

PAOPAO & OPUNOHU VALLEYS

From Mo'orea's two great bays, valleys sweep inland, meeting south of the coastal bulk of Mt Rotui. In the pre-European era the valleys were densely populated and the Opunohu Valley was dotted with *marae,* some of which have been restored and maintained.

A small *fare* at the **Lycée Agricole** (Agricultural College; Map p364; ⊘8am-4.30pm Mon-Thu, 8am-3.30pm Fri, 9am-2.30pm Sat) sells jams in local flavours and on occasion, ice cream. If you've got itchy feet, there's a small network of **walking trails** that leads through the estate, in the basin of the caldera.

Past the agricultural college, the valley road comes to a parking area beside the huge **Marae Titiroa** (Map p364). From there the track continues to the **Marae Ahu-o-Mahine**, a more recent *marae* of round stones with an imposing three-stepped *ahu* (altar). A short way up the road from Marae Titiroa is **Marae Afareaito** and an adjacent **archery platform**. Beyond Marae Afareaito the road continues to climb steeply, winding up to the excellent *belvédère* (lookout).

Horse Riding

Ranch Opunohu Valley HORSE RIDING
(Map p364; ☎56 28 55, 78 42 47; 2hr rides 5000 CFP; ⊘by reservation) Two-hour guided rides into the island's interior are available mornings and afternoons. The ranch is up in the Paopao Valley (it's signposted).

Surfing & Kite Surfing

The most popular spot is **Haapiti** (May to October), which has the regularity and strength of reef waves with the security of a beach wave. Other spots include **Temae** (a difficult right-hander), **Paopao** (Cook's Bay) and **Opunohu Bay**; and the expert-only left-hander at **Intercontinental Moorea Resort**.

On windy days you'll see dozens of kites whipping across the lagoon in front of the Intercontinental Moorea Resort.

Whale & Dolphin Watching

This activity has exploded in recent years. You can count on finding dolphins year-round but it's the whales, who migrate to Mo'orea from July to October, who draw in the crowds. Trips cost 8000 CFP and kids under 12 are half price. Most dive centres run whale-watching trips, or you can contact the following outfits.

Dr Michael Poole WHALE WATCHING
(☎56 23 22; www.drmichaelpoole.com) A world specialist on South Pacific marine mammals and an advocate for their protection, Dr Poole began the first whale- and dolphin-watching tours and continues to lead the best ones available.

Moorea Deep Blue WHALE WATCHING
(☎76 37 27; www.moorea-deepblue.com) A former dive instructor runs small-group whale- and dolphin-watching trips with environmental awareness and minimal impact to the animals.

🛏 Sleeping

COOK'S BAY TO HAURU POINT

Magnificent Cook's Bay does not have any beach, and so is the quieter, less touristy sister to Hauru Point.

Hilton Moorea Lagoon Resort & Spa RESORT $$$
(Map p364; ☎55 11 11; www.hilton.com/worldwide; PK14; bungalows d from 38,000 CFP; ❃🖧🌊) The beach here is particularly attractive (with top snorkelling) and the activities desk is great – both of these aspects are important since the hotel is quite isolated from the main areas of the island. Amenities include a water-sports centre, a dive shop, a pool, a spa, a gym, two bars and two restaurants.

Moorea Pearl Resort & Spa RESORT $$$
(Map p367; ☎55 17 50; www.pearlresorts.com; PK5; bungalows d from 30,000 CFP; ❃🖧🌊) The infinity pool here is the island's best. The artificial, white-sand beach is smaller than those at other resorts but the Pearl's vibe is more intimate and relaxed. Facilities include a restaurant, a spa and a dive centre.

Motu Iti BUNGALOW, DORM $
(Map p364; ☎55 05 20, 74 43 38; www.pension motuiti.com; dm 1700 CFP, bungalows d 10,500-12,000 CFP; @) A good bet for unfussy

travellers, despite the odd layout of the compound. The five bungalows are tightly packed together on a small property overlooking the lagoon. The dorm is airy (but not very social) with a view of the sea. Swimming is not *that* tempting, with very shallow waters and a profusion of algae.

Club Bali Hai
RESORT **$$**
(Map p367; ☑56 13 68; www.clubbalihai.com; PK8; r & bungalows d from 16,000 CFP; ✳@🕏☎) Club Bali Hai sits on the eastern shore of Cook's Bay with a picture-postcard view of Mt Rotui. One of Mo'orea's few mid-price accommodation options, it has a range of spick-and-span rooms in a two-storey, motel-like building as well as an assortment of local-style bungalows, including a handful of over-water units which are among the least expensive in French Polynesia.

Motel Albert
BUNGALOW **$**
(Map p367; ☑56 12 76; www.ile-tropicale.com/motelalbert; PK8; studios 6500-7600 CFP, bungalows q 11,000 CFP; 🕏) A good budget choice, this modest place has a handful of serviceable bungalows with open terraces, as well as a row of uninspiring studios with mini terraces closed in with mosquito screens. All options have kitchens and there's a minimum stay of two nights. Cash only.

HAURU POINT
Unlike Cook's Bay, Hauru Point has a beach. Though narrow, it's pretty spectacular with turquoise water, a few *motu* (islets) out front to swim to and good snorkelling.

Les Tipaniers
RESORT **$$**
(Map p369; ☑56 12 67; www.lestipaniers.com; PK25; d 8500 CFP, bungalows d 15,500-17,000 CFP; 🕏) Scattered amid a flowery garden, the 22 bungalows aren't going to win any architectural awards but are big, practical and clean. Budget tip: it also harbours four cheaper rooms (book well ahead). The resort also features two restaurants (half board is optional), a bar, a dive shop and a small watersports centre. Free bikes and kayaks.

Fare Miti
BUNGALOW **$$**
(Map p369; ☑56 57 42, 21 65 59; www.mooreafaremiti.com; PK27.5; bungalows q 13,000-15,000 CFP; @🕏) With only eight few-frills but functional bungalows (that can sleep up to four people) and a friendly relaxed atmosphere, this is a great place to veg out on the beach in a low-key environment. Kayaks and snorkel gear are available for rent.

Domloc
VILLAS **$$**
(Map p369; ☑72 75 80; www.domlocpolynesie.com; PK25; bungalows from 12,000 CFP; ✳🕏) Domloc is actually a time-share vacation club, but it's run like a hotel – a cool hotel indeed, with nine well-appointed villas of varying sizes and shapes. The beach is just a few steps away from the property. Prices fluctuate wildly according to seasons and school holidays.

Intercontinental Moorea Resort & Spa
RESORT **$$$**
(Map p369; ☑55 19 19; www.tahitiresorts.intercontinental.com; PK25; r & bungalows d from 28,000 CFP;

Cook's Bay & Maharepa

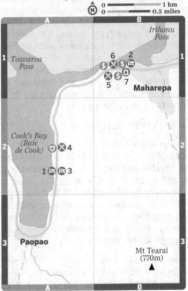

Cook's Bay & Maharepa

✳☎☱) Spread out over 4.5 hectares along the seashore, Mo'orea's biggest resort features a host of facilities and amenities, including two pools, two restaurants, two bars, a well-respected spa, a watersports centre, a full dive shop, a marine turtle rehabilitation centre and a Dolphin Centre. With its varied accommodations it's appropriate for couples and families alike. It's a member of Earthcheck.

Camping Nelson CAMPGROUND, BUNGALOW $
(Map p369; ☑56 15 18; www.camping-nelson.pf; PK27; campsites per person 1500 CFP, dm/d with shared bathroom from 1800/4300 CFP, bungalows d from 6300 CFP; @) Camping Nelson boasts a spiffing lagoon frontage in a green location. Pitch your tent on the grassy plot within earshot of the gentle surf, or choose one of the slightly claustrophobic cabins. A handful of more comfortable bungalows, with private bathrooms, were under construction at the time of writing. Precious perks include a kitchen for guests' use and hot water in the shared bathrooms. Prices are valid for a minimum stay of two nights.

HAAPITI TO TEMAE

TOP CHOICE **Green Lodge** INN $$
(Map p364; ☑56 31 00, 77 62 26; www.greenlodge. pf; d incl breakfast from 16,000 CFP, bungalows d incl breakfast from 18,500 CFP; ✳☎) This relaxing cocoon with a boutique feel features well-designed bungalows that orbit around an alluring pool and a nicely laid out tropical garden. Temae Beach is a five-minute walk away. Bikes are free.

Résidence Linareva BUNGALOW $$
(Map p364; ☑55 05 65; www.linareva.com; PK34.5; studios & bungalows d from 16,000 CFP; ✳@☎) Résidence Linareva has a wide variety of well-furnished bungalows in a lush garden by the lagoon. Bicycles, kayaks and snorkelling equipment are all provided free of charge. No beach, but there's great swimming and snorkelling off the long pontoon jutting out over the lagoon.

Tehuarupe BUNGALOW $$
(Map p364; ☑56 57 33; www.moorea-paradise.com; PK 22.2; bungalows d 12,000 CFP; ☎☱) On the mountain side of the road, these sea-view bungalows are a home away from home, with lovingly finished interiors, wooden decks and tastefully chosen furniture. There's no beach nearby, but guests are provided with free kayaks to paddle to coral gardens.

There's a green touch – rainwater is recycled and there's a waste management policy.

Fare Maeva BUNGALOW $$
(Map p364; ☑74 10 14; www.faremaevamoorea. com; bungalows d 10,200 CFP) This charming, isolated place is dominated by coconut trees and coral gravel. All the tidy, tastefully done-out bungalows have a bathroom with hot water and kitchen. For swimming, head to Temae Beach, which is 500m away. Cash only.

Sofitel Moorea Ia Ora Beach Resort RESORT $$$
(Map p364; ☑55 12 12; www.sofitel-frenchpolynesia. com; bungalows d from 35,000 CFP; ✳☎☱) This excellent modern Polynesian resort is on the best beach on the island. The list of facilities is prolific, with two restaurants, a wonderful spa, a small pool, a jewellery shop and a reputable diving centre.

Mark's Place Moorea BUNGALOW $$
(Map p364; ☑56 43 02, 78 93 65; www.marks placemoorea.com; PK23.5; bungalows s/d from 6000/8000 CFP; @☎) The open, lush garden and creative, smartly finished bungalows – it helps that the American owner is a carpenter – make this a good option on Mo'orea, but we've heard the odd grumble about variable service. It's away from the beach and just about everything else besides the Haapiti surf break, but bike and kayak rentals (1000 CFP per day) make getting around less of a chore.

✕ Eating

Cook's Bay and Hauru Point are the dining epicentres. Most places close around 9pm and are open for lunch and dinner.

MAHAREPA & COOK'S BAY

Lilikoi Garden Café POLYNESIAN $$
(Map p364; ☑29 61 41; PK13.5; mains 1100-1900 CFP; ☺breakfast & lunch daily, dinner Fri) Lilikoi Garden Café is that easy-to-miss 'secret spot' that locals like to recommend. It serves meals made with locally sourced ingredients. It also has a takeaway counter.

Allo Pizza PIZZERIA $$
(Map p367; ☑56 18 22; Cook's Bay; mains 1400-1900 CFP; ☺11am-2pm & 5-9pm) Despite its unpromising location across the road from the *gendarmerie* (police station), Allo Pizza is a great place to taste wood-fired pizzas. There's also a fine selection of salads and steaks as well as a limited dessert menu. Takeaway is available.

Caraméline SNACK $$
(Map p367; ☑56 15 88; Maharepa; breakfast from 1100 CFP, mains 900-2100 CFP; ⊘7am-4pm) Get all-day American-, French- or Tahitian-style breakfasts, burgers, pizzas, salads, ice-cream treats and more at this affordable and popular cafe. Don't miss the French-style coffee, pastries and crêpes.

Le Sud FRENCH $$$
(Map p367; ☑56 42 95; Maharepa; mains 1600-3000 CFP; ⊘lunch Tue-Sat, dinner Mon-Sat) The airy French-plantation decor is inviting, despite the unassuming location on the main road. The menu lurches between Mediterranean, Polynesian and Italian, but has a lightness of touch missing from many of its nearby peers.

HAURU POINT

TOP CHOICE **Le Mayflower** FRENCH, INTERNATIONAL $$$
(Map p369; ☑56 53 59; PK27; mains 1900-3300 CFP; ⊘lunch Tue, Thu & Fri, dinner Tue-Sun) The G-spot for local gourmands. Everything here is special, but a personal recommendation is the duck breast served in a mango sauce.

Snack Mahana POLYNESIAN $$
(Map p364; ☑56 41 70; PK23.2; mains 1500-2100 CFP; ⊘11am-3pm Mon-Sat) In a sublime location overlooking the turquoise lagoon, breezy Mahana is a heart-stealing open-air snack. Linger over burgers, a plate of grilled mahi mahi or tuna sashimi while savouring the lagoon views. Cash only.

Crêperie Toatea CREPERIE $$
(Map p364; ☑55 11 11; Hilton Moorea Lagoon Resort & Spa, PK14; mains 1300-3400 CFP; ⊘dinner) Here you can dine on lip-smackingly good crêpes prepared to order by an Alsatian chef. Another draw is the setting – it's inside the Hilton Moorea, on the pontoon that leads to the over-water bungalows (nonguests are welcome).

PKO JAPANESE $$$
(Map p369; ☑22 84 01; www.pkomoorea.com; PK27.3; mains 1900-3300 CFP; ⊘lunch & dinner Tue-Sun) Another dash of culinary flair in cosy surrounds (wooden floors, tropical plants, tapa-adorned walls and teak furniture), the PKO offers delectable Japanese-inspired dishes with a twist.

Les Tipaniers FRENCH, POLYNESIAN $$$
(Map p369; ☑56 12 67; PK25; mains 1100-2600 CFP; ⊘lunch & dinner) Lunch is served at the

Beach Restaurant which, as the name suggests, has a fabulous beach frontage. Dinner is at the less well located but elegant roadside restaurant, where Italian and French-inspired dishes feature prominently on the menu.

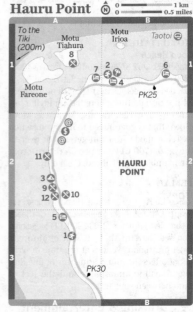

Hauru Point

Hauru Point

⊕ **Activities, Courses & Tours**

TAHITI & FRENCH POLYNESIA MO'OREA

Coco d'Isle
POLYNESIAN, FRENCH **$$**

(Map p369; ☑56 59 07; PK27; mains 1400-2600 CFP; ☺dinner Mon-Sat) The food is a crowd-pleasing mix of steaks, fish dishes, salads and pizzas.

La Paillotte
SANDWICHES **$**

(Map p369; ☑56 48 49; PK27.3; mains 400-1300 CFP; ☺lunch & dinner) Serves good, cheap and wholesome snacks and mains.

MOTU TIAHURA
Coco Beach
POLYNESIAN **$$**

(Map p369; ☑72 57 26; Motu Tiahura; mains 1000-2200 CFP; ☺lunch Wed, Thu, Sat & Sun, lunch daily during school holidays) This friendly eatery with a casual atmosphere has an idyllic setting on Motu Tiahura (also known as Motu Moea) that is guaranteed to help you switch to 'relax' mode. You can get a boat over to the *motu* (700 CFP per person return) from the mainland – call ahead. Cash only.

TEMAE
 Le K
POLYNESIAN, INTERNATIONAL **$$$**

(Map p364; ☑56 39 95; Sofitel Moorea Ia Ora Beach Resort, Temae; mains 2100-3900 CFP; ☺dinner Mon-Wed, Thu & Fri) Ah, Le K. One of Mo'orea's most prestigious venues at the time of writing, it offers the intoxicating mix of fine dining, romantic atmosphere and the feel of sand between your toes.

 Drinking & Entertainment

The big hotels have bars where all are welcome to enjoy a predinner drink, and many of the restaurants listed earlier, such as Les Tipaniers, are good spots for a sunset tipple. A couple of times a week, the bigger hotels organise excellent Polynesian music and dance performances by local groups.

 Shopping

The coastal road is littered with souvenir places. For *pareu*, T-shirts and other curios, try the Maison Blanche between Cook's Bay and Maharepa. The major black-pearl specialists have outlets on Mo'orea.

 Information

INTERNET ACCESS Many hotels and pensions have wi-fi access.

Magic Photo (Map p369; ☑56 59 59; PK26.5, Hauru Point; per hr 540 CFP; ☺8am-6pm Mon-Sat) Also has wi-fi access (same rates).

Tiki@Net (Map p369; ☑31 39 72; Le Petit Village shopping centre, Hauru Point; per hr 500 CFP; ☺8am-5pm Mon, 8am-6pm Tue-Sat) Also has wi-fi access (same rates).

MEDICAL SERVICES There's a medical centre in Afareaitu as well as several private doctors and two pharmacies.

MONEY The Banque Socredo across from the quay at Vaiare has an ATM. There are banks and ATMs clustered around the small shopping centre in Maharepa near PK6. In Le Petit Village (the Hauru Point shopping centre) there is a Banque de Polynésie and an ATM.

POST Mo'orea has a post office in Maharepa and another in Papetoai, just before Hauru Point.

TOURIST INFORMATION The **Mo'orea Tourist Bureau** (☑56 29 09; ferry quay, Vaiare; ☺8am-1pm Mon-Sat) has a small kiosk at the ferry quay. Mildly helpful.

 Getting There & Away

There's less than 20km of blue Pacific between Tahiti and Mo'orea, and getting from one island to the other is simplicity itself.

AIR Air Tahiti (☑86 42 42; www.airtahiti. pf) flies between Mo'orea and Pape'ete (4200 CFP one way), Bora Bora (19,000 CFP one way, daily), Huahine (14,000 CFP one way, three weekly) and Ra'iatea (14,000 CFP one way, three weekly).

BOAT It's a breezy ride between Tahiti and Mo'orea. First departures in the morning are usually around 6am; the last trips are in the afternoon at around 4.30pm or 5.30pm. All fares are about 1450 CFP each way (900 CFP for children). If you are bringing a car (from 3100 CFP) it's best to reserve in advance.

Aremiti 5 (☑50 57 91, 56 31 10; www.aremiti. pf) This catamaran jets to and from Mo'orea in about 35 minutes five to seven times daily.

Aremiti Ferry (☑50 57 91, 56 31 10; www. aremiti.pf) Runs two to four times daily and takes about 75 minutes to cross.

ⓘ Getting Around

The coastal road is about 60km around. It's best to rent a scooter, car or bicycle to get around Mo'orea: distances are long and there is no public transport. Hitching may be another option, which is usually safe provided the usual precautions are taken, but we don't recommend it.

To/From the Airport & Quay
Buses (400 CFP) meet all *Aremiti 5* arrivals and departures but not the Aremiti Ferry. Mo'orea's taxis are notoriously expensive: from the airport to the Intercontinental Moorea Resort & Spa will cost about 4500 CFP.

The airport is in the island's northeastern corner. Most hotels offer airport transfers.

Car

On Mo'orea having your own wheels is very useful but expensive. Generally, you'll pay from around 9500 CFP per day including liability insurance and unlimited mileage.

Albert Rent-a-Car (☑56 19 28, 56 33 75) Has three outlets around the island and can deliver to your hotel.

Avis (☑56 32 61, 56 32 68; www.avis-tahiti. com) At the ferry quay at Vaiare, at Intercontinental Moorea Resort & Spa and at Club Bali Hai.

Europcar (☑56 34 00, 56 28 64; www.europ carpolynesie.com) At Le Petit Village shopping centre (Hauru Point) and at the ferry quay at Vaiare.

Scooter & Bicycle

Bikes can be rented or are sometimes offered for free by many hotels and pensions.

Albert Rent-a-Car (☑56 19 28, 56 33 75) Rents scooters (6000 CFP for 24 hours).

Europcar (☑56 34 00, 56 28 64; www.europ carpolynesie.com) Rents bikes for 1700 CFP for 24 hours.

Magic Photo (☑56 59 59; PK26.5, Hauru Point; per 8/24hr 5500/6000 CFP) Has mountain bikes (1200 CFP for eight hours).

Rent a Bike – Rent a Scooter (☑71 11 09) Rents bikes (1600 CFP for 24 hours) and scooters (5500 CFP for 24 hours).

HUAHINE

POP 5750 / AREA 75 SQ KM

With its snoozy Polynesian charm, Huahine is the perfect spot to break from city blues, dump the watch and let the days flow by like the pages of a romance novel. If you do care to pick up the pace, there's a slew of activities available in the outlandishly aquamarine lagoon, a few hikes to tackle up the low, lush mountains and archaeology buffs will love Maeva, one of the most extensive complexes of pre-European *marae* in French Polynesia. With only one real resort, Huahine remains undeveloped and unpretentious, far from the hype of Bora Bora and much less expensive.

Huahine comprises two islands of fairly similar size: Huahine Nui (Big Huahine) to the north and Huahine Iti (Little Huahine) to the south. Huahine Nui is more developed, home to most of the main tourist and administrative facilities. Huahine Iti offers the island's best beaches, most azure lagoons and a serene, get-away-from-it-all atmosphere.

◉ Sights

HUAHINE NUI

This 60km clockwise circuit of the larger island starts at Fare.

Fare TOWN

Fare is the image of a sleepy South Seas port. Check out the colourful little waterside **market** and the few creative boutiques, sign up for a dive or otherwise rent a ramshackle bicycle and just pedal around.

Maeva ARCHAEOLOGICAL SITE

Prior to European influence, Maeva village, about 7km east of Fare, was the seat of royal power on the island. It's mostly famous for its concentration of pre-European archaeological sites, including a host of *marae* scattered along the shoreline and also up the slopes of Matairea Hill. Given the lack of signboards and proper waymarks, it makes sense to hire a guide. Contact American anthropologist Paul Atallah, from **Island Ecotours** (☑71 30 83; www.islandecotours.net). Count on 5000 CFP for the tour (about three hours).

Beside the bridge coming off Motu Ovarei are a number of V-shaped **fish traps**, made from rocks. They have been here for centuries and some are still in use.

La Cité de Corail BEACH

This secluded beach at the southern tip of Motu Ovarei, just off the now defunct Sofitel, features shade trees, white sand, calm waters and healthy coral gardens a few finstrokes away.

FREE **Huahine Pearls & Pottery** PEARL FARM

(☑78 30 20; www.huahine-pearlfarm.com; ☺10am-4pm Mon-Sat, 10am-noon Sun) Peter Owen, the owner, is a potter as well as a pearl farmer and his work is shown in Pape'ete's galleries. His studio is on his pearl farm in the middle of the lagoon. From Faie a ferry departs for the studio every 15 minutes from 10am to 4pm. Upon arrival you'll be given a demonstration of pearl farming and have an opportunity to browse the collection of pearls inside the shop.

Faie VILLAGE

The coast road turns inland beside narrow Faie Bay to the village of Faie. Inland from Faie it's a steep climb to the **belvédère** on the slopes of Mt Turi. From this high point, the road drops even more steeply to the shores of Maroe Bay.

Huahine

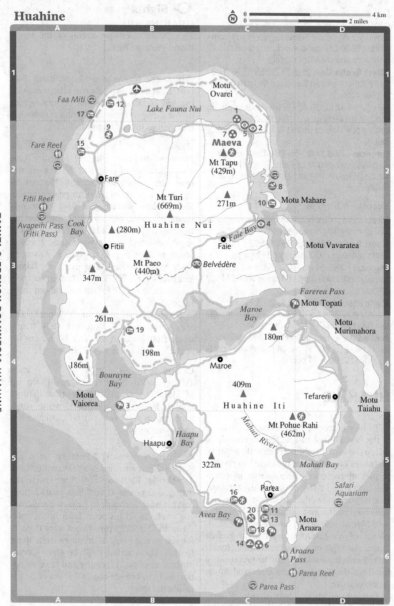

Faa Miti
17
12
9
Fare Reef
15
Fitii Reef
Avapeihi Pass
(Fitii Pass)
Cook
Bay
Fare
Fitiii
Lake Fauna Nui
Motu
Ovarei
1
7 5 2
Maeva
Mt Tapu
(429m)
8
10 Motu Mahare
4
Faie Bay
Faie
Motu Vavaratea
Belvédère
Mt Turi
(669m)
271m
Huahine Nui
(280m)
Mt Paeo
(440m)
347m
261m
19
198m
186m
Bourayne
Bay
Motu
Vaiorea
3
Farerea Pass
Motu Topati
Maroe
Bay
180m
Motu
Murimahora
Maroe
409m
Huahine Iti
Tefarerii
Motu
Taiahu
Mt Pohue Rahi
(462m)
Mahuti Bay
Haapu
Bay
Haapu
322m
Mahuti River
Safari
Aquarium
Parea
16
20 11
13
Avea Bay
18
14 6
Motu
Araara
Araara
Pass
Parea Reef
Parea Pass

HUAHINE ITI

Start at the village of Maroe, on the south side of Maroe Bay, and head clockwise to **Marae Anini**, the community *marae* on the island's southern tip. Made of massive coral blocks, this large coastal *marae* was dedicated to 'Oro (the god of war) and Hiro (the god of thieves and sailors) and is a great stop for a picnic. Some of the best **beaches** around Huahine are found on the southern peninsula and along its western shore around Avea Bay.

Huahine

🏃 Activities

Diving & Snorkelling

Huahine has three scuba centres offering magnificent dives for all experience levels. For more information on diving off Huahine, see p32. Snorkelling is no less impressive. On the east coast, near the visitor car park at the now defunct Sofitel, you'll find **La Cité de Corail**, which offers superb snorkelling among coral pinnacles and rich marine life only a few metres offshore. **Motu Topati**, at the entrance to Maroe Bay, and **Motu Vaiorea**, at the entrance to Bourayne Bay, are magnificent sites for snorkelling that are accessible by boat.

Mahana Dive   DIVING
(☎73 07 17; www.mahanadive.com) In Fare, this outfit charges 7000 CFP for an introductory dive, 6200 CFP for a single dive and 23,200 CFP for a four-dive package.

Pacific Blue Adventure   DIVING
(☎68 87 21; www.divehuahine.com; ☺Mon-Sat) A friendly centre on the quay at Fare. Same prices as Mahana Dive.

Heremiti Dive   DIVING, SNORKELLING
(☎27 90 57, 68 86 49; www.heremitidive.com) At Mauarii on Huahine Iti. It charges 7000 CFP for an introductory dive, 6500 CFP for a single dive and 22,000 CFP for a four-dive package. Also organises dedicated snorkelling trips (6500 CFP).

Lagoon Excursions

Various lagoon tours are offered on Huahine, with stops for snorkelling, swimming, fish or shark feeding, a pearl-farm visit and a *motu* picnic. Departures are at around 9am or 10am, returning towards 4pm. Tours cost from 8500 CFP. A minimum number of participants are required, so book ahead through your pension.

Horse Riding

La Petite Ferme   HORSE RIDING
(☎68 82 98; lapetiteferme@mai.pf; 2hr trips from 7500 CFP) To see the island from the back of a horse, head to this equestrian centre on the main road between Fare and the airport. The two-hour ride along the beach, through coconut plantations and around the shore of Lake Fauna Nui is truly enchanting.

Hiking

There are no clearly marked trails on Huahine and the occasional paths in the interior grow over quickly if they're not maintained (which is usually the case) so DIY hikes are limited. **Huahine Randonnée** (☎73 53 45; teriitetumu@mail.pf; Camping Hiva Plage; half-day hikes per person 4500 CFP) offers hikes to the tops of either Mt Tapu on Huahine Nui or Mt Pohue Rahi on Huahine Iti, as well as a walk on Matairea Hill and around Avea Bay.

WORTH A TRIP

HANA ITI BEACH

Here's a secret, only known to locals (whisper it softly): the beach of the former Hana Iti Hotel. This dream-like cove lapped by lapis lazuli waters offers a nice patch of sand backed by lush hills. There's no access road; get there by kayak or rent a dinghy with **Huahine Lagoon** (☎68 70 00; boat rental per 2/4hr 5000/7000 CFP). No licence required. Fuel costs extra.

Surfing

Huahine has some of the best and most consistent surf in French Polynesia, best tackled by experienced surfers. Local surfers can be very possessive, however, so be respectful.

Kayaking

Huahine provides distinctive opportunities to dip a paddle around the quiet lagoon. You can steer to Hana Iti Beach, Motu Araara or any other *motu*. Most places to stay either rent or offer free sea kayaks for guests' use. In Fare, **Huahine Lagoon** ([☎]68 70 00) hires out kayaks for 4000 CFP per day.

🛌 Sleeping

HUAHINE NUI

The places listed here are either right in town or a few kilometres to the north or south.

TAHITI & FRENCH POLYNESIA HUAHINE

Au Motu Mahare TOP CHOICE BUNGALOW $
([☎]77 76 97; www.aumotumahare.blogspot.com; bungalows d/tr 8000/9900 CFP) Run by a French-English couple (no language barrier here), this lovely retreat on a peaceful *motu* has two handsomely designed bungalows that were built using local materials in authentic Polynesian style (cold-water showers). Solar panels provide the electricity and rainwater is recycled. No meals are served but there's an impeccable communal kitchen. Free kayaks and free airport transfers. Cash only.

Maitai Lapita Village RESORT $$$
([☎]68 80 80; www.hotelmaitai.com; bungalows d from 27,000 CFP; [❄][☎][≋]) Opened in 2011, the Maitai is not just another luxury resort. No fancy over-water units here, but an array of creatively designed bungalows around a small lake complete with water lilies. All units mimic *fare va'a* (outrigger-canoe huts). There's a solar-powered energy system, part of the food is grown organically and green waste is composted.

Rande's Shack BUNGALOW $$
([☎]68 86 27; randesshack@mail.pf; bungalows 10,000-15,000 CFP; [☎]) Great for families and a long-time surfer favourite American expat Rande and his lovely Tahitian wife give a warm welcome and offer two great-value self-catering beachside houses, the larger of which sleeps up to six people. They're ideally located on a small beach perfect for swimming and snorkelling. Bikes and kayaks are

complimentary. Airport transfers are 600 CFP (one way).

Fare le Fare LUXURY TENTS $$
([☎]60 63 77; www.tahitisafari.com; tents d incl breakfast 16,500 CFP; [☎]) By far the most unusual sleeping option on Huahine, this good find offers two giant African-themed luxury safari tents. Spacious and airy, the tents are uniquely decorated and comfortable, featuring wooden floors, creative artwork and large beds with fluffy quilts. Right on a good swimming beach, the place has a funky, self-catering, gnarled-wood kitchen, and free snorkels, masks, kayaks and bicycles. Airport transfers are free.

Chez Guynette GUESTHOUSE $
([☎]68 83 75; www.pension-guynette-huahine.com; dm 1800 CFP, s/d with shared bathroom 4900/5900 CFP) This excellent-value place on the main street offers seven simple but comfortable rooms which have fans and bathrooms (with hot water). The eight-bed dorm is spacious and clean (though not at all private) and there's a big communal kitchen. Airport transfers are 500 CFP per person (one way) and breakfast costs 800 CFP. Minimum stay of two nights.

Meherio PENSION $
([☎]60 75 71, 60 61 35; meherio.huahine@mail.pf; s/d incl breakfast 8500/10,600 CFP; [☎]) A reliable abode. Room exteriors are woven bamboo, interiors have lots of colourful local fabrics, there are plenty of plant-filled common areas and you're a stone's throw from Fare's nicest beach and snorkelling. Bikes and kayaks are free for guests. Meals are available on request. Airport transfers are free.

Fare Maeva HOTEL $$
([☎]68 75 53; www.fare-maeva.com; d/bungalows 7500/12,800 CFP; [❄][☎][≋]) On a coral rock beach (not good for swimming), this place has 10 elementary bungalows sleeping two to four people, all with kitchens, private bathrooms (with hot water) and mosquito screens. It also rents out five adjoining rooms that are smaller, less expensive versions of the bungalows. There's a room-plus-car deal from 14,600 CFP per day for two people.

Tupuna PENSION $$
([☎]68 70 36, 79 07 94; www.pensiontupuna.com; bungalows d incl breakfast 8000-12,000 CFP; [☎]) On an isolated property, the four rustic Polynesian-style bungalows, each with a private

hot-water bathroom, are in a lush tropical garden bursting with all sorts of exotic trees. Mostly organic meals (dinner 3500 CFP) are served family-style; kayaks and snorkelling equipment are free. Note that there's no beach and the waters are murky at low tide. Airport transfers are 1500 CFP. Cash only.

HUAHINE ITI

The (marginally) smaller island has several ideally situated places, as well as the most beautiful beaches and widest lagoon.

Fare Ie Parea LUXURY TENTS $$
(☑60 63 77; www.tahitisafari.com; tents d incl breakfast from 16,500 CFP) The beach here is about on par with the Fare location but it's much quieter over this side. Manager Marguerite is charming, helpful and adds some Polynesian flair. The four tents are the same style as those at Fare Ie Fare and are well spaced out in a neat garden. Free bikes and kayaks, and free airport transfers. Cash only.

Mauarii PENSION $
(☑68 86 49; www.mauarii.com; bungalows d incl breakfast 9200 CFP; @☎) Mauarii is in a fabulous beachside location but some travellers have complained that it tries so hard to exude shabby chic, it sacrifices comfort. There are several different room-and-bungalow options, some fancier than others, but all crafted from local materials and enhanced with creative touches. There's an on-site dive shop. Free kayaks. Airport transfers cost 2000 CFP per person return.

Hiva Plage CAMPGROUND, GUESTHOUSE $
(☑68 89 50, 73 53 45; teriitetumu@mail.pf; campsites s/d 1300/1800 CFP, s/d with shared bathroom 2800/5000 CFP; ☎) This place is a dependable bet for budgeters. Pitch your tent on the grassy plot or choose one of the basic rooms in a separate house. Precious perks include a kitchen for guests' use, surfboard, scooter and tent hire, laundry service and complimentary bikes and kayaks. Meals are available on request (from 1500 CFP). Airport transfers are 2000 CFP per person return. Cash only.

Relais Mahana RESORT $$$
(☑68 81 54; www.relaismahana.com; bungalows d 23,000-34,000 CFP; @☎⛱) This upscale hotel is on what's arguably the best beach on Huahine, and there's a sensational coral garden just offshore. Bungalow interiors are tastefully decorated with local art and all bathrooms (except in the rooms) have

indoor-outdoor showers in private mini-gardens. Airport transfers are 4200 CFP per person return.

Chez Tara BUNGALOW $$
(☑68 78 45; bungalow d incl breakfast 12,000 CFP) Next to the eponymous restaurant, this place has a wonderfully rustic bungalow overlooking the beach. Free kayaks.

Hiva One PENSION $$
(☑90 01 83; www.hivaone.com; bungalows d incl breakfast 15,600 CFP; ☎) Three simple bungalows facing a lovely bay fringed with a coral and sand beach lapped by turquoise waters. There's a communal kitchen. Free kayaks.

✖️ Eating

Most of Huahine's places to eat are found near Fare. Around the rest of the island, eating options are limited to restaurants in pensions – some of which are fabulous – and casual *snack* eateries.

FARE & AROUND
New Te Marara RESTAURANT $$
(☑68 70 81; mains 1600-2400 CFP; ☺lunch & dinner Mon-Sat) In a great location right on the lagoon, this lively restaurant is a favourite local watering hole and the best place to eat around Fare. It has a beach-bar vibe and the menu is meat- and seafood-based.

Chez Guynette SNACK $
(☑68 83 75; mains 800-1500 CFP; ☺breakfast & lunch Thu-Tue) Fare's best coffee plus fresh fruit juices, breakfast dishes and light meals are served on a lively open-air terrace. The tuna steak and the skewered mahi mahi certainly won our heart. Brilliant value.

Le Mahi Mahi RESTAURANT $$
(mains 1100-2200 CFP; ☺lunch Tue-Sun, dinner Tue-Sat) Right in downtown Fare, this surf-style eatery has a live lobster tank (a meal of them is 3500 CFP) and a stunning mural on the wall of the namesake fish. The menu is creative with dishes like duck breast with pineapple, plenty of seafood, an excellent fish burger, a great pastry counter, cocktails from 900 CFP and a good wine list.

Roulottes FOOD VANS $$
(mains 1000-1500 CFP; ☺lunch & dinner) The quayside *roulottes* are Huahine's best bargain for cheap eats. Huge portions of fish, chicken, burgers, steaks and chips are the order of the day, but there are also pizzas, crêpes and ice cream.

Super Fare Nui – Super U

SUPERMARKET $

(☺6am-6.30pm Mon-Sat, 6-11.30am Sun) If you're preparing your own meals, head to this well-stocked supermarket opposite the waterfront.

Market

MARKET $

(☺Mon-Sat) For organic fruits and vegetables, as well as fresh fish, nothing can beat the market on the waterfront.

AROUND THE ISLAND

Once you've left Fare there aren't too many places to eat, apart from the hotels and a few scattered, inexpensive *snacks*.

TOP CHOICE ## Chez Tara

RESTAURANT $$

(☑68 78 45; mains 1300-3800 CFP; ☺lunch & dinner) One of Huahine's unexpected gems, Chez Tara is easily the best place on the island to sample Tahitian specialities. Head here on Sundays for its legendary *ma'a Tahiti* (served buffet-style; 3500 CFP) served at lunchtime. It's in a great location, right on the lagoon. Bookings essential.

Mauarii

RESTAURANT $$$

(☑68 86 49; mains 1500-4500 CFP; ☺lunch & dinner) Not only is this one of the only places in French Polynesia where you can consistently order *ma'a Tahiti* à la carte, but it's also one of the only places you'll find delectable local crab on the menu. It's also terrific for hearty sandwiches (600 CFP). The setting is in a Polynesian-style hut overlooking an expanse of turquoise water.

ⓘ Information

There are private doctors and a pharmacy in Fare. Visiting yachties can obtain water from Pacific Blue Adventure (p373), on the quay.

Ao Api New World (per hr 900 CFP; ☺8.30am-7pm Mon-Fri) Internet access with a view of Fare's port. It's upstairs.

Banque de Tahiti (☺8.15am-noon & 1-3.30pm Mon-Fri) Currency exchange, and has an ATM.

Banque Socredo (☺7.30-11am & 1.30-4pm Mon-Fri) Currency exchange, and has an ATM.

Comité du Tourisme (tourist office; ☑68 78 81; ☺9am-2pm Mon-Fri) On Fare's main street.

Post office (OPT; ☺7am-3pm Mon-Thu, 7am-2pm Fri, 7.30-8am Sat) Has internet and wi-fi access (with the Manaspot network).

ⓘ Getting There & Away

Huahine, the first of the Leeward Islands, is 170km west of Tahiti and 35km east of Ra'iatea and Taha'a.

Air

Air Tahiti (☑68 77 02, 86 42 42; www.airtahiti.pf; ☺7.30-11.30am & 1.30-4.30pm Mon-Fri, 8-11.30am Sat) has an office on the main street in Fare. Destinations include Pape'ete (12,600 CFP, 35 minutes, four to five daily), Ra'iatea (7100 CFP, 15 minutes, daily), Bora Bora (9500 CFP, 20 minutes, daily) and Mo'orea (14,000 CFP, 30 minutes, daily).

Boat

The passenger boat **Aremiti 4** (☑50 57 57; www.aremiti.pf) runs once a week between Pape'ete and Bora Bora (9500 CFP), stopping at Ra'iatea and Huahine en route. It generally departs on Friday and returns on Sunday.

Two cargo ships, the *Hawaiki Nui* and the *Taporo*, make two trips a week between Pape'ete and Bora Bora (via Huahine, Ra'iatea and Taha'a), leaving Pape'ete on Tuesday and Thursday around 4pm. Note that it's pretty difficult for tourists to get passage aboard the *Taporo* as it's usually booked out by locals. See p428 for more information.

ⓘ Getting Around

To/From the Airport

Huahine's airport is 2.5km north of Fare. Pensions and hotels will arrange taxi transfers (sometimes included in the tariff).

Car

A sealed road follows the coast all the way around both islands. Public rates are exorbitant – about 9500 CFP to 12,600 CFP – but discounts are available if you book through your hotel or pension.

Avis-Pacificar (☑68 73 34)

Europcar (☑68 82 59; kake@mail.pf)

Fare Maeva (☑68 75 53; www.fare-maeva.com)

Scooter & Bicycle

You can hire bicycles from **Europcar** or **Huahine Lagoon** (p373) for about 2000 CFP a day. For scooters, check with Europcar, which charges 6200 CFP for 24 hours.

RA'IATEA & TAHA'A

The twin islands of Ra'iatea and Taha'a, though encircled by a common lagoon, are far from identical; from geography to history and general vibe, it's even hard to believe they're related at all! Ra'iatea is vast and mountainous with a regal past yet has never really been a hit with the tourism crowd; meanwhile shy, short Taha'a quietly sits in Ra'iatea's shadow and is drawing in

an increasing number of visitors with her white-sand *motu* and lush views of Bora Bora. Neither island, however, is very touristy and both offer a glimpse of a self-reliant Polynesia and a more authentic way of life.

Ra'iatea

POP 12,030 / AREA 170 SQ KM

No other French Polynesian island feels as intensely mysterious as Ra'iatea. As the ancient seat of Polynesian spirituality and home to Taputapuatea, the site that many consider to be the queen of all Polynesian *marae,* this island has more than its share of *mana* (spiritual force). Perhaps this intensity comes from the dark, brooding mountains that shade the deep valleys and the country's only navigable river, or its emblem flower, the *tiare apetahi,* that simply won't grow anywhere else in the world except the Temehani Plateau.

◉ Sights

We'd recommend renting a vehicle and driving the entire 98km sealed circuit around Ra'iatea.

Uturoa is the second-largest town in French Polynesia. Take some time to wander around: the place provides a sample of the local flavour, plus there's some funky little shops and great deals on black pearls.

Drive along the east coast, to the south. Soon after you've passed the mouth of the **Faaroa River**, a turn-off heads to the south coast. Turn right here to climb to a **belvédère** with great views of Faaroa Bay. Or turn left to reach **Marae Taputapuatea**, which had immense importance to the ancient Polynesians.

At **Tevaitoa** village, on the northwestern side of the island, massive stone slabs stand in the 50m-long wall of **Marae Tainuu**, behind the church (the church was built on the *marae*). Then the road passes the **Apooiti Marina**, the airport and returns to Uturoa.

🏃 Activities

Diving & Snorkelling

There are about 15 dive sites along the east and west coasts and around Taha'a. Highlights include the superb Teavapiti Pass and the *Nordby,* the only real wreck dive in French Polynesia. For more information, see p32.

Some of the reef *motu* are splendid and perfect for swimming or snorkelling. Ask at your hotel about renting a boat or joining a lagoon tour.

Ra'iatea has two diving centres.

Hemisphere Sub   DIVING
(☑66 12 49, 72 19 52; www.hemispheresub.com) This operation based at the Apooiti Marina charges 7000 CFP for an introductory dive, 6200 CFP for a single dive, 11,700 CFP for a two-tank dive and 29,000 CFP for a five-dive package. The centre also has a base at Raiatea Hawaiki Nui.

Te Mara Nui   DIVING
(☑66 11 88, 72 60 19; www.temaranui.pf) This small outfit offers personalised service and charges 6200 CFP for an introductory dive, 6000 CFP for a single dive and 37,000 CFP for a certification course.

Hiking

Good walking opportunities include the walk up to the **Temehani Plateau**; the short climb up **Mt Tapioi**, near Uturoa; and the **Three Waterfalls walk**, near Manava pension.

DON'T MISS

MARAE TAPUTAPUATEA

The most important *marae* (traditional temple) in French Polynesia, sprawling Marae Taputapuatea dates from the 17th century. This was the centre of spiritual power in Polynesia when the first Europeans arrived, and its influence was international: *ari'i* (chiefs) from all over the Maohi world, including the Australs, the Cook Islands and New Zealand, came here for important ceremonies.

The main part of the site is a large paved platform with a long *ahu* (altar) stretching down one side. At the very end of the cape is the smaller **Marae Tauraa**, a *tapu* (taboo) enclosure with a tall 'stone of investiture', where young *ari'i* were enthroned. The lagoonside **Marae Hauviri** also has an upright stone, and the whole site is made of pieces of coral.

Ra'iatea & Taha'a

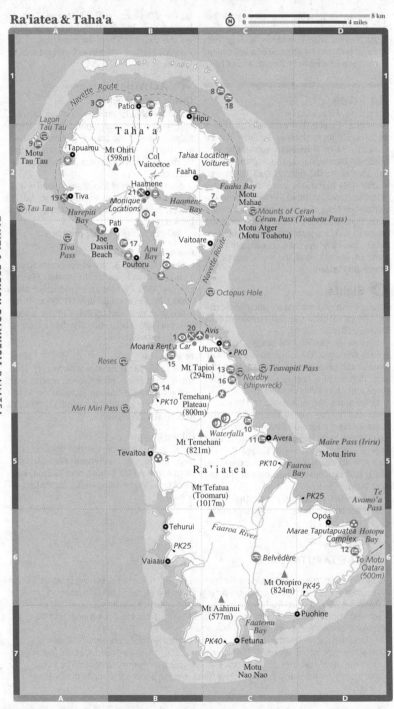

Ra'iatea & Taha'a

Sights
1 Apooiti Marina.................................B4
2 Ferme Perlière Champon B3
3 Love Here.......................................A1
4 Maison de la Vanille B2
5 Marae Tainuu B5

Activities, Courses & Tours
Hemisphere Sub ....(see 1)
Hemisphere Sub ....(see 13)

Sleeping
6 Fare Pea Iti....................................B1
7 Hibiscus...C2
8 La Pirogue.....................................C1
9 Le Taha'a Private Island & Spa A2
10 Manava...C5
11 Opeha...C5
12 Opoa Beach D6
13 Raiatea Hawaiki Nui........................C4
14 Raiatea Lodge B4
15 Sunset Beach Motel B4
16 Tepua...C4
17 Titaina..B3
18 Vahine Island Private Island
    Resort..C1

Eating
19 Chez Louise...................................A2
20 Le Napoli......................................B4
Le Nordby ....(see 13)
Opoa Beach ....(see 12)
Raiatea Lodge ....(see 14)
21 Tahaa Maitai.................................B2

With the exception of the walk to Mt Tapioi, a guide is required. Try **Thierry Laroche** (66 20 32, 77 91 23; raiatearando@mail.pf), who charges 4000 CFP per person (8000 CFP for Temehani Plateau).

Yachting
Ra'iatea's central position in the Society Islands, and its fine lagoon, have helped make it the yacht-charter centre of French Polynesia. Most operations will offer whatever a customer demands and prepare fully stocked and equipped boats. The following Ra'iatea-based companies are recommended.

Dream Yacht Charter   YACHT CHARTERS
(66 18 80; www.dreamyachtcharter.com) Offers catamaran and monohull cruises in the Leeward Islands.

Moorings   YACHT CHARTERS
(66 35 93; www.moorings.com) This international outfitter has about 20 monohulls and catamarans on offer.

Sunsail   YACHT CHARTERS
(60 04 85; www.sunsailtahiti.com) Operates a variety of bare-boat charters and crewed cruises in the Leeward Islands and the Tuamotus.

Tahiti Yacht Charter   YACHT CHARTERS
(66 28 86; www.tahitiyachtcharter.com) Has catamarans and monohulls.

Lagoon Excursions
Boat tours are very popular in Ra'iatea. Most tours actually spend the majority of their time on the island of Taha'a, but most companies are based on Ra'iatea and pick up from the pier in Uturoa. Two companies run dedicated trips on Ra'iatea.

Temehani   BOAT TOUR
(66 12 88, 77 54 87; www.vacances-tahiti.com) Half-/full-day trips aboard a monohull cost 7500/9500 CFP.

Arii Moana Tours   BOAT TOUR
(79 69 72) The only operator that offers full-day tours of Ra'iatea that include snorkelling and swimming stops and a visit to Marae Taputapuatea (9000 CFP, including lunch).

Sleeping
UTUROA & AROUND
Raiatea Hawaiki Nui   RESORT $$$
(60 05 00; www.hawaikinuihotel.com; PK2; r from 15,000 CFP, bungalows d from 20,000 CFP; ✳️🛜🌊) This small complex on the outskirts of Uturoa consists of several different accommodation options, including plain rooms, garden bungalows, 'semi-lagoon' (read: partially over-water) bungalows and over-water units. Amenities include a restaurant, a bar and a dive shop. Good deals can usually be found online.

Tepua   PENSION $$
(66 33 00; www.pension-tepua.com; PK2.5; dm/s/d with shared bathrooms 2500/5000/7500 CFP, bungalows d 10,000-13,000 CFP; @🛜🌊) This is a good base for budget travellers. The four rooms are bare and the partition walls are thin but they're clean and colourfully decorated, the shared bathrooms have hot showers, and the 12-bed dorm is spartan and compact but kept clean. For more privacy, opt for one of the well-equipped bungalows.

TAHITI & FRENCH POLYNESIA RA'IATEA

Society Islands

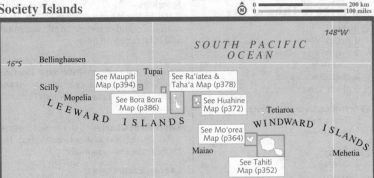

Bike and kayak rental is available. Airport transfers are 1000 CFP return.

AROUND THE ISLAND

Sunset TOP CHOICE

Beach Motel   BUNGALOWS, CAMPGROUND **$$**
(☑66 33 47; www.sunset-raiatea.pf; PK5; campsites per person 1300 CFP, bungalows s/d 11,000/12,000 CFP; ☎) Just the location (on an expansive coconut plantation fronting the lagoon) alone would make this one of Ra'iatea's best options, but the 22 bungalows – which are perhaps better described as small homes – make this one of the best deals in the islands. Bikes, snorkelling equipment and airport transfers are free. A grassy, shady plot is set aside for campers, who have their own ablution block and kitchen.

Opoa Beach   RESORT **$$$**
(☑60 05 10; www.hotel-raiatea.com; PK37; bungalows d from 25,000 CFP; ☎☒) This small resort with a boutique feel is one of Ra'iatea's top hotels. The collection of cottages set amid beautifully landscaped gardens appeals to couples looking for creature comforts and style without an exorbitant price tag. The property also has a highly respected restaurant.

Raiatea Lodge   HOTEL **$$**
(☑66 20 00; www.raiateahotel.com; PK8.8; s 14,000 CFP, d 16,500-20,000 CFP; ☒☎☒) Raiatea Lodge pays elegant homage to colonial architecture, with a two-storey plantation-style building sitting quietly at the back of a coconut plantation. It attracts holidaymakers looking for comfortable rooms and amenities, including a restaurant, a bar and

a pool. Add 4000 CFP (up to four people) for return airport transfers. Bikes, snorkelling gear and kayaks are free, and English is spoken.

Opeha   PENSION **$**
(☑66 19 48; www.pensionopeha.pf; PK10.5; bungalows d incl breakfast 10,000 CFP; ☒☎) A crisp and compact waterfront abode, Opeha has a handful of very white, very clean, kitchen-equipped bungalows, lined up in a row in a tiny, immaculate property. Airport transfers are 1000 CFP per person return. Cash only.

Manava   PENSION **$**
(☑66 28 26; www.manavapension.com; PK6; d with shared bathrooms 5000 CFP, bungalows d 8500 CFP; ☎) This is a friendly, well-managed place with four spacious bungalows, all with kitchens and private bathrooms (hot water), dotting a tropical garden. If you're scratching the pennies, opt for one of two adjoining rooms that share bathrooms (hot water) and a communal kitchen. Airport transfers are free.

✕ Eating

You'll find small *snack*-style places and a few *roulottes* dotted around the island.

UTUROA & AROUND

Uturoa has several well-stocked supermarkets, open Monday to Saturday and some on Sunday morning. A handful of *roulottes* open at night along the waterfront strip at the north end of the marina.

Le Nordby   RESTAURANT **$$$**
(☑60 05 00; PK2.5; mains 1500-3000 CFP; ☺breakfast, lunch & dinner) The restaurant

inside the Raiatea Hawaiki Nui resort has a good reputation, and the convivial bar serves good cocktails.

Le Napoli
RESTAURANT, PIZZERIA $$
(☑66 10 77; www.pizzerianapoli.com; Uturoa; mains 1400-2400 CFP; ⊙lunch Tue-Fri, dinner Tue-Sun) In a reed hut decorated with loads of flowers, this congenial pizzeria near the Avis agency offers a long list of Italian dishes including pasta, wood-fired pizzas, and meat and fish specials.

Brasserie Maraamu
BISTRO $$
(☑66 46 54; Uturoa; mains 1300-2200 CFP; ⊙lunch Mon-Sat, breakfast & dinner Mon-Fri) This popular joint serves huge plates of reasonably priced food.

AROUND THE ISLAND
Bring a picnic if you're travelling around the island as there aren't many opportunities to find a meal during the day.

TOP CHOICE Opoa Beach
RESTAURANT $$$
(☑60 05 10; PK37; set menu 5000 CFP; ⊙dinner by reservation) At the Opoa Beach hotel, this is Ra'iatea's glammest dinner spot. The chef earns raves for his high-flying creative dishes combining fresh produce and spices. The menu changes daily. Hotel guests have priority, so reserve early.

Raiatea Lodge
RESTAURANT $$$
(☑66 20 00; PK8.8; mains 2200-2900 CFP; ⊙lunch & dinner) The Raiatea Lodge's on-site restaurant is a great place for a drink as well as a meal. There's sure to be a dish on the extensive menu that suits your palate but leave room for dessert.

❶ Information
The following places are all found within Uturoa.

Banque de Polynésie (⊙8.15am-noon & 1-3.30pm Mon-Fri) Currency exchange, and has an ATM.

ITS (per hr 1000 CFP; ⊙8am-noon & 1-5pm Mon-Fri, 8-11.30am Sat) Internet access. Inside the gare maritime (boat terminal).

Post office (OPT; ⊙8am-12.30pm & 2-4pm Mon-Fri, 8-10am Sat) North of the centre, towards the airport. Internet and wi-fi access (with the Manaspot network). Has an ATM.

Raiatea visitors information centre (☑60 07 77; ⊙8am-4pm Mon-Fri) In the gare maritime in Uturoa. It's also open on weekends when visiting cruise ships are in port.

Socredo (⊙8.15am-noon & 1-3.30pm Mon-Fri) Currency exchange and has an ATM.

❶ Getting There & Away
Ra'iatea is 220km northwest of Tahiti and 40km southeast of Bora Bora.

Air
Air Tahiti (☑60 04 44, 86 42 42; www.airtahiti.pf) operates direct flights from Tahiti (14,200 CFP, 40 minutes, seven to eight daily) with connections via Mo'orea (14,000 CFP) and Huahine (7100 CFP). There are also direct flights to Bora Bora (7800 CFP, 20 minutes, daily) and Maupiti (8500 CFP, 20 minutes, three weekly).

Boat
Ra'iatea is separated from Taha'a by a 3km-wide channel.

TAHA'A The navette (shuttle boat) services on the **Te Haere Maru** (☑65 61 33) run between Uturoa and various stops on Taha'a twice a day, at 5.30am and 11.30am. There is no service on Saturday afternoon or Sunday. The one-way fare is 650 CFP.

There is also a **taxi-boat service** (☑79 62 01) between the two islands, which operates daily. It costs 6600 CFP to go to southern Taha'a and 12,600 CFP to get to the north of the island (prices are for two people).

OTHER ISLANDS The passenger boat **Aremiti 4** (☑50 57 57; www.aremiti.pf) runs once a week between Pape'ete and Bora Bora, stopping at Ra'iatea en route. It generally departs on Friday and returns on Sunday. Pape'ete–Ra'iatea costs 6300 CFP, while Ra'iatea–Bora Bora is 5250 CFP one way.

The **Maupiti Express** (☑67 66 69; www.maupitiexpress.com) travels between Bora Bora, Taha'a and Ra'iatea three days a week. The one-way/return fare is 4000/5000 CFP; it costs 500 CFP to go from Ra'iatea to Taha'a.

The cargo ships Taporo and Hawaiki Nui also make a stop at Ra'iatea; see p428.

❶ Getting Around
A sealed road hugs the coast all the way around the island. Point kilométrique (PK; kilometre point) distances start in Uturoa near the gendarmerie (police station) and then run south to Faatemu Bay. The options for getting around are to hire a car or hitchhike (although we don't recommend the latter).

The airport, which also serves Taha'a, is on the northern tip of the island. Most island accommodation will pick you up if you have booked (although there may be a charge).

Some hotels and guesthouses hire out bicycles. **Avis** (☑66 34 06; avis.raiatea.loc@mail.pf) hires out bicycles/scooters for 3500/6500 CFP for 24 hours. For car rental, contact **Avis** (☑66 34 06; avis.raiatea.loc@mail.pf), **Hertz** (☑66 35 35; hertz.raiatea@mail.pf) or **Moana Rent a**

Car (☎75 08 30; www.moanarentacar.com). An economy car costs 10,000 CFP for 24 hours.

Taha'a

POP 4850 / AREA 90 SQ KM

As sweet and pretty as its hibiscus flower shape, Taha'a is about as low-key an island as you'll find in the Society Archipelago. Most people visit on a day trip from Ra'iatea; however, if you really want to get away from it all, stop longer. The economy putters along on pearl farming and vanilla production, but tourism, particularly in the luxury sector, is adding a new dimension to the charming simplicity. There are some fabulous sleeping options on the lush, though mostly beachless island (this is where you'll find the budget choices), as well as the sandy *motu* that are blessed with sunset views over the iconic Bora Bora silhouette.

◉ Sights

A 70km sealed road winds around the island and the population is concentrated in eight villages on the coast. **Tapuamu** has the main quay, **Patio** is the main town, and **Haamene** is where the roads around the southern and northern parts of the island meet, forming a figure eight.

Ferme Perlière Champon   PEARL FARM
(☎65 66 26; www.champonperles.com) This well-run pearl farm is known for its high-quality mounted and unmounted pearls. It's at the southern end of Apu Bay.

Maison de la Vanille   VANILLA FARM
(☎65 67 27; ⊙by reservation) On the right of the road into Haamene is this small family-run operation where you can see vanilla preparation and drying processes and also purchase vanilla pods.

Love Here   PEARL FARM
(☎65 66 67; www.loveherepearlfarm.com) At this family-run pearl farm right on the seashore, visitors learn how pearls are prepared for grafting, as well as the varieties and their characteristics. It has a gift shop that sells mounted and unmounted pearls as well as jewellery.

🏃 Activities

Diving & Snorkelling

Taha'a has one dive centre. The dive centres on Ra'iatea regularly use the dive sites to the east of the island, and will collect you from lodgings in the south of Taha'a. See p377 for more details. Like Ra'iatea, you have to go to the *motu* for swimming and snorkelling. Some guesthouses will drop you on a *motu* for the day or you can join an organised *pirogue* tour. The healthiest coral gardens are off **Motu Tau Tau**, **Motu Toahotu** and **Motu Atger**.

Tahaa Diving   DIVING, SNORKELLING
(☎65 78 37, 24 80 69; www.tahaa-diving.com) This low-key operation in Tapuamu charges 6000 CFP for an introductory dive or a single dive and 11,000 CFP for a two-tank dive. Snorkelling trips are also on offer. Cash only.

☞ Tours

Tours allow you to get out to those sandy *motu* and provide easy access to local pearl farms and vanilla plantations. Many tour operators are based in Ra'iatea and offer pick-up services from Ra'iatea. Full-day tours range from 8500 CFP to 10,500 CFP and can be arranged through your hotel or pension. Book ahead as a minimum number of people (usually four) is required.

🛏 Sleeping

THE ISLAND

Titaina TOP CHOICE   PENSION $$
(☎65 69 58, 29 17 13; www.pension-titaina.com; Poutoru; bungalows d 11,700-14,500 CFP; ☎) At the end of the asphalted road north of Poutoru, this delightfully secluded retreat has three bungalows that are spread out on grassy grounds. They're far from fancy but are prettily decorated and kept scrupulously clean. Your courteous hosts speak English and go above and beyond to ensure you enjoy your stay. There are (free) bikes and kayaks. No pick-up at Ra'iatea's airport, but the quay at Poutoru (for the *Maupiti Express 2*) is just 200m down the road. Cash only.

Hibiscus   HOTEL $$
(☎65 61 06; www.hibiscustahaa.com; Haamene Bay; bungalows d from 10,600 CFP; ☎) The haphazardly run Hibiscus gets mixed reviews but its promo deals ('stay three nights, pay for two') make it a bargain. Seven simply built bungalows of varying sizes and shapes are clustered in an Eden-like garden on a hillside overlooking Haamene Bay. Transfers from Raiatea cost 6000 CFP per person return.

Fare Pea Iti   PENSION $$$
(☎60 81 11, 76 98 55; www.farepeaiti.pf; Patio; bungalows d garden or beach 18,000-36,000 CFP; ☎▨)

Fare Pea Iti has three well-designed and capacious bungalows with spiffing lagoon frontage. Hint: aim for the smaller, cheaper unit which is slightly set back from the waterfront. Swimming is not *that* tempting, with very shallow waters and a profusion of algae at certain times of year. Perks include a small pool and complimentary kayaks, bikes and DVDs. Transfers to Raiatea's airport cost 10,400 CFP per person return.

THE MOTU

Motu digs are set in private paradises that rival (and some would say exceed) the settings of Bora Bora's better resorts.

TOP CHOICE **Vahine Island**

Private Island Resort RESORT $$$
(65 67 38; www.vahine-island.com; Motu Tuuvahine; bungalows d from 60,000 CFP; ✳🐕) In a picturesque location with white-sand beaches and translucent water, this intimate resort caters to couples seeking exclusivity. It has nine French Polynesian–style bungalows – three of which are perched over a shallow lagoon speckled with healthy coral formations. Kayaks and snorkelling equipment are available for free. Airport transfers cost 8000 CFP per person return. Look out for internet deals.

La Pirogue RESORT $$$
(60 81 45; www.hotel-la-pirogue.com; Motu Rootava; bungalows d from 30,000 CFP; 🐕) This small, secluded *motu* resort is famous for its gorgeous sunsets over Bora Bora out on the horizon. It's intimate and friendly, and appeals to couples looking for a bit of luxury without an exorbitant price tag. Airport transfers are 8400 CFP per person return.

Pension Atger PENSION $
(28 26 81; atgertheodore@mail.pf; Motu Atger; bungalows with full board per person 9000 CFP; 🐕) This well-priced retreat on secluded Motu Atger has four bungalows that are comfortably furnished, have private facilities and open onto the lagoon. The atmosphere is delightfully chilled out, swimming and snorkelling are excellent, and kayaks are complimentary. Cash only.

Le Taha'a Private Island & Spa RESORT $$$
(60 84 00; www.letahaa.com; Motu Tau Tau; bungalows d from 85,000 CFP; ✳@🐕🏊) This is one of the most exclusive resorts in the country, in an exceptional setting on Motu Tau Tau. Every option is designed with luxurious creativity and offers space and a supreme level

WORTH A TRIP

JOE DASSIN BEACH

If you're willing to take a bit of a walk you can get to deserted Joe Dassin Beach, on the southwest side of the island, a 15-minute walk along the coast north of Pati. Ask a local in Pati to show you the trailhead, pack a lunch and get lost in paradise for the day. Oh, and don't forget your snorkel gear for there's fantastic snorkelling just offshore.

of privacy. Le Taha'a is definitely a destination resort (it's very isolated) but the place offers enough activities to keep most guests entertained for days.

✕ Eating

There are shops in each village and a few *roulottes* open around the island at night, but the dining options are very limited. The *motu* resorts all have their own restaurants and bars, and are open to nonguests by reservation.

Tahaa Maitai RESTAURANT $$$
(65 70 85; Haamene; mains 1300-3500 CFP; ⊙lunch Tue-Fri & Sun, dinner Tue-Sat) Travellers recommend this restaurant right on Haamene Bay not only for its fabulous views but also for its delicious cuisine. The menu features lots of fresh seafood, local fruits and vegetables, and delicious French desserts.

Chez Louise RESTAURANT $$$
(71 23 06; Tiva; mains 1400-1900 CFP; set menu 4900 CFP; ⊙lunch & dinner) This is one of the best stops for lunch on a tour of Taha'a. Louise cooks simple but palatable Polynesian specialities and is famous for her 'marina menu', which includes lobster, shrimps and raw fish served in bamboo plates. Cash only.

ℹ Information

The post offices in Patio and Haamene have an ATM. The Banque Socredo in Patio also has an ATM.

ℹ Getting There & Away

There is no airport on Taha'a. From the southern tip of Taha'a, the airport on Ra'iatea is only 15 minutes across the lagoon and some hotels will pick up guests from the airport or from the ferry quay at Uturoa on Ra'iatea.

See p381 for information on the *navette* service between Ra'iatea and Taha'a.

The **Maupiti Express** (☑67 66 99; www.maupitiexpress.com) operates on Wednesday, Friday and Sunday between Bora Bora, Taha'a (Poutoru) and Ra'iatea.

Interisland ships stop at Tapuamu on Taha'a en route from Ra'iatea to Bora Bora, but not on every voyage.

ⓘ Getting Around

There is no public transport on Taha'a. Hiring a car or bike are the only ways to see the island independently. **Monique Locations** (☑65 62 48) hires out cars for 11,000/14,000 CFP for eight/24 hours, while **Tahaa Location Voitures** (☑65 66 75, 72 07 71; www.hotel-tahaa.com) charges 9500/10,000 CFP for four/24 hours. You can save money on Taha'a's ridiculously expensive car costs by hiring a scooter on Ra'iatea and bringing it across on the *navette*.

BORA BORA

POP 8900 / AREA 47 SQ KM

Tell someone you're heading to Bora Bora, one of the world's most famous dream destinations, and prepare for a jealous response and cries of 'Can I come too?' Indeed, there are worse things in life than splashing about in a huge glinting turquoise swimming pool, snorkelling amid pristine coral reefs, sipping a cocktail on your private terrace, and sampling gourmet fare in a fancy restaurant. The good thing is that you can mix slow-paced sun-and-sand holidays with action-packed experiences. Diving, water sports and hiking are available.

◎ Sights

Bora Bora's 32km coast road hugs the shoreline almost all the way around the island. We describe an anticlockwise tour that starts in Vaitape; as it's flat except for the decent hill around Fitiiu Point it makes a good bicycle ride, though it's not a bad idea to join a 4WD tour because some sights are not easy to find (due to lack of signage).

Vaitape   TOWN
If arriving by air you'll be transported from the Motu Mute airport to Vaitape, the island's main settlement. It's a great place to do a bit of shopping, take care of banking and internet needs and just get a feel for the way locals really live. Vaitape is at its liveliest on Sunday morning, when numerous food stalls selling such delicacies as *pahua*

taioro (clams marinated in coconut seawater sauce) and *firifiri* (doughnuts) take position along the main road.

Matira Beach & Matira Point   BEACH
Matira Beach graces both sides of Matira Point, a narrow peninsula that extends south into the lagoon. Bora Bora's only real beach, it's a stunning stretch of snow-white sand that's perfect for relaxing, swimming and evening up your sunburn. Though it's dotted with a few *snacks* and places to stay, its sheer size means that finding your own square of paradise is a snap.

Fitiiu Point   HISTORIC SITE
Up a small hill at Fitiiu Point, a track peels off to the right and leads to well-preserved **WWII coastal guns**. The walking trail along the ridge starts behind the first house, at the sharp bend in the road. Ask permission to take the trail.

Faanui Bay   HISTORIC SITE
Faanui Bay was the site of the US military base during WWII. At the end of Tereia Point, a rectangular concrete water tank marks the position of another **coastal gun**.

Marae Fare-Opu is squeezed between the roadside and the water's edge. Two of the slabs are clearly marked with petroglyphs.

Note the picturesque **church**, slightly inland.

Pahua Point   HISTORIC SITE
Two **coastal defence guns**, placed here to guard the shipping route into the lagoon, overlook Pahua Point. The access road is not well marked, so ask around if you get lost, or join a 4WD tour.

🏃 Activities

All operators listed here organise free pick-ups and drop-offs from hotels and pensions.

Diving & Snorkelling
Bora Bora provides enthralling diving for the experienced and novices alike. A few favourites include Tapu, famous for its lemon shark encounters; Anau, renowned for its manta ray sightings; and Toopua and Toopua Iti, which feature numerous eagle rays. Outside the reef, to the north, Muri Muri (La Vallée Blanche) offers guaranteed sightings of grey sharks, turtles and barracudas, in less than 20m. See p32 for more information on diving.

No visit to Bora Bora would be complete without a bout of snorkelling. Alas, the best

snorkelling spots can't be reached from shore – you'll have to rent a boat or opt for a lagoon tour. At the site called Anau, you'll have the opportunity to observe majestic manta rays in the morning.

There are two professional diving outfits on Bora Bora.

Bora Diving Centre DIVING
(☑67 71 84, 77 67 46; www.boradiving.com) Has introductory dives (9000 CFP), single dives (8000 CFP), two-tank dives (15,000 CFP), six-/10-dive packages (40,000/64,000 CFP) and Nitrox dives. At Matira Point and at Le Méridien Bora Bora.

Topdive DIVING
(☑60 50 50; www.topdive.com) Charges 9000 CFP for an introductory dive, 8500/15,000 CFP for a single-/two-tank dive and 43,000/70,000 CFP for a six-/10-dive package. The main base is on the northern edge of Vaitape, and there are two annexes at Intercontinental Resort & Thalasso Spa Bora Bora and Bora Bora Pearl Beach Resort.

Lagoon Excursions
Taking a cruise around Bora Bora's idyllic lagoon will be one of the main highlights of your trip to French Polynesia and it's well worth the expense.

It will cost about 6000 CFP to 7000 CFP for half-day trips and 9500 CFP for whole-day trips.

Tours typically stop to feed the sharks at the southern edge of the lagoon, and to feed and swim with the rays off Motu Toopua (whether it's a good idea or not is debatable), and include snorkelling stops at coral gardens. Full-day tours include a *motu* barbecue.

There are plenty of operators available. You can book through your pension or hotel.

Undersea Walks
Aqua Safari UNDERSEA WALKS
(☑28 87 77; www.aquasafaribora.com; trips 8500 CFP) This company provides the unique experience of walking underwater, wearing a diver's helmet and weight belt. Pumps on the boat above feed air to you during the 35-minute 'walk on the wet side', in less than 4m of water. Walks are available to everyone over the age of eight.

Kite Surfing
The steady winds that buff Matira Point mixed with the reef-sheltered lagoon are the perfect combination for kite surfing. Chat to Alban at **Kitesurf School** (☑29 14 15; www.kitesurf-school-polynesie.com) to get hooked up with the how-to.

Walking
You don't have to get all your thrills on or in the water. Draped in thick forest and dominated by bulky basaltic mountains, the island's interior has exceptional green treats. Arrange any hike with **Polynesia Island Tours** (☑29 66 60) or **Bora Bora Mountain Trek** (☑73 61 23), which have professional walking guides who speak passable English. Count on 6500 CFP for a half-day walk and anything between 12,000 and 14,500 CFP for the Mt Pahia ascent.

 Tours
A couple of operators organise island tours aboard open 4WDs. Half-day trips visit American WWII sites along with locally important (and hard-to-find) archaeological

 MAKING THE MOST OF THE MOTU

Aah, the tantalising *motu* on Bora Bora. All are private, so don't treat the land as yours to explore without permission. We've found a few options, though:

Manu Taxi Boat (☑79 11 62; ⊙9am-4.30pm) can arrange transfers to **Motu Fanfan**, at the southernmost tip of Motu Piti Aau, for 3000 CFP.

Rohivai Tours (☑67 54 26, 32 60 46) can drop you off on private **Motu Ringo** (Motu Piti Uu Tai) for 2500 CFP. It departs at 12.30pm and returns at 3.30pm.

La Plage (☑67 68 75, 28 48 66; laplage.bora@hotmail.com) can transfer you to a *motu* adjoining Motu Fanfan (3500 CFP per person, minimum two people).

Bora Bora Lagoonarium (☑67 71 34, 79 73 67; ⊙Sun-Fri) can drop you off on its private *motu* at the northern tip of Motu Piti Aau (2500 CFP). You may not like the 'lagoonarium' – a sort of fenced water park where you can swim with (or observe) captive turtles, rays and sharks.

Bora Bora

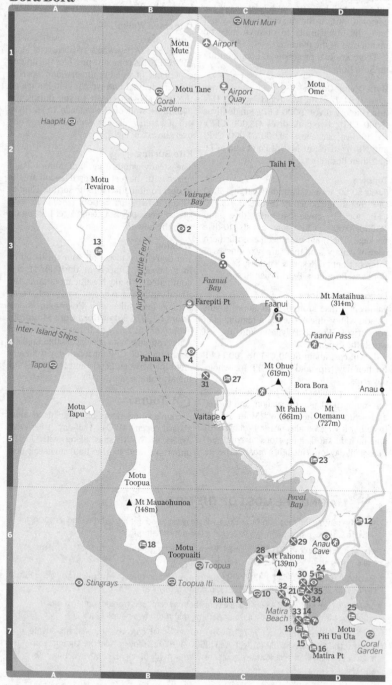

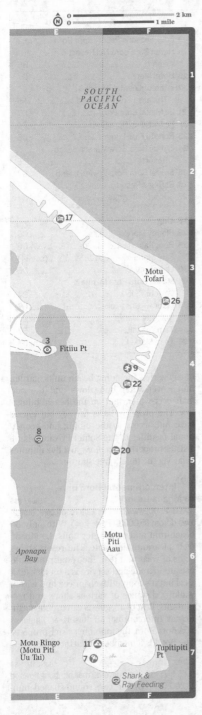

areas and a few stops at lookouts. At about 7600 CFP per person, these tours are good value if you don't want to rent a car. Contact **Tupuna Mountain Safari** (☑67 75 06) or **Vavau Adventures** (☑72 01 21). Free pick-ups.

🛌 Sleeping

Glossy brochures and promotional literature focus on Bora Bora's ultra-swish resorts, which are as luxurious and as expensive as the hype leads you to believe. That said, there's a smattering of affordable pensions that have sprung up over the last two decades (and are still largely ignored by most first-time visitors).

WEST COAST

TOP CHOICE **Sunset Hill Lodge**   BUNGALOW $$
(☑79 26 48; www.sunset-hill-borabora.biz; Vaitape; bungalows d 7000-12,000 CFP; 🖥) This is a real find if you're working to a tight budget. It features three immaculately furnished bungalows, one of which – *pilotis* ('on stilts') – has air-con, a full kitchen and lovely views of Vaitape bay. The whole place is centred on pleasantly landscaped grounds. The owner offers the most unbiased information in town and will take the time to explain all the options to travellers. Also on offer: bikes and kayaks for hire. On the northern outskirts of Vaitape. Cash only.

Rohotu Fare Lodge   BUNGALOW $$
(☑70 77 99; www.rohotufarelodge.com; Povai Bay; bungalows 19,000 CFP; 🖥) Find yourself brilliantly poised in three local-style, fully equipped bungalows hidden in a verdant array of tropical flora, with cracking views over Povai Bay. There's no beach nearby, but Matira Point is an easy bike ride away. If you don't fancy cooking, there's a number of excellent restaurants nearby.

MATIRA POINT

Much of the island's accommodation is clustered around Matira Point, at the southern toe of Bora Bora. This area also features the island's best beach.

Hotel Matira   BUNGALOW $$$
(☑67 70 51, 60 58 40; www.hotel-matira.com; bungalows d from 22,000 CFP) Like many of the places along this stretch, the lagoon setting is spectacular, and the bungalows facing this direction are priced accordingly. They occupy a grassy property overlooking the beach. Pity about the concrete wall at the entrance, though.

Bora Bora

🖊 Le Maitai Bora Bora
RESORT $$$

(☎60 30 00; www.hotelmaitai.com; r/bungalows d incl breakfast from 20,000/35,000 CFP; ✱@⊛) This option is a good deal with its nicely furnished rooms, and the over-water bungalows are the cheapest on Bora Bora. Best of all, it's close to the action. Don't get carried away – this is no exclusive experience but, at the price, it's hard to find a comparable bargain, especially if you can score promotional rates. It's a member of Earthcheck.

Bungalows Temanuata
BUNGALOW $$$

(☎67 75 61; www.temanuata.com; bungalows d from 20,000 CFP; ⊛) This popular venture is ideally positioned on Matira Point but only two units have full lagoon views. The rest are tightly packed together on a verdant property. Check out the website for off-season discounts.

Sofitel Bora Bora
Marara Beach Resort
RESORT $$$

(☎60 55 00; www.sofitel-frenchpolynesia.com; bungalows d from 30,000 CFP; ✱⊛⊛) This matriarch of the Bora Bora luxury hotel dynasty offers a wide range of facilities, including an infinity pool, a small spa and two restaurants. The bungalows come in a large range

of categories, including beach units, garden units, over-water bungalows and the odd 'half over-water, half on the beach' bungalow. The property lacks privacy but guests have full access to the dining and recreational facilities of the Sofitel Private Island, a sister property on a *motu* just five minutes away via the hotel's free shuttle.

🖊 Intercontinental Bora Bora
Le Moana Resort
RESORT $$$

(☎60 49 00; www.borabora.interconti.com; bungalows d from 35,000 CFP; ✱⊛⊛) With only 60 beachfront and over-water units, Le Moana feels pleasantly intimate. The resort shows signs of wear and tear, the restaurant could use an upgrade and service is a bit lackadaisical but it's competitively priced and within walking distance of various shops and restaurants. Best of all, guests can use the facilities at Intercontinental Resort & Thalasso Spa Bora Bora, the top-notch sister property. The hotel is a member of Earthcheck.

Chez Nono
BUNGALOW $$

(☎67 71 38; nono.leverd@mail.pf; bungalows d 13,200 CFP) Of the two round-shaped bun-

galows, one is right on Matira Beach; the other is just behind. They're both no-frills, the bathrooms are separated from the bedrooms by a curtain and the property needs some TLC, but overall it's not bad value given the irresistible location. Bonuses: free kayaks.

Chez Robert & Tina PENSION $
(☎67 72 92; pensionrobertettina@mail.pf; d with/without bathroom 9500/8400 CFP) Right on the point, this is surely one of the most divinely situated pensions in Bora Bora. Sadly, we've heard reports of variable service, indifferent owners and lack of maintenance. Rooms are in three functional, fan-cooled homes, all with shared kitchen. A few rooms have private facilities (cold-water bathrooms). The shore isn't sandy but Matira Beach is just a coconut's throw away.

EAST COAST

Bora Bora Ecolodge & Spa PENSION $$
(☎21 54 07; www.sejour-en-polynesie.com; Anau; bungalows d 10,000-12,000 CFP) The name is misleading – there's nothing vaguely 'eco' or 'lodge' in this modest pension featuring six self-contained bungalows. The location sucks (the lagoon is muddy, there's no beach and it's isolated) but it's an acceptable plan B provided you keep your expectations in check. Transfers from the Vaitape quay are free.

THE MOTU

Staying on a *motu* ensures unrivalled tranquillity, a complete escape and great views of Bora Bora.

TOP CHOICE **Intercontinental Resort & Thalasso Spa Bora Bora** RESORT $$$
(☎60 76 00; www.tahitiresorts.intercontinental.com; Motu Piti Aau; bungalows d from 80,000 CFP; ✳@☎☒) Seen from above, the layout of the 80 over-water bungalows resembles two giant crab's claws. The wow factor continues inside, with Starck-inspired decor. The seawater air-conditioning system is the pride of the hotel, and justifiably so: it saves 90% of the electricity consumed by a conventional cooling system of similar capacity. The spa (www.deepoceanspa.com) ranks as the most attractive in French Polynesia. It's been a member of Earthcheck since 2006.

Sofitel Bora Bora Private Island RESORT $$$
(☎60 56 00; www.sofitel-frenchpolynesia.com; Motu Piti Uu Uta; bungalows d from 45,000 CFP; ✳@☎) This Sofitel strikes a perfect balance between luxury, seclusion, privacy (there are only 31 units) and convenience – on hilly Motu Piti Uu Uta, it's just five glorious minutes by shuttle boat from the main island, so you're not too far from the action. Due to its position, it gets plenty of sunshine, even late afternoon.

Le Méridien Bora Bora RESORT $$$
(☎60 51 51; www.borabora.lemeridien.com; Motu Piti Aau; bungalows d from 55,000 CFP; ✳@☎☒) Renovated in 2011, Le Méridien is one of the best cures for winter blues. The vast glass floors in the over-water bungalows are mesmerising, the boat-shaped bar is fabulous and the infinity-edge pool is adorable. Le Méridien is strongly involved in sea-turtle protection work (check out www.boraboraturtles.com). Though artificial, the beach has chalk-white sand.

St Régis Resort RESORT $$$
(☎60 78 88; www.stregis.com/borabora; Motu Ome; bungalows d from 95,000 CFP; ✳@☎☒) The darling of stylish travel mags, the St Régis is a romantic resort, extremely quiet and popular with couples. The 90 over-water and beach villas have an artistic and casual elegance that let the luxury sneak up on you. Its two restaurants are of very high standard.

Bora Bora Pearl Beach Resort & Spa RESORT $$$
(☎60 52 00; www.spmhotels.com; Motu Tevairoa; bungalows d from 60,000 CFP; ✳@☎☒) Of all Bora Bora's top-end options, the Pearl has the strongest Polynesian feel. The 80 units are all built from bamboo, thatch and wood

---

EXPLORING THE LAGOON DIY-STYLE

If you prefer setting your own pace and fancy tootling around the lagoon yourself, consider exploring it in your own boat. **La Plage** (☎67 68 75, 28 48 66; laplage.bora@hotmail.com), based on the beach near hotel Maitai Polynesia Bora Bora, rents small four-seater motor boats that are easy to drive; no licence is required. A detailed map featuring the lagoon is provided, as well as life jackets. Plan on 14,000/20,000 CFP per half/full day for the boat, petrol and transfers included. Bring a picnic and your snorkelling gear.

and blend perfectly into the landscaped property. Other highlights include the dazzling infinity pool and the tropical spa. One grumble: it's exposed to the prevailing winds. It's a member of Earthcheck.

Hilton Bora Bora Nui Resort & Spa
RESORT $$$

(☑60 33 00; www.boraboranui.com; Motu Toopua; bungalows d from 60,000 CFP; ❄@🛜🌊) This splendid resort with a dizzying array of accommodation options extends along a ravishing stretch of porcelain sand, on hilly Motu Toopua. It boasts 120 glorious units, including over-water bungalows and lovely hillside villas, as well as top-notch amenities.

Bora Bora Camping
CAMPGROUND $

(☑31 55 33; boraboracamping@gmail.com; Motu Piti Aau; campsites per person 2000 CFP; 🛜) You couldn't possibly get a more idyllic position for a relaxing sojourn – swaying palm trees, gin-clear waters, a fantastic coral garden a few finstrokes away and mesmerising views. Amenities are very limited – cold showers and basic self-catering facilities – but at this price and in such an enviable location nobody's complaining. Transfers to Matira Point are 2000 CFP per person return.

✖ Eating

Nearly all the independent restaurants (excluding *snack* bars), as well as some of the resort restaurants, offer free transport to and from your hotel.

All of the luxury hotels have dance performances with buffet dinners several times a week. Expect to pay around 7500 CFP to 9500 CFP.

WEST COAST

In Vaitape, there's a string of cheap eateries along the main road that sell sandwiches and cool drinks. In the evening, several *roulottes* along the main road serve simple dishes.

TOP CHOICE Bora Kaina Hut
RESTAURANT $$

(☑67 54 06; mains 1500-3500 CFP; ⊙dinner Sat-Thu) A great place for a *diner à deux*. The Kaina Hut exudes romantic vibes at dinner with candlelit tables, wooden furniture, a sand floor and a soothing soundtrack. Be sure to try the divine homemade *uru* (breadfruit) gnocchi or the mahi mahi with passionfruit sauce cooked on volcanic stones – Kaina Hut's signature dishes. The catch of the day is equally popular.

Maikai Bora Bora Marina & Yacht Club
RESTAURANT $$

(☑60 38 00; www.maikaimarina.com; mains 1600-2500 CFP; ⊙lunch & dinner, closed Sun & Mon in low season) This highly rated eatery offers excellent Polynesian cuisine with a refined twist, savoured in a vast local-style yet elegant dining room overlooking the lagoon. Same location as Topdive.

Bloody Mary's
RESTAURANT $$

(☑67 72 86; mains 2500-3700 CFP; ⊙dinner Mon-Sat) The stage is set: a backdrop featuring lots of exotic plants, a thatched roof, sand floors and coconut stools. Grilled lagoon fish and pelagics take centre stage. Guest stars include meat dishes cooked the American-barbecue way. It's a concept that has been cult since 1979, so you can't go wrong.

MATIRA POINT & AROUND

Matira – Chez Julie
SNACK $

(☑67 77 32; dishes 500-2000 CFP; ⊙10am-3pm Tue-Sun) The decor is nonexistent at this no-frills eatery but the lagoonside location more than makes up for it. Fish, steaks, burgers and sandwiches are the order of the day.

Tama'a Maitai
HOTEL RESTAURANT $

(☑60 30 00; mains 1500-2800 CFP; ⊙11.30am-9pm) Part of Le Maitai Bora Bora, Tama'a Maitai overlooks the lagoon and catches lots of breeze. All the usual suspects are featured on the menu including salads, pizza, fish and meat dishes, as well as a few vegetarian options.

Fare Manuia
RESTAURANT $$

(☑67 68 08; mains 1500-3900 CFP; ⊙breakfast, lunch & dinner) The hardest thing about eating at this local favourite is deciding between the excellent meat or fish dishes, crunchy salads, filling and delicious pasta and mouth-watering pizzas. Big appetite? Opt for the huge wood-fired prime rib or the rack of New Zealand lamb.

La Bounty
RESTAURANT $$

(☑67 70 43; mains 1300-3500 CFP; ⊙lunch & dinner) This buzzy restaurant in an open-air thatched-roof building is a good place to soak up the tropical climes and indulge in fine dining without breaking the bank. The menu is eclectic, with an emphasis on French specialities – salads and pasta sit happily alongside flavoursome pizzas and even *fondue bourguignonne* (Burgundy fondue). Alas, no lagoon views to speak of.

Roulotte Matira
SNACK $

(mains 1200-1800 CFP; ⊙breakfast, lunch & dinner) This popular hang-out serves honestly prepared dishes such as burgers, grilled fish and beef steaks in a sand-floor dining room. It's just across the road from Hotel Matira.

Tiare Market
SUPERMARKET $

(⊙6.30am-7pm Mon-Sat, 6.30am-1pm & 3-6pm Sun) This local supermarket is well stocked with all the necessities – from wine and fresh bread to sunscreen and toothpaste.

THE MOTU

Free shuttles, which generally operate until 11pm or midnight, allow you to enjoy the restaurants at most luxury hotels on the *motu* around Bora Bora. Note that reservations are mandatory, and you won't be allowed over if the hotel is fully booked. The Four Seasons, which is dubbed 'the fortress' on Bora Bora, has the most restrictive policy and usually doesn't accept outside guests on its premises.

By popular opinion, the restaurants at St Régis Resort and Intercontinental Resort & Thalasso Spa Bora Bora offered the best gourmet fare at the time of research.

Drinking & Entertainment

Dinner and a show in one of the big hotels are about the limit of nightlife on Bora Bora; make the most of the daytime activities and have an early night.

Any of the luxury hotels will provide a cold beer or cocktail (about 1000 CFP) by the lagoon. The *motu* hotels run free shuttles until about midnight. The bar at Bloody Mary's is popular.

Don't miss a traditional dance performance by a local group in one of the luxury hotels. Some places allow you in for the price of a drink at the bar. For about 8000 CFP to 12,000 CFP, you can combine the performance with a sumptuous buffet dinner. Performances take place two or three times weekly.

Other than that, nightlife is as restrained as it is on the other islands of French Polynesia.

Shopping

Black pearl jewellery is sold in many places around Bora Bora, and you will find numerous retail shops. Apart from pearls, shopping on Bora Bora tends to mean hopping between the many galleries and boutiques that are scattered around the island, wrapping yourself in various brightly coloured *pareu* (sarongs), finding the perfect Marquesan woodcarving or perhaps getting yourself a traditional Marquesan-designed tattoo.

❶ Information

Most services are in Vaitape. There's a medical centre in Vaitape as well as numerous private doctors and a pharmacy.

Aloe Cafe (per hr 1000 CFP; ⊙6am-6pm Mon-Sat) Internet access. Wi-fi is also available (same rates). At the back of a small shopping centre.

Banque de Polynésie (⊙8am-noon & 1.15-4.30pm Mon-Thu, 8am-noon & 1.15-3.30pm Fri) Currency exchange and has an ATM.

Banque de Tahiti (⊙8am-noon & 1-4pm Mon-Fri) Currency exchange and has an ATM.

Banque Socredo (⊙7.30-11.30am & 1.30-3.30pm Mon-Fri) Currency exchange and has an ATM.

Bora Bora visitor information centre (⌨67 76 36; info-bora-bora@mail.pf; ⊙9am-noon & 1-4pm Mon-Fri, 9am-noon Sat) The office is on the quay at Vaitape. It has pamphlets and other info. Mildly helpful.

Bora Spirit Matira (per hr 500 CFP; ⊙9am-7pm) Near Matira Point. Internet and wi-fi access.

Post office (OPT; ⊙7am-3pm Mon-Thu, 7.15am-2.15pm Fri) Internet and wi-fi access (with the Manaspot network). Has an ATM.

❶ Getting There & Away

Bora Bora is situated 270km northwest of Tahiti and can be reached by air or boat from there.

Air

Air Tahiti (⌨67 53 53, 86 42 42; www.airtahiti.pf; Vaitape; ⊙7.30-11.30am & 1.30-4.30pm Mon-Fri, 8-11am Sat) flies between Bora Bora and Tahiti (16,700 CFP, 50 minutes, up to 10 flights daily), Huahine (9500 CFP, 20 minutes, one to two flights daily), Maupiti (8500 CFP, one to two flights weekly), Mo'orea (19,500 CFP, one hour, one to three flights daily) and Ra'iatea (7800 CFP, 15 minutes, one to three flights daily). Air Tahiti also has direct flights from Bora Bora to the Tuamotus, with a very handy flight to Rangiroa (26,000 CFP, 1¼ hours, five to six flights weekly) and onward connections to other atolls, including Tikehau, Fakarava and Manihi.

Boat

The passenger boat **Aremiti 4** (⌨50 57 57; www.aremiti.pf) runs once a week between Pape'ete and Bora Bora (9500 CFP), stopping at Ra'iatea and Huahine en route. It generally departs on Friday and returns on Sunday.

Two cargo ships, the *Hawaiki Nui* and the *Taporo*, make two trips a week between Pape'ete and Bora Bora (via Huahine, Ra'iatea and Taha'a). See p428 for more information.

The **Maupiti Express 2** (☎67 66 69; www.maupitiexpress.com; Vaitape) runs between Bora Bora and Maupiti on Thursday and Saturday (4000/5000 CFP one way/return, two hours). The boat also serves Ra'iatea/Taha'a on Wednesday, Friday and Sunday (4000/5000 CFP one way/return, 1½ hours).

ⓘ Getting Around

Bora Bora's 32km coast road hugs the shoreline almost all the way around the island.

To/From the Airport

The airport is on Motu Mute, at the northern edge of the lagoon; transfers are offered to and from the Vaitape quay on two large catamaran ferries (included in the cost of your ticket). There's a regular bus from the quay to the hotels at Matira Point (500 CFP).

When leaving by air, you need to be at the quay at least 1¼ hours before the flight. The top hotels transfer their visitors directly to and from the airport; all other passengers are picked up at the quay by the catamaran ferries (the cost of this is included in the ticket).

Car & Bicycle

There are two petrol stations in Vaitape.
Bora Bora Rent a Car – Avis (☎67 70 15, 67 56 44; www.avis-tahiti.com; ⏰7.30am-5.30pm Mon-Sat) Has its main office in the centre of Vaitape, as well as a desk near Matira Point. Cars cost from a whopping 13,500 CFP per 24 hours. Bikes cost 2000 CFP per 24 hours.
Bora Spirit Matira (⏰9am-7pm) At Matira Point. Rents bike for 1000 CFP per day.

MAUPITI

Bora Bora's discreet little sister, Maupiti, is one of the most ravishing islands in French Polynesia. Yet it still remains a hideaway where insiders come to revel in an unblemished tropical playground and to drop out of sight in a handful of quaint pensions, where you can enjoy fantastic views of the shimmering aqua lagoon without even leaving your bed. Maupiti offers complete relaxation – there's only one road, and virtually no cars, just bicycles. And when you want to play, there's plenty of scope for activities on the water, such as kayaking, snorkelling and diving.

⊙ Sights

THE MOTU

Maupiti's star attractions are its five idyllic *motu*, spits of sand and crushed coral dotted with swaying palms, and floating in the jade lagoon that surrounds the main island. Besides acting as quiet retreats, the *motu* also offer good beaches.

Motu Paeao, at the northern end of the lagoon, is ideal for swimming and snorkelling. There's an important melon-production plantation on **Motu Auira**, as well as a lovely coral sand beach. At low tide you can reach it from the mainland by wading across the lagoon – the water is warm and only waist high, but keep an eye out for rays.

Motu Tiapaa has beautiful, sandy, white beaches and good snorkelling on its ocean and lagoon sides. It's also the most developed *motu*, with several pensions. If you have a kayak, you can paddle across to the completely isolated **Motu Pitihahei**, but be sure to steer way to the north of Onoiau Pass, which is very dangerous due to strong currents near the pass.

The airport and a few pensions are found on **Motu Tuanai**, another picture-friendly islet. However, the lagoon is shallow along this *motu*, which doesn't make it good for swimming bar for young children.

THE MAIN ISLAND

Tereia Point   BEACH
Fringed by a placid turquoise lagoon and backed by arching coconut trees, small Tereia Beach, on the northern coast, is a wonderful place to sunbathe or have friendly splash-wars in the translucent water, but it's not ideal for swimming as the lagoon is too shallow.

Marae Vaiahu   ARCHAEOLOGICAL SITE
Just northeast of the main quay (it's sign-posted), make a beeline for Marae Vaiahu, Maupiti's most important *marae*. This features a large coastal site covered with coral slabs and a fish box made of coral blocks.

Activities

Snorkelling & Lagoon Tours

Maupiti's magnificent lagoon is crystal clear, bath-warm and packed with colourful species fluttering around healthy coral gardens, which provides great snorkelling opportunities. The best sites are the reefs stretching north of Onoiau Pass (but beware of the currents) and Motu Paeao.

Most guesthouses have masks and snorkels you can borrow. The pensions also run lagoon tours with snorkelling stops (3000 CFP to 5000 CFP). In season, the pensions also offer snorkelling trips to the manta rays' cleaning station (about 2000 CFP). One reputable operator is **Sammy Maupiti Tour** (☑76 99 28; half-/full-day trip 3000/5000 CFP), which promises a memorable day of snorkelling, fishing and shark feeding.

Diving

There are outstanding dive sites outside the lagoon, including a stunning drop-off just north of the pass. Another calling card for divers on Maupiti is Manta Point, which is home to a cleaning station visited by manta rays. It's in the lagoon, near the pass, and, in principle, they're here every morning between April and mid-September (but sightings can't be guaranteed).

See p32 for more information on diving in French Polynesia.

Maupiti Nautique   DIVING
(☑67 83 80; www.maupiti-nautique.com) This low-key diving venture specialises in small groups (maximum four divers). Single dive trips or introductory dives cost 6500 CFP including gear and two-tank trips are 12,000 CFP. An open-water course costs 41,000 CFP. Book well ahead. Cash only.

Kayaking

Sea kayaking is another popular activity of the DIY variety. Paddling around the quiet lagoon offers the chance to discover hidden spots, search for leopard rays and manta rays, or just put down the oar, lie back and sunbathe. Most places to stay either rent or offer free sea kayaks for guests' use.

Walking

Maupiti has some good walking, including the superb climb to the summit of **Mt Teurafaatiu** (380m), the island's highest point. It's a fairly arduous hike but the 360-degree panoramas are phenomenal. Allow three hours for the return trip. The track is not properly waymarked, so it's best to go with a guide – contact your pension to secure one (about 3000 CFP).

Whale & Dolphin Watching

Apparently, humpback whales find Maupiti attractive too. Every year during the austral winter, from mid-July to October, they frolic off Maupiti's barrier reef. Whale-watching trips are available through the pensions. You may have the privilege of swimming right alongside these graceful giants, but don't stress them and follow the guide's instructions. Dolphins can be spotted all year round along the reef. A three-hour excursion costs 7500 CFP.

Sleeping & Eating

For the full Robinson Crusoe experience, places on the *motu* are hard to beat. If island life is your top priority, stay on the main island. Most people opt for half or full board at their accommodation; if you're staying on the *motu* this will likely be your only option. Several small village shops sell basic supplies.

Maupiti Residence   PENSION $$
(☑67 82 61; www.maupitiresidence.info; Tereia Beach; bungalows d 11,000-14,000 CFP, q 15,000-18,000 CFP; ☀☜) With a well-deserved reputation as one of the best-value pensions on Maupiti, this venture delivers all the hedonist essentials: two large and comfortable villas that are fully self-contained, a spiffing Tereia beach frontage and plenty of perks, including free bicycles and kayaks. And not to mention soul-stirring sunsets. Air-con is extra. Credit cards are accepted.

Poe Iti – Chez Gérald & Joséphine   PENSION $
(☑74 58 76; maupitiexpress@mail.pf; Motu Tuanai; bungalows s/d 5500/9500 CFP; ☀) This highly affable and efficient pension has two big windmills attesting to its commitment to preserving the environment. Four well-proportioned bungalows (with hot water and air-con) are scattered in a well-tended property right by the lagoon. Gourmet palates, you're in luck: Joséphine will treat you with tasty Polynesian dishes at dinner (2600 CFP). Free kayaks.

Kuriri Village   PENSION $$
(☑67 82 23, 74 54 54; www.maupiti-kuriri.com; Motu Tiapaa; bungalows with half board per person 12,600 CFP; ☜) A series of simply designed yet tastefully arranged bungalows is scattered amid lovely gardens and coconut palms. It's intimate and laid-back, and appeals to couples looking for a bit of style without an exorbitant price tag. As befits a French-run outfit, you can expect to eat divinely. Free kayaks and fishing rods. Credit cards are accepted.

Maupiti

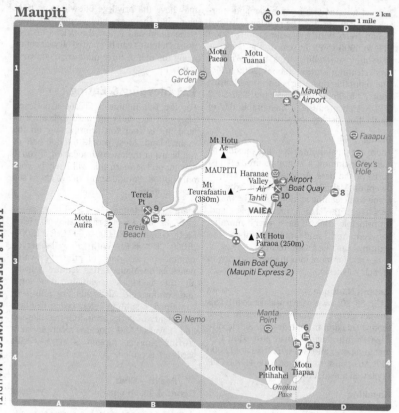

Pension Papahani – Chez Vilna PENSION $$
(☑60 15 35; pensionpapahani@hotmail.fr; Motu Tiapaa; bungalows with half board per person 9500-12,600 CFP; 🛜) Informality is the name of the game at this place – so you'll immediately shift down a few gears here. The five bungalows are set in attractive tropical gardens. Try for one of the newer, slightly more expensive bungalows as the two units at the rear look a bit tired.

Maupiti Village PENSION $
(☑67 80 08; Motu Tiapaa; dm/r/bungalows with full board per person 6000/7000/12,000 CFP) Digs are in three particle-board rooms with a shared outside bathroom, a bare-bones 10-bed dorm or a few teensy cabins with saggy mattresses. However, visitors usually forgive its shortcomings for the top-notch location on the ocean side of Motu Tiapaa, affordable rates, laid-back vibes and lovely food. Kayaks are free.

Auira – Chez Edna PENSION, CAMPGROUND $
(☑67 80 26; Motu Auira; campsites per person 2100 CFP, garden bungalows 5000 CFP, beach bungalows with half board per person 9000 CFP) Chez Edna has the reputation of being haphazardly run but the truly magical setting offers some compensation. While the garden bungalows are teeny and fairly ramshackle, the beach bungalows with private terrace cut the mustard. It's a good bargain for those who have a tent, with a sandy area and plenty of shade, but you'll have to deal with hordes of mosquitoes in the evening.

Mareta – Chez Manu PENSION $
(☑67 82 32; chezmanu@mail.pf; s/d with/without bathroom 6000/3000 CFP; @) Nice prices, plain rooms and a family atmosphere make this place a viable port of call for budgeteers. Guests may use the cooking facilities for an extra 300 CFP or order a meal for about 1500 CFP.

Maupiti

Tarona SNACK **$$**
(☏67 82 46; mains 1200-1700 CFP; ☺lunch & dinner Mon-Sat) Just north of the village, this place comes recommended for its hearty portions of traditional French Polynesian dishes such as raw fish, tuna sashimi, braised beef, and pork with taro.

Chez Mimi SNACK **$**
(Tereia Beach; mains 800-1200 CFP; ☺9am-3pm) Feel the sand between your toes at this oasis of a place soothingly positioned right on Tereia Beach. It's an ideal spot for a filling lunch after (or before) working your tan. The menu concentrates on sandwiches and simply prepared fish dishes.

❶ Getting There & Away

Maupiti is 320km west of Tahiti and 40km west of Bora Bora.

Air

Air Tahiti (☏60 15 05, 67 81 24, 86 42 42; www.airtahiti.pf; ☺8-11am Mon, Wed & Thu, 8.45am-1pm Tue & Fri) flies from Maupiti to Tahiti (17,000 CFP, 1½ hours, five flights weekly), Ra'iatea (8500 CFP, 25 minutes, three flights weekly) and Bora Bora (8000 CFP, 20 minutes, one or two flights weekly).

Boat

The **Maupiti Express 2** (☏67 66 69, 78 27 22; www.maupitiexpress.com) runs between Maupiti and Bora Bora on Thursday and Saturday (4000/5000 CFP one way/return). Leaving Vaitape (Bora Bora) at 8.30am, it arrives at Maupiti at 10.15am then departs for the return trip at 4pm, arriving back at Bora Bora around 6pm.

❶ Getting Around

If you've booked accommodation you'll be met at the airport, although some places charge for the trip (around 2500 CFP return).

It's simple to arrange a boat out to the *motu* from the village and vice versa. All the pensions on the mainland or *motu* can arrange these transfers.

TUAMOTU ISLANDS

Anyone who loves the water will adore this archipelago; so you can expect wrinkly fingers and toes because there is a good chance you will be in the water more often than out. These atolls are veritable underwater playgrounds that are teeming with so many fish you could practically put an empty hook down and they'll still bite. It is a pared-down way of life out here in the Tuamotu Islands and you will find only a few trees, shrubs and coconut palms that are able to thrive in the coral soils, and man-made development is minimal. Fruit, vegetables and modern conveniences are few but the plentiful fish, smiling locals, silent nights with knock-you-out starry skies and the nearly blinding colours from the white beaches and blue lagoon make most visitors change their schedules and stay longer.

The archipelago is made up of 77 atolls scattered over a stretch of ocean that are 1500km northwest to southeast and 500km east to west.

❶ Getting There & Away

AIR Flying is by far the easiest, fastest and most comfortable way to get to the Tuamotus, with **Air Tahiti** (www.airtahiti.pf) serving no less than 32 atolls. Most of the traffic is to and from Pape'ete, but there are also transversal connections between Bora Bora and the more tourist-oriented atolls, including Fakarava, Rangiroa and Tikehau, which eliminates the need to backtrack to Pape'ete. Within the archipelago, Rangiroa is the major flight hub.

BOAT Starting from Pape'ete, there is a network of cargo vessels that runs between the atolls. See individual island listings for more on travelling by cargo ship.

❶ Getting Around

Public transport is virtually nonexistent in the Tuamotu. Outboard motorboats, bicycles and scooters are the most convenient ways to get around. Only Rangiroa and Fakarava have sealed roads; elsewhere, roads are often just crushed-coral tracks.

Tuamotu Islands

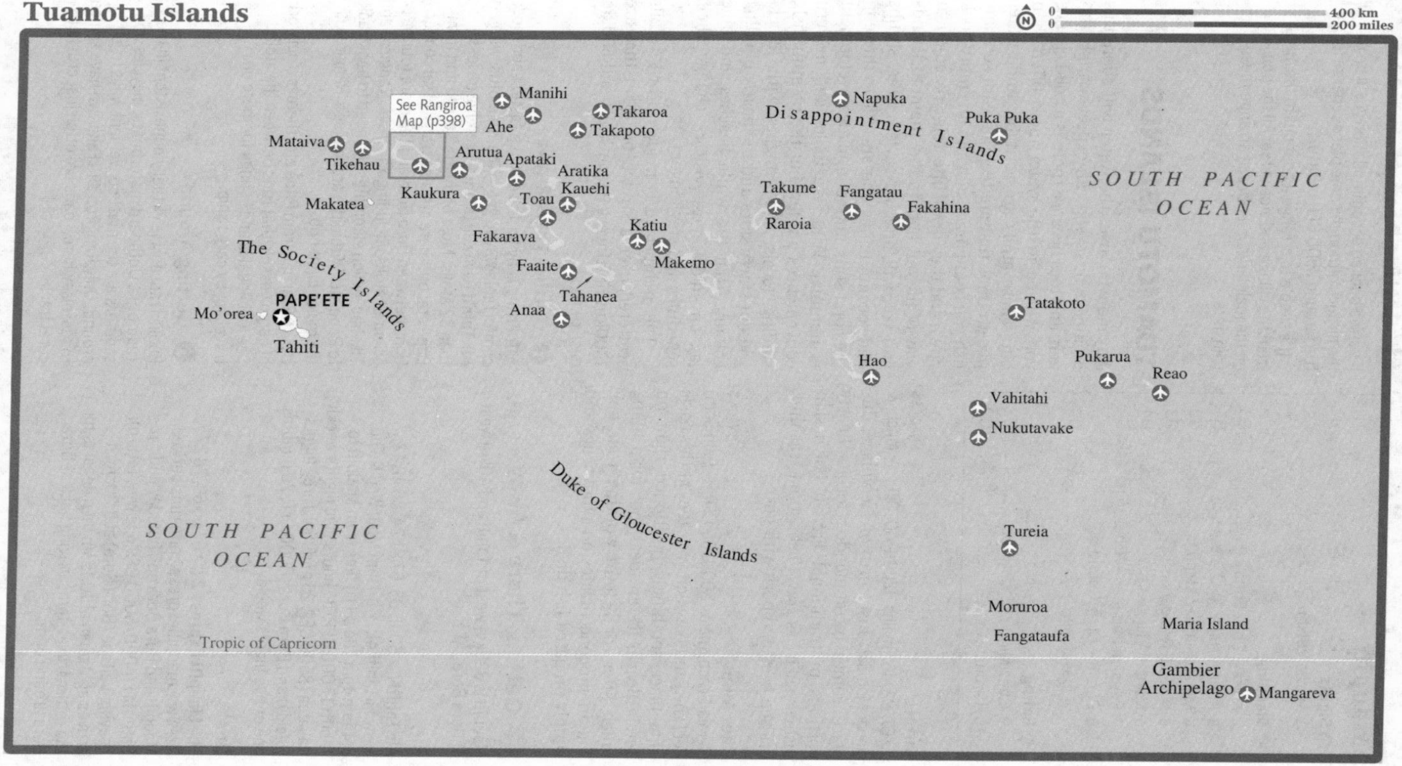

400 km
200 miles

SOUTH PACIFIC OCEAN

Gambier
Archipelago Mangareva

Maria Island

Reao

Pukarua

Tatakoto

Vahitahi
Nukutavake

Tureia

Moruroa
Fangataufa

Puka Puka

Disappointment Islands

Napuka

Fangatau
Fakahina

Takume
Raroia

Hao

Duke of Gloucester Islands

Takaroa
Takapoto

Mamihi

Ahe

Aratika
Arutua Kauehi
Apataki
Toau

Katiu
Makemo

Faaite
Tahanea

Fakarava

Anaa

See Rangiroa
Map (p398)

Kaukura

Mataiva
Tikehau

Makatea

The Society Islands

PAPE'ETE

Tahiti

Mo'orea

SOUTH PACIFIC OCEAN

Tropic of Capricorn

Airports are sometimes near the villages, or sometimes on remote *motu* on the other side of the lagoon. If you have booked accommodation, your hosts will come and meet you but transfers are not necessarily free.

Rangiroa

POP 3245

The Tuamotu Archipelago's 'Big Smoke' is wondrously languorous and its biggest developments are two resorts, a middle school, an airport and 12km of paved road. If this is the city, just imagine what the other atolls are like! What is big about Rangiroa, however, is its lagoon, which at 1640 sq km is said to be the second largest in the world. It's so big that you can't see the other side as you fly over it and you could spend years exploring its never-ending expanses of coral gardens.

The main village of Avatoru, spread out between the two main passes (Avatouru and Tiputa), is where most people stay and this is very convenient if you've come here to dive as most sites will be just beyond your doorstep. Do be warned, however, that beaches are scarce. For landlubbers the never-ending string of remote *motu* are the real draw and trips across the lagoon to the stunning Île aux Récifs and Lagon Bleu are not to be missed.

Sights

Île aux Récifs
TOP CHOICE | NATURAL SITE
South of the atoll, an hour by boat from Avatoru, Île aux Récifs (Island of Reefs) is an area dotted with raised *feo* (coral outcrops), weathered shapes chiselled by erosion into petrified silhouettes on the exterior reef. They stretch for several hundred metres, with basins and channels that make superb natural swimming pools. There's a good *hoa* (shallow channel) for swimming and a picturesque coconut grove by the beach.

Lagon Bleu
NATURAL SITE
Lagon Bleu is a popular spot about an hour away from Avatoru by boat. This is what many people visualise when imagining a Polynesian paradise: a string of *motu* and coral reefs has formed a natural pool on the edge of the main reef, a lagoon within a lagoon. The lagoon isn't deep and offers safe snorkelling among the myriad little fish, but don't expect much from the coral.

Avatoru
VILLAGE
Avatoru won't leap to the top of your list of preferred villages in French Polynesia but its location, right by Avatoru Pass and the lagoon, is stunning. It's a modern and bustling place by Tuamotu standards. The two churches – one Catholic and one Mormon – are about the only buildings of interest.

Tiputa
VILLAGE
Around the middle of the day, you could pretty safely fire a gun along the main street in Tiputa and not hit anyone. It's a charming little village; getting a boat across the Tiputa Pass adds to the whole experience. After the village the track continues east through coconut plantations until it's halted by the next *hoa*.

Gauguin's Pearl
PEARL FARM
(93 11 30; www.gauguinspearl.com; guided tours 8.30am, 10.30am & 2pm Mon-Fri) Free tours are offered of the pearl farm directly next to the boutique.

Plage Publique
BEACH
This artificial beach near Kia Ora Resort & Spa is nothing special but has a few shady trees and a good vibe from a mix of locals and tourists.

Activities

Diving & Snorkelling
The number-one activity on Rangiroa is diving, and it's no wonder. The Tiputa and Avatoru Passes have reached cult status in the diving community and offer some of the best drift dives in the world. Sharks and manta rays are the big attraction, but you'll also encounter countless reef species as well as shoals of barracuda and trevally. See p32 for details.

Snorkelling is another great way to visit the lagoon. You can just grab a snorkel and splash around near your hotel or guesthouse, but to really experience life under the sea it's necessary to sign up with Rangiroa Plongée, the Six Passengers or any boat tour operator and go out to further marine wonderlands.

Rangiroa Plongée
DIVING, SNORKELLING
(77 65 86, 27 57 82; www.rangiroaplongee.pf) This small dive outfit charges 6800 CFP for an introductory dive or a single dive and 5000 CFP for a dedicated two-hour snorkelling trip through the Tiputa Pass.

Rangiroa

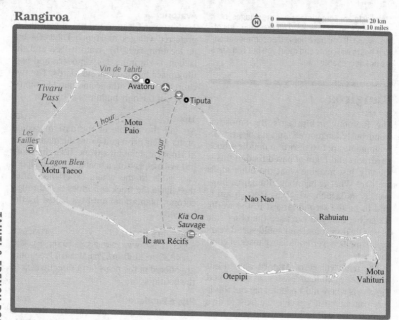

The Six Passengers
DIVING, SNORKELLING

(☑96 02 60; www.the6passengers.com) The Six Passengers offers introductory dives (7900 CFP), single dive trips (7000 CFP), snorkelling trips, dive packages and certification courses.

Topdive
DIVING

(☑96 05 60; www.topdive.com) Introductory dives go for 8000 CFP while single dives cost 8500 CFP. Dive packages are also available.

Y'aka Plongée
DIVING

(☑20 68 98; www.yakaplongeerangiroa.com) Has introductory dives (7500 CFP), single dive trips (7500 CFP), dive packages and courses.

Boat Excursions

Organised tours are really the only way of exploring the most scenic spots on the lagoon and, if you happen upon a nice group, make for a wonderful day. The most popular excursions – the Lagon Bleu and Île aux Récifs – are to the opposite side of the lagoon from Avatoru, which takes at least an hour to cross and can be uncomfortable if the sea is rough. When the weather's bad or the winds are too high, excursions are cancelled. Usually a minimum of four to six people is required.

Full-day trips cost around 7500 CFP including lunch. All bookings can be made through your hotel or pension. Transfers are provided.

Sleeping

Rangiroa has lots of simple, family-run pensions (only a sample is listed here) and a few more luxurious places.

Tevahine Dream
PENSION $$

(☑93 12 75; www.tevahinedream.com; bungalows d with half board per person 12,500-16,500 CFP; ☎) Five rustic-chic bungalows are designed in a Zen-meets-Polynesia style, which are dripping with wood and draping white fabrics. Bathrooms are mini oases with ferns and coral gravel, and the garden units, built of pine planks, have their own tiny pool. Excellent Polynesian and Chinese dishes are served in an appealing dining room overlooking the lagoon. Prices include bikes and kayaks. Minimum stay of two nights. Cash only.

Kia Ora Resort & Spa
LUXURY HOTEL $$$

(☑93 11 11; www.hotelkiaora.com; bungalows d from 55,000 CFP; ✳☎☒) One of the swankiest options in French Polynesia, with 50 plush bungalows, including 10 enormous overwater units. The ravishing garden villas come with their own pool and are dotted around

a magnificent coconut plantation situated on a fine li'l stretch of white sand. It incorporates a restaurant, a bar, a spa and a swimming pool. For the ultimate escape, book a couple of days at **Kia Ora Sauvage**, on Motu Avearahi, about an hour away by boat.

Raira Lagon   HOTEL $$

(☎93 12 30; www.raira-lagon.pf; bungalows incl breakfast/half board per person from 11,600/13,700 CFP; ✳☎) A cross between a family-run place and a hotel, Raira Lagon features 10 bungalows that meet modern standards. They're spread throughout a garden fringed by one of the better swimming areas on the atoll, and the more expensive ones come with a lagoon view. The restaurant balcony faces the lagoon. Bonuses: free kayaks and snorkelling gear.

Chez Cécile   PENSION $

(☎93 12 65; pensioncecile@mail.pf; bungalows with half board per person 7500-8500 CFP; ☎) This very pleasant place run by a charming Paumotu family features nine spacious wood bungalows (with cold-water bathrooms) in a flowery garden. Most units line the 'beach', which is actually a breakwater filled in with coral gravel, but you can swim off a pier extending over the lagoon.

Le Merou Bleu   PENSION $$$

(☎79 16 82; www.merou-bleu.com; bungalows s/d with half board 16,000/30,000 CFP; ☎) An agreeable option in a magical garden setting right on Avatoru Pass in front of the surf-break (but forget about swimming). Bungalows are creatively made from woven coconut thatch and other natural materials but manage to maintain a fair level of comfort, and have hot water, good mosquito nets and lovely terraces. It's a bit isolated, but this actually adds to the charm. Credit cards are not accepted.

Turiroa Village – Chez Olga   BUNGALOW $$

(☎96 04 27, 70 59 21; pension.turiroa@mail.pf; dm 2500 CFP, bungalows tr 10,500 CFP) Popular with budget-minded divers, this venture features an airy, six-bed dorm with an ace location on the lagoon and four modern bungalows that are modern. No meals are provided except breakfast (500 CFP) but you can whip up something in the clean guest kitchen. Kayaks are free.

Le Maitai Rangiroa   HOTEL $$$

(☎93 13 50; www.hotelmaitai.com; bungalows d incl breakfast from 26,000 CFP; ✳☎) This midrange hotel has 38 bungalows that are tightly packed on a small property, but otherwise it's well run and serviceable. Bar a small sunbathing patch of crushed coral, Le Maitai doesn't have any beach (the shoreline is craggy) nor a swimming pool, but there's a pontoon with lagoon access. The on-site restaurant is a plus.

Pension Bounty   PENSION $$

(☎96 05 22; www.pension-bounty.com; s/d incl breakfast 12,500/17,000 CFP; ☎) Lodging here is in four adjoining rooms rather than bungalows, but these are well scrubbed and modern, and have mosquito screens and hot water. They're slightly claustrophobic but the whole place is kept shipshape. A coral path leads to a small beach beside the Kia Ora Resort & Spa. Dinner is available but you also have your own equipped kitchen. English, Spanish and Italian are spoken.

Tuanake   PENSION $$

(☎96 03 52; www.tuanake.pf; bungalows s/d with half board 10,500/16,800 CFP; ☎) Tuanake is a haven of peace set in a coconut plantation on the coral gravel-lined lagoon. Some bungalows (with hot-water showers) show signs of wear and tear (there are plans to renovate them) but the congenial atmosphere and excellent cuisine more than make up for this. Bikes are free.

Chez Loyna   PENSION $

(☎96 82 09, 29 90 30; www.pensionloyna.com; r/ bungalows with half board per person 6500/7500 CFP; ☎) Although it's not directly beside the lagoon, this venture popular with unfussy

---

CORAL WINE

A vineyard? On an atoll? While completely surreal, it's true. Vin de Tahiti has a 20-hectare vineyard planted on a palm-fringed *motu* about 10 minutes by boat from Avatoru village. This is the only atoll vineyard in the world making wines, the only ones produced from coral soil. It produces coral white wine, dry white and rosé. Since October 2010, the wine has been made using the principles of biodynamic agriculture. Vin de Tahiti should be awarded organic certification by the time you read this. Most restaurants on the atoll have it, and it's also on sale at the supermarkets.

For more on Vin de Tahiti's history go to www.vindetahiti.pf.

divers is a bargain, with three modest yet clean rooms with bathroom (hot water) and a handful of larger bungalows out the back. Food here is a definite plus, with generous meals using local ingredients.

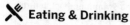 Eating & Drinking

Most visitors opt for half board at their hotel or pension but there are also a few good independent eating options. Avatoru has a few supermarkets.

Raira Lagoon –
Beach Raira   RESTAURANT $$
(☎93 12 30; mains 1600 CFP, menu 3500 CFP; ⊙breakfast, lunch & dinner) Lunch is a good bet if you need to recharge the batteries post-diving, or are just looking for a good meal in a friendly spot blessed with cracking lagoon views. The menu is short but concentrates on well-prepared fish dishes.

Lagoon Grill   RESTAURANT $$$
(☎96 04 10; mains 1600-3500 CFP; ⊙lunch & dinner Wed-Mon) The well-respected Lagoon Grill is a terrific spot for a lagoonside meal, with alfresco tables under large shade trees. It majors on flawlessly cooked grilled beef rib and *magret de canard* (duck breast) but also offers a good selection of seafood dishes. Offers pick-up service at dinner.

Moetua – Ohotu   SNACK $$
(☎78 30 38; mains 1000-1400 CFP; ⊙lunch Mon-Sat) Talk about location! The dining deck of this buzzing *snack* at the eastern tip of Avatoru is on the lagoon, literally. The menu concentrates on simply prepared fish and meat dishes served in generous portions. Sandwiches (from 400 CFP), burgers and salads are also available. It's a good place to catch local vibes and enjoy plenty of local colour.

Puna   SNACK $$
(☎73 76 10; mains 400-2000 CFP; ⊙lunch & dinner Tue-Sun) A local favourite that serves excellent, fresh food in massive portions. Light eaters can order single fish *brochettes* (400 CFP each) or big side orders of salad, fries and more. At the marina.

Le Kai Kai   RESTAURANT $$
(☎96 03 39; mains 1200-2600 CFP; ⊙lunch & dinner Fri-Wed) French garden restaurant along the main road (no views). Beautifully grilled fresh tuna, mahi mahi and meat specialities are embellished with flavours such as orange and ginger, and then dished up with a medley of vegetables. Transfers from your pension or hotel are free. Credit cards are not accepted.

Vaimario   RESTAURANT, PIZZERIA $$$
(☎96 05 96; mains 1400-3000 CFP; ⊙closed Wed & lunch Sat) The extensive menu takes in seafood, meat and pizza and combines French tradition with an eye to local flavours. The weak point is its unassuming position along the road, with no sea views. Free transfers are offered (at dinner only).

Heirani   RESTAURANT $$
(☎28 65 61; mains 1100-2000 CFP; ⊙lunch Tue-Sun, dinner Tue-Sat) Wholly unpretentious and bearing not an ounce of belabored design, this popular locale next to the Six Passengers dive centre whips up cheap eats that make the perfect lunch on a budget.

ⓘ Information

Note that there are only two ATMs on Rangiroa – one in Avatoru and one in Tiputa.

Banque de Tahiti (Avatoru; ⊙8-11am Mon, Tue, Fri & Sat, 1-4pm Mon & Fri) Currency exchange.

Banque Socredo (Avatoru; ⊙7.30-11.30am & 1.30-4pm Mon, Wed & Fri, 1.30-4pm Tue & Thu) Currency exchange. Has a 24-hour ATM.

Centre Médical d'Avatoru (☎96 03 75; ⊙7.30am-3.30pm Mon-Fri) Medical centre. There are also two private doctors in Avatoru.

Gendarmerie (police station; ☎96 73 61)

Le Kai Kai (per hr 700 CFP; ⊙lunch & dinner Fri-Wed) Internet access.

Post office Avatoru (OPT; ⊙7am-3pm Mon-Thu, 7am-2pm Fri) Internet and wi-fi access (with the Manaspot network); Tiputa (OPT; ⊙7am-12.30pm Mon-Thu, to 11.30am Fri) Has a 24-hour ATM.

The Six Passengers (per hr 500 CFP; ⊙8am-noon & 2-5pm) This dive shop offers internet and wi-fi access.

ⓘ Getting There & Away

AIR The airport is smack in between Avatoru (to the west) and Tiputa (to the east). **Air Tahiti** (☎93 14 00, 86 42 42; www.airtahiti.pf) offers two to three flights daily between Pape'ete and Rangiroa (one hour, 19,000 CFP). Rangiroa is also connected by air to Bora Bora and other atolls in the Tuamotus. One-way fares on offer include Bora Bora–Rangiroa 26,000 CFP, Rangiroa–Tikehau 7500 CFP and Rangiroa–Fakarava 7500 CFP.

BOAT The *Dory, Mareva Nui* and *Saint-Xavier Maris-Stella* are the only cargo ships serving Rangiroa (see p429).

❶ Getting Around

A sealed road runs the 10km from Avatoru village at the western end of the string of islets to the Tiputa Pass, at the eastern extremity.

If you have booked accommodation, your hosts will be at the airport to welcome you. If your pension is near the hotel, transfers will probably be free; places further away tend to charge (ask when you book).

Car, Bicycle & Scooter Hire

The easiest way to get around is to hire a bicycle or a scooter (as it's hardly worth getting a car).

Arenahio Location (🖉96 82 45) Hires out cars/scooters/bicycles for 8500/5500/1300 CFP for a full day.

JJ Loc (🖉27 57 82) Rents bikes/scooters for 1400/5500 CFP for a full day.

Rangi Rent a Car (🖉96 03 28) Rents cars from 6500 CFP per day.

Taxi Boat

Manu Taxi Boat (🖉78 13 25) Offers a shuttle service between Ohotu wharf and Tiputa village for 500 CFP return.

Fakarava

POP 800 / LAGOON AREA 1121 SQ KM

Welcome to paradise. One of the largest and most beautiful atolls in French Polynesia, Fakarava is the stuff of South Seas fantasy. Heavenly white and pink sand, ruffled coconut trees and a surreal palette of lagoon blues are the norm here. The atmosphere is supremely relaxed and the infrastructure is quite good, with an assortment of well-run pensions and a few swish options.

Garuae Pass, in the north of the atoll, is the widest pass in all of French Polynesia. There's also a second pass, Tumakohua in the far south.

Fakarava is a great place to unwind, but for those looking for more than a suntan, it offers a number of high-energy distractions. The fantastic diving and snorkelling is legendary among divers, who come for a truly exhilarating experience in the two passes.

❍ Sights

TOP CHOICE Les Sables Roses   NATURAL SITE

A double crescent of dreamy beaches split by a narrow spit of white-and-pink coral sands, Les Sables Roses seems to come right out of central casting for tropical ideals. The turquoise water laps both sides of the sandy strip. It's near the southernmost tip of the atoll, not far from Tetamanu, and is reached only by boat.

Lagon Bleu (Motu Tehatea)   NATURAL SITE

Near the northwestern corner of Fakarava, and reached only by boat, Lagon Bleu features an indescribably lovely stretch of white-sand coral beach, robin-egg blue water, palm trees leaning over the shore – and not a soul in sight.

Rotoava   VILLAGE

Most islanders live in Rotoava village at the northeastern end of the atoll, 4km east of the airport. Aside from Rangiroa's Avatoru, this is the most developed and busy town in the Tuamotus but it's still pretty quiet by most people's standards.

PK10.5   NATURAL SITE

The PK10.5 marks the end of the dirt road, just on the edge of the phenomenal **Garuae Pass**. By incoming or outgoing current, the pass gets really rough, with waves that can easily exceed 2m in the middle of the pass.

Plage du PK9   NATURAL SITE

A bit of a local's secret, Plage du PK9 is – you guessed it – 9km northwest of Rotoava. It's a thin, laid-back, postcard-perfect stretch of white coral sand backed by palms and lapped by calm, sparkling turquoise waters. It's equally good for sunning and swimming and there's excellent snorkelling not far offshore.

Tetamanu   HAMLET

A handful of inhabitants also live in Tetamanu village, a tiny settlement on the edge of **Tumakohua Pass**, which is as backwater as backwater gets. It has a cute coral **chapel** built in the 19th century and an old **graveyard** with coral tombstones.

🏄 Activities

Diving & Snorkelling

Divers can't gush enough about the fabulous fish life, especially grey sharks, blacktip sharks, manta rays, tuna and barracuda, that can be found in the Garuae Pass (also known as 'Northern Pass') and Tumakohua Pass (also known as 'Southern Pass'). For details, see p32. Another draw is the coral, which is much healthier than on Rangiroa. If you're based in or near Rotoava, day trips to the Southern Pass are regularly organised by local dive shops but they're weather-dependent and require a minimum of divers.

Fakarava Diving Center DIVING
(🖉93 40 75, 73 38 22; www.fakarava-diving-center.
com) In Rotoava. Charges very reasonable
prices – 7000 CFP for an introductory dive,
6500 CFP for a single dive and 18,000 CFP
for a day trip to Tumakohua Pass (including
two dives and lunch).

Tetamanu Diving by Eleuthera DIVING
(🖉77 65 68, 77 10 06; www.dive-tahiti.com) At
Tetamanu village. Offers introductory dives
(6100 CFP), single dives (6100 CFP), courses
and packages.

Topdive DIVING
(🖉98 42 50, 29 22 32; www.topdive.com) In Rotoava. Also has an annex on a *motu* near
Tetamanu Pass. This reputable outfit has
introductory dives (from 8500 CFP), one-/
two-tank dives (8500/15,500 CFP) and can
arrange day trips to Tumakohua Pass for
23,000 CFP including lunch.

Boat Excursions

Like in Rangiroa, organised tours are the
only way of exploring the idyllic, remote
spots on the lagoon, including Lagon Bleu,
Tetamanu (if you're based in the north) and
Sables Roses. Usually a minimum of four to
six people is required.

Half-/full-day trips to Lagon Bleu cost
around 7000/8500 CFP. A full-day excursion taking in Sables Roses, Tetamanu and
a snorkelling stop in the Southern Pass usually costs 12,000 CFP, including a barbecued
lunch at Sables Roses. All bookings can be
made through your hotel or pension.

Note that it's at least a 90-minute boat
ride to get to the southern sites from Rotoava. For Lagon Bleu, it takes about 30 minutes by boat from Rotoava.

🛏 Sleeping & Eating

Raimiti PENSION $$$
(🖉71 07 63; www.raimiti.com; s/d bungalow with full
board for 2 nights from 54,000/99,000 CFP) Cru-
soe-chic and very isolated, the bungalows on
this sandy private *motu* to the south of the
atoll ooze romance. Meals are excellent, es-
pecially considering the beachside location.
Oil lamps light the scene at night and dur-
ing the day; if you're not off on an organised
activity, you can walk for hours along the
empty lagoon or exterior reef. Prices include
transfers and activities.

Relais Marama BUNGALOW, CAMPGROUND $
(🖉98 42 51, 76 12 29; www.relais-marama.com;
campsite incl breakfast per person 2600 CFP, bunga-

low with shared bathroom per person incl breakfast
6000 CFP, @🖙) A good-value, backpacker-
like option with simple yet immaculate
bungalows with shared bathroom (cold
water). All prices include breakfast, while
for other meals you can use the communal
kitchen or go to nearby eateries. Campers
share the same facilities as the bungalows.
There's a fee of 1000 CFP for internet and
wi-fi access (valid for the length of your
stay). Bikes are free.

Havaiki Pearl Guesthouse PENSION $$
(🖉93 40 15, 74 16 16; www.havaiki.com; bunga-
lows s/d with half board from 13,000/20,000
CFP; 🖙) On the southern end of the village,
this is the liveliest pension on Fakarava.
The beachfront bungalows are very simple
wooden structures but they offer a lovely
lagoon frontage. If you're seeking space, opt
for the two-bedroom garden units. Good
English is spoken and airport transfers cost
2000 CFP return. Bikes and kayaks are free.
There's a three-night minimum stay. Cash
only.

Tokerau Village PENSION $$
(🖉98 41 09, 70 82 19; www.tokerau-village.com;
bungalows s/d with half board 12,600/23,400 CFP;
🖙) This is one of the most comfortable pen-
sions on Fakarava, in a manicured garden.
Each unit has a big terrace, mosquito net
and TV but for the price you'd expect a fan.
Some English is spoken and the whole place
runs on solar energy. Kayaks are free. Air-
port transfers are 2000 CFP return. It's 7km
south of Rotoava.

Paparara PENSION $$
(🖉98 42 66; www.fakarava-divelodge.com; bunga-
low s with half board 9500-12,600 CFP, bungalow d
with half board 17,000-21,000 CFP) You have two
options here: one of two small and basic
fare that are right on the water and share a
cold-water bathroom (ask for the 'Robinson'
unit, which is as cosy as a bird's nest), or
four better-equipped beachside bungalows
with private bathrooms. It's 7km south of
Rotoava.

Fare Kohei BUNGALOW $$
(🖉28 89 26, 79 88 14; http://farekohei.jimdo.com;
bungalow d 12,000 CFP) Opened in 2012, this
venture sports a self-contained bungalow
right in Rotoava village. It's nothing fancy
but well managed and well priced, and it's
conveniently close to shops, restaurants and
dive centres.

White Sand Beach Resort
RESORT $$

(☏93 41 50; www.whitesandfakarava.com; bungalows with half board per person 16,000-23,000 CFP; ✳@@☏) With 30 spacious wooden bungalows and a restaurant, this is the biggest option on Fakarava. The beach is good and there's a picturesque pontoon with fabulous snorkelling ops but the hotel is understaffed, the garden needs some TLC and some bungalows are in need of a lick of paint. Despite its shortcomings, it's not a bad deal considering the price and location. It's 7km south of Rotoava.

TOP CHOICE Snack Te Anuanua
RESTAURANT $$

(☏93 40 65; Rotoava; mains 1600-3500 CFP; ⊘lunch daily, dinner Wed-Sun) A surprisingly hip open-air restaurant with swoon-worthy lagoon views, this culinary outpost specialises in *tartares* (raw meat or fish), grilled meat and fish dishes served in a variety of sauces, healthy salads and lip-smacking desserts. Cash only.

🅘 Getting There & Away

The atoll is 488km east-northeast of Tahiti.

AIR Air Tahiti (☏93 40 25, 86 42 42; www. airtahiti.pf) flies from Pape'ete to Fakarava every day (20,000 CFP one way), twice weekly from Fakarava to Rangiroa (7500 CFP), four times weekly from Rangiroa to Fakarava (7500 CFP) and once or twice weekly to/from Manihi (12,200 CFP).

BOAT The *Saint-Xavier Maris-Stella* and *Mareva Nui* stop at Fakarava and take passengers (see p429).

🅘 Getting Around

The airport is 4km west of Rotoava. There's a 20km road from the airport to the southeast side of the atoll. From the airport, a dirt track goes as far as the edge of Garuae Pass.

Faka Location (☏78 03 37) hires out bikes for 2000 CFP per day and scooters (8000 CFP per day).

Tetamanu is accessible by boat only.

Tikehau

POP 510 / LAGOON AREA 461 SQ KM

If it's endless stretches of empty white- and pink-sand beaches you're looking for, Tikehau should be your first stop. The atoll is geologically different from many others in the archipelago: its baroque bays and craggy nooks have been whittled by the sea both into the lagoonside shores and along the exterior reef. The result, surrounded by the bluest of lagoons, is better than a postcard-come-to-life, yet the only things that seem to flock to Tikehau are seabirds and a huge variety of fish.

👁 Sights

Tuherahera
VILLAGE

Most islanders live in Tuherahera, in the southwest of the atoll. Find peace in this pretty village, bursting with *uru* (breadfruit), coconut trees, bougainvillea and hibiscus. It's easy to bike your way around – follow the dirt track that skirts the picturesque ocean side of the *motu* until the airstrip and pedal back to the village taking the lagoon side road.

Fancy a dip? Head to one of Tuherahera's coral **beaches**. The best one lies east of the village, near the airstrip, and is lined up by several pensions. Another beauty lies at the western tip of the village; this strip is lapped by a glassy turquoise *hoa* and has pinkish sands.

Les Sables Roses
BEACHES

(Pink Sands) Southeast of the atoll the shores are fringed with truly amazing 'Pink Sands Beaches' which really do glow a light shade of pink, a result of finely pulverised coral.

Motu Puarua
ISLAND

(Île aux Oiseaux, or Bird Island) Lying almost in the middle of the lagoon, the rocky Motu Puarua hosts several species of ground-nesting birds including brown noddies and *uaau* (red-footed boobies) that can easily be approached.

Île d'Eden
ORGANIC FARM

It's hard to describe Île d'Eden (Eden Island). It's not a traditional tourist site per se, but a working farm operated by a handful of families belonging to the Church of the New Testament. They have created a vibrant, organic garden in the infertile sands of their superb *motu*.

🏃 Activities

Diving & Snorkelling

The extraordinary Tuheiava Pass, to the west of the atoll, about 30 minutes by boat from Tuherahera village, is an unspoilt underwater idyll teeming with all sorts of fish and marine life; see p32 for more information. Inside the lagoon, the Ferme aux Mantas is another killer site.

Topdive

DIVING, SNORKELLING

(☎96 22 40, 96 23 00; www.topdive.com) Based at Tikehau Pearl Beach Resort, but transfers from most pensions can be arranged. This small yet well-organised dive outfit has introductory dives (9000 CFP), single dives (7800 CFP), two-tank dives (15,000 CFP) and six-/10-dive packages (37,500/70,000 CFP). At most dive sites, snorkelling is also possible.

Lagoon Excursions

All pensions and hotels can organise excursions, sometimes through an outside operator, and trips cost from 7500 CFP per person. They usually take in La Ferme aux Mantas, Motu Puarua and Île d'Eden, and include a barbecue picnic on one of many paradisiacal *motu* dotted along the Sables Roses.

🛏 Sleeping & Eating

All pensions on Tikehau are on white-sand beaches on the lagoon side of the atoll and a handful are on private *motu*.

TOP CHOICE Ninamu Resort

RESORT $$$

(☎73 78 10; www.motuninamu.com; bungalows with full board per person 30,000 CFP; ☎) Anchored on a private white- and pink-sand *motu* a 10-minute boat ride from the village, this Australian-run venture is the kind of haven stressed-out city slickers dream about. The massive bungalows are built from gnarled hunks of wood, coral stonework and coconut thatch, and the restaurant is another Crusoe-with-style masterpiece. Prices also include daily excursions. The ethos here is laid-back, ecological and activity-oriented.

Tikehau Village

PENSION $$

(☎96 22 86, 76 67 85; www.tikehauvillage.com; bungalows s/d with half board 13,000/20,000 CFP; ☎) You can't argue with the location. It's right on the beach, so your biggest worry is tracking sand into your bungalow. The shady terraces look out over white-sand and turquoise-lagoon bliss. There are kayaks and bikes for guests' use. Some English is spoken. The restaurant at the Tikehau village is one of the prettiest spots around, overlooking the water with cool breezes and a social vibe – nonguests are welcome.

Tikehau Pearl Beach Resort

RESORT $$$

(☎96 23 00; www.spmhotels.com; bungalows d from 59,000 CFP; ❄☎☀) A hot favourite with Italian honeymooners, this intimate resort (only 38 units) boasts a stunning position between endless white- and pink-sand beaches and bright blue waters. All options except the over-the-water standard bungalows have air-con. There's a dive centre on-site.

🍴 Hotu

PENSION $

(☎96 22 89; www.pensionhotu.com; bungalows with half board per person 9500 CFP; ☎) Deservedly popular and occupying a divine stretch of sand, pension Hotu is a great place to enjoy the coral beach in a low-key surrounding. It features five fan-cooled bungalows with private facilities (hot showers, that are heated with solar energy). Kayaks and bikes are available for hire (500 CFP for the duration of your stay).

Chez Justine

PENSION, CAMPGROUND $

(☎96 22 87, 72 02 44; campsite for 2 persons incl breakfast 4000 CFP, bungalows half board per person 8000 CFP; @☎) Ask for one of the three big beachfront bungalows that cost the same as the four basic, humbly furnished rooms behind. They all feel a little past their prime on the inside, but they're clean, and the location, on a wide beach lapped by topaz waters, is divine. Campers can pitch tents on a sandy, shady plot just 10m from the lagoon. Kayaks and bikes are complimentary.

Chez Cindy

SNACK $

(☎96 22 67; mains 1200-1400 CFP; ☺lunch & dinner Sun-Fri) This modest eatery in the village serves massive portions of good *poisson cru* (raw fish), *steak frites* (steak and chips), chow mein and more.

ℹ Information

There is no bank or ATM on Tikehau. There's wi-fi access near pensions Hotu and Chez Justine.

ℹ Getting There & Away

Tikehau lies 300km northeast of Tahiti and 14km north of Rangiroa.

AIR The airport is about 1km east of the village entrance. **Air Tahiti** (☎96 22 66, 86 42 42; www.airtahiti.pf) has daily flights between Pape'ete and Tikehau (18,500 CFP). There are also several weekly flights between Bora Bora and Tikehau (26,000 CFP), via Rangiroa. The Tikehau–Rangiroa flight costs 7500 CFP.

BOAT The *Mareva Nui* and *Saint-Xavier Maris-Stella* offer transport to Tikehau (see p429).

ℹ Getting Around

A 10km track goes around Tuherahera, and passes by the airport. Bicycles can be hired (1200 CFP per day) at your pension or if you stay at Chez Justine they're free.

Manihi

POP 800

Considered the birthplace of the Tahitian pearl industry, Manihi is a classically gorgeous atoll with one deep pass in the southwest and great fishing. Since pearl prices began to plummet around 2000, approximately 50 farms have gone out of business but there's still a smattering of pearl farms dotted around the lagoon.

Shaped like an ellipse, the atoll is 28km long and 8km wide. The best beaches and picnic spots are at the south of the lagoon where white sand, ruffled palms and sapphire waters make for the perfect escape. Swimming and sunbathing will be big on the daily checklist for most visitors, but energetic types can fill their holiday with diving, kayaking and snorkelling.

Sights

The not-very-pretty village of **Turipaoa** takes about five minutes to wander round but is a good place to get a sense of atoll life. Manihi is now eclipsed by its quiet neighbour Ahe in terms of numbers of pearls produced but it's still a great place to visit a **pearl farm** – ask at your pension or at the hotel.

 Activities

Diving & Snorkelling

The novice diver will find Manihi's waters fascinating and filled with life, but those who have travelled to other atolls might find

---

WORTH A TRIP

AHE & MATAIVA

Most tourists tend to visit only Rangiroa, Tikehau, Fakarava and Manihi, which have the bulk of tourist infrastructure, but it's also possible to explore lesser-known beauties like Ahe and Mataiva.

Ahe

This 20km-long by 10km-wide ring of coral is a charmer. The many hues of its pure aqua-blue water, the foaming breakers around the reef and the thin strips of coral sand beach of its many deserted *motu* (islets) make for an enchanting scene.

The aim of the game on Ahe is to relax – but if you're keen to get the blood flowing a bit there are a few options available. It's also a great place to buy pearls direct from the pearl farm.

In a coconut plantation facing the lagoon, **Cocoperle Lodge** (☑96 44 08; www. cocoperlelodge.com; bungalows with half/full board per person from 11,000/13,000 CFP) has a handful of comfy ecochic bungalows. Excellent meals are served in a *fare* by the lagoon and the bar is open all day. Activities include snorkelling, kayaking and excursions to the nearby bird *motu* or to a pearl farm. The lodge is run on solar power. **Chez Raita** (☑96 44 53; www.pension-raita.com; bungalows with half/full board per person 9500/12,500 CFP) is a friendly and charming place on a white-sand *motu* on the east side of the atoll.

Air Tahiti (☑86 42 42; www.airtahiti.pf) flies from Pape'ete to Ahe three to four days weekly (22,200 CFP one way). Twice-weekly flights to Manihi are 5900 CFP one way.

Mataiva

Like stepping into a time machine, this tiny, picturesque atoll is the sort of hideaway that you search your whole life to discover. Despite the limited tourist infrastructure, it provides a delightful escape holiday. There are superb coral beaches, numerous snorkelling spots, lots of fish and one of the few noteworthy archaeological sites in the Tuamotus.

You can stay at **Ariiheevai – Chez Alphonsine** (☑76 73 23, 96 32 50; bungalows with full board & excursions per person 8500 CFP; ✳). This place is one of the best deals in the Tuamotus. Alphonsine, the owner, lovingly tends the six well-organised bungalows all on the edge of the white-sand-fringed emerald lagoon. The food is great and there are plenty of activities included.

Air Tahiti (☑96 32 48, 86 42 42; www.airtahiti.pf) operates two weekly flights to/from Pape'ete (18,500 CFP one way), and one flight to/from Rangiroa (7500 CFP one way).

that it compares unfavourably. That said, the sites near Tairapa Pass are excellent, as is Le Cirque, inside the lagoon, where manta rays can regularly be spotted. See p32 for more information on diving in French Polynesia. The coral reefs and coral outcrops that are dotted around the lagoon are perfect for snorkelling.

Topdive
DIVING

(☎96 42 17; www.topdive.com) Based at Manihi Pearl Beach Resort, this is the only dive outfit on the atoll. It has introductory dives (9000 CFP), single dives (7800 CFP), two-tank dives (15,000 CFP) and six-/10-dive packages (37,500/70,000 CFP).

Boat Excursions
All the places to stay can organise lagoon excursions which include snorkelling stops and picnic lunch on a deserted *motu*.

🛏 Sleeping & Eating

Manihi Pearl Beach Resort   RESORT $$$
(☎96 42 73; www.spmhotels.com; bungalows d from 48,000 CFP; ✳🛜🌊) Embedded in a thick tropical garden near the airport, this well-run resort is one of the older establishments in the Tuamotus. Accommodation ranges from a smattering of individual bungalows on the beach to over-water units. The faux beach is no great shakes but a slew of daily activities on offer, ranging from village visits to lagoon excursions to pearl farm visits, will keep you occupied. It has a restaurant, a bar, a spa and a dive shop.

Nanihi Paradise   PENSION $$
(☎93 30 40; www.nanihiparadise.com; bungalow with full board per person 13,500 CFP; 🛜) On a tiny *motu*, this quirkily laid-out place has three clean, flower-bedecked, two-bedroom bungalows with fully equipped kitchen and outdoor bathrooms (cold-water showers). Various excursions and lagoon tours can be arranged. Round-trip airport transfers are 2500 CFP per person.

ℹ Information
There is no bank on the atoll, so bring a wad of cash. The post office in Turipaoa village has internet and wi-fi access (with the Manaspot network).

ℹ Getting There & Away
AIR Air Tahiti (☎96 43 34, 86 42 42; www.airtahiti.pf) has almost daily flights be-tween Pape'ete and Manihi (22,100 CFP one

way), direct or via Rangiroa, Tikehau or Fakarava (11,000 CFP one way). There's also a twice-weekly flight to Fakarava (12,200 CFP one way).

BOAT The *Mareva Nui* and *Saint-Xavier Maris-Stella* service Manihi and accept passengers (see p429).

ℹ Getting Around
The only track on Manihi links Motu Taugarau-fara to the airport, covering a total distance of only about 9km. The Manihi Pearl Beach Resort has bicycles.

MARQUESAS ISLANDS

Whether you believe in legends or not, this archipelago looks like something from the pages of a fairy tale. Here, nature's fingers have dug deep grooves and fluted sharp edges, sculpting intricate jewels that jut up dramatically from the cobalt-blue ocean; waterfalls taller than skyscrapers trickle down vertical canyons; the ocean thrashes towering sea cliffs like a furious beast; sharp basalt pinnacles project from emerald forests; and scalloped bays are blanketed with desert arcs of white or black sand.

No wonder that over the last 170 years the Marquesas have been an escape for artists, writers, adventurers and musicians, includ-

Marquesas Islands

See Nuku Hiva Map (p408)

See 'Ua Pou Map (p413)

See Hiva Oa & Tahuata Map (p414)

> **DON'T MISS**
>
> ## THE ARANUI
>
> If there's an iconic trip in French Polynesia, it must be on the *Aranui*. For nearly 25 years, this 104m-long boat has been the umbilical cord between Tahiti and the Marquesas and a hot favourite with tourists. Its 14-day voyage, departing from Pape'ete, takes it to one or two atolls in the Tuamotus and the six inhabited islands of the Marquesas. There are 16 to 17 trips per year. It's very convenient because you get an overview of the archipelago in a relatively short time at a fraction of what you'd pay if you had to do it independently.
>
> It's both a freighter and a passenger vessel, with four classes of accommodation, from large cabins with balcony, double bed and bathroom (€3500 to €4900 per person) to dorm-style beds with shared bathroom facilities (€2100 per person). Foreigners are not supposed to use deck class, used by islanders, but if you are just going from one island to the next and there's room, there shouldn't be a problem.
>
> For more information, contact your travel agency or the shipowner directly at **Compagnie Polynésienne de Transport Maritime** (CPTM; ☎42 62 42, in Papeete 43 48 89; www.aranui.com).

ing Paul Gauguin, Herman Melville and Jack London.

It's not all about inspiring landscapes, though. The Marquesas are culturally intense and offer plenty of sites dating from pre-European times.

If you've got energy to burn, hiking, horseback riding, diving and snorkelling will keep you busy.

❶ Getting There & Away

AIR Nuku Hiva and Hiva Oa are well connected with Tahiti, with almost daily direct flights from Pape'ete. Flights to 'Ua Huka via Nuku Hiva run four days a week, and 'Ua Pou has flights six to seven days a week via Nuku Hiva or Hiva Oa.

BOAT The *Taporo IX* and *Aranui* (www.aranui.com) service the Marquesas, departing from Pape'ete and travelling via the Tuamotus (Fakarava and/or Rangiroa). Note that the *Taporo IX* doesn't take passengers. For more on travelling by cargo ship, see p428.

❶ Getting Around

The easiest and quickest way to island hop within the archipelago is by regular Air Tahiti flights, with Nuku Hiva and Hiva Oa being the hub islands. Tahuata and Fatu Hiva are only accessible by boat (both from Atuona).

You can hop on the cargo ship *Aranui* if your timing is right (ask your hosts about arrival dates), but it's at the captain's discretion.

On the islands, there's no public transport and you'll have to charter taxis to get around the islands' web of 4WD tracks (and, increasingly, surfaced roads). It is also possible to rent your own vehicle on Nuku Hiva and Hiva Oa.

Nuku Hiva

POP 2640 / AREA 340 SQ KM

This huge (the second largest in French Polynesia after Tahiti), sparsely populated island boasts a fantastic terrain, with razor-edged basaltic cliffs pounded by crashing waves, deep bays blessed with Robinson Crusoe beaches, dramatic waterfalls and timeless valleys that feel the end of the world.

If you've got itchy feet for active pursuits, you'll find some of the most inspirational hikes and rides in Polynesia. Culture vultures will get a buzz with plenty of archaeological sites scattered around the island.

◉ Sights

TAIOHAE

The only town of any size on Nuku Hiva, Taiohae is strung along the horseshoe-shaped Taiohae Bay. It has a handful of sights.

Tohua Koueva   ARCHAEOLOGICAL SITE

(off Map p409) The neatly restored *tohua* Koueva, a sacred place venerated by the ancient Marquesans, is about 1.5km up the Pakiu Valley on the road to Taipivai. The almost mystical hush that shrouds this extensive paved esplanade, surrounded with banyan trees, is reason enough to come here.

Pae Pae Piki Vehine   ARCHAEOLOGICAL SITE

(Map p409) On the seafront, the *pae pae* Piki Vehine contains modern sculptures and a dozen magnificent *tiki* (sacred statues) made by local sculptors and artisans from Easter Island.

Nuku Hiva

TAHITI & FRENCH POLYNESIA NUKU HIVA

Notre-Dame Cathedral
of the Marquesas Islands   CATHEDRAL
(Map p409) This well-proportioned cathedral is built from stones that come from the archipelago's six inhabited islands.

AROUND THE ISLAND

TOP CHOICE Hakaui Valley   WATERFALL, HIKE
(Map p408) About 8km west of Taiohae, the river has cut vertical walls of nearly 800m into the basalt and the **Vaipo Waterfall** (Map p408) plunges an awesome 350m into a basin. From Taiohae, the valley can be reached by speedboat (about 40 minutes). From Hakaui Bay, where the boat anchors, allow about 2½ hours to reach the waterfall on foot, on a flat path which follows the river. A guide is required. Contact **Marquises Plaisance** (☎92 08 75, 73 23 48; e.bastard@mail.pf), which can arrange day trips to the waterfall from Taiohae (13,500 CFP for two people).

Paeke   ARCHAEOLOGICAL SITE
(Map p408) The reason to stop in **Taipivai**, about 16km northeast of Taiohae, is to visit this site, with two well-preserved paved platforms flanked by a set of brick-coloured *tiki*. It's on a hillside at the exit of the village on the way to Hatiheu.

Hatiheu   VILLAGE
(Map p408) is a graceful little village dominated by a crescent of black sand, soaring peaks and colourful gardens. It is renowned for its powerful archaeological sites, including **Hikokua**, **Kamuihei**, **Teiipoka** and **Tahakia**, all located nearby Hatiheu. They feature vast esplanades (*tohua*), *tiki* and petroglyphs.

Aakapa   VILLAGE
(Map p408) In the northwest, this village is in a superb setting below high peaks; it can be reached by 4WD from Hatiheu.

🏃 Activities

Hiking
Hiking is *the* very best Nuku Hiva has to offer, and is a dizzying experience (literally). The catch? A guide is essential because trails are not marked.

Other excellent walking options include the hikes to the Vaipo Waterfall and from Hatiheu to Anaho.

Marquises Rando   GUIDED HIKES
(☎92 07 13, 29 53 31; www.marquisesrando.com) This operation is run by a professional guide who offers ultra-scenic hikes which take in some awe-inspiring viewpoints. Hikes range

from five to six hours, are suitable for all levels and cost from 6600 CFP per person.

Horse Riding

Horse riding is another good way to soak up the drop-dead gorgeous scenery.

Sabine Teikiteetini   HORSE RIDING
(☑92 01 56, 25 35 13; half-day rides incl transfers 8000 CFP) Sabine is a qualified guide who can arrange lovely rides on Toovii Plateau.

Diving

There are a dozen magnificent diving sites, which are very different from those of the Society group or the Tuamotus. The Marquesas don't boast coral reefs, peaceful lagoons or crystalline waters. The water is thick with plankton, and visibility is consequently reduced (generally 10m to 20m). All kinds of rays – mantas, eagles and stingrays – also swim close to the shore.

Most sites require a half-hour or so boat trip.

Centre Plongée Marquises   DIVING
(Map p409; ☑92 00 88; marquisesdives@mail.pf) This small operation runs on a charter basis only. An outing costs 35,000/45,000 CFP for up to three/four divers. Prices include equipment and two successive dives. Book ahead.

Quad Biking

Revving up the motor and hitting the trail on a quad bike (ATV) is a great way to explore the area around Taiohae.

Marquises Quad Aventure – ATV Tours   QUAD
(☑32 18 37; ☺by reservation) This quad-biking operator runs a variety of guided tours that visit Colette Bay, Taipivai and Hatiheu. Guided trips for two-person quads cost 12,000/15,000 CFP per half-/full day.

Whale Watching

If you've ever fancied snorkelling with a pod of melon-headed whales *(Peponocephala electra)*, this is your perfect chance. These intriguing creatures congregate off the east

Taiohae

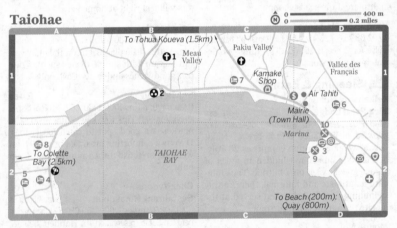

Taiohae

ANAHO & HAATUATUA BAY

One of the best-kept secrets in the Marquesas is **Anaho** (Map p408). This serene hamlet is only accessible by speedboat (15 minutes from Hatiheu, 7000 CFP) or a little less than 1½ hours by foot from Hatiheu. It's a popular anchorage for visiting yachts and, with the only coral reef on Nuku Hiva, the bay is lagoon-like and inviting.

From Anaho, a 30-minute stroll along an easy-to-follow path to the east leads to **Haatuatua Bay** (Map p408). The reward? A crescent-shaped bay fringed with a yellow scimitar of sand, framed by lofty volcanic ridges.

coast in the morning. While an encounter is not exactly guaranteed, the operator claims a success rate of 70%. Note that the 45-minute journey to get to the site can be a nightmare if the sea is choppy.

Marquises Plaisance WHALE WATCHING
(☑92 08 75, 73 23 48; e.bastard@mail.pf; half-day cruise for 2 people 15,000 CFP) Runs whale-watching excursions.

🛏 Sleeping & Eating

Keikahanui Nuku Hiva Pearl Lodge HOTEL $$$
(Map p409; ☑92 07 10; www.pearlodge.com; bungalows d 26,000-31,000 CFP; ✻@🛜🏊) Nuku Hiva's swankiest option comprises 20 Polynesian-style bungalows hidden in a sea of spruce greenery set on a hillside. The ambience is intimate and informal, there's a tiny swimming pool and the food served at the on-site restaurant is flavoursome.

Moana Nui HOTEL $$
(Map p409; ☑92 03 30; pensionmoananui@mail. pf; s incl breakfast/half board 6500/9000 CFP, d incl breakfast/half board 9900/16,000 CFP; ✻🛜) This is the perfect headquarters for the budget-conscious traveller who's not looking for fancy trimmings. The eight rooms are utilitarian but clean and well organised, with private facilities and daily cleaning. Note that prices may change significantly as there are plans to upgrade the place. The on-site restaurant serves a wide range of French and Polynesian specialities as well as pizzas.

Paahatea Nui – Chez Justin & Julienne PENSION $
(Map p409; ☑92 00 97; paahateanui@mail.pf; bungalows s/d incl breakfast 6000/10,000 CFP) On the western side of the bay, this well-priced establishment has six bungalows set in a fragrant garden. No meals are available, except breakfast, but you can use the kitchen.

Mave Mai PENSION $$
(Map p409; ☑92 08 10; pension-mavemai@mail. pf; s/d incl breakfast 9000/11,000 CFP, with half board 11,000/15,000 CFP; ✻🛜) All eight rooms are light and well appointed, with private facilities (hot water) and air-con, as well as a kitchenette in two of the rooms. But they're not terribly Polynesian.

Hee Tai Inn HOTEL $$
(Map p409; ☑92 03 82; www.marquesas-hinn. com; s/d 9000/10,500 CFP; ✻🛜) Here the accommodation is in a rather characterless building, but the eight motel-like rooms are spacious and meticulously clean. It's run by an American lady, so English-speaking visitors will feel right at home here.

Café Vaeaki CAFE $
(Map p409; mains 800-1100 CFP; ⊘closed dinner Sun) At this little place right on the quay you can fuel up with simple dishes such as raw fish, sandwiches and fruits. Cash only.

Snack Tuhiva CAFE $
(Map p409; mains 1000-1200 CFP; ⊘breakfast & lunch Mon-Sat) This low-key venue inside the market is a good spot to catch local vibes. Devour a comforting breakfast or munch on well-prepared fish dishes at lunchtime. Cash only.

Chez Yvonne – Restaurant Hinakonui RESTAURANT $$
(☑92 02 97; mains 1700-3000 CFP; ⊘lunch & dinner Mon-Sat, by reservation) In Hatiheu, be sure to stop by this place, which has a magnificent terrace that opens directly onto the seafront. The menu brims with local flavours.

❶ Information

The following are in Taiohae.
Banque Socredo (Map p409; ☑92 03 63; ⊘7.30-11.30am & 1.30-4pm Mon-Fri) Currency exchange, as well as two ATMs.
Hospital (Map p409; ☑91 20 00) Has a dentist, too.
Keikahanui Nuku Hiva Pearl Lodge (Map p409; ☑92 07 10; ⊘7am-9pm) Internet and wi-fi access.

Moetai Marine – Yacht Services (☎92 07 50; ⊙8am-12.30pm Mon-Fri) On the quay. Has internet and wi-fi access (900 CFP per hour), laundry service (1000 CFP) and can help yachties with formalities.

Post office (Map p409; ⊙7-11.30am & noon-3.30pm Mon-Thu, 7-11.30am & noon-2.30pm Fri) Internet access and wi-fi (with the Manaspot card). Has an ATM.

Tourist office (Map p409; ☎92 08 25; ⊙7.30am-12.30pm Mon-Fri) Has a few brochures and can help with simple queries.

ⓘ Getting There & Away

AIR Air Tahiti (☎91 02 25, 92 01 45, 86 42 42; www.airtahiti.pf; ⊙8am-noon & 1.30-4.30pm Mon-Thu, 8am-noon & 1.30-3.30pm Fri) has up to nine weekly flights between Pape'ete and Nuku Hiva (33,000 CFP one way, three hours). Within the Marquesas there are daily flights from Nuku Hiva to Hiva Oa (12,500 CFP one way), and four to five flights per week from Nuku Hiva to 'Ua Huka and 'Ua Pou (both cost 8200 CFP one way). These flights connect with the Pape'ete flights through Nuku Hiva.

BOAT The **Aranui** (www.aranui.com) stops at Taiohae. See the boxed text, p407.

ⓘ Getting Around

To/From the Airport

It takes at least 1¼ hours to reach the airport from Taiohae along a winding road, longer if it has rained and the ground is muddy.

Licensed 4WD taxis generally wait for each flight. It is nevertheless wise to book through your hotel or pension. Transfers to Taiohae cost 4000 CFP per person.

4WD

4WDs without a driver can be rented from 11,500 CFP to 13,500 CFP per day. Rates include insurance and unlimited mileage but not petrol. Contact the hotel **Moana Nui** (☎92 03 30; pensionmoananui@mail.pf).

'Ua Huka

POP 590 / AREA 83 SQ KM

This low-key, less-visited island remains something of a 'secret' and you'll probably have it all to yourself. Here's your chance to buy carvings from master artisans, zigzag up the flanks of an extinct volcano to reach mysterious archaeological sites tucked away in the jungle, take a boat excursion to offshore islets and delve right into Marquesan life.

⊙ Sights

Vaipee VILLAGE
The island's main settlement, Vaipee is at the end of the very narrow, deep and aptly named Invisible Bay. The **museum** (admission free, donations appreciated) displays pestles, *tiki*, sculptures, *pahu* (drums), jewellery and period photos, as well as a traditional house.

Hane VILLAGE
The number-one reason to stop in Hane is the **Meiaute archaeological site**, higher up in the valley. It includes three 1m-high red-tuff *tiki* that watch over a group of stone structures, *pae pae* and *me'ae*.

Hokatu VILLAGE
About 4km east of Hane, Hokatu is so mellow and scenic that you may never want to leave. It lies in a sheltered bay edged with a pebble beach pounded with frothy azure seas, and offers direct views of imposing, sugar-loafed Motu Hane. On the waterfront there's a small **petroglyph museum** (admission free).

Vaikivi Petroglyphs ARCHAEOLOGICAL SITE
A little-visited archaeological site on the Vaikivi Plateau that's well worth the detour, if only for the walk or horse ride to get there. The petroglyphs represent an outrigger canoe, a human face and various geometric designs.

Manihina BEACH
Near the airport, Manihina Beach is a wonderfully scenic pebbly beach framed by basaltic cliffs. Sadly there are lots of *nonos*. It's accessible by a dirt road.

TAHITI & FRENCH POLYNESIA 'UA HUKA

ⓘ IMPORTANT! READ THIS...

The Marquesas are *not* a beach destination, although there are a few enticing beaches.

As appealing as these beaches may look, the reality is they are invariably infested with *nono* – a small, aggressive biting fly. Fortunately they are found almost exclusively on beaches and in a few valleys and do not carry diseases. Cover yourself in lightweight trousers and long-sleeve shirts and whip out the jungle juice.

✻ Activities

From Hane or Vaipaee, it's a memorable three-hour **walk** inland to the Vaikivi Petroglyphs, hidden in the jungle. Ask at your pension for a guide. Other walks include the Small Crater and the Big Crater, near Vaipaee, and the Hokatu to Hane inland track.

Horse riding trips can also be organised through your pension. A ride typically costs 5000 CFP for a half-day or 10,000 CFP for a full day, including a guide.

🛏 Sleeping & Eating

Chez Maurice et Delphine   PENSION $
(☎92 60 55; Hokatu; bungalows with half board per person 6500 CFP) This pension has five ramshackle and very simply furnished bungalows on a little knoll on the village outskirts. Airport transfers are 2000 CFP return.

Le Reve Marquisien   PENSION $$
(☎79 10 52; revemarquisien@mail.pf; Vaipaee; s/d half board 16,400/21,000 CFP) A perfect escape situated in a secluded clearing at the far end of the village, and surrounded by a lush coconut grove. The four bungalows are of a high standard but the place feels a bit isolated (it's a 2km walk to Vaipee). Transfers included.

❶ Information

Infrastructure is very limited on 'Ua Huka. Bring a wad of cash – there's no bank and no ATM, and credits cards are not accepted.

❶ Getting There & Away

AIR Air Tahiti (☎91 60 16, 92 60 44, 86 42 42; www.airtahiti.pf) has regular flights to Nuku Hiva (8200 CFP), Hiva Oa (9800 CFP) and 'Ua Pou (8200 CFP). For Pape'ete (36,000 CFP), you'll have to change on Nuku Hiva.

BOAT The **Aranui** (www.aranui.com) stops at Vaipaee. See the boxed text, p407.

❶ Getting Around

A surprisingly good 13km road links Vaipaee to Hokatu via Hane.

'Ua Huka's airport is on an arid plateau midway between Vaipaee and Hane. Some pensions charge 2000 CFP return for airport transfers. The pension owners can take you by 4WD to visit the three villages (10,000 CFP per day).

'Ua Pou

POP 2110 / AREA 125 SQ KM

'Ua Pou's jewel-like natural setting will frame everything you do here, from hiking across the island to visiting secluded hamlets. A collection of 12 pointy pinnacles seem to soar like missiles from the basaltic shield. Almost constantly shrouded in swirling mist and flecked by bright sunlight, they form one of the Marquesas' most enduring images. The island also offers up a handful of powerful archaeological sites.

◉ Sights

Hakahau   TOWN
'Ua Pou's largest settlement, Hakahau has few charms but it's blessed with a photogenic location and it's a convenient base to start your island adventures. The stone-and-timber **Catholic church** in the south of town displays noteworthy sculptures by local artisans. From Hakahau, it's a 30-minute walk east to deserted **Anahoa Beach**.

Hakanai Bay   BEACH
Shortly after the airport at Aneou, Hakanai Bay appears like a mirage from around a sharp bend: a long curve of wave-lashed beach. It has been named Plage aux Requins (Shark Beach) because of the sharks that are occasionally seen in the cove (it's safe for a dip nonetheless).

Hohoi   VILLAGE
Time seems to have stood still in picturesque little Hohoi in the southeast of the island, 13km from Hakahau. Above the village, the magnificent **tohua Mauia** comprises a huge L-shaped stone platform and numerous *pae pae* dotted around the main complex.

Hakahetau   VILLAGE
Charming Hakahetau in the island's northwest springs up like an oasis after driving along the dusty track. At the far end of the village, make a beeline for the grandiose **Tetahuna archaeological site**. Continue higher in the valley until you reach **Cascade Vaiea**, suitable for a refreshing dip.

✻ Activities

You can walk along the 4WD tracks that connect the villages. For deeper exploration, it's advisable to hire a guide since it's easy to get lost. Ask at your pension. Recommended hikes include the cross-island path from Hakahau to Hakahetau (about three hours) and the more challenging Poumaka loop (about four hours). Both hikes afford hauntingly beautiful panoramas of the interior of the island. A full-day guided walk is about 12,000 CFP for two.

🛏 Sleeping & Eating

Pukuéé   PENSION, RESTAURANT **$**
(☑92 50 83, 72 90 08; pukuee@mail.pf; Hakahau;
r with half board per person 9000 CFP; 🛜🖥) Reliable, friendly and fabulously situated on a hillside with swooning views of Hakahau Bay, Pukuéé offers four smallish rooms with shared bathrooms (hot water) in a wooden house surrounded by greenery. Owner Jérôme is great with excursion organisation and his wife Elisa is a real cordon bleu cook.

Pension Leydj   PENSION **$**
(☑92 53 19; Hakahetau; r with half board per person 5500 CFP) In a plum setting on a hill at the edge of Hakahetau, this mellow pension offers clean, well-swept, yet impersonal rooms with shared bathrooms (cold water), at a nice price. Owner Tony is a renowned master carver and his spouse Célestine can cook some seriously good Marquesan meals. Cash only.

ℹ Information

There's a small medical centre with a doctor and dentist in the south of the village.
Banque Socredo (⊙7.30am-noon & 1-3pm Mon-Fri) Currency exchange, as well as an ATM.
Post office (OPT; ⊙7-11.30am & 12.15-3pm Mon-Thu, 7-11.30am & 12.15-2pm Fri) On the seafront. Internet and wi-fi access (with the Manaspot network). Has an ATM.

ℹ Getting There & Away

AIR Air Tahiti (☑91 52 25, 86 42 42; www.airtahiti.pf) has regular flights from Nuku Hiva to 'Ua Pou (8200 CFP one way). Flights connect with the Pape'ete–Nuku Hiva flight (Pape'ete to 'Ua Pou costs 36,000 CFP one way). There are also five weekly flights from Hiva Oa to 'Ua Pou (9800 CFP one way) and from 'Ua Huka to 'Ua Pou (8200 CFP).
BOAT The **Aranui** (www.aranui.com) stops at Hakahau and Hakahetau.

ℹ Getting Around

One dirt 4WD track runs most of the way around the island, with the only inaccessible bit being the section between Hakamaii and Hakatao.

The airport is at Aneou, about 10km west of Hakahau. Your hosts will come to collect you if you have booked accommodation; it usually costs 4000 CFP per person return.

Ask at your pension about hiring a 4WD with driver; expect to pay 15,000 CFP to 20,000 CFP per day.

'Ua Pou   ⓝ   0 —— 5 km   0 —— 3 miles

Hakanai Bay
Tetahuna Archaeological Site
Aneou Airport
Anahoa Beach
Hakahetau
Cascade Vaiea
Mt Poutemoka ▲ (683m)
Hakamoui Valley
Hakahau
Haakuti
▲ Mt Oave (1203m)
Mt Poumaka ▲ (973m)
Hakamaii
Tohua Mauia
Hohoi
Hikeu
Hakatao
Motu Oa

Hiva Oa

POP 2010 / AREA 320 SQ KM

Sweet Hiva Oa. Nowhere is the Marquesas' verdant, moody beauty better captured than here. This oh-so-mellow island is a picturesque mix of lush jungle, sea-smashed coastal cliffs and lofty volcanic peaks. No wonder that French painter Paul Gauguin and singer-songwriter Jacques Brel were won over by the island's powerful landscapes and serenity and chose to live out their lives in Atuona.

👁 Sights

TOP CHOICE Smiling Tiki   ARCHAEOLOGICAL SITE
Hiva Oa's most bizarre statue can be found near the road to the airport, about 10km from Atuona. About 1m in height, it stands alone in a clearing. To find it (no sign), ask for the little sketch map that's on sale at the tourism office.

Espace Culturel Paul Gauguin   MUSEUM
(adult/child 600/300 CFP; ⊙8-11am & 2-5pm Mon-Thu, 7.30am-2.30pm Fri, 8-11am Sat) In the centre of Atuona, this refurbished museum has digital exhibits of the painter's work. Outside, have a look at the **Maison du Jouir** (House of Pleasure), a replica of Gauguin's own house.

Centre Jacques Brel   MUSEUM
(adult/child 600/300 CFP; ☺8-11am & 2-5pm Mon-
Thu, 7.30am-2.30pm Fri, 8-11am Sat) Behind the
Espace Culturel Paul Gauguin you'll find a
hangar that houses this collection. In the
centre is Brel's plane, *Jojo;* posters tracing
the musician's life adorn the walls and his
music plays dreamily over the sound system.

Calvaire Cemetery   CEMETERY
Another must-see for Gauguin and Brel devotees is the Calvaire Cemetery, perched on
a hill overlooking Atuona. You will find this
frangipani-filled graveyard an appropriately
colourful place for Paul Gauguin's tomb.
Jacques Brel's grave is a bit below, near the
access steps, on the left.

Tehueto petroglyphs   ARCHAEOLOGICAL SITE
Hidden high up in the Tahauku Valley, the
Tehueto petroglyphs are a good walk from
Atuona but it's usually quite overgrown and
the path is confusing; we suggest hiring a

guide (ask at your pension). You'll find a
massive rock with prolific carvings on two
sides, including stylised human figures.

AROUND THE ISLAND

TOP CHOICE **Iipona**   ARCHAEOLOGICAL SITE
One of the best-preserved archaeological
sites in French Polynesia, Iipona lies on
the outskirts of **Puamau**, a two-hour drive
northeast of Atuona. You'll be moved by the
eeriness of the site and impressed by the
five monumental *tiki,* including **Tiki Takaii**
which, at 2.67m, is the largest *tiki* in French
Polynesia, and the reclining **Tiki Maki Taua
Pepe**, representing a woman lying on her
stomach, her head stretched out and arms
pointing to the sky.

Tohua Upeke   ARCHAEOLOGICAL STE
Near the village of **Taaoa**, 7km southwest of
Atuona, the eerie Tohua Upeke, with more
than 1000 *pae pae*, some of which are re-

stored, is a definite must see for culture buffs.

Hanapaaoa
VILLAGE

It's a winding but scenic 1½-hour journey by 4WD to wild and beautiful Hanapaaoa from Atuona. Ask a local to take you to the **Tiki Moe One**, hidden in a forest on a hillside. One of the quirkiest statues in the Marquesas, it features a carved crown around the head.

Hanaiapa
VILLAGE

Another gem of a village, Hanaiapa is cradled by striking mountains carpeted with shrubs and coconut trees. At the entrance of the village (coming from Atuona), you'll find some well-preserved **petroglyphs**.

Hanatekuua Bay
BEACH

One of Hiva Oa's best-kept secrets is this impossibly scenic bay fringed with a pristine stretch of white-sand beach and backed by a lovely coconut grove. This slice of paradise is accessible by foot only (or by boat). From Hanaiapa, it's a fairly easy 90-minute walk, although the path is not waymarked.

Activities

Hiking

There are some truly excellent hiking possibilities on Hiva Oa, including the strenuous cross-island trek from Atuona to Hanamenu (about 11 hours). Sadly, there's no waymarked trail and no guide was available on the island at the time of writing. Ask at your pension or contact Paco, from Hamau Ranch – Chez Paco, who may organise something for you.

Horse Riding

A network of trails leading to some of the most beautiful sites can be explored on horseback.

Hamau Ranch – Chez Paco HORSE RIDING
(☑92 70 57, 28 68 21; hamauranch@mail.pf; rides 7000-14,000 CFP) Paco organises three-hour jaunts on the plateau near the airport. No previous experience is necessary. The ultimate is a full-day ride to Hanatekuua Bay, in the north of the island.

Diving

Hiva Oa is certainly not possessed of dazzling tropical reefs (there's no barrier reef and no turquoise lagoon in the Marquesas, remember), but there are many excellent diving sites along the crumpled coastline of Hiva Oa and Tahuata. See p32.

SubAtuona DIVING
(☑92 70 88, 27 05 24; eric.lelyonnais@wanadoo.fr; Atuona) Including all gear, the cost of a single-/two-tank dive is 7000/13,000 CFP (minimum two divers). SubAtuona also offers day trips to Tahuata that combine one dive and a tour of Tahuata's main villages (15,000 CFP). Note that the owner had plans to sell his operation at the time of writing.

Boat Excursions

Taking a boat excursion to nearby Tahuata is well worth the expense (especially given the lack of reliable boat services to Tahuata). Day-long trips usually include stops at Hapatoni and Vaitahu and a picnic lunch at Hanamenino Bay or Hanahevane Bay. Your pension will make arrangements with a local operator. Plan on 11,500 CFP per person.

Sleeping

Accommodation options on Hiva Oa are fairly limited. All places are in (or near) Atuona, bar one in Puamau. Unless otherwise noted, credit cards are accepted.

TOP CHOICE **Temetiu Village** PENSION $
(☑91 70 60; www.temetiuvillage.com; bungalows standard s/d 7100/9000 CFP, large 10,200 CFP; ☎☒) Efficient hosts, a homely atmosphere, top-notch location and high standards of cleanliness all add up to a winning formula. Digs are in four bungalows perched on a lush hillside. There are also two older (and slightly cheaper) bungalows, but they lack the wow factor. Other pluses include a small pool and high-quality meals.

DON'T MISS

MARQUESAS ARTS FESTIVAL

Powerful, grandiose, visceral – words do little justice to the Marquesas' premier festival, which lasts about one week and is held once every four years, usually in December, either on 'Ua Pou, Nuku Hiva or Hiva Oa. It revolves around a series of music, dance and cultural contests, with dance performances being the highlights. Most dancing contests take place on restored archaeological sites, which adds to the appeal.

Bookmark December 2015 for the next festival, on Hiva Oa.

Hotel Hanakéé Hiva Oa
Pearl Lodge
HOTEL $$$

(☎92 75 87; www.pearllodge.com; bungalows d 26,000-31,000 CFP; ✳@🛜🏊) Hiva Oa's upscale resort, the Hanakéé boasts 14 well-designed bungalows adorned with fancy touches and lots of tropical flowers. The location is ace, on a mound overlooking Tahauku Bay.

Pension Kanahau – Chez Tania
PENSION $$

(☎91 71 31, 70 16 26; http://pensionkanahau.com; s/d incl breakfast 10,000/12,500 CFP; 🛜) Location-wise, this pension plays in the same league as nearby Temetiu Village, with a flower-filled garden and stupendous views of Tahauku Bay and the mountain amphitheatre. The four bungalows are well furnished, spacious and sparkling clean (hot water is available). Cash only. There's a 15% drop in price if you stay more than three nights.

Pension Moehau
PENSION $$

(☎92 72 69; www.relaismoehau.pf; s/d incl breakfast 8100/12,200 CFP; 🛜) All rooms here are scrupulously clean, amply sized and well appointed (hot water, fan and plump bedding) but avoid the ones at the back – they face the dark hill behind. Ask for an oceanside room.

Areke – Chez Kayser
GUESTHOUSE $$

(☎92 76 19, 23 48 17; www.pension-hivaoa.com; r with half board per person 10,500 CFP; 🛜🏊) This eyrie affords glorious views of Tahauku Bay and has a nice little pool in the garden. The modern house is charmless but this place enjoys a good reputation for its delicious home cooking and convivial atmosphere. Prices drop by 10% if you stay more than three nights. Cash only.

✖ Eating

Most restaurants provide free transport for their dinner guests (call ahead). In Atuona, you will find several well-stocked grocery stores.

Hotel Hanakéé Hiva Oa
Pearl Lodge
RESTAURANT $$$

(☎92 75 87; mains 1500-3900 CFP; ⊙lunch & dinner) The sweeping views from the terrace are impressive enough, but the excellent French-influenced cuisine is better still, and makes imaginative use of the island's rich produce.

Relais Moehau
RESTAURANT $$

(☎92 72 69; mains 1400-2500 CFP; ⊙lunch & dinner) It's worth stopping in one night for a pizza at this terrace restaurant (go for the fish pizza). There are also good fish and meat dishes available.

Temetiu Village
RESTAURANT $$$

(☎91 70 60; set menu 3000 CFP; ⊙lunch & dinner, by reservation) What's the draw here? The panoramic views from the open-air dining room? The convivial atmosphere or the delectable (and copious) Marquesan specialities? Come and see for yourself.

Areke –
Chez Kayser
RESTAURANT $$$

(☎92 76 19, 23 48 17; www.pension-hivaoa.com; set menu 2500 CFP; ⊙by reservation) The Kaysers are *bons viveurs* and Madame knows her stuff when it comes to cooking lip-smacking Marquesan specialities, such as goat with coconut sauce or chicken with papaya sauce. Cash only.

Snack Make Make
SNACK $$

(☎92 74 26; mains 1300-2300 CFP; ⊙lunch Mon-Fri) Opposite the post office, this long-standing joint serves inexpensive fish and meat dishes. It may also be open for dinner certain days (call ahead). Cash only.

ⓘ Information

Banque Socredo (☎92 73 54; Atuona; ⊙7.30-11.30am & 1.30-4pm Mon-Fri) Currency exchange. Has a 24-hour ATM.

Cyberservices (☎92 79 85, 23 22 47; VHF 11; Atuona) Laundry service, wi-fi and can help yachties with formalities (just give a call to be picked up).

Post office (Atuona; ⊙7am-noon & 12.30-3pm Mon-Thu, 7am-noon & 12.30-2pm Fri) Internet and wi-fi access (with the Manaspot card, available at the counter). Has an ATM, too.

Tourism office (☎92 78 93; Atuona; ⊙8.30-11.30am & 2-4pm Mon-Fri) Hands out useful brochures and sells sketch maps of most tourist sites. Opening hours are erratic.

ⓘ Getting There & Away

AIR Air Tahiti (☎91 52 25, 86 42 42; www.airtahiti.pf) offers daily flights (not always direct) to Pape'ete (36,000 CFP), Nuku Hiva (12,500 CFP, daily), 'Ua Pou (9800 CFP, five weekly flights) and 'Ua Huka (9800 CFP, five weekly flights).

BOAT The **Aranui** (www.aranui.com) stops at Hiva Oa. See p407.

ⓘ Getting Around

The airport is 13km from Atuona. If you have booked your accommodation, your host will come and collect you for about 3600 CFP return.

Atuona Rent-a-Car (📞92 76 07, 72 17 17) and Hiva Oa Location (📞92 70 43, 24 65 05) rent 4WDs without driver for about 13,000 CFP per day, with unlimited mileage.

Fatu Hiva

POP 690 / AREA 80 SQ KM

With no landing strip and only poorly serviced by the *bonitiers* from Hiva Oa (75km), Fatu Hiva is not a bad place to play castaway for a few days, if not weeks.

When arriving by boat, expect a visual shock: wrinkled cliffs tumble into the ocean and splendid bays, including the iconic Bay of Virgins, indent the coastline.

There are only two villages (Omoa and Hanavave), one good pension and one dirt track, so there are plenty of opportunities to move into slow gear.

◎ Sights

Omoa   VILLAGE

Omoa is famous for its two **giant petroglyphs**, in two different locations. The first site is easily accessed after a 10-minute walk from the main road (ask around) and features a huge fish (probably a dorado) as well as a few small anthropomorphic designs inscribed on big basaltic boulders. The second site is a 20-minute walk from Chez Lionel Cantois. It has a clearly outlined whale incised on a big slab – an eerie sight.

Hanavave   VILLAGE

On the seashore, Hanavave is at the mouth of a steep-sided valley leading into the **Bay of Virgins**, a favourite of passing yachties. With its towering basaltic cones drenched in purple at sunset, it ranks as one of the most scenic bays in the South Pacific. This phallic skyline was originally (and aptly) named Baie des Verges in French (Bay of Penises). Outraged, the missionaries promptly added a redeeming 'i' to make the name Baie des Vierges (Bay of Virgins).

🛏 Sleeping & Eating

Chez Lionel Cantois   PENSION $

(📞92 81 84, 70 03 71; chezlionel@mail.pf; Omoa; s/d incl breakfast 4500/6500 CFP; bungalow s/d incl breakfast 6500/9500 CFP; dinner from 1500 CFP; @) This pension at the far end of Omoa has an air of *Little House on the Prairie*. The well-equipped bungalow with bathroom (hot water) in the manicured garden is welcoming but, if funds are short, the two rooms in the owners' house can fit the bill.

TAHUATA

Tahuata is accessible only by boat (there's no landing strip) from Hiva Oa. Given that there's no regular service, most travellers visit Tahuata on a day tour from Hiva Oa, which includes visits of Hapatoni, Vaitahu and a picnic on a beach at idyllic Hanamenino Bay, Hanamoenoa Bay or Hanahevane Bay.

Lionel is a treasure trove of local information and can take you virtually anywhere on the island.

❶ Information

Bring a stash of cash – there's no bank on the island and credit cards are not accepted.

❶ Getting There & Away

Fatu Hiva is the most difficult island to get to in the Marquesas, but sorting out transport is manageable if you're flexible. In Hiva Oa, find out if boat charters to Fatu Hiva are being organised during your stay and you may be able to share the costs. There's no regular service. Another option is to hop on the **Aranui** (www.aranui.com) when it stops at Atuona, Omoa or Hanavave; see the boxed text, p407. The crossing between Hiva Oa and Atuona takes anything between three and five hours, depending on the sea conditions. The journey can be very uncomfortable if the sea is choppy.

❶ Getting Around

The only dirt road is 17km long and links Hanavave with Omoa, but it's quicker (and cheaper) to hire a speedboat to travel between the two villages.

Inquire at your pension about renting a 4WD; expect to pay 15,000 CFP a day with driver.

THE AUSTRAL ISLANDS

Fly south towards the Tropic of Capricorn to find the blustery Austral Archipelago (Map p419), where it's cool enough to grow peaches yet warm enough for bananas, coconut palms and turquoise, coral-laden lagoons. On these outrageously fertile islands you'll find some of the most authentic Polynesian culture in all of French Polynesia. If, after visiting the Australs, you still feel the urge for more off-the-beaten-track adventures,

consider travelling to the Gambier, where visitors are an absolute rarity.

Rurutu

Vertical limestone cliffs pockmarked with caves line Rurutu's coast, while the volcanic interior is a fertile, mind-bogglingly abundant jungle. The island is a *makatea*, a geologic phenomenon where a coral atoll has been thrust from the sea by volcanic activity to wall in the island it once encircled. While there's very little fringing reef, there are plenty of white-sand beaches. From July to October migrating humpbacks draw in visitors who come to see the mammals in some of the clearest waters on the planet.

One of the best places to stay is **Manôtel** (☑93 02 25; www.lemanotel.com; bungalows s/d with half board per person 11,100/15,600 CFP; ☜), which sports seven very pretty bungalows with fans, good bathrooms and particularly inviting terraces. Equally reliable is **Rurutu Lodge** (☑93 03 30; www.hotelrurutulodge.com; bungalows s with half board 7000-14,200 CFP, bungalows d with half board 9000-19,500 CFP; ☜), with a clutch of bungalows near a white-sand beach, and **Teautamatea** (☑93 02 93, 70 34 65; pension.teautamatea@mail.pf; s/d with half board 8500/13,000 CFP; ☜), run by a British-Rurutu couple.

Tubuai

Tubuai is flatter than most French Polynesian high islands, and its stretches of fertile plains, mixed with the ideal climate, have made it the fruit bowl and vegie bin for all of French Polynesia. The lagoon is as blue as Raivavae's but is consistently windy (an average of 300 days per year!). You can base yourself at **Wipa Lodge** (☑93 22 40, 73 10 02; maletdoom@mail.pf; campsites per person 2500 CFP, s/d 4500/7500 CFP; ☜).

Raivavae

This is a paradise not only because of the sweeping blue lagoon, idyllic white-sand *motu* or the mountainous interior dominated by square-topped Mt Hiro (437m), but also because of the ultra-warm Polynesian welcome and extraordinary glimpse into a traditional way of life. Amazingly, though considered one of the great beauties of the South Pacific, the island receives only a trickle of tourists.

You can stay at **Raivavae Tama** (☑95 42 52; www.raivavaetama.com; Anatonu; d with half board per person 6500 CFP, bungalows s/d with half board 8500/13,000 CFP), which has three rustic, coconut-thatched bungalows with bathrooms on a skinny stretch of white sand and two basic rooms without bathroom in the family's home. Another good option is **Chez Linda** (☑95 44 25, 78 80 24; www.pensionlindaraivavae.pf; Rairua; s/d with half board 7400/10,600 CFP, bungalows s/d with half board 10,600/16,200 CFP; ☜), with three Polynesian-style bungalows with private bathrooms and three tiny, modest rooms in the owner's house.

THE GAMBIER ARCHIPELAGO

All the makings of an island holiday paradise can be found in the Gambier Archipelago (Map p419), but it's so far away (1700km southeast from Tahiti) and expensive to get to that it remains one of the least developed regions in French Polynesia. The geology here is unique: one reef, complete with sandy *motu*, encircles a small archipelago of lush high islands dotting a blue lagoon that's as clear as air. Adding to the allure, the Gambier is the cradle of Polynesian Catholicism and houses some of the most eerie and interesting post-European structures in the country. It's also famous for its lustrous and colourful pearls.

Mangareva, the main island, has a couple of places to stay, including **Maro'i** (☑97 84 62; www.pensionmaroi.com; bungalows 9600 CFP; ☜).

Tempted? Contact **Air Tahiti** (☑86 42 42; www.airtahiti.pf), which has regular flights to the Australs and the Gambier Islands. Cargo ships also serve the Australs and the Gambier Islands (see p428).

UNDERSTAND TAHITI & FRENCH POLYNESIA

French Polynesia Today

Political instability hinders economic development and keeps potential investors at bay. Since 2004 the country's government has been in turmoil as the main political parties battle it out, call each other names, and try

Austral Islands & Gambier Archipelago

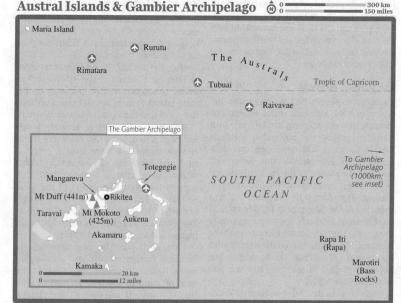

Maria Island

Rurutu

The Australs

Rimatara

Tubuai

Tropic of Capricorn

Raivavae

The Gambier Archipelago

Totegegie

SOUTH PACIFIC OCEAN

To Gambier Archipelago (1000km; see inset)

Mangareva

Mt Duff (441m) — Rikitea

Taravai — Mt Mokoto (425m) — Aukena

Akamaru

Rapa Iti (Rapa)

Kamaka

Marotiri (Bass Rocks)

0 — 20 km
0 — 12 miles

0 — 300 km
0 — 150 miles

to woo members of the assembly to flip-flop the balance of power. When there is a fragile majority, which is usually the case, one or two allegiance changes can overturn the entire government. From 2004 to 2009 this happened eight times but since 2010 things have stabilised a bit; Oscar Temaru, the pro-independence leader, has been in power since April 2011.

Now that Oscar Temaru has seemingly secured his presidential seat, he has begun to work on his lifelong goal: independence from France. Throughout 2011 to early 2012 Temaru tried to muster support to get French Polynesia on the UN's decolonisation list. If French Polynesia gets added to this list (the UN denied the entry in 2011 but Temaru is continuing to bid), the UN would monitor and help implement the territory's road to independence. Unfortunately for Temaru, he has gained little international backing aside from some Pacific island nations and his support from home is shaky and oft-criticised.

On the economic front, the situation is not rosy in French Polynesia. While elsewhere in the Pacific tourism is back on the rise, Tahiti's 2011 stats plummeted to equal those of 1996 (under 150,000). This grim situation is mostly due to the global recession,

the expensive airfares and a lack of better-targeted promotional campaigns – so far most publicity campaigns have been based on luxury resorts and honeymoons, while the country has so much more to offer.

The pearl industry – which was once the second most important asset (tourism is the first) in French Polynesia's economy – is also in a shambles. Today, with the price of Tahitian pearls at one quarter of what it was in 2000, only a few larger farms and a scattering of small family-run farms are still in business.

With the county's top products, tourism and Tahitian pearls, in tatters and a firm reliance on France for everything from imports to education, popular opinion is that the country is not ready to separate itself from France's teat. Meanwhile Paris presses that French Polynesia has the highest level of autonomy of any French territory and the US$2 billion it gets from France every year is what keeps the country going.

History

Modern theories have Polynesian voyages originating from the Philippines or Taiwan, spurred on by territorial disputes or over-population. Whatever the reason, ancient

Polynesians packed up their outriggers with coconuts, *uru* (breadfruit), taro, sugar cane, dogs, pigs and chickens and headed out into the blue. These were feats of maritime prowess, not to be matched by Europeans for more than 1000 years.

European Arrival

European explorers first ventured into the region in 1595, although major expeditions didn't really get under way until the late 18th century. Lacking the navigation methods that Polynesians had developed over millennia of Pacific travel, the Europeans searched for islands in the Pacific by means of a rather random needle-in-a-haystack method. Don Alvaro de Mendaña y Neyra came upon the Marquesas Islands in 1595 on his second search for *terra australis incognita*, the nonexistent great southern continent. Mendaña named the islands after his patron, Marquesas de Mendoza, but his visit resulted in open warfare and 200 islanders were killed.

With his ship the *Dolphin,* Samuel Wallis anchored at Matavai Bay in Tahiti's lagoon in late June of 1767. He only stayed in Matavai Bay for a few weeks, just long enough to name the island King George's Land and to claim it for Britain.

With his ships *La Boudeuse* and *L'Étoile,* Louis-Antoine de Bougainville arrived on Tahiti in April 1768, less than a year after Wallis. At this time Wallis was still homeward bound, so Bougainville was completely unaware he was not the first European to set eyes on the island.

Unaware that the Union Jack had already flown over the island, Bougainville took time out to claim Tahiti for France but, like Wallis, he was soon overshadowed when the greatest Pacific explorer of them all, James Cook, arrived on the scene. In three great expeditions between 1769 and 1779, James Cook filled the map of the Pacific so comprehensively that future expeditions were reduced to joining the dots.

Already firmly established in South America, the Spanish looked upon the Pacific as their backyard and were less than happy to hear about other European navigators' visits. In 1772 Don Domingo de Boenechea sailed the *Aguilla* from Peru and anchored in the lagoon off Tautira on Tahiti Iti (Small Tahiti). For the third time, the island was claimed by a European nation.

Bounty Mutineers

In 1789 the infamous mutiny on the *Bounty* occurred after Bligh's crew had spent six long comfortable months on Tahiti. See p529 for more about the *Bounty*.

After the mutiny the mutineers returned to Tahiti and Tubuai in the Australs before sailing to a more remote hideaway on Pitcairn Island. Sixteen stayed behind on Tahiti, a move that changed the course of history.

Before the Europeans arrived, power had been a local affair. No ruler was strong enough to control more than a patch of land, and Tahiti was divided into a number of squabbling groups. However, once they realised the persuasive power of European weaponry, Tahitians pressed the *Bounty* mutineers to take sides in local conflicts. The mutineers became mercenaries to the highest bidder, the Pomare family.

That deal was the beginning of the Pomares' metamorphosis into a ruling dynasty. Pomare I, known as Tu, controlled most of Tahiti by the time he died in 1803; his son Pomare II took over, a trend that was to continue through the century.

Whalers, Missionaries & Depopulation

The London Missionary Society (LMS) landed at Tahiti's Point Vénus in March 1797 and did its best to rid the islanders of their wicked ways. Dancing, 'indecent' songs, tattoos, nudity, indiscriminate sex and even wearing flowers in the hair were banned once the missionaries got their patron, Pomare II, on their side.

Whalers and traders arrived in Polynesia in the 1790s, spreading diseases, encouraging prostitution and introducing alcohol and more weapons.

Plagued by diseases against which they had no natural immunity, the population plummeted. When Cook first visited, Tahiti's population was about 40,000. In 1800 it was less than 20,000 and by the 1820s it was down to around 6000. In the Marquesas the situation was even worse – the population dropped from 80,000 to only 2000 in one century.

Pomares & the Missionaries

After 1815 the Pomares ruled Tahiti, with Protestant missionaries advising them on government and laws, and trying to keep whalers and Australian traders at arm's length. Pomare II died in 1821, leaving his

son Pomare III to rule until his death six years later in 1827, at which point the young Queen Pomare IV assumed the throne for the next 50 years.

English Protestant missionaries were the major advisers to chiefs in the Society, Austral and Tuamotu Islands. But in the Gambier Archipelago and the Marquesas Islands, French Catholic missionaries were in control. In 1836 two French missionaries, Laval and Caret, visiting Pape'ete from the Gambier Archipelago, were caught up in this rivalry when the British promptly arrested and deported them.

French Takeover

The French saw the deportation of Laval and Caret as a national insult. Demands, claims, counterclaims, payments and apologies shuttled back and forth. In 1842 Admiral Dupetit-Thouars settled matters by turning up in *La Reine Blanche* and pointing the ship's guns at Pape'ete, forcing Queen Pomare to yield. French soldiers promptly landed, along with Catholic missionaries.

The French arrested and deported George Pritchard, the British missionary who was the queen's consul and unofficial chief adviser. Queen Pomare, still hoping for British intervention, fled to Ra'iatea in 1844 and a guerrilla rebellion broke out on several islands. The rebels were subdued and by 1846 France controlled Tahiti and Mo'orea. The queen returned to Tahiti in 1847 as a mere figurehead.

Queen Pomare died in 1877; her son, Pomare V, had little interest in the position and abdicated in 1881. French power extended to include most of the other Society Islands in 1888, although rebellions continued to rumble on Ra'iatea until almost the end of the century. The Gambier Archipelago was annexed in 1881 and the Austral Islands in 1900–01.

20th Century

Soon after the turn of the century an economic boom attracted colonists, mostly French. By 1911 there were about 3500 Europeans in the islands, adding to Chinese immigration, which had begun in 1864 with cotton production at Atimaono on Tahiti.

French Polynesia was directly involved in both world wars. In WWI almost 1000 Tahitian soldiers fought in Europe, and on 22 September 1914 two German cruisers patrolling the Pacific sank the French cruiser *Zélée* and shelled the Pape'ete market. In WWII, 5000 US soldiers were based on Bora Bora, and a 2km runway was built in 1943. Tahitian volunteers in the Pacific Battalion fought in North Africa and Europe.

In 1946 the islands became an overseas territory within the French Republic, sparking agitation for independence. A political party, the Rassemblement Démocratique des Populations Tahitiennes (RDPT; Democratic Assembly of Tahitian Populations), took centre stage on the political scene for about 10 years.

On 22 July 1957, the territory officially became French Polynesia. The 1960s were a real turning point. In 1961, Faa'a airport was built, opening French Polynesia to the world. Shortly after, the filming of *Mutiny on the Bounty* on Tahiti poured millions of dollars into the economy. In 1963 the nuclear-testing Centre Expérimentation du Pacifique (CEP; Pacific Experimentation Centre) was established at Moruroa and Fangataufa.

From 1977 to 1996, French Polynesia took over internal management and autonomy from France. The nuclear testing of the era shook Polynesia physically, socially and economically: violent protests rocked Pape'ete in 1987 and 1995, and the CEP made French Polynesia economically dependent on France. The end to nuclear testing in 1996 also meant the end of the prosperity of the previous 30 years.

The Culture

The National Psyche

If French Polynesia had a national slogan it might be '*haere maru*' (take it slow), words that often fall off the lips of Tahitians when addressing their busy French and Chinese cohabitants. It's hard not to take it slow in the islands. With one road encircling the main island of Tahiti, it's easy to get caught driving behind an old pick-up truck at 40km/h with no chance of passing; national holidays seem to close up the shops and banks once every week or so; and getting served in a restaurant can take an eternity. This can be frustrating to anyone in a hurry, but somehow it all works out: you make it to wherever you were going even if it did take twice as long, the bank can wait till tomorrow and your food arrives once you are really, really hungry. The Tahitian people know this and always seem slightly amused by anyone who tries to break the rhythm of calm.

Regardless of 'Tahiti time', Pape'ete manages to move at a pace fitting for a capital: there are traffic jams, everyone is on a mobile phone and the nightlife shakes on till 5am. The modern world is quickly infiltrating the slow pace of life and this is most evident in the younger generations.

Lifestyle

The traditional Tahitian family is an open-armed force that is the country's backbone. Although modern girls are increasingly less likely to stay home and have baby after baby, an accidental pregnancy is considered more of a blessing than a hindrance and babies are passed along to another eager, infant-loving family member. *Faamu* (adopted children) are not thought of as different from blood brothers and sisters to either the parents or siblings – although the real mother, and occasionally the father, sometimes remain a peripheral part of the child's life.

This family web is vitally important to an individual. When people first meet, the conversation usually starts with questions about family and most people are able to find a common relative within minutes. This accomplished, they are 'cousins' and fast friends.

It's not all roses in what appears to be such a warm, fuzzy family framework. Domestic violence and incest are prevalent. This is closely connected with high rates of alcoholism.

Although religion has been teaching people to think otherwise, homosexuality is generally viewed as a natural part of human existence. This tolerance is displayed most strongly by the presence of *mahu* (or the more flamboyant, transvestite-like *raerae*), effeminate men who live their lives as women. Lesbians are rare but are generally accepted.

Pakalolo (marijuana) and the Bob Marley lifestyle have been thoroughly embraced in French Polynesia, but harder drugs are rare. The exception is ice, a highly addictive meth-amphetamine that has rapidly gained popularity in the upper classes of Pape'ete.

Population

Paralleling worldwide patterns of urbanisation, French Polynesia's people have migrated towards the city and main island: 69% of the population currently make their home on Tahiti and 75% of those on Tahiti live in Pape'ete or its suburbs.

On all the islands the majority of the population lives in coastal zones. The rugged interior is virtually uninhabited.

Language

See the Language chapter on p591 for Tahitian basics.

Arts

The zealous missionaries endeavoured to wipe out all forms of 'primitive' Polynesian art and culture. They destroyed temples and carvings, banned tattooing and dancing, and generally took a lot of the joy out of life. Fortunately some traditions survived this period of cultural censorship, and in recent years there has been a revival of Polynesian culture, particularly in music, dance and tattooing.

Dance

The dances that visitors see in French Polynesia are not created for tourists: they are authentic performances and play a major part in spreading the influence of Tahitian culture. In this land of oral traditions, dance is not merely an aesthetic medium but also a way to preserve the memory of the past.

The luxury hotels offer quality dance shows about twice a week. On Tahiti and Mo'orea they are performed by semiprofessional groups, but on other islands the companies are more amateur. The best dance performances are held at the annual Heiva festival in July.

The most common forms of dance are the Otea, with fast gyrating hip action for the women and scissor-like leg movements for the men; and the Aparima, a free-flowing and graceful dance that tells a story using hand movements and song.

Music

Traditional Polynesian music, usually performed as an accompaniment to dance, is heard reverberating through the islands. Ukuleles and percussion instruments dominate this style of music, which is structured by a hypnotic and an often quite complex drum beat. Song, both traditional and religious, is also popular and important.

Modern Polynesian music by local artists is the blaring soundtrack to everyday life, whether it's in a bus, at a cafe or on the radio. Some groups also perform in hotels and bars.

Painting & Sculpture

Even today, well over a 100 years after his arrival on Tahiti, painting in the South Pacific is synonymous with Paul Gauguin, the French post-Impressionist painter. Gauguin spent much of his later life in Polynesia, and presented Europe with images of the islands that moulded the way Europeans viewed (and, arguably, continue to view) Polynesia. In his wake a number of predominantly European artists – working in media ranging from watercolour to line drawing – have also sought inspiration in the region.

Jacques Boullaire, a French artist who first travelled to Tahiti in the 1930s, produced many magnificent watercolours; reproductions of his work are readily available today.

Traditionally the best sculpture and woodcarvings have come out of the Marquesas, where fine *tiki* (sacred statues), bowls, mortars and pestles, spears and clubs are carved from rosewood, *tou* wood or in stone.

Tattoos

Since the early 1980s, tattooing has enjoyed a strong revival, becoming one of the most expressive and vibrant vehicles of Polynesian culture. Young Tahitians have delved into their ancient traditions and have brought this ancestral form of bodily adornment, with its undisputed artistic qualities, completely up to date. Today many Polynesian men and women sport magnificent tattoos as symbols of their identity.

Modern tattooing is completely for the sake of style or beautification; in ancient times it was a highly socially significant and sophisticated art.

Environment
The Land

French Polynesia is a vast, scattered collection of 118 islands and atolls that stretch across five million sq km of ocean. However, most of these volcanic blips are small and the five archipelagos have a total land area of barely 3500 sq km.

The Society Islands, the westernmost archipelago, has mountains and lagoons protected by barrier reefs, sometimes dotted with small fringing islets known as *motu*. Subdivided into the Windward and Leeward Islands, the Societies are home to more than three-quarters of French Polynesia's population.

The Tuamotus, east of the Society Islands, are classic low-lying coral atolls. The remote Marquesas, north of the Tuamotus and not far from the equator, are rugged high islands but lack barrier reefs or lagoons. Finally, there are the even more remote and scattered Australs, also high islands, and the tiny Gambier Archipelago.

Wildlife

Basically, anything that couldn't swim, float or fly to French Polynesia has been introduced; therefore the flora and fauna is limited compared with that of the west Pacific. There are no snakes but plenty of insects and about 100 species of *manu* (birds). Seabirds include terns, petrels, noddies, frigate birds and boobies.

Any dismay about the lack of animal diversity on land is quickly made up for by the quantity of underwater species – it's all here. The coral reefs provide a rich environment for sea creatures including *rori* (sea cucumber), sharks, *ono* (barracuda), manta rays, moray eels, dolphins and the endangered *honu* (turtle). In Nuku Hiva, in the Marquesas, electra dolphins, also known as pygmy orcas or melon-headed whales, gather in their hundreds in a unique phenomenon; while on Rurutu, Tahiti and Mo'orea it's possible to swim with humpback whales.

Ancient Polynesian navigators brought plants and fruits that flourished. In the 19th century missionaries and settlers imported other ornamental and commercial plants. Vegetation varies significantly from one archipelago to another. On the atolls, where the soil is poor and winds constant, bushy vegetation and coconut palms predominate. On the high islands, plant cover is more diverse and changes according to the altitude.

Marine reserves in French Polynesia are few: Scilly and Bellingshausen (remote islands in the Leeward group of Society Islands) and eight small areas within Mo'orea's lagoon are the only ones protected by the country itself. Fakarava and its surrounding atolls are a Unesco biosphere reserve. The only terrestrial reserves are the Marquesan Nature Reserves, which include the remote uninhabited islands of Motu One, Hatutu, Eiao and Motane. Several species are protected and there are limits placed on the fishing of some fish and crustaceans. Unfortunately fish continue to be caught indiscriminately and shells are still collected. Although turtles are highly protected, they

continue to be poached for their meat and their shells.

Environmental Issues

Atolls and high islands are ecologically fragile but French Polynesia has been slow to implement environmental protection. Despite a limited number of 'green' establishments that are springing up, and the rigorous requirements of public buildings and hotels to blend in with the landscape, pollution is steadily chipping away at the picture of paradise.

Although there are many low-lying atolls in French Polynesia, the effects of climate change, including rising sea level, have so far been minimal. Higher water temperatures are one of the biggest threats to the health of the country's coral reefs and, during El Niño years in particular, huge amounts of coral die, affecting the entire ecosystem.

The environmental repercussions of French nuclear testing are still hotly debated. It was confirmed in 1999 that Moruroa and Fangataufa were fissured by tests and that radioactivity has been allowed to escape from cracks in the atolls' coral cones. Evidence has been found of low-level activity in certain areas of the Gambiers but long-ranging conclusive evidence has yet to come forth.

SURVIVAL GUIDE

Directory A–Z

Accommodation

Although the brochures show exotic overwater bungalows, French Polynesia has everything from camping and hostel dormitories to five-star accommodation. However, in all categories, the balance between price and quality can be discouraging. Expect it to be expensive and enjoy the fabulous locations, if not the rooms and service.

PRACTICALITIES

» **Media** There are two Tahitian dailies, *Les Nouvelles de Tahiti* and *La Dépêche de Tahiti*, both in French.

» **Electricity** 220V, 60Hz, some deluxe hotels may have 110V supply for electric shavers.

» **Weights & measures** Metric system

Air-conditioning is often not supplied, even in some quite expensive places, but the night breeze means you can usually live without it. Many cheaper places don't supply towels or soap.

Credit cards are welcome at luxury resorts, and many midrange places accept them; however, budget places rarely do. The prices quoted in this chapter include taxes, but many places will quote you pretax prices and the add-ons might horrify you.

CAMPING & HOSTELS
Camping options aren't common in French Polynesia, but beyond the handful of places that are set up for campers, guesthouses will sometimes allow you to pitch your tent and use their facilities; you'll pay anywhere from 1200 CFP to 2500 CFP per person. Camping is possible on Tahiti, Mo'orea, Huahine, Ra'iatea, Taha'a, Bora Bora, Maupiti, Rangiroa, Tikehau, Mataiva and Tubuai. You may need to rethink camping if it's raining too hard. Some guesthouses have dorm beds ranging from 2000 CFP to 3500 CFP per person per night.

HOTELS
A hotel that is neither a resort nor a pension is a rare beast in French Polynesia. Anything in the top-end price category is a resort, while midrange and budget offerings are most often pensions. There are a few business-oriented hotels in Pape'ete that are not enticing to anyone on a real holiday (think no beach, no garden and lots of traffic).

PENSIONS
Pensions are a godsend for travellers who baulk at the prices (and gloss) of the big hotels. These little establishments, generally family affairs, are great places to meet locals and other travellers. At the lower end of the scale, brace yourself for cold showers, lumpy pillows and thin walls, but lap up the charm, interesting discussions and artistic touches that are often part and parcel of the experience. Upmarket pensions can be private, have lots of amenities and be downright luxurious.

Many pensions, particularly on islands where there are few to no other eating options available, offer half board (or demi-pension), which means breakfast and dinner. Young children usually stay for free, and children up to about 12 usually pay half price.

Think ahead in terms of money as many pensions do not take credit cards.

RESORTS

If you are ever going to pamper yourself silly, French Polynesia is a great place to do it. Some of the top hotels are on isolated *motu* and can only be reached by boat. Four- and five-star hotels are found on Tahiti, Mo'orea, Bora Bora, Huahine, Ra'iatea, Tikehau, Taha'a, Rangiroa, Hiva Oa, Manihi and Nuku Hiva. You can expect restaurants, bars, swimming pool, a shop or two and a well-organised activities desk. Glass-bottomed coffee tables, which look straight down into the lagoon, have become standard features of the over-water bungalows. The prices are just as dazzling: expect to pay from 45,000 CFP to 250,000 CFP a night, not including meals.

PRICE RANGES

The following price ranges refer to a double room with bathroom in high season. Unless otherwise stated tax of 14% is included in the price.

$ less than 10,000 CFP

$$ 10,000–20,000 CFP

$$$ more than 20,000 CFP

Business Hours

The following are common business hours in French Polynesia; exceptions are noted in reviews.

Banks & post offices 8am to noon and 1.30pm to 5pm Monday to Thursday, 8am to noon and 1pm to 3pm Friday.

Restaurants 11am to 10pm (on touristy islands).

Shops 7.30am to 11.30am and 1.30pm to 5pm Monday to Friday, 7.30am to 11.30am Saturday.

Children

Fire the babysitter and bring the kids: French Polynesia is a great destination to explore with children. There are no major health concerns, the climate is good and the food is easy to navigate. Most locals have a number of children themselves and will not be troubled by a screaming child at the next table, should the treasure be throwing a tantrum over dinner.

Consulates

Given that French Polynesia is not an independent country, there are no foreign embassies, only consulates, and many countries are represented in Pape'ete by honorary consuls.

The following honorary consuls and diplomatic representatives are all on Tahiti. Many are just single representatives and do not have official offices, so you'll have to call them.

Australia & Canada (☏46 88 53; service@mobil.pf; Pape'ete)

New Zealand (☏54 07 40; nzcgnou@offra tel. nc; c/- Air New Zealand, Vaima Centre, Pape'ete)

USA (☏42 65 35; usconsul@mail.pf; US Info, Centre Tamanu, Puna'auia)

Festivals & Events

Chinese New Year (January or February) Usually falling between late January and mid-February, the New Year is ushered in with dancing, martial arts displays and fireworks.

Festival international du film documentaire océanien (FIFO; January) A reputable film festival with a focus on South Pacific countries.

Tahiti Nui Marathon (February) One thousand runners gather on Mo'orea for this long-established fundraising event along a flat course past spectacular scenery.

Arrival of the First Missionaries (5 March) The landing of the first LMS missionaries is re-enacted at Point Vénus on Tahiti Nui. Celebrations are held at Protestant churches on Tahiti and Mo'orea, and in Tipaerui and Afareaitu.

Beauty Contests (April–May) Many contests are held ahead of the Miss Tahiti and Miss Heiva i Tahiti contests in June (Mr Tahiti contests are also held).

Miss Tahiti & Miss Heiva i Tahiti contests (June–July) Winners of beauty contests around the archipelago in the last 12 months gather in Pape'ete to vie for the chance to represent French Polynesia around the world. Miss Heiva reigns for the month-long Heiva celebrations.

Heiva i Tahiti (July, August) This major Polynesian festival, held in Pape'ete, includes traditional demonstrations throughout July. Mini-Heiva events take place on other islands in August.

Billabong Tahiti Pro Surfing Tournament (August) Three days of international-level surfing in the big waves of Teahupoo (Tahiti).

Hawaiki Nui Canoe Race (November) The major sporting event of the year.

All Saints' Day (1 November) Graves are cleaned and decorated in an explosion of flowers; families sing hymns in candlelit cemeteries.

Tiare Tahiti Days (1–2 December) The national flower is celebrated.

Marquesas Arts Festival (December) A major arts festival at either 'Ua Pou, Nuku Hiva or Hiva Oa, celebrating Marquesan identity. It's held once every four years – the next edition is scheduled in 2015.

Food

Restaurant review price indicators are based on the cost of a main course.

$ less than 1200 CFP

$$ 1200–2000 CFP

$$$ more than 2000 CFP

Internet Access

Internet cafes can be found on all the major islands – although the ones on the smaller islands often have only ancient computers and slow connections. Most post offices also have internet posts. Many top-end hotels offer internet access to their guests (sometimes at ridiculously high prices), and access elsewhere is fairly straightforward. You'll generally pay around 900 CFP per hour.

If you're toting your own computer through the Society, Marquesas or Austral Islands, consider buying a prepaid **Mana Pass** (per hr 500 CFP; available at www.manaspot. pf or local post offices) to access the internet at 'Mana Spots' (wi-fi zones) in post offices and at some hotels, restaurants and public areas. You'll find other networks that enable wi-fi access, such as **Iaoranet** (www.iaoranet.pf) and **Hotspot-wdg** (www.webdatagest-tahiti.com). Check the website for locations.

Internet Resources

Lonely Planet (www.lonelyplanet.com/tahiti-and-french-polynesia)

Tahiti Explorer (www.tahitiexplorer.com)

Tahiti Heritage (www.tahitiheritage.pf)

Tahiti Tourisme (www.tahiti-tourisme.com)

Money

The unit of currency in French Polynesia is the Cour de Franc Pacifique (CFP), referred to in English as 'the Pacific Franc'. There are coins of one, two, five, 10, 20, 50 and 100 CFP; and notes of 500, 1000, 5000 and 10,000 CFP. The CFP is pegged to the euro.

Tipping and bargaining are not traditionally part of Polynesian culture.

All prices given in this book are inclusive of tax.

ATMs ATMs will give you cash via Visa, MasterCard, Cirrus or Maestro networks. International cards generally work only at Banque Socredo ATMs; luckily most islands have at least one of these. You'll need a four-digit pin number.

Credit Cards All top-end and midrange hotels, restaurants, jewellery shops, dive centres and the bigger supermarkets accept credit cards, sometimes exclusively Visa or MasterCard. You can also pay for Air Tahiti flights with a card. Most budget guesthouses and many tour operators don't accept credit cards. Check with your bank before you leave home to ensure that the card you plan to use to withdraw cash doesn't have a low daily or weekly limit.

Moneychangers Banque de Tahiti, Banque de Polynésie and Banque Socredo will change money in most major currencies, but expect fairly hefty bank charges for changing money (at least 550 CFP per transaction). You are better off exchanging larger sums of money (that is, making fewer transactions) than smaller amounts.

Telephone

Public phone boxes requiring a prepaid phonecard are becoming harder to find; buy phonecards from post offices, newsagencies, shops and even some supermarkets in 1000 CFP, 2000 CFP and 5000 CFP denominations.

There are no area codes in French Polynesia. From a landline, local phone calls cost 17 CFP per minute or 22 CFP per minute to a mobile phone. To call overseas, dial ☏00 plus the country code followed by the phone number. French Polynesia's country code is ☏689.

Mobile (Cell) Phones Mobile phone services operate on 900 GSM and 98% of the inhabited islands have cellular coverage. SIM cards are available for 5900 CFP at most post offices on main islands bearing a 'Vini' sign and this price includes one hour of local minutes. Talk isn't cheap however: calls from a mobile cost 30 CFP to 50 CFP per minute. Many foreign

mobile services have coverage in Tahiti but roaming fees are usually quite high.

Time

French Polynesia is 10 hours behind London, two to three hours behind Los Angeles and three hours ahead of Sydney; the region is just two hours east of the International Date Line. The Marquesas are a half-hour ahead of the rest of French Polynesia (noon on Tahiti is 12.30pm in the Marquesas). Gambier Archipelago time is one hour ahead of Tahiti time.

Tourist Information

The main and only real tourist office is the **Gie Tahiti Manava visitors information centre** (☑50 57 00; www.tahiti-tourisme.com; Fare Manihini, Blvd Pomare; ⊘7.30am-5pm Mon-Fri, 8am-noon Sat & public holidays) in the centre of Pape'ete.

For information before you leave home, go to the **Tahiti Tourisme** (www.tahiti-tourisme.com) website, which has several international tourism office links.

Visas

Everyone needs a passport to visit French Polynesia. The regulations are much the same as for France: if you need a visa to visit France then you'll need one to visit French Polynesia. Anyone from an EU country can stay for up to three months without a visa, as can Australians and citizens of a number of other European countries, including Switzerland.

Citizens of Argentina, Canada, Chile, Japan, Mexico, New Zealand, the USA and some other European countries are able to stay for up to one month without a visa. Other nationalities need a visa, which can be applied for at French Embassies.

Apart from permanent residents and French citizens, all visitors to French Polynesia need to have an onward or return ticket.

Women Travellers

French Polynesia is a great place for solo women. Local women are very much a part of public life in the region, and it's not unusual to see Polynesian women out drinking beer together or walking alone, so you will probably feel pretty comfortable following suit.

It is a sad reality that women are still required to exercise care, particularly at night,

but this is the case worldwide. As with anywhere in the world, give drunks and their beer breath a wide berth.

Perhaps it's the locals getting their own back after centuries of European men ogling Polynesian women, but there is reportedly a 'tradition' of Peeping Toms in French Polynesia, mainly in the outer islands. Take special care in places that seem to offer opportunities for spying on guests, particularly in the showers, and make sure your room is secure.

Getting There & Away

Air

Faa'a International Airport (www.tahiti-aeroport.pf), on Tahiti, is the only international airport in French Polynesia. It's on the outskirts of Pape'ete, about 5km west of the capital.

A number of international airlines serve French Polynesia. Airline offices in Pape'ete

Aircalin (www.aircalin.nc)

Air France (www.airfrance.com)

Air New Zealand (www.airnz.com)

Air Tahiti Nui (www.airtahitinui.com)

Hawaiian Airlines (www.hawaiianair.com)

Lan (www.lan.com)

Flights go to Tahiti direct from Los Angeles, Honolulu, Sydney, Auckland, Tokyo, Easter Island (with connections to Santiago, Chile) and New Caledonia. The interior airline, **Air Tahiti** (www.airtahiti.pf), has flights once a week to the Cook Islands. Tahiti is a popular stop on round-the-world (RTW) tickets (see p582).

There is no departure tax within French Polynesia.

Sea

Travelling to French Polynesia by yacht is entirely feasible: you can often pick up crewing positions from North America, Australia or NZ, or in the islands; ask at yacht clubs in San Diego, LA, San Francisco, Honolulu, Sydney, Cairns or Auckland.

It takes about a month to sail from the US west coast to Hawai'i and another month south from there to the Marquesas; with stops, another month takes you west to Tahiti and the Society Islands. Then it's another long leg southwest to Australia or New Zealand.

Getting Around

Getting around French Polynesia is half the fun. Travelling between islands involves flights or boat travel and, thanks to French Government financial support, travel to the larger and more densely populated islands is relatively easy and reasonably priced.

Air

With the exception of a few charter operations, flying within French Polynesia means **Air Tahiti** (☎86 42 42; www.airtahiti.pf). Air Tahiti flies to 47 islands in all five of the major island groups.

Flight frequencies ebb and flow with the seasons, and in the July–August peak season, extra flights are scheduled. Air Tahiti publishes a useful flight schedule booklet (available from the airport domestic check-in counter), which is essential reading for anyone planning a complex trip around the islands. If you are making reservations from afar, you can reserve online and pay by credit card.

Note that Air Tahiti and Air Tahiti Nui are different airlines; Air Tahiti Nui is the international carrier, while Air Tahiti operates domestic flights only.

AIR PASSES

Several passes allow you to save on visiting multiple islands: all require you to begin your trip in Pape'ete and limit the number of transits through Pape'ete. You are only allowed one stopover on each island but you can transit on an island as long as the flight number does not change. Stopping at an island to change flights counts as a stopover.

Passes are valid for 28 days and all flights (except between Pape'ete and Mo'orea) must be booked at the beginning. Once you've taken the first flight, the routing cannot be changed and the fare is nonrefundable. There may be restrictions on which 'colour' flights you can use.

Check Air Tahiti's website for all details about air passes.

DISCOUNT CARDS

Air Tahiti offers several cards that let you buy tickets at reduced prices, depending on whether the flight is classified as blue, white or red.

If you're aged under 25, a *Carte Jeunes* (Youth Card), and if you're over 50 a *Carte Marama* (Third Age Card), gives you up to 50% reductions (depending on the colour of the flight) and costs 1500 CFP. A *Carte*

Famille (Family Card) gives adults up to 50% and children up to 75% discount. It costs 2500 CFP. You need a passport and photos and for the Family Card the kids' birth certificates.

These cards are issued on the spot, only in Pape'ete.

Bicycle

French Polynesia is an ideal region to explore by bike. Distances are manageable, the coast roads are generally flat, traffic is light (outside Pape'ete) and you can travel at your own pace. Bicycles can often be rented for about 1500 CFP per day, and many guesthouses have bicycles for their guests, sometimes for free, though you might be riding an old rattler. A mountain bike is ideal for some of the rougher roads and it's even worth bringing your trusty steed with you; they're accepted on all the interisland ships.

Boat

Boat travel within the Society group isn't as easy as you'd hope unless you're only going to Mo'orea or taking a cruise or sailboat. A number of companies shuttle back and forth between Tahiti and Mo'orea each day; other routes between the islands are less frequent but served at least twice a week by cargo vessels.

In the other archipelagos travel by boat is more difficult. If you are short on time and keen to travel beyond the Society Islands you may need to consider flying at least some of the way.

Cargo ships, also known as *goélettes,* are principally involved in freight transport. Some take passengers, however, and for those who want to get off the beaten trail such a voyage can, depending on the circumstances, be anything from a memorable experience to an outright nightmare.

FERRY & CARGO SHIP

Aranui (www.aranui.com) This is a veritable institution, taking freight and passengers on 16 trips a year from Pape'ete to the Marquesas (see the boxed text, p407).

Aremiti V & Aremiti Ferry (www.aremiti. net) The Aremiti Ferry is a car ferry while the *Aremiti V* is a high-speed catamaran. The two boats jet between Tahiti and Mo'orea six or more times daily. It takes between 30 minutes and an hour.

Aremiti 4 (www.aremiti.net) This on and off service relaunched at the end of 2011

and hopefully, it will stay in business. The Pape'ete–Huahine–Ra'iatea–Bora Bora round trip leaves Pape'ete once a week.

Cobia III (☑43 36 43) A small cargo boat (think lots more wave movement) that travels Pape'ete–Kaukura–Arutua–Apataki–Fakarava–Pape'ete once a week.

Hawaiki Nui (☑54 99 54) This cargo ship travels the Society Islands on a twice-weekly schedule.

Kura Ora II & Kura Ora IV (☑45 55 45) These boats make a trip every 15 days to the remote atolls of the central and eastern Tuamotus, including Anaa, Hao and Makemo. The complete trip takes two to three weeks.

Mareva Nui (☑42 25 53) Runs a circuit from Pape'ete taking in Makatea, Mataiva, Tikehau, Rangiroa, Ahe, Manihi, Takaroa, Takapoto, Raraka, Kauehi, Aratika, Fakarava, Arutua, Apataki, Niau and Kaukura.

Maupiti Express (www.maupitiexpress.com) This passenger boat takes regular trips between Bora Bora and Maupiti, and Bora Bora to Taha'a and Ra'iatea.

Nuku Hau (☑54 99 54; contact@stim.pf) Once a month this boat takes a 15-day circuit from Pape'ete to Rikitea in the Gambier Archipelago via a few eastern Tuamotu atolls.

Saint-Xavier Maris-Stella (☑42 23 58; maris-stella@mail.pf) Travels a circuit from Pape'ete every 15 days, taking in Mataiva, Tikehau, Rangiroa, Ahe, Manihi, Takaroa, Takapoto, Arutua, Apataki, Aretika, Kaukura, Toau, Fakarava, Kauehi, Raraka and Niau. This is the most comfortable option for the Tuamotus but it's still pretty grubby.

Taporo VI & VII (☑41 25 35, 42 63 93) This boat runs cargo to Huahine, Ra'iatea, Bora Bora and Tah'aa twice per week. It rarely takes tourists.

Tuhaa Pae IV (☑50 96 05, 41 36 06; snathp@mail.pf) This new boat started chugging to the Australs in early 2012, leaving Pape'ete three times a month. It stops at Rurutu, Tubuai, Rimatara and Raivavae on every trip, Rapa once every two months. You can choose between berths and air-con cabins.

YACHT
French Polynesia is a popular yachting destination. See p379 for more information.

Bus

French Polynesia doesn't have much of a public transport system, and Tahiti is the only island where public transport is even an option. The colourful, old *le trucks* (trucks with bench seats in the back for passengers) have been almost entirely replaced now by a less personable, but more modern fleet of proper air-con buses. Buses stop at designated spots (marked with a blue clock) and supposedly run on a schedule – although times are hardly regular.

Car & Scooter

If you want to explore the larger islands of the Society group at your own pace, it is well worth renting a car.

DRIVING LICENCE

Car-hire agencies in French Polynesia only ask to see your national driving licence, so an international driving licence is unnecessary.

HIRE

There are many different car-hire agencies on the more touristy islands, but the prices really don't vary much. For a small car, expect to pay from 10,000 CFP per day, which includes unlimited kilometres and insurance.

At certain times of year (July, August and New Year's Eve), it's wise to book vehicles a few days in advance; on the smaller islands it's best to always book ahead as the number of cars are limited. You'll need a credit card, of course.

On the Marquesas, rental vehicles are mainly 4WDs complete with a driver. Rental without a driver is possible only on Atuona (Hiva Oa) and Taiohae (Nuku Hiva).

Avis and Europcar both hire scooters on a number of islands. You'll pay around 6000 CFP a day. After numerous accidents there are no scooters for hire on Tahiti.

ROAD RULES

Driving is on the right-hand side in French Polynesia. Although the accident statistics are pretty grim, driving in French Polynesia is not difficult, and the traffic is light almost everywhere apart from the busy coastal strip around Pape'ete on Tahiti. However, the overtaking habits of locals can sometimes get the heart rate up. Beware of drunk drivers at night, and of pedestrians and children who may not be used to traffic, particularly in more remote locations.

Tonga

Best Eco-Accommodation

» 'Eua'iki Island Eco-Resort (p461)
» Hideaway (p444)
» Port Wine Guest House (p455)
» Serenity Beaches (p450)
» Matafonua Lodge (p449)

Best Cafes

» Friends Café (p439)
» Mariner's Cafe (p448)
» Café Tropicana (p458)
» Aquarium Café (p458)
» Café Escape (p440)

Why Go?

Say goodbye to tourist hype – you're now in the Kingdom of Tonga. This is a country that survives on international aid and remittances sent from Tongans living overseas. You may get the impression that most Tongans would prefer visitors to donate their dollars and not leave the airport; expats seem determined to build a tourist industry, but most of the locals just don't seem to care. In some ways, this is incredibly refreshing and in others incredibly frustrating. You won't have to try to gain a cultural experience – it's all around.

There's no doubting the natural beauty of Tonga. Travellers choose the pace of their adventure here, mixing sun-and-sand holidays with unique and intrepid experiences. Throw away any preconceived ideas, slow down to the pace of local life, and you'll love the place. Expect too much and you'll likely go away frustrated.

When to Go
Nuka'alofa

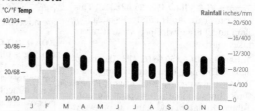

Jun–Oct Humpback whales frolic in the waters throughout Tonga. A rare chance to swim with whales!

May–Oct The cooler, dryer, less humid season when yachties turn up to play.

Nov–Apr Warm and wet but fine for water sports. Cyclone season, but they rarely hit Tonga.

Connections

Most visitors fly into Tonga's only international airport on the main island of Tongatapu. From there, air is the fastest and most comfortable way to head to the other islands. Chathams Pacific is the sole domestic airline, offering friendly, reliable service and various options with its Kingdom air passes.

After Tonga's disastrous ferry tragedy of 2009, visitors may balk at the idea of boarding a boat. The good news is that a new ferry, donated by the Japanese government, now plies the waters between Tongatapu and Vava'u (via Ha'apai) weekly. Other ferries connect Tongatapu with nearby 'Eua.

Boat travel is the way to reach outer islands in Ha'apai and Vava'u.

ITINERARIES

One Week

After a bit of recovery time in Friends Café in Nuku'alofa, explore the main island of Tongatapu and its sights. This is easiest as part of an island day tour. Fly north to Vava'u and experience this magical group of islands, beaches, reefs and turquoise waterways. All sorts of water activities and adventures await. Fly back to Tongatapu the day before your international flight out.

Two weeks

With a bit more time, throw in a visit to Ha'apai on your way back south from Vava'u. One of Tonga's best-kept secrets, the islands of Ha'apai offer plenty to the intrepid traveller. Once back on Tongatapu, make the effort to visit 'Eua, a unique ecotourism destination known for its hiking, rainforest and red shining parrot.

One Month

Consider using ferries to get between islands and slip into 'Tonga time'. A stay out at Ha'atafu Beach is a great option on Tongatapu. Lengthen your stays in Vava'u, Ha'apai and on 'Eua. A trip to the Niuas could even be on the cards.

Top Tonga Travel Tips

» Patience is a virtue...and Tongan time is a flexible entity! Slow down.

» Respectful dress is important to Tongans.

» Swimsuits should be worn only at resorts. Tongans swim fully dressed.

» Tongan law prohibits being in a public place without a shirt.

» 'Keeping face' is extremely important in Tonga. If things don't meet your expectations, don't make things worse by waving and shouting about it.

» Tonga closes down on Sundays.

AT A GLANCE

Currency Tongan pa'anga (T$)

Language Tongan, English

Mobile phones Good coverage.

Money ATMs on Tongatapu, Vava'u only; banks open Monday to Friday.

Visas 31 days for most nationalities without a visa.

Fast Facts

» **Capital** Nuku'alofa
» **Country code** 676
» **Emergency** 911
» **Land area** 747 sq km
» **Population** 106,000

Exchange Rates

Australia	AU$1	T$1.80
Canada	C$	T$1.75
Europe	€1	T$2.25
Japan	¥100	T$2.25
New Zealand	NZ$	T$1.45
UK	UK£1	T$2.80
USA	US$1	T$1.80

For current exchange rates see www.xe.com.

Set Your Budget

» **Budget hotel room** T$60
» **Two-course evening meal** T$25
» **Beer at a bar** T$6
» **Whale-watching tour** T$250
» **Tongatapu–Vava'u flight** T$230

Tonga Highlights

1 Swim with the **humpback whales** (p452)

2 **Kayak** (p454 and p454) among pristine waterways, islands and deserted beaches

3 Hike through **'Eua's** (p443) tropical rainforests

4 Marvel at the imposing **Ha'amonga 'a Maui Trilithon** (p442), the 'Stonehenge of the South Pacific'

5 Taste the suckling pig and enjoy the fire dance at the **Oholei Beach Feast & Show** (p441)

6 Swim into **Swallows' Cave** (p459) on Kapa island in Vava'u

7 Explore remote **Niuafo'ou** (Tin Can Island; p461) that resembles a doughnut floating in the sea

8 Laze on **Uoleva's** (p450) spectacular beach and, if you're lucky, watch whales breaching offshore

9 Take a photo of the infamous **fishing pigs** (p441) on Tongatapu's northeastern coast

10 Sail the turquoise waters of **Vava'u** (p453), one of the most popular cruising areas in the world

176°W · 174°W

7 Niuafo'ou

NIUA GROUP

Tafahi

Niuatoputapu

16°S

SOUTH PACIFIC OCEAN

⊕ N

0   100 km
0   50 miles

Fonualei

18°S · Toku

VAVA'U GROUP

2
10 Vava'u
⊙ Neiafu

Late ⊙

6

Swallows' Cave

20°S

'Ofolanga

Kao
Tofua
Ha'ano

HA'APAI GROUP

Ha'afeva
Pangai
Foa
⊙ Lifuka

Kotu
Tungua

8 Uoleva

Tokulu
'O'ua Uiha

Nomuka
Fonuafo'ou
Nomuk'iki
Telekivava'u

Hunga Tonga

Hunga Ha'apai

2

Ha'amonga'a Maui Trilithon

NUKU'ALOFA ✪ **4** 'Eue'iki

Tongatapu **5** **9** Fishing Pigs

Oholei Beach

3 'Eua

TONGATAPU GROUP

Tonga Trench

'Ata ⊙

⊙ Vityaz Deep (10,882m)

To Minerva Reef (300km, See Inset)

Same Scale as Main Map

Minerva Reef

Inset

TONGATAPU

POP 75,000 / AREA 260 SQ KM

Tongatapu (Sacred South) is the main island – the landing and launching pad for most activity in Tonga.

Most of the island's population lives in bustling Nuku'alofa (Abode of Love) and its surrounding villages. Outside of the capital, the island is comprised of plots of agricultural land, small villages and plenty of churches.

Most archaeological sights – such as Lapaha and Ha'amonga 'a Maui Trilithon – are found on Tongatapu's eastern side, which also features caves, calm sandy coves and the airport. To the west is the wilder surf coast and the Mapu'a Vaca blowholes.

ⓘ Information

INTERNET ACCESS

Nuku'alofa has many internet cafes. Tops are the following:

Café Escape (Map p436; free for customers)

Friends Café (Map p436; free for customers)

MEDICAL SERVICES

Vaiola Hospital (off Map p436; ☎23200; Taufa'ahau Rd) Recommended only for emergencies and after-hours needs.

Village Mission Pharmacy (Map p436; ☎27522; vmissp@hotmail.com; 'Unga Rd; ⊙8.30am-5pm Mon, Tue, Thu & Fri, 9am-noon Wed & Sat) There is a doctor either here or at its sister clinic, the Village Mission Clinic (Map p434; ☎29052) in Ha'ateiho, 5km south of Nuku'alofa. The central pharmacy is well stocked.

MONEY

ANZ (Map p436; www.anz.com/tonga) ANZ has two branches and nine ATMs around Tongatapu.

Westpac Bank of Tonga (Map p436; www.westpac.to) Three branches and six ATMs around Tongatapu, including an ATM outside arrivals at Fua'amotu International Airport.

POST

Post office (Map p436; Taufa'ahau Rd) This office has a poste restante window next to the main entrance; address to: Post Restante, GPO, Nuku'alofa, Kingdom of Tonga.

TOURIST INFORMATION

Friends Tourist Centre (Map p436; ☎26323; www.friendstonga.com; Taufa'ahau Rd; ⊙8am-10pm Mon-Fri, 8am-7.30pm Sat) A switched-on private tour-booking office with plenty of details on what's happening around the kingdom.

Tonga Visitors Bureau (TVB; Map p436; ☎25334; www.thekingdomoftonga.com; Vuna Rd; ⊙8.30am-4.30pm Mon-Fri, 9am-12.30pm Sat) A government-run institution with information on Tonga.

TRAVEL AGENCIES

Jetsave Taufonua (Map p436; ☎23052; www.taufonua.com; Fund Management Bldg, Taufa'ahau Rd) Books day tours and domestic package holidays to all island groups.

Jones Travel & Tours (Map p436; ☎23423; www.tonga-travel.travel; cnr Taufa'ahau & Wellington Rds)

Teta Tours (Map p436; ☎23363; www.teta tourstonga.to/tetatourstonga.to; cnr Wellington & Railway Rds)

ⓘ Getting There & Away

See p469 for information on transport between Tongatapu and other countries.

AIR Fua'amotu International Airport is 21km southeast and a 30-minute drive from Nuku'alofa.

Chathams Pacific (Map p436; ☎28852; www.chathamspacific.com) Services 'Eua, Ha'apai, Vava'u and the Niuas from the domestic terminal. Transfers between the international and domestic terminals cost T$5 for a taxi.

Offices in Nuku'alofa of airlines connecting Tongatapu with other Pacific destinations:

Air New Zealand (Map p436; ☎23192; www.airnz.co.nz; Vuna Rd) The Air New Zealand Travel Centre is down on the waterfront.

Fiji Airways (formerly Air Pacific; Map p436; ☎23423; www.airpacific.com; Vuna Rd) Down opposite the wharves on the waterfront.

Virgin Australia (formerly Pacific Blue; Map p436; ☎26033; www.virginaustralia.com; Taufa'ahau Rd)

BOAT MV *'Otuanga'ofa* connects Tongatapu with Ha'apai, Vava'u and the Niuas. Other vessels provide frequent services between Tongatapu and 'Eua. See p470 for details of schedules and fares.

ⓘ Getting Around

TO/FROM THE AIRPORT Taxis meet all incoming flights, charging T$40 between the airport and Nuku'alofa. Watch out for drivers taking you to a different guesthouse than you asked for when you arrive in Nuku'alofa. Many hotels and guesthouses arrange transfers if you pre-book (some for free). Shuttles will take you into town for T$15 to T$25 per person.

The international and domestic airports are separate; it's a T$5 taxi fare between them. The Flying Fox Cafe is at the domestic airport.

BICYCLE Some guesthouses have bicycles for guest use. **Bicycle Rental** (Map p436; Vuna Rd; half-/full-day bicycle hire T$8/15) is next to the International Dateline Hotel. Ask for the newest bicycle they've got.

Tongatapu

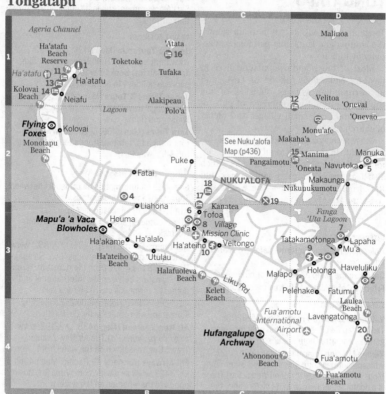

BOAT The offshore island resorts (see p443) all provide boat transport.

BUS Buses are run privately. There are no public buses and no fixed timetables. Nuku'alofa's two bus terminals are on the waterfront on Vuna Rd.

Buses to outlying areas of Tongatapu depart from the western bus terminal (Map p436), close to Vuna Wharf. Nuku'alofa buses leave from the eastern bus terminal (Map p436), opposite the TVB. Fares range from 70 *seniti* to T$1.70. Bus services run from about 8am to 5pm, and there are no buses on Sunday. In urban areas, bus stops are marked with a small sign reading '*Pasi*'. Elsewhere, flag down a bus by waving.

CAR & MINIBUS Legally, you must get a Tongan driving licence from the police (costing a whopping T$60) before heading out. Contact Fab and Sunshine by telephone, as they can deliver rental cars to you.

Avis (Map p436; ☎21179; www.avis.com; Fund Management Bldg, Taufa'ahau Rd) From T$80 per day.

Fab Rentals (☎23077; leeintonga@gmail.com) Cars and vans from T$50 per day, including insurance and door-to-door service.

Sunshine Rental Cars (☎23848; sunshineren talcars@gmail.com) Cars from T$50 per day.

TAXI Taxis charge a minimum fare of T$3 for the first kilometre and T$1.50 for each additional kilometre. Ask for the fare to your destination before you agree to pay or get in. Taxis have a 'T' on the licence plate. They're not permitted to operate on Sunday, but some guesthouses know secret Sunday taxi suppliers.

Atelaite Taxi (☎23919)

Holiday Taxi (☎25655)

Wellington Taxi (☎24744)

Nuku'alofa

POP 23,000

Nuku'alofa is the kingdom's seat of government and the home of the royal family. While it may not fulfil a vision of Pacific

Tongatapu

◎ Top Sights

◎ Sights

◔ Activities, Courses & Tours

◚ Sleeping

◙ Eating

◔ Entertainment

paradise, Tonga's 'big smoke' (sometimes unkindly referred to as 'dirty nuke') still has a little charm and promise if you blow the dust from its surface and ignore the still-visible scars of the 2006 pro-democracy riots. Its broad waterfront strip provides impressive views across the bay to beautiful coral islands (just a boat ride away); there's a bustling market and enviable-quality dining options for a place its size. You'll still find plenty of pigs and chickens roaming the back streets.

◎ Sights

Royal Palace   PALACE
(Map p436) Surrounded by large lawns and Norfolk pines, the white Victorian-style Royal Palace, erected in 1867, is a symbol of Tonga to the rest of the world. The palace grounds are not open to visitors but you can get a good view from the waterfront area on the west side.

Royal Tombs   TOMBS
(Map p436) Mala'ekula, the large park-like area opposite the basilica, has been the resting place of the royals since 1893. It's off limits to the public but you can peer through the crested perimeter fence.

Centenary Chapel   CHURCH
(Map p436) Royal watchers and rubber-neckers (regardless of denomination) head here to catch a glimpse of members of the royal family at a Sunday service and to hear the magnificent, booming singing of the congregation. Dress well; you can expect a friendly reception if you do.

Nuku'alofa

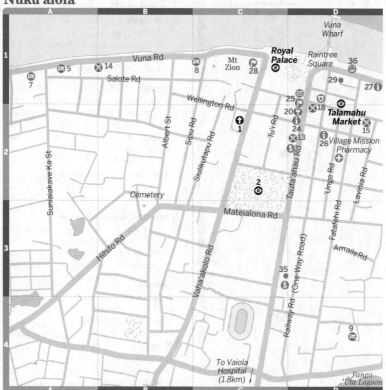

Talamahu Market MARKET

(Map p436; Salote Rd; ⊙early morning-4.30pm Mon-Sat) One of Nuku'alofa's most interesting sights is Talamahu, the kingdom's main fresh-produce hub. You'll find produce in handmade woven-frond baskets, branches of bananas, colourful pyramids of weighed-out produce and a few food stands – plus excellent Tongan arts and crafts. It's a hive of activity, particularly on Saturday mornings.

🏃 Activities

Subaquatic adventures around Tongatapu range from snorkelling around the wreck off Pangaimotu Island to diving 'Eua's unique sea caves. Tongatapu's northwest coast, off Ha'atafu Beach, is renowned for its surf.

On land, Tongatapu is relatively flat so exploring by bicycle is an option for the energetic. See p469 for info on bicycle hire.

You can also head out to the islands you can see from Nuku'alofa – Pangaimotu, Fafá or 'Atata (see p443) – for a day trip that could include transfers, swimming, snorkelling and lunch. They're a good option on Sunday, when Tonga takes a 24-hour break.

Deep Blue Diving DIVING, FISHING

(Map p436; ☑27676; www.deepbluediving.to; Faua Jetty) Offers a number of diving options, its major drawcards being 'Eua's enormous sea caves and the beautiful, uninhabited islands north of Tongatapu. Full-day bottom-fishing tours are A$300 for up to four anglers. Deep Blue also runs whale-swim trips out of Tongatapu (A$150) and 'Eua (A$110) and has Deep Blue Lodge, providing accommodation five minutes' walk from central Nuku'alofa.

Tonga Charters FISHING

(☑8832052; www.tonga-charters.com) Game fishing (half/full day T$720/1000 per person) and spear-fishing (full day T$180 per person) are on offer here.

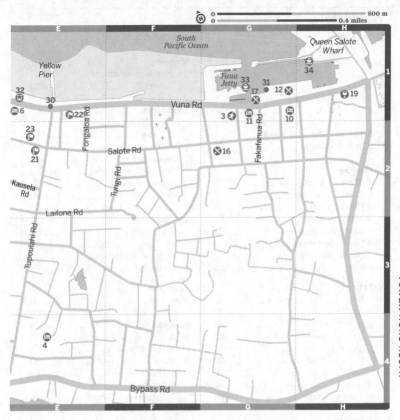

Golf course GOLF
(Map p434; ☏8704194) Take a swing at Tonga's only golf course, a relaxed nine-hole affair at 'Atele on the way to the airport. Green fees are T$20/30 for nine/18 holes with rental gear included.

Fatai Kayak Adventures KAYAKING
(Map p434; ☏7745832; www.fataiglobal.com) Based in Holonga Village in eastern Tongatapu, this company runs kayak adventure tours and kayak rentals. Its Island Hop Adventure takes paddlers out to Pangaimotu and Makaha'a islands (a 6½-hour tour with two hours of paddling is US$138 per person). Rental kayaks cost US$20/30 per half/full day.

Seastar Yacht Charters SAILING
(☏22800; www.seastarsailing.com) Head out for day or overnight cruising, or charter for a week. Look at the website for all the options.

Ha'atafu Beach Resort SURFING
(Map p434; ☏41088; www.surfingtonga.com) Steve Burling knows it all from his 28 years' surfing in Tonga. Check out his informative website.

☞ Tours

Tongatapu's main sights can be comfortably covered in a day tour of the island. There are a number of operators charging about the same rate and most of the sleeping options will have one they recommend in particular. Considering the cost of getting a Tongan driving licence, taking an island tour beats getting a rental car and trying to do it yourself. An island tour is a good option for Sunday.

Toni's Tours GUIDED TOUR
(☏21049, 7748720; www.tonisguesthouse.com; tours T$57.50) Toni's popular island tours run daily (minimum three people) and take in

Nuku'alofa

all the Tongatapu sights. Take a sun hat, sunscreen and swimming gear.

Supa Tours   GUIDED TOUR
(☑7716450; phlatohi@kalianet.to) Big John's island tours operate daily.

🛏 Sleeping

Rental houses and flats are listed at the TVB and on the bulletin board at Friends Tourist Centre (see p445).

Ali Baba's Guest House   GUESTHOUSE $$
(Map p436; ☑25154, 8786076; www.alibaba guesthouse.com; off Tupoulahi Rd, Ngele'ia; shared bathroom s/d/f incl breakfast T$60/80/110, private bathroom d/f incl breakfast T$110/130; ⓅⓈⒸ) This place is funky and friendly. Floors are in chequered gold, and the rooms have their own colour schemes and themes. The facili-

ties are ultraclean, and a festive ambience breezes through the communal lounge to the pretty gardens. There's internet, satellite TV and a book exchange to keep you busy. It's about 1.5km from the post office.

Waterfront Lodge   LODGE $$$
(Map p436; ☑24692; www.waterfront-lodge. com; Vuna Rd; garden/sea-view d incl breakfast T$184/200, extra bed T$50; ⊛⊚) The boutique-style Waterfront's elegance colours its spacious rooms, which are furnished in teak and cane. There is an excellent restaurant and watering hole featuring Gauguin prints downstairs.

Winnie's Guest House   GUESTHOUSE $
(Map p434; ☑25215; winnies@kalianet.to; Vaha'akolo Rd; r per person incl breakfast T$50; ⊚) This home-ly five-room house about 2km from town out

near the hospital has a well-equipped kitchen, shared bathroom and a comfy lounge. Run by 91-year-old Winnie and her son Marc, it's popular with international medical students, so book in advance.

Emerald Hotel
HOTEL $$$
(Map p436; ☎22888; www.emerald-tonga.com; Vuna Rd; tw/ste T$250/345; ❋☎) Tonga's newest boutique hotel also has the best rooms around. Everything you could possibly want is here and there is a fully licensed Chinese restaurant downstairs that's open daily 7am to 10pm.

'Utu'one Bed & Breakfast
B&B $$
(Map p436; ☎24811; www.utuonebedandbreakfast. to; Vuna Rd; d/tw with shared bathroom T$95, d/tw with private bathroom T$180; ❋☎) Down on the waterfront, this place is bright and cheerful with a large lounge and kitchen. Many long-term guests stay here.

Captain Cook Apartments
APARTMENTS $$
(Map p436; ☎25600; www.captaincooktonga. com; Vuna Rd; d T$160, extra person T$25; ❋☎) Two-bedroom serviced apartments with full kitchen and living area on the waterfront. Long-stay discounts.

Toni's Guest House
GUESTHOUSE $
(Map p434; ☎21049, 48720; www.tonisguesthouse. com; Tofua; dm T$15-20; @) Toni's is an expanding budget favourite, virtually overtaking the neighbourhood in Tofoa, 3km south of Nuku'alofa. It's renowned for regular kava sessions, popular tours (p437) and brightly coloured buildings. There are a lot of options so check out the website. Toni's offers a shuttle service to and from town for T$1 and airport transfers for T$10.

Sela's Guest House
GUESTHOUSE $$
(Map p436; ☎25040; mettonga@kalianet.to; off Fatafehi Rd; dm T$25, s/d T$80/100; ☎) Stable-like rooms open off a central courtyard, and guests have use of the kitchen. There are also rooms that share a bathroom (single/double/triple T$40/60/90). Lavish cooked breakfasts with fruit are available (T$15). It's 1.5km from the post office.

Seaview Lodge
LODGE $$$
(Map p436; ☎23709; www.seaview-lodge.com; Vuna Rd; standard/garden/sea-view d T$207/247/282; ❋☎) This reliable favourite for regulars has large balconied rooms decorated with local crafts. The lodge sits in immaculate gardens behind its popular Seaview Restaurant, around 1km west of the post office.

Little Italy Hotel
HOTEL $$$
(Map p436; ☎25053; www.littleitalytonga.com; Vuna Rd; pool view/ocean view T$230/290 incl breakfast; ❋☎) Two floors of Tonga's top rooms sit atop Little Italy restaurant on Vuna Rd west of the palace. Rooms boast air-conditioning, coffee maker, refrigerator and free wi-fi.

 ## Eating

Nuku'alofa's decent spread of cafes and restaurants are mostly stretched along waterfront Vuna Rd and on or nearby the main drag, Taufa'ahau Rd. Nuku'alofa's supermarkets stock a reasonable range of products.

TOP CHOICE Friends Café
CAFE $
(Map p436; breakfast from T$6, mains T$10-20; ☺breakfast, lunch & dinner Mon-Sat; ☎) With a breezy charm and dependably good food, Friends, on the opposite corner from the post office in the centre of town, is deservedly popular with visitors and locals alike. Everything from panini to seafood chowder to stacked burgers. Free wi-fi for customers.

Fiesta Seafood
SEAFOOD $$
(Map p436; ☎56062; mains T$15-40; ☺lunch & dinner Mon-Sat) Reasonably priced and exceptionally good seafood. A tad hard to find back on Salote Rd, but well worth the effort. Licensed and open until 11pm daily.

THE SUNDAY EXPERIENCE

All visitors need to remember that Tonga comes to a screeching halt at midnight each Saturday night for 24 hours – Sunday is a day of rest and it is enshrined in Tongan law that it is illegal to work. There are no international or domestic flights, shops are closed, the streets are empty, sports are prohibited, and Tongans are going to church, feasting and resting. The tourism industry is starting to make inroads though and you'll find some restaurants open.

No visitor should miss the amazing cultural experience of attending a church service in Tonga. The singing is unbelievable – as are the fiery sermons and the length of the service! – whether you're at the Centenary Chapel in Nuku'alofa (p435) or in a small village church on a remote island.

TONGA NUKU'ALOFA

Luna Rossa Restaurant ITALIAN $$
(Map p434; ✆26324; mains T$20-40; ☺dinner Mon-Fri) You'll need a car or taxi to get here, but for sophisticates it will be worth it. This is intimate fine dining on authentic Italian cuisine, with the bonus of ultrafresh and well-prepared seafood.

Café Escape CAFE $$
(Map p436; breakfast from T$7, mains T$10-20; ☺breakfast, lunch & dinner Mon-Fri, to 4.30pm Sat; ☎) Slick Café Escape could be anywhere but it provides a refined, air-con oasis and infuses the tropics into its mixed menu. Free wi-fi for customers.

Beach Hut Café (Juice Bar) CAFE $$
(Map p436; breakfast from T$7, mains T$12-20; ☺breakfast & lunch Mon-Sat; ☎) A popular spot down on the waterfront that does a roaring trade with locals at lunchtime. Tasty juices and cold drinking coconuts await.

Emerald CHINESE $$
(Map p436; mains T$6-25; ☺breakfast, lunch & dinner) Part of the new Emerald Hotel, this place gets the nod for top Chinese restaurant in town. Good value, it's licensed, takeaway is available and it's open Sunday.

Cottage Breeze INTERNATIONAL $$
(Map p436; ✆28940; mains T$20-30; ☺dinner) Earning a glowing reputation, this place on Vuna Rd to the west of the palace offers consistently good food and service. Has everything from pork ribs to seafood grills. Open seven days a week.

Waterfront Café INTERNATIONAL $$
(Map p436; www.waterfront-lodge.com; mains T$20-40; ☺breakfast & dinner Mon-Sun) Soak up the stylishly breezy mood and follow sun-downers with meals of pasta, steak, lobster and seafood.

Talamahu Market MARKET $
(Map p436; ☺early morning-4.30pm Mon-Sat) Fruit and vegetables are sold by the pyramid (around T$2 to T$3) or woven-frond basket (for root crops and coconuts) with prices generally marked.

Fish market MARKET $
(Map p436; Tuimatamoana Harbour; ☺from early morning Mon-Sat) Starts when the boats come in at around 5am. Get there early.

Cowley's Bakery BAKERY $
(The Bread Bin; Map p436; Salote Rd; ☺24hr Mon-Sun) Does a brisk trade in baked goods including meat pies, savoury breads, muffins, doughnuts and lurid pineapple-iced cupcakes.

🍷 Drinking

Tongans drink with enthusiasm and Nuku'alofa has a spirited bar scene, ranging from upmarket to unashamedly seedy. Recently introduced laws see bars closing by 1am Monday to Friday and at midnight on Saturday.

Enquire locally about recommended kava circles (which you may be invited to join). Ordinarily a male-only affair, both men and women are welcome around the kava bowl at Toni's Guest House (p439).

Billfish Bar & Restaurant BAR
(Map p436; Vuna Rd) This relaxed open-air place down by the wharves is a long-time locals' favourite. There are decent pub-style meals and the Billfish regularly has live music.

IT'S SUNDAY IN NUKU'ALOFA

What to do, when nothing stirs on a Sunday (see p439) and even mangy dogs have deserted the streets?

» Go to Church – the magnificent singing lifts the soul and almost the roof. A favourite activity with visitors is to attend Centenary Chapel (p435) to worship with the king and the royal family.

» Take a round-the-island tour (p437) and explore Tongatapu's sights and attractions.

» Hire a bicycle (p469) and explore at your own pace.

» Visit one of the offshore island resorts (p443) and enjoy the sandy beaches and snorkelling.

» Head out to Ha'atafu Beach (p442) and relax.

» Sleep and eat – that's what most of the locals will be doing!

CONCRETE PARKS?

No, those are not vast concrete parks in downtown Nuku'alofa – they are the result of the November 2006 pro-democracy riots (see p464) when reportedly half the city was set alight. A huge number of buildings burnt to the ground (or to their concrete foundations) and these swaths of concrete, now overgrown with weeds, are the most visible scars of the riots.

They have started to disappear though. Those new buildings that dot the landscape in downtown Nuku'alofa were made possible because the old buildings were incinerated. And all that new construction producing the dust... thank the pro-democracy rioters.

Reload BAR
(Map p436; Tafa'ahau Rd) A popular lively new place serving ice-cold beer opposite Friends Café in the middle of town.

🔒 Shopping

Impressive Tongan arts, crafts and carvings are sold on both floors of the **Talamahu Market** (p436) and at the **Langafonua Handcrafts Centre** (Map p436), a non-profit cooperative next to Friends Café.

Around the Island

Buses are sporadic and taxis expensive, so the best way to see the sights is by island tour (see p437) or rental car. The following points of interest run in a clockwise direction around the island.

⊙ Sights & Activities

EASTERN TONGATAPU

Royal Residences LANDMARK
(Map p434) South of Nuku'alofa, between Tofoa and Pe'a, you'll pass the royal residences of the Princess, adorned with white tigers and cannons, and the King, an austere European-style hilltop palace opposite. Apparently it is a total coincidence that the Princess's cannons appear to be pointing directly at the King's palace.

Captain Cook Landing Site HISTORIC SITE
(Map p434) A cairn above a mangrove inlet near Holonga village marks the spot where Captain Cook came ashore in 1773 and

Queen Elizabeth popped by to commemorate it in 1970.

Mu'a (Lapaha) ARCHAEOLOGICAL SITE
(Map p434) The Mu'a area contains the richest concentration of archaeological remnants in Tonga. In AD 1200 the 11th in the Tu'i Tonga line of kings, Tu'itatui, moved the royal capital from Heketa (near present-day Niutoua) to Lapaha, now known as Mu'a. There are 28 royal stone tombs *(langi)* in the area, built with enormous limestone slabs. Turn towards the sea on the dirt road just north of the Catholic church to reach a grassy area with two monumental mounds. This is Tonga's most imposing ancient burial site. The structure closest to the main road is the **Paepae 'o Tele'a** (Platform of Tele'a), a pyramid-like stone memorial. Tele'a was a Tu'i Tonga who reigned during the 16th century. The other, the **Langi Namoala**, has a fine example of a *fonualoto* (vault for a corpse) on top.

Fishing Pigs LANDMARK
(Map p434) As you round the coast to the north of Mu'a keep an eye out for the infamous fishing pigs. These unusual porkers head out in search of seafood and the word is they taste saltier than their land-based brethren. Well worth a photo!

DON'T MISS

OHOLEI BEACH & HINA CAVE FEAST & SHOW

(Map p434; ☎11783; www.oholei beachresort.com; T$40 buffet & show) Tops in entertainment on Tongatapu, Simana Kami's Feast and Show is the place to go. The evening starts with entertainment on sandy Oholei Beach, followed by a tasty Tongan feast, including suckling pig roasted on a spit. The highlight though is the dancing in open-topped Hina Cave, enthusiastically performed and culminating in a captivating fire dance.

Runs on Wednesday and Friday nights, with buffet only on Sunday afternoon at 2pm. Accommodation places throughout Tongatapu will book and organise transport for you to this southeast-coast location. If partying until late and staying over appeals, arrange to stay in one of Simana's Oholei Beach Resort *fales* (see the website).

Ha'amonga 'a Maui Trilithon
ARCHAEOLOGICAL SITE

(Map p434) The South Pacific's equivalent of Stonehenge, the Ha'amonga 'a Maui (Maui's Burden) trilithon near Niutoua, is one of ancient Polynesia's most intriguing monuments. Archaeologists and oral history credit its construction to Tu'itatui, the 11th Tu'i Tonga. The structure consists of three large coralline stones, each weighing about 40 tonnes, arranged into a trilithic gate.

A walking track winds northward past several *langi* (tombs; known as the Langi Heketa), including 'Esi Makafakinanga, supposedly Tu'itatui's backrest. Such chiefly backrests were common in Polynesia, and apparently Tu'itatui used this one as a shield against attack from behind while he watched construction.

'Anahulu Cave
CAVE

(Map p434; admission T$5) Tongatapu's most famous cave is an over-loved, slightly eerie place full of stalactites and stalagmites, and blackened from the soot of flaming-frond torches and too much traffic. It features an underground freshwater pool suitable for swimming.

WESTERN TONGATAPU

Heading around the southern coast and turning to the west, there are some interesting spots along the rugged coastline.

Hufangalupe Archway
LANDMARK

(Map p434) This impressive arch on the southern coast, also known as 'the pigeon's doorway', is a natural land bridge over pounding waves that was formed when the roof of a sea cave collapsed. It can be traversed and there are spectacular views west along the coast.

Mapu'a 'a Vaca Blowholes
LOOKOUT

(Map p434) On an especially good day at Mapu'a 'a Vaca (Chief's Whistles), hundreds of blowholes spurt at once. They are best viewed on a windy day with a strong swell, when the water, forced up through natural vents in the coralline limestone, can shoot 30m into the air. The blowholes stretch 5km along the southwestern coast, near the village of Houma.

Double-headed Coconut Tree
LANDMARK

(Map p434) If you think we must be scratching for highlights to include a double-headed coconut tree then think again. Locals swear that this is the only coconut tree with two separate heads in Tonga...some say in the whole South Pacific. It's well worth the obligatory photo. Located on Loto Rd, just past Liahona.

Flying Foxes
LANDMARK

(Map p434) While you'll get the opportunity to see flying foxes (*peka*; fruit bats) in many places in Tonga, one spot renowned for their presence is the village of Kolovai, up near the western tip of the island. They cling to the trees upside down in their hundreds and if you haven't seen bats before they are quite enthralling.

Abel Tasman Landing Site
HISTORIC SITE

(Map p434) At the northwestern tip of Tongatapu is a monument commemorating the spot where Abel Tasman became the first European to discover Tongatapu. He was on his way back to Batavia (present-day Jakarta) after discovering firstly Tasmania, then New Zealand. With great European sensibility he named Tongatapu 'Amsterdam'.

Ha'atafu Beach Reserve
BEACH

(Map p434) On the sunset side of the island, the Ha'atafu Beach Reserve encompasses Ha'atafu's clean, sandy beach and surrounding reef. There's protected swimming and reasonable snorkelling at high tide in the broad lagoon, and the reef breaks offer some of the best surfing in Tonga (suitable for more experienced surfers). If your timing is good, you may see whales swimming outside the reef from the beach (June to November).

🍴 Sleeping & Eating

📷 Blue Banana Beach House
CABINS $$

(Map p434; ✆41575; www.bluebananastudios.com; small cabin per night/week A$100/660, big cabin per night/week A$130/860, min 3 nights; ⓟ) Looking for an attractive, secluded, self-contained studio cabin nestled among trees on the beach edge all to yourself? The beautifully decorated Blue Banana *fale* provide the beauty of an offshore island with the convenience of the mainland. Great for self-caterers.

Heilala Holiday Lodge
BUNGALOWS $$

(Map p434; ✆41600; www.heilala-holiday-lodge.com; s/d T$70/95, s/d fale T$105/135, s/d superior fale T$145/175; ⓟ🛜) Cute, thatched *fale* are spaced through tropical gardens in Heilala's new home at Ha'atafu Beach. Rates include breakfast, and delicious meals are available in the evening. Sven and his team are very helpful and will arrange anything you need.

Ha'atafu Beach Resort
BUNGALOWS $

(Map p434; ☑41088; www.surfingtonga.com; dm A$65, garden/beachfront fale per person A$75/90, child 2-12yr A$45; ℗@) Mainly catering to all-inclusive surfing holidays, this family-run set-up is laid-back and peaceful. Paths connect thatched-roof bungalows to clean, shared facilities and the dining room. Rates here include full breakfast and buffet dinner, but not 15% tax. Facilities, including snorkelling gear and paddle skis, are for guest-use only. Owner Steve is a Tonga surfing guru.

Offshore Islands

To the north of Tongatapu are a number of gorgeous islands that make for a great day trip or extended stay. All are only a short boat ride from Nuku'alofa.

🛏 Sleeping & Eating

Pangaimotu Island Resort
RESORT $

(Map p434; ☑7715762; www.eco-islands.info; Pangaimotu Island) The closest island resort from Nuku'alofa, Pangaimotu is best as a day trip. Daily departures, including Sunday, leave from the domestic wharf beside the fish market at 10am and 11am, returning at 4pm and 5pm. The trip (adult/child return T$20/10) takes about 10 minutes. There's a nice beach, a good restaurant, decent snorkelling and it's a good spot to take the kids.

Big Mama Yacht Club (VHF Channel 08) is here and yachties can anchor offshore and use its facilities, including restaurant, bar, showers, laundry, internet and transfers to town.

Fafá Island Resort
RESORT $$$

(Map p434; ☑22800; www.fafaislandresort.com; Fafá Island; s & d superior fale €170, deluxe fale €220, half/full board €47/56; ☎) The most elegant of Tongatapu's island resorts is set on a magnificent beach. The traditional-style *fale* are perfect in their simplicity, with wood-shingle roofs and walls of woven palm leaves. The restaurant features plenty of local seafood and also hosts a weekly culture show and feast. One-way airport-to-island transfers cost €20.

Day trips to Fafá (T$69 including lunch) depart Faua Jetty at 11am and return at 4.30pm daily.

Royal Sunset Island Resort
RESORT $$$

(Map p434; ☑21254; www.royalsunset.biz; 'Atata; d east side/west side/superior T$250/330/350, half/full board T$100/112; ☎▨) 'Atata, 10km from Tongatapu, has lovely beaches, a local village and the Royal Sunset Island Resort. New owners are renovating and refurbishing beachfront bungalows on this beautiful island. A stroll through the local village is a must. Snorkelling, diving and fishing are all possible from here. Sunday day trips including lunch, a snorkelling trip and boat transfers (30 minutes) cost T$70. The boat leaves Nuku'alofa from the wharf by the fish market at 10am and returns at 4pm.

'EUA

POP 5000 / AREA 87 SQ KM

Rugged 'Eua, 40km southeast of Tongatapu, is a slice of natural paradise all its own. Known as 'the forgotten island', it is

TROUBLE IN PARADISE

Minerva Reef, Tonga's southernmost extremity, 350km southwest of Tongatapu, has long served as a rest point for yachts travelling between Tonga and New Zealand. Awash most of the time, it contains a safe anchorage in an almost perfect circle of reef, and has a colourful history. Tonga first claimed the unpopulated reef in 1972 after the Phoenix Foundation, founded by a Las Vegas property developer, tried to create a tax-free republic there. The Tongan king himself sailed south to tear down the republic's flag.

As of 2011, yachties have been warned to keep away after a fracas between neighbours Fiji and Tonga. The latest flare-up is thanks to a high-ranking Fijian military man who fled the dictatorship in his homeland and escaped to Tonga, where he received Tongan citizenship and a Tongan passport. More than slightly peeved, the Fijian regime retaliated by reiterating its objections to Tongan claims to Minerva Reef (that are recognised by the Pacific Forum) and placed a navy warship in the lagoon. The Tongans then dispatched two navy patrol boats which apparently 'chased away' the Fijian warship. The two neighbours have now gone to the UN for help to sort it all out. In the meantime it is suggested that yachties avoid Minerva Reef. Yachties should check www.noonsite.com for updates.

geologically the oldest island in Tonga (40 million years old!) and one of the oldest in the Pacific. There are 'mountains', cliff-top lookouts, hidden caves, sinkholes, a limestone arch and jungle-like rainforest to explore. With its own species of plants, trees and the endemic red shining parrot, 'Eua has a growing awareness of itself as a unique ecotourism destination.

The people are fascinating, too. In times past 'Euans had a reputation as the fiercest warriors in Tonga. The sparsely populated island also became a haven for migrants moved from other islands. In 1860, when King Tupou I heard that European ships were capturing Tongans at the remote southern island of 'Ata for use as slaves he resettled the island's entire population to 'Eua for their own protection. In 1946, after a nasty volcanic eruption at Niuafo'ou (see p461) in the Niuas, Queen Salote moved that island's population to 'Eua also.

⊙ Sights & Activities

'Eua's interesting activities are best booked at your guesthouse. Discuss what you want to do and everything will be arranged for you. 'Eua is the second-largest island in Tonga and while fairly easy to navigate, with one long main road and 15 villages along it, there is no public transport and distances are deceiving. Rely on advice from your guesthouse; the best option is to take a guided day tour.

'Eua is becoming known for its **hiking**, particularly in **'Eua National Park** in the 'mountains' along the island's eastern coast. There are a number of options so discuss

SPOTTING WHALES

Craig McLachlan

The flight from Tongatapu to 'Eua may be the world's shortest scheduled commercial flight at only 10 minutes, but it may also be one of the best for spotting whales. Whatever you do, don't doze off! When my wife and I flew over to the 'forgotten island', the pilot zigged and zagged his way across the straits at a little over 1000 feet in altitude, pointing out one group of whales after another. Cameras clicked and passengers positively squealed with delight to look down on families of humpback whales frolicking below.

things where you are staying, get a map and organise a ride to the trailhead. Better yet, hire a guide for the day.

Wildlife watchers will find that 'Eua has a lively **bird** population, the star of which is the *koki*, or red shining parrot. Others include *ngongo* (noddies), white-tailed *tavake* (tropic birds) and *pekapeka-tae* (swiftlets). The *peka* (fruit bat) is also commonly seen. **Whales** come in very close to land here and can often be seen from the restaurant at Hideaway. Failing that, there are both whale-watching and whale-swim tours on offer from June until October.

For a **cultural encounter**, Hideaway offers the chance for guests (and nonguests) to participate in community-orientated experiences such as **kava ceremonies** and **basket weaving** in the local village, as well as church visits and *umu* (earth oven) feasts on Sunday. Hideaway also runs **4WD tours** to parts of 'Eua that are virtually inaccessible any other way. It's a great way to see the island.

'Eua has some of the best **diving** in Tonga and its huge **Cathedral Cave** is becoming legendary. Book through your guesthouse. **Deep Blue Diving** (p436), based in Nuku'alofa, also offers diving from its 'Eua base in Ohonua near the ferry quay.

🛏 Sleeping & Eating

All accommodation on 'Eua is of the budget variety. 'Euans don't eat out, so the only place for visitors to dine is at guesthouses, where cooked meals are available daily. The most popular is Hideaway's ocean-view bar-restaurant (dinner from T$20).

Hideaway [TOP CHOICE]   GUESTHOUSE $
(☑50255; www.kalianet.to/hideawayeua; Tufuvai village; campsite T$25, s/d/tr/q incl breakfast T$55/70/85/100; ☎) Tongan-owned and operated, Taki's place is the first choice for most travellers to 'Eua. Its viewing platform, built over the rocky shore, makes for fantastic sunset viewing and whale watching. Comfortable motel-style rooms have hot showers and the restaurant-bar looks out on the ocean and is an easy spot to while away a few hours. Optional tours for the next day are listed nightly and can be booked on the spot. Rates include continental breakfast and transfers.

Taina's Place   GUESTHOUSE $
(☑50186; www.tainasplace.com; camping per person T$20, cabin s/d/tr T$40/55/80; ☎) Cute

houses are arranged in gardens inland near the forest. Bathroom facilities are nearby, and the communal lounge/kitchen area is an easy spot to relax in. Taina's works with Hideaway when it comes to booking optional tours. Breakfast is T$12, transfers to the wharf are T$10 return, and airport transfers are T$6 return.

❶ Information

MOBILE PHONES There is coverage in the villages but none on most of the hiking trails.

MONEY There are two banks but no ATMs on 'Eua. Bring enough cash with you. Hideaway is the only place that accepts credit cards.

TOURIST INFORMATION www.eua-island -tonga.com

❶ Getting There & around

AIR Chathams Pacific (p469) makes the 10-minute flight from Tongatapu, reputedly the world's shortest scheduled commercial service, at least twice daily (one way T$70).

BOAT On a calm day there is nothing to the two-to-three-hour ferry trip between 'Eua and Tongatapu (T$28 one-way). The ferry leaves Nuku'alofa four times weekly (Tuesday, Thursday, Friday and Saturday) at 12.30pm. The return ferry is at the rather nasty hour of 5am! (Monday, Wednesday, Friday and Saturday).

CAR & BICYCLE Accommodation hosts will pick you up at the wharf or airport. Bikes can be hired at Hideaway (T$20 per day).

HA'APAI GROUP

POP 8200 / AREA 110 SQ KM

Virtually untouched and one of Tonga's best-kept secrets, the Ha'apai islands are sprinkled across the kingdom's central waters. With 62 islands, 45 of which are uninhabited, Ha'apai appears like the idyllic South Pacific paradise: palm-fringed islands, vibrant reefs, breaching whales, deserted white beaches and even a couple of massive volcanoes.

TONGA HA'APAI GROUP

Ha'apai Group

For adventurous travellers searching for a special South Seas experience, Ha'apai is the place to head to. It's a sleepy, seductive place and you get the feeling the locals would prefer to keep it that way.

An increasing number of tourists visit with each year. There is no ATM so turn up with cash if you are arriving at the weekend. Best advice: be like the locals and 'don't worry, be Ha'apai!'

History

Archaeological excavations in southern Lifuka island reveal settlement dating back more than 3000 years.

The first European to turn up was Abel Tasman in 1643. He stopped for supplies at Nomuka and called the island Rotterdam. Later, several notable events in Tongan history took place in Ha'apai. Captain Cook narrowly escaped the cooking pot in 1777 (see p464), the mutiny on the *Bounty* occurred just offshore from Tofua in 1789 (see p451), and the *Port-au-Prince*, with William Mariner aboard, was ransacked in 1806 (see p446).

In 1831 Ha'apai was the first island group in Tonga to be converted to Christianity following the baptism of its ruler Taufa'ahau. He took the name of Siaosi (George) after the King of England, and adopted the surname of Tupou. His wife was baptised Salote after Queen Charlotte. As King George Tupou I he united Tonga and established the royal line that continues through to the present day.

Nuku'alofa's main street, Taufa'ahau Rd, is named after him.

ⓘ Information

Check out www.haapai.to.

ⓘ Getting There & Away

AIR Ha'apai's Pilolevu Airport is 3km north of Pangai on Lifuka. The island's main road passes right through the middle of the runway, meaning that the road is closed when aircraft are arriving or departing.

Chathams Pacific (p469) flies daily (except Sunday) between Ha'apai and Tongatapu, and three or four times a week between Ha'apai and Vava'u. Make the most of your flight by ensuring you are on their DC3 (see p470) for the flight from Tongatapu to Ha'apai.

BOAT MV *Otuanga'ofa* stops weekly at Pangai on both its northbound and southbound runs between Tongatapu and Vava'u. See p470 for ferry details.

There are protected anchorages along the lee shores of Lifuka, Foa, Ha'ano and Uoleva.

ⓘ Getting Around

TO/FROM THE AIRPORT & WHARF Tom's taxi (it's the only one!) charges T$10 between the airport and Pangai. If you arrive at the airport and Tom's not there, ask someone heading into town for a lift. Head to Mariner's Cafe (p448) and sort yourself out there. If you're making a booking at a guesthouse in Pangai, ask to be picked up at the airport or wharf. The Foa Island resorts (p449) will arrange transfers for you at a cost. Make sure to ask about this when you book.

WILLIAM MARINER

Thanks to a series of serendipitous incidents, the world has an extensive account of the customs, language, religion and politics of pre-Christian Tonga.

In 1805, 15-year-old William Mariner went to sea on the privateer *Port-au-Prince*. The voyage took the ship across the Atlantic, around Cape Horn, up the west coast of South America, to the Sandwich (Hawaiian) Islands and finally into Tonga's Ha'apai Group. The crew anchored at the northern end of Lifuka (see p447) and was immediately welcomed with yams and barbecued pork. Their reception seemed friendly enough (see p464), but on 1 December 1806 an attack was launched while 300 Tongans were aboard the ship.

Young Mariner, dressed in uniform, was captured and escorted ashore. Finau 'Ulukalala I, the reigning chief of Ha'apai, seeing the well-dressed young man, assumed that Mariner was the captain's son and ordered that his life be spared.

Mariner was taken under the wing of Finau and became privy to most of the goings-on in Tongan politics over the following four years. He learned the language well and travelled with the chief, observing and absorbing the finer points of Tongan ceremony and protocol.

After the death of Finau, the king's son permitted Mariner to leave Tonga on a passing English vessel. Back in England, an amateur anthropologist, Dr John Martin, was fascinated with Mariner's tale and suggested collaboration on a book. The result, *An Account of the Natives of the Tonga Islands*, is a masterpiece of Pacific literature.

HA'APAI TOURS

Sandy, deserted beaches and uninhabited islands may be all you need for a perfect trip to Ha'apai, but for more active visitors, a number of operators are running excellent tours both on and off the water.

Each operator tends to offer a number of options so check out their websites before you go. They will do pick-ups at accommodation on Foa and Uoleva islands.

The waters around Ha'apai teem with humpback whales from July to October.

Fins 'n' Flukes (☑60015, 8870141; www.finsnflukes.com) Based over the road from the Tonga Visitors Bureau in Pangai, Fins 'n' Flukes, run by Brian and Sabine, offers popular diving and snorkelling tours, whale-watching/swimming tours, island transfers, and kayak and bicycle rentals. Also runs tours in German.

Friendly Islands Kayak Company (☑70173; www.fikco.com) Friendly Islands Kayak offers superb tours in Ha'apai, such as the 13-day package including nine days of kayaking through the island group. It also has a seven-day resort-based kayaking tour and an 'adventure week' that includes kayaking, sailing and whale watching. Kayaking in Ha'apai has been named 'one of the 25 greatest adventures in the world' by *National Geographic Adventure* magazine.

Ha'apai Whale & Sail (☑60374, 8885800; www.uoleva.com) Run out of Mariner's Cafe in Pangai by Craig Airey, Ha'apai Whale & Sail offers whale-watching/swimming tours and sailing tours on the yacht *Gwendolin*. Craig is the Uoleva island specialist (see p450), runs Uoleva day tours and can tell you what you need to know. He also runs the **Ha'apai Yacht Club** (VHF Channel 16).

Whale Discoveries (☑8737676; www.whalediscoveries.com) Dave and Tris run excellent whale-watching/swimming tours and snorkelling tours on *Tropic Bird*, a specially designed inflatable, and live-aboard sailing tours on their catamaran, *Wildlife*. Contact Dave if you want to know about kite surfing in Ha'apai. This enterprising couple have sailed the world and have plenty of stories to tell.

BICYCLE Lifuka and Foa are flat, and a bicycle is a great option for exploring. Mariner's Cafe (p448) and Fins 'n' Flukes (p447) rent out bikes for T$15 per day.

BOAT The TVB in Lifuka may assist in arranging boat transport around the Ha'apai group – though you may be told to ask at Mariner's Cafe!

TAXI Tom runs the only taxi. Book through Mariner's Cafe or at your guesthouse.

Lifuka Group

Most visitors to Ha'apai stay within the Lifuka group of islands found along the eastern barrier reef of Ha'apai. The airport, main ferry wharf and almost all accommodation and services are located within the Lifuka group – with most of the action for visitors based on Lifuka, Foa and Uoleva islands.

It will take planning and a determined effort to get out to remote islands in the Ha'apai group, many of which are uninhabited.

LIFUKA
Pangai, Lifuka's main town, has basic services but struggles to be described as attractive.

It's hardly the highlight of a visit to Ha'apai. On hot afternoons the wharf is a writhing mass of drenched, cooling-down kids.

◉ Sights
The best way to get around the Lifuka island sights is by rental bicycle. The 14km (one-way) ride to **Houmale'eia Beach** (p449) at the northern tip of Foa island is a good option.

Shirley Baker Monument & European Cemetery   CEMETERY
About 800m north of Pangai, the grave and monument of Reverend Shirley Baker, Tonga's first prime minister and adviser to King George Tupou I, stands amid the graves of various 19th- and early-20th-century German and English traders and missionaries. A Tongan cemetery, with decorated sand and coral mounds, is directly opposite.

Port au Prince Massacre Monument   MONUMENT
A few hundred metres north of the airport runway is a signed turn-off west to the beach where a monument commemorates the spot

HEAD TO MARINER'S CAFE

Ha'apai is a superb place to visit, and there are a couple of ways to do it.

For those who come to dive, snorkel, whale watch or sit on the beach as part of a relaxing holiday and want a bit of comfort, book yourself into one of the Foa island resorts – upmarket Sandy Beach Resort (p449) or the more affordable Matafonua Lodge (see p449). Alternatively, make a booking at Serenity Beaches on Uoleva island (see p450).

For adventurous types who are out exploring, your initial arrival on Ha'apai may be a bit of a surprise, whether you arrive by plane or ferry. Simply put, there isn't much here. If you were trying to get away from it all, pat yourself on the back – you've succeeded!

The best advice is to head straight to **Mariner's Cafe** (☑60374; VHF Channel 16; marinerstonga@yahoo.co.uk; ⊙breakfast, lunch & dinner Mon-Sat, dinner Sun; @) in Pangai. Yachties take note: this is also the base for the **Ha'apai Yacht Club**.

This relaxed social hub, named for William Mariner (p446), is Lifuka's only real restaurant and bar and has a good range of tasty and fresh dishes. It's a good place to come for advice. Sit down with a beer or coffee and absorb some local knowledge before heading out for adventure. Internet access is available for T$3 for 30 minutes.

where the *Port au Prince* was ransacked and its crew massacred in 1806 (see p446). The ship's original anchor was discovered offshore in 2009.

Hihifo's Archaeological Sites
ARCHAEOLOGICAL SITE

Hihifo, the village south of Pangai, hides some archaeological relics seemingly of more interest to rooting pigs than anyone else. Hidden behind a low wire fence in a grove of ironwood is **Olovehi Tomb** (Loto Kolo Rd), the burial ground for people holding the noble title of Tuita.

About 1.2km south of Pangai, a turning towards the east leads to the circular **Velata Mound Fortress**, a type of ring ditch fortification found throughout Tonga, Fiji and Samoa.

Southern Lifuka
AREA

From Hihifo, the road continues to **Hulu'ipaongo Point**, with its sweep of white beach and views south to Uoleva island. About 200m short of the point is **Hulu'ipaongo Tomb**, the burial site of the Mata'uvave line of chiefs.

🛏 Sleeping

Accommodation options on Lifuka are basic, most with shared bathrooms and kitchens. Expect an early rise – Lifuka's rooster population is boisterous.

'Evaloni's Guesthouse
GUESTHOUSE $

(☑8660029; evaloniguesthouse@yahoo.com; s/d T$25/35, d with private bathroom from T$75) With fan-cooled rooms downstairs and two spacious rooms upstairs, 'Evaloni's has a tapa-lined verandah on which to shoot some pool. Order meals in advance (breakfast/dinner T$15/25) or head to nearby Mariner's Cafe. 'Evaloni includes airport and port transfers in the price. A bonus of staying here is that she has what is left of the Ha'apai Museum on site, including some shards of 3000-year-old Lapita pottery.

Billy's Place
GUESTHOUSE $

(☑8660029; evaloniguesthouse@yahoo.com; small fale incl breakfast T$45, large fale T$65) If you're OK with isolation and want to have a whole east-side beach to yourself, this place is a decent option. There are secluded bungalows with clean, shared bathrooms and kitchen use for T$5 per day. Northeast of Pangai, it's a 10-minute 1.5km bike ride (free bikes are available for guests). Billy is 'Evaloni's brother and 'Evaloni handles its bookings.

Fifita Guesthouse
GUESTHOUSE $

(☑60213; marinerstonga@yahoo.co.uk; Fau Rd, Pangai; s/d T$35/50, s/d with private facilities T$65/75) Fifita's central location next to Mariner's Cafe and just a short walk from the wharf makes it a popular choice. It's basic but friendly, with plenty of travel banter exchanged in the communal kitchen. Rates include breakfast.

Lindsay Guesthouse
GUESTHOUSE $

(☑60107; fehiwa@gmail.com; cnr Loto Kolo & Tuita Rds; s/d/f incl breakfast T$30/45/55) A clean and friendly spot, with a broad verandah and communal sitting room and kitchen. The scent of baking bread wafts across the lawn from the bakery. Bikes are available for guests.

Fonongava'inga (Langilangi) Guesthouse
GUESTHOUSE $

(☎8820701; vimahi@kalianet.to; s/d/tr T$15/25/45) The light-filled communal lounge make this place worth the few minutes' walk from the centre of town. Be warned: there's little signage and it's hard to find. Your host Langilangi enjoys teaching local crafts to guests. Most guests head to Mariner's Cafe for meals. Kitchen use is available for T$3 per day.

✗ Eating

The only real option for eating out in Pangai is Mariner's Cafe (p448).

A number of shops with limited food supplies are around town, but they can't be described as supermarkets – more as limited markets.

Matuku-ae-tau Bakery
BAKERY $

(Lindsay Guesthouse, cnr Loto Kolo & Tuita Rds; ⊙8am-5pm Mon-Sat, 5-8pm Sun) The bakery's two ovens keep the island in bread, jam-filled rolls and *keki* (similar to doughnuts). There's a mad rush on Sunday afternoon.

Pangai Market
MARKET $

(cnr Waterfront & Palace Rd; ⊙9am-5pm Mon-Sat) Head down early in the day for fresh produce.

ⓘ Information

The town water supply in Ha'apai should be used only for washing and bathing. Drink only bottled or rain water.

Niu'ui Hospital (☎60201; Hihifo) Basic facilities. The pharmacy is open 8.30am to 4.30pm.

Post office (cnr Waterfront & Palace Rds) Mail can be sent c/o Post Office, Pangai, Ha'apai. The **Customs & Inland Revenue** office is also based here.

Tonga Visitors Bureau (TVB; ☎60733; www.thekingdomoftonga.com; Holopeka Rd; ⊙8.30am-12.30pm & 1.30-4.30pm Mon-Fri) May assist with accommodation bookings, boat transport or other queries.

Westpac Bank of Tonga (Holopeka Rd; ⊙9am-12.30pm & 1.30-3.30pm Mon-Fri) Exchanges foreign currencies (cash and travellers cheques), gives cash advances on Visa and MasterCard and also deals with MoneyGram cash transfers. There is no ATM.

FOA

To the north of Lifuka and connected by a potholed causeway that you can cycle over, Foa is a heavily wooded island. **Houmale'eia Beach**, on the northern tip, is the best beach on the 'Ha'apai mainland', with sandy water access, sublime views of Nukunamo and some beautiful snorkelling.

🛏 Sleeping

TOP CHOICE ★ **Matafonua Lodge**
BUNGALOWS $$$

(☎69766; www.matafonua.com; fale incl breakfast T$200; ☎) These attractive elevated *fale* have water views over foreshore foliage and are very comfortable. They have freshwater showers in well-designed shared bathrooms and kids are welcome. A kiosk-style cafe-bar, open 7.30am to 8.30pm and open to the public, has a good variety, reasonable prices and overlooks Nukunamo island. The sandy swimming beach is superb. Rental kayaks and bicycles are available for hire. The lodge also runs a **cultural tour** to Ha'ano island (see p449).

Sandy Beach Resort
RESORT $$$

(☎69600; www.sandybeachresort.de; s/d per person €80; ☎) Long regarded as one of Tonga's best resorts, Sandy Beach's comfortable bungalows are oriented for sunset views over the magnificent white-sand Houmale'eia Beach. The resort can organise a number of activities daily. Breakfast/dinner costs €15/38. The restaurant is open to house guests only. Return airport transfers cost €25 per person.

ⓘ Getting There & Around

If you are staying at either of the sleeping options, the operators will arrange to get you there. By bicycle from Pangai it takes around one hour; the taxi fare is about T$35.

NUKUNAMO

The small, enticing picture-postcard island viewed from the tip of Foa is Nukunamo, an uninhabited island with a shining white beach covered with beautiful shells. You can snorkel to Nukunamo over the life-filled coral heads between the islands. Only confident swimmers should attempt this, and only with local advice, as the currents through the pass can be powerful. Talk to Matafonua Lodge before you go.

HA'ANO

Cultural travellers will get a good dose of traditional Tongan life on the strikingly clean and friendly island of Ha'ano that lies to the north of Foa and Nukunamo.

Matafonua Lodge runs **cultural day tours** here along with the Ha'ano Women's Group. For T$125, which is paid directly to the Women's Group, you get a big day out that includes boat transfers, a school visit,

kava ceremony, handicraft demonstrations, a Tongan feast, some snorkelling and transport in a horse and cart around the island (there are only two cars on Ha'ano!). Participants rave about it.

UOLEVA

If you're looking to really get away from it all, the island of Uoleva, to the south of Lifuka, is the place to come. Uninhabited apart from the accommodation providers – there's no village on Uoleva – it offers up a real South Seas experience with little to do other than swim, snorkel, fish, read and relax. At the time of research, whales were breaching about 400m offshore from the perfect white-sand beach this Lonely Planet writer was relaxing on!

Activity operators based on Lifuka will pick you up here if you are booked on their tours. See www.uoleva.com for more information.

🛏 Sleeping

Uoleva now has two levels of accommodation. The budget options both have unbeatable, absolute beachfront positions on a perfect, white-sand beach. They have no electricity and only rudimentary cold showers. Both places receive rave reviews from intrepid travellers, but not-such-rave reviews from those expecting too much in the way of facilities. Bring your own drinks, food, a book and mosquito repellent; inform owners in advance if you want meals.

Serenity Beaches   BUNGALOWS $$$
(☑13010, 8734934; www.serenitybeaches.com; small/large fale T$190/290, half/full board

T$70/90) Fresh on the scene at the southern end of Uoleva, Serenity Beaches features beautifully constructed *fale* with private facilities on both sides of the island. Food is well prepared and there are all sorts of recreational options on offer; check out the website. Transfers from Pangai cost T$50 per person one-way. If you've got the loot, stay here.

Captain Cook Hideaway   CABINS $
(☑60014, 8791144; s/d T$30/45) Soni's place has basic beachfront cabins just back from the waves. Savour the peace and solitude. Meals are available (breakfast/lunch/dinner T$10/15/20) and you can use the kitchen for T$5 per day. Transfers from Pangai cost T$25 per person each way.

Taiana's Beach Resort   CABINS $
(☑60612, 8831722; s/d/f T$35/45/75) Ponder the stars and lapping waves at this absolute beach-bum paradise. Tapa-lined *fale* have mats over sandy floors and enclosed sitting areas. Rates are similar to Captain Cook Hideaway for meals, kitchen use and transfers.

'UIHA

The conservative, traditional island of 'Uiha, to the south of Uoleva, is a friendly place with two villages: 'Uiha, with a wharf, and Felemea, about 1.5km south.

In the centre of 'Uiha village is a large, elevated burial ground containing several **royal tombs**. The burial ground of the Tongan royal family was on 'Uiha until the move to Nuku'alofa. At the village church are two **cannons**, souvenirs taken from a Peruvian

---

DISAPPEARING ISLAND: FONUAFO'OU

The Ha'apai group is home to Tonga's mysterious disappearing island, Fonuafo'ou. From 1781 to 1865 there were repeated reports of a shoal 72km northwest of Tongatapu and 60km west of Nomuka in the south of the Ha'apai group. An island was confirmed by the HMS *Falcon* in 1865 and given the name Falcon Island. In 1885, the island was 50m high and 2km long. Amid great excitement, Tonga planted its flag and claimed it as Fonuafo'ou, meaning 'New Land'.

Then in 1894 Fonuafo'ou went missing! Two years later it reappeared 320m high before disappearing again. In 1927 it re-emerged and in 1930 was measured at 130m high and 2.5km long! By 1949 there was again no trace of Fonuafo'ou, which had once more been eroded by the sea. Fonuafo'ou came back again, but at last report this geographical freak had once more become submerged.

The island is a submarine volcano that alternates between building itself up above sea level and being eroded down below it. At present, its summit elevation is estimated at 17m below sea level. If the 'New Land' does come back, your best chance of spotting it is if you are on a yacht.

blackbirding (slaving) ship that was attacked and destroyed by the locals in 1863.

'Esi-'o-Ma'afu Homestay HOMESTAY $
(☑60605, 60438; fale s/d T$20/25) You'll get a good introduction to village life at this welcoming place right on the beach at Felemea. Shared bathrooms are clean, and there's a small kitchen (T$3) or, with notice, the owners will prepare Tongan food. Talk to the TVB in Pangai (p458) about bookings and boat transport.

TOFUA & KAO
Seventy kilometres west of Lifuka are pyramidal Kao (1046m) and its smoking partner, Tofua (507m). On a good day this uninhabited pair is clearly visible from Lifuka.

Tofua is a flat-topped volcanic island that, like Niuafo'ou in the Niuas, is shaped like a huge floating doughnut. It started life as a classic pyramid-shaped volcano but the top blew off in a violent eruption. In the middle of the doughnut of land is a freshwater lake 38m above sea level. The crater rim is a tough one-hour climb from the Hokala landing site on the northern side of the island.

Adding to Tofua's intrigue, champion Swiss snowboarder Xavier Rosset decided to be a modern-day Robinson Crusoe there in 2008 and spent 10 months on the island in survival mode. He took a satellite phone and regularly updated a blog on his adventures – see www.xavierrosset.ch.

The four-hour hike up uninhabited Kao, 4km north of Tofua, is not recommended without a guide. The 1046m volcano is the highest point in Tonga, but there is no marked track and the vegetation is dense.

Reaching Tofua or Kao is not easy without your own boat. Talk to the TVB (p458) or operators in Pangai if you are keen. It should be considered a major expedition, not a day trip, and taking along a local guide is a smart move. Locals from the southern Ha'apai islands occasionally head to Tofua and Kao to harvest kava.

VAVA'U GROUP

POP 17,000 / AREA 119 SQ KM

Shaped like a giant jellyfish with its tentacles dangling south, Vava'u (pronounced va-VA-ooh) is picturesque at every turn. Those tentacles are made up of spectacular islands (61 in all!) intertwined with turquoise waterways and encircling reefs

BLIGH SURVIVES TOFUA

Not far from Tofua is where the infamous mutiny on the *Bounty* occurred. On 28 April 1789, Captain Bligh and 18 loyal seamen landed on Tofua having been set adrift by Fletcher Christian and his mutineers. Islanders – Tofua was inhabited in those days – clubbed quartermaster John Newton to death. Bligh and the rest narrowly escaped and embarked on a 6500km journey to Timor in an open boat, desperately short of food and water, having not discovered Tofua's large freshwater lake.

that have created one of the most popular sheltered cruising grounds on the planet.

To really experience it you have to get out on the water. Long regarded as one of the world's great sailing locations, Vava'u has it all: charter sailing, sea kayaking, game fishing, surfing, diving and swimming with whales are all possible here. Stay in town or head out to one of the islands to enjoy the stunning scenery and activities that Vava'u offers in abundance.

Vava'u plays host to around 500 visiting yachts each year, mainly during the May to October season as trans-Pacific yachts pass through on their way west. A number of yachts also hole up in Port of Refuge – considered one of the safest harbours in the South Pacific – for the cyclone season from November to April.

History
Vava'u is believed to have been settled for around 2000 years. The capital, Neiafu, looks out onto Port of Refuge, christened by Don Francisco Antonio Mourelle of Spain who sighted Vava'u on 4 March 1781 en route from Manila to Mexico. Mourelle claimed the new-found paradise, one of the last South Pacific islands to be contacted by Europeans, for Spain. Captain Cook missed it a decade earlier when the Ha'apai islanders convinced him that there were no safe anchorages north of Ha'apai.

William Mariner (see p446) spent time here during Finau 'Ulukala I of Ha'apai's conquest of Vava'u in 1808. Later, on the death of 'Ulukala III, King George Tupou I added Vava'u to his realm when he formed a united Tonga in 1845.

TONGA VAVA'U GROUP

WHALE ENCOUNTERS

Tonga is an important breeding ground for humpback whales, which migrate to its warm waters between June and October; it's one of the few places in the world where you can swim with these magnificent creatures. They can be seen raising young in the calm reef-protected waters and engaging in elaborate mating rituals.

Humpbacks are dubbed 'singing whales' because the males sing during courtship routines, and the low notes of their 'songs' can reach 185 decibels and carry 100km through the open ocean.

As Tonga's whale-watching industry has grown, so has concern over its possible impact. At the centre of the debate is the practice of swimming with whales, which some say disturbs the mothers and calves just when they are most vulnerable – and may force them to alter their natural behaviour.

Humpback populations around the world have declined rapidly over the past 200 years, from 150,000 in the early 1800s to an estimated 12,000 today. The same predictable migration habits that once made the giants easy prey for whalers nowadays make them easy finds for whale watchers.

There are whale-watch and whale-swim operators in all of Tonga's island groups. Two big points: make sure you go with a licensed operator, and give yourself a few days to do it so that there is no pressure on the operator to 'chase' whales in order to keep you happy. If you feel your whale-swim operator has breached the boundaries and 'hassled' the whales, make sure you report this to the Tongan Visitors Bureau.

ⓘ Information

Check out www.vavau.to for all you need to know, including a free cruising guide.

ⓘ Getting There & Away

AIR Lupepau'u Airport (Map p454) is a 15-minute drive north of Neiafu.

Chathams Pacific (Map p456; ☑28852; www.chathamspacific.com) Flies daily between Tongatapu and Vava'u, and three or four times weekly between Ha'apai and Vava'u. You can also fly north from here to the Niuas (see p469).

BOAT See p470 for interisland ferry information.

ⓘ Getting Around

TO/FROM THE AIRPORT Some accommodation, including island resorts, offers airport transfers for a price. Taxis charge T$25 for the airport–Neiafu trip.

BICYCLE Vava'u is hilly but fairly manageable by bicycle. Adventure Backpackers (p457) rents out good bikes (half/full day T$13/20).

BUS Buses run from Sailoame and 'Utakalongalu Markets (Map p456) to most parts of Vava'u and its connected islands, leaving when full. They usually make the run into town in the morning and return in the afternoon, so they're not very convenient for day trips from town.

CAR A rental car probably isn't necessary in Vava'u, but they are available. A Tongan driver's licence is a must; available for T$60 from the police station (see p458). There are an incredible number of cars in Vava'u with broken or cracked windscreens. Do not park your rental vehicle under a coconut tree. When driving, watch out for kids, pigs, chickens and dogs.

Pasifika Rentals (Map p456; ☑70781) has a few rental cars for T$60 to T$80 per day. Call ahead or get the TVB (p458) to arrange one for you.

TAXI Taxis charge T$5 around Neiafu, and T$25 to the airport, 'Ano and Hinakauea Beaches, and Talihau village.

Neiafu

POP 6000

Overlooking Port of Refuge, surely one of the world's most amazing and protected harbours, Neiafu may or may not appeal. Home to a surprising number of good restaurants and bars along the waterfront, the town itself is more than a tad ramshackle and run down. With visiting yachties and a steady flow of visitors flying in during the same period (many who are here to swim with the whales), the busy season of June to October sees the small town transformed into a hive of activity.

◉ Sights

Taking in the Port of Refuge view of yachts bobbing at their moorings from a cafe or bar may be the only sight you need to see in Neiafu.

St Joseph's Cathedral   CATHEDRAL
(Map p456; Fatafehi Rd) Standing high above Port of Refuge, this colonial-style cathedral is Neiafu's most prominent building. The stretch of road along the waterfront cliff below the cathedral is **Hala Lupe** (Way of Doves), named for the mournful singing of the female prisoners (convicted of adultery by the church) who constructed it.

Mt Talau National Park   MOUNTAIN
(Map p454) The flat-topped mountain dominating Port of Refuge, 131m Mt Talau (Mo'unga Talau), is protected in the Mt Talau National Park. From the centre of Neiafu, travel west along Tapueluefu Rd for around 2km, until the road narrows into a bush track that leads up to the summit. Keep an eye out for flying foxes, the Tongan whistler and *fokai* (banded lizard).

Old Harbour   HARBOUR
(Map p456) Turning left in front of the cathedral will take you down to Old Harbour and boat access to the eastern islands.

🏃 Activities
Boating & Sailing
Vava'u is a world-famous yachtie paradise. Charter a yacht, either bareboat or skippered, and cruise the islands, stopping to snorkel and wander beaches at will.

Moorings   YACHT CHARTER
(Map p456; ✆70016; VHF Channel 72; www.tonga sailing.com) Charters out catamarans and monohulls that sleep up to 10 passengers. Prices vary according to the season; check the website for details.

Sailing Safaris   YACHT CHARTER
(Map p456; ✆70650; VHF Channel 68) Offers a host of options, including whale-watching, bareboat and skippered charters, and learn-to-sail courses. Also operates a full marine centre for boat repairs.

Melinda Sea Adventures   YACHT CHARTER
(Map p456; ✆8897586; VHF Channel 16; www.sailtonga.com) Fully crewed, minimum three-day charters. Rates depend on the season and number of passengers. Whale-watching trips are also available.

Port of Refuge Yacht Club   YACHT CLUB
(Map p456; ✆70016; www.portofrefugeyachtclub.com) On a balmy Friday afternoon you can't beat knocking back a beer or rum and watching a relaxed yacht race around Port of Refuge. If you want to crew, turn up at Mango Cafe (p458) when the skippers meet at around 4pm between June and November. Spectators can watch from the bar at the 5pm race start. There's a ton of fun to be had afterwards.

Vava'u Island Express   BOAT RENTALS
(Map p454; ✆70911, 7716848; www.vavauhouseboats.com; Toula) Operates water taxis, charters, tours and boat hire to get you where you want to go.

Diving
Vava'u's dive sites range from hard and soft coral gardens and encrusted wrecks to vast sea caves and other geological marvels. There is a wide variety of diving for all levels and abilities.

The dive operators all also offer whale-swim tours and there are myriad options. Check the websites for what is on offer.

Dive Vava'u   DIVING
(Map p456; ✆70492; www.divevavau.com) Operates from down on the waterfront below Tonga Bob's.

Dolphin Pacific Diving   DIVING
(Map p456; ✆70292; VHF Channel 71; www.dolphinpacificdiving.com) Prides itself on being a relaxed, friendly operation. Down on the waterfront beside the Puataukanave Hotel.

Beluga Diving   DIVING
(Map p456; ✆70327; VHF Channel 09; www.beluga divingvavau.com) Further along the waterfront, next to Moorings.

Fishing
Vava'u is regarded as one of the best game-fishing destinations in the Pacific and a prime site for catching marlin. Keen fishers may like to head to the dedicated fishing lodge on Hunga island (p460).

Hakula Sport Fishing Charters   FISHING
(Map p454; ✆70872; www.fishtonga.com) Operates out of Hakula Lodge (p457).

Poppin' Tonga   FISHING
(✆71075; www.talihaubeach.com) Kurt, who also runs Lucky's Beach Houses, specialises in fishing for Giant Trevally, either land or boat based.

Karting
Vava'u Adventures Kart Safaris   KARTS
(Map p456; ✆8746248) Exciting three-hour guided kart tours all over the main island. Take it all in, including wind-blown dust and dirt, while driving your own one- or two-seater kart (US$200/300).

Vava'u Group

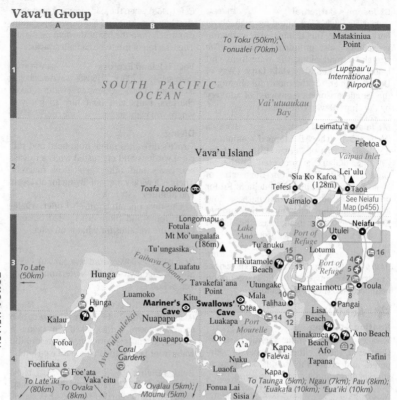

Water Sports

Island resorts and beachside accommodation generally provide or rent out kayaks for guest use. Note that surfing in Vava'u is not for beginners.

TOP CHOICE Friendly Islands Kayak Company SEA KAYAKS
(Map p454; ☎70173; www.fikco.com) This eco-friendly outfit has been revealing some of Tonga's magic to kayaking adventurers on its camping and paddling expeditions around Vava'u (and Ha'apai) since 1991. It provides truly unique experiences (and supplies excellent equipment) on five-/nine-/11-/13-day packages. There's a friendly local Tongan guide on every trip, providing a great way to become friends with and learn about the life of the locals.

Whale Watching

Vava'u has become one of the world's top whale-watching destinations, particularly due to the opportunity to swim with humpbacks. The activity is not without controversy (see p452).

There are 13 commercial whale-watching licensees in Vava'u, all with similar prices (T$250 to T$300 per person per day), so you have plenty of options. The whales are generally around from June to late October. Diving operators (p453) offer whale-swims and are suitably licensed.

A great option is to stay out where the whales are at 'Euaiki island (see p461).

☞ Tours

Land-based tours are the best way, along with Kart Safaris (p453), to see the main island of Vava'u, while a number of operators run day boat excursions that typically include Swallows' and Mariner's Caves, picnicking on an uninhabited island and snorkelling at an offshore reef.

TONGA NEIAFU

Vava'u Tours
ISLAND TOURS

(☎8740000, 8874744; www.vavau.to/portofrefuge villas) Salesi Paea proudly shows visitors all over his home island for T$75.

Cultural Bike Rides
CYCLING

(☎8746247) Jason's rewarding half-day bike tours (T$75) take you to a local village to visit weaving circles, schools, churches, Tongan homes and even cemeteries.

Aquarium Adventures
BOAT TOUR

(☎8771053; www.saildivetonga.to) Stu and Fran offer day tours out on the water on their 45ft catamaran that include sailing, snorkelling at Swallows' Cave, drinks and a barbecue lunch for T$150.

Hakau Adventures
BOAT TOUR

(☎7558164; www.hakauadventures.com) Half- and full-day glass-bottomed boat trips that include swimming, snorkelling, swimming and beach time from T$130 per person.

🎉 Festivals & Events

Regatta Vava'u & Festival
REGATTA

(www.regattavavau.com) Held in late August or early September each year, Regatta Vava'u is a blossoming party week with all sorts of things going on for yachties and landlubbers alike.

🛏 Sleeping

There's a good range of accommodation around Neiafu and its causeway-connected islands (see also p459). Bookings are advised between June and October.

For rentals, look online at www.vavau. to and www.vavauholidayhomes.com. Also, check the noticeboards at Adventure Backpackers (p457) and Café Tropicana (p458).

TOP CHOICE **Port Wine Guest House** GUESTHOUSE $
(Map p456; ☎70479; www.portwineguesthouse. com; r per person with shared/private bathroom T$60/90; P🛜) For a great Tongan

Neiafu

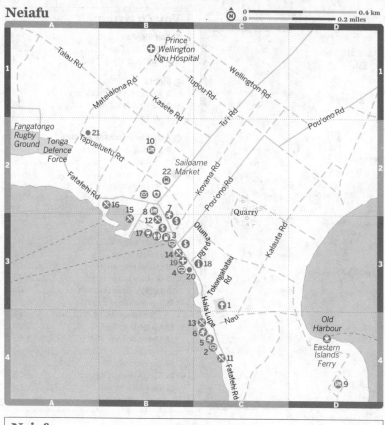

N   0 ━━━━━━━ 0.4 km
0 ━━━━━━━ 0.2 miles

TONGA NEIAFU

experience head to Port Wine, run by kindly Lu'isa Tuiniua and her son Tai. Just back from town in Neiafu, there are two options – the original guesthouse (T$60 per person) or the new guesthouse, Lakemba, which Tai has built out the front (T$90 per person). The latter includes breakfast, use of the kitchen, wi-fi and private bathrooms. There's always a cold coconut in the fridge and fruit comes straight out of the garden. An *umu* is a Sunday highlight for guests.

Port of Refuge Villas   VILLAS $
(Map p456; ☑8740000; www.vavau.to/portof refugevillas; dm T$30, d T$50, house T$150; ⓟ) Four fully furnished clean vacation houses with kitchens only a short walk from town up behind the cathedral. Run by Salesi and Yvette, these homes are a great deal and totally flexible depending on how many of you there are. You can opt for a bed, a private bedroom or take a whole house. Free airport transfers for guests. Salesi also runs Vava'u Tours (see p455).

Harbour View Resort   BUNGALOWS $$$
(Map p454; ☑70687, 7512149; www.harbourview resort.com; cabin T$180, 2-bedroom unit T$230; ⓟ�ⓢ) Set in tropical gardens south of Neiafu, this place has detached cabins, each with kitchenette and verandah. It's a relaxed, family-oriented place run by expat Kiwis. Taxis cost T$10 from Neiafu, T$30 from the airport.

Twin View Motel   MOTEL $$
(Map p454; ☑70597; www.twinview.to; 2-bedroom units T$100-180; ⓟ) Up on the hill with magnificent views 1.5km south of town, this place has good two-bedroom motel units with kitchens that are spacious and tastefully decorated. It also has backpacker rooms (single/double T$40/60).

Hakula Lodge   LODGE $$$
(Map p454; ☑70872; www.fishtonga.com; s/d/tr A$200/225/275; ❄ⓢ) Two top-end units opening onto a full-length verandah overlooking Port of Refuge. Guests can head down the tropical garden path to swim off the private jetty, from which the owners' whale-watching and fishing trips depart (see p453). It's located 2km south of Neiafu.

Vava'u Guest House   GUESTHOUSE $
(Map p454; ☑70300; Fatafehi Rd; s/d T$20/30, fale s/d $75/95) Located 1.5km south of Neiafu and in conjunction with Ovava Restaurant (see p458), the backpacker building down

CHANGE IS IN THE WIND

Not much changes fast in Tonga except businesses in Vava'u. These start up, close down and change ownership and/ or management at a frantic pace. It seems that many come to these islands with a South Pacific dream, buy or start a business, stick at it for a while, then decide it wasn't for them after all. It has been said that 'for every beach in Tonga, a *palangi*'s dreams lie buried in the sands'. During research, it seemed that every second business was up for sale. Keep this in mind if things turn out differently from the description in this book – and send us some feedback.

the front isn't flash, but the four *fale* behind are good value.

Adventure Backpackers   HOSTEL $
(Map p456; ☑70955; www.visitvavau.com/back packers; dm T$30, s/d from T$89/99) This central, modern hostel in the middle of Neiafu makes a handy base to spring into Vava'u's myriad activities and nightlife. Fan-cooled rooms are bright, clean and secure, and there's a shared kitchen and communal area, and a sun-soaked terrace.

Eating

Neiafu has a swath of dining options, many of which double as bars.

Joining a Tongan feast is the best way to experience Tongan food – much of which is cooked in an *umu* – and get a good dose of traditional Tongan music and dance at the same time. Contact the TVB or your accommodation for current feasts. Expect to pay around T$40.

Neiafu's supermarkets stock a reasonable range. On Sunday afternoon, just follow your nose through town to the bakeries.

Aquarium Café   CAFE $$
(Map p456; www.aquariumcafevavau.com; VHF Channel 16; mains T$15-25; ⓑbreakfast, lunch & dinner; @ⓢ) A great one-stop shop, you can get it all here at Aquarium with tasty meals, a fully stocked bar and wi-fi for customers. There are superb views out over the harbour from the deck and excellent service. They also have 12 **moorings** available for rent and can provide wi-fi to the whole harbour.

Top spot in town – you can tell because all the locals and the yachties are here!

Café Tropicana
CAFE $

(Map p456; www.vavau.to/tropicana; sandwiches T$6; ☺breakfast & lunch Mon-Sat; @☺) Nab a table in the cool interior or slouch into a deckchair on the harbour-view terrace at this central cafe next to Adventure Backpackers. Tasty options range from sandwiches and burgers to Tongan dishes. Pies, cookies and cakes line the front cabinet. Wi-fi and computers are on hand (T$3 per 30 minutes) and there's a book swap bookshelf.

Mango Cafe
CAFE $$

(Map p456; www.vavau.to/food3.html; daily specials T$15; ☺breakfast, lunch & dinner) Right on the water and a favourite with yachties who can tie up their tenders here. Good regular menu plus great-value daily specials. The menu is on the website. Mango is also the home of the Port of Refuge Yacht Club (see p453).

Ovava
PIZZA, POLYNESIAN $$

(Map p454; Fatafehi Rd; mains T$15-40; ☺dinner Mon-Sat) Under a huge ovava (banyan) tree 1.5km south of town, Laurence's place produces Vava'u's only wood-fired-oven pizza and top pan-polynesian dishes using local seafood.

Rooster Bistro & Marina Bar
BISTRO $$

(Map p456; mains T$15-35; ☺lunch & dinner Mon-Sat) This waterfront spot offers dishes served with finesse from a Swiss chef. Portions are generous and options include everything from local seafood to international cuisine.

'Utukalongalu Market
MARKET $

(Map p456; ☺8.30am-4.30pm Mon-Fri, 7am-noon Sat) The best place for fresh produce. Close to Halaevalu Wharf.

Vava'u Fish Market
MARKET $

(Map p456; Halaevalu Wharf; ☺8.30am-4.30pm Mon-Fri, to noon or 1pm Sat) The freshest fish can be found here.

Drinking

All the cafes and restaurants mentioned have a brew on offer, but the most dedicated drinking establishment in Neiafu is...

Tonga Bob's
BAR

(Map p456) As laid-back as it comes. Head to Tonga Bob's (run by Matt the Aussie) for everything you could ask for – a sand floor to sink your toes into, ice-cold beers, views over the harbour and a highly entertaining

fakaleiti show (see p465) each Wednesday night. Tonga Bob's is a haven for entertainment, with quiz nights and a big screen for sporting events.

Shopping

Superbly made Tongan handicrafts are sold at the market and at the **Langafonua Handcrafts Shop** next to the TVB on Fatafehi Rd.

Information

Vava'u has its own eclectic English radio station: PIG FM, at 89.3FM. Greg plays what he likes – where else can you still hear Frank Zappa on the radio? A yachties' information net is on VHF Channel 26 at 8.30am each day. There is a Cruising Guide at www.vavau.to.

The **Westpac Bank of Tonga**, **ANZ**, **Western Union** and **MBF**, all on Fatafehi Rd, change cash and travellers cheques. Westpac and ANZ have 24-hour ATMs. Westpac is open Saturday mornings (9am to 11.30am).

Aquarium Café (Map p456; per 15min T$3; ☺8am-11pm) An excellent option for internet access that's open all day. Free wi-fi for customers.

Café Tropicana (Map p456; per 15min T$3; ☺6.30am-6pm Mon-Sat) Internet access and wi-fi.

Police station (Map p456; ☎922; ☺24hr)

Post office (Map p456) Poste restante mail (c/o General Delivery, Post Office, Neiafu, Vava'u).

Prince Wellington Ngu Hospital (Map p456; ☎70201; Mateialona Rd; ☺24hr) For emergencies.

Tonga Visitors Bureau (TVB; Map p456; ☎70115; ☺8.30am-4.30pm Mon-Fri) A well-stocked office with helpful staff happy to assist with bookings and accommodation reservations.

Vava'u Pharmacy & Health Centre (Map p456; ☎70213; pharmacy@kalianetvav.to; ☺8.30am-4pm Mon, Tue, Thu & Fri, to 11.30am Sat) New Zealand–trained doctor and pharmacist. Also retails health products.

Around Vava'u

The best way to see the villages and scenic points on the main island is to take an **Island Tour** (p454) or a **Kart Safari** (p453).

⊙ Sights & Activities

'Ene'io Botanical Garden
BOTANICAL GARDEN

(Map p454; ☎8671048; www.eneio.com) Developed by former Minister of Agriculture, Haniteli Fa'anunu, these gardens will appeal

to those with a botanical bent. With its own restaurant and bar, it's like a secret hideaway. The gift shop sells everything from handicrafts to nonu juice to organic taro chips. Book and they'll find a way to get you there. 'Ene'io Beach is near the eastern extremes of the main island.

'Ano & Hinakauea Beaches BEACHES

(Map p454) Near the southern end of Pangaimotu are beautiful and very quiet beaches, with sheltered turquoise water, abundant vegetation, good snorkelling and a safe anchorage.

Floating Ark Gallery GALLERY

(Map p454; 8887998; VHF Channel 10) This unique gallery, at anchorage 11, features paintings, prints and local arts and crafts. Landlubbers should take a taxi to 'Ano Beach and you'll be picked up there, or if you're on a yacht, sail up and use one of the Ark's moorings. You get one night's free mooring with a purchase from the gallery.

Kurt's Surfing Adventures SURFING

(71075; www.talihaubeach.com) Vava'u's reef surfing gets the thumbs up from Kurt Carlson – check out his website and contact him for details. He only offers surfing trips to guests staying at his Lucky's Beach Houses.

Sleeping & Eating

The long, thin island of 'Utungake is connected by a causeway to Pangaimotu and offers up some good sleeping options.

Tongan Beach Resort RESORT $$$

(Map p454; 70380; VHF Channel 71; www.the tongan.com; bungalows NS$295;) On Hikutamole Beach, this is a relaxed place looking out onto the main channel into Port of Refuge. Under energetic new ownership, it has recently renovated rooms, a lovely sand-floor *fale* bar and beachfront restaurant. Yachties are welcome for dinner.

Mystic Sands MOTEL $$$

(Map p454; 7584148, 7584027; www.mystic sands.net; d & tw T$235, 2-bedroom house T$440;) Offers self-contained motel-like units on the beachfront. There is no restaurant on site but the town, with its restaurants and markets, is 10 minutes away by taxi. Activity operators will pick you up at the jetty out front.

Lucky's Beach Houses BUNGALOWS $

(Map p454; 71075; www.talihaubeach.com; fale T$65, beach house T$140;) Overlooking the water at Talihau Beach at the tip of 'Utungake, this place is run enthusiastically by Kurt and Lynn. There are two houses and two *fale* right by the water. Guests can launch a kayak off the beach to explore the islands and paddle over to nearby Mala. Meals are available. Kurt is the man to talk to about surfing in Vava'u and giant trevally fishing. Look at his website.

Southern Vava'u Islands

If you study the map on p454 you will see that Vava'u has an incredible number of islands and waterways to the south. Visitors can head out to one of the growing number of island resorts or take it all in by boat, by sail, or on a multiday kayak tour.

Vava'u Island Express (70911, 7716848; www.vavauhouseboats.com) operates water taxis, charters, tours and boat hire to get you where you want to go.

MALA

Just south of 'Utungake, the small island of Mala is only a few minutes by boat from the road end. It has a sandy swimming beach and a small resort, **Mala Island Resort** (Map p454; www.malaisland.com).

The **Japanese Gardens** is a beautiful snorkelling spot between Mala and Kapa, though a strong current flows between these two islands and 'Utungake.

KAPA

Kapa island's main attraction, **Swallows' Cave** ('Anapekepeka; Map p454), cuts into a cliff

HELPING OUT

Kurt and Lynn at Lucky's Beach Houses have a good thing going to help out their local village. They request that guests who come to stay with them bring some basic school supplies to be donated to the village primary school. The school and the local children are always in need of things like pencils, crayons, paper and reading materials. They've had a great response and the Talihau village school is all the better for it. This great idea will be greatly appreciated at schools throughout Tonga, especially in the more isolated villages.

on the west side of the island. It's actually inhabited by hundreds of swiftlets, and is easy to swim into. The water is crystal clear with the floor of the cave 18m below the surface. A popular inclusion in day tours, the only access is by boat.

Reef Resort (Map p454; ☎8659276; VHF Channel 71; www.reefresortvavau.com; r T$480, full board T$150) is a top boutique resort that receives excellent reviews. With a perfect beachfront location and spacious, clean rooms, things look bright at Reef Resort. The accommodating owners also run Fafá Island Resort (p443) off Tongatapu. Return airport transfers cost T$100 per person.

HUNGA & FOFOA

To the west, a large, sheltered lagoon formed by Hunga, Kalau and Fofoa offers excellent anchorage and impressive snorkelling.

Ika Lahi Lodge (Map p454; ☎70611; www.tongafishing.com; tw NZ$275, full board NZ$165) is a **fishing-focused resort** (*ika lahi* means 'big fish, many fish'). It's handily close to the deep ocean and has log-cabin-like units with en suite bathrooms and balconies. There's plenty of interest for nonfishing partners. Check out the website for options.

FOE'ATA & FOELIFUKA

The island of Foe'ata, immediately south of Hunga, offers glorious white **beaches** and good snorkelling.

Blue Lagoon (Map p454; ☎8671300; VHF Channel 16; www.bluelagoontonga.com; fales T$335, full board T$130) is a one-of-a-kind ecolodge that enjoys an idyllic beach position on Foe'ata. Each of the eight bungalows is uniquely constructed from local materials, and the food is some of Vava'u's best. Airport transfers cost T$155.

NUAPAPU

Nuapapu is best known for **Mariner's Cave** (Map p454), a hidden underwater cave at its northern end. The main entrance is a couple of metres below the surface and the tunnel is about 4m long; use the swell to pull you towards it, then exit when the swell pushes you out. Make sure you're with someone who knows what they are doing; snorkelling gear is recommended.

'EUA'IKI & 'EUAKAFA

The small raised island of 'Eua'iki has easy boat access to the stunning white **beach**, and a **coral garden** located off the northern shore.

A sandy beach rings the north side of uninhabited 'Euakafa. From its eastern end a trail leads through the forest and mango trees to the summit (100m) and the overgrown tomb of Talafaiva.

MOUNU & 'OVALAU

Mounu and 'Ovalau are two more of the perfect islands Vava'u has in abundance.

Mounu Island Resort (off Map p454; ☎8866403; VHF Channel 77; www.mounuisland.com; from T$550 per night, full board per person T$150) has ecofriendly wooden *fale* spaced around the island for privacy. It has developed a glowing reputation as a place to get away from it all and relax. Whale-watching tours are run by the owners.

Eastern Vava'u Islands

The **Eastern Islands Ferry** (Map p456; ☎7574393; www.southpacifichouse.to) is the best way to see Vava'u's eastern islands. Operates daily to Mafana and 'Ofu islands from the Old Harbour Wharf in Neiafu and also has a five-island day tour.

MAFANA & 'OFU

These islands are well worth a day's exploration. 'Ofu's surrounding waters are the primary habitat of the prized but endangered *'Ofu* shell – note that buying them will only encourage their collection.

Budget accommodation on outer islands in Vava'u is scarce. **Mafana Island Beach Backpackers** (Map p454; ☎8897679; www.mafanaislandbeach.com; tents s/d T$35/55, fales s/d T$55/75) is located on a tranquil secluded beach with tents and *fale* (beds and linen provided). Guests self-cater, with a communal cooking area on the beach, and there are beach showers. Swim, snorkel, kayak and explore the many island tracks. Boat transfers from Neiafu cost T$10 per person.

NIUA GROUP

Tongan tradition remains very much alive on these three small volcanic islands in Tonga's extreme northern reaches. These were the first Tongan islands to be seen by Europeans (Dutchmen Schouten and Le Maire in 1616); it may seem like little has changed since. The main islands of Niuatoputapu and Niuafo'ou are about 100km apart.

STAY WHERE THE WHALES ARE

If the idea of watching whales frolic while you eat your breakfast appeals, stay out where the whales are at Mark Belvedere's **'Eua'iki Island Eco-Resort** (off Map p454; ☑7512935; www.tongaislandresort.com; fale T$400, full board per person T$150).

Previously known as Treasure Island, this is a magical setting on 'Eua'iki island. Its thatched bar-restaurant perches on a white, sandy beach, and solid *fale* with water views are spaced along the beachfront. Snorkelling equipment and kayaks are available.

There are deep channels on both sides of the island that the whales use, and if you hear Mark's dog barking on the beach, you know it's time to look out for the whales. He can hear them when you can't!

Meals generally feature fish (the day's catch), and are available to yachties if booked ahead. Mark is a specialist in the maritime history of the Pacific and makes your visit an educational experience by explaining the seafaring migration of the Pacific. Check out his website (www.kaliafoundation.org) for information on the Polynesian seafaring tradition.

Unless you are on a yacht, any trip to the Niuas should be approached with flexibility in mind as weather conditions often cause delays and cancellations of flights and ferry services.

ⓘ Getting There & Away

AIR Chathams Pacific (p469) flies weekly to Niuatoputapu (T$258 one-way from Vava'u) and fortnightly to Niuafo'ou (T$298 one-way from Vava'u).

BOAT The ferry supposedly makes a trip from Vava'u to Niuatoputapu and Niuafo'ou, then back to Vava'u once a month. The unpredictable schedule is reliant on a number of unreliable factors. Enquire at the TVB in Tongatapu (p445).

Most visitors arrive on private yachts. Both islands are ports of entry to Tonga. Niuafo'ou lacks a decent anchorage or landing site (see boxed text p462). Niuatoputapu has a pass in the reef on the northwest side of the island.

Niuatoputapu

POP 1400 / AREA 18 SQ KM

Niuatoputapu (Very Sacred Coconut) has a squashed sombrero shape made up of a steep and narrow central ridge 130m high and surrounding coastal plains. The north coast is bounded by a series of reefs, but there is a passage through to Falehau Wharf.

In 2009, following the Samoa earthquake, Niuatoputapu suffered extensive tsunami damage and nine people died.

The island is surrounded by magnificent white beaches and is easily circumnavigated on foot. **Boat trips**, including to nearby Tafahi, can be negotiated with local fishermen. There's good **diving** outside the reef,

but no diving equipment is available on the island.

Hihifo, the Niuas' 'capital', has a police station, a post office and a small store. Cash and travellers cheques can be changed at the Treasury, though it sometimes runs out of cash so it's advisable to bring *pa'anga* with you. There is no ATM.

Kalolaine Guesthouse (☑85021; s/d T$20/25) offers up warm hospitality in a village home with a spacious lounge and neat rooms. Guests can use the kitchen or book meals in advance. To find it, just ask a local to point the way.

Tafahi

POP 150 / AREA 3.4 SQ KM

Nine kilometres north of Niuatoputapu is the perfect cone of the extinct volcano Tafahi (656m). On the right tide you can cross to Tafahi in the morning and return in the afternoon. It's a good climb to the summit, from which on a good day you can see Samoa! You'll have to negotiate boat transfers with a local fisherman.

Niuafo'ou

POP 735 / AREA 49 SQ KM

Remote Niuafo'ou, about 100km west of Niuatoputapu, resembles a doughnut floating in the sea. It is a collapsed volcanic cone thought to have once topped 1300m in height. Today, the highest point on the caldera is at 210m, and the enclosed lake is nearly 5km wide and 23m above sea level.

TIN CAN ISLAND

Niuafo'ou is the 'Tin Can Island' legendary for its unique postal service. In days of old, since there was no anchorage or landing site, mail and supplies for residents were sealed up in a biscuit tin and tossed overboard from a passing supply ship. A strong swimmer from the island would then retrieve the parcel. Outbound mail was tied to the end of metre-long sticks, and the swimmer would carry them balanced overhead out to the waiting ship. This method persisted until 1931, when the mail swimmer was taken by a shark.

In keeping with its postal tradition, special Niuafo'ou postage stamps, first issued by the Tongan government in 1983, are highly prized. To stamp collectors, Tin Can Island is legendary. The post must go through...

During the past 150 years, Niuafo'ou has experienced 10 major volcanic eruptions. After a particularly nasty one in 1946, the government evacuated the 1300 residents to 'Eua island, and Niuafo'ou was uninhabited until 200 homesick locals returned in 1958.

Niuafo'ou has no coral reef and no sandy beaches, just open ocean surrounds. A track leads right around the doughnut-shaped volcanic cone and its impressive freshwater lake, **Vai Lahi** (Big Lake). Keep an eye out for Niuafo'ou's most unusual inhabitants, the **megapode birds**, which use the warm volcanic soil to incubate their eggs. Efforts to save the threatened Tongan megapode have included transplanting chicks to the uninhabited volcanic island of Late, one of Vava'u's outlying islands.

There are good campsites on the crater, although you should ask for permission first. A handful of village houses offer guest rooms; contact the TVB in Tongatapu for details. There are several small shops scattered through the villages, but it would be wise to bring plenty of food with you.

Money can be changed at the Treasury. There is no ATM.

UNDERSTAND TONGA

Tonga Today

Politically, Tonga is in the midst of exciting times.

Before King George Tupou V was crowned on 1 August 2008, his Lord Chamberlain announced that the new King would relinquish much of his power to meet the democratic aspirations of his people. Changes were subsequently made to the electoral system, and in the November 2010 elections, the general population of 106,000 Tongans gained the right to vote for 17 spots out of 26 in Parliament. The other nine members are elected by the noble class from among themselves (there are 33 noble titles in Tonga).

Eighty-nine per cent of eligible voters turned out to cast their ballots in this historic election with the Democratic Party of the Friendly Islands, led by long-term pro-democracy leader Akilisi Pohiva, winning 12 of the 17 seats available to commoners. This wasn't quite enough however. The other five seats were won by independents and they joined the nine nobles for a 14 to 12 majority in parliament and elected a noble, Lord Tu'ivakano, to be Prime Minister. This irked a number of political commentators. Democracy is taking root though, and the next elections in 2014 are sure to be keenly fought.

Economically, Tonga is in the doldrums. Remittances from Tongans living abroad are dropping as worldwide recession hits and second-generation Tongans abroad need their hard-earned cash to raise their own families – rather than sending it back to Tonga. International aid is also apparently dropping, though aid from China, in the form of Chinese workers building new roads in Tonga, is plainly visible. Tonga's local economy depends on tourism, agriculture and fishing.

Psychologically, as this is written, Tonga is on a high. Ikale Tahi, the national rugby team, had the honour of playing New Zealand in the opening match of the 2011 Rugby World Cup in front of enthused fans and a worldwide TV audience. The team then topped that by beating eventual finalists France 19–14, igniting wild celebrations through the islands with an effort that will be talked about for generations. All this excitement has done much to gloss over Tonga's various problems.

History

Tonga has a rich mythological tradition, and many ancient legends relate to the islands' creation. One tells that the Tongan islands were fished out of the sea by the mighty Polynesian god Tangaloa. Another story has Tonga plucked from the ocean by the demigod Maui, a temperamental hero well known throughout the Pacific.

The earliest date confirmed by radiocarbon testing for settlement of the Tongan group is 1100 BC. On Tongatapu, the Lapita people had their first capital at Toloa, near present-day Fua'amotu International Airport. Archaeological excavations in the village of Hihifo in Ha'apai unearthed Lapita pottery that has carbon dated settlement of this area to more than 3000 years ago. The Vava'u Group has been settled for around 2000 years.

The first king of Tonga, known as the Tu'i Tonga, was 'Aho'eitu. He came to power some time in the middle of the 10th century AD and was the first in a line of almost 40 men to hold the title.

During the 400 years after the first Tu'i Tonga, the Tongans were aggressive colonisers, extending their empire over eastern Fiji, Niue and northward as far as the Samoas and Tokelau.

European Arrival

The first European arrivals in Tonga were Dutch explorers Willem Schouten and Jacob Le Maire, who discovered the Niuas group in 1616.

Tongatapu's first European visitor was Dutchman Abel Tasman, who spent a few days trading with islanders in 1643. He named the island 'Amsterdam'. In the same year, Tasman was also the first European to visit the Ha'apai group.

The next European contact came in 1773 with James Cook, who became close friends with the 30th Tu'i Tonga, Fatafehi Paulaho.

Vava'u remained undiscovered by Europeans until Don Francisco Antonio Mourelle of Spain showed up in 1781, making it one of the last South Pacific islands to be contacted by Europeans.

House of Tupou

In 1831 missionaries baptised the ruling Tu'i Tonga, who took the Christian name George. As King George Tupou I, he united Tonga and, with the help of the first prime minister, Reverend Shirley Baker, came up with a flag, a state seal and a national anthem, then began drafting a constitution, which was passed in 1875. It included a bill of rights, a format for legislative and judicial procedures, laws for succession to the throne and a section on land tenure. It is also responsible for Tonga's heavily Christian laws today.

The second king, George Tupou II, who took over in 1893, lacked the charisma, character and fearlessness of his predecessor. He signed a Treaty of Friendship with Britain in 1900, placing Tonga under British protection and giving Britain control over Tonga's foreign affairs. When he died at the age of 45 in 1918, his 18-year-old daughter Salote became queen.

Queen Salote

A popular figure, Queen Salote's primary concerns for her country were medicine and education. With intelligence and compassion she made friends for Tonga throughout the world and was greatly loved by her subjects and foreigners alike. Her legendary attendance at Queen Elizabeth's coronation in 1953 won many hearts as she took part in the procession bareheaded in an open

STOP PRESS: THE KING IS DEAD, LONG LIVE THE KING

In what was a shock to all Tongans, King George Tupou V died suddenly in Hong Kong on 18 March, 2012. A hundred and fifty pallbearers carried him to his grave and the country mourned. Tongans may be mourning more than his death, however, as his deeply religious and staunchly conservative younger brother is the new King Tupou VI. The former Crown Prince, Tupouto'a Lavaka Ata has previously voiced his opposition to democracy for Tonga and has a chequered history in charge, including a stint as Prime Minister that ended in his resignation. Tonga's economy plummeted during his leadership, leading to growing calls for democracy. He was also involved in the demise of Royal Tongan Airlines, which lost the country millions. While many worry about the future under the new king, others feel that as a family man with a wife and children – his brother was a bachelor – he will be a more caring king.

THE 'FRIENDLY ISLANDS' – A MISNOMER?

On Captain James Cook's third voyage – he later died in Hawai'i on this same trip – he spent from April to July 1777 in the Tongan islands. While visiting Lifuka in the Ha'apai group, Cook and his men were treated to lavish feasting and entertainment by chief Finau, inspiring Cook to name his South Seas paradise the Friendly Islands.

It was later learned, through William Mariner (p446), that the celebration had been part of a conspiracy to raid the two ships *Resolution* and *Discovery* for their plainly visible wealth. The entertainment had been planned in order to gather the Englishmen in one spot so that they could be quickly killed and their ships looted. There was, however, a last-minute dispute between Finau and his nobles, and the operation was abandoned. Cook never learned how narrowly they had escaped – if he had, he may have changed his name for the 'friendly islands'.

carriage through London, smiling resolutely at the crowds despite the pouring rain.

World's Heaviest Monarch

King Taufa'ahau Tupou IV took over as ruler of Tonga on his mother's death in 1965. He re-established full sovereignty for Tonga on 4 June 1970 and oversaw Tonga's admission to the Commonwealth of Nations and to the UN. In his later years, however, he made a number of unpopular decisions, including selling Tongan passports to anyone who wanted one and appointing an American to the dual role of financial advisor and official court jester who oversaw the loss of T$50 million in funds.

An imposing figure who was renowned as the world's heaviest monarch, the 210kg king became a health role model for Tongans when he shed more than 75kg in weight. He was 88 when he died in September 2006.

In the last years of his life, the king resisted growing calls for democracy, which peaked in a 2005 strike by public servants that lasted for months and resulted in a huge growth of pro-democracy sentiment. Two months after his death, riots in Nuku'alofa killed eight, destroyed much of the business district, shocked the world and led to Australian and New Zealand troops being sent to the supposedly peaceful Pacific paradise.

King George Tupou V

Following in the footsteps of his father, King George Tupou V was crowned in a lavish ceremony on 1 August 2008. The monocled bachelor, a graduate of Oxford and Sandhurst, came to power with the Lord Chamberlain making the following statement before his coronation: 'The sovereign of the only Polynesian kingdom...is voluntarily surrendering his powers to meet the democratic aspirations of many of his people...the people favour a more representative, elected parliament. The king agreed with them. He planned to guide his country through a period of political and economic reform for the 21st century.' See Tonga Today (p462) for what has happened since.

The Culture

Tonga is a largely homogenous, church- and family-oriented society. Although, on the whole, Tongans are open and extremely hospitable, due to cultural nuances many foreigners feel a bit at arm's length.

Population

Tongans are proud Polynesians with a unique culture, different from other South Pacific nations. Tongans make up the vast majority of the people – there are a few *palangi* (Westerners) and a small but significant population of Chinese immigrants.

Tonga's total resident population is around 106,000. Tongatapu has more than 65% of the total population, with approximately 30% of the total living in and around Nuku'alofa (the island's and the nation's capital).

Estimates suggest there are as many Tongans living abroad as there are in the kingdom, mostly in New Zealand, Australia and the US. There are now many second- and third-generation Tongans living in these countries.

Religion

Tonga is, on the surface at least, a very religious country. Ninety-nine per cent of the country identifies itself as being of Christian

faith. The Free Wesleyan Church (which is the royal family's church of choice) claims the largest number of adherents, followed by the (Methodist) Free Church of Tonga, the Church of England, the Roman Catholics, Seventh Day Adventists and the wealthy and increasingly prominent Mormons.

Churches are central to everyday life and, as they are seen as social and community organisations, Tongans donate a lot of money to them. Because of this, Tongans are very conservative and bring religion into all kinds of aspects of their daily lives. Many Tongans, especially women, may go to church two, three or even four times every Sunday. Public displays of affection between the sexes are a no-no.

Many Tongans still believe in the spirits, taboos, superstitions, medical charms and gods of pre-Christian Polynesia. One such belief is that if a family member is suffering a serious illness, it is because the bones of their ancestors have been disturbed. Many will return to old family burial sites, dig up remains and rebury relatives to remedy their own ill health.

Lifestyle

Family is very important in Tongan life, with each member playing a role and elders commanding respect. A family unit often consists of all sorts of extras including adopted children, cousins and other relatives living alongside the parents, children and grandparents. Everything is communal, from food to sleeping arrangements and everyone is looked after. The patriarch is usually the head of the family and jobs are distributed according to gender.

You'll often see Tongans in conservative dress wearing distinctive pandanus mats called *ta'ovala* around their waists. In place of a *ta'ovala*, women often wear a *kiekie*, a decorative waistband of woven strips of pandanus. Men frequently wear a wraparound skirt known as a *tupenu* and women an ankle-length *vala* (skirt) and *kofu* (tunic).

Education

Tongans highly value education. The literacy rate is 99%, reflecting the large investment that Tonga – and some highly visible religious groups – have made in the people. English is taught in schools throughout the islands.

Visitors may be surprised at the colourful array of school uniforms worn by Tongan students. Children at government primary schools wear red and white, government secondary school students wear maroon, blue is the colour for Wesleyan schoolkids, orange for Church of Tonga schools, and Mormon school students wear green. This is standard throughout the country.

Language

See the Language chapter on p591 for Tongan basics.

Arts

Handicrafts

Tongan handicrafts are handmade from local materials and each piece is unique, not mass produced. A lot of time and effort has gone into making all those bone-carved necklaces, wooden carvings, woven baskets

---

FAKALEITI

One of the most distinctive features of Tongan culture are *fakaleiti*, a modern continuation of an ancient Polynesian tradition, known as *fa'afafine* in Samoa and *mahu* or *rae rae* in French Polynesia.

The term *fakaleiti* is made up of the prefix *faka-* (in the manner of) and *-leiti* from the English word *lady*. Traditionally, if a Tongan woman had too many sons and not enough daughters she would need one of the sons to assist with 'women's work' such as cooking and housecleaning. This child would then be brought up as a daughter. These days, becoming a *fakaleiti* can also be a lifestyle choice. There is little stigma attached to *fakaleiti*, and they mix easily with the rest of society, often being admired for their style.

On Tongatapu, the Tonga Leitis' Association is an active group – note that members prefer to call themselves simply *leiti* (ladies). The association sponsors several popular, well-attended events, including the international Miss Galaxy competition in early July.

Visitors to Vava'u can't help but enjoy the *fakaleiti* show on Wednesday nights at Tonga Bob's (see p458).

and *tapa* mats that you see at markets and handicraft shops.

Women's groups often work together making handicrafts and especially *tapa* and woven mats, which are treasured possessions in every household and used for important occasions like weddings and funerals.

Tapa is made from beaten bark of the mulberry tree, and as women usually work together in a mat-making group to produce a large piece, it is often divided up later. Woven mats are made from pandanus leaves and used for floor coverings or as *ta'ovalas,* to be worn around the waist.

Visitors should avoid buying handicrafts made from turtleshell or whalebone while in Tonga.

Music & Dance

Tongans love to sing and they do so enthusiastically in church, at festivals and dances, and even in small kava circles. They also love brass marching bands and every high school has one. Young Tongans, however, increasingly listen to imported Western music, including rap and whatever can be downloaded from the internet.

The most frequently performed traditional dance in Tonga is called the *lakalaka*. The *tau'olunga,* a female solo dance, is the most beautiful and graceful of all Tongan dances, while the most popular male dance is the *kailao* – the war dance.

At feasts that visitors may go to, female dancers are often lathered in coconut oil and, as they dance, members of the audience approach and plaster paper money to the sticky body. This is good form and 'tips' given in this manner will be greatly appreciated.

Environment

The Kingdom of Tonga is made up of 171 islands, scattered across 700,000 sq km of ocean. Geographically Tonga is composed of four major island groups, which are, from south to north: Tongatapu and 'Eua, Ha'apai, Vava'u and the Niuas.

Tonga sits on the eastern edge of the Indo-Australian plate, which has the Pacific tectonic plate sliding under it from the east, creating the Tonga Trench. This 2000km-long oceanic valley that stretches from Tonga to New Zealand is one of the deepest in the world – if Mt Everest was placed in the deepest part of the Tonga Trench,

there would still be more than 2km of water on top of it. Tonga is moving southeast at 20mm a year, meaning that the region is a particularly volatile area for volcanic and earthquake activity.

Ecology

While Tonga's national flower is the heilala, colourful and scented hibiscus, frangipani, bird of paradise and other flowers create an oasis of colour. There are coconut groves and banana plantations amid fields of taro, cassava and yams. Papaya are everywhere. Huge rain trees, mango trees and banyans dot the landscape, while mangroves cover the mudflats.

Dolphins and migrating humpback whales swim in the waters around Tonga. The humpbacks come from June to October and can often be seen offshore from the major islands.

The only land mammal native to Tonga is the flying fox (fruit bat; *peka*). Interesting birdlife includes the *henga* (blue-crowned lorikeet); the *koki* (red shining parrot) of 'Eua; and the *malau* (megapode or incubator bird), originally found only on the island of Niuafo'ou, but introduced in recent years to uninhabited Late Island to the west of Vava'u in an effort to save it from extinction.

Conservation Issues

A number of murky conservation issues cloud the waters of Tonga. These are mainly based around the environment being compromised for economic gain and include the following:

Swimming with whales There are arguments that swimming with whales alters their behaviour and has a detrimental affect on both the mothers and babies.

Green turtle conservation Tongans eat green turtles, often as part of religious ceremonies, but turtle numbers are dwindling.

Sea cucumbers Asian culinary tastes mean that big dollars can be earned by exporting sea cucumbers to Asia. There is a fear that they are being overfished.

Aquarium fish It has been suggested that exporting brightly coloured aquarium fish to the USA is to the detriment of populations around Tongan reefs.

National Parks

Tonga has eight officially protected areas, including six national marine parks and

reserves, and two national parks – the 449-hectare 'Eua National Park and the Mt Talau National Park in Vava'u.

Food & Drink

Being an island nation, Tonga is surrounded by the sea and Tongans will eat just about anything that comes out of it, from shellfish to shark to sea turtle. *'Ota'ika,* raw fish in coconut milk, is an island-wide favourite.

Pigs are prized possessions and roam the streets along with chickens. For feasts, smaller pigs are roasted on spits over open fires while bigger ones are cooked in *umu* (underground ovens).

Root crops such as taro, sweet potato and yams are easy to grow in Tonga, so take precedence over other vegetables, which are much harder to produce.

Tropical fruits are everywhere, with coconuts, bananas and papaya available year-round. Summer is the season for mango, pineapple, passionfruit and guava.

Unfortunately, imported goods are having detrimental effects on Tongan diets and obesity is a problem. One of the worst offenders is fatty mutton *(sipi)*, imported from New Zealand, and canned meats.

There are bakeries throughout Tonga producing a wide variety of goodies. Tongans love *keki* (doughnuts).

Beer is available everywhere, but is imported and expensive. As in other South Pacific countries, Tongan men drink kava, made from pepper roots. This is done as a social activity by groups of men in kava circles, usually in the evenings and late into the night.

SURVIVAL GUIDE

Directory A–Z
Accommodation

'Resort' is an extremely loose term in Tonga. If prices are surprisingly cheap, don't expect much in the way of facilities. Even if prices are expensive, don't expect too much. Check the websites but don't believe everything you see.

Tonga does not have a range of good hotels. Smaller boutique-style accommodation is a much better option. There is boutique-style accommodation with plenty of comforts on Tongatapu and its nearby islands, on Foa in Ha'apai and throughout the Vava'u group.

Good budget and midrange guesthouse options are available – many with cooking facilities. They'll be cheaper with shared bathroom, more expensive with private bathroom.

Camping is generally discouraged and is illegal in Ha'apai and Vava'u unless part of a guided trip. Some guesthouses allow camping on their property. Ask first!

PRICE RANGES

The following price ranges refer to a double room with bathroom. Unless otherwise stated tax is included in the price.

$ less than T$80

$$ T$80 to T$150

$$$ more than T$150

Business Hours

Here are some standard business hours, but remember, time is a flexible entity in Tonga. Virtually everything is closed on Sunday.

Banks 9am to 4pm Monday to Friday.

Bars 11am to 12.30am Monday to Friday, to 11.30pm Saturday.

Cafes early to 10.30pm Monday to Saturday.

Post offices & government offices 8.30am to 4pm Monday to Friday.

Shops 8am to 5pm Monday to Friday, to 1pm Saturday.

Children

Tonga is a great destination for families. There is plenty to keep kids entertained and Tongans love children.

Bring your essentials with you. Disposable nappies (diapers) and powdered milk are widely available. Bring children's snorkelling gear and your own child car seat.

Embassies & Consulates

The following foreign diplomatic representatives are found in Nuku'alofa:

Australia (Map p436; ☑23244; www.tonga. embassy.gov.au; Salote Rd) High Commission.

China (Map p436; ☑24554; Vuna Rd) Embassy.

EU (☑23820; eutonga@kalianet.to; Taufa'ahau Rd) European Commission.

Japan (Map p436; ☏22221; National Reserve Bank Bldg, Salote Rd)

New Zealand (Map p436; ☏23122; nzhcnuk@kalianet.to; Taufa'ahau Rd) High Commission.

UK (Map p436; ☏24395; britcomt@kalianet.to; Vuna Rd) High Commission.

US (Peace Corps; ☏25466) Nearest US Embassy is in Suva, Fiji.

Food

See p467 for information on what is available in Tonga. The following prices ranges for a main course were used in the Eating options in this chapter:

$ less than T$15

$$ T$15 to T$30

$$$ more than T$30

Gay & Lesbian Travellers

Homosexuality is an accepted fact of life in Tonga. You'll see plenty of gay men around. The fine old Polynesian tradition of *fakaleiti* (see p465) is alive and well. The lesbian population is much more underground. Public displays of sexual affection are frowned upon, whether gay or straight.

Internet Access

Internet cafes are throughout Tonga, with more in Tongatapu and Vava'u. Charges are around T$6 per hour. Many accommodation houses have wireless and/or computers available. Slow connections are the norm.

Money

Cash is king. Be sure to take it with you to Ha'apai and 'Eua where there are no ATMs. There are ATMs in Tongatapu and Vava'u, including an ATM outside Arrivals at Fua'amotu International Airport. It's easy

PRACTICALITIES

» **Customs regulations** You may bring two cartons of cigarettes and 2.25L of spirits or 4.5L of wine or beer into Tonga duty free.

» **Currency** Notes in denominations of one, two, five, 10, 20 and 50 *pa'anga* (T$) and coins in denominations of one, five, 10, 20 and 50 *seniti*.

» **Electricity** 240 volts AC Hz/50 cycle.

to change major currencies at banks and money exchanges.

Credit cards are accepted at many tourist facilities but often attract a 4% to 5% fee on transactions. Visa and MasterCard are the most common.

Tongans don't expect tips but you won't cause any offence by rewarding special service with one. *Fakapale* (gifts of money) are often given to performers at cultural events.

Public Holidays

In addition to New Year's Day, Easter, Christmas Day and Boxing Day (see p579 for dates), public holidays in Tonga include the following:

Anzac Day 25 April

Emancipation Day 4 June

Crown Prince Tupouto'a-Lavaka's Birthday 12 July

Official Birthday of the King of Tonga 1 August

Constitution Day 4 November

King George Tupou I Commemoration Day 4 December

Safe Travel

Tonga, in general, is a safe country to visit, though late nights and alcohol can be a bad mix and brawls are not uncommon in bars.

Dogs can be aggressive. Do as the Tongans do and pretend to throw a stone; the dogs will cower away.

Telephone

The country code for Tonga is ☏676, and there are no local area codes. Dial ☏913 for the international operator and ☏910 for directory enquiry. The emergency phone number is ☏911.

Public phones are located throughout Tonga. You can use phonecards (readily available in denominations of T$5, T$10 and T$20) to make local and overseas calls.

Mobile (cell) phones are the must-have accessory in Tonga. Most foreign phones set up for global roaming will work here and coverage is reasonably good throughout the islands. The two telecommunication companies are **Tonga Communications Corporation** (TCC; UCall Mobile Shop; ☏27006; www.tcc.to) and **Digicel** (☏8761000; www.digiceltonga.com), and a cheap local phone, including SIM, will cost you around T$50. Digicel also offers a T$10 Visitor SIM that expires after 30 days.

Time

Tonga is 20 minutes east of the 180th meridian, placing it 13 hours ahead of Greenwich Mean Time. Tonga does not observe daylight savings. At noon in Tonga, the time is:

» 9am the same day in Sydney
» 11am the same day in Auckland
» 11pm the previous day in London
» 3pm the previous day in Los Angeles.

Tourist Information

Tonga Visitors Bureau (www.thekingdom oftonga.com)

Vavu'a Islands (www.vavau.to)

Ha'apai Islands (www.haapai.to)

'Eua Island (www.eua-island-tonga.com)

Matangi Tonga (www.matangitonga.to) Online newspaper.

Lonely Planet (www.lonelyplanet.com/tonga) Planning advice, recommendations and reviews.

Visas

Most countries' citizens are granted a 31-day stay on arrival. You'll need a passport with at least six months' validity and an onward ticket. One-month extensions are granted at the immigration department for up to six months at T$46 per month. Contact the **Tonga Immigration Department** (☎26969; visatonga@gmail.com).

Those intending to fly in and depart Tonga by yacht require a letter of authority from a Tongan diplomatic mission overseas or the immigration division.

Getting There & Away
Air

Three airlines fly into Tonga. Access is easy from New Zealand, Australia and Fiji with direct flights. Coming from anywhere else, you'll need to make connections at Auckland, Sydney or Nadi. The cheapest flights are booked early and online.

Air New Zealand (Map p436; ☎23192; www. airnewzealand.com; Air NZ Travel Centre, Vuna Rd)

Fiji Airways (Map p436; ☎23422; www. airpacific.com; Vuna Rd) Formerly known as Air Pacific.

Virgin Australia (Map p436; ☎24566; www. virginaustralia.com; Taufa'ahau Rd)

Sea

Trans-Pacific yachts arrive on the trade winds from Samoa, the Cook Islands and French Polynesia. Others come north from New Zealand. All vessels calling on Tonga must give customs 24-hour advance notice of arrival. To summon the harbour master and for emergencies in Tonga use VHF Channel 16. It is no longer necessary to formally clear in and out of each island group (see www.noonsite.com).

Ports of entry are Nuku'alofa (Tongatapu), Neiafu (Vava'u), Pangai (Ha'apai), Falehau (Niuatoputapu) and Futu (Niuafo'ou).

Getting Around
Air

Flying is by far the easiest, fastest and most comfortable way to get around Tonga.

Chathams Pacific (Map p436; ☎23192; www.chathamspacific.com; Air NZ Travel Centre, Vuna Rd) operates all domestic flights in Tonga. Bookings can be made and paid for online and flights are scheduled to work in with arriving and departing international flights (no flights on Sundays). There are three price levels – EasyGo, Standard or Flexi fares. Book early to get the cheapest fares. Some example fares:

ROUTE	EASYGO FARE	DURATION/ FREQUENCY
Tongatapu–Vava'u	T$231	45min/2 daily
Tongatapu–Ha'apai	T$153	30min/daily
Tongatapu–'Eua	T$70	10min/2 daily
Ha'apai–Vava'u	T$143	30min/3–4 weekly
Vava'u–Niuafo'ou	T$298	1hr/fortnightly
Vava'u–Niuatoputapu	T$255	1hr/weekly

KINGDOM AIR PASSES

There are four kinds of Kingdom Air Pass:

AIR PASS	DESTINATIONS	FARES DEC-MAY/ JUN-NOV
Fonu (Turtle) Pass	Tongatapu– Ha'apai–'Eua	T$390/ T$458
Anga (Shark) Pass	Tongatapu– Ha'apai–Vava'u	T$438/ T$541
Tolofini (Dolphin) Pass	Tongatapu– Vava'u–'Eua	T$540/ T$602
Tofua'a (Whale) Pass	Tongatapu–Ha'apai– Vava'u–'Eua	T$564/ T$693

AVIATION BUFFS READ THIS!

Aviation buffs have started turning up in Tonga from all over the world to ride one of the last remaining DC3s on a scheduled commercial service. Officially named *Tanagaloa*, this fully restored DC3 first flew as part of the New Zealand Air Force in 1944! It has been cruising the skies ever since, and after being lovingly restored by **Chathams Pacific** (p469; see the photos on its website), has been flying the Tongatapu–Ha'apai route. If you are requesting your flights as part of a Kingdom Air Pass, be sure to ask for a seat on the *Tanagaloa*, surely the most photographed aircraft flying the South Pacific skies.

INTERISLAND FERRY SCHEDULE:

DEPARTS	ARRIVES
Nuku'alofa, 10pm Mon	Pangai (Ha'apai), 8.30am Tue
Pangai (Ha'apai), 10am Tue	Neiafu (Vava'u), 5pm Tue
Neiafu (Vava'u), 10am Wed	Pangai (Ha'apai), 5pm Wed
Pangai (Ha'apai), 6pm Wed	Nuku'alofa, 6am Thu

NUKU'ALOFA TO 'EUA

The ferry trip (two to three hours, T$28 one-way) on either **MV Alaimoana** (☏21326) or **MV 'Ikale** (☏23855) leaves Nuku'alofa at 12.30pm on Tuesday, Thursday, Friday and Saturday. The return trip departs 'Eua at 5am Monday, Wednesday, Friday and Saturday.

OTHER VESSELS

Smaller islands off the main ferry routes in all island groups can be reached by smaller boats.

Boat

INTERISLAND FERRY

The **Tonga Visitors Bureau** (TVB; www.thekingdomoftonga.com) lists ferry schedules, which must be rechecked prior to intended travel.

Steer clear of the MV *Pulupaki*, which also sails between Tongatapu and Vava'u. One look should have you running the other way from this rusty tub, which in the past has sailed despite an order of detainment of vessel from the Ministry of Transport for being unsafe.

Friendly Islands Shipping Company (Map p436; ☏22582; www.fisa.to; Queen Salote Wharf, Nuku'alofa) operates the MV *'Otuanga'ofa*, a relatively sparkling beauty donated by the Japanese government in 2011. It plies the waters between Tongatapu and Vava'u, and occasionally heads to the Niuas. Check the timetable before you turn up.

APPROXIMATE ECONOMY FARES:

(Note that the following are adult fares; children aged 4–12 years pay half price.)

ROUTE	FARE
Nuku'alofa–Pangai (Ha'apai)	T$68
Nuku'alofa–Neiafu (Vava'u)	T$88
Pangai (Ha'apai)–Neiafu (Vava'u)	T$60
Neiafu (Vava'u)–Niuatoputapu	T$214
Neiafu (Vava'u)–Niuafo'ou	T$224

Bus

Buses run on Tongatapu, and in a more limited capacity on Vava'u and its causeway-linked islands. Fares range from T$0.50 to T$1.70 depending on the island and the distance travelled. Don't expect to get where you're going in a hurry but riding a local bus is a cultural experience in itself.

Car

Rental cars are available on Tongatapu and Vava'u. To be legal, you need a Tongan driving licence from the police; simultaneously produce your home driving licence, your passport and T$60 cash. Hiring a car or van with a driver is another option.

People drive very slowly on the left-hand side of the road. The speed limit is 40km/h in villages and 65km/h elsewhere. When driving, watch out for children, dogs, chickens and pigs and don't park under coconut trees – you will be liable for the broken windscreen.

Taxi

Taxis have a 'T' in front of the numbers on the licence plate. There are plenty of taxis on Tongatapu and Vava'u, though it may not be

2009 FERRY TRAGEDY

Tragedy struck Tonga in August 2009 with the sinking of the *Princess Ashika* and the loss of more than 70 lives. The *Ashika* was a stop-gap measure. The previous main ferry, the MV *'Olovaha,* had been deemed unseaworthy and the *Ashika* brought in to replace it until the arrival of a new ferry from Japan in 2011.

As it turned out, the *Ashika* was 10 years older and less seaworthy than the *'Olovaha* – and went down in a disaster that touched virtually every family in Tonga. To make matters worse, the new king, in a move that did not endear him to his people, headed overseas on holiday the next day without comment, despite being aware of the tragic events.

Subsequent investigations have seen government officials resign, payouts to victims' families and a number of civil court cases. If there is any positive outcome from this awful event, it is that all ferries and aircraft have come under intense scrutiny, and safety standards have risen dramatically. The new ferry, the MV *'Otuanga'ofa,* donated by the Japanese government, should induce confidence in all who ride upon it.

There is a wall of remembrance, featuring the faces of those who died on the *Ashika,* on the inland side of Vuna Rd, opposite the domestic ferry terminal in Nuku'alofa.

an 'official' taxi that picks you up. If you ask someone to organise a taxi, it may be their husband, brother or nephew who comes to get you. Just pay the going rate.

Passengers should always ask the rate before getting in the taxi and ask for the going rate at your accommodation before you leave so you have a ballpark figure.

Vanuatu

Includes »

Why Go?

Where else can you jump from a tropical fish- and coral-filled blue hole into a 4WD truck to watch an active volcano spit out lava high above you? Contrasts like these make Vanuatu a country well worth taking the time to explore. The ni-Van take life in smiling strides, and as you adjust to their early mornings and dark evenings, you'll wonder why you've ever lived life in a rush. It's all thatched-roof accommodation in the outer islands but glitzy resorts abound on Efate and Santo. These islands also boast great roads, giving you round-island access on Efate and smooth access to stunning beaches and blue holes on Santo. Add to that scented balmy breezes and several best-in-the-world experiences that few people know about: a luxury liner shipwrecked in clear waters, gigantic banyan trees, pounding waterfalls, an ancient living culture with extraordinary ceremonies and picture-perfect beaches.

Best Places to Stay

» Rocky Ridge Bungalows (p495)
» Havannah (p487)
» Oyster Island Restaurant and Resort(p513)
» Traveller's Budget Motel (p481)

Best Places to Eat

» Mangoes Restaurant (p483)
» Deco Stop Restaurant (p510)
» Jill's Cafe (p483)
» Kelsorn's Exotic Thai Kitchen (p483)

When to Go
Port Vila

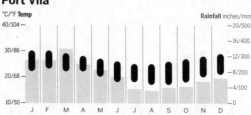

Late Sep–Oct Avoid Australian school holidays and enjoy warm weather without the rain.	**Apr–Jun** Cyclone season is over. Pentecost's land diving is in full swing.	**Nov–Dec** Christmas time; accommodation is plentiful.

Connections

Regular passenger ferries head north weekly from Port Vila and cost two-thirds the price of an airfare. Cargo ships stop at most villages on their route, and are often more comfortable and cheaper than truck travel along rutted roads. Most villages have speedboats, and interisland travel is possible (for example, between Ambae, Maewo and Pentecost).

Air Vanuatu flies to 26 airports, and Air Safaris and Air Taxi fly charters (see p524).

ITINERARIES

One Week

Take the morning flight from Port Vila to **Tanna**. Cross the incredible ash plain by 4WD truck and find your tree-house haven beneath rumbling **Mt Yasur**. Climb the active volcano before dusk then witness the fireworks. Back at **Port Vila**, explore the **cascades** then head to northern Efate to **Pele** or **Nguna** for some rustic island time. Return to Vila and visit one of its three islands for lunch, dinner and snorkelling. Fly north to **Santo** to explore Million Dollar Point and relax at **Oyster Island**, taking a day trip to stunning **Champagne Beach**.

Two Weeks

As above, with more time to enjoy Port Vila's organised activities. Fly to **Ambrym** to hike its two volcanoes, witness a Rom dance and stock up on local carvings. Between April and June, head to **Pentecost** and witness the famous land diving. Enjoy the isolation and beauty of **the Maskelynes**, off Malekula, before heading up north of **Norsup** to see original cannibal sites.

Keeping Costs Down

Flexibility is the key to travelling Vanuatu's islands cheaply.

Catch passenger ferries and the odd cargo ship and always go with the regular transport (both speedboat and truck) instead of expensive charters.

Shop for fresh food at local markets and self-cater in Port Vila and Luganville.

AT A GLANCE

Currency Ni-Vanuatu Vatu (VT)

Language Bislama, French

Mobile phones Local SIMs can be used in unlocked European and Australian phones.

Money ATMs are only found in Luganville and Port Vila. Travellers cheques can be cashed on some islands, but cash is preferable.

Visas 30-day visas are issued at the border for most nationalities. Extensions are available.

Fast Facts

» **Capital** Port Vila (Efate)
» **Country code** ☑678
» **Emergency** ambulance ☑25566; police ☑22222
» **Land area** 12,200 sq km
» **Population** 234,000

VANUATU

Exchange Rates

Australia	A$1	94VT
Canada	C$1	90VT
Europe	€1	116VT
Japan	¥100	116VT
New Zealand	NZ$1	73VT
UK	UK£1	144VT
USA	US$1	20VT

For current exchange rates see www.xe.com.

Set Your Budget

» **Budget hotel room** 3500–8000VT
» **Two-course meal** 4500VT
» **Museum entrance** 700VT
» **Bottle of beer** 500VT
» **Transport ticket** 150VT

Vanuatu Highlights

1 Camping near **Mt Marum** (p501), an active volcano, while surrounded by the jungle, cane forests, lava beds and ash plains on Ambrym

2 Swimming through an underwater world of luxury liners, coral gardens and encrusted caves off **Luganville** (p507)

3 Connecting with people's savagery and mysticism at cannibal sites off the **Dog's Head** (p498) on Malekula

4 Talking to the gods and hearing their thunderous replies punctuated with brilliant volcanic fireworks at **Mt Yasur** (p493) on Tanna

5 Relaxing 'resort style' at the delightful **Oyster Island** (p513) on Santo

---

166°E   168°E   170°E

TORRES ISLANDS

Hiu
Tegua
Linua
Loh
Toga
Kamilisa Guesthouse
Ureparapara
Waterfall Bay Yacht Club & Waterfall Bungalows
Rah Paradise Beach Bungalows
Rah
Mota
Mota Lava
Sola
Leumerous Guesthouse & Yacht Club
Vanua Lava
BANKS ISLANDS
Gaua (Santa Maria)
Wongrass Bungalow
Fresh Wind Bungalow
Lake Letas
Mt Garet (797m)
Mere Lava

TORBA PROVINCE

PENAMA PROVINCE

Big Water Waterfall
Sanasom
Maewo
Mule Ocean View Guesthouse
Laone
Ambae
Lonorore
Pentecost

Espiritu Santo
Port Olry
Oyster Island **5**
Champagne Beach 6
Luganville **2**
Malo

SANMA PROVINCE

Dog's Head **3**
Norsup
Malekula

Craig Cove
Mt Marum 1
Lamap
Ambrym
Paama

16°S

MALAMPA PROVINCE

Ulei
Ramen Bay
Valesdir
Epi **8**

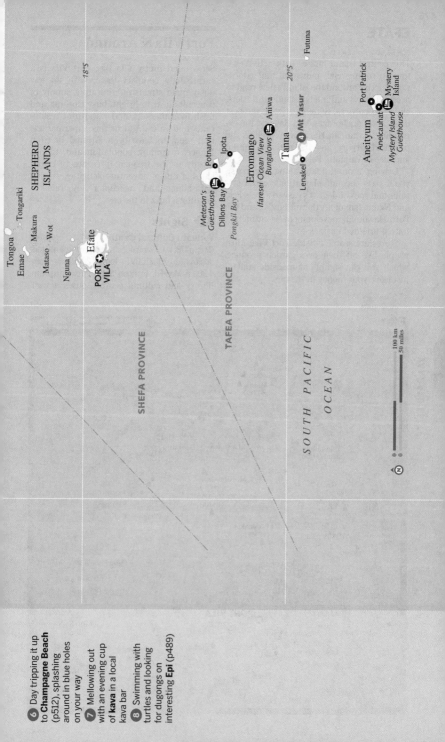

6 Day tripping it up to **Champagne Beach** (p512), splashing around in blue holes on your way

7 Mellowing out with an evening cup of **kava** in a local kava bar

8 Swimming with turtles and looking for dugongs on interesting **Epi** (p489)

18°S

Tongoa
Emae · Tongariki
Makura
Mataso · Wot
Nguna

SHEPHERD
ISLANDS

Efate

PORT ☆
VILA

SHEFA PROVINCE

TAFEA PROVINCE

Meteson's
Guesthouse
Dillons Bay
Pongkil Bay

Potnarvin
Ipota

Erromango
*Ifaresel Ocean View
Bungalows*

Aniwa

Tanna

4 Mt Yasur

Lenakel

SOUTH PACIFIC

OCEAN

20°S

Futuna

Aneityum

Port Patrick
Anelcauhat
Mystery
Island
*Mystery Island
Guesthouse*

100 km
50 miles

0
0

Ⓝ

EFATE

POP 66,000 / AREA 915 SQ KM

This central island buzzes with activities – tourist, commercial, industrial and educational. Drive around the island's new road to access its bays and inlets, islands and islets, cliffs and crevices. Efate has two of the best deep-water anchorages, Vila Bay and the expanding Havannah Harbour, as well as the principal airport, and the national capital and face of Vanuatu, Port Vila.

Driving around Efate along the coast, you'll pass coconut plantations, cattle stations and rocky inlets. It's easy to access Pele and Nguna (small northern islands), and the Port Havannah development is attracting tourist-oriented businesses.

Stores are scarce outside Port Vila. Most people live off their own garden produce, which you can sample at roadside stalls – just leave your money in the box.

Port Vila & Around

POP 44,000

Set around pretty Vila Bay, Port Vila is a surprisingly compact town, with its few dusty main streets offering up a supply of souvenirs next to bright, busy clothing and fresh food markets, and waterfront restaurants and cafes. Add to this supermarkets that seem to have been airlifted in from France, a smiling population and, thanks mostly to the frequent presence of cruise ships, a raft of adventure activities – think parasailing and helicopter joy rides – creating a buzz in the bay.

◉ Sights

Vanuatu Cultural Centre   MUSEUM
(Map p478; www.vanuatuculture.org; off Rue d'Artois; adult/child 700/100VT, tours 200VT; ⊙9am-4.30pm Mon-Fri, to noon Sat) This museum, library and cultural centre houses a well-

Efate

displayed selection of traditional artefacts, including *tamtam* (slit drums), massive outrigger canoes, ceremonial headdresses and examples of Lapita and Wusi pottery. There are photographic displays, and you can watch videos about traditional ceremonies and legends. Tours include a traditional instrument demonstration and sand drawing.

Markets
MARKET

Vila's colourful waterfront **outdoor market** (Map p484; Lini Hwy; ☺Mon-Sat) is open round the clock from Monday morning to noon on Saturday with women from all over the country wearing beautiful island dresses selling their fruit and vegetables. Along the harbour wall past the playground is the **Nambawan Market** (Map p484), just as colourful, where the women will braid your hair and sell you jewellery, woodcarvings, souvenirs and clothes. Between the two, across the road, is **Hebrida Market Place** (Map p484; Lini Hwy). This market buzzes with the sound of sewing machines, as women make island dresses to order. There's a range of hand-painted clothes, hand-made souvenirs, woven bags, mats and trinkets for sale.

Erakor
ISLAND

(Map p476; www.erakorislandresort.com; next to Le Lagon Resort; ☺24hr) Day trippers can hire snorkels and swim at the shallow white-sand beach or stay dry and gaze at fish from Aqua Restaurant. It's possible to hire kayaks and zoom around the little island; children will enjoy the beachside trampoline. Guests staying at Lagoon Beach Resort Apartments get free kayak and snorkel hire. It's a quick taxi trip south of the centre.

Hideaway Island
ISLAND

(Map p476; www.hideaway.com; opposite Mele Beach; ☺24hr) The ferry (adult/child 1000/500VT) putts out from busy Mele Beach taking you quickly to Hideaway Island where you can snorkel (snorkel hire 500VT), scuba dive or post a waterproof postcard (400VT) at Vanuatu's underwater post office. The beachside cafe serves fast food and cold beer.

Efate

Iririki Island ISLAND

(Map p478; www.iririki.com; opposite Grand Hotel & Casino; ⏱24hr) This is the green, bungalow-laden island you spot from Port Vila's water-front; head over for dinner (try Melanesian night on Tuesdays), or swim (in the pool or beach), snorkel and kayak by day. The 24-hour ferry takes three minutes and departs from beside the Grand Hotel and Casino. The trip's 1500VT, which is redeemable on food and drinks.

Mele Cascades WATERFALL

(Map p476; adult/child 1500/750VT; ⏱8.30am-5pm) Only 10km from Port Vila are these pools of stunningly clear aquamarine water that have formed below a 35m waterfall. A little path with guide ropes wobbles up to the top – it's steep and slippery in places. There are toilets and change rooms at the entrance. Go out by local bus (200VT), or take a guided tour with **Evergreen** (Map p484; ✆23050; www.evergreenvanuatu.com; Lini Hwy; tours 3000VT; ⏱9am & 2pm) with drinks and tropical fruit included.

Tanna Coffee Factory COFFEE FACTORY

(Map p476; ✆23661; Devil's Point Rd, Mele; ⏱9am-4.30pm Mon-Fri) Near the cascades is this coffee-roasting factory, with adjoining cafe. Learn the story of Tanna Coffee then enjoy a 100% arabica coffee in the cafe (350VT).

Ekasup Cultural Village VILLAGE

(off Map p476) Futuna islanders talk about and demonstrate their traditional lifestyle at their *kastom* village. Book a tour to this stunning cultural experience through **Nafonu Tatoka Tours** (✆24217, 7746734; tatokatours@vanuatu.com.vu; adult/child 3850/1900VT; ⏱9am & 2pm Mon-Fri, 9am Sat). There's original local music and *kastom* dancing shows off the colourful costumes. **Feast nights** (adult/child 3100/1550VT; ⏱5pm Fri) include shells of kava, fun entertainment and interesting food. Book a day in advance.

🏃 Activities

Abseiling & Parasailing

Edge Abseiling ADVENTURE SPORTS

(Map p484; ✆5553153; www.edgevanuatu.com; abseiling 8800VT; ⏱9am Mon, Wed & Fri) The team here takes you down the Mele Cascades like one wild shower-bath.

Port Vila Parasailing ADVENTURE SPORTS

(Map p484; ✆7742331; www.portvilaparasailing.com; s/tandem 8000/6000VT) Takes you out over the sparkling waters. Like, wow!

Diving & Snorkelling

Local dive sites include wrecks, coral reefs, deep drop-offs, thermal vents, caverns and swim-throughs. These include the Cathedral, a warren of underwater holes, stipples and tunnels; Paul's Rock, with sheer walls of coral down an extinct submarine volcano; small plane wrecks; and the *Star of Russia*, an iron-hulled schooner with masts and hull still intact that's home to thousands of colourful fish. For the brightest coral, try offshore-island or boat dives.

Introductory dives start from 8000VT, double dives for certified divers from 11,000VT and gear hire from 3000VT. Bus or boat trips and meals are extra. All operators offer Professional Association of Diving Instructors (PADI) courses from 32,000VT.

Big Blue Vanuatu DIVING, SNORKELLING

(Map p484; ✆27518, 7744054; www.bigblue vanuatu.com; ⏱8am-4pm) Discover Scuba Diving courses are free and the Snorkel Sa-

Greater Port Vila

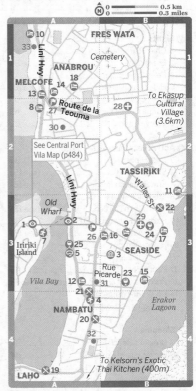

fari shows you the local hot spots. Divers can sign up for multidive packs; the 10-dive package is 50,000VT.

Hideaway Island
DIVING, SNORKELLING

(Map p476; ☑22963; www.hideaway.com.vu; Hideaway Island) Beside a marine sanctuary, offering 15 dive sites.

Nautilus Watersports
DIVING

(Map p478; ☑22398; www.nautilus.com.vu; Lini Hwy) Great resources: five-star PADI dive centre, dive boat and skills pool. Also offers bunkhouse or studio accommodation.

Fishing

Vanuatu's waters and the available choices (game and reef, live aboard, remote island) mean your time on the deep blue will be memorable.

Harbour Fishing Charters
FISHING

(Map p476; ☑7739539; www.melebeach.com. vu; half/full day 40,000/70000VT) Head out with Mitch and fish for marlin on a 6.7m Stabicraft. Trips over six hours' duration include lunch.

Wild Blue Fishing
FISHING

(Map p478; ☑22398, 7743288; www.nautilus.com. vu; full day per person from 44,000VT) Shimano tackle on a 10.2m Blackwatch or 9m Reefmaster. Offers great packages including accommodation on an island.

Flying

Port Vila's harbour makes a magnificent backdrop to a short sightseeing tour but, hey, take off to rainforests, lagoons, volcanoes – just keep flying.

Vanuatu Seaplanes
SCENIC FLIGHTS

(Map p478; ☑5554200; www.vanuatuseaplanes.com; Iririki Island Resort; flights from 11000VT) Choose your own adventure; up to four passengers.

Vanuatu Helicopters
SCENIC FLIGHTS

(Map p484; ☑7744106; www.vanuatuhelicopters. com; Numbawan Cafe; Vila/Efate/volcano flights 7000/20,000/135,000VT) Adventure, romance, elegance: this offers it all.

Horse Riding

Clip clop through the rainforest, ride along the beach, go bareback into the sea, take

Greater Port Vila

VANUATU PORT VILA & AROUND

a sunset trail, sit at the bar while the kids ride a pony, have a picnic or ride to a village: there's all sorts of adventures from 9.30am to 5.30pm all week except Monday.

Hippo-Campus
Seahorse Ranch   HORSE RIDING
(Map p476; ☑5540102; www.hippo-campus.com. vu; Mele Beach; half hr 5000VT) On a farm by Mele Bay, think best horse, best beach or rainforest, best experience.

Club Hippique   HORSE RIDING
(Map p476; ☑23347, 5566947; 1hr 4000VT; ☺9.30am & 2.30pm) Offers morning and afternoon horse rides by the lagoon, and tube rides on weekends.

Swimming & Surfing
Surfers can get up-to-date info on www. surf-forecast.com. Beaches are unexpectedly hard to find. Catch a bus to the following:

Devil's Point Rd   BEACH
(off Map p476) All along here is white-sand beach.

Breaka's Beach Resort   BEACH
(off Map p476) Good surfing and swimming right along to Pango Point.

Erakor Island   BEACH
(Map p476) Intermediate surfing out at the point.

Eratap Beach Resort   BEACH
(Map p476) Swim here, or canoe across to Eratap Island to surf. There's a left-hander at the resort.

Water Sports
Island Time Kayaking   KAYAKING
(☑5695140; www.islandtimekayaking.net; 2½hr tour adult 4000VT) Kayaking trips around the nearby island of Ifira.

U-Power Zego
Sea Adventures   WATER SPORTS
(Map p484; ☑7760495; www.upowerzegovanuatu. com; Port Vila Market; tours from 3500VT) Grab a friend and take to the bay in a high-speed Zego sports boat, playing follow the leader as you check out Vila's beaches.

Land-Based Activities
Wet 'n' Wild Zorbing   ADVENTURE SPORTS
(☑26847, 5552604; wetnwildvanuatu@gmail.com; Devils Point Rd; adult/child 5900/4500VT; ☺Tue & Fri) Roll down a hill in a giant water-filled ball. You'll get wet! 'Chickens' can try the chicken run.

Port Vila Golf & Country Club   GOLF
(Map p476; ☑22564; www.pvgcc.vu; Rte de Mele; 18 holes 3000VT, club & buggy hire 2000VT, caddie 1000VT) A challenging course with palm-tree and ocean-front hazards, and an excellent 19th hole overlooking Mele Bay. Visitors very welcome.

 Tours

There are stacks of tours departing from Port Vila, from half a day to five days. Around Efate tours include swimming at Eton Blue Hole, visiting WWII relics, river cruises and firewalking. Take a sunset cruise, a helicopter flight, a glass-bottom boat glide or an evening extravaganza of feasting and dancing at a cultural village. Try birdwatching or river kayaking. Visit Efate's small offshore islands for superb beaches and great coral reefs. Get grounded on an overnight tour to an island bungalow.

Best of all, have a grand adventure to the outer islands: to Tanna's or Ambrym's volcanoes, to Santo's magnificent shipwreck, to Epi's dugongs, to Malekula's cannibal site.

Vanuatu Ecotours   ECOTOUR
(☑5403506; www.vanuatu-ecotour.com.vu; half-day tours from 4900VT) Pascal Guillet leads you through lush gardens, down cascades, into rock pools and along riverbanks. Cycling tours are grand adventures through villages, across rivers and up mountain tops. There's a bike tour to Tanna and you can hire bikes (per day 2500VT). Book as far in advance as possible.

Buggy Fun Adventures   GUIDED TOUR
(Map p478; ☑22775, 7744092; www.buggyfunren tal.com.vu; beach/safari rides 8000/6500VT) Your guide buggy leads kids between six and 106 on wicked trails.

Meridian Charters Sunset Cruise   BOAT TOUR
(Map p478; ☑7743352; adult 5000VT; ☺5-7pm Tue-Sun) *Caraid,* a handsome 20m motor yacht, sails from Le Café du Village. French wines and cheeses are included; it's very romantic.

Coongoola Day Cruise   BOAT TOUR, SNORKELLING
(Map p484; ☑25020; www.southpacdivecruise. com.vu; adult/child/diver 8900/4450/13,650VT) Sail to Tranquillity Island on *Lady of the Sea,* once the mother ship for the Sydney–Hobart yacht race. Picnic on the beach, visit the turtle sanctuary, snorkel – you'll love it all.

Vanuatu Discovery   GUIDED TOUR
(Map p484; 23167,46312; www.vanuatudiscov ery.com.vu; Lini Hwy) Tours include Pentecost land-diving day tours and Tanna volcano tours.

Vanuatu Adventures in Paradise   GUIDED TOUR
(Map p478; 25200, 23135; www.adventuresin paradise.vu; Lini Hwy) Local tours as well as Tanna overnight and full-day Pentecost land-diving packages.

Lelepa Island Day Tours   GUIDED TOURS
(23144, 7742714; www.lelepatours.com; adult 7800VT; ☺8am Sun-Fri) A family adventure in-cluding fishing and snorkelling.

Bali Hai Charters   BOAT CHARTER
(5522126; www.balihaicharters.com) Has a 11m trimaran, *Witchitit* (50,000VT per 24 hours).

Sleeping

There's stacks of accommodation in Vila and surrounds. Many places offer free accommo-dation for children under 12, so always ask. Most rooms have a fridge.

Eratap Beach Resort   RESORT $$$
(Map p476; 5545007; www.eratap.com; Eratap; d incl breakfast from 50,000VT; ❄🛜🏊) This is one of Vanuatu's top resorts, boasting honey-moon rooms with private plunge pools and baths with views. All 12 waterfront villas have locally made bathroom goodies, flat-screen TVs, outdoor showers and the all-important coffee plunger for a great start. There are kids activities during Australian school holidays (the only time children aged five years and over are accepted), and boats, kayaks and DVDs are available year-round.

TOP CHOICE Traveller's Budget Motel   HOTEL $
(Map p478; 23940, 7756440; www.thetravel lersmotel.com; Ave du Stade; dm/d 3500/8000VT; ❄🛜🏊) Jack and Janelle have created a place you'll be hard-pressed to leave, with spotless motel-style rooms surrounding a pool, ter-rific homemade breakfasts and plenty of as-sistance in planning your ongoing travel. It's a great place to meet other travellers.

Lagoon Beach Resort Apartments   APARTMENTS $$$
(Map p476; 25505; www.lagoonbeachvanuatu. com; Teouma Rd, Tassiriki; 2-bedroom apt/villas 30,000/34,000VT; ❄@🏊) Smart and modern two-bedroom apartments sit in spacious gar-dens and have lagoon glimpses. All are fully

self-contained. Kids will love the swimming pool, sandy lagoon beach and free snorkel and kayak use; there's also a kindergarten on site that they can join for their holidays.

Paradise Cove Resort & Restaurant   BOUTIQUE RESORT $$
(Map p476; 22701; www.paradisecoveresort. net; 1-/2-bedroom bungalows incl breakfast 18,150/26,600VT; 🏊) Ten self-contained, spacious bungalows with every luxury, locat-ed way out Pango way. Snorkel gear is avail-able, and diving is on offer if you're certified. The restaurant offers an international menu (mains 1300VT to 2800VT, open all day) and breakfast is served until early afternoon.

Tropicana Lagoon Village   HOTEL $
(Map p476; 22202; www.tropicana-lagoon. com; Teouma Rd; studios/2-bedroom apt 20,000/32,000VT; 🛜🏊) This friendly spot has self-contained rooms with natural ven-tilation, timber floors and barbecues. Guests can use the kayaks, outrigger canoe or mo-torboat and try their luck at fishing in the adjoining lagoon.

Sportsmen's Hotel   HOTEL $
(Map p478; 25550; info@thesportsmenshotel vanuatu.com; Rue d'Artois; s/d 2000/4000VT; ❄) This new hotel, run by larger-than-life character Bob, offers up small, cheap rooms downstairs, and larger rooms upstairs (per person 2500VT), most with shared

bathrooms. You won't get hungry; Emily's Takeaway is on site and it's open 24 hours.

Kaiviti Motel HOTEL $
(Map p478; ✆24684; www.kaivitimotel.com; studios/apt 9100/13,600VT; ✳✆✆) The rooms look good and are self-contained (there's a huge supermarket nearby), and the location is just right. Enjoy a drink at the poolside bar while the kids splash up a storm in the pool.

Room with a View GUESTHOUSE $
(Map p478; ✆23703, 7751327; roomwithaview@yahoo.com.au; cnr Renee Pujol & Rte de la Teouma; s/d incl breakfast 4600/5100VT; ✆) This lovely colonial building just a few minutes from the centre has a balcony with great views – it's the perfect place to eat your breakfast, then just sit to watch the fascinating range of people. Hire mountain bikes for around 700VT.

Coconut Palms Resort HOTEL $
(Map p478; ✆23696; www.coconutpalms.vu; Rue Cornwall; dm/d/tw incl breakfast 5250/9600/10,880VT, r/apt with air-con 13,600/16,200VT; ✳@✆✆) Welcome to the place with everything – a full range of interesting rooms, excellent communal areas, spacious dining room, sports bar, lounge bar, sparkling big pool, kitchen and barbecue area. The deluxe room is great for families.

Warwick Le Lagon RESORT $$
(Map p476; ✆22313; www.lelagonvanuatu.vu; Erakor; d/bungalows/ste incl breakfast from 17,500/21,000/47,000VT; ✳@✆) This accommodation, ranging from simple motel-style doubles to more traditional bungalows, sprawls amid lawns, restaurants, a watersports centre, three swimming pools, tennis courts and 12-hole golf course. There's a kids club and free stays for children under 13.

Hideaway Island Resort RESORT $
(Map p476; ✆22963; www.hideaway.com.vu; d & tw 8800VT, bungalows from 22,310VT; ✳✆) On an island on the edge of a marine sanctuary, Hideaway attracts divers, snorkellers and day trippers. The bungalows look out over Mele Bay; the rooms with shared facilities are simple fan-cooled affairs. Budget dorm beds in grubby rooms are also available for 3750VT. There's heaps to do on Hideaway: kayak, swim, snorkel or learn how to scuba dive. Western-style mains at the restaurant are 1600VT to 1800VT.

Fatumaru Lodge LODGE $$
(Map p478; ✆23456; www.fatumaru.com; Lini Hwy; d/f 17,500/16,500VT; ✆✆) Close to town and fronting the lagoon, Fatumaru is on the airport road and ideal for your first or last night in Port Vila. Borrow a kayak for a peaceful

NO PITTER PATTER

Child-free? Take advantage of the following peaceful retreats (note that children are usually welcome for dinner). Some spots also have separate child-free accommodation and some only accept children during school holiday periods (Eratap Beach Resort). Check when you book.

Mangoes Resort (Map p478; ✆24923; www.mangoesresort.com; bungalows from 20,000VT; ✳✆✆) You'd never guess there were 29 bungalows here, but there are, and 10 of those have plunge pools. There are three swimming pools if you miss out on a plunge. Four bungalows are self-catering, but the restaurant is a stunner, so why bother? The views are grand and the vibe is definitely 'sophisticated'.

Vila Chaumières (Map p476; ✆22866; www.vilachaumieres.com; r from 14,000VT; ✳@✆) Garden bungalows, lagoon-side rooms with views and a little palm-fringed beach. The restaurant juts out over the water; feed the fish before dining in the candlelight.

Breaka's Beach Resort (Map p476; ✆23670; www.breakas.com; garden/beachfront bungalows 21,620/29,800VT; ✳✆✆) Traditional bungalows styled to delight any eye. Surf out the front, visit nearby Pango caves, play bocce, tennis and table tennis, or relax, have a massage and dine alfresco. Neighbouring villas (where children are allowed) start from 54,000VT.

Sunset Bungalows (Map p476; ✆29968; www.sunset-bungalows.com; studios/superior bungalows incl breakfast 20,500/25,500VT; ✳✆✆) Cool timber floors, over-water balconies, cathedral ceilings and four-post beds make for a delightful, if slightly cramped, spot. Slit carvings watch as you swim in the pool and you can borrow kayaks to explore the big 'pool' (the lagoon).

exploration of your 'front yard' then settle in your comfortable timber Melanesian-style room with kitchenette.

Tradewinds Resort
HOTEL $$

(Map p478; ✏26018, 7727018; www.tradewinds. com.vu; Captain Cook Ave; studios/2-bedroom apt 14,500/22,700VT; ❄🔊❄) Self-contained Western-style apartments catch the trade winds for tropical comfort. It's a home away from home and great for families. Cute pool beside the barbecue, too.

Seachange Lodge
APARTMENTS $

(Map p478; ✏26551; www.seachangelodge.com; Captain Cook Ave, Seaside; studios/cottages/lodge 9000/15,000/23,000VT; ❄❄) Orchids line your path as you meander down to your waterside spot, with glass-bottomed kayaks awaiting and recliner chairs offering. Higher up, near the pool, the studios are unique and homey.

Holiday Inn Resort
RESORT $$$

(Map p478; ✏22040; www.ichotelsgroup.com/ holidayinnresorts; Tassiriki Park; d incl breakfast from 21,500VT; ❄🔊❄) Set on 24 hectares, the rooms here have great views and are beautifully presented. Head over the rope walkway to the gorgeous over-water villas. This resort also has a free kids club, a golf course and an on-site casino.

Erakor Island Resort
RESORT $$$

(Map p476; ✏26983; www.erakorislandresort.com; Erakor Island; dm/superior/deluxe/f bungalows 8550/26,500/29,250/31,050VT; @) Walk along a lantern-lit path to your own bit of waterfront on this 6.5-hectare island. There's catamarans, outrigger canoes, glass-bottomed kayaks and snorkel gear (for hire or free for guests) at Get Wet Water Sports. Starfish Lodge has dorm rooms and a large kitchen; no matter what your budget, you can enjoy Erakor.

Chantilly's on the Bay
HOTEL $$

(Map p478; ✏27079; www.chantillysonthebay.com; Lini Hwy; studios/apt d 18,500/22,000VT; ❄❄) A sparkling hotel sitting prettily on Fatumaru Bay with its own jetty (ideal for drinks on the pier). Rooms have balconies, the famous bay views and kitchenettes. Ask for one of the 'sunlover' apartments for an extended deck. Middle rooms are quieter.

Moorings Hotel
RESORT $$

(Map p478; ✏26800; www.mooringsvanuatu.com; Lini Hwy; d/f 16,000/18,000VT; ❄🔊❄) Still flush with newness, Moorings sits on the waterfront and around a large pool. It also

houses Rumours Nightclub and Moos Bar & Grill (open 7am to 9.30pm).

Eating

TOP CHOICE Jill's Cafe
AMERICAN $

(Map p484; mains 350-900VT; ⊙7am-5pm Mon-Fri, 7am-1.30pm Sat) This mighty American eatery has American-flag action on its sign and piñata action above the tables. It's great value and the fresh food is excellent; try Jill's homemade earthquake chilli and famous Port Vila thick shakes.

Nambawan Café & Juice Bar
CAFE, PIZZA $

(Map p484; mains 480-1950VT; ⊙6.30am-8pm; 🔊) The place to hang out, this outside eatery on the harbour has free wi-fi, a simple menu and, oh joy, free film nights on Wednesday, Friday and Sunday. The night lights of the harbour behind the screen plus pizzas and beer in front equals top night.

Mangoes Restaurant
RESTAURANT $

(Map p478; ✏24923; mains 1200-2500VT; ⊙breakfast, lunch & dinner Mon-Sat) The chef here is a hero, cooking everything to perfection using the best seafood and other local produce, then adding his special touch. Try the KFC (Kokonut Fried Chicken). Even your children will clean their plates.

L'Houstalet
FRENCH $$

(Map p478; ✏22303; meals 1200-2700VT; ⊙dinner) Famous for its menu featuring flying fox and wild pigeon, L'Houstalet offers much more: great atmosphere and exciting food – including swords of flaming prawns – or takeaway pizza and pasta (from 900VT) if you prefer.

TOP CHOICE Kelsorn's Exotic Thai Kitchen
THAI $

(off Map p478; ✏29949; mains 1500-2200VT; ⊙lunch & dinner Mon-Sat, dinner Sun) Fabulously fresh flavours perfect for a delicious takeaway or a pleasant dine-in (outside) experience under the swishing fans. Next to Peter Pan School.

Kanpai
JAPANESE $

(Map p478; mains 1000-2500VT; ⊙lunch & dinner, Mon-Sat) Look out over the town (and tiny pool) as you enjoy perfectly cooked Japanese dishes as well as sushi and sashimi. The lunch boxes offer a taste treat, and they're served into the evening.

Au Péché Mignon
CAFE $

(Map p484; Lini Hwy; meals 500-1300VT; ⊙6am-6pm) A very French patisserie that spills

VANUATU PORT VILA & AROUND

Central Port Vila

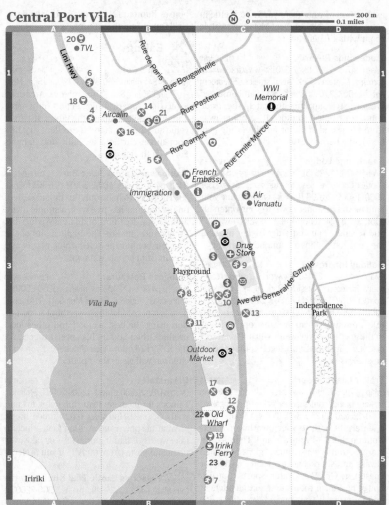

0   200 m
0   0.1 miles

out onto the street. Wonderful pastries and sweet treats to take away or eat in.

Island Time Fish & Chips   FISH & CHIPS $
(Map p484; Lini Hwy; mains 950VT; ⊙7am-9.30pm) This busy little spot has sea glimpses and serves only locally grown produce. The chicken burger is popular, or try a 'big fella' burger.

Flaming Bull Steakhouse   STEAKHOUSE $$
(Map p484; mains 1000-2700VT; ⊙noon-11pm) Great locally sourced steak, and if you hit this steakhouse on the right night you might find live music.

La Casa   PIZZA $
(Map p478; ☑26969; Nambatu; meals 1450-2200VT; ⊙lunch & dinner Mon-Sat, dinner Sun) Family-friendly restaurant with great pizzas (1450VT, take away). There's English comfort food and French delicacies, which makes for an interesting menu. Also does delivery.

Chill   SEAFOOD $$
(Map p484; ☑22578; mains 2100-4000VT; ⊙11am-late) Top location, upstairs, next to the market and looking over the harbour. It's a fun place with excellent food; the 1200VT lunch special is a treat if you're not too hungry.

Central Port Vila

Tilly's RESTAURANT $$
(Map p478; mains 2100-2800VT; ⊙breakfast, lunch & dinner) Downstairs at Chantilly's on the Bay, between the pool and the harbour. Sit back, relax in these lovely surroundings and enjoy fine dining, tapas, French, fusion or simply a piece of fish cooked just right.

Seaview Takeaway FAST FOOD $
(Map p484; 200-500VT; ⊙7am-9.30pm) The place for chicken 'n' chips, with tables and chairs set right on the sea wall.

🍷 Drinking

Port Vila has a few atmospheric bars and an abundance of kava bars where the bamboo walls and earth floors create their own atmosphere. The sunset **kava cup** (small/large 50/100VT), served in a coconut shell or plastic bowl, is a ritual. Try it out at **Ron's Nakamal** (Map p478; Nambatu) or **Seaside Kava Strip** (Map p478; behind the hospital).

Hemisphere LOUNGE
(Map p484; ⊙5-11.30pm Mon-Sat) A lush bar on the rooftop of the Grand Hotel. Everyone comes to happy hour from 5pm Friday, but it's got top Port Vila views at anytime.

Office Pub PUB
(Map p484; ⊙noon-midnight Tue-Sat, 5pm-midnight Sun-Mon) The town centre's only true pub has a cosy atmosphere: booths, wooden sculptures and an old-style 'Kelly Bar' where people chat and listen to live music.

Waterfront Bar & Grill PUB
(Map p478; ⊙11am-late) Live music plays well into the night and everyone just kicks back, enjoying the ambience. It's a spot for sun-kissed yachties and expats unwinding after work.

Anchor Inn SPORTS BAR
(Map p484; ⊙11am-11pm Mon-Sat, 4-8pm Sun) A great beer barn that buzzes, especially when international sports are on. There's live music on Friday nights. It's home to the **Vanuatu Cruising Yacht Club** (☑24634; www.vanuatucruisingyachtclub.org; ☎), and there's lunch, dinner and free wi-fi.

☆ Entertainment

Check out the information centre (p486) for a list of the Melanesian nights on offer. Most large resorts have one a week (often on a Thursday night) that includes kava tasting, string bands and *kastom* dancers. Prices range from 2400VT to 4500VT.

Rumours NIGHTCLUB
(Map p478; Moorings Hotel, Lini Hwy; ⊙8.30pm-late Tue-Sat) The town's tourist nightclub with a great sound system, live bands in the garden, Foxtel showing all sports and free entry except for special events.

🔒 Shopping

When you've bought up the markets, you'll find a number of shops selling duty-free products on Lini Hwy. They're reasonable for alcohol, perfume, fine china and jewellery.

Goodies
SOUVENIRS

(Map p484; Lini Hwy; 8am-5.30pm Mon-Fri, to 1pm Sat, 8.30am-noon Sun) The perfect combination: exchange your money here then buy up the nontacky souvenirs it sells.

Diana Tam Gallery
ARTS & CRAFTS

(Map p476; 23038; www.dianatam.info; near Erakor Island Jetty; 1.30-5pm Mon-Fri, 2-4pm Sat) Check out Diana's stunning oil paintings, prints and glassware. See examples on the website.

Information

MEDICAL SERVICES

Drug Store (Map p484; 22789; 7.30am-6pm Mon-Fri, to noon Sun, 8.30am-noon Sun) A well-stocked pharmacy. If you can't get it here, try Healthwise Pharmacy opposite.

Pro Medical (Map p478; 25566) A 24-hour paramedic service with Vanuatu's only decompression chamber.

Vila Central Hospital (Map p478; 22100)

MONEY

You'll need cash in vatu for almost everything, including accommodation, away from Port Vila. Foreign exchange is provided by **ANZ** (Map p484; Lini Hwy; 9am-3.30pm Mon-Fri) and **Westpac** (Map p484; Lini Hwy; 9am-3.30pm Mon-Fri). Both have ATMs.

Goodies Money Exchange (Map p484; goodies@vanuatu.net.vu; cnr Lini Hwy & Rue Pasteur; 8am-5.30pm Mon-Fri, 8am-1pm Sat, 8.30am-noon Sun) Generally gives the best rates. Has three offices on Lini Hwy in the centre of town.

National Bank of Vanuatu (NBV; Map p484; Rue de Paris) Can also handle foreign exchange.

POST

Post office (Map p484; Lini Hwy; 7.30am-5pm Mon-Fri, 8am-noon Sat)

TOURIST INFORMATION

Vanuatu Tourism Office (VTO; Map p484; 22813; vanuatu.travel; Lini Hwy; 7.30am-4.30pm Mon-Fri, 8am-noon Sat, 8am-3pm cruise ship days) Free maps and information about accommodation, activities, tours and the outer islands.

TRAVEL AGENCIES

Air Vanuatu (Map p484; 23848; www.air vanuatu.com; Rue de Paris) Organises international and domestic flights.

Vanuatu Hotels (24444; www.vanuatu-hotels.vu) Organises tours & adventures.

Getting There & Around

See p524 for details of airline and shipping services to and from Port Vila.

TO/FROM THE AIRPORT Taxis charge around 1300VT (shared) from the airport; **Melanesian Tours** (26847, 7772729; www.melanesian tours.com) has reliable pick-ups and drop-offs from Port Vila hotels (1100VT per person), which are great for early or late flights. If you don't have much luggage and arrive during the day, you can catch a minibus (150VT) from outside the neighbouring domestic terminal.

CAR & MOTORCYCLE Port Vila's car-hire companies include **Budget** (Map p478; 23170, 25700; www.budgetvanuatu.com; Nambatu) and **World Car Rentals** (Map p478; 26515; www.vanuaturentalcars.com). A small car costs around 6000VT (including VAT and 1500VT insurance) a day.

Go 2 Rent (Map p478; 22775, 7744092; go2rent@vanuatu.com.vu; Nambatu; 7.30am-5.30pm) rents cars from 5500VT per day and scooters (half/full day 2900/4000VT).

MINIBUS & TAXI The main roads are usually thick with minibuses between 6am and 7.30pm. In most cases, it's first in, first dropped off. Fares are a uniform 150VT around town. To travel further afield to, say, Hideaway Island or the Mele Cascades, costs 200VT. Vila's main taxi stand is beside the market.

White Sands Beach

East of Vila, past Teouma River (Efate's largest), a right-hand turn takes you down to the coastal road where the Pacific Ocean is fringed with screw-trunked pandanus palms. If you feel like swimming, be careful of currents.

You'll find six luxurious French-colonial cottages with little love-nest porches at **Tamanu on the Beach Resort & Restaurant** (Map p476; 27279, 7743454; www. tamanu.vu; planters/beachfront incl breakfast 24,000/29,000VT; @). Use the bikes, then swim or snorkel in rock pools. The restaurant is well known for its great meals and romantic setting, and it's right on the beach and open for breakfast, lunch and dinner. The road here is a little bumpy.

Eton

Continue around the east coast to **Eton Blue Hole** (Map p476; admission 300VT), a lovely garden with picnic tables, toilets and change rooms. Step down the bank into the blue, blue water for fun swimming and canoeing.

Another pretty picnic area 2km along the coast is **Eton Beach** (Map p476; admission 300VT), famous for its gurgling river and white-sand beach.

Takara

The waters out from Takara, with the prevailing southeast winds, offer ideal conditions for **kite surfing**. Ring ☑23576 for daily weather reports.

Two **US WWII fighter planes** lie in the shallows near **Baofatu**. They ran out of fuel coming in to land at Quoin Hill. Erik will take you out in a boat to see them, and show you the not so impressive **Matanawora WWII Relics** (☑5427057; 2000VT). Alternatively, ask him about an ecoadventure boat ride out to Emao for walking and snorkelling.

Siviri

At Undine Bay is white-sand **St Lawrence Beach** (Map p476; admission 300VT). It's isolated and inviting and fringed with palm trees. Nearby is pretty Siviri known for its fragrant flowers. Explore **Valeva Cave** (Map p476; admission 500VT) in a kayak (1000VT). It has chambers, tunnels and an underground lake. The villagers will show you the massive limestone boulder that was somehow moved by people, and the strange footprints engraved in the rock floor.

Havannah Harbour

This area, best known for its underwater WWII memorabilia finds and as a *Survivor* TV show location, has taken off in recent years. Have some fresh fish at the **Wahoo Bar** (Map p476; www.wahoobar.com.au; Efate Ring Rd; mains from 1950VT; ☺lunch & dinner Thu-Sun) or head out from there on a fishing charter with **Sport Fish Vanuatu** (☑5552434; www.sportfishvanuatu.com.vu; full day A$700, max 3 people).

The **Havannah** (Map p476; ☑5518060; www.thehavannah.com; Efate Ring Rd; d incl breakfast 50,000VT; ✳🕲) is a luxurious child-free resort with 16 villas. Those enjoying the Waterfront Villas can wrap themselves in their 'welcome sarong' and mosey on down the few steps from their king-sized bed to their private infinity plunge pool that looks out over Havannah Bay. Even those in the

cheaper Garden Sunset Villas will love the polished floors, ice-cold air-con and spacious bathrooms. There's a tennis court and restaurant (with dress code), though, after a free sunset catamaran cruise, guests can have their dinner on the beach or jetty (book in advance).

West Coast Offshore Islands

Three very different islands offer an interesting range of activities. Tranquillity (Moso) Island has a turtle sanctuary, dive base and rustic resort; Lelepa has spectacular **Feles Cave** (Map p476), cave drawings and fishing adventures; Hat (Eretoka) Island is the **burial ground of Chief Roimata** (Map p476), a sacred place. The coral reefs around here are bright, healthy and include **Paul's Rock** (Map p476). To dive these waters see p480.

At **Tranquillity Island Resort** (Map p476; ☑25020, 22560; www.tranquillitydive.com; dm 14,100VT per person, s bungalows/lodge 19,400/23,200VT; d bungalows/lodge 32,000/38,800VT; 🕲), rates include transfers, meals, kayaks, snorkel gear and two days on this rambling island. The traditional bungalows have homemade beds and ooze atmosphere; if you're after a little more luxury choose the lodge. Or bring your own tent and camp for 1400VT per night. Check out the little turtle sanctuary on the island and try a discovery scuba dive (4000VT).

At **Tranquillity Island Dive Base** (Map p476; ☑25020, 23271; www.tranquillitydive.com; 🕲) near 16 dive sites you can expect to see loads of turtles and the occasional dugong.

Albert Solomon's crew from **Lelepa Island Fishing Charter** (☑23144, 7742714; www.lelepatours.com; half/full day 39,000/48,000VT; ☺4.30am Sun-Fri) can take you where the big fish are in a 7m banana boat with Shimano tackle. Tours include transfers and, on the full-day tour, also lunch.

Sailaway Cruises (Map p484; ☑25155, 23802; www.sailawayvanuatu.com; adult/child 9000/4500VT) offers a fab day with a small group on the *Golden Wing* (per 24 hour charter 75,000VT), a 13m long trimaran. Includes snorkelling and diving (2500VT per dive) around Hat Island and Paul's Rock, top spots for healthy coral and colourful fish, and lunch on Survivor Beach (of TV fame).
Sailaway Cruises Dive (☑23802, 7723802; cruise with lunch, transfers, 2 dives & gear hire

15,500VT) takes qualified divers to Hat Island, Paul's Rock and Turtle Reef.

There are day tours to Lelepa and Tranquillity Island from Port Vila.

Nguna & Pele

POP 1200 & 300

Only 45 minutes' drive from Port Vila is the wharf leading to these two lovely islands. Both have protected marine reserves (www.marineprotectedarea.com.vu) and terrific snorkelling. Nguna has a line-up of places to stay, all fronting the marine reserve, while Pele has three different bungalows to choose from, all located in different parts of the island but within walking distance.

⊙ Sights & Activities

Nguna has ordered streets, a long white-sand **beach** and a labelled **snorkel trail** through exotic coral gardens. Pele is more remote, with a **Giant Clam Garden** (Map p476), inspired by the one in the Maskelynes.

Guided **hikes** (guides 1500VT) take you through village gardens to mountain peaks. Utanlangi, by a sheltered cove, is the best place from which to climb Nguna's extinct volcano (593m) **Mt Taputaora** (Map p476; admission 1000VT); the climb is arduous, but you'll be rewarded with superb panoramas over the Shepherd Islands and much of Efate. Go partly by truck for 4000VT return.

Head out in an outrigger canoe to see the villagers **turtle tagging**. Sponsor your own turtle, name it and see it back into the ocean.

LAPITA UNEARTHED

Decorative Lapita pottery, with its fine geometric patterns, has been found throughout the Pacific, as the Lapita people were seafarers. The site at Teouma, on Efate, is the oldest cemetery to be found in the Pacific. For cultural reasons the heads of those buried had been placed in large Lapita pots and some are still almost intact. Some bones at the dig site show the existence of turtles as large as those in the Galapagos Islands.

If you're staying out on Tranquillity Island (Moso; p487), ask about the old Lapita cooking site the owners found when they were building the new bungalow. It even included a shell axe.

🛏 Sleeping & Eating

PELE

TOP CHOICE **Napanga Bungalows** BUNGALOWS $
(Map p476; ☑5630315, 7107607; Pele; s/d incl meals 3500/7000VT) Kenneth has two colourful bungalows set apart from the small village on the cutest little bay in Pele. Sit on a deck chair and watch for dugong while you sip juice from a coconut. He's a good cook too.

Simoa Bungalow BUNGALOWS $
(Map p476; ☑5686685, 5407386; Pele; s/d incl meals 3500/7000VT) Mark and Miriam run this beach-fronting set-up beautifully. Dine alfresco on fresh fish while watching the hermit crabs come out to play, before retiring to your simple, Western-style bungalow with your solar-powered lamp.

Wora-Namoa Bungalow BUNGALOWS $
(Map p476; ☑7790881; Pele; s/d incl meals 3500/7000VT) This grand beach bungalow is very much part of the community as it sits in the middle of the village. It was built by Australian kids as a school project and is made from local timbers and decorated with hand-dyed materials.

NGUNA

TOP CHOICE **Uduna Cove Beach** BUNGALOWS $
(Map p476; ☑22219, 5432202; Nguna; per person 3000VT) These four bright blue and yellow bungalows sit in a landscaped garden and come complete with mosquito nets. The bathrooms are shared, and there's a kitchen guests can use (otherwise meals are 500VT). The black-sand beach is lovely.

Vat-Vaka Beach Bungalows BUNGALOW $
(Map p476; ☑771916, 29995; Nguna; s/d incl meals 3500/7000VT) Two lovely 'bush' bungalows with lino floors and mosquito nets have a great kitchen and dining area, or stay in the original beachfront bungalow.

Juboes Bungalows BUNGALOWS $
(Map p476; ☑5667322; Nguna; s incl meals 3000VT) Edward and Susan Sisi run this spacious Western-style guesthouse with a kitchen, across from two bungalows that share outside facilities. There's also a simple bungalow a few steps from the sea.

❶ Getting There & Around

Transport trucks to Emua Wharf depart from the **bus stop** (Map p484) near Port Vila's police station between 1.30pm and 4.30pm, from Monday

to Saturday (500VT). Ask people to point it out or ring ahead (☑7757410). The truck connects with an often-crowded boat to Nguna (500VT). The return trip departs at 5am. Ask your accommodation to organise a private charter if you are not arriving by bus; it's usually 2000VT to Pele, 3000VT to Nguna (one-way).

Two companies run day trips to Pele: **Sandy Beach Pele Island** (☑5407386, 7755193; www.sandybeachpeleisland.com.vu; adult/child 7800/3900VT) and **Evergreen** (Map p484; ☑25418, 23050; www.evergreenvanuatu.com; adult/child 7800/3900VT). Both offer barbecue lunches, time for snorkelling, and transfers to and from Port Vila.

EPI

POP 5200 / AREA 444 SQ KM

Epi's **Lamen Bay** is a great spot for peaceful dugong spotting, swimming with huge sea turtles and chilling out. It's a place where you can cheer at the day's fishing haul, listen to the local lads pounding the kava ready for you to drink in the dusky *nakamal* (men's clubhouse) and chat to the ladies of the village as they prepare their ground ovens and wrap the *laplap* in banana leaves. Swim with young Bondas the dugong if he's in town.

🛏 Sleeping & Eating

Paradise Sunset Bungalows BUNGALOW $
(☑5649107; Lamen Bay; breakfast & dinner per person 3500VT) A relaxed and friendly place 15 minutes' walk from the airfield. The rooms and shared facilities are basic, but the food (fish, and plenty of it) and the bay views are lovely. Tasso has snorkel gear, and will arrange tours to Laman Island (opposite) and transfers. A truck to the air strip is 200VT. The restaurant (buffet 500VT; open breakfast, lunch and dinner), otherwise known as the Lamen Bay Yacht Club, is often full of yachties, which makes for a fun evening (the neighbouring kava bar is rather more subdued).

TOP CHOICE Epi Island Guesthouse LODGE $$
(☑5528225; epiguesthouse@gmail.com; Valesdir Plantation; adult/child incl meals 13,000/6500VT; 🕭) Down south in Valesdir (the name of a plantation), the plane lands in a field of cows, but it's the organic food and relaxed lodge life of Epi Island Guesthouse that draws people here. This arty lodge is powered by a microhydro turbine and run by the delightful Alix and Rob Crapper. Sit around the central room full of fascinating bits

CUTE DUGONGS

Bondas, Lamen Bay's resident dugong, has been going to sea for months at a time, but if he's around you may find yourself snorkelling near him, watching his fat little snout swishing around on the ocean floor as he separates out his food. He'll roll over to get a better look at you. The experience is extraordinary – you realise in one mind-blowing moment what conservation is all about.

Dugongs inhabit warm tropical and subtropical coastal waters. But, worldwide, populations are declining due to overhunting, drowning in fishing nets, pollution and loss of food resources. In fact, dugong are considered vulnerable to extinction. Fortunately, by being so cute, they've turned themselves into a major tourist attraction. Hopefully, this will help protect them.

(such as 1865–75 Enfield guns once owned by blackbirders) and chat about island life, self-sufficiency and *Survivor*. Sleep in a beach hut (or camp for 1000VT per person) if you like, but be back for the excellent meals that Alix whips up.

ⓘ Getting There & Around

AIR A good plan when visiting Epi is to fly to **Lamen Bay Airfield**, make your way down the west coast by truck (8000VT) and then fly out of Valesdir (or vice versa). Epi's roads are basic, and there are only walking tracks in the east.

Air Vanuatu (☑23848) flies from Port Vila to Valesdir on Monday, Wednesday and Friday, and to Lamen Bay on Thursday and Saturday. You'll need to pay 200VT departure tax (per person).

Air Safaris (☑7745207; www.airsafaris.vu) runs overnight trips (per person 66,000VT) to Epi Island Guesthouse; rates include accommodation, flights and meals.

Air Taxi (☑5544206; airtaxivanuatu.com) runs half-day tours (per person 42,000VT) including flights and lunch.

BOAT Fresh Cargo (☑7760660; freshcargovanuatu@gmail.com; 4500VT) calls into Epi twice a week, as does the faster **Big Sista** (Map p478; ☑23461, 5663851; 5500VT) though you arrive in the early hours. See p525.

For yachts, there are several good anchorages in north Epi: **Lamen Bay**, **Mapuna Bay**, **Rovo Bay**, **Walavea** and **Cape Foreland**. All can be unsuitable depending on the wind direction.

Epi

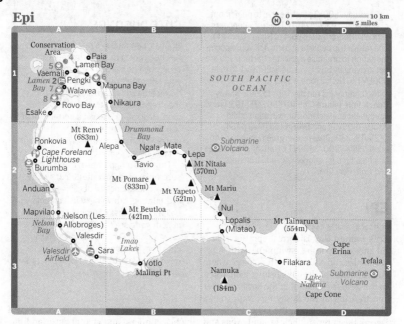

Epi

🛏 Sleeping
1 Epi Island Guesthouse A3
2 Paradise Sunset Bungalows...............A1

ℹ Transport
3 Cape Foreland Anchorage.................A2
4 Lamen Bay Airfield A1
5 Lamen Bay Anchorage.......................A1
6 Mapuna Anchorage A1
7 Rovo Bay Anchorage...........................A1
8 Walavea Anchorage.............................A1

TANNA

POP 29,000 / AREA 565 SQ KM

Black-sand Tanna is one of Vanuatu's most popular destinations, especially for those wishing to gaze into the red-hot lava depths of an active volcano. Apart from the fuming, furious Mt Yasur (the world's most accessible volcano), there are undisturbed rainforests, coffee plantations, plains where wild horses run with their foals, mountains, hot springs, blue holes and waterfalls. Local chiefs have formed marine and wildlife sanctuaries. Christianity, cargo cults (John Frum, in particular) and *kastom* are important, and all

natural phenomena have a fourth dimension of spirituality and mystique.

When the volcano has finished working its magic on you, there are horses to ride, forests to trek through, waterfalls to stand under and a kilometre-deep drop-off tumbling with coral to snorkel along. Meet *kastom* villagers wearing *namba* (penis sheath) and grass skirts, watch age-old festivals or just laze on a tropical island beach and watch the sun set.

Lenakel is the main town with a market, port, several shops and hospital, and it's near here that Tanna's more upmarket accommodation is located.

To see the volcano you'll need to take the hairy road trip to Tanna's centre; it's unforgettable, especially when the volcano looms up in front of you. You may pass through a central fertile, dense forest, aptly called Middlebush, with coconut, coffee, vegetables and fruit grown here for export. Kava is a major cash crop. To get to the volcano the 'road' crosses Mt Yasur's remarkable ash plain, which is dotted with rocks that were only recently in the belly of the volcano. Continue past the volcano's entrance (37km from Whitegrass Airport) to get to the coastal region of East Tanna. Mt Yasur, Sharks Bay and quiet Port Resolution are within hiking, horse-riding or walking distance of each other.

Tanna

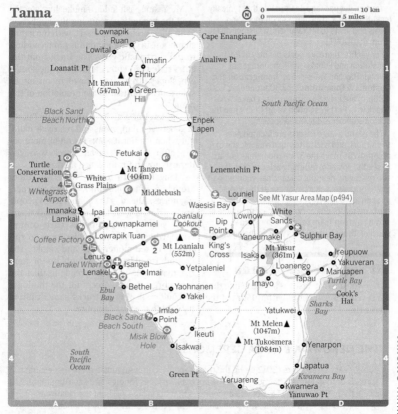

ⓘ Information

You'll need to take enough cash (vatu) for your whole time here as you can change travellers cheques only at the NBV in Lenakel. Credit cards are accepted at the large resorts.

Ambulance (☏88659)

Emergencies (☏112)

Hospital (☏88659) At Lenakel.

Internet access (Map p491; per hr 500VT; Lenakel; ☺8-11.30am & 1.15-4pm Mon-Fri) At TVL next to the NBV.

Police (☏88658) At Isangel.

ⓘ Getting There & Around

Air Vanuatu flies its ATR72 between Vila and Tanna most mornings, flying from the international airport. It also flies on Tuesday, Wednesday, Friday and Saturday afternoons. Its much smaller Harbin Y12 makes the trip four times a week. Taxis (4WD utes) and a rundown yellow minibus meet incoming flights. The fare to Lenakel is 2000/300VT by truck/bus.

Tanna

⊙ Sights
1 Blue Hole A2
2 Giant Banyan B3

🛏 Sleeping
3 Rocky Ridge Bungalows A2
4 Tanna Evergreen Bungalows A2
   Tanna Evergreen Restaurant ..... (see 4)
5 White Beach Bungalows A3
6 White Grass Ocean Resort A2
   White Grass Restaurant .... (see 6)

Air Safaris (p491) runs volcano tours (per person 46,500VT); imagine landing on the ash plain and getting a bird's eye view of the crater. **Air Taxi** (p491) also runs day trips (per person 35,000VT) from Port Vila to the volcano. A scenic flight over the volcano is an extra 4000VT per person.

You can get package deals in Vila that typically include airfares, transfers, accommodation, meals and visits to Mt Yasur and a *kastom* village (from 45,000VT).

For yachts, there are ports of entry at Port Resolution and Lenakel, and anchorages at Sulphur Bay and Waesisi Bay. **Immigration** and **Customs & Quarantine** (⊙7.30am-noon & 1.30-4.30pm) are in Lenakel, opposite Lenakel Wharf. Check with Port Resolution Yacht Club when the customs officer is due (a fee applies).

The island's large resorts are located near the airport, and each afternoon a cavalcade of resort 4WDs make the 37km trip to take guests to see the volcano, returning after sunset. If you're staying near the volcano ask your bungalow to organise a charter, or ask at the airport as soon as you arrive. Expect to pay 5000VT for the transfer for one or two people. At the time of writing a steep 16km section of the road was a shocker, though roadworks were in the pipeline.

Mt Yasur & East Tanna

Active volcano Mt Yasur is so accessible that 4WD vehicles can get to within 150m of the crater rim.

Mt Yasur's ash-laden smoke has smothered the vegetation, reducing the landscape to an alien prehistoric desert, with the gaunt shapes of surviving pandanus palms adding to the surrealistic view. The track from the entry gate then enters a gully on the southern slopes. Tree ferns crowd in on either side, a lush contrast to the desolation of the plains.

The level of activity within Yasur fluctuates between dangerous and relatively calm, but when it's hot it's hot. It's often more active after the wet season; check www.geohazards.gov.vu for the latest alert level.

Along the path to the crater rim, there are whiffs of sulphur and whooshing, roaring noises. Ahead is the silhouette of people on the rim, golden fireworks behind them. Then you're looking into a dark central crater where three vents take turns to spit rockets of red-molten rock and smoke. The ground trembles and a fountain of fiery magma shoots up and spreads against the sky. All turns quiet, except for the thudding of boulders as big as trucks somersaulting down into the vast campfire.

THE NEKOWIAR & TOKA CEREMONY

About every three years (2012 being the most recent), come August, a great restlessness spreads across Tanna. The men scour the bush and villages for pigs and kava, counting, calculating. Finally one of the chiefs announces that his village will host the Nekowiar. Hooray! Romance is in the air. It will be a three-day extravaganza of song, dance and feasting during which the leaders of neighbouring villages organise marriages. Negotiations for the marriages continue for months afterwards.

Preparations for the Nekowiar are exhaustive. Three complex dances are practised, and beauty magic takes over. Men, women, boys and girls use powders mixed with coconut oil to colour their faces a deep red, with black and yellow stripes.

Finally, as many as 2000 people assemble while the hosts display around 100 live, squealing pigs, tied by the feet and suspended on poles.

The ceremony begins with the host village's young men dancing an invitation to the women. They respond with the Napen-Napen, a spectacular dance that represents their toil in the fields, and continues throughout the first night.

The male guests watch and wait for dawn, when they dance the Toka, a pounding, colourful dance that shows scenes of daily life. The Toka reaches its climax that night. If the Toka dancers make a circle around a woman, she's tossed up and down between them. During this stage a man may have sex with any woman who is willing.

On the third day the chief of the host village produces the *kweriya*, a 3m bamboo pole with white and black feathers wound around it and hawks' feathers on top. It announces that the Nao – the host village's dance – is to begin. This men's dance enacts events such as hunting and wrestling.

The climax is in the afternoon. Pigs, kava roots, woven mats, grass skirts and massive quantities of *laplap* (Vanuatu's national dish) are brought out. The pigs are ceremonially clubbed and cooked, and a huge feast begins.

If you get a chance to attend, go for it. You may need to camp out, like the villagers. It costs 8000VT to watch, plus 10,000VT to video it.

Just when you're getting used to it, there's a gasp and a bang, the ground shakes, and lumps of red-hot magma shoot high overhead. Black smoke boils upwards in a dense column, lightning flashes inside the crater, and magma splashes in the central vent and subsides again.

Some visitors find Yasur terrifying; it's definitely unforgettable.

◉ Sights & Activities

Mt Yasur
VOLCANO

(Map p494; admission 3350VT) Mt Yasur dominates the landscape as you travel east across the ash plains. There are many tours up to see the old man; arrange them through your host in Tanna or through a Port Vila tour operator.

Take a horse ride up the volcano. Horses are available at Mountain Brezze, or simply walk, listening to the rumble as you go.

Don't go up to the rim when the volcano is reaching levels three and four, and make sure you buy some special singed cards to post at **Volcano Post** (www.vanuatupost.vu), the world's only postbox on top of a volcano. It's possible (and very enjoyable) to walk up to the rim from the main road; it takes around 45 minutes.

Cargo Cults
CULTURAL TOUR

Check out Namakara's **John Frum Village** (Map p494), which is one of the biggest on the island. Dances are held on Friday nights, when songs of praise are sung to the tunes of American battle hymns. An offshoot of John Frum, the Unity Movement, sees women in trances twirling themselves into the water at Yakuveran (near Port Resolution). Head there on Wednesday for a peek. See the boxed text on p495 for more on John Frum.

Port Resolution
HARBOUR

Tanna's best anchorage is this beautiful bay with magnificent cliffs. The 'village' has a souvenir/fruit shop and a couple of basic restaurants. To the left, a road leads up to the pared-back version of your average yacht club and to a **marine sanctuary** (Map p494) at Yewao Point where you can snorkel in the calm water just before the coral reef finishes.

Another path reaches an attractive whitesand beach at **Ireupuow**, and the last path brings you to a top **surf beach** (Map p494), with deep swells along 2.5km to Yankaren Para (watch your board; make sure it travels

on the same plane as you). Port Resolution is 8km from the volcano entrance. A truck makes a return trip on Monday, Wednesday and Friday mornings from Port Resolution to Lenakel (2000VT), otherwise walk, ride a horse or organise a charter.

🛏 Sleeping & Eating

There's a bunch of places to stay below the volcano itself – most offer camping spots, meals and basic bungalow or tree-house accommodation. Accommodation in the east is basic, with generators usually providing electricity in the evenings (but don't expect it). If you can't get through by phone don't worry, just arrive and find a room.

There's a little store in Port Resolution with handicrafts, fruit and vegetables, and two very basic restaurants.

Jungle Oasis
BUNGALOWS $

(Map p494; ☑7754933; www.jungle-oasis.com; Loanengo; bungalows s/d 3500/4500VT, camping 1000VT) Kelson is very active in the local tourism industry, and helped start things off with these simple bungalows, set in blacksand gardens. There's also a tree house. Book ahead for meals in the dining room, which doubles as a church (lunch/dinner 750VT/1200VT).

Mountain Brezze
BUNGALOWS $

(Map p494; ☑5410134; tannavolcano@gmail.com; Loanengo; s & d incl meals 2500VT) This is a peaceful spot, even with old Yasur roaring. Spacious bungalows are set in an unusual, meandering garden, and a nearby cave has been turned into a natural sauna (1000VT). You can camp too (500VT). Ask for Joseph. Organise a horse ride to the volcano (1500VT one-way or 3000VT return), or a biggest banyan tree tour (500VT) here.

Tanna Banian Paradise Treehouse
BUNGALOWS $

(Map p494; ☑5417737; Loanengo; d incl breakfast 2500VT) If you don't sleepwalk, you might like to try the tree house at this place, which has two doubles way up high with glorious views. Neighbouring Volcano Whispering Lodge has a restaurant and was being renovated at the time of research.

Banyan Castle
BUNGALOWS $

(Map p494; ☑5415931, 7795622; www.banyancastle.info; Loanengo; s/d incl breakfast 2500/5000VT) This place has heaps of rooms (and views) to choose from, including three tree houses, two bungalows and camping sites. The rustic

Mt Yasur Area

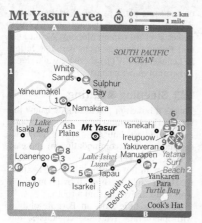

0 —— 2 km
0 —— 1 mile

SOUTH PACIFIC OCEAN

White Sands
Sulphur Bay
Yaneumakel
Namakara
Lake Isaka Bed
Ash Plains
Mt Yasur
Yanekahi
Ireupuow
Yakuveran
Loanengo
Lake Isiwi Luan
Manuapen
Yatana Surf Beach
Tapau
Yankaren Para Turtle Bay
Imayo
Isarkei
South Beach Rd
Cook's Hat

dining room (lunch/dinner 700/1000VT) is a good spot to catch up with other travellers.

Port Resolution Yacht Club BUNGALOWS $
(Map p494; ☑88791, 5416989; portresolution@ vanuatu.com.au; Port Resolution; s/d/tr incl breakfast 2000/4000/5000VT, camping 1500VT) Up on a bluff, three bungalows have views of the bay. A fourth more Western version is set apart from the others and has an en suite. Werry turns on the electricity in the evenings, and there are warm showers. The dining room (meals from 500VT to 1200VT) has cold beer and comfy old couches.

Sunrise Bungalows BUNGALOWS $
(Map p494; ☑88050, 68022; www.sunrise bungalows.netfast.org; Turtle Bay; s/d incl breakfast 3600/5000VT) Wild-cane bungalows teeter amid jungle and cliff, with the ocean just below. Ask about camping up on a hill with volcano views. Volcano tours are 5550VT. Your tropical breakfast is served in a spacious restaurant; lunch and dinner are 1000/1500VT. Return airport transfers are 10,000VT.

Ianiuia Surf Beach Restaurant RESTAURANT $
(Map p494; ☑547990; Port Resolution; 3-course buffet 750VT; ☺by arrangement) Chef Lea serves a range of chicken or vegetable dishes using a huge array of local produce, fresh herbs and flair. Book a day in advance (ask someone to help you find Lea) and bring your own lighting for the evening feast.

Avoka Restaurant RESTAURANT $
(Map p494; Port Resolution; meals 700VT; ☺by arrangement) This cute spot by the large oval serves basic meals (chicken or fish) if you

ask beforehand, and local Tanna coffee. The owners live next door.

West Tanna

Visible from the aeroplane as you come in to land are the coral reefs and rock pools of the west coast. The main town is Lenakel, which has mains electricity, some stores, bakeries and colourful markets on Monday and Wednesday afternoons, and Friday. The kava bars provide a meeting place. Note that Tanna's kava is potent – probably the strongest in the country.

⊙ Sights & Activities

All experiences start with Mt Yasur volcano (p492). Tours leave from the west in the midafternoon and return for dinner at about 8pm. If you're not on a package from Port Vila, your host will arrange your tour.

Visit **Yakel** or **Ipai**, where you see village life that hasn't changed in centuries, or **Namakara**, a John Frum settlement where they raise the American flag daily. There's *kastom* dancing, colourful *namba* and grass skirts, *laplap* and artefacts. People gather nightly under a huge banyan at Yakel to drink kava, and dancing nights occur on a regular basis.

Jungle trails take you past villages to a **giant banyan** (Map p491) as big as a soccer field. It's near Lowrapik Tuan.

Sea kayaks are available at several resorts. Guided walks (book through your accommodation) take you through rainforests and coffee plantations, among the wild horses, along stunning coastlines and under two grand waterfalls.

There's excellent snorkelling right along the west coast, with the reef face cascading down covered in coral, in and out of its pocketed volcanic surface. A **Blue Hole** (Map p491) just north of White Grass Ocean Resort is like a fish nursery with coral wall decorations, and there's another **private blue hole** (Map p491) in front of Rocky Ridge Bungalows.

Surfing at the **black-sand beach** (Map p491) north of Louniel is fun.

🛏 Sleeping & Eating

TOP CHOICE **Rocky Ridge Bungalows** BUNGALOWS $
(Map p491; ☏ 5417220; www.rockyridgebungalows.wordpress.com; s/d/f incl breakfast 4000/8000/10,000VT) Tom and Margaret run this friendly place to stay; the three simple bungalows have en suites and small balconies for gazing out seawards. Dinnertime sees Tom preparing filling meals like beef curry, and breakfast (included) sets you up for the whole day. Tours to Mt Yasur are 12,000VT per person, airport transfers are 1000VT (or it's a 3km walk).

Tanna Evergreen Bungalows BUNGALOWS $$
(Map p491; ☏ 88774; www.tevergreenresort-tours.vu; PO Box 151; budget s/d incl breakfast 4250/8500VT, d/f 14,250/16,800VT; camping 1000VT; @) These bungalows hide in lush gardens; some are en suite, others ocean view or both. The honeymoon bungalow is so romantic. Snorkel at the end of the garden along the drop-off. Snorkel gear, babysitting, laundry, massage, glass-bottomed kayaks, tours – it's all here. Don't miss the Magic Tour (4800VT). At **Tanna Evergreen Restaurant** (meals 1000-2100VT; ⏱ 6am-11pm) the deck sweeps out to show fab views, the meals are always a treat and it's fun chatting to other guests.

White Grass Ocean Resort BUNGALOWS $$$
(Map p491; ☏ 30010; www.whitegrassvanuatu.com.vu; s/d/tr/f incl breakfast 16,500/23,100/28,000/27,500VT; @🏊) A cosy resort where bungalows look out onto tiny rocky inlets, which are linked with timber bridges. There's a bar, hammocks, tennis, *pétanque* (boule) and a three-hole golf course. Snorkelling gear and golf clubs are available. **White Grass Restaurant** (meals 2000-2500VT; ⏱ lunch & dinner) is on site, set in lovely surroundings, overlooking the ocean – a spread of light and colour at sunset – and with reliably good food.

White Beach Bungalows BUNGALOWS $
(Map p491; ☏ 5949220; s/d incl breakfast 2000/4000VT) Head down the road to the Tanna Coffee Factory and keep going to find these pleasant beachfront bungalows. There's snorkelling gear to borrow and a simple on-site restaurant offering basic meals (beef/fish 700/1000VT).

VANUATU WEST TANNA

THE JOHN FRUM MOVEMENT

Magic is a central force in ni-Vanuatu lives. So in 1936, when John Frum came from the sea at Green Point and announced himself to some kava drinkers, they could see that he was the brother of the god of Mt Tukosmera. He told the men that if the Europeans left Tanna, there would be an abundance of wealth. They spread the word. It was the beginning of a neopagan uprising, with followers doing things the missionaries had banned, such as traditional dancing – but not cannibalism, fortunately.

When US troops arrived a few years later, many Tannese went to Efate and Santo to work for them. There they met African American soldiers, who were colourful, with theatrical uniforms, decorations, badges, belts and hats. The African Americans had huge quantities of transport equipment, radios, Coca-Cola and cigarettes. But most of all, they were generous and friendly, treating the ni-Van as equals. Here was the wealth and way of life the ni-Van had been told about – John Frum was connected to America, they decided.

Some supporters made radio aerials out of tin cans and wire to contact John Frum. Others built an airfield in the bush and constructed wooden aircraft to entice his cargo planes to land. Still others erected wharves where his ships could berth. Small red crosses were placed all over Tanna and remain a feature in John Frum villages, where flags are raised daily to this god of their collective imagination.

MALEKULA

POP 20,000 / AREA 2023 SQ KM

Shaped like a sitting dog, Malekula has two highland areas connected by 'the dog's neck'. The uplands are extremely rugged and inhospitable, rising to over 800m and crisscrossed by narrow valleys.

Two of Malekula's major cultural groups are the Big Nambas and Small Nambas, named because of the size of the men's *namba*. Small Nambas men wear one leaf of dried fibre wound around the penis and tucked into a bark belt. Their semi-*kastom* communities are built around *tamtam*, ready to beat a rhythm, and a dance area.

Big Nambas men wind large purple pandanus fibres around their penis, securing the loose ends in a thick bark belt and leaving the testicles exposed. They had such an awesome warlike reputation that no foreigner dared venture into their territory. Even police expeditions, which came to punish them for killing traders, were ambushed and dispersed. They kept a stone fireplace where unwelcome outsiders were ritually cooked and eaten. Cannibal sites that travellers can visit change; at the time of writing travellers could see cannibal sites on the island of Rano only.

Big Nambas *erpnavet* (grade-taking) ceremonies are preceded by lengthy rehearsals. The men cover themselves in charcoal and

THE SMALLER SOUTHERN ISLANDS

Mystery Island 'Welcome to Paradise', the pilot will say as you clamber out of the tiny plane onto Aneityum's grass airstrip on Mystery Island. And it's true: this beautiful sandy islet off Aneityum is surrounded by a broad sandbank and dazzling coral in an azure sea...just like in the movies. Garden paths crisscross the island, many leading to little thatched loos. Snorkelling is fantastic off the end of the airstrip, as the island is a marine sanctuary. Aneityum people believe Mystery Island is the home of ghosts, so no one will live there.

Cross to Anelcauhat, Aneityum's main village, to see fascinating ruins of whaling-industry equipment, missionary Geddie's church and old irrigation channels. Take stunning walks from Anelcauhat to picturesque Port Patrick, impressive **Inwan Leleghei Waterfall** or to the top of **Inrerow Atahein** (853m), an extinct volcano.

Mystery Island Guesthouse (☑88888, 88896; www.mysteryislandbungalows.com; beds 2500VT) has colourful bungalows and a central kitchen with a gas refrigerator. You need to bring your own food, although someone will row across from Aneityum each day to see if you need anything. Cruise ships call in regularly, hence the little loos.

Erromango The 'land of mangoes' is mountainous, with almost all the people living in two main villages on its rugged coast. Each village has a fertile garden, where taro, tomato, corn and sweet potato thrive among huge mango, coconut and pawpaw trees.

Dillons Bay is Erromango's largest settlement, with a huge crystal-clear swimming hole formed by the Williams River as it turns to the sea. Sandalwood trees still grow in the rainforest, and a rock displays the outline of Williams, the first missionary here. They laid his short, stout body on this rock and chipped around it prior to cooking him.

Guided walks from Dillons Bay include trips to the **kauri reserve** (admission 2000VT) to see ancient 40m-high trees, and a three-day walk south and across to Ipota. There's magnificent scenery as you drop in and out of deep, fjordlike valleys, pass taro gardens, carve through tropical rainforests and trek down a 300m-high escarpment to scenic Pongkil Bay. Then you follow the coastal cliffs to a final steep descent to South River, situated beside a picturesque estuary. Boulder-hop and ford South River as you follow it to the Ipota road. A guide will cost you about 1500VT per day, plus food.

At the mouth of Williams River, **Meteson's Guesthouse** (☑68792, 68993; s/d incl breakfast 4200/5600VT) sleeps 10. Chief William arranges fishing trips and guides for treks.

Aniwa This island is set around beautiful, clear-blue Itcharo Lagoon, with 1.5km of white-sand beach, coconut palms, a marine sanctuary, great snorkelling, gorgeous coral and stacks of fish. Stay at one of two bungalows at **Ifaresei Ocean View Bungalows** (☑5616506; s incl meals 3500VT). They're in a quiet spot facing Tanna. Joshua also organises tours.

Malekula

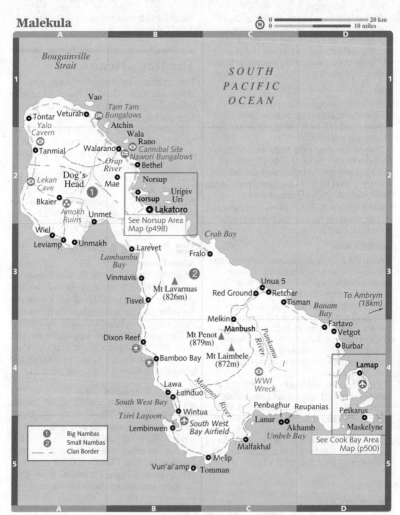

VANUATU MALEKULA

coconut oil, tie nut rattles around their ankles and wear feathers in their hair. At the highest level, a man has the powerful characteristics of a hawk, and a hawk dance is performed by a spirit man. The outfit, the movement and the spirit are stunning and unforgettable.

ℹ Information

There are no ATMs and nowhere will take your credit card. The NBV in Lakatoro will change travellers cheques and Australian dollars, but you can't access cash through your accounts, so take heaps of vatu.

The **Malampa Tourism Office** (Map p498; ☎48491, 48888; malampatourism@gmail.

com), near the police station in Lakatoro, can help with any aspect of tourism in the province and also offers an accommodation booking service. It's the place to go to organise the Manbush Trail Tour (see p499).

Check the internet on the computers at the **TVL Internet Vilaj** (Map p498; 1hr 500VT).

There's a **hospital** (☎48410) at nearby Norsup. Malekula's mountainous central regions are malaria free, whereas the coast is infested with it.

ℹ Getting There & Around

AIR

There are daily flights with **Air Vanuatu** (☎23748, 23878) from Port Vila and Santo

to Norsup, and three a week from Craig Cove. There are flights between Lamap and Norsup on Mondays and Thursdays. This may be the only way to travel between the two places during the wet season (and the flight can be cheaper than a boat or 4WD charter).

BOAT

A chartered speedboat ride from Wala in northern Malekula to Luganville on Santo costs around 20,000VT. From Craig Cove on Ambrym to Lamap it costs 10,000VT.

The passenger ferry **Big Sista** (Map p498; to Port Vila 7500VT, to Santo 3000VT) stops en route to Santo and Port Vila; check the office behind the market for times and days. **Fresh Cargo** (p491; to Santo 2500VT) stops here too.

All inhabited islands are linked to the mainland by speedboats or canoes. Ask at local stores if you wish to charter one.

CAR, BUS & TRUCK

A road runs from Norsup around the north coast and down the east coast to Lamap. The road south is rough and rutted and fords many rivers; in the wet season it's often closed.

It costs 300/100VT by taxi/minibus from Norsup airport into Lakatoro, but on weekends there aren't many around. Boats often arrive at Litslits south of Lakatoro in the early evening, and a taxi then is also unlikely, so try to hitch if you see a vehicle. Otherwise you may have to walk, bring a torch.

Jump in the tray of a **truck** (☑5499748; 4hr) to travel between Lakatoro and Lamap (1000VT) on weekdays. It leaves Lamap between 3.30am and 5am and returns from Lakatoro at 1pm. At weekends you'll need to charter a truck from Levi's Store (22,000VT). Trucks/charters run more frequently between Lakatoro and Veturah in the north (1 hour, 500/6500VT).

Most public transport leaves Lakatoro from the MDC General Store.

The Dog's Head

The culture-filled, Frankophone zone of Malekula's Dog's Head is home to several cannibal sites as well as the Big and Small Nambas tribal groups.

Kastom dancing tours go to Vao to see Small Nambas dances; to Unmet and Mae to see Big Nambas. Other tours go to the spectacular **Yalo Cavern** near Tanmial and the islets of Wala (a cruise-ship favourite) and Vao.

Most northern accommodation can arrange tours to the **cannibal site** on the island of Rano – worth a visit to sate your cannibal appetite.

🛏 Sleeping & Eating

Nawori Bungalows   LODGE $
(Map p497; ☑5685852, 48888; Wala Mainland; d incl breakfast 2500VT) Etienne hosted the film crew for the *Last One Standing* TV series so his lodge is quite swish: there's a generator, flush toilet and mosquito nets. Fall asleep to the sound of the sea lapping at the cliff below. His wife Lyne will cook for you. Cannibal tours to nearby Rano are 2000VT per person, plus 1500VT to charter the boat.

Tam Tam Bungalows   BUNGALOW $
(Map p497; ☑5548926, 5548927, 48888; Veturah; bungalows 7000VT) These pink bungalows have recently been updated and make a peaceful base for joining a tour and exploring the cannibal site at Rano and Small Nambas in Vao. There's snorkel gear and spear/canoe fishing, electricity from 6pm to 9pm, a *nakamal* for drinking kava and

Norsup Area

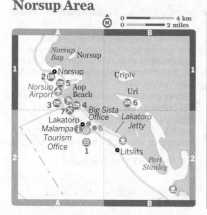

Norsup Area

MANBUSH TRAIL TOUR

If you have five days spare, a zest for hiking and good fitness, consider taking on Malekula's Manbush Trail Tour. **Malampa Travel** (☎48888) has put together an itinerary that includes guides, porters (one for two people), accommodation and meals, for 30,000VT per person. As usual for travel in Vanuatu's remote islands, transport costs are high, but the 37,000VT for truck and boat transfers can be reduced when divided between a maximum of eight travellers. It's no picnic; expect to walk six hours a day along bush tracks. You'll be starting at Red Ground and heading to the bush village of **Melkin**. Tour Melkin before walking to **Lambur**, where you spend the first night. Enjoy views of surrounding islands on the next day's walk to **Mt Laimbele**, where you camp out in a bush shelter.

The next village is **Lebongbong**, an old trading centre where you could exchange goods for pigs. It's so beautiful that it's seriously worth the agony. Visits to caves, waterfalls and a *nakamal* are included. The walking part of the trail tour finishes at Lawa, where you catch a boat to Lambumbu and a truck back to Norsup/Lakatoro where you can recuperate.

a restaurant (meals start at 1200VT). Transfers from Lakatoro are 6500VT.

Lakatoro

Lakatoro is a busy town with decent roads, shops and power supply. Set on two levels divided by a steep slope, this attractive place with many shady trees is Malampa province's administrative capital. On the top level is the **Cultural Centre** (Map p498; adult/child 300/100VT), which has fascinating exhibits – Malekula is well known for its terrific carvings – and photos and a library. You can buy traditional carvings here. At the northern end of town is the LTC Co-op, NBV bank, post office, bakery and Air Vanuatu office. The southern end has the MDC General Store and market. Ask here about taking a boat out to Uripiv and Uri islands.

Across from the airport terminal is sandy **Aop Beach**, with palms and turquoise water making it a pretty spot to wait for your plane. A long stretch of beautiful coral reef stretches southwards from Aop Beach to Litslits, the main port for this area.

Tours to Small and Big Nambas cultural villages and to cannibal sites can be arranged through your hosts (5000VT per person plus transfers), or ask about treks around the Dog's Head.

🛏 Sleeping & Eating

Lakatoro Palm Lodge LODGE $
(Map p498; ☎7721027, 48888; Lakatoro; s/d incl breakfast 2500/5000VT) A short walk from Lakatoro is this lovely lodge. Under the traditional thatched roof are three tiled-floor bedrooms, a shared lounge and kitchen (it's self-catering). Local spears decorate the inside walls and there's a nice coral-floored chill-out spot out front. There's also 24/7 solar electricity.

Ameltoro Resort & Restaurant BUNGALOWS $
(Map p498; ☎48431, 7742724, 48888; Lakatoro; bungalows 6500VT) Cute egg-shaped bungalows and a gorgeous restaurant where Rona cooks a French-influenced meal (by arrangement, from 500VT) for you.

Nabelchel BUNGALOWS $
(Map p498; ☎7740482, 48888; hoseatessi@gmail. com; Norsup; d incl breakfast 2500VT) These bungalows share a pleasant central sitting area and are handily located near the airport and a stunning beach. Meals are 800VT.

LTC Holiday Units MOTEL $
(Map p498; ☎549825; apt fan/air-con 6500/ 8500VT; ❄) These eight self-contained, one-bedroom Western-style units are set in grassland behind the LTC Co-op. Go for the air-conditioned ones.

Kimberly's Restaurant RESTAURANT $
(Map p498; Lakatoro; meals 350VT; ⊘breakfast & lunch Mon-Fri) A little place opposite the LTC Co-op with colourful tablecloths and curtains. The drinks are cold, Kimberly's cooking is excellent (staples include rice, steak and omelette) and the locals are often ready to chat.

Uripiv & Uri

These little islands have **marine reserves** proclaimed by the chief. These have everything for snorkellers, with beautiful coral,

Cook Bay Area

Cook Bay Area

0 ⸻ 4 km
0 ⸻ 2 miles

SOUTH PACIFIC OCEAN

Asuk Bay

2 Peunoamp Pt
Lamap

Port Sandwich (Ballande Wharf) Merivar

Barias Wreck of SS Per Vance Lamap-Orovail Airfield Dravai Lake Orovail

Boats to Maskelyne

Pt Doucere

Gaspard Bay

Cook Bay Sakao

Sakao Beach The Maskelynes

Bagatelle 5 1 Metai

Avokh Pellonk

Lembong Peskarus 4 3

Awei Lutes Batghutong

Sugarlump Reef Maskelyne (Uliveo) Khuneveo

Pt Baneuv Vulai

days; check the night before. Stay at **Lulu's Guesthouse** (Map p500; ☏5959552; per person 1000VT) near the church up the hill, which is also the town's tiny bakery (yum, fresh bread!).

The Maskelynes

The road from Lamap ends at a sandy beach, **Point Doucere** (transport from Lakatoro 1500VT) where canoes and speedboats head out to the Maskelynes (2500VT). It's a 20-minute walk south from the airport through coconut plantations.

The Maskelynes are just gorgeous. Most islands have coral reefs with excellent **diving** and **snorkelling**, especially at Sakao Beach. But be *very* careful of strong currents between the islands. Some of the islands are very rugged; others have patches of mangrove-lined coast or sandy beaches. The main island, **Maskelyne (Uliveo)**, is a friendly, busy place – watch the villagers make canoes, weave, string necklaces and hunt for edible sea creatures when the tide is out. You're welcome at the kava bars, and you can hire outrigger canoes for free (1000VT with a guide).

Take a tour to **Ringi Te Suh Marine Conservation Area** (Map p500; 1300VT), a 100-hectare reef protected by the villagers of Pellonk (the name itself means 'leave it alone'). You can snorkel over the beautiful giant clams and picnic on an artificial island.

Take a **Mangrove Discovery Tour** (1000VT) to learn about this ecologically rich resource, or a half-day **fishing expedition** (11,000VT) to catch yellow-fin tuna, or travel by outrigger to an island to see **kastom dances** (5000VT). Contact **Cedrik** (☏7751463) or **Stewart** (☏7103496) of the local tourism group (www.maskelynetourism.blogspot.com.au) for tour and travel information.

colourful fish and turtles. The sanctuary at Uri protects the mangroves and reef, and you'll see colourful giant clams.

Lines and Jake run the isolated **Nan Wat Bungalows** (Map p498; ☏5938523; Uri; s/d incl meals 2500/5000VT). It's 1000VT to get a boat transfer to this little spot on quiet Uri (the neighbouring island of Uripiv is a bustling city in comparison), and once you're there there's little to do but relax, snorkel and enjoy the fresh fruits that your hosts will prepare for you. Rooms are comfortable, with mosquito nets and pretty decorations.

You can get to Uripiv and Uri by speedboat from the Lakatoro jetty. Plenty of boats travel across between 4pm and 4.30pm (200VT) or you can charter a speedboat for 1000VT.

Lamap

Lamap is the entry point to the Maskelynes in the south. There's not much to it. It has an airport and a church. There's one surprisingly well-stocked shop, **Levi's Store** (☏5499748), which also arranges transfers from the airport (500VT), 'port' at Point Doucere (500VT) and Lakatoro (1000VT weekdays, charter 22,000VT). The truck departs between 3.30am and 5am on week-

🍴 Sleeping & Eating

Some of the hosts may be away picking fruit in New Zealand when you visit, but their families will step in to look after you.

TOP CHOICE Malaflaf

Beach Bungalow BUNGALOWS $
(Map p500; ☎7103474; www.maskelynetourism.blogspot.com.au; Lutes; s/d incl meals 2500/5000VT) Ambong has built one bungalow with two rooms in a sandy, delightfully remote, spot a walk away from the village. The basic rooms front a seagrass-filled lagoon with a coral reef. Enjoy your meals (ask for the local oysters) at a table on the beach while watching the sunset.

Malog Bungalows BUNGALOWS $
(Map p500; ☎5656056; www.maskelynetourism.blogspot.com.au; Peskarus; s/d incl breakfast 2500/5000VT, camping 500VT) Kalo has three traditional rooms on the muddy shore between the mangroves, with shared flush toilets and showers plus generator lighting till 9pm. If he's around, ask him to take you in an outrigger boat to a reef for beginners' snorkelling; it's shallow, clear, still and pretty.

Tohorhilau Eco Bungalow BUNGALOWS $
(Map p500; ☎7735737; Pellonk; s/d all meals 2500/5000VT) This eco-bungalow looks out onto mangroves and, thanks to the Australian High Commission, boasts composting toilets and solar power.

AMBRYM

POP 7300 / AREA 680 SQ KM

Ambrym (called the Black Island because of its volcanic soils) has amazing twin volcanoes, Mt Marum and Mt Benbow, which keep volcanologists all over the world on the alert. Other attractions include Vanuatu's best tree-fern carvings and *tamtam*, Rom dances of northern and western Ambrym, and Lake Fanteng Conservation Reserve.

Magic in Vanuatu is strongest on the islands with active volcanoes, and Ambrym is considered the country's sorcery centre. Sorcerers (*man blong majik* or *man blong posen*) are feared and despised. Many ni-Van have seen too many unexplained happenings, and would treat anyone who was found practising black magic severely. Tourists can visit villages that feature traditional magic, but magic for tourists is not considered black.

Ambrym is also the island for sand drawings, with 180 sand designs, each referring to a specific object, legend, dance or creature.

◉ Sights & Activities

VOLCANOES

The dark, brooding outlines of Mt Benbow and Mt Marum are about a kilometre apart, shrouded in smoke and cloud but dominating the vast, grey ash plain that lies within the old caldera. At night, the sky above them glows red.

Mt Benbow & Mt Marum VOLCANOES
Look over the smoky gullet of Mt Marum and see the red-hot magma boiling below like a satanic pot of tomato soup. It spews molten rock and dense black smoke from its vents. Both volcanoes are closely monitored, and evacuation plans are always ready.

To go up, you have to be fit and used to walking on steep terrain, and you need a good guide (see p507) to hack your way through jungle, cross glassy strips of old lava, push through wild bamboo forest and trudge along steamy gorges. And when you reach the caldera, the hard work starts.

There's no shade, just wave after wave of barren grey ridges. Skin protection and plenty of drinking water are essential. There's a dry, slippery crust around both volcanoes so your boots need to be strong enough to kick toe holes. Ankle support is also necessary as there's some boulder hopping. Between the mountains, the walk over the razor-backed ridge gets very narrow and snakes nastily upwards, while vents all around spurt acrid smoke. Mother Nature does her best to be daunting.

Access Points

The best idea is to go up the volcanoes one way and down another (different guides will meet you on the caldera). Trek prices depend on the distance travelled by truck (up to 5000VT return), local fees (1500VT per person), whether you stay overnight and how many guides you use (2000VT per person).

The four routes (three via Craig Cove airport, route four via Ulei airport) are as follows:

» **Emiotungun or Polipetagever** Truck it to the road's end, then walk along sand cliffs with no major slopes. If you come back this way, go direct with the truck to the hot pools at Baiap. Very relaxing!

Ambrym

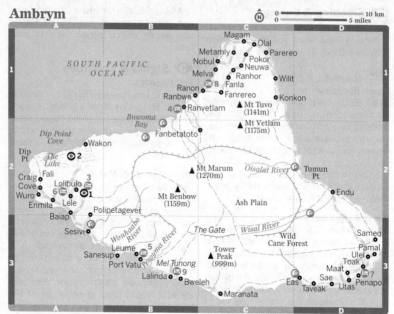

Ambrym

◎ Sights

🛏 Sleeping

» **Ranon or Ranvetlam** A complete experience – truck to Fanbetatoto, three hours of jungle, views, ash plain – return or continue down south.

» **Lalinda or Port Vatu** The slopes are fierce, but this way is the quickest: a truck trip, then a three-hour slog from the end of the road. The sudden break from forest to ash plain is stunningly beautiful.

» **Endu or Toak** From Endu, it's a four-hour trek to the ash plain, across Wisal River, and back through a wild cane forest. From Toak, you'll camp on the ash plain, returning along black-sand beaches and pools.

WEST AMBRYM

Ambrym's tiny commercial centre, **Craig Cove**, has a market, an NBV (you can't access cash so bring plenty of vatu), and a co-op that sells fresh bread, canned food, alcohol and hardware.

Emiotungun   VILLAGE
Emiotungun has lovely old carvings in the *nasara* (*nakamal*; admission 300VT). Polipetagever villagers perform Rom dances (5500VT), magic shows (500VT), sand drawing (500VT) and string band concerts (300VT). Or you can take a historical tour for 1500VT.

**Lake Fanteng
Conservation Area**   NATURE RESERVE
(local fee 500VT) At Dip Point north of Craig Cove, this is a beautiful spot, with many wild ducks and more than 30 bird species. Organise a trip (4000VT and 500VT entrance) with Sam from Sam's Guest Bungalows.

NORTH AMBRYM

Most of Ambrym's northern coast has high volcanic cliffs rising straight out of the sea. The motorboat journey north from Craig Cove burbles past sheer angled cliffs, forests, rock caves, hot pools, coral reefs, turtles, dolphins and wild ducks.

The best Rom dances and magic (admission 4500VT) can be seen inland at **Fanla**, a 45-minute walk from Ranon. An island feast can be prepared for a group, and locals will bring out a terrific array of carvings for your perusal. It was prohibited to access the volcano from here during yam season, but in line with the rest of the island it is no longer taboo.

Chief Joseph at Ranvetlam is the *kastom* owner of the northern approach to the volcanoes; the guides also live in this village.

EAST AMBRYM

Ulei is also an entry point to the volcanoes. **Toak**, near the airfield, is a large village where you'll see very traditional sand drawing, magic, *kastom* stories, dances, caves and waterfalls. Taxis can be hired here.

Tours

Your volcano tour guides usually have gear (tents, sleeping bags, hard hats, gloves, gas masks) should you want to hire anything. Ask if you need to bring your own food. Some options:

Dolven Bong HIKING
(☑7749486) Operates volcano tours out of Emiotungun.

Isaiah Bong HIKING
(☑7783480) Operates volcano tours out of Ranvetlam.

Joseph Talo HIKING
(☑23167, 46312; vandiscovery@vanuatu.com.vu) Organises three-night packages from Port Vila.

Sam David HIKING
(☑7767129) Operates volcano tours out of Craig Cove.

Solomon Douglas HIKING
(☑5637502, 5412896) Operates volcano tours out of Ranon.

Festivals

North Ambrym loves a good festival. Homestay accommodation (1500VT) is organised for tourists, crafts are for sale and stalls are heaped with food. For details, check with **Mayumi** (☑37365; mayumi@wreckstorainforest.com) on Santo, or **Chief Sekor** in Olal.

There are three main festivals (**Fanla Art Festival** and **North Ambrym Magic Festival** in July, and **Back to my Roots** in August), each an annual extravaganza of cultural demonstrations, ceremonies, fashion shows, Rom dances, magic and cooking lessons with guides and explanations in English and French.

🛏 Sleeping

WEST AMBRYM

Sam's Guest Bungalows BUNGALOW **$**
(☑7767129; Craig Cove; s/d incl meals 2500/5000VT) Small bungalows and bathrooms are behind Sam's family compound so you can enjoy family and village life. You'll find Sam working at the airfield; he can arrange tours and transport.

Bae Luke Guesthouse GUESTHOUSE **$**
(☑7730530; Emiotungun; s/d incl meals 2000/4000VT) This Western-style house by a friendly village has a kitchen with gas stove and an

VANUATU AMBRYM

THE ROM DANCE

Ambrym's most striking traditional ceremony, the Rom dance combines *maghe* (grade-taking) elements with magic. When a man wishes to move up in the village structure, he must find someone who owns the design of a mask and ask to buy it, with pigs and cash. The owner makes his *nakamal* (men's clubhouse) *tabu* (taboo), and the buyer comes to discuss the purchase and learn the rules determining the colours and shapes of the mask. Once the design has been bought, the buyer invites men to pay to enter this *nakamal* where they practise the dance for days, cooking the food the buyer has provided. Finally there's a feast, and the next morning the dancers perform wearing the extraordinary costume: a tall, conical, brightly painted banana-fibre mask and a thick cloak of banana leaves.

Only those men who paid to enter the *nakamal* will have seen the Rom costume being made. Anyone who disobeyed this *tabu* would be fined a pig and have their backs whipped with *nanggalat* (a native plant that burns the skin for days) or wild cane. Wild cane also marks the entrance to the *tabu* area. Be careful!

Costumes are burnt following the dance, to ensure that the spirit of the dance doesn't stay to make trouble in the village. Most tourists see only a pretend dance.

inside shower and toilet, but humidity is taking its toll. Arrange volcano tours here (per person 4000VT for same-day return, or stay overnight for an extra 1000VT per person).

SOUTH AMBRYM

Island Experience Eco Tours   GUESTHOUSE $
(7742661; tassojohn@yahoo.com; Port Vatu; per person incl meals 2000VT) Stay in the simple, multibed guest bungalow and prepare yourself for John Tasso's overnight volcano tour (6200VT including tent, entry fee and food). A truck charter is 5000VT from Craig Cove. Tasso also organises tours across the island.

Wola Volcano Guesthouse   BUNGALOWS $
(5487405; Lalinda; per person incl meals 2500VT) This thatched bungalow has two rooms and six beds, with a hole-in-the-ground toilet behind. Joses and his family will make you feel welcome and organise your volcano tour.

NORTH AMBRYM

Solomon Douglas Bungalows   BUNGALOWS $
(5637502, 5412896; Ranon; d incl breakfast 3000VT) Stay in traditional bungalows on the beach or up the cliff where there are stunning views. Meals are 600VT. Douglas organises tours to Rom dances in Fanla and volcano truck-and-treks. He also runs speedboat transfers to and from Craig Cove (12,000VT); ask him to stop while you snorkel along the coral-bedecked shoreline, or bask in the hot springs. Note that others in the boat may remove large megapode eggs while you're bathing, so consider the environmental impact before deciding on a hot spring stop. (The megapode is a large ground-dwelling bird, listed as vulnerable.)

Bang Were Bungalows   BUNGALOWS $
(7716903, 5398857; Ranvetlam; s/d incl meals 2500/5000VT) These simple but bright bungalows have great views looking over a bay. Enjoy flush toilets and a 'real' shower. Only accessible by foot or boat (transfer from Craig Cove 12,000VT).

EAST AMBRYM

The **Savuli Community Bungalows** (546-4208; Toak; per person incl meals 3000VT), made of stone and bamboo, are set along the black-sand beach; ask for Jeppy (transfers 1500VT). Overnight volcano treks including tents and campfire-cooked meals are 6500VT.

ⓘ Getting There & Around

AIR Air Vanuatu (23748) flies from Port Vila to Craig Cove four times a week (once a week from Santo), and to Ulei on Saturdays (on Tuesdays from Santo). Tour companies in Port Vila (p480) offer volcano adventure flights to Ambrym.

BOAT The *Brisk* cargo ship makes its way from Vila to Santo on Saturdays, stopping at both Craig Cove and Ranon.

The best anchorages are at Craig Cove and Sanesup in the south (Port Vatu is OK in good weather), and Buwoma Bay, Ranvetlam, Ranon and Nobul in the north.

If you aren't concerned about deep ocean swells and fierce currents, you can travel with Douglas of Solomon Douglas Bungalows by speedboat from north Ambrym to Pangi in southwest Pentecost (13,000VT). It's also possible to travel from Craig Cove to Lamap in Malekula (10,000VT) with Sam of Sam's Guest Bungalows (see p503).

Speedboats also travel between Craig Cove and Ranvetlam or Ranon (12,000VT one-way). Ask your bungalow host to arrange transport. Avoid a stop off at the hot springs if you'd prefer not to encourage the removal of megapode eggs.

TRUCK If you're heading south from Craig Cove to Port Vatu, try to get a lift from the airport on one of the trucks heading there, otherwise it can be a long wait for an expensive charter. If landing at Ulei, trucks run from Ulei to Endu on the east coast.

SANTO

POP 31,000 / AREA 3677 SQ KM

Far from having a one-track 'diving mind', Santo is out to prove it suits landlubbers, too. Weekly direct flights from Brisbane, Australia, bring in those in search of 'island resort' escapes (and Santo has plenty to choose from), hikers keen to explore the Millennium Cave as well as those with flippers attached to their feet. Military buffs can swoon over remnants of WWII, and even nonbuffs will marvel at the amazing Million Dollar Point site as they scramble over rusting military tanks at low tide. With blue holes seemingly around every corner, and one of the world's most stunning beaches stretching out in the northeast, you do need your bathers, and if a snorkel piques your interest, go further and consider diving the world's best wreck, the SS *Coolidge*, as elegant as the *Titanic*.

Santo's people live mainly on the southern and eastern coastal strips. Fanafo, north of Luganville, was where, in 1963, charismatic Jimmy Stevens formed the Nagriamel

movement (see p518). Then, on 27 May 1980, eight weeks before national independence, he and his supporters staged a coup known as the Coconut Rebellion. Armed mainly with bows and arrows, they occupied Luganville and proclaimed Santo's independence, calling their new country Vemarana. However, the new nation collapsed with Stevens' arrest on 1 September.

Inland, villages are isolated and the locals totally self-sufficient, even dressing in clothes woven from the leaves of the jungle. Southwest Santo has Vanuatu's highest mountains: Mt Tabwemasana (1879m), Mt Kotamtam (1747m), Mt Tawaloala (1742m) and Santo Peak (1704m). About 5000 people live in tiny villages that interrupt these thickly wooded mountains tumbling abruptly into the sea. As *kastom* demands, there are important *nimangki* ceremonies throughout the villages.

ⓘ Getting There & Around

AIR Pekoa International Airport (Map p511) is big, bright and new. It welcomes weekly international flights to and from Brisbane, Australia, and there are at least two return flights daily to Port Vila. It's also the feeder airport for Vanuatu's northern islands. Contact Air Vanuatu at its **town office** (Map p508; ☎36421; Main St) and **airport office** (Map p511; ☎36506).

BOAT Luganville has **Customs and Quarantine** (Map p508; ☎36225) and **Immigration** (Map p508; ☎36724) facilities for yachts at or near the **Main Wharf** (Map p508). Segond Channel, with its sandy bottom, is the town's main anchorage but Aore Island is the safest: 40m deep and away from the southeasterlies that hit the mainland.

Big Sista (☎23461; 9000VT) has a weekly service between Santo and Port Vila, leaving Port Vila on Mondays, returning Wednesdays, and **Fresh Cargo** (p491; 7500VT) stops here too.

CAR Santo has a lovely new sealed road connecting Luganville with the north and east coasts; elsewhere travel by boat, 4WD truck, or walk. Hire cars at the **Espiritu** (Map p508; ☎36061), where an around-town five-seater costs 6200VT per day including tax and insurance. Go wild and get an old Jeep from **Jeep Rental** (Map p508; ☎5619105; jeeprental@vanuatu.com.vu; per day incl tax from 9000VT).

MINIBUS & TAXI A minibus will pass you every minute in Luganville between 7am and 5.30pm. Hail one and you'll be dropped at your destination. Around Luganville is 150VT. It's 200VT from the airport.

A minibus runs up the east coast from Luganville to Port Olry (600VT) from Monday to Saturday, leaving Unity Shell Garage in Luganville between 1pm and 4pm. To return, stand by the roadside in Port Olry before 6.30am.

Cute, colourful taxis zip around Luganville, costing 150VT around town or 1000VT to the airport.

Luganville & Around

POP 13,200

Luganville, Vanuatu's northern capital, has a long, languid main road running parallel to the waterfront. It's a mixture of cheap Chinese shops, cool cafes, French-inspired restaurants, and tourism and dive operators. Combine this with some great new bargain accommodation and you've got the beginnings of a travellers'' centre. A sister festival to Port Vila's musical Fest' Napuan (Lukaotem Gud Santo) takes place in Luganville each November, see www.festnapuan.org for details.

◉ Sights

Millennium Cave   CAVE
(Map p508) Join a tour from Luganville and prepare yourself for some hard walking work. Trek and trudge through the jungle, across creeks, along bamboo bridges and through cascades to this massive cave, 20m wide and 50m high. Climb down a bamboo ladder, and through a rocky pool dodging cascades and little bats, then out into the sunlight and into icy water to zap down the rapids on a kids blow-up floaty thingy past amazing towering rocks, gorgeous rainforest and waterfalls. Scramble out all wet and shivery to climb back up to your bus. It's an awesome experience.

WWII sites   RUINS
There are lots of WWII remains in town, such as the caterpillar-like corrugated-iron American WWII **Quonset huts** (Map p508) at Main Wharf and near Unity Park, and the rusting **steel sea walls** (Map p508) that are evidence of busier times. **Million Dollar Point** (Map p511; admission per car 500VT) shows its coral-encrusted machinery to snorkellers, divers and low-tide walkers.

Leweton Cultural Village   VILLAGE
(Map p511; ☎5671114; admission 3000VT) Listen to women making water music and see other traditions from the Banks Islands.

Ransuck Cultural Village   VILLAGE
(Map p511; ☎5443973; admission 2500VT) Community members from Pentecost take you

VANUATU LUGANVILLE & AROUND

Santo

0 ————————————— 20 km
0 ————————————— 10 miles

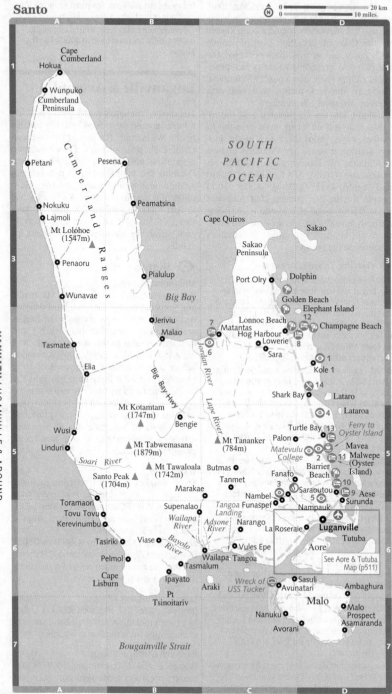

VANUATU LUGANVILLE & AROUND

Cape Cumberland
Hokua

Wunpuko
Cumberland Peninsula

Cumberland Ranges

Petani

Pesena

SOUTH
PACIFIC
OCEAN

Nokuku
Lajmoli
Mt Lolohoe (1547m)

Peamatsina

Cape Quiros

Sakao

Penaoru

Pialulup

Sakao Peninsula

Port Olry

Dolphin

Wunavae

Big Bay

Golden Beach
Elephant Island

Jeriviu
Malao

7
Matantas
6

Lonnoc Beach
Hog Harbour
Lowerie
Sara

12
Champagne Beach

Tasmate

Jordan River

8

Elia

1
Kole 1

Big Bay Hwy

Lape River

14
Shark Bay

Lataro

Mt Kotamtam (1747m)

Bengie

4
Lataroa

Wusi
Linduri

Mt Tabwemasana (1879m)

Mt Tananker (784m)

Turtle Bay 13
Palon
Matevulu College

Ferry to Oyster Island

Soari River

Mt Tawaloala (1742m)
Santo Peak (1704m)

Butmas
Tanmet

Mavea
11 Malwepe (Oyster Island)

Marakae

Barrier Beach

Toramaori
Tovu Tovu
Kerevinumbu

Supenalao

Fanafo
3
Nambel

Tangoa Landing
Funaspef

10

Saraoutou
5
9 Aese
Surunda

Tasiriki
Viase

Wailapa River
Adsone River

Narango

Nampauk

Bayolo River

Vules Epe

La Roseraie

Luganville
Tutuba

Pelmol

Wailapa
Tasmalum
Tangoa

Aore

See Aore & Tutuba Map (p511)

Cape Lisburn

Ipayato
Araki

Wreck of USS Tucker

Sasuli
Avunatari

Ambaghura

Pt Tsinoitariv

Nanuku

Malo

Malo Prospect
Asamaranda

Avorani

Bougainville Strait

Santo

through a lush garden and show you how their beautiful mats are made.

Luganville Market   MARKET
(Map p508; Main St; ☉24hr) Villagers come from all over to sell their produce. It's near the Sarakata Bridge.

🏃 Activities

Diving & Snorkelling

Snorkelling here is excellent – totally brilliant – but you shouldn't come to Santo without trying a dive. The coral's bright and healthy, the wrecks are world class, prices are fantastic and dive operators extremely professional. Look at operators' websites for some amazing images, such as MV *Henry Bonneaud*, one of the world's top night dives; SS *President Coolidge*, lying in 21m to 67m of water; and Tutuba Point, a spectacular drift dive with brilliant corals and marine life.

There are boat and offshore dives for beginners to gurus. An intro dive costs about 10,000VT; double dives offshore/boat are 8200/12,600VT; diver certification courses cost from 48,000VT; equipment hire is 1500VT.

Allan Power Dive Tours   DIVING
(Map p508; ☎36822; www.allan-power-santo.com; Main St, Luganville) A favourite since 1969.

Aore Island Dive   DIVING
(Map p511; ☎36705; www.aoreresort.com) In-house diving at Aore Island Resort (p509).

Aquamarine   DIVING
(Map p508; ☎36196; www.aquamarinesanto.com; Luganville) Big and popular. Sit on the deck to study your notes.

Bokissa Island Dive   DIVING
(Map p511; ☎30030; www.bokissa.com) Just for guests of Bokissa Eco Island Resort (p510).

Santo Island Dive & Fishing   DIVING, FISHING
(Map p508; ☎7758082, 58080; www.santodive. com; Main St, Luganville) Choose your own adventure with this small, professional operator. Great picnic lunch too.

This operator also stays close to shore for reef fishing, snorkelling and a picnic lunch (half/full day 25,000/35,000VT), or heads out in search of tuna, mahi-mahi and wahoo.

Golf

Palikulo Golf Club   GOLF
(Map p511; ☉Sat & Sun) This golf club at Palikulo Bay welcomes visitors, but you'll need your own clubs. The course runs along the seafront with fine views of Aese Island and Palikulo Point. There's a tournament on the last Sunday of every month.

Horse Riding

Lope Lope Adventure Lodge   HORSE RIDING
(Map p506; ☎7774700; megan@splashextreme. com; 1-2hr incl transfers & photo 8550VT) Enjoy a waterfront horse-riding adventure around 11km north of Luganville.

Swimming

The best place to swim is at the beach in front of Beachfront Resort, where you're welcome. There's a beach on the way to Palikulo Point (about 1200VT by taxi return). But for gorgeous beaches, go up the east coast to Champagne Beach and Lonnoc Beach.

Hiking

Favourite Santo treks are through the Vatthe Conservation Area (p512) and the Loru Conservation Area (p512) but Wrecks to Rainforest (p508) are good for trekking closer to Luganville.

🤙 Tours

There are many operators with minivans or taxis ready with tours (from 3000/4000VT per half/full day). A typical day trip includes

VANUATU LUGANVILLE & AROUND

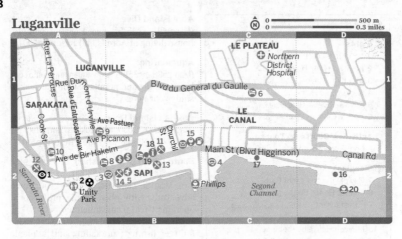

Luganville

◎ Sights
1	Luganville Market	A2
	Quonset Huts	(see 20)
2	Steel sea walls	A2

⊕ Activities, Courses & Tours
3	Allan Power Dive Tours	B2
4	Aquamarine	C2
5	Santo Island Dive & Fishing	B2
	Wrecks to Rainforest	(see 7)

⊟ Sleeping
6	Deco Stop Lodge	C1
7	Espiritu	B2
8	Hotel Santo	A2
9	Le Motel Hibiscus	A2
10	Tropicana Motel & Backpackers	A2

⊗ Eating
	Deco Stop Restaurant	(see 6)
11	Le Jardin Des Saveurs	B2
12	Market Meal Booths	A2
13	Natangora Café	B2
14	Vittoria Café	B2

⊙ Drinking
15	Roys	B2

ⓘ Information
16	Customs & Quarantine	D2
17	Immigration Office	C2
18	VTO Office	B2

ⓘ Transport
19	Air Vanuatu Office	B2
20	Main Wharf	D2
	The Espiritu	(see 7)

a visit to Champagne Beach and Matevulu Blue Hole. Discuss where you will go: some cultural highlights can be a real fizzer, some guides can't access Champagne Beach, some places require long bus trips. Tailored tours offer hiking, WWII relics, culture and nature.

An absolute must-do is Millennium Cave (p505), high in the hills inland from Luganville. Another is Riri Riri River and Blue Hole, a grotto of tree ferns overhanging a white-sand and crystal-blue pool.

Wrecks to Rainforest GUIDED TOUR
(Map p508; ☏37365, 5547001; www.wreckstorain forest.com) Owner Mayumi Green is a terrific source of knowledge and can organise

four-day treks (per day from 6000VT) taking you through rainforest, gardens, along and across Wailapa River to Marakae. A three-day trek to Funaspef includes the Millennium Cave. You'll sleep in traditional villages where the MalMal people still use Stone Age equipment. Mayumi also runs tours to the northern islands (four-day tours to Rah Island are 34,300VT) and Malekula and Ambrym.

Butterfly Adventure Tours GUIDED TOUR
(☏5660290; tourvanuatu@gmail.com) Glenn runs tours ranging from bushwalking to seeing wild orchids and WWII relics.

Heritage Tours
GUIDED TOUR

(☑36862, 7740968; www.espiritusantotourism.com/santoheritagetours.html) These tours have been running for over 20 years; speak to Tim.

Little Paradise of Port Olry
GUIDED TOUR

(☑5424893; PO Box 115) Ask for Tarcisius. Offers tours and accommodation on the pretty beaches way up north.

Paradise Tours
GUIDED TOUR

(☑7747159; www.paradisetourssanto.com) Luke has been running tours for years. He picks you up from your accommodation and offers a mix of one- and half-day tours.

Santo Island Tours
GUIDED TOUR

(☑36601, 7742151; www.tropicanasanto.com.vu) Kenneth has a good range of tours and can customise them for individuals.

Santo Safari Tours
GUIDED TOUR

(☑7742178; www.santosafaritours.com) Erick has fab new buses and loads of tours, including bird-spotting ones.

🛏 Sleeping

These are just a few of the places in and around Luganville.

TOP CHOICE Le Motel Hibiscus
MOTEL $

(Map p508; ☑36727; Rue Dumount D'Urville; lemotelhac@gmail.com; tr 3500VT; 🐾) These terrific rooms, all with bathrooms and kitchenettes, sleep three and are set around a central area. It's close to everything, bargain priced and has terrific hosts.

TOP CHOICE Aore Island Resort
RESORT $$

(Map p511; ☑36705; www.aoreresort.com; bungalows incl breakfast from 12,000VT; @🐾) Spacious bungalows (some in a child-free area), grassy slopes to the water, snorkel gear and kayaks: all are good, and the restaurant (mains 1400VT to 3000VT) is a grand area. The ferry leaves from Phillips Wharf; ask for the schedule when you book. Nonguests can hang out at the resort as long as they buy lunch here. There's a dive shop, too (p507).

Village de Santo
APARTMENTS $$

(Map p511; ☑36123; www.villagedesanto.com; Red Corner; d incl breakfast 12,500VT; 🐾) Swish self-contained family units nestle around a pool. It's very close to the beach, the lovely Restaurant 1606 (p511) is on site and it's just a stroll into town. The weekly local music gigs here have led to the annual Lukaotem Gud Santo Festival (held in November).

Tropicana Motel & Backpackers
MOTEL $

(Map p508; ☑36036; www.tropicanasanto.com.vu; Cook St; dm/s/d 2000/3000/4500VT; 🐾) Clean, modern rooms with en suite bathrooms surround a lovely garden, while the amazing kitchen has to be seen (and used) to be believed.

Beachfront Resort
LODGE $

(Map p511; ☑36881; www.thebeachfrontresort.com; lodge dm/d/tr 4200/8200/10,400VT, bungalows s/d air-con 8800/11,000VT; ❄🐾🐾) Budget rooms at the lodge are custom built for divers, with secure wash facilities, six-bed

---

LOCAL KNOWLEDGE

ALLAN POWER, DIVER

Experienced diver Allan Power runs dive tours around Santo (p507).

You've just been initiated into the International Scuba Diving Hall of Fame. How long have you been diving Santo? Since 1969. Everyone comes to Santo to see the SS *Coolidge*, Allan Power and other Santo wrecks.

What's your favourite dive near Santo? The *Coolidge*, of course.

What's the best dive for expert divers? The *Coolidge* again. It's good for everyone from beginners to experienced, with a deep depth to 60m.

How many dives have you clocked at the Coolidge? It's about 28,000 dives over 42 years. Each dive is better – it's such a big wreck, so there's so much to see.

Tell me about the coral garden you made. The *Coolidge* is a shore dive; the divers follow a big rope to the wreck, and they used to spread out all over the coast, so I built a coral garden to keep them all together. It's big enough for 15 divers to fit on. The garden's been completely wiped out four times from cyclones. We start again. A bit breaks off and you put it on and, within months, it fuses. It's a colony and just keeps growing. We're always at it.

dorm rooms and a sparkling clean kitchen. The neighbouring modern bungalows are squeaky clean with kitchenettes. Its beach is the best place to swim, even if you aren't staying.

Bokissa Eco Island Resort RESORT $$$

(Map p511; ☑30030; www.bokissa.com; d 48,000VT; ✷@✷) Fluffy-white-towel luxurious with bungalows 10 footsteps away from astounding snorkelling over plate corals piled high, branches of soft coral, and anemones with their 'Nemos'. It's a busy dive base, but nondivers can kayak up a river, walk, turtle watch and swim in the pool with a swim-up bar.

Ratua Private Island Resort RESORT $$$

(Map p511; ☑30020; Ratua; www.ratua.com; d 45,000VT; ✷@✷) This private island resort some 30 minutes' speedboat ride from Santo has 200-year-old Bali-sourced bungalows and an eco bent (ceiling fans, not air-con, for instance). Horse riding is popular, or laze away the day reading in the Yacht Club or being pampered at the on-site spa.

Deco Stop Lodge LODGE $$

(Map p508; ☑36175; www.decostop.com.vu; dm/units 4900/12,300VT; ✷) High on the ridge behind Luganville overlooking Segond Channel, Deco Stop has a huge deck floating around a grand swimming pool. Behind some of the rooms is set a secure wash area for divers' gear.

Espiritu HOTEL $

(Map p508; ☑37539; www.the-espiritu.com; Main St; d 8500VT; ✷☎@) Rooms are fresh from a renovation (expect all mod cons) and the

spirit is refreshed from a name change. There's a Chinese restaurant out the front (Ocean King Restaurant; mains 1100VT to 2100VT; closed Wednesday) and its central location is a bonus.

Coral Quays Fish & Dive Resort BUNGALOWS $$

(Map p511; ☑36257; www.coralquays.com; fan/air-con r incl breakfast 11,300/12,600VT; ✷☎) Eighteen attractive bungalows with soaring ceilings sit in a veritable tropical forest. Use the private jetty across the road to snorkel or dive over coral gardens and the *Tui Twaite* shipwreck, 800m away. A minibus/taxi from town costs 150/400VT.

Hotel Santo HOTEL $$

(Map p508; ☑36250; www.hotelsanto.com.vu; s/d 7250/8290VT, upstairs s/d/tr 12,000/13,200/14,500VT; ✷☎) It's a bit of a time warp, but that's part of the appeal of this retro '70s hotel, with its fabulous huge *tamtam* in the foyer. Fan-cooled rooms open onto the pool area; or head upstairs for air-conditioning.

 Eating

Le Jardin Des Saveurs FRENCH $$

(Map p508; mains 2000-2900VT; ⊗breakfast, lunch & dinner) This spot has two menus: one a snack-bar menu for the front and the other a grander menu (think frog's legs and lobster salad) for the restaurant further back. Popular with local expats.

TOP CHOICE Deco Stop Restaurant RESTAURANT $

(Map p508; mains 1500VT; ⊗7am-9pm) You're on top of the world, sitting around the beautiful pool, gazing way out over the channel, and

---

JUNGLE TO CITY TO DIVING HUB

Segond Channel was the Allies' base during WWII. For three years to September 1945, more than half a million military personnel, mainly Americans, were stationed here waiting to head into battle in the Pacific. There were sometimes 100 ships moored off Luganville.

Roads were laid. There were 40 cinemas, four military hospitals, five airfields, a torpedo boat base, jetties and market gardens. Quonset huts were erected for use as offices, workshops and servicemen's accommodation. More than 10,000 ni-Van came to work for the troops. To them, the servicemen seemed fabulously wealthy and generous.

Unfortunately, SS *President Coolidge*, a luxury liner turned troopship, hit a friendly mine. It's since become the world's largest accessible and diveable shipwreck.

After the war, the USA offered the Condominium government the surplus equipment but they didn't respond, so the lot was dumped. Everything from bulldozers, aeroplane engines and jeeps to crates of Coca-Cola went into the sea at what is now Million Dollar Point. The coral-encrusted equipment makes the point a popular diving and snorkelling spot.

Aore & Tutuba

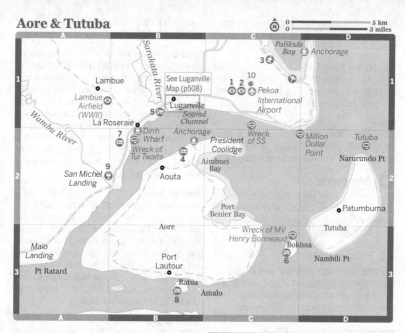

choosing from an excellent menu. Get stuck into the crab or organic Santo beef.

Restaurant 1606   RESTAURANT $
(Map p511; Red Corner; mains 1800-2700VT; ☺breakfast, lunch & dinner) Head here to 'build your own sandwich' at lunch, or enjoy grilled scallops or crispy pork belly (organic Santo-grown pork, of course) for dinner.

Market Meal Booths   MARKET $
(Map p508; meals 350VT; ☺7.30am-10pm) Sit at a bright little table and a cheery lady appears at the booth window with a glass of red cordial. There's a choice of dishes, but steak's the best. You can watch it being cooked and the fresh herbs added – delicious.

Natangora Café   CAFE $
(Map p508; Main St; meals 450-1250VT; ☺7.30am-4.30pm Mon-Fri, 8am-1pm Sat; 🛜) Specialises in breakfast, house-roasted coffee, hamburgers, juices and salads. The alfresco setting and reasonable prices make it popular with locals, expats and tourists alike.

Vittoria Café   PIZZA $
(Map p508; mains 1000-1900VT; ☺7.30am-4.30pm Mon-Sat) With pizza slices and meals 'ready to go' (and great coffee), this place is perfect for a quick top-up to stave off hunger and coffee-withdrawal.

🍷 Drinking & Entertainment

The entertainment scene is pretty light on in Luganville. Deco Stop Lodge is your best bet, and another is the weekly live music at

Village de Santo (p509). Kava bars are open from 6pm to 10pm – look for a red or green light.

San Michel Kava Bar BAR
(Map p511; South Santo Rd) A seaside kava bar popular with locals. It's a bit out of town; buy your taxi driver a cup.

Roys BAR
(Map p508; Main St) This spot, behind Unity Shell Service Station, is where the internationals working in Santo often head.

Shopping
Shopping is small-town style, but there's a range of boutique clothes and accessories, along with the diving gear at **Santo Island Dive & Fishing** (p507; ✆7758082; Main St).

Information
The **VTO** (Map p508; ✆36984; santo@tourism. travel; Main St; ⏰7.30am-4.30pm) has plenty of info. Also check www.espiritusantotourism.com.

Luganville's main street has commercial banking facilities with ATMs.

Ambulance (Map p508; ✆36112)

ANZ Bank (Map p508; ✆36711; ⏰8am-3pm Mon-Fri) Has an ATM.

Club de Sanma (Map p508; ✆36039; Main St; ⏰9am-midnight) The money exchange here offers good rates.

National Bank of Vanuatu (NBV; Map p508; ✆36441; ⏰8am-3pm Mon-Fri)

Northern District Hospital (Map p508; ✆36345) Perched above the town in Le Plateau, usually hosts 'baby docs' (international doctors-in-training)

Police (Map p508; ✆36222)

Post office (Map p508; ⏰8.30am-5pm Mon-Fri) There's a cardphone outside.

Westpac Bank (Map p508; ✆36625; ⏰8am-4pm Mon-Fri) Has an ATM.

The East Coast Road

With its upgraded road beckoning, staying at one of the terrific places on the east coast is a must. The following are ordered approximately by distance from Luganville.

Sights & Activities

Blue Holes SWIMMING
(Map p506) Stop at **Matevulu Blue Hole** (admission per car 1000VT) and take the pretty plunge, or continue on to the lovely **Nanda Blue Hole** (admission per car 1000VT), which

has good facilities and friendly faces just off the main road.

Loru Conservation Area NATURE RESERVE
(Map p506; admission 500VT) Covering 220 hectares, Loru Conservation Area contains one of the last patches of lowland forest remaining on Santo's east coast. There are several excellent nature walks, many coconut crabs and a bat cave, which the villagers use as a cyclone shelter. If you've come without a guide, ask for Kal at Kole 1 village. For more details, see www.positiveearth.org/bunga lows/sanma/loru_pa.htm.

Lonnoc Beach BEACH
(Map p506) In a beautiful coastal setting is this lovely beach, all white and turquoise, with stunning views of Elephant Island. A guide (600VT per person) from Lonnoc Beach Bungalows will take you to visit local gardens, to Hog Harbour, or to swim at a local blue hole. Go out in a canoe to fish or see turtles, or take a half-day canoe trip (1000VT) to Elephant Island.

Champagne Beach BEACH
(Map p506; admission 2000VT per car) Champagne Beach is a stunner. You may have this horseshoe of fine white sand and turquoise water to yourself (unless the cruise ships are docked).

Vatthe Conservation Area NATURE RESERVE
(Map p506; admission 600VT) Those seeking a wilderness experience can head west to Vatthe Conservation Area, a protected area of 2276 hectares.

Sleeping & Eating
Lope Lope
Adventure Lodge BOUTIQUE LODGE $$$
(Map p506; ✆36066; www.lopelopeadventure lodge.com; d fan/air-con 38,500/41,000VT; ☏) Lope Lope Adventure Lodge has three very fancy bungalows resting on the water's edge. The hammocks and beds are placed to get the great views, and there's a free bottle of champagne in your room on arrival. No kids. Also has a horse riding/adventure centre (yes, kids).

Moyyen House
by the Sea BOUTIQUE ACCOMMODATION $$$
(Map p506; ✆30026; www.moyyan.com; d incl breakfast 28,000VT) On Barrier Beach is this cool dark timber and glass place over white sand and blue water. It comes complete with a day spa and frequently sighted dugong.

THE ALMIGHTY OYSTER

Stop when you see a turnoff to **Oyster Island** (Malwepe; Map p506). Summon the boat by banging on the gas cylinder, and in two minutes you'll be kicking back with a drink and a meal on a sweep of deck. You must try the oysters because, guess what, there's a stack of oysters. It's part of the magical **Oyster Island Restaurant and Resort** (Map p506; ☑36283; www.oysterisland. com; d basic/standard/delux incl breakfast 9000/15,600/17,600VT; ☎). Use your cute bungalow as a base to explore the nearby blue hole by kayak, or go snorkelling or diving. It's a social, friendly and busy spot.

Turtle Bay Lodge   LODGE $$
(Map p506; ☑37988; www.turtlebayresort.vu; dm/d/f incl breakfast 3000/10,600/11,600VT; ☎☒) Has bright and cheery dorm rooms and units with private verandahs. There's a restaurant and kayaks to borrow. If Matt's around, ask about circus classes.

Lonnoc Beach
Bungalows & Restaurant   BUNGALOWS $
(Map p506; ☑5416456; www.lonnocbeach bungalows.com; s/d/honeymoon incl breakfast 5500/7000/12000VT) Each traditional bungalow here has a cute porch, but electricity is only in the restaurant. Spend your evenings at the bar, or take an oil lamp down to the beach. Airport transfers are 3500VT per person.

Towoc Restaurant &
Bungalows   BUNGALOWS $
(Map p506; ☑5636173; www.towocresto@hot mail.com; s/d incl breakfast 2500/4500VT) Keep going down the road from Lonnoc Beach Bungalows to these simple but perfectly adequate bungalows. Stay in one of the bungalows and enjoy free access to the nearby world-class beach (it's in the family).

Bay of Illusions Yacht Club   BUNGALOWS $
(Map p506; ☑5612525; d incl breakfast 2500VT) Get in touch with Purity at this Bay of Illusions Yacht Club, which has three bungalows near the beach at Matantas. Three-course meals here are 1700VT. Head out on a coconut crab tour, village tour or check out the bat cave.

Velit Bay Plantation   SEAFOOD $$
(Map p506; www.velitbayplantation.com) For something quite unusual and unexpected, drive down the rocky road of Velit Bay Plantation (you can't miss the sign!), to sample the edible delights of **15 South**. It's a lovely little restaurant with a fridge full of icy cold champagne. There's a bunch of water activities in the cute bay, too, or just have a game of beach volleyball.

🛈 Getting There & Away

MINIBUS, TAXI & TRUCK There's a daily minibus service along the east coast (see p505). Taxis cost about 2000VT (shared) to Oyster Island, 5000VT to Lonnoc Beach. A truck to Matantas from Luganville costs 8000VT (one-way), it's cheaper to catch the daily minibus to Sara Village from Unity Shell Petrol Station, Luganville (500VT), then travel by local truck from Sara to Matantas (2500VT; Monday to Friday).

Ambae

Ambae has **Mt Lombenben** (1496m) on the rim of a semiactive volcano that rumbles dynamically. A cone rose out of blue **Lake Manaro Lakua**, one of its famous crater lakes, in 2005, creating world news, then went bad down. Hot and lime-green **Lake Vui** also sends volcanologists into a frenzy whenever it boils. **Lake Manaro Ngoru**, the third crater lake, is mostly dry with a central cold-water spring.

In Longana stay at **NTJ Guesthouse** (☑7760250, 7745864; Longana; s 1800VT), which has a well-stocked shop, electricity till 9pm and three nice rooms. Lake access from the

Ambae

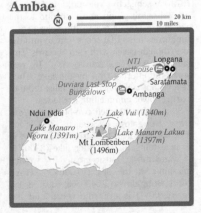

north is a four-hour trek along an overgrown track stay at **Duviara Last Stop Bungalows** (☑5949740; Ambanga; s 1500VT), where you can organise a guide. Guides and entry fees cost 1000VT each, transfers 5000VT, and meals 1000VT.

REMOTE NORTHERN ISLANDS

Maewo

The 'Island of Water' has rivers, hot springs, deep cold pools, magnificent waterfalls and water-taro terraces. It is only accessible by boat from Ambae or Pentecost (10,000VT). **Big Water waterfall**, in the north, is thought of locally as the Eighth Wonder of the World.

Down south, at **Sanasom**, is magnificent **Hole of the Moon cave** (admission 1500VT) and **Malangauliuli**, a cave with spectacular petroglyphs. Chief Jonah is *kastom* owner of the cave. **Justin Ihu** (☑7727897) can get you there on his boat (7000VT). He and Ericka run **Mule Ocean View Guesthouse** (☑7721287; Asanvari; s incl breakfast 1500VT) near the fading Yacht Club. Swim at the lovely Lavoa Cascade, which is home to the new Sparkling Waters Bar. This is a very popular spot for yachts.

Gaua (Santa Maria)

Gaua offers spectacular hikes, including a two-day test around the island's three major sights: pretty **Lake Letas**, one of the largest freshwater lakes in the Pacific; Mt Garet (797m), a semiactive volcano; and fabulous **Siri Waterfall**. Wind and climb up to the lake and canoe across to the volcano – a sulphurous mess that seeps orange into the lake (though check with Geo Hazards Vanuatu first; www.geohazards.gov.vu). It's well worth the effort. Camp by the lake. Then it's a vicious trek down to the falls, 120m of roaring power pummelling to the sea.

Stay at the thatched two-bedroom **Wongrass Bungalow** (☑5690831, 7712879; incl meals 3500VT), near the airport. Charles will arrange tours to the crater lake (3500VT) or water music, music created by women splashing in the sea (10,000VT). **Fresh Wind Bungalow** (☑5400366, 5393538; incl meals 2500VT) is near the ocean and has

comfortable dormitory-style rooms. Collet Vanva prepares very nice meals with local ingredients. Airport-boat transfers are 1500VT.

Vanua Lava

Sola, the island's capital, is the centre for excellent walks, such as the glorious day's walk via Mosina across the plateau overlooking Vureas Bay, through water-taro gardens, over streams and rapids to **Waterfall Bay**, where spectacular **Sasara Falls** tumbles over the cliff into the bay. A speedboat from Sola to Waterfall Bay costs around 26,000VT return (entrance fee 1000VT).

In Sola, stay at **Leumerous Guesthouse** (☑7733426, 5391846; Sola; s incl meals 2500VT, camping 500VT) where thatched bungalows sit along a garden path. On the beach is the **Leumerous Yacht Club** (meals 300VT to 900VT), everybody's favourite spot. Enjoy breakfast, lunch or dinner with yachties and locals.

At Waterfall Bay, only minutes from the falls, is **Waterfall Bay Yacht Club** (meals 400VT) in a grand bungalow with artefacts and handicrafts for sale. Stay at **Sara Waterfall Bungalows** (incl meals 2500VT). The rumbling waterfall will lull you to sleep.

Motalava & Rah

Rah Paradise Beach Bungalows (incl meals 3000VT) is on a beautiful beach on this tiny island located next to Motalava mainland. It's run by Father Luke and his wife Rona, who work closely with the village. Airport transfers cost 5000VT one-way. Father Luke organises a bunch of activities, including a snake dance (5000VT), treks to the sleeping mountain (2000VT), a legend tour of Rock of Rah (1000VT) as well as reef-island trips (31,000VT).

Torres Islands

These are the most remote islands of Vanuatu. They feature dazzling white-sand beaches, with good surfing, especially when the trade winds are blowing. There's excellent snorkelling on most islands: **Linua**, which is unpopulated except for tourist accommodation; **Loh**, across a tidal sandbank; **Tegua** and **Hiu** to the north (you can see the Solomon Islands from here on a clear day!); and **Toga** where most of the people live.

Everyone gets around in outrigger canoes. The delightful **Kamilisa Guesthouse** (Linua; s incl meals 3000VT) is in a delicate rainforest, right on the lagoon. Butterfly lovers will find this place amazing. There's no phone coverage here, but owner Whitely greets every flight, looking for guests.

PENTECOST

POP 16,800 / AREA 438 SQ KM

Pentecost has the *naghol* (land diving), the most remarkable custom in all of Melanesia, where men make spectacular leaps of courage from high towers as a gift to the gods to ensure a bountiful yam harvest. Pentecost also has great scenery, significant waterfalls and lots of festivals and ceremonies. Most of the population lives along the west coast, which has a high rainfall, attributed to local rainmakers. Sceptical Westerners say it's because the island's mountainous spine catches the southeasterlies, causing precipitation.

A rocky beach extends 12km from just before Lonorore airfield south to Ranputor. The south is the home of the *naghol,* and you can witness this amazing celebration during the *naghol* season during April, May and June. Pangi is very basic, with just a kava bar, clinic and couple of stores.

⊙ Sights & Activities

Land Diving CULTURAL TOUR

Land-dive towers are erected at **Lonorore Airport**, **Londot**, **Pangi** and **Rangusuku** (sites change and they're announced annually). **Luke Fargo** (☏7734621) arranges tours to the land diving (adult/child 12000/6000VT). Most tourists come on day packages (per person including flights 50,000VT) with Port Vila tour companies, including **Vanuatu Discovery** (p481).

Take adventure walks to waterfalls and banyans and the stone ruins of a feasting hall, where 100 people were killed by the eel spirit. Other tours include visits to villages to see *kastom* dances. Or walk up a river with your host and help him catch river prawns. How fresh will they be! Swimming and snorkelling are relatively safe in Bay Homo because of the reef.

North of the airstrip is magnificent **Waterfall Falls**, tumbling down behind Waterfall Village into pretty rock pools.

⨶ Sleeping & Eating

Sara and Alice have **restaurants** (meals 300VT; ⊗6am-9pm Mon-Fri) in Pangi. Both women cook the one dish and stay open until it's all sold. There's no knowing what

THE LAND DIVERS OF PENTECOST

The men of Pentecost spend many weeks building towers by binding tree trunks, saplings and branches to a tall tree with vines. The towers are the shape of a man or woman up to 35m high. The tower sighs as it bends in the wind; you'll sigh, as you see the men make their spectacular leaps to ensure a successful harvest.

Each diver carefully selects his own liana vines, then an experienced elder checks to ensure that it's strong and elastic enough. The soil in front of the tower is cleared of rocks, then loosened. Fathers teach their young sons to dive from their shoulders. Boys practise diving from boulders into the sea. At age eight they are circumcised; then they can make their first jump.

Between 10 and 20 males per village will dive. Each man prepares in turn while his friends tie his vines. The women sing and dance below. As he raises his hands he tells the crowd his most intimate thoughts; the people stop their singing and dancing, and stand quietly – these could be his last words.

Finally the diver claps his hands, crosses his arms and leans forward. In slow motion, falling, he arches his back. The platform breaks away. Snap. The vines abruptly stop him. Only his hair will touch the soil, to fertilise the yam crop. The crowd roars its appreciation, dancing, stomping and whistling in tribute.

It is such a celebration. The colour and sounds add to the atmosphere: men wearing small red-dyed *namba* (penis sheath), clearly visible from so high above; women wearing white grass skirts made from wild hibiscus, spinning and twirling – a sea of swirling white grass. It's a huge drawcard for tourists, and has (controversially) transformed from an event that happened each weekend for a month, to one that occurs almost daily for three months from April to June.

Pentecost

your next meal will be, but it will be fresh and tasty.

Noda Guesthouse BUNGALOWS $
(☎5473071, 7727394; www.pentecostisland.net/noda; Waterfall Village; s incl meals 3200VT) A great place to stay while you play in the cascades. This well-kept house has six bedrooms (12 beds), friendly folk running it and electricity in the evenings. A bunch of tours (1000VT) run from here.

Mari Bungalows BUNGALOWS $
(☎773462; Wali; s/d incl breakfast 3000/4000VT) These new bungalows are set into the hills beside a land-dive site and opposite the friendly Londot beachfront restaurant. It's self-catering or 600VT per meal.

Bebe Bungalow BUNGALOWS $
(☎7106845, 5929397; Pangi; s incl meals 2500VT) Right in front of the Pangi land-dive site (you can hear the screams!) are these two simple bungalows with single beds. There's electricity, too.

Vanambil Guesthouse BUNGALOWS $
(☎5348846, 7723374; Baravet; d incl breakfast 3000VT) A short drive north of the airstrip, this guesthouse has four rooms. Jonas arranges land-diving, snorkelling, waterfall and cave tours.

ⓘ Getting There & Away

TO/FROM THE AIRPORT Transport from Lonorore airfield to Pangi by truck or boat is 4000VT. For transport around the south, ring **Jonas** (☎7723374).

AIR Lonorore airfield is the main point of entry for Pentecost. **Air Vanuatu** (☎23748) flies here from Port Vila and Santo five times a week.

BOAT Pentecost has good protection from the southeastern trade winds along the west coast, with many anchorages and landing places. Panas and Loltong are popular.

Cargo ships including *Tina 1* and *Brisk* make stops at Pangi and Baravet.

UNDERSTAND VANUATU

Vanuatu Today

Since independence in 1980, the ni-Vanuatu government's desire has been for development that benefits everyone equally, while preserving customs and traditions. There were years with many political parties, much infighting and some high-profile scandals. Kalkot Matas Kelekele had five years of presidency before, after three rounds of voting in 2009, Iolu Johnson Abil defeated six other candidates to become president. Vanuatu's prime minister is Sato Kilman of the People's Progress Party. His election came after the previous prime minister was ousted in a vote of no confidence. Sato Kilman himself was ousted in 2011, though it was later reversed, and he was elected by parliament as the prime minister a month later.

In 2005 Vanuatu qualified for the **US Millennium Challenge** (www.mcc.gov), a grant available to countries that show they will use it for sustainable economic growth. It was the only South Pacific country to be selected. The US$65 million was used to seal the Efate Ring Rd and the East Coast Rd on Santo.

Recent economic growth has been attributed to the services sector (including tourism) and the growth of aid programs. Other encouraging economic trends are the 2 billion vatu earned by 3000 ni-Van workers under New Zealand's Registered Seasonal Employer (RSE) scheme annually; the rising interest in copra (coconut fibre); the demand for Vanuatu beef, which consistently outstrips supply; and the increased variety of Vanuatu crops now allowed into New Zealand. Vanuatu joined the World Trade Organisation in October 2011.

History

In 2004 an archaeological dig at Teouma, near Port Vila, unearthed evidence of a Lapita culture dating back 3000 years. The site provided archaeologists with insights into the beliefs and rituals of these first people to settle, establish crops and have domestic animals in Vanuatu. Lapita people are the ancestors of all Polynesian people, from Tahiti to Hawai'i to New Zealand. They had crossed the sea from the Solomon Islands.

Between the 11th and 15th centuries AD, many Polynesians arrived from the central Pacific in sailing canoes holding up to 50 people, live animals, and gardens growing in the boats. Vanuatu's traditions tell of cultural heroes arriving around this time from islands to the east, bringing with them new skills and customs.

Ancient Vanuatu

The people traditionally lived in clan-based villages, each with its own language because villages were separated by impassable mountains and rocky coastlines. Everyone lived in the shadow of their ancestors' spirits. Some spirits were benevolent, but others were hostile: famines, cyclones, enemy attack and other misfortunes could result if they became displeased. Magic was the main defence against angry spirits.

Interisland trade networks were established using large sailing canoes. Otherwise, villagers regarded their neighbours with deep suspicion. Skirmishes between villages were frequent, and usually the victor captured one or more male prisoners. It gave a chief great status to present a victim, ready for the pot, to chiefs of other villages. The victims' relatives would mount reprisals, so hostilities continued indefinitely.

Alongside this, the culture was steeped in agriculture. Yam cultivation decided the cycle of the year, and months were named after yams.

European Explorers

The first Europeans to visit Vanuatu, in May 1606, were on a Spanish expedition led by Pedro Fernández de Quirós, who was convinced that Santo was the fabled *terra australis incognita*. It was not until May 1768 that Louis-Antoine de Bougainville sailed between Malekula and Santo, proving that Vanuatu's largest island was not *terra australis*.

James Cook arrived on 16 July 1774, on his second Pacific expedition. He drew the first charts of the region and named places he visited, including Tanna, Erromango, Ambrym and the Shepherd Islands.

In 1789, shortly after the famous mutiny on the *Bounty,* William Bligh sailed through the northern Banks group in his longboat.

He sighted several previously unrecorded islands, and returned three years later to confirm his discoveries.

Missionaries & Traders

The first Christian missionary on the scene was the Reverend John Williams from the London Missionary Society (LMS). In 1839 he stepped ashore on Erromango, and was promptly eaten. After this inauspicious beginning, the church sent Polynesian teachers from Samoa, hoping they would be more acceptable. However, a number of them were also killed or died of malaria.

In 1848 the Reverend John Geddie arrived on Aneityum and made it the headquarters for the Presbyterian mission in Vanuatu, the major Christian denomination on the southern islands. The Anglican Diocese of Melanesia followed in 1860 and became influential in the northern islands. Catholicism arrived in 1887.

Meanwhile, traders heard about the sandalwood trees on Erromango. There was great demand for the wood in China, where it was used for incense. Islanders traded tree trunks for guns, tobacco or men from enemy villages to be eaten at ceremonies. The best study of the turbulent times of the 19th-century sandalwood trade is Dorothy Shinberg's *They Came for Sandalwood* (1967).

Blackbirding (see p547) developed as cheap labour was needed for the sugar-cane industries, coconut plantations and nickel mines of nearby countries. Blackbirders kidnapped shiploads of ni-Vanuatu (ni-Van; Vanuatu people) but the missionaries stepped in, campaigning relentlessly until the practice was banned.

European Settlement

The first European settler was a cattle rancher who arrived in 1854 and other settlers arrived to set up cotton plantations. Intense rivalry existed between the French and English. Brawls were commonplace, as were clashes between settlers and ni-Vanuatu, who resented the loss of their land.

As elsewhere in the Pacific, the local inhabitants were decimated by European diseases. Some say Vanuatu's population was about one million in the early 19th century, but in 1935 only 41,000 ni-Vanuatu remained.

Condominium

With the Germans becoming influential in the region, the British and French governments established the Anglo–French Condominium of the New Hebrides, in an awkward moment of togetherness in 1906. Vanuatu would be ruled equally by the two colonial powers.

Cynics called the Condominium 'the Pandemonium', as the dual administration produced a bizarre duplication of authorities. Road rules were an issue, as the English drove on the left, the French on the right. Anglo–French rivalry reached new extremes of farce, as the height of each flag up each ministerial flagpole was measured every morning. At least the food was edible in the French jail.

To Kill a Bird with Two Stones (1981) by Jeremy MacClancy is available at the Vanuatu Cultural Centre (p476) in Port Vila. It's an excellent history from Vanuatu's earliest beginnings through the Condominium period (the 'two stones' of the title).

WWII

US forces arrived in Vanuatu in early 1942 and constructed bases, first at Havannah Harbour and Port Vila on Efate, then in southeastern Santo. With Japan's defeat in 1945, the US forces withdrew, leaving behind huge quantities of equipment. Some was sold, the remainder dumped into the sea near Luganville on Santo, at Million Dollar Point.

Cargo cults appeared on several islands as ni-Van sought to secure the kind of wealth they'd seen in the camps – they believed that if they acted like Europeans, then 'cargo' would come their way.

Independence

Land ownership had become Vanuatu's major political issue by the mid-1960s. It was the spark that spurred the country to seek independence.

At this time European settlers 'owned' about 30% of the country's land area. A movement based on *kastom* (custom; rules relating to traditional beliefs) called the Nagriamel sprang up under the leadership of the charismatic Jimmy Stevens. Operating from Santo, its aims were to protect ni-Vanuatu claims to their traditional land. By the late 1960s, Nagriamel had expanded to other islands in northern Vanuatu.

Another great leader, Father Walter Lini, formed the New Hebrides National Party in 1971. It was later called the Vanua'aku Party. His book *Beyond Pandemonium: From*

New Hebrides to Vanuatu (1980) tells of the lead-up to his country's independence.

The Condominium authorities agreed to hold the country's first general election in November 1979. The Vanua'aku Party were clear winners. Independence was fixed for mid-1980.

Serious threats of secession were being made by the ni-Van on Santo and Tanna in early 1980; late in May matters came to a head. An insurrection on Tanna split that island between government supporters and rebels. On Santo, secessionists seized Luganville and hoisted the flag of the Independent Republic of Vemarana. Several other northern islands proclaimed their own secessions during June. They merged and announced the Provisional Government of the Northern Islands, under Jimmy Stevens.

Order was not restored until the new government brought in soldiers from Papua New Guinea following independence on 30 July, after which the secessionist ringleaders were arrested and the rebellion collapsed.

The Culture

Vanuatu's culture and customs vary widely. Dances, funerals, weddings, initiations, systems of authority, artistic styles, and animal and crop husbandry all differ from island to island. Yet there are common themes, particularly the obligation to pay for all services rendered and the finality of any area labelled *tabu*, which means 'sacred' as well as 'forbidden'. If a part of a traditional ceremony, a section of beach, a cave, anywhere at all, is *tabu*, it must be respected.

The lavishly illustrated *Arts of Vanuatu* (1996), edited by Joel Bonnemaison et al, is a fabulous introduction to the diversity of Vanuatu's culture, connecting historic and contemporary influences.

The National Psyche

Ownership of ancestral land, sea and reefs, and everything that comes from them, is fundamental to ni-Vanuatu life. It is held by ni-Van for the future, and the rhythm of the seasons dictates how those resources are used. They viewed with horror the European way of using the land; disputes over use and ownership are still serious issues. Always carry at least 1000VT with you as you never know when you'll have to pay a fee for swimming, fishing, or looking at or walking on a property. This is despite the fact that ni-Van

are very hospitable and generous. It is a matter of respect for the value of the resource.

Everyone has a role to play in society. Each village is run by a chief who acts as a justice of the peace and village delegate. His word is law. Even politicians must do what the chief says when visiting his home villages.

In a place where Mother Nature provides for all needs, society has developed new challenges. In many areas, chiefs achieve their rank through *nimangki* (grade-taking) ceremonies, which include a lavish feast. Villagers who eat at the feast are then indebted to the chief, becoming a party of supporters who look to him for leadership and guidance. Each step up the village social ladder is accompanied by the ritual killing of pigs, so only men who have acquired enough pigs can hope to reach society's highest levels.

A young man needs a wife to care for his pigs, but he cannot look for a wife until he has built himself a house.

Lifestyle

The centre of village life is the *nakamal*, a men's clubhouse and clan museum, where men meet to discuss village and national issues. A traditional *nakamal* is always strictly *tabu* to women, and tourists may still be barred from entering in *kastom*-oriented areas. Women, too, have a meeting house, where they produce goods for sale, such as woven sections of roof.

Women spend many hours in the family garden and watching over the husband's pigs, while men tend their cash crops, fish, hunt, build boats, carve artefacts and discuss village matters. While the women prepare the evening meal, the men talk in the *nakamal* and drink kava.

There are strict rules in every village regarding dress. Islanders do not wear scant or revealing clothing, and women's thighs are always covered.

BON ANNÉE

All through January, to welcome the new year, villagers prepare flower-embedded posts and set out together to walk as far as they can, dancing along, stopping at each village they pass to sing songs and chant, 'Happy, Happy, Bon Année'. Then they dust their listeners with talcum powder and set off to the next village.

VANUATU THE CULTURE

Overall, the most pressing problem for ni-Van families is finding the money to pay their children's school fees each quarter.

Population

Vanuatu's population is almost entirely ni-Vanuatu (Melanesian, although some islands have a strong Polynesian heritage). There are a few Europeans, Asians and other Pacific islanders.

Most people live in rural areas, in villages of fewer than 50 people, along narrow coastal strips or on tiny offshore islets. There is a drift into towns, particularly Port Vila, by ni-Vanuatu in search of work.

Language

See the Language chapter on p591 for Bislama basics.

Arts

The population is spread over 83 islands, and Vanuatu's art and traditions vary from island to island; this diversity contributes to the country's unique cultural identity.

The most common subject matters in ni-Vanuatu arts are the human form and traditional interpretations of what ancestral figures looked like. The most important artefacts are made for *nimangki* (grade-taking ceremonies). The Vanuatu Cultural Centre in Port Vila (p476) is an excellent place to learn more about art and culture in Vanuatu.

Carvings

While wood is the main carved material, objects are also made from tree fern, stone and coral. Serious carving is almost entirely created for ceremonies, while items for sale to tourists are usually small copies of the real thing.

Cinema

Vanuatu has a small but lively cinema scene, led by Port Vila's **Wan Smol Bag Theatre** (www.wansmolbag.org).

Dances & Ceremonies

Traditional dances in Vanuatu require constant rehearsals. The timing is exquisite and the movements regimented; everyone turns, leaps and stomps together. Thus harmony and cooperation develop between people and villages. There are two major styles of dance: impersonation and participation. Impersonation dances require more rehearsal, as each dancer pretends to be an ancestor or legendary figure and wears an elaborate mask or headdress, such as in the Rom dances of Ambrym (see p503). In participatory dances, several people – or even several villages – take part to enact traditional themes such as hunting, war and death, as in the Toka dances of Tanna.

Music

String bands developed during WWII, when ni-Van heard the US soldiers playing bluegrass. The singing is done with a pinched throat, forming a high-pitched lyrical note. Musicians are getting recognition, and sound studios and training rooms are being established on many islands. Most local music tends to be a blend of reggae, country and rock, with an off beat that is a typical Toka dance rhythm. Check the Fest' Napaun website (www.festnapaun.org) to see who's striking the right chords in Vanuatu's con-

---

CHOOSE YOUR CARVING

The best carvings come from northern Ambrym. Malekula also has amazing carvings, and some can be bought at Malekula's Cultural Centre (p499). Items to look out for:

» Carved bows and arrows, and traditional ceremonial spears.

» War clubs made to designs attributed to ancestral cultural heroes.

» Pig-killing clubs shaped like mattocks, with two stylised faces carved on either side.

» Large platters and bowls in which yams and kava are pounded, or in which *laplap* (Vanuatu's national dish) is also served.

» Model canoes, some with figureheads, others with sails made from dried pandanus leaves.

» Statues made from tree ferns, representing ancestral figures.

» *Tamtam* (the slit-gong drums with faces carved above the slit).

temporary music world. If you're in town in November, don't miss the festival itself.

Vanuatu's *tamtam* (slit drums) are logs with hollowed-out slits and carved human faces (up to five, one above the other) set above the drum part. *Tamtam* are the largest free-standing musical instruments in the world.

Painting & Sand Drawing

Petroglyphs and rock paintings are the country's most ancient forms of pictorial art. The former are common and widespread, although their meanings have been lost and their main significance these days is to archaeologists. Several islands have caves where the walls are decorated with hand stencils and simple paintings of animals.

Styles of painting include bark art and body painting, a part of traditional ceremonies.

Ni-Van create beautiful sand drawings on beaches and sandy spots, making many delicate loops and circles without raising their fingers, to leave messages or illustrate local legends, songs or ceremonies. The most elaborate and picturesque versions are made in Ambrym. Drawings may be public or sacred, and they have World Heritage status.

Traditional Dress

It's less common now, but in *kastom*-oriented parts of Tanna and Pentecost, men wore *namba* (penis sheaths) every day, while women dressed in grass skirts. On Santo, the men wore *mal mal* (loincloths), while some women wore an apron of leaves. In southern Malekula, women of the Small Nambas people traditionally wore raffia skirts, woven from banana-tree fibres.

In other parts of Vanuatu, grass skirts are fashioned from the bark of the *burao* (wild hibiscus). Once it's stripped, the bark is placed in sea water, dried, measured into lengths and, if necessary, dyed.

Most ni-Van wear traditional dress only to attend ceremonies, when elaborate headgear is also worn. Masks are usually made from tree-fern material and represent the faces of demons and ancestral spirits. Others are constructed out of clay reinforced with coconut fibres and layered onto a wickerwork frame.

Painted tree-fern face masks in southern Malekula are decorated with feathers and carved pigs' tusks.

Weaving

Baskets and mats are made throughout the country, as are traps for fish, shellfish and birds. Weaving is done mostly by women, using pandanus leaves and *burao* stalks. Wicker, coconut leaves and rattan are used when a more robust item is required.

Environment

Vanuatu lies squarely on the Pacific Ring of Fire, so it gets frequent earth tremors, and rises or subsides by up to 2cm per year in some areas. There are nine active volcanoes (seven on land), and fumaroles (volcanic steam vent) and thermal springs are found throughout the archipelago.

Animals

Cats, dogs, cattle, horses, pigs and goats were all introduced to Vanuatu and have since run wild. Rats are the bane of village life and do much damage to the copra industry.

Native land mammals are restricted to four flying-fox species and eight other bat species. Marine life includes more than 300 species of coral and 450 species of reef fish. The country's largest mammal is the dugong, the world's only herbivorous marine mammal.

Of Vanuatu's 121 bird species, 55 can be found on Santo, including all seven of the country's endemic species (those found nowhere else). One interesting species is the mound-building, fowl-like megapode (*namalao* in Bislama) that uses the warm volcanic soils to incubate its eggs.

There are 19 native lizards, all small skinks and geckos, and one land snake, the harmless Pacific boa, which grows to 2.5m. While the yellow-bellied and banded sea snakes are extremely venomous, their small mouths and teeth aren't suitable for savaging humans.

The saltwater (or estuarine) crocodiles that live in Vanua Lava have probably swum down from the Solomon Islands after losing their bearings during cyclones.

Plants

About 75% of Vanuatu is natural vegetation, including rainforest and rain-shadow grasslands. Cyclones tear at the jungle regularly, renewing it. Logging and subsistence farming hacks into a bit, but much of the country is a botanical wonderland.

The lord of most forests is the banyan tree, whose crown can be 70m or more across. Forests of mighty kauri trees are found on Erromango, while cloud forests dripping with moss and moisture are a magnificent feature of highland areas.

Vanuatu has around 20 species of palm, of which 14 are endemic. Orchids festoon the trees in many areas; there are 158 orchid species. Less enchanting are the introduced weeds, such as lantana and the widespread 'mile-a-minute' vine.

Conservation Areas

There are four official conservation areas in Vanuatu: Vatthe (p512) and Loru (p512) on Santo, the kauri reserve (p496) on Erromango, and the cloudforest area around Lake Manaro on Ambae (p513).

Chiefs and *kastom* landholders often proclaim conservation areas as a means of protecting a valuable resource, such as turtles or coconut crabs, from over exploitation.

SURVIVAL GUIDE

Directory A–Z
Accommodation

Budget accommodation is plentiful in Vanuatu, but you may find communication difficult (the owner may have dropped their mobile phone in the ocean); bungalows deserted (the owner's headed off to New Zealand for seasonal grape picking); or simply not there (it takes time to reroof a bungalow after a cyclone). 'Just go' is the best motto in Vanuatu; you'll find somewhere to stay. Many places will let you camp (for a fee). Ask the local chief for permission if you want to pitch your tent somewhere other than at a bungalow.

A guesthouse is often a concrete building with a very basic kitchen. Bungalows are usually thatched rooms with pandanus-leaf walls. Budget for a minimum of 2500VT per night, which may include meals. Showers and toilets are usually separate from the bungalows and vary in cleanliness and usefulness. Remember that the humid jungle environment takes its toll on buildings and infrastructure. Travel with some food supplies, toilet paper and a torch. Impressive resorts and hotels abound on Efate and Santo and there's a handful on Tanna. Many lovely hotel rooms cost under 8000VT, while luxury resorts start at around 18,000VT per double.

The following price ranges refer to a double room.

$ less than 10,000VT

$$ 10,000–20,000VT

$$$ more than 20,000VT

Activities

It's easy to be lazy here, but it's also difficult to ignore the excellent diving, snorkelling, hiking, horse riding, fishing, sailing and extreme sports on offer. You'll find you're easily immersed in the culture and natural environment.

DIVING

Vanuatu has several world-class dive sites (see p36). Vila has a great range of underwater topography and a Corsair WWII fighter plane wreck near Pele, amid fan corals and healthy reefs, while Santo has USS *President Coolidge* among others. *The Lady and the President* (1997), by Peter Stone, covers the tragedy of war and delights of scuba diving.

For details of dive operators, see the text in the Efate (p478) and Santo (p507) sections.

FISHING

World-standard game fishing, river fishing and spear fishing are on offer in Vanuatu – if it lives in water you can enjoy chasing it, with string and a bent pin or the latest hi-tech gear. Always check who owns the water, though, and pay them first. See p479 for operators.

HIKING

The country has many fine walks, including strenuous two- to five-day hikes on Ambrym, Santo, Pentecost, Vanua Lava, Gaua and Malekula. Organise a guide yourself (around 1000VT to 3000VT a day) or through your host or a tour operator. Don't set out alone with a map – sorry, all roads change dramatically during cyclones and mudslides, or can disappear under a metre-high layer of vine. Without a guide, you'll quickly be up you know where.

Always wear long pants in the jungle to protect yourself from stinging plants. Sandals and runners are not suitable for jungle treks or volcano climbs.

SWIMMING

Port Vila isn't brilliant for swimming, but further afield there are glorious beaches: white or black sand, volcanic rock or coral. Sharks, stonefish and strong currents are a danger in some areas. Seek advice before plunging in.

YACHTING

Vanuatu is a popular yachting destination, especially around Maewo, Tanna and Epi. It's possible to charter a cruising trimaran with skipper and crew from Port Vila (see p480).

Business Hours

Reviews in this chapter don't list business hours unless they differ from these standards.

Government offices 7.30am to 11.30am and 1.30pm to 4.30pm Monday to Friday, and sometimes on Saturday morning.

Shops 7.30am to 6pm Monday to Friday; some close for lunch; to 11.30am Saturday. Chinese stores open all weekend.

Children

Children will enjoy the freedom of being in this laid-back environment. There's plenty to do, from hermit-crab hunting to mango dislodging, and the ni-Van kids make wonderful companions.

Embassies & Consulates

Australia (Map p478; ☎22777; www.vanuatu. embassy.gov.au; Winston Churchill Ave, Port Vila)

France (Map p484; ☎22353; fax 22695; ambafra@vanuatu.com.vu; Lini Hwy, Port Vila)

New Zealand (Map p478; ☎22933; kiwi@ vanuatu.vu; Lini Hwy, Port Vila)

Food

The following price ranges refer to a standard main course.

$ less than 2000VT

$$ 2000–3000VT

$$$ more than 3000VT

Health

Malaria is prevalent on most islands so take precautions. Stick to bottled water, which is available in most places.

Internet Access

There are internet cafes in Port Vila, Luganville, Lenakel and Lakatoro, and free wi-fi at most hotels.

Internet Resources

Lonely Planet (www.lonelyplanet.com/vanuatu)

Vanuatu Geohazards Observatory (www.geohazards.gov.vu)

Vanuatu Government (www.government ofvanuatu.gov.vu)

Vanuatu Hotels (www.vanuatu-hotels.vu)

Vanuatu Tourism Office (www.vanuatu.travel)

Wantok Environment Centre (www.positiveearth.org)

Money

You'll find ANZ and Westpac ATMs dotted around Port Vila (including one at the international airport to help those in transit), and one of each in Luganville.

Take plenty of vatu everywhere outside Port Vila and Luganville as you won't be able to change foreign currencies or access any accounts, not even over the counter at a bank. Resorts/hotels often charge a 3 to 5% surcharge on credit cards.

Public Holidays

New Year's Day 1 January

Lini Day 21 February

Custom Chiefs' Day 5 March

Good Friday, Easter Monday March/April

Labour Day 1 May

Ascension Day 17 May

Children's Day 24 July

Independence Day 30 July

Assumption Day 15 August

Constitution Day 5 October

Unity Day 29 November

Christmas Day 25 December

Family Day 26 December

Telephone

Almost the entire country is now covered. Buy a local SIM card from TVL (p478) or Digicel. A Smile SIM card package is 3000VT including 2500VT of calls, or you can get a Digicel phone with card for 2000VT. You can buy top-up cards everywhere.

Time

Vanuatu time is GMT/UMT plus 11 hours. Noon in Port Vila is 1am in London, 6pm in Los Angeles and 1pm in Auckland.

Tourist Information

The **VTO** (Vanuatu Tourism Office; Map p478; ☎22813; www.vanuatu.travel; Lini Hwy;

⊙7.30am-4.30pm Mon-Fri, 8am-noon Sun) has a very informative website.

Visas

Visitors must have a passport valid for a further six months. Entry visas are not required for nationals of the British Commonwealth and EEC; see www.governmentofvanuatu. gov.vu. You're allowed an initial stay of up to 30 days, extended for up to four months (6000VT) at the Department of Immigration.

Nonexempt visitors should contact the **Principal Immigration Officer** (☑22354; earukelana@vanuatu.gov.vu; PMB 092, Port Vila) to organise their visa application (3600VT fee). This must be finalised *before* you arrive.

Getting There & Away
Air

South Pacific Travel (Map p484; ☑22836; spts@vanuatu.com.vu; Lini Hwy, Port Vila; ⊙8am-5pm Mon-Fri, 8-11am Sat) in Vila is an agent for Virgin Australia, Fiji Airways and Air Vanuatu.

The following airlines have regular scheduled flights to Vanuatu.

Air New Zealand (☑22666; www.airnew zealand.co.nz) Direct flights from Auckland (from NZ$200) to Port Vila.

Air Vanuatu (Map p484; ☑23848; www.air vanuatu.com; Rue de Paris, Port Vila) Air Vanuatu/Qantas (code-share) operates direct flights from Brisbane and Sydney to Port Vila, and flies from Melbourne to Port Vila most Thursdays. Return fares start from A$650. There are also direct flights to Espiritu Santo from Brisbane. From New Zealand, Air Vanuatu/Qantas flies direct from Auckland (from NZ$200) to Port Vila; and has flights from Auckland via Nadi and Suva (Fiji), Honiara (Solomon Islands) and Noumea (New Caledonia).

Aircalin (Map p484; ☑22739; www.aircalin.com; Lini Hwy, Port Vila) Has flights to Port Vila from Nadi and Noumea.

Fiji Airways (formerly Air Pacific; Map p484; ☑22836; www.airpacific.com; South Pacific Travel, Lini Hwy, Port Vila) Flies to Port Vila from Nadi and Noumea.

Virgin Australia (Map p484; ☑22836; www. virginaustralia.com; South Pacific Travel, Lini Hwy, Port Vila) Direct flights from Brisbane and Sydney to Port Vila. Return fares start from A$650.

AIRPORTS

Port Vila's Bauerfield International Airport has an ANZ ATM, an NBV branch for currency exchange, a cafe and duty-free shopping. Santo's Pekoa International Airport has an ANZ ATM, cafe and duty-free shop.

Sea

The passenger and cargo boat **MV Havannah** (☑25225; carvanuatu@vanuatu. com.vu) sails out of Noumea for Port Vila, Malekula and Santo once a month (adult/child 13,000/9500VT). You'll need to ask as there's no regular departure date. It departs Noumea on the Monday at 8pm and arrives in Port Vila on Wednesday noon, stopping at Lakatoro, Malekula on Thursday morning and Santo in the afternoon. It heads back to Noumea from Port Vila on Friday, arriving Saturday afternoon. If you can't get through to the Vanuatu office try **New Caledonia's MV Havannah office** (☑687 27 04 05; cmis@lagoon.nc).

The best source of general information on yachting matters is **Yachting World Vanuatu** (Map p478; ☑/fax 23273, VHF16; www. yachtingworld-vanuatu.com; Lini Hwy). It has a sea-wall tie up and diesel dock; it'll arrange customs and quarantine inspections to your buoy; there are hot showers, wi-fi and the Waterfront Bar & Grill is next door.

The authorised ports of entry for touring yachts are Port Vila (Efate), Luganville (Santo), Lenakel (Tanna) and Sola (Vanua Lava). There are hefty fines if you make landfall in or depart from Vanuatu before customs and immigration have been cleared. The landing fee is 7000VT for the first 30 days and 100VT per day thereafter. Quarantine clearance is 4000VT.

Port Vila Boatyard (Map p476; ☑23417; www.portvilaboatyard.com) has many amenities and facilities in sheltered Pontoon Bay.

Getting Around
Air

Download Air Vanuatu's domestic flight schedule from www.airvanuatu.com. You can book Santo and Tanna flights online. Email requests for flights to other islands then purchase tickets at **Air Vanuatu** Port Vila (Map p478; ☑23848; www.airvanuatu.com; Rue de Paris; ⊙7.30am-5pm Mon-Fri); Luganville (Map p508; ☑36421; Main St). Show your international flight ticket with Air Vanuatu to receive a 20% discount. Children aged under

12 and students receive a 50% and 25% discount respectively (take your student card). It pays to book well in advance.

Unity Airlines (Map p478; ☎24475, 23242; www.unity-airlines.com; Nambawan, Port Vila; ☺7.30am-5pm Mon-Fri, 8am-noon Sat & Sun) flies tour groups to outer islands and is available for charter. **Air Safaris** (☎7745207; www.air safaris.vu) and **Air Taxi** (☎5544206; airtaxivan uatu.com) also run tours and are available for charter.

Boat

CANOE & SPEEDBOAT
When ni-Vanuatu talk of speedboats, they mean outboard-powered dinghies. Canoes are dugout craft with outriggers, paddle-powered. Speedboat prices are high, so it's best to wait for a scheduled service rather than charter.

PASSENGER BOAT
Big Sista (Map p478; ☎23461, 5663851; 9000VT) has a weekly service between Santo and Port Vila, leaving Port Vila on Mondays, returning Wednesdays. It stops at Epi (5500VT) and Malekula (7500VT).

Fresh Cargo (Map p478; ☎7760660, 5553670; freshcargovanuatu@gmail.com) carries 70 people in a substantial catamaran. It heads north from Port Vila on Efate to Epi (4500VT), Malekula (5500VT) and Santo (7500VT) twice a week and is available for charter. Also heads to Tanna (6500VT) and Erromango.

Bus & Taxi

Minibuses with a red 'B' on their number-plates operate in Port Vila, Luganville and northeast Malekula. They don't run fixed routes but zoom to your destination. Flag them down by the roadside (150VT for short trips).

Taxis in Port Vila and Luganville are mostly sedans, but elsewhere they're 4WD trucks. Charges depend on distance, but also on the state of the road. Ask your driver for a price. It will usually be honest and reasonable. A short trip in Port Vila might cost 400VT, but a day charter will cost between 8000VT and 12,000VT. Local taxis (usually 4WD truck) meet flights at island airstrips, but may not be around on Sunday, public holidays or when there's no fuel on the island.

Car & Motorcycle

You can hire cars, 4WDs and scooters in Port Vila (p488) and in Luganville (p505). The minimum age for renting a car is 23; for a scooter it's 17, provided you've held a valid driving licence for over a year. You don't need an International Driving Licence.

There's a speed limit of 50km/h in Port Vila and Luganville. Vehicles drive on the right.

Other Pacific Islands

Far-Flung Gems

The South Pacific islands listed here are as remote as they are distinct. In some cases, long boat trips are the only means of access – there are no flights. And where flight options do exist, they're infrequent and usually involve getting to another South Pacific access point first. However, the dedicated traveller who does make the journey will be rewarded with places of great natural beauty: the coral atolls of Tokelau, palmed-topped outer islets of Tuvalu or the rugged, scenic coast of Niue. Even more rewarding for the traveller, the islands' very isolation has preserved cultures that are unique in the South Pacific. We were unable to visit these islands this edition. This information is based on our previous research trips to the islands, and has been verified and updated using local contacts and other sources.

Niue

Niue (*new*-ay) may be the world's smallest independent nation, but the Pacific island known as the 'Rock of Polynesia' packs in plenty of surprises for the intrepid traveller. Don't expect palm-fringed beaches or languid lagoons, but look forward to a rugged landscape of limestone caverns, hidden sea caves and a rocky, untamed coast. Ditch the deck chair and pack your walking shoes and sense of adventure instead.

From June to September get face to face with humpback whales nursing their calves in the safe haven of Niue's warm waters. Descend further to the indigo depths for some of the best diving in the Pacific.

🏃 Activities

Niue's capital Alofi stretches for several kilometres along the west coast. Alofi's southern area was badly damaged during Cyclone Heta in 2004 and abandoned structures punctuate the cliff top.

You will need to walk, climb and sometimes swim to see the attractions hugging Niue's outrageously scenic perime-

ter. Rent a car or motorcycle and get exploring the numerous caves, snorkelling spots and cliff-encircled chasm pools.

Niue Dive DIVING
(☑4311; www.dive.nu) Runs dive trips (two dives from NZ$160) and snorkelling trips (adult/child NZ$40/25) to sites around the island, including Snake Gully. You can also swim and snorkel with spinner dolphins (April to December) and humpback whales (June to October).

Kayak Niue KAYAKING
(☑4224, after hrs 4097; www.kayakniue.nu) Explore beyond Niue's reef. Half-day tours NZ$75.

Misa Kulatea NATURE TOURS
(☑4381) Conducts nature walks in the forest, explaining traditional Niuean customs. Misa's tours can be booked through the visitor information centre.

🛏 Sleeping & Eating

Budget and midrange guesthouses cluster in Alofi. Apart from Matavai Resort, accommodation includes kitchen facilities, often on a shared basis in cheaper places.

Namukulu Cottages & Spa BUNGALOWS $$
(☑3001; www.namukulu-motel.nu; bungalows from NZ$175; ☒) Four spacious bungalows, each with a double bed, two single beds and fully equipped kitchen, cluster near a swimming pool with picnic tables and a barbecue. The newest bungalow has two bedrooms. Look for humpback whales cruising by.

Matavai Resort RESORT $$$
(☑4360; www.matavairesort.com; r with ceiling fan/air-con NZ$200/255; ☺☒@☒) Niue's premier resort has a restaurant, two bars and two swimming pools cascading to a reef with turtles and dolphins. All rooms have a verandah and include a fridge and ISD phone.

TOP CHOICE **Washaway Café** BAR, RESTAURANT $$
(☑4822; meals NZ$14; ☺from 11am Sun) This is the self-proclaimed 'only self-service bar in the Pacific', so help yourself to drinks and settle the bill with Willy at the end of the night.

❶ Information

Currency NZ dollar (NZ$)
Languages English and Niuean
International telephone code ☑683
Internet Free wi-fi patchy but island-wide
Website www.niueisland.com

DON'T MISS

NIUE HIGHLIGHTS

❶ Diving with tangles of sea snakes at **Snake Gully** or negotiating twin underwater chimneys at **Ana Mahaga**

❷ Floating calmly as a **humpback whale** and her calf swim beneath you

❸ Experiencing the Pacific Ocean's power at **Togo Chasm** and **Talava Arches**

❹ Exploring the fish-laden **reef pools** near Matapa Chasm

❶ Getting There & Away

AIR Air New Zealand (www.airnewzealand.com) has a once-weekly service to/from Auckland.
YACHT The **Niue Yacht Club** (☑4017; www.nyc.nu) has 20 well-maintained moorings available. Harbour fees are NZ$10 per day per yacht.

Pitcairn Island
POP 50 / 4.5 SQ KM

What's rarely mentioned about Pitcairn Island, between the infamous *Bounty* story and the 2004 sex trials gossip, is that it's a place of incredible natural beauty. The island's 4.5 sq km surface is almost entirely sloped and has a varied landscape – from desolate rock cliffs that look over an infinite expanse of sea to lush hillsides bursting in tropical plenty.

The nearest inhabited island to Pitcairn is Mangareva in French Polynesia, 480km or a 36-hour boat ride away. Besides a few hundred cruise ship passengers per year (who often only spend an hour or two on Pitcairn when the ship passes), the only visitors are a few yachts, occasional groups of boat-chartering birders and a handful of ham radio enthusiasts.

In January 1790 the *Bounty* mutineers arrived on Pitcairn after a long search for a remote hideaway, far from the long arm of British naval justice. Led by Fletcher Christian, the party was made up of eight other mutineers, six Tahitian men, 12 Tahitian women and a child. Once they were settled on the island, the *Bounty* was burnt both to prevent escape and to avoid detection. Chaos and bloodshed ruled the first years, largely due to the English mutineers' slave-like treatment of the Polynesian men. By 1800, Adams (who had recently discovered

religion), was the sole surviving man along with 10 women and 23 children.

Adamstown was a neat little settlement of God-fearing Christians when American Captain Mayhew Folger rediscovered Pitcairn Island in 1809, solving the 19-year mystery of what had happened to Christian and the *Bounty* after the mutiny. By this time British attention was focused on Napoleon and there was no interest in the surviving mutineer who was guilty of a decades-old crime.

Pitcairn didn't hit world headlines again till 2004 when six men, including most heads of the community, were found guilty of a string of sex offences, including rape and indecent assault, on young girls. Life on Pitcairn changed irrevocably. Deep within the closest knit society imaginable, sisters, daughters and wives were pitted against uncles, fathers and brothers and, just as often, each other. In response, Britain has paid more attention to this speck of a colony than it has since the days of Bligh. From a new jetty on the opposite side of the island to Bounty Bay, to a state-of-the-art telephone system, the island has gotten back on its feet and everyone hopes the years of sex abuse have ended.

Although Pitcairn's population grew to 223 before WWII, depopulation rather than overpopulation has become the major concern. With British funds being poured into the island for development since 2004, a few ex-islanders are being lured home. The presence of British officials and government workers has raised the population to around 60.

Sights & Activities

There's a **museum** with some *Bounty* artefacts as well as several historical sights around the island. **Down Rope** is the is-

---

DON'T MISS

PITCAIRN HIGHLIGHTS

1 Taking a cool dip in the electric blue, glass-clear waters of **St Paul's Pool**

2 Climbing the precipice to **Christian's Cave** and imagining what must have gone through the mutineer's head as he sat there hundreds of years ago

3 Mingling with locals on Friday nights at **Christian's Café**

4 Watching a flightless Henderson rail trundle by as you relax on the mosquito-free shores of **Henderson Island**

---

land's only beach. **St Paul's Pool** is a stunning, cathedral-like rock formation encircling a sea-fed pool and an ecotrail leads up to **Christian's Cave**, which overlooks Adamstown. The only **mutineer's grave** is that of John Adams, in Adamstown.

HENDERSON ISLAND

Uninhabited Henderson Island is 168km northeast of Pitcairn and is the largest island of the Pitcairn group. The usual landing spot is long North Beach and, during certain tides, there is sometimes a freshwater spring in a cave at the north of the island.

Henderson Island is populated by four species of endemic land birds – the flightless Henderson rail, the colourful Stephen's lorikeet, the territorial Henderson fruit dove and the Henderson warbler. Because of its pristine condition and rare birdlife, Henderson Island was declared a Unesco World Heritage site in 1988. Visitors require a licence to visit, which is dependent on approval by the Pitcairn Island Council.

The wrecking of the whaling ship *Essex* on the island in 1820, after a charge by a sperm whale near the Marquesas, is believed to have provided the inspiration for Herman Melville's *Moby Dick*.

Shopping

The islanders do a busy trade turning out curios for visiting ships, including the signature woven round pandanus baskets, the famous models of the *Bounty* and a variety of *miro* wood carvings. Honey (NZ$11 for a small pot on the island) and Pitcairn Island stamps are also specialities.

Limited food supplies are available from the **Government Store** in Adamstown, which opens three times a week for a few hours or on request.

Information

Currency NZ dollar (NZ$; official); US dollar (US$; for tourist goods and services)
Languages English and Pitkern
International telephone code ☑64
Websites www.government.pn and www.visitpitcairn.pn

Getting There & Away

PASSENGER/CARGO VESSEL Pitcairn Island now has an excellent tourism website (www.visitpitcairn.pn) with information about all available passenger/cargo vessel transportation, visas (US$35) and lodging with locals (US$70 per night per person including all meals).

MUTINY ON THE BOUNTY

On 28 April 1789 Captain William Bligh and 18 crewmen of the HMS *Bounty* were involuntarily relieved of their duties and set adrift in an open boat off the island of Tofua in Tonga, with minimal supplies. It became the most famous naval mutiny in history.

The *Bounty*'s mission was to fetch breadfruit from Tahiti to feed England's African slave population in the Caribbean. Under the command of Bligh, an expert navigator who had trained under Captain James Cook, the expedition arrived in Tahiti in September 1788 after a particularly arduous 10-month journey. The breadfruit season was over and they had to wait six months in Tahiti before returning. Three weeks into the return journey, the crew, led by the master's mate Fletcher Christian, mutinied.

Whatever problems Bligh had with people skills, he was a brilliant navigator. Against the odds, he managed to get the longboat and most of his loyal crew 7000km from Tonga to Timor in the Dutch East Indies (modern-day Indonesia).

Under Christian's command the mutineers returned to Tahiti, then eventually split into two groups: Fletcher took a group of sailors and Tahitians off in search of Pitcairn Island, while a second group of 16 sailors stayed behind on Tahiti.

After Bligh returned to England, Captain Edward Edwards (a tyrant who made Bligh look like a saint) was sent in the *Pandora* to search for the mutineers. Edwards sailed past Ducie Atoll in the Pitcairn group, but he didn't see the larger island 470km to the west. However, Edwards did find and capture 14 of the 16 mutineers who had remained on Tahiti. Unfortunately, Edwards's sailing skills were not up to Bligh's standards and he ended up sinking the *Pandora* on the Great Barrier Reef. Of the surviving prisoners, three were ultimately hanged for the mutiny.

An American duo, Nordhoff and Hall, wrote three books on the *Bounty* mutiny and its aftermath in 1934. Several other books and films have ensued.

CRUISE SHIP About 10 cruise ships call at Pitcairn every year. Like cargo vessels, they anchor well offshore and, seas permitting, passengers are ferried to Bounty Bay.

YACHT Pitcairners are happy to sell fresh fruit and supply fresh water to yachts, but other supplies generally have to be imported from New Zealand and may be in short supply. There is no sheltered anchorage at Pitcairn and boats must be moved when the winds change.

Tokelau

In a world where travel has become easy and accessible to the masses, travelling to Tokelau still requires a dedication that dissuades all but the most committed visitors. It takes upwards of 24 hours to reach Tokelau by boat from its nearest neighbour, Samoa, and you can forget about flying – there's no airstrip. Once you're there, the ship that brought you is your only means of getting between the nation's three atolls; it takes nine hours to travel between the two most distant ones. This ship will be your only ticket home, so you'll have to be prepared to stay for at least five days until it's ready to leave, or wait for the next one in a couple of weeks.

Environment

Consisting only of low-lying coral atolls rising to a maximum of 5m, Tokelau faces great risk from global warming. It is predicted that all three atolls will be uninhabitable by the end of the 21st century, though some estimates give only another 30 years. While some Tokelauans regard these predictions as overly dramatic, others foresee the end to their 1000-year-old history.

On a more positive note, Tokelau has set the goal of being self-sufficient in its energy needs through sustainable sources. A pilot program in solar energy on Fakaofo has been such a success that the people of Tokelau are considering extending it to the other atolls.

Land shortages have long forced emigration from Tokelau, and most of the country's people live overseas, predominantly in Samoa, New Zealand and Australia.

🛏 Sleeping & Eating

Accommodation on Tokelau must be arranged before arrival through the **Tokelau Apia Liaison Office** (TALO; ☑685-20822; www.tokelau.org.nz; PO Box 865, Apia; ☺8am-5pm Mon-Fri) in Samoa. This is also where you'll need to apply for your NZ$20 visitor's permit.

DON'T MISS

TOKELAU HIGHLIGHTS

❶ Descending beneath the clear waters of any of the lagoons for memorable **snorkelling** or **diving**

❷ **Pitching your tent** on an uninhabited speck of an island for a genuine castaway experience

❸ Boogying down with the locals at a community **disco**

❹ Heading out **fishing** with the experts

On Nukunonu try **Te Mahina** (☏4190; zak-p @lesamoa.net; per person NZ$60), which has some en suite rooms (NZ$30 extra), or **Luana Liki Hotel** (☏4140; hei_perez@hotmail.com; per person NZ$60) which can organise lagoon outings and snorkelling expeditions.

Atafu has one small **accommodation house** (☏2146; fax 2108; per person NZ$60), run by master fisherman Feleti Lopa.

❶ Information

International telephone code ☏690
Currency NZ dollar (NZ$)
Languages Tokelauan and English
Website www.tokelau.org.nz

❶ Getting There & Away

BOAT Several ships service Tokelau from Apia in Samoa, with one departure every 12 days or so. You can get the schedule about two months out and book tickets through Yevonna (yevonna@ lesamoa.net) at the TALO office. Cabin fare is NZ$528 return and deck fare is NZ$286.

YACHT There are no harbours and anchoring offshore is not easy, especially in an offshore wind. The sea floor drops off sharply outside the coral reef, and the water is too deep for most anchor chains. There is one anchorage beyond the reefs at each atoll. The channels blasted through the coral are shallow and intended for dinghies only.

Tuvalu

Approaching these islands by plane – after endless miles of dull ocean – a dazzling smear of turquoise and green appears, ringed with coral and studded with tiny, palm-topped islets, bobbing vulnerably in the surrounding waters. The landmass of Fongafale, Tuvalu's main island, is so startlingly narrow that as the plane nears the airstrip it seems as if it's about to tip into the ocean.

Environment

Unfortunately, environmental concerns have focused international attention on Tuvalu. As an atoll nation, the major long-term ecological threat to Tuvalu comes from global warming (see p554) and rising sea levels. As well as shoreline erosion, water bubbles up through the porous coral on which the islands are based, and causes widespread salt contamination of areas used to grow staple crops. Over the past few years, king tides – the biggest swells of the year – have been higher than ever. If sea levels continue to rise as predicted, the islands could be wiped off the face of the earth.

What will happen to the population if Tuvalu does start to go under? The government has been in talks with Australia, which has twice rejected Tuvalu's pleas to open a migration channel. New Zealand currently accepts 75 migrants a year and has said it will absorb Tuvalu's population if it comes to that.

Population pressures and changing lifestyles also present a problem. Tiny 2.8 sq km Fongafale islet, only about a third of which is habitable, is crammed with some 4500 people. Pits end up filled with waste, due to a lack of adequate garbage disposal and the reliance on imported packaged food.

FUNAFUTI ATOLL & FONGAFALE ISLET
POP 4500 / AREA 2.8 SQ KM

Tuvalu's capital and the only place in the country where tourists can change money, make international phone calls or use the internet, Fongafale (also spelt Fogafale or Fagafale) is Tuvalu's answer to a metropolis, the seat of government, and the largest islet in Funafuti Atoll. Funafuti's must-sees include the sublime marine conservation area to the west and Funafala Islet to the south, which is lined with talcum-powder beaches and has basic accommodation right by the water.

◉ Sights & Activities

The best thing about a visit to Fongafale is simply soaking up the slow-paced island way of life. Take a stroll around town or hop on a bike or motorcycle to explore the islet from top to toe. There are also a handful of WWII relics.

Airstrip AREA

People play ball games on the runway in the late afternoons, young men race up and down it on their motorcycles and, on steamy summer nights, whole families may drag their sleeping mats and pillows out to spend the night on the tarmac (in the stifling heat it's the best place to catch breezes).

Funafuti Conservation Area MARINE RESERVE

It would be a shame to visit Tuvalu without experiencing the Funafuti Conservation Area, a half-hour motorboat ride across the lagoon. If you book through the town council, it should cost you around A$160 for a return boat trip (maximum 12 people), including time on one or two of the islets and perhaps some snorkelling.

Sleeping & Eating

There's a small selection of accommodation on Fongafale that includes a hotel, a lodge, a motel and some family-run guesthouses. There's also a basic guesthouse on Funafala Islet.

Most restaurants on Tuvalu sell cheap, filling plates of Chinese-style food. Restaurants sometimes suffer from shortages when shipments don't arrive. Thursday to Saturday is party night on Fongafale, when the old timers go to 'twists' (discos) and the youngsters go 'clubbing'.

Filamona Moonlight Lodge LODGE $

(20 983; s/d incl breakfast A$70/80;) The most conveniently located lodgings in Vaiaku (the main town), right next to the *maneapa* (meeting hall) by the airport. This family-run lodge has a dorm, several doubles and one of the island's most popular restaurants.

TOP CHOICE Vaiaku Lagi Hotel HOTEL $$

(20 500; fax 20 503; s/d A$125/180;) It's not the facilities that make Tuvalu's only hotel the pick of the bunch – it's the location. Sitting on the edge of the lagoon, some 100m northwest of the airport, rooms have small balconies with outstanding views over the water.

OUTER ISLANDS

A trip to be made only if you've plenty of time to spare, Tuvalu's beautiful and remote outer islands have very little infrastructure for visitors. The cargo ships do a round trip lasting several days to each of the three island groups – the northern group comprises Nanumea Atoll, Niutao Atoll, Nanumaga Atoll and Nui Atoll; the central group is Vaitupu, Nukufetau Atoll and Fongafale Islet; and the southern group comprises Nukulaelae Atoll and Niulakita. The ships call in at each island for the best part of a day to unload and load supplies and passengers. So if you're prepared to spend your nights on board ship, you can explore the islands during the daytime. If you choose to get off the boat and plan to stay, be warned; it might be some weeks before the next transport arrives! Give advance warning of your arrival and come prepared to be pretty much self-sufficient.

Information

International telephone code 688
Currency Australian dollar (A$)
Languages Tuvaluan, Gilbertese and English
Website www.timelesstuvalu.com

Getting There & Away

AIR Fiji Airways (20 737; www.airpacific.com) ploughs the Suva–Funafuti route on Tuesdays and Thursdays (from F$1181 return; two hours, 20 minutes).

BOAT Government-owned cargo/passenger ships travel to Suva, Fiji, every three months or so (the trip takes about four days). One-way fares are around A$85/350 for deck/double cabin, with meals. **Pacific Agencies** (679-331 5444; info@pacship.com.fj) is the agent in Suva. The **Marine Department** (20 055; Government Offices) handles schedules and bookings in Funafuti.

The cargo boat *Nei Matagare* makes trips several times a year between Tuvalu and Fiji. **Williams & Goslings** (679-331 2633; www.wgfiji.com.fj) are its Suva agents.

DON'T MISS

TUVALU HIGHLIGHTS

1 Realising the desert-island fantasy of your wildest dreams and exploring the clear waters and palm-covered islets of the stunning **Funafuti Conservation Area**

2 Experiencing traditional life on a remote island with the few remaining families of **Funafala Islet**

3 Joining the locals for a sunset or early morning dip in the luminous waters of the **Funafuti lagoon**

4 Taking in a unique performance of Tuvalu's national dance, **fatele**

TE ANO

While in Tuvalu, try to watch, or better still join in, a game of Tuvalu's unique sport, *te ano*. Almost completely incomprehensible to a first-timer, it's great fun and one of the few games that men and women play together.

To play *te ano* you need two round balls, about 12cm in diameter and woven from dried pandanus leaves. Two opposing teams face each other about 7m apart in five or six parallel rows of about six people, and nominate their *alovaka* (captain) and *tino pukepuke* (catcher), who stand in front of each team.

Team members hit the ball to each other with the aim of eventually reaching the catcher. Only the catcher can throw the ball back to the captain to hit back to the other team. To keep the game lively, two balls are used simultaneously. When either ball falls to the ground the other team scores a point, and the first to 10 points wins the game.

Wallis & Futuna

These two little-known French-funded volcanic specks lie smack in the centre of the Polynesia/Melanesia region. Islanders drive flashy 4WDs to and from their taro fields and enjoy satellite TV at night after a beer or some kava, but the culture and its intricate *coutume* (customs) have remained remarkably intact.

Wallis and Futuna, which lie 230km away from each other, are linked through French colonialism and that's all. Wallis has ancestral connections with Tonga, while Futuna traces its roots to Samoa. This is evident in the languages, which are quite different, although mutually comprehensible, as well as the Samoan-like tapa designs of the Futunans and the Tongan-influenced designs found on Wallis. The two islands remain competitive with each other, but Wallis, being more populous and the centre of government, retains the upper hand.

WALLIS ISLAND
POP 9080 / AREA 77.9 SQ KM

What Wallis lacks in lofty emerald peaks and pearly white beaches it makes up for with its outrageously clear-blue lagoon, weird crater lakes and extensive archaeological sites tucked back in the bush. It's a big, flat jungle of a place where traditional life is played out behind plain, modern cement walls.

Mata'Utu is the country's sprawling administrative and business centre. The 35km island-circuit road is unsealed and at times fairly rough. It never actually runs along the coast, although in a few places there are detours that run along the water's edge. Unmarked side roads lead to impressive archaeological sites and lush crater lakes.

The calm, turquoise waters and impressive variety of islets of Wallis' lagoon are as much a reason to visit this island as the sights of the interior.

🏃 Activities

Evasion Bleue   DIVING
(☎72 13 68; www.evasionbleuewallis.com) A dive centre (including lake and night dives) that also provides taxi-boat service to islets in the lagoon (from 1500 CFP to 3000 CFP) and lagoon excursions.

🛏 Sleeping & Eating

Aside from a few restaurants, simple snack bars dot the island. There's a supermarket in the Fenuarama shopping centre.

Hôtel Lomipeau   HOTEL $$
(☎72 20 21; hotel.lomipeau@wallis.co.nz; s/d incl breakfast 12,500/14,500 CFP; 🕸🖭) Centrally located in Mata'Utu, this standard hotel-style place has great views of the lagoon, but the funny noises coming from the old plumbing pipes might keep you awake. Has friendly staff.

FUTUNA & ALOFI
FUTUNA: POP 4400 / AREA 64 SQ KM
ALOFI: POP 0 / AREA 51 SQ KM

Loaded with flowers, sparkling beaches, traditional houses and vistas over Pacific blue, Futuna is storybook Polynesian pretty. Yet since the islanders here have firmly decided not to develop tourism in order to preserve their lifestyle, it's a particularly difficult place to get around. It's divided into two kingdoms, Alo and Sigave, which today live in peaceful, if quite competitive, harmony with each other.

Uninhabited Alofi, with its tropical forest and beach, is just as gorgeous and more wild. A strait less than 2km wide separates the two islands.

All practicalities are in Leava, Futuna's major centre, on the south coast. There are a couple of supermarkets, the island's administrative headquarters (there's even a library) and a wharf.

It's a 33km circuit around Futuna but, with speed bumps on the good roads and potholes on the bad ones, it'll take at least 1½ hours to go round. Along the route, you'll come across a handful of some of the most beautiful churches in the Pacific, including the towering **Pierre Chanel Church** (called Petelo Sanele in Futunan), painstakingly decorated throughout with white-and-brown tapa. The chapel includes relics of the saint, including some of his clothes and the war club that is said to have dispatched him (see p546).

Boats run across to idyllic, uninhabited Alofi from Vele beach (for the whole boat 4000 CFP, 15 minutes), beside the airport.

🍴 Sleeping & Eating

The few hotels on Futuna all have bar-restaurants. Futuna's shops and supermarkets are stocked with an amazing but expensive variety of imported goods. A new hotel, Lalovi, was planned to open in 2013.

Somalama Park Hôtel HOTEL **$$**
(☎72 31 20; somalama@mail.wf; s/d/tr incl breakfast 9000/10,000/11,000 CFP; ✳@) Located on the northwest tip of Futuna, this beautiful, isolated place has a hacienda feel and the only sounds you'll hear are the waves lapping up on the palm-fringed beach.

Hôtel Fiafia HOTEL **$$**
(☎72 32 45; fax 72 35 56; hotel_fiafia@yahoo.fr; d incl breakfast 12,000 CFP; ✳) Right in Leava, the rooms here are nice and the not-so-pretty central setting puts you in the heart

WALLIS & FORTUNA HIGHLIGHTS

❶ Visiting Wallis' paradisaical lagoon islets like **Île Fenua Fo'ou**

❷ Gazing down the steep walls of Wallis' **Lake Lalolalo**

❸ Finding shards of Lapita pottery in the king's path at **To'oga Toto**

❹ Marvelling at the imposing tower and graceful tapa decorations at **Pierre Chanel Church** on Futuna

of what little action there is on Futuna. The owner sometimes offers free island tours.

ℹ Information

International telephone code 681
Currency Cour de Franc Pacifique (CFP)
Languages Wallisian, Futunan and French
Website www.outre-mer.gouv.fr, in French (select Wallis and Futuna on the map)

ℹ Getting There & Away

AIR Aircalin (☎72 00 05; www.aircalin.com) flies from Noumea, New Caledonia, to Wallis three times per week (return 64,000 CFP) and onwards to Nadi, Fiji, from Noumea once a week (return 33,000 CFP). There are about 10 weekly Aircalin flights between Wallis and Futuna (27,000 CFP return).

SEA No regular ferries or cruise ships docking.

YACHT Yachts don't visit Wallis that often, despite its welcoming lagoon. Because there is not much room around the Mata'Utu wharf, yachts are encouraged to moor near the petroleum wharf at Halalo in the south of Wallis.

Understand
South Pacific

population per sq km

SOUTH PACIFIC | SOLOMON ISLANDS | AMERICAN SAMOA

👤 ≈ 20 people

South Pacific Today

Mumblings Around the Kava Bowl

The Pacific Islands are a varied bunch and in the ocean's vastness, it's not all kava and cocktails. This region has a mindset all of its own that's at once sleepy, stubborn and ingenious. Despite the islands harbouring little violence or danger, corruption is rife. Old customs continue even as islanders face a rapidly modernising world.

You'll hear mumblings about Fiji and the Solomon Islands, which have both seen unrest. RAMSI (Regional Assistance Mission to the Solomon Islands) troops arrived in the Solomon Islands in 2003 to police the nation, while coup-prone Fiji struggles to maintain diplomatic relations with other Pacific nations who don't like the idea of skipping elections and military-based rule.

Shifting Colonial Power & New Democracy

There are also new freedoms in the islands. A referendum for New Caledonia's independence from France is scheduled to take place between 2014 and 2019. Meanwhile French Polynesian president Oscar Temaru has pushed for independence for his country with rocky support. Tongans voted for the first time in 2010 elections – while monarchy-linked nobles (that have reigned for centuries) won that election, there will be another election in 2014.

Ex-colonies like Australia and New Zealand exert considerable influence in the Pacific through their membership of the Pacific Islands Forum, while France and the USA still finance their island territories. Lobbying from Australia resulted in the suspension of Fiji from the Pacific Islands Forum in 2010 for its failure to host elections. Australia continues to lobby for greater regionalism, whereby Pacific nations will act collectively on trade, fishing, waste management and air transport. Under the

---

Surface of earth covered by the Pacific: 28%

Islands in the Pacific: 25,000

Highest peak in this book: Mt Popmanaseu, Solomon Islands (2335m)

Population of islands in this book: 2,504,445

Landmass in this book: 87,337 sq km

Largest island in this book: Grand Terre, New Caledonia (6467 sq km)

Top Three Reads

» *Blue Latitudes* (Tony Horwitz) The author retraces some of Cook's voyages and compares the past with the present; lively and informative.

» *The Sex Lives of Cannibals* (J. Maarten Troost) Hysterical tales of the author's escapades on an atoll; you'll get it more once you're on Pacific soil.

» *Mutiny on the Bounty* (Nordhoff & Hall) Page-turning saga of love, adventure and piracy with a historical backdrop.

Big-Screen Scenes

» *Cast Away* (2000) Fiji

» *Couples Retreat* (2009) Bora Bora

» *The Blue Lagoon* (1980) Fiji

» *Mutiny on the Bounty* (1935, 1962 & 1984) Tahiti, Bora Bora and Mo'orea

» *Rapa Nui* (1994) Easter Island

belief systems

(% of population)

71
Protestant

25
Catholic

4
Other

if the South Pacific were 100 people

81 would be Pacific Islanders
15 would be of Asian origin
4 would be of European origin

Forum's Pacific Plan, nations would remove barriers to trade within the region and trade externally as a collective group.

As old colonies change their roles in the Pacific, new powers are appearing. In 2006 China signed the catchily titled Action Plan of Economic Development and Cooperation offering trade with and aid to several Pacific nations. Today China is one of the largest trading partners in the South Pacific after Australia and New Zealand. While many nations have imposed sanctions on Fiji for its military government, Beijing has offered it increasing support. Some diplomats have been critical of the move, suggesting it's an attempt to get a stake in the region's natural resources (such as fishing rights) as well as a tactical foothold. Still the South Pacific – particularly Fiji, Vanuatu, the Solomon Islands and Tonga – is benefiting with building programs and access to Chinese markets.

Climate Change Concerns

There is one issue on which the South Pacific agrees: climate change. While small islands like Tuvalu and Tokelau are at risk of sinking, other environmental issues are also a factor. Reduced land anywhere in the Pacific means less space for agriculture, and the precious corals of Fiji and French Polynesia are bleaching as water temperatures rise.

UN Secretary-General Ban Ki-moon was the first UN leader to attend the Pacific Islands Forum (in 2011), where the hottest topic was reducing the region's reliance on fossil fuels. The US Deputy Secretary of State also attended the forum where many nations pledged aid for research about climate change and its impact in the region; to improve food and water security; and for ecosystem protection. Ironically, the South Pacific is one of Earth's lowest emitters of greenhouse gases yet is among the hardest hit by the effects.

Greet everyone, from a nod and a smile when passing strangers on the street to the local customary greeting when being introduced to someone. If you get invited to someone's home or a party, greet everyone in the room.

Myths & Facts

Myth Island societies are sexually free paradises.
Fact Today people are bound by church and family to behave more conservatively than those from most Western countries.

Myth If you wear a flower behind your right ear everyone will know you're single.
Fact No one really follows this old tradition anymore.

Myth The South Pacific is chock-full of tourist-filled resorts.
Fact Most places to stay are local-style and humble; aside from a few hot spots, the region receives little tourism.

History

The Great Polynesian Migration is one of the world's most outlandish yet mysterious historical events. Imagine families and clans tossing chickens, dogs, pigs, vegies and the kids into canoes and sailing into an unknown, empty blue. Then they found islands, lots of them, using celestial navigation as well as now-forgotten methods of reading cloud reflections, wave formations and bird flight patterns.

More than 3000 years after the people we now know as Melanesians and Polynesians dominated the Pacific, European explorers finally achieved the marine technology to 'discover' these tropical paradises. By the late 1700s, explorers' tales of the idyllic way of life and the beauty of the landscapes turned the region into a dream destination for Europe that, in many ways, retains the same allure today. Unfortunately the majority of Europeans who reached the South Pacific through the 1800s were sailors and traders who brought disease, alcohol and guns. Within a hundred years of first contact, the population of most islands had plummeted, some by as much as 95%, as islanders died of diseases they had no immunity against, drank themselves to death or, some say, died of sadness watching their cultures die.

Meanwhile missionaries began to evangelise the archipelagos from the early 1800s. By converting chiefs, using the widespread death and disease to instil hope for an afterlife and by portraying faith as a path to European wealth, the missionaries achieved great success. While their teachings brought literacy, via the need for written language to translate the Bible, and buffers to the vices brought in by traders and explorers, the missionaries also destroyed many parts of the existing cultures by prohibiting traditional dance, song and tattooing.

European colonisation followed the need to protect trade and religion in the region, and the islands became strategic ports in WWII. Battles with the Japanese took place in Micronesia. Though Polynesia was never invaded, many islanders went to war in support of their colonisers.

TIMELINE	50,000 years ago	1500 BC	200 BC
	The Papuans, related to Australia's Aborigines, settle the Pacific in PNG and the Solomon Islands but are unable to travel further due to lack of technology.	Long-distance seafaring begins in earnest by the Lapita people in Vanuatu, New Caledonia, Fiji and central Polynesia, where they develop the culture now known as Polynesian.	Polynesians spread east to the Society and Marquesas Islands (modern-day French Polynesia). Melanesians following from New Guinea and the Solomon Islands come to dominate Vanuatu, New Caledonia and Fiji.

Fighting side by side in war helped to equalise races and led many nations to question their subservience to colonial powers, eventually leading to independence. Meanwhile the Marshall Islands in the North Pacific and French Polynesia in the South Pacific became nuclear testing grounds for the USA and France, respectively.

Getting There is Half the Fun

About 50,000 years ago the first people reached the Pacific islands, arriving in New Guinea from Southeast Asia via Indonesia. These people, now known as Papuans, share ancestry with Australia's Aborigines. Moving slowly east, the Papuans' progress halted in the northern Solomon Islands about 25,000 years ago, due to the lack of marine technology needed to cross the increasingly wide stretches of ocean. Subsequent people, collectively known as Austronesians, moved into the area from the west, mingling with the Papuans and eventually becoming the highly diverse group of people known as 'Melanesians'. New Guinea and the Solomons were the only inhabited islands in the Pacific for many thousands of years.

The wide seas from the Solomons to Vanuatu were finally crossed in about 1500 BC by the Lapita people, who later gave rise to Polynesian culture.

The Melanesians of New Guinea and the Solomons mingled a little with the Lapita and followed them across the Pacific. Melanesians came to dominate New Guinea, the Solomons, Vanuatu, New Caledonia and Fiji.

The development of the outrigger canoe, with its additional support, called *ama* in many Polynesian languages, allowed Austronesian people to journey vast distances across the Pacific.

HISTORY GETTING THERE IS HALF THE FUN

THE ANCIENT LAPITA CULTURE

The ancient race of people known as the Lapita is thought to be responsible for the wide distribution of Polynesian culture and Austronesian languages in the Pacific. It was in Tonga and Samoa that the Lapita developed into the people we now call Polynesians.

The Lapita had an enormous influence from 1500 BC to 500 BC over a vast area of the Pacific, where their influence can be traced through the far-flung dispersal of their unique pottery. Lapita pottery has been found in Papua New Guinea, New Caledonia, in parts of Micronesia and in Fiji, Tonga, Samoa and Wallis and Futuna.

The Lapita were skilled sailors and navigators, able to cross hundreds of kilometres of open sea, and trade and settlement were important to them. They were also agri-culturists and practised husbandry of dogs, pigs and fowl. Regarded as the first cultural complex in the Pacific, they were an organised people who traded obsidian (volcanic glass used in tool production) from New Britain (an island off PNG) with people up to 2500km away in Tonga and Samoa.

You can see Lapita artefacts in the national museums of Vanuatu (p476) and in Suva (p88) and Sigatoka (p81) in Fiji.

AD 300–900	1568	1768–79	1785
The final major wave leaves the Societies and Marquesas: north to Hawai'i, southwest to the Cooks and southeast to Easter Island and, lastly, to New Zealand.	Don Alvaro de Mendaña y Neyra lands on Santa Isabel Island finding traces of gold and, believing he has discovered King Solomon's Mines, names the islands the Solomons.	Captain James Cook 'boldly goes' on three voyages through the Pacific to explore more of the earth than anyone in history, before being killed in Hawai'i.	French explorer La Pérouse sets off to explore the Pacific. He visits Tonga, Samoa and Australia before mysteriously disappearing. His wrecked ship is discovered in the Solomons in 2005.

The Lapitas' Polynesian descendants waited on Samoa and Tonga for a thousand years or so, until developing more advanced ocean vessels and skills. Some time around 200 BC, they crossed the long ocean stretches to the east, reaching the Society and Marquesas island groups (in modern French Polynesia). From there, voyaging canoes travelled southwest to Rarotonga and the southern Cook Islands, southeast to Rapa Nui (Easter Island) in AD 300, north to Hawai'i around AD 400 and southwest past Rarotonga to Aotearoa (New Zealand) in AD 900.

Although the predominant direction of human movement was from west to east, population pressure and the occasional religious disagreement prompted constant movement of people across the oceans. So Polynesians can be found today in Melanesia's eastern islands, while the largely Melanesian Fiji is also home to many Polynesians and Micronesians.

Compared to the coast hugging of contemporary Europeans, the settlement of the Pacific Ocean was the most remarkable feat of ocean sailing up to that time. All but the farthest-flung islands of the massive Pacific were colonised by 200 BC. By contrast it was more than 1000 years later that the Vikings crossed the (relatively small) Atlantic to make Europe's first cross-ocean settlement.

Melanesians embarked on regular trade and some war missions, but Polynesians travelled the broader stretches of open ocean. Almost no Pacific islands were cut off entirely from other cultures, and the presence of the *kumara* (sweet potato) in the Pacific islands confirms that at least some journeys were made as far east as South America, probably from the Marquesas or Austral Islands. Traditional stories also indicate exploratory journeys into Antarctic waters 'not seen by the sun'.

Voyaging & Navigation

Ancient Pacific islanders' voyages were motivated by war, trade, colonisation and the search for resources, or sometimes merely by curiosity and pride. The Tongans, known as the 'Vikings of the Pacific', ruled Samoa, Niue and eastern Fiji with an iron fist, and raided from Tuvalu to the Solomon Islands, 2700km to the west.

At the time of European contact, prodigious feats of navigation and voyaging still occurred, although not on as grand a scale as previously. The navigator-priest Tupaia, who boarded Cook's *Endeavour* in Tahiti, could name around 100 islands between the Marquesas and Fiji, and he directed Cook's search for islands west of Tahiti. For the entire circuitous journey to Java in Indonesia, Tupaia could always point in the direction of his homeland.

Canoes

The term 'canoe' (*vaka* or *va'a*) is misleading. The same word describes small dugouts used for river navigation, giant war vessels accommodating

1789

Fletcher Christian famously relieves Captain Bligh of his duties. Christian, eight mutineers and a handful of Tahitian men and women leg it to Pitcairn Island; 16 mutineers remain on Tahiti.

1812

King Pomare II of Tahiti seeks conversion to Protestantism, which leads to European support of his rule and allows him to centralise power; the missionaries essentially become the government.

» Modern traders at Bounty Bay, Pitcairn Island

MODERN VOYAGING

The voyaging skills of today's Pacific islanders may not match those of their ances-tors, but the traditional knowledge of navigation is still put to everyday use. Both small interisland trips and long-distance voyages have been used to test many theories about ocean voyaging.

Kon Tiki

Probably the most famous such voyage was that of Thor Heyerdahl's *Kon Tiki* from South America to the Tuamotus in 1947. The journey attempted to prove that Polynesia could have been populated from South America. While that theory has since been disproved by genetic evidence, the 8000km trip caused many historians to rethink their ideas about ancient Polynesian technology and ability to sail between islands.

Exploring Tradition

Modern voyages along traditional routes have refined theories about canoe construc-tion and navigational methods. Among such journeys, the 25m-long outrigger canoe *Tarratai* was sailed from Kiribati 2500km south to Fiji in 1976. That same year the voyage of the 20m *Hokule'a*, which used traditional navigation methods for the 4250km trip from Hawai'i to Tahiti, sparked a resurgence of interest in traditional navigation.

Other voyaging canoes include the 21m *Hawaiki Nui*, which sailed 4000km from Tahiti to Aotearoa in 1985. In 1995 *Te Au o Tonga*, captained by former prime minister of the Cook Islands Sir Thomas Davis (Papa Tom), sailed from Rarotonga to Tahiti, on to Hawai'i and back to Rarotonga. Part of the cargo on the last leg was less than traditional: Papa Tom's new 1200cc Harley-Davidson. The *Hokule'a* and *Te Au o Tonga*, among other great *vaka* (outrigger canoe), continue to make long voyages.

Te Mana O Te Moana

More recently a group of seven traditional voyaging canoes, each skippered by a different Polynesian nation and calling themselves Te Mana O Te Moana (The Spirit of the Sea), set sail from New Zealand in April 2011. Voyaging through Polynesia, the canoes arrived in Hawai'i for the Kava Bowl Summit that addressed the effects of cli-mate change in the Pacific, then travelled onward to the West Coast of the USA, and eventually headed back through Polynesia to Pacific Arts Festival in the Solomon Islands in 2012. Their overall goal: to raise environmental awareness of the great ocean.

hundreds of men and 25m-long ocean-voyaging craft. Ocean-voyaging craft – either double canoes or single canoes with outriggers – carried one or more masts and sails of woven pandanus. Captain James Cook and con-temporary observers estimated that Pacific canoes were capable of speeds greater than their own ships; probably 150km to 250km per day, so that trips of 5000km could be comfortably achieved with available provisions.

1838	1841	1845	1864
After French Catholic missionaries are kicked off Tahiti, France sends in a gunboat, leading to bloody battles and the island being declared a French protectorate in 1842.	Pierre Louis Marie Chanel becomes patron saint of the Pacific islands after being killed for eroding the traditional power structure and gaining too many converts in Futuna.	Tonga's King George Tupou I takes the throne over a newly united nation and creates a governing system with a little help from his prime minister, Reverend Shirley Baker.	The first 'black-birded' labourers from Vanuatu and the Solomons arrive in Fiji. Meanwhile, the first 329 Chinese workers are brought to Tahiti to work at American-run cotton fields.

Navigation Techniques

Initial exploratory journeys often followed the migratory flights of birds. Once a new land had been discovered, the method of rediscovery was remembered and communicated mostly by which stars to follow. Fine-tuning of these directions was possible by observing the direction from which certain winds blew, the currents, wave fronts reflecting from islands and the flight of land birds.

European Arrival

Like Pacific islanders, European explorers came in search of resources (gold and spices initially), driven by curiosity and national pride. Europeans were also inspired by one overpowering myth: a great southern continent, Terra Australis.

Since the time of Ptolemy, scientists predicted the presence of a huge landmass in the southern hemisphere to counter the earth's northern continents. Otherwise, it was believed, the globe would be top heavy and fall over. In the absence of hard facts, Terra Australis was believed to be peopled with strange heathens and magical creatures, and rumoured to be rich in gold. The biblical tale of King Solomon had included vast gold mines in some unknown location. What could be a better spot than Terra Australis?

Spanish

In 1521 the Portuguese Ferdinand Magellan led a Spanish expedition that discovered, at the southern tip of the Americas, an entrance to the ocean he named Mar Pacifico – the Pacific Ocean – for its calmness. Magellan spotted only two small, uninhabited islands until he had sailed north-west almost the entire ocean to Guam in Micronesia.

On Guam the first contact between Pacific islanders and Europeans followed a pattern that would become all too familiar. The islander belief that all property was shared meant that Guam's islanders helped themselves to one of the expedition's small boats and Magellan retaliated – seven islanders were killed. Magellan himself was killed two months later while in the Philippines, but not before he became the first person to circumnavigate the globe (having previously visited the Philippines from the other direction).

Spaniard Don Alvaro de Mendaña y Neyra sailed west across the Pacific in search of Terra Australis in 1567. On the Solomon Islands, conflict with the locals arose when islanders were unable to supply the resources Mendaña needed to resupply.

It took Mendaña nearly 30 years to gain approval for his disastrous second voyage during 1595. An estimated 200 islanders were killed in the

1879

Following the outlawing of 'black-birding', Britain introduces the first Indian indentured labourers to Fiji to work in the sugar-cane fields of the main island.

1889–94

'Here he lies where he longs to be' – Robert Louis Stevenson abandons the chilly moors of Scotland for the warm delights of Samoa via French Polynesia.

» Sugar plantation workers on Viti Levu, Fiji

DAVID SANGER PHOTOGRAPHY / ALAMY ©

Marquesas when conflict broke out. There was even more conflict with locals when the ship reached the Solomons, and fighting also spread to the crew. Mendaña himself died of malaria, and the expedition limped to Peru under the command of the more humane Pedro Fernández de Quirós. Quirós led another expedition to the Pacific in 1605, discovering the Tuamotu Islands and Vanuatu.

Dutch

Jacob Le Maire and Willem Schouten's 1616 search for Terra Australis introduced Europe to the Tongan islands and Futuna. Jacob Roggeveen spotted Bora Bora in the Society Islands in 1722, and Tutuila and Upolu in Samoa. Abel Tasman became the most famous Dutch explorer after charting Tasmania and the east coast of New Zealand in 1642, then landing on the islands of Tonga and Fiji.

French

The most famous French explorer, Louis-Antoine de Bougainville, came upon Tahiti and claimed it for France in 1768 (he didn't realise that Wallis had claimed it for England less than a year before). He went on to the Samoan islands, then continued to Vanuatu and Australia's Great Barrier Reef. Bougainville's impact was greater than dots on a map, however; his accounts of the South Pacific sparked massive interest back in Europe and created the myth of a southern paradise.

In 1827 Dumont d'Urville sailed the Pacific searching for his lost countryman, the comte de la Pérouse, whose boat had sunk near the Solomon Islands in 1788. D'Urville's writings of this and another journey (10 years later) were to establish the concept of the three great subdivisions of the Pacific: Melanesia, Micronesia and Polynesia.

English

In 1767 Samuel Wallis – *still* searching for Terra Australis – landed on Tahiti, but the greatest of the English explorers was James Cook.

Cook's three journeys into the region – the first (1768–71) most famously 'discovered' Australia and New Zealand – saw detailed mapping and exploration that would later allow others to follow. His third and final journey was the first European visit to Hawai'i where Cook was killed. His legacy can be seen throughout the Pacific with his detailed maps used until the 1990s and several places bearing his name, most notably the Cook Islands.

Following the most famous of maritime mutinies, Fletcher Christian captained the *Bounty* to discover Rarotonga in the southern Cook Islands in 1789 (see p529).

HISTORY EUROPEAN ARRIVAL

Passing European seafarers reported Easter Island's famous *moai* had toppled over between 1722 and 1868 with oral stories pointing to a civil war that saw the statues pushed over to indicate defeat.

The Cook Islands were originally called the Hervey Islands by the modest Captain Cook. It was only after his death in the 1820s that the new name appeared in his honour on a Russian naval chart.

1890–1903	1899	1914	1918–19
French post-Impressionist Paul Gauguin retreats to Tahiti and the Marquesas to devote his life to art. His paintings strengthen the idyllic image of the South Pacific in the Western world.	Tripartite Treaty splits the Samoas between Germany and America; Britain steps out of the Samoas in exchange for the renunciation of German claims on Tonga, the Solomon Islands and Niue.	Concerned about the proximity of an enemy territory during WWI, New Zealand sends troops to occupy German territories in Samoa and meets no opposition.	Spanish influenza, an H1N1 virus that caused one of the biggest worldwide pandemics in history, ravages Tonga, Tahiti, Fiji and Samoa, wiping out approximately 20% of their populations.

Evangelisation of the Pacific

ON A MISSION

After a few largely unsuccessful Spanish Catholic forays into Micronesia during the 17th century, the first major attempt to bring Christianity to the Pacific was by English Protestants. The newly formed London Missionary Society (LMS) outfitted missionary outposts on Tahiti and Tonga, and in the Marquesas in 1797. These first missions failed – within two years the Tongan and Marquesan missions were abandoned. The Tahitian mission survived but its success was limited. For a decade there were only a handful of islanders who were tempted to join the new religion.

Other Protestants soon joined the battle. The new players in the South Pacific were the Wesleyan Missionary Society (WMS), fresh from moderate success in New Zealand, and the American Board of Commissioners for Foreign Missions (ABCFM), following their Christianising of Hawai'i. The WMS and ABCFM both floundered in the Marquesas, but fared better in Tonga.

When French Catholic missionaries were kicked off Tahiti in 1836, France sent a gunboat in 1838, which led to the island being declared a French protectorate in 1842.

In the 1830s French Catholic missions were established in the Marquesas and Tahiti. Catholic missionaries were often as pleased to convert a Protestant as a heathen, with the fierce rivalry between the different denominations extended to their island converts. Religious conflicts fitted easily into the already complex political melee of Pacific society, and local chiefs manipulated the two Christian camps for their own purposes.

Despite the slow start, missionary success grew. By the 1820s missionary influence on Tahiti was enormous. The Bible was translated into Tahitian, a Protestant work ethic was instilled, tattooing discouraged, promiscuity guarded against by nightly 'moral police' and the most 'heathen' practices such as human sacrifice were forbidden. From Tahiti, Tonga and Hawai'i, Christianity spread throughout the Pacific.

The missionaries' success was due to three major factors. Clever politics played a part, particularly the conversion of influential Tongan chief Taufa'ahau and the Tahitian Pomare family. The perceived link between European wealth and Christianity also played a part: missionaries 'civilised' as well as Christianised, and islanders obtained European tools and skills, such as literacy. Finally, the message of afterlife salvation fell on attentive ears as European arrival coincided with the massive depopulation through the spread of disease.

Missionaries shielded islanders from the excesses of some traders, and it was missionary pressure that finally put an end to the blackbirding trade (see p547). Putting Pacific languages into written form, initially in translations of the Bible, was another major contribution. While many missionaries deliberately destroyed 'heathen' Pacific artefacts and beliefs, others diligently recorded myths and oral traditions that would otherwise have been lost. A substantial portion of our knowledge of Pacific

1942–43	**1944**	**1946**	**1947**
Japanese and American forces battle post-Pearl Harbor on Guadalcanal in the Solomon Islands. The American win marks a turning point of WWII and halts Japanese expansion in the Pacific.	Fijian Corporal Sefanaia Sukanaivalu is posthumously awarded the Victoria Cross after heroically rescuing two men and giving his life to save others in a WWII battle in the Solomon Islands.	The first atomic testing in the Pacific begins: two bombs the size of those dropped on Nagasaki are detonated by the US on Bikini Atoll in the Marshall Islands.	Thor Heyerdahl sails the balsa raft *Kon Tiki* from Peru to the Tuamotus to prove that the Pacific was populated from the Americas. His theory is later disproved by genetics.

CAPTAIN JAMES COOK *Tony Horwitz*

If aliens ever visit earth, they may wonder what to make of the countless obelisks, faded plaques and graffiti-covered statues of a stiff, wigged figure gazing out to sea from Alaska to Australia, from NZ to North Yorkshire, from Siberia to the South Pacific. James Cook (1728–79) explored more of the earth's surface than anyone in history, and it's impossible to travel the Pacific without encountering the captain's image and his controversial legacy in the lands he opened to the West.

For a man who travelled so widely, and rose to such fame, Cook came from an extremely pinched and provincial background. The son of a day labourer in rural Yorkshire, he was born in a mud cottage, had little schooling and seemed destined for farm work. Instead, Cook went to sea as a teenager, worked his way up from coal-ship servant to naval officer, and attracted notice for his exceptional charts of Canada. But Cook remained a little-known second lieutenant until, in 1768, the Royal Navy chose him to command a daring voyage to the South Seas.

In a converted coal ship called *Endeavour,* Cook sailed to Tahiti, and then became the first European to land at New Zealand and the east coast of Australia. Though the ship almost sank after striking the Great Barrier Reef, and 40% of the crew died from disease and accidents, the *Endeavour* limped home in 1771.

On a return voyage (1772–75), Cook became the first navigator to pierce the Antarctic Circle and circled the globe near its southernmost latitude, demolishing the ancient myth that a vast, populous and fertile continent surrounded the South Pole. Cook also crisscrossed the Pacific from Easter Island to Melanesia. Though Maori killed and cooked 10 sailors, the captain remained sympathetic to islanders. 'Notwithstanding they are cannibals', he wrote, 'they are naturally of a good disposition.'

On Cook's final voyage (1776–79), in search of a northwest passage between the Atlantic and Pacific, he became the first European to visit Hawai'i, and coasted America from Oregon to Alaska. Forced back by Arctic pack ice, Cook returned to Hawai'i, where he was killed during a skirmish with islanders who had initially greeted him as a Polynesian god. In a single decade of discovery, Cook had filled in the map of the Pacific and, as one French navigator put it, 'left his successors with little to do but admire his exploits'.

But Cook's travels also spurred colonisation of the Pacific, and within decades of his death, missionaries, whalers, traders and settlers began transforming – and often devastating – island cultures. As a result, many indigenous people now revile Cook as an imperialist villain who introduced disease, dispossession and other ills to the Pacific (hence the frequent vandalising of Cook monuments). However, as islanders revive traditional crafts and practices, from tattooing to *tapa,* they have turned to the art and writing of Cook and his men as a resource for cultural renewal. For good and ill, a Yorkshire farm boy remains the single most significant figure in the shaping of the modern Pacific.

Tony Horwitz is a Pulitzer-winning reporter and nonfiction author. His latest book is Midnight Rising: John Brown and the Raid that Sparked the Civil War. He retraced Cook's voyages in his 2002 book Blue Latitudes: Boldly Going Where Captain Cook Has Gone Before.

HISTORY EVANGELISATION OF THE PACIFIC

1958	**1962**	**1963**	**1970**
'Wash that man right out of my hair' – the camp musical *South Pacific,* based on James Michener's short story of the same title, is unleashed upon the world.	Western Samoa becomes the first Pacific nation to be given independence after being a UN Trust Territory administered by New Zealand since the end of WWII.	The first South Pacific Games (now called Pacific Games), a multisport mini Olympics, was held in Suva, Fiji. It is first played in three-year intervals then expanded to four years.	After 96 years of colonial rule Fiji becomes independent, adopting a British model of parliament with two houses including a 'House of Lords' made up of Fijian chiefs.

ST PIERRE CHANEL OF OCEANIA *Errol Hunt*

Pierre Louis Marie Chanel was born into a French peasant family in 1802, and trained as a priest. He embarked for the Pacific islands with the newly formed Catholic Society of Mary (Marist) in 1836 and, the following year, was the first missionary to set foot on Futuna. The ruling king, Niuluki, welcomed him.

As the missionaries gained converts and thus eroded the traditional power structure of the island, Niuluki became less keen on the newcomers. When Niuluki's own son asked to be baptised, the king issued an edict that the missionaries cease their activities. On 28 April 1841 a band of warriors, probably condoned by Niuluki, attacked Pierre Chanel and killed him.

Despite this (or perhaps because of it) the island soon became fully Catholic as other Marist priests took up the challenge.

Pierre Chanel was declared venerable in 1857, beatified in 1889 and finally canonised as the patron saint of Oceania in 1954. He is also recognised as the first martyr to lay his life down for Oceania (Rev John Williams had been dead for two years at this stage, but he was a Protestant – and that doesn't count).

history and traditional culture comes from the work of missionary historians.

The church remains an important political player in many islands on the basis of its strong history. Ruling dynasties in Tonga, Tahiti and Fiji all owed their success to missionary backing, just as missionary success owed a lot to those dynasties.

Gold of the South Seas

Whaling

European whalers enthusiastically hunted in the Pacific from the late 18th century. Trade peaked in the mid-19th century, then declined as whale products were superseded by other materials. The effect on the Pacific's whale population was catastrophic, but the effect on Pacific islanders was complex. There were opportunities for lucrative trade as ships resupplied and many Pacific islanders, as always fond of travel, took the opportunity to travel on whaling ships. Some islanders, however, were effectively kidnapped and forced to travel without consent; whalers of the Pacific were not the most gentle of men.

Bêches-de-Mer

Also known as *trepang,* sea cucumbers or sea slugs, *bêche-de-mer* is a marine organism related to starfish and urchins. An Asian delicacy, Pacific

1971	1978	1978	1980
Establishment of the South Pacific Forum (now Pacific Islands Forum). Its aims include government cooperation to work towards economic and social well being of the peoples of the South Pacific.	More than 20 years after crushing the nationalist movement, Britain grants independence for the Solomon Islands with Chief Minister Sir Peter Kenilorea automatically assuming the role of prime minister.	After separating from the Ellis and Gilbert Islands (now Kiribati) under the commonwealth and changing its name from Ellis Island to Tuvalu in 1974, Tuvalu becomes entirely independent.	The islands known as the New Hebrides (which were co-governed by France and Great Britain) become independent with the new name of Vanuatu.

bêches-de-mer were sought by early-19th-century Europeans to trade for Chinese tea. *Bêches-de-mer* were relatively abundant, and important trading relations were forged with islanders. For the most part trade was mutually beneficial, with islanders trading eagerly for metal, cloth, tobacco and muskets. The trade in *bêches-de-mer* was largely nonviolent, in contrast with the sandalwood trade.

Sandalwood

Nineteenth-century Europeans trading with China found another valued Pacific resource in fragrant sandalwood, used in China for ornamental carving and cabinet making, as well as incense. By the 1820s these traders had stripped the sandalwood forests of Hawai'i, and looked to islands to the south. Extensive sandalwood forests on Fiji, Vanuatu, the Solomons and New Caledonia became the focus for traders keen to satisfy the demands of the Chinese market.

On each new island, payment for sandalwood was initially low. A small piece of metal, a goat or a dog was sometimes sufficient to buy a boatload of the aromatic wood. But as the supply of slow-growing sandalwood dwindled, the price rose – islanders demanded guns, ammunition, tobacco or assistance in war as payment.

While the sandalwood trade in Fiji was fairly orderly under the supervision of local chiefs, spheres of chiefly influence in the Solomons, Vanuatu and New Caledonia were much smaller and traders had difficultly establishing lasting relationships with islanders. Sandalwood was the most violent of any trades in the Pacific, and Melanesia's savage reputation in Europe was not improved. There were many attacks on ships' crews, sometimes motivated by a greed for plunder, but often a response to previous atrocities by Europeans. Melanesians assumed that all Europeans belonged to the one kin group, and thus were accountable for another's crimes.

The sandalwood trade was far from sustainable. Island after island was stripped of its forests, and the trade petered out in the 1860s with the removal of the last accessible stands.

Blackbirding

In the late 19th century, cheap labour was sought for various Pacific industries, such as mines and plantations. Pacific islanders were also 'recruited' to labour in Australia, Fiji, New Caledonia, Samoa and Peru. Satisfying the demand for labour was a major commercial activity from the 1860s.

In some cases islanders were keen to sign up, seeking to share the benefits of European wealth. Often, though, islanders were tricked into boarding ships, either being deceived about the length of time for which

KIDNAPPED

'Once the people were on board they locked them up and sailed away. Two men escaped and swam back to shore, but the rest were never seen again.' Kelese Simona, in *Time and Tide: The Islands of Tuvalu*, recalls his father's account of blackbirders kidnapping 70% of the island's population.

1987

Bloodless Fijian coups return power to an elite minority: Rabuka takes over government; the 1970 constitution is invalidated, Fiji is declared a republic and dismissed from the Commonwealth.

1996

The end of nuclear testing in the Pacific: last bombs detonated at Moruroa Atoll after anti-testing riots sweep through Pape'ete. The first bombs were tested on the atoll in 1966.

AFP / GETTY IMAGES ©

» A memorial to the first nuclear test at Moruroa, Pape'ete

they were contracted, or sometimes enticed aboard by sailors dressed as priests. In many cases no pretence was attempted: islanders were simply herded onto slaving ships at gunpoint.

The populations of many small, barely viable islands were devastated by blackbirders (a term used for the co-opting and sometimes kidnapping of islanders) – Tokelau lost almost half its population to Peruvian slave ships in 1863, while the Tongan island of 'Ata lost 40% of its population, and as a result is today uninhabited. People were also taken as slaves from Tuvalu, New Caledonia, Easter Island, Vanuatu and the Solomon Islands.

Blackbirding was outlawed by Britain's Pacific Islanders' Protection Act in 1872, largely due to persistent lobbying by missionaries. Their campaigns resulted in the banning of overseas-labour recruitment to Australia (in 1904), Samoa (in 1913) and Fiji (in 1916). The British government followed up the law with regular patrols of the region to prevent unscrupulous blackbirders, marking the beginning of a colonialist mentality of protection.

While some islanders returned to their homelands, others remained – such as the large Melanesian population in Queensland, Australia. In Fiji the large plantation economy looked elsewhere for cheap labour, transporting indentured labourers from India, who remain an important part of Fiji today (see p139).

Flag Follows Trade

Once European traders were established in the Pacific, many began agitating for their home countries to intervene and protect their interests. Missionaries also lobbied for colonial takeover, hoping that European law would protect islanders from the lawless traders. European powers began following a policy of flag following trade by declaring protectorates and then by annexing Pacific states.

Between 1878 and 1899 Germany annexed the Marshall Islands, northern Solomons and Samoa. The latter treaty ceded American Samoa to the US, joining the Phoenix Islands (now in Kiribati), which the US and Britain had claimed in 1836. After annexing French Polynesia (1840s) and New Caledonia (1853), the French lost interest for a while before claiming Wallis and Futuna (1880s) and going into partnership with Britain in Vanuatu in 1906.

Contrary to popular opinion, Britain was a reluctant Pacific-empire builder. However, it ended up with the largest of all Pacific empires, after being forced by various lobby groups to assume responsibilities for the Phoenix Islands in 1836, then Fiji, Tokelau, the Cooks, the Gilbert and Ellice Islands (modern Kiribati and Tuvalu), the southern Solomons and Niue between 1874 and 1900, and finally Vanuatu in 1906. Between 1900

1999	1999	2000	2001
Tuvalu laughs all the way to the bank when it begins selling its '.tv' internet domain name to TV shows around the world.	Civil war breaks out in the Solomon Islands, and hundreds die in the fighting. Following mediation by Australia and New Zealand, a peace agreement is signed between the two factions in October 2000.	George Speight heads a Fijian coup with hostages held in parliament for eight weeks; Speight is eventually charged with treason and given a life prison sentence.	Australia begins its Pacific Solution (2001–07), moving asylum seekers arriving to Australia by boat, to detention camps in PNG and Nauru rather than let them land in Australia.

and 1925, Britain happily offloaded the Cooks, Niue and Tokelau to eager New Zealand.

Colonialism brought peace between warring European powers but an increase in tensions with islanders. The arrival of settlers brought diseases that had been unknown in the Pacific or had been experienced only in limited contact with explorers or traders, and these took a horrific toll. Cholera, measles, smallpox, influenza, pneumonia, scarlet fever, chickenpox, whooping cough, dysentery, venereal diseases and even the common cold had devastating effects. Most Polynesian populations were halved, while Micronesia and Melanesia's populations suffered even more. Some islands of Vanuatu were among the worst hit, dropping to just 5% of their original populations.

War in the Pacific

WWI had little impact on the Pacific, though German colonial rulers in Micronesia, Samoa and Nauru were exchanged for Japanese, New Zealand, Australian and British rule. Germany, slightly preoccupied with events in Europe at the time, didn't resist these Pacific takeovers.

In contrast, the Pacific was a major arena of conflict during WWII. The war with Japan was fought through the Micronesian territories Japan had won from Germany in WWI, in Papua New Guinea and in the Solomon Islands.

Initially Japan expanded south from its Micronesian territories almost unhindered and captured the Solomons in 1942. They began building an airfield on Guadalcanal (which today is Henderson Airport) that would supply further advances south. Allied forces staged a huge offensive that saw more than 60 ships sunk in the surrounding waters that became known as Iron Bottom Sound. From 1944, US and Australian forces pushed the defending Japanese back, island by island. US bombers based in the Marianas punished Japanese cities for 10 months until 6 August 1945, when *Enola Gay* took off from Tinian (Northern Marianas) to drop an atomic bomb on Hiroshima. Days later another was dropped on Nagasaki and the Pacific war was over.

The suffering of islanders during the Pacific war was immense: Japanese forces in Micronesia forced the transport of large numbers of islanders between various islands, seemingly without motive. People were concentrated in areas without adequate food, thousands died from hunger and thousands more were executed by the Japanese as an Allied victory became apparent.

Soldiers from Fiji, the Solomons, Samoa, Tonga, French Polynesia and New Caledonia served in the armed forces, seeing action in the Pacific, Africa and Europe. Their valour cemented relations with other allies.

WWII Reminders

» Diveable shipwrecks in Vanuatu (p510)

» Wreckage across the Solomons' Western Province (p338)

» Guadalcanal (p320)

2002	2003	2006	2006
US reality series *Survivor* comes to French Polynesia with *Survivor Marquesas* – later seasons bring world attention to Fiji, Vanuatu and the Cook Islands.	As the Solomons again descend into lawlessness, the RAMSI, an Australian-led coalition of police from Pacific island states, is deployed to restore order.	On 16 November, riots erupt in the Tongan capital of Nuku'alofa as pro-democracy supporters express their anger at government inaction despite earlier promises for reform.	After making demands about upcoming bills, Commodore Frank Bainimarama begins military manoeuvres that eventually depose the Fiji government, and declares himself acting president in a coup.

WWII had a lasting effect on the region. Most obviously, Japan's Micronesian colonies were taken over by the US, becoming the Trust Territory of the Pacific islands. However, the war also left a legacy of more widespread and subtle effects. There was a huge improvement in roads and other infrastructure on many islands. There was also an input of money, food and other supplies that contributed towards the development of so-called cargo cults, whose devotees believed the goods were gifts from ancestral spirits.

WWII also hastened the end of traditional colonialism in the Pacific, the relative equality between white and black US soldiers prompting islanders to question why they were still subservient to the British and the French. Many independence leaders were influenced by wartime experiences.

Military Playground

In 1946, a US military officer met the people of the tiny Bikini Atoll in the Marshall Islands and asked if they'd be prepared to leave their island for 'the good of mankind and to end all world wars'. Over 160 Bikinians left their home to make way for 42,000 US personnel who would begin nuclear testing on this remote island.

Along with Enewetok and Kwajalein atolls, the area became known as the Pacific Proving Grounds where 105 atmospheric tests were conducted until 1962. The most disastrous test occurred in 1954, when a hydrogen bomb code-named Bravo was detonated in an intense 32km-high fireball that stripped branches from trees on surrounding islands. It was the largest US test, with fallout washing over other Marshall Islands along with a Japanese fishing boat, *Daigo Fukuryu Maru* (Lucky Dragon No 5). It was a beacon that blazed around the world, and eventually, in 1963, the Partial Test Ban Treaty was signed.

Some nations, however, didn't sign up. France began nuclear testing in 1966 on Moruroa Atoll, an isolated part of French Polynesia. More than 40 tests were conducted until 1974 when international pressure pushed testing literally underground. The French abandoned testing on Moruroa and drilled into the island itself, detonating a further 147 nuclear devices here and later at Fangataufa. The tests began to crack the atolls themselves and there were concerns that nuclear material would leak into the open seas. Protests (including those by Greenpeace ship *Rainbow Warrior,* which was bombed by French intelligence agents in 1985) eventually brought international condemnation and the last test was conducted in 1996 when France signed the Comprehensive Nuclear Test Ban Treaty.

While some French military who worked at the test sites have been compensated for health problems, Roland Oldham, President of Moruroa

2007	2007	2008	2009
Samoa's King Malietoa Tanumafili II dies and the nation becomes a republic, electing Tuiatua Tupua Tamasese Efi as head of state for a five-year term.	The Solomons are struck by an earthquake and tsunami killing 54 and making many thousands homeless; another devastating quake and tsunami hit in 2010 destroying some 200 homes.	On August 1, George Tupou V is officially crowned king of Tonga. Three days before, he indicates his intention of relinquishing much of his power to the Prime Minister.	A 4.5m tsunami generated from an earthquake near Apia affects Tonga but devastates Samoa and American Samoa, killing more than 170 people and wiping out entire villages.

E Tatau which represents former test site workers in French Polynesia, claims that red tape and complicated court cases have prevented islanders from getting help from France. As for environmental clean up, the French government has been strict about who it allows to the atolls and what information is given to the public so it's difficult to gauge the impact of the tests or how any possible damage has been dealt with.

The impact of the testing in the area was huge. In 1968, the US declared Bikini Atoll habitable again and returned Bikinians to their homeland. They remained there for 10 years until a team of French scientists investigated reports of birth defects and cancer among Bikinians. A second evacuation followed and the US made a payment of US$150 million, which was spent removing and destroying the top half-metre of soil. Compensation claims are still being made today as Bikinians attempt to discover the half-life of US responsibility.

Postcolonial Pacific

From Samoa in 1962 through to Vanuatu in 1980, most Pacific island states gained independence (or partial independence) from their former colonial rulers. This was a relatively bloodless transition, with colonial masters as keen to ditch their expensive responsibilities as islanders were to gain independence. It took longer for the US to dismantle its Trust Territory of Micronesia, slowed by their desire to maintain a military presence in the region.

Only a handful of South Pacific territories remain in the hands of the US (American Samoa), France (New Caledonia, French Polynesia), Chile (Easter Island) and New Zealand (Rarotonga and the Cook Islands), with some gradually returning power to islanders. Self-government has not always been easy for Pacific nations with Fiji and the Solomons offering bellicose examples. Tonga, which was never officially colonised, remains the last monarchy in the Pacific, though the former king, who passed away in March 2012, had begun to relinquish his power in favour of democracy. Today the Pacific's governments face new challenges including environmental problems like global warming, particularly for smaller islands such as Tuvalu and Kiribati, which are at great risk from these effects.

To hop aboard the *Rainbow Warrior* as it journeyed through the Pacific protesting against nuclear testing, read NZ journalist David Robie's *Eyes of Fire: The Last Voyage of the Rainbow Warrior* (1986).

2010	2011	2012	2012
Tonga holds its first democratic elections. Nobles from the monarchy that has ruled for generations win when fringe parties join their ranks but another election is set for 2014.	Samoa and Tokelau jump forward one day on the Date Line to make it easier for the countries' business relations with Australia and Asia.	Commodore Frank Bainimarama lifts martial law in Fiji and announces he will open a national consultation process for developing a new constitution.	King George Tupou V of Tonga dies on 18 March.

Environmental Issues

The South Pacific has three types of islands: continental, high and low. The 'high' ones are mostly the peaks of volcanoes, extinct or active, and 'low' islands, or atolls, are formed by fringing reefs that encircle lagoons where volcanic islands have eroded and sunk. Melanesia has the only large continental islands in the region.

The most severe ecological danger to the nations of the South Pacific is attributed to the developed world. Waste management of litter, from both the islands themselves and rubbish drifting ashore, is another major concern. Rising sea levels due to global warming is a critical issue for Pacific islands and low-lying coral atolls are especially vulnerable. King tides are already threatening Tuvalu's nine low-lying atolls and islanders from Papua New Guinea's Carteret group have had to relocate to Bougainville – we may soon see whole Pacific populations on the move as climate-change refugees. In 2012 the Micronesian nation of Kiribati got the go ahead to buy 23 sq km on Fiji's Viti Levu in case their country becomes uninhabitable.

Mangroves are an important lynchpin in Pacific ecosystems and are also vulnerable to rising sea levels.

Fishing

Commercial fishing fleets in the Pacific catch around half of the world's fish – an annual harvest that approaches 100 million tonnes. While many seem to believe that the ocean is an infinite resource because of its vast size, others claim this catch is unsustainable. The UN has found that most commercially exploited fisheries worldwide are being fished beyond their capacity to recover, and has stated that the industry is 'globally nonsustainable' and that 'major ecological and economic damage is already visible'.

It is not only fish caught for consumption that are endangered – fishing fleets worldwide claim a 'bycatch' of almost 30 million tonnes per year. These are unwanted species such as dolphins, sharks and turtles that are pulled up along with the target species and then dumped. The infamous drift nets, which are legally limited to 2.5km in length but are often much longer, claim a huge bycatch.

Remnants of drift nets are often found wrapped around dead whales that wash ashore. Nets and lines that have broken loose continue to drift through the oceans, catching and killing as they go. Longlines drifting loose on the surface of the South Pacific have decimated albatross populations, bringing some species near to extinction. Closer to the coast, blast fishing and cyanide fishing – both illegal – kill everything nearby including coral and shellfish rather than just their target species.

To resource-poor Pacific island nations, selling licences to fish their relatively large Exclusive Economic Zones (EEZ) is one of their few economic options.

Whaling

Australia and New Zealand have for years been trying to raise enough support among member countries in the International Whaling Commission (IWC) to declare a South Pacific whale sanctuary, but have failed to gain the required three-quarters majority. The IWC pronounced a moratorium on commercial whaling in 1986, although Japan was allowed to continue to hunt whales under an agreed scientific-research clause (heavily criticised by opponents of whaling as being commercial whaling in disguise). Japan has tried to have the ban overturned, and won a vote on the 'eventual return of commercial whaling' by one vote in 2006; however, the ban was not lifted.

All three major players in the debate (Japan, Australia and New Zealand) are significant suppliers of foreign aid to Pacific nations, raising accusations of 'vote buying' at the IWC on both sides of the disagreement. Each year Japan plans a catch list of around a thousand whales that incorporates both endangered and nonendangered species.

Twelve Pacific countries and territories protect whales within economic exclusion zones. This area of 12 million sq km between French Polynesia and Australia is a de facto whale sanctuary.

Deforestation

Easter Island led the world in its deforestation efforts a thousand years before Magellan sailed into the Pacific. The resources put into constructing the famous *moai* statues of Easter Island turned the island into a desolate wasteland.

In modern times many South Pacific governments, with few other economic options, have embraced logging as a necessary evil. Logging is usually done by offshore companies and it's widely reported that graft and corruption is often involved in the granting of logging concessions by Pacific governments. Foreign logging companies often have no long-term interests in Pacific countries beyond the harvesting of timber resources and sometimes operate at every edge of what's legal. Local people rarely see net benefits from their traditional lands laid to waste. Only larger Pacific islands like those in the Solomons, Vanuatu, New Caledonia, Fiji and Samoa have sufficient timber reserves to interest such companies. The Solomons' timber is perilously overharvested – by some accounts accessible timber will be exhausted within the next decade. Much of this logging is illegal, run by well-organised international syndicates and this fuels corruption, exploitation and violence. In 2007 the Anglican Church of Melanesia reported on widespread child sexual exploitation associated with an Asian logging company around Arosi in Makira Province in the Solomons.

As well as loss of habitat for native birds and animals, deforestation leads to massive soil loss, which is particularly serious on small coral islands such as Niue, whose soil quality has never been good. Increased runoff from deforested land also leads to pollution of waterways and muddying of coastal waters, which can severely retard the growth of coral.

Nuclear Issues

The Pacific Ocean has seen more than its fair share of nuclear explosions. In fact, in one respect it all started here: the world's only hostile uses of nuclear weapons, on Hiroshima and Nagasaki in 1945, were launched from the Northern Marianas. Subsequently, the US, UK and France have conducted nuclear testing here.

In 1971 the nuclear-testing issue loomed large at the first meeting of the South Pacific Forum (SPF; now Pacific Island Forum). In 1986 the

CLIMATE CHANGE & GLOBAL WARMING *Saufatu Sopoanga*

Tuvalu began to voice its concern about climate change internationally in the late 1980s. Our key concern then, and now, is sea-level rise, which has the potential to submerge the islands we call home. Successive governments in Tuvalu have amplified warnings of this threat.

Over 35 years ago, scientists hinted that manmade emissions of carbon dioxide and other greenhouse gases may be raising the earth's atmospheric temperature, causing glaciers and polar ice to melt and sea levels to rise.

Now, is the sea rising? We think it is, and this view is supported by a broad scientific consensus. Estimates of sea-level rise in the southwest Pacific range between 1mm and 2mm per year. This is what science tells us, and anecdotal evidence here in Tuvalu – just south of the equator, and west of the international dateline – suggests the same.

What we see in Tuvalu is marginally higher (peak) sea levels when tides are highest. This means annual high tides are creeping further ashore. There is crop damage from previously unseen levels of saltwater intrusion, and a higher incidence of wave washover during storms or periods of strong tidal activity.

Some commentators, journalists and scientists have attributed these phenomena to construction too close to fragile lagoon foreshores or ocean fronts, or to the loss of natural coastal protection from cutting down shoreline trees and shoreline mining. Whether or not this is true is debatable. If the sea is rising, no amount of natural or artificial coastal protection that is not prohibitively expensive will fend it off. So-called 'adaptation' measures, however beneficial, merely delay the inevitable. Unless, of course, the worldwide volume of greenhouse gas production is cut drastically, and cut fast.

Tuvalu's nine small atolls and reef islands are geographically flat, rising no more than 4m above sea level. We cannot move away from our coastlines as all the land we inhabit is coastline. We have no continental interior to which we can relocate; no high interior, as is found on a volcanic island.

Confronting the Issues

Successive governments in Tuvalu have adopted the concept of sustainable development. But however much we try to put this concept into action locally, we also know it will not solve the problem of rising sea levels. So what else can we do?

As much as we try to meet the expectations of the international community, which demands that we include sustainable development in our national policy, our efforts on the ground have been mostly unsuccessful. (Other developing countries around the world share the same experience.)

In the context of climate change, it has become obvious to us that sustainable development is clearly not a defence against sea-level rise, no matter how hard the international debate tries to connect the two. As the former chairman of the Association of Small Island States, Tuiloma Neroni Slade, said: 'It may be that we manage to get our sustainable development polices right. Yet we will still face the risk that all will be undermined by climate change.' This reality is the situation we face in the Pacific. Manmade climate change is not a Pacific invention, nor are rising sea levels our problem to fix. There is only this: Tuvalu and other Pacific island countries will be among the first to suffer the catastrophic consequences of sea-level rise.

SPF's Treaty of Rarotonga established the South Pacific Nuclear-Free Zone, banning nuclear weapons and the dumping of nuclear waste. This was ratified 10 years later by France, the US and the UK.

France's Pacific nuclear-testing program commenced with atmospheric tests in 1966 at Moruroa and Fangataufa in French Polynesia. Their early atmospheric tests caused measurable increases in radiation in several Pacific countries and as far away as Fiji, 4500km to the west. Atmospheric testing was abandoned in 1974 under severe international pressure, but underground tests (totalling 127 on Moruroa and 10 on Fangataufa) continued until 1996.

The effects of US atmospheric nuclear testing, which ceased in 1970, have rendered Rongelap and Bikini uninhabitable (although short-term visits are fine); their people live in unhappy exile on neighbouring islands.

Fragile coral atolls were always a questionable place to detonate underground nuclear weapons, and the French Atomic Energy Commission confirmed the appearance of cracks in the coral structure of Moruroa and Fangataufa atolls, and leakage of plutonium into the sea from Moruroa. The effect of large amounts of radioactive material leaking into the Pacific Ocean would be catastrophic and far reaching. Claims of high rates of birth defects and cancer on neighbouring islands of French Polynesia are denied by the French, but are impossible to confirm because of the secrecy attached to government health records.

El Niño

The prevailing easterly trade winds tend to send warmer surface water towards the western Pacific, resulting in more rainfall in that region (Melanesia, Australia and NZ) than in the east.

An El Niño (more correctly El Niño Southern Oscillation, or ENSO) event occurs when the annual Christmas-period reversal in wind direction combines with high air pressure in the western Pacific and low air pressure in the east. The warm surface water is then blown back towards the eastern Pacific, carrying rain along with it: western Pacific countries experience droughts at this time, while eastern islands suffer unusually heavy rains or cyclones.

While El Niño (the Boy) develops in the Pacific, its effects on weather are felt worldwide. El Niños are often followed by La Niña (the Girl), which reverses El Niño – bringing storms to the western Pacific and droughts to the east.

El Niños usually last for about a year and recur irregularly every four or five years – they are currently impossible to predict.

Culture, Lifestyle & Religion

Pacific culture is as diverse as the islands in this vast ocean from the Solomon Islands to Easter Island. Each is isolated enough to have evolved a distinctive lifestyle. This diversity means that every generalisation is paired with its own exception, and the more you try to define the South Pacific, the more it invites you to the kava bowl and tells you to relax.

The region breaks down into Polynesia (from Greek, meaning 'many islands'), the un-PC-named Melanesia ('black islands') and the oft-forgotten Micronesia ('small islands'). The Polynesian people of the Pacific share a common ancestry in the Lapita people (see the boxed text, p539), though from this shared history each nation has developed a unique culture.

The Pacific Psyche

Ever since Europeans have been journeying to the Pacific, they've been idealising its islands as paradise on earth.

Rousseau to Gauguin

Eighteenth-century French philosopher Jean-Jacques Rousseau fantasised that the islands were a return to the innocence of Eden, populated by angelic beings who knew no guilt, ambition or social strictures. He dubbed these people 'noble savages', believing their lifestyle to be a panacea to the Industrial Revolution infecting Europe at the time. When, almost a century later, Rousseau's countryman Paul Gauguin returned from Tahiti and the Marquesas with images of idyllic islands and angelic women, the islands were confirmed an earthly paradise.

Ironically for people believed to be living in heaven on earth, islanders converted to Christianity in great numbers. While tourist brochures will echo that the Pacific is a paradise, its denizens are far more diverse than Rousseau's fantasies suggested, and more complex than the cherubic faces Gauguin depicted. For a look at the individual societies read the Understand section in each country chapter.

Contrary to Rousseau's idea of a simple life free from rules, most Pacific islands share the common notion of *tapu* (or taboo, as it became pronounced in English), which holds certain objects or practices as sacred. You only need to see how seriously some islanders observe the Sabbath to lose your ideas about a carefree people.

Hierarchy & Reciprocity

Melanesian communities were generally small – less than a few hundred people – with a 'bigman' as ruler. Hereditary factors were important in

ISLAND IDYLL

The most widely read anthropology book of all time is Margaret Mead's *Coming of Age in Samoa*, a brilliant but rose-tinted study that describes Utopian society on the Samoan island of Ta'u in the 1920s.

selecting a Melanesian bigman, but the individual's ambition and nous in politics and war were equally important.

Power was hereditary on the male side only in some Polynesian societies, with the most senior male serving as *ariki, ari'i* or *ali'i* (chief) and with subchiefs and commoners beneath them, and it was strictly hierarchical in the islands of Tonga and Tahiti.

After the arrival of Europeans, these societies became single-ruler 'countries', resembling traditional monarchies. In egalitarian Samoa, *matai* (chiefs) were selected on the grounds of political acumen and ability rather than lines of descent. Today, the power of chiefs and monarchies has waned, with Tonga the only remaining kingdom.

The central role of reciprocity in Melanesian culture has created a reputation for generosity and friendliness. In the past, aid in the form of food or labour would be given out of a sense of duty, with the expectation of the favour being returned in the future. In Polynesia, the lack of a sense of ownership has diminished but you still might be offered an object if you comment that you like it, or be expected to give something of yours away when an islander praises it.

Family Unit

Family is key to islanders' perceptions of themselves, even when migrating to other countries. Ancestor worship took this reverence of kin to a spiritual level and many Pacific islanders still believe strongly in the family unit, often sending money or gifts home to family when they emigrate.

Similarly, Polynesians have a strong respect for the family. Their tribal groups were based on extended family and the introduction of Christianity strengthened these ties. Today many small businesses are run by families, with extended families serving as additional employees or affiliates; don't be surprised if a guesthouse owner's cousin offers tours or other complementary services.

Lifestyle

The family is a vital element of islander society, reflecting the traditional clan basis of many Pacific communities. You can expect to be asked about your own family on numerous occasions, and some visiting couples become annoyed by the ubiquitous question: 'When are you going to have children?' Raising children is a shared activity in many Pacific-island countries, with children often invited to join in communal activities. Disciplining by other parents is not uncommon.

Many islanders are seeing their traditions challenged by globalisation as they become more urbanised. The struggle between *kastom* (custom)

TIPS ON MEETING LOCALS

Want to get chatting with the locals? A good conversation starter is often sports such as rugby or netball: 'Can Fiji/Samoa/Tonga knock over the Kiwis at the next Commonwealth Games?' Given that many islanders travel around the world, they may want to talk about where you're from and they're almost guaranteed to have a relative who moved to Auckland, Sydney or Utah. Observe these simple rules when visiting traditional villages:

» Remove your shoes when entering a home.
» Sit cross-legged on the floor, rather than with your feet pointing out.
» Avoid entering a house during prayers.
» Avoid walking between two people in conversation.
» Try to remain on a lower level than a chief to show respect.

and capitalism continues and can be seen in the abandonment of traditional diet in favour of processed Western food, which has led to high rates of obesity and type 2 diabetes among islanders.

Women

The role of women in the South Pacific is improving, though everyday sexism, such as being leered at while swimming or having the answers to their questions directed to male companions, can still be disturbing to female travellers. For South Pacific women the effects are more far reaching. They are less likely to be employed and are typically poorer paid. In fact, some studies estimate that less than a third of the female populations of Fiji and Tuvalu work outside of the home. A darker side of gender relations is that it's well documented the region is plagued by domestic violence. In some countries like French Polynesia, however, women hold positions of political power and are gaining more equality.

The role of women in the Pacific is complex. Many cultures are matrilineal and women can wield considerable power in village affairs even if they're not highly visible.

Homosexuality

Attitudes to homosexuality in the Pacific vary considerably, and in some parts of the region it is technically illegal (see the Directory, p577). In more conservative areas, religious leaders work themselves into a lather about it, as witnessed in Fiji when 3000 Methodists took to the streets protesting 'ungodly acts' in 2005.

Elsewhere, attitudes are more tolerant. Tahitian *mahu* (men who act like women), for example, are respected within their culture. Similarly, in Tonga the 'third-gendered' *fakaleiti* can be bisexual and their cross-dressing skills are celebrated in the Miss Galaxy Pageant (see p465). Their equivalent in Samoa are called *fa'afafine*.

Sport

From the cities to the smallest communities, recreational sport is an integral part of Pacific culture. Around sundown everyone seems to come out and play.

Rugby & Football

The Pacific has made a name for itself based on the success of its rugby players. Football of several varieties is played throughout the islands during winter but it is rugby union that is most popular, with teams from Tonga, Fiji and Samoa competing in the fiercely competitive Pacific Tri-Nations and Pacific Nations Cup. The Pacific's other rugby-obsessed countries include Vanuatu, Niue, the Cook Islands, Solomon Islands and, to a lesser extent, French Polynesia. American NFL football holds sway in American Samoa.

Netball (Volleyball)

In villages across the Pacific, Saturday is the day for inter-village (and sometimes interisland) netball, with games mostly in the winter season, though they can be played year-round. There's strong grassroots support in Samoa, Vanuatu, Tonga, Niue and the Solomon and Cook Islands, and the countries often fight it out on the netball court in the Pacific or Commonwealth Games. While netball provides an important way for women to keep up contact with other villages, it is also becoming popular among men, even in macho Samoa.

Cultural Hot Spots

» Easter Island

» The Marquesas Islands, French Polynesia

» Pentecost, Vanuatu

» Navala, Fiji

» The Niuas, Tonga

» Ta'u, American Samoa

» Mitiaro, Cook Islands

» Fongafala Islet, Tuvalu

Cricket

Cricket remains a summer colonial legacy and it's most popular in Fiji and the Cook Islands, though you'll also hear the cracking of willow in Tonga. In Samoa there's a pitch in almost every village but it's usually used for the local game, *kirikiti,* which has a lot in common with cricket but throws in an extra bowler and commonly features singing and dancing from the batting team (see the boxed text, p273). Tokelau's brand of cricket, *kilikiti,* uses a three-sided bat and has teams that include most of the village. In Tonga, *lanita* (a bat and ball game) is another variation on traditional cricket.

Canoeing

Not surprisingly, canoeing is another sport common to most Pacific nations. The sport is a great source of national pride at events such as the annual Hawaiki Nui *va'a* (canoe) race in French Polynesia and the Pacific Games. Tahiti took home 11 of 12 gold medals in the 2011 Pacific Games.

Religion

Traditional Beliefs

Before the Europeans arrived, ancestor worship and magic were common beliefs in Melanesia, while in Polynesia a variety of gods were worshipped.

Melanesia's ancestor worship and sorcery were essential to every aspect of daily life, with spells cast for success in war, fishing and health. Headhunting and cannibalism were practised as sacred rituals as late as the 1950s, and in the Solomons and Vanuatu *kastom* continues to preserve the sacredness of traditions that have remained the same for centuries and which it is forbidden to question.

Across Polynesia, religious beliefs were remarkably similar because of the islands' common ancestry. The Polynesian pantheon was ruled by Tangaroa (Tangaloa or Ta'aroa) and included several lesser gods who divvied up the duties for the seas, forests, war, crops and other important aspects of life. While there were many commonalities within Polynesia, each myth had a different interpretation or elaboration.

Existing as a separate class alongside Polynesian chiefs, and often sharing their power, the priests known as *tohunga* (*tohu'a* or *kahuna*) were the keepers of Polynesian religion. As well as having divine knowledge such as creation myths or rituals, these priests were also interpreters of the gods' wills for the village. They could act as vital checks to ambitious chiefs or form an alliance of considerable political power by joining with them.

Christianity

Christianity arrived in various forms in the early 19th century, and the race to convert the Pacific was on (see p544). Many countries have

FESTIVE SPIRIT

French Polynesia's Heiva festival in July features plenty of canoe racing but also highlights other traditional sports including coconut husking, rock lifting, fruit carrying and javelin throwing.

MAUI: DEMIGOD, COMEDIAN

Many Polynesian legends feature the demigod Maui – a trickster, fool, hero, Polynesian Prometheus and first-rate fisherman. Each island has its variations on the traditional tales but Maui's contributions to humanity included stealing fire from the gods, slowing the path of the sun and creating the first dog. One of his major appeals to Polynesian society seems to be the use of trickery to defeat force. No Hollywood-style hero, Maui is fondly remembered as being particularly ugly.

several different denominations, including Anglican, Catholic, Mormon and Jehovah's Witness.

Traditional beliefs were incorporated but, overall, Christianity has come to dominate spiritual life in the South Pacific. The popularity of church singing in both Micronesia and Polynesia is testament to the missionaries' early efforts and a visit to church to hear it is not to be missed, no matter what your beliefs. Only Fiji, with its large Hindu and Muslim Indo-Fijian population, has significant numbers of non-Christians, though there is some tension between the two groups (see p139).

Island Life

Pacific island life is slow and graceful and it's hard not to follow suit. Every moment seems to be marked – whether by the hint of flowers in the air or by the last second of orange sun before it disappears below the horizon. The cultures that have evolved in this balmy, plentiful region are diverse, but they all share a happy, seafaring spirit. Expect locals in floral fabrics, nights of singing and big meals of fresh fish.

Youngsters bedecked in tropical blooms for Independence Day, Fiji

TOM COCKREM / LONELY PLANET IMAGES ©

People, History & Culture

Over 1700 years before the Vikings, Chinese merchants or European explorers had the technology to travel over great distances of ocean, Polynesian and Melanesian ancestors reached the South Pacific in their sailing canoes. Over the next several hundred years they populated island groups spanning a stretch of over 10,000km, using navigational and boat building savvy and, one can presume, an uncommon amount of determination and courage.

Within each island group, different cultures evolved. Complex hierarchical social systems kept order and life revolved around strong spirituality and ceremony. Most islands were made up of a collection of villages independently run by their own chief and priests – it wasn't until Europeans arrived with their advanced weapons that most 'kings' and 'queens' were able to take over and rule entire islands. In many nations, these rulers eventually abdicated power to their colonisers.

Today, many Pacific island nations have independence or are working towards it. Christianity has mostly replaced the old beliefs but it's practised with similar, heartfelt devotion of the old religion of times past. Beautiful harmonies emanate from churches on Sunday, dress for the most part is conservative and in some countries it's even illegal to fish on the day of the Lord.

Clockwise from top left
1 Attending church on White Sunday, 'Upolu, Samoa
2 Woodcarvings in the jungle, Vanuatu 3 Rarotongan man playing nose flute, Cook Islands

Music & Art

Pacific islanders cherish their fun. Despite the cultural restrictions early missionaries enforced on 'lewd' dancing, tattooing or even singing, none of these activities were ever entirely squelched and today many art forms are making a comeback.

Nights of ukulele music are the norm from local parties to resort dining rooms; Polynesians in particular are reviving their intricate, stunning tattoo designs; and get any Pacific islander on the dance floor and you're likely to see moves that would make 19th-century evangelists turn in their graves. Big dance shows from the soft sway of Fiji to the high-speed hip blur of French Polynesia are as much a part of cultural revival as they are a way to keep tourists entertained.

While performing arts are evolving and flourishing with the times, other crafts such as tapa (cloth made from tree bark) are becoming less and less common due to the work these types of products take to produce and the availability of substitutes, such as imported fabrics. Shell necklaces are still prized but decline in shell populations make them more difficult to make and not sustainable – some shell necklaces you see today may be made in the Philippines.

Fortunately other arts like wood carving and woven hats and mats are still in demand and the finest ones, that take uncountable hours to create, bare a merited hefty price tag.

Clockwise from top left

1 Making *siapo* (bark cloth) on Savai'i, Samoa 2 A Malaita Islander playing bamboo panpipes, Solomon Islands 3 Welcoming ceremony dance on Tanna island, Vanuatu

Food & Drink

Bring an empty stomach because Pacific islanders love nothing more than to fill you up with their hearty, bone-building cuisine of fish, pork, taro, cassava and plenty of fresh fruit. And what makes this all better than a heavy topping of coconut cream?

Alongside traditional favourites you'll find fiery curries in Indian-influenced Fiji, béchamel in the French territories of New Caledonia and French Polynesia or modern New Zealand flair in the Cook Islands; nearly everywhere you'll find Chinese food from chow mein to lemon chicken.

Down all these delicacies with quaffable regional blond beers like Samoa's Vailima, Tahiti's Hinano or Fiji's Fiji Bitter, or go for a cocktail (try a Mai Tai) made from local rum. Fresh juices can be hard to find but when you do they will probably be made from outrageously sweet pineapples or perhaps refreshing green-skinned oranges, and of course the best drink around is the electrolyte-filled, thirst-quenching water inside a coconut.

In many islands in the Eastern regions you'll surely be offered kava, a muddy, slightly bitter, narcotic beverage that will mellow you out even more than the pace of life. Kava plays a very important ceremonial role so take a small courteous sip even if you don't like it. In most cases it will be acceptable to pass on a second bowl. The experience of sitting with locals, passing around a half coconut shell filled with kava and the accompanying protocol, be it clapping or spilling a bit for the spirits, makes trying the drink a must.

Right
1 A French Polynesian dish of raw fish and coconut milk
2 Fijian men preparing a traditional kava drink

Art & Influence

The Arts

Dance

Dance was extremely important to Polynesian and Melanesian culture in ancient times. After being condemned by Christian leaders for over a century it's now making a comeback, sometimes with a modern twist.

Siva, the traditional Samoan dance, has a Hawaiian feel with slow hand movements that often relate a narrative. Fijian *meke* are melodic oral histories of battles, appointments of chiefs or gossip that use spears and fans as props. In the Cook Islands the rhythmic *hura* dance resembles the Hawaiian hula. The fast hip movements of *oro tahiti* (Tahitian dance) make it the most seductive dance of the Pacific and shows involve lavish costumes, live percussion orchestras and troupes of up to hundreds of dancers.

Music

Diversity is the byword for Pacific music, with enough variety to dispel any stereotyped grass-skirt preconceptions you might have had. Group dancing is a part of many rituals across the islands, and with the arrival of Christianity, church singing became popular.

Contemporary music often draws on traditional sound, as you can hear in the tunes of acoustic guitar groups and those that fuse traditional with pop sounds. But increasingly islanders are nodding their heads to reggae or tuning into hip hop. The New Zealand music scene has benefited from Pacific migration to such a degree that New Zealand-based band Nesian Mystik coined the term *Polysaturated* for an album title that could describe New Zealand's recording industry. Internationally, Samoans have inspired local rappers. Small production studios are appearing in the Pacific enabling recording by local groups and creating a burgeoning gangsta scene in Suva.

Tapa

No art form is as characteristic of the Pacific as the beating of mulberry bark to create tapa cloth. Whether it's called *siapo* in Samoa, *mahute* on Easter Island or *masi* in Fiji, this is much more than an everyday fabric. Fijian *masi* is essential to almost every stage of life: newborn babies are swaddled in it, coffins are covered with it and brides' mothers covet top pieces for their girls' wedding garb. In Tahiti it was made in huge sheets 3m wide and hundreds of metres in length, and signified the power of a chief.

Bark was stripped from mulberry (or sometimes breadfruit) trees then beaten into sheets on a specialised anvil. The thin sheets were then glued together using a substance such as manioc root.

Traditionally, the real value of tapa was based on the ritual surrounding its creation and the community that produced it. It was made exclusively

South Pacific Playlist

» **Jonah Lomu** Tyson (Cook Islands)

» **Tama'i** Matato'a (Easter Island)

» **I Love the Islands** Savage (Samoa)

» **Paradisia** Fenua (Tahiti)

» **Soamako** Mala'e Fenua (Futuna)

» **Mane Paina** Narasirato (Solomon Islands)

» **Nesian Style** Nesian Mystik (Pacific Islands/ New Zealand)

FILM

by women in a communal ritual that revealed the strength of a tribe. When given to another tribal group it placed the group in debt to the giver, and the receiver would have to honour this debt.

With the arrival of calico and accompanying European values, the making of tapa declined. Tapa's legacy remains on several islands, though it is not made in the quantities it once was.

Tattoos

Go to www.ica. pf (Institut de la Comminication Audiovisuelle, in French) for pod-casts and videos of everything cultural in French Polynesia. Down-load or buy old films, and watch music videos, Tahitian news, clips of Tahitian dance and more.

Pacific islanders of both sexes were tattooed to mark the onset of puberty and arrival into adulthood, and later to signify status within their tribal groups.

The most outrageous were seen on Marquesan warriors who 'wore' a full-body armour of tattoos, including on their eyelids and tongues. In Tahiti, Samoan and Tongan tattoos were elaborate designs worn on the buttocks and hips; the natural pigments were pounded into the skin with shell or bone tools. In Melanesia, scarring of the body was a popular alternative to tattooing, although tattoos also bestowed status.

While tattoos became popular with passing European seamen in the 19th century, Christian missionaries discouraged or forbade tattooing; Fijian tattooing (with its strong links to sexuality) became virtually extinct.

Samoan *tofuga* (tattooists) remain strongly traditional (see the boxed text, p307). The tattoo revival has seen full arm and leg designs becoming popular and even the full-body patterns are en vogue, particularly among Tahiti's traditional dancers. Tongans' *tatatau* (tattoos) were thought to be almost extinct, until a revival in 2003 by Samoan artist Su'a Sulu'ape Petelo.

Sculpture & Carving

Adorning the World: Art of the Marquesas Islands, published by the Metropoli-tan Museum of Art, is a gorgeous coffee-table book exploring Marquesan art from collections around the world.

Whether in wood, stone, coral or bone, distinctive sculpture is found across the Pacific. Canoes were the most common source of inspiration; a prow's stylised bow could reveal an arrival's spiritual beliefs before they reached land. On war canoes the depiction of gods of battle and death would have explicitly declared the visitor's intentions. Other objects, such as bailers and paddles, were inlaid with symbolic motifs to bring protection or prosperity in fishing or conflict.

Objects of war were also crafted with considerable aesthetic skill. Marquesan *u'u* (war clubs) are prized by collectors for the fine-relief images of war gods carved into the hardwood. In Polynesia, woven or wooden shields often depicted protection deities.

Masks and headgear from around the region were not meant to be worn but to be destroyed in funeral pyres or preserved for hundreds of years and used in ongoing rituals. Other effigies and masks were built for long-dead ancestors to inhabit and watch over the clan.

Vanuatu was famous for its over-modelling of skulls, with clay, fibres or other materials being added to the bones to create elaborate effigies with eyes, teeth and hair, sometimes including earrings or other ornamentation.

The most recognisable icons of Pacific art are the enormous *moai* of Easter Island (see the boxed text, p54). *Moai* are similar to other eastern Polynesian statues, particularly the large stone *tiki* of the Marquesas and Tuamotu Islands.

Most wooden sculptures of the Pacific were either burnt by mission-aries as idols or looted by souvenir-hunting Europeans. Many of the Pacific's most impressive artworks are in North American or European museums, such as the Marquesas collection at New York's Museum of Metropolitan Art or the pan-Pacific holdings of the British Museum.

Architecture

Traditional architecture throughout the Pacific was constructed knowing it would have to be rebuilt after storms or war. Samoan *fale* (houses) are designed without walls, but with woven blinds that can be lowered for harsher weather, while Fijian *bure* have walls and roofs of reeds or woven palms. Modern building materials are used today, with only large ceremonial buildings or hotels being constructed in the traditional fashion.

In Polynesia the *marae* (or *malae*) was the village meeting point. In western Polynesia, *marae* were village greens, possibly walled off with matting, while in the east they became elaborate structures. In Easter Island, the Societies, Australs and Marquesas *marae* were impressive open-air, paved temples with altars, carved-stone seating, platforms and walls, though only ruins and petroglyphs remain today.

Men's houses are still widespread throughout Melanesia and are often a village's dominant building. With intricate carvings, towering facades and detailed interiors, they're made with complex joinery not using a single nail or screw. Throughout Melanesia secret councils of men still convene in these houses.

In terms of modern architecture a highlight is undeniably New Caledonia's Tjibaou Culture Centre in Noumea, which draws on traditional village architecture and mythology. Elsewhere in the Pacific you can see the vestiges of colonial architecture, including at Levuka on Ovalau in Fiji or Nuku'alofa's Royal Palace in Tonga.

Survivor in the South Pacific

» *Survivor Marquesas* (2002)
» *Survivor Vanuatu* (2004)
» *Survivor Cook Islands* (2006)
» *Survivor Fiji* (2007)
» *Survivor Samoa* (2009 & 2011)

Cinema & TV

Film-makers have long been drawn to the locations of the Pacific, though many films only superficially explore its culture. Hollywood's take on James Michener's novels *Return to Paradise* (1953) and *South Pacific* (1958) have plenty of postcard images, even if the latter was filmed in Hawai'i, Malaysia and, ahem, Spain. The original *Blue Lagoon* (1949) and the Brooke Shields remake (1980) both feature the Yasawa Islands, while

SIA FIGIEL: AUTHOR

Samoan poet and novelist Sia Figiel is the recipient of the Commonwealth Writers Prize for her book *Where We Once Belonged*.

What are your favourite books by South Pacific writers? If I had room in my suitcase for ONE book, *Tales of the Tikongs* (Epeli Hau'ofa) would be it! *Tales* is Epeli's masterpiece. It's a fabulous satirical look at island living that had me laughing hysterically from page one. An absolute must from our most gifted and sagacious storyteller.

Then there's *Sons for the Return Home* (Albert Wendt), the book that made me want to be a writer. Published over 40 years ago, it's an intimate history of Samoans and Pacific people that continues to be relevant today. It's an in-depth look into the Pacific migrant experience and the complexities of love, racism and cultural identity in a new country – then how that identity is changed upon return to the motherland. Compelling and provocative!

Last is *The Shark that Ate the Sun* (John Pule). *The Shark* devours you with its fast-paced rhythm and raw sensuality, and drowns you with its poetic vision. John Pule's memories and imagination are intertwined in a haunting story that flows between Niue and the land of the long white cloud. Illuminating and mesmerising!

And your novels? I wrote the first line to *Where We Once Belonged* on a napkin while travelling between Prague and Berlin. That was almost 20 years ago. It's an intimate look at what our lives were like in Samoa in the '70s. I've only reread the whole thing once, about five years ago, and I was overwhelmed by its understanding of *alofa* – that love really is what glues Samoan and Pacific peoples across this vast ocean.

Tom Hanks was *Cast Away* (2000) on location in Fiji. More recently, *Couples Retreat* (2009) was filmed on location in Bora Bora.

Increasingly documentaries are exploring beneath the postcard veneer and showing the world the real Pacific. Highlighting this welcome genre is the Annual International Oceania Documentary Film Festival (FIFA) held in Pape'ete, which features films made by Pacific islanders.

One of the most successful Pacific islander ventures is the animated TV series by a troupe calling themselves Naked Samoans, *bro'Town,* a politically incorrect look at the life of Samoan boys growing up in South Auckland that ran through five series. Several of the Naked Samoans appear in the feature films *Sione's Wedding* (2006), *Sione's Wedding 2* (2012) and *Children of the Migration* (2004), which have different takes on Pacific islanders in NZ. In the US, Fijian Vilsoni Hereniko shows the real Pacific to Hollywood with his feature *Pear Ta Ma 'on Maf (The Land Has Eyes;* 2005).

But for many visitors the Pacific remains the land of the *Survivor* TV series, with several series made in the region. In the same reality TV vein, Britain's *Meet the Natives* (2007) followed villagers from Tanna in Vanuatu as they journeyed to the UK to meet their idol, Prince Philip.

Legendary Authors in the Pacific

» Herman Melville 1841–1844

» Robert Louis Stevenson 1888–1894

» Jack London 1907–1915

» James A Michener 1944–1946

Literature

The Pacific has a small but lively writing culture. Writers such as the influential Samoan Albert Wendt have found success in NZ and based themselves there. Other Pacific writers were born in NZ but have drawn on their Pacific heritage in their work. Tusiata Avia's first book of poetry, *Wild Dog Under My Skirt,* takes a humorous look at her Samoan roots, while the Samoan novelist Sia Figiel received great praise for her debut title *Where We Once Belonged.* Maori-language publisher Huia (www.huia.co.nz) also publishes islander books, including *Island of Shattered Dreams* by Tahitian Chantal Spitz and the excellent anthology *Niu Voices.*

Hawai'i is another powerhouse of Pacific literature, with small presses like Tin Fish Press (www.tinfishpress.com) publishing and championing Pacific writers.

Of course, Westerners have been scribbling about the Pacific for centuries, from Jack London to Paul Theroux. Robert Louis Stevenson relocated to Samoa, while Herman Melville based his *Typee* on four months' desertion from a whaling boat on the Marquesas Islands.

Coconuts & Kava

The food of the South Pacific is as sturdy, jovial and inviting as the people who cook it. It's fulfilling comfort fare, so don't worry about consuming thousands of extra calories or piling your plate too high – the more you eat, the more the islanders will love you for it.

While staples were once dictated by what the ancient navigating peoples brought in their canoes, each island nation now has a distinctive culinary style, influenced by French, English or US colonisation and the presence of Chinese and Indian labourers. Root tubers, fish and pork now share a plate with pasta, rice and a smorgasbord of canned foods, from corned beef to foie gras.

Staples & Specialities

Starch, meat and fish make up the bulk of the South Pacific diet. Vegetables have never played much of a part in traditional cuisines, although foreign influences have added some colourful touches incorporating a wider variety of ingredients.

Breadfruit

Breadfruit is typically eaten unripe and roasted till charred on an open fire; its flavour is somewhere between a potato and a chestnut. It can also be fried into chips, boiled or baked in the oven. The addition of coconut cream, kneaded into the cooked flesh, makes a sweet, doughy paste that can be eaten as is or wrapped in leaves and baked to create a starchy pudding.

Many traditional cultures fermented breadfruit (and a few still do), both as a preservation technique and to add flavour to an otherwise bland diet (the fermented fruit develops a strong, sour taste).

Taro

There are several varieties of taro, all producing an oblong root tuber that is boiled in water or steamed in a traditional earthen pit oven. It's a firm, starchy, potato-like food that has a slightly gooey exterior when cooked just right. Covered with coconut milk it exudes a hearty, gotta-be-good-for-you quality and makes a satisfying side dish.

The leaves of certain species of taro can also be eaten, usually mixed in savoury stews or eaten with coconut milk. They resemble spinach when cooked, and are the only traditional leafy green in Polynesia.

Coconut

Nothing invokes the flavours of the South Pacific more than the versatile coconut. It's an all-in-one food: meat, sugar, oil and water, all conveniently presented in its own bowl and cup. Each of the nut's four growth stages provides a different form of food or drink. The first stage is ideal for drinking because there's no flesh inside, except for a tasty jelly-like substance. The best eating stage is the second, when the flesh is firm but

Do

» ...try at least one meal cooked in a traditional earthen oven.

» ...wash your hands: you might be eating with your fingers.

Don't

» ...eat turtle. It's endangered and you'll be promoting illegal business.

» ...just dig in. Many people say grace before a meal.

thin and succulent. After this, the flesh becomes thick and hard – ideal for drying into copra. At its fourth stage, the milk inside goes spongy, making what is sometimes known as 'coconut ice cream'.

Fruit

While the Polynesian islands are generally dripping in fresh fruit (think mangoes, papayas, pineapples, giant grapefruit and the world's sweetest bananas), some parts of Melanesia are less well endowed but you will still find tropical fruit as well as avocados and tomatoes. A few varieties of plantains and regular bananas are cooked and served as a side dish, sometimes topped with coconut cream. Most locals source fruit from their own trees or from family and friends, so it can be surprisingly hard to buy local fruit throughout the Pacific. When possible, the best and cheapest places to buy it are at markets and roadside stalls.

A single coconut has about as much protein as 125g of beef. The tasty water inside is sterile and can be used in medical procedures including IVs.

SUPER FOOD

Fish & Meat

Fresh fish and shellfish are found on nearly every restaurant menu and, as a rule, are fabulous. Pigs were traditionally more highly valued than seafood and dog was once eaten but that's now a rare occurrence.

Regional meats include flying foxes (fruit bats) in eastern Polynesia and Melanesia, venison in New Caledonia and goat in the Marquesas Islands. High-quality lamb and beef imported from New Zealand (NZ) is often available, as are low-quality frozen chicken legs from the US.

Canned Influences

Ever-popular canned meat is cheap, easy and tasty – unfortunately, it's also full of fat, nitrites and empty calories. The effect of this and other imports, such as soft drinks and fast food, on the weight and health of native Pacific peoples has been devastating. Heart problems, hypertension and diabetes are rife throughout the region.

Drinks

Nothing is better on a hot South Pacific day than an ice-cold coconut. It's slightly sweet and full of electrolytes. Fresh juices can be difficult to find, and you'll often have to choose a bottle or can that has been imported from somewhere far less appealing. Otherwise go for filtered, boiled or bottled water – stay away from the tap water unless you've been assured by a reliable source that it's OK (see p590).

Coffee is found everywhere, but the further you get from the major towns, the more likely it will be instant coffee.

Kava is the most important drink on many Pacific islands, both for ceremonial and mind-calming reasons.

Kava

The drinking of kava remains a strong social tradition in many Pacific cultures, and is practised throughout almost all of Polynesia and much of Melanesia. As well as a form of welcome, it's used to seal alliances, start chiefly conferences and to commemorate births, deaths and marriages. To decline kava when it is offered is to decline friendship – so even though it may taste disgusting to you, try to gulp it down and appear impressed.

In many countries kava has helped retain ancient customs. Many people attribute a low crime rate to the calming, sedative effects of the drink, which, unlike alcohol, does not produce aggressive behaviour.

Ceremony

In more traditional areas, kava root is prepared by chewing it into a mush and spitting the hard bits onto leaves. Water is added to the mush,

then it's all filtered through coconut fibres. This method produces a more potent brew, as saliva triggers the root's active ingredients. Modern techniques involve pounding the kava root in a bucket, and it can even be prepared from a commercially produced powder.

Kava is served in a coconut-shell cup and the chief and honoured guests usually drink first. Some cultures expect drinkers to down the kava in a single gulp, any remaining liquid being poured onto the ground. In Samoa a small amount is tipped out of the bowl before drinking. Sometimes kava is drunk in silence, but some cultures prefer a great deal of slurping to show appreciation. Your companions will sometimes clap while you drink, but other noises and conversation are generally kept to a minimum.

In some areas, particularly the more touristy ones where customs have become more lenient, both men and women drink kava. In most places, though, it is an exclusively male activity – some say the original kava plant sprang from the loins of a woman, hence the *tapu* (taboo).

Kava makes the drinker's eyes sensitive to glare, so any strong lights, especially flashbulbs, are very intrusive.

Experiential Effects

Kava has a pungent, muddy taste and you'll begin to feel its effects within 10 to 25 minutes. If it's a strong brew, it'll make your lips go numb and cold like you've had a Novocaine injection, then your limbs will get heavy and your speech will slow. If it's really strong, you might get double vision and want to go to sleep. Even from the mildest form of the drink, you will feel slightly sedated and have a general sense of wellbeing. Some islanders claim to have repeated religious experiences after drinking kava.

Medicinal Uses

Broken down, kava is a cocktail of up to 14 analgesics and anaesthetics that work as natural pain and appetite suppressants. The root also has antibacterial, relaxant, diuretic and decongestant properties. Studies showing that kava may help to combat depression, reduce anxiety and even lower blood pressure led to a short-lived kava boom in Western countries during the 1990s. However, other studies have claimed the root could potentially cause liver damage, which has resulted in bans or warnings on kava beyond the South Pacific while research is continuing.

Alcoholic Drinks

The detrimental effects of alcohol, such as domestic violence, have convinced some communities to ban alcohol completely, but in most countries it's freely available. Most nations brew their own beers, and Australian, NZ and US beers are also widely available. There aren't too many happening bars or nightspots on most islands, but at swank hotels and resorts you'll find all the tropical, coconut and pineapple cocktails you could dream of imbibing. The French colonies offer a surprising selection of fine French wines.

Celebrations

Traditionally, celebrations meant feasts prepared in traditional earthen ovens – the size of a feast was a way for chiefs to show off their power and wealth as well as to share it with their people. Today, throughout the Pacific, a celebration still usually means an earthen *umu* (*ahima'a* in French Polynesia, *lovo* in Fiji), but nowadays anyone can throw a party. In general, Christian holidays, birthdays and weddings are the main reasons to celebrate.

Beers of the Pacific
» Hinano (Tahiti)
» Fiji Bitter
» Ikale (Tonga)
» Vailima (Samoa)
» Matutu (Cook Islands)
» Solbrew (Solomon Islands)
» Tusker (Vanuatu)
» Mahina (Easter Island)

WE DARE YOU!

If you've got the guts, give these regional favourites a try:

» **Fafaru** (French Polynesia) Raw fish marinated in rotting-fish-infused seawater; it smells like road kill but the texture is divine.

» **Palolo** (Vanuatu and Samoa) Collected from coral reefs, *palolo* looks like blue worms and is quite salty and served on toast.

» **Sea** (Samoa) This incredibly salty, oyster-like delicacy of sea-slug innards leaves a metallic aftertaste.

Every island has its own method of preparing the feast, but the common theme is that food, ranging from meat and fish to taro and cabbage, is neatly wrapped in leaves or a wet cloth and cooked in a stone-lined, wood-fired pit covered with earth. The flavours and juices mingle for several hours and the resulting meal is steamy, tender and delectable.

In most island groups there are tourist-oriented local feasts of earthen cooked food (called 'Island Nights' in the Cook Islands, *fiafia* in Samoa, *meke* in Fiji, *laplap* in Vanuatu, *ma'a tahiti* in French Polynesia or *bougna* in New Caledonia) that usually involve dance performances and make a great night out.

Where To Eat & Drink

In most cases Pacific islanders don't patronise restaurants, so eating establishments mostly serve the tourist or expat population and are concentrated in highly touristed areas. Bars aren't overly common, although some restaurants double as watering holes.

Restaurants in the French territories can be superb, but they are very expensive. In Fiji there are sumptuous, reasonably priced Indian restaurants and most islands have at least a handful of Western and Chinese places.

Markets are your source of the freshest and cheapest foodstuffs, while shops often rely on canned goods.

Vegetarians & Vegans

Fish, pork and chicken form the basis of most Pacific dishes, so vegetarians will have to either pick through their food or get creative with self-catering. The exception to this is Fiji, which has a large Indian population and great vegetarian options.

Habits & Customs

Ways of eating in the Pacific islands vary according to the fare: Chinese and Japanese food is eaten with chopsticks; you should use your hands when eating traditional Pacific fare and some Indian specialities; and you can finally pick up a knife and fork for Western food. But for the most part, no one will complain if you fork through everything.

While many islanders eat copious breakfasts of fish or meat and rice, breadfruit or taro, visitors in hotels are more likely to encounter light breakfast fare, like breads, coffee and sometimes fruit.

If you are invited to someone's home for dinner or a barbecue, it's not uncommon for the hosts to wait to eat until their guests have finished – so don't be shy, dig in.

Survival Guide

Directory A–Z

This South Pacific Directory covers region-wide information but for country-specific information, see the Directory section for each country chapter. Some subjects are covered in both directories; for example, activities in the region are given in this directory, but specific activities are covered in the country directories. When seeking information, consult both directories and note the cross-references.

Accommodation

For information on accommodation types, see the Which Island? chapter on p26, or for detailed listings and reviews see the individual country chapters.

Business Hours

Most family businesses in the South Pacific have relaxed opening hours – grocery stores may open early in the morning and stay open until late. Banks have more formal opening hours: 9.30am to 3pm Monday to Friday is average, but depending on the country they may close even earlier. Some banks open on Saturday morning, but they're an exception to the rule. In general, businesses and government offices open from 9am to 4pm or 5pm Monday to Friday, but in countries with French ties (New Caledonia and French Polynesia, for example), they get going as early as 7.30am. Many businesses will shut at lunch for an hour (or two in those French-connection countries). For more information on opening hours, see the country chapter directories. We don't list opening hours in this guide unless they differ significantly from the norm.

Dangers & Annoyances

The islands of the Pacific are safer than most countries in the world and the people are some of the friendliest you'll ever meet. But, as with travel to anywhere, it pays to exercise common sense.

Even in the larger cities, assaults and violent crime are uncommon, but they do occur. Be aware when walking around at night and try to stick to well-lit areas where there are others around – avoid situations where you might be vulnerable.

Grazes, coral cuts and even insect bites can quickly become infected in tropical climes. Treat any lesions liberally with antiseptic. Have great respect for the sun and keep yourself hydrated.

Marine Hazards

Many Pacific islands have sheltered lagoons that offer safe swimming and snorkelling, but currents can be strong around passages that empty into the open sea. These are typically near river mouths where a falling tide can cause the swift movement of water out of a lagoon. If there are no other swimmers around, always seek local advice about the conditions before plunging in. Avoid swimming alone.

Stay alert for venomous sea life (see p590) – the lionfish is perhaps the most significant of these because it's mobile (though not aggressive) and has long venomous spines that cause extremely painful wounds. Most other beasties – sea urchins, stonefish and cone shells – sit placidly on the seafloor. The simple rule is look but don't touch – reef shoes (or old runners) can be useful. Stings and bites are extremely rare.

Shark attacks, too, are extremely rare and swimming inside a reef offers protection. Blacktip reef sharks look menacing, can grow to 2m long and sometimes swim in groups (shiver) in shallow waters, but are harmless unless provoked.

Mosquitoes

Malaria exists in western regions of the South Pacific – particularly the Solomons and Vanuatu – but even where mosquitoes don't carry malaria, their bites can cause discomfort and, in some cases, dengue fever (p589). Mosquitoes are less of a problem around the coast where sea breezes keep them away, but inland they can be a pest. For more information see p590.

Theft

Petty crime exists and thefts from hire cars and beach bags do occur. Look after your valuables and keep them out of sight. Particularly guard your passport, papers, tickets and money, in that order. Money belts are a hassle – an ordinary wallet is better for cash – while you should keep your documents and passport with you and remain vigilant about security (stow document photocopies separately, in your luggage). Valuables are normally safe in a locked hotel room if you're heading out for the day, but tuck them out of sight. Many Pacific cultures have relaxed attitudes to property, but it's best not to leave expensive gear lying around. Most hotels have safes or secure places for valuables.

Electricity

The first plug shown is used in French Polynesia, New Caledonia and Easter Island while the second one is used in all the other main countries in this book except American Samoa which uses an American, two square-pronged plug.

240V/50Hz

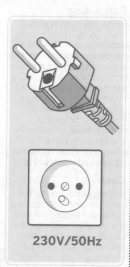

230V/50Hz

Embassies & Consulates

The Directory sections of the individual country chapters list the addresses and contact details of embassies and consulates.

As a visitor you are bound by the laws of the country you're visiting and your embassy is powerless to intervene. So if you've committed a crime in another country, embassy staff will show no sympathy, even where such actions are legal in your home country. The onus is on the visitor to be aware of and adhere to local laws.

However, if you are in a dire emergency you might get some assistance, and if your passport has been stolen, your embassy will help you get a new one. In other genuine emergencies you might get some assistance once all other avenues have been exhausted. A crime committed against you would be a matter for the local police. Stolen money, tickets or valuables are normally covered by insurance and your embassy would (reasonably) expect you to have travel insurance. Your embassy may be able to help you seek assistance elsewhere with local government agencies. But it will normally only evacuate citizens in the event of a major natural disaster, war or sudden civil upheaval, such as a violent coup where all citizens of its country are affected.

Gay & Lesbian Travellers

Attitudes towards homosexuality in the Pacific are multilayered and complex. Due to the conservative influence of the Christian church, homosexuality is on one level regarded as unnatural, and some religious and community leaders can get vociferous in their opposition to it. Yet in Polynesia there are long traditions of male cross-dressing and transgenderism that are usually, though not always, associated with homosexuality – see the boxes on p465 and p422 for more information. Melanesian countries tend to be less tolerant of homosexuality, but this stance has noticeably softened over the last decade or so.

Male homosexuality is technically illegal (although this is rarely enforced) in many Pacific countries, including the Cooks, Fiji, Niue, the Solomon Islands, Tokelau and Tonga. Female homosexuality only gets an official mention in Samoa, where it is also illegal. In the more liberal French colonies of New Caledonia and French Polynesia, homosexuality is legal. Excessive public displays of affection – both heterosexual and homosexual – are frowned upon in most Pacific societies.

Insurance

Travel insurance that covers theft, loss and medical problems is essential. There's a wide variety of policies available, and those handled by

STA Travel and other student travel organisations are usually good value. There's strong competition among travel insurers – most of which have websites where you can take out policies online – so shop around and compare like with like. See the Health chapter (p589) for details on medical insurance.

Some policies exclude 'dangerous activities', which can include scuba diving, motorcycling and even hiking. A locally acquired motorcycle licence is also not valid under some policies. See p587 for details on car and motorcycle insurance.

Internet Access

In theory, there are various ways you can connect to the internet while travelling in the South Pacific. Wi-fi-enabled laptop users will find increasing numbers of wi-fi hot spots in major tourist and urban centres. Prepaid wi-fi is easy to use and inexpensive. Many upper-end hotels offer wi-fi or LAN-based internet access for laptop users (often for free) and have resident computers for others. And with the proliferation of internet cafes, travellers without their own computers are never far from internet access in the main islands at least. Some more remote islands may not have any internet at all while others may surprise you with fast connections.

See the individual country chapters for information about internet access in each country.

Money

The South Pacific has some very exotic-sounding currencies – Vanuatu's vata, Samoa's tala and the Tongan pa'anga. However, some of the countries of the South Pacific use US, Australian or New Zealand dollars, while the Pacific franc (the Cour de Franc Pacifique, or CFP) is legal tender in the French territories of New Caledonia and French Polynesia. The individual country directories have all the practical information you need, including what currencies are used in the country you're visiting.

Exchange rates can fluctuate substantially. As an indication of what to expect we've included the exchange rates that were correct at time of publication in the opening pages of each country chapter. XE (www.xe.com) is a useful website for up-to-date currency exchange rates.

Be aware that using money in foreign countries will cost you, whether that's in fees for buying and cashing travellers cheques, exchanging hard currency, withdrawing money from overseas ATMs or international currency fees charged for overseas credit-card transactions. With internet banking, its much easier to transfer money between accounts while you're away from home.

When taking money overseas it's best not to put all your eggs in one basket; give yourself a few options. A combination of credit and/or debit card, travellers cheques and a stash of cash gives you options to fall back on if an ATM swallows your card or the banks in an area are closed.

ATMs & Credit Cards

Withdrawing cash against your home bank or credit account from Cirrus, Maestro and Visa-enabled ATMs is the easiest way of getting money in South Pacific countries.

Credit cards allow you to pay for expensive items (eg airline tickets) without carrying lots of cash, and you get the best exchange rate (often lower than the advertised rate) on transactions. They also allow you to withdraw cash at selected banks and from the many ATMs that are linked internationally. However, if an ATM swallows a card that was issued outside the Pacific, it can be a major headache. Most major credit cards can withdraw cash from Cirrus, Maestro and Visa-enabled ATMs, but it's always prudent to check with your bank. ATMs are common in major Pacific centres, but are unknown in outer islands and rural areas.

Cash cards can be used in the South Pacific at ATMs linked to international networks.

Charge cards, such as American Express (Amex), have offices in many countries that will replace a lost card within 24 hours. However, Amex offices in this part of the Pacific are limited to Australia, French Polynesia, New Caledonia and NZ. Charge cards are not widely accepted off the beaten track.

Be warned: fraudulent shopkeepers have been known to quickly make several imprints of your credit card when you're not looking, and then copy your signature from the one that you authorise. Try not to let your card out of sight, and always check your statements upon your return.

Bargaining

Bargaining is not practised in any South Pacific country and it may also offend. While it is becoming more common in tourist shops and markets in major cities, village people will take their goods home rather than accept a lower price than what's asked. Protracted haggling is considered extremely rude. The one exception is Fiji where Indo-Fijians expect to bargain and will initiate it.

Cash

Nothing beats cash for convenience...or risk. If you lose it, it's gone forever and very few travel insurers will come to your rescue. Those that will compensate you limit the amount to somewhere around US$300.

For tips on carrying your money safely, see Theft (p577).

Moneychangers

Fees, commissions and buy/ sell exchange rates mean that every time you change money, you lose. If you're travelling to three South Pacific countries, buy all three currencies before you leave home rather than changing one for another. Even big-city bank branches in your home country may not hold cash in the Pacific currency you're after but can usually order it in for you. Banks and moneychangers in major gateway cities, such as Auckland, Brisbane, LA and Honolulu, are more likely to have obscure Pacific currencies.

The Cook Islands dollar is now discontinued since the country switched to New Zealand dollars (although you may end up with a few strays) and it's the only currency that cannot be changed outside the country. All other Pacific currencies are fully convertible, but you may have trouble exchanging some of the lesser-known ones at small banks. Currencies of countries with high inflation have poor exchange rates. To redeem anything like its face value, it is best to get rid of any cash in Pacific currencies before you leave the region.

Most airports and big hotels have banking facilities that are open outside normal office hours, and sometimes ATMs on a 24-hour basis. However, hotels are almost always the worst places for exchanging money. The best exchange rates are offered at banks. Exchange bureaus generally offer worse rates or charge higher commissions. American Express and Thomas Cook usually don't charge a commission for changing their own travellers cheques, but may offer a less favourable rate than banks.

Tipping

Attitudes to tipping vary in the Pacific but, in general, tipping is not expected. In Polynesian countries leaving a tip is fine if you feel so disposed; however, in Melanesian countries the issue is more complicated. In traditional Melanesian societies, a gift places obligation on the receiver to reciprocate somehow, and this can cause confusion and embarrassment when you're just trying to say thanks to the lady who cleans your hotel room – particularly if you're about to leave. You can always ask if unsure.

Travellers Cheques

The only reason for carrying travellers cheques rather than cash is the security they offer from loss and theft, but they're losing popularity as more travellers withdraw money from ATMs. American Express and Thomas Cook travellers cheques are accepted at banks but less frequently elsewhere and have efficient replacement policies. American Express has the greatest chance of being accepted.

Ask about fees and commissions as well as the exchange rate when you change cheques. There may be a per-cheque service fee, a flat transaction fee or a fee charged as a percentage of the total transaction. Some banks charge fees (often exorbitant) to change cheques and not cash. Others do the reverse. Since some banks and moneychangers charge a per-cheque fee, get your cheques in large denominations.

Keep a record of cheque numbers – without these, replacing lost cheques will be a slow process.

Value-Added Tax

Value-added tax (VAT), known as TVA (taxe sur la valeur ajoutée) in French-speaking countries, is levied in some Pacific nations such as French Polynesia, New Caledonia, the Cook Islands and Fiji. It's added to the price of goods and services, including hotel and restaurant bills, and is usually included in the prices quoted. Throughout this guide, all prices include VAT unless otherwise stated.

Post

Postage costs vary from country to country, as does post office efficiency: the 'slowest post' award must go to Pitcairn Island – expect three months for letters either way. Wonderful, colourful stamps are usually available.

Major post offices still provide poste-restante services. Ask people writing to you to print your name, underline your surname and mark the envelope 'Poste Restante (General Delivery)' with the name of the city and country. Your passport may be required for identification when collecting mail and a fee may be charged. Check under your first name as well as your surname. Post offices usually hold letters for a month.

If you're arriving by yacht, letters should have the name of the vessel included somewhere in the address. Mail is normally filed under the name of the vessel, rather than by surname.

Public Holidays

Most Western holidays are observed in South Pacific islands. Month by Month (p19) shows the main festivals and events in the region. The following is a list of some standard public holidays:

New Year's Day 1 January
Easter March/April
Labour Day 1 May
Whit Sunday & Monday May/June (Pentecost)
US Independence Day 4 July

Bastille Day 14 July
Assumption Day 15 August
All Saints' Day 1 November
Veterans' (Armistice) Day
11 November
Christmas Day
25 December
Boxing Day 26 December

Telephone

Mobile Phones

Your mobile telephone carrier may have global-roaming agreements with local providers in the South Pacific, but the costs of calling home can be staggering. Mobile coverage in some South Pacific countries is limited to major urban areas although it's rapidly expanding. See the individual country chapters for more information on how you can get mobile phone coverage.

Phone Cards

Public telephones can be rare in Pacific countries, but it's usually not hard to find a shop owner who will let you use their phone for a local call. Some top-end hotels charge steeply for the privilege of using their phones. Phonecards are used in various Pacific countries – even Pitcairn Island, with just one public telephone, has its own phonecards. Refer to the directories in individual country chapters for details.

Phone Codes

For international calls, you can dial directly from most countries in the South Pacific to almost anywhere in the world. This is usually cheaper than going through the operator. To call abroad, simply dial the international access code (IAC) for the country you are calling from (most commonly ✆00 in the Pacific, but 05 in Fiji and 19 in Wallis and Futuna), then the international telephone code (ITC) for the country you are calling (see the opening pages in each country chapter), the local area code (if there is one, and usually dropping the leading zero if there is one) and finally the number. If, for example, you are in the Cook Islands (IAC ✆00) and you want to make a call to the USA (ITC ✆1), San Francisco (area code ✆212), number ✆123 4567, then you dial ✆00-1-212-123 4567. To call from Fiji (IAC ✆05) to Australia (ITC ✆61), Sydney (area code ✆02), number ✆1234 5678, then you dial ✆05-61-2-1234 5678 (dropping the zero from Sydney's area code). There are no area codes in countries of the South Pacific.

Other country codes include: Australia ✆61, Canada ✆1, France ✆33, Germany ✆49, Hong Kong ✆852, Indonesia ✆62, Japan ✆81, Malaysia ✆60, New Zealand ✆64, Papua New Guinea ✆675, Singapore ✆65, South Africa ✆27, UK ✆44, USA ✆1.

Time

Local time relative to Greenwich Mean Time (GMT, which is the same as Coordinated Universal Time – UTC) is specified in each of the country chapters. Most South Pacific islands don't use daylight savings time, except for Vanuatu and Pitcairn Island in summer. Check your airline tickets and itinerary carefully if a country on your route is starting or finishing daylight saving.

The International Date Line splits the region in half and makes time zones complicated – flying east across the International Date Line will have you arriving at your destination before you left. Crossing from east to west, you will lose a day. The International Date Line runs along the 180-degree longitude, detouring 800km to the east around Fiji and Tonga, and 3600km to the east to accommodate all of Kiribati in one day.

At Noon in Fiji:

COUNTRY	TIME
American Samoa, Niue	1pm, previous day
Cook Islands, Society Islands, Tahiti, Tokelau, Honolulu	2pm, previous day
Marquesas Islands	2.30pm, previous day
Gambier Archipelago	3pm, previous day
Pitcairn Island	3.30pm, previous day
Los Angeles	4pm, previous day
Easter Island	6pm, previous day
New York	7pm, previous day
London	Midnight, same day
Paris, Berlin	1am, same day
Singapore	8am, same day
Tokyo	9am, same day
Sydney	10am, same day
New Caledonia, Solomon Islands, Vanuatu	11am, same day
New, Zealand Tuvalu, Wallis & Futuna	Midday, same day
Samoa, Tonga	1pm, same day

Tourist Information

The quality and quantity of information varies from one country to another, but thanks to the internet, even the most remote islands now have websites (though these may not be up-to-date). See country chapters for details.

The **South Pacific Tourism Organisation** (SPTO; ✆679-330 4177;

www.south-pacific.travel) is an intergovernmental organisation that fosters regional cooperation in developing and promoting tourism. The SPTO serves as a tourist office for a few countries, however, it doesn't offer a lot in the way of services to independent travellers.

Travellers with Disabilities

Pacific countries generally have poor facilities for disabled travellers. Wheelchair users will find getting around a problem since small domestic planes have steps and narrow doors, and ships may not have ramp access. Some larger international resorts offer rooms with disabled access, but it's not common. That said, Pacific cultures look after their elderly, disabled and infirm as integrated members of the community – they have no special schools or aged-care facilities. So islander people won't simply look away if you need to get into a taxi or up some stairs; they'll call helpers, pitch in and assist people with disabilities.

Get in touch with your national support organisation (preferably the 'travel officer' if there is one) to enquire about the countries you plan to visit.

Visas

More often than not in the Pacific, you will get a visa or tourist permit at the airport or seaport on arrival, but not always. See the individual country chapters for details. It's worth checking with the embassies or consulates of the countries you plan to visit before travelling, as visa requirements can change.

With a valid passport from most Western countries, you can visit most Pacific countries for up to three months, provided you have an onward or return ticket and sufficient means of support.

Volunteering

Volunteering is a great way to get to know a country and have an adventure while doing something worthwhile. Many volunteers find their work profoundly rewarding, and there's a strong movement among travellers towards making a contribution to the countries they visit. There are all sorts of volunteering organisations, some requiring long-term commitments and experience or tertiary qualifications in specific fields and others based around the notion of short-term working holidays and community projects.

Lonely Planet's **volunteering website** (www.lonelyplanet.com/volunteer/index.cfm) has excellent resources for those interested in making a contribution to the South Pacific or elsewhere.

Volunteer organisations active in the Pacific region include the following:

Australian Volunteers International (☎03-9279 1788; www.australianvolunteers.com; Australia)

Global Volunteers (☎1 800 487 1074; www.globalvolunteers.org; USA)

Madventurer (☎0845 121 1996; www.madventurer.com; UK)

Projects Abroad (☎21 674 4449; www.projects-abroad.org; South Africa) With offices worldwide.

South Pacific Projects (☎679 869 9744; www.southpacificprojects.org; offices in London & Fiji)

UN Volunteers (☎228-815 20 00; www.unv.org; Germany)

US Peace Corps (☎1 800 424 8580; www.peacecorps.gov; USA)

Voluntary Service Overseas (VSO; ☎020-8780 7200; www.vso.org.uk; UK) There are also offices in Canada, Ireland and the Netherlands.

Volunteer Service Abroad (VSA; ☎04-472 5759; www.vsa.org.nz; New Zealand)

World Wildlife Fund (WWF; ☎Secretariat 22 346 91 11; www.panda.org; Switzerland) With offices worldwide.

Work

Generally it's hard to get a work visa for South Pacific countries. To find out the rules and regulations regarding work in a particular country, contact the relevant embassy, consulate or immigration office, or check their website.

Transport

This chapter has the practical information about travel to and around the island states of the South Pacific. For the detailed nuts and bolts of travelling within Pacific countries, see the Transport section of the individual country chapters. Flights and tours can be booked online at www.lonelyplanet.com/bookings.

GETTING THERE & AWAY

Air

Due to vast expanses of open ocean and the relatively small number of travellers visiting the region, just getting to the South Pacific can be expensive. The main gateways are the US, Australia, New Zealand and Japan, and large international airlines fly routes between these countries that link a number of South Pacific destinations. There are also several smaller local airlines that only service the Pacific region. For airlines that will get you around once you are in the region, see p585.

Airlines

Join the mailing lists of most airlines for last-minute deals on flights that can be very attractive.

Air France (☑in France 08 20 82 08 20; www.airfrance.com) Flies from Paris to New Caledonia via Tokyo and Seoul and to French Polynesia via Los Angeles.

Air New Zealand (☑in NZ 0800 737 000; www.airnz.co.nz) Flies between New Zealand and most Pacific countries.

Air Niugini (☑675-327 3444; www.airniugini.com.pg) Has flights between Port Moresby and Nadi to Honiara.

Air Rarotonga (☑22888; www.airraro.com) Code-share flights on Thursdays with Air Tahiti linking Tahiti with Rarotonga.

Air Tahiti (www.airtahiti.aero) Code-share flights on Thursdays with Air Rarotonga linking Tahiti with Rarotonga.

Air Tahiti Nui (☑689-46 02 02; www.airtahitinui.com) Flies between French Polynesia, the USA, France, Australia, New Zealand and Japan.

Air Vanuatu (☑678-23848; www.airvanuatu.com) Flies to Australia (Brisbane, Melbourne and Sydney), New Zealand, Fiji, New Caledonia and the Solomon Islands.

Aircalin (☑687-26 55 00; www.aircalin.nc) Flies from New Caledonia to Australia, New Zealand, Japan, Indonesia, Singapore, South Korea, Vanuatu, Fiji and French Polynesia. It is the only airline that flies to Wallis and Futuna.

Fiji Airways (☑679-672 0888; www.airpacific.com) Fiji's national carrier, formerly known as Air Pacific, flies between Fiji, Hong Kong, Australia, New Zealand and the US (LA and Honolulu), with connections to New Caledonia, Samoa, Tonga, Vanuatu, Tuvalu and the Solomon Islands.

Hawaiian Airlines (☑in Hawai'i 808-838 3700; www.hawaiianair.com) Connects mainland US cities through Honolulu to American Samoa and Tahiti (French Polynesia).

Japan Airlines (☑in Japan 0120 25 5931; www.jal.co.jp) Flies from Japan to French Polynesia on a code share with Air Tahiti Nui.

Jetstar Airways (www.jetstar.com) Flies between Australia and Fiji.

Korean Air (☑850-2-2667 0386; www.koreanair.com) Flies from South Korea to Fiji.

LAN Chile (☑56-2-526 2000; www.lan.com) Flies between Chile and French Polynesia, with stops at Easter Island.

Our Airline (☑674-444 3746; www.ourairline.com.au) Formerly Air Nauru, flies between Australia, Solomon Islands and Nauru.

Qantas (☑in Australia 13 13 13; www.qantas.com) Code shares with some Pacific airlines, flying from Australia, New Zealand and the US to New Caledonia, Vanuatu, Tahiti (French Polynesia) and Fiji.

Solomon Airlines (☑677-20031; www.flysolomons.com) Connects the Solomons

to PNG, Australia, Fiji and Vanuatu.

United (☑in the US 1 800 538 2929; www.united.com) Flies or code shares with Star Alliance partners from the US and Japan to the Cook Islands, French Polynesia, Fiji and Samoa.

Virgin Australia (☑672 0777; www.virginaustralia. com) Previously Virgin Blue. Flies from Australia and New Zealand to the Cook Islands, Fiji, Tonga, Samoa, Vanuatu, PNG and the Solomons.

Virgin Samoa (☑685-22172; www.virginsamoa.com) Partnership between Virgin Australia and the Samoan government. Flies from Australia and New Zealand to Samoa.

Tickets

South Pacific destinations tend to be relatively expensive to get to, and flying between Pacific islands is costly too. Because transport to and between islands is almost exclusively by plane, you'll need to have it planned up front. Many people come to the Pacific as a stopover on a round-the-world (RTW) ticket, or you might consider an air pass (see p583) that allows stops on several Pacific islands.

Don't automatically discount tours and packages from travel agents that include flights, transfers and accommodation. Agents buy fares and accommodation wholesale and can bundle packages together at very competitive prices. Also

consider specialist dive-tour agencies and other activity-based tours. These packages typically include flights and accommodation, plus activities and tours.

For long-term travel, there are plenty of discount tickets valid for 12 months, allowing multiple stopovers with open dates.

The (return) airfares quoted in this book should be used as a guide only. Airport taxes, surcharges and the like are not included and these can quickly add up to hundreds of dollars. Full-time students and those under 26 with a valid International Student Identity Card (ISIC) may have access to better deals than other travellers – they may not always be cheaper fares but may include more flexibility to change flights or routes.

ROUND-THE-WORLD TICKETS

Various airline alliances offer RTW tickets, which give travellers an almost endless variety of possible airline and destination combinations. RTWs can be excellent value; expect to pay from US$3000, AU$3500, €2000 or UK£1350. **Star Alliance** (www.staralliance.com) – a code-sharing group of airlines that includes Air New Zealand – and **OneWorld** (www.oneworld.com) – a group including Qantas – offer some of the best RTWs for the South Pacific region.

Fiji is the most popular destination for travellers on

RTWs, but Samoa, French Polynesia, Tonga and the Cook Islands can all be visited on these tickets.

CIRCLE PACIFIC TICKETS

Circle Pacific fares are similar to a RTW ticket except that they're used for travel only between Pacific Rim countries – the USA, South Pacific nations, South America, Southeast Asia, New Zealand and Australia. They can be great value if you're combining a Pacific journey with destinations in Australasia and the Americas. As with RTW tickets, there are advance-purchase restrictions, as well as limits on how many stopovers you can make. Fares are based on mileage.

You should expect to pay about US$3700 for a fare that includes Los Angeles–Tahiti (Pape'ete)–Cook Islands (Rarotonga)–Auckland–Brisbane–Singapore–Los Angeles. Air New Zealand and its Star Alliance partners offer these tickets, as does Qantas and the One World affiliates.

AIR PASSES

Inter-country flights in the Pacific can be prohibitively expensive. A good way to travel to a handful of countries is by using an air pass. Seating availability for heavily discounted fares can be quite limited, so book early. Note that most air passes have to be bought well in advance. Air passes come and go with some frequency, so seek

CLIMATE CHANGE & TRAVEL

Every form of transport that relies on carbon-based fuel generates CO_2, the main cause of human-induced climate change. Modern travel is dependent on aeroplanes, which might use fuel per kilometre per person than most cars but travel much greater distances. The altitude at which aircraft emit gases (including CO_2) and particles also contributes to their climate change impact. Many websites offer 'carbon calculators' that allow people to estimate the carbon emissions generated by their journey and, for those who wish to do so, to offset the impact of the greenhouse gases emitted with contributions to portfolios of climate-friendly initiatives throughout the world. Lonely Planet offsets the carbon footprint of all staff and author travel.

up-to-date information from airlines and travel agents.

In addition to air passes offered by airlines and their affiliates, travel agencies and wholesalers can blend air sectors into interesting combinations. **Air Brokers International** (www.airbrokers.com), **World Travellers' Club** (www.around-the-world.com) and **Travelscene** (www.travelscene.com), for example, offer excellent Circle Pacific fares out of the US.

Circle Asia & Southwest Pacific This air pass, sold by One World, allows travel that begins and terminates in Australia, New Zealand and several Asian countries to include one or more stopovers in the southwest Pacific, including Tonga, Vanuatu, Fiji and New Caledonia. Routes must also take in both northeast and Southeast Asia.

Virgin Australia Air Pass These passes (www.virginblueairpass.com) are geared to people travelling to/from Australia and New Zealand and can also include flights to Asia. Internal Australia and New Zealand flights can be included from AU$90 per flight and international legs from AU$199. Flights to Fiji, Tonga, Samoa, Vanuatu, the Solomon Islands and the Cook Islands are eligible but there are no flights between islands, so you'll have to hop back to Australia or New Zealand and this can add up.

Asia

Flying from Japan, there are direct flights to Fiji (Nadi; around ¥115,000 return), French Polynesia (Pape'ete; around ¥195,000 return) and New Caledonia (around ¥169,000). There are also direct flights from South Korea to Fiji (starting from US$1300) and New Caledonia (around ¥62,216). Travellers from other Asian destinations will find it easiest to fly to Australia or New Zealand and connect there with onward flights to the South

Pacific. Most Asian countries offer fairly competitive airfare deals – Bangkok, Singapore and Hong Kong are some of the best places to shop around for discount tickets.

Australasia

Although close to Australia and New Zealand, the South Pacific is still reasonably expensive to get to as there's not a lot of competition on these routes and they're generally flown by small national airlines. There's not much difference between seasonal fares, except during Christmas holidays when fares increase considerably.

Brisbane and Sydney have excellent connecting flights to Melanesia (Solomon Islands, Vanuatu, Fiji and New Caledonia), while Auckland is the main gateway into Polynesia (Cook Islands, Samoa, Tonga and French Polynesia).

Australia's east coast and New Zealand are included in several air pass routes (see p583).

Some Australian travel agents specialise in discount South Pacific air tickets, and some, particularly smaller ones, advertise cheap airfares in the travel sections of weekend newspapers, such as the *Age* (in Melbourne) and the *Sydney Morning Herald*.

Travel agencies that specialise in South Pacific holidays include **Hideaway Holidays** (☎02-8799 2500; www.hideawayholidays.com.au) and **Pacific Holidays** (☎02-9080 1600; www.pacificholidays.com.au).

Return fares from Australia's east-coast capitals to Fiji cost from AU$640/900 in the low/high season, to French Polynesia from AU$1350/2000 and to Vanuatu from AU$555/900.

The *New Zealand Herald* has a travel section in which travel agents advertise fares. Both **Go Holidays** (☎09-914 4700; www.goholidays.co.nz) and **Air New Zealand** (☎0800 737 000; www.airnewzealand.co.nz) offer a range of fares and packages

from New Zealand to most South Pacific destinations.

You can get year-round return fares to Fiji from about NZ$650 and return fares to the Cook Islands from NZ$770. To French Polynesia, return fares start from about NZ$1225.

UK & Europe

There are flights from most major European cities to LA, Honolulu, Sydney and Auckland, from where connecting flights into the South Pacific are frequent. London, Paris and Frankfurt have the most flight options, but there's not much variation in fares between these cities. Flights from Europe via Japan and South Korea are shorter if you're going to the west side of the South Pacific while it's quicker to get to French Polynesia via the US.

The South Pacific is almost exactly on the other side of the globe from Europe, so a RTW ticket (see p583) is probably the most economical way to get into the region.

Discount air travel is big business in London. Advertisements for travel agencies appear in the travel pages of the weekend broadsheet newspapers, as well as *Time Out*, the *Evening Standard* and in the free magazine *TNT*. Recommended travel agencies that offer good South Pacific products include **Trailfinders** (☎0845 058 5858; www.trailfinders.co.uk).

From the UK, flights via LA are generally the easiest and cheapest option for travel to the South Pacific. Air New Zealand or Qantas flights from London to Australia or New Zealand often allow for stopovers in the South Pacific and flights from London via Seoul and Tokyo are another possibility.

Return fares from London to Nadi (Fiji) and Rarotonga (Cook Islands) start from £1050/1400 in the low/high season, and flights to Pape'ete (Tahiti) cost from £1400/1750.

In Germany, **Adventure Travel** (☎0911 979 95 55; www.adventure-holidays.com) and **Art of Travel** (☎089-21 10 76-13; www.artoftravel.de, in German) specialise in South Pacific travel.

In the Netherlands, try **Wereldcontact** (☎0343 530 530; www.wereldcontact.nl) and **Pacific Island Travel** (☎020-626 13 25; www.pacific islandtravel.com) for flight/accommodation deals.

Travel agencies in France that specialise in South Pacific travel include **Ultramarina** (☎08 25 02 98 02; www.ultramarina.com). From Paris and Frankfurt, low-season return fares to Pape'ete (Tahiti) start from €2000, while fares to Noumea (New Caledonia) start from €1450.

North America

LA and Honolulu are the gateway cities for travel to the South Pacific, with direct flights to the Cooks, Fiji, French Polynesia and Samoa. There are also flights to Australia and New Zealand for connections to other Pacific destinations.

In Canada, the *Toronto Globe & Mail, Toronto Star, Montreal Gazette* and *Vancouver Sun* are good places to start looking for cheap fares. **Goway** (☎800 387 8850; www.goway.com) is a Toronto-based travel agency specialising in trips to the South Pacific.

Fares from Vancouver to Nadi (Fiji) start from C$1500/2300 in the low/high season, or C$2000/3000 to Pape'ete (Tahiti). From Toronto and Ottawa, return low season fares to Nadi start from C$2200 and C$2500 to Pape'ete.

In the US, the *Los Angeles Times, New York Times, San Francisco Examiner* and *Chicago Tribune* have weekly travel sections with ads and information on discounted flights. US travel agents who specialise in the South Pacific region include **Travel2** (www.travel2-us.com), **Pacific for Less** (☎808 875 7589; www.pacific-for-less.com) and

South Seas Adventures (☎800 576 7327; www.south -seas-adventures.com).

Low/high season fares start from US$1250/1400 to Pape'ete (Tahiti) and Nadi (Fiji). From New York and other east-coast cities, return low/high season fares start from US$1600/2500 to Pape'ete and US$1500/2000 to Nadi.

South America

LAN (www.lan.com) flies between Santiago (Chile) and Pape'ete (French Polynesia), and one flight a week stops on Easter Island. Return fares (Pape'ete to Easter Island) cost around US$805 and a round trip (Pape'ete to Santiago with a stop in Easter Island) is around US$3300.

Sea

Cruise ships are an expensive way of seeing the South Pacific – they only ever call into major tourist islands and rarely stay longer than a few hours. For details on travelling around the region by cargo vessel or yacht, see Getting Around (p586) and the boxed text on p586.

Tours

It's worth considering the many and various packages offered by travel agents and airlines – these can be off-the-shelf or tailored to your requirements. Tours – that can include flights, airport transfers, accommodation, meals and activities – can be very cost effective. It's quite possible to book a package and extend your stay with independent travel.

GETTING AROUND

Air

Flying in light aircraft is the primary way of getting be-

tween islands – don't expect cabin crew and complimentary meals. These small aircraft often land on grass airstrips on remote islands, where the terminal is a tin shed and a guy with a two-way radio. Some interisland flights might operate just once or twice a week and can be heavily booked, so don't assume you can make travel arrangements on the spot. Details of domestic air travel are given in the Transport section of individual country chapters.

The most cost-effective way of travelling to more than one or two South Pacific nations is by buying an air pass. There are several international and domestic air passes available (see p583) that can make air travel more affordable.

Airlines in the South Pacific

Good places to start planning your adventure are with the local airline websites to see where they fly, schedules and the cost. The following airlines fly between and within South Pacific countries. Check the Transport section of the individual country chapters for schedules, fares and details on domestic airlines.

Air Niugini (www.airniugini.com.pg) Has flights between Port Moresby and Nadi to Honiara.

Air Tahiti (☎689 86 40 23; www.airtahiti.aero) Flies between French Polynesia and the Cook Islands.

Air Vanuatu (☎678-23848; www.airvanuatu.com) Flies from Vanuatu to Fiji, New Caledonia and the Solomon Islands.

Aircalin (☎687-26 55 00; www.aircalin.nc) Flies from New Caledonia to Fiji, French Polynesia, Vanuatu, and Wallis and Futuna.

Fiji Airways (☎679-672 0888; www.airpacific.com) Fiji's national carrier, formerly known as Air Pacific, flies from Fiji, the

Solomon Islands, Samoa, Tonga, Tuvalu and Vanuatu.

Inter-Island Airways (☎684-699 5700; www.inter islandair.com) Flies between American Samoa and Samoa.

Polynesian Airlines (☎685-22172; www.polynesian airlines.com) Flies between Samoa and American Samoa.

Solomon Airlines (☎667-20031; www.solomonairlines. com.au) Flies from the Solomon Islands to Vanuatu and Fiji.

Boat

There are a few possibilities for those romantics taken with the idea of travelling the Pacific by sea. It's certainly much slower than flying and

not necessarily any cheaper. For information about yacht chartering or sailing on a tall ship, see the boxed text.

Cargo Ship & Ferry

If you've got lots of time and don't mind seriously roughing it, check the supply ship schedules. Interisland shipping routes connect many remote islands that are not serviced by aeroplane. Cargo vessels, some of which carry passengers, travel between far-flung island groups and the main trading island of the country they belong to, while other ships carry cargo across international borders.

Cargo and dual-purpose cargo/passenger ships ply between the following countries: Tuvalu and Fiji, Vanuatu and New Caledonia, Samoa and Tokelau, Samoa and the

Cook Islands. There's also a car ferry operating between Samoa and American Samoa. See the Transport section of individual country chapters for detailed information on these services.

Cruise Ship

Cruise-ship fares vary enormously, but generally prices run upwards from US$200 per day. Major ports of call are Noumea (New Caledonia), Port Vila (Vanuatu), Rarotonga (Cook Islands) and Pape'ete, Mo'orea and Bora Bora (all in French Polynesia). Melanesian cruises usually depart from Australia's east coast, mostly from Sydney and Brisbane. Other cruises depart from the US west-coast ports like Seattle, San Francisco, LA or Honolulu.

CREWING ON A YACHT

Yachties are often looking for crew, and for those who'd like a bit of adventure, this can be a great opportunity. Most of the time, crew members will only be asked to take a turn on watch – to scan the horizon for cargo ships, stray containers and the odd reef – and possibly to cook or clean up the boat. In port, crew may be required to dive and scrape the bottom, paint or make repairs. In most cases, sailing experience is not necessary and crew members can learn as they go. Most yachties charge crew around US$20 per day for food and supplies.

If you'd like a crewing berth, try to find a yacht that has wind-vane steering, since the tedious job of standing at the wheel, staring at a compass all day and all night is likely to go to the crew members of the lowest status (that's you). Comfort is also greatly increased on yachts that have a furling jib, a dodger to keep out the weather, a toilet and shower. Yachts rigged for racing are usually more manageable than simple liveaboards. As a general rule, about 3m of length for each person aboard affords relatively uncrowded conditions.

If you're trying to find a berth on someone else's yacht (or trying to find crew for your own boat), ask at local yacht clubs and check noticeboards at marinas and yacht clubs. In the US, Honolulu and the west coast – San Francisco, Newport Beach and San Diego – are the places to start looking. Australia's northeastern seaboard is good and so are Auckland, Whangarei and the Bay of Islands in New Zealand. In the South Pacific, ask around in Pape'ete, Pago Pago, Apia, Nuku'alofa, Noumea or Port Vila. **Latitude 38** (www.latitude38.com) is a great resource for finding boats that need crew.

Some companies that organise sailing trips around the South Pacific are:

» **Ocean Voyages** (www.oceanvoyages.com) Organises yacht charters in the South Pacific. It's possible to charter a whole boat or book a berth on a yacht sailing a particular route. A charter is about the only way to get to some remote islands and atolls if you don't have your own yacht.

» **Tallship Soren Larsen** (www.sorenlarsen.co.nz) This 45m tall ship sails from Auckland to various South Pacific countries between March and November. It's possible to join the crew in Auckland or at any of the ports on its trip. Count on about NZ$260 per day.

Contact travel agents, or the cruise companies themselves, well in advance if you are planning on taking a South Pacific cruise. A few companies include:

Adventure Life (www.adventure-life.com) Specialises in smaller, off the beaten path cruises.

Crystal Cruises (www.crystalcruises.com)

Holland America (www.hollandamerica.com)

P&O (www.pocruises.com)

Princess Cruises (www.princess.com)

ResidenSea (www.residensea.com)

Yacht

The South Pacific is a favourite playground for yachties and many people tour the region aboard their own vessel (or someone else's). Between May and October, the harbours of the South Pacific swarm with cruising yachts from around the world. Almost invariably, yachts follow the favourable westerly winds from the Americas towards Asia, Australia or New Zealand.

Popular routes from the US west coast take in Hawai'i and Palmyra Atoll before following the traditional path through Samoa and American Samoa, Tonga, Fiji and New Zealand. From the Atlantic and Caribbean, yachties access the South Pacific via Panama, the Galápagos Islands, the Marquesas, the Society Islands and the Tuamotus. Possible stops include Suwarrow (northern Cook Islands), Rarotonga and Niue.

The cyclone season begins in November and most yachties try to be well on their way to New Zealand by the early part of that month.

The yachting community is quite friendly and yachties are a good source of information about world weather patterns, navigation and maritime geography. They're also worth approaching to ask about day charters, diving and sailing lessons.

RED TAPE

You must enter a country at an official 'port of entry' (usually the capital). If this means sailing past a dozen beautiful outlying islands on the way to an appointment with an official in a dull capital city, bad luck. Ports of entry are listed in the Transport section of the country chapters.

When you arrive, hoist your yellow quarantine flag (Q flag) and wait for the appropriate local official to contact you. Often, you are expected to alert them by VHF radio (usually on channel 16). Some countries charge visiting yachties entrance fees. Ask customs officials at the port of entry about requirements for visiting other islands in the country. Bear in mind that you are legally responsible for your crew's actions as well as your own.

Local Transport

Bicycle

On flat South Pacific islands, riding a bicycle can be an excellent way to get around. For specific information and bicycle rentals, see the individual country chapters. Most rental bikes won't come with a helmet or lock unless you ask for them. Watch for poor road surfaces, and check your travel insurance for disclaimers about hazardous activities. If you're bringing your own bike, ask the airline about costs and rules regarding dismantling and packing the bike.

Boat

Within a country, ferries and cargo boats are often the only way to get to some outer islands. See individual country chapters for details.

Bus

Large and populous islands usually have some kind of bus service. However, South Pacific public transport is rarely described as ruthlessly efficient. Buses are often privately (or sometimes fam-

ily) owned. It is not unusual for owner-drivers to set their own schedules. If there aren't many people travelling on a particular day, the buses may stop altogether. Build flexibility into your plans.

Car & Motorcycle

Larger islands and tourist destinations will usually have some car- or motorcycle-hire companies – see the individual country chapters for more details.

Driving in some Pacific countries is on the right-hand side of the road, while it's on the left in others. Roads in rural areas may be no more than dirt tracks used mostly for foot traffic. Be careful of people or animals on the road and drive especially carefully near villages. Road conditions can be dreadful in undeveloped areas and worse if there's recent cyclone or flood damage.

When you rent a car, ask about petrol availability if you're heading off the main routes, and make sure you get the insurance rules and conditions explained. Check your own travel insurance policy too; some do not cover unsealed roads or riding a motorcycle.

Prior to travel, check whether you need an International Driving Permit for the countries you're visiting.

Hitching

In some Pacific countries hitching is an accepted way of getting where you're going, and is practised by locals and tourists alike. In others, it's not the local custom and only tourists are seen trying it.

The main difficulty on a Pacific island is that rides won't be very long, perhaps only from one village to the next, and it could take you a while to travel a longer distance. Hitching can be a great way to meet locals and is an option for getting around when the buses aren't running. You might be expected to pay a small fee for a ride, so offer what

you think the ride is worth – although offers of payment will often be refused.

Keep in mind that hitching is never entirely safe. If you do choose to hitch, it is safer to travel in pairs.

Tours

Many travellers now seek activity-based holidays, and several of these types of trips are available as organised tours. Local companies often specialise in activity-based tours – see the Tours sections in the individual country chapters.

Package Tours

The South Pacific lends itself to the package tour. Given the high price of flights to the region, and the often inflated price of accommodation once there, a package tour can work out to be a financial godsend. On the downside, package tours don't give much leeway to explore at will. Although most tours offer the opportunity to visit more than one island, you will have to prebook one hotel or *pension* for each destination before departure (meaning you can't swap resorts halfway through if you're not happy).

There's a variety of tour packages available from travel agents and online booking agencies in all Western countries. If you want more than a straightforward combo package, a good travel agent is essential – they can negotiate better prices at the larger hotels and handle the internal flight bookings. In addition to the traditional tour operators, there are agencies that specialise in diving tours. These packages typically include flights, accommodation and diving tours.

Surf Tours

A few tour operators specialise in surfing holidays in the South Pacific, including **South Pacific Surfing Holidays** (USA 0208 123 8622, in Australia 02 8005 1232; www.surfing-pacific.com) and **World Surfaris** (617 5444 4011; www.worldsurfaris.com).

Where to Book

Plenty of agents book packages to the South Pacific but a good place to search and get a feel for pricing is on the websites of the airlines that service the region (see p582).

Note that most packages quote double-occupancy pricing. Solo travellers have to pay a single-person supplement. Extra people can usually share a room, but there's a charge for the extra bed, which varies enormously from resort to resort.

Health

The health risk to travellers to the Pacific region is low. The Solomon Islands and Vanuatu share the one serious health hazard: malaria. Elsewhere the main danger is from mosquito-borne dengue fever.

BEFORE YOU GO

A little planning before departure, particularly for preexisting illnesses, will save trouble later. A signed and dated letter from your physician describing your medical conditions and medications, including generic names, is a good idea.

Insurance

Make sure that your health insurance has provision for evacuation. Under these circumstances, hospitals will accept direct payment from major international insurers, but for all other health-related costs cash upfront is usually required.

American Travellers Check whether your health plan covers expenses in American Samoa.

EU Travellers You have the same rights in French Polynesia, New Caledonia, and Wallis and Futuna as you do in France, but remember to obtain the European Health Insurance Card (EHIC) before leaving home.

New Zealand Travellers You may have free access to public but not private facilities in the Cook Islands.

Required Vaccinations

For all countries in the region, vaccinations are recommended for hepatitis A, hepatitis B and typhoid fever.

IN THE SOUTH PACIFIC

Availability & Cost of Health Care

In Fiji, French Polynesia and American Samoa there are doctors in private practice, and standard hospital and laboratory facilities with consultants in the major specialities. In the Cook Islands, New Caledonia, Samoa, Solomon Islands, Tonga and Vanuatu specialised services may be limited but private general practitioners, dentists and pharmacies are present. On smaller islands there may be no services at all or perhaps just a nurse. Cost varies between countries but is generally similar to Western prices.

Infectious Diseases

Dengue Fever

Risk All countries, especially in the hotter, wetter months

Symptoms & Treatment Mosquito-borne dengue fever causes a high fever, headache and severe muscle pains. There might also be a fine rash. Self-treatment includes paracetamol (do NOT take aspirin), fluids and rest. Danger signs are prolonged vomiting, blood in the vomit, a blotchy dark red rash and/or bruising.

Eosinophilic Meningitis

Risk Cook Islands, French Polynesia, Fiji, Tonga

Symptoms & Treatment An illness manifested by scattered abnormal skin sensations, fever and sometimes meningitis symptoms (headache, vomiting, confusion, stiffness of the neck and spine). Eosinophilic meningitis is caused by a microscopic parasite – the rat lungworm – that contaminates raw food. There is no proven treatment, but symptoms may require hospitalisation. For prevention, pay strict attention to advice on food and drink.

Leptospirosis

Risk American Samoa, Fiji, French Polynesia, possibly elsewhere

Symptoms & Treatment Also known as Weil's disease, leptospirosis produces fever, headache, jaundice and, later, kidney failure. It's caused by the spirochaete organism found in water contaminated by rat and pig urine. Often confused with dengue fever, this disease is the more

serious of the two. The organism penetrates skin, so swimming in flooded areas is a risk. If diagnosed early, it's cured with penicillin.

Malaria

Risk Solomon Islands (except the outlying atolls and Honiara), Vanuatu (except Port Vila and Futuna, Tongoa, Aneityum and Mystery Islands)

Symptoms & Treatment Both malignant (falciparum) and less threatening but relapsing forms are present. Avoid getting bitten by mosquitoes and take anti-malarial drugs before, during and after risk exposure. No antimalarial is 100% effective and there's no vaccine. The essence of the disease is fever. In a malarial zone it is best to assume that fever is due to malaria unless blood tests rule it out. This applies to up to a few months after leaving the area as well. Malaria is curable if diagnosed early.

Yaws

Risk Solomon Islands
Symptoms & Treatment A bacterial infection that causes multiple skin ulcers. Once thought to have been eliminated, there has been a recent resurgence. Infection is by direct contact. Treatment with penicillin produces a dramatic cure.

DRINKING WATER

To prevent diarrhoea, avoid tap water unless it has been boiled, filtered or chemically disinfected (with iodine tablets), and steer clear of ice. This is a sensible overall precaution, but the municipal water supply in capital cities in the region can be trusted.

Environmental Hazards

Threats to health from animals and insects are rare indeed, but travellers need to be aware of them.

Bites & Stings

Jellyfish Watch out for the whip-like stings of the blue-coloured Indo-Pacific man-of-war. If you see these floating in the water or stranded on the beach, it is wise not to go in the water. The sting is very painful and is best treated with vinegar or ice packs. Do not use alcohol.

Cone Shells Poisonous cone shells abound along shallow coral reefs. Avoid handling them. Stings mainly cause local reactions, but nausea, faintness, palpitations or difficulty in breathing are signs that medical attention is needed.

Sea Snakes As in all tropical waters, sea snakes may be seen around coral reefs. Unprovoked, sea snakes are extremely unlikely to attack and their fangs will not penetrate a wet suit.

Coral Ear

This is a fungal infection caused by water entering the ear canal. Apparently trivial, it can be very, very painful and can spoil a holiday. Apart from diarrhoea it is the most common reason for tourists to consult a doctor. Self-treatment with an antibiotic-plus-steroid eardrop preparation (eg Sofradex, Kenacort Otic) is very effective. Stay out of the water until the pain and itch have gone.

Staph Infection

Infection of cuts and scrapes is very common and cuts from live coral are particularly prone to infection. As soon as you can, cleanse the wound thoroughly (getting out all the little bits of coral or dirt if needed), apply an antiseptic and cover with a dressing. You can get back in the water but healing time will be prolonged if you do. Change the dressing regularly, never let it sit wet and check often for signs of infection.

Diving Hazards

Because the region has wonderful opportunities for scuba diving, it is easy to get overexcited and neglect strict depth and time precautions. See p31 for more information on diving in the region.

Fish Poisoning

Ciguatera poisoning is characterised by stomach upsets, itching, faintness, slow pulse and bizarre inverted sensations – cold feeling hot and vice versa. Ciguatera has been reported in many carnivorous reef fish, including red snapper, barracuda and even smaller reef fish. There is no safe test to determine whether a fish is poisonous or not and, although local knowledge is not entirely reliable, it is reasonable to eat what the locals are eating. Deep-sea tuna is perfectly safe.

Treatment consists of rehydration and if the pulse is very slow, medication may be needed. Healthy adults will make a complete recovery, although disturbed sensation may persist for some weeks – sometimes much longer.

Heat

Sunburn Use sunscreen liberally.

Heat Exhaustion Stay hydrated. Heat exhaustion is a state of dehydration associated to a greater or lesser extent with salt loss.

Heat Stroke More dangerous than heat exhaustion, heat stroke happens when the cooling effect of sweating fails. This condition is characterised by muscle weakness and mental confusion. Skin will be hot and dry. If this occurs, 'put the fire out' by cooling the body with water on the outside and cold drinks for the inside. Seek medical help.

WANT MORE?

For in-depth language information and handy phrases, check out Lonely Planet's *South Pacific Phrasebook* and *Pidgin Phrasebook*. You'll find them at **shop.lonelyplanet.com**, or you can buy Lonely Planet's iPhone phrasebooks at the Apple App Store.

Language

Which Language Where?

Here's an overview of the main languages of the South Pacific and where they are spoken, followed by some handy basics for the ones you're most likely to come across.

American Samoa	Samoan, English
Cook Islands	Rarotongan/Cook Islands Maori, English
Easter Island	Rapa Nui, Spanish
Fiji	Fijian, Fijian Hindi, English
New Caledonia	Kanak languages/Melanesian-Polynesian dialects, French
Rarotonga	Rarotongan, English
Samoa	Samoan, English
Solomon Islands	Solomon Islands Pijin, indigenous languages, English
Tahiti & French Polynesia	Tahitian (and others such as Austral, Marquesan & Tuamotuan), French
Tonga	Tongan, English
Vanuatu	Bislama, indigenous languages, English, French

Other Pacific Islands:

Niue	Niuean, English
Pitcairn Islands	Pitkern, English
Tokelau	Tokelauan, English
Tuvalu	Tuvaluan, Gilbertese, English
Wallis & Futuna	Wallisian, Futunan, French

BISLAMA

Bislama, a form of pidgin English, is Vanuatu's national language. English and French are also widely spoken, and schools teach in French or English. Vanuatu also has the greatest number of local languages per capita in the world, with about 120 still spoken.

Hello.	Alo.
Hello.	Alo olgeta.
Goodbye.	Bae.
See you.	Mi lukem yu.
How are you?	Olsem wanem?
I'm well, thanks.	I gud nomo, tankyu tumas.
Please.	Plis.
Thank you.	Tankyu tumas.
Sorry.	Sore.
Yes./No.	Olraet./No.
Do you speak English?	Yu tok tok Engglis?
I don't understand.	Mi no save.

COOK ISLANDS MAORI

See Rarotongan.

FIJIAN & FIJIAN HINDI

The majority of the local people in Fiji you're likely to come in contact with speak English, and all signs and official forms are also in English. However, indigenous Fijians speak Fijian at home. There are two major groups of Fijian dialects – western and eastern. The form understood throughout the islands is popularly known as *vosa vakabau* (Bauan).

Hello.	Bula.
Goodbye.	Moce.
Please.	Mada.
Thank you.	Vinaka.
Sorry.	Ni vosota sara.
Yes.	Io.
No.	Sega.
Do you speak English?	Oni kilaa na vosa vakavaalagi?
I don't understand.	E sega ni macala.

Indo-Fijians speak Fijian Hindi (also known as Fiji-Hindi or Fiji Hindustani). Note that in Fijian Hindi there are no equivalents for 'please' and 'thank you'. To be polite in making requests, people use the word *thoraa* (a little) and a special form of the verb ending in *-naa*, eg *thoraa nimak denaa* (please pass the salt). For 'thanks', people often just say *achhaa* (good).

Hello. (for Hindus)	Namaste.
Hello. (for Muslims)	Salaam alaykum.
Goodbye.	Fir milegaa.
How are you?	Kaise?
I'm well.	Tik.
Sorry.	Maaf karnaa.
Yes.	Ha.
No.	Nahi.
Do you speak English?	Aap/Tum English boltaa? (pol/inf)
I don't understand.	Ham nahi samajhtaa.

FRENCH

French is the official language in New Caledonia/French Polynesia, where indigenous Kanak (Melanesian-Polynesian) dialects are also spoken. French will also come in handy in Vanuatu and Tahiti, as well as Wallis and Futuna.

Hello.	Bonjour.
Goodbye.	Au revoir.
How are you?	Comment allez-vous?
I'm well, thanks.	Je vais bien, merci.
Please.	S'il vous plaît.
Thank you.	Merci.
Sorry.	Pardon.
Yes.	Oui.
No.	Non.
Do you speak English?	Parlez-vous anglais?
I don't understand.	Je ne comprends pas.

NEW CALEDONIAN

More than 30 indigenous Kanak (Melanesian-Polynesian) dialects are spoken in New Caledonia alongside French. There are 28 distinct Kanak languages (not counting dialects) and all belong to the Melanesian branch of the Austronesian language family, except for Faga Uvea (spoken on Uvea), which is a Polynesian language. The following are the basics for Drehu, the most widely spoken Kanak language (spoken in the Loyalty Islands).

Hello.	Bozu./Talofa.
Goodbye.	Tata./Iahni.
How are you? (only asked by an adult)	Hapeu laï?
I'm well.	Kaloi./Egöcatr.
Do you speak English?	Hapeu nyipë a qene papaale?

RAPA NUI

Spanish is the official language on Easter Island and it will get you by. The indigenous language is Rapa Nui, an eastern Polynesian dialect closely related to the languages of French Polynesia and Hawai'i. These days the language increasingly bears the influence of English and Spanish. Any attempt at a few basic phrases in Rapa Nui will be greatly appreciated by the locals.

The apostrophe (') in written Rapa Nui indicates a glottal stop (like the pause in the middle of 'uh-oh').

Hello.	'Iorana.
Goodbye.	'Iorana.
How are you?	Pehē koe/kōrua? (sg/pl)
I'm well.	Rivariva.
Thank you.	Mauuru.

RAROTONGAN

Rarotongan (or Cook Islands Maori, as it's also known) is a Polynesian language similar to New Zealand Maori and Marquesan (from French Polynesia). There are minor dialectal differences between many of the islands, and some northern islands have their own languages. English is spoken as a second (or third) language by virtually everyone.

In Rarotongan, the glottal stop replaces the 'h' of similar Polynesian languages; for example, the Tahitian word for 'one', *tahi* (pronounced 'ta-hee'), is *ta'i* (pronounced 'ta-ee') in Rarotongan.

Hello.	Kia orana.
Goodbye. (if staying)	'Aere ra.
Goodbye. (if leaving)	'E no'o ra.

How are you?	Pe'ea koe?
Please.	Ine.
Thank you.	Meitaki.
Yes.	Ae.
No.	Kare.

SAMOAN

Samoan is the main language spoken in Samoa and American Samoa, although most people also speak English.

In Samoan, the 's' replaces the 'h' of many other Polynesian languages, 'l' replaces 'r', and a glottal stop replaces 'k'. Therefore, the Tahitian word for 'one', *tahi*, is *tasi* in Samoan, *rua* (two) is *lua*, and *ika* (Rarotongan for 'fish') is *i'a*. The soft 'ng' sound in Samoan is written as a 'g' (*palagi*, for example, is pronounced 'pah-lah-ngee').

Hello.	Tālofa.
Goodbye.	Tōfā soifua.
How are you?	'O ā mai 'oe?
I'm well, thanks.	Manuia lava, fa'afetai.
Please.	Fa'amolemole.
Thank you.	Fa'afetai.
Yes.	Ioe.
No.	Leai.

SOLOMON ISLANDS PIJIN

Officially, there are 67 indigenous languages and about 30 dialects in the Solomon Islands, so people from different villages often speak mutually incomprehensible languages. As a result, the national language is Solomon Islands Pijin, or Pijin for short. Educated people generally also speak English, which is the official language of the administration.

Hello.	Halo.
Goodbye.	Bae-bae.
How are you?	Oraet nomoa?
I'm well.	Oraet nomoa.
Please.	Plis.
Thank you.	Tanggio tumas.
Yes.	Ia.
No.	Nomoa.

SPANISH

Spanish is the official language on Easter Island. The indigenous population also speaks Rapa Nui.

Hello.	Hola.
Goodbye.	Adiós.

How are you?	¿Cómo está? (pol)
	¿Cómo estás? (inf)
I'm well, thanks.	Bien, gracias.
Please.	Por favor.
Thank you.	Gracias.
Sorry.	Perdón.
Yes./No.	Sí./No.
Do you speak English?	¿Habla inglés? (pol)
	¿Hablas inglés? (inf)
I don't understand.	No entiendo.

TAHITIAN (REO MAOHI)

The official languages of French Polynesia are French and Tahitian. Other languages on the islands include Austral, Marquesan and Tuamotuan, and much of the tourist industry uses English. If you venture to the more remote and less touristy islands, it's useful to know some French. On all islands, at least trying a few words in French – and even more so, Tahitian – will be appreciated.

Tahitian, also known as Reo Maohi, is a Polynesian language very similar to Hawaiian and Cook Islands Maori.

In Tahitian, a glottal stop replaces the consonants 'k' and 'ng' – for example, the Polynesian word *vaka* (canoe) is *va'a* in Tahitian.

Hello.	Ia ora na, nana.
Goodbye.	Pārahi, nana.
How are you?	E aha te huru?
Thank you.	Māuruuru roa.
Sorry.	E'e, aue ho'i e.
Yes.	E, 'oia.
No.	Aita.
I don't understand.	Aita i ta'a ia'u.

TONGAN

Tongan is a Polynesian language. It is the official language of Tonga, along with English, and the language most often used in everyday communication.

Note that the glottal stop is represented by an apostrophe (').

Hello.	Malo e lelei.
Goodbye. (if staying)	'Alu a.
Goodbye. (if leaving)	Nofo ā.
How are you?	Fefe hake?
I'm well, thanks.	Sai pe, malo.
Please.	Faka molemole.
Thank you.	Malo.
Yes.	'Io.
No.	Ikai.

GLOSSARY

'aiga – extended family (Samoa)

'ava – see *kava* (Samoa)

ahima'a – earth/stone oven

ahu – raised altar on ancient *marae* (Polynesia)

aitu – spirit (Polynesia)

ali'i – see *ariki*

ari'i – see *ariki*

ariki – paramount chief; members of a noble family

atoll – low-lying island built up from deposits of coral

aualuma – society of unmarried women (western Polynesia)

aumaga – society of untitled men who do most fishing and farming (Polynesia)

Austronesians – people or languages from Indonesia, Malaysia and the Pacific

barrier reef – a long, narrow coral reef that is separated from the land by a deep lagoon and shelters the land from the sea

bêche-de-mer – lethargic, bottom-dwelling sea creature; sea cucumber

bigman – chief (Solomons, Vanuatu)

bilibili – bamboo raft (Fiji)

blackbirding – a 19th-century recruitment scheme little removed from slavery

bougna – *Kanak* meal of root vegetables and coconut milk with chicken, fish or seafood, wrapped in banana leaves and cooked in an earth oven (New Caledonia)

bula – Fijian greeting

burao – wild hibiscus tree

bure – thatch dwelling (Fiji)

cagou – New Caledonia's national bird

Caldoche – white people born in New Caledonia with ancestral ties to the convicts or early French settlers

cargo cults – religious movements whose followers hope for the delivery of vast quantities of modern wealth (cargo) from supernatural forces or faraway countries

case – traditional *Kanak* house (New Caledonia); see also *grande case*

CFP – Cour de franc Pacifique (Pacific franc)

dalo – see *taro* (Fiji)

'ei – necklace (Cook Islands)

fa'a – see *faka*

fa'afafine – see *fakaleiti* (Samoa)

fafine – see *vahine*

faka – according to (a culture's) customs and tradition, eg *fa'a Samoa* or *faka Pasifika*

fakaleiti – man who dresses and lives as a woman (Tonga)

fale – house with thatched roof and open sides; often used to mean any building

fale fono – meeting house, hall or parliament building

fare – see *fale*

fatele – music and dance performance (Tuvalu)

fenua – land

fiafia – dance performance (Samoa)

fono – governing council (Polynesian)

gîte – group of bungalows used for tourist accommodation (French territories)

grade-taking – process by which Melanesian men progress through castes, proving worth through feasts and gifts; see *nimangki*

grande case – big house where chiefs meet; see *case*

heilala – Tonga's national flower

honu – turtle (French Polynesia)

hôtel de ville – see *mairie*

i'a – see *ika*

ika – fish

kai – food

Kanak – indigenous New Caledonians

kastom – custom; rules relating to traditional beliefs (Solomons, Vanuatu)

kastom ownership – traditional ownership of land, objects or reef

kava – mud-coloured, mildly intoxicating drink made from the roots of the *Piper methysticum* plant

kikau – thatch-roofed

kilikiti – see *kirikiti*

kirikiti – cricket with many players on each side (French Polynesia, Samoa)

koutu – ancient open-air royal courtyard (Cook Islands)

kumara – sweet potato

la coutume – custom (New Caledonia); see *kastom*

Lapita – ancestors of the Polynesians

laplap – Vanuatu national dish

lava-lava – sarong-type garment; wide piece of cloth worn as a skirt

lei – see *'ei*

LMS – London Missionary Society

lovo – traditional feast (Fiji)

mahu – see *fakaleiti* (French Polynesia)

maire – aromatic leaf (Cook Islands)

mairie – town hall (French Polynesia, New Caledonia)

makatea – a raised coral island; coral coastal plain around an island

mal mal – *T-piece* of cotton or *tapa* cloth worn by male dancers (Vanuatu)

malae – see *marae*

malo – Polynesian greeting

man blong majik/posen – sorcerers

mana – spiritual power

maneapa – community meeting house (Tuvalu)

manu – birds
Maohi – see *Maori*
Maori – indigenous people (Cook Islands, Society Islands)
marae – community village green (western Polynesia); pre-Christian sacred site (eastern Polynesia); ceremonial meeting ground (Cook Islands)
masi – bark cloth with designs in black and rust (Fiji)
matai – senior male, political representative of a family (Samoa, Tokelau and Tuvalu)
mataiapo – see *matai* (Cook Islands)
me'ae – see *marae*
meke – dance performance enacting stories (Fiji)
Melanesia – the western Pacific: Papua New Guinea, Solomons, Vanuatu, New Caledonia and Fiji; the name is Greek for 'black islands'
Métro – someone from France (New Caledonia)
Micronesia – the northwestern Pacific: Palau, Northern Mariana Islands, Guam, FSM, Marshall Islands, Nauru and Kiribati; the name is Greek for 'small islands'
moai – large stone statues (Easter Island)
motu – island, islet

naghol – land-diving ritual (Vanuatu)
nakamal – men's clubhouse (New Caledonia, Vanuatu)
namalao – megapode bird
namba – traditional sheath (Vanuatu)
natsaro – traditional dancing ground (Vanuatu)
nguzunguzu – carved wooden canoe figurehead (Solomons)
nimangki – status and power earned by *grade-taking* (Vanuatu)
niu – coconut
ni-Vanuatu – people from Vanuatu
nono – small gnats, sandflies (French Polynesia)
nuku – village (Polynesian)
nu'u – see *nuku*

ono – barracuda

pa'anga – Tongan currency
PADI – Professional Association of Dive Instructors
pae pae – paved *marae* floor
pakalolo – marijuana (French Polynesia)
palagi – see *palangi*
palangi – white person, westerner (Polynesia)
Papuans – ancient people who are among the ancestors of modern Melanesians
pareu – *lava-lava* (Cook Islands, French Polynesia, New Caledonia and Vanuatu)
pe'a – see *peka* (Samoa)
peka – bat, small bird
pelagic – creatures in the upper waters of the ocean
pilou – *Kanak* dance, performed for important ceremonies or events
Polynesia – a huge area bound by Hawai'i, New Zealand and Easter Island; includes the Cook Islands, French Polynesia, Niue, Pitcairn Island, the Samoas, Tokelau, Tonga, Tuvalu, and Wallis and Futuna; the name is Greek for 'many islands'
Polynesian Outliers – the islands of eastern Melanesia and southern Micronesia populated by Polynesians
pukao – topknot
pulenu'u – head man, village mayor (Polynesia)

quonset hut – WWII military storage shed

rae rae – see *fakaleiti* (French Polynesia)
rangatira – chief, nobility (Polynesia)
ratu – chief (Fiji)
rori – see *bêche-de-mer* (French Polynesia)

sevusevu – presentation of a gift to a village chief and, by extension, to the ancestral gods and spirits (Fiji)
siapo – *tapa* (Samoa)
snack – cheap cafe (French Territories)

SPF – South Pacific Forum
SPTO – South Pacific Tourism Organisation
swim-through – tunnel big enough to swim through

tabu – see *tapu*
tamtam – slit-gong, slit-drum; made from carved logs with a hollowed-out section (Vanuatu)
ta'ovala – distinctive woven pandanus mats worn around the waist (Tonga)
tapa – see *masi*
tapu – sacred, prohibited
taro – plant with heart-shaped leaves, cultivated for its leaf and edible rootstock
tatau – tattoo
taupou – title bestowed by high-ranking chief upon a young woman of his family (Polynesia)
tiki – carved human figure (Polynesia)
tivaevae – colourful intricately sewn appliqué works (Cook Islands)
to'ona'i – Sunday lunch (Samoa)
trepang – *bêche-de-mer*
tu' – see *tui* (Tonga)
tufuga – priest, expert (Samoa)
tui – paramount king (central Pacific)
tumunu – hollowed-out coconut-tree stump used to brew bush beer; also bush-beer drinking sessions

umu – earth oven
umukai – feast cooked in an *umu*

va'a – see *vaka*
vahine – woman (Polynesia)
vaka – canoe
vale – see *fale* (Fiji)

wantok – one talk; the western Melanesian concept that all who speak your language are allies (Solomon Islands)

yaqona – see *kava* (Fiji)

behind the scenes

SEND US YOUR FEEDBACK

We love to hear from travellers – your comments keep us on our toes and help make our books better. Our well-travelled team reads every word on what you loved or loathed about this book. Although we cannot reply individually to postal submissions, we always guarantee that your feedback goes straight to the appropriate authors, in time for the next edition. Each person who sends us information is thanked in the next edition – the most useful submissions are rewarded with a selection of digital PDF chapters.

Visit **lonelyplanet.com/contact** to submit your updates and suggestions or to ask for help. Our award-winning website also features inspirational travel stories, news and discussions.

Note: We may edit, reproduce and incorporate your comments in Lonely Planet products such as guidebooks, websites and digital products, so let us know if you don't want your comments reproduced or your name acknowledged. For a copy of our privacy policy visit lonelyplanet.com/privacy.

OUR READERS

Many thanks to the travellers who used the last edition and wrote to us with helpful hints, useful advice and interesting anecdotes:

Patricia Aros, Victor Blum, Richard Bowerbank, Jessica Carpelan, Duval Claude, Efrat Elron, Kip Freytag, James Gray, Reinhard Hannak, James Hunter, Ute Keck, Jennifer McKay, Rosie Randall, Rainer Roth and Jason Thompson.

AUTHOR THANKS
Celeste Brash

Most thanks to my kids, Jasmine and Tevai, and to my husband Josh for putting up with my absences. In Fiji, *vinaka* to Sharon and Scott, Colin and Janine, Harry my taxi driver, Ursula (Mila), Tuvununu, Peiro and Vuli, Richard at Matava, Richard at Mai Dive, Christian, Seru and Sala, my new Fijian family, and Serai. In Samoa, thanks to the Martel family, Christina Gale, Gabor and Fiona and Ocean. In American Samoa, huge thanks to John and Luao Wasko, my Ta'u host Lesi'i and Sia Figiel.

Brett Atkinson

Meitaki ma'ata to all the friendly Cook Islanders I met on my travels, especially Papatua Papatua in Rarotonga, Marshall and Jéanne Humphreys on 'Atiu, and Tangata and Teata Ateriano on Ma'uke. On tiny Mitiaro, thanks to Papa Neke – and a big hug to Aunty Mii – and on Aitutaki, thank you to Tutai Clark. Back in Auckland, Kelly Hansen and Michal McKay were both very helpful, and love and thanks to Carol for holding the fort at Casa Loma.

Jean-Bernard Carillet

Heaps of thanks to the *South Pacific* team at LP, especially Maryanne and Errol, for their trust and support, and to the editorial and cartography teams. A heartfelt *mauruuru roa* to coordinating author Celeste, with whom I share the same passion for that trippy *fenua*; she was utterly helpful and patient throughout the process. In French Polynesia, a special mention goes to my second family, the Peirsegaeles in Mahina – thanks Yan, Vai, Sean, Majo, Hubert for having open all doors and the infectious *aroha* (despite a broken car). A big thanks also to all people who helped out and made this trip so enlightening, including Alain Buzenet (next time we'll be off to the *motu*!), Katou, Verly, Heikura, Moearii, Pam, Reata, Tepupu, Lucile, Céline, Lionel and Pascale, among others. And how could I forget my daughter Eva and Christine, who shared some of my Polynesian adventures and give direction to my otherwise roving life?

Jayne D'Arcy

Thanks to wonderful, patient Sharik Billington – what a honeymoon! Thanks also to young Miles, who swam, snorkelled and harassed hermit crabs on some 30 islands. In Vanuatu, thanks Tony Houlahan, Olivia Johnson, Jessica Sherry, Werry Narua, Carolyn Donald, Karen Henry, Alice and Ugo, Charlotte Connell, Mayumi Green, Bev Anti, Allan Power, Howard Iseli, Pascal Gavotto, and Jack and Jeanne at Travellers Budget Motel (an oasis). In New Caledonia, thanks to Nathalie Mermoud from the Office de Tourism, Christéle and Arnaud, tree-climbing Alan, Willy from Ouvéa and the folks at Auberge de Jeunesse.

Virginia Jealous

Vinaka vakalevu to Hugh, Cristelle and Tahi for my Suva home away from home, Mafa for language skills and laughs, Sashi for my Lautoka home away from home, Elenoa from SSC and the boat crews who every day treated me like a long-lost friend, Sushil from Rosie's, the GVI crew on Nacula, Bulou for the gift of bananas and Tui who shared an unexpectedly long 4WD trip with me (lucky we had the bananas).

Craig McLachlan

A huge *malo 'aupito* to all those who helped me out in Tonga this time around. Special mention to Bruno in Vava'u – I hope all your piglets are doing well. Cheers to Sandra at the TVB, Luisa and Tai, Craig, and to my good mate Kava. Double-special thanks to my exceptionally beautiful wife, Yuriko, for putting up with the mess.

ACKNOWLEDGMENTS

Climate map data adapted from Peel MC, Finlayson BL & McMahon TA (2007) 'Updated World Map of the Köppen-Geiger Climate Classification', *Hydrology and Earth System Sciences*, 11, 1633–44.
Cover photograph: The view from a hut on Lifou's Luengoni beach in the Loyalty Islands, New Caledonia/Yves Talensac/Photononstop/Photolibrary
Many of the images in this guide are available for licensing from Lonely Planet Images: www.lonelyplanetimages.com.

BEHIND THE SCENES

THIS BOOK

This 5th edition of Lonely Planet's *South Pacific* guidebook was researched and written by Celeste Brash, Brett Atkinson, Jean-Bernard Carillet, Jayne D'Arcy, Virginia Jealous and Craig McLachlan. Celeste, Brett, Jean-Bernard and Craig also worked on the previous edition, alongside Rowan McKinnon, Peter Dragicevich, Jocelyn Harewood, Nana Luckham and Dean Starnes. Dr Michael Sorokin was the original contributor for the Health content, which was updated for this edition by Celeste Brash. George Dunford wrote the previous edition's History and Culture chapters, with Tony Horwitz contributing the Captain James Cook boxed text in the History chapter; both these chapters were updated and repurposed for this edition by Celeste Brash. Former Tuvaluan prime minister Saufatu Sopoanga wrote the Climate Change & Global Warming boxed text in the Environmental Issues chapter.

This guidebook was commissioned in Lonely Planet's Melbourne office, and produced by the following:
Commissioning Editor Maryanne Netto
Coordinating Editor Catherine Naghten
Coordinating Cartographers Peter Shields, Jacqueline Nguyen
Coordinating Layout Designer Wibowo Rusli
Managing Editors Bruce Evans, Annelies Mertens
Managing Cartographers Shahara Ahmed, Corey Hutchison, Adrian Persoglia
Managing Layout Designer Jane Hart
Assisting Editors Janet Austin, Carolyn Bain, Anne Mulvaney, Tasmin Waby, Helen Yeates
Assisting Cartographers Rachel Imeson, Alex Leung, Joelene Kowalski, Andrew Smith
Cover Research Naomi Parker
Internal Image Research Claire Gibson
Language Content Branislava Vladisavljevic
Thanks to Anita Banh, Sasha Baskett, Barbara Delissen, Ryan Evans, Karusha Ganga, Joshua Geoghegan, William Gourlay, Larissa Frost; Laura Jane, Andi Jones, Wayne Murphy, Susan Paterson, Trent Paton, Kirsten Rawlings, Averil Robertson, Dianne Schallmeiner, Gerard Walker

ACKNOWLEDGMENTS

NOTES

NOTES

index

how to use this book

These symbols will help you find the listings you want:

👁	Sights	👉	Tours	🍷	Drinking
🐟	Beaches	🎆	Festivals & Events	☆	Entertainment
🏃	Activities	🛌	Sleeping	🛍	Shopping
🎓	Courses	🍴	Eating	ℹ	Information/Transport

These symbols give you the vital information for each listing:

📞	Telephone Numbers	📶	Wi-Fi Access	🚌	Bus
⏰	Opening Hours	🏊	Swimming Pool	🛥	Ferry
🅿	Parking	🥗	Vegetarian Selection	Ⓜ	Metro
🚭	Nonsmoking	ⓘ	English-Language Menu	Ⓢ	Subway
❄	Air-Conditioning	👨‍👩‍👧	Family-Friendly	🚋	Tram
@	Internet Access	🐾	Pet-Friendly	🚆	Train

Reviews are organised by author preference.

Look out for these icons:

TOP CHOICE	Our author's recommendation
FREE	No payment required
🌱	A green or sustainable option

Our authors have nominated these places as demonstrating a strong commitment to sustainability – for example by supporting local communities and producers, operating in an environmentally friendly way, or supporting conservation projects.

Map Legend

Sights
- ⚫ Beach
- ⚫ Buddhist
- ⚫ Castle
- ⚫ Christian
- ⚫ Hindu
- ⚫ Islamic
- ⚫ Jewish
- ⚫ Monument
- ⚫ Museum/Gallery
- ⚫ Ruin
- ⚫ Winery/Vineyard
- ⚫ Zoo
- ⚫ Other Sight

Activities, Courses & Tours
- ⚫ Diving/Snorkelling
- ⚫ Canoeing/Kayaking
- ⚫ Skiing
- ⚫ Surfing
- ⚫ Swimming/Pool
- ⚫ Walking
- ⚫ Windsurfing
- ⚫ Other Activity/Course/Tour

Sleeping
- ⚫ Sleeping
- ⚫ Camping

Eating
- ⚫ Eating

Drinking
- ⚫ Drinking
- ⚫ Cafe

Entertainment
- ⚫ Entertainment

Shopping
- ⚫ Shopping

Information
- ⚫ Bank
- ⚫ Embassy/Consulate
- ⚫ Hospital/Medical
- @ Internet
- ⚫ Police
- ⚫ Post Office
- ⚫ Telephone
- ⚫ Toilet
- ⚫ Tourist Information
- ⚫ Other Information

Transport
- ⚫ Airport
- ⚫ Border Crossing
- ⚫ Bus
- ⚫ Cable Car/Funicular
- ⚫ Cycling
- ⚫ Ferry
- Ⓜ Metro
- ⚫ Monorail
- 🅿 Parking
- ⚫ Petrol Station
- ⚫ Taxi
- ⚫ Train/Railway
- ⚫ Tram
- ⚫ Other Transport

Routes
- Tollway
- Freeway
- Primary
- Secondary
- Tertiary
- Lane
- Unsealed Road
- Plaza/Mall
- Steps
- Tunnel
- Pedestrian Overpass
- Walking Tour
- Walking Tour Detour
- Path

Geographic
- ⚫ Hut/Shelter
- ⚫ Lighthouse
- ⚫ Lookout
- ▲ Mountain/Volcano
- ⚫ Oasis
- ⚫ Park
-)(Pass
- ⚫ Picnic Area
- ⚫ Waterfall

Population
- ⚫ Capital (National)
- ⚫ Capital (State/Province)
- ⚫ City/Large Town
- ⚫ Town/Village

Boundaries
- International
- State/Province
- Disputed
- Regional/Suburb
- Marine Park
- Cliff
- Wall

Hydrography
- River, Creek
- Intermittent River
- Swamp/Mangrove
- Reef
- Canal
- Water
- Dry/Salt/Intermittent Lake
- Glacier

Areas
- Beach/Desert
- +++ Cemetery (Christian)
- ××× Cemetery (Other)
- Park/Forest
- Sportsground
- Sight (Building)
- Top Sight (Building)

welcome to the South Pacific

The Dream

The South Pacific is synonymous with paradise. This lofty reputation began when the first European explorers returned to their home shores with tales of a heaven on earth, where the soil was fertile, life was simple and people were beautiful. And while these island nations have modernised since that time, their allure hasn't changed. You'll still find the bluest waters, smiling bronzed locals in flowery fabrics and humid, gardenia-scented air. But what's most amazing is how refreshingly untainted by tourism most regions are. Blame it on their remoteness or the price of getting here but few people who fantasise about the South Pacific ever actually go. This is a great gift to those who book a ticket to this magical place that generations have dreamed about.

Diversity

Even the biggest geography buffs crinkle their brows when it comes to this many islands. On a map all those little dots look the same and their many-vowelled names get lost on the tongue. But get to know these places and you'll find diversity that would be fitting for any expanse of this size. Yes, there are Polynesian nations and Melanesian nations but within these headings are myriad languages, customs, histories and landscapes that make each island unique. No, it's not just a homog-

ON THE ROAD

PAGE 42

YOUR COMPLETE DESTINATION GUIDE
In-depth reviews, detailed listings

D1155093

Equator

Solomon Islands p316

Samoa p250

American Samoa p295

Vanuatu p472

New Caledonia p145

Fiji p60

Rarotonga & the Cook Islands p196

Tahiti & French Polynesia p346

Tonga p430

Tropic of Capricorn

Easter Island (Rapa Nui) p44

SOUTH PACIFIC OCEAN

Other Pacific Islands 526

SURVIVAL GUIDE

PAGE 575

VITAL PRACTICAL INFORMATION TO
HELP YOU HAVE A SMOOTH TRIP

Health

health risk to travellers to Pacific region is low. The Solomon Islands and Vanuatu are the one serious health rd: malaria. Elsewhere main danger is from mos borne dengue fever.

RE YOU GO
ng before depar
y for presid
e trouble
d letter

in France, but remember to obtain the European Health Insurance Card (EHIC) before leaving home.
New Zealand Travellers You may have free access to public but not private facilities in the Cook Islands.

Required Vaccinations For all countries

THIS EDITION WRITTEN AND RESEARCHED BY

Celeste Brash,

Brett Atkinson, Jean-Bernard Carillet, Jayne D'Arcy,

Virginia Jealous, Craig McLachlan